"It's rare that one sees a handbook about humanity's relationship with, and activities in outer space, that goes beyond a few widely discussed themes focussed on science, technology, economics, law or geopolitics. Yet, as this unique collection of different perspectives clearly shows, space is so multi-faceted and touches every person on the planet. To see in one book the many other diverse 'voices' on space – from indigenous, to anthropological, to spiritual, to archaeological, to aesthetic, just to name a few – allows us to begin to comprehend the true 'wonder' of space and recalibrate our thinking about our responsibilities to respect and protect space for the future generations. A wonderful book co-edited by two amazing thought leaders about the future of humanity and its place in the galaxy around us."

Emeritus Professor Steven Freeland, *Western Sydney University & Bond University, Vice-Chair of UNCOPUOS Working Group on Legal Aspects of Space Resource Activities*

"This volume captures the capacious work and thinking that comes under the title 'social studies of outer space.' It excels at orienting the reader to the field's formations and setting an ambitious and welcome vision for future work that embraces the multivocality of the cosmos. The contributing authors creatively and insightfully draw from numerous ontologies and epistemologies to animate what space is and can be. This generates an exciting collection that will no doubt inspire many new avenues of research."

Lisa Messeri, *Assistant Professor of Anthropology, Yale University, Author of Placing Outer Space: An Earthly Ethnography of Other Worlds*

"This ambitious and timely book brings outer space studies into the 21st century, bringing together cutting-edge critical theory with insights from voices marginalized by traditional space studies – voices that speak to the most pressing issues of today and open up genuine alternatives for future relations with earth and other planets. Weaving together issues of power, violence, social and ecological justice, and (inter-)planetary crises, it offers newcomers to the field a nuanced understanding of the complexities of engaging with outer space in theory and practice, while experts will benefit from the richness of disciplines, knowledge systems, perspectives, and innovative research found throughout its chapters. This book will make a lasting and critical impact on the field for years to come."

Audra Mitchell, *Professor, Canada Research Chair in Global Political Ecology, Wilfrid Laurier University*

"Outer space is not outside. It is inside. Inside the slipstreams of colonialism, capitalism, and the Cold War. But look to this extraordinary book to find countercurrents of the decolonial, antiracist, and communitarian – zones not of a universal universe, but of possible pluriverses, outside the orbits of cosmography as usual."

Stefan Helmreich, *Elting E. Morison Professor of Anthropology, MIT*

"Urgent, provocative, inspiring, troubling, and sure to be of enduring significance. With rich discussions of theories, methods, questions and interventions coming from across the social sciences and humanities, this mind-expanding compendium surveys some of the growing terrain of social studies of outer space and offers a robust welcome to newcomers to this vibrant and growing field."

Julie Klinger, *Assistant Professor in the Department of Geography and Spatial Sciences, University of Delaware*

"Alice Gorman and Juan Francisco Salazar are two of the most interesting and innovative writers and thinkers about outer space. They are legends in this field, both in Australia and internationally, and have inspired so many others to follow their lead in exploring this rich and endlessly fascinating topic. In this Handbook, they have brought together such an extraordinary range of diverse voices and perspectives on space. The publication of this Handbook is a watershed moment for all of us interested in using the social sciences and humanities to craft new approaches to human imaginings and futures in space."

Ceridwen Dovey

"This is a welcome contribution to the growing library of the social sciences, arts, and humanities on outer space that provides challenging socio-political perspectives in a field often dominated by narrow technical and bureaucratic histories."

Bleddyn Bowen, *University of Leicester*

"This meticulously curated collection offers critical and creative techniques to think-with space, to learn from earth's predicaments, and to invent unforeseen modes of planetary habitation. In examining how space is bounded to Earth in the practices of everyday life, the rich and pluriversal space-making interventions presented here act as catalysts for remembering the past and for reinventing our social, cultural, political, and environmental relations."

Marie-Pier Boucher, *Assistant Professor of Media Studies at the Institute of Communication, Culture, Information, and Technology, University of Toronto*

THE ROUTLEDGE HANDBOOK OF SOCIAL STUDIES OF OUTER SPACE

The *Routledge Handbook of Social Studies of Outer Space* offers state-of-the-art overview of contemporary social and cultural research on outer space. International in scope, the thirty-eight contributions by over fifty leading researchers and artists across a variety of disciplines and fields of knowledge, present a range of debates and pose key questions about the crafting of futures in relation to outer space. The *Handbook* is a call to attend more carefully to engagements with outer space, empirically, affectively, and theoretically, while characterizing current research practices and outlining future research agendas. This recalibration opens profound questions of intersectional politics, race, equity, and environmental justice around the contested topics of space exploration and life off-Earth. Among the many themes included in the volume are the various infrastructures, networks and systems that enable and sustain space exploration; space heritage; the ethics of outer space; social and environmental justice; fundamental debates about life in outer space as it pertains to both astrobiology and SETI; the study of scientific communities; the human body and consciousness; Indigenous astronomical systems of Knowledge; contemporary space art; and ongoing critical interventions to overcome the legacies of colonialism and dismantle hegemonic narratives of outer space.

Juan Francisco Salazar is an interdisciplinary researcher and documentary filmmaker. He is a Professor of Communications, Media, and Environment at Western Sydney University, Australia.

Alice Gorman is an archaeologist and heritage consultant. She is an Associate Professor at Flinders University in Adelaide, Australia.

ROUTLEDGE ANTHROPOLOGY HANDBOOKS

THE ROUTLEDGE HANDBOOK OF ANTHROPOLOGY AND REPRODUCTION
Edited by Sallie Han and Cecília Tomori

THE ROUTLEDGE COMPANION TO CONTEMPORARY ANTHROPOLOGY
Edited by Simon Coleman, Susan B. Hyatt and Ann Kingsolver

THE ROUTLEDGE HANDBOOK OF ANTHROPOLOGY AND THE CITY
Edited by Setha Low

THE ROUTLEDGE HANDBOOK OF MEDICAL ANTHROPOLOGY
Edited by Lenore Manderson, Elizabeth Cartwright and Anita Hardon

THE ROUTLEDGE HANDBOOK OF THE ANTHROPOLOGY OF LABOR
Edited by Sharryn Kasmir and Lesley Gill

THE ROUTLEDGE COMPANION TO MEDIA ANTHROPOLOGY
Edited by Elisabetta Costa, Patricia G. Lange, Nell Haynes and Jolynna Sinanan

THE ROUTLEDGE HANDBOOK OF SOCIAL STUDIES OF OUTER SPACE
Edited by Juan Francisco Salazar, Alice Gorman, and Paola Castaño

https://www.routledge.com/Routledge-Anthropology-Handbooks/book-series/RANTHBK

THE ROUTLEDGE HANDBOOK OF SOCIAL STUDIES OF OUTER SPACE

Edited by
Juan Francisco Salazar and Alice Gorman

LONDON AND NEW YORK

Designed cover image: Juan Francisco Salazar, from a photograph taken in 2018 from a wall in SoHo, New York City, of an original graffiti art work signed by B.D. White.

First published 2023
by Routledge
4 Park Square, Milton Park, Abingdon, Oxon OX14 4RN

and by Routledge
605 Third Avenue, New York, NY 10158

Routledge is an imprint of the Taylor & Francis Group, an informa business

© 2023 selection and editorial matter, Juan Francisco Salazar and Alice Gorman; individual chapters, the contributors

The right of Juan Francisco Salazar and Alice Gorman to be identified as the authors of the editorial material, and of the authors for their individual chapters, has been asserted in accordance with sections 77 and 78 of the Copyright, Designs and Patents Act 1988.

All rights reserved. No part of this book may be reprinted or reproduced or utilised in any form or by any electronic, mechanical, or other means, now known or hereafter invented, including photocopying and recording, or in any information storage or retrieval system, without permission in writing from the publishers.

Trademark notice: Product or corporate names may be trademarks or registered trademarks, and are used only for identification and explanation without intent to infringe.

British Library Cataloguing-in-Publication Data
A catalogue record for this book is available from the British Library

ISBN: 9781032248615 (hbk)
ISBN: 9781032248745 (pbk)
ISBN: 9781003280507 (ebk)

DOI: 10.4324/9781003280507

Typeset in Bembo
by codeMantra

CONTENTS

List of Figures   *xi*
List of Tables   *xiii*
Preface   *xiv*
Foreword   *xvii*
List of Contributors   *xx*
Acknowledgements   *xxx*

1 Social Studies of Outer Space: Pluriversal Articulations   1
   Juan Francisco Salazar and Alice Gorman

PART I
Fields   23

2 Trilogie Terrestre   25
   Frédérique Aït-Touati and Bruno Latour

3 Refielding in More-Than-Terran Spaces   31
   Valerie A. Olson

4 Space and Time through Material Culture: An Account of Space Archaeology   44
   Alice Gorman

5 Anthropology and Contemporary Space Exploration, with a Note on Hopi Ladders   57
   Istvan Praet

6 Planetary Ethnography in a "SpaceX Village": History, Borders, and the Work of "Beyond"   71
   Anna Szolucha

7	The Spaces of Outer Space Oliver Dunnett	84
8	Sociological Approaches to Outer Space Paola Castaño and Álvaro Santana-Acuña	96
9	Space Ethics Tony Milligan and J. S. Johnson-Schwartz	108
10	Other Worlds, Other Views: Contemporary Artists and Space Exploration Nicola Triscott	121

PART II
Intersections and Interventions — 137

11	As Above, So Below: Space and Race in the Space Race Rasheedah Phillips	139
12	A Chronopolitics of Outer Space: A Poetics of Tomorrowing Juan Francisco Salazar	142
13	Feminist Approaches to Outer Space: Engagements with Technology, Labour, and Environment Réka Patrícia Gál and Eleanor S. Armstrong	158
14	The Iconography of the Astronaut as a Critical Enquiry of Space Law Saskia Vermeylen	172
15	Diversity in Space Evie Kendal	185
16	*Mare Incognito:* Live Performance Art Linking Sleep with the Cosmos through Radio Waves Daniela de Paulis, Thomas Moynihan, Alejandro Ezquerro-Nassar, and Fabian Schmidt	199

PART III
Colonial Histories and Decolonial Futures — 215

17	Celestial Relations with and as Milŋiyawuy, the Milky Way, the River of Stars Bawaka Country, including Dr Laklak Burarrwanga, Ritjilili Ganambarr, Merrkiyawuy Ganambarr-Stubbs, Banbapuy Ganambarr, Djawundil Maymuru, Lara Daley, Sarah Wright, Sandie Suchet-Pearson, and Kate Lloyd with Naminapu Maymuru-White and Rrawun Maymuru	217

18 Coloniality and the Cosmos 226
    Natalie B. Treviño

19 Safeguarding Indigenous Sky Rights from Colonial Exploitation 238
    Karlie Alinta Noon, Krystal De Napoli, Peter Swanton, Carla Guedes, and Duane Hamacher

20 Anishinaabeg in Space 252
    Deondre Smiles

21 Earthless Astronomy, Landless Datasets, and the Mining of the Future 263
    Katheryn M. Detwiler

22 Reconstellating Astroenvironmentalism: Borders, Parks, and Other Cosmic Imaginaries 281
    Alessandra Marino

23 Divergent Extraterrestrial Worlds: Navigating Cosmo-Practices on Two Mountaintops in Thailand 295
    Lauren Reid

PART IV
Objects, Infrastructures, Networks, and Systems — 309

24 A Glitch in Space 311
    Juan Francisco Salazar

25 Preparing for the "Internet Apocalypse": Data Centres and the Space Weather Threat 313
    A. R. E. Taylor

26 Space Infrastructures and Networks of Control and Care 328
    Katarina Damjanov

27 Mexico Dreams of Satellites 339
    Anne W. Johnson

28 Space Codes: The Astronaut and the Architect 351
    Fred Scharmen

PART V
Cultures in Orbit/Life in Space — 363

29 Cosmic Waters 365
    Julie Patarin-Jossec

30 Unearthing Biosphere 2, Biosphere 2 as Un·Earthing *Ralo Mayer*	371
31 Living and Working in "The Great Outdoors": Astronautics as Everyday Work in NASA's Skylab Programme *Phillip Brooker and Wes Sharrock*	388
32 Adapting to Space: The International Space Station Archaeological Project *Justin St. P. Walsh*	400
33 An Ethnography of an Extraterrestrial Society: The International Space Station *David Jeevendrampillai, Victor Buchli, Aaron Parkhurst, Adryon Kozel, Giles Bunch, Jenia Gorbanenko and Makar Tereshin*	413
34 Plant Biologists and the International Space Station: Institutionalising a Scientific Community *Paola Castaño*	427
35 Whiteboards, Dancing, Origami, Debate: The Importance of Practical Wisdom for Astrophysicists and Instrument Scientists *Fionagh Thomson*	441
36 Understanding the Question of Whether to Message Extraterrestrial Intelligence *Chelsea Haramia*	454
37 Astrobiology and the Immanence of Life amidst Uncertainty *Dana Burton*	468
38 A Post-Geocentric Gravitography of Human Culture *Alice Gorman*	480
Index	*493*

FIGURES

1.1	*Refugee Astronaut II*, 2016. Yinka Shonibare CBE. Fibreglass mannequin, Dutch wax printed cotton textile, net, possessions, astronaut helmet, moon boots, and steel baseplate. 210 × 90 × 103 cm. © Yinka Shonibare CBE. All rights reserved, DACS/Artimage 2022. Image courtesy James Cohan Gallery. Photo: Stephen White & Co	3
2.1	INSIDE. © Zone Critique Company. Reproduced with permission of the artist	25
2.2	INSIDE. © Zone Critique Company. Bruno Latour performing INSIDE. Reproduced with permission of the artist	26
2.3	INSIDE. © Zone Critique Company. Bruno Latour performing INSIDE Reproduced with permission of the artist	27
2.4	MOVING EARTHS © Zone Critique Company. Bruno Latour performing INSIDE Reproduced with permission of the artist	28
2.5	VIRAL. © Zone Critique Company. Image of Bruno Latour rehearsing VIRAL at the Theatre des Amandiers, in Nanterre. The image projected on the table is the surface of Mars. Reproduced with permission of the artist. © Zone Critique Company. Reproduced with permission of the artist	29
4.1	Image of Surveyor 3 on the lunar surface in 1967. Image courtesy of NASA	48
5.1	Walapi Antelope Kiva of the Hopi Indians in the village of Mishongnovi, ca. 1901. Photo by Pierce, C.C. (Charles C.), 1861–1946. USC Libraries Special Collections. Public Domain	58
6.1	End of Highway 4, looking onto SpaceX launch site near Boca Chica beach, 17 June 2022. Photo by the author	74
6.2	The different styles of the border wall in Brownsville, 22 September 2022. Photo by the author	79
7.1	*Dead Satellite with a nuclear reactor, Eastern Arizona (Cosmos 469)*, 2011. C-print 48 × 60 in. © Trevor Paglen. Courtesy of the artist, Altman Siegel Gallery (San Francisco), and pace gallery	87
10.1	Nahum, *Voyage: A session for remembering*, 2015. Cajarc, France. Photo: Yohann Gozard	123
10.2	Living the Cosmos (2020), a KOSMICA institute educational programme for vulnerable kids in San Luis Potosí, Mexico	124
10.3	*Vortex of Infinity*, Unseen Amsterdam 2019 © Andres Pardo. Tabita Rezaire, *Satellite Devotion* (2019), installation view from Unseen Amsterdam 2019. Photo: Andres Pardo. Courtesy of the artist and Goodman Gallery	129

Figures

12.1	Video still from the film *Nightfall on Gaia*, (2015) directed by Juan Francisco Salazar, with the character of astrobiologist Xûe Noon played by performance artist Victoria Hunt. Image by Juan Francisco Salazar, 2014	144
12.2	Video still from the film *Cosmographies*, directed by Juan Francisco Salazar, in production during 2023. The film is a sequel to the 2015 film *Nightfall on Gaia*. The image portrays the character of astrobiologist Xûe Noon played by performance artist Victoria Hunt. Image by Juan Francisco Salazar, Atacama Desert, Chile, 2022	151
16.1	Daniela de Paulis (Mare Incognito, 2022). Video still from Mare Incognito. Credits: Mirjam Somers, Bas Czerwinski	199
17.1	Naminapu Maymuru-White, *Milŋiyawuy #1*. Reproduced with permission	218
17.2	Naminapu Maymuru-White, *Milŋiyawuy #2*. Reproduced with permission	219
17.3	Naminapu Maymuru-White, *Milŋiyawuy #3*. Reproduced with permission	221
17.4	Naminapu Maymuru-White, *Milŋiyawuy #4*. Reproduced with permission	222
17.5	QR Code to listen to Guwak	223
19.1	Image of Venus and the Pleiades open star cluster featuring tracks of Starlink satellites. Credit Torsten Hansen/IAU OAE. Public domain	241
21.1	Event Horizon Telescope Collaboration: Supermassive black hole in M87 Galaxy, 2017	268
21.2	Schematic of Chuquicamata block cave mine	268
21.3	*Pago* ceremony at the 2013 inauguration of the Atacama Large Millimeter/Submillimeter Array on Chajnantor/Thaknatur. Source: ESO	278
24.1	*Space Glitch Astronaut #3*. Image by Juan Francisco Salazar, 2022	312
24.2	*Space Glitch Afronaut #5*. Image by Juan Francisco Salazar, 2022	312
25.1	News coverage of the threat that space weather poses to the internet. Screenshots by author	318
25.2	VMCloud's "space weather-proof" server room. Photo by author	320
27.1	"México... ¡Me subo a tu nave!" by Federica Sánchez y Carrillo Bernal. 1er. Concurso de Arte Espacial "México Hacia la Luna", Agencia Espacial Mexicana. Used with permission	339
27.2	NanoConnect-2 appears on the platform as an image that visually represents the transmission of its signal, a long rectangle in tones of blue and green: "the cascade"	346
29.1	*Cosmic Waters #1*. Image by Julie Patarin-Jossec, 2022	366
29.2	*Cosmic Waters #2*. Image by Julie Patarin-Jossec, 2022	367
29.3	*Cosmic Waters #3*. Image by Julie Patarin-Jossec, 2022	368
29.4	*Cosmic Waters #4*. Image by Julie Patarin-Jossec, 2022	369
29.5	*Cosmic Waters #5*. Image by Julie Patarin-Jossec, 2022	370
30.1	Collapsed model of Biosphere 2 at the abandoned visitor centre. Photo: Ralo Mayer/Bildrecht, 2009	373
30.2	Crew of Biosphere 2 and Biospherian trainer Kathelin Gray after a performance of *The Wrong Stuff*, 1991. Photo courtesy of the Institute of Ecotechnics	378
30.3	Biosphere 2 at night. Still from *Extra-Terrestrial Ecologies*. Photo: Ralo Mayer/Bildrecht, 2018	382
32.1	NASA astronaut Kayla Barron takes a photograph of one of the sample areas for the SQuARE experiment in the US Node 1 galley area (dotted lines indicate the sample area boundaries). Credit NASA	409
34.1	Diagram of plant space scientists at the intersection of social circles. By Paola Castaño	434
35.1	Above the clouds: Cumbrecita Ridge (2,426 m), Parque Nacional de la Caldera de Taburiente, La Palma, location of sixteen observatories. Photo by author	441
36.1	The Arecibo message sent in 1974 from the Arecibo Observatory. Author Arne Nordmann. Public Domain. Wikimedia Commons	462
38.1	Crew training in the Marshall space flight center neutral buoyancy simulator, 1967. Image courtesy of NASA	485

TABLES

38.1 Comparative gravity of solar system bodies. Source: edited from Wikipedia   483
38.2 Post-geocentric gravitography   490

PREFACE

"The world's been nightmarished", once wrote Lemony Snicket. From its conception in 2019 on a muggy New Orleans late summer afternoon, over three inconceivable years, to its conclusion at a series of events in Paris in October 2022, where the editors gave the book its final impulse, this book developed slowly yet relentlessly during prolonged periods of grief for people and nature.

Because books are never written and edited in a vacuum, the process of making this book was an intricate oscillation between forces simultaneously boosting and slowing it down, in the context of the extraordinary events which 'took place', locally and globally, on and off Earth, during this three-year period. A stark reminder of the intricate ways in which knowledges of outer space are always situated.

The origins of the book can be traced to a series of academic panels that Paola Castaño and Juan Francisco Salazar convened during the 2019 annual meeting of the Society for Social Studies of Science (4S) in New Orleans in September 2019. This meeting took place exactly fourteen years on the day after the Hurricane Katrina Disaster, where 80% of New Orleans was flooded, over fifteen hundred people died, and over two hundred thousand people were displaced. This panel in 2019 was synchronic with wider endeavours set in motion by the Social Studies of Outer Space Network, which had formed a year earlier in 2018 in Lancaster, UK, with the aim of developing social and cultural research and methods to engage critically with the broad topic of outer space. Another contiguous precedent for this edited collection is the special issue coedited by Istvan Praet and Juan Francisco Salazar for the journal *Environmental Humanities* in 2017 titled "Familiarizing the Extraterrestrial/Making Our Planet Alien", which offered a broad overview of anthropologically inflected social scientific perspectives on outer space.

With this in mind, this *Handbook* has been carefully and patiently curated and nurtured over three years. Many authors started the journey in 2019 but were not able to finish it. Others came very late in the process. Probably every single one of the over fifty authors hereby included were infected with coronavirus or were deeply distraught by the COVID-19 pandemic. Many were directly affected by extreme weather events, and by the war in Ukraine. Many, especially emerging scholars, had to deal with the precarity of academic labour across the neoliberal university system of knowledge production, and some contributors relocated to new universities or even new countries. Whether they made it to the end or not, everyone remains part of this book in spirit.

Other spirits and forces also intruded with intense verve. Between October 2019 and January 2020, the worst wildfire crisis in recorded history was declared along Australia's east coast, where I have lived since 1998. Over the course of a few months, 26 lives were lost, 2448 homes were destroyed, and 5.5 million hectares of land and forests were burnt. The impact on communities, farmers, wildlife, and bushland was unprecedented. Nearly 3 billion animals—mammals, reptiles, birds, and frogs—were killed or displaced according to the WWF. NASA's Earth Observatory captured these events in dramatic pictures, showing the scale of the devastation through images taken from satellites in lower Earth orbit. This unprecedented event was followed by two summers of the worst floods ever recorded in the very same areas. At the time of writing this preface, China had just recorded the worst heatwave on record, Pakistan the worst floods on record, and Europe the worst drought in recent times. The climate emergency that started in the second half of the twentieth century had a dramatic intensification in these last three years, where the acceleration of the climate and ecosystem breakdown has brought the planet dangerously close to irreversible change.

During this period of extreme wildfires, I found myself in the streets of Santiago de Chile during the unprecedented events that came to be known as the "estallido social" or social outburst. During these months, thirty-five people died as a result of police brutality and over two hundred were blinded. For the following three years, a unique constitutional process ensued with the task of drafting a proposal for a new constitution to replace the current one dating back to the military dictatorship of Augusto Pinochet. This participatory process was led by social movements, Indigenous leaders and Elders, and feminist organisations and sexual dissidences, only to be defeated at the very end in a referendum in September 2022 where the proposed New Constitution was rejected.

By February 2020, when I was returning from Antarctica to Australia, where together with a group of young leaders we had launched an Antarctic Youth Coalition, a platform for young people from Antarctic gateway cities to come together, the world was beginning to close down as COVID-19 was becoming a global pandemic. By April 2020, most cities globally had gone into severe lockdown. At the time of writing, 6.7 million people had died of Covid and 625 million had been infected.

In the northern hemisphere's spring of 2020, while I was in hospital on the other side of the world recovering from a serious bike accident, massive protests erupted across the US calling for justice after George Floyd was murdered by a white police officer in Minneapolis on 25 May. In astronomy, a field where Black academics make up about 1% of the people in the field, the organisers of Black In Astro forged a movement and a supportive space. Massive Black Lives Matter protests also erupted in Sydney and across Australia, revitalising the struggles against the ongoing harms of colonialism against Aboriginal and Torres Strait Peoples and Nations in this country.

On 6 April 2020, only a few weeks before the events that led to the murder of George Floyd and the #icantbreathe moment, the US released an executive order signalling that US citizens and companies have the right to engage in the commercial exploration, recovery, and use of resources in outer space. It also allowed the US secretary of state to negotiate bilateral and multilateral arrangements with foreign states regarding future public and private recovery and use of space resources. This edict prompted a fundamental legal and policy question about the real prospects of governing the mining and use of space resources by governments and enterprises.

In November 2020, as some of the first abstracts began to arrive from contributors, and while a large number of people across the world were still in lockdown, the concentration of CO_2 went above 400 ppm for the first time in several million years, pretty much at the same time as the International Space Station marked twenty years since its first residents arrived to live and work there. Since then, it has hosted 241 crew from 19 countries.

Over the course of 10 days in February 2021, three missions arrived on Mars: first, the United Arab Emirates' Hope orbiter, followed by China's Tianwen-1 mission with an orbiter, lander, and rover, and finally NASA's Perseverance rover, whose goals include to collect and set aside samples to be returned to Earth by NASA's next mission to Mars. In December 2021, the James Webb Space Telescope (JWST) was launched on an Ariane 5 rocket from Arianespace's ELA-3 launch complex at Europe's spaceport located near Kourou, French Guiana—a location and infrastructure that has been well documented by scholars working on social studies of outer space in the context of ongoing forms of colonialism. The telescope arrived at L2—one of the Sun–Earth Lagrange points, or gravitationally stable locations in space—on 24 January 2022, one year after robotic technologies were making themselves at home on Mars and sending back astonishing images, and a few weeks before Russia invaded Ukraine in February 2022, in a major escalation of the Russo-Ukrainian conflict begun in 2014. Roscosmos announced it could well end its participation in running the International Space Station, a move that would most likely disrupt an enduring symbol of international cooperation. As the Russian invasion of Ukraine escalated, the first images from the JWST began to be published, illuminating in astounding detail whole areas of the universe never before seen with this level of clarity. The telescope is a collaboration between NASA, the European Space Agency, and the Canadian Space Agency. While close to three hundred universities, companies, space agencies, and organisations are involved, it is imperative to remember that it is named after the NASA administrator who was directly associated with the persecution of queer people in the "lavender scare" of the 1950s and 1960s. Despite requests to rename the telescope, NASA persevered and declined to change its name. The telescope's first full-colour images and spectroscopic data were released during a televised broadcast on 12 July 2022, a few weeks after *Nature* magazine had published an editorial titled "Science Must Overcome Its Racist Legacy" in which the guest editors were invited to advise on the production of a series of special issues on racism in science, in an effort to "decolonize research and forge a path towards restorative justice and reconciliation".

Soon after, during August and September 2022 as celebrations were underway for the forty-fifth anniversary of the launch of Voyager I and Voyager II, carrying that Golden Record with greetings, sounds, images, and music from Earth, NASA released audio of transposed sound waves flowing out of a supermassive black hole located 250 million light-years away at the core of the Perseus cluster of galaxies, just as thousands of people were preparing to attend the largest ever International Astronautical Congress (IAC) in Paris. As the celebrations of NewSpace at the IAC drew to a close, following the failure of the launch of the Artemis I mission, NASA's DART mission hit an asteroid in the first-ever planetary defence test, as it was called, and NASA astronaut Nicole Mann became the first Native American woman in space.

These brief words are a welcome to our *Handbook*. The message is simple: it matters immensely from where one thinks of space, when, and why (and with whom). The production of perspectives and positionings are both grounded in and mobilised by historical and present conditions, by the politics of location of who writes, and whom they write for. Readers of this book will hopefully agree that thinking about outer space is necessarily a rethinking of life on Earth. Its vicissitudes and predicaments. Its ongoing struggles to fight racism, colonialism, forced migration, and social inequality. And its never-ending fight against the extinction of human and non-human life in a period that is seeing, in slow-motion, the catastrophic collapse of entire ecosystems on Earth.

Juan Francisco Salazar
Santiago de Chile
14 November 2022

FOREWORD

Dr. Lucianne Walkowicz

The ultimate, hidden truth of the world is that it is something that we make, and could just as easily make differently.

David Graeber

Human imaginings of outer space are stories told by shadow puppets: in the foreground, our material present is held up to the light as is or bent into the many shapes of hope and desire. Space, its infinite depths flattened by our perspective from Earth, functions as the projection screen onto which these long shadows are cast. Thus, while imaginings of our space futures might seem insubstantial, we must remember that they take their shape from the very concrete project of world-building in the here and now, which in turn has its roots in history.

Many people wonder what current social and economic orders here on Earth have to do with space. After all, at the time of this writing, there are no humans on other planets, and very few humans in space at all—so some might argue that space is a realm beyond earthly influences. However, even from a purely technical perspective, space activities on Earth and those that actually take place in space are not neatly separable. When planetary scientists and engineers build Mars rovers, for example, they test them on Earth first. Similarly, aspects of proposed social order—or continuations of existing social orders—are practised on Earth, even if they are accompanied by a narrative that places them as being "for space". In this sense, space is always liminal: it is both a conceptual, imaginative realm and a literal physical place. If we understand space as occupying this multinature, we can start to understand the bridge that provides nutrient flow between nascent plans for space and their actualisation in the physical realities that humans exist in, both for people in the professional space sector and those who live and work outside it.

In the past few decades, the idea of space as a realm of human presence and activity has come to the forefront in a variety of new ways. Space missions like NASA's Kepler Mission or the Transiting Exoplanet Survey Satellite (TESS) have discovered thousands of planets orbiting other stars, each discovery accompanied by press releases that hold up every new world in comparison to our home planet, Earth. While the data that astronomers like myself use to make these discoveries is decidedly unphotogenic—all bone-dry graphs of squiggly lines—artists embedded within press teams bring these worlds to life, creating illustrations that invite the viewer to imagine themselves there. Images like these have historically been effective tools in convincing people that not only *can* humans live and work in space, they *must*.

Of course, scientific discoveries are not the only ones vying for attention: alongside these imaginings of potentially "Earth-like" planets around other stars are those of closer-to-home space locales, particularly Mars. The past several years have given us a deluge of marketing pushes from private space companies; whether it's Blue Origin's Jeff Bezos displaying newly redrawn space habitats cribbed from Gerard X. O'Neill, or SpaceX's Elon Musk chortling on late-night talk shows about using thermonuclear weapons to melt the Martian ice caps, there is no shortage of dusted-off (or half-baked) space futures wafting about in the zeitgeist.

The motivation for private industry to wield popular imaginings of space is obvious: to cement space as a realm of capitalist expansion, a new place where fortunes might be further amassed. However, profiteering doesn't play nearly as well as saying that you're going to save humanity. Alongside the profusion of inviting new images that beckon people to imagine a life beyond Earth, we are faced with compounding crises here on this planet, where climate change, widening inequality, resource hoarding, and other human-made disasters intertwine and accelerate one another. Never to miss an opportunity, many space companies have capitalised on this very warranted dread about the future of our world, threading the narrowest needle's eye between offering salvation via a future beyond Earth, and avoiding any mention of how people might have created (or might address) the very conditions that threaten to tear us apart. Easier to point to an asteroid strike, or to remind us all that the Sun will evolve and engulf the Earth billions of years from now. We should hope to have that long.

Modern iterations of colonial capitalism would have us all believe that it is only natural that humanity go to space, that we have no choice but to abandon our home planet in service of a lazily reanimated manifest destiny with a better graphics department… but far from being visionary, or daring, those futures are small, and bankrupt. Earth is not some discardable cradle for our species—it is the place that fosters space exploration by providing an abundance of resources, even if human beings do not distribute those resources equitably. Going to space is one of many things humanity could do, and choosing our path forward is not up to a handful of billionaires, no matter how loud.

What is to be done about a future held hostage?

Certainly, our world does face existential threats. But largely, those threats are of our own creation, and most—like the climate crisis and colonial violence—cannot be solved by moving off world. If human beings can imagine thousands of exoplanets in compelling detail, we can do better than a death cult set on Mars. Individually—and more importantly, collectively—we all know that we could imagine something else, and what's more, we could build something else.

Currently, the vast majority of so-called "space" activities take place here on Earth—whether it is astronomy research, the planning, and testing of both physical and ideological technologies, or the imaginative world-building that informs how we interpret astronomical data *and* communicate discoveries. Of course, Earth is also the place in which peoples' rights to create, sculpt, and participate in various space imaginaries are either nourished or circumscribed.

This book is an invitation to step into that nutrient stream between our lives here on this planet and our dreams of space—and as we wade forward, to let the eddies around our ankles trouble old dilemmas, to mix and remix with the prismatic perspectives offered here. Discussions of space are always haunted by its unwieldy scale, spanning the personal, to the planetary, the galactic, the cosmic—but by bringing the many voices in this book into conversation with one another, one may find opportunities, fresh lenses, and old passageways to new doors. These chapters form a mesh of ideas that hold both the cosmic and the human.

Foreword

When I co-founded the JustSpace Alliance with my friend and fellow astronomer Erika Nesvold, we set out not because the two of us hold any kind of magical knowledge about what space futures will be or even should be. Similarly, you'll notice that no chapter in this volume bears the title "How to Solve Everything". However, we did know that human beings, even in the most dire circumstances, are capable of imagining better futures for themselves, and the greatest things happen when people come together to do exactly that. I hope readers will take the invitation in these pages to "think-with" the cosmos.

Remember: whether on this planet or beyond it, we are always in space.

CONTRIBUTORS

Editors

Juan Francisco Salazar is an interdiciplinary researcher, author, and filmmaker. He is a Professor of Media and Environment at Western Sydney University and an Australian Research Council Future Fellow (2020–2024). His work is interested in the politics of socioecological change, art–science collaborations, and social justice, with a recent focus on Antarctica and outer space. He is co-editor of three volumes including *Anthropologies and Futures: Researching Emerging and Uncertain Worlds* (Bloomsbury, 2017), *Media Cultures in Latin America: Key Concepts and New Debates* (Routledge, 2019), and *Thinking with Soils: Material Politics and Social Theory* (Bloomsbury, 2020). Credits as film director and co-director include *Anatomia Monumental* (Chile, 1999), *De la Tierra a la Pantalla* (Chile, 2004), *Nightfall on Gaia* (Australia-Chile, 2015), *The Bamboo Bridge* (Australia-Cambodia, 2019), and *Cosmographies* (in production for release in 2024). His creative work has screened at Serpentine Gallery, London (2022); Biennale of Sydney (2022); London International Documentary Film Festival (2021); Vision du Réel (Nyon 2020); CPHDOX (Copenhagen 2015); Antenna Film Festival (Sydney 2015 and 2019); Casula Powerhouse Arts Centre (Sydney 2008); Museo de las Américas (Denver 2005); and Museo Nacional de Bellas Artes (Santiago 1999).

Alice Gorman is an internationally recognised leader in the field of space archaeology. Her research focuses on the archaeology and heritage of space exploration, including space junk, planetary landing sites, off-Earth mining, rocket launch pads, and antennas. She is an Associate Professor at Flinders University in Adelaide and a heritage consultant with over twenty-five years' experience working with Indigenous communities in Australia. In collaboration with NASA and Chapman University, she is conducting the first archaeological study of the International Space Station. She is a mentor in the United Nations Office of Outer Space Affairs' Space4Women Mentor Network. Her book *Dr Space Junk vs the Universe: Archaeology and the Future* (MIT Press, 2019) won the Nib Literary Award People's Choice for Non-Fiction and the John Mulvaney Book Award. She tweets as @drspacejunk and blogs at Space Age Archaeology.

Contributing Authors

Frédérique Aït-Touati is a historian of science and literature, a theatre director, and a CNRS Research Fellow at the Ecole des Hautes Etudes en Sciences Sociales in Paris. Her work explores connections between the sciences and the arts. She was awarded the 2012 MLA Prize in Comparative Literature for her book *Fictions of the Cosmos* (Chicago University Press, 2011) and the Prix Gegner de l'Académie des Sciences Morales et Politiques for *Contes de la Lune, essai sur la fiction et la science modernes* (Gallimard, 2011). She is the director of the theatre company Zone Critique and of the Experimental Programme in Political Arts (SPEAP) founded by Bruno Latour with whom she created performances, including *the Terrestrial trilogy: INSIDE* (2016–2018), *Moving Earths* (2019–2020), and *VIRAL* (2021), recently presented at FIAF Crossing the Lines Festival in New York.

Eleanor S. Armstrong (she/her) is a Postdoctoral Researcher at Stockholm University (Sweden), taking a critically queer feminist approach to informal science education and cultural geographies of space science. She has held a Postdoctoral Fellowship at the University of Delaware (USA) and Visiting Scholar positions at the University of Cambridge (UK) and the Canadian Aviation and Space Museum (Canada). She developed the Queering the Science Museum (2018) and Bridging Binaries (2019) programmes at Whipple Museum for the History of Science and the Sedgewick Earth Science Museum. She co-organises the virtual conference Space Science in Context (2020, 2023), which has been noted in NASA decadal reviews for its gender-inclusive practices.

The Bawaka Collective (also known as the Gay'wu Group of Women) is an Indigenous and non-Indigenous, more-than-human research collective. The collective is led by Bawaka Country and includes human authors Dr. Laklak Burarrwanga, Ritjilili Ganambarr, Merrkiyawuy Ganambarr-Stubbs, Banbapuy Ganambarr, Djawundil Maymuru, Kate Lloyd, Sarah Wright, Lara Daley, and Sandie Suchet-Pearson.

Bawaka Country is the diverse land, water, human, and non-human animals (including bäru and the human authors of this chapter), plants, rocks, thoughts, and songs that make up the Yolŋu homeland of Bawaka in North East Arnhem Land, Australia.

Black Quantum Futurism (BQF) was co-founded by Rasheedah Phillips and Camae Ayewa in 2016 as a new approach to living and experiencing reality by way of the manipulation of space-time in order to see into possible futures, and/or collapse space-time into a desired future in order to bring about that future's reality. This vision and practice derive its facets, tenets, and qualities from quantum physics and Black/African cultural traditions of consciousness, time, and space. Through various writing, music, film, visual art, and creative research projects, BQF Collective also explores personal, cultural, familial, and communal cycles of experience and solutions for transforming negative cycles into positive ones using artistic and holistic methods of healing. BQF's work focuses on recovery, collection, and preservation of communal memories, histories, and stories.

Phillip Brooker is a Lecturer in Sociology at the University of Liverpool. He is currently working on a project about NASA's Skylab 3 mission with a focus on work-related disputes and has created the podcast *Living and Working in Space* as part of his research process.

Victor Buchli is Professor of Material Culture within the Material Culture Group at University College London. Victor is PI of the ERC-funded project ETHNO-ISS. His research focuses on the new material culture and manufacturing economy emerging in low Earth orbit. Victor's previous interests have been the anthropology of architecture and the material culture and architecture of utopian planning in the Soviet Union and post-socialist Kazakhstan.

Giles Bunch is a social anthropologist and PhD student at UCL. His research focuses on the training of Flight Controller teams and the culture of human spaceflight at the European Space Agency (ESA). In his fieldwork at ESA-affiliated centres in Germany, he is exploring themes of simulation and creativity, organisational structure, and time.

Dr Laklak Burarrwanga is a Datiwuy Elder, Caretaker for Gumatj, and eldest sister. As such she has both the right and the cultural obligation to share certain aspects of her knowledge and experiences with others. She has many decades' experience sharing this knowledge with children and adults through teaching, art, and tourism. She is a senior member of the Bawaka Collective and the Gay'wu Group of Women.

Dana Burton is an anthropologist who investigates scientists' search for evidence of life in outer space and how they imagine, theorise, and evaluate this evidence in their mission-related work. Her fieldwork follows scientists, documents, microbes, and machines across the Atacama Desert, Chile, NASA facilities, and interplanetary space. Dana's work was funded by Wenner-Gren Foundation, National Science Foundation, and Society for the History of Technology.

Paola Castaño is a sociologist and a Research Fellow at the Egenis Centre for the Study of Life Sciences at the University of Exeter. Her research focuses on the International Space Station as a platform for science, and her book *Beyond the Lab: The Social Life of Experiments on the International Space Station* is in process of completion.

Lara Daley is a Research Fellow in Human Geography at the University of Newcastle. Her research engages Indigenous-led geographies and ongoing colonisation in urbanising and changing environments. She is a member of the Bawaka Collective and Yandaarra, two Indigenous-led collaborations with a focus on Indigenous sovereignties and Indigenous-led ways of caring for Country and addressing socio-environmental change.

Katarina Damjanov is a Senior Lecturer in Digital Media and Communication Design at the University of Western Australia. Katarina's research revolves around considerations of the changing relationships between humans, technologies, and environments. Some of her work situates these inquiries in outer space and features in journals such as *Science, Technology & Human Values*, *Environment and Planning D*, *Leonardo*, and *Mobilities*.

Katheryn M. Detwiler is a Teaching Assistant Professor of Science and Technology Studies at the Stevens Institute of Technology. Her research explores how contemporary and emerging data practices forge intersections among computing and prospecting, cosmology and instrumentality, and mineral extraction and astronomical observation in Chile's Atacama Desert.

Krystal De Napoli is a Gomeroi author, astrophysicist, and science communicator devoted to the advocacy of Indigenous knowledges and equity in STEM. She is co-author of *Astronomy: Sky Country* (Thames & Hudson, 2022), which explores the significance of astronomy in Aboriginal and Torres Strait Islander knowledge systems. Krystal is the host of the weekly radio programme *Indigenuity* on Triple R 102.7 FM (Melbourne), where she holds conversations with Aboriginal and Torres Strait Islander knowledge holders to platform their ingenuity.

Contributors

Daniela de Paulis is a media artist working internationally and a licensed radio operator. Her artistic practice is informed by space in its widest meaning. Since 2009 she has been implementing radio technologies in her art projects. She is currently the recipient of the Baruch Bloomberg Fellowship in Astrobiology at the Green Bank Observatory in West Virginia. She is a member of the IAA SETI (Search for Extraterrestrial Intelligence) Permanent Committee.

Oliver Dunnett is a Senior Lecturer in Human Geography at Queen's University Belfast specialising in cultural, historical, and political geography. His research focuses on the ways in which the cultures and politics of outer space, science, and technology are connected to questions of place, landscape, and identity in a variety of local, regional, and (inter-)national contexts. He is the author of *Earth, Cosmos and Culture: Geographies of Outer Space in Britain, 1900–2020* (Routledge, 2021).

Alejandro Ezquerro-Nassar recently completed a PhD in Psychology at the Consciousness and Cognition Lab, University of Cambridge (2021). His research involves the use of EEG and statistical modelling techniques to investigate the neural-cognitive dynamics of the sleep onset period as well as the phenomenology of hypnagogic states. He also serves as Research Impact Manager for Dream in Cosmos, generating and maintaining collaborations between researchers and artists.

Réka Patrícia Gál is a PhD candidate at the Faculty of Information at the University of Toronto (Canada) and a Fellow at the McLuhan Centre for Culture and Technology. Her work brings together feminist media theory, decolonial technoscience, and environmental history to explore how technological tools and scientific methods are employed to purportedly solve socio-political problems. She is the co-editor of *Earth and Beyond in Tumultuous Times: A Critical Atlas of the Anthropocene* (meson press, 2021).

Banbapuy Ganambarr grew up at Guluruŋa. She is a bilingual student who completed her degree at Bachelor College through the Northern Territory University. Banbapuy is now a Senior Indigenous Teacher at Yirrkala School. She is an influential author, artist, weaver, and teacher. She is a senior member of the Bawaka Collective and the Gay'wu Group of Women.

Ritjilili Ganambarr is a second eldest daughter, a Datiwuy elder, and caretaker for Gumatj. She works hard on health issues in the community and is passionate about working with mothers and children—teaching and educating them that strong mothers create strong children. She is a weaver and writer/illustrator. She is a senior member of the Bawaka Collective and the Gay'wu Group of Women.

Merrkiyawuy Ganambarr-Stubbs is a proud Yolŋu woman and leader from North East Arnhem Land. She has written six books. Her children's books are written in Yolŋu Matha for use in primary schools as Walking Talking Texts. She plays an important role in the bilingual education movement in Arnhem Land working with Yolŋu Elders to develop both-ways learning. She is a senior member of the Bawaka Collective and the Gay'wu Group of Women.

Jenia Gorbanenko is a PhD candidate in anthropology at UCL. She specialises in the nascent field of anthropology of religion in space. Prior to joining the ETHNO-ISS project, Jenia's research focused on the post-Soviet religious revival in Russia. In her doctoral research, she interrogates the Russian Orthodox Christian perspective on space exploration.

Contributors

Carla Guedes is a passionate and experienced anthropologist, Sydney-based Scientia PhD Candidate at the University of New South Wales, and cultural astronomy researcher. With over two decades' experience in communications, journalism, copywriting, and creative direction, Carla has dedicated her career to the exploration of culture, diversity, communication, and creativity.

Duane Hamacher is an Associate Professor of Cultural Astronomy at the ARC Centre of Excellence for All Sky Astrophysics in 3 Dimensions (ASTRO 3D) and the School of Physics at the University of Melbourne. Duane researches cultural astronomy, dark sky studies, astronomical heritage, and the history and philosophy of science and wrote the trade book *The First Astronomers: How Indigenous Elders Read the Stars* (Allen & Unwin, 2022). He serves as Secretary of the International Society for Archeoastronomy and Astronomy in Culture (ISAAC), as Chair of the International Astronomical Union's (IAU) Working Group on Ethnoastronomy & Intangible Heritage, and serves on the IAU Working Group for Star Names.

Chelsea Haramia is an Associate Professor of Philosophy at Spring Hill College and a Senior Research Fellow at the University of Bonn, Germany. She is the author of several articles and book chapters on space ethics and the search for extraterrestrial intelligence, and she is currently conducting research for the collaborative project between the Universities of Cambridge and Bonn titled *Desirable Digitalisation: Rethinking AI for Just and Sustainable Futures*.

David Jeevendrampillai is an anthropologist of outer space. His research focuses on emerging notions of planetary citizenship with particular reference to Earth imagery from the International Space Station. He is a postdoctoral researcher on the ETHNO-ISS project and is the Director of the Centre for Outer Space Studies at UCL.

Anne W. Johnson is a Professor in the Graduate Program in Social Anthropology at the Universidad Iberoamericana in Mexico City. Her research interests include the social study of science and technology, the anthropology of the future, performance, memory, and material culture. Her current project, based on research with the Mexican Space Agency, a space instrumentation laboratory, and various art collectives, revolves around Mexican imaginaries of outer space and the future.

Evie Kendal is a bioethicist and public health researcher in the School of Health Sciences and Biostatistics, Swinburne University of Technology, Australia. Evie's research interests include ethical dilemmas in emerging biotechnologies, space ethics, and public health ethics.

Adryon Kozel is an anthropologist and PhD candidate at UCL Anthropology. Her research examines the ways in which communities of space enthusiasts emerge and how people relate to place, science projects, and extreme environments through the virtual. Her research interests include the anthropology of outer space, diverse narratives of the future, storytelling, virtual reality, digital co-presence, enthusiasm, home, place, and identity.

Bruno Latour (1947–2022) was a philosopher, sociologist, and anthropologist. Member of several academies, he was the recipient of the Holberg Prize in 2013 and the Kyoto Prize in 2021. He was especially known for his work in the field of science and technology studies (STS). After teaching at the École des Mines de Paris (Centre de Sociologie de l'Innovation) from 1982 to 2006, he became Professor at Sciences Po Paris (2006–2017), where he was the scientific director of the Sciences Po Medialab. He was the author and editor of more than thirty books and published more than one hundred and fifty articles, notably *Laboratory Life* (with Steve Woolgar, 1979), *Science in Action* (1987), *We Have Never Been Modern* (1993), *Facing Gaia* (2017), and *Down to Earth* (2018).

Kate Lloyd is an Associate Professor in Human Geography at Macquarie University. Kate's work focuses on several projects which take an applied, action-oriented, and collaborative approach to research characterised by community partnerships, co-creation of knowledge, and an ethics of reciprocity. She is a member of the Bawaka Collective and the Gay'wu Group of Women.

Alessandra Marino works as Senior Research Fellow in International Development within AstrobiologyOU. Her research addresses how postcolonial and decolonial studies can contribute to current debates on knowledge production within space science. She also explores how space technologies are designed and used in international development programmes funded by space agencies. She has been a Co-Principal Investigator on two UKSA-funded projects and is involved in other projects on space research and policy.

Ralo Mayer is an artist and filmmaker based in Vienna. His research-based works delineate ecologies on Earth and beyond through multilayered storytelling across various media. In his artistic research PhD on "Space Un·Settlements", Mayer explored a range of examples of humans living in outer space in fiction, scientific speculation, and actual experiments.

Djawundil Maymuru is a Maŋgalili woman raised by a Gumatj elder. She is a Yolŋu mother and grandmother from the beautiful homeland of Bawaka in North East Arnhem Land. She is a co-author of three books and works with Bawaka Cultural Experiences, a highly successful Yolŋu-owned and -run Indigenous tourism business. She is a member of the Bawaka Collective and the Gay'wu Group of Women.

Rrawun Maymuru comes from a long line of Yolŋu songmen from Yirrkala in North East Arnhem Land and his songs reflect a love for Country and culture as well as his distinct perspective on the modern world. In 2012, Rrawun was awarded the G. R. Burarrwanga Memorial Award for best new talent at the National Indigenous Music Awards. Rrawun also fronts the Aboriginal rock band, East Journey. In the Songspirals exhibition, Rrawun sings and shares the Guwak Songspiral. He is Wäŋa Wataŋu, the custodian of the songspiral, and it is his responsibility to care for this songspiral through his father, who is from the Maŋgalili clan.

Naminapu Maymuru-White is a contemporary artist of the Maŋgalili clan whose homeland is at Djarrakpi at the base of Cape Shield, the northern perimeter of Blue Mud Bay, Arnhem Land in the Northern Territory. Naminapu's work references Maŋgalili country, and particularly the 'outside story' or origin story of the Maŋgalili using the miny'tji or sacred clan design for the sandscapes of Djarrakpi. The outside story places the night sky and sea at the centre, whereby the soul's journey from life to death to rest to rebirth is conducted through water. The night sky is an astral body of water where Maŋgalili souls, both deceased and yet to be born, are seen today in the Milky Way.

Tony Milligan is a UK-based researcher and author. He holds a DPhil from Oriel College, Oxford, and is currently a Visiting Researcher at Cambridge University's Centre for the Study of Existential Risk. He studies the history of ideas: primarily the ways changing theories about the wider universe have transformed human self-conceptions and practical priorities throughout the past, as a building sense of our placement within wider ranges of space and time has been pieced together.

Contributors

Thomas Moynihan is a UK-based researcher and author. He holds a DPhil from Oriel College, Oxford, and is currently a Visiting Researcher at Cambridge University's Centre for the Study of Existential Risk. He studies the history of ideas: primarily the ways changing theories about the wider universe have transformed human self-conceptions and practical priorities throughout the past, as a building sense of our placement within wider ranges of space and time has been pieced together.

Karlie Alinta Noon is a Gamilaroi astronomer and science communicator working with audiences around Australia for the past decade promoting Indigenous astronomical knowledge systems and advocating for more women and girls in STEM. Karlie is co-author of *Astronomy: Sky Country* (Thames & Hudson, 2022) and co-host of ABC's astronomy podcast *Cosmic Vertigo*, and was the first Aboriginal woman in Australia to graduate with combined degrees in mathematics and physics. She has an advanced Masters of Astronomy and Astrophysics and is currently undertaking a PhD in Astrophysics at the Australian National University.

Valerie A. Olson is an environmental anthropologist and Associate Professor of Anthropology at the University of California at Irvine. Her projects focus on the political ecologies of outer space, ocean subsurfaces, and watersheds. She serves on UCI interdisciplinary research teams and campus initiatives such as Water UCI, the Salton Sea Initiative, the UCI OCEANS Initiative, and the UCI Community Resilience programme.

Aaron Parkhurst is an Associate Professor of Biosocial and Medical Anthropology at UCL. His current projects include an ethnography of the human body on board the International Space Station and the complex networks of life-science research conducted on the ISS. He works at the intersection of health, wellbeing, and culture, with a focus on chronic illness, bioethics, the intersection of technology and the human body, and outer-space studies. He is editor of the journal *Anthropology and Medicine*.

Julie Patarin-Jossec holds a PhD in Sociology and is a lecturer, professional diver, light aircraft pilot, photographer, and documentary filmmaker. Her dissertation, the first ethnographic study of the International Space Station, included three years of fieldwork at ESA, CNES, and Roscosmos, archival research, and interviews with astronauts/cosmonauts. She has taught at French and Russian universities and has led several research or technical committees dedicated to visual politics or habitability in outer space. In 2022, she became a certified professional technical diver to expand her academic skillset for analysing astronauts' activities and the operational challenges of space exploration.

Rasheedah Phillips is a lawyer, housing policy advocate, parent, and interdisciplinary artist. Phillips is the founder of The AfroFuturist Affair, a founding member of Metropolarity Queer Speculative Fiction Collective, co-founder of Black Quantum Futurism, and co-creator of the Community Futures Lab. As part of BQF and as a solo artist, Phillips has been a CERN Artist Resident, Vera List Center Fellow, Knight Arts + Tech Fellow, Pew Fellow, and A Blade of Grass Fellow.

Istvan Praet is an anthropologist based at Durham University. He has regional expertise in Latin America, where he worked with Chachi Indigenous people in Ecuador. More recently, he has conducted ethnographic research with astrobiologists and planetary scientists. He focuses on how the sciences are being rethought for the Anthropocene and has a particular interest in how scientists remake objectivity itself.

Contributors

Lauren Reid is a PhD candidate in social and cultural anthropology at the Freie Universität with the research project "Thinking Beyond the Final Frontier: Cosmic Futures in Thailand". Her research interests include anthropology of outer space, the Anthropocene, posthumanism, animism, futures, PSI experiences, and decolonial theory. Lauren is additionally an independent curator, Co-director of the curatorial collective 'insitu', and a Lecturer in Curatorial Practice at Node Centre for Curatorial Studies.

Álvaro Santana-Acuña is an Associate Professor of Sociology at Whitman College, where he teaches courses in cultural sociology, social theory, political sociology, and the sociology of big data. He is the author of *Ascent to Glory: How* One Hundred Years of Solitude *Was Written and Became a Classic* (Columbia University Press, 2020).

Fred Scharmen teaches architecture and urban design at Morgan State University's School of Architecture and Planning. He is the co-founder of the Working Group on Adaptive Systems, an art and design consultancy based in Baltimore, Maryland. His work circles around questions about how and why we make spaces for the future, and who is invited into them. His books include *Space Settlements* (Columbia University Press, 2019) and *Space Forces* (Verso 2021). His writing has appeared in the *Journal of Architectural Education*, *New Geographies*, *Places Journal*, *Atlantic CityLab*, *Slate*, *Log*, *CLOG*, *Volume*, and *Domus*.

Fabian Schmidt is a scientific staff member (Forschungsgruppenleiter) at the Max Planck Institute for Astrophysics, Garching (near Munich), Germany. He is interested in all aspects of cosmology, but particularly in using large-scale structures to learn about gravity, dark energy, and the early universe.

J. S. Johnson-Schwartz is an Associate Professor of Philosophy at Wichita State University who specialises in the philosophy and ethics of space exploration. She is author of *The Value of Science in Space Exploration* (Oxford University Press, 2020), editor (with Tony Milligan) of *The Ethics of Space Exploration* (Springer, 2016), and editor (with Linda Billings and Erika Nesvold) of *Reclaiming Space: Progressive and Multicultural Visions of Space Exploration* (Oxford University Press, forthcoming).

Wes Sharrock is an Emeritus Professor at the University of Manchester, UK. He has spent his entire career since 1965 in sociology until his retirement in 2017 at the University of Manchester. His main interests have been in the philosophy of social science and in ethnomethodology, and he has published widely on issues of sociological principle and empirical research in these areas.

Deondre Smiles (Leech Lake Band of Ojibwe) is currently an Assistant Professor in the Department of Geography at the University of Victoria, in British Columbia, Canada. His research interests lie at the intersection of several fields, including critical Indigenous geographies, human–environment interactions, political ecology, tribal cultural resource preservation, and science and technology studies. Other academic interests include Indigenous geographies of outer space, Indigenous futures, research ethics with Indigenous communities, and interdisciplinary collaborations, including with scholars in fields such as rhetoric, linguistics, history, and quantitative social science.

Sandie Suchet-Pearson is an Associate Professor in Human Geography at Macquarie University in Sydney. Her research and teaching experiences over the last twenty years have been in the area of Indigenous rights and environmental management. She is a member of the Bawaka Collective and the Gay'wu Group of Women.

Peter Swanton is a Gamilaraay man and astronomer at The Australian National University. Peter's work in astronomy initially began with research around black holes and cosmology, but he has since shifted his focus to cultural astronomy and dark sky preservation. Peter's work looks to highlight the scientific importance of Indigenous star knowledges and what we need to do in order to preserve these knowledges on Country, as well as in the night sky.

Anna Szolucha is the Principal Investigator of the ARIES (Anthropological Research into the Imaginaries and Exploration of Space) project at the Institute of Ethnology and Cultural Anthropology at the Jagiellonian University in Krakow, Poland. Her research interests focus on the intersections of natural resources, technology, and society. Her current project investigates the role of space resources and technologies in creating and sustaining imaginaries of 'multiplanetary' communities. She is the author of *Real Democracy in the Occupy Movement* (Routledge, 2016) and editor of *Energy, Resource Extraction and Society: Impacts and Contested Futures* (Routledge, 2018).

A. R. E. Taylor is a Lecturer in Communications at the University of Exeter and a Marconi Fellow in the History and Science of Wireless Communication at the University of Oxford. He works at the intersection of social anthropology and science and technology studies and his research focuses on the material infrastructure that underpins internet and space services. He is Editor of the *Journal of Extreme Anthropology* and co-founder of the Social Studies of Outer Space network.

Makar Tereshin is an anthropologist, documentary photographer, and a PhD candidate at UCL, where he is part of the ETHNO-ISS project. His doctoral research focuses on the political ecology of the Russian space programme, space debris, and communities affected by space launches from the Baikonur Cosmodrome in Central Kazakhstan.

Fionagh Thomson is a visual ethnographer, human geographer, ecologist, and philosopher. She explores how we move through and make sense of our everyday world, drawing on the objects/tools we find around us, including our bodies/senses. Fieldwork includes rainforests, peatbogs, hospitals, microscope labs, and astronomical observatories. Currently, Fionagh is a Senior Research Fellow in Physics, at Durham University, UK (Centre for Extragalactic Astronomy; Centre for Advanced Instrumentation).

Natalie B. Treviño is a postdoctoral researcher at the Open University, UK, where she studies the ethics of space exploration. Her primary work examines the colonial production of human in the modern space–earth ecosystem.

Nicola Triscott, PhD, is a contemporary art curator, writer, producer, and administrator. She is currently Director/CEO of FACT Liverpool, the UK's leading organisation for the support and exhibition of art, film, and new media. Her curatorial work and research focuses on the intersections between art, science, technology, and society. Previously, she was the founding Director of the art and research organisation Arts Catalyst (1994–2019).

Saskia Vermeylen is a socio-legal scholar and curator, who studies and critiques property theories. She finished a Leverhulme Fellowship on space law and utopian literatures and is currently working on a monograph on utopian and dystopian arts practices and space law. In 2022, she curated the international exhibition EXTR-Activism: Decolonising Space Mining at Kunsthalle Exnergasse in Vienna.

Lucianne Walkowicz is an astronomer and co-founder with Erika Nesvold of the JustSpace Alliance, an organisation established in 2018 to advocate for a more inclusive and ethical future in space. They study the ethics of space exploration, stellar magnetic activity, how stars influence a planet's suitability as a host for alien life, and how to use advanced computing to discover unusual events in large astronomical data sets. They are a practising artist, working in a variety of media, from performance to sound, and until 2022 an astronomer at the Adler Planetarium in Chicago.

Justin St. P. Walsh is an Associate Professor of Art History and Archaeology at Chapman University. He has co-directed the International Space Station Archaeological Project since 2015 and is an invited expert member of the International Astronautical Federation's Space Habitat Technical Committee.

B.D. White is a New York-based artist who entered the art scene by painting hundreds of streetlight bases throughout New York City. Despite his spinal injury, he earned a reputation as a prolific street artist using spray paint and stencils as his main medium. He has shown in group exhibitions in New York, Los Angeles, Las Vegas, Chicago, Miami, and Berlin and his continued work on the streets of New York has garnered him a strong and growing collector base.

Sarah Wright is a Professor of Human Geography at the University of Newcastle. She is a member of the Bawaka Collective and the Gay'wu Group of Women. She also works in the Philippines with a network of subsistence organic farmers and is part of Yandaarra, a Gumbaynggirr-non-Gumbaynggirr collective seeking to shift camp together to care for and as Country where she lives on Gumbaynggirr Country on the mid-north coast of New South Wales.

ACKNOWLEDGEMENTS

This book was inspired by the confluence of many people across several places in Australia, Chile, the United States, and France and as part of many conversations over several years which coalesced around the annual meetings of the Society for Social Studies of Science (4S) in Sydney in 2018 and in New Orleans in 2019. From initial musings at these events Juan Francisco Salazar and Paola Castaño conceived this book together and invited Alice Gorman as co-editor. We are infinitely appreciative of Paola and her spearheading vision during the first stages of assembling this book during the Covid-19 pandemic.

We wish to thank Lucianne Walkowicz for offering an inspiring foreword to the book and to Rasheedah Phillips for generously allowing us to reprint an excerpt of their work. We are immensely grateful to Frédérique Aït-Touati and Bruno Latour for sharing glimpses of their performance collaboration as part of our book. We pay our respects to the late Bruno Latour who passed away during the final stages of editing of this book while both editors were in Paris.

The cover image is a digital manipulation of a photograph taken by Juan Francisco Salazar in December 2018, of an original graffiti artwork by B.D. White in The Bowery, Manhattan. We are most grateful to B.D. White for the permission to use his work in this way. Our profound gratitude goes of course to all the contributors who worked caringly with us in the development of this collective volume and for their generous time and thought-provoking chapters, which contribute in significant ways to advancing these fertile fields of social studies of outer space, space humanities, and space art.

Our most sincere appreciation to our academic editor, Mona-Lynn Courteau, who provided expert and caring editing, copyediting, and proofreading services for all the chapters. She is an outstanding, patient, caring, and creative collaborator who engaged way beyond the duties of a copyeditor, and without whom this book might not have seen the light of day.

We wish to thank Routledge's editorial team for their support of our project, especially Dr. Meagan Simpson, Editor, Anthropology; Eleanor Catchpole Simmons, Editorial Assistant, Gender Studies; and Katherine Ong, former Editor, Anthropology & Religion (Research).

We are very thankful to those who have offered feedback on this project over the years, to the anonymous reviewers and the many wonderful endorsements the book has received.

Juan Francisco Salazar

This book was supported with funding from an Australian Research Council Future Fellowship (FT190100729 [25/05/2020–24/05/2024]). I am grateful to the Fondation Maison des Sciences de l'Homme (FMSH) in Paris, for supporting my work through the DEA Programme 2022. The School of Humanities and Communication Arts and the Institute for Culture and Society at Western Sydney University (WSU) have been my academic home for the past twenty-five years. I sincerely thank my colleagues at WSU: Heather Horst, Peter Hutchings, Gay Hawkins, Katherine Gibson, Brett Neilson, Ned Rossiter, Hart Cohen, Matt McGuire, Alison M. Downham Moore, Rachel Morley, Liam Magee, Tsvetelina Hristova, Terence Fairclough, Flora Zhong, Michelle Kelly, Cheryl D'Cruz, Simone Casey, and Sally Byrnes. I have benefited immeasurably from ongoing conversations with a range of academics and artists, especially Steven Freeland, Ceridwen Dovey Clemencia Rodríguez, Céline Granjou, Matthew Kearnes, Marisol de la Cadena, Manuel Tironi, Sarah Pink, Victoria Hunt, Jason de Santolo, Flora Vilches, Cirecie West-Olatunji Lisa Stefanoff, Elisa Tironi, Sebastián Martín-Valdez, and Robert Nugent. And foremost and everywhen, to the bright stars that always shine in my night sky, Alejandra Canales, Dominga Salazar, and Martina Salazar.

Alice Gorman

I would especially like to acknowledge the inspiration and contributions of Paola Castaño in shaping our vision for new approaches to space humanities and social sciences in this book. Justin Walsh has been my research collaborator for many years and discussions with him have been an important part of my thinking about space cultures. I'd also like to thank my colleagues Heather Burke, Lynley Wallis, Sumen Rai, Claire Smith, Jane Lydon, Ian Moffat, Ralo Mayer, and Amy Roberts, who have always been ready to listen to my musings about space.

1
SOCIAL STUDIES OF OUTER SPACE
Pluriversal Articulations

Juan Francisco Salazar and Alice Gorman

The Space Conjuncture

At a crucial moment of cascading planetary-scale political, health, and ecological crises, when precarity has become the condition of our time, questions emerge around the possibilities and prospects of human individuals, groups, or communities living, working, reproducing, and being in orbit and in outer space. Over the past two decades a second space age and a new 'space race' have noisily kicked off, shouldering brusquely on against the context of the Covid-19 pandemic, unrelenting social and political unrest triggered by ongoing forms of racism and colonialism, growing inequalities, and a life-threatening acceleration of climate breakdown recorded across the entire planet.[1]

In spite of these arresting conditions, since the late 1990s, under the auspices of economic liberalism and globalisation, there has also been a strident push to commercialise and militarise space (Geppert et al. 2021). This renewed intensification of space activities and decisions continues to be based on a narrow set of market values in which space is a resource frontier[2]—values that are still driven by geopolitical rivalry, national prestige, and scientific practices that have yet to fully shift away from understandings of space as a place to be 'conquered', as a quest for finding other planets to 'settle', as a 'hunt' for life in the universe.[3] In the last thirty years, around five hundred humans—mostly male and white—have travelled to space and lived temporarily in orbit. Spacecraft orbit Earth from upper reaches of the atmosphere to more than 36,000 km away—only a few thousand kilometres less than the circumference of Earth. They also orbit the Moon, Sun, Venus, Mars, and several other celestial bodies. Robotic instruments rove the surface of Mars. Landing sites exist on the Moon, Mars, Venus, Titan, asteroids, and comets. As of 2022 when this book was being assembled nine missions are being proposed and developed to return to the Moon as early as 2024. And this time, it is to develop space habitats for humans. A lunar orbiting space station, the Lunar Gateway, is in the works, and the logistics and infrastructures to extract lunar resources, including oxygen and water, are in an advanced state of development. A Mars sample-return (MSR) mission is also being developed with the purpose of collecting rock and dust samples on Mars and bringing them to Earth by the end of this decade.

While the scientific value of understanding past life on Mars is not in question, by the end of this decade life on Earth might well be unrecognisable. In late October 2022 several United Nations agencies warned there was "no credible pathway to 1.5°C … in place" (UNEP 2022) and that urgent and collective action is imperative to cut down emissions by about half by 2030 to meet the internationally agreed target of a temperature rise limit of no more than 1.5°C. This appears against record profits gained in 2022 and 2023 by fossil fuel companies and more rockets are launched into space than ever before.

We chose two images to introduce the volume to illustrate these predicaments. First is the cover image, which draws on political art techniques as well as the history of the term *glitch* associated with the early space-age infrastructures in Earth's lower orbit and in outer space. The image uses software data manipulation and databending to glitch an original photograph taken in December 2018 by Juan Francisco Salazar of an original graffiti artwork created by artist B. D. White in The Bowery, Manhattan, around the corner from the iconic CBGB music club, now turned into a clothing store.[4] Second, we chose the well-known artwork *Space Refugee II* by British-Nigerian artist Yinka Shonibare CBE. (Figure 1.1) The 'refugee astronaut' is a metaphor for environmental breakdown, a critique of race, and an exploration of Nigerian cultural heritage, subverting the notion of space exploration as a white endeavour. It can be read as the participation of diverse communities of peoples in space sciences and discovery. For Shonibare, the figure is both a warning and a celebration. Clothed in traditional Nigerian textiles, it is a nomadic astronaut seeking a place that's still habitable. On Earth. Off-Earth. The refugee astronaut dislocates the colonial figure of the astronaut and the cosmonaut. It is not on a quest to conquer space. It is a nomad in space-time finding a place to make a home in times of rising water levels and the mass displacement of people.

Our purpose in this introductory chapter is not to trace the genealogies of social studies of outer space. Since the 1990s, an outstanding body of original work on outer space has emerged and crystallised across the social sciences, humanities, engaged planetary sciences, and contemporary art.[5] Our purpose is rather to offer an overview of emerging openings and challenges across cultural and social studies of outer space and the nascent interdisciplinary field of space humanities, by introducing the key topics that the diversity of contributors in this book brings together through a range of critical responses and apertures to space studies. As a compendium of contemporary critical thinking and critical making, this collection of chapters is a call to attend more carefully to the ways in which we craft engagements with outer space, and space futures, empirically, affectively, aesthetically, and theoretically. This broad body of work loosely assembled around the notion of social studies of outer space often examines critically the convergent and divergent tendencies shaping power relations in the broad field of outer space. Much of this work, however, continues to be produced, read, and exhibited within discrete, often unconnected fields of knowledge production and knowledge making. We argue that a different set of "pluriversal articulations" (Kothari et al. 2019: xxviii) are needed to rethink outer space in relation to current predicaments on Earth. By pluriversal articulations we mean perspectives which may illustrate empirical research work, artistic experimentation, political theorisation, activism, and policy-making from around the world, to counter modernist colonial, capitalist, and racial perspectives of universalism in space—what sociologist John Law (2015) has called "the one-world world"—and to illustrate that other worlds are possible, both in outer space and on Earth—what Zapatista communities in Mexico have called 'Un Mundo Donde Quepan Muchos Mundos' ('A World Where Many Worlds Fit'). This book is a small step in that direction, as an invitation to think aloud together about other kinds of futures in space that could be enacted.

This is the 'conjuncture' that this *Routledge Handbook of Social Studies of Outer Space* addresses. In reference to Stuart Hall's use of the term, this book aims to offer an analysis of the make-up of the particular political-ecological conjunctures of outer space at the beginning of the twenty-first century. Tony Bennett notes that for Stuart Hall a conjuncture is "both a moment of danger and one of opportunity; it is something to intervene in, a configuration whose components were to be rearranged through practice. It [is] a call to action—intellectual, social, cultural, political" (Bennett 2016: 284). Drawing on Farhana Sultana's analysis of approaches in political ecology to power relations across scales, a conjunctural approach to outer space may

Figure 1.1 *Refugee Astronaut II*, 2016. Yinka Shonibare CBE. Fibreglass mannequin, Dutch wax printed cotton textile, net, possessions, astronaut helmet, moon boots, and steel baseplate. 210 × 90 × 103 cm. © Yinka Shonibare CBE. All rights reserved, DACS/Artimage 2022. Image courtesy James Cohan Gallery. Photo: Stephen White & Co.

bring to the fore "processual and interconnecting factors, exposing the contours of uneven differentiations and coproductions, while offering possible alternative futures" (2021: 1721) of and in outer space.

Practices of Spacemaking—Stories of Outer Space So Far

Through this conjunctural approach, each contribution in the book provides insights into what we call here 'practices of spacemaking'. These are essential parts in the production of sociotechnical and socioecological imaginaries of outer space, and of novel subjectivities, both inside and outside the unequal and caustic social and power relations organised by capitalism. The book is therefore conceived as an ensemble of perspectives that converge but also diverge. It also attempts to underscore the polysemic nature of outer space. There is no single definition of where outer space begins. For some, Earth ends, and outer space starts, just above the mesosphere, at a point called the Kármán line, some one hundred kilometres above the planet's surface. For others, this boundary is a little bit lower, in the mesopause, which is the outermost physical boundary of Earth's atmosphere, where meteors typically burn up. And of course, the atmosphere itself expands and contracts with variations in solar weather. Technically, the International Space Station is still within the atmosphere in its orbit at about four hundred kilometres above Earth. The boundary between Earth and space is relevant for demarcating the territory of aeronautical law from space law but in other areas, the distinctions between Earth and space are starting to make less and less sense. The polysemic nature of outer space entails that space does not have the same meaning for everyone.

As a project to intervene in the current political-ecological space conjuncture, this book aims to bring to the fore the urgency of questioning how the hegemonic formations of outer space might be broken apart, and be given new meanings and political directions. Michael Oman-Reagan's (2017) points out that "as venture capitalist space entrepreneurs and aerospace contractors compete to profit from space exploration, we're running up against increasingly conflicting visions for human futures in outer space". Therefore, this book highlights this need for imagining a diversity of futures in space while querying those frameworks that reproduce ongoing historical harms from the exploitation of people and nature on Earth.[6]

A core orientation for us has been to generate a space of conversation, dialogue, and debate, across a diversity of disciplines, practices, and perspectives, around how we might better calibrate our academic, scientific, and artistic work towards biocentric, sustainable, caring, just, and inclusive approaches to outer space. As such, this book was assembled through a process of curation and driven by an impulse to establish a dialogue among the authors, researchers, and artists hereby included and their interlocutors. A dialogue, Deborah Bird Rose observes, is an "intersubjective exchange of ideas, stories, empathy, imagery, and much more" (Rose 2015: 127). Affirming its holistic intent, the title of this book takes this same framing of 'social studies of outer space' but expands it to related interdisciplinary fields in space humanities, art–science collaborations, critical Black and Indigenous studies, and contemporary space art and space visual cultures. As Lisa Messeri posited in her landmark book *Placing Outer Space*, social studies of outer space seek to understand "what the cosmos can tell us about ourselves" (2016: 16). But this 'ourselves' needs to be unpacked and undone to acknowledge ongoing questions of colonialism, racism, sexism, and ableism in space affairs. This move to see off-Earth spaces as a site for diverse forms of social science, ethnographic, and humanities enquiry has contributed to critical efforts to destabilise western, humanist, extractivist engagements with the pervasive narrative of space-as-frontier. This work has opened up multiple lines of enquiry that demonstrate both the interrelation between the development of off-Earth science and technologies—and the imaginaries that anticipate the prospects of both privatised space exploitation and state-backed military-industrialisation of extraplanetary spaces—and contemporary geo- and ecopolitics.

Anna Tsing (2003) demonstrated long ago how in the last two decades of the twentieth century the formation of new 'resource frontiers' across the world was made possible by Cold War militarisation and the growing power of corporate transnationalism, where "resource frontiers grew up where entrepreneurs and armies were able to disengage nature from its previous ecologies" (p. 5100). This is precisely the work at play today in outer space as it is inexorably rendered as a new resource frontier.

What seems striking, though, across this growing body of work in the social studies of outer space is the degree to which the construction of outer space as a "site of sociality" (Messeri 2016: 17) relies on, and indeed reinforces, a universalising figure of the human. What is notable in much of this literature—and indeed broader literatures that address human planetary sociality—is a referent human subject; that we have always been in space; that space is already occupied by an amorphous human subject. Here the tensions between the imagined *we* invoked to produce a depiction of space as already human and therefore implicitly social—indeed to resist the more radical claim of the inhumanness of off-Earth spaces (Clark 2011; Yusoff 2015)— and what Yusoff (2016) terms the "universalising impetus of the Anthropocene" appear clear. Clark's provocation to attend to Earth's inhumanness, to "come to terms with a planet that constantly rumbles, folds, cracks, erupts, irrupts" (2011: xiv), also extends to the cosmos. As Gorman puts it:

> Despite the common perception of space as a vacuum, it is a rich and complex environment. Beyond the atmosphere are high energy cosmic rays emanating from the far reaches of the galaxy, the constant stream of sub-atomic particles that is the solar wind, charged clouds of high temperature gases, swarms of meteors, and atoms of hydrogen, helium and oxygen.
>
> *(Gorman 2014: 89)*[7]

Inspired by the influential work of geographer Doreen Massey, we invite readers to engage with these chapters as 'stories of outer space so far', where a return to the Moon and voyages to the expanse beyond will require a new terrestrial, grounded, geologic politics both on and off Earth. These stories of outer space so far may allow us to remake worlds on Earth, in a period of ecological breakdown, one which US science fiction writer and cultural theorist Kim Stanley Robinson portrayed in his novel *2312* (2012). In the novel, the character of Charlotte, a historian, defines the period of 2005–2060 as "the Dithering", to describe our current epoch as "a state of indecisive agitation" over climate change, and the failure to preempt what came next: the 2060–2130 period known as "the Crisis" (Robinson 2012: 144–45; see also Salazar et al. 2017).

In her book *Into the Extreme: U.S. Environmental Systems and Politics Beyond Earth*, Valerie Olson (2018) notes a lack of critical attention to "outer space as environment" (p. 30) in the social sciences. She sees this as an effect of a "surface bias" that fails to "adequately account for the post-terrestrial scaling of social ecological and economic space" and calls for analysis to engage with the fact that space is "known as an environment that links Earth and space weather, as a system of forces, and low Earth orbit is considered polluted by orbital technology debris" (p. 30). Gorman (2005b) has pointed out that this lack of attention has consequences in how industry sees its responsibilities towards the environmental management of Earth orbit, arguing that the concept of space as an environment is very poorly developed.

A polysemic understanding of outer space thus entails taking note of the intricately entangled vertical political ecology that traverses from Earth's inner core and mantle, through and across Earth's oceans and surfaces, up into lower Earth orbit, further on to the Moon, and into deep space. As Bruno Latour suggests in his book *Down to Earth* (2018), instead of an abstract and only horizontal version of a ground criss-crossed by lines as on a map, we must deal rather with a vertical ground, which limits (and delimits) human ambitions quite differently.

Space as Method

This *Handbook* approaches outer space as a site and as a research object, but not only. Drawing from the work of Marisol de la Cadena (2018), we highlight the potential emergences that come to challenge what we know about outer space, the ways outer space is known, and even, as de la Cadena would suggest, the impossibility of knowing outer space.[8] Second, drawing on the work of political theorists Sandro Mezzadra and Brett Neilson, we invite readers who engage with this book to regard outer space as an epistemic framework. Taking up Mezzadra and Neilson's proposal to attend to borders as method (2013), we are also interested in the expediency of space as method in ways that enable new perspectives on the accelerating current phase of space activities, in order to reassess the cultural, social, and political concepts we use and associate with space. We are tempted to ask whether outer space is not so much a new frontier as a new border,[9] a border along Earth's orbit full of space debris and space junk, "the spread of our scorched-earth habits into space" (Ellery 2019). Space as a manufactured border now extends into outer space concurrently with new and ongoing borders proliferating on Earth as a product of the deeply heterogeneous space and time of global capitalism (Mezzadra and Neilson 2013). We are also tempted to think with Mary Louise Pratt here and see outer space as an emergent "contact zone", not only as a resource frontier and as more than a border—a site where "cultures meet, clash and grapple with each other, often in contexts of highly asymmetrical relations of power, such as colonialism, slavery, or their aftermaths" (Pratt 1991: 34). For archaeologists, the contact zone results in hybrid expressions of materiality where everyday objects are mobilised into supporting or subverting social hierarchies and power dynamics (Rubertone 2000). The border is spatial but also personal at the level of individual interactions across it.

Understanding outer space as method is also a provocation to highlight the violence of colonialism and racism that still envelops so much work on and in space. Paraphrasing Farhana Sultana we might speak of the "unbearable heaviness" (Sultana 2022) of space coloniality.[10] As astrophysicist Chanda Prescod-Weinstein (2021) observes in relation to decolonising the space sciences, "[s]cience has instead wholeheartedly embraced the view that intent matters more than historical context or impact". This is something that astronomer Lucianne Walkowicz has also advocated in some of her recent work and which she presents in the Foreword to this book. Decolonising planetary sciences towards multiplanetary ethics, for Walkowicz, is a question of social justice in space, and a political act of reclaiming the notion of justice from ongoing co-optation as a way to highlight urgent processes of collective imagination for inclusive futures.

The contrasting, often dissimilar, yet mutually intelligible chapters across the volume all propose grounded insights into recent advances in space research by simultaneously urging us to reorient politics towards the 'terrestrial'. Imagining space futures implies also thinking-with Earth, as a broad body of work and scholarship in feminist theory, critical Indigenous studies, and science and technology studies have shown, where scientific practices affect and are affected by questions of race, ethics, politics, and justice in the production and reproduction of social, political, and ecological imaginaries. This book project of thinking-with space is also based on an assumption about deep connectivity between humans and Earth and between Earth and the cosmos. Deeper understandings of the cosmos must involve processes of re-earthing. Prospects of humans making themselves at home off-world are deeply connected to ongoing inequalities across human societies on Earth. How else might we think of human habitation in space at a time of crises of habitation on an Earth becoming ever less hospitable to most forms of life? We can't inhabit the cosmos until we learn to remember how to coinhabit on Earth, or, as Bruno Latour eloquently put it in some of his last works, until we crash land back on Earth, to come to terms with living bound to Earth (Latour 2017). Futures in space can't continue to be imagined and anticipated without tackling reparations for colonialism and slavery in an age of climate breakdown, allowing for practices of reparations as worldbuilding, as Olúfẹ́mi O. Táíwò proposes in his work *Reconsidering Reparations* (2022), in reference to the too many peoples who have inherited the moral liabilities of past injustices.

Structure of the *Handbook*

The book curation involved a process of working athwart disparate disciplines and knowledge practices, engaging with emerging and established academics, artists, and curators who were invited to think across theory, method, and practice transversely and intersectionally.[11] Not all chapters easily coexist, and not all chapters are concerned with these issues we hope to bring to the fore in this introduction. Many of the chapters would usually not be read together in one single volume. In this book, they 'take place' within an epistemic trading zone that we as editors have created to offer a non-essentialist, non-normative yet dynamic theoretical and empirical proposal to glance outwards, inwards, and sideways towards life in space.

The *Handbook* contains 38 Chapters divided into five parts which are preceded by a foreword by astronomer Lucianne Walkowicz. Each section begins with moments of interference, and disruption; with five invited intrusions.

Fields

The first section is *Fields*. It opens with a very unique intervention across the fields of history of science, theatre, and philosophy featuring a series of photographs and excerpts from *Trilogie Terrestre*, a programme of three lecture-performances cowritten by theatre director and historian of science Frédérique Aït-Touati and philosopher Bruno Latour, who make the stage a place for "scenic essays" and philosophical experimentation.[12] The images and texts by Aït-Touati show Latour on stage between 2016 and 2021 reflecting on the critical zone and surface of the Earth and the surface of Mars, drawing a parallel between the old Earth and this new moving Earth through the figure of Gaia and the work of Margulis, and drawing a lesson from viruses to explore the Earth as an entanglement of living beings.

This section is followed by eight chapters by renowned scholars of outer space who offer diverse critical-analysis provocations around research methods and approaches, across anthropology, space archaeology, geography, sociology, space ethics, and space art.

In "Re-fielding: On More-Than-Terran Spaces", Valerie Olson shows how social scientific research is being 're-fielded' to include transplanetary and stellar fields. She surveys methods, problems, innovations, and politics addressing the more-than-terran dynamics of geopolitics and place-making, racial hierarchy and empire, Indigeneity and colonisation, and the enclosures and openings of experimentation and sovereign becoming.

Archaeology is a field-based discipline, and thus extending it into outer space, where it is impossible to work 'in the field', has posed a new challenge. Alice Gorman, in "Space and Time Through Material Culture: An Account of Space Archaeology", reviews methods used to counter this limitation, and describes the value of taking an archaeological approach to understanding the nature and distribution of human materials throughout the solar system.

Istvan Praet argues in his chapter "Anthropology and Contemporary Space Exploration, with a Note on Hopi Ladders" that an outstanding characteristic of the emerging field of outer space studies is the radical breaking of boundaries between social and natural scientists. Scholars in outer space studies have refused to accept the convention that they have nothing to say about 'the cosmos itself'. Praet characterises off-Earth anthropologists as "metaphysical troublemakers" emboldened by the realisation that their colleagues in the natural sciences can no longer safely ignore them.

In "Planetary Ethnography in a 'SpaceX village'", Anna Szolucha unpacks the notion of planetary ethnography as an approach that aims to bring forth ethnography's potential to challenge hermetically closed meanings, accepted theories, and power relations. Szolucha uses ethnographic material from the diverse and multivocal terrain that is the village of Boca Chica, where SpaceX has been developing its new spaceship, to show how paying attention to the planetary perspective of their research can bring researchers close to the promise of ethnography. This topic has acquired renewed attention after the explosion of SpaceX's Starship rocket in April 2023, with debris affecting surrounding state parks, National Wildlife Refuge lands and the fact that Boca Chica is central to the creation story of the Carrizo/Comecrudo Nation of Texas where communities are often cut off from their ancestral lands by SpaceX's facilities.

Oliver Dunnett, in "The Spaces of Outer Space", explores geographical approaches to understanding the social, cultural, political, and environmental meanings of outer space, and how outer space relates to Earthly spaces. He focuses on the key geographical concepts of place and landscape, mobility, and circulation. Finally, he proposes future directions for geographical research into outer space.

Paola Castaño and Álvaro Santana-Acuña, in "Sociological Approaches to Outer Space", ask which subfields of sociology have taken outer space as an object of inquiry, what specific aspects and units of analysis have been examined, which types of methodological and theoretical approaches have been incorporated in these studies, and what kinds of interventions within and outside the discipline these studies have enabled. They outline future research agendas and some challenges for the role of sociologists.

Tony Milligan and J. S. Johnson-Schwartz in their chapter "Space Ethics" summarise the origins of space ethics within the space community, with professional philosophers and ethicists joining the discussion more recently.[13] Typical concerns include space mining; risk, disclosure, and justice in space; and iconic topics such as the settlement and terraforming of Mars. Milligan and Johnson-Schwartz highlight the importance of ongoing ethical engagement at all stages of space exploration programmes.

Contemporary space art also features in important ways in this volume.[14] We invited a series of contributions from space artists and curators who discuss their aesthetic and critical responses to themes of outer space and space exploration, and how these might contribute but also disrupt ingrained understandings of humans' relations to the cosmos. Focusing on recent works by several internationally recognised contemporary artists, art curator, and author Nicola Triscott, in her chapter "Other Worlds, Other Views: Contemporary Artists and Space Exploration", explores how contemporary artists' aesthetic and critical responses to themes of outer space and space exploration interweave histories and imaginaries of space with contemporary thought, drawing out four main lines of inquiry: decolonisation, Afrofuturism, Indigenous perspectives, and planetarity. The perspective developed here by Triscott is further developed—from different perspectives—in the chapters by Gál and Armstrong, Vermeylen, Salazar, Treviño, Noon et al., and Smiles.

Intersectional Interventions

The second section is titled *Intersectional Interventions* and opens with a well-known and generative text by the collective Black Quantum Futurism (BQF) titled "As Above, So Below: Space and Race in the Space Race". BQF is an exceptional multidisciplinary collaboration between Camae Ayewa (Rockers!; Moor Mother) and Rasheedah Phillips (The AfroFuturist Affair; Metropolarity) exploring the intersections of futurism, creative media, DIY aesthetics, and activism in marginalised communities through an alternative temporal lens. Originally published as part of the *Black Space Agency* art exhibition and community programme in 2018, this work by BQF is inspired by the legacy of the Fair Housing Act, the Civil Rights and Black Liberation movements, and the space race in North Philadelphia during the 1960s. When Rev. Leon H. Sullivan, a civil rights leader and minister at Philadelphia's Zion Baptist Church, established Progress Aerospace Enterprises (PAE) shortly after the death of Martin Luther King Jr. in 1968, PAE was one of the first Black-owned aerospace companies in the world.

The international space community in recent years has recognised that the human future in space is not served well by the entrenchment of a white, heteronormative monoculture. In 2016 the International Astronautical Federation developed the 3G platform (Geography, Generation, Gender) to address equality and diversity. Nonetheless, the pace of change is slow: the number of women in the space sector, for example, has not risen above 20% globally. Planetary scientists and astronomers have also entered the debate with notable interventions in the field of the ethics of space observation and space exploration. Emily Martin et al. for instance, in the current context of expansion in private industry-led space exploration, argue that "as the population of Earth's orbital environment and human exploration of space intensifies, it is critical to have a strong ethical framework in place so that mistakes of the past are learned from and not repeated" (Martin et al. 2022: 641). For Tavares et al. the planetary sciences must engage in a "robust reevaluation" of how discussions about crewed and uncrewed missions to the Moon, Mars, and elsewhere in the solar system ought to "resist colonial structures" and their rootedness in the violence of colonialism that has served exploration off-Earth (Tavares et al. 2020). In the incisive work *The Disordered Cosmos*, Prescod-Weinstein (2021) shows how her cosmological work is in part a product of a form of settler colonialism that asserts control over territory by replacing its Indigenous population and manufacturing a disconnection of Indigenous knowledge from its larger cosmology. A growing number of scientists, artists, scholars, and activists alike are vigorously calling for a substantial and emancipatory shift in the way space exploration is spoken and written about (Walkowicz in Drake 2018). As Prescod-Weinstein (2021) puts it,

> Perhaps the way we think about the universe can still provide a way to step outside of our usual language and think abstractly about our society. We must have care in making this kind of move; there is always the potential for misrepresentation.
>
> (p. 99)

The section is then followed by five chapters, starting with "A Chronopolitics of Outer Space: A Poetics of Tomorrowing", where Juan Francisco Salazar argues that outer space is not only a topos but also a chronos of production of capitalist value and imaginaries of the future. Centring their analysis on the expediency of the notion of 'futurity' as an epistemic angle, they describe different narrative framings that articulate the horizons of space exploration. On the one hand are the neoliberal imaginaries grounded in linear temporalities that enact and enforce a commoning spatio-temporal strategy for anticipating space futures; on the other are differing modes of counter-futuring—Black, Indigenous, feminist, and queer futurisms—which variously transform, refuse, and contest hegemonic imaginaries by setting in motion uncommoning tactical interventions that point to a different and emancipatory chronopolitics of outer space.

Aspects of this discussion are taken up in more detail and depth by Réka Patrícia Gál and Eleanor S. Armstrong in their chapter "Feminist Approaches to Outer Space: Engagements with Technology, Labour, and Environment". They demonstrate how feminist methods, theories, and analysis reveal how intersecting social hierarchies—including gender, race, and class—have been affected by and reinforced through the space sciences, engineering, and space-related popular culture. They focus on labour, technology, and the environment as areas of feminist intervention.[15]

In the chapter "The Iconography of the Astronaut as a Critical Enquiry of Space Law", Saskia Vermeylen contends that despite the recognition of how race matters in the space 'race', barely any attention has been given to the silencing of women and people of colour in space law. This chapter juxtaposes astronauts as envoys of humankind with afronauts as harbingers of lost and regained utopias. Focusing on the iconography of the afronauts' spacesuits, Vermeylen exposes how spacesuits simultaneously are sites of critique but also embody hope for a more inclusive, just, and progressive body of space law.

Evie Kendal in the chapter "Diversity in Space" argues that astronaut selection criteria generally exclude the differently abled or those with mental health issues. Women, people of colour, and older candidates are underrepresented among space travellers and astronomers.[16] Kendal then considers the contribution these different groups can and do make to the space sector, focusing on the importance of real and fictional role models to inspire the next generation of workers in the space industry.

This section ends with a special type of intersection across art and science with an interdisciplinary project exploring the poetic and philosophical aspects of transitional states of consciousness during sleep. In their chapter "*Mare Incognito*: Live Performance Art Linking Sleep with the Cosmos through Radio Waves", artist Daniela de Paulis with colleagues Thomas Moynihan, Alejandro Ezquerro-Nassar, and Fabian Schmidt share their reflections on *Mare Incognito*, a series of live performances poetically highlighting the gradual dissolution of consciousness and of the thinking process while falling asleep, shifting from the subjective to the cosmic perspective. During each performance, the brain activity of sleep is transmitted into space in real time by an antenna of the Square Kilometre Array in Cambridge, United Kingdom.

Colonial Histories/Decolonial Futures

The third Section is titled *Colonial Histories/Decolonial Futures* and comprises six Chapters following an opening essay by Bawaka Country titled "Celestial Relations with and as Milŋiyawuy, the Milky Way, the River of Stars". Through the paintings reproduced in the chapter and their story, Bawaka Country shares ongoing Yolŋu connections with and as Milŋiyawuy that challenge dominant imaginaries of 'outer' space and its exploration. They show why celestial relations, as Milŋiyawuy points out, with respect to existing laws, protocols, beings, and systems of relations already inhabit the night sky.

In Australia, Indigenous astronomers have a continuous tradition of scientific knowledge and stories based on precise observation of the skies dating back at least thirty thousand years. Many astronomical discoveries which have been attributed to western astronomers in the last few centuries were in fact long known. As shown by Duane Hamacher in *The First Astronomers* (2022) and by Krystal De Napoli and Karlie Noon in their book *Astronomy: Sky Country* (2022), oral traditions by Aboriginal and Torres Strait Island peoples in Australia describe rare phenomena, such as solar eclipses, meteorite impacts, and supernova, that only occur on a timescale of hundreds to thousands of years. As Lempert (2021) notes, centring Indigenous astronomies amidst current "astro-colonialism" is crucial for decolonising outer space, which needless to say entails challenging colonial assumptions and ethical protocols within astronomy as a scientific practice.[17]

This third section continues with "Coloniality and the Cosmos", where Natalie Treviño contends that it is coloniality, rather than curiosity, that lies at the heart of westernised conceptions of space exploration. The future that mostly US-centric space advocates envision simply reproduces the norms, systems, and myths of oppression and violence of the European colonial order. This cosmic order separates nature from humanity, enforces a hierarchy of humans, and renders nature, and those denied personhood, fully exploitable.

Next is "Safeguarding Indigenous Sky Rights from Colonial Exploitation", where astronomers Karlie Noon, Krystal De Napoli, Peter Swanton, Carla Guedes, and Duane Hamacher engage with how Indigenous and Black communities have fostered deep cultural and intellectual connections to the sky since time immemorial. The authors show how Indigenous sky rights are fundamental for safeguarding traditional knowledge and heritage. These engaged cultural astronomers poignantly illustrate in their chapter how human connection to the cosmos is increasingly being affected by the loss of dark skies due to the ongoing colonial exploitation of land, sea, sky, and space. This has particularly damaging effects as Indigenous cultures, land rights, and knowledge systems such as identity, knowledge, relationships, and survival are dependent on being able to see the stars.

Continuing this theme, Deondre Smiles critically interrogates settler colonial logics of space exploration in the chapter "Anishinaabeg in Space" by directly comparing these logics to

Indigenous conceptions of outer space exploration. Rather than subscribing to the myth that human exploration of outer space is necessary due to environmental degradation, this chapter works against both the 'inevitability' of ecological collapse and the accompanying impetus to look to the stars for humanity's salvation, challenging society to reflect on why we go to space, and how we might be able to do so in an ethical manner.[18]

Continuing with the chapters in this section, in "Reconstellating Astroenvironmentalism: Borders, Parks, and Other Cosmic Imaginaries", Alessandra Marino shifts the discussion on coloniality to the notion of orientalism to examine the spatial imaginaries of what she terms astroenvironmentalism. Marino contends that bordering processes, the encircling of parks, and the use of wilderness thinking are colonial tools of earthly governance that have been exported into outer space and raises questions about the possibility that colonial tropes and modes of environmental management can initiate a more just relationship with space.

Persisting in this topic, Katheryn M. Detwiler describes how large-scale mining and astronomical observation in Chile come to interact on the terrain of optimisation and automation—of extraction, on the one hand, and observation, on the other. In the chapter "Earthless Astronomy, Landless Datasets, and the Mining of the Future", Detwiler points to the production of complex, large, and mobile astronomical datasets at the ALMA observatory, to argue that not only are astronomical datasets not "free" but also that, in an optimisation economy, extraction is optimised, not displaced.

The last chapter in this section is "Divergent Extraterrestrial Worlds: Navigating Cosmopractices on Two Mountaintops in Thailand", where Lauren Reid explores cosmic aspirations, plans, and imaginaries within Thailand's emergent space-interested communities. Drawing on grounded ethnographic fieldwork among Thai scientific, religious, and creative communities, including the National Astronomical Research Institute of Thailand and the extraterrestrial-believer group UFO Kaokala, Reid describes how as Thailand's first astronomical institute opens and space science and space entrepreneurism there rapidly expand, Buddhist and animist ontologies are offering alternatives to pervasive colonial and western metaphysical approaches to outer space.

These chapters in one way or another all investigate how perspectives on space environmentalism are growing (Marino and Cheney 2022). Many of these point to how space colonisation is entwined within an "extractive gaze" (Gómez-Barris 2017) where evangelical dreams of humanity becoming an interplanetary species depend on moons, planets, asteroids, and any other celestial bodies to become just another territory of extraction under some form of capitalism. As Julie Klinger (2021a) reminds us, human engagement with outer space is a problem of environmental justice, where the "environmental geopolitics of Earth and outer space are inextricably linked by the spatial politics of privilege and the imposition of sacrifice—among people, places, and institutions" (p. 667). As she notes,

> On Earth, environmental (in)justice unfolds on multiple scales: local and stratospheric emissions from space launches, the placement of outer space related infrastructure in so-called peripheral places, and the role of power in determining whether the use of such infrastructure aids socio-environmentally constructive or destructive practices.
>
> (p. 676)

Writing on similar themes, Micha Rahder (2019) asserts that "privatized space research mobilizes fears of ecological, political, or economic catastrophe to garner support for new utopian futures, or the search for Earth 2.0" (p. 158), an argument echoed by Richard Tutton, who describes how these "'extraplanetary imaginaries' ... [are] situated at the nexus of two opposing futures that feed into each other: one characterized by sociotechnical optimism and the other by a planetary pessimism about global environmental change" (2021: 439).[19]

Objects, Infrastructures, Networks, and Systems

Part 4 is *Objects, Infrastructures, Networks, and Systems* opens with an visual intervention by Juan Francisco Salazar who experiments with a series of digital photomontages using an artificially intelligent (AI) text-to-image generator. The section then follows with another four chapters. From parallel perspectives, all are concerned with the objects, infrastructures, networks, and systems shaping practices of spacemaking. All in one way or another deal with what Gál et al. (2021) call 'space media', to refer to "technologies, techniques, ways of knowing, and modes of existence that bring humans into contact with outer space… [and] the means by which human and outer space are bound together" (p. 645). It is relevant to point out that data from the early generation of satellites following the International Geophysical Year of 1957–1958 was the first ever to be collected at a global scale, creating what might be termed a "satellite gaze". Data derived from satellites in Earth orbit has been integral to "the very apprehension of what is now being called the 'anthropocene'" (Gorman 2014: 87). Over seventy years the human material-culture footprint in orbit has become substantial. The Space Age has transformed the way humans live on Earth. Earth's orbit is becoming a new border. However, this orbital divide is not so neatly defined along national borders. For Justin St. P. Walsh, Alice Gorman, and Wendy Salmond (2021) this marks the "emergence and evolution of a particular kind of space station culture with implications for future habitat design" (p. 804).

The first chapter of the section is "Preparing for the 'Internet Apocalypse': Data Centres and the Space Weather Threat", where A. R. E. Taylor shows how, over the last decade, space weather has become a key target of critical infrastructure protection efforts. Drawing from fieldwork and tracing the expanding security cosmology of critical infrastructure protection, Taylor examines how the space weather threat is being addressed in the data centre industry and how it is rendered as both a threat and a marketing opportunity.

From a different perspective, Katarina Damjanov begins the next chapter with a brilliant provocation. Various beings and things have left the Earth, often never to return. In the chapter "Space Infrastructures and Networks of Control and Care", Damjanov analyses how great efforts are taken to keep them safe and sound amidst the perils of space. The precarious circumstances of these space envoys propel the evolution of more-than-planetary networks of control and care, conditioning the manners and means by which human societies pursue their prospects "out there".

Continuing with a focus on satellites, and based on ethnographic and documentary sources, Anne Johnson describes in the chapter "Mexico Dreams of Satellites" how satellites occupy a privileged place within the imaginary and the practices of the so-called "space community" in Mexico as fundamental elements in infrastructural assemblages that connect and co-construct subjects and objects.

The section ends with the chapter "Space Codes: The Astronaut and the Architect", where Fred Scharmen invites us to seek out the hidden rules that make space visible by surveying existing recommendations, regulations, codes, and standards that apply to the design and construction of human habitable spaces in outer space.

Cultures in Orbit/Life in Space

The fifth and last section is *Cultures in Orbit/Life in Space*.[20] It opens with a commissioned photographic intervention by Julie Patarin-Jossec titled *Cosmic Waters*, a series of black-and-white photographs and text linking underwater worlds and outer-space worlds.[21]

The section includes another nine chapters beginning with "Unearthing Biosphere 2, Biosphere 2 as Un·Earthing", where artist Ralo Mayer looks at Biosphere 2, the closed ecological system experiment conducted in the early 1990s as a test for future crewed space inhabitation. Through methods of artistic research, and proposing the notion of "un·Earthing" as the transformations that humans undergo when leaving Earth, Mayer examines how this unique experiment at the intersections between science, technology, and culture displays narratives and storytelling of possible trajectories of human life in space.

In "Living and Working in 'The Great Outdoors': Astronautics as Everyday Work in NASA's Skylab Programme", Phillip Brooker and Wes Sharrock look at how NASA's post-Apollo vision, beginning with Skylab, aimed to develop space stations that would not only sustain human life but also afford a large populace a means of living well and undertaking productive work—in short, that would make space an everyday (social) setting.

This section includes contributions from some of the most renowned social researchers currently writing about the International Space Station (ISS) and spearheading novel research projects on orbital cultures. The ISS is humanity's most expensive piece of infrastructure ever built. It is a "large-scale space ecosystemic object" (Olson 2018: 30) and "a singular outpost of the species at the very edge of our planetary environment" (Damjanov and Crouch 2019: 77). The ISS is also one of two occupied space stations in low Earth orbit, the other being the first module of the Chinese station Tiangong, which launched in April 2021 and is crewed intermittently as it develops. Launched in 2000, the ISS will be decommissioned by the end of the 2020s, marking a new era of space stations and orbit culture. NASA plans to develop further commercial space stations following an earlier proposal by Axiom Space, which may well be the "first attempts to create places for humans to live and work in space outside the framework of government space agencies [representing] a major shift in how space will be used" (Walsh and Gorman 2021).

The first of three concurrent Chapters on the International Space Station is "Adapting to Space: The International Space Station Archaeological Project", where Justin St. P. Walsh discusses the International Space Station Archaeological Project (ISSAP), the first full-scale, systematic archaeological investigation of material culture from a site of human activity in space. This chapter tells the story of ISSAP from concept to execution, providing a view into the reality of space archaeology as a social science in the early twenty-first century.

This is followed by another project, ETHNO-ISS, where David Jeevendrampillai, Victor Buchli, Aaron Parkhurst, Adryon Kozel, Giles Bunch, Jenia Gorbanenko, and Makar Tereshin look at the ISS for its invaluable insights into fundamental questions at the heart of the social sciences. As the authors argue in their chapter "An Ethnography of an Extraterrestrial Society", the ISS affords the opportunity to critically reexamine our terrestrially based theories regarding such things as religion; cosmology; transcendence; territoriality; habitability, infrastructure, and architecture; materiality; and the body and technology.

From a different yet related perspective, Paola Castaño in the chapter "Plant Biologists and the International Space Station: Institutionalising a Scientific Community" provides a sociological characterisation of scientific work, a long-standing object of interest in social studies of science, describing analytically how to conceptualise communities of scientists working with living plants in the ISS.

Moving on from the ISS, the next chapter, "Whiteboards, Dancing, Origami, Debate: The Importance of Practical Wisdom for Astrophysicists" by Fionagh Thomson, continues Paola Castaño's interest in working with scientific communities. Drawing on ethnographic fieldwork with astrophysicists and instrument scientists, Thomson offers an alternative view of how these communities make sense of the world 'up and out there', with a focus on temporary, dynamic interactions, through technologies and the importance of being human and getting it wrong.

The section then continues with two chapters on astrobiology and the search for extraterrestrial life. First, Dana Burton in the chapter "Astrobiology and the Immanence of Life amidst Uncertainty" poses core questions about life and asks what possibilities are immanent in moments when science cannot claim a result with certainty. Her chapter is an invitation to imagine the encounter of Viking and Mars during the 1976 NASA mission to search for life.

Chelsea Haramia in the chapter "Understanding the Question of Whether to Message Extraterrestrial Intelligence" also posits a fundamental philosophical question about whether we should be trying to communicate with aliens, questioning both the issue of the referents involved—of 'we' and 'aliens'—and the issue of the message itself. As she contends, not all messages are created equal.

This section and the volume wrap up with Alice Gorman's essay "A Post-Geocentric Gravitography of Human Culture", which examines the role of gravity in shaping human culture. Gorman speculates about the required adaptations in bodies, material culture, and social forms that gravity environments beyond Earth's surface impose.

Conclusions

The chapters hereby curated offer only a glimpse into the many themes and perspectives across a wide-ranging body of work. All established and emerging authors across the social studies of outer space, space humanities, and space art were invited not only to think about space but to *think-with* it. Through this programme of thinking-with, we seek to underline how concerns and hopes around outer space call for an urgent reimagination of humanity's place—and humanity's time—in outer space. This entails an interrogation of who counts and is counted in this notion of humanity. With the aim of contributing to this expanding, increasingly urgent, interdisciplinary formation of sociocultural research, this book wishes to intervene critically and productively in ongoing political debates, engaging with outer space as part of an entangled cosmic ecology. This is crucial at a critical moment of cascading and overlapping planetary-scale political unrest, health pandemics, and ecological breakdown. And it entails resisting the notion that the politics of outer space are decoupled from Earthly politics and a recognition of a need to slow down the reasoning about the future shape of space exploration and the socionatural relations this engenders. Neoliberal subjectivities, the language of frontiers and extraction, and the accelerated temporalities of NewSpace all overshadow the urgency of developing a different awareness of the problems and situations rallying us towards outer space. This reassessment is crucial to offer a shift in understandings of space and ways of reorienting an ethics of caring for space as environment, as cosmos, to ramp up the critique of framings of space as a resource frontier where outer space 'territories' also become, as Martín Arboleda argues in *Planetary Mine* (2020), "geographies of extraction … entangled in a global apparatus of production and exchange that supersedes the premises and internal dynamics of a proverbial world system of cores and peripheries defined exclusively by national borders" (p. 5).

While characterising current research practices and outlining future research agendas, this much-needed recalibration certainly exceeds the chapters contained in the volume. A plethora of work in the social sciences, the humanities, the arts, and engaged space sciences are opening profound questions of inclusion, race, equity, and sustainability around the contested topics of space exploration and life off-Earth. As outer space has become an arena where stratified and spatialised terrestrial socioeconomic, environmental, and political relations are expanding (Battaglia, Valentine, and Olson 2015), this book develops a foundation for interdisciplinary dialogue grounded in novel perspectives and old dilemmas, with critical interventions in a wide range of debates about the social and political histories and futures of and in outer space. The volume therefore represents a comprehensive effort to contribute to more systematic and materially sensitive engagements with space, bringing into dialogue theoretical and empirical contributions, art practices, and case studies across several regions and disciplines. Ultimately, this book is designed as an opportunity to think both creatively and earnestly, not only about the space in which we live and are part of but also about space worlds yet to come.

Notes

1 Almost twenty years ago Alice Gorman characterised the 'Space Race' model as

> a popular and compelling version of space history, [where] the interests of largely white male American astronauts, space administrators, scientists and politicians are presented as universal human values. The military, nuclear, nationalist and colonial aspirations of space-faring nations are eclipsed by a 'master narrative' in which heroic acts of discovery in space are the outcomes of a natural human urge to explore.
>
> (Gorman 2005a: 86)

2 Here we draw on Anna Tsing, for whom "frontiers are projects in making geographical and temporal experiences ... made of visions and vines and violence ... [that] reach backward as well as forward in time energising old fantasies, even as they embody their impossibilities" (2003: 5100).

3 This is clear in NASA's articulation of its new Artemis missions. On its website NASA proclaims:

> With Artemis missions, NASA will land the first woman and first person of color on the Moon, using innovative technologies to explore more of the lunar surface than ever before. We will collaborate with commercial and international partners and establish the first long-term presence on the Moon. Then, we will use what we learn on and around the Moon to take the next giant leap: sending the first astronauts to Mars. We're going back to the Moon for scientific discovery, economic benefits, and inspiration for a new generation of explorers: the Artemis Generation. While maintaining American leadership in exploration, we will build a global alliance and explore deep space for the benefit of all.
>
> (NASA 2022)

4 See Salazar's space glitch intervention in this volume.

5 It is important for us to acknowledge some of the seminal work that informs this *Handbook* and several of the chapters in it, even as we can't do justice to this growing body of work. Edge and Mulkay (1976) produced one of the first detailed sociological studies of the development of radio astronomy in Britain. During the 2000s sociological studies of space-related activities also emerged through work on the "cosmic society" (Dickens and Ormrod 2007) and "astrosociology" (Pass 2006) and the ground-breaking work of Janet Vertesi (2014; 2020). Alexander C. T. Geppert, in the introduction to *Imagining Outer Space: European Astroculture in the Twentieth Century* (2012), similarly sought to frame space ideologies as a particular form of culture, addressing the question: "How did the idea of outer space, spaceflight and space exploration develop over the course of the twentieth century into a central element of the project of Western and in particular European modernity?" (p. 6). Related work around this time also includes environmental historian Peder Anker's (2005) work on the ecological colonisation of space. Magoroh Maruyama and Arthur Harkins's 1975 *Cultures Beyond Earth: The Role of Anthropology in Outer Space* was a very early effort to think outer space anthropologically. Early ethnographic accounts developed in Europe with work such as Stacia Zabusky's *Launching Europe: An Ethnography of European Cooperation in Space Science* (1995). By the late 1990s anthropologist Peter Redfield developed a body of work that examined the colonial contexts of space exploration in French Guiana in *Space in the Tropics* (2000). Positioning his critique at the intersection between postcolonial studies and science studies, Redfield's work was among the earliest to develop a contemporary critical approach to social studies of outer space. Redfield's interests lay in 'provincialising' outer space, unmasking the "colonizing impulse" that has dominated narratives of space exploration since the 1950s. For the past twenty years, the anthropology of outer space has become a booming field of theorising and ethnographic critical description. The works of Stefan Helmreich (2009, 2012, 2017), Valerie Olson (2018), and David Valentine (2012; Valentine, Olson, and Battaglia 2009, 2012) are paramount in this field. Some of this is captured in Praet and Salazar (2017). In the Foreword to that special issue, Stefan Helmreich (2017) offers a partial genealogical tracing of some of the many lineages of social studies of outer space. He argues that the special issue might work for the readers as a novel wrinkle in space—where he uses wrinkle, following the *Oxford English Dictionary*, as "a crease, fold, or ridge caused by the folding, puckering, or contraction of a ... pliant substance," "a minor difficulty or irregularity", "a clever or adroit expedient or trick", or "a piece or item of useful information, knowledge, or advice". See also Savannah Mandel (2021). Tamara Álvarez et al. (2019) argue that from the 1980s science and technology studies (STS) research developed alongside the emergence of the 'space sciences'. This work also developed alongside—and in reference to—foundational work in STS, such as Donna Haraway's 1989 *Primate Visions: Gender, Race, and Nature in the World of Modern Science* or Sandra Harding's 1993 edited volume *The 'Racial' Economy of Science: Towards a Democratic Future*. Work

in political geography and political ecology has also been extensive and wide-ranging (Beery 2012; Dunnett et al. 2019; Macdonald 2007; Sage 2008; Klinger 2021a, 2021b). Since the early 2000s archaeologists began turning their gaze upwards to examine the material culture of space through the study of lunar landing sites (O'Leary 2009; Spennemann 2004), orbital debris (Gorman 2005b), and Indigenous intersections with space at terrestrial launch sites (Gorman 2007). These studies analysed how material culture related to ideologies of space travel and contributed to the formation of distinct space cultures.

6 Julie Klinger's work has been instrumental within a new field of work at the intersection of environmental geopolitics and outer space demonstrating how these "are inextricably linked by the spatial politics of privilege and the imposition of sacrifice—among people, places, and institutions" (Klinger 2021b: 667).

7 Gorman goes beyond this to also describe the effects of human-induced changes on the composition of interplanetary space. She notes how

> The interpolation of spacecraft has added elements, minerals and molecules that are not 'naturally' found in interplanetary space. The most common material in spacecraft manufacture is aluminium, the third most abundant element in the Earth's crust, but absent in the predominantly hydrogen/helium environment of space. Other common materials are titanium, carbon fibre composites, silicon in photovoltaic cells, fuels such as hydrazine, nickel and cadmium used in batteries. If the anthropocene on Earth has involved the redistribution of elements such as carbon and nitrogen, this is also true of the movement of elements from terrestrial environments into space.
>
> (2014: 89)

8 de la Cadena uses the term *not only* as an ethnographic concept. We use it here conceptually, as she does, in relation to the incommensurability of outer space, to perform ontological openings towards the historically unthinkable, or that which challenges the established real.

9 See Praet and Salazar (2017) for a discussion of frontiers as borders of a very specific kind where Earth is being transformed into a "natural laboratory" of sorts, allowing scientists to experiment with and theorise about alien life. For Praet and Salazar, "while borders are conventionally portrayed as spaces of profound, intimate, flowing interaction, frontiers both recapitulate and challenge borders, such as those between nature and culture or between science and art" (p. 310).

10 Farhana Sultana is speaking here about the "unbearable heaviness of climate coloniality" that "seeps through everyday life across space and time, weighing down and curtailing opportunities and possibilities through global racial capitalism, colonial dispossessions, and climate debts" to work against "the reproduction of ongoing colonialities through existing global governance structures, discursive framings, imagined solutions, and interventions" (2022: n.p.).

11 We evoke here the work of Stefan Helmreich, for whom an approach that works athwart theory is one where theory is thought of "neither as set above the empirical nor as simply deriving from it but, rather, as crossing the empirical transversely" (2011: 133).

12 This work started in 2016 with the lecture-performance INSIDE, followed in 2019 by Moving Earths and in 2020 by VIRAL. See https://www.zonecritiquecie.org/trilogie-terrestre for more information on the project as a reflection on the need for a profound renewal of our representations of the terrestrial world, biotic and abiotic. See also Frédérique Aït-Touati and Bruno Latour, *Trilogie Terrestre* (Éditions B42, 2022) where the authors reflect on why the major cosmological upheaval we are currently experiencing cannot do without the introduction of a new character, Earth, or Gaia, onto the world stage.

13 See also work in this field by Baird Callicott (1986), Arnould (2001), Livingston (2003), Milligan (2013), Rolston (1986), and Williamson (2003).

14 French art curator and author Annick Bureaud, director of Leonardo/Olats, observes that the first space art–related article in *Leonardo*, "On the Visual Fine Arts in the Space Age" by Frank Malina, was published in 1970. Since its inception in 1968, *Leonardo* has shown a special interest in space art, firstly because "it is a perfect example of the tumultuous, sometimes difficult, always challenging relations between art, science and technology" (Bureaud 2005: 374). Contemporary space art (Malina 1991) is today troubling the pervasive hegemonic narratives coming out of space evangelists and entrepreneurs that insist on how the 2020s will be recognised as the decade humans transitioned into a truly spacefaring species that utilises space resources to survive and thrive both in space and on Earth (Triscott 2016; Vermeylen 2021; King 2022).

15 The "queering" of outer space allows for an interrogation of prevalent and recalcitrant heteronormative assumptions that may move beyond an "inclusion and diversity" framing of LGBT space researchers and space workers. Michael Oman-Reagan calls for the need to go further than

> Academically interrogating the military and corporate narratives of space 'exploration' and 'colonization' [to] water, fertilize, and tend the seeds of alternative visions of possible futures in space, not only seeking solutions to earthly problems of the moment, but actively *queering* outer space and challenging the future to be even more queer.
>
> (Oman-Reagan 2017: 1, italics in original)

16. As De Witt Douglas Kilgore (2003) shows in his work on astrofuturism in the United States, the exclusion of women and racial minorities from the pioneering astronaut programs of the 1950s and 1960s was "a deliberate gesture", founded in the imperial politics and utopian schemes of modernist visions of outer space as an endless frontier.
17. See also Chanda Prescod-Weinstein et al. (2020).
18. The implications of decolonising space go far beyond redressing historical inequities in space exploration. Work in this space is also asking, for instance, how cultural bias distorts the search for extraterrestrial intelligence (SETI) and attempts at messaging extraterrestrial intelligence (METI). Chelsea Haramia and Julia DeMarines (2021) contend that ethically responsible searches for extraterrestrial intelligence require careful reflection and propose an expansive and inclusive understanding of moral considerability, drawing on ecological and ethical reasoning and arguing for a planetocentric and ecosystemic approach to SETI and METI debates. See also Denning (2010); Race et al. (2012); Lempert (2021).
19. Similar arguments have been made by numerous other authors; see, e.g., Mitchell (2017).
20. Here the title is in reference to Lisa Parks's landmark interdisciplinary study, *Cultures in Orbit* (2005), of how satellite practices, such as remote sensing, live transmission of global events, and astronomical observation have altered humanity's image of itself and our planet within the cosmos. See also Gorman (2016), Damjanov (2017) and Gál et al. (2021).
21. Interestingly, the origins of the space suit can be traced to the first diving helmets in the 1820s, where the diver gazed outward from a window in a spherical helmet and was connected to the atmosphere by an umbilical. Deep water tanks are used by NASA to create neutral buoyancy environments to simulate the free fall of microgravity for astronaut training.

References

Aït-Touati, Frédérique, and Bruno Latour. 2022. *Trilogie Terrestre*. Paris: Éditions B42.
Álvarez, Tamara, Michael Clormann, Craig Jones, A. R. E. Taylor, Richard Tutton, and Matjaz Vidmar. 2019. "Social Studies of Outer Space." In *Innovating STS Digital Exhibit*, curated by Aalok Khandekar and Kim Fortun. Society for Social Studies of Science. August. https://stsinfrastructures.org/content/social-studies-outer-space-1/essay.
Anker, Peder. 2005. "The Ecological Colonization of Space." *Environmental History* 10 (2): 239–68. https://doi.org/10.1093/envhis/10.2.239.
Arboleda, Martín. 2020. *Planetary Mine: Territories of Extraction Under Late Capitalism*. New York: Verso.
Arnould, Jacques. 2001. *La Seconde Chance D'ICARE: Pour une Éthique de l'Espace*. Paris: Cerf.
Baird Callicott, J. 1986. "Moral Considerability and Extraterrestrial Life." In *Beyond Spaceship Earth: Environmental Ethics and the Solar System*, edited by Eugene C. Hargrove, 227–59. San Francisco, CA: Sierra Club Books.
Battaglia, Debbora, David Valentine, and Valerie Olson. 2015. "Relational Space: An Earthly Installation." *Cultural Anthropology* 30(2): 245–56. https://doi.org/10.14506/ca30.2.07.
Beery, Jason. 2012. "State, Capital and Spaceships: A Terrestrial Geography of Space Tourism." *Geoforum* 43 (1): 25–34. https://doi.org/10.1016/j.geoforum.2011.07.013.
Bennett, Tony. 2016. "The Stuart Hall Conjuncture." *Cultural Studies Review* 22 (1): 282–86. http://doi.org/10.5130/csr.v22i1.4917.
Bureaud, Annick. 2005. "Did You Say Space Art? Leonardo's Commitment to Space Art, 35 Years On." *Leonardo* 38 (5): 374–75. https://doi.org/10.1162/leon.2005.38.5.374.
Clark, Nigel. 2011. *Inhuman Nature: Sociable Life on a Dynamic Planet*. London: Sage.
Damjanov, Katarina. 2017. "Of Defunct Satellites and Other Space Debris: Media Waste in the Orbital Commons." *Science, Technology, & Human Values* 42 (1): 166–185. https://doi.org/10.1177/0162243916671005
Damjanov, Katarina, and David Crouch. 2019. "Orbital Life on the International Space Station." *Space and Culture* 22 (1): 77–89. https://doi.org/10.1177/1206331217752621.

de la Cadena, Marisol. 2018. "Earth-Beings: Andean Indigenous Religion, But Not Only." In *The World Multiple: The Quotidian Politics of Knowing and Generating Entangled Worlds*, edited by Keiichi Omura, Grant Jun Otsuki, Shiho Satsuka and Atsuro Morita, 20–36. London and New York: Routledge.

De Napoli, Krystal, and Karlie Noon. 2022. *Astronomy: Sky Country*. Sydney: Thames & Hudson.

Denning, Kathryn. 2010. "Unpacking the Great Transmission Debate." *Acta Astronautica* 67 (11–12): 1399–405. https://doi.org/10.1016/j.actaastro.2010.02.024.

Dickens, Peter, and James S. Ormrod. 2007. *Cosmic Society: Towards a Sociology of the Universe*. Abingdon: Routledge.

Drake, Nadia. 2018. "We Need To Change the Way We Talk about Space Exploration." National Geographic, 10 November. https://www.nationalgeographic.com/science/article/we-need-to-change-way-we-talk-about-space-exploration-mars.

Dunnett, Oliver, Andrew S. Maclaren, Julie Klinger, K. Maria D. Lane, and Daniel Sage. 2019. "Geographies of Outer Space: Progress and New Opportunities." *Progress in Human Geography* 43 (2): 314–36. https://doi.org/10.1177/0309132517747727.

Edge, David O., and Michael J. Mulkay. 1976. *Astronomy Transformed: The Emergence of Radio Astronomy in Britain*. New York: Wiley.

Ellery, Alex. 2019. "We Need New Treaties to Address the Growing Problem of Space Debris." *The Conversation*, 26 May. https://theconversation.com/we-need-new-treaties-to-address-the-growing-problem-of-space-debris-115757.

Gál, Réka Patrícia, Leon M. Wilkins, Yuxing Zhang, Marie-Pier Boucher, Tero Karppi, and Jeremy Packer. 2021. "Space Media." *Canadian Journal of Communication* 46 (3): 645–62. https://doi.org/10.22230/cjc.2021v46n3a4085

Geppert, Alexander C. T. 2012. "European Astrofuturism, Cosmic Provincialism: Historicizing the Space Age." In *Imagining Outer Space: European Astroculture in the Twentieth Century*, edited by Alexander C. T. Geppert, 3–28. London: Palgrave Macmillan. https://doi.org/10.1057/978-1-349-95339-4_1.

Geppert, Alexander C. T., Daniel Brandau, and Tilmann Siebeneichner, eds. 2021. *Militarizing Outer Space: Astroculture, Dystopia and the Cold War*. London: Palgrave Macmillan.

Gómez-Barris, Macarena. 2017. *The Extractive Zone: Social Ecologies and Decolonial Perspectives*. Durham, NC: Duke University Press.

Gorman, Alice C. 2005a. "The Cultural Landscape of Interplanetary Space." *Journal of Social Archaeology* 5 (1): 85–107. https://doi.org/10.1177/1469605305050148.

Gorman, Alice C. 2005b. "The Archaeology of Orbital Space." In *Australian Space Science Conference 2005*, 338–57. Conference Proceedings 5th NSSA Australian Space Science Conference: 14 to 16 September 2005. Melbourne: RMIT University. ISBN 0864593740

Gorman, Alice C. 2007. "La Terre et l'Espace: Rockets, Prisons, Protests and Heritage in Australia and French Guiana." *Archaeologies: Journal of the World Archaeological Congress* 3 (2): 153–68. https://doi.org/10.1007/s11759-007-9017-9.

Gorman, Alice C. 2014. "The Anthropocene in the Solar System." In "Forum: Anthropology of the Anthropocene." *Journal of Contemporary Archaeology* 1 (1): 87–91. https://doi.org/10.1558/jca.v1i1.73.

Gorman, Alice C. 2016. "Culture on the Moon: Bodies in Time and Space." *Archaeologies* 12 (1): 110–28. https://doi.org/10.1007/s11759-015-9286-7.

Hamacher, Duane. 2022. *The First Astronomers: How Indigenous Elders Read the Stars*. Crows Nest: Allen & Unwin.

Haramia, Chelsea, and Julia DeMarines. 2021. "An Ethical Assessment of SETI, METI, and the Value of Our Planetary Home." In *Astrobiology: Science, Ethics, and Public Policy*, edited by Octavio Alfonso Chon Torres, Ted Peters, Joseph Seckbach, and Richard Gordon, 271–91. Beverly, MA: Scrivener. https://doi.org/10.1002/9781119711186.ch13.

Haraway, Donna. 1989. *Primate Visions: Gender, Race, and Nature in the World of Modern Science*. New York: Routledge.

Harding, Sandra, ed. 1993. *The 'Racial' Economy of Science: Toward a Democratic Future*. Bloomington, IN: Indiana University Press.

Helmreich, Stefan. 2009. *Alien Ocean*. Los Angeles: University of California Press.

Helmreich, Stefan. 2011. "Nature/Culture/Seawater." *American Anthropologist* 113 (1): 132–44. https://doi.org/10.1111/j.1548-1433.2010.01311.x.

Helmreich, Stefan. 2012. "Extraterrestrial Relativism." *Anthropological Quarterly* 85 (4): 1125–39. https://doi.org/10.1353/anq.2012.0064.

Helmreich, Stefan. 2017. "Foreword: A Wrinkle in Space." *Environmental Humanities* 9 (2): 300–08. https://doi.org/10.1215/22011919-4215306.

Kilgore, De Witt Douglas. 2003. *Astrofuturism: Science, Race, and Visions of Utopia in Space*. Philadelphia, PA: University of Pennsylvania Press.

King, Barbara Amelia. 2022. "The Limitless Horizons of Space Art." In *Outer Space and Popular Culture*, edited by Annette Froelich, 53–73. Southern Space Studies. Cham: Springer.

Klinger, Julie M. 2021a. "Critical Geopolitics of Outer Space." *Geopolitics* 26 (3): 661–65. https://doi.org/10.1080/14650045.2020.1803285.

Klinger, Julie. M. 2021b. "Environmental Geopolitics and Outer Space." *Geopolitics* 26 (3): 666–703. https://doi.org/10.1080/14650045.2019.1590340.

Kothari, Ashish, Ariel Salleh, Arturo Escobar, Federico Demaria, and Alberto Acosta, eds. 2019. *Pluriverse: A Post-Development Dictionary*. New Delhi: Tulika Books and AuthorsUpFront.

Latour, Bruno. 2017. *Où Atterrir? Comment S'orienter en Politique*. Paris: La Découverte.

Latour, Bruno. 2018. *Down to Earth: Politics in the New Climatic Regime*. Cambridge: Polity.

Law, John. 2015. "What's Wrong With a One-World World?" *Distinktion: Journal of Social Theory* 16 (1): 126–39. https://doi.org/10.1080/1600910X.2015.1020066.

Lempert, William. 2021. "From Interstellar Imperialism to Celestial Wayfinding: Prime Directives and Colonial Time-Knots in SETI." *American Indian Culture and Research Journal* 45 (1): 45–70. https://doi.org/10.17953/aicrj.45.1.lempert.

Livingston, David. 2003. "A Code of Ethics for Conducting Business in Outer Space." *Space Policy* 19 (2): 93–94. https://doi.org/10.1016/S0265-9646(03)00015-8.

Macdonald, Fraser. 2007. "Anti-*Astropolitik*—Outer Space and the Orbit of Geography." *Progress in Human Geography* 31 (5). https://doi.org/10.1177/0309132507081492.

Malina, Roger F. 1991. "In Defense of Space Art: The Role of the Artist in Space Exploration." *International Astronomical Union Colloquium* 112: 145–52. https://doi.org/10.1017/S0252921100003894.

Mandel, Savannah. 2021. "Three Cheers for Pioneers: A Review of Outer Space Anthropology." *Anthropology Now* 13 (2): 111–22. https://doi.org/10.1080/19428200.2021.1973332.

Marino, Alessandra, and Thomas Cheney. 2022. "Centring Environmentalism in Space Governance: Interrogating Dominance and Authority Through a Critical Legal Geography of Outer Space." *Space Policy*. Published ahead of print, 2 November 2022, article 101521. https://doi.org/10.1016/j.spacepol.2022.101521.

Martin, Emily C., Lucianne Walkowicz, Erika Nesvold, and Monica Vidaurri. 2022. "Ethics in Solar System Exploration." *Nature Astronomy* (6): 641–42. https://doi.org/10.1038/s41550-022-01712-0.

Maruyama, Magoroh, and Arthur M. Harkins, eds. 1975. *Cultures Beyond Earth: The Role of Anthropology in Outer Space*. New York: Vintage Books.

Messeri, Lisa. 2016. *Placing Outer Space*. Durham, NC: Duke University Press.

Mezzadra, Sandro, and Brett Neilson. 2013. *Border as Method, or, the Multiplication of Labor*. Durham, NC: Duke University Press.

Milligan, Tony. 2013. "Scratching the Surface: The Ethics of Mining Helium-3." In *Proceedings of the 8th IAA Symposium on the Future of Space Exploration: Towards the Stars*. Torino, Italy, July 3–5, 2013.

Mitchell, Sean T. 2017. *Constellations of Inequality: Space, Race and Utopia in Brazil*. Chicago: University of Chicago Press.

NASA 2022. *Artemis*. Accessed 31 October 2022 at https://www.nasa.gov/specials/artemis/.

O'Leary, Beth. 2009. "The Evolution of Space Archaeology and Heritage." In *Handbook of Space Engineering, Archaeology and Heritage*, edited by Ann Garrison Darrin and Beth Laura O'Leary, 29–48. Boca Raton, FL: CRC Press.

Olson, Valerie. 2018. *Into the Extreme: U.S. Environmental Systems and Politics Beyond Earth*. Minneapolis, MN: University of Minnesota Press.

Oman-Reagan, Michael P. 2017. "Queering Outer Space." SocArXiv. January 23. https://doi.org/10.31235/osf.io/mpyk6.

Parks, Lisa. 2005. *Cultures in Orbit*. Durham, NC: Duke University Press.

Pass, Jim. 2006. "Astrosociology as the Missing Perspective." *Astropolitics* 4 (1): 85–99. https://doi.org/10.1080/14777620600762865.

Praet, Istvan, and Juan Francisco Salazar. 2017. "Introduction: Familiarizing the Extraterrestrial/Making Our Planet Alien." *Environmental Humanities* 9 (2): 309–24. https://doi.org/10.1215/22011919-4215315.

Pratt, Mary Louise. 1991. "Arts of the Contact Zone." *Profession*1991: 33–40. https://www.jstor.org/stable/25595469.

Prescod-Weinstein, Chanda. 2021. *The Disordered Cosmos: A Journey into Dark Matter, Spacetime, and Dreams Deferred*. New York: Bold Type Books.

Prescod-Weinstein, Chanda, Lucianne M. Walkowicz, Sarah Tuttle, Brian Nord, and Hilding R. Neilson. 2020. "Reframing Astronomical Research Through an Anticolonial Lens—for TMT and Beyond." *Arxiv preprint*, last revision date 3 January 2020. https://arxiv.org/abs/2001.00674.

Race, Margaret, Kathryn Denning, Constance M. Bertka, Steven J. Dick, Albert A. Harrison, Christopher Impey, Rocco Mancinelli, and Workshop Participants. 2012. "Astrobiology and Society: Building an Interdisciplinary Research Community." *Astrobiology* 12 (10): 958–65. https://doi.org/10.1089/ast.2011.0723.

Rahder, Micha. 2019. "Home and Away: The Politics of Life after Earth." *Environment and Society* 10 (1): 158–77. https://doi.org/10.3167/ares.2019.100110.

Redfield, Peter. 2000. *Space in the Tropics: From Convicts to Rockets in French Guiana*. Berkeley: University of California Press.

Robinson, Kim Stanley. 2012. *2312*. New York: Orbit Books.

Rolston, Holmes, III. 1986. "The Preservation of Natural Value in the Solar System." In *Beyond Spaceship Earth: Environmental Ethics and the Solar System*, edited by Eugene C. Hargrove, 140–82. San Francisco, CA: Sierra Club Books.

Rose, Deborah Bird. 2015. "Dialogue." In *Manifesto for Living in the Anthropocene*, edited by Katherine Gibson, Deborah Bird Rose, and Ruth Fincher, 127–32. Brooklyn, NY: Punctum Books.

Rubertone, Patricia E. 2000. "The Historical Archaeology of Native Americans." *Annual Review of Anthropology* 29 (1): ruber425-446.

Sage, Daniel. 2008. "Framing Space: A Popular Geopolitics of American Manifest Destiny in Outer Space." *Geopolitics* 13 (1): 27–53. https://doi.org/10.1080/14650040701783482.

Salazar, Juan Francisco, Céline Granjou, Anna Krzywoszynska, Manuel Tironi, and Matthew Kearnes. 2017. "Thinking-With Soils: An Introduction." In *Thinking With Soils: Material Politics and Social Theory*, edited by Juan Francisco Salazar, Céline Granjou, Matthew Kearnes, Anna Krzywoszynska and Manuel Tironi, 1–13. London: Bloomsbury.

Spennemann, Dirk H. R. 2004. "The Ethics of Treading on Neil Armstrong's Footprints." *Space Policy* 20 (4): 279–90. https://doi.org/10.1016/j.spacepol.2004.08.005.

Sultana, Farhana. 2021. "Political Ecology II: Conjunctures, Crises, and Critical Publics." *Progress in Human Geography* 45 (6): 1721–30. https://doi.org/10.1177/03091325211028665.

Sultana, Farhana. 2022. "The Unbearable Heaviness of Climate Coloniality." *Political Geography* 102638. Published ahead of print, 28 March 2022. https://doi.org/10.1016/j.polgeo.2022.102638.

Táíwò, Olúfẹ́mi O. 2022. *Reconsidering Reparations*. New York: Oxford University Press.

Tavares, Frank, Denise Buckner, Dana Burton, Jordan McKaig, Parvathy Prem, Eleni Ravanis, and Natalie Treviño, et al. 2020. "Ethical Exploration and the Role of Planetary Protection in Disrupting Colonial Practices." *Arxiv preprint*, arXiv:2010.08344. https://doi.org/10.48550/arXiv.2010.08344.

Triscott, Nicola. 2016. "Transmissions from the Noosphere: Contemporary Art and Outer Space." In *The Palgrave Handbook of Society, Culture and Outer Space*, edited by James S. Ormord and Peter Dickens, 414–44. London: Palgrave Macmillan.

Tsing, Anna Lowenhaupt. 2003. "Natural Resources and Capitalist Frontiers." *Economic and Political Weekly* 38 (48): 5100–06. https://www.jstor.org/stable/4414348.

Tutton, Richard. 2021. "Sociotechnical Imaginaries and Techno-Optimism: Examining Outer Space Utopias of Silicon Valley." *Science as Culture* 30 (3): 416–39. https://doi.org/10.1080/09505431.2020.1841151.

UNEP (United Nations Environment Programme) 2022. *Emissions Gap Report 2022: The Closing Window—Climate Crisis Calls for Rapid Transformation of Societies*. Nairobi. https://www.unep.org/emissions-gap-report-2022.

Valentine, David. 2012. "Exit Strategy: Profit, Cosmology, and the Future of Humans in Space." *Anthropological Quarterly* 85 (4): 1045–67. http://doi.org/10.1353/anq.2012.0073.

Valentine, David, Valerie A. Olson, and Debbora Battaglia. 2009. "Encountering the Future: Anthropology and Outer Space." *Anthropology News* 50 (9): 11–15. https://doi.org/10.1111/j.1556-3502.2009.50911.x.

Valentine, David, Valerie A. Olson, and Debbora Battaglia. 2012. "Extreme: Limits and Horizons in the Once and Future Cosmos." *Anthropological Quarterly* 85 (4): 1007–26. https://doi.org/10.1353/anq.2012.0066.

Vermeylen, Saskia. 2021. "Space Art as a Critique of Space Law." *Leonardo* 54 (1): 115–24. https://doi.org/10.1162/leon_a_01990.

Vertesi, Janet. 2014. *Seeing Like a Rover: How Robots, Teams, and Images Craft Knowledge of Mars*. Chicago: University of Chicago Press.

Vertesi, Janet. 2020. *Shaping Science: Organizations, Decisions, and Culture on NASA's Teams*. Chicago: University of Chicago Press.

Walsh, Justin St. P., and Alice Gorman. 2021. "Private Space Stations Are Coming. Will They Be Better than Their Predecessors?" *The Conversation*, 6 December. https://theconversation.com/private-space-stations-are-coming-will-they-be-better-than-their-predecessors-170871.

Walsh, Justin St P., Alice C. Gorman, and Wendy Salmond. 2021. "Visual Displays in Space Station Culture: An Archaeological Analysis." *Current Anthropology* 62 (6): 804–18. https://doi.org/10.1086/717778.

Williamson, Mark. 2003. "Space Ethics and Protection of the Space Environment." *Space Policy* 19 (1): 47–52. https://doi.org/10.1016/S0265-9646(02)00064-4.

Yusoff, Kathryn. 2015. "Geologic Subjects: Nonhuman Origins, Geomorphic Aesthetics and the Art of Becoming *In*human." *Cultural Geographies* 22 (3): 383–407. https://doi.org/10.1177/1474474014545301.

Yusoff, Kathryn. 2016. "Anthropogenesis: Origins and Endings in the Anthropocene." *Theory, Culture & Society* 33 (2): 3–28. https://doi.org/10.1177/0263276415581021.

Zabusky, Stacia E. 1995. *Launching Europe: An Ethnography of European Cooperation in Space Science*. Princeton, NJ: Princeton University Press.

PART I
Fields

2
TRILOGIE TERRESTRE

Frédérique Aït-Touati and Bruno Latour

The *Terrestrial Trilogy* began in 2016 with a lecture-performance, INSIDE, followed in 2019 by another, Moving Earths, and in 2020 by VIRAL. The trilogy is a reflection on the need for a profound renewal of our representations of the terrestrial world, biotic and abiotic. INSIDE explores visual alternatives to the haunting and deceptive image of the 'Globe'; Moving Earths immerses us in the experience of a moving, reactive earth; VIRAL is an exploration of contagion as an essential process of our closed world, and the political consequences of this expanded definition of life. The three lecture-performances are the result of a singular process of creation and long-term research developed at the Théâtre Nanterre Amandiers, where philosopher Bruno Latour and director Frédérique Aït-Touati make the stage a place for 'scenic essays' and philosophical experimentation (Figure 2.1). In 2022 Frédérique Aït-Touati and Bruno Latour published the book *Trilogie Terrestre*.

Figure 2.1 INSIDE. © Zone Critique Company. Reproduced with permission of the artist.

INSIDE

The Terrestrial Trilogy|INSIDE
Lecture-performance produced in November 2016 at Théâtre Nanterre-Amandiers
Conception by Frédérique Aït-Touati and Bruno Latour
Direction and set design by Frédérique Aït-Touati
With Bruno Latour or Duncan Evennou
Images and animation by Alexandra Arènes, Axelle Grégoire, Sonia Lévy
Video and lights by Patrick Laffont de Lojo
Music by Éric Broitmann, with the support of IRCAM
Lighting design by Rémi Godfroy
© Zone Critique Company

Each lecture-performance in the *Trilogy* tests a hypothesis. The first, in INSIDE, could be formulated as follows: "We do not live on a globe but rather in its critical zone"—that is, that very thin external layer where water, soil, subsoil, and life can interact. Can we change the way we see the Earth? Our way of walking on Earth? INSIDE suggests seeing ourselves as standing not on the globe but in this "critical zone" that scientists speak of.

Our common representations of the Earth are global, unifying representations that do not take into account the variety of modes of existence and cosmologies. When we think of the Earth, it is an image of the globe that appears, the famous *Blue Marble* photograph taken by NASA's Apollo 17 crew in 1972. In order to understand what it means to "live in" rather than "live on", the conference-performance engages a series of tests and visual hypotheses (Figure 2.2).

INSIDE is a lecture in which the philosopher plays his own role of philosopher but is seen as if immersed in his Powerpoint. Each "slide" thus becomes a scene, a dramatic image that is deployed not just in two dimensions but in all the dimensions of the stage.

This first step is to shatter the image of the globe, which cannot engage with ecological issues, too large and too remote to comprehend. The second step is to bring us inside (hence the title) this

Figure 2.2 INSIDE. © Zone Critique Company. Bruno Latour performing INSIDE. Reproduced with permission of the artist.

particular layer, fragile and complex, but with few images to latch onto. The dramatic experiment consists in sharing with the audience a variety of images created by scientists, artists, and architects: dynamic maps, diagrams, and sound and light to test new ways of situating ourselves. The important point is that *we don't know exactly where we are* (in this photo Bruno Latour shows a blurred image of Gaia projected on the ground), or rather, *in what we are*. Theatre, architecture, photography, stratigraphy, and even music are brought to the stage, but without any hope of coming up with definitive answers. At best we can come close. The lecture's key trigger is the lack of images to replace the image of the globe. A recurring phrase, and sometimes a recurring joke, during the lecture, is that the images we create are actually not very spectacular. There is an explicit tension in the idea of a show about Gaia when Gaia is so difficult to represent, so unspectacular (Figure 2.3).

This lecture-performance is part of a larger project in which Bruno and I engage with scientists around the notion of the "critical zone" and what we call "Gaia-graphy". The aim is to create new representations of territories—superimposed, multidimensional, fluctuating, exceeding the limits they are assigned—by observing them through various disciplinary lenses: stratigraphy, geochemistry, geophysics, architecture. In this image, Bruno describes the diagram behind him, drawn by an architect, Alexandra Arènes, while geologist Jérôme Gaillardet explains the concept of the critical zone, choosing to define it like this:

> At the intersections of geology, hydrology, geochemistry, geophysics, ecology, and soil science, a new discipline, or a new set of collaborations between disciplines, has recently emerged for the study of critical areas. The term "critical zone" refers to a network of observatories around the world dedicated to studying the various layers, from canopy tops down to the undisturbed bedrock below. In a broader sense, the term refers to the thin, porous area of the Earth's surface that hosts life, whose geochemical cycles have been sufficiently altered to create a very special zone, far from a state of equilibrium, that forms a kind of skin, varnish, veneer, or film on the surface of the globe.

Figure 2.3 INSIDE. © Zone Critique Company. Bruno Latour performing INSIDE Reproduced with permission of the artist.

Figure 2.4 MOVING EARTHS © Zone Critique Company. Bruno Latour performing INSIDE Reproduced with permission of the artist.

While the word globe or Earth refers to the planet as a whole, primarily as an object of celestial mechanics and viewed from outside, the concept of the critical zone is closer to that of Gaia or Earth system science. The word "zone" emphasises its uncertain status, different from other, older concepts: planet, nature, biosphere, etc. The word "critical" foregrounds the physical property of being far from equilibrium, and thus the zone's fragility—a fragility that is, of course, felt all the more acutely due to the impacts of the actions of humans on the Earth system, dubbed the "Anthropocene", a contested but broadly convenient label (Figure 2.4).

Moving Earths

> The Terrestrial Trilogy|Moving Earths
> Lecture-performance produced in December 2019 at Théâtre Nanterre-Amandiers
> Text by Bruno Latour and staging by Frédérique Aït-Touati
> Set design by Patrick Laffont de Lojo
> With Bruno Latour or Duncan Evennou

When in 1609 Galileo pointed his telescope to the sky, he discovered mountains on the surface of the Moon, making it another Earth, and the Earth a star among others. He thus upset not only the cosmic order but also the political and social order of his time. Four centuries later, the role and position of our planet are once again being turned on its head by new science, which is revealing how human action leads it to respond in unexpected ways. Galileo taught us that the Earth is in motion. Scientists James Lovelock and Lynn Margulis are discovering an Earth "in motion" in another sense: they describe a planet where space and time are the product of the actions of living people. This leads us to change our worldview and our understanding of the cosmos. And, once again, the whole structure of society seems to be called into question. Whereas in 1610 we had to absorb the shock that "the earth moves", in 2019 we have to accept the shock, even more surprising, that "the earth moves", that it shakes and reacts to the actions of humans to the point of interfering with all our projects to develop it.

Trilogie Terrestre

Figure 2.5 VIRAL. © Zone Critique Company. Image of Bruno Latour rehearsing VIRAL at the Theatre des Amandiers, in Nanterre. The image projected on the table is the surface of Mars. Reproduced with permission of the artist. © Zone Critique Company. Reproduced with permission of the artist.

From the Earth to the Moon and back: we invite the audience to test the hypothesis of a parallel between that time of astronomical revolution and our own. Are we experiencing a global transformation as profound and radical as that of Galileo's time? One thing is certain: we no longer know exactly what planet we live on, nor how to describe it. What we see now is not a single, fixed, stable Earth but rather a multitude of planets that we must explore in order to determine which to land on (Figure 2.5).

VIRAL

The Terrestrial Trilogy | VIRAL
Produced in April 2022 at the Tangram (Évreux) as part of the Festival Les Anthroposcènes, then in October 2022 at the Crossing the Line Festival in New York City
Text by Bruno Latour; directed by Frédérique Aït-Touati
Set, video, and lighting design by Patrick Laffont de Lojo
Original music by Grian Chatten
With scientific support from Déborah Bucchi, Emanuele Coccia, and Nikolaj Schultz

With the pandemic, we have once again realised the extent to which we are caught in material dependencies, coevolving with pathogens and viruses. These dependencies, which we tend to forget in normal times, make themselves felt in times of crisis.

Is it possible, with the exhaustion of the pandemic, to view isolation positively? The show offers this paradox: we are "isolated" in the critical zone, that thin layer on the surface of the Earth where those that are alive and the resources they need are concentrated. And what is more, we are unable to survive without other living beings superimposed on us and intertwined with us. Unable to survive, in other words, without contagion. Isolation and contagion characterise our earthly condition. VIRAL attempts to reveal—and perhaps make bearable—this seemingly untenable paradox.

The audience is welcomed on the stage, transformed into a museum room. They wander freely through an exhibition of Martian landscapes that evoke the various dreams inspired by the red planet: extraterrestrial life, exploration of Mars, panoramic shots taken by rovers, terraforming projects… Suddenly, on the central table, faces appear in a video projection and begin to speak. They express different opinions about the recent expeditions to Mars: enthusiasm, suspicion, irony.

The voices stop and a guide enters the exhibition. A strange guide: he will try to dismantle, image by image, the fascination that underlies the whole exhibition. In this museum of our dreams of elsewhere, the exhibition highlights an outdated imagining, that of the conquest of space and the colonisation of Mars, the deep causes of which the guide explores: a desire for freedom, the glamour of the aesthetics of science fiction, a morbid attraction for a dead planet, a desire to leave the Earth, a thirst for conquest… he explores and probes the whole imaginary of space. The exhibition becomes a performance, a discussion, a debate: why do we like these images of Mars so much? What fascinates us in what is basically a lifeless desert?

Then everything changes: the iron curtain opens. We are no longer in a museum but in a theatre, where we see shifting clouds and lights of terrestrial landscapes. It is the Earth, in all its viral strangeness, that our guide invites us to discover. The exhibition table becomes a billiard table and then a dissection table: on it, different models of the world collide. The model of classical physics gives way to a new model, one made of virality and composite beings.

References

Aït-Touati, Frédérique, and Bruno Latour. 2022. *Trilogie Terrestre*. Paris: Editions B42.

3
REFIELDING IN MORE-THAN-TERRAN SPACES

Valerie A. Olson

Spaces outside Earth's atmosphere are, for unaided humans, unsurvivable. And yet all societies include those outer spaces—and their things and entities—within the bounds of shared experience. Scholars who do work on social space and place know this, but most have assumed their earthly research fields to be separate *a priori* from those outer spaces. This had made outer spaces ambiguous in social scientific terms. They are apart but not disconnected, here but not here. It is in this ambiguous mode that spaces beyond Earth's surface are becoming legitimate social research project sites.

This chapter surveys how scholars of outer spaces do fieldwork on ambiguous ground. I pluralise "outer space" to counter the hegemonic western concept of an epistemologically and ontologically singular outer space. There is a broadening range of social, scientific and humanities work on outer spaces, but I focus here on scholars who do their research by situating themselves in sites in which outer spaces matter—in other words, I focus on scholars who do fieldwork. When these fieldworkers set out to follow the fundamental social science dictum that spaces shape social experience, they immediately face two problems. The first is the methodological problem of what counts as "the field" and "fieldwork". Outer space studies scholars need to engage spaces that they can't directly experience in the manner of conventional fieldwork, and that exist outside the standard disciplinary geopolitical coordinates of the "local", "global", and "terrestrial". The second problem is conceptual. Outer space studies scholars must figure out ways to theorise processes of experience, power, identity, relations of beings and things, and histories, following Marisol de la Cadena, *Earthly-but-not-only* (de la Cadena 2014, 2015). In order to make this broadened spatiality visible in their projects, they have to reconfigure what counts as a legitimate social science field. They must refield their projects in a different kind of space.

In addressing this problem of refielding the category of space, I join scholars such as de la Cadena who have refielded "the human" by decentring it in relation to the more-than-human (see, inter alia, Abram 1996; TallBear 2011; Todd 2018; Povinelli 2020), beyond-human (Kohn 2013), and human-but-not-only (de la Cadena 2014). Scholars using these categories signal a vital departure from the western positivist notion of human that maps onto liberal and scientific Man. They also hold that such ways of perceiving human relatedness extend to organismal as well as nonliving entities. However, even if the resulting accounts of more-than-human relations include other-than-Earthly things like suns, stars, moons, and other material formations and worlds, they still often keep E/earth as a de facto perspectival and analytic boundary. Scholars of outer spaces do not work in this de facto Earthly space. They attempt to shift into modes of perceiving and working that include but do not centre Earth or dominant conceptualisations of space and boundaries.

I offer "more-than-terran" to call attention to this broad spatiality. And I deliberately use the term "terran" rather than "earthly" or "terrestrial". *Terra* is at the etymological root of western discourses that associate earthliness and terrestriality (Latin *terra*) with ground, matter, and home locality as well as claimed territory, inert materiality, spatial nullity, and the possessable frontiers of an enclosable commons (Peters, Steinberg, and Stratford 2018; Squire, Mould, and Adey 2021; Jones 2021). As such, "terran" can index the various nonpossessive and possessive ways that social groups include outer space things, matter, and being. It can also call attention to what is at stake when scholars make analytic or political claims that "the Earth itself" is the only proper place or ground of social and political experience (Ingold 1993; Latour 2018). More-than-terran is, like more-than-human, a phrase that can foster new critiques and open multidimensional research spaces (Peterson and Olson forthcoming). Among other things, it can help to shift fieldworkers outside of hierarchical binary spatial schemas centred on Man and globe (Wynter 2003; Zhan 2009; Ferreira da Silva 2007).

Although the process of refielding in the more-than-terran points most obviously to the methodological task of extending a project workspace beyond normative spatial boundaries, it also includes theoretical and political tasks. Scholars including outer spaces in their fieldwork immediately confront a set of normative spatialised assumptions about core social science concepts: space itself, relations, subjectivity, and temporality. In a nutshell, these assumptions promote the idea that the field should always anchor in disciplinarily defined terran surface geographies (like nations or geopolitical regions), that the field's structural and relational objects of study originate on and move outward from Earth, that the field is only what is directly experienced by fieldworkers on their cultural terms, and that the field's temporality must synchronise with dominant terran modes. For outer space studies, scholars engaged in critical work, as it is for scholars in other disciplines, regard the Earth as set within a broader physical or cultural field, those methodological and conceptual assumptions don't easily stay in place and out of the question.

In what follows, I survey how scholars of outer spaces refield in the more-than-terran by attending to the more-than-terran dimensions of territories, infrastructures, and environments, of subjectivities of being and belonging, and of industrial and evolutionary models of temporal existence. The set of projects I examine here is by no means comprehensive or representative and the emerging subfield of outer space studies is transforming constantly.

Outer space studies doing critical more-than-terran refielding work are important not just because they challenge what counts as the field or establish the disciplinary contours of a new subfield. These studies also call attention to the contemporary and unequal more-than-terran extents of material-semiotic power. And increasingly, they are addressing the more-than-terran dynamics of geopolitics and place-making, racial hierarchy and empire, indigeneity and colonisation, and the enclosures and openings of experimental forms of collective life. In calling attention to some of this work, I advocate for the value of social scientific refielding in spaces outside earthly surfaces, and also for what might be possible when analysts design their projects in a more-than-terran mode even though they don't specifically focus on "outer space".

Getting Out of the Field

Over the past three decades, historians and social scientists have critically reimagined "the field" as a situated space and concept. Science and technology studies (STS) scholars trace the nineteenth-century emergence of scientific fieldwork in its outside relation to laboratory centres of power, showing how field-based scientists established the legitimacy of their embodied data collection practices in uncontrolled out-of-bounds spaces (Kohler 2002). From the mid-twentieth century onward, social scientists, particularly anthropologists, turned their capacity to physically *be there in the field* into an emblem of truth-production. The social scientist's aim was to be emplaced within a field they could fully occupy, engage, and traverse, whether it was familiar or unfamiliar to them. Since the early twentieth century, Black, feminist, and Indigenous studies scholars have examined the political dimensions of fields as spaces of scientific occupation and positivist ideology, as well as questioning whether fields and fieldworking positions are considered legitimate. Critiques in this tradition analyse how fieldwork can replicate imperial and colonial practices and how it unequally affects bodies subject to racialised violence and exclusions (e.g., Hurston 1991; Haraway 1988; Berry et al. 2017).

In the last two decades, "the field" has become a constructed political form (Amit 2000; Moser 2007; Rogers and Swadener 1999). Fieldwork in virtual worlds and of speculative or imaginative social experiences have challenged what counts as the sensed emplacement and interactive space of analysts and interlocutors—both human and more-than-human (Boellstorff et al. 2012). Nevertheless, these studies still tend to anchor in geopolitically defined terran areas, in the name of identifying one's area specialisation or of organising into mappable subdisciplines.

Some of the first acts of more-than-terran refielding, as I detail below, were conducted to escape hidden disciplinary forces that make "the field" inherently earthbound, and to reject fieldwork's horizontal local/global geometry. While all of these works orient in earth-based territory for incontrovertible reasons, they open portals into new spatial and theoretical configurations of structure, relations, subjectivity, and time. In particular, Indigenous studies and other critical studies of setter colonial outer spatiality analyse dominant constructs of western social and scientific fields. They reveal how those fields perpetuate the concept of a *cosmos nullius* within which Western definitions of life, intelligence, and sociality stand as unexamined political inventions.

More-Than-Terran Spaces and Structures

Ordinarily, social scientists select field sites that are recognisable as experientially "local" places for human and more-than-human subjects. The upper limits of such field sites are commonly understood to be spatially and methodologically global. In these schemas, "global" refers to the whole of the geopolitically defined earthly surface area. When scholars reject this standard local/global field scope, they usually focus on how such terms erase the spatial complexities of interlocutor experience. But all social experience is usually assumed to be centred on an identifiable area of coordinates. As a result, scholars operating within normative institutional frameworks such as those established in the US often tie their field sites to the disciplinary coordinates of geographic "area studies" that map onto professional job titles and divisions of expertise.

Scholars whose fields now include volumetric spaces above or below earthly planetary surface areas—such as undergrounds, airspaces, atmospheres, and orbital spaces—still typically anchor their work in the geopolitical surface areas that make claims on those spaces, such as Hong Kong, China, or the US (Redfield 2000; Jasanoff and Martello 2004; Choy 2011; Bebbington and Bury 2013; Zee 2015; Howe and Boyer 2015; Rand 2016). Typically outer space studies follow this established area-study-based mode of project description. In anthropology and in STS, those studies are often described in terms of their geographic fieldwork centre, e.g., rocket launching from Guyana, space science in Nigeria, and space ports in the US. There are currently no disciplinarily legitimate lunar, Martian, solar systemic, or galactic "area studies" categories. Nevertheless, outer space studies scholars end up refielding their projects to give equal analytic weight to nongeographic areas, such as planetary orbits or Martian or lunar landing sites. In doing so, they refield the standard social scientific categories of place, environment, and ecology with uncanny prefixes like alien, extraterrestrial, and outer.

The social sciences and humanities disciplines most likely to refield projects to include outer spaces as inherently social spaces are archaeology and Indigenous studies, which, more so than other disciplines, conceptualise the field as politically cosmological. I begin this survey by discussing archaeology's attention to more-than-terran technical structures and space studies work that calls attention to shifting political economies and ecologies of outer space. I then move to work in Indigenous studies, which analyses the cosmopolitical research field schemas that structure settler colonisation ventures and sciences of all kinds, including social science.

In this discipline, outer space things, such as the sun, moon, stars, and meteors/meteorites are legitimately linked to earthly fieldsites through symbolic and material cultural associations. Since the turn of the twenty-first century, Alice Gorman and associated colleagues have invented methods and concepts that allow them to study technoscientific outer spaces as extended social artefactual spaces with rapidly accreting pasts (Gorman 2005a, 2005b; Gorman and O'Leary 2013). Launch sites, landing sites, and spaceflight material culture can be described, compared, interpreted, and even preserved.

The methodological more-than-terran challenges that outer spaces present to archaeologists reveal how such spaces are paradoxically tied and untied to earthly territory. Space archaeologists must access sites and artefacts tied to Earthly property rights and territorial security, but which are also conceptually and physically outside of them.

First, archaeology doesn't require the analyst to "be there", temporally or physically. As a result, space archaeology fieldworkers and space programme ethnographers are refielding their methods in a broad more-than-terran "spacescape" (Gorman 2005b). They use or deploy remotely controlled device data, such as spacecraft reconnaissance images, to map and track changes to spaceflight objects, sites, and social processes that reflect changes in social relationships to space as a territory or temporary habitat (Buchli 2020; Gorman 2005a). In addition, they use remote audio recordings and data, such as mission-control conversations, to evaluate changes in the linguistic forms or interrelational practices associated with off-surface sociality.

Archaeologists of outer spaces are also devising ways to examine spaceflight as a vehicle for understanding the more-than-terran conceptual and material extensions of imperialism and militarism. They also study the relationship of those processes to Indigenous senses of space and belonging that make space launch sites, spacecraft landings, and crash debris into violent spaces of occupation and dispossession (Gorman 2005b). This work shows how doing fieldwork on the social production of extraterrestrial spaces as paradoxically grounded in and unbounded from Earth presents new possibilities for fieldwork on colonisation, decolonisation, science, and technology.

In the past thirty years, territorialisation has become visible as more-than-terran via scholars interested in the production of planet-scale power. In the late twentieth century, scholars of geopolitical technologies and colonisation began to refield geopolitics as "earthly politics", calling attention to the territorial occupation of low Earth orbit and the ways global north planet-scale knowledge is used to dominate nations with less spacefaring capacity (Redfield 2000; Jasanoff and Martello 2004; DeLoughrey 2014). Alongside this critical look at the production of geopolitical planetarity, ethnographers of imperial, scientific, and corporate spaceflight were positioning themselves in the sites where this work was being done: launch sites, space analogues, and space ports.

A group of ethnographers have been refielding geopolitical space by treating colonial and military infrastructures as more-than-terran. In these works, outer spaces, such as orbital space, can be recognised as "high grounds" for technologies that define contemporary colonies, localities, and global power (Rand 2016). Peter Redfield's groundbreaking work to examine the unfinished project of French colonial spatial conquest in Guiana included a rocket launch site as a contradictory locality (Redfield 2000). Redfield argues that, on one hand, the launch site enrolled local peoples in the rejuvenation of imperial Europe's reach through the building of roads and the construction of rocket trajectories outward into orbit. On the other hand, those projects faltered in the face of local resistance, showing how colonial efforts to unbound empires reveal the paradoxical limits and infinite aspirations of their politics and cosmologies.

Along with launch sites, ethnographers began to situate themselves in paradoxically here-but-there versions of typical fieldsites—communities, labs, and ports—to investigate the production of more-than-terran infrastructures of knowing and territorialisation. Space studies ethnographers highlighted the more-than-terran spatiality of contemporary US and Soviet religious cosmologies. Debbora Battaglia (2006) conducted ethnographic work within the Raelian religious community, where authorities were viewed as being on the threshold of an interstellar post-human evolution. Deana Weibel and Glen Swanson (2006) examined the ways Soviet cosmonauts enacted a sense of their participation in Russian cosmism's more-than-terran domain of spirit and nation. In the case of Soviet spaceflight, space became not only an empire-building venture but a distributed technical venture that created a sense of local territorial connections to outer spaces across the Soviet Union (Sivkov 2019).

Other ethnographers examined the more-than-terran scopes of contemporary US laboratory work and structures. Constance Penley's (1997) work juxtaposing the speculative off-world sensibilities of NASA engineers and sci-fi fan fiction writers showed how influential spaceflight science fiction—namely *Star Trek*—was in the production of everyday US consumer goods, from cell phones to novels. Stefan Helmreich's (2009) work to understand the production of new microbial knowledge and economies showed how deeply and broadly more-than-terran these life forms were, linguistically and practically. Microbes on earth are understood to be inherently terrestrial-but-alien, which justifies national projects to search for life on other planets and corporate projects to exploit them as consumer goods (Salazar 2017b).

In ethnographies of space ports and "analogue" spaceflight practice sites, scholars refield standard social scientific assumptions about the geocentricity and horizontality of modern western infrastructures. Historian Maria Lane (2010) documents the historical sources of this process in her work on the co-development of modern geography and astronomical "areology". In their work on the construction of the Spaceport America tourism launchsite in the American Southwest, Katherine Sammler and Casey Lynch (2021) argue that outer space portal constructions are anchored in colonial co-appropriations of Indigenous lands and cosmological sovereignty. David Valentine's work (2012, 2016) among the space capitalists who build such ports show how these sites become speculative portals for unbounding capitalism's material and ethical limitations. Moving capitalism offworld gives it a vertical exit from the gravitational drag of concerns about resource limits, the degradation of earthly space, and the finitude of the market as a theoretical structure. Valentine's work reveals how western economic theory and practices have an implicit more-than-terran spatiality.

Space studies work goes beyond the concept of space, as scholars investigate the more-than-terran fields and methods of contemporary scientific placemaking. In her work on exoplanetary science in analogue sites—field sites that represent the planetary terrains—Lisa Messeri (2016) shows how outer space has become outer place. Placemaking, for scientists trying to adapt their methods and sensibilities beyond earth, involves refielding their embodied and technical methods to give them a sense of being both on and off earth. The consequent production of "resonant" knowledge about planets as "other Earths" gives scientific practice a broader comparative field.

In addition, to launch sites, ports, and analogues, scholars are examining telescopes as more-than-terran structures that support and legitimate colonialism as eternally unfinished. Hi'ilei Julia Hobart (2019) documents Indigenous resistance to measurement-based near–far colonial extensions in telescope-building on Mauna Kea. In this case, she examines how the appropriation of unceded Indigenous sacred space extends into extraterrestrial space via space-object discovery and naming projects. She writes about the ways that these colonial extensions rely on what she notes as "measurements of absence". Depictions of the relative absence of qualities of life and of air, on the Hawaiian mountain top, and in extraterrestrial spaces, create a de facto appropriation of a near and far *terra nullius*. Hobart's analysis shows how the west's "terra" concept scales across and beyond the terrestrial.

In decentring western assumptions about more-than-terran spaces and being, Indigenous scholars and leaders also work to advance ways of knowing and relating to them. Scholars who critically engage with settler science projects to see and listen for "intelligence" or "life" reveal how those concepts are operationalised in ways that re-inscribe imperial bids to annex, diminish, and control otherness (Atalay et al. 2021; Charbonneau 2021). David Uahikeaikaleiʻohu Maile shows how astronomy is an industrial activity structured by desires for "time and territory" (Maile 2021: 99). Suzanne Kite's efforts to make "contact" with other life- or mind-forms are structured by fears about "the unknowability of Terran (human native or resident of the planet Earth) nature and nonhuman beings" (Kite 2021: 138). These scholars call for new processes of engaging outer spaces from positions that do not centre scientific objectives but rather axiological intentions, and from a sense of already existing shared copresence (Atalay et al. 2021; Lempert 2021; Shorter and TallBear 2021). In a collaborative scholarly and story-making article, Bawaka Country presents an Indigenous disposition *within* interconnected sky-earth worlds that differ completely from western dispositions *toward* "outer space" (Bawaka Country 2020; see Bawaka Country this volume).

In all these outer space studies projects, including ethnographic projects, researchers must refield social theories of infrastructure, imperialism, religion, scientific practice, place-making, and capitalism to include more-than-terran versions of nation, soul, life, company, knowledge, and belonging. This move opens new theoretical horizons on more-than-planetary experience of social life. A visionary version of this comes from Achille Mbembe, who states that "colonial expansion was a planetary project" (Mbembe 2019). His thoughts on the urgency of decolonisation and debounding include a more-than-terran description of the "world" concept:

> We might dream about colonising Mars or Venus or other unknown planets in the future, but for the time being that is not part of our actuality. We only have one world, one solar system and for this world to last as long as possible and for this solar system to not calcinate life as such, we need to become a bit more intelligent and wiser.
>
> *(Mbembe 2019)*

This is a call to examine the paradoxical conditions of actual planetarity in the face of solar-systemic-scaled imperialism and capitalism, but also in the face of new understandings of space as unboundedly relational.

More-Than-Terran Relationalities

In addition to refielding social scientific understandings of space, place, and infrastructure, scholars who include outer spaces in their work have also refielded the relational concepts of environment and ecology. Haunting contemporary global north spaceflight expansionist and survivalist projects are, as Mbembe notes, not just the spectre of an uninhabitable earth but a totally uninhabitable solar system. Clifford Siskin's history of the system concept shows that it was, from its seventeenth-century inception, a post-Copernican more-than-terran idea that the distributions of things in space was not a matter of platonic geometry but of dynamic relations (Siskin 2016). Writings by Peder Anker (2005), Patrick McCray (2012), and me (Olson 2018) detail the history of midcentury artificial ecological system development and show how the concept of the closed system, and the methods to make such systems, support western imperialist projects to control and enclose all relational spaces, even and especially those deemed too "extreme" to support human life.

Istvan Praet and Juan Francisco Salazar (2017) argue that analogue fieldsites, especially in extreme and extraterritorial areas of planet Earth, are places in which geocentric earth science gives way to interplanetary-scaled environmental science and thought. Lisa Messeri and I (2015) locate the rise of today's most broadly scaled earth-system concepts—a global climate and the Anthropocene—to the emergence of midcentury comparative planetary sciences. This means that Earth's environmental scales have always unfolded in a paradoxically unearthly field.

Technoscientific efforts to know and control Earth as one planet among many have made it into an ecologically relational rather than exceptional object. This relational Earth in relational space is the object of state-sponsored annexations of outer space, but it can also be an object of liberatory potential (Battaglia, Valentine, and Olson 2015). My ethnography (Olson 2018) of the NASA human spaceflight project Constellation is a study about the making of national environmental power via the production of systems of systems within an unbounded environment. The Constellation programme approached the solar system as the proper spatial container in which to envision projects of control, such as asteroid-impact mitigation projects, that remap earth's surface into new regions of technological and ecological survival and sacrifice. This kind of system-building work is what makes the solar system practically rather than just conceptually an ecological and economic system. However, I also argue (see Olson 2012, 2013) that the production of a dually ecological and economic solar ecosystem is as much a project of imperial statecraft as it is of communities of practitioners, and in this way, spaceflight inaugurates new extensions of power as well as new perspectives on the communal necessity of thinking and acting from a more-than-terran perspective.

As spatial, structural, and relational refielding efforts, all of the outer space studies projects surveyed above invite social scientists to rethink what they include in a project's field. In these projects, "earth" is conceptually and technically re-situated within broader structural and relational spaces. This makes it possible to imagine projects on infrastructure, spatialisation, and place that do not automatically assume a terran boundary. It also presents opportunities for new projects that focus specifically on how orbits, gravity, the sun and solar weather, other planets, solar systemic energies and materials, galactic energies, and stellar configurations and meanings are being incorporated into contemporary social spaces. In what follows I examine how outer space studies work refields the social spaces of subjecthood and identity.

More-Than-Terran Subjectivities: Beings, Belonging, and Becoming

In addition to including outer spaces and things in their projects, outer space studies scholars have also been examining historical and emerging experiences of more-than-terran subjectivity. In large part, these examinations include work on senses of identity, being, community, and becoming that are shaped by engagements with the alien and cosmic. Some of these projects are concerned with subjectivities that have emerged within governmental and industrial spaceflight workspaces. Other projects focus on "otherwise" (Povinelli 2014) senses of terran-but-more-than-terran embodiment, affinity, being, becoming, and belonging. In all of these projects, scholars have spatially unbounded the field in which they consider gender, race, ability, and precarity. Their projects have generated new theorisations of the ways that extreme and remote more-than-terran spaces are shaping modern understandings of embodiments and selves.

Space studies' work complicates theories of human embodiment by highlighting how labour, gender, and ability are constituted in extremely inhuman environments. The first spacefarers were highly constrained animals, and subsequent spacefaring bodies were equally controlled and contained (Gaard 2013). In studies of human astronauts and cosmonauts as government labourers, scholars show how astronauts are only paradoxically elite and privileged figures. Matthew Hersch (2012) shows that the hypermasculine and frontier-traversing figure of the midcentury astronaut was also a worker highly constrained by labour laws, institutional control, and even constricting spacesuit fabrication techniques invented in the modern lingerie industry. I have argued against the assumption that astronaut bodies are hypernormative, finding through ethnography that they are instead impaired and vulnerable by western biomedical and social standards (Olson 2012). This highlights the hidden earthbound spatiality of ability and disability.

Not all spacefarers are humans in space, as scholars show in studies of robotic space missions. Janet Vertesi (2012) argues that robotic spaceflight missions produce new modes of human-technology hybridity, creating the need for human labourers to identify with and embody their remote machines in order to operate them effectively. In their work on human and robotic spaceflight, scholars have shown how space exploration is, at its limits, an activity of human proxies. In this way, space studies work on more-than-terran embodiments presaged work on human proxies on earth (Mulvin 2021).

One particularly visible more-than-terran body is that of the alien, which sits at the intersection of diverse representations of territorial, racial, and species otherness. In work on belief in the presence of outer space aliens in the US, scholars map tales of alien abduction, mind control, and control of governments onto communal perceptions of economic precarity and governmental tyranny (Dean 1998; Lepselter 2016). This work expands theorisations of capitalist subjectivity, providing a way to understand how contemporary capitalist alienation has a more-than-terran spatiality.

While outer spaces can be sites for extensions of economic and racial subjectification, Black and Indigenous scholars also emphasise their potential for exploring liberatory and unalienated modes of being, belonging, and becoming. Astronomer Chanda Prescod-Weinstein (2021) takes her dislocated African indigeneity and blackness as a basis for her work to explore the politics of cosmological and biological theories of "darkness". Arguing that her expertise in theorisations and explanations of cosmic dark matter is concomitant with her work to expose scientific racial inequities, Prescod-Weinstein invokes the more-than-terran dimensions of blackness and indigeneity. Her work shows how Black queer feminist physics opens up new avenues for studying the universe (Prescod-Weinstein 2020). Works in Black speculative writing and art break through the space-time enclosures of imperial and slave geographies to create what Sherese Francis describes as an unbounded connection between an "inner and greater cosmos" (Francis 2019: 140). This connects with works by Black feminist authors calling attention to the spatialisations of embodied fieldwork as well as those of interlocutors in which outer spaces can be included in analyses of fugitivities, marronages, embodiments, and futurisms (Berry et al. 2017).

Deondre Smiles (2020) expands the question of field politics by addressing the emergence of Indigenous representations of space travel and futurity as a continuation of existing traditions. Citing Young's (1987) work on Indigenous responses to space exploration, Smiles points to the unbounded dimensions of Indigenous spatiality in which human beings are already here and there as a model for futures outside of colonial enclosure. Smiles's work draws forward the temporality of more-than-terran spaces, which are as paradoxical and multifaceted as more-than-terran spatialities, relationalities, and subjectivities.

More-Than-Terran Space-Times: Presence and Co-Existence

Outer spatial temporalities can be structured by science and industries as frontiers for knowledge and markets (McCray 2012), but, in different contexts, they can also be space-times of historical continuity, radical co-presence, and emergent futures (Salazar et al. 2017). A foundational model for the inclusion of outer space-times in critical social theory is Afrofuturism, which, as Sofia Samatar (2017) describes it, emphasised the planetary scale and borderlessness of blackness, rather than national belonging, as a mode of escape and reclamation. Afrofuturism rejects evolutionist models of progress and development, "prizing instead time-traveling leaps, sidesteps into alternate universes, and the reanimation of history" (p. 176). Notable among new critical works on outer space-times are studies that critique the potentialising temporality of space enterprises, argue for nighttime studies, and focus on emerging postcolonial and Indigenous futurity. The latter works are unbounded in form as well as space; they can be written, visual, sonic, and tactile (Salazar 2017a; Lempert 2014). In those forms, they are exactly spatialised acts of historical reanimation, space-time travel, and stepping into different universes.

Pursuing an understanding of the International Space Station (ISS) as a unique scientific setting in terms of time, Paola Castaño (2021) refields pragmatism and hermeneutics in low Earth orbit in order to theorise the orbital laboratory as an extreme case of anticipatory valuation. Calling the ISS an "iridescent institution", Castaño observes that it "exists in the realm of possibility" in which its job is to never fulfil its capacity to be nearly valuable (p. 694). Her work refields political economic theory, showing how governmental and corporate outer space-times provide new venues for promissory science (Fortun 2008). Studies like this call attention to the ways that outer space-time opens new research foci, and nowhere is this more clear than when it comes to the associations of outer spaces with night.

In recent calls for attending to and rectifying the pervasive daytime bias in social science by foregrounding nighttime, scholars are gesturing to a period of time when assumptions about separation of terrestrial and extraterrestrial space are eclipsed. In an article focusing on this problem, Kyba et al. (2020) cite emerging work in night studies that refer to night as much as a space as it does a time. When scholars describe night in spatial terms, it is clear that terran space can be regarded as implicitly diurnal and outer spaces as implicitly nocturnal. A more-than-terran temporal perspective on social experience does not separate daytime and nighttime, and can refield theories of power, race, gender, economy, territoriality, and embodiment. What is at stake in this is a recognition of the political geography of time-space.

Citing this notion of an unbounded social geography that moves beyond dominant understandings of spatial scalarity, Laura Harjo (2019) describes pathways toward sovereign Indigenous community futures. In *Spiral to the Stars: Mvskoke Tools of Futurity*, Harjo draws readers into the potentiality of what she calls "jumping scale", by which she means not just scaling up from body to community, but thinking about the nonlinear scalar relations of what she calls emergence geographies. In such geographies, it is possible to jump conventional scalar nodes to connect with powers acting at larger levels. In this model, Harjo proposes another way to experience ranges of things and spaces, one that is spirally shaped and unbounded. In this work, Indigenous perceptions of space-time can take the form of an imaginary or social action. The emergence of global south space programmes is one area in which the social stakes of more-than-terran space-time are emerging.

In Anne Johnson's study (2020) of the cosmopolitics and cosmopoetics that animate the Mexican space industry (see also Johnson this volume), she calls attention to reanimations of Mexican cosmic pasts in relation to imagined futures. Her work among Mexican engineers, scientists, and policymakers tracks how Mexican state-sponsored imaginaries of outer space "conquest" as a way to generate national autonomy and power provide ways to understand how global south discourses of modernity can include paradoxical understandings of spatial conquest and liberation. In this way, outer space studies scholarship can refield theories of colonisation and decolonisation in order to investigate different social imaginaries of the kinds of social experiences that outer space-times evoke.

Conclusion

In sum, outer space studies opens a more-than-terran spatiality that refields social scientific and humanities sites, methods, and concepts. Among the many potentials of working with more-than-terran space-times is that outer spaces are no longer defined by western or global north understandings of outer or otherness. Considering a project's fieldspace to be more-than-terran can call attention to coexisting, and patently contradictory, forms of social experience. Namely: that human social earthliness is inalienable, but that societies are in terrestrial/extraterrestrial transboundary coexistence in more-than-earthly spaces and in subatomic and imagined kinship with more-than-earthly entities. It can be argued that any fieldworker's body is already outside of and within outer space, and that projects that open to this experience may reveal, like the night sky, otherwise understandings of what it means to be together and apart.

References

Abram, David. 1996. *The Spell of the Sensuous: Perception and Language in a More-than-Human World*. New York: Vintage Books/Random House.
Amit, Vered, ed. 2000. *Constructing the Field: Ethnographic Fieldwork in the Contemporary World*. London: Routledge.
Anker, Peder. 2005. "The Ecological Colonization of Space." *Environmental History* 10 (2): 239–68. http://www.jstor.org/stable/3986114.
Atalay, Sonya, William Lempert, David Delgado Shorter, and Kim TallBear. 2021. "Indigenous Studies Working Group Statement." *American Indian Culture and Research Journal* 45 (1): 9–18. https://doi.org/10.17953/aicrj.45.1.atalay_etal.
Battaglia, Debbora, ed. 2006. *E.T. Culture: Anthropology in Outerspaces*. Durham, NC: Duke University Press.
Battaglia, Debbora, David Valentine, and Valerie Olson. 2015. "Relational Space: An Earthly Installation." *Cultural Anthropology* 30 (2): 245–56. https://doi.org/10.14506/ca30.2.07.
Bawaka Country (including A. Mitchell et al.). 2020. "Dukarr Lakarama: Listening to Guwak, Talking Back to Space Colonization." *Political Geography* 81: 102218. https://doi.org/10.1016/j.polgeo.2020.102218.
Bebbington, Anthony, and Jeffrey Bury. 2013. *Subterranean Struggles: New Dynamics of Mining, Oil, and Gas in Latin America*. Austin: University of Texas Press.
Berry, Maya J., Claudia Chávez Argüelles, Shanya Cordis, Sarah Ihmoud, and Elizabeth Velásquez Estrada. 2017. "Toward a Fugitive Anthropology: Gender, Race, and Violence in the Field." *Cultural Anthropology* 32 (4): 537–65. https://doi.org/10.14506/ca32.4.05.
Boellstorff, Tom, Bonnie Nardi, Celia Pearce, and Tina L. Taylor. 2012. *Ethnography and Virtual Worlds: A Handbook of Method*. Princeton, NJ: Princeton University Press.
Buchli, Victor. 2020. "Extraterrestrial Methods: Towards an Ethnography of the ISS." In *Lineages and Advancements in Material Culture Studies: Perspectives from UCL Anthropology*, edited by Timothy Carroll, Antonia Walford and Shireen Walton, 17–32. London: Routledge.
Castaño, Paola. 2021. "From Value to Valuation: Pragmatist and Hermeneutic Orientations for Assessing Science on the International Space Station." *The American Sociologist* 52 (4): 671–701. https://doi.org/10.1007/s12108-021-09515-y.
Charbonneau, Rebecca A. (2021). "Imaginative Cosmos: The Impact of Colonial Heritage in Radio Astronomy and the Search for Extraterrestrial Intelligence." *American Indian Culture and Research Journal* 45 (1): 71–93. https://doi.org/10.17953/aicrj.45.1.charbonneau.
Choy, Timothy. 2011. *Ecologies of Comparison: An Ethnography of Endangerment in Hong Kong*. Durham, NC: Duke University Press.
Dean, Jodi. 1998. *Aliens in America: Conspiracy Cultures from Outerspace to Cyberspace*. Ithaca, NY: Cornell University Press.
de la Cadena, Marisol. 2014. "Runa: Human But Not Only." *HAU: Journal of Ethnographic Theory* 4 (2): 253–59. https://doi.org/10.14318/hau4.2.013.
de la Cadena, Marisol. 2015. *Earth Beings: Ecologies of Practice Across Andean Worlds*. Durham, NC and London: Duke University Press.
DeLoughrey, Elizabeth. 2014. "Satellite Planetarity and the Ends of the Earth." *Public Culture* 26 (73): 257–80. https://doi.org/10.1215/08992363-2392057.
Ferreira da Silva, Denise. 2007. *Toward a Global Idea of Race*. Minneapolis: University of Minnesota Press.
Fortun, Michael A. 2008. *Promising Genomics: Iceland and deCODE Genetics in a World of Speculation*. San Francisco: University of California Press.
Francis, Sherese. 2019. "'The Electric Impulse': The Legba Circuit in Ralph Ellison's Invisible Man." In *The Black Speculative Arts Movement: Black Futurity, Art+Design*, edited by Reynaldo Anderson, and Clinton R. Fluker, 131–49. Lanham, MD: Lexington Books.
Gaard, Greta. 2013. "Animals in (New) Space: Chimponauts, Cosmodogs, and Biosphere II." *Feminismo/s* 22: 113–45. https://doi.org/10.14198/fem.2013.22.08.

Gorman, Alice C. 2005a. "The Archaeology of Orbital Space." In *5th NSSA Australian Space Science Conference 2005*, 338–57. RMIT University, Melbourne, 14–16 September 2005.

Gorman, Alice C. 2005b. "The Cultural Landscape of Interplanetary Space." *Journal of Social Archaeology* 5 (1): 85–107. https://doi.org/10.1177/1469605305050148.

Gorman, Alice C., and Beth Laura O'Leary. 2013. "The Archaeology of Space Exploration." In *The Oxford Handbook of the Archaeology of the Contemporary World*, edited by Paul Graves-Brown, Rodney Harrison and Angela Piccini, 409–24. Oxford: Oxford University Press.

Haraway, Donna. 1988. "Situated Knowledges: The Science Question in Feminism and the Privilege of Partial Perspective." *Feminist Studies* 14 (3): 575–99. https://doi.org/10.2307/3178066.

Harjo, Laura. 2019. *Spiral to the Stars: Mvskoke Tools of Futurity*. Tucson: University of Arizona Press.

Helmreich, Stefan. 2009. *Alien Ocean: Anthropological Voyages in Microbial Seas*. Berkeley: University of California Press.

Hersch, Matthew H. 2012. *Inventing the American Astronaut*. London: Palgrave Macmillan.

Hobart, Hi'ilei Julia. 2019. "At Home on the Mauna: Ecological Violence and Fantasies of Terra Nullius on Maunakea's Summit." *Native American and Indigenous Studies* 2 (6): 30–50. https://doi.org/10.5749/natiindistudj.6.2.0030.

Howe, Cymene, and Dominic Boyer. 2015. "Aeolian Politics." *Distinktion: Journal of Social Theory* 16 (1): 31–48. https://doi.org/10.1080/1600910X.2015.1022564.

Hurston, Zora Neale. 1991. *Dust Tracks on a Road*. New York: Harper Perennial.

Ingold, Tim. 1993. "Globes and Spheres: The Topology of Environmentalism." In *Environmentalism: The View from Anthropology*, edited by Kay Milton, 31–42. London: Routledge. https://doi.org/10.4324/9780203449653.

Jasanoff, Sheila, and Marybeth Long Martello, eds. 2004. *Earthly Politics: Local and Global in Environmental Governance*. Boston, MA: MIT Press.

Johnson, Anne W. 2020. "A Mexican Conquest of Space? Cosmopolitanism, Cosmopolitics, and Cosmopoetics in the Mexican Space Industry." *Review of International American Studies* 13 (2): 123–44. https://doi.org/10.31261/rias.9808.

Jones, Craig H. 2021. "Enclosing the Cosmos: Privatising Outer Space and Voices of Resistance." *Society and Space*, 24 May. https://www.societyandspace.org/articles/enclosing-the-cosmos-privatising-outer-space-and-voices-of-resistance.

Kite, Suzanne. 2021. "'What's on the Earth Is in the Stars; and What's in the Stars Is on the Earth': Lakota Relationships with the Stars and American Relationships with the Apocalypse." *American Indian Culture and Research Journal* 45 (1): 137–56. https://doi.org/10.17953/aicrj.45.1.kite.

Kohler, Robert E. 2002. *Landscapes and Labscapes: Exploring the Lab–Field Border in Biology*. Chicago: University of Chicago Press.

Kohn, Eduardo. 2013. *How Forests Think: Toward an Anthropology Beyond the Human*. Berkeley: University of California Press.

Kyba, Christopher M., Sara B. Pritchard, A. Roger Ekirch, Adam Eldridge, Andreas Jechow, Christine Preiser, and Dieter Kunz, et al. 2020. "Night Matters—Why the Interdisciplinary Field of 'Night Studies' Is Needed." *Multidisciplinary Science Journal* 3 (1): 1–6. https://doi.org/10.3390/j3010001.

Lane, K. Maria D. 2010. *Geographies of Mars: Seeing and Knowing the Red Planet*. Chicago: University of Chicago Press.

Latour, Bruno. 2018. *Down to Earth: Politics in the New Climatic Regime*. Translated by Catherine Porter. London: Polity.

Lempert, William. 2014. "Decolonizing Encounters of the Third Kind: Alternative Futuring in Native Science Fiction Film." *Visual Anthropology Review* 30 (2): 164–76. https://doi.org/10.1111/var.12046.

Lempert, William. 2021. "From Interstellar Imperialism to Celestial Wayfinding: Prime Directives and Colonial Time-Knots in SETI." *American Indian Culture and Research Journal* 45 (1): 45–70. https://doi.org/10.17953/aicrj.45.1.lempert.

Lepselter, Susan. 2016. *The Resonance of Unseen Things: Poetics, Power, Captivity, and UFOs in the American Uncanny*. Ann Arbor: University of Michigan Press.

Maile, David Uahikeaikalei'ohu. 2021. "On Being Late: Cruising Mauna Kea and Unsettling Technoscientific Conquest in Hawai'i." *American Indian Culture and Research Journal* 45 (1): 95–121. https://doi.org/10.17953/aicrj.45.1.maile.

Mbembe, Achille. 2019. "Thoughts on the Planetary: An Interview with Achille Mbembe." Interview by Sindre Bangstad and Torbjørn Tumyr Nilsen. *New Frame*, 5 September. https://www.newframe.com/thoughts-on-the-planetary-an-interview-with-achille-mbembe/.

Messeri, Lisa. 2016. *Placing Outer Space: An Earthly Ethnography of Other Worlds*. Durham, NC: Duke University Press.

McCray, W. Patrick. 2012. *The Visioneers: How a Group of Elite Scientists Pursued Space Colonies, Nanotechnologies, and a Limitless Future*. Princeton, NJ: Princeton University Press.

Moser, Stephanie. 2007. "On Disciplinary Culture: Archaeology as Fieldwork and Its Gendered Associations." *Journal of Archaeological Method and Theory* 14 (3): 235–63. https://doi.org/10.1007/s10816-007-9033-5.

Mulvin, Dylan. 2021. *Proxies: The Cultural Work of Standing In*. Cambridge: MIT Press.

Olson, Valerie. 2012. "Political Ecology in the Extreme: Asteroid Activism and the Making of an Environmental Solar System." *Anthropological Quarterly* 85 (4): 1027–44. https://doi.org/10.1353/anq.2012.0070.

Olson, Valerie. 2013. "NEOecology: The Solar System's Emerging Environmental History and Politics." In *New Natures: Joining Environmental History with Science and Technology Studies*, edited by Dolly Jørgensen, Finn Arne Jørgensen and Sara Pritchard, 195–211. Pittsburgh, PA: University of Pittsburgh Press.

Olson, Valerie. 2018. *Into the Extreme: US Environmental Systems and Politics Beyond Earth*. Minneapolis: University of Minnesota Press.

Olson, Valerie A., and Lisa Messeri. 2015. "Beyond the Anthropocene: Un-Earthing an Epoch." *Environment and Society: Advances in Research* 6 (1): 28–47. https://doi.org/10.3167/ares.2015.060103.

Penley, Constance. 1997. *NASA/TREK: Popular Science and Sex in America*. New York: Verso.

Peters, Kimberley, Philip Steinberg, and Elain Stratford. 2018. *Territory Beyond Terra*. London: Rowman & Littlefield.

Peterson, Kristin, and Valerie Olson. Forthcoming. *The Ethnographer's Way: A Multidimensional Research Design Handbook*. Durham, NC: Duke University Press.

Povinelli, Elizabeth A. 2014. "Geontologies of the Otherwise." Editors' Forum: Theorizing the Contemporary. *Fieldsights*, 13 January. Society for Cultural Anthropology. https://culanth.org/fieldsights/geontologies-of-the-otherwise.

Povinelli, Elizabeth A. 2020. "The Ancestral Present of Oceanic Illusions: Connected and Differentiated in Late Toxic Liberalism." *E-flux Journal* 112, October 2020. https://www.e-flux.com/journal/112/352823/the-ancestral-present-of-oceanic-illusions-connected-and-differentiated-in-late-toxic-liberalism/.

Praet, Istvan, and Juan Francisco Salazar. 2017. "Familiarizing the Extraterrestrial/Making Our Planet Alien." *Environmental Humanities* 9 (2): 309–24. https://doi.org/10.1215/22011919-4215315.

Prescod-Weinstein, Chanda. 2020. "Making Black Women Scientists under White Empiricism: The Racialization of Epistemology in Physics." *Signs: Journal of Women in Culture and Society* 45 (2): 421–47. https://doi.org/10.1086/704991.

Prescod-Weinstein, Chanda. 2021. *The Disordered Cosmos: A Journey into Dark Matter, Spacetime, and Dreams Deferred*. New York: Bold Type Books.

Rand, Lisa Ruth. 2016. *Orbital Decay: Space Junk and the Environmental History of Earth's Planetary Borderlands*. PhD Dissertation, History and Sociology of Science, University of Pennsylvania.

Redfield, Peter. 2000. *Space in the Tropics: From Convicts to Rockets in French Guiana*. Berkeley: University of California Press.

Rogers, Linda J., and Beth Blue Swadener. 1999. "Reframing the 'Field.'" *Anthropology and Education Quarterly* 30 (4): 436–40. https://doi.org/10.1525/aeq.1999.30.4.436.

Salazar, Juan Francisco. 2017a. "Antarctica and Outer Space: Relational Trajectories." *The Polar Journal* 7 (2): 259–69. https://doi.org/10.1080/2154896X.2017.1398521.

Salazar, Juan Francisco. 2017b. "Microbial Geographies at the Extremes of Life." *Environmental Humanities* 9 (2): 398–417. https://doi.org/10.1215/22011919-4215361.

Salazar, Juan Francisco, Sarah Pink, Andrew Irving, and Johannes Sjöberg, eds. 2017. *Anthropologies and Futures: Researching Emerging and Uncertain Worlds*. New York and London: Bloomsbury.

Sammler, Katherine G., and Casey R. Lynch. 2021. "Spaceport America: Contested Offworld Access and the Everyman Astronaut." *Geopolitics* 26 (3): 704–28. https://doi.org/10.1080/14650045.2019.1569631.

Shorter, David Delgado, and Kim TallBear. 2021. "An Introduction to Settler Science and the Ethics of Contact." *American Indian Culture and Research Journal* 45 (1): 1–8. https://doi.org/10.17953/aicrj.45.1.shorter_tallbear.

Siskin, Clifford. 2016. *System: The Shaping of Modern Knowledge*. Infrastructures. Cambridge, MA: MIT Press.

Sivkov, Denis. 2019. Shagi i Skachki: Antropologiia Kosmosa v Poiskakh Masshtaba [Steps and Leaps: The Anthropology of Space in Search of Scale]. *Etnograficheskoe Obozrenie* 6: 29–33. https://doi.org/10.31857/S086954150007766-2.

Samatar, Sofia. 2017. "Toward a Planetary History of Afrofuturism." *Research in African Literatures* 48 (4): 175–91. https://doi.org/10.2979/reseafrilite.48.4.12.

Squire, Rachael, Oli Mould, and Peter Adey. 2021. "The Final Frontier? The Enclosure of a Commons of Outer Space." *Society and Space*. https://www.societyandspace.org/forums/the-final-frontier-the-enclosure-of-a-commons-of-outer-space.

Smiles, Deondre. 2020. "The Settler Logics of (Outer) Space." *Society and Space*, 26 October. https://www.societyandspace.org/articles/the-settler-logics-of-outer-space

TallBear, Kim. 2011. "Why Interspecies Thinking Needs Indigenous Standpoints." *Fieldsights*, 18 November. Society for Cultural Anthropology. https://culanth.org/fieldsights/why-interspecies-thinking-needs-indigenous-standpoints.

Todd, Zoe. 2018. "Refracting the State Through Human-Fish Relations: Fishing, Indigenous Legal Orders and Colonialism in North/Western Canada." *Decolonization: Indigeneity, Education & Society* 7 (1): 60–75.

Valentine, David. 2012. "Exit Strategy: Profit, Cosmology, and the Future of Humans in Space." *Anthropological Quarterly* 85 (4): 1045–67. https://doi.org/10.1353/anq.2012.0073.

Valentine, David. 2016. "Atmosphere: Context, Detachment, and the View from Above Earth." *American Ethnologist* 43 (3): 511–24. https://doi.org/10.1111/amet.12343.

Vertesi, Janet. 2012. *Seeing Like a Rover: How Robots, Teams, and Images Craft Knowledge of Mars*. Chicago, IL: University of Chicago Press.

Weibel, Deana L., and Glen E. Swanson. 2006. "Malinowski in Orbit: 'Magical Thinking' in Human Spaceflight." *Quest: The History of Spaceflight Quarterly* 13 (3): 53–61.

Wynter, Sylvia. 2003. "Unsettling the Coloniality of Being/Power/Truth/Freedom: Towards the Human, After Man, Its Overrepresentation—An Argument." *The New Centennial Review* 3 (3): 257–37. https://doi.org/10.1353/ncr.2004.0015.

Young, M. Jane. 1987. "'Pity the Indians of Outer Space': Native American Views of the Space Program." *Western Folklore* 46 (4): 269–79. https://doi.org/10.2307/1499889.

Zee, Jerry. 2015. "Breathing in the City: Beijing and the Architecture of Air." *Scapegoat* 8 (8): 46–56. http://www.scapegoatjournal.org/docs/08/ZEE_6.pdf.

Zhan, Mei. 2009. *Other-Worldly: Making Chinese Medicine through Transnational Frames*. Durham, NC: Duke University Press.

4
SPACE AND TIME THROUGH MATERIAL CULTURE
An Account of Space Archaeology

Alice Gorman

Introduction

Space archaeology can be defined as the study of "the material culture relevant to space exploration that is found on earth and in outer space (i.e., exoatmospheric material) and that is clearly the result of human behavior" (Darrin and O'Leary 2009: 5). While it may seem counter-intuitive to call the study of materials so recent "archaeology", the field is defined by its methods rather than the age of the material. Archaeology investigates the relationship between human culture, objects, and the built and natural environments, in order to understand change and adaptation over time. Patterns of behaviour can be found in the spatial and chronological relationships between things and used to discern the intangible worlds of human existence. The age of the material is irrelevant, although bringing these methods into the realm of living people creates tensions between conceptions of time and identity: the present is as slippery as the future "best before" date on discarded food packaging.

Space archaeology is situated in the subdiscipline called the archaeology of contemporary past, which is generally considered to be the period after the Second World War (Harrison and Schofield 2010). In this era, there is an increase in mobility with the expansion of international air travel; an accelerated process of globalisation; mass manufacture and mass discard; new technologies, such as electronics and computing; and new materials, including plastics and nuclear products. Following Augé (1992), González-Ruibal (2008) characterises this archaeology as "supermodernity" in its excesses and destructiveness. The human movement into space, starting from the launch of Sputnik 1 in 1957, adds another strand of distinctive material culture to this period with the subsequent growth of space industries providing Earth observation, telecommunications, navigation, and timing. Satellite services have radically altered terrestrial spatial behaviour (Isaacson and Shoval 2006; Speake and Axon 2012) and are implicated in constructing the subject in the contemporary world (Olsen 2003: 100).

Space archaeology seeks to illuminate the impacts of these new technologies on human behaviour, in much the same way that other archaeologies trace the cultural changes resulting from the introduction of agriculture or iron-working into a society. Its geographic range extends beyond Earth to celestial bodies such as the Moon and the asteroids. In these places, humans have never lived; yet human intent has created archaeological sites and robotic landscapes with their own distinct qualities in response to the planetary environments they were designed for. With the global growth in orbital industries and a renewed push for a human presence on the Moon and Mars, these places are now under threat from off-Earth activities. Thus their heritage value for present and future generations is also considered part of space archaeology (Barclay and Brooks

2002; Butowsky 1984; Fewer 2002; Gorman 2005a, 2005b, 2007a, 2009a, 2021; Idziak 2013; O'Leary 2009a, 2009b, 2009c; Spennemann 2004, 2007a; Walsh 2012; Westwood, O'Leary, and Donaldson 2017).

There is much in common with industrial and historical archaeology, which study the post-Medieval growth of capitalist markets and the impacts of colonialism (Croucher and Weiss 2011; Orser 1996), incorporating historical sources into the interpretation of data. The use of remote sensing to image planetary landing sites or orbital objects is another key method shared with terrestrial archaeology. However, the methods and theories of space archaeology have had to adapt to nonterrestrial environments, the absence of legislation or international norms around heritage outside Earth, and the impossibility, generally, of undertaking fieldwork to collect data (Walsh and Gorman 2021).

Where the Spacecraft Are

Much like the "out-of-Africa" hypothesis of human origins, the origins of space exploration converge on a single geographic region and time period. The V2 rocket, developed in the 1930s in Germany and deployed as a weapon in the Second World War, is the ancestor of most contemporary space programmes. During the Cold War (1946–1991), space technology was mobilised as an ideological weapon in the conflict between the western and eastern blocs (Gorman and O'Leary 2007: 73). The diaspora of German rockets and rocket scientists after the end of the war led to a proliferation of space sites, such as launch facilities in the late 1940s, followed in the 1950s by Earth-orbiting satellites and their tracking stations, and from the 1960s, spacecraft sent to Mars, Venus, and beyond. By the 2010s, spacecraft had travelled outside what is considered the limit of the solar system into interstellar space.

Space places can be characterised by their mobility or velocity in relation to a notionally immobile Earth's surface. Ground facilities usually stay in one location (although there are mobile rocket launchers and tracking stations too). Rockets can be suborbital, their range confined to within Earth's atmosphere, or orbital, in which case they shed components such as boosters on the journey and leave other components in freefall around Earth. Depending on their altitude above Earth, some of these will fall back into the atmosphere, mostly incinerating but with the more robust elements sometimes surviving to reach solid land or drown in the ocean depths. Others still transit to high altitudes, such as geostationary orbit, where only the most chaotic dynamics can cause their orbits to decay towards Earth. From high Earth orbits, other spacecraft reach the Moon or the Earth–Moon Lagrange points where they become "stationary" again. The movement between these locations resembles the sessile and motile phases of sea creatures such as sponges and sea jellies.

Hypothetically, a single spacecraft launch can resonate out to leave parts scattered between Earth, sea, orbit, and celestial body. Describing the relationship between these positions is perhaps best done by conceptualising them as points on a Riemann manifold (Gorman 2009d). Our naïve geocentric geometry, intuitively Euclidean, is a poor framework for understanding the stratigraphy of this archaeological record.

The temporality of these components also defies an easy assignment into past or present. Old satellites or space junk in Earth orbit are not resting quietly with the dead; they have a terrible agency and destructive power in the present and future, and a capacity to fragment and self-propagate like the heads of the hydra. Conservative estimates calculate approximately 25,000 pieces of space junk larger than 10 cm are circulating above our heads at average speeds of 7000 km/hr (NASA n.d.). Taphonomy, the study of post-depositional environmental effects on the materials and spatial relations between artefacts at archaeological sites, has a very different complexion at these speeds.

In evolutionary terms, the vast geographic spread of human material culture, achieved in less than a century, is remarkable in itself. It may be ambitious from the perspective of our immersion in it to try and understand what this means; nevertheless, such an endeavour must surely be attempted. From the seabed, where fallen spacecraft lie "full fathom five", to the cold emptiness of the outer solar system where the Sun's rays are quenched by darkness, the archaeological record of space encompasses a range of different gravities, mediums, and electromagnetic environments far beyond the narrow rind of temperature and pressure to which humans and their ancestors have adapted over the last 3 million years.

The entire solar system is now a cultural landscape (Gorman 2005a), shaped by the conditions of the natural space environment, and the elements and processes added to it by human actions. This distribution can also be conceptualised as a hyperobject (Campbell 2021; Gorman 2019a: 247–52; Morton 2010), as most of this landscape cannot be seen or experienced at the human level. Edgeworth (2010) has argued that the contemporary archaeological record is characterised by extremes of scale, where nano- and mega-scale objects and views, enabled by new technologies, challenge the ability of human perceptions to comprehend them.

Until the launch of Sputnik 1, every human object made on Earth stayed on Earth. While objects in archaeological deposits below the surface of the Earth are not visible to us, they are not lost: they have never left Earth and have the immanent quality of being "discoverable" if they are excavated before decomposing into the soil matrix. Things that leave Earth and escape our tracking are truly lost. And they are practically immortal: the Voyager 1 and 2 spacecraft, for example, have an estimated lifetime of 5 billion years, older than Earth itself (Bartels 2021).

The Archaeological Record in Space

The archaeological record of space technology on Earth includes places related to the development, manufacture, launch, and administration of spacecraft. For every object beyond Earth, there is an associated ground segment that supports its function. Without wanting to violate the reader's tolerance for metaphor, another one seems appropriate here: the ground segment resembles a spider sitting in the geocentre of its web, its senses extending through electromagnetic threads between the planets to respond to the slightest tremor. As yet, there are no ground segments on other celestial bodies; but this is poised to change in coming decades with plans for bases on the Moon and Mars. For a future-looking discipline such as space archaeology, what is absent can be almost as informative as what is present.

Antenna facilities used for tracking, surveillance, and downlink purposes range from extensive installations to domestic satellite dishes adorning urban skylines from Melbourne to Marrakesh (Gorman 2009b: 175). Terrestrial facilities may be remote enclaves or networked into the landscape and infrastructure of non-space urban and rural communities. A mighty launch tower or a monumental paraboloid dish will share the landscape with the residences of the people who build and maintain them. The faceless rockets are fuelled by the everyday lives of ordinary people.

Off-Earth, the oldest human artefacts in space are the Vanguard 1 satellite and its upper stage rocket, launched in 1958 by the USA and now over sixty years old. It was the fourth satellite to reach orbit, but its predecessors, Sputnik 1 and 2 and Explorer 1, have long since reentered the atmosphere. In an eccentric orbit with a perigee of 649 km in altitude, Vanguard 1 is predicted to be stable for another 240 years.

Spacecraft of various kinds are in orbit around the Moon, Mars, Ceres and Vesta (planetoids in the asteroid belt), Venus, and the Sun, bouncing around in Lagrange points, jostling among the asteroid belt or Kuiper belt, or sailing out into the galaxy, like the Voyagers and Pioneers, and eventually New Horizons. Others grace the surfaces of the Moon, Mars, Venus, Mercury, Titan (a moon of Saturn), the asteroids Eros, Itokawa, and Ryugu, and the comet

Churyumov–Gerasimenko. Some have flown on after leaving craters or scratches on small bodies such as comet Tempel 1 and asteroid Bennu.

The Moon currently has over one hundred places where human material culture has been deposited, since the impact of the USSR Luna 2 probe in 1959. Combined, this is over one hundred metric tons of terrestrial material moved from Earth to the Moon by various missions from the USSR, USA, Japan, India, China and Israel. Many of these sites are craters from deliberate or accidental crash impacts—the types of places which quickly become obscured on Earth, as the V2 rocket craters have been, but are exposed for eternity on an airless body. We might call the crashed rockets and probes "cultural meteorites" to distinguish them from the nonhuman material which constantly bombards the Moon; but in another sense, this is now a phase in lunar environmental history.

Capelotti (2010) argues that the Apollo (1969–1972) remains constitute a distinct culture in archaeological terms, as a suite of objects and behaviours bounded in space and time, and peculiar to the technology and ideologies of the 1960s. For space archaeologists, the iconic Apollo 11 bootprints are as evocative as the fossil trackway created by ancestral hominids in the volcanic ash of Laetoli in Tanzania, 3.6 million years ago (Díaz-Martínez et al. 2021; Meldrum et al. 2011).

Mars is the next most densely populated with human materials. The USSR's Mars 2 orbiter, launched in 1971, was the first successful mission to the planet and remains in orbit over fifty years later. There are at least nineteen archaeological sites created by the USA, European Space Agency, USSR/Russia, China, India, and the United Arab Emirates landing missions. If the Moon is known for its human landing sites, Mars is the planet of autonomous rovers, with six including the functioning Perseverance, Curiosity, and Zhurong, and nine if you count the never-deployed Mars 2 and 3 rovers, still encased in their landing craft. On Venus, the Cold War was won by the USSR: there are thirteen Russian Venera landing vehicles, and only one US landing mission. Mercury bears the 2015 impact crater of the Messenger spacecraft and nothing more until BepiColombo impacts sometime after 2028.

With the exception of the six Apollo missions to the Moon, these are all robotic or mechanical sites. To return to what is absent: at this point in time, there are no human remains beyond excreta and biomolecules in space. The cultural landscape of space is also a machine landscape (Gorman 2019b). Young describes machine landscapes as "sites, architectures and infrastructures of a system not built for us, but whose form, materiality and purpose is configured to anticipate the logics of machine vision and habitation rather than our own" (2019: 10). There are many machine landscapes on Earth—"server farms, telecommunications networks, distribution warehouses, unmanned [sic] ports and industrialised agriculture" (Young 2019: 10) which underpin the functioning of contemporary society but are not intended for humans to occupy or visit. The staples of the archaeological record on Earth, such as bones, ceramics, houses, burials, factories, and farms, are missing from the space machine landscape.

A perennial debate in the space community is whether a human presence in space is required at all when machines or robots can do what is needed at less expense. Science fiction writers (e.g., Stanislaw Lem (1974) and Greg Egan (1997)) have imagined futures where humans are no longer the dominant sentience in the solar system, having been superseded by robots who easily adapt to variable gravity conditions and can be radiation-hardened in ways that soft human bodies cannot. In such futures, Spennemann (2007b) has considered how self-aware robots and artificial intelligences (AIs) might create their own archaeology and heritage—highlighting that the concept of heritage value is species-specific.

Overview of the Development of Space Archaeology

On 19 November 1969, the Apollo 12 mission touched down 180 metres away from Surveyor 3, which had soft-landed in 1967 (Figure 4.1). In order to gain data on the effects of the lunar

Figure 4.1 Image of Surveyor 3 on the lunar surface in 1967. Image courtesy of NASA.

environment on human materials, the astronauts documented the site by photographs, noted the condition of the probe, and collected several pieces for analysis, much as a terrestrial archaeologist would take samples (O'Leary 2009a: 30). Effectively, this was the first taphonomic study in space, and Capelotti (2004: 49) suggests that it could be interpreted as the first archaeological fieldwork on the Moon.

That the contemporary era of space travel could be the focus of archaeological enquiry was presaged by US doyen of historical archaeology James Deetz, in his 1967 book *Invitation to Archaeology*, in which he posited that spaceships may one day be examined as archaeological artefacts. In 1974, Anthony Haden-Guest explored the archaeological significance of places on the "space coast" of Florida, noting that "the space project has already accumulated a history of Byzantine complexity" (1974: 37). Other archaeologists flagged the potential too. Ben Finney (1992) suggested the comparison of space sites created by the USA and USSR. William Rathje (1999), who pioneered the study of contemporary archaeology in his famous Tucson garbage project (Rathje and Murphy 1992), identified orbital debris as an archaeological record.

In 1999, NASA funded Beth Laura O'Leary's Lunar Legacy Project to document the assemblage of artefacts left behind by the Apollo 11 crew, and to investigate the relevant US federal preservation laws and regulations (New Mexico Space Grant Consortium/Lunar Legacy Project 2000). The project identified over 106 artefacts, structures, and features at Tranquility Base. This is the only one of the six Apollo sites for which this foundational work has been done. Identifying and documenting the archaeological record in space could be regarded as a necessary first stage in establishing the purview of space archaeology. Capelotti (2010) continued this work with a "desktop" survey of material remains throughout the solar system, using the NASA Space Science Data Coordinated Archive (NSSDCA) catalogue.

Gorman (2007a, 2009a) evaluated extant satellites in Earth orbit in the period between the launch of Sputnik 1 in 1957 and the launch of the first geostationary satellite in 1963, identifying technological trajectories such as a move from passive to active telecommunications and from spherical forms to more diverse designs. She described the increase in spacecraft orbiting Earth as an Anthropocene process of redistributing elements, such as aluminium, into new contexts (Gorman 2014). While space junk is viewed as discarded or abandoned material, it could also be seen as an assemblage with emergent properties that may only become evident over time (Gorman 2015).

In 2015, recognising that no systematic analysis of space artefacts or sites had yet been undertaken, Walsh and Gorman started the International Space Station Archaeological Project, using the NASA image archive and a legacy version of the ISS Inventory Management System to map human–object interactions (see Walsh this volume). Although "human factors" in space have been extensively studied from biomedical, psychological, and engineering perspectives, a material culture approach was missing. A pilot analysis of icons and other images placed by the crew in an ad hoc display in the Zevzda module showed that they changed over time in relation to political events in Russia and drew on a much older USSR tradition of venerating the three "space heroes", Tsiolkovsky, Korolev, and Gagarin (Salmond, Walsh, and Gorman 2020).

More recently, Westwood, O'Leary, and Donaldson (2017) undertook a comprehensive overview of the cultural significance, interconnectedness, and context in the contemporary archaeological record of Apollo-related sites on Earth and in space, noting that the terrestrial components were often crumbling into ruins. It's not impossible that one day the most intact remnants of Apollo culture will be on the Moon, long after Apollo vestiges have vanished from Earth. As a result of these studies and many others, space archaeology has developed from a barely acknowledged specialisation to "one demanding attention in a world increasingly reliant on space-based services" (Gorman and O'Leary 2013: 409). When the case no longer has to be made that this is archaeology, there is room to develop innovative theoretical approaches to understanding space and time through material culture.

Interpretations, Potentials, and Theoretical Approaches

Archaeology lies at the intersection of science, social science, and humanities. Modern historical archaeology encompasses the study of colonialism in settler nations, the growth of global capitalist societies, and social inequality (e.g., Hall and Silliman 2006; Leone 2016; Lightfoot and Martinez 1995; Orser 1996). If, as is often said, history is written by the victors, the strength of historical and contemporary archaeology is the ability, through the focus on material culture, to investigate sectors of a society absent or poorly represented in the documentary record, such as Indigenous people, women, children, working classes, and unfree labourers. These groups are also frequently absent from standard space histories. Redfield (2002: 791) has argued that the space industry, with its narrative of conquering the "high frontier", is the last bastion of unapologetic colonialism.

The space industry has tended to valorise a pseudo-Darwinian narrative which could be called the "Space Race Model":

> In this popular and compelling version of space history, the interests of largely white male American astronauts, space administrators, scientists and politicians are presented as universal human values. The military, nuclear, nationalist and colonial aspirations of space-faring nations are eclipsed by a "master narrative" in which heroic acts of discovery in space are the outcomes of a natural human urge to explore.
>
> *(Gorman 2005a: 86)*

Archaeology can be used to "decolonise" space exploration through a critical approach to the spatiality and materiality of these places and objects. The impacts of space technology on Indigenous people have been explored by Gorman (2005a, 2007b, 2009b, 2009c, 2019a) at the launch sites of Woomera (Australia), Kourou (French Guiana), and Colomb-Béchar (Algeria), using a cultural landscape approach in which the presence of material remains from different occupiers highlights changing power relationships. Launch sites are frequently located in colonies or former colonies, which colonial processes have constructed as "empty" and hence safe for dangerous installations. The juxtaposition of archaeological sites and contemporary technology is often framed as a contrast between the Stone Age and Space Age, in which Indigenous people's agency in the present is erased.

While material culture in space is dominated by the "spacefaring" nations, there are alternative narratives represented in the material culture. In orbit, the origins of CubeSats can be traced to the amateur satellite programmes of the early 1960s, which continue to provide low-cost access to space for "non-spacefaring" nations, students, and other groups (Gorman 2009c). Beyond the big-ticket space hardware items, the traces of non-elite individuals and groups can be discerned in the interstices and at the small scale.

An Australian example provides a web of connections centred around the boomerang, an object which has immense cultural resonances but is not normally thought of as a space artefact. It starts from Ngarrindjeri scientist David Unaipon's 1914 proposal of boomerang aerodynamics to build a helicopter (twenty-two years before the first operational helicopter) and continues to a boomerang given to Yuri Gagarin in 1961, new boomerang designs based on NASA data in the 1980s, a 2013 paper boomerang experiment in microgravity, a Kaurna boomerang flown on the ISS in 2019, to finally, a helicopter on Mars. Taking an artefact as the central focus rather than a spacecraft allows other stories to be told, such as the intersection of Indigenous science with space technology in this instance.

In more general terms, Gorman and O'Leary (2013) proposed behavioural archaeology as the theoretical framework which best fits space archaeology. Behavioural archaeology interprets material culture as components in systems of meaning, in which technology can be used to investigate how humans shape and are shaped by the material world (e.g., Binford 1978; Rathje and Schiffer 1982; Schiffer 1976). This approach has much in common with STS (science and technology studies) (e.g., Ferguson 1974; Winner 1977). However, while "things" are an essential category of inquiry in STS, there has been limited engagement with archaeological theories and data (Geselowitz 1993; Webmoor 2013). Space archaeology offers deep-time perspectives on innovation and technology transfer, adaptations to new environments, and the role of material culture in the construction of social identity.

"Creative Re-Imaginings": Methods for Space Archaeology

Like historical archaeology, space archaeology takes full advantage of the documentary and oral record to augment or explore divergences in interpretations of the material record. Unlike history, the focus is on human behavioural interactions with the material culture that are often not captured in documents or recollections. Despite an abundance of documentary sources, there are large gaps; and the objects themselves often provide the only evidence of decisions and design processes (Westwood, O'Leary, and Donaldson 2017). Ground truthing in space is not possible at the time of writing, except to a limited extent by remote sensing data from orbiters. Remote sensing enables mapping of the nature and extent of sites on planetary surfaces, without affecting the physical integrity of these places. The Lunar Reconnaissance Orbiter (LRO) imaged the Apollo archaeological sites on the Moon in 2009 and 2011, as well as identifying sites like the USSR Lunokhod 2 rover. In 2022, the LRO located the crash site of a Chinese Long March rocket on the far side.

In Earth orbit, tracking data can be used to model the distribution and evolution of discarded spacecraft over time, in conjunction with technical manuals, engineering prototypes and back-up spacecraft, blueprints, and photographs, to "interrogate the space object as an artefact" (Gorman and O'Leary 2013: 413). But as atmospheric reentry causes the regular demise of spacecraft, often documents have to stand in for the object (Walsh 2015), and spatial relations read from between the lines. This is also the case with inaccessible places, for example, the numerous landing sites on asteroids, and sites on the Moon. The Lunar Legacy Project used records, photographs, films, and maps of the Apollo 11 location to create its inventory of artefacts, although O'Leary observed that it is probably not yet complete without visiting the site (O'Leary 2009b: 763). The project established one of the key methods of conducting archaeology from Earth on places off-Earth. Of course, the documents and images are cultural products themselves, and much has been written on the anthropology of the photograph (e.g., Lydon 2020).

The International Space Station has been studied as a space habitat using the NASA image archive (Walsh and Gorman 2021; Walsh, Gorman, and Salmond 2021). The International Space Station Archaeological Project (ISSAP) uses "creative re-imaginings" of traditional archaeological fieldwork techniques to overcome the limitations of studying an inaccessible site. Machine learning was used to model the distribution of crew in different modules according to gender and space agency affiliation (Hamza et al. 2022). In 2022, the project flew an archaeological experiment on the ISS in which six sample squares of approximately 1 × 1 m were photographed each day for two months in order to map the movement of objects in this unique microgravity environment (see Walsh this volume). This is a very basic archaeological survey method usually used for surface survey or excavation. The astronauts became temporary archaeologists for the purpose of this experiment.

The application of archaeological methods to space places and objects is based on the core idea that the material culture can tell stories that are not represented in the documentary records, illuminating social and ideological factors which shape space technologies and larger-scale patterns of behaviour. The materials show what actually happened rather than what was supposed to happen, offering new perspectives even in the contemporary era with an overabundance of information.

Research Directions

The small number of space archaeologists has meant that many research directions have barely been pursued. Nonetheless, there is a rich potential in investigating the material record of space. Cultural changes during the Space Age include the 1991 end of the Cold War, a period in which national prestige was a primary motivation for space exploration (Hays and Lutes 2007), a move in the last decade away from nation-states as the agent of technological change (McDougall 1982: 1022) to private companies or New Space (Valentine 2012) as the drivers of off-Earth endeavours, and the growth of "emerging space nations" from the Global South. The Space Age progressed at the same time as a decolonising process, which saw the proliferation of new nations after the Second World War (Gorman 2009c).

Within the technical constraints of launch, tracking, and satellite design, space infrastructure expresses cultural differences and continuities. The space programmes of the USA, USSR, France, and Britain were built on the common origin of German rocketry, each nation co-opting local science, landscapes, and aspirations into industrial complexes to produce distinct traditions of space design. The study of local material expressions of this global technology can illuminate the technological and social choices made in the construction of space hardware.

Human–machine interfaces created by space suits, spacecraft and space stations, the control room, and personal devices, such as navigation units and smartphones, have another story to tell. They affect perceptions of space and personal distance as choices are based on "physical worlds available to human consciousness only through technological prostheses" (Fischer 1999: 468), rather than direct experience. Space archaeology can investigate how technologies that interface between humans and the space environment structure actions and embodiment on Earth. The reliance of the Apollo astronauts on machines to keep them alive exemplified, according to Mindell (2008: 15), "broad changes in human–machine relationships", in constantly negotiated boundaries between what was appropriate for computers and software to do and the assertion of autonomy by human actors, entangled with conceptions of gender and ideology in masculine bodies epitomising the ideal communist or capitalist (Gerovitch 2007).

There are wide-reaching cultural impacts of access to satellite services on Earth that can also be considered from the perspective of space archaeology. Space-based Earth observation, navigation, and telecommunications have changed patterns of resource extraction, production, trade, and consumption. Effectively, contemporary material culture on Earth can no longer be studied without taking the impacts of the space industry on everyday life into account. This extends to popular culture which reflects mundane responses to space technology in the form of vernacular and popular design, manifested in architecture, furniture, souvenirs, toys, clothes, utensils, food, and music. The ideologies of space exploration are translated and consumed in ways which reflect everyday aspirations for the future.

Popular cultural expressions of space technology demonstrate acculturation and accommodation between state-sponsored technological complexes and the everyday world, outside scientific elites (e.g., Gorman 2018; Macdonald 2008). Public support for expensive Cold War human spaceflight programmes in the USA and its allies, such as Australia, was generated by the domestication of outer space—creating products that promised participation through their consumption, such as the plastic astronauts offered in cereal boxes and the playground rockets that enticed children to dream of space. Macdonald (2008) argues that space toys were a way of reconciling the opposing values of military and civil spaceflight.

The ideologies of space exploration are visible in material remains of artefacts and landscapes that weave place and people together. The television camera which was one of the first objects placed on the lunar surface is surely one of the most significant artefacts at the Apollo 11 site because it enabled the participation of millions of viewers on Earth. Connected to domestic televisions and living rooms across the globe, its presence on another planet is evidence of a shared spectacle which has shaped how people envisage future human planetary landings. Most cameras in space are designed to collect scientific data; this one performed a social function.

Settings such as planetary landing sites and space stations remove variables which make the interpretation of human behaviour on Earth complex. For example, a longstanding issue in terrestrial archaeology is the degree to which environmental changes drive cultural change. While environmental determinism has been out of favour as an explanation of cultural change for some time, new techniques and data are reopening questions about human–environmental interactions (e.g., Arponen et al. 2019). The rate of environmental change on the Moon is so slow that it offers an opportunity to test the causes of technological and social change in isolation. The reverse applies to gravity. On Earth, it is a constant, so its role in shaping human behaviour is rarely examined. In variable gravity contexts, it is possible to assess which aspects of behaviour are dependent on particular kinds of gravity. This perspective may enable new interpretations of terrestrial material culture, but more importantly, can provide critical knowledge for the creation of new societies off-Earth in the much longer term.

Conclusion

The increase of mobility between Earth and space means that it no longer makes sense to view the material culture of the late industrial age as solely terrestrial. Space industries have been implicated in everyday life across the globe since the mid-twentieth century. One could even argue that the boundaries of Earth need to be redefined by cultural rather than scientific measures, to incorporate the geostationary ring at around 35,000 km in altitude. The archaeological study of the material record of space broadens the range of enquiry into human behaviour outside the normal spatial and temporal boundaries, and initiates an "investigative disintegration" (Meneganzin and Currie 2022) of the concept of behavioural modernity: what makes us human.

References

Ali, Rao Hamza, Amir Kanan Kashefi, Alice C. Gorman, Justin St. P. Walsh, and Erik J. Linstead. 2022. "Automated Identification of Astronauts on Board the International Space Station: A Case Study in Space Archaeology." *Acta Astronautica* 200: 262–69. https://doi.org/10.1016/j.actaastro.2022.08.017.

Arponen, Vesa P. J., Walter Dörfler, Ingo Feeser, Sonja Grimm, Daniel Groß, Martin Hinz, Daniel Knitter, Nils Müller-Scheeßel, Konrad Ott, and Artur Ribeiro. 2019. "Environmental Determinism and Archaeology: Understanding and Evaluating Determinism in Research Design." *Archaeological Dialogues* 26 (1): 1–9. https://doi.org/10.1017/S1380203819000059.

Augé, Marc. 1992. *Los no Lugares: Espacios del Anonimato, una Antropología de la Sobremodernidad*. Barcelona: Gedisa.

Barclay, Robert L., and Randall Brooks. 2002. "*In Situ* Preservation of Historic Spacecraft." *Journal of the British Interplanetary Society* 55 (5/6): 171–81.

Bartels, Megan. 2021. "Scientists' Predictions for the Long-Term Future of the Voyager Golden Records Will Blow Your Mind." *Space*.com, February 23. https://www.space.com/predicting-voyager-golden-records-distant-future.

Binford, Lewis R. 1978. *Nunamiut Ethnoarchaeology*. New York: Academic Press.

Butowsky, Harry A. 1984. *Man in Space: A National Historic Landmark Theme Study*. Washington, DC: US National Park Service, US Department of the Interior.

Campbell, Peter B. 2021. "The Anthropocene, Hyperobjects and the Archaeology of the Future Past." *Antiquity* 95 (383): 1315–30. https://doi.org/10.15184/aqy.2021.116.

Capelotti, P. J. 2004. "Space: The Final (Archaeological) Frontier." *Archaeology* 57 (6): 48–55.

Capelotti, P. J. 2010. *The Human Archaeology of Space: Lunar, Planetary and Interstellar Relics of Exploration*. Jefferson, NC: McFarland.

Croucher, Sarah K., and Lindsay Weiss, eds. 2011. *The Archaeology of Capitalism in Colonial Contexts: Postcolonial Historical Archaeologies*. New York: Springer.

Darrin, Ann G., and Beth L. O'Leary. 2009. "Introduction." In *Handbook of Space Engineering, Archaeology, and Heritage*, edited by Ann G. Darrin and Beth L. O'Leary, 3–15. Boca Raton, FL: CRC Taylor & Francis.

Deetz, James. 1967. *Invitation to Archaeology*. Garden City, NY: Natural History Press.

Díaz-Martínez, Ignacio, Carlos Cónsole-Gonella, Paolo Citton, and Silvina de Valais. 2021. "Half a Century After the First Bootprint on the Lunar Surface: The Ichnological Side of the Moon." *Earth-Science Reviews* 212: 103452. https://doi.org/10.1016/j.earscirev.2020.103452.

Edgeworth, Matt. 2010. "Beyond Human Proportions: Archaeology of the Mega and the Nano." *Archaeologies* 6 (1): 138–49. https://doi.org/10.1007/s11759-010-9125-9.

Egan, Greg. 1997. *Diaspora*. London: Millennium.

Ferguson, Eugene S. 1974. "Toward a Discipline of the History of Technology." *Technology and Culture* 15 (1): 13–30. https://doi.org/10.2307/3102758.

Fewer, Greg. 2002. "Toward an LSMR and MSMR (Lunar and Martian Sites & Monuments Records): Recording Planetary Spacecraft Landing Sites as Archaeological Monuments of the Future." In *Digging Holes in Popular Culture: Archaeology and Science Fiction*, edited by Miles Russell, 112–20. Oxford: Oxbow Books.

Finney, Ben R. 1992. *From Sea to Space*. Palmerston North: Massey University.

Fischer, Michael M. J. 1999. "Emergent Forms of Life: Anthropologies of Late or Postmodernities." *Annual Review of Anthropology* 28: 455–78. https://doi.org/10.1146/annurev.anthro.28.1.455.

Gerovitch, Slava. 2007. "'New Soviet Man' Inside Machine: Human Engineering, Spacecraft Design, and the Construction of Communism." *Osiris* 22 (1): 135–57. https://doi.org/10.1086/521746.

Geselowitz, Michael N. 1993. "Archaeology and the Social Study of Technological Innovation." *Science, Technology and Human Values* 18 (2): 231–46. https://doi.org/10.1177/016224399301800207.

González-Ruibal, Alfredo. 2008. "Time to Destroy: An Archaeology of Supermodernity." *Current Anthropology* 49 (2): 247–79. https://doi.org/10.1086/526099.

Gorman, Alice C. 2005a. "The Cultural Landscape of Interplanetary Space." *Journal of Social Archaeology* 5 (1): 85–107. https://doi.org/10.1177/1469605305050148.

Gorman, Alice C. 2005b. "The Archaeology of Orbital Space." In *5th NSSA Australian Space Science Conference*, 14–16 September 2005, 338–57. Melbourne: RMIT University.

Gorman, Alice C. 2007a. *Leaving the Cradle of Earth: The Heritage of Low Earth Orbit, 1957–1963*. Paper presented at Extreme Heritage: Australia ICOMOS Annual Conference, James Cook University.

Gorman, Alice C. 2007b. "La Terre et l'Espace: Rockets, Prisons, Protests and Heritage in Australia and French Guiana." *Archaeologies: Journal of the World Archaeological Congress* 3 (2): 153–68. https://doi.org/10.1007/s11759-007-9017-9.

Gorman, Alice C. 2009a. "Heritage of Earth Orbit: Orbital Debris—Its Mitigation and Cultural Heritage." In *Handbook of Space Engineering, Archaeology, and Heritage*, edited by Ann G. Darrin and Beth L. O'Leary, 381–97. Boca Raton, FL: CRC Taylor & Francis.

Gorman, Alice C. 2009b. "Beyond the Space Race: The Significance of Space Sites in a New Global Context." In *Contemporary Archaeologies: Excavating Now*, edited by Angela Piccini and Cornelius Holtorf, 161–80. Frankfurt: Peter Lang.

Gorman, Alice C. 2009c. "The Archaeology of Space Exploration." In *Space Travel and Culture: From Apollo to Space Tourism*, edited by David Bell and Martin Parker, 129–42. Sociological Review Monographs. Oxford: Wiley-Blackwell.

Gorman, Alice C. 2009d. "The Gravity of Archaeology." *Archaeologies* 5 (2): 344–59. https://doi.org/10.1007/s11759-009-9104-1.

Gorman, Alice. 2014. "The Anthropocene in the Solar System." *Journal of Contemporary Archaeology* 1 (1): 89–93. https://doi.org/10.1558/jca.v1i1.87.

Gorman, Alice C. 2015. "Robot Avatars: The Material Culture of Human Activity in Earth Orbit." In *Archaeology and Heritage of the Human Movement into Space*, edited by Beth L. O'Leary and P. J. Capelotti, 29–47. Heidelberg: Springer. https://doi.org/10.1007/978-3-319-07866-3_3.

Gorman, Alice C. 2018. "Gravity's Playground: Dreams of Spaceflight and the Rocket Park in Australian Culture." In *Defining the Fringe of Contemporary Australian Archaeology: Pyramidiots, Paranoia and the Paranormal*, edited by Darran Jordan and Rocco Bosco, 92–107. Newcastle upon Tyne: Cambridge Scholars Publishing

Gorman, Alice C. 2019a. *Dr Space Junk vs the Universe: Archaeology and the Future*. Cambridge, MA: MIT Press.

Gorman, Alice C. 2019b. "Ghosts in the Machine: Space Junk and the Future of Earth Orbit." In *Machine Landscapes: Architectures of the Post-Anthropocene*, edited by Liam Young. Special issue, *Architectural Design* 89 (1): 107–11. https://doi.org/10.1002/ad.2397.

Gorman, Alice C. 2021. "Space Debris, Space Situational Awareness and Cultural Heritage Management in Earth Orbit." In *Commercial and Military Uses of Outer Space*, edited by Melissa de Zwart and Stacey Henderson, 133–51. Singapore: Springer. https://doi.org/10.1007/978-981-15-8924-9_10.

Gorman, Alice C., and Beth Laura O'Leary. 2007. "An Ideological Vacuum: The Cold War in Outer Space. In *A Fearsome Heritage: Diverse Legacies of the Cold War*, edited by John Schofield and Wayne Cocroft, 73–92. Walnut Creek, CA: Left Coast Press.

Gorman, Alice C., and Beth Laura O'Leary. 2013. "The Archaeology of Space Exploration." In *The Oxford Handbook of the Archaeology of the Contemporary World*, edited by Paul Graves-Brown, Rodney Harrison and Angela Piccini, 409–24. Oxford: Oxford University Press. https://doi.org/10.1093/oxfordhb/9780199602001.013.040.

Haden-Guest, Anthony. 1974. "An Archaeology of the Space Age: Traveling in an Already Antique Land." *Harper's Magazine*, May, 37–40.

Hall, Martin, and Stephen W. Silliman, eds. 2006. *Historical Archaeology*. Malden, MA: Blackwell.

Harrison, Rodney, and John Schofield. 2010. *After Modernity: Archaeological Approaches to the Contemporary Past*. Oxford: Oxford University Press.

Hays, Peter L., and Charles D. Lutes. 2007. "Towards a Theory of Spacepower." *Space Policy* 23 (4): 206–9. https://doi.org/10.1016/j.spacepol.2007.09.003.

Idziak, Luke A. 2013. "Cultural Resources Management in Outer Space: Historic Preservation in the Graveyard Orbits." *Synesis: A Journal of Science, Technology, Ethics, and Policy* 4: 61–75.

Isaacson, Michal, and Noam Shoval. 2006. "Application of Tracking Technologies to the Study of Pedestrian Spatial Behavior." *The Professional Geographer* 58 (2): 172–83. https://doi.org/10.1111/j.1467-9272.2006.00524.x.

Lem, Stanislaw. 1974. *The Cyberiad: Fables for the Cybernetic Age*. New York: Seabury Press.

Leone, Mark P. 2016. *Critical Historical Archaeology*. London: Routledge.

Lightfoot, Kent, and Antoinette Martinez. 1995. "Frontiers and Boundaries in Archaeological Perspective." *Annual Review of Anthropology* 24: 471–92. https://doi.org/10.1146/annurev.an.24.100195.002351.

Lydon, Jane. 2020. *Photography, Humanitarianism, Empire*. London: Routledge.

Macdonald, Fraser. 2008. "Space and the Atom: On the Popular Geopolitics of Cold War Rocketry." *Geopolitics* 13 (4): 611–34. https://doi.org/10.1080/14650040802275479.

McDougall, Walter A. 1982. "Technocracy and Statecraft in the Space Age—Toward the History of a Saltation." *The American Historical Review* 87 (4): 1010–40. https://doi.org/10.2307/1857903.

Meldrum, D. J., Martin G. Lockley, Spencer G. Lucas, and Charles Musiba. 2011. "Ichnotaxonomy of the Laetoli Trackways: The Earliest Hominin Footprints." *Journal of African Earth Sciences* 60 (1–2): 1–12. https://doi.org/10.1016/j.jafrearsci.2011.01.003.

Meneganzin, Andra, and Adrian Currie. 2022. "Behavioural Modernity, Investigative Disintegration & Rubicon Expectation." *Synthese* 200 (1): 47 (1–28). https://doi.org/10.1007/s11229-022-03491-7.

Mindell, David A. 2008. *Digital Apollo: Human and Machine in Spaceflight*. Cambridge, MA: MIT Press.

Morton, Timothy. 2010. *The Ecological Thought*. Cambridge, MA: Harvard University Press

NASA Orbital Debris Program Office n.d. *Frequently Asked Questions*. https://orbitaldebris.jsc.nasa.gov/faq/#.

New Mexico Space Grant Consortium/Lunar Legacy Project 2000. http://spacegrant.nmsu.edu/lunarlegacies.

O'Leary, Beth. 2009a. "The Evolution of Space Archaeology and Heritage." In *Handbook of Space Engineering, Archaeology, and Heritage*, edited by Ann G. Darrin and Beth L. O'Leary, 29–48. Boca Raton, FL: CRC Taylor & Francis.

O'Leary, Beth. 2009b. "One Giant Leap: Preserving Cultural Resources on the Moon." In *Handbook of Space Engineering, Archaeology, and Heritage*, edited by Ann G. Darrin and Beth L. O'Leary, 757–80. Boca Raton, FL: CRC Taylor & Francis.

O'Leary, Beth. 2009c. "Historic Preservation at the Edge: Archaeology on the Moon, in Space and on Other Celestial Bodies." *Historic Environment* 22 (1): 13–18.

Olsen, Bjørnar. 2003. "Material Culture after Text: Remembering things." *Norwegian Archaeological Review* 36 (2): 77–104. https://doi.org/10.1080/00293650310000650.

Orser, Charles. 1996. *A Historical Archaeology of the Modern World*. New York: Plenum.

Rathje, William. 1999. "An Archaeology of Space Garbage." *Discovering Archaeology* 1 (5): 108–12.

Rathje, William, and Cullen Murphy. 1992. *Rubbish! The Archaeology of Garbage*. New York: HarperCollins.

Rathje William L., and Michael B. Schiffer. 1982. *Archaeology*. New York: Harcourt Brace Jovanovich.

Redfield, Peter. 2002. "The Half-Life of Empire in Outer Space." *Social Studies of Science* 32 (5–6): 791–825. https://doi.org/10.1177/030631270203200508.

Salmond, Wendy, Justin Walsh and Alice C. Gorman. 2020. "Eternity in Low Earth Orbit: Icons on the International Space Station." *Religions* 11 (11): 611. https://doi.org/10.3390/rel11110611.

Schiffer, Michael B. 1976. *Behavioral Archeology*. New York: Academic Press.

Speake, Janet, and Stephen Axon. 2012. "'I Never Use "Maps" Anymore': Engaging with Sat Nav Technologies and the Implications for Cartographic Literacy and Spatial Awareness." *The Cartographic Journal* 49 (4): 326–36. https://doi.org/10.1179/1743277412Y.0000000021.

Spennemann, Dirk H. R. 2004. "The Ethics of Treading on Neil Armstrong's Footsteps." *Space Policy* 20 (4): 279–90. https://doi.org/10.1016/j.spacepol.2004.08.005.

Spennemann, Dirk H. R. 2007a. "Extreme Cultural Tourism from Antarctica to the Moon." *Annals of Tourism Research* 34 (4): 898–918. https://doi.org/10.1016/j.annals.2007.04.003.

Spennemann, Dirk H. R. 2007b. "On the Cultural Heritage of Robots." *International Journal of Heritage Studies* 13 (1): 4–21. https://doi.org/10.1080/13527250601010828.

Valentine, David. 2012. "Exit Strategy: Profit, Cosmology, and the Future of Humans in Space." *Anthropological Quarterly* 85 (4): 1045–67. https://doi.org/10.1353/anq.2012.0073.

Walsh, Justin St P. 2012. "Protection of Humanity's Cultural and Historic Heritage in Space." *Space Policy* 28 (4): 234–43. https://doi.org/10.1016/j.spacepol.2012.04.001.

Walsh, Justin St P. 2015. "Purposeful Ephemera: The Implications of Self-Destructing Space Technology for the Future Practice of Archaeology." In *Archaeology and Heritage of the Human Movement into Space*, edited by Beth L. O'Leary and P. J. Capelotti, 75–90. Heidelberg: Springer. https://doi.org/10.1007/978-3-319-07866-3_6.

Walsh, Justin St. P., and Alice Gorman. 2021. "A Method for Space Archaeology Research: The International Space Station Archaeological Project." *Antiquity* 95 (383): 1331–43. https://doi.org/10.15184/aqy.2021.114.

Walsh, Justin St. P., Alice Gorman, and Wendy Salmond. 2021. "Visual Displays in Space Station Culture: An Archaeological Analysis." *Current Anthropology* 62 (6): 804–18. https://doi.org/10.1086/717778.

Webmoor, Timothy. 2013. "STS, Symmetry, Archaeology." In *The Oxford Handbook of the Archaeology of the Contemporary World*, edited by Paul Graves-Brown, Rodney Harrison and Angela Piccini, 105–20. Oxford: Oxford University Press. https://doi.org/10.1093/oxfordhb/9780199602001.013.039.

Westwood, Lisa, Beth Laura O'Leary, and Milford Wayne Donaldson. 2017. *The Final Mission: Preserving NASA's Apollo Sites*. Gainesville, FL: University Press of Florida.

Winner, Langdon. 1977. *Autonomous Technology: Technics-Out-of-Control as a Theme in Political Thought*. Cambridge, MA: MIT Press.

Young, Liam. 2019. "Neo-Machine: Architecture without People." *Architectural Design* 89 (1): 6–13. https://doi.org/10.1002/ad.2381.

5
ANTHROPOLOGY AND CONTEMPORARY SPACE EXPLORATION, WITH A NOTE ON HOPI LADDERS

Istvan Praet

"Beautiful ladder beam, beautiful ladder rungs, fastened to the ladder with turquoise. Thus we came out." —*Muyingwa*, the kachina responsible for the germination of seeds, during an initiation ritual for Hopi children.

(Geertz 1994: 234)

At first sight, anthropology has no business in outer space. So far, no alien humanities have been discovered (Figure 5.1). Within anthropology's traditional remit—academic scholarship about human beings—the study material is very limited: a handful of astronauts and cosmonauts in the International Space Station and nowadays also the occasional ultra-rich space tourist. From this vantage point, the anthropology of humans beyond Earth appears like a niche interest, and the potential contribution of the discipline to the broader endeavour of contemporary space exploration seems marginal. In this chapter, I make the case that 'off-Earth anthropology' has much more to offer than the major space agencies have fathomed so far. The long-standing expertise of anthropologists with questions of inclusion and exclusion (colonialism, racism, sexism, etc.) also has pertinence across the terrestrial/extraterrestrial divide. In what follows I provide an overview of how that expertise shapes the emerging field of outer space studies and outline its prospective relevancy for the space sciences more widely. I pay particular attention to the way in which anthropologists reconfigure debates regarding human exceptionalism. Outer space studies, it should be noted, is distinct from the comparative study of human conceptions of the cosmos, which has a long tradition in anthropology and is commonly known as *cultural astronomy* (e.g., Baity 1973; Ruggles and Saunders 1993; Holbrook, Medupe, and Urama 2008; Urton and Ruggles 2010; Kelley and Milone 2011). To begin this overview, it is useful to dwell on this distinction for a moment. Consider a classic example in the cultural astronomy genre: the role of *kachina* star-beings in Hopi cosmology.

In the ethnographic literature, Hopi ceremonialism is routinely characterised as staggeringly complex, eerily beautiful, and mesmerisingly alien. The various annually recurring ceremonies are timed according to the position of certain star constellations and involve a colourful cast of kachinas, impersonated by dancers pertaining to specific clans. They take place in Hopi villages perched on three adjoining mesas in northern Arizona. The whole area is envisaged as the axis of the world and indeed the centre of the cosmos. The open-roofed kivas where the ceremonies

Figure 5.1 Walapi Antelope Kiva of the Hopi Indians in the village of Mishongnovi, ca. 1901. Photo by Pierce, C.C. (Charles C.), 1861–1946. USC Libraries Special Collections. Public Domain.

are performed also function as sky observatories. In fact, the kiva connects multiple worlds, for the present one is the fourth in a sequence of seven, according to one strand of Hopi cosmology (the seven stars of the Pleiades—*chööchökam*, 'the stars that cling together'—represent those seven worlds). As visitors from the stars and from other worlds, the kachinas descend from the sky and enter the kiva via a ladder through the roof. At winter solstice, the turquoise-helmeted *soyal kachina* and the black-masked *mastop kachina* appear—they come from very far away, as testified by the three white stars painted on each side of the latter's head, representing the three stars in Orion's belt. In fact, dozens if not hundreds of these 'visitors from afar' emerge during the ceremonial season, each with their own antics, their own clownish tricks and ritual powers, their own costumes, masks, body decorations, and accessories. Taken as a whole, the ceremonies constitute a veritable cosmology—they can be interpreted, as a number of ethnographers have done, as the cyclical reenactment of cosmic history and the emergence of life (e.g., Waters 1977 [1963]; Geertz 1984). This cursory sketch suffices to highlight a key characteristic of the cultural astronomy approach: natural scientists—whether they are space researchers, planetary scientists, or astrobiologists—can safely ignore it (but see Hamacher 2011 for a study in cultural astronomy that attempts to break with that template).

By definition, cultural astronomy limits itself to examining *representations* of the cosmos. The cosmos itself—the 'actual' cosmos—is quite happily left to physical cosmologists, scientific astronomers, and assorted natural scientists. One can say there exists a tacit entente between cultural astronomers and space scientists: the former restrict themselves to how reality is represented, the latter can claim sole ownership of the domain of reality itself without having to fear any interference. The tasks are neatly divided: the first only deal with culture, the second exclusively study nature. That the modern divide between culture and nature may be equally provincial and equally as exotic as the costumes of kachina dancers is a thought that neither side seems to have given much attention. At any rate, no cultural astronomer has ever challenged that convenient division of labour as far as I know. The upshot of their line of thinking is this: Hopi cosmology is interesting, to be sure, but can only be taken seriously up to a certain point. The idea that one can travel between worlds by means of a humble ladder, rather than by using rockets or high-tech spacecraft, is dismissed out of hand. And so are the Hopi tales wherein kachinas journey across the sky piloting *paatuwvota*, flying shields made of lightweight cotton woven in the manner of Hopi wedding dresses (cf. Malotki and Gary 2001: xi). The social scientist/cultural astronomer and the natural scientist/modern space explorer are in perfect agreement on all this; human fictions and proper facts can and must be kept separate at all times. Kachinas 'returning home' to their otherworldly abodes at summer solstice, kitted out with ritually procured spruce branches and eagle feathers, are of a different order than NASA astronauts in their next-generation space suits. An unbridgeable gulf divides religious belief and scientific exploration.

If the emerging field of outer space studies has one outstanding characteristic it must be that it radically breaks with this traditional, mutually agreed division of labour between social scientists and natural scientists. What unites scholars in outer space studies is that they refuse to accept the cultural astronomers' self-imposed constraint, namely that they have nothing to say about 'the cosmos itself'. Whatever it is that off-Earth anthropologists are after, it is not limited to meta-level representations of a supposedly more fundamental reality ('nature'). They are metaphysical troublemakers who have come to realise that they cannot be 'safely ignored' by their colleagues in the natural sciences. In their hands, outer space is no longer the exclusive domain of accredited space researchers based at major space agencies or elite universities. What connects them is that they systematically challenge the age-old prerogatives of space scientists working under the rules of modern metaphysics. What distinguishes them is an awareness that the access to nature of an astrophysicist, a planetary geologist, or an astrobiologist is not more direct than anyone else's. Modern scientists' apprehension of the cosmos is commonly hailed as supremely objective, but outer space studies scholars know that objectivity did not fall from the sky ready-made—it has both a history and an anthropology. What scientists deem 'objective', and which criteria they use to define that epistemic virtue, changes over time and across disciplines, sometimes subtly and sometimes quite abruptly—rival notions of objectivity may even coexist within a single discipline.

The anthropologists Sophie Houdart and Christine Jungen have done pathbreaking work to overcome the divide between what they refer to as the cosmologists' cosmos and the anthropologists' cosmos. In "Cosmos Connections" Houdart and Jungen (2015) refrain from making a hard distinction between the physical mechanisms that constitute the 'actual' cosmos and its 'subjective' representations. Instead, they foreground various possible *connections* with the cosmos. What is radical about their move is that no single connection is privileged. In essence, Houdart and Jungen show that there are many valid (and I dare add 'objective') ways of connecting with the cosmos. The rather droll image they invoke is that of a plumbing system: researchers have a plethora of tubes, pipes, and conduits at their disposition. The preeminence of visual connections, of which the famed blue marble picture is the prototype, is not set in marble. As a consequence, the history of cosmological science has to be reimagined:

> We arrive at something that is very different from a linear history, very different from a history that goes from a closed world to the infinite universe, as Alexandre Koyré phrased it in the mid-twentieth century. We are no longer dealing with the progression from a subjective, anthropocentric cosmos to a more objective comprehension of an endless cosmos with laws of its own. The cosmos now appears as a fragile and equivocal object, something one can easily lose track of as one approaches it. An object with a remarkable tendency to dodge those who investigate it, an elusive object which only ever reveals itself partially, an object that requires a lot of work in order to stabilise it, however provisional that stabilisation may be. Whatever one's way of approaching it, the cosmos is a matter of connections, canals, and tubes, of wavelengths, vibrations, and tuning.
>
> (Houdart and Jungen 2015: 7, my translation)

Such connections are key to apprehending the immensely large but are equally determinant to fathoming the infinitely small: they apply both at the galactic scale and at the molecular scale. Methodologically, macrocosm and microcosm confront researchers with perfectly comparable problems of capture and representation. In a complementing publication Tiziana Beltrame, Houdart, and Jungen (2017) again emphasise the endless *work* that is involved to stabilise evanescent minuscule beings: techniques of amplification, sensorial translation, operations of capture, visualisation, manipulation, and transformation. All of this, they are at pains to explain, is never merely a matter of automatically zooming in or zooming out.

In fact, insights in the same vein had already been acquired in the early 2000s by anthropologists such as Gísli Pálsson and Stefan Helmreich. In "Celestial Bodies: Lucy in the Sky", a seminal text for outer space studies, Pálsson (2009) focussed on the cross-disciplinary recurrence of idioms of voyaging and mapping, and on the remarkable, more-than-metaphorical similarities between research into what is often referred to as 'the universe within' (i.e., the human body, particularly the genome) and the exploration of outer space. And in subsequent work, he has consistently endeavoured to bridge the divide between the social and the natural sciences, notably by means of the theoretical concepts of biosociality and geosociality (cf. Ingold and Pálsson 2013; Pálsson and Swanson 2016). Helmreich, for his part, has pioneered social scientific research on so-called extreme life in analogue environments. It may seem a little odd to refer to his *Alien Ocean: Anthropological Voyages in Microbial Seas* (2009)—essentially a fine-grained ethnographic study of marine biologists and oceanographers—as one of the foundational books of outer space studies. Yet insofar as it is the first sustained anthropological interrogation of how contemporary scientists employ the category of 'the alien' it unquestionably merits pride of place. Just as critics of cultural astronomy may formulate doubts on whether Hopi kachinas necessarily have to be envisaged as mere make-believe aliens, Helmreich makes one wonder whether oceans are best captured as terrestrial (the modern habit) or as extraterrestrial (a novel metaphysical option, increasingly toyed with in fields such as astrobiology). A key lesson is that what counts as extreme or alien may be in the eye of the beholder—it should never be considered a given; such designations must always be the target of anthropological enquiry. From the standpoint of a luminescent octopus living in the dark, high-pressure depths of the Atlantic, we, non-shiny surface dwellers, may be the extremophiles. What makes Helmreich's work stand out is that it has the temerity to systematically question some of the most basic conceptual underpinnings of modern thought. By asking deceptively simple and seemingly unanthropological questions (e.g., "What is water?") Helmreich in effect *provincialises* modern science as it developed since the so-called Scientific Revolution in the sixteenth and seventeenth centuries. It is a technique he perfects in *Sounding the Limits of Life*, which offers—among other things—an ethnographically informed portrayal of the scientific search for extraterrestrial life (Helmreich 2016).

In the United States, the anthropology of outer space came of age with the appearance of groundbreaking books such as *Placing Outer Space: An Earthly Ethnography of Other Worlds* and *Into the Extreme: U.S. Environmental Systems and Politics Beyond Earth*. In the former Lisa Messeri (2016) describes how planetary scientists and astronomers familiarise faraway celestial bodies through specific practices of mapping and visualising—the strange and the unknown are translated into the sensorially relatable. By making outer space "rich with place", as she puts it, scientists are able to scale the infinite cosmos down to the level of human experience—this announces a metaphysical regime change of sorts, "a new vision of the universe" (p. 23). In the latter Valerie Olson (2018) investigates how North American scientists and engineers have redefined the solar system in environmental terms. Her book's central innovative feature is that it shows how outer space is increasingly grasped through the lens of political ecology and is no longer thinkable just in terms of political geography or political economy. The heliosphere, the wider solar neighbourhood, is de facto becoming an ecosystem. But the originality of authors such as Messeri and Olson also sits in their methodology and, more particularly, in their unconventional choice of field sites: a Mars analogue site in Utah, an astronomical observatory in the Atacama Desert of Chile, the MIT laboratories where exoplanet hunters visualise super-Earths and mini-Neptunes, an undersea astronaut training facility off the Florida coast, the NASA Johnson Space Center in Houston. With hindsight, this move may seem straightforward, but a decade ago—when outer space anthropology was deemed a frivolous fantasy by all but a handful of their colleagues—it was actually quite bold (if only in terms of career prospects!). The gamble seems to have paid off, and their lead has since been followed by a number of scholars: in US academia there now exists a thriving scene of anthropologists focussing on space exploration. David Valentine (2012, 2017) has written on prospective Mars settlement schemes and continues to develop critical angles on the (extra)geopolitics of commercial space ventures. Zara Mirmalek (2020) has published *Making Time on Mars*, in which she describes how mission scientists and engineers who remotely control the Mars rovers struggle to synchronise Earthly and Martian temporalities and reflects on what it takes to make an interplanetary workplace function well. Micha Rahder (2020) has published *An Ecology of Knowledges*, a book on how conservation practices and scientific knowledge are enabled by remote sensing technologies (e.g., satellite imagery) in the context of Guatemala's Maya biosphere reserve. Iokepa Casumbal-Salazar (2017) has written about the conflict between native Hawaiians and the astronomers who seek to build yet another huge telescope on the summit of the sacred Mauna Kea volcano. From this angle, he develops the provocative argument that the logics of colonial settlement remain inherent to Western science to this day. Janet Vertesi is the author of *Seeing like a Rover* (2014), a ethnographically informed book on how NASA teams and their robotic rovers visualise the Martian surface and thus create knowledge of Mars. More recently (2020) she also published *Shaping Science: Organisations, Decisions, and Culture on NASA's Teams*.

In Europe, the anthropology of outer space has taken root as well in the past five years or so. There are two main clusters: one in London and one in Paris. At University College London Victor Buchli has initiated ETHNO-ISS (see Jeevendrampillai et al. this volume), an EU-funded project which aims to provide the first systematic and comparative ethnographic study of what is in effect the oldest extraterrestrial society in low Earth orbit: the International Space Station (ISS). Buchli (2020a, 2020b) and his team have set up a direct video link with the space station and are particularly interested in microgravity material cultures and radically new forms of human habitation. David Jeevendrampillai, who directs the newly established Centre for Outer Space Studies at UCL, and Aaron Parkhurst, who focuses on medical and bodily aspects of human spaceflight, have extended this anthropological examination of habitability and materiality to all forms of off-Earth architecture, including designs for prospective Mars settlements (Parkhurst and Jeevendrampillai 2020). At the Université Paris Sciences et Lettres Perig Pitrou is one of the principal coordinators of the PSL IRIS OCAV project, which seeks to investigate the origins and the conditions of the appearance of life from a variety of disciplinary perspectives spanning the natural and the social sciences. It arguably constitutes the first long-term collaboration between planetary scientists, astrobiologists, anthropologists, STS scholars, and historians of science. The emphasis on 'life' (rather than materiality or systems or place-making) is one of its characteristic features. Another specificity of the French group is that many of its members and associates came to outer space studies indirectly. Pitrou himself, for example, did not start out as an anthropologist of science but as an Americanist with a focus on non-Western notions of vitality and on indigenous conceptions of the relation between microcosm and macrocosm—only later onwards did he develop an interest in modern scientific ideas of life (see, e.g., Pitrou 2012, 2014, 2015). Yet it turns out that this extensive comparative scope has distinctive advantages that benefit the joint effort of outer space studies scholars to nuance dominant narratives of cumulative progress and to provincialise modern forms of space exploration in unexpected ways. The group also has significant expertise in human–robot relations, biomimicry, and the modelling of artificial life in closed environments, all of which are relevant to scholarship on space travel and extraterrestrial settlement. Joffrey Becker (2015, 2019, 2022) may be the only anthropologist in the world who has not only written about living *with* robots but also about living *in* robots. Lauren Kamili (2020), for her part, has reexamined the life/non-life divide through a study of a biomimetic lamp modelled on a luminescent fungus. Finally, I cannot fail to mention Charlotte Bigg and Elsa De Smet, two historians of science with a strong interest in visual anthropology (see especially Bigg 2012, 2015, 2018; De Smet 2018). Their idea of studying space exploration after the manner of art history is one that I myself have also strived to put into practice in some of my latest work, albeit in a slightly idiosyncratic way (Praet 2017, 2021, forthcoming).

Elsewhere in Europe and in the rest of the world, the anthropology of outer space is going strong as well. Valentina Marcheselli (2020, 2022) has conducted ethnographic research at astrobiological analogue sites in Sardinia and in Iceland and has also written about 'weird life' and 'shadow biospheres' from a sociological perspective. Filippo Bertoni (2018, 2020) has used the notion of *mesocosm*—miniaturised environments with characteristics that mirror the real-life-scale cosmos at large, but more tractable and open to experiment and control—in his studies of earthworms, 'global worming', and the potential role of worms in soiling Mars. Davide Chinigò and Cherryl Walker (Walker and Chinigò 2018; Chinigò and Walker 2020) have studied the Square Kilometre Array radio telescope project in South Africa's Karoo region, critically reflecting on the manifold tensions between big science and local development concerns. Tamara Álvarez (2020) has ethnographically investigated Euro-American schemes to settle the Moon, 'our eighth continent'. Juan Francisco Salazar (2017, 2020) has used his fieldwork experience in Antarctica to rethink how space scientists engage with extreme environments and terrestrial analogue sites (see also Praet and Salazar 2017). Matthew Kearnes and Thom van Dooren (2017) have started to think about 'an ethic of interstellar flourishing' in the context of meteorite mining and the unfolding corporate 'gold rush in space' (see also Klinger 2018). Denis Sivkov has conducted ethnographic research on 'amateur cosmonautics'—non-commercial and non-professional DIY projects of space exploration in contemporary Russia. Space amateurs, Sivkov argues, are the 'hidden figures' in the history of space research and exploration: in light of their manifold yet generally ignored contributions to the space sciences, further neglecting them is unjustified (Sivkov, pers. comm.). And Julie Patarin-Jossec (2020) has written on the training of foreign astronauts in Russia, showing that becoming an astronaut implies cultivating a 'legitimate body' in line with cultural and gendered models informed by Soviet heritage and ideals of 'heroic' masculinity.

Last but not least, an increasing number of Native American scholars are engaging with some of the burning questions of the so-called Space Age in distinctive ways. Lou Cornum (2015), who has written on Black and Indigenous science fiction, has shown how authors of colour use sci-fi to subvert a genre that has always been prone to reproducing colonial imaginaries. Writing from the standpoint of the "colonizee", they seek to reverse "the telescope's gaze of who is exploring who". This is not a mere literary gimmick, Cornum emphasises, but a profound rethinking of how we moderns imagine time, progress, and who is worthy of the future. As they put it: "In the colonial imaginary, Indigenous life is not only separate from the present time but also out of place in the future, a time defined by the progress of distinctively western technology". Why, Cornum wonders, can't indigenous peoples also project themselves among the stars? And: might their visions of the cosmos forge less harmful relationships than colonial visions of a final frontier, both here on Earth and beyond? In a similar vein, the cultural geographer Deondre Smiles (2020) has examined various possible ways of viewing outer space through a 'decolonial' lens and to avoid replicating colonial frameworks of space occupation and resource extraction when exploring celestial bodies such as Mars. Besides the direct and active involvement of Indigenous peoples in contemporary space exploration, Smiles points to another option which has been ignored so far: engaging with alternative, non-Western ways of thinking 'space' here on Earth. The basic idea is that understanding how Indigenous people make and remake space "can provide another blueprint for how we might engage with space beyond Earth". Recent archaeological studies of Hopi walking trails exemplify this line of reasoning. In cooperation with anthropologists and archaeologists, Leigh J. Kuwanwisiwma (Kuwanwisiwma et al. 2019; Ferguson, Berlin, and Kuwanwisiwma 2004) has examined *kukhepya*, a Hopi notion that can be translated "to go along looking for footprints". Such footprints are ruins, petroglyphs, potsherds, and shrines left behind long ago by the ancestors during their epic migrations towards the current Hopi homelands, which are conceived of as the centre of the cosmos (cf. Colwell-Chanthaphonh and Ferguson 2006). They embody "the faraway" both in terms of time and in terms of space—they are generally understood as entry points to or from other worlds. As such they may be a reasonably close equivalent to modern notions of the extraterrestrial. The so-called Salt Trail to the Grand Canyon and the trail to the Zuñi Salt Lake are ancient and are associated with ceremonial pilgrimages and trading expeditions. That these trails often lead to what astrobiologists refer to as extreme environments (the halophilic organisms that inhabit them can be studied as analogues to lifeforms on early Mars or elsewhere) is interesting in itself. But these trails also suggest that the modern metaphysics that became dominant from the seventeenth century onwards has configured the cosmos in a highly peculiar way, in the sense that outer space is by and large associated with the alien and the unfamiliar. Hopi pilgrims, however, travelled in a cosmos that was never conceived of as a totally alien space, a terra nullius, or a cosmic wilderness but as a cosmos stuffed with things one can relate to, by ancient kin and old friends, by star-beings.

For all their quirks and idiosyncrasies, outer space studies scholars share at least one conviction: they have realised that knowing the cosmos is as much a conceptual adventure as it is a collective effort to grasp the workings of nature with ever greater exactitude. Understanding it merely as the inexorable accumulation of ever more precise data—along the lines of which it is invariably covered in journals such as *Nature* or *Science*—is reductive and fails to do it full justice: space exploration is about physics, yes, undeniably, but also about metaphysics—i.e., about something that modern scientists thought they had evacuated long ago, once and for all (the conviction that its conclusions are or at least should be 'certified metaphysics-free' has indeed *defined* modern science ever since the so-called Scientific Revolution). Outer space studies scholars have begun to realise that this traditional conception of science is no longer fit for purpose, in the sense that it does not adequately reflect what is actually happening in the space sciences. Anthropologists who conduct ethnographic research with astronomers, planetary geologists, or astrobiologists are starting to notice that the meanings of 'science' itself are mutating. And there is an emerging consensus that the exploration of outer space—notwithstanding its global entanglements, its high-tech infrastructure, and its cosmic reach—is also very much a provincial endeavour which takes place within highly specific and historically contingent metaphysical circumstances. Understanding that peculiarly modern conceptual framework, and the surprising ways in which it is currently changing, is the common purpose of outer space studies scholars and off-Earth anthropologists. A number of received ideas may turn out to be much more fragile than scientists typically realise.

To conclude I would like to illustrate this by homing in on a notion that is essential to how modern scientists, and modern thinkers in general, conceive of their place in the cosmos: human exceptionalism. That there is only one known humanity is commonly deemed an incontestable fact. As scientists like to express it: $n=1$. Astrobiology tells us that we, members of the species *Homo sapiens*, are alone in the universe until further notice: so far, no alien humanoids have been reported; Search for Extraterrestrial Intelligence (SETI) research which for many years now has aimed to pick up signals of extraterrestrial intelligence is vexingly inconclusive. If one goes along with that view, off-Earth anthropology is indeed a vain enterprise: a scholarly field without subject matter (save for the odd astronaut). Yet could it be that this grim predicament of cosmic loneliness is self-imposed in the sense that it has been built into modern modes of scientific thinking by default? Or, to put it more crudely: does our habitual way of looking prevent us, moderns, from spotting alien humans? By way of experiment I propose to tackle this at-first-sight rather preposterous question not by taking recourse to SETI radio telescopes but by employing another highly sophisticated yet unjustly underestimated technological device: Hopi ladders. These ladders, I would suggest, are the structural equivalent of spacecraft and modern rockets in the Space Age: they are a means to travel between worlds. It is along these ladders that the kachina star-beings enter the kivas during the great ceremonies. If the kiva is a veritable microcosm, the ladder sticking out of the opening in its roof symbolises the *axis mundi*. In fact, each kiva has two openings: besides the one towards the sky, there is also the *sipaapu*, a small hole in the floor usually covered by a wooden plug—it refers to the place where the Hopi first emerged from the flowery underworld. The current world is conceived of as just one world somewhere in the middle of a stack of multiple superposed worlds, all connected via ladders. The anthropologist Patrick Pérez (2012) rightfully speaks of a "metaphysical cathedral"; some interpreters envisage the Hopi cosmos as a Klein bottle—go up long enough and you arrive back at the bottom (cf. Geertz 1984: 219).

At any rate, ladders are omnipresent in Hopi cosmology. They are closely associated with flight, with celestial travel, and with birds. When a previous world became too chaotic the clan chiefs decided it was time to escape: "They had heard some sounds away up, as of footsteps, as if somebody was walking there … they wanted to investigate above and see how it was there" (Geertz 1994: 375). In their kiva, they manufactured a bird, a 'strong one', which they instructed to fly straight upwards into the firmament. The strong one perched on top of the ladder, went up, and discovered an opening that exactly resembled a kiva hatchway. That was the entrance to our present world. On hair-washing day, an initiation ritual for Hopi children, this ascent is ceremonially enacted by planting spruce trees and reeds (which are also ladders; every node of the reed being a rung of the ladder). The Hopi did indeed emerge into the present world through a reed in some myths. That is why—as a follow-up to the hair-washing—they used to undertake arduous pilgrimages to a reed-bordered waterhole/sacred salt cave in the Grand Canyon which they refer to as *sipaapu*, just like the hole in the kiva floor. In fact, the entire landscape is littered with such places of emergence: this goes from ancient Pueblo ruins to oddly coloured rocks, red-flowered cactuses, or even anthills. On the night of the hair-washing, as specific constellations have risen into view through the ladder opening, star-masked kachinas would descend from the roof into the kiva, visitors from far away who hum eerily. As their low humming became louder and more intense and the ritual reached a climax, all those present would strip naked and riotously "leap for the ladder to get out unscathed before the world is destroyed" (Waters 1977 [1963]: 145). Ladders, in other words, are instruments to leap between worlds; they are Hopi rockets. Otherworldly visitors—whether they are eagle kachinas, parrot kachinas, hummingbird kachinas, cloud kachinas, corn kachinas, snow kachinas, or any other clownish star-being—invariably use ladders to arrive on this world, but also to depart from it. The captured eaglets that were traditionally sacrificed at the midsummer sending-back ceremonies, when the kachinas return to their heavenly abodes, were always buried with a wooden stick that represents the ladder by means of which the star-beings ascend.

I no longer need to labour the point: Hopi cosmology is suffused by ladders. But what is the point of dwelling on all this, some readers are bound to wonder with increasing impatience. What does all this have to do with *actual* space travel, or with the idea of human exceptionalism for that matter? Surely one cannot seriously advise NASA to invest in ladders rather than rockets or—to co-opt a phrase from Armin W. Geertz (1984)—to grow reeds that pierce the sky? Of course not. Yet I still contend that Hopi ladders cannot be reduced to safely ignorable cultural fluff. That would amount to giving in to the cultural astronomy position. What is much more productive, in my view, is to consider why the Hopi do not seem to suffer from the same sense of cosmic loneliness that plagues modern scientists and modern thinkers more generally. The ethnographic record is unequivocal: no sane-minded Hopi would ever ask something along the lines of "Are we alone?" From their perspective, the question that is so central to current astrobiology is downright silly. Within Hopi cosmology, the existence of humanoid aliens is blatantly obvious: all kachinas, even the most grotesque ones, qualify as such. All the star-beings—butterfly kachina, bean kachina, ant kachina, gourd kachina, frog kachina, thunder kachina, moon kachina, sun kachina, the entire pantheon of kachinas—are Hopi-like aliens. Any entity that is "a ladder away" from the Hopi is on the one hand deeply unfamiliar and clownishly weird but on the other hand fundamentally convergent: they have arms and legs, and heads with eyes and mouths; they sing and dance and behave in ways that are instantly recognisable and relatable. Hopi metaphysics posits a cosmos populated by convergent aliens, by 'Hopi-oids'. For the Hopi it leaves no doubt that they are in no way unique or special: nothing could be more incompatible with their outlook than the idea of human exceptionalism. The originality of Hopi metaphysics, with its emphasis on convergent aliens, cannot be overemphasised. Modern metaphysics has long been and continues to be premised on the opposite axiom: that of divergent familiars. All human beings, and indeed all living beings, are ultimately related through evolutionary processes. Organisms may be different from each other, but only just a little bit. To speak of terrestrial aliens is forbidden under the terms and conditions of modern metaphysics. The Hopi manifestly have no such qualms. Bumblebees, corn, parrots, prickly pear cactuses, bears: all are star-beings, and all are conceived of as alien humanoids.

If modern metaphysics is essentially about connecting familiars (through DNA), Hopi metaphysics centres on separating aliens (through ladders). If modern science has been built around the biological notion of the organism, Hopi cosmology attributes a central role to the idea of the kachina. Connection is the default setting in the former (terrestrial life envisaged as one unified whole—hence the *we* in "Are we alone?"), separation is the preferred option in the latter (the Gruyère cheese cosmos and its cavernous, kiva-like worlds are suffused by Hopi-like aliens—the kachinas). Crucially, I use the concepts of the organism and the star-being at eye level here: thinking with kachinas is in no way inferior to thinking with organisms. Cultural astronomers are bound to protest here, of course: they will point out that kachinas are merely make-believe aliens. To encounter 'actual' aliens, these detractors will say, one needs to cross the interplanetary medium to Mars or Venus at a very minimum, and to contact alien humanoids even that will not do: here one is obliged to look into SETI-style interstellar communication. This is not the place to go into Space Age moderns' strange and protracted obsession with the interplanetary and the interstellar mediums as the only thinkable serious boundaries: suffice it to say that they have for some reason convinced themselves that to meet aliens, you require rocketry and fancy space suits or radio telescopes and suchlike. How curiously folkloristic this dominant Western idea is was already noted by an artistic researcher who happens to work in the Hopi territories-of-old: "We [modern Americans] are so literal," James Turrell famously complained, "we actually have to go to the Moon: we can't just look at a rock".[1] Or, to slightly reframe this lament for off-Earth anthropology purposes: to find alien humans, we have to beam messages to Sirius; we can't just have a look at, say, parrots or clowns. Under the regime of modern metaphysics—it is worth repeating as the move is far from self-evident—terrestrial aliens have been banned quite effectively. All those who dwell on Earth, all DNA-based organisms, are taken to be 'like us'. But my response to the stance that kachinas are just make-believe aliens is not denial: rather, I retort that organisms are every bit as much make-believe familiars. And that should not be read as an attempt to devalue the perfectly honourable concept of 'the organism' or as a critique of the venerable academic discipline of biology—outer space studies scholars are not in the business of debunking science. It is only to say that the modern sciences, including all space sciences, are inescapably premised on particular metaphysical choices. To view the Earth as one unified planet populated by divergent familiars who are without exception connected to the terrestrial tree of life and as a celestial globe beyond which everything is alien by default (e.g., 'biodiversity', 'blue marble', 'the extraterrestrial') is indeed a choice. It does not directly mirror nature but rather reflects a specific *anthropology of nature*. It is an eminently provincial way of looking at the cosmos (and I underline, again, that this is not meant as a critique—there simply is no way around this provincialism; only moderns implausibly insist there is). To view the world as a disunity of 'macro-kivas' populated by convergent aliens and disconnected by ladders is an equally reasonable and I daresay an equally objective choice. What the Hopi are hinting at, then, is the possibility of a different *mode* of objectivity and the prospect of another *style* of space exploration, one that replaces the tenet of human exceptionalism by a principle of humanoid abundance.

What intrigues off-Earth anthropologists is that such alternative styles of space exploration are by no means restricted to Hopi or other Indigenous cosmologies—they have begun to blossom within the fields of astrobiology and planetary science as well. Astrobiologists' notable fascination with octopuses is a case in point. They study them as analogues for intelligent aliens, and their capacity to 'speak' to each other through cutaneous colour changes has been taken as a possible model for extraterrestrial forms of communication. Cephalopods, an astrobiologist once told me, are the primates of the sea. Some are even inclined to describe them as marine humanoids. The philosopher Vinciane Despret (2021), for one, has interpreted octopuses' well-known habit of spouting ink as a form of wilful expression rather than as just an evolutionary adaptation—as an otherworldly form of writing. Think of the ink cloud as a poem you have not (yet) learnt to read, or as a joke you do not (yet) get. Octopuses, Despret insists, are consummate poets and comedians—in other words, they are convergent aliens just as kachinas are for the Hopi. Or consider another alien humanoid and playful comic, as described by an early-twentieth-century observer:

"They seem to be ever on the look-out for mischief; and, when a good joke is in view, they take good care not to lose it" (Marriner 1908: 65). These mischievous humanoids may be olive green, but they are able to walk like humans (albeit with an odd, skipping gait); they eat like humans (they are omnivores who know how to hunt); they relish novelty and are unstoppably inquisitive; and they even have the equivalent of facial expressions: by fluffing their head feathers in certain ways they can do 'submissive' or 'aggressive' and a number of subtle emotions in between. I am referring to an alpine parrot of New Zealand, the kea, who in the words of the ornithologists Judie Diamond and Alan B. Bond (1999: 1) is endowed with "an extraordinary, alien intelligence". And this reference to the alien is not a slip of their pen, for Diamond and Bond immediately add that New Zealand, because of its geological isolation, "is as close as we will get to the opportunity to study life on another planet" (p. 2, quoting Jared Diamond). Keas, 'the clowns of the mountains', as they are also referred to, are here explicitly staged as convergent aliens and not as divergent familiars, along the exact same lines as the Hopi stage kachina clowns. Why go to outer space if New Zealand is just a ladder away? More examples in the same vein are easy to find: suffice it to say that it is not a coincidence that astrobiologists champion a growing list of 'honorary humans' such as octopuses and parrots; nor is it by chance that they are showing such a marked interest in questions of convergent evolution (e.g., Conway-Morris 2003). What these scientists intuit is that 'shadow humanities' may be all around us; it is just that they have not yet learnt how to look for them. Helping them in this endeavour is a key task for outer space studies. At present, there are many signs that a major metaphysical rearrangement is upon us. Some of the most creative researchers, both in the space sciences and in the environmental humanities, have de facto already abandoned the notion of human exceptionalism. Today anthropologists look back with some embarrassment at the colonial and racist attitudes exhibited by their predecessors in the Victorian epoch. One day they may well find themselves a touch embarrassed that the pages of the great journals of their discipline, until well into the twenty-first century, were exclusively reserved for articles on members of the genus *Homo*. If there is anything that unites off-Earth anthropologists it surely must be that they are imbued with a specific sense of urgency: a dedicated *Journal for Alien Humanities* is long overdue.

Acknowledgements

I warmly thank Perig Pitrou and Joffrey Becker, with whom I undertook a short but memorable trip to the Hopi territories in 2018. The discussions we had at the time inspired the present chapter a great deal.

Note

1 James Turrell interview, 2013, available on YouTube at https://www.youtube.com/watch?v=1-gmHA7KbcU.

References

Álvarez, Tamara. 2020. *The Eighth Continent: An Ethnography of Twentieth-First Century Euro-American Plans to Settle the Moon*. PhD Dissertation, The New School, New York.
Baity, Elizabeth Chesley. 1973. "Archaeoastronomy and Ethnoastronomy So Far." *Current Anthropology* 14 (4): 389–431. https://doi.org/10.1086/201351.
Becker, Joffrey. 2015. *Humanoïdes: Expérimentations Croisées Entre Arts et Sciences*. Paris: Paris Ouest University Press.
Becker, Joffrey. 2019. "Éléments Pour une Anthropologie de la Robotique." In *Techniques & Cultures. Anthropologie de la Vie et des Nouvelles Technologies*, special issue edited by Morgan Meyer and Perig Pitrou. http://journals.openedition.org/tc/10214.

Becker, Joffrey. 2022. "Anthropology, AI and Robotics." In *The Routledge Social Science Handbook of AI*, edited by Anthony Elliott. Abingdon: Routledge.

Beltrame, Tiziana N., Sophie Houdart, and Christine Jungen. 2017. "Parler Depuis L'infime." *Techniques & Culture* 68: 10–25. https://doi.org/10.4000/tc.8552.

Bertoni, Filippo. 2018. "Global Worming: Politics of Nature and Earth(Worm) Systems." In *The SAGE Handbook of Nature*, edited by Terry Marsden, 892–912. London: SAGE Publications. https://doi.org/10.4135/9781473983007.n47.

Bertoni, Filippo. 2020. "Soiling Mars: 'To Boldly Grow Where No Plant Has Grown Before'?" In *Thinking with Soils: Material Politics and Social Theory*, edited by Juan Francisco Salazar, Céline Granjou, Matthew Kearnes, Anna Krzywoszynska and Manuel Tironi, 107–22. London: Bloomsbury Academic.

Bigg, Charlotte. 2012. "Les Études Visuelles des Sciences: Regards Croisés Sur les Images Scientifiques." *Revue Histoire de l'Art* 70: 95–101. https://doi.org/10.3406/hista.2012.3394.

Bigg, Charlotte. 2015. "Sciences du Portrait Céleste." In *Tout ce que le Ciel Permet (En Cinéma, Peinture, Photographie et Vidéo)—Collection Théorème nr. 24*, edited by Barbara Le Maître and Bruno Nassim Aboudrar, 119–26. Paris: Presses de la Sorbonne Nouvelle.

Bigg, Charlotte. 2018. "Of Blurs, Maps and Portraits: Photography and the Moon." In *Selene's Two Faces: From 17th Century Drawings to Spacecraft Imaging* (Nuncius Series, vol. 3), edited by Carmen Pérez González, 114–46. Leiden: Brill. https://doi.org/10.1163/9789004298873_006.

Buchli, Victor. 2020a. "Extraterrestrial Methods: Towards an Ethnography of the ISS." In *Lineages and Advancements in Material Culture Studies*, edited by Timothy Carroll, Antonia Walford and Shireen Walton, 17–32. London and New York: Routledge.

Buchli, Victor. 2020b. "Low Earth Orbit: A Speculative Ethnographer's Guide." In *Anti-Atlas: Towards a Critical Area Studies*, edited by Tim Beasley-Murray, Wendy Bracewell and Michał Murawski. London: UCL Press.

Casumbal-Salazar, Iokepa. 2017. "A Fictive Kinship: Making 'Modernity,' 'Ancient Hawaiians,' and the Telescopes on Mauna Kea." *Native American and Indigenous Studies* 4 (2): 1–30. https://doi.org/10.5749/natiindistudj.4.2.0001.

Chinigò, Davide, and Cherryl Walker. 2020. "Science, Astronomy, and Sacrifice Zones: Development Trade-offs, and the Square Kilometre Array (SKA) Radio Telescope Project in South Africa." *Social Dynamics* 46 (3): 391–413. https://doi.org/10.1080/02533952.2020.1850626.

Colwell-Chanthaphonh, Chip, and T. J. Ferguson. 2006. "Memory Pieces and Footprints: Multivocality and the Meanings of Ancient Times and Ancestral Places among the Zuni and Hopi." *American Anthropologist* 108 (1): 148–62. https://doi.org/10.1525/aa.2006.108.1.148.

Conway Morris, Simon. 2003. *Life's Solution: Inevitable Humans in a Lonely Universe*. Cambridge: Cambridge University Press.

Cornum, Lou. 2015. "The Space NDN's Star Map." *The New Inquiry*, 26 January. https://thenewinquiry.com/the-space-ndns-star-map/.

De Smet, Elsa. 2018. *Voir L'espace: Astronomie et Science Populaire Illustrée (1840–1969)*. Strasbourg: Strasbourg University Press.

Despret, Vinciane. 2021. *Autobiographie d'un Poulpe et Autres Récits D'anticipation*. Arles: Actes Sud.

Diamond, Judie, and Alan B. Bond. 1999. *Kea, Bird of Paradox: The Evolution and Behavior of a New Zealand Parrot*. Berkeley, CA: University of California Press.

Ferguson, T. J., G. Lennis Berlin, and Leigh J. Kuwanwisiwma. 2004. "Kukhepya: Searching for Hopi Trails." Presentation at the 103rd AAA Annual Meeting. https://www.sas.upenn.edu/~cerickso/from_ccat/Roads/Papers/Ferguson%20et%20al2.pdf.

Geertz, Armin W. 1984. "A Reed Pierced the Sky: Hopi Indian Cosmography on Third Mesa, Arizona." *Numen* 31 (2): 216–41. https://doi.org/10.2307/3269955.

Geertz, Armin W. 1994. *The Invention of Prophecy: Continuity and Meaning in Hopi Indian Religion*. Berkeley: University of California Press.

Hamacher, Duane Willis. 2011. *On the Astronomical Knowledge and Traditions of Aboriginal Australians*. PhD Thesis, Macquarie University, Sydney.

Helmreich, Stefan. 2009. *Alien Ocean. Anthropological Voyages in Microbial Seas*. Berkeley: University of California Press.

Helmreich, Stefan. 2016. *Sounding the Limits of Life: Essays in the Anthropology of Biology and Beyond*. Princeton and Oxford: Princeton University Press.

Holbrook, Jarita, R. Thebe Medupe, and Johnson O. Urama, eds. 2008. *African Cultural Astronomy*. Astrophysics and Space Science Proceedings, vol. 6. Springer.

Houdart, Sophie, and Christine Jungen. 2015. "Cosmos Connections." *Gradhiva. Revue D'anthropologie et D'histoire des Arts* 22: 4–23. https://doi.org/10.4000/gradhiva.3016.

Ingold, Tim, and Gísli Pálsson. 2013. *Biosocial Becomings: Integrating Social and Biological Anthropology*. Cambridge: Cambridge University Press.

Kamili, Lauren. 2020. "The Lamp, the Fly, and the Fungus: Observing and Experimenting with Living Organisms in a Biomimetic Artifact." *Supplement, Techniques et Cultures* 73. https://doi.org/10.4000/tc.13727; https://journals.openedition.org/tc/13727?lang=en

Kearnes, Matthew, and Thom van Dooren. 2017. "Rethinking the Final Frontier: Cosmo-Logics and an Ethic of Interstellar Flourishing." *GeoHumanities* 3 (1): 178–97. https://doi.org/10.1080/2373566X.2017.1300448.

Kelley, David H., and Eugene F. Milone. 2011. *Exploring Ancient Skies: A Survey of Ancient and Cultural Astronomy*. New York: Springer.

Klinger, Julie M. 2018. *Rare Earth Frontiers: From Terrestrial Subsoils to Lunar Landscapes*. Ithaca, NY: Cornell University Press.

Kuwanwisiwma, Leigh J., T. J. Ferguson, and Chip Colwell, eds. 2019. *Footprints of Hopi History: Hopihiniwtiput Kukveni'at*. Tucson, AZ: University of Arizona Press.

Malotki, Ekkehart, and Ken Gary. 2001. *Hopi Stories of Witchcraft, Shamanism, and Magic*. Lincoln; London: University of Nebraska Press.

Marcheselli, Valentina. 2020. "The Shadow Biosphere Hypothesis: Non-knowledge in Emerging Disciplines." *Science, Technology, & Human Values* 45 (4): 636–58. https://doi.org/10.1177/0162243919881207.

Marcheselli, Valentina. 2022. "The Exploration of the Earth Subsurface as a Martian Analogue." *Tecnoscienzia: Italian Journal of Science & Technology Studies* 13(1): 25–46.

Marriner, George R. 1908. *The Kea: A New Zealand Problem; Including a Full Description of This Very Interesting Bird, Its Habitat and Ways, Together with a Discussion of the Theories Advanced to Explain Its Sheep-Killing Propensities*. Christchurch: Marriner Bros. & Co.

Messeri, Lisa. 2016. *Placing Outer Space: An Earthly Ethnography of Other Worlds*. Durham, NC: Duke University Press.

Mirmalek, Zara. 2020. *Making Time On Mars*. Cambridge, MA: The MIT Press.

Olson, Valerie. 2018. *Into the Extreme: U.S. Environmental Systems and Politics Beyond Earth*. Minneapolis, MN: University of Minnesota Press.

Pálsson, Gísli. 2009. "Celestial Bodies: Lucy in the Sky." In *Humans in Outer Space—Interdisciplinary Odysseys*, edited by Luca Codignola, Kai-Uwe Schrogl, Agnieszka Lukaszczyk and Nicolas Peter, 69–81. Vienna; New York: Springer. https://doi.org/10.1007/978-3-211-87465-3_9.

Pálsson, Gísli, and Heather Anne Swanson. 2016. "Down to Earth: Geosocialities and Geopolitics." *Environmental Humanities* 8 (2): 149–71. https://doi.org/10.1215/22011919-3664202.

Parkhurst, Aaron, and David Jeevendrampillai. 2020. "Towards an Anthropology of Gravity: Emotion and Embodiment in Microgravity Environments." *Emotion, Space and Society* 35: 100680. https://doi.org/10.1016/j.emospa.2020.100680.

Patarin-Jossec, Julie. 2020. "The Politics of Heroes' Body: Ethnographying the Training of Foreign Astronauts in Russia." *Corpus Mundi* 1 (2): 14–36. https://doi.org/10.46539/cmj.v1i2.12.

Pérez, Patrick. 2012. "De Maison en Sanctuaire, une Petite Histoire de la Kiva des Hopi." *Les Nouvelles de l'Archéologie* 127: 54–58. https://doi.org/10.4000/nda.1363.

Pitrou, Perig. 2012. "Figuration des Processus Vitaux et Co-Activité Dans la Sierra Mixe de Oaxaca (Mexique)." *L'Homme* 202: 77–111. https://doi.org/10.4000/lhomme.23025.

Pitrou, Perig. 2014. "La Vie, un Objet Pour L'anthropologie? Options Méthodologiques et Problèmes Épistémologiques." *L'Homme* 212: 159–89. https://doi.org/10.4000/lhomme.23786.

Pitrou, Perig. 2015. "Life as a Process of Making in the Mixe Highlands (Oaxaca, Mexico): Towards a 'General Pragmatics' of Life." *Journal of the Royal Anthropological Institute* 21 (1): 86–105. https://doi.org/10.1111/1467-9655.12143.

Praet, Istvan. 2017. "Astrobiology and the Ultraviolet World." *Environmental Humanities* 9 (2): 378–97. https://doi.org/10.1215/22011919-4215352.

Praet, Istvan. 2021. "The Global Biosphere and Its Metaphysical Underpinnings: Ecumenical Alternatives in Animism and Astrobiology." *Sociologus: Journal for Social Anthropology* 71 (1): 55–72. https://doi.org/10.3790/soc.71.1.55.

Praet, Istvan. n.d. "Styles of Contemporary Space Exploration: Columbian and Vespuccian Modes of Researching Alien Worlds." In *Anthropology Off Earth*, edited by Perig Pitrou and Istvan Praet. Under review with Oxford University Press.

Praet, Istvan, and Juan Francisco Salazar. 2017. "Familiarizing the Extraterrestrial/Making Our Planet Alien." *Environmental Humanities* 9 (2): 309–24. https://doi.org/10.1215/22011919-4215315.

Rahder, Micha. 2020. *An Ecology of Knowledges: Fear, Love, and Technoscience in Guatemalan Forest Conservation.* Durham, NC: Duke University Press.

Ruggles, Clive L. N., and Saunders, Nicholas J., eds. 1993. *Astronomies and Cultures.* Niwot, CO: University Press of Colorado.

Salazar, Juan Francisco. 2017. "Antarctica and Outer Space: Relational Trajectories." *The Polar Journal* 7 (2): 259–69. https://doi.org/10.1080/2154896X.2017.1398521.

Salazar, Juan Francisco. 2020. "Speculative Fabulation: Researching Worlds to Come in Antarctica." In *Anthropologies and Futures: Researching Emerging and Uncertain Worlds*, edited by Juan Francisco Salazar, Sarah Pink, Andrew Irving and Johannes Sjöberg, 151–70. London: Routledge.

Smiles, Deondre. 2020. "The Settler Logics of (Outer) Space." Essay in *Society and Space*, 26 October. https://www.societyandspace.org/articles/the-settler-logics-of-outer-space.

Urton, Gary, and Clive Ruggles. 2010. *Skywatching in the Ancient World: New Perspectives in Cultural Astronomy.* Boulder: University Press of Colorado.

Valentine, David. 2012. "Exit Strategy: Profit, Cosmology, and the Future of Humans in Space." *Anthropological Quarterly* 85 (4): 1045–67. https://doi.org/10.1353/anq.2012.0073.

Valentine, David. 2017. "Gravity Fixes: Habituating to the Human on Mars and Island Three." *Journal of Ethnographic Theory* 7 (3): 185–209. https://doi.org/10.14318/hau7.3.012.

Vertesi, Janet. 2014. *Seeing Like a Rover: How Robots, Teams, and Images Craft Knowledge of Mars.* Chicago, IL: University of Chicago Press.

Vertesi, Janet. 2020. *Shaping Science: Organizations, Decisions, and Culture on NASA's Teams.* Chicago, IL: University of Chicago Press.

Walker, Cherryl, and Davide Chinigò. 2018. "Disassembling the Square Kilometre Array: Astronomy and Development in South Africa." *Third World Quarterly* 39 (10): 1979–97. https://doi.org/10.1080/01436597.2018.1447374.

Waters, Frank 1977 [1963]. *Book of the Hopi: The First Revelation of the Hopi's Historical and Religious Worldview of Life.* New York: The Viking Press.

6
PLANETARY ETHNOGRAPHY IN A "SPACEX VILLAGE"
History, Borders, and the Work of "Beyond"

Anna Szolucha

Introduction

The city of Brownsville is tucked away at the very southern tip of Texas, bordering the Gulf of Mexico to the east and the Mexican city of Matamoros to the south. Highway 4 that runs through the city is the only throughway that connects it with the small village of Boca Chica, terminating at the sand dunes of Boca Chica Beach. This characteristic location had served as the basis of Brownsville's slogan, "On the Border By the Sea", since 1966 (Oliveras González 2015). Aimed mainly at domestic tourists from more northern states, the city offered "[t]ropical palms of every variety, sparkling sunshine and beautiful girls [which were] ... only three ingredients in the well-spiced recipe for winter fun and relaxation", as a local newspaper put it at the time (*The Brownsville Herald*, 26 Oct. 1966, cited in Popik 2008). The city changed its motto in 2008, but more recently, it revived the old slogan, adding that Brownsville was now "On the Border By the Sea and Beyond". The "beyond" part is a tribute to SpaceX and its interest in the area and signals the city's ambitions to become a hub for the aerospace industry.

SpaceX (Space Exploration Technologies Corporation) was co-founded in 2002 by Elon Musk, who remains its main, if often controversial, public face and CEO. In 2014, the company started to set up its facilities in Boca Chica, thirty-seven kilometres east of Brownsville, where it is currently developing and testing its Starship system—the biggest ever spacecraft that is to take humans and cargo to the Moon and Mars. As the nearest urban area to SpaceX, Brownsville is set on capitalising on this newfound purpose, as the new slogan aptly demonstrates. When conducting ethnographic research in the area, however, one is quickly confronted with the realisation that going "beyond" has a much more complex meaning and broader significance than just its reference to space travel and exploration. In fact, it may serve as a metaphor for the myriad of projects, ventures, and socioeconomic relations that have moulded the area throughout history.

"Beyond" is a somewhat ambiguous concept, yet one with virtually unlimited creative potential because it often connotes notions of adventure and passionate exploration that characterises venturing into uncharted waters. The work of "beyond" may require that one leaves the old, the familiar, and the problematic behind in order to make a leap into the new, the unfamiliar, and the (seemingly) unproblematic. In Southeast Texas, "beyond" may be seen as a metaphor used to imagine social and commercial initiatives that would help the area build local prosperity and overcome the multiple socioeconomic issues that it has been experiencing. However, as a concept of the unbounded, "beyond" necessarily passes over into its opposite—the border, the limit, the boundary. "Beyond" and the border are immanent in each other, just like the future imaginaries of Brownsville residents are shaped by the conditions of living on the international border. The concept of "beyond" destabilises limits and boundaries, without necessarily erasing them; it may even reestablish them in a different guise, so it is never an innocent formation, free-floating, and entirely originary. Nevertheless, thinking about "beyond" is often about reimagining borders so it has a potentially transgressive character, especially when all boundaries are revealed to be porous and indistinct.

The anthropology of outer space (Timko et al. 2022; Valentine, Olson, and Battaglia 2009; Praet and Salazar 2017) is inherently interested in the work of "beyond" as we confront our imaginations, social systems, and theories with analyses that pertain to cosmic scales, extraterrestrial realms, and potentially new forms of historicity. In recent decades, and following the dominant narratives, social scientists have talked (often in a critical way) about the "beyond" of space exploration as encapsulated in the notion of the frontier (see, e.g., McCurdy 2011; Messeri 2017). They have also employed the trope of the extreme as an analytic of both limits and horizons that are to be overcome (Valentine, Olson, and Battaglia 2012). Prompted by Brownsville's slogan and its reference to the "beyond" (rather than the frontier or the extreme), in this chapter, I would like to open up this discussion to potentially new insights and explore their significance for developing novel methodological approaches in the social studies of outer space.

Brownsville would be a great example of the uncanny landscape of a space frontier where fancy restaurants and new bars sit near empty storefronts under tangled powerlines and freshly painted murals adorn buildings in the downtown area that is struggling to keep its function as a civic and social heart of the city. At the same time, Brownsville—just as much as the Lower Rio Grande Valley that it is part of—also defies the two-sidedness of any narratives that one would want to impose on it. Its status "On the Border By the Sea and Beyond" is highly multivocal, shaped by decades and centuries of multinational flows, porous borders, and recurring cycles of hope and vision, unequal development, injustice, economic or natural adversity, and societal resolve.

Brownsville's multivocality demonstrates how the work of "beyond" presents particular challenges to ethnographic methods and anthropology of outer space. First, the breadth and the multiplicity of perspectives and the social, historical, and cultural material that we need to take into consideration to attempt a comparative exploration of how people imagine and relate to space are not to be ignored. Second, there is also a risk of slipping into certain modes of interpretation that may simplify people's relation to space. This may generate potential silences, but even more so, it may also contribute to the polarisation and conflict in society that we have already seen the effects of. Finally, while attending to the multiple and sometimes conflicting ways in which the "beyond" manifests itself in local relations and landscapes, one cannot lose sight of the fact that our own approaches and modes of analysis are deeply shaped by historically and terrestrially determined ways of theorising and researching. The question then remains—to what extent is it justified to start talking about new forms of historicity and extraterrestrial theory that may emerge in response to the current era of space exploration?[1] Those are some of the challenges that drove me to search for something like a planetary ethnography. I have been wondering if there is a way of talking about and acknowledging these difficulties, some of which are quite specific to our current social and political moment, which also charts a way forward. This way forward should not be treated as a universal blueprint but an intervention into researching space, into anthropology and into our societies and politics more broadly, and into where we are heading as societies in the future.

In this chapter, I will use my ongoing fieldwork to illustrate some of the ethnographic challenges that anthropology of outer space may be facing and offer some ideas about what the potential implications for planetary ethnography might be. Planetary ethnography is an approach that aims to bring forth ethnography's potential to challenge hermetically closed meanings, accepted theories, and power relations (Szolucha 2022; Szolucha, Korpershoek et al. 2022). As we are working towards a more detailed definition and practice, we draw on the planetary as a perspective that includes differences yet aims at a more general understanding—one that would not be locally determined but able to tell us something interesting about what is common for humans everywhere. In this risky endeavour, we tap into the tension that is fundamental to the discipline of anthropology in particular, but I hope that

> [T]hinking about the planet may help us escape our everyday assumptions and open us up to understanding one another as humans. Since a planetary view can be seen as a universalising moment, it can also lie at the heart of the constant revival and transformation of societies.
>
> *(Szolucha, Tabas et al. 2022)*

The Magic Valley

"Now everyone knows where Brownsville is", one Brownsville resident tells me passionately. He works in sales and reflects on how in the past, he always had to explain to his suppliers where the city was. This changed when SpaceX moved into the area, he claims. Indeed, local residents that I have talked to seem to be clued in on what the company is doing in Boca Chica, and they often ask me for more information when they learn that I "research SpaceX". It seems that SpaceX has brought a new sense of recognition to the area, and with the various rebranding projects already on the way, the company is likely to influence its official identity in the coming years.

The evolving identity of the area is tightly connected to the ongoing relationship of exchange that the local authorities have with the company. Texas officials have granted SpaceX about US$15 million worth of economic incentives and a local economic development agency added another US$5 million (Etter 2015). Legislators altered the Texas Open Beaches Act to allow Boca Chica Beach to be closed during SpaceX rocket launches. The city has also agreed to abandon specific portions of public roads in Boca Chica as requested by SpaceX. Furthermore, the SpaceX site is located in a Texas Enterprise Zone and as such may be eligible for tax refunds as well as capital gains tax abatement due to its location within a special Opportunity Zone created by the federal administration's Tax Cuts and Jobs Act. In return, the Musk Foundation donated US$4.5 million to the Brownsville Independent School District (KRGV Channel 5 News 2022) and pledged US$10 million to the City of Brownsville for downtown revitalisation (Duffy 2021). These exchanges have been accompanied by other sociocultural phenomena that speed up the process of rebranding the city as a space hub. For example, many people from all over the United States and abroad have flocked to Boca Chica and Brownsville as tourists to visit and witness firsthand how Starship is being built. A sizeable group of photographers, filmmakers, sound engineers, music makers, and artists have moved to the area on a more permanent basis to document the developments. There are also those who have recently arrived to work at SpaceX, usually easily identifiable by the out-of-state licence plates on their mid-range and upscale cars parked outside the production or launch sites in Boca Chica. In conversations with locals, SpaceX seems to offer them hope not only for the long-term survival and a multiplanetary future of the human species—as Musk sees it (Musk 2017)—but also for the development of the entire area. As one city commissioner put it:

> To have always believed that something very, very special was going to happen to Brownville and to have been able to witness it and to know that future generations are going to be able to have this opportunity, to have this incredible future at their fingertips, makes me so incredibly happy. So believe in the future and believe in Brownsville because incredible things are happening here every day.
>
> *(Sandoval 2022)*

Figure 6.1 End of Highway 4, looking onto SpaceX launch site near Boca Chica beach, 17 June 2022. Photo by the author.

This narrative of development-led growth resonates with the ongoing attempts to revitalise the area. Brownsville has been infamous for its high poverty rates. It has consistently ranked as one of the cities with the highest poverty rates in the country (DePietro 2021). It is estimated that in 2021, 22% of the population lived below the poverty line (down from 38.6% in 2010) (United States Census Bureau n.d.). Over the years, Boca Chica has also had a bad reputation, with Boca Chica Beach being referred to as the poor people's beach (Figure 6.1). The dominant language spoken in Brownsville is Spanish and the population of the city is 94% Hispanic or Latino (United States Census Bureau 2021). The area of the Lower Rio Grande Valley—the floodplain named after the main river that serves as the border between the United States and Mexico in the southmost part of Texas—has been plagued with complex economic and social problems, including lack of access to adequate healthcare, lack of basic infrastructure in colonias (unincorporated communities of mainly Latino immigrants) (Gomez 2015), social and economic isolation and cultural marginalisation of undocumented immigrants (Hilfinger Messias et al. 2017), and persisting segregation and exploitation of Hispanic immigrants (Ryabov and Merino 2017).

It is highly unlikely that SpaceX alone will solve all or any of these problems, but its activity in the area revives historical tropes and narratives that animated the region in the past. Those narratives celebrated the incredible potential of the area, which was supposed to encourage new investors and residents to bind their personal fate to that of the Valley. As early as the beginning of the twentieth century, with the completion of the railway to Brownsville (which does not exist anymore), some reported that prosperity had arrived in the Valley, brought about by the fertility of the local soil and efficient irrigation as well as the new arrivals who were seeking a milder climate to live in. This period came after years marked by several outbreaks of cholera and yellow fever epidemics as well as severe storms that struck the area in the second half of the nineteenth century (Pierce 1917).

In the 1920s to 1940s, the Valley was referred to as the Magic Valley, where Anglo farmers could benefit financially and live a good life thanks to the natural climate of the area and a landscape transformed by the work of cheap labour of segregated Hispanic workers. These narratives relied on many of the tropes that we would now recognise as part of the SpaceX appeal—business ingenuity, hard work, reliance on local resources, and labour. A promotional pamphlet from the era struck a familiar if also a slightly prophetic chord; the title of the first chapter read: "What everyone should know about the richest frontier in the world today, the Lower Valley of the Rio Grande". It continued: "Vision is the first requisite of accomplishment, the vital essence of all true success. Attribute of every pioneer soul, it sets him high above his fellows, starbound" (Montgomery 1928: 3). The publication was referring to the construction of the railroad to the region and portrayed it as a bold and visionary undertaking that would bring investment and wider prosperity to the area:

> Accepting the premise that development follows transportation facilities, it is reasonable to conclude that the entry of the Southern Pacific at this stage of the Valley's progress will greatly stimulate investment of large capital, more intensive cultivation of lands already under the plow, promote the building of new communities and clearing of hundreds of new farms, rapidly increase population, and guarantee the excellence of transportation service in a country fast demanding the utmost of every developing agency.
>
> *(p. 4)*

This extraordinary endeavour was justified by the "magical" qualities of the Valley:

> Almost invariably men who come to the Valley are seized with *The Spirit of the Valley*, that contagious, infectious, breathing, palpitating *Something*, which in itself embodies *Magic*, a word fitly applied to the strip of silt-laden soils stretching, rainbow-like, from the Gulf of Mexico at Point Isabel to a setting in the hills of Starr County, a distance of a possible hundred and twenty-five miles.
>
> *(p. 5, emphasis in original)*

The Valley offered unparalleled climate, a good place to live and bring up a family, and a "magic of irrigation" so strong that at one point the Rio Grande Potato Growers Association of the Rio Grande Valley of Texas challenged the Egyptian government to a world comparison between the Nile and the Rio Grande as to their respective potentials for food production. The food production in the Valley was touted as a potential solution for the "Nation's food problem". The local authorities were portrayed as facilitating good access to various public utilities. The only thing that the area was lacking was investment capital, but the publication announced: "[t]hey are coming, men of means and vision" because "[w]isdom plants investments where growing conditions are best. The Valley offers a golden, fertile field. Let the rich man escape it, if he can" (p. 64).

The images of the "Magic Valley" were largely aspirational and created through such texts as that referenced above as well as other performances as a type of a place myth to boost land and water sales in the area (Brannstrom and Neuman 2009). Another publication from the period makes this goal plainly clear: "TO THE LAND BUYER. Raw land, that can be relied upon to produce good crops each consecutive year, is becoming very scarce in this country and will certainly increase in value" (Shary 1918). Driven largely by the Anglo elites, land and water sales marginalised the position of native Hispanics. In the promotional materials and performances, the Valley featured as a place of abundance of resources and labour, investment security, and good life—quite contrary to its enduring images as a place of semiarid wilderness and lawlessness (Brannstrom and Neuman 2009).

Nevertheless, over those years, the Valley did turn into an important horticultural and citrus-producing region. In 1930, an article in the journal *Economic Geography* reported:

> The production and marketing of early vegetables, citrus fruits, and cotton gives such abounding prosperity that immigration is attracted from other sections of the United States; and the population has increased rapidly during the last two decades. Modern homes, business houses, school and church buildings, and recently constructed highways and railroads impart a vigorous, progressive aspect to urban and rural landscapes, while areas occupied by mesquite, chaparral, prickly pear, and prairie grasses, in many cases used as cattle range, give a striking conception of the recent past of the region.
>
> *(Chambers 1930: 364)*

However, problems with the efficient use and conservation of water soon surfaced (Chambers 1930). In 1940, another article concluded that the prosperity promised by the developers of the irrigation systems did not follow. Additionally, natural factors such as severe frosts and the area's relative lack of experience in managing citrus production also impeded its development. Production surpluses and issues with adequate transport and distribution were common. These problems had the biggest impact on the poorly paid Mexican workers (Cline 1940). Publications from the period praised the abundance of cheap labour in the area (Chambers 1930; Montgomery 1928; Shary 1918). Of course, there were also contemporary observers who criticised the injustices that the workers sustained (Brannstrom and Neuman 2009), but these injustices culminated in 1954 with Operation Wetback. It was claimed that under this programme as many as over 1 million temporary Mexican workers were deported from the United States following military-style round ups (History, Art & Archives 2022). However, other analyses seem to acknowledge a greater role of voluntary repatriations and legalisation of undocumented labourers in the process (Hernández 2016). Although after World War II the narrative of the Magic Valley dissipated under activist challenges to the system of segregation and lawsuits against the overappropriation of water (Brannstrom and Neuman 2009), a similar narrative about the Valley as a land of opportunity and good life returned again, and this time directly to Boca Chica (which was not called that at the time).

In 1963, a man called John Caputa—a radio personality and land developer from Chicago—partnered with Harold Caldwell, who owned land on the Gulf Coast (Garza 1995). Caputa pitched his new venture to working-class Polish immigrants by running advertisements in Polish newspapers and on Polish-language radio programmes (Miller 2016). The village was supposed to become a retirement community and a new Fort Lauderdale of sorts (Herguth 2022). Over two thousand people signed up for land with Caputa and many first-generation Polish immigrants trusted him with their life savings (Garza 1995); some seemed to have signed documents that they did not understand (Herguth 2022). Houses sold for US$12,500 and unstaked lots for US$1200 (Garza 1995). Caputa named the place Kennedy Shores after John F. Kennedy. Thirty-two ranch-style houses were built as well as a restaurant, a hotel, and a sand-filtered water treatment plant. However, shortly after completion, in 1967 Hurricane Beulah flooded the area, destroying the restaurant and the utility system (Garza 1995), and to this day water needs to be trucked in from Brownsville. There are no stores or facilities at the nearby beach. One of the the residents summed it up that the developers "promised everything, but they wanted only money" (The Associated Press 1994).

In 1975, the village changed its name to Kopernik Shores after the Polish astronomer Nicolaus Copernicus (and preserving the Polish spelling of his name). The renaming was part of an effort to incorporate the village, which ultimately failed. County workers used to refer to the village as "Los Polacos" (Jmon 2021). After Caputa's death in 1979, many residents discovered that they did not have a clear title to their land (Garza 1995). In 1980, another hurricane struck the settlement. According to some accounts, residents climbed to their attics to survive (Jmon 2021). The population of the village remained low throughout the 1990s and 2000s, numbering fewer than thirty inhabitants, many of whom were seasonal, which probably led Musk to claim that "we've got a load of land with nobody around, so if it blows up, it's cool" (Solon 2021). Not without controversy, most of the houses in the village have now been bought by SpaceX and its subsidiary; they have been refurbished and made available to SpaceX employees. Elon Musk has its main residence in the village as well. Before SpaceX set up shop in the village, Boca Chica seems to have undergone several cycles of development and financially or naturally led decline. In 1998, one visitor to the area described the site as follows:

> The drive out is a boulevard of broken dreams: a roadside marker commemorating the last battle of the Civil War, a scattering of homes in a failed subdivision (Kopernik Shores, marketed to Polish immigrants from Chicago), the crumbling gates of another development that never got under way, and the most recent failure, Playa Del Rio, envisioned as a mega-resort of hotels and golf courses when it was announced in 1986. Now the U.S. Fish and Wildlife Service owns most of Boca Chica, as part of the Lower Rio Grande Valley National Wildlife Refuge.
>
> *(Patoski 1998)*

The ebbs and flows of various land and property development projects in the area would lend themselves particularly well to a critical analysis of development-led growth and persisting social injustices. The situation is further compounded by a myriad of other local and national factors and processes that come into play. To mention just a few, the mouth of the Rio Grande river and the areas surrounding it are not only recognised wildlife refuge areas but also sacred, unceded territories of the Esto'k Gna, also known as the Carrizo/Comecrudo Tribe of Texas. Sites such as Garcia Pasture in Southeast Texas are unfortunately poorly documented, but it has been found that they contained burial sites, and thousands of pieces of archaeological collection have been found in the area. SpaceX sites in Boca Chica are located in the area of the old fishing villages of the Esto'k Gna. According to their accounts, the villages were not permanent because the tribe had a good knowledge of the weather and climate and migrated with the seasons. Since the Carrizo/Comecrudo tribe, despite being the original Indigenous people of Texas, are not a federally recognised tribe, they lack the kinds of protections that other tribes may have. This means that when the area around Boca Chica village is closed for SpaceX testing of their prototypes, they have no access to their land. The area in Boca Chica is particularly important to them because the mouth of the Rio Grande is where the first woman was created: "It's like the uterus," one tribe member told me. Since the river flows from the Rocky Mountains of Colorado and into the Gulf of Mexico at Boca Chica Beach, every animal of every Carrizo/Comecrudo clan was built into and shaped the first woman. Not only has the value of life and life-giving been entrenched in their history and language (for example, when they say "give life" instead of goodbye), but the life-giving qualities are inextricably connected to the land and the river. In the past, the Esto'k Gna's villages sprang up next to the river; today, confronted by SpaceX they find themselves reaffirming the intrinsic value of land and have partnered with environmental groups to oppose the company. This is as much about empathising with their ancestors as making a connection in order to grow and to understand their teachings and lifeways at a time when they are being challenged in multiple ways, not unlike those they had experienced at the hands of colonial powers five centuries ago.

In this context, SpaceX's project to build Starship may fit into a broader landscape of controversial commercial development in the immediate area. Parts of the sacred Garcia Pasture have been fenced off and slated for a fracked-gas export terminal—one of originally three, now two, LNG export terminals planned for this area. Since the Carrizo/Comecrudo tribe is not federally recognised, it was not one of the official consultees on the project. This means that the land that contains Carrizo/Comecrudo burial sites is claimed by the port of Brownsville and fenced off, and if members of the tribe wanted to enter, they would most likely be treated as trespassers. This is happening in, as I have been told, "deep, deep Texas"—a very militarised zone, due to not only the gun culture but also its proximity to the border with Mexico. While in the area, one is regularly reminded of this condition by the presence of the border patrol checkpoint located on Highway 4, approximately twenty-four kilometres from Boca Chica as well as of multiple agencies' vehicles, aircraft, drones, and boats that surveil the area day and night.

Despite these long histories of colonisation, extractivism, and militarisation in the area, it is hard to ignore the fact that the Starship project has been a source of awe, true inspiration, and income to a lot of people. The Boca Chica village is now frequently called Starbase by SpaceX and people who support the company. It has also become a focus point for space fans worldwide as well as attracting a devoted following from long-term rocket watchers and newbies alike. Supporting this ephemeral online community are people who document the progress at Starbase using various digital technologies and channels. These are often individuals who have moved to the area to do this work—as part of either self-employment or a contract for a bigger social media channel or a news website. They are part of a very intricate local ecosystem as well as an international economy that span actual and virtual realms. What is also interesting about this entirely new ecosystem is that it is created by people, not unlike those who might be the first to go to and live on Mars, if that becomes a reality. Just like everyone else, these people have to navigate the complex landscapes and relationships of Southeast Texas that are marked by historical and persisting social and environmental injustices as well as the captivating and recurring, if inherently uncertain, narratives of opportunity and good life.

Porous Borders and Beyond

Visitors to Starbase often marvel at how close they could actually get to the parts of Starship that SpaceX is developing in Boca Chica. They can easily peek into some of the assembly buildings and behind open gates, just by standing on a public road. Many see this level of public access as unprecedented and incomparable to the tightly controlled admittance regimes of NASA, for example. However, those who are regulars at Starbase (photographers, YouTubers, filmmakers, etc.) do not take this access for granted, and some have noticed it being gradually constrained. They have also engaged in self-imposed practices that are aimed at ensuring that their actions do not provoke the company to limit public access further, thus possibly jeopardising the photographers' and livestreamers' ability to do their job.

In reality, this relatively open access to Starbase is predicated on its opposite—namely, a type of boundary setting that is negotiated with SpaceX and enforced by an unusual private–public arrangement between the company and the local authorities. Members of the public can observe the developments at Starbase as long as there is no road closure scheduled for the day. The road closures are announced on the County website and usually arranged in three-day slots. Most closures are planned to last twelve hours, but they can be extended, delayed, or cancelled altogether—often with no previous notice and no explanation given. The closures serve as a public safety measure to make sure that the public is evacuated from the area when the company is planning to test its hardware. Much has been said in the press about how this limits the public's access to the beach—a constitutional right in the state of Texas—which had to be subtly worked around to facilitate SpaceX. Furthermore, the public has no access to the parts of public roads that the County abandoned in favour of the company. Despite these limitations, photographers and YouTubers working at Starbase have found creative ways to continue doing their work, even when roads are closed, once again demonstrating that all boundaries are permeable.

Just like Starbase, the Lower Rio Grande Valley can be a prime example of this porousness of the border, which is manifested not only in the continuous migratory flows between the United States and Mexico but also in the social and cultural relations and imaginaries that have shaped the area over

Planetary Ethnography in a "SpaceX Village"

centuries. The river that constitutes the border between the two countries has both divided and connected them. In Mexico, it is called El Río Bravo del Norte. It has served people on both banks as a source of water for irrigation and crop growing. As we have seen above, it is considered to be a source of life and used to be directly connected to the livelihood and lifeways of the Indigenous inhabitants of these lands. The river is flowing and constantly changing, making it practically impossible to know exactly where the borderline is at any given time: "As a creature of climate and topography, it is indifferent to the destiny of nations" (Casey and Watkins 2014: 102). According to the 1848 Treaty of Guadalupe Hidalgo, the borderline between the United States and Mexico is demarcated by the middle of the river's deepest channel, which inevitably changes with seasons and weather.

This porous nature of the border should not be seen as a mere consequence of a natural phenomenon; the border is also permeable by design. Even the border wall in the area seems to attest to the highly porous and incomplete status of this international boundary—it comes in different styles and sizes throughout Brownsville (see Figure 6.2); at some places, it is set apart from the actual borderline, creating a no man's land in between; and in other places, it appears to come to a stop, creating a gaping hole in what is otherwise supposed to seem like a mighty deterring technology (Casey and Watkins 2014).

The incompleteness of the border wall is an accurate symbol of this area between the United States and Mexico that has been characterised by constant movement, cultural continuity, and cross-border sociality, which are evident throughout the area at all times of the year. Charro Days, for example, is an annual cultural celebration organised in Brownsville in cooperation with Matamoros. The fiestas recognise Mexican culture and attract locals and tourists to participate in a street parade, dances, and concerts (Robinson 2008). Brownsville and Matamoros coordinated or co-organised similar celebrations over many decades of the twentieth century. Local folktales often refer to the common Mexican-American histories of the area or engage with the motive

Figure 6.2 The different styles of the border wall in Brownsville, 22 September 2022. Photo by the author.

of the border (Kearney, Knopp, and Zavaleta 2008). Many families still travel between the two countries and businesses operate across the border. As one migrant concluded:

> I don't know if it's because we live close to the border. It's as if we lived apart, like there's a difference ... I don't feel like we live in the US. We are only divided by a bridge and a border agent that checks my papers when I cross, but it's basically the same as if we were living on the other side.
>
> *(Hilfinger Messias et al. 2017: 272)*

The indistinct nature of the border in the Lower Rio Grande Valley sustains the hybrid "mestizaje" culture as well as language varieties that do not always conform to textbook versions of Spanish or English (Christoffersen 2019). As such, it is also a place of contradictions, which may capture individuals in an uncomfortable place in-between cultures where they are trying to negotiate multiple, hybrid, or flexible identities (Anzaldúa 2012). Their experience of the borderlands is one of struggle against essentialism, dualism, and exclusion.

If borders are always porous and a site of contestation of either/or identities and dualistic thinking, then is there perhaps also space to rethink the work of "beyond" as a practice that is not about establishing new borders but redefining social and environmental relations and seeking more just alternatives? In the case of the Lower Rio Grande Valley, thinking about "beyond" could be seen as connecting rather than dividing very different social groups that experienced hope, hardship, struggle, and injustice (albeit in very unequal ways that should not be forgotten). The struggle for the "beyond" of one's current conditions reveals perhaps some form of longing for a good life—defined by different, culturally and historically determined means. The challenge lies in bringing together these multiple meanings of what good life is and how it should be pursued. In answering this challenge, one may be guided by local historical experience that shows that visions of good life will not last if they are built on socioeconomic injustices and unsustainable use of resources. Are there also specifically ethnographic ways in which we could explore and analyse the work of "beyond"? This is a question for planetary ethnography.

Conclusion: Planetary Ethnography Under Construction

One of the impulses of planetary ethnography[2] is to reimagine social relationships, resisting various particular positions. In the concrete case analysed in this chapter, this rethinking of social relations may be undertaken by exploring the shared and contradictory dynamics of borders in the area as they are experienced and mediated by various groups and individuals. The work of "beyond" can be performed by exploring the conflicting everyday assumptions of different groups, thus opening space up for new social possibilities and human creativity. One way to accomplish this aim may be, for example, through trying to conceive of new economies by exploring how the space media individuals around Boca Chica are mediating and inventing various economic and moral principles in a vastly unequal landscape.

I hope that planetary ethnography can fulfil one of the promises of anthropology, that is to break with any particular position to be able to see the totality of what seems to be going on (Bruce Kapferer in Szolucha, Tabas et al. 2022). This is not a detached vision, but it necessarily emerges from a comparative analysis of how different people in different situations or places relate to the phenomenon of space exploration. Understanding of planetary ethnography as something that emerges from a comparative, multisited, and multiscalar analysis has the potential to change and transform things in all directions, and can really open up new perspectives for anthropology and for our societies more broadly.

There are many ideas to draw from to develop the conceptual tools of planetary ethnography, including planetarity (Spivak 2014) from which one can borrow its focus on the margins as an ethical disposition; epistemic disconcertment (Verran 2013)—learn how to be mindful of unhelpful allegories; planetary social thought (Clark and Szerszynski 2020)—expand ways of thinking about social life through earthly processes; planetary imaginations (Messeri 2016)—understand the role of imagination in creating places; the planetary (Masco 2010)—consider multiple ways in which the planetary becomes an object of insecurity and analysis; the more-than-terran (Olson 2022)—question the terracentrism of research; and the post-planetary (Tabas 2020)—critically assess the histories of planetary thinking. Some of these are more compatible with one another than others (Szolucha, Korpershoek et al. 2022), and we need to be careful so that this recent "planetary turn" in social sciences and humanities does not lead us to a situation where the planetary becomes another word for the global, that is, a particular view of the world. However, what all of these works point to is the necessity to do the work of "beyond", regardless of whether we are talking specifically about anthropology of outer space or humanities and social sciences more broadly. I would suggest that this means exploring the possibility of new modes of analysis and perspective, including speculative exploration and experimenting with various forms of temporal and spatial parallax. There are some big epistemological and methodological questions that would necessarily become part of this endeavour, such as the role of fieldwork in creating new historical and analytical categories.[3] I hope that by bringing the case of Boca Chica into the discussion, we may gain a better understanding of the types of challenges and potentials that the work of "beyond" and planetary ethnography may offer us to reimagine what borders, societies, and planets could be like.

Acknowledgements

Research for this article received funding from the National Science Centre, Poland, project number 2020/38/E/HS3/00241.

Notes

1 I owe this perspective to the discussion at the Planetary Conversation workshop organised at the Jagiellonian University, 19 May 2022.
2 Planetary ethnography is a concept and method that is being developed as part of the ARIES project (Anthropological Research into the Imaginaries and Exploration of Space). The overarching goal of the ARIES project is to analyse space exploration as socially produced. Our team aims to conduct research that is international and comparative, i.e., we are working simultaneously in multiple places and scales to test the universalising narratives about space exploration with real, on-the-ground experience of diverse groups of people who would be affected by it. We are focusing primarily on three different groups: space scientists and engineers, space activists and lobbyists, and local communities that live in the vicinity of space infrastructure.
3 I owe this insight to the discussion at the Ethnographies of Outer Space: Methodological Opportunities and Experiments workshop, organised at the University of Trento, 1–2 September 2022. https://webmagazine.unitn.it/evento/sociologia/109969/ethnographies-of-outer-space

References

Anzaldúa, Gloria. 2012. *Borderlands/La Frontera: The New Mestiza*. San Francisco, CA: Aunt Lute Books.
Brannstrom, Christian, and Matthew Neuman. 2009. "Inventing the 'Magic Valley' of South Texas, 1905–1941." *Geographical Review* 99 (2): 123–45. https://doi.org/10.1111/j.1931-0846.2009.tb00423.x.
Casey, Edward S., and Mary M. Watkins. 2014. *Up Against the Wall: Re-Imagining the U.S.-Mexico Border*. Louann Atkins Temple Women & Culture Series, Book 35. Austin: University of Texas Press.
Chambers, William T. 1930. "Lower Rio Grande Valley of Texas." *Economic Geography* 6 (4): 364–73. https://doi.org/10.2307/140529.

Christoffersen, Katherine. 2019. "Linguistic Terrorism in the Borderlands: Language Ideologies in the Narratives of Young Adults in the Rio Grande Valley." *International Multilingual Research Journal* 13 (3): 137–51. https://doi.org/10.1080/19313152.2019.1623637.

Clark, Nigel, and Bronislaw Szerszynski. 2020. *Planetary Social Thought: The Anthropocene Challenge to the Social Sciences*. Cambridge: Polity.

Cline, C. L. 1940. "The Rio Grande Valley." *Southwest Review* 25 (3): 239–55. https://www.jstor.org/stable/43466522.

DePietro, Andrew. 2021. "U.S. Poverty Rate By City In 2021." *Forbes*, 26 November 2021. https://www.forbes.com/sites/andrewdepietro/2021/11/26/us-poverty-rate-by-city-in-2021/.

Duffy, Kate. 2021. "Elon Musk Takes Texas City by Surprise by Tweeting He's Going to Donate $30 Million to Boost the Area." *Business Insider*, 1 April 2021. https://www.businessinsider.com/elon-musk-surprise-texas-brownsville-donation-revitalize-area-spacex-2021-4.

Etter, Lauren. 2015. "Musk Makes Enemies Fast in Texas Town Hosting Space-X Launches." *Chicago Daily Herald*, 13 September 2015, sec. Business. https://www.chicagotribune.com/news/sns-wp-blm-news-bc-spacex09-20150909-story.html.

Garza, Alicia A. 1995. "Kopernik Shores, TX." *Texas State Historical Association*, 1 February 1995. https://www.tshaonline.org/handbook/entries/kopernik-shores-tx.

Gomez, Madeline M. 2015. "Intersections at the Border: Immigration Enforcement, Reproductive Oppression, and the Policing of Latina Bodies in the Rio Grande Valley." *Columbia Journal of Gender and Law* 30 (1): 84–118. https://doi.org/10.7916/cjgl.v30i1.2727.

Herguth, Robert. 2022. "Elon Musk's Space Program Grows in Texas on Land Once Pitched to Chicago Retirees." *Chicago Sun-Times*, 9 April 2022. https://chicago.suntimes.com/2022/4/8/23002733/spacex-starbase-elon-musk-texas-caputa-boca-chica-village-chicago.

Hernández, Kelly Lytle. 2016. *A Two-Minute History of 'Operation Wetback'*. CNN, 14 January 2016. Video, 1:51. https://www.cnn.com/videos/politics/2016/01/14/a-history-of-operation-wetback-origwx-gr.cnn.

Hilfinger Messias, DeAnne K., Patricia A. Sharpe, Lourdes del Castillo-González, Laura Treviño, and Deborah Parra-Medina. 2017. "Living in Limbo : Latinas' Assessment of Lower Rio Grande Valley Colonias Communities." *Public Health Nursing* 34 (3): 267–75. https://doi.org/10.1111/phn.12307.

History, Art & Archives, U.S. House of Representatives. *Depression, War and Civil Rights*. https://history.house.gov/Exhibitions-and-Publications/HAIC/Historical-Essays/Separate-Interests/Depression-War-Civil-Rights/.

Jmon. 2021. "(Kennedy) Kopernik Shores Was Incorporates in 1975." *El Rrun Rrun* (blog), 5 March 2021. https://rrunrrun.blogspot.com/2021/03/kennedy-kopernik-shores-was.html.

Kearney, Milo, Anthony Knopp, and Antonio Zavaleta, eds. 2008. *Additional Studies in Rio Grande Valley History*. Vol. 8. The UTB/TSC Regional History Series. Brownsville: The University of Texas at Brownsville and Texas Southmost College.

KRGV Channel 5 News 2022. *Brownsville ISD Gets Second Round of Funding from Elon Musk Foundation*. 27 January 2022. http://www.krgv.com/videos/brownsville-isd-gets-second-round-of-funding-from-elon-musk-foundation/.

Masco, Joseph. 2010. "Bad Weather: On Planetary Crisis." *Social Studies of Science* 40 (1): 7–40. https://doi.org/10.1177/0306312709341598.

McCurdy, Howard E. 2011. *Space and the American Imagination*. 2nd edition. Baltimore, MD: Johns Hopkins University Press.

Messeri, Lisa. 2016. *Placing Outer Space: An Earthly Ethnography of Other Worlds*. Durham, DC: Duke University Press.

Messeri, Lisa. 2017. "We Need to Stop Talking About Space as a 'Frontier'." *Slate Magazine*, 15 March 2017. https://slate.com/technology/2017/03/why-we-need-to-stop-talking-about-space-as-a-frontier.html.

Miller, Tom. 2016. *On the Border: Portraits of America's Southwestern Frontier*. Reprint edition. New York Open Road Distribution.

Montgomery, Julia Cameron. 1928. *A Little Journey Through the Lower Valley of the Rio Grande: The Magic Valley of Texas*. Houston, TX: Southern Pacific Lines.

Musk, Elon. 2017. "Making Humans a Multi-Planetary Species." *New Space* 5 (2): 46–61. https://doi.org/10.1089/space.2017.29009.emu.

Oliveras González, Xavier. 2015. "Estrategias de Marketing Territorial en una Región Transfronteriza: Tamaulipas-Texas." *Si Somos Americanos* 15 (2): 97–122. https://doi.org/10.4067/S0719-09482015000200005

Olson, Valerie. 2022. "Refielding in More-Than-Terran Spaces." *Keynote Presented at Ethnographies of Outer Space: Methodological Opportunities and Experiments, Trento*, 2 September 2022.

Patoski, Joe Nick. 1998. "The Wild Coast." *Texas Monthly* 26 (6): 94–101.

Pierce, Frank C. 1917. *A Brief History of the Lower Rio Grande Valley*. Menasha, WI: The Collegiate Press, George Banta Publishing Company.

Popik, Barry. 2008. "On the Border by the Sea (Brownsville Slogan)." *The Big Apple* (blog), 16 September 2008. https://www.barrypopik.com/index.php/new_york_city/entry/on_the_border_by_the_sea_brownsville_slogan/.

Praet, Istvan, and Juan Francisco Salazar. 2017. "Introduction: Familiarizing the Extraterrestrial/Making Our Planet Alien." *Environmental Humanities* 9 (2): 309–24. https://doi.org/10.1215/22011919-4215315.

Robinson, Robin. 2008. "Short Stories and Sound Bites from the UTB Hunter Room's Brownsville Chamber of Commerce Files." In *Additional Studies in Rio Grande Valley History*, Vol. 8, edited by Milo Kearney, Anthony Knopp, and Antonio Zavaleta, 363–75. The UTB/TSC Regional History Series. Brownsville: The University of Texas at Brownsville and Texas Southmost College.

Ryabov, Igor, and Stephen Merino. 2017. "Recent Demographic Change in the Rio Grande Valley of Texas: The Importance of Domestic Migration." *Journal of Borderlands Studies* 32 (2): 211–31. https://doi.org/10.1080/08865655.2016.1195704.

Sandoval, Freddy. 2022. "Video: Great Things Happening in Brownsville, Part Two, with Commissioner Jessica Tetreau." *Rio Grande Guardian*, 20 May 2022. https://riograndeguardian.com/video-great-things-happening-in-brownsville-part-two-with-commissioner-jessica-tetreau/.

Shary, John H. 1918. *The Treasure Land of the Lower Rio Grande*. Omaha: Omaha Printing Co.

Solon, Olivia. 2021. "Disgruntled Neighbors and Dwindling Shorebirds Jeopardize SpaceX Expansion." *CNBC*, 8 December 2021. https://www.cnbc.com/2021/12/08/disgruntled-neighbors-and-dwindling-shorebirds-jeopardize-spacex-expansion.html.

Spivak, Gayatri Chakravorty. 2014. "Planetarity." In *Dictionary of Untranslatables: A Philosophical Lexicon*, edited by Barbara Cassin, 1223. Princeton, NJ: Princeton University Press.

Szolucha, Anna, Karlijn Korpershoek, Chakad Ojani, and Peter Timko. 2022. "Planetary Ethnography: A Primer." *SocArXiv*, Last modified 25 March 2022. https://doi.org/10.31235/osf.io/sy2gh.

Szolucha, Anna, Brad Tabas, Kseniia Khmelevska, Virginia Sanz Sanchez, Marek Pawlak, Iva Ramuš Cvetkovič, and Sundar Sarukkai, et al. 2022. "Planetary Conversation: A Multidisciplinary Discussion about Ethnography and the Planetary." *Unpublished Workshop Transcript*.

Tabas, Brad. 2020. "Hatred of the Earth, Climate Change, and the Dreams of Post-Planetary Culture." *Ecozon@: European Journal of Literature, Culture and Environment* 11 (1): 63–79. https://doi.org/10.37536/ECOZONA.2020.11.1.3188.

The Associated Press 1994. "Around Texas." *Austin American-Statesman*, 21 November 1994.

Timko, Peter, Karlijn Korpershoek, Chakad Ojani, and Anna Szolucha. 2022. "Exploring the Extraplanetary: Social Studies of Outer Space." *Anthropology Today* 38 (3): 9–12. https://doi.org/10.1111/1467-8322.12726.

United States Census Bureau 2021. *U.S. Census Bureau QuickFacts: Brownsville City, Texas*. https://www.census.gov/quickfacts/brownsvillecitytexas.

United States Census Bureau n.d. *S1701: Poverty Status in the Past 12 Months—Census Bureau Table*, 24 September 2022. https://data.census.gov/cedsci/table?t=Income%20and%20Poverty&g=1600000US4810768&tid=ACSST1Y2021.S1701&moe=false.

Valentine, David, Valerie A. Olson, and Debbora Battaglia. 2009. "Encountering the Future: Anthropology and Outer Space." *Anthropology News* 50 (9): 11–15. https://doi.org/10.1111/j.1556-3502.2009.50911.x.

Valentine, David, Valerie A. Olson, and Debbora Battaglia. 2012. "Extreme: Limits and Horizons in the Once and Future Cosmos." *Anthropological Quarterly* 85 (4): 1007–26. https://doi.org/10.1353/anq.2012.0066.

Verran, Helen. 2013. "Engagements between Disparate Knowledge Traditions: Toward Doing Difference Generatively and in Good Faith." In *Contested Ecologies: Dialogues in the South on Nature and Knowledge*, edited by Lesley Green, 141–61. Cape Town: HSRC Press.

7
THE SPACES OF OUTER SPACE

Oliver Dunnett

Introduction: Geography and the Language of Outer Space

A geographical approach to outer-space research is about understanding context, scale, and perspective, and the interrelations between people, place, and environment that also encompass cosmic spaces. Indeed, space, as a postmodern analytical term in geography, has come to be understood not in the absolute, mathematical sense, but relationally, such that "no space is free from human intent, human desire, and human imagination" (Mitchell 2000: 214). Scholarship in geography and related disciplines has begun to apply such understandings of space to cosmic subjects. In this work, a rich history of engagement between geography (or 'earth-writing') and extraterrestrial space, which has recognised Earth's place in its broader cosmic environment and the significance of this in ways of life and the use of power, is drawn upon.

A classic work of geography from the mid-nineteenth century epitomises the cosmic reach of geographical study: Alexander von Humboldt's *Cosmos: A Sketch or Physical Description of the Universe* (1858). Informed by his lengthy travels in South and Central America, Humboldt's most comprehensive work aimed to form a descriptive account of the entire known natural world, not just Earth but also its setting in the cosmic environment of stars, planets, and other extraterrestrial phenomena. In doing this, his writings effectively synthesised romantic and scientific approaches to describing and explaining the natural world. Some have argued that this historically close relationship between geography and cosmology, which stretches back to the Classical era, was interrupted by Enlightenment ideals of science, progress, and human agency (Cosgrove 2003); however, geography's postmodern turns, including new geographies of outer space, have acknowledged these older influences on the discipline, while employing the diverse perspectives and theoretical underpinnings that drive contemporary research in cultural, historical, and political geography (Dunnett et al. 2019).

A renewed focus on the spaces of outer space, as this chapter argues, has the potential to expand and deepen understandings of the social and cultural aspects of humanity's relation to the cosmos. This spatial approach can refer not only to the diversity of spaces, places, and landscapes beyond Earth—for example in orbital trajectories, the atmospheres of other worlds, or zero-gravity space habitats—but also to the terrestrial relational spaces that generate and derive meaning from outer space, including the colonial, experimental, or imagined spaces whose connections to the cosmic environment are particularly evocative. Here an awareness of how geographical knowledge has been "implicated in relationships of power" is essential to interpreting critically the language of colonial practice in the present day (Driver 1992: 23; Livingstone 1992). In highlighting recent research in critical geographies of outer space, while pointing out earlier foundational works, this chapter also seeks to acknowledge and develop the argument that outer space has become an "ordinary" part of the lives of millions of people around the world, by focusing on a diverse range of specific places, landscapes, and environments and their individual meanings in relation to cosmic space (MacDonald 2007: 594).

With this contextual, relational approach, it becomes necessary to reach beyond a simple binary classification of terrestrial space and outer space in geographical writing. As Ingrid Medby writes, there is a need to "reassess the value of language as both analytical topic and academic practice" in geographical scholarship, thereby thinking critically about terminologies and nomenclature used in descriptions of Earth and space, but also applying the languages of spatial enquiry to consider a range of research subjects (Medby 2020: 148). Some have favoured a revised terminology of 'off-world' spaces and activities that breaks conspicuously from invocations of capitalist and colonialist language found in terms such as exploration, frontier, and even 'space' itself (Sammler and Lynch 2021). While this chapter uses a mixture of terms for the cosmic realm and its variety of spaces, it is structured according to certain themes in contemporary geographical scholarship. As such, the first section examines concepts of place and landscape in terrestrial contexts, focusing on spaces that convey meaning in relation to outer space and invoke powerful critiques of colonialism, both terrestrial and interplanetary. The second section attends to an emerging focus on mobility and circulation in understandings of outer-space practices and processes, including the geopolitics of satellite trajectories and new understandings of atmospheres as socially and culturally affective spaces, on this and other planets. This chapter concludes with reflections on the sublime, the history of geography, and their relation to new geographies of outer space.

Place and Landscape

Understanding human relations with the spaces of outer space can inform deeper and more socially just engagements among societies here on Earth. Indeed, while universalising themes of space exploration pervade Western scientific culture, there is a growing appreciation that human interactions with cosmic subjects take place in specific places and landscapes on the ground, whether in terms of space-launch facilities, Earthly analogues for extraterrestrial environments, or other centres of calculation for outer-space science and technology.

Geography's extensive engagement with place and landscape can offer new perspectives on the spaces of outer space. As such, while the term 'place' generally refers to subjective, human understandings of certain spaces, or "a way of relating to the world" (Cresswell 2008: 54), landscape can be thought of as more of a confluence of discourse and power in space, typically associated with representations or experiences of particular environments (Wylie 2007). While landscapes have been understood to be bounded by the limits of the horizon (Casey 2001), for Humboldt, "the expression 'landscape' evoked cosmic dimensions", hinting at a more expansive understanding (Buttimer 2003: 130). Such analyses foreground the social and cultural construction of outer-space knowledges, which, as Jason Beery explains, involves "questioning the 'global' character of these [outer-space] natures" that are often established by space industry and legal frameworks (Beery 2016: 93; Redfield 1996). In this section, a set of examples, including from the southwestern United States, South America, and central Australia, demonstrates how focusing on place and landscape can help to structure critical interpretations of outer-space culture, addressing the colonial basis of outer-space science and technology in the late-modern period.

The southwestern United States is home to a variety of places and landscapes that have evoked cultures of space exploration, including as sites of scientific endeavour in rocketry and astronomy, as places of esotericism and UFO culture, but perhaps most notably as analogues for the planet Mars. The anticipated human colonisation of Mars is a trope that has been circulating in Western science and culture for well over a century, from the literary exploration fantasies of Edgar Rice Burroughs to the personified tweets of NASA's Mars rovers Curiosity and Perseverance. Indeed, NASA's plans to return humans to the Moon in the 2020s are presented as a "stepping stone" to the eventual human exploration of the Red Planet (NASA 2020: 8). While the language of colonialism has long been associated with space exploration programmes (Dittmer 2007; Dunnett 2017; Sage 2014), a critical geographical perspective on analogous Martian places and landscapes in this part of the United States is especially attuned to historic and ongoing colonial acts.

As scholars including Natalie Koch and Lisa Messeri have pointed out, space research projects including the Mars Society's Desert Research Station in Utah and Biosphere 2 habitation domes in Arizona "mobilize the desert aesthetic" in promoting the "human exploration and habitation of Mars" (Koch 2021: 39), as part of a process of "encountering Mars on Earth" (Messeri 2017: 134). Here, terrestrial desert landscapes mirror the images of Mars sent back by probes, from NASA's Viking landers in the 1970s to the current crop of mobile robotic explorers, with the visual landscape acting as the primary register of relation. Such landscapes also offered Martian analogues for some early Hollywood science-fiction films including *Rocketship X-M* (1950) and *Robinson Crusoe on Mars* (1964), both filmed in California's Death Valley (Miller 2016). As such, making sense of Mars in the popular and scientific imagination takes place as much on Earth as it does in interplanetary space.

In the case of Biosphere 2 in the early 1990s, a community of settlers contrived to live for two years in an ecological bubble outside Oracle, Arizona, in what was presented as a pioneering social-scientific experiment to inform prospective Martian settlements has been interpreted as little more than a media spectacle with settler-colonialist underpinnings (Mayer 2016, this volume). Crucially, Koch identifies the relevance of the broader historical geography of the region, and the interplay between colonial and scientific practices, such that "beyond naturalizing a colonial perspective of Mars itself", projects such as Biosphere 2 "also naturalize colonialism" in the United States (Koch 2021: 38). Part of this process involves framing the desert landscape as barren, empty, and free of prior human influence, contrary to the ongoing presence of Indigenous communities in this region. Similar imaginative geographies of desert landscapes as pristine, vacant, experimental areas have been noted as significant in the cultural construction of early space-launch facilities in the mid-twentieth century, including in Algeria and Australia (Gorman 2005). However, the southwestern United States stands out as a region that has continued to host a variety of imaginative and scientific engagements with the landscape of outer space consistently since at least the nineteenth century.

Geographers have demonstrated how such landscapes have acted as a confluence for discourses of colonialism, astronomy, space exploration, and the sublime throughout modern US history. For Maria Lane, the "isolation and purity" of the Sierra Nevada in California helped to legitimise nineteenth-century sightings of Mars by prominent astronomers, as part of a narration of the sublime in elevated natural landscapes that could only be told through heroic masculine scientific endeavour (Lane 2008: 127). A century later, the proving grounds at White Sands, New Mexico, acted as the launch pad for the V-2 tests that first pictured the curvature of Earth's surface from space. The latter became part of what Fraser MacDonald evocatively has called "rocketry's accelerating sublime", foregrounding the cultural and geopolitical hegemony of the United States in the postwar period (MacDonald 2010: 210). More recently, the 'two frontiers' of historic US colonialism and the exploration of space have been juxtaposed in the landscape photography of Trevor Paglen (Figure 7.1), which takes as its frame of reference the militarised night skies of the US southwest, set in the context of the violent dispossession of these lands from their first inhabitants (Gustafsson 2013: 151). In recognising this duplicity of landscape, Paglen's photographs visually reference historic frontier photography in this region, while being calibrated to expose the orthogonal trails of military satellites orbiting overhead.

The Spaces of Outer Space

Figure 7.1   Dead Satellite with a nuclear reactor, Eastern Arizona (Cosmos 469), 2011. C-print 48 × 60 in. © Trevor Paglen. Courtesy of the artist, Altman Siegel gallery (San Francisco), and pace gallery.

While Paglen's works address directly the colonial logic of the US military–outer-space nexus, further critical readings are required to interpret the establishment of Spaceport America, a public–private venture led by the State of New Mexico that hit the headlines in July 2021 with the Virgin Galactic test flight that reached the borders of space, carrying the business magnate Richard Branson. Katherine Sammler and Casey Lynch argue that, notwithstanding its role as a centre of prospective space tourism, Spaceport America "is performative, linking political economic models, technological systems, and cultural imagination in an ongoing production of the present-future of offworld access" (Sammler and Lynch 2021: 709). Similarly, David Valentine has recognised Spaceport America as a confluence of libertarian, free-market outer-space ideologies and the historic colonialism of the United States, noting that "the gravitational pull of history and empire is powerful in this desert" (Valentine 2017: 186). As such, Spaceport America represents a neoliberal salvo in the contested production of outer space in the twenty-first century, an imaginary that is ultimately couched in a colonial imagination of outer space. Central to such imaginative geographies is the spaceport itself and its place in the desert landscape, designed to a retro-futurist aesthetic to appeal to the fantasy of space exploration as much as the reality of its use as a base for a limited number of suborbital test flights.

As well as offering critical accounts of space-related discourse and practice in specific spatial contexts, studies attuned to broader geographies of empire and colonial enclosure have highlighted modes of local resistance to outer-space projects, their harmful impacts in specific communities, and their extended global networks of power. Here, the process of enclosure, often understood in relation to the privatisation of common land in the Middle Ages, has been recognised as "a key dimension of our colonial present" (Shaw-Taylor and Vasudevan 2009: 192). In a classic study, Peter Redfield demonstrated how a local controversy over a section of road bisecting the European Space Agency's Centre Spatial Guyanais in Kourou, French Guiana, became embroiled in wider anticolonial political protests in the 1990s. Here, the Mouvement de Décolonisation et d'Émancipation Sociale led a campaign against the new road, emphasising the desire for local, democratic decision-making in one of France's five remaining overseas departments, or de facto colonies (Redfield 2002). As well as highlighting the colonial basis of the European Space Agency's principal launch facility, which regularly deploys orbital payloads using the Ariane rocket system, Redfield's study demonstrates the locality of outer-space networks on the ground, and their impacts in specific places and communities.

Such impacts can be physical as well as sociopolitical, in the form of falling debris down-range from rocket launch sites. While the majority of the world's main space-launch sites are eastern-facing coastal locations that allow launch debris to fall more safely into the ocean, a number of sites including Woomera in South Australia (an experimental range for the precursor of the European Space Agency in the 1960s) and Baikonur in Kazakhstan (the long-standing launch site of the Russian Space Agency) have enrolled their surrounding landscapes as 'drop-zones' or debris fields (Dunnett 2017; Bichsel 2021). These landscapes are effectively brought into the broader processes of colonial enclosure that affect local populations, and on several occasions have provoked acts of protest or resistance. The wider landscape of Woomera, for example, prior to its use as a monitoring and recovery zone for rocket testing during the postwar years, became the focus of protests by representatives of the Kokatha and Pitjantjatjara people, the Traditional Owners of parts of the land bisected by the Woomera rocket range that extended hundreds of miles into central Australia. For these Indigenous communities, the central Australian desert was not the barren wasteland of the rocketry drop-zone but a landscape of cultural, environmental, and cosmic importance. As Alice Gorman points out, "the colonial aspects of space exploration are a mirror of those same aspirations played out on Earth", enacted through processes of imaginative framing, experimentation, and enclosure (Gorman 2005: 99).

While it is important to acknowledge colonial discourse and acts of protest in the landscapes of outer space on Earth, it is equally important to highlight alternative ways of understanding human relationships with the cosmic realm. Speaking to such debates, research at the nexus of critical geography and Indigenous cosmology has emerged recently to deepen anticolonial understandings of outer space. Bawaka Country, a research collective with members drawn from Indigenous and non-Indigenous communities in Australia, has sought to counter dominant discourses of space colonisation by highlighting alternative ways of valuing the landscape of outer space (Bawaka Country et al. 2020, this volume). Such approaches reject implicitly the popular language of space exploration and space colonisation, in a shift towards appreciating cosmic spaces as intimately connected to societies on Earth rather than subject to the exploratory impulses of the most powerful in society. As noted in many of the examples in this chapter, nomenclature and terminology are important in such debates, and the Bawaka collective's use of the term 'Sky Country' as an alternative to 'outer space' helps to convey the relational meanings that are assigned to landscape and skyscape alike in Indigenous cosmologies (Gorman 2015; Noon and De Napoli 2022).

Narrative geographies are also at play, with the traditional song spiral identified as one of the ways in which the interconnected environment of human and nonhuman—land, sea, and sky—are drawn together ceremonially to mark the passing of the dead. For the Yolŋu people, the song spiral "provides the map through space and time needed for spirits to travel safely through Sky Country", such that "Sky Country is and always has been a richly known, mapped, governed and cared-for place" (Bawaka Country et al. 2020: 6). As such, the collective explains how space exploration practices have materially harmed Sky Country, countering assumptions that 'outer space' remains empty and devoid of life, that it is distinct from and separate to Earth, and that space exploration presents no ethical or moral barriers to justification. However, as the co-creation practice of the Bawaka collective illustrates, rather than establish a Western/Indigenous binary of mutually incompatible conceptualisations of outer space, it is possible to draw together ways of thinking about the cosmic environment that are mutually beneficial, seeking to establish more careful stewardship of our home planet, generating and sustaining more meaningful relationships between people and the night skies, and avoiding the most damaging aspects of space exploitation. Place and landscape are central to such conceptualisations, foregrounding the relational understandings of space and the specificities of scale that are generated in critical geographical approaches.

Mobility and Circulation

Studying the spaces of outer space presents certain challenges to conceptualising key terms in geography, such as mapping, timekeeping, and gravitational forces, as even the very notions of 'up' and 'down' are spun out of their familiar context. An iconic photograph of Earth taken from the orbit of the Moon by Apollo astronaut William Anders in December 1968 illustrates this point, as its orientation was rotated by ninety degrees in postproduction to give the semblance of a traditional landscape composition, later named *Earthrise*, with the Earth appearing in the 'sky' and the lunar surface as the 'ground' (Cosgrove 1994). Here, a sense of terrestrial order was applied to the three-dimensional motion of planetary bodies in space, in a way that calls into question the fixity of photographic representation.

Notwithstanding the significance of images of humans on the Moon, Denis Cosgrove (2001) has argued that the cultural and political power of the Apollo programme largely lay with its iconic imagery of the whole Earth from space, drawing meaning from a planetary scale that invoked far older imaginative geographies. Further interpretations of such 'Apollo's eye' visions have noted how they also serve to obscure the "differences, divergences and discriminations that shape our planet" (Peters 2021: 251), while their ubiquity in visual culture tends to erase the "enormous flows of resources" involved in their "extraction, production and consumption" (Sidaway 2005: 72). As such, a move towards critical understandings of mobility and circulation helps to extend geographical enquiry to the spaces of outer space in ways that reach beyond the purely representational and iconographic.

Outer-space mobilities take account of Earth's place in a dynamic solar system—not only the movement of Earth around its axis and the Sun, but also the ways in which it interacts with extraterrestrial phenomena, including meteors and other planetary bodies, radiative and electromagnetic space weather, and other types of fluid and solid motion (Szerszynski 2016). These mobilities also affect human activity in space, making orbital mechanics and weightlessness key factors in the geographies of spaceflight. As several examples in this section show, recognising outer space as being part of Earth's dynamic environment can add further depth to conceptualising the spaces of outer space in geographical enquiry.

Understandings of orbital circulation are central to both the scientific and political importance of satellite technologies. The popular shock of Sputnik in 1957 was tied intimately to the demonstration of the fact that, once an artificial satellite had reached low Earth orbit, it could circumnavigate the globe at high speed, in this case visibly traversing the landmass of the United States several times each day (Bulkeley 1991). The devastating potential of intercontinental ballistic missiles to deploy atomic weapons from the borders of space was made clear, triggering the early 'space race' that proceeded rapidly during the pre-treaty period of the Cold War (Mieczkowski 2013).

Notwithstanding their geopolitical significance, the environmental impacts and applications of space rockets and artificial satellites are manifold, bringing understandings of landscape, atmosphere, and biosphere into synthesis, and blurring the boundaries between Earth and space.

An early example of the potential of orbital and suborbital human activity to convey and affect geopolitical atmospheres was the US atomic weapons testing that occurred beyond the boundaries of space in the early 1960s. This activity not only materially damaged some of the early communications satellites, including Telstar 1, the world's first commercial communications satellite, and Ariel 1, the first US–UK collaborative satellite, but it also delivered charged particles and radiation into the ionosphere, the uppermost region of Earth's atmosphere, which then circulated around the world (Godwin 2010). As well as causing a diplomatic incident that strained the limits of trans-Atlantic military and technological cooperation in this period, these atomic tests were decried by the British scientist Bernard Lovell, director of the Jodrell Bank radio telescope, as a moral transgression of Earth's environment (Dunnett 2021). Here, the nature of events that occurred both in a specific place and as a mobile atmospheric phenomenon had the power to affect geopolitical, environmental, and moral understandings of the upper atmosphere, Earth-orbital space, and the planet as a whole.

Human activity in the near-Earth spaces of outer space can inform wider discussions about the ways in which orbital, atmospheric, and terrestrial spaces are coproduced by natural, commercial, and political processes. It has widely become acknowledged that artificial satellites, although designed to "annihilate space via instantaneous communications", have distinct geographies that relate both to the physical properties of the orbital environment and to cultural and political realities on Earth's surface (Warf 2007: 391). Therefore, equatorial geostationary orbits hold specific value in terms of global communications and monitoring, while polar orbits favour low-level reconnaissance and geographical positioning systems, and a range of other orbital trajectories suit their own scientific, cultural, and political imperatives. Each of these orbital configurations has a corresponding surface geography of space-launch facilities and monitoring stations, amid wider networks of governance, data sharing, and protection, forming a global assemblage of technology and power to which artificial satellites belong.

One of the ways in which satellites have altered human understandings of Earth has been through their use for environmental monitoring, from the very first satellites advancing knowledge of the upper atmosphere as part of the 1957–1958 International Geophysical Year to the long-running Landsat programme of Earth-imaging satellites from 1972 onwards. Furthermore, since the mid-1980s NASA has been influential in the development of Earth system science, a study of "the interactions that bind the Earth's components into a unified, dynamical system", using a combination of orbital and in situ remote sensing technologies (ESSC 1986: 15). A recent addition to this programme has been the Jason-3 satellite, which was launched in 2016 to gather planetary-scale oceanographic data on sea-level changes, oceanic circulation, and other ocean–climate interactions from a low Earth orbit. In charting its role as an essential actant in contemporary Earth system science, Julie Saperstein has contrasted this satellite's regular, predictable orbits with the lauded "Apollonian gaze" of the omniscient outer-space perspective, highlighting a circulatory geography that becomes part of "the co-constitution of 'outer' space and terrestrial space" in international collaborative research, while sustaining the scope of environmental science at the planetary scale (Saperstein 2021: 729).

As well as carrying scientific and political agency, satellites are also subject to decay in terms of their functional and orbital degeneration. While some satellites are moved into graveyard orbits as they become redundant 'space junk', others burn up as they reenter Earth's atmosphere, and in some rare cases component parts have been known to fall unpredictably to impact the surface. Such acts of decay are partly related to the expansion of Earth's atmosphere that occurs during periods of increased solar activity, a process that operates as "a planetary self-cleaning mechanism, sweeping lower orbital altitudes clear of uncontrolled junk" (Rand 2019: 82; Fedrizzi, Fuller-Rowell, and Codrescu 2012). Redundant objects that remain in Earth's orbit increasingly pose hazards to other satellites, including the International Space Station, and may restrict access to space for emerging spacefaring nations as launch pathways become increasingly obstructed. In any case, rather than representing a transcendent break from the terrestrial realm, the Earth-orbital field constitutes a "repository of human ideologies and values" that is shaped by natural as well as cultural and political forces (Gorman 2019: 108).

Mobile and circulatory geographies of outer space also reach beyond Earth's orbit to encompass the diverse spaces of the solar system and beyond, as well as their relation to Earth and their meanings for humankind. Just as "there is a constant flow of material and energy between the various layers of Earth's atmosphere", suggests environmental historian Dagomar Degroot, "other flows also connect Earth to the rest of the cosmos" (Degroot 2017: 25). As such, events in the solar system have been monitored and discussed in amateur observation, professional astronomy, and popular culture, from the transits of Venus in the eighteenth and nineteenth centuries that drew the attention of Western scientists and explorers to a solar eclipse in 1919 that helped to prove the theory of relativity, and a comet crash on Jupiter in 1993 that informed concepts about the movement of meteors and their possible threat to Earth. Here, human mobilities interact with cosmic circulations and flows, as scientists and other observers have traversed the globe in search of optimal viewing conditions, facilitated and limited by global networks of travel and empire (Mawhinney 2018).

More directly, deep-space probes, launched in synchrony with favourable planetary alignments, have extended understandings of processes in the cosmic environment, as well as the physical, magnetic, and radiative qualities of the outer planets of the solar system. Here the relative mobilities of spacecraft, planetary bodies, and data telemetry have come together to enrich the wealth of human knowledge about the universe, with Voyager 1 becoming the first human artefact to move beyond the heliopause, marking the outer extent of the solar system, in 2012. Acknowledging cosmic mobilities such as these contributes to a sense in which, rather than outer space being a static backdrop to human endeavour, Earth and space can be recognised together as part of a moving, energetic, and active cosmic environment.

Space weather is a phenomenon that encompasses changes in solar radiation, magnetism, and flows of particulate matter throughout the solar system, affecting Earth's upper atmosphere and aurora. Researchers have also applied atmospheric understandings of weather to the circulations of gases that increasingly have become detectable on other planets. The sound of wind on Mars, for example, has recently been conveyed via NASA's Perseverance rover, while the weather of Neptune has been recognised as the most powerful in the solar system. Kimberley Peters argues that understandings of weather on other planets do not just represent the accumulation of scientific data about interplanetary space; they also help humans to form affective relational understandings of our place in the universe, as part of "a 'sticky web' of bindings between our planet and a wider network and assemblages of deep spaces, sites and energies" (Peters 2021: 256). Such work takes inference from the rich social and cultural meanings of terrestrial weather, which are "embedded in sensory and affective memories" (Edensor, Barry, and Borovnik 2021: 12; Mahony and Randalls 2020). Understandings of planetary weather, therefore, enable us to imagine what life is like on other worlds, and the potential for human experience of extraterrestrial environments.

Among the most captivating of all outer-space missions, the Pioneer and Voyager probes, sent by NASA in the 1970s to explore the outer solar system, deepened scientific knowledge of the atmospheres of the gas giants, especially Jupiter. In relaying a series of data that codified multiple consecutive images of Jupiter, a sense of the motion of the planet's atmosphere was achieved, alongside the monitoring of electromagnetic data during the planetary flyby (Burgess 1982). With much NASA-derived data being freely available to the scientific community worldwide, members of the British Interplanetary Society were able to interpret these studies of Jupiter's weather. As part of their Interstellar Studies series of research papers in the 1980s, data from the Pioneer and Voyager programmes informed speculative plans to mine the Jovian atmosphere for helium-3 and deuterium isotopes, determined to be the best way of accumulating fuel for an interstellar voyage to the planetary companions of Barnard's Star, the fourth closest to the solar system (Dunnett 2021). Here, space weather became a medium through which to imagine future geographies of exploration in space, notwithstanding the prospect of detecting atmospheres on more remote worlds.

In such ways, notional understandings of the first exoplanets to be discovered further engendered imagined futures of human exploration beyond the solar system, considering the atmospheric properties of worlds orbiting distant stars (Messeri 2016). Over four thousand exoplanets have been discovered since the mid-twentieth century, using a variety of observational methods including most recently from the Kepler and TESS space telescopes, with the prospect of many more to come from the James Webb space telescope. Central to this research is analysing the constitution of exoplanetary atmospheres, including the detection of water vapour in so-called 'habitable-zone planets' of distant stars (Tsiaras et al. 2019). As such, whether considering flows of matter through space, the winds of Mars, or the atmospheric composition of distant planets, conceptualising weather beyond our home planet has provoked imaginative geographies of life in the cosmos and the potential for human colonisation of other worlds.

Conclusion: Writings of Earth and Cosmos

This chapter has offered a summary of some approaches in contemporary critical geography and related fields that have sought to extend interpretations of conceptual space to the cosmic realm while understanding their synergies and connections with and among the terrestrial world that are inherent to geographical study. Each of the two main sections has focused on strands of thinking in critical geography that have their own much broader set of theoretical contributions and fields of engagement. While studies of place and landscape have long been central components of geographical study, a renewed focus on mobility and circulation has emerged to complement this approach and ensure that geographical enquiry takes into consideration the movements and processes that connect places and convey meanings. As such, some of the specific places and landscapes in which outer-space knowledge has been configured have been identified, and the interplay between science and colonialism has been probed through focusing on case studies in the southwestern United States, South America, and Australia. Furthermore, the importance of orbital motion and atmospheric circulation has been explained in configuring the geographies of outer space, with work highlighting the conceptualisation of outer space and Earth being seen as part of the same natural and cultural environment. The importance of language has been emphasised throughout, with new terminologies highlighted alongside established terms, utilising the productive specificities of geographical description while acknowledging the role of geography in the growth of empires, both historically and in the present day, and the potential of language to subvert such imperatives.

Such approaches have particular meanings and associations when applied to the realm of outer space: landscapes of other worlds come into view, while flows of cosmic matter make connections in space. These broad, almost limitless parameters of the study are correlated with the postmodern nature of contemporary geographical research, just as the intense specialisation of geographical subdisciplines since the Enlightenment gave way to a more holistic appreciation of the human and natural environment that can be seen to extend beyond Earth's immediate boundaries. In the words of Alexander von Humboldt, sublime encounters can be manifested

> Whether we float on the surface of the great deep, stand on some lonely mountain summit enveloped in the half-transparent vapoury veil of the atmosphere, or by the aid of powerful optical instruments scan the regions of space, and see the remote nebulous mass resolve itself into worlds of stars.
>
> *(Humboldt 1997 [1858]: 40)*

It is in the spirit of Humboldt that geographies of outer space are presented in this chapter: considering a relational, synthesised approach to understanding Earth and Cosmos together.

References

Bawaka Country et al. 2020. "Dukarr Lakarama: Listening to Guwak, Talking Back to Space Colonization." *Political Geography* 81: 102218. https://doi.org/10.1016/j.polgeo.2020.102218.

Beery, Jason. 2016. "Unearthing Global Natures: Outer Space and Scalar Politics." *Political Geography* 55: 92–101. http://doi.org/10.1016/j.polgeo.2016.04.003.

Bichsel, Christine. 2021. "When Things Fall from the Sky: Understanding Rocket Stages on the Kazakh Steppe as Imperial Debris." *Society + Space Magazine*, 24 May 2021. https://www.societyandspace.org/articles/when-things-fall-from-the-sky-understanding-rocket-stages-on-the-kazakh-steppe-as-imperial-debris.

Bulkeley, Rip. 1991. *The Sputniks Crisis and Early United States Space Policy*. London: Macmillan.

Burgess, Eric. 1982. *By Jupiter: Odysseys to a Giant*. New York: Colombia University Press.

Buttimer, Anne. 2003. "Renaissance and Re-membering Geography: Pioneering Ideas of Alexander von Humboldt 1769–1859." *South African Geographical Journal* 85 (2): 125–33. https://doi.org/10.1080/03736245.2003.9713792.

Casey, Edward. 2001. "Between Geography and Philosophy: What Does It Mean to Be in the Place-World?" *Annals of the Association of American Geographers* 91 (4): 683–93. https://doi.org/10.1111/0004-5608.00266.

Cosgrove, Denis. 1994. "Contested Global Visions: *One-World*, *Whole-Earth*, and the Apollo Space Photographs." *Annals of the Association of American Geographers* 84 (2): 270–94. https://doi.org/10.1111/j.1467-8306.1994.tb01738.x.

Cosgrove, Denis. 2001. *Apollo's Eye: A Cartographic Genealogy of the Earth in the Western Imagination*. Baltimore, MD: John Hopkins University Press.

Cosgrove, Denis. 2003. "Globalism and Tolerance in Early Modern Geography." *Annals of the Association of American Geographers* 93 (4): 852–70. https://doi.org/10.1111/j.1467-8306.2003.09304006.x.

Cresswell, Tim. 2008. "Space and Place (1977): Yi-Fu Tuan." In *Key Texts in Human Geography*, edited by Phil Hubbard, Rob Kitchin and Gill Valentine, 53–60. London: Sage.

Degroot, Dagomar. 2017. "'A Catastrophe Happening in Front of Our Very Eyes': The Environmental History of a Comet Crash on Jupiter." *Environmental History* 22: 23–49. https://doi.org/10.1093/envhis/emw067.

Dittmer, Jason. 2007. "Colonialism and Place Creation in *Mars Pathfinder* Media Coverage." *Geographical Review* 97 (1): 112–30. https://doi.org/10.1111/j.1931-0846.2007.tb00282.x.

Driver, Felix. 1992. "Geography's Empire: Histories of Geographical Knowledge." *Environment and Planning D: Society and Space* 10 (1): 23–40. https://doi.org/10.1068/d100023.

Dunnett, Oliver. 2017. "Geopolitical Cultures of Outer Space: The British Interplanetary Society, 1933–1965." *Geopolitics* 22 (2): 452–73. https://doi.org/10.1080/14650045.2016.1247267.

Dunnett, Oliver. 2021. *Earth, Cosmos and Culture: Geographies of Outer Space in Britain, 1900–2020*. Abingdon: Routledge.

Dunnett, Oliver, Andrew S. Maclaren, Julie Klinger, K. Maria D. Lane, and Daniel Sage. 2019. "Geographies of Outer Space: Progress and New Opportunities." *Progress in Human Geography* 43 (2): 314–36. https://doi.org/10.1177/0309132517747727.

Edensor, Tim, Kaya Barry, and Maria Borovnik. 2021. "Introduction: Placing Weather." In *Weather: Spaces, Mobilities and Affects*, edited by Tim Edensor, Kaya Barry and Maria Borovnik, 1–22. London: Routledge.

ESSC (Earth System Sciences Committee) 1986. *Earth System Science: Overview*. Washington, DC: NASA.

Fedrizzi, Mariangel, Tim J. Fuller-Rowell, and Mikhail V. Codrescu. 2012. "Global Joule Heating Index Derived from Thermospheric Density Physics-Based Modeling and Observations." *Space Weather* 10(3). https://doi.org/10.1029/2011SW000724.

Godwin, Matthew. 2010. "'Britnik': How America Made and Destroyed Britain's First Satellite." In *New Spaces of Exploration: Geographies of Discovery in the Twentieth Century*, edited by Simon Naylor and James Ryan, 173–95. London: I. B. Tauris.

Gorman, Alice. 2005. "The Cultural Landscape of Interplanetary Space." *Journal of Social Archaeology* 5 (1): 85–107. https://doi.org/10.1177/1469605305050148.

Gorman, Alice. 2015. "Australian Aboriginal Place Names in the Solar System." *Astrosociological Insights* 4 (2): 14–15.

Gorman, Alice. 2019. "Ghosts in the Machine: Space Junk and the Future of Earth Orbit." *Architectural Design* 89 (1): 106–11. https://doi.org/10.1002/ad.2397.

Gustafsson, Henrik. 2013. "Foresight, Hindsight and State Secrecy in the American West: The Geopolitical Aesthetics of Trevor Paglen." *Journal of Visual Culture* 12 (1): 148–64. https://doi.org/10.1177/1470412912468711.

Koch, Natalie. 2021. "Whose Apocalypse? Biosphere 2 and the Spectacle of Settler Science in the Desert." *Geoforum* 124: 36–45. https://doi.org/10.1016/j.geoforum.2021.05.015.

Lane, K. Maria D. 2008. "Astronomers at Altitude: Mountain Geography and the Cultivation of Scientific Legitimacy." In *High Places: Cultural Geographies of Mountains, Ice and Science*, edited by Denis Cosgrove and Veronica Della Dora, 126–44. London: I. B. Tauris.

Livingstone, David N. 1992. *The Geographical Tradition: Episodes in the History of a Contested Enterprise*. Oxford: Blackwell.

MacDonald, Fraser. 2007. "Anti-*Astropolitik*: Outer Space and the Orbit of Geography." *Progress in Human Geography* 31 (5): 592–615. https://doi.org/10.1177/0309132507081492.

MacDonald, Fraser. 2010. "High Empire: Rocketry and the Popular Geopolitics of Space Exploration, 1944–62". In *New Spaces of Exploration: Geographies of Discovery in the Twentieth Century*, edited by Simon Naylor and James Ryan, 196–221. London: I. B. Tauris. http://doi.org/10.5040/9780755620555.ch-009.

Mahony, Martin, and Samuel Randalls, eds. 2020. *Weather, Climate, and the Geographical Imagination: Placing Atmospheric Knowledges*. Pittsburgh, PA: University of Pittsburgh Press.

Mawhinney, Rory. 2018. "Astronomical Fieldwork and the Spaces of Relativity: The Historical Geographies of the 1919 British Eclipse Expeditions to Príncipe and Brazil." *Historical Geography* 46: 203–38. http://doi.org/10.1353/hgo.2018.0032.

Mayer, Ralo. 2016. "Beyond the Blue Marble: Artistic Research on Space and Ecology." *Acta Astronautica* 128: 573–79. http://doi.org/10.1016/j.actaastro.2016.08.015.

Medby, Ingrid. 2020. "Political Geography and Language: A Reappraisal for a Diverse Discipline." *Area* 52 (1): 148–55. https://doi.org/10.1111/area.12559.

Messeri, Lisa. 2016. *Placing Outer Space: An Earthly Ethnography of Other Worlds*. Durham, NC: Duke University Press.

Messeri, Lisa. 2017. "Resonant Worlds: Cultivating Proximal Encounters in Planetary Science." *American Ethnologist* 44 (1): 131–42. https://doi.org/10.1111/amet.12431.

Mieczkowski, Yanek. 2013. *Eisenhower's Sputnik Moment: The Race for Space and World Prestige*. Ithaca, NY: Cornell University Press.

Miller, Thomas Kent. 2016. *Mars in the Movies: A History*. Jefferson, NC: McFarland & Co.

Mitchell, Don. 2000. *Cultural Geography: A Critical Introduction*. Oxford: Blackwell.

NASA 2020. *NASA's Lunar Exploration Program Overview*. https://www.nasa.gov/sites/default/files/atoms/files/artemis_plan-20200921.pdf.

Noon, Karlie, and Krystal De Napoli. 2022. *Sky Country*. First Knowledges: Astronomy. Port Melbourne: Thames & Hudson.

Peters, Kimberley. 2021. "Writing (Extra)Planetary Geographies of Weather-Worlds." In *Weather: Spaces, Mobilities and Affects*, edited by Kaya Barry, Maria Borovnik and Tim Edensor, 250–62. Abingdon: Routledge.

Rand, Lisa Ruth. 2019. "Falling Cosmos: Nuclear Reentry and the Environmental History of Earth Orbit." *Environmental History* 24 (1): 78–103. https://doi.org/10.1093/envhis/emy125.

Redfield, Peter. 1996. "Beneath a Modern Sky: Space Technology and Its Place on the Ground." *Science, Technology, and Human Values* 21 (3): 251–74. https://doi.org/10.1177/016224399602100301.

Redfield, Peter. 2002. "The Half-Life of Empire in Outer Space." *Social Studies of Science* 32 (5/6): 791–825. https://doi.org/10.1177/030631270203200508.

Sage, Daniel. 2014. *How Outer Space Made America: Geography, Organization and the Cosmic Sublime*. Farnham: Ashgate.

Sammler, Katherine, and Casey Lynch. 2021. "Spaceport America: Contested Offworld Access and the Everyman Astronaut." *Geopolitics* 26 (3): 704–28. https://doi.org/10.1080/14650045.2019.1569631.

Saperstein, Julie. 2021. "Opening the Black Box of Outer Space: The Case of Jason-3." *Geopolitics* 26 (3): 729–46. https://doi.org/10.1080/14650045.2020.1806241.

Shaw-Taylor, Leigh, and Alexander Vasudevan. 2009. "Enclosure." In *The Dictionary of Human Geography*, 5th ed., edited by Derek Gregory, Ron Johnston, Geraldine Pratt, Michael Watts, and Sarah Whatmore, 191–92. Oxford: Wiley-Blackwell.

Sidaway, James. 2005. "*Empire's* Geographies." *ACME: An International E-Journal for Critical Geographies* 3 (2): 63–78. https://acme-journal.org/index.php/acme/article/view/718/580.

Szerszynski, Bronislaw. 2016. "Planetary Mobilities: Movement, Memory and Emergence in the Body of the Earth." *Mobilities* 11 (4): 614–28. https://doi.org/10.1080/17450101.2016.1211828.

Tsiaras, Angelos, Ingo P. Waldmann, Giovanna Tinetti, Jonathan Tennyson, and Sergey N. Yurchenko. 2019. "Water Vapour in the Atmosphere of the Habitable-Zone Eight-Earth-Mass Planet K2–18 b." *Nature Astronomy* 3: 1086–91. https://doi.org/10.1038/s41550-019-0878-9.

Valentine, David. 2017. "Gravity Fixes: Habituating to the Human on Mars and Island Three." *HAU: Journal of Ethnographic Theory* 7 (3): 185–209. https://doi.org/10.14318/hau7.3.012.

Von Humboldt, Alexander. 1997 [1858]. *Cosmos: A Sketch or Physical Description of the Universe*. Vol. 1. Baltimore, MD: Johns Hopkins University Press.

Warf, Barney. 2007. "Geopolitics of the Satellite Industry." *Tijdschrift voor Economische en Sociale Geografie* 98 (3): 385–97. https://doi.org/10.1111/j.1467-9663.2007.00405.x.

Wylie, John. 2007. *Landscape*. London: Routledge.

8
SOCIOLOGICAL APPROACHES TO OUTER SPACE

Paola Castaño and Álvaro Santana-Acuña

Introduction

This chapter examines how sociologists have approached outer space as an object of inquiry. As a multiparadigmatic discipline, sociology has long-standing debates about its scientific or humanistic character. In Abbott's words (2001: 6): "[F]or every sociologist who thinks causal analysis is important there is another who pursues narrative explanation. For every sociologist who believes in objective knowledge, another denies it. For every reflective interpretivist there is a rigorous positivist." These lines of contention and their implications are likely to be revisited and reinvigorated as sociologists undertake research related to the various social dimensions of outer space.

From this general premise about the discipline and acknowledging that outer space has not been a major part of sociology's objects of inquiry, in this chapter we ask: Which kinds of sociology have so far taken outer space as an object of study? Which subfields have engaged with it? What specific aspects and units of analysis have been examined? What types of methodological and theoretical approaches have been incorporated into these studies? And what sorts of interventions inside and outside the discipline have these studies enabled?

Based on these questions, this chapter identifies three major lines of inquiry to date: (1) the astrosociological approach that seeks the multidisciplinary study of the relationship between space exploration and societies; (2) a perspective that offers a historical materialist explanation of the relationship between human society and the cosmos; and (3) most recently, lines of inquiry stemming from organisational sociology and sociology of science where sociologists have also carved a dominion of pertinence, most notably inside NASA. The three approaches point to different explanatory ambitions and modes of engagement in the discipline of the study of outer space. As such, they differ in their levels of analysis, conceptual interlocutors, theoretical implications, and agenda-setting ambitions. Amongst this diversity, and with different tools for its achievement, there is a shared goal: to make sociology relevant to contemporary discourses and practices related to outer space. This chapter concludes by outlining future research directions in the discipline as well as some challenges in terms of sociologists' role in this area of study outside the discipline.

Astrosociology

Futurist and scientist Allen Tough coined the term astrosociology in 1998, and, as a field, astrosociology came into existence in 2004. Beyond the use of the term and the acknowledgment of its source, there is no substantive intellectual genealogy or current relationship between future studies and astrosociology. To this day, the field's trajectory is mainly connected to the efforts of its leading exponent: sociologist Jim Pass, founder and CEO of the non-profit organisation Astrosociology Research Institute (ARI).

In its different iterations, Pass (2004, 2012, 2015, 2018) has defined astrosociology as the sociology-grounded multidisciplinary study of the relationship between space exploration and societies in both an academic and applied manner. Seeking to become a specialised academic field, with its own literature and practitioners, along with the ARI, astrosociology has its own journal, *The Journal of Astrosociology*, newsletter, *Astrosociological Insights*, and social media presence.

To date, astrosociology's contributions have primarily been at the programmatic level. Two of its key premises are the recognition of the "human dimension" of the "relationship between outer space and society" (ARI 2008–2022) and the notion that outer space exploration requires unprecedented levels of cooperation among the sciences. This exploration would be handicapped if undertaken by reproducing the divisions of knowledge already existing on Earth. "Rocket science", Pass (ARI 2008–2022) argues, "is no longer adequate on its own", and the natural and physical sciences cannot monopolize the study of outer space leaving aside the humanities, the social sciences, and the arts (Pass 2018). Accordingly, he claims that astrosociology "fills a void that spans nearly the entire Space Age" (Pass 2015: 536) and is the best-suited field to achieve such an integration. From this perspective, "astrosocial phenomena" are not reducible to a disciplinary label but rather are "social, cultural, and behavioral patterns related to outer space" (ARI 2008–2022). However, astrosociology, we contend, has not yet developed the specifics of how that integration between the sciences will happen.

Equipped with this integrative aim, which arguably echoes Auguste Comte's efforts to create the "science of Society" as the "link by which all our varied observations of phenomena can be brought into one consistent whole" (2015 [1844]: 1–2), astrosociology seeks to be a holistic scientific approach, an umbrella field for the behavioural and social sciences, the humanities, and the arts. Its promise is to build a pan-disciplinary platform so that social scientists interested in outer space issues do not work in isolation among themselves and from other fields of knowledge. The desired outcome of interdisciplinary cooperation is that astrosociology closes the "Great Divide" between the main branches of science. Such closure would result in a body of knowledge beneficial to "humanity in both extraterrestrial *and* terrestrial environments" (ARI 2008–2022, original emphasis).

Building on Wright Mills's notion of the sociological imagination, Pass proposes the "astrosociological imagination", defined as "an insightful way of looking at the world that allows a person possessing and exercising it to make connections between his or her personal world of experiences and the macro-level ... existence of astrosocial forces" (Pass and Harrison 2016 cited in Pass 2020). In connection to this term is that of "applied astrosociology", namely, "the application of astrosocial knowledge to the attempt to solve social problems relevant to both space concerns and all aspects of terrestrial social life" (ARI 2008–2022) and to produce "empirical knowledge to inform decision makers" (Pass 2018: 162). Such knowledge is part of what astrosociology calls "space assets", which are "created or used for space exploration or space-related purposes" (ibid.: 165).

On the ethical side, for astrosociology, "astrosocial change" (another of its terms) is inevitable because space exploration will increasingly influence Earthly society. For example, findings about the atmospheres of other planets could "provide insights about severe weather patterns in Earth's atmosphere that can save lives" (ibid.: 154) or the popularisation of faster transportation on Earth thanks to breakthroughs in space transportation (ibid.: 156). Hence, the need to get rid of the "Earth-centric view", as Pass (2020) claims, has finally come, and astrosociology is committed to "solving social problems with space assets" (ARI 2008–2022) because space exploration is having an impact on human beings on Earth. As the exploration of outer space expands, this impact will accelerate.

With two issues published in 2015 and 2017 on the ARI webpage, the *Journal of Astrosociology* poses the question, "Can we bring astrosociology into the mainstream among the social sciences?" (vol. 1, p. 1). The heterogeneous pieces published in this journal—a total of eight papers, three essays, and one book review—cover topics like the inspirational role of space, space debris, and sustainability, the economic feasibility of asteroid mining, the psychology of space exploration, and of boredom in Mars exploration, the space-age narrative in Southern music in the United States, and the use of social media to promote space awareness. In these pieces, there is a predominantly blanket use of the adjective "social", and only one addresses broader sociological issues and engages with social scientific literature (Wilson 2017).

In terms of interventions outside sociology, Pass has participated in several events of the Mars Society, a nonprofit organisation founded by Mars enthusiast Robert Zubrin in 1998 that advocates for human Mars exploration and, in their own words, "colonization", a term that Pass uses uncritically. Building on Zubrin's ideas, Pass sees Mars as astrosociology's first laboratory. In his words, astrosociology is equipped to help "plan for social life on Mars" (Pass 2020). This planet's colonisation cannot be reduced to the development of a successful physical habitat because it is not enough for a safe social environment (ibid.). Mars research should successfully include "the monitoring of social interactions and other forces associated with the complexities generated by a growing population existing in an isolated and dangerous ecosystem on another planet" (ibid.). Martian colonisation, if executed with the astrosociological imagination, could bring the two branches of science together: on the one hand, the physical and natural sciences and STEM and, on the other hand, the social sciences, the humanities, and the arts. "Lacking [the astrosociological imagination] on Mars can become injurious or even fatal" (ibid.: 7).

According to Pass, astrosociologists should be doing astrosociology about Mars while being on Mars. They are needed, first, to help set up Martian "social institutions" and, second, to study the behaviour of the social systems created on Mars, paying special attention to population increase (ibid.: 6). Pass believes that without astrosociologists' "input on Mars, chaos and conflict in addition to other forms of deviant behavior is much more likely to occur, as the stressors generated by confinement and isolation on another planet can cause great behavioral disruptions" (Pass 2020). In that sense, astrosociologists should provide guidance on all dimensions of social life on Mars from the rights of alien microbes to the regulation of human colonisers' behaviour and emotions to the overseeing of new religious cults and forms of governance. Nothing could escape astrosociology's study of "Martian society" as the first "space society", the foundational social system erected in an extraterrestrial environment (ibid.).

From a critical standpoint, astrosociology remains a conceptually thin and normatively problematic approach with very limited empirical use. Its main—and perhaps only—exponent does not go beyond an understanding of sociology in its most generic terms, and of astrosociology as full of Comtean intentions. After almost two decades, astrosociology is still yet to make empirical, methodological, and conceptual contributions to the discipline of sociology beyond adding the prefix "astro" to several sociological terms. Its generic view of sociology, while attractive for people outside the discipline, has certainly not galvanised support from mainstream professional sociologists and organisations who would, rightfully, have reservations about many of the terminologies and goals that astrosociology embraces.

Pass's ideas have made their way into the communities of professional and amateur space enthusiasts where the broad questions and insights posed by him about "the social" are well received. In our view, this sociological approach easily resonates with these communities because it—naïvely—subscribes to their view of the "human cultural drive to explore the unknown" and space exploration as "the logical continuation of the expansion of the human presence from its starting point" (Pass 2015: 537). A field that seeks to create a body of knowledge beneficial to "humanity" (Pass 2020) cannot simply embrace "exploration" and "colonization" as the suitable strategies to arrive on Mars given the problematic history of human colonialism on Earth, as several pieces in this volume show.

Furthermore, the search in space for the ultimate knowledge synthesis seems unattainable as astrosociology has not developed a methodological trajectory, a set of systematic empirical studies, or a conceptual framework, but rather a discourse imbued with science-fiction utopianism and perilous colonialism.

Historical Materialism and "The Cosmos"

Using a historical materialist and dialectical approach, sociologists Peter Dickens and James S. Ormrod (2007: 2; 2016) have put "social power" and "capital" front and centre in their study of outer space, with which they engage at the broad level of "the cosmos". Their focus has been theoretical and conceptual, and not so much empirical.

A fundamental premise for these authors, building on the ideas of the young Karl Marx about nature and "species-being", is that the human species is a "universal species"—a claim that, for them, means that our species have had "the whole of the universe, including their own and other species, as part of their consciousness and scientific activity" (Dickens and Ormrod 2007: 2). For this reason, the human species has always been cosmic, even if the actual human exploration of outer space is a recent, ongoing event.

In these authors' broad view of history, outer space started to be "colonized"—again, the term is used uncritically here—through the imagination several millennia ago and in different cultures. They rely on general ideas about how human beings' interpretation of the natural world, including the stars and planets, shapes their own self-understanding. From this observation, they claim that there are "dialectical relationships between the universe and society on Earth" (ibid.: 177). Accordingly, human history can be understood as a series of cosmologies, that is, specific ways in which societies interact with the universe, and the cosmos has consistently played a major role in the organisation of terrestrial life. From this perspective, all human societies have been in different degrees (for instance, depending on their worship of specific extraterrestrial objects) "cosmic societies". Along these lines, the current age, marked by the space race, is not entirely new in its social characteristics. Rather, it is an *acceleration* of three preexisting social processes: the rise of the nation-state, the prevalence of the private sector, and the expanding capitalist commodification of the universe.

For Dickens and Ormrod (2007: 177) societies "interact with a cosmos that has been socially constructed", particularly by elites, who have long used it to justify power inequality and social orders on Earth. But to this standard and known argument, in an expansive twist of classical historical materialism, this approach argues that each ruling elite has claimed that the source of its power comes from its monopoly over the use of the cosmos and not only from the appropriation of Earth of the means of production, its rule over oppressed classes, and its control of the legal superstructure. In consequence, human elites are not only materialist but also cosmic. Several of the most powerful humans and institutions in history, from Babylonian priests to Louis XIV, the Sun King, to NASA and Elon Musk, derive a significant portion of their power from their proximity to the cosmic. Such a connection is marked by a massive mobilisation of economic resources. For instance, Babylonian priests built the ziggurats, Louis XIV ordered the construction of a new palace and garden in Versailles, and, with the support of NASA and private investors, Musk founded the pioneering cosmic company SpaceX. Whether they are priests, kings, national space agencies, or private companies, they are, simply put, the powerful "cosmic elite". In the very broad-brush strokes about historical processes that characterises this approach, history would then repeat itself, but with different elite members in command.

The familiar Marxist conceptual repertoire is set in motion characterising the launch of networks of satellites as a mechanism of control at the planetary-cosmic scale fuelled by the cooperation between the private and military sectors. Devices such as satellites are becoming elites' agents of social control, part of an "orbital panopticon" (Dickens and Ormrod 2007: 11). Space tourism is also seen as an arena for the expression of class inequalities, with an elite that has the resources to travel to space. Finally, capitalism's alienation of human relations is affecting the universe with the growing amounts of space junk—a cosmic risk society, in their words (ibid.: 11).

Building on Gramscian Marxism, Dickens and Ormrod claim that political and economic elites do not operate in isolation, and intellectuals are necessary to perpetuate hegemony (ibid.: 188). Their hegemonic ideas in our present cosmology are about "individualism, imperialism, and capital accumulation" (ibid.: 12). In another classical materialist move, they claim that spatial colonialism is accelerating the contradictions within "cosmic capitalism". The rise of counter-hegemonic social movements, they argue, can be a useful antidote. With their support, another humanisation of the universe could be possible, one in which "the universe "does not further empower the already powerful" (ibid.: 190). Such humanisation "could attempt to emulate the early twentieth-century Russian cosmists by spreading a socialist or communist society throughout the whole of nearby outer space" (ibid.: 190).

Dickens and Ormrod are active scholars inside and outside sociology. In the 2016 *Palgrave Handbook of Society, Culture and Outer Space* they brought together a group of scholars that first met during a conference at the University of Brighton in 2010 titled "Power in Outer Space". In this volume, the Marxist framework now incorporates a Lefebvrian account of the "production of space" (namely, the recognition that space is an undertheorised site of power relations) and the ideas of geographer David Harvey (especially on the global circulation of capital), and the areas of inquiry also broaden to incorporate chapters about gender, science, indigenous cultures, activism, science fiction, and SETI. More recently, Ormrod (2020: 243) engaged with environmental sociology examining arguments that treat outer space as an environment and drawing lessons from terrestrial environmental sociology that "can improve our relationship with the space environment in pivotal times". In 2020, Dickens published a piece in the online magazine *Futures of Work* where he discussed the social relations of spacecraft production and argued for a return to the old NASA model of work and state intervention.

Critically speaking, the approach outlined by Dickens and Ormond is the most theoretical amongst the three in this chapter, yet its theoretical grounding is rigid and its empirical agenda, so far, is not developed. This perspective relies on a long-standing intellectual tradition in the social sciences that tackles capitalism, alienation, and power, issues whose importance given the nature of contemporary space activities is beyond question. However, its approach only sees these contemporary space activities as evidence of the adequacy of the framework and as a confirmation of its predicted trajectories. More fundamentally, this approach overgeneralises and extrapolates to outer space a narrow view of social life, which adds nothing substantially new to the theorisation of historical materialism. Rather, it reproduces several key shortcomings of the materialist tradition. Amongst them are the mechanistic understanding of the relationship between the ideational and the material aspects of social life, and an understanding of elites as a cohesive homogeneous action group—an abstract and superficial view that hides how elites are empirically speaking a far more complex heterogeneous group.

Sociology of Organisations and Science at NASA

The last line of work is represented by the work of two sociologists who have studied and collaborated with NASA: Diane Vaughan and Janet Vertesi. Vaughan's *The Challenger Launch Decision* (1996) now stands as a classic in sociology that has also had a significant impact outside the discipline. Her book locates the social causes of the 1986 Space Shuttle *Challenger* disaster, which killed all seven crew members on board, within NASA's organisational practices. Through detailed analysis and mostly drawing on organisational sociology, Vaughan shows how the failure leading to *Challenger*'s explosion seconds after launch was not simply "a technical matter" in the seal of the solid rocket boosters, but a complex "social problem" linked to perceptions of risk at different levels within this organisation. Among the empirical questions the book illuminates are the following: "Why [did] NASA managers, who not only had all the information on the eve of the launch but also were warned against it, decid[e] to proceed"? (Vaughan 1996: xii) and "Why did worried engineers repeatedly recommend launching in the face of continued and worsening signals of potential danger?" (ibid.: 196).

Vaughan's book is known for a central concept, "normalization of deviance", which encapsulates the answer to the former questions. What led to the decision to launch was "a definition of the situation that allowed [engineers and managers] to carry on as if nothing was wrong when they continually faced evidence that something *was* wrong" (ibid.: 62). Normalisation of deviance has had a life of its own in sociology and other fields (Hutter and Power 2005; Paletz et al. 2009; Prielipp et al. 2010; Bogard et al. 2015; Courtois and Gendron 2017; Gerstle 2018; Petruzzeli 2020; Wright, Polivka, and Clark 2021), and later on also became pertinent within NASA as members of the agency made sense of this disaster. What leads to this concept is Vaughan's examination of how the decision sequences that preceded the launch were embedded in the complexity and multidimensionality of NASA's culture. In this context, three factors explain the normalisation of deviance: production pressure under economic strain at different levels of the organisation, the way in which work group cultures produce shared mental models about situations and the lack of transparency in the handling of information within the agency. These three factors defined how the boundaries of acceptable risk increasingly became more expansive as managers and engineers interpreted the various elements leading to the launch (Vaughan 1996: 124).

The *Challenger* book turned Vaughan into an expert on NASA and shuttle accidents, which prompted her participation in 2003 in the Accident Investigation Board of NASA's next major accident: the disintegration of Space Shuttle *Columbia* as it reentered the atmosphere, killing all seven crew members. As Vaughan (2006: 358) states, "I was not surprised by the accident: in the last paragraph of my book, I predicted another because the systemic social causes of the shuttle's technical failure were being reproduced even as I wrote". Throughout this experience, and in her own words, "sociology mattered" as the similarities between the two tragedies were evident. Vaughan was consulted by the press, called to testify before the board, and invited to join it as a consultant and staff researcher, and authored a chapter in the final report.

In a paper about this involvement with the board and the agency, Vaughan (2006) addressed how sociological knowledge was disseminated and gained credibility and acceptance leading to the institutionalisation of the accident's sociological explanation: the disaster was a failure of NASA's organisational system. This piece shows the ways in which the analogy between *Challenger* and *Columbia* was not self-evident, and sociological theory moved across the disciplinary boundary to public and policy domains through perceptions of professional legitimacy sustaining her voice as an expert, the board's authority and influence, conversation, technologies, time, networks, and social support. She also unpacks the conflicts in the interstices between academic and public sociology where, as her involvement deepened, her "ability to speak as an autonomous expert was increasingly compromised" (ibid.: 385). In the problematic language of some ethnographic reflections, she became "native" (ibid.: 370) as she started sharing the board's goals and institutional commitments. But the process was far from linear, something that she characterised drawing on Burawoy's (2005) distinctions between professional, critical, public, and policy sociology and their relational complexities (Vaughan 2006: 355).

After publishing the report, Vaughan was invited by the NASA administration for a translation task when it came to implementing the report's recommendations for "cultural change" in the agency. In her words, "the space agency that I once studied from the safe distance of historical ethnography opened its doors, enlisting my advice about how to make the organisational changes recommended in the report" (ibid.: 354). However, in this instance, she declined the offer, acknowledging the limitations in her training to actually implement organisational change and, more broadly, of sociology as a "policy science" (ibid.: 378).

Inspired by Vaughan's questions about the role of organisations in shaping knowledge practices, Vertesi's ethnographic work centred on NASA's robotic spacecraft teams in planetary science. Her initial two-year examination of the work of scientific representation in Mars robotic exploration resulted in *Seeing Like a Rover* (2015). Her book studies how scientists and engineers work "with the digital images their robots take on Mars to make sense of the distant planet and work together to explore its surface" (ibid.: 7). In her analysis, these images are labour-intensive products that result from digital manipulations that entail crafting, interpretation, selection, and negotiations to make claims about the planet. All these activities are implemented while working with the constraints of remote operations not only between the teams on Earth and the robots on the Martian surface but also within the team as well. Vertesi uses the notions of embodiment and calibration to conceptualise the stakes in scientific visualisation, which is not about accuracy per se, but rather is

> A practical activity of *drawing* a natural object *as* an analytical object, inscribing a value into the very composition of what that object is and what makes it interesting, so that subsequent viewers and image makers will see, draw, and interact with that same object in the same way.
> *(ibid.: 103, original emphasis)*

More recently, in *Shaping Science* (2020) Vertesi's gaze expands from Mars to Saturn, from science and technology studies (STS) to organisational sociology, and from scientific visualisation to the organisation of scientific teams. The central argument of her book is that the organisation of scientific teams shapes the knowledge they produce. Empirically, Vertesi substantiates this claim by comparing the consensus-based, flat-hierarchy mode of organisation that she observed in the Mars rovers teams with an orbital mission to Saturn. While the first is centralised and interdependent, the second is decentralised and modular. Drawing from the constructivist repertoires of STS scholarship, which leads her also to characterise "the planets themselves as organizationally constituted" (ibid.: 246) and to pseudonomise these clearly identifiable missions, she makes the case about how these types of organisations shape "the kinds of things we know about the world" (ibid.: 5). Vertesi shows how each organisational mode produces different visions of a planet. The Mars team uses data from various instruments to study a region generating a "multi-instrumental collectivism" (ibid.: 155), while the Saturn team (in which instrument-team affiliation is the salient organisational mode) focuses on findings from single instruments, resulting in "a patchwork quilt that pulls together single instrument and target observations" (ibid.: 259). The science in these two missions is indeed different—not better or worse, something that is not the sociologist's task to elucidate—because of how it comes through in these organisational processes. According to Vertesi (ibid.: 267, original emphasis), "both missions are astonishing successes, but we might qualify this statement by adding that they each do an outstanding job of producing *different types of knowledge*".

Analytically, these missions and their teams are Vertesi's units of analysis, and they are treated as organisations with particular features: "routines, rituals, practices, and interactional norms that members use to conduct their scientific and technical work", and, more concretely, rules for decision-making that members accept as legitimate, strategies for observational allocations, patterns of authority, status-based interactions, and lines of accountability (ibid.: 5, 11, 75). Based on this premise, she articulates a framework of organised science that has three features or principles, as she calls them. First, scientific organisations shape scientific outcomes; second, these outcomes in turn shape scientific organisations; and third, scientific outcomes affect scientific organisations in a looping effect.

Beyond the ethnographic and analytical neatness of these descriptions and typifications—which we see sometimes as too unidirectional, going from "the organization" to "the science"—Vertesi's work offers an empathetic window into the challenges these scientists face in their careers. Amongst those challenges are the competing temporalities of long-term missions and short-term pressures, which means working on different missions while also writing proposals and crafting collaborations to bring the next one into existence. Vertesi also describes the misalignments in their different institutional affiliations, the international politics of citation, and the many uncertainties in the funding cycles that sustain scientists' work. This world of institutional demands and accountabilities is what some participants actually describe to Vertesi as "the sociology" of their work (ibid.: 127, 130, 132–33, 142).

As in Vaughan's case, Vertesi's sociology matters to NASA (Witze 2020), and she has continued her engagement with the agency studying other planetary missions, doing so with funding from the agency in 2015 and 2018 to study the Europa Clipper Mission. "How to integrate large groups of people with a range of expertise in order to solve complex problems?" (Vertesi 2020: 3). This is a crucial question for the agency and the planetary science community, as they think about their research agenda for the future. Recently, Vertesi coauthored five white papers with planetary scientists for the Planetary Science and Astrobiology Decadal Survey 2023–2032 (2021). Amongst them, a piece devoted to human factors for long-duration space missions provides insights from her work about lessons learned and best organisational practices regarding multigenerational succession in teams, data management, planning, and adopting bureaucratic–hierarchical forms, bringing Max Weber to bear in future robotic planetary exploration (Vertesi and Rymer 2021: 1).

Vaughan's sociological translation work for NASA has gone from the agency's language of human factors to social causes, and Vertesi also incorporates the opposite direction going from social organisation to human factors in her more practice-oriented engagement with the agency. These involvements can be invisible to the profession (Vaughan 2006: 383), yet the translations that can make sociological work relevant for those whom we study deserve serious and careful attention. Vaughan's and Vertesi's work counters the notion that policymakers prefer research that is free of theoretical baggage (Lauder et al. 2004: 5, 17, cited in Vaughan 2006). Indeed, the *Columbia* report and Vertesi's recommendations are clearly informed by theory and concepts. And finally, they confirm ethnography's capacity "to describe social life in sufficiently vivid detail that the relevant elements become alive for others. An account in ethnographic thick description can persuade because, despite a unique setting, it resonates with other events or circumstances" (Vaughan 2006: 379).

Organisational sociology has opened an accessible path for sociologists in the halls of NASA, as exemplified by Vaughan and Vertesi. The depth and detail of their research are beyond question, as well as the fact that they situate their insights in the body of literature of organisational sociology that—while undoubtedly anchored in a set of core assumptions—is open to contributions and reformulations. Moreover, from NASA's side, these sociologists offer agency insights that are perceived as rigorously researched, important, and implementable, while staying within the perimeter of their mandate as an organisation. Using Vaughan's own distinctions between public sociology and academic sociology following Burawoy (2005), their research can be translated into "policy sociology". As Vaughan has put it, "being useful is seductive in its own right" and becomes a wish for the sociologist (2006: 385). And as Vertesi has shown, this usefulness also means caring for those that one studies and the bonds created in the process of research.

Conclusion

The three approaches outlined in this chapter delineate outer space in fundamentally different ways. The first two do so in an impressionistic and almost generic manner, whereas for the third the objects of inquiry are specific institutional settings, actors, and modes of action. This delineation marks sharp contrasts regarding the empirical depth, theoretical framing, and aspirations of the pertinence of the three approaches. However, one feature in which these fundamentally different approaches converge is their lack of engagement with contemporary developments in other social sciences regarding critical reflections about space. While there are some instances of collaboration (Messeri and Vertesi 2015; Walsh, Gorman, and Castaño 2022), for the most part, sociologists who have addressed outer space have done so in an isolated manner from other social sciences that have been more actively engaged with this area, particularly anthropology.

Currently, there is sociological research about past and present space stations (Brooker, Castaño, and Le Moignan 2021). Philip Brooker (2019–2020, this volume, forthcoming) uses an ethnomethodological approach to examine written and audiovisual records from NASA's first space station, Skylab. His work focuses on labour and the use of Taylorist management techniques in the execution of astronaut's activities. The International Space Station (ISS) is another research site that exemplifies the diversity of approaches in the discipline. Julie Patarin-Jossec's (2021) ethnography of the ISS centres on European and Russian training facilities and the figures of the astronaut and cosmonaut. Building on sociological scholarship on the body and gender, her object of inquiry is "the social logic of an exceptional profession" (ibid.: 65, our translation) with its dominant cultural and gendered models, bodily practices, particularly during the process of training, and reliance on ground support personnel. Taking a different direction, Castaño (2021, this volume, in preparation) examines the ISS as a peculiar platform for science with a mixture of theoretical resources and ethnographic, interview, and documentary methods. In particular, she characterises the process of conducting experiments on the station and accounts for each experiment as a series of events of varying locations and temporalities which, in addition, is being assessed by the divergent criteria of several stakeholders and observers. Even when looking at a similar kind of object—even the same object—sociological approaches are diverse in their foci of attention, methods, and conceptual underpinnings.

Looking ahead, we see three decisive areas of research for sociologists: space as a domain of economic expansion, knowledge production, and environmental concern. Regarding the first area, one key challenge to which sociologists are yet to respond is the detailed study of the current commercialisation in space affairs. With the exception of sociological interest in the utopias of Silicon Valley (Tutton 2021), prevailing explanatory frameworks about space commercialisation belong to one of two ends of the spectrum: "business-school" styles of economics exemplified by Weinzierl (2018, 2021) and orthodox historical materialist perspectives like the one exemplified by Dickens and Ormrod (2007, 2016). Whereas the first framework embraces a teleological view of history that leads to the commercialisation of space and sees governmental involvement either as background infrastructure or even an obstacle, the other overlooks the multidimensional complexities of this process with the conceptual and political steamroller of Marxism. If commercialisation is more than the mere "unfolding of history"—both in the triumphant and voluntaristic view of the first and in the fatalistic overdetermined view of the second—there are plenty of tasks for sociologists here. For instance, as is the case in many other industries that need to protect their interests via legislation, lobbying is a central practice for space companies to pave the way for "commercialization". In this context, political and legal sociologists would be uniquely equipped to see this process as facilitated by multiple and intricate institutional arrangements that have not been adequately studied.

Returning to Vaughan's (2006: 388) reflection about the seductions of being useful, sociology, as a diverse and multiparadigmatic discipline, requires its practitioners to ask themselves why and how external organisations and individuals find our research pertinent, how they benefit from it, and to what ends sociological research will be put to work outside academia. One path here is academic research that positions itself as sharply critical of the prevailing logics of outer space affairs and makes that critique in an academic language that is only comprehensible to some colleagues. Another path is to claim the scientific status of the discipline—with echoes of nineteenth-century anxieties of wanting to belong to the "actual" (i.e., natural or physical) sciences—and promising our relevance to space agencies, companies, and organisations along those lines from the start. This path entails remaining within the given boundaries of the mandate of these institutions, taking their concrete problems as our disciplinary research problems, and offering practical and doable insights about them. And then there is the never-ending and vital effort to find a path with languages for cross-domain intelligibility while balancing all key elements of the research process and its outputs: rigour, critique, and pertinence both for our disciplinary debates and for the actors that we study. There are many unresolved questions here for sociologists' aspirations to usefulness for which there are no formulas, and only particular research trajectories—with their relationships forged during the process—can find their singular answers.

As outer space exploration continues to grow, from scientific enterprises to tourism, the most likely scenario is a multiplication of research interests in sociology, which would parallel the diversification of space activities. This abundance of activities will turn outer space into "just another" domain in which to be a political sociologist, economic sociologist, sociologist of science, culture, ethnicity, gender, crime, or morality, in a practice less defined by the geographical domain as is the case in other disciplines—most saliently anthropology—but by the focus on the social relations under examination. And as in any sociological research, each sociologist would bring to the task their own combination of the will to learn something about the actions of some humans in given institutional settings, a few proven and prospective tools of elucidation, and some disillusionment or hope about the relevance of that undertaking.

References

Abbott, Andrew. 2001. *Chaos of Disciplines*. Chicago, IL: University of Chicago Press.
ARI, Astrosociology Research Institute 2008–2022. Accessed 10 August 2022 at http://www.astrosociology.org.
Bogard, Kevin, Timothy D. Ludwig, Chris Staats, and Danielle Kretschmer. 2015. "An Industry's Call to Understand the Contingencies Involved in Process Safety: Normalization of Deviance." *Journal of Organizational Behavior Management* 35 (1–2): 70–80. https://doi.org/10.1080/01608061.2015.1031429.
Brooker, P. (Forthcoming). *Living and Working in Space: An Ethnomethodological Study of Skylab*. Manchester: Manchester University Press.Brooker, Philip. 2019–2020. *Skylab 3: Living and Working in Space*. Podcast series, 9 episodes.
Brooker, Philip, Paola Castaño, and Effie Le Moignan. 2021. "Living and Working in Space: Expanding the Human Factors Framework." *The Sociological Review Blog,* May 2021. Accessed 10 August 2022 at https://thesociologicalreview.org.
Burawoy, Michael. 2005. "For Public Sociology." *American Sociological Review* 70 (1): 4–28. https://doi.org/10.1177/000312240507000102.
Castaño, Paola. 2021. "From Value to Valuation: Pragmatist and Hermeneutic Orientations for Assessing Science on the International Space Station." *American Sociologist* 52: 671–701. https://doi.org/10.1007/s12108-021-09515-y.
Castaño, Paola. "Beyond the Lab: The Social Life of Experiments on the International Space Station." In preparation.
Comte, Auguste. 2015. *A General View of Positivism [1844]*. Routledge Revivals. Abingdon, Oxon: Routledge.
Courtois, Cynthia, and Yves Gendron. 2017. "The 'Normalization' of Deviance: A Case Study on the Process Underlying the Adoption of Deviant Behavior." *Auditing: A Journal of Practice and Theory* 36 (3): 15–43. https://doi.org/10.2308/ajpt-51665.
Dickens, Peter. 2020. "Making Spacecraft: Skills, Labour-Processes and Cosmic Society." *Futures of Work* (online magazine), October 2020. Accessed 22 December 2021 at https://futuresofwork.co.uk/2020/10/01/making-spacecraft-skills-labour-processes-and-cosmic-society/.
Dickens, Peter, and James Ormrod. 2007. *Cosmic Society: Towards a Sociology of the Universe*. London: Routledge.

Dickens, Peter, and James S. Ormrod, eds. 2016. *The Palgrave Handbook of Society, Culture and Outer Space.* New York: Palgrave.

Gerstle, Claudia R. 2018. "Parallels in Safety between Aviation and Healthcare." *Journal of Pediatric Surgery* 53 (5): 875–78. https://doi.org/10.1016/j.jpedsurg.2018.02.002.

Hutter, Bridget M., and Michael Power, eds. 2005. *Organizational Encounters with Risk.* Cambridge: Cambridge University Press.

Messeri, Lisa, and Janet Vertesi. 2015. "The Greatest Missions Never Flown: Anticipatory Discourse and the 'Projectory' in Technological Communities." *Technology and Culture* 56 (1): 54–85. https://doi.org/10.1353/tech.2015.0023.

Ormrod, James. 2020. "Outer Space and New Frontiers to Environmental Imaginations." In *The Cambridge Handbook of Environmental Sociology*, Vol. 1, edited by Katharine Legun, Julie C. Keller, Michael Carolan and Michael M. Bell, 243–61. Cambridge: Cambridge University Press. https://doi.org/10.1017/9781108554510.017.

Paletz, Susannah B. F., Christopher Bearman, Judith Orasanu, and Jon Holbrook. 2009. "Socializing the Human Factors Analysis and Classification System: Incorporating Social Psychological Phenomena into a Human Factors Error Classification System." *Human Factors* 51 (4): 435–45. https://doi.org/10.1177/0018720809343588.

Pass, Jim. 2004. "Inaugural Essay: The Definition and Relevance of Astrosociology in the Twenty-First Century (Part One: Definition, Theory and Scope)." *Astrosociology Research Institute* (webpage). Accessed 27 November 2021 at http://www.astrosociology.org/Library/Iessay/iessay_p1.pdf.

Pass, Jim. 2012. "What Is Astrosociology?" *Astrosociology Research Institute* (webpage). Accessed 27 November 2021 at http://www.astrosociology.org.

Pass, Jim. 2015. "An Astrosociological Perspective on the Societal Impact of Spaceflight." In *Historical Studies in the Societal Impact of Spaceflight*, edited by Steven Dick, 535–76. Washington, DC: NASA Office of Communications and NASA History Program Office.

Pass, Jim. 2018. "Astrosociology: Social Problems on Earth and in Outer Space." In *The Cambridge Handbook of Social Problems*, edited by A. Javier Treviño, 149–68. Oxford: Oxford University Press. https://doi.org/10.1017/9781108656184.010.

Pass, Jim. 2020. "Astrosociology on Mars." In *Mars Exploration: A Step Forward*, edited by Giuseppe Pezzella and Antonio Vivani, 1–38. London: IntechOpen. https://doi.org/10.5772/intechopen.93309.

Patarin-Jossec, Julie. 2021. *La Fabrique de L'astronaute: Ethnographie Terrestre de la Station Spatiale Internationale.* Paris: Éditions PETRA.

Petruzzeli, Emily. 2020. "Normalization of Deviance in the Time of COVID-19." *Chemical Engineering Progress* 116 (8): 3.

Prielipp, Richard C., Maria Magro, Robert C. Morell, and Sorin J. Brull. 2010. "The Normalization of Deviance: Do We (Un)Knowingly Accept Doing the Wrong Thing?" *Anesthesia and Analgesia* 110 (5): 1499–502. https://doi.org/10.1213/ANE.0b013e3181d5adc5.

Tutton, Richard. 2021. "Sociotechnical Imaginaries and Techno-optimism: Examining Outer Space Utopias of Silicon Valley." *Science as Culture* 30 (3): 416–39. https://doi.org/10.1080/09505431.2020.1841151.

Vaughan, Diane. 1996. *The Challenger Launch Decision: Risky Technology, Culture, and Deviance at NASA.* Chicago: University of Chicago Press.

Vaughan, Diane. 2006. "NASA Revisited: Theory, Analogy, and Public Sociology." *American Journal of Sociology* 112 (2): 353–93. https://doi.org/10.1086/506413.

Vertesi, Janet. 2015. *Seeing Like a Rover: How Robots, Teams, and Images Craft Knowledge of Mars.* Chicago: University of Chicago Press.

Vertesi, Janet. 2020. *Shaping Science: Organizations, Decisions, and Culture on NASA's Teams.* Chicago: University of Chicago Press.

Vertesi, Janet, and Abigail Rymer. 2021. "Human Factors for Long Duration Space Missions." Whitepaper #457 submitted to the Planetary Science and Astrobiology Decadal Survey 2023–2032. *Bulletin of the American Astronomical Society* 53(4). Planetary/Astrobiology Decadal Survey Whitepapers. https://doi.org/10.3847/25c2cfeb.06f5cb52.

Walsh, Justin St P., Alice C. Gorman, and Paola Castaño. 2022. "Postorbital Discard and Chain of Custody: The Processing of Artifacts Returning to Earth from the International Space Station." *Acta Astronautica* 195: 513–31. https://doi.org/10.1016/j.actaastro.2022.03.035.

Weinzierl, Matthew. 2018. "Space, the Final Economic Frontier." *Journal of Economic Perspectives* 32 (2): 173–92. https://doi.org/10.1257/jep.32.2.173.

Weinzierl, Matt, and Mehak Sarang. 2021. "The Commercial Space Age Is Here." *Harvard Business Review Digital Articles*. Accessed 12 February 2021 at https://hbr.org/2021/02/the-commercial-space-age-is-here.

Wilson, Fergus. 2017. "Postcards from the Cosmos: Cosmic Spaces in Alternative Religion and Conspiracy Theories." *Journal of Astrosociology* 2: 133–48. http://www.astrosociology.org/joa.html.

Witze, Alexandra. 2020. "Lessons in Teamwork from the Heart of NASA." *Nature* 587: 359–60. https://doi.org/10.1038/d41586-020-03222-3.

Wright, M. Imelda, Barbara Polivka, and Paul Clark. 2021. "Exploring Normalization of Deviance among Perioperative Registered Nurses in the Operating Room." *Western Journal of Nursing Research* 44 (2): 116–24. https://doi.org/10.1177/0193945921999677.

9
SPACE ETHICS

Tony Milligan and J. S. Johnson-Schwartz

An Abbreviated History of Space Ethics

As the term is used here, "space ethics" refers to research conducted by members of a larger community of people who work in systematic ways on the ethical dimensions of questions concerning human activities in space. This is a large and growing community, though it is worth pointing out that the majority of scholars who self-identify as space ethicists are professional philosophers. Until the second decade of the new millennium, the majority of space ethics was carried out by well-informed scientists and institutionally embedded members of the spaceflight community who shared a sustained interest in ethical questions. Several publications classifiable as space ethics can, however, be traced back to at least the 1960s. The best known is Hannah Arendt's famous essay "The Conquest of Space and the Stature of Man", which raised the possibility of a negative overview effect in which human goals and humanity itself might seem diminished when viewed from above (see Arendt 1963, but also Ginsberg 1971; Beck 1971–1972). However, the idea of space ethics as a subject of organised research, and eventually, as an applied ethical *discipline* (akin to engineering, environmental, or medical ethics in bringing philosophical and ethical tools to bear on questions prompted by activities taking place *within* its subject of analysis) received its first clear instantiations in the 1980s, with the activities leading up to the publication of *Beyond Spaceship Earth: Environmental Ethics and the Solar System* (1986), edited by Eugene Hargrove, founder of the journal *Environmental Ethics*.[1]

During the 1980s, advances in planetary science, particularly in light of Mars and Venus exploration programmes, led to the realisation that it might be possible to terraform Mars, that is, to use geophysical engineering technologies to transform Mars into a planet that is hospitable for human life. To the credit of many of the natural scientists and engineers engaged in research related to terraforming, deliberate attempts were made to include ethical and other humanities and social science perspectives in broader conversations about terraforming. In this respect, the first questions of space ethics were: Is terraforming Mars morally permissible? And, if so, when should we attempt to do so? Questioning of this sort could go either way, leading to a rejection of terraforming, or enabling terraforming by posing a problem about *timeliness*. A wildcat attempt to melt portions of the Mars icecaps to boost the atmosphere could, after all, go badly wrong. This would compromise a future polar resource and opportunities for planetary engineering when more effective technologies could be in place.[2]

There was some gathering of the pace of research in the 1990s, with David Duemler's schematic application of philosophical ethics in *Bringing Life to the Stars* (1993), a schematic text written at some distance from actual space programmes, but nonetheless an important milestone in the sense that it showed that there need be no assumed ethical hostility to even the most ambitious human activities in space. An ethical approach could be both constraining and enabling. A more precise and detailed study of ethical issues surrounding the Space Shuttle then appeared in Rosa Pinkus et al.'s *Engineering Ethics: Balancing Cost, Schedule, and Risk* (1997), a text more in tune with the broader move within ethics towards detail, and in tune with growing institutional concern about the potential impact of perceived failures of safety and ethics upon public support for space programmes. Momentum was added by the discussion surrounding the premature (and ultimately mistaken) 1996 announcements about the Alan Hills 84001 Martian meteorite fragment, which some scientists (briefly) thought might contain evidence of microbial Martian life—a prospect which raised a number of ethical concerns as well as those associated with worries about contamination.

The volumes just mentioned exemplify significantly different approaches towards ethics. For instance, within a more theory-centred approach, one first commits to a particular normative ethical theory (e.g., utilitarianism, Kantianism, and virtue ethics) which can then be "rolled out" in different contexts (e.g., animals, the environment, and space). The appeal of this sort of approach is its strong academic fit, continuity of method with at least some established ethical discourses in other areas, and clear connections to classic ethical discourse from Aristotle to Mill and onwards. The downside is that space agencies do not actually roll out ethical theories of this sort. They do not apply a consequentialist approach, a rights-based approach, or an approach which asks, "What would a virtuous agent would do when faced with this problem?" Indeed, we might object if space agencies or policymakers began rolling out their own preferred ethical theory, no matter how well argued and how well constructed the theory might be, given that disputes within normative ethics can be at least as controversial as disputes about specific issues in space ethics (Stoner 2017; Green 2020). Consequentialists might begin to object to the funding of programmes driven by virtue ethics, rights theorists might argue that policy driven primarily by consequences was insufficiently constrained.

On the other hand, there is a more situational and problem-driven approach towards space ethics. Its downside is that it is harder to fit into the more general ethical discussions within the tradition of philosophical ethics, even though it is usually informed by a detailed knowledge of the latter. The upside is that this more situational kind of approach offers more opportunities for integration into policy and into the work of space agencies. There also tends to be more pragmatic constraining of this kind of problem-driven ethics, because it involves a good deal of detailed knowledge about how space technologies, policy, and space law actually work. Space ethics of this sort tends to be not only closer to the concerns of actual space programmes but also more informed by the latter. There is, as a result, greater clarity about the distinction between thought experiments and prospects for actual activities in space.

While there is an emerging and interesting literature which focuses upon the application of special normative ethical theories (e.g., Sparrow 1999; McArthur and Boran 2004; Reiman 2009; Baum 2016; Wilks 2016), the majority of contributions to space ethics have belonged to the more situational and problem-driven approach. There have also been some crossovers, though, such as Brian Green's *Space Ethics* (2022), which applies a foundational approach (the philosophical idea of Natural Law) to a variety of questions in a detailed manner. The overall concern for a more situated space ethics has not been the result of ethicists bringing ethics from the outside and squeezing it into the discussions of a reluctant space community. Rather, it has emerged out of a two-way movement. Space ethicists have tried to draw out the ethical dimensions of particular problems, while scientists from NASA and from the broader space community have begun to engage more consistently with questions of the sort posed by Carl Sagan when he asked whether or not rudimentary Martian life could have some sort of moral standing (Sagan 1994).

As questions of this sort have emerged, a number of figures from the science side have recognised that interdisciplinary work with ethicists can be important for thinking clearly about such matters, especially the ethics of discovering rudimentary extraterrestrial life. After all, it is difficult to say just *what it would mean in practice* to value rudimentary alien life, especially when the very idea sounds far removed from our existing sense of our responsibilities. It would probably involve saying that we have certain duties to protect and conserve rudimentary alien life (on Mars or anywhere else we might discover it). But would these duties be excessively constraining? Would they get in the way of science, commerce, or both? The involvement of ethicists has helped to make it clearer that accepting responsibilities of this sort need not involve embracing a theory of equal moral standing. It is one thing to say that microbial life may be due protection, but something quite different to call for "Equal rights for Martians!" or even to say, with Sagan, that Mars would belong to the Martians even if they happened to be microbial (Sagan 1994). There may be a sense in which we can say that microbial life belongs to a planet, without saying that the planet belongs to microbial life. Clarifying problems of this sort is the kind of thing that ethicists are familiar with and do well (Smith 2009; Persson 2012). They know the terrain.

These discussions have continued into the present century, with institutional involvement helping to flesh out views of ethics that might make room for the novelty of encountering microbial alien life, without simply subsuming it into existing kinds of ethical discourse geared to life forms such as humans and other animals, or even subordinating it to familiar kinds of environmental ethical discussions based around complex ecosystems. This provisional phase of the discipline culminated in the Pompidou report for the European Space Agency and UNESCO, *The Ethics of Space Policy* (2000), which contained an impressive mixture of speculations, forward-looking pragmatism, and commitment to the practical value of ethics, with involvement by the pioneering space ethicist Jacques Arnould (2011). Work by Arnould was, again, problem-focused, and sought to bridge the gap between the ways ethicists work and the ways scientists and policymakers think. This gap is a familiar difficulty for ethicists who do embed work in any domain where science plays a major role (Rollin 2006). Arnould's solution was to draw upon a shared narrative, the myth of Icarus, in order to set out both the dangers and the opportunities afforded by space flight. His volume *La seconde chance d'Icare* (2001) was structured around this approach.

From a historical point of view, Arnould's texts appeared at a junction point when a number of other professional philosophers and ethicists were only beginning to work on space, and when the majority of contributors to discussions remained well-informed scientists and institutionally embedded members of the space community, such as Linda Billings (1997), Charles Cockell (2004), Robert Haynes (1990), Mark Lupisella (1997), Christopher McKay (1990), Margaret Race (Randolph, Race, and McKay 1997), and John Rummel (Rummel and Billings 2004). All are respected, recognised researchers with appropriate connections to organisations such as NASA, ESA, and COSPAR. McKay, for instance, had been involved in some of the earliest environmental ethical discussions and had refined his approach, producing one of the seminal essays on the ethics of terraforming (McKay 1990). These individuals, working on ethical concerns since the turn of the millennium, could be considered key "early adopters" of using philosophical techniques and ethical insights to explore the possible discovery of alien life, the environmental side to the protection of the Martian landscape, and the human and cultural significance of space exploration.

In the 2010s, as the space ambitions of Elon Musk of SpaceX and Jeff Bezos of Blue Origin were gaining momentum and bringing increased attention to space activities, the early adopters were joined by scholars from related disciplines such as anthropology and sociology, and a growing cluster of more specialised space ethicists, often concerned with matters of inclusion and the potential for human practices in space to reproduce or diverge from familiar commercial activities and societal norms (Valentine 2012). This led to the formation of what could be called a "societal dimensions of space" resource community, or an ELSI community, looking at ethical, legal, and societal implications of human activities in space. A notable organisational development here was the 2016 founding of the Society for Social and Conceptual Issues in Astrobiology by philosopher Kelly Smith.

The result of this convergence of scholars has been a flowering of research and publications specifically on space ethics, with key publications including an expanded translation of Arnould's text as *Icarus' Second Chance: The Basis and Perspectives of Space Ethics* (2011) from the original French (though Arnould's pioneering work dates back to the Pompidou report), Tony Milligan's *Nobody Owns the Moon: The Ethics of Space Exploitation* (2015), James Schwartz's and Milligan's edited volume *The Ethics of Space Exploration* (2016), Charles Cockell's three-volume edited series on extraterrestrial liberty (2015a, 2015b, 2016), Konrad Szocik's edited volumes *The Human Factor in a Mission to Mars* (2019) and *Human Enhancements for Space Missions* (2020), Schwartz's *The Value of Science in Space Exploration* (2020), Kelly Smith and Carlos Mariscal's edited collection *Social and Conceptual Issues in Astrobiology* (2020), Brian Green's *Space Ethics* (2022), and Margaret Boone Rappaport and Konrad Szocik's *The Human Factor in the Settlement of the Moon* (2021). There are various other volumes that might be added to the above list, as well as hundreds of shorter publications on matters of space ethics philosophy, space policy, and space science journals with regular contributions from space ethicists such as Erik Persson and strong crossovers with scholars such as David Dunér (Capova et al. 2018) and NASA historian Steven J. Dick (2012), and others who work on astrobiology and the history and philosophy of science. The conversation across this community started in Western Europe and the USA but rapidly spread to Eastern Europe, Latin America, Japan, and a number of countries across Asia where space programmes are also progressing. As the discipline has grown geographically, it has also grown beyond an initial tendency to focus exclusively upon the Western ethical canon. Meanwhile, on the curricular side, some universities have begun offering course topics and even dedicated courses on space ethics as part of a broader curriculum development.

What Space Ethics Is Not

With this brief historical sketch, we hope it is clear that *space ethics has emerged primarily as an offshoot of spaceflight itself*, as opposed to something with an outsider backstory. Matters could have been different. Space ethics could have emerged within the academy and could mostly have looked like Duemler's text, with strong gearing to an audience of academic philosophers. The character and value of the discipline would then have been somewhat different. Occasionally, a text will take this path, e.g., Adam Morton's *Should We Colonize Other Planets?* (2018), which poses some interesting questions for classroom discussions but is more of an *outsider* text and notable primarily because of the author's exceptional work in other areas of philosophy. This has not become the main line of development for space ethics. Space ethics might equally have emerged in much the same way that environmental ethics emerged, i.e., as a critique of processes and with strong links to activist communities opposed to the rolling out of various technologies, and with broadly communitarian background assumptions. Or, it may have developed in the way that animal ethics emerged, as a critique of longstanding practices and presuppositions about human entitlements, rooted in liberal individualist assumptions. However, while space ethics has drawn upon these kinds of discourses, it emerged in neither of these ways. Most of the key texts cited above were written by scholars with an independent interest in space (such as Schwartz) or whose work was rooted in philosophical traditions that emphasised agent experience and the limits of appeals to any single philosophical or ethical theory (such as Milligan).

We say this because of the unavoidable emergence of narratives of suspicion which seem to be part and parcel of any rigorous, scholarly attempt to discuss the ethics of space exploration. They are the other side of the coin, and it seems that we cannot put space ethics into circulation without also creating opportunities for such narratives. There have been texts which advance what might be called "space scepticism". Hannah Arendt's paper, mentioned above, would be one obvious example. And scepticism of this sort can interlock with broader political critiques of advanced technologies and where they might take humanity (Deudney 2020; Williams 2010). Nonetheless, space ethics has emerged as a discourse of evaluation and process formation and not as a narrative of restriction and control, in some way hostile to human activity in space. It is not, as Robert Zubrin (2020) suggested in an editorial for *The National Review*, a sort of "wokeist" move that might threaten human activity in space. Rather, it has emerged (mostly over the course of four decades) as a discourse about space as a societally important arena of human activity. Space ethics poses various challenges and dilemmas, as well as opportunities, as we discuss below in more detail. To ignore the challenges and dilemmas is to be poorly prepared. It is a little like trying to go to Mars before the proper technology is in place, and without any means of return—a proposal that has been made more than once. Such an approach would itself pose numerous ethical problems. Preparation for future human activities in space, as on Earth, is a many-sided endeavour, and ethics is part of the preparatory process.

However, it is noteworthy that the influence of space ethics lags far, far behind the influence of dedicated space advocacy groups like the Mars Society and the National Space Society and the more unitary voice of advocacy. That some might perceive "space ethics" as a threat probably says something about the discipline's comparative newness, which can make the boundary between core contributors and online bloggers hard for nonspecialists to recognise. But it also says something about a problematic expectation that we must all either be unqualified enthusiasts for space or else wholehearted sceptics about the whole thing. Apparently, we must be the best of friends in space exploration, or else its enemies. This is an excessively binary view of the world, one which is far removed from the mixed ways in which most of us actually experience it. This touches upon a central concern of space ethics from Jacques Arnould onwards, that of keeping the ethics close to our actual ways of experiencing the world. While it is certainly conceivable that some or other particular ethicist might happen to reject space activity in some general way, it is simply not the day job of ethicists to be hostile to human activity in space, or to be committed to "progressive space activism", to coin a phrase, even if our day job does require some of us to consider both sceptical approaches and progressive ideas and proposals as part of a larger, and inclusive, conversation about the set of practices involved in space exploration. Indeed, there has been a conspicuous lack of ethicists among the most prominent space sceptics since the beginning of spaceflight. (Arendt comes closest, but she is more of a political theorist and political philosopher than an ethicist in the strict sense.)

To deepen this point about "what ethicists do", we might draw a contrast with the kinds of things that well-informed space advocates such as Rand Simberg do. Simberg's book *Safe Is Not an Option* (2013) is a detailed insider's view of the risks associated with space and a committed statement of why they should be downgraded, based upon a solid technical understanding of the issues and a broad analogy with the opening of other frontiers by humans. Risk is part of the process. It will always be part of the process. People will die. Simberg is, of course, correct in many of the things that he says. There is a price. His book is, however, a very different sort of treatment of risk from Pinkus et al. (1997), and not just because it appeals to historic instances of expansion which might themselves be regarded as problem cases (such as the US frontier). There is also a significantly different sense of relevance and a difference in the ways that attention is directed. Like Simberg, Pinkus et al. acknowledge the ongoing dangers of the space environment, but their work carries much more of a sense of *the ways in which ethical failings over safety can themselves get in the way of space exploration*, as they eventually did with the Shuttle programme. As Diane Vaughan's analysis of the *Challenger* disaster (Vaughan 1997) noted, NASA, bowing to pressures to meet an overly ambitious launch schedule, effectively became incentivised to overlook major safety concerns (a professional ethical failing), even overlooking concerns raised by its own engineers as well engineers at contracted firms. The malfunctions which doomed *Challenger* had also occurred on previous flights. The problems were known. How one chooses to *run* a space programme is just as important to interrogate as what missions one supports with that programme, but these are distinct tasks that may call for different kinds of ethical assessment.

We are not suggesting that one of these two books is better than the other, but rather that they are performing different sorts of tasks, and an understanding of this difference between the tasks can help us to tell a provisional story about the day job of ethicists. Both texts take what we might think of as an engineering point of view, but Pinkus et al. fuse this with more of an ethicist's point of view. From a more strictly engineering view, risk is an extension of familiar problems of tolerances and probabilities of failure. These can be quantified, at least in principle. From more of an ethicist's point of view, it is important to consider not only the level of risk, measured as probability of failure, but also the potential societal and institutional impact of failures, the importance of informed consent, and the *disclosure* of risks to those most directly affected. In this way, ethics can help to paint a nuanced picture of the kinds of things that matter. And it brings an awareness of problems which might not otherwise be clear. Disclosure and consent, for example, raise a host of ethical issues, given that disclosure always occurs under a description (O'Neill 2008). A doctor might describe a "procedure" to a patient, or they can talk about slicing the patient open and cutting off bits of their body. Both descriptions might be accurate enough, and suitable for particular purposes. But they will direct the patient's attention in very different ways. As consent is given under one description of an operation but not another, it is particularly important that an *appropriate* but still sufficiently detailed description of the operation and of its risks is given. This has to involve something more than telling the patient a number or saying that "ninety-six percent of the time it all goes fine". The consent of astronauts, and people who aspire to become astronauts, requires an appropriate description of the risks. In the case of the Shuttle, astronauts needed to be aware that there was a switch in mission control that could blow the craft up, to avoid a greater disaster on the ground. But they deserved, and needed, to know a good deal more than this.

Ethicists are focused upon matters of justice and injustice, which help us to understand what meaningful consent involves in the case of spaceflight. And so when they look at risks they are particularly interested in the ways in which risks and rewards are distributed. When unnecessary and programme-threatening risks are taken, in the interests of agents who do not themselves go into space, and with the dangers improperly explained to those who do go, then it is very much the day job of ethicists to say "we have a problem". Again, the problem is not the sheer presence of risks, or that they are higher than we might like. Rather, the problem is about how reasonably or unreasonably risks are faced (Athanassoulis and Ross 2010), how the burden of risk is carried, whether or not it is distributed in a way that is fair or unfair, and how any unfairness compares to regular workaday kinds of unfairness. Is it better, worse, or much the same as the routine injustices of human life? This is recognisably ethical territory but also territory about which there may be a growing, wider, understanding. One of the recurring features of risk discussions from the early stages of the COVID-19 epidemic onwards was the varying distribution of risks, and how different policy measures would have an uneven, and sometimes unfair, effect upon risk levels across populations (Fowers et al. 2021).

Attention to these matters is not the same as risk aversion or hostility to processes that involve vulnerability to harm. To avoid all risk would involve living a life unlike any that we know. Another way of saying this would be to point out that recognition of vulnerability will be built into any plausible account of what it means to be human, a point which (along with deliberation about luck) has played an important role in general ethical theory for some time (Nagel 1979; Williams 1981; Nussbaum 1986). Nor is this idea of a distinctly ethical approach towards risk the same as rolling out a preferred special sort of ethical theory, e.g., some direct application of ideas from Immanuel Kant or John Stuart Mill, that might struggle to engage directly with space policy, institutional practice, and questions of space law. It is closer to a difficult balancing out of considerations, or (in more philosophical terms) an informed search for practical wisdom.

What Do Space Ethicists Do?

So what, then, do space ethicists actually do? At the highest level of generality, we are simply here to ask the ethical questions that, sooner or later, will need to be asked. And it is a feature of the practice of ethics, and not a bug, that doing so results in *productive* disagreements about the answers. To fill out the point, and the scope there is for reasonable and well-argued disagreement, we identify four broad roles that characterise the vast majority of space ethics research. There are no doubt others that will emerge in the future, as space ethics is an evolving discipline, but, for the foreseeable future, *doing* space ethics will continue to involve these roles: balancing value considerations, enhancing decision-making, stress-testing concepts and frameworks, and doing these (and other things) in an ongoing way rather than as a "one-off" exercise.

Balancing Value Considerations

Space exploration is not a monolith; it is not just "one thing". And this makes "supporting spaceflight" and "opposing spaceflight" ambiguous notions, compatible with a great many specific positions. Space exploration includes a diverse range of activities representing a diverse range of goals and objectives—Earth observation for scientific, economic, political, and defence purposes; satellite telecommunications; space tourism; scientific research and exploration (crewed and robotic); and possibly in the future, manufacturing, geoengineering, space mining, and space settlement. These activities compete over territory and resources, and they are coming increasingly into conflict with one another, especially with the scaling up of commercial spaceflight activities over the last decade. In Earth orbit, we are already at the point where push comes to shove: there are only so many positions in which satellites can be placed, massive satellite constellations interfere with astronomical observations, and with the increasing debris threat, the long-term sustainability of satellite operations is in doubt. The Moon could soon face a similar crowding problem, as many of the landers planned for the next decade target the same few locations (Elvis, Krolikowski, and Milligan 2021). The long debate about whether Mars should be protected for the sake of scientific research (or for the sake of any life that might exist there), conflicting with the goals of aspiring space miners and settlers, is heating up as plans such as those of Musk move closer to becoming realities.

How do we balance these conflicting interests? What values should be recognised? Whose interests matter most? Which spaceflight objectives are likely to serve the greater human good, and which might further inequality and carry various kinds of societal risk? What concerns are likely to appeal to future generations who will decide whether or not the projects that we begin are continued or abandoned? In a very direct sense, space ethics exists to *help us figure out matters of this sort and what is worth doing in space*. For large classes of new activities, and even for familiar activities in the unfamiliar context of space, there is little justification for claiming that we already have the answers.

Enhancing Decision-Making

That space exploration is important, worthwhile, necessary, or misguided is not in any way a basic assumption of space ethics. These are conclusions that might be reached by individual space ethicists, depending upon how they reason about the value, importance, or risks involved in space exploration. But, often, the positions that occur may be less binary, less prone to some single judgement about everything that we might call space exploration. Some activities are more important, necessary, and valuable than others. Space ethicists might validate the importance of Earth-observing satellites but deny the value of space tourism. Or they might validate space tourism as a unique way to enhance the human experience. Ethics is especially well suited to addressing issues of this sort, without lapsing into slogans, convenient fallacies, or a "one view fits all" approach.

Interestingly, this view of space ethics is distinct from the take of Joel Sercel (CEO of Trans Astronautica Corporation) and Lt. Gen. Steven Kwast on space ethics in an op-ed published in *Politico* in November 2020 (Sercel and Kwast 2020). They anticipated that space ethics would automatically affirm the need to "update international space law to recognise property ownership and salvage rights" and that it would answer the "call to move forward as fast as feasible to ethically explore space and do the research that will enable settlement of the high frontier". These are legitimate points of view, and various things can be said in their favour. There are space ethicists who would argue along these lines, but others who would argue differently. Neither would have to step outside of the discipline in order to do so. Part of the value of ethics is that it allows us to look at problems from different points of view, a feature that it shares with law. But we are often more ready to acknowledge that dissenting opinions and cases for and against are integral, and that the practice of law would be impoverished without them. Ethics is like this too. For nontrivial matters where almost everyone is likely to agree, it is important that justifications are given in the face of opposing positions. And this is one of the ways in which we arrive at the view that a particular justification for doing x or for not doing x is a good one.

In terms of actual cases, even the oft-invoked justification for clarifying property rights in space (as it will enable space mining and space settlement) is itself a contentious matter, given that mining and settlement both have downsides as well as upsides. These downsides need a voice, just as the upsides do. And the balance between upsides and downsides may also shift from place to place in ways that good examples of space ethics will try to track. The same ethical story will not fit the different cases of mining the Moon, Mars, and the Main Asteroid Belt. Similarly, there are informative, and action-guiding, ethical arguments both for and against space settlement, and for attempting it sooner or else taking a cautious approach. Good arguments against, as well as good arguments for, will inform settlement if it ever occurs, by drawing attention to various matters that we would do well to address, such as behaviour in life-and-death situations, and the responsibilities of those back on Earth to any prospective group of settlers with regard to rescue and return. This constructive role for the opposing view again makes ethics (and space ethics) a little like law, but very unlike politics. In politics, it is a normal rhetorical view to present (or misrepresent) the opposing view. Good ethics, by contrast, follows a *principle of charity*: we must represent opposing views in their best form, even if it involves reformulating criticisms in more effective terms. The ability to withstand well-formulated critique is, again, a way to test an ethical position.

To think of space ethics as constructive and productive is not, however, the same as holding that it exists for the purpose of validating anyone's preconceived opinion on complex issues where different value considerations are simultaneously in play. Moreover, a decision to go ahead with some activity in space, in spite of any "all-things-considered" justification, need not result in a further series of unjustified actions all along the line. Suppose, for example, that we have agreed to exploit the water ice deposits in the permanently shadowed regions on the Moon and to do so *in this generation*. And suppose that we have grounded this ethically by agreeing that there is some obligation to act, and to act now. At this point, we would face an entirely new set of ethical questions: *How should it be done? What is a tolerable efficiency level for extraction and waste? Who should be permitted to conduct the exploitation?* And so on. If we later realised that the decision was an irreversible blunder, we would face a further series of ethical questions that would only arise because of the initial error. We might then have to face ethical problems that would not otherwise emerge. At such points, it may be no use to pretend that we are still in an ideal situation where all the things that we value can still be protected to the same level that would otherwise be possible. At points when things go wrong, ethics can provide us with a non-arbitrary background for decisions about *how to go on* because examining situations of this type is part of the day job for ethicists, and it is difficult to look over multiple cases of this sort without learning something.

Stress-Testing Concepts and Frameworks

An aspect of the way that ethics improves our deliberation processes was touched upon above: the way in which the clash of multiple viewpoints can result in stronger and clearer justifications. This "testing" of viewpoints by space ethicists warrants consideration in its own right and is worth extending beyond disputes about mining or settlement, to the idea that space ethics is an area where differing conceptual frameworks can meet. It is rare that US space advocates ever have to grapple with non-US, non-European, and non-libertarian value systems or ways of seeing the world. But examining a broader spectrum of human cultures and perspectives is absolutely vital for increasing our confidence that we are doing the right things, for the right reasons, in the best ways. If we fail to do this, we invite the risk that the projects we begin will not be continued by others. In the case of multigenerational projects such as human expansion into space, this is particularly important. What we do should at least make sense to those who come after, and one of our best guides to whether it will do so or not is its appeal across multiple perspectives and across multiple cultures. This is not politically correct wokeness *du jour* but a concern for the stability of projects, given the strong likelihood of cultural and political change over time.

Here, it is worth noting that space advocacy in the past has had a tendency to marginalise the perspectives of women; persons of colour; Indigenous persons; persons from African, Asian, European, and Middle Eastern cultures; disabled persons; and members of the LGBTQIA community. Taken together, these are not an irascible minority but a clear majority of humans on our planet. If space truly promises a boon to all of humanity, then it should be possible to demonstrate this without relying solely on our own default approach, or upon some fairly narrow perspective from either end of the political spectrum, or upon perspectives which show an unhealthy obsession with the state-versus-market debates of twentieth-century Europe and North America (important though they were a generation ago). A broader generality of appeal is a good indication that some approach stands a good chance of stabilising over time, and across different generations of humans. As a qualification to this, while space ethics teaches us to seek a wider perspective, it does not need to be territorially ambitious in a disciplinary sense. We should also seek insights from anthropologists, historians, political scientists, sociologists, astronomers, engineers, poets, artists, musicians, and dancers exploring the limits of the human body. At certain points, as collaboration intensifies, it may even be difficult to tell whether we are doing one thing, or another, or both at the same time. Few fields of inquiry or modes of creative expression will fail to add value to our understanding of space exploration *as a civilisation-changing human endeavour*.

Ongoing Ethical Engagement

Ethics, for space or otherwise, is not something that you do only "before" you pursue a project. It is something you have to do while you are continuing and completing it. In this respect, space ethics is indeed analogous to bioethics, as Sercel and Kwast also point out. Like the analogy with the law and the disanalogy with partisan politics, this analogy also has obvious limits. Spaceflight (the main focus of space ethics) and medical care (a major focus of bioethics) are very different things. But they are similar in that each pursues large-scale, expensive, multigenerational projects that have the potential to affect the well-being of the wider public in beneficial and injurious ways. As a result, there are revealing similarities between the ethical questions we ought to raise when evaluating new projects and proposals, whether they are spaceflight proposals or medical care proposals. In this narrow sense, planning a new space mission is a lot like planning new construction on a hospital.

We need to ask ethical questions during the planning phase in which we are figuring out *what* to do: Where is the best location for the hospital? Where are the patients in most need? Which services should the hospital provide? Should it be public or for-profit (and if healthcare involves both, how will the two combine)? How do we keep it open once it has been built? To what degree is it permissible for "all-things-considered" cost reduction and economic sustainability to override community health needs and priorities given that funds are not infinite and hard decisions must sometimes be taken? Comparably, for a space activity or mission, we would need to ask: What is the target destination? What objectives should be prioritised? Which instruments or capabilities should be included? To what degree is it permissible to trade off or sacrifice goals because of cost limitations? What are the risks involved, who are the risk takers and potential beneficiaries, and how do we make sure that risk takers know all that they need to know for informed judgement?

Ethical evaluation continues through the design and construction phase, where we are determining *how* to do things: How well should the designers and construction workers building a hospital be paid, given a possible trade-off between fairness in construction and long-term quality of care? What if something unexpected happens during construction? To what degree can cost overruns justify design changes which might have later and undesirable consequences? What levels of process automation should be anticipated during the design? Ethical questions also persist long after the hospital opens: Which patients should receive which treatments? Does it matter whether a patient has insurance? Is euthanasia ever permissible, what should triage look like, and what should be done when the latter starts to look suspiciously like the former? In each case, there are analogous questions we might pose during the construction of the spaceflight kit and hardware, during the preparation stage for flight, and throughout the implementation of the mission or activity. In both cases, matters of life and death are continuously in play. Space ethicists try to make sure that our deliberation about such matters is sound, that the different things we value are given their due, and that deliberation takes ongoing account of well-formulated criticisms. And while it may sometimes seem, from the standpoint of the individual ethicist, that they are searching for the one right narrative, what goes on, at a higher level of description, is a continuous and productive dialogue.

Conclusion

Given that spaceflight activities are expected to increase over the coming decades, possibly significantly so, so too will the salience and importance of critically engaging with the ethics of space exploration. While it is fortunate that space ethics has a substantial history, one that has developed organically out of spaceflight itself, nevertheless its continued salience depends on the growth of the space ethics community, especially through a growth in the number of professionally trained ethicists and philosophers who research space topics. We would like to close this chapter by highlighting possible pathways into this space ethics community from different areas of our home discipline, philosophy.

In our decade-plus experience in space ethics, what has become apparent is that *no matter what area of philosophy you work in, there is a fruitful opportunity to apply your specialisation to the case of space*. The main reason for this is the underlying interdisciplinarity of space exploration. Space exploration as it has been conducted to date has taken advantage of nearly every scientific discipline, from anthropology to astronomy, from psychology to political science, from engineering to entomology, and from biology to biomedicine. Moreover, plans for future space exploration activities include attempts to construct new human communities, even societies, in space. It is difficult to identify any areas of scholarly inquiry that *will not* prove significant to this ambitious endeavour.

However, the context of space presents many disanalogies to the terrestrial case. Various scientific disciplines will benefit from the conceptual resources that philosophers can bring to bear in order to understand this shift in context. Philosophers by training are especially adept at recognising the limitations of conceptual frameworks, and how they change in the face of novel circumstances. This applies even to the concepts of science and space science. Many people know how to do good science, but telling a plausible story about what science is, or what space science is, and what makes it different from non-science, draws us towards the more philosophical territory and to the possibility that a good story about science or space science will need to exclude some things but still be open-ended enough to allow for new practices to emerge in the context of space. The value of philosophy, and philosophical ethics, has already been seen in the development of the research methods and questions of astrobiology where conceptual questions about the nature of life and our ethical duties have a place alongside biochemistry and physics (Capova et al. 2018). The traffic is not one-way. Space ethics draws upon a multiplicity of other disciplines in order to frame questions in realistic ways (Smith 2021), improve our decision-making, and make sense of space exploration as a socially transformative process—one that may change humanity for better or for worse, depending upon the pathways chosen.

Acknowledgements

This chapter is part of a project that has received funding from the European Research Council (ERC) under the European Union's Horizon 2020 research and innovation programme (Grant Agreement No. 856543).

Notes

1 The philosophy journal *The Monist* also dedicated its January 1988 issue (Vol. 71, No. 1) to topics related to space exploration. See also Scherer (1982), Hartmann (1984), Kavka (1985), Regis (1985), and Munévar (1998), which draws upon materials published as early as the 1980s and examines space issues in the light of the philosophy of science.
2 Two other seminal terraforming ethics works are Haynes (1990) and McKay (1990). See Schwartz (2013) for a review of additional philosophical and ethical work related to terraforming.

References

Arendt, Hannah. 1963. "The Conquest of Space and the Stature of Man." In *Between Past and Future*, edited by Hannah Arendt, 260–74. New York: Penguin Books.
Arnould, Jacques. 2001. *La Seconde Chance D'ICARE: Pour une Éthique de L'espace*. Paris: Les Éditions du Cerf.
Arnould, Jacques. 2011. *Icarus' Second Chance: The Basis and Perspectives of Space Ethics*. New York: Springer.
Athanassoulis, Nafsika, and Allison Ross. 2010. "A Virtue Ethical Account of Making Decisions about Risk." *Journal of Risk Research* 13 (2): 217–30. https://doi.org/10.1080/13669870903126309.
Baum, Seth. 2016. "The Ethics of Outer Space: A Consequentialist Perspective." In *The Ethics of Space Exploration*, edited by James S. J. Schwartz and Tony Milligan, 109–23. New York: Springer. https://doi.org/10.1007/978-3-319-39827-3_8.
Beck, Lewis White. 1971–1972. "Extraterrestrial Intelligent Life." *Proceedings and Addresses of the American Philosophical Association* 45: 5–21.
Billings, Linda. 1997. "Frontier Days in Space: Are They Over?" *Space Policy* 13 (3): 187–90. https://doi.org/10.1016/S0265-9646(97)00020-9.

Capova, Klara A., Erik Persson, Tony Milligan, and David Dunér, eds. 2018. *Astrobiology and Society in Europe Today*. New York: Springer.
Cockell, Charles. 2004. "The Rights of Microbes." *Interdisciplinary Science Reviews* 29 (2): 141–50. https://doi.org/10.1179/030801804225012635.
Cockell, Charles, ed. 2015a. *The Meaning of Liberty beyond Earth*. New York: Springer.
Cockell, Charles, ed. 2015b. *Human Governance beyond Earth: Implications for Freedom*. New York: Springer.
Cockell, Charles, ed. 2016. *Dissent, Revolution and Liberty beyond Earth*. New York: Springer.
Deudney, Daniel. 2020. *Dark Skies: Space Expansionism, Planetary Geopolitics, and the Ends of Humanity*. New York: Oxford University Press.
Dick, Steven J. (2012). "Critical Issues in the History, Philosophy, and Sociology of Astrobiology." *Astrobiology* 12 (10): 906–27. https://doi.org/10.1089/ast.2011.0786.
Duemler, David. 1993. *Bringing Life to the Stars*. Lanham, MD: University Press of America.
Elvis, Martin, Alanna Krolikowski, and Tony Milligan. 2021. "Concentrated Lunar Resources: Imminent Implications for Governance and Justice." *Philosophical Transactions of the Royal Society A* 379 (2188): 20190563. https://doi.org/10.1098/rsta.2019.0563.
Fowers, Blaine J., Lukas F. Novak, Alexander J. Calder, and Robert K. Sommer. 2021. "Courage, Justice, and Practical Wisdom as Key Virtues in the Era of COVID-19." *Frontiers in Psychology* 12: 647912. https://doi.org/10.3389/fpsyg.2021.647912.
Ginsberg, Robert. 1971. "The Future of Interplanetary Ethics." *Journal of Social Philosophy* 2 (2): 5–7. https://doi.org/10.1111/j.1467-9833.1971.tb00205.x.
Green, Brian. 2020. "Convergences in the Ethics of Space Exploration." In *Social and Conceptual Issues in Astrobiology*, edited by Kelly C. Smith and Carlos Mariscal, 179–96. New York: Oxford University Press. https://doi.org/10.1093/oso/9780190915650.003.0011.
Green, Brian. 2022. *Space Ethics*. Lanham, MD: Rowman and Littlefield.
Hargrove, Eugene, ed. 1986. *Beyond Spaceship Earth: Environmental Ethics and the Solar System*. San Francisco, CA: Sierra Club Books.
Hartmann, William. 1984. "Space Exploration and Environmental Issues." *Environmental Ethics* 6 (3): 227–39. https://doi.org/10.5840/enviroethics19846325.
Haynes, Robert. 1990. "Ecce Ecopoiesis: Playing God on Mars." In *Moral Expertise: Studies in Practical and Professional Ethics*, edited by Don MacNiven, 161–83. London: Routledge.
Kavka, Gregory. 1985. "Space War Ethics." *Ethics* 95 (3): 673–91. https://doi.org/10.1086/292666.
Lupisella, Mark. 1997. "The Rights of Martians." *Space Policy* 13 (2): 89–94. https://doi.org/10.1016/S0265-9646(97)00009-X.
McArthur, Dan, and Idil Boran. 2004. "Agent-Centered Restrictions and the Ethics of Space Exploration." *Journal of Social Philosophy* 35 (1): 148–63. https://doi.org/10.1111/j.1467-9833.2004.00222.x.
McKay, Christopher. 1990. "Does Mars Have Rights? An Approach to the Environmental Ethics of Planetary Engineering." In *Moral Expertise: Studies in Practical and Professional Ethics*, edited by Don MacNiven, 184–97. London: Routledge.
Milligan, Tony. 2015. *Nobody Owns the Moon: The Ethics of Space Exploitation*. Jefferson, NC: McFarland and Co.
Morton, Adam. 2018. *Should We Colonize Other Planets?* Hoboken, NJ: Wiley.
Munévar, Gonzalo. 1998. *Evolution and the Naked Truth: A Darwinian Approach to Philosophy*. London: Routledge.
Nagel, Thomas. 1979. *Mortal Questions*. Cambridge: Cambridge University Press.
Nussbaum, Martha. 1986. *The Fragility of Goodness: Luck and Ethics in Greek Tragedy and Philosophy*. Cambridge: Cambridge University Press.
O'Neill, Onora. 2008. *Autonomy and Trust in Bioethics*. Cambridge: Cambridge University Press.
Persson, Erik. 2012. "The Moral Status of Extraterrestrial Life." *Astrobiology* 12 (10): 976–84. https://doi.org/10.1089/ast.2011.0787.
Pinkus, Rosa, Larry Shuman, Norman Hummon, and Harvey Wolfe. 1997. *Engineering Ethics: Balancing Cost, Schedule, and Risk—Lessons Learned from the Space Shuttle*. Cambridge: Cambridge University Press.
Pompidou, Alain. 2000. *The Ethics of Space Policy*. Paris: UNESCO World Commission on the Ethics of Scientific Knowledge and Technology.
Randolph, Richard, Margaret Race, and Christopher McKay. 1997. "Reconsidering the Theological and Ethical Implications of Extraterrestrial Life." *CTNS Bulletin* 17 (3): 1–8.
Rappaport, Margaret Boone, and Konrad Szocik, eds. 2021. *The Human Factor in the Settlement of the Moon: An Interdisciplinary Approach*. New York: Springer.
Reiman, Saara. 2009. "Is Space an Environment?" *Space Policy* 25 (2): 81–87. https://doi.org/10.1016/j.spacepol.2009.03.005.

Regis, Edward, ed. 1985. *Extraterrestrials: Science and Alien Intelligence*. Cambridge: Cambridge University Press.
Rollin, Bernard. 2006. *Science and Ethics*. Cambridge: Cambridge University Press.
Rummel, John, and Linda Billings. 2004. "Issues in Planetary Protection: Policy, Protocol and Implementation." *Space Policy* 20 (1): 49–54. https://doi.org/10.1016/j.spacepol.2003.11.005.
Sagan, Carl. 1994. *Pale Blue Dot*. New York: Random House.
Scherer, Donald. 1982. "Anthropocentrism, Atomism, and Environmental Ethics." *Environmental Ethics* 4 (2): 115–23. https://doi.org/10.5840/enviroethics19824220.
Schwartz, James. 2013. "On the Moral Permissibility of Terraforming." *Ethics and the Environment* 18 (2): 1–31. https://doi.org/10.2979/ethicsenviro.18.2.1.
Schwartz, James. 2020. *The Value of Science in Space Exploration*. New York: Oxford University Press.
Schwartz, James, and Tony Milligan, eds. 2016. *The Ethics of Space Exploration*. New York: Springer.
Sercel, Joel, and Steven Kwast. 2020. "To Boldly Go… Responsibly." *Politico*, 20 November 2020. https://www.politico.com/news/2020/11/20/space-ethics-opinion-438526.
Simberg, Rand. 2013. *Safe Is Not an Option: Overcoming the Futile Obsession with Getting Everyone Back Alive That Is Killing Our Expansion into Space*. Jackson, WY: Interglobal Media.
Smith, Kelly. 2009. "The Trouble with Intrinsic Value: An Ethical Primer for Astrobiology." In *Exploring the Origin, Extent, and Future of Life: Philosophical, Ethical, and Theological Perspectives*, edited by Constance M. Bertka, 261–80. Cambridge, UK: Cambridge University Press.
Smith, Kelly, ed. 2021. "Philosophers on Space Exploration." *Daily Nous* (blog), 22 February 2021. https://dailynous.com/2021/02/22/philosophers-on-space-exploration/.
Smith, Kelly, and Carlos Mariscal, eds. 2020. *Social and Conceptual Issues in Astrobiology*. New York: Oxford University Press.
Sparrow, Robert. 1999. "The Ethics of Terraforming." *Environmental Ethics* 21 (3): 227–45. https://doi.org/10.5840/enviroethics199921315.
Stoner, Ian. 2017. "Humans Should Not Colonize Mars." *Journal of the American Philosophical Association* 3 (3): 334–53. https://doi.org/10.1017/apa.2017.26.
Szocik, Konrad, ed. 2019. *The Human Factor in a Mission to Mars*. New York: Springer.
Szocik, Konrad, ed. 2020. *Human Enhancements for Space Missions*. New York: Springer.
Valentine, David. 2012. "Exit Strategy: Profit, Cosmology, and the Future of Humans in Space." *Anthropological Quarterly* 85 (4): 1045–67. https://doi.org/10.1353/anq.2012.0073.
Vaughan, Diane. 1997. *The Challenger Launch Decision: Risky Technology, Culture, and Deviance at NASA*. Chicago: University of Chicago Press.
Wilks, Anna Frammartino. 2016. "Kantian Foundations for a Cosmocentric Ethic." In *The Ethics of Space Exploration*, edited by James S. J. Schwartz and Tony Milligan, 181–94. New York: Springer. https://doi.org/10.1007/978-3-319-39827-3_13.
Williams, Bernard. 1981. *Moral Luck*. Cambridge: Cambridge University Press.
Williams, Lynda. 2010. "Irrational Dreams of Space Colonization." *Peace Review* 22 (1): 4–8. https://doi.org/10.1080/10402650903539828.
Zubrin, Robert. 2020. "Wokeists Assault Space Exploration." *The National Review*, 14 November 2020. https://www.nationalreview.com/2020/11/wokeists-assault-space-exploration/.

10
OTHER WORLDS, OTHER VIEWS
Contemporary Artists and Space Exploration

Nicola Triscott

Introduction

Artists have long helped to shape social imaginaries of outer space. Since the early twentieth century and earlier, artists' representations of space have had a significant impact on how space activities have been dreamed up, advocated for, and manifested in different cultures (Triscott 2016). The richly illustrated novels of Jules Verne (1828–1905) influenced aviation pioneers, rocketry innovators, and astronomers across Europe, the USA, and Russia. In the USA, artist Chesley Bonestell, working closely with Wernher von Braun—the German scientist who led the US Army's rocket development team after World War Two—produced a series of seemingly 'realistic' visual representations of outer space that contributed significantly to a climate of opinion that supported a large-scale space programme (Dickens 2014). Whilst art was also used systematically in the 1950s and 1960s in Soviet Russia to construct a visual universe for its citizens to absorb the mythologies that the country built around its space programme (Franetovich 2019), Russia's long fascination with space travel was underpinned by deep intricate links between religious, artistic, and political ideologies, with space travel understood as a revolutionary quest for new worlds (Science Museum n.d.).

Space enthusiasts and proponents, including NASA (Pendle 2016) and science fiction writer Arthur C. Clarke (Clarke 1989), often consider the primary importance of space art to be its capacity to inspire space travel—Dickens worries that "Space Art" as a genre merely aims to stimulate governments and economies through generating popular imaginaries (2014). However, I believe that the real value of contemporary art to our understanding of outer space lies in the ability of artists to challenge prevailing ideologies and envisage alternative worlds.[1] During the 1950s and 1960s, when many people were inspired and excited by the constructed space imagery and visions of the future in the mass media, several artists, among them Yves Klein and Gustav Metzger, questioned Western notions of progress through their art. As the Apollo programme progressed, there was a particularly strong counternarrative in African-American newspapers and magazines and by African-American artists characterizing the Moon landings as a giant step in the wrong direction (Spigel 2001). Famously, the poet and musician Gil Scott-Heron mocked the Apollo programme in his 1970 song "Whitey on the Moon".

In the contemporary moment—marked by the climate emergency, the sixth great extinction, the renewed global movement to address legacies of empire and slavery, and increasing conflict—how are artists responding to themes of outer space and space exploration? What do their aesthetic and critical responses contribute to understandings of our relationship to space, at a time when the increasing commercialization and militarization of space—activities promoted heavily by corporations, billionaires, presidents, and space agencies—threatens the fundamental principles of international space law?

In this chapter, I give a short critical overview of several contemporary artists' responses to themes of space exploration and space travel, and explore some of the movements, concepts, and theories influencing contemporary artists today. Focusing on artworks from the 2010s to the present (2022), the chapter is structured around four strands of contemporary thought: decolonisation, Afrofuturism, Indigenous perspectives, and planetarity. Decolonisation refers to the process of deconstructing and offering alternatives to colonial ideologies of the superiority of Western thought and approaches that permeate institutions and systems, which is now being applied to space. Afrofuturism is a cultural movement, manifesting through music, art, literature, film, and other expressive forms, that interweaves black history and culture with science fiction and futuristic themes. Indigenous perspectives emphasise the acknowledgement of complex relationships between Indigenous people and their homelands, waters, cosmologies, ancestral connections, ceremonies, languages, and the natural world of nonhuman animals and plants. Planetarity is a concept conceived by Spivak (2003) as a counter to prevailing notions of the world, the globe, and globalisation, and offers the opportunity to consider our planet from the outside: "The planet is in the species of alterity, belonging to another system; and yet we inhabit it, on loan" (p. 72). Within these broader contextualisations, I discuss how the artists' subjectivity and often detailed research unfold in their artworks and consider the insights and knowledge this presents.

Today, the divide between space enthusiasm and space scepticism seems more blurred in contemporary art than it was during the Space Age, with artists engaging critically with this theme less prone to proselytise either for or against space exploration. Their works, rather than overt critiques of space activities, draw on histories and imaginaries of outer space and interweave them with contemporary ideas. In doing so, they exist in tension between space as a place of possibility and imagination and one of exploitation and potential destruction. I am interested in how contemporary artists are questioning discourses around space exploration and the governance of outer space from decolonial, new materialist, and Indigenous perspectives, as well as accessing and appropriating the technologies of space to challenge and disrupt dominant narratives of colonisation and globalisation, and expose the processes and controls at work in the military–industrial and private–public partnerships that drive the space industry.

Decolonising Space

The structures created by colonialism are still alive today, influencing the scientific community and political and commercial institutions, both in the West and in other parts of the world. The five-hundred-year-old language of colonialism—"colonising Mars", "conquering space", "the final frontier"—has long been part of the space exploration community's rhetoric around human spaceflight, and continues to be used uncritically by politicians, journalists, and even artists. Now, as commercial and private–public partnerships become increasingly central to the future of space exploration and military interest continues to grow, these structures are worryingly apparent in plans for human space exploration and resource extraction (Smiles 2020; Tavares et al. 2020; Treviño 2020; Walkowicz 2018).

There is a disturbing and strange contradiction between the rhetoric of the space community around outer space being for the "benefit of all mankind", a concept that underpins much international space law, and the persistent use of these terms with their violent, often genocidal, histories. Treviño notes that these rhetorical habits and tropes "are drenched in the worship of technology, individualism, the bootstrap mentality, and colonial ambitions" (Treviño 2020: 17). More than rhetoric, she argues, the motivations for space are "mere extensions of the logic of capital and the continuation of coloniality" (p. 17). Dickens and Ormrod (2007) claim that the desire to go into space is "cosmic narcissism", a sort of projection of capitalist individualism onto the universe.

The repetitiveness of a colonial, expansionist imaginary, Treviño argues, "can be understood as both violence and a lack of imagination" (p. 26). It also seems to be a strange blind spot for the space agencies, at a time when ideas of decolonisation and posthumanism are becoming mainstream, for example, in officially sanctioned renaming or removing memorials and place names from a racist, colonial past, and in debate and law-making around personhood and rights of animals and rivers.

Whilst a conversation around the language of space exploration has started within the space agencies—NASA, for example, has been weeding out the gendered language of the USA's space programme (changing "manned" human space missions to gender-neutral terms like "piloted" or "crewed", for example)—this scrutiny of language has not yet, it seems, been applied to colonialism. A recent article on the NASA website (NASA n.d.) blithely discusses space colonisation moving closer to "a reality" and even bizarrely suggests that the worldwide Covid pandemic has revalidated "the urgency to establish humanity as a multi-planet species".

One of the most sustained artistic interventions into the space world is the cultural space agency Kosmica, founded and led by Mexican artist Nahum. Kosmica aims to create "critical, cultural and poetic discourse on our relationship with outer space, space exploration and the impact of these activities here on Earth" (Kosmica n.d.). Kosmica organises festivals and educational activities and initiates and promotes new discourse around humanity's relationship with outer space. It can be said that the institute follows a curatorial model of co-inquiry (Triscott 2017), constructing an ecology of practices with practitioners from different disciplines to inquire into a matter of concern and co-produce and share transdisciplinary knowledge concerning humanity's relationship with outer space and space activities (Figures 10.1 and 10.2).

Figure 10.1 Nahum, *Voyage: A session for remembering*, 2015. Cajarc, France. Photo: Yohann Gozard.

Figure 10.2 Living the Cosmos (2020), a KOSMICA institute educational programme for vulnerable kids in San Luis Potosí, Mexico.

As an artist, Nahum has made significant connections with several major space agencies including NASA, ESA, Roscosmos, and SpaceX, both to progress artistic projects and to embed himself and introduce cross-disciplinary discourse into the heart of the space industry. As well as launching an interactive artwork into space (*The Contour of Presence*, SpaceX/ISS, 2018), for several years Nahum was chair of the International Astronautical Federation's Technical Activities Committee for the Cultural Utilisation of Space (ITACCUS), a committee that I founded in 2007 with astronomer Roger Malina.[2] He is also a member of the adjunct faculty of the International Space University.

Holding critical agency in these embedded roles is challenging and is only achievable, I suggest, because Nahum combines a genuine fascination for space exploration with a critical mindset and because his position as an artist gives him some licence and autonomy not to act as others feel they need to act. Thus, his work can embrace the dream of space whilst remaining critical of many aspects of the space industry.

Nahum's art weaves together space technologies, illusionism, music, and hypnosis to guide audiences on unsettling journeys. His hypnotic performance *Voyage: A Session for Remembering* (2016), also performed as *Evocations of a Forgotten Voyage*, explores the possibilities of producing an intimate experience about a trip to the Moon. It addresses the limitations of such travels, that so far have been reserved to a group of twelve white American men. Over the course of one year, Nahum, a trained hypnotist, led several hypnosis sessions with participants in a series of venues in Mexico and the United Kingdom. Through these, he planted a false memory in people's minds, a fiction of a personal trip to the Moon. The memory was carefully crafted with the guidance of astronomers and geologists.

Born and raised in Mexico, Nahum understands the trauma of a country and nationality that is subjected to the attitudes of colonising countries. He sees many of those structures and mental processes still present in how those countries leading the exploration of space approach and think about this endeavour (Nahum 2019). He considers his work an act of decolonisation. Artworks such as *Evocations of a Forgotten Voyage*, for example, broaden the experience of space travel to a far wider group of people than the small elite who get travel physically into space. In this way, Nahum reframes space exploration as a potential anticolonialist and inclusive undertaking. Reaching further than this, Kosmica's extensive work with young people in Mexico and refugee children in Europe contributes actively to opening space to non-Westerners.

Working with children and young people as participants and audiences is also central to the work of Bahamian artist Tavares Strachan (2020). Raised in Nassau, Strachan's dreams of escaping the confines of the island drove a fascination for space exploration. Later, as an artist based in New York, he decided to undertake cosmonaut training at the Gagarin Cosmonaut Training Centre in Star City, Russia. This research contributed to a remarkable multiphase body of work, *Orthostatic Tolerance* (Strachan 2010). Orthostatic tolerance refers to a person's ability to tolerate gravitational stress, through which Strachan also understood his experience of standing upright in the face of extreme social stress, from his upbringing in the Bahamas to his experience as a displaced person in New York. *Orthostatic Tolerance* includes videos, drawings, and photography from his cosmonaut and deep-sea-diver training, as well as sculptures of exploded astronauts, a life-size blown-glass diver submerged in mineral oil, and sugarcane-fuelled glass rockets (made from Bahamas sand), with documentation of their launches. These are juxtaposed with his dreams of establishing the Bahamas Aerospace and Sea Exploration Center (BASEC), an educational centre in his homeland.

Strachan's work continues to explore themes of science and knowledge, particularly the control of histories and how certain members of society are overlooked in traditional historical narratives. His work in the 2019 Venice Biennale, *Works Related to Robert Henry Lawrence Jr.* (2018), included a neon sculpture, *Robert* (2018), of the body of astronaut Robert Lawrence, the first African-American astronaut, who died in a training accident in 1967 and who has remained largely invisible in standard histories of US space travel. In 2018, Strachan launched an artwork, *Enoch*, named after the biblical figure who could transcend death, into orbit (2018).[3] The work, a gold bust of Lawrence, was encased in metal and will stay in orbit for seven years. Strachan's work about Lawrence, and his own experiments in cosmonaut training, expose the humanity, fragility, and mortality underlying the mythology of space frontierism and underline the history of space travel as also being one of race.

Syrian artist Halil Altındere's work *Space Refugee* (2016–2019), shown in the 2019 Venice Biennale, presents a part-cynical, part-optimistic reframing of space travel, proposing that those who might go to Mars be refugees rather than the rich and powerful. Muhammed Ahmed Faris, a Syrian air force colonel who joined the Soviet cosmonaut programme in 1985 and flew to the Mir Space Station in 1987, is the subject of a twenty-minute video by Altındere interweaving Faris's story (in 2011, when the revolution in Syria broke out, Faris protested, calling for reform, and the next year defected to Turkey) with the notion of enabling the world's refugees to settle on Mars. In the video, Faris describes his journey out of Syria and expresses his hopes of returning or, if not, that "we can rebuild cities for them [refugees] in space, where there is freedom and dignity and where there is no tyranny, no injustice". The video portrays three astronauts— two of them children—as they explore the Martian desert juxtaposed with scientists discussing how to settle the planet. A VR piece gives the viewer an immersive and isolating experience of joining the astronauts in their lonely exploration of the desert, filmed in Cappadocia in Turkey. Altındere draws on old-fashioned space iconography—the exhibition design reminiscent of an old space museum—and futuristic ideas that echo the myth of colonisation that the space industry continues to present, but the work's content, that of a new Syrian diaspora, sets it firmly in the present day. It is a humorous yet poignant work that entwines old and new imagery, ideas, and technologies to unsettle any easy acceptance of the "space for the benefit of all humanity" ideal that underpins most space law. When society is so divided on Earth, why would it be any different in space?[4]

Mona Benyamin's short film *Moonscape* (2020), a reflection on love, hope of escape, and despair, tells a story through a song, composed by the artist. Images from space are juxtaposed with the artists' parents dancing to the music. As the narrator in the film, Benyamin comments on being startled, when reading about a company called the Lunar Embassy that purports to sell land on the Moon, by a realisation that it would be more possible for a Palestinian refugee to own land on the Moon than to return to their own homeland. She starts an email exchange with the Lunar Embassy, initially enquiring about the number of people from Arab countries who have purchased land on the Moon—no one from Syria, only a handful of buyers from Israel, UAE, and Saudi Arabia. One of the Lunar Embassy's customers worries about future neighbours on the Moon. "What if they don't like me?" they ask the embassy. The embassy replies that they can always move back to Earth if they don't like the neighbours.

While the singer in Benyamin's work (the artist is the composer) states that the Moon is "a long way from colonialism", it is indicative of the pervasiveness of the language of 'colonising space' that one arts reviewer, although clearly understanding the intention of the film, still refers to it misleadingly as reflecting on "colonizing space". The artist herself, whilst embracing the notion of individual ownership of pieces of space, is talking—or singing—about escape, psychologically at least, from the constraints of colonisation and occupation. Yet it seems the reviewer cannot escape the grip of a space rhetoric based on ideas that are five hundred years old.

Afrofuturism

Afrofuturism is a term that encompasses the way in which black artists have used outer space and the science fiction genre to reflect on the black experience and history and imagine alternative futures. Ekow Eshun (2021) notes:

> One of the significant things about Afrofuturism is that it enables us to understand that we can be more than the Western world has given us. We can leave this behind. We can live in our dreams. We can reach into space. The cosmic, the outer space, the infinite can be our home.

Afrofuturism reaches back to black science fiction writers and jazz musicians of the 1960s and 1970s, including musician Sun Ra and writer Octavia Butler, although 'Afrofuturism' wasn't coined as a term until 1994, when white critic Mark Dery used the word in his essay "Black to the Future" (Dery 1994). "The human-machine interface became both the condition and the subject of Afrofuturism", wrote Kodwo Eshun in 1998 (Eshun 2018), underlining the connection of this cultural movement to debates at the time around cyberculture and postmodernism linked to posthumanism. Seminal works from the 1990s include the film *The Last Angel of History* (1996) by John Akomfrah and Black Audio Film Collective.

As a cultural aesthetic, Afrofuturism has continued to exert a powerful influence on black artists and scholars, including those from Africa and the African diaspora. In her ongoing project *Afrogalactica* (begun in 2011), Canadian artist Kapwani Kiwanga imagines herself as an anthropologist from the future lecturing on Afrofuturism and the role of its ideas in creating the United States of Africa. *Afrogalactica* takes the form of a series of lecture performances, one of the earliest being presented at Arts Catalyst[5] in 2011 as part of the inaugural Kosmica event series, and has since evolved and been performed at multiple venues internationally.[6] In her *Afrogalactica* series, Kiwanga draws on mythology, pop culture, film, poetry, science, and scholarly discourse to challenge Eurocentric historical narratives around colonial struggle and the African diaspora and cultural constructions of gender and race. She regards history as creative and mutable, and mixes fact and fiction to generate new stories while speculating on the future.

Despite Afrofuturism's popularity, US artist Martine Syms is sceptical of what she considers to be its escapist imaginaries. Her outspoken and funny piece *The Mundane Afrofuturist Manifesto* (2013–2015), first published by digital art organisation Rhizome, criticises some of the fundamental notions and more whimsical elements of Afrofuturism, and is suspicious of its utopian ideas. She writes:

> We did not originate in the cosmos. The connection between Middle Passage and space travel is tenuous at best. Out of five hundred thirty-four space travellers, fourteen have been black. An all-black crew is unlikely. Magic interstellar travel and/or the wondrous communication grid can lead to an illusion of outer space and cyberspace as egalitarian. This dream of utopia can encourage us to forget that outer space will not save us from injustice and that cyberspace was prefigured upon a 'master/slave' relationship.
>
> *(Syms 2017)*

As a reframing as well as a reimagining of the past, present, and future of African and African diaspora contributions to the advancement of science, technology, and culture through music, art, and literature, Afrofuturist thought has an ever-expanding reach. A recent symposium, Claiming Space: A Symposium on Black Futures—Past, Present, and Potential, organised by the Smithsonian Afrofuturism Series,[7] brought together panels to consider Afrofuturism as applied across oceans, land reclamations, cyberspace, inner space, and outer space. The cross-disciplinary panel on outer space (Aganaba et al. 2022) discussed how Afrofuturist perspectives might counter the dominant narratives and assumptions behind the imagined futures of space, and whether ideas of indigeneity and decolonisation could be brought into the activities of space to challenge increasingly commercial, extractive, and militaristic approaches to outer space.

Afrofuturism has also influenced the emergence and expression of other "futurisms". Lama Suleiman (2016) writes: "(Afro)futurism can offer diasporic cultures a way to deconstruct and reconstruct history in a manner that infiltrates territorial and mental borders." She argues that interest in Arabfuturism is growing through conferences, art exhibitions, and discussions on Arab science fiction in literature and film.

Indigenous Perspectives on Space

Anthropologist Jane Young cites a colleague who worked in Alaska with Inuit peoples. Speaking to them about the Apollo Moon landings, the Inuit replied, "We didn't know this was the first time you white people had been to the moon. Our shamans have been going for years. They go all the time" (Young 1987: 272).

Mitchell et al. (2020) point out that the space sector assumes that there are no beings in outer space and that outer space, separate from Earth, is therefore considered a place where extraction can be carried out without harm to life, and that colonisation can happen without violence or displacement. However, as we have noted, many formerly colonised and currently occupied people have painful associations with this language and feel excluded by its use. For Indigenous people in North America, terms like 'pioneer' and 'manifest destiny', the latter used by former US President Donald Trump in his 2020 State of the Nation address, as well as the related concept of 'terra nullius', have deep meanings, resonant of the violence that was inflicted on their peoples, cultures, and nations.

The attitude that space colonisation is harmless also assumes that there is no impact of space activities on those on Earth, or at least only positive impacts, for example through the use of satellites or the acquisition of scientific knowledge. Yet, Indigenous lands have been annexed and Indigenous people displaced for installations that enable space exploration, and the launch of satellite megaconstellations, such as SpaceX's Starlink, are adding to the light pollution that acts to disconnect Indigenous people from that land where they live, as so much Indigenous knowledge is based on star lore and observations of the sky (Neilson and Ćirković 2021). Mitchell et al. (2020) emphasise that outer space is the ancestral domain of many Indigenous cultures throughout the world. The understanding of the Aboriginal Australian Yolŋu Peoples, for example, is that Land, Sea, and Sky Country are all connected. For the Yolŋu, there is no such thing as 'outer space' or 'Outer Country'. What is done in one part of Country affects all others.

This disjunction is a topic that contemporary artists and filmmakers are starting to address through their work. Navajo filmmaker Nanobah Becker's 2014 short film *The Sixth World* is based on a Navajo origin story. It centres on a female Navajo astronaut piloting the first spaceship to "colonize Mars". Omnicorn, a genetically modified corn, will be used to produce enough oxygen for the journey. An older Navajo astronaut asks, "Corn with no husks? No stalks or tassels?" "They're genetically engineered to have very few unusable parts", he is told. "That's creepy", the astronaut replies, "Some people use those parts. If they have use on Earth, they can be used on Mars." Three months into the mission, the GMO corn fails. The sacred corn pollen taken on board saves the colony and humanity's future. Becker's film, which has been held as an example of Indigenous futurisms, a term first characterised by Grace Dillon (2012), uses the notion of space colonisation to represent the Navajo as a technologically advanced and culturally strong nation, whilst emphasising the importance of origin stories and traditional knowledge, and warning against the disruption and ignorance of this knowledge.

Traditional or Indigenous knowledge refers to the distinctive understandings, rooted in cultural experience, that Indigenous peoples around the planet have gathered and preserved, that guide relations among human, non-human, and other-than-human beings in specific ecosystems (Bruchac 2014). Indigenous epistemologies and cosmologies offer ways of thinking that break from the human–non-human distinction (Leonard 2020), and Indigenous studies scholarship has developed theories about the agency of non-human things (Rosiek, Snyder, and Pratt 2019). Hokowhitu (2021) argues that posthumanist and new materialist thinking—which decentre the human subject and acknowledge the agencies of a full array of human and non-human actors—are not new and need to engage with Indigenous knowledges and scholarship. Neilson and Ćirković (2021), among others, call for Indigenous thinking to be brought into conversations around space.

Part of Neilson and Ćirković's argument stresses the importance of the Moon and Mars as part of the cultures and knowledge systems of Indigenous peoples around the world, an attitude that is understood by many artists. French Guianese artist Tabita Rezaire's *Satellite Devotion* (2019), "an invitation to build intimacy with the Moon, an opportunity to experience her depth, and an ode to her glow" (Rezaire 2019), incorporates aspects of Indigenous thinking. The installation comprises twelve videos placed on a circular unit, the videos featuring a series of interviews with experts about the Moon from across the planet: a shaman from the Amazon rainforest, an astrophysicist from Guyana, a traditional herbalist from the Democratic Republic of Congo, a Druid leader, and others. Accompanying their lessons are video portraits of the Moon, filmed through the artist's telescope. The work's range of cultural and disciplinary perspectives reminds us that we need to draw on many understandings, meanings, and connections about the Earth's satellite—ecological, scientific, cultural, and spiritual—at a time when it is increasingly seen as a strategic asset within global spatial politics (Figure 10.3).

Satellite Devotion raises issues of how we relate to, and therefore behave towards, non-human entities, in this case, 'non-living' entities such as celestial bodies, the atmosphere, oceans, and our mineral commons. In 2014, Arts Catalyst's exhibition *Republic of the Moon* was triggered by the rise of logics of resource extraction and militarisation of outer-space bodies. The exhibition was shown in London in 2014,[8] a month after China's Chang'e 3 robotic exploration mission landed

Figure 10.3 *Vortex of Infinity*, Unseen Amsterdam 2019 © Andres Pardo. Tabita Rezaire, *Satellite Devotion* (2019), installation view from Unseen Amsterdam 2019. Photo: Andres Pardo. Courtesy of the artist and Goodman Gallery.

a lunar rover on the Moon. Named after the goddess of the Moon in Chinese mythology, the objectives of the mission included a survey of potential mineral resources on the Moon. The title of the exhibition—in which we declared a Moon republic, set up a Moon embassy on Earth, and invited a group of international artists to create and show new mythologies for the Moon in the contemporary era—was drawn from a conversation the exhibition's curator, Rob La Frenais, and I had with Ciro Arévalo-Yepes, then chair of the United Nations Committee on the Peaceful Uses of Outer Space about Moon protection, during which Arévalo-Yepes commented: "No one is calling for a republic of the Moon".

Drawing on Indigenous thinking, Neilson and Ćirković (2021) suggest that the Moon, Mars, and other solar system objects have their own rights and that we have an ethical duty to consider them. Noting that legal personhood is already extended to many non-human entities, including rivers and corporations, space archaeologist Alice Gorman has also suggested that the Moon might be granted legal personhood, which would give it the right to enter into contracts, own property, and sue other persons. In the case of environmental features already given personhood, trustees are appointed to act on their behalf. In practice, Gorman notes, this could mean trustees would determine whether and to what extent the Moon's resources could be extracted or set conditions on activities which alter the qualities of the Moon irreversibly (Gorman 2020).

Satellite Planetarity

Spivak's notion of planetarity (2003) offers the opportunity to consider our planet from the outside, contextualised by planets other than the one we inhabit. Spivak draws on the aerial view from her plane as she flies across invisible borders from Asia into Europe to describe how the land (by implication, its geology, geography, and climate) underpins her understanding of planetarity: "The view of the Earth from the window brings this home to me" (p. 93).

Whilst the aerial perspective—the view of a landscape as if seen from far above—has been part of human imagination since ancient times, it was the phenomenon of human flight that profoundly changed the way that the environments in which we live were seen and had a vast impact on visual culture. Today, how we imagine and visualise the Earth and its environment is tied closely to images produced by space activities, specifically photographic representations by satellites and from spaceships. As aerospace technologies developed through the twentieth century, the aerial view could zoom further and further out. High-altitude rocketry, satellites, and orbital space flight produced overview images of the Earth, the direct experience of which, it has often been reported, may bring about a cognitive shift in awareness in astronauts.[9] Images from space, such as those dubbed *Earthrise* (1968) and *The Blue Marble* (1972), are said to have propelled the environmental movement with a new consciousness of the planetary biosphere, although these images are deeply connected to the history of Cold War militarisation.

DeLoughrey (2014) brings together Cosgrove's theory of an Apollonian vision of the globe (2003), in which these images of a spherical earth are inextricably linked to Western notions of control and processes of globalisation, and Spivak's concept of "planetarity" (2003), a way of understanding the world as a planet, containing multitudes of ecologies and cultures. This is what DeLoughrey calls 'satellite planetarity': "a vision of the globe that arose after the development of artificial satellite imagery ... which also produces an understanding of the planet as alterity in which human vision is both connected to and disconnected from the earth" (2014: 265). It is through this lens of 'satellite planetarity' and the question of how it is possible to use satellite imagery "to unsettle figures of totality and regulation in order to attend to the incommensurate, the unjust, and the yet to be recognized" (Gabrys 2018) that I look at the work of a number of artists working with the "inverted astronomy"—to use Sloterdijk's phrase (1990, cited in Sachs 1999: 111)—of satellite images and sensing.

Forensic Architecture is a multidisciplinary research group at Goldsmiths, University of London. The group investigates human rights abuses, political violence, and environmental destruction and crimes employing a range of techniques in spatial and architectural analysis. Their investigatory works make use of remote data such as satellite images, enabling comparative analysis of 'before' and 'after' images to help them identify transformations on the ground. Whilst Forensic Architecture is not foremost an arts collective, the group includes several artists, regularly exhibits work in international art museums and exhibitions,[10] and was one of four nominees for the 2018 Turner Prize, a major UK contemporary art prize. Members or former members of the Forensic Architecture group also have their own artistic practices, including Susan Schuppli and Nabil Ahmed.

In Forensic Architecture's *The Bombing of Rafah* (2014), smartphone footage and satellite imagery are used to map the destruction of the town of Rafah, after an Israeli soldier was captured and taken into tunnels below the town, as over two thousand munitions were fired into the city in a single day. 'Before' and 'after' images were used to assess changes in site conditions at attack sites under analysis. Three satellite images were used in this project, dated 30 July, 1 August, and 14 August. The group's research supported the conclusions by Amnesty International that "there is overwhelming evidence that Israeli forces committed disproportionate, or otherwise indiscriminate, attacks which killed scores of civilians in their homes, on the streets, and in vehicles and injured many more".

Nabil Ahmed's work as an artist and researcher is strongly influenced by his long-term affiliation with the Forensic Architecture research group. He leads Inter-Pacific Ring Tribunal (INTERPRT), a group of researchers, architects, and spatial designers who undertake long-term investigations focused on environmental justice. In 2017, I curated INTERPRT's work on the Grasberg mine as part of the exhibition *Conflict Minerals* (2017).[11] The open-pit Grasberg mine, operated by Freeport-McMoRan, is one of the world's largest copper and gold mines. It occupies the ancestral land of the Amungme and Kamoro people of the Melanesian land of West Papua and is the site of a long-term conflict between Indonesia and Indigenous Papuans seeking self-determination. For decades, pollution from mining has devastated one of the most biodiverse places on the planet. The exhibition included maps, satellite imagery including vegetation analysis, a sculptural representation of the mine, drawings, videos, and other archival material from INTERPRT's documentation of the gradual destruction of rainforest, mangroves, rivers, and coastal waters between 1987 and 2014. INTERPRT's painstaking research contributes towards building a case of ecocide against the Indonesian state, which includes Indonesian military campaigns of mass killings of Indigenous Papuans, soil contamination and deforestation from the Grasberg mine, industrial land grabs, and intentional forest fires that together show the deliberate destruction of Papuan social, cultural, and natural environments.

Slovenian artist Marko Peljhan has theorised, and used as a tactic, the concept of 'conversion'—the adoption of military–industrial technologies by citizens—through a series of highly ambitious projects since the early 1990s. In Peljhan's view, much technology is developed and applied in the military; tools and equipment developed there then have to go through the long process of conversion through civil industry into civil usage, and only then do they become available to the artist (Čufer 2019: 61). Rothe and Shim note that satellite imagery, previously restricted to the defence and intelligence communities, has only recently become available to a range of non-state actors leading to the rise of what they call "satellite-based activism" (2018). To counter this delay in conversion, as early as 1995, Peljhan established the technological arm of his arts organisation Projekt Atol called PACT Systems where he developed a global navigation satellite system based on a participatory networked mapping project. He has continued to develop tactics to circumvent the slow process of technological conversion in order to use space and military technologies at an early stage in their development as an artist. Using these technologies, he creates images and ideas about their impact on humanity, most recently *System 317* in the 2019 Venice Biennale, which called attention to the rise of hypersonic weapons.

An overview of satellite planetarity and art should not neglect the issue of the increasingly congested, contested, and competitive built environment of near-Earth space. The number of satellites in low Earth orbit is predicted to grow from around two thousand to an astounding one hundred thousand over the next ten years. This rapid increase in satellite numbers is enabled by the reduction in size, weight, and cost of satellites, and the number of spacefaring states and private corporations entering the sector. There is also a shift in interest from the conventional (high) geostationary orbit to low and medium Earth orbits, but the lower the orbit, the more satellites are required for coverage. Some proposed systems consist of hundreds and even thousands of satellites. This rapid increase in satellite constellations, Venkatesan et al. (2020) argue, is a simmering crisis silently approaching a point of no return. This increase in access and affordability of satellite technologies is not without benefits to many fields, including scientific research, climate, and environmental monitoring, rescue operations, land stewardship, and indeed radical projects of visual activism, such as those of Forensic Architecture. However, Venkatesan et al. (2020) argue that the pace and manner of 'occupying' near-Earth space, in addition to their direct impact on astronomy (the authors' speciality), raises the risk of repeating the mistakes of colonisation in space, and that consideration must be given to the impact of new satellite megaconstellations on "the essential human right to dark skies and on cultural sky traditions across all peoples" (p. 1043).

In this context, artists who place or plan to place artworks in orbit[12] can be—and have been—criticised for adding to the clutter, even though their contribution to the congestion is relatively miniscule. The defence of artist Trevor Paglen—whose *Orbital Reflector*, in the end, was unable to deploy fully—is that his purpose as an artist is to invite people to look at the heavens and the stars above, which stands in contrast to the military and commercial use of satellites, which Paglen has studied extensively (Paglen 2018). Indeed, Paglen has been pioneering in documenting and exposing the unseen political geographies in hidden and remote parts of the planet, including in lower Earth orbit. His photographic series *The Other Night Sky* (2007) resulted from years of research conducted in the desert valley below the Sierra Nevada mountains, where he used advanced telescopic equipment to track and photograph the nearly two hundred classified American spacecraft that were orbiting the Earth at that time.

Conclusion

Art is a highly varied set of practices that often, and increasingly, include varied research methods—including ethnography, archival work, critical analysis, technological development, data mining, and data visualisation—both in production and as artistic mediums, forming part of installations or exhibitions. Artists may be academics, but, for many artists, including Kapwani Kiwanga, research is simply where the process of art-making begins: "I start with a spark of interest in the subject matter, or an anecdote I overhear, or an event, and then I do what I like doing best—research" (Nathan 2016). There are also many artist groups outside the academy, and particularly in non-Western cultures, that call their work 'research'. Given artists' increasing focus on research, as well as the extensive discourse around art, it is unsurprising that art has much to contribute to emerging ideas and conversations around multiple topics, and that scholars from an ever-widening range of disciplines are reaching to the arts for new perspectives. Art, whilst hopefully free from being framed as corporate–academic 'research outputs', can generate new insights, experiences, communities, and trans- or non-disciplinary forms of knowledge, as well as points of critique for the academy as much as the arts (see Hawkins 2021; Hughes et al. 2021).

The current unstable and uncertain planetary situation is pushing artists, as well as researchers in many other disciplines, to develop expositional strategies to address fundamental questions, such as what we value, how control and ownership systems work, and whose stories and histories are made visible, and to communicate that research to publics. A key strategy in the works of artists such as Nahum, Tavares Strachan, Kapwani Kiwanga, and Tabita Rezaire is to revisit and rethink past events—Moon landings, the history of astronautics, ancient forms of cosmology, colonial histories—and to consider them in relation and as still belonging to our current time. Intervening in and appropriating today's space communities and technologies is a tactic used by several artists discussed to research and reveal unseen events and political geographies happening today (Forensic Architecture, Paglen, Ahmed, Peljhan) and, ambitiously, to attempt to reshape space as a more inclusive decolonised undertaking (Kosmica).

For some groups, showing their work in an arts context is a strategy to communicate their research to the public. Forensic Architecture, argues its founder and director, Eyal Weizman, uses arts venues such as documenta and the ICA as a means of representation, adding that this is vital to multiplying the real-life impact of their work. For others, like Kosmica, intervening in non-arts spaces is a tactic to make the influence of their critical ideas more direct.

Whatever their tactics as individual artists or collectives, the combined effect of their work is to offer new possibilities to think in a more progressive way about the culture of space and the future of space activities. As difficult as it might be to create a code of ethics for space exploration, words and concepts are a starting point and images are a key communicator. Outer space has become a site for black, Indigenous, and other oppressed people to reimagine and re-present their histories and to consider other futures, despite the exclusionary tropes of colonisation and conquest with their language of violence and their histories written primarily by white males. If the space sector believes that space should be for the benefit of all humanity, it needs to work harder to eliminate these ideologies and embrace ideas expressed by artists and thinkers from cultures and communities who have historically not controlled space activities or written those histories. And if it doesn't, it is up to the rest of us to reclaim it as such.

Artworks

Ahmed, Nabil. 2017. Inter-Pacific Ring Tribunal (INTERPRT). *Maps, Drawings, Model, Videos, and Archival Material*. London. Arts Catalyst.

Akomfrah, John, and Black Audio Film Collective 1996. *The Last Angel of History*. Film.

Altındere, Halil. 2016–2019. *Space Refugee*. Video and Installation, 2019. Italy. Venice Biennale.

Becker, Nanobah, dir. 2014. *The Sixth World*. Film. https://vimeo.com/256611676.

Benyamin, Mona, dir. 2020. *Moonscape*. Film. UK. Sheffield Doc Fest.

Forensic Architecture 2015. *The Bombing of Rafah*. Videos, Schematics, and Photographs. London. Institute of Contemporary Arts.

Kiwanga, Kapwani. 2011. *Afrogalactica*. Performance. London. Arts Catalyst.

Nahum. 2016. *Voyage: A Session for Remembering*. Performance. Liverpool. FACT.

Nahum. 2018. *The Contour of Presence*, SpaceX/ISS.

Paglen, Trevor. 2007. *The Other Night Sky*. Photographs. Washington, DC. Smithsonian America Art Museum.

Paglen, Trevor. 2012. *The Last Pictures*. Gold-plated disc housing a silicon wafer with 100 images, EchoStar XVI communications satellite. New York. Creative Time.

Paglen, Trevor. 2018. *Orbital Reflector*. Inflatable mylar balloon with reflective surface. Reno, Nevada. Nevada Museum of Art.

Peljhan, Marko. 2019. *System 317*. Installation. Italy. Slovenian Pavilion at the 58th Venice Biennale 2019.

Rezaire, Tabita. 2019. *Satellite Devotion*. Installation. London. Arebyte Gallery.

Robert, 2018. *Tavares Strachan*. Blue neon, purple neon, pyrex, transformers, MDF box. 58th Venice Biennale 2019.

Strachan, Tavares. 2010. *Orthostatic Tolerance*. Sculptural works, photographs, videos, and installations. "The Orthostatic Tolerance: Launching into Infinite Space", Grand Arts, Kansas City, MA; "Orthostatic Tolerance: It Might Not Be Such a Bad Idea if I Never Went Home", MIT List Visual Arts Center, Cambridge, MA.

Strachan, Tavares. 2018. *Enoch*. Bronze, 24k gold, sand, steel, aluminium, sacred air blessed by Shinto priest. USA. The Los Angeles County Museum of Art (LACMA).

Strachan, Tavares. 2018. *Works Related to Robert Henry Lawrence Jr*. Installation. Italy. 58th Venice Biennale 2019.

Notes

1 An ability that Dickens recognises in space fiction.
2 https://www.iafastro.org/about/iaf-committees/technical-committees/committee-for-the-cultural-utilisation-of-space-itaccus.html.
3 In a collaboration with SpaceX and the LACMA Art+Technology Lab. The satellite launched via Spaceflight's SSO-A: SmallSat Express mission from Vandenberg Air Force Base on a SpaceX Falcon 9 rocket.
4 *Space Refugee* was exhibiting in the USA when Donald Trump issued an immigration ban excluding the citizens of seven majority Muslim countries from entering the United States.
5 The nonprofit arts organisation of which I was, at the time, director and that I had founded in 1994.
6 Including Villa Arson, Nice (2012); Centre Pompidou, Paris (2013); Tate Project, Lagos (2014); documenta 14, Athens (2017); Momentum Nordic Biennial of Contemporary Art, Sweden (2017); and Illingworth Kerr Gallery, Calgary (2018).
7 The Smithsonian Afrofuturism Series is a collaboration between the National Air and Space Museum, the National Museum of African American History and Culture, and the National Museum of African Art.
8 *Republic of the Moon* initially opened at FACT Liverpool in 2011. It was re-curated for its London showing in 2014.

9 In 1973, after his expedition to the Moon, Apollo 14 astronaut Edgar Mitchell founded a New Age think tank, the Institute of Noetic Sciences, to explore crosscurrents of science and mysticism. Russell Schweickart (Apollo 9) embraced Zen Buddhism, and Jim Irwin (Apollo 15) became a born-again Christian, leaving NASA in order to launch the evangelical High Flight Foundation.
10 Including Haus der Kulturen der Welt, Berlin, 2014; documenta 14, Kassel, 2016; Barcelona Museum of Contemporary Art, 2017; Institute of Contemporary Arts, London, 2018; Whitney Biennial, New York City, 2019; and ZKM Center for Art and Media Karlsruhe, Karlsruhe, 2020.
11 *Conflict Minerals*, Arts Catalyst, London, 2017.
12 Successful launches, if not full deployment, include Trevor Paglen's *The Last Pictures* (2012) and *Orbital Reflector* (2019) and Tavares Strachan's *Enoch* (2018).

References

Aganaba, Timiebi, Elizabeth Hamilton, Chanda Prescod-Weinstein, and Danielle Wood. Discussant: André M. Carrington. 2022. *Outer Space: Projecting Histories and Futures onto the Stars*. Panel discussion at Claiming Space A Symposium on Black Futures—Past, Present, and Potential, 29 January. https://nmaahc.si.edu/events/claiming-space-symposium-black-futures-past-present-and-potential.
Bruchac, Margaret. 2014. "Indigenous Knowledge and Traditional Knowledge." In *Encyclopedia of Global Archaeology*, edited by Claire Smith, 3814–24. New York: Springer. https://doi.org/10.1007/978-1-4419-0465-2_10.
Clarke, Arthur C. 1989. "Foreword." In *Visions of Space: Artists Journey Through the Cosmos*, edited by David A. Hardy. London: Belitha Press.
Cosgrove, Denis E. 2003. *Apollo's Eye: A Cartographic Genealogy of the Earth in the Western Imagination*. Baltimore, MD: Johns Hopkins University Press.
Čufer, Eda. 2019. "War in a Mousetrap: System 317." In *Marko Peljhan: Here We Go Again… System 317: A Situation of the Resolution Series*, 33–64. Exhibition catalogue. Pavilion of the Republic of Slovenia at the 58th International Art Exhibition—La Biennale di Venezia and Moderna Galerija Ljubljana. http://www.projekt-atol.si/wp-content/uploads/2019/09/Catalogue-System-317_spreads.pdf
DeLoughrey, Elizabeth. 2014. "Satellite Planetarity and the Ends of the Earth." *Public Culture* 26 (2): 257–80. https://doi.org/10.1215/08992363-2392057.
Dery, Mark. 1994. "Black to the Future: Interviews with Samuel R. Delany, Greg Tate, and Tricia Rose." In *Flame Wars: The Discourse of Cyberculture*, edited by Mark Dery, 179–222. New York: Duke University Press. https://doi.org/10.1515/9780822396765-010.
Dickens, Peter. 2014. "Alternative Worlds in the Cosmos." In *Alternative Worlds: Blue-Sky Thinking since 1990*, edited by Ricarda Vidal and Ingo Cornils, 255–81. Oxford: Peter Lang.
Dickens, Peter, and James S. Ormrod. 2007. *Cosmic Society: Towards a Sociology of the Universe*. New York and London: Routledge.
Dillon, Grace L. 2012. *Walking the Clouds: An Anthology of Indigenous Science Fiction*. Tucson, AZ: University of Arizona Press.
Eshun, Ekow. 2021. *Dark Matter: A History of the Afrofuture*. Radio broadcast, 17 May 2021. BBC.
Eshun, Kodwo. 2018. *More Brilliant than the Sun: Adventures in Sonic Fiction*. London: Verso.
Franetovich, Alessandra. 2019. "Cosmic Thoughts: The Paradigm of Space in Moscow Conceptualism." *E-flux Journal*. Issue 99: 1–16 https://www.e-flux.com/journal/99/263593/cosmic-thoughts-the-paradigm-of-space-in-moscow-conceptualism/
Gabrys, Jenifer. 2018. "Becoming Planetary." *E-flux Architecture*. https://www.e-flux.com/architecture/accumulation/217051/becoming-planetary/.
Gorman, Alice. 2020. "Can the Moon Be a Person? As Lunar Mining Looms, a Change of Perspective Could Protect Earth's Ancient Companion." *The Conversation*, 27 August. https://theconversation.com/can-the-moon-be-a-person-as-lunar-mining-looms-a-change-of-perspective-could-protect-earths-ancient-companion-144848.
Hawkins, Harriet. 2021. *Geography, Art, Research: Artistic Research in the Geohumanities*. Abingdon, Oxon: Routledge.
Hokowhitu, Brendan. 2021. "Indigenous Materialisms and *Disciplinary Colonialism*." *Somatechnics* 11 (2): 157–73. https://doi.org/10.3366/soma.2021.0349.
Hughes, Rolf, Rachel Armstrong, Peter Peters, Peter De Graeve, and Veerle Van der Sluys. 2021. "The Postresearch Condition: Five EARN Working Groups." In *The Postresearch Condition*, edited by Henk Slager, 27–42. Utrecht: Metropolis M Books.

Kosmica. n.d. *Kosmica—About Us.* Accessed 20 January 2022 at https://www.kosmicainstitute.com/about-us/.

Leonard, Nicholas. 2020. "The Arts and New Materialism: A Call to Stewardship through Mercy, Grace, and Hope." *Humanities* 9 (3): 84. https://doi.org/10.3390/h9030084.

Mitchell, A., S. Wright, S. Suchet-Pearson, K. Lloyd, L. Burarrwanga, R. Ganambarr, M. Ganambarr-Stubbs, B. Ganambarr, D. Maymuru, and R. Maymuru. 2020. "Dukarr Lakarama: Listening to Guwak, Talking Back to Space Colonization." *Political Geography* 81 (August): 102218. https://doi.org/10.1016/j.polgeo.2020.102218.

Nahum. 2019. "Outer Space on Earth." Interview by Nina Kruschwitz. *Journal of Beautiful Business*, 27 May. https://journalofbeautifulbusiness.com/q-a-nahum-71fde537cfd8.

NASA n.d. *Space Colonization.* Accessed 22 January 2022 at https://www.nasa.gov/centers/hq/library/find/bibliographies/space_colonization.

Nathan, Emily. 2016. "Up and Coming: Armory Artist Kapwani Kiwanga Explores the Social and Political Economy of Gift-Giving." *Artsy*, 24 February. https://www.artsy.net/article/artsy-editorial-up-and-coming-meet-kapwani-kiwanga-the-emerging-artist-challenging-what-you-learned-in-history-class.

Neilson, Hilding, and E. E. Ćirković. 2021. "Indigenous Rights, Peoples, and Space Exploration: A Response to the Canadian Space Agency (CSA) Consulting Canadians on a Framework for Future Space Exploration Activities." *ArXiv:2104.07118 [Astro-Ph, Physics:physics]*, April. https://doi.org/10.48550/arXiv.2104.07118.

Paglen, Trevor. 2018. "Trevor Paglen Responds to Astronomers Who Criticize Space-Based Art—and Has a Few Pointed Questions for Them, Too." Interview by Sarah Cascone. *Artnet*, 23 August. https://news.artnet.com/art-world/trevor-paglen-responds-to-angry-astronomers-1337462.

Pendle, George. 2016. "Space Art Propelled Scientific Exploration of the Cosmos—But Its Star is Fading Fast." *Atlas Obscura*, 20 September 2016. https://www.atlasobscura.com/articles/space-art-propelled-scientific-exploration-of-the-cosmosbut-its-star-is-fading-fast.

Rezaire, Tabita. 2019. "Tabita Rezaire—Waning Moon from Moon Meditation Series as Part of the Satellite Devotion Exhibition at Arebyte Gallery 2019." *Vimeo*, 11 June 2020. https://vimeo.com/428103433.

Rosiek, Jerry Lee, Jimmy Snyder, and Scott L. Pratt. 2019. "The New Materialisms and Indigenous Theories of Non-human Agency: Making the Case for Respectful Anti-colonial Engagement." *Qualitative Inquiry* 26 (3–4): 331–46. https://doi.org/10.1177/1077800419830135.

Rothe, Delf, and David Shim. 2018. "Sensing the Ground: On the Global Politics of Satellite-Based Activism." *Review of International Studies* 44: 414–37. https://doi.org/10.1017/s0260210517000602.

Sachs, Wolfgang. 1999. *Planet Dialectics: Explorations in Environment and Development.* London: Zed Books.

Science Museum n.d. *Cosmonauts: Birth of the Space Age.* Accessed 28 January 2022. https://artsandculture.google.com/story/wQXhbpPvWOZ3JQ.

Smiles, Deondre. 2020. "The Settler Logics of (Outer) Space." *Society+Space*, October 2020. https://www.societyandspace.org/articles/the-settler-logics-of-outer-space

Spigel, Lynn. 2001. *Welcome to the Dreamhouse: Popular Media and Postwar Suburbs.* Durham, NC: Duke University Press.

Spivak, Gayatri Chakravorty. 2003. *Death of a Discipline.* New York: Columbia University Press.

Strachan, Tavares. 2020. "Tavares Strachan: 'I Grew up Not Feeling Empowered by Art.'" Interview by Louisa Buck. *The Art Newspaper*, 8 September. https://www.theartnewspaper.com/2020/09/08/tavares-strachan-i-grew-up-not-feeling-empowered-by-art.

Suleiman, Lama. 2016. "Afrofuturism and Arabfuturism: Reflections of a Present-Day Diasporic Reader." *Tohu Magazine*, 12 June. http://tohumagazine.com/article/afrofuturism-and-arabfuturism-reflections-present-day-diasporic-reader.

Syms, Martine. 2017. "The Mundane Afrofuturist Manifesto." *The Third Rail* 3. http://thirdrailquarterly.org/martine-syms-the-mundane-afrofuturist-manifesto/.

Tavares, Frank, Denise Buckner, Dana Burton, Jordan McKaig, Parvathy Prem, Eleni Ravanis, and Natalie Treviño, et al. 2020. "Ethical Exploration and the Role of Planetary Protection in Disrupting Colonial Practices." *ArXiv:2010.08344 [Astro-Ph]*, 27 October 2020 revision. https://doi.org/10.48550/arXiv.2010.08344.

Treviño, Natalie B. 2020. *The Cosmos Is Not Finished.* PhD Dissertation, The University of Western Ontario.

Triscott, Nicola, 2016. "Transmissions from the Noosphere: Contemporary Art and Outer Space." In *The Palgrave Handbook of Society, Culture and Outer Space*, edited by James Ormrod and Peter Dickens, 414–44. London: Palgrave Macmillan.

Triscott, Nicola. 2017. *Art and Intervention in the Stewardship of the Planetary Commons: Towards a Curatorial Model of Co-Inquiry.* PhD Dissertation, University of Westminster.

Venkatesan, Aparna, James Lowenthal, Parvathy Prem, and Monica Vidaurri. 2020. "The Impact of Satellite Constellations on Space as an Ancestral Global Commons." *Nature Astronomy* 4 (11): 1043–48. https://doi.org/10.1038/s41550-020-01238-3.

Walkowicz, Lucianne. 2018. "We Need to Change the Way We Talk about Space Exploration." Interview by Nadia Drake. *National Geographic*, November 2018. https://www.nationalgeographic.com/science/article/we-need-to-change-way-we-talk-about-space-exploration-mars.

Young, M. Jane. 1987. "'Pity the Indians of Outer Space': Native American Views of the Space Program." *Western Folklore* 46 (4): 269–79. https://doi.org/10.2307/1499889.

PART II

Intersections and Interventions

11
AS ABOVE, SO BELOW
Space and Race in the Space Race[1]

Rasheedah Phillips

Black Quantum Futurism (BQF) is a new approach to living and experiencing reality by way of the manipulation of space-time in order to see into possible futures, and/or collapse space-time into a desired future in order to bring about that future's reality. This vision and practice derive its facets, tenets, and qualities from quantum physics and Black and Afrodiasporian conceptions of reality, time, and space. Under a BQF intersectional time orientation, the past and future are not cut off from the present—both dimensions have influence over the whole of our lives, who we are, and who we become at any particular point in space-time. Through various interdisciplinary writing, music, performance, film, visual art, and creative research projects, we also explore personal, cultural, familial, and communal cycles of experience, and solutions for transforming negative cycles into positive ones using artistic and wholistic methods of healing. Our work focuses on recovery, collection, and preservation of communal memories, histories, and stories.

As long-time residents of the area, we often focus on North Philadelphia as an active site of Black futurist liberation that has forged and sustained its own temporality in the midst of hostile visions of the futures of the low-income and marginalised Black communities concentrated within its boundaries. In a 2019 BQF exhibition called *All Time is Local* we consider time's intimate relationship to space and locality through a text, object, and video installation. Including select pieces from our *Dismantling the Master's Clock*, *Temporal Disruptors*, and *Black Space Agency* series, the works meditate on the complex, contested temporal and spatial legacies of historical, liberatory Black futurist projects based primarily in North Philly. Some of these projects, like Progress Aerospace Enterprises, have been all but forgotten, while others still survive and thrive, such as Progress Plaza, Berean Church, and Zion Gardens. Others still, like Berean Institute, have monuments at the sites where they once stood, while other monuments and murals commemorating these legacies have been covered or removed by luxury and student housing. In spite of the status of the physical remnants of many of these Black futurist projects, their implications stretch backward and forward in the Afrofuturist timescapes undergirding North Philly. It is a temporality that challenges exclusionary narratives of North Philly painting the residents in the area as complicit in their own poverty and disinvestment, and thus deserving of a gentrification that will wipe out the past and move the community into the future of the government's visions. BQF works to recover and amplify the historical memory of these autonomous Black communal space-times embedded in North Philly.

One of the Black futurist projects we explore is Progress Aerospace Enterprises (PAE). Based in North Philadelphia during the 1960s, Reverend Leon H. Sullivan, a civil rights leader and minister at Philadelphia's Zion Baptist Church, established PAE days after the death of Martin

Luther King Jr. PAE was one of the first Black-owned aerospace companies in the world. With the Moon landing being seen as one of the ultimate milestones of progress of western society and a quintessential symbol of humankind's arrival into "the future", Sullivan stated in an interview that "when the first landing on the Moon came, I wanted something there that a black man had made". PAE had strong connections to the civil rights and Black liberation movements, affordable housing, economic stability, the April 1968 passage of the Fair Housing Act, and the space race. Sullivan also founded the Zion Gardens Apartments affordable housing project with members of his church, purchasing the building from the owner after learning that Black applicants had been denied housing there based on their race. He also organised boycotts, workers' strikes, and community police boards. With members of his church, he founded Progress Plaza (the first Black-owned supermarket plaza that still exists today), Progress Garment Factory, Opportunities Industrialization Center, Inc., Zion Investment Association, and other innovative organisations and programmes around the country and world. Throughout all of his organisations and at PAE in particular, Rev. Sullivan emphasised hiring of women and young, unskilled labourers and provided them with training opportunities and jobs in engineering and building parts for NASA and, controversially, weapons for war.

Although Rev. Sullivan was a controversial figure, critiqued by anti-capitalists and more radical Black liberation movements in Philadelphia as being respectable and pro-cop, his futurist vision of progress in the Progress Movement was nonetheless inclusive and innovative for its time. His co-opting of the "progress" narrative and usage of the "future" in slogans were specific forms of temporal reclamation. As Helga Nowotny notes, "temporal control is symbolized by the idea of progress, of economic boom" (1996: 23). Sullivan seemed to grasp the close associations between temporal control, sustainable Black communities existing within the American imperialist project, and the notion of linear progress well. The technology built at PAE and through other Rev. Sullivan projects allowed for a hacking into future histories where Black people had already been largely erased—such as in the space race—and helped to ensure our appearances in those histories as they play out on the linear, progressive timeline. Or, as Kodwo Eshun puts it, "chronopolitically speaking, these revisionist historicities may be understood as a series of powerful competing futures that infiltrate the present at different rates" (2003: 297).

During that decade, the civil rights and Black liberation movements and space race would collide, with a lot of resistance to the space race from the Black community, such as the Poor People's March at Cape Canaveral. Black leaders across wide and varying political stances from Martin Luther King Jr. to Eldridge Cleaver commented on the race to land on the Moon, juxtaposed to the neocolonialism and urban renewal causing displacement of entire Black communities. In a 1966 speech, Dr. King remarked that "there is a striking absurdity in committing billions to reach the Moon where no people live ... while the densely populated slums are allocated miniscule appropriations", and ended his speech questioning "on what scale of values is this a program of progress?" MLK could not determine a sense of progress where Black people had not yet achieved racial justice and social equity. Reflecting on the archives of Black newspapers and magazines like *Jet* and *Ebony*, and even national news publications, reveals widespread critiques of the lack of diversity in NASA employees, and the destruction and displacement of Black communities in order to build subsidised housing for NASA employees. Partly in response to such critiques, NASA created programmes that designed and utilised spaceship materials in "urban" housing, as well as campaigns to increase diversity in hiring.

Meanwhile, destruction, segregation, and displacement of Black communities across the United States (the space race on the ground) led to riots and uprisings around the country during the 1960s, including North Philly. Columbia Avenue, now known as Cecil B. Moore Avenue after the late Philadelphia civil rights attorney and activist, was the site of race riots and uprisings in 1964 that destroyed a once vibrant, multiethnic community with a strong economic base—the reverberations of which continue to echo throughout that communitydecades later. In the present day, gentrification, racialised segregation, and targeted disinvestment have disrupted the landscape, vibrancy, and texture of the neighbourhood, forcing its memories and residents to the edges of the city.

Housing and cultural displacement are usually framed in terms of spatial inequality and displacement or erasure from location. However, hierarchies of time, inequitable time distribution, and uneven access to safe and healthy futures inform intergenerational poverty in marginalised communities in some of the same ways that monetary wealth passes between generations in privileged communities. Sociologist Jeremy Rifkin says that "temporal deprivation is built into the time frame of every society", where people living in poverty are "temporally poor as well as materially poor" (1989: 192). Inevitably, marginalised Black communities are disproportionately impacted by both material, spatial, and temporal inequalities in a linear progressive society. The implications of time and of space in gentrification, displacement, and redevelopment are integrated into the pre-established temporal dynamics of the impacted community, layered over and within the communal historical memory and the shared idea of the future(s) of that community. Nested within those layers are individual, subjective temporalities and the lived realities of the residents, often at odds with the linear, mechanical model of time on which their external spatial-temporal constructs are etched.

But as Giordano Nanni points out, "time has long played a role as one of the channels through which defiance towards established order can be manifested" (2015). By exploiting those temporal tensions, there are several opportunities to develop practical strategies for achieving Black temporal autonomy and spatial agency. Some of these strategies include unearthing afro/retrofuturist technologies and quantum time capsules buried by our forebears.

Note

1 Editors' note: This text first emerged in the context of Black Quantum Futurism's art exhibition and community programming Black Space Agency in April 2018 at Icebox Project Space, Philadelphia, which was "inspired by the legacy of the Fair Housing Act, Civil Rights and Black Liberation movements, and the space race in North Philadelphia during the 1960s". Black Space Agency addressed issues of affordable and fair housing, displacement/space/land grabs, redlining, eminent domain, and gentrification through the lens of afrofuturism, oral histories/futures, and Black spatial-temporal autonomy and featured five community-based events and artworks by Betty Leacraft, Black Quantum Futurism, Bryan O. Green, and Sammus. The text was also republished in *Maarav* on 2 June 2020, http://maarav.org.il/english/2020/06/02/space-race-space-race-black-quantum-futurism-rasheedah-phillips-camae-ayewa/. *Maarav* is an online art and culture magazine established in 2004. Sections of this reprint also appeared in Rasheedah Phillips, "The Nowness of Black Chronopolitical Imaginaries in the Afro/Retrofuture" (2019), in *The Funambulist*, https://thefunambulist.net/magazine/24-futurisms/nowness-black-chronopolitical-imaginaries-afro-retrofuture-rasheedah-phillips.

References

Eshun, Kodwo. 2003. "Further Considerations on Afrofuturism." *CR: The New Centennial Review* 3 (2): 287–302. https://doi.org/10.1353/ncr.2003.0021.
Nanni, Giordano. 2015. *The Colonisation of Time: Ritual, Routine, and Resistance in the British Empire*. Studies in Imperialism. Manchester: Manchester University Press.
Nowotny, Helga. 1996. *Time: The Modern and Postmodern Experience*. Cambridge: Polity.
Rifkin, Jeremy. 1989. *Time Wars: The Primary Conflict in Human History*. New York City: Touchstone Books.

12
A CHRONOPOLITICS OF OUTER SPACE
A Poetics of Tomorrowing

Juan Francisco Salazar

Introduction

Something significantly striking across the diverse interdisciplinary work in social and cultural research on outer space is how scant attention has been paid to the pervasive narrative of space as temporal frontier. The construction of outer space as a site of sociality also relies on, and indeed reinforces, the universalising hegemonic temporality of colonialism and capitalism. As a new space age takes shape in the 2020s it is crucial to interrogate the ways in which space futures continue to be normalised through technoutopian social imaginaries, to ask what institutional conditions, creative practices, and political interventions might craft different openings of outer space futures. The intention here is not to impose a dualism between spatiality and temporality. On the contrary, it is to highlight the relational onto-epistemics of time-space—the chrono-topos. Drawing on the work on 'chronopolitics' developed by Kodwo Eshun (2003) and Rasheedah Phillips (2019). I discuss the politics of time in—and politicised futures of—outer space. The notion of critical chronopolitics is not posed as an alternative to critical geopolitics but acknowledges both as already at work within each other.

A primary aim in this chapter is to critically analyse the social imaginaries of outer space in NewSpace narratives, not only as topos but also as chronos of production of capitalist value. I depart from Bakhtin's concept of the chronotope, which captures the narrative construction of social imaginaries of the world and reveals their connection to everyday practices and economic relations, but reifies the figure of the human at the centre of its epistemology (Valentine 2017). This leads to the second aim, which is to draw from, and think with, varied spheres of Black and Indigenous futurisms and diverse forms of space feminisms and queer radical futurisms, to stress and embrace projects that evoke a more interwoven anticolonial and emancipatory account of space-time and space futures. Taken together, the purpose is to foment a discussion between disparate knowledge traditions, drawing on Helen Verran, as a way of "doing difference generatively" (2013: 141).[1]

This chapter is divided into four parts. In the first part, I describe the expediency of the notion of futurity as method and epistemic framework. It is then followed by two sections where I look at differing futuring strategies of outer space, from hegemonic and co-opted forms of 'commoning' space futures to radical forms of contesting and 'uncommoning' these futures. In the first of these sections, the 2022 International Astronautical Congress serves as a case study of sorts, to illustrate how hegemonic sociotechnical imaginaries at play, in the largest space event held every year since 1951, enacts a neoliberal mode of commoning outer space.[2] The focus of analysis is on the influence that NewSpace narratives and imaginaries have had in recent years and draws on recent perspectives that critique these technoutopian narratives, particularly in terms of how they impose colonial linear temporalities. As Craig Henry Jones (2021) observes, the "New Space Economy" seeks to legitimise extractivist efforts "not only through the physical and legislative enclosure of Outer Space but [also] through the enclosure of imaginative spaces ... through process(es) of disimagination" (n.p.). This chapter continues with an engagement with a diversity of radical futurisms that are crafting diverse ways of futures-making. have termed *ways of futures-making*, by re-storying and counterimagining outer space. Reading athwart Indigenous, Black, and feminist scholarship and practice, I discuss how these approaches highlight the ways capital and race mediate the temporalities of outer space. In doing so the aim is to raise questions about the urgency of disrupting, interfering with, and ultimately uncommoning technoutopian imaginaries of capital expansion. This chapter concludes with a general discussion on the chronopolitics of space futures.

Futurity as Method

Helga Nowotny once wrote that "everyone is a practitian and theoretician of time" (1994: 6). But within that 'everyone', time is practised and theorised in radically different ways. Kodwo Eshun (2003) has stressed how "inquiry into production of futures becomes fundamental, rather than trivial" as "capital continues to function through the dissimulation of the imperial archive, as it has done throughout the last century" (p. 289). Rasheedah Phillips (2019, 2020, 2021) has produced notable work on how the concept of time has been weaponized, and specifically, how while the "settler colonial project is often referred to as one that successfully colonized space, it also necessarily involved a conquering of the temporal domain of the future" (Phillips 2021). The seminal work of Alondra Nelson (2000) has been most influential in tackling mainstream hegemonic conceptions of a raceless future, with Afrofuturism exploiting culturally distinct approaches to technology and digital worlds. For Rasheedah Phillips, "Afrofuturist methodologies provide weapons for disrupting the messages that Black people won't survive into and thrive in the future(s)" (2020: 48). From a different perspective, Manu Karuka notes how "the future of the corporation presupposes the future of the colonial state, and the law of the corporation colonizes the future" (2019: 153). In part, this colonisation of the future is not only spatial. Phillips notes how thinking or talking about the future "involves a spatialization of time", a process of "space-time mapping" where the future is preconceived spatially—near or far, but always in front. Phillips puts it starkly:

> Rarely do we take account of where the future is, who has access to it, its plurality, and whether we are all accelerating at the same rate and pace into that future. We seldom think about how gender, race, and income shifts or limits access to the future and even the past.
>
> *(2020: 10)*

For Elizabeth Grosz, temporality and futurity are "modalities of difference" (1998: 38). Or perhaps, drawing on Isabelle Stengers's work, they could be thought as modalities of divergence. Mario Blaser and Marisol de la Cadena explain Stengers's notion of divergence in this way: it

> Does not refer to difference between people, practices, or cultures conceived as discrete entities that share constitutive properties and therefore can be compared (and thus be similar or different). Rather, divergence constitutes the entities (or practices) as they emerge both in their specificity and with other entities or practices.
>
> *(Blaser and de la Cadena 2018: 9)*

These ideas above, in one way or another, relate to the politics of time, or chronopolitics, as I discuss later in this chapter. They point to how space futures in this case are constituted through difference and divergence, where practices of spacemaking emerge both in their specificity and with other entities or practices. In academic and creative work undertaken in Antarctica over a decade (Salazar 2015, 2017a, 2017b, 2017c) I developed an interest in what I called 'a poetics of tomorrowing' (2017a), to refer to creative experimentations using futurity as an epistemic framework. The meaning here is derived from *poiesis*, the practices of making or bringing things into being—in this case of bringing tomorrows into being.[3] But these tomorrows are not immutably fixed before us. They are not only the not-as-yet but also point to a conception of time as spiralling and in motion. The impulse across this body of work was to use futurity as a method for researching Antarctic imaginaries and narratives, but also, to deconstruct and destabilise the heteronormative and colonial fantasies that plague the history of human engagement with the icy continent, and to open up the discussion of the cosmopolitics of humans making themselves at home in extreme environments. This was carried forward especially through the film *Nightfall on Gaia* (Salazar 2015), a speculative feature-length documentary film made over four years returning each summer to undertake fieldwork in the Antarctic Peninsula. Drawing from feminist speculative fiction and Indigenous futurisms, the film depicts the relational conditions of life in extreme environments, while simultaneously using the device of a fictional character in the future (that of Māori astrobiologist Xuê Noon) as a diffractive approach, to invite audiences to recognise nontangible and yet-to-be worlds that are nevertheless always immanent to the present and ingrained with the past (Figure 12.1).

Mobilising futurity as method entails taking a processual approach, one that is inexorably tentative, diffractive, and fluid. In using futurity as method to discuss the chronopolitics of outer space, the intent is to avoid the prescriptive archetype of fully imagined futures in space that is so prevalent in technoutopian imaginaries (Tutton 2018, 2021). Kodwo Eshun (2003) has observed how control in the early twenty-first century has come to be performed through prediction, where power "operates predictively as much as retrospectively … [and] functions through the envisioning, management, and delivery of reliable futures" (p. 289). As unpacked in more detail later in the chapter, NewSpace, the term coined around 2006 by US-based Space Frontier Foundation advocate Rick Tumlinson (Berinstein 2002), imposes a distinctive colonial chronopolitics that operates as an accepted designation of the new types of space exploration projects. NewSpace inexorably builds a narrative where the category of the future is rendered invisible and is replaced by an extended present.

Figure 12.1 Video still from the film *Nightfall on Gaia*, (2015) directed by Juan Francisco Salazar, with the character of astrobiologist Xûe noon played by performance artist Victoria Hunt. Image by Juan Francisco Salazar, 2014.

Against the Commoning Temporalities of NewSpace

The International Astronautical Federation (IAF) was established in 1951, several years before the International Geophysical Year of 1957–1958 and the launch of the Sputnik satellite by the Soviet Union in 1957. Anticipating the space age yet to come, the first International Astronautical Congress (IAC) was hosted in Paris in the same year. Seven decades on, in September 2022, the 73rd IAC returned to Paris, this time with the motto "Space for @ll". The event had over 9000 delegates from 130 countries and attracted 250 exhibitors from a range of governments, space companies, and venture-capital start-ups. Heads of the most important space agencies were present, including NASA, ESA, JAXA, and CSA, but with the notable exceptions of Roscosmos and the China National Space Administration (CNSA). Hosted by the IAF together with the Centre national d'études spatiales (CNES), the motto captures well the intention of the contemporary global space sector:

> We will be reaching beyond the space community to bring together all communities along with the burgeoning global ecosystem of start-ups, entrepreneurs, laboratories, research scientists and manufacturers likely to get involved in space activities or benefit from them. We will offer great opportunities for networking and forging contacts and potential partnerships.
> *(IAC Prospectus 2022: 3)*

The first thing to note here is both the use of the term 'space community' and the motto 'Space for @ll'. In speaking univocally about space futures at the opening plenary forum, also titled "Space for All", the interventions by the participating national heads of agencies confirmed that space is constructed as an inherently optimistic and future-oriented set of activities that entail precise tactics, technologies, and institutions for anticipating futures, for preparing in advance, and for organising the present according to the logics of NewSpace. At IAC 2022, the silence about both the Covid-19 pandemic and the climate emergency was deafening. Framing outer space was not only performed by what Daniel Sage (2008) called the popular geopolitics of American manifest destiny in outer space. At play here is a new chronopolitics of a *global* manifest destiny in outer space and not only the cosmology of profit and the exit narratives that David Valentine (2012) has described. We hear from the heads of the space agencies about how "we" are "returning to the Moon to stay" and that "space delivers the living standards 'we' have", and how one-third of the European economy depends on weather forecasts and 95% of weather forecasting is performed by satellites. At the IAC the hegemonic temporalities of NewSpace are projected on 8K-resolution screens across massive rooms redolent of buoyant optimism as well as across hundreds of exhibition booths, all chasing business opportunities in space, and where handshakes abound as multi-million-dollar contracts are discussed. David Valentine (2012) observed in his genealogy of NewSpace how

> Despite the industry's diversity, they are united by a common—and apparently extreme—vision of the future and of capitalism: that entrepreneurial activity will radically and positively transform the future evolution of society and of our species itself by establishing human settlements in the solar system and beyond.
> *(p. 1047)*

At IAC 2022, government and industry actors' perceptions of the future in space are steeped in relations of power and are interwoven with the hegemonic ideologies of NewSpace. NewSpace operates under a 'commoning framework'. In the global space sector, what is termed the 'democratisation' of space has allowed for the entry of private actors, the proliferation of extractivist ambitions that range from Moon and asteroid mining to space data mining, and a technocapitalist vision of perpetual and unlimited innovation and growth under the umbrella of space for all, and space as commons.[4] Anishinaabeg scholar and activist Leanne Simpson describes clearly the link between assimilation and extractivism when she says that in the 'extraction-assimilation system' "the act of extraction removes all of the relationships that give whatever is being extracted meaning" (quoted in Klein 2013). Frédérique Aït-Touati has described in extensive detail how modern science became gradually defined in the seventeenth century according to the narrative scheme of exploration, invention, and discovery. She traces the motto "Plus Ultra: Always Further", said to have been originally coined by Emperor Charles V, and which Francis Bacon gave to modern science as a programmatic wayfinding maxim. Today it illustrates how contemporary scientific imaginaries of space exploration, discovery, and exploration are still imbued in narratives of conquest and appropriation where "progress, arrow of time and conquest of new territories go hand in hand" (Aït-Touati 2019: 7). As Audra Mitchell observes, the visions outlined by NewSpace entrepreneurs to colonise outer space have important implications for human security and will likely have profound impacts in terms of gender, race, the vulnerability of migrants and workers, and the rights of Indigenous peoples (Mitchell 2018).

The motto "Space for @ll" is the early twenty-first century's version of the "Plus Ultra" of the seventeenth century, carrying the same narrative of enclosing the global commons of outer space (Squire, Mould, and Adey 2021; Jones 2021). At play at IAC 2022 was a twenty-first-century version of Marshall McLuhan's "global village" projected onto the expanse of outer space, "narrated as a global-collective experience for all of humanity with an identifiable beginning, common horizon, and shared fate" (Amoureux and Reddy 2021: 929) and, as mentioned earlier, buoyed by what Alondra Nelson calls a "raceless future paradigm" (2002: 1) akin to the mode in which the digital revolution of the 1990s was promoted, and akin to what Manu Karuka argues regarding outer-space investors who imagine "financial accumulation as autonomous from labor, whiteness as autonomous from blackness and indigeneity" (2019: 150).

"Geopolitics has its ideological foundations in chronopolitics", wrote Johannes Fabian in *Time and the Other* (Fabian 1983: 156). This technoimaginary of space ages has created an "allochronic distancing" effect (p. 156) against other, older, vibrant imaginaries and stories of outer space, while reinscribing onto the world what Faye Ginsburg, drawing on Fabian, calls an "'allochronic chronopolitics' … in which 'the other' exists in a time not contemporary with our own" (Ginsburg 2008: 300). Swarm, accelerate, boost, unlock, infinite, persevere, adventure, quest, mission, and agile. These most repeated words in presentations, booths, advertisements, and events at the IAC demonstrate the unambiguous aspirations of a global space sector: visions of an endless common frontier of progressive scientific and technological development. Valerie Olson has shown how dominant outer-space imaginaries in the US are enacted by highlighting limits and extremes, where space itself denotes "not a spatial limit but a political horizon" (2018: 28).

NewSpace displays a pervasive commoning of outer space as 'space for all', as a tabula rasa for resource extraction, as a solution to earthly woes, and for endless scientific discovery for the benefit of all humankind. As I develop in more detail in the next sections and thinking with Blaser and de la Cadena's work on uncommoning the commons, it is imperative to uncommon the imaginaries and practices depicting outer space as a "common good" which ends up being appropriated by corporations, or the state, in pursuit of national the "common good". Blaser and de la Cadena (2017) propose that we "think of uncommons as constitutive of the commons, and that 'uncommoning' might be crucial for giving shape to solid commons" (p. 185). As Laura Bear (2016) has argued, the techniques of time in capitalist modernity are a source of accumulation and spatiotemporal inequality that reduces time to a mere tool to create and increase capital. The call for uncommoning outer space is also a call for uncommoning temporalities, for uncommoning futures. David Valentine and Amelia Hassoun (2019) remind us of the perils of the excesses of neoliberal capitalism and the ways they pervade contemporary attempts at theorising futurity.

Developing an anthropological theorisation of futures, they call for temporal multiplicities and collective future imagining—temporal pluralisation, or an opening up of futures. In earlier work, Valentine (2012) argues that beyond the possibilities for new forms of capital investment and profit enabled by commercial space enterprise, it is this promise of a radically transformed human social future that underwrites NewSpace discourses and activities (p. 1049).

NewSpace creates a 'temporal disjunction'. As a technology of imagination, it is an instance of time that has been "colonised, racialised and economised" (Phillips 2020). As this futural mode aims to create space futures in the present it has been incredibly pervasive in imposing certain imaginaries of the future over others. Eshun notes how in the first half of the twentieth century, "avant-gardists from Walter Benjamin to Frantz Fanon revolted in the name of the future against a power structure that relied on control and representation of the historical archive" (2003: 289). For Eshun, today we observe a reversal, where it is the structures of power that employ futurists to "draw power from the futures they endorse, thereby condemning the disempowered to live in the past. The present moment is stretching, slipping for some into yesterday, reaching for others into tomorrow" (p. 289). For Laura Bear, "to create new times would require a combination of critical analysis, attritional activism, and embodied assertions that the future can be different— now" (2016: 497). As Yusoff (2019) observes, "imaginaries of temporality produce racial subsidies alongside a conception of the earth" (p. 7)—and by extension conceptions of the off-Earth. This suggests that attending to the possible ways in which diverse futurisms provide a vantage point for refiguring the assumed subject of the social studies of outer space entails attending to the overlapping spatial and temporal logics of this subject. Black Quantum Futurism (BQF), most notably, through a number of generative projects and critical writings, has argued how "an ontological framework and alternative theory of temporal-spatial consciousness can facilitate and make possible Black temporal agency, temporal and spatial reparations, and spatial liberation" (Time Zone Protocols n.d.). This work brings to the fore the imposition of colonial and Western temporal regimes that mobilise Eurocentrism as chronocentrism. For Michel Serres, "time can be schematized by a kind of crumpling, a multiple, foldable diversity" (Serres and Latour 1995: 59) where different timescapes coexist and where "we are always simultaneously making gestures that are archaic, modern, and futuristic" (p. 60). NewSpace imaginaries negate not only the pluriversal but also the polychronic nature of outer space. As Serres argued, "every historical era is likewise multitemporal, simultaneously drawing from the obsolete, the contemporary, and the futuristic. An object, a circumstance, is thus polychromic, multitemporal, and reveals a time that is gathered together, with multiple pleats" (p. 60).

In the lecture-performance project INSIDE by Frédérique Aït-Touati and Bruno Latour (2018; see this volume), Latour takes aim on stage at the image of the 'blue marble' taken from orbit in 1972 by the crew of Apollo 17. Latour reflects on it with regard to NASA's drive to escape our terrestrial "inside" and to a rejection of the nefarious effects of globalisation as a dominant image of the West's ravenousness for totality, abstraction, and global domination. Latour had this in mind when writing many years earlier that "what is at stake is precisely what is *common* in the common world to be built" (2004: 455, emphasis in original). Latour insisted: "A common world is not something we come to recognize, as though it had always been here (and we had not until now noticed it)" (p. 455). Think for a moment about the recognition of outer space as a global commons for humankind as reflected in the 1967 Outer Space Treaty. "A common world, if there is going to be one", warns Latour, "is something we will have to build, tooth and nail, together" (p. 455).

Uncommoning Outer Space: Or, a Commons through Divergent Futurisms

In 1909, on the front page of the French newspaper *Le Figaro*, Filippo Tommaso Marinetti published his Futurist Manifesto. In one passage Marinetti calls for the destruction "of museums, libraries, and academies of every sort, and for fighting against moralism, feminism, and every form of utilitarian or opportunistic cowardice" (Marinetti 1909: 51 in Doutreligne 2020: 39). A few years later he developed his ideas further, writing: "We male Futurists have felt ourselves abruptly detached from women, who have suddenly become too earthly or, better yet, have become a mere symbol of the Earth that we ought to abandon" (Marinetti 1915: 89 quoted in Doutreligne 2020: 40). It is striking to see the similitude between the desire for detachment from women who 'have suddenly become too earthly' and a mere symbol of the Earth to be abandoned, and the contemporary practices of SpaceX, Blue Origin, and Virgin Galactic, which are also framed around exit strategies and visions of abandonment for certain humans to become a multiplanetary species and finally detach themselves from those peoples who remain too earthly. It is also interesting to counterpose Marinetti's declaration from a hundred years ago against calls to provincialise outer space (Redfield 2002) and to come back down to Earth (Latour 2018) to learn how to live with (or stay with) the wreckage produced by centuries of capitalism and continuing colonialism on Earth.

Sophie Doutreligne has traced the work of female Futurist and Dadaist artists including Valentine de Saint-Point, Mina Loy, Giannina Censi, Sophie Taeuber, and Emmy Hennings, whose work and lives countered the misogyny within the historical European avant-gardes in which they practiced their art. Doutreligne also shows how Marinetti's controversial ideas spread quickly among avant-gardists while the work of several female artists was suppressed, appropriated, and erased. A few years after Marinetti's glorification of war and scorning of women, Mina Loy published *Aphorisms on Futurism* (1914) and Valentine de Saint-Point wrote and performed publicly her militant *Manifesto of the Futurist Woman* (1912) as a direct attack on Marinetti's misogynist statements and defending women's equality.

Space feminisms (Boucher 2022) draw from feminist speculative fiction and feminist technoscience to develop an ethical-political attitude in approaching feminist experiments in imagining outer space otherwise (Olufemi 2021). Rather than drawing from literature or social studies of science and technology, the notion of space feminisms emerges as more closely aligned to art-science practices. In this sense, it carries on the struggles of European feminist futurists a century ago. Space feminisms is a generative trope across several related "cluster concepts" (Scott 2021: 147) which might also relate to queer futurisms, trans temporalities, and perspectives calling for the future to be a site of resistance. All of these, Scott argues, have their own "aesthetic potency and political efficacy" (p. 154), of course, but come together around the tensioning of the notion of the future as a crucial position of inquiry. Michael P. Oman-Reagan, for instance, asserts that "queerness has been discussed and debated in terms of the concept of 'no future'. When thinking about outer space, this could mean the freedom to disrupt normative futures—to remix, twist, adjust, tear, collage and *queer* the future" (2017: 15, emphasis in original). Trans-temporality (Fisher, Phillips, and Katri 2017: 1) also acquires political efficacy as trans-specific narratives shape alternative, intersectional, and multidisciplinary theorisations of time, and by extension, of outer space. As Elizabeth Freeman has argued, the critique of temporality is crucial to queer politics, where temporal and sexual dissonance are intertwined and chrononormativity is deployed as a hegemonic use of time in the organisation of individual human bodies for maximum productivity. Or as she puts it: "'Chrononormativity' describes the process by which subjects are interpellated into temporalities of development and production naturalized through heterosexual discourses of genealogy and progress" (2010: 3).[5]

A plethora of critical ideas, practices, and political interventions for 'uncommoning' space futures have been galvanising over the past few decades through a number of polychronic tropes and practices of radical futurisms that have emerged and re-emerged with a pledge to "decolonise the not-yet", as T. J. Demos (2021) puts it. Lynch and Gunkel (2019) speak about the "currency of a black visioning of a future that is political and cultural, and proposes practices, identities, and a way of being in the world" where despite the fact that "some of these outcroppings have become branded and sold back to us through the capitalist system, a radical strain of black fictions, visions, and imaginings surface and retain collective resonance" (p. 24), mostly through a focus on posing a deep political-ecological concern with speculative visions of times past and times to come using alternative modes of science fiction.

With this framework in hand, I briefly signal towards the counterfuturing chronopolitics of spacemaking within vast and diverse modes of what I see as a critical move to 'uncommon' outer space. These might be loosely organised for the purpose of this summary around theories and practices, stories, and knowings stemming from Indigenous futurisms (Dillon 2012), and Black futurisms (van Veen and Anderson 2018; Phillips 2019, 2020; Gunkel and lynch 2019). As with space feminisms mentioned above, all, with their own uncommonalities, intersect, interrupt, intrude, and recalibrate critical thinking and critical doing, on and in outer space.

As has been widely documented, dominant Western narratives, whether in science, cinema, literature, or NewSpace, the story of outer space is one of colonisation. Of course, one needn't look too far for examples. For instance, in the US alternative history and science fiction TV series *For All Mankind* (Apple TV), whose title is inspired by the lunar plaque left on the moon by the astronauts of Apollo 11, the US built, in 1983, a moon base called Jamestown. The literal reference here is to the Jamestown settlement in the Colony of Virginia in the early 1600s, which was the first permanent English settlement in today's US—an obvious embracing of the spirit of settler-colonialism now exported into outer space. First Nations stories and peoples are once again "stripped of the temporality of the present" (Loncon Antileo 2019); Indigenous spacetime is enclosed by "settler time" (Rifkin 2017) and either muted and rendered totally invisible or consigned to the past and inserted into the present in ways that normalise non-Indigenous spacetime.

As a vast body of work by First Nations scholars has shown, Indigenous storytelling is a process of decolonisation (Mita 2000), of "assertive self-determination" (Behrendt 2019), of truth-telling (Bodkin-Andrews et al. 2022), or of "survivance", where storytelling, as "narratives of Native presence" (Vizenor 2008), becomes a way of overcoming the lived experience of tragedy, dominance, and victimhood. In part, this is where the notion of Indigenous futurisms emerges from. In *Walking the Clouds*, Grace Dillon (2012) uses the term Indigenous futurisms to refer to science fiction works from a growing movement of First Nations authors and artists, mostly from North America, spanning literature, cinema, visual arts, and video games.[6] For Dillon, Indigenous futurisms arise from an impulse to subvert what she terms "reservation realisms" as a category imposed on First Nations literatures. Michelle Raheja in *Reservation Reelism* (2011) traces and outlines the notion of 'visual sovereignty' in a radical rethinking of Native cultural production in cinema and video. Today, Raheja argues, cultural artists are providing nuanced and complex forms of self-representation against the powers of the state, while "imagining a futurity that militates against the figure of the vanishing Indian, and engaging in visual sovereignty on virtual reservations of their own creation" (2011: 240). The state and its politics of recognition reproduce the colonisation of Indigenous imaginaries of time, temporality, and futures. Rifkin refers to struggles for "temporal sovereignty", drawing on Sara Ahmed's queer phenomenology, to argue that a fundamental element of temporal sovereignty is what he terms "Indigenous orientations" toward time (2017: 1). Drawing on the language of science fiction, Dillon develops the notion of 'Native slipstream' as a "hallmark of Native storytelling tradition" to describe how time exists simultaneously as "pasts, presents, and futures that flow together like currents in a navigable stream" (Dillon 2012: 3) through which narratives often traverse in multiple directions. Each of these articulations of Indigenous space-time assert 'temporal sovereignty' as they imagine ways to move 'beyond settler time'.

As Kyle Powys Whyte eloquently demonstrates, "important emerging scholarship discusses how concepts and narratives of crises, dystopia, and apocalypse obscure and erase ongoing oppression against Indigenous peoples and other groups" (2018: 234). In Indigenous futurism and Indigenous science fiction, uncommoning works for intentionally dislodging Native slipstream from settler time and to "empower women and nonhuman protagonists" (Medak-Saltzman 2017; see also Whyte 2018; Mitchell and Chaudhury 2020). In *Spiral to the Stars: Mvskoke Tools of Futurity* Laura Harjo (2019) uses Mvskoke and Indigenous feminist epistemologies, conceptions of Indigenous space, place, and mapping in a community praxis of futurity, to outline the notion of "kin-space-time" constellations. This operates as a pluriversal chronopolitics to overcome trauma and re-story memory and futures in spiral ways, connecting a past, present, and future, by looking up at the same constellations that ancestors and future relatives will see. Similarly, Bawaka Country has consistently shown how the colonial cosmologies of NewSpace "assume that there are no people or other beings Indigenous to 'outer space', and that there is no life there to harm" (2020: 2). They dispute that there is an 'outer' space separate from Earth where the harmful effects of extraction can be externalised (Collis 2017), and point out that the annexation of Indigenous lands and displacement of Indigenous peoples is enabled for the development of infrastructures and logistical projects that promote space exploration (Bawaka Country 2020). Country—and indeed sky Country—is seen as woven with notions of land and time that can be visited.

Outer space narratives continue to be the subject of techniques and practices that concretise an "uneven distribution of futurity" (Grove et al. 2022) that signals "how the modern experience of futurity ... has been conditioned by historically specific *de-futuring* practices that violently deny these same possibilities to the racialised Others of the modern Self" (p. 7, emphasis in original). NewSpace is paradigmatic of a 'temporal ghetto' of "racial capitalism" that unevenly distributes spatiotemporal mobility, agency and determination" (Phillips 2020). T. J. Demos comments on BQF's work as capable of unleashing the force of radical reversibility. Here I think it is also relevant to pick up on William Lempert's observation that "the hubristic delusion of linearity (i.e., progress) is a key component in the rendering of colonization as morally coherent" (Lempert 2021: 48).

This is a similar approach to the one we developed with Māori performance artist Victoria Hunt in *Nightfall on Gaia* (Salazar 2015), using Indigenous futurisms as a device to craft past-present-future worlds in Antarctica (Figure 12.2) As Lou Cornum observes, it is crucial to recognise how science fiction by Black and Indigenous authors act as models of world building, and as a "theoretical elaboration of a concrete spacetime transformed from the here and now" (Cornum 2021). Black and Indigenous speculative fiction provides a mode of "decolonial speculation" (Cornum and Moynagh 2020) where paraliterary genres outline a critique of temporality that "furthers the challenge to Eurochronology posed by the Black and Indigenous intellectual and creative traditions" (p. 12). Decolonial speculation here works against utopian imaginaries of a whiteness unencumbered by earthly entanglements as in Marinetti's Manifesto mentioned earlier.

Of course there are too many convergences and divergences among and across all these terms and approaches. But they perhaps all share the fact that they are all historically situated. Afrofuturism for Eshun could be described as a "multimedia project distributed across the nodes, hubs, rings, and stars of the Black Atlantic" and as a

> As a program for recovering the histories of counter-futures created in a century hostile to Afrodiasporic projection and as a space within which the critical work of manufacturing tools capable of intervention within the current political dispensation may be undertaken.
> *(2003: 301)*

In discussing the reemergence and reappropriation of Black visions of political and cultural futures, Damion Kareem Scott (2021), for instance, argues that there are important ontological and semantic differences between Afrofuturism and Black Futurism. It is way beyond the scope of this chapter to address these debates properly, an undertaking that certainly must be done in informed ways based on lived experience.[7] In this section I refer to both as powerful counter-narratives to space futures and as futuring methods. Following Eshun (2003), Afrofuturism is a

Figure 12.2 Video still from the film *Cosmographies,* directed by Juan Francisco Salazar, in production during 2023. The film is a sequel to the 2015 film *Nightfall on Gaia*. The image portrays the character of astrobiologist Xûe noon played by performance artist Victoria Hunt. Image by Juan Francisco Salazar, Atacama Desert, Chile, 2022.

diverse approach that "does not seek to deny the tradition of countermemory. Rather, it aims to extend that tradition by reorienting the intercultural vectors of Black Atlantic temporality towards the proleptic as much as the retrospective" (p. 289). T. J. Demos echoes Eshun, writing that Black futurisms "revolt against being de-futured, elaborated in a proleptic tense of the present-impending—a chronopolitics of prefiguration" (2021: 58). Writing in the context of yet another imagined end of history—the winding down of the Cold War and the emergence of the internet-enabled age in the 1990s—and indeed the creation of novel avenues for social science scholarship, Alondra Nelson (2002) critically analyses the popular rhetoric that characterised the late-1990s dot-com boom and "the promise of a placeless, raceless, bodiless near future enabled by technological progress" (p. 1). At stake here is a parallel between two visions whereby a supposed ending provides the setting for an imagining of a technologically enabled future where (some) humans would no longer be limited by the biophysical, ecological, and geopolitical limits of both the Earth itself and the old order. This figure of the amorphous human subject of the social studies of outer space—and planetary thinking more generally—appears for Nelson as a more familiar (if undesignated) face of technology more generally. What Nelson identifies in this human subject is that in these visions of a technological future untethered from history itself, we see "paradigms for understanding technology [that] smack of old racial ideologies" (p. 1). In response, and drawing on histories of Afrofuturist thought, Nelson questions the "myth of black disingenuity with technology", insisting on the "centrality of black people's labour in modernisation and industrialisation as well as the historical truths of black participation in technological development" (p. 6). Writing on Black futurist imaginaries and the relationship between politics and time, Rasheedah Phillips argues that to change the linear fatalistic future to which Black people have been told they do not belong, Black people have forcefully had to fight for space on the collective timeline. This is crucial for interrogating why and how outer space futures have been pre-empted and anticipated since the 1950s as a project of modernity, where, as Hodari Davis (2022) argues, "conceptions, forecasts, and projections of the future [have] been built on ideas that are fundamentally anti-Black ... [for] anti-Blackness in the futures space serves to preserve colonial ideologies and epistemologies into the future, sustaining the anti-Blackness that fuels it" (p. 94). Relatedly, Black Quantum Futurism's (BQF) work brings to the fore the need to adopt "alternative temporal orientations and frameworks, opening up access to the future" (Phillips 2020: 41). T. J. Demos writes extensively about how BQF "graphs the techno-optimism of past space travel, dramatized in astronaut iconography and mirrored helmets reflecting Black faces, onto newspaper clippings reporting unfulfilled dreams of urban housing justice, resonating with the goals of BQF's Community Futures Lab in North Philadelphia" (Demos 2021; see BQF this volume).

The metanarrative of NewSpace has co-opted notions of commoning, leaving little room for divergence. A hegemonic vision of space commons neutralises and dismisses alternative configurations of outer space futures. This, of course, is also a core technique in mainstream science fiction cinema and literature. This is one reason why I think that to think with Marisol de la Cadena and Mario Blaser here is pertinent when they highlight the analytical and political purchase of processes of uncommoning, which are crucial for building other commons by making visible the divergence in those 'heterogeneous assemblages of life' that are often concealed by science, the state, and other "hegemonic commoning agents" (Chua et al. 2021), including, I would add, the film and music industries, and, of course, the global and national space sectors. Drawing on Isabelle Stengers (2005) and what she calls "interests in common which are not the same interests", Blaser and de la Cadena regard the 'uncommons' as a "negotiated coming together of heterogeneous worlds (and their practices) as they strive for what makes each of them be what they are, which is also not without others" (2018: 4). Acknowledging the uncommons, they argue, is a way of conceiving of a world of many worlds.

Concluding Remarks: An Emancipatory Chronopolitics of Outer Space

In concluding, I wish to bring the attention to what Kyle Powys Whyte calls "the allyship of innocence" (2018) which more often than not refuses to acknowledge –and cancels– the fluidity of "post-apocalyptic and ancestrally dystopian spaces of Indigenous spiraling time, intergenerational dialogue, and science (fiction)" (p. 237). In bringing in counterfuturing perspectives that offer deep framings of the spiral temporalities of outer space, this chapter essays a notion of futuring as an epistemic angle to critically describe chronopolitical tensions and controversies that both inform and arise from narratives framing the horizons of anticipation, hope, and speculation through which space exploration is articulated. To decentre and interrogate this all-encompassing trope of "we in space, space for all", this chapter aligns with efforts that call for, as Mitchell and Chaudhury put it: "worlding beyond 'the' 'End' of 'the world'". In doing so I have engaged with—and walked alongside—a number of diverse considerations and political interventions being put forward by vital energies of diverse scholarship and practice in Black, Indigenous, feminist, and queer futurisms, which ponder different, anticolonial modes of futuring outer space.

Commoning, in all forms, Miller and Gibson-Graham (2019: 15) propose, is "the ongoing production of a shared space of mutual exposure to the ethical demands of interdependence", as the "collective politicization of livelihood", and as the sites from where "*oikoi* (habitats) overlap, converge, and become sites" for asking a crucial and transformative question: how will we live together—in this case, in outer space? In this chapter, I have attempted to outline how NewSpace has co-opted the language of the commons and stripped commoning from its more emancipatory qualities to argue, along with Marisol de la Cadena, that a way forward might be for uncommoning the futures projected by NewSpace through what she calls "commons through divergence" (2019: 51). The "Space for @ll" motto of the IAC 2022 comes to illustrate what John Law called the one-world world (OWW) (2015), which in a sense resembles this project of commoning, understood as the making of one shared domain within which all differences that NewSpace advances exist. I have argued that futurity-as-trope and method can be a pertinent approach to rethinking, remembering, and re-storying forms of human sociality in space that are yet to be fully imagined. I have striven to highlight the utmost significance of embracing an emancipated chronopolitics of outer space that may be cultivated not in relation to the prescribed narrow futures conveyed by the technoutopias of NewSpace, and not only to an undetermined not-yet, but most importantly to a "radical infinitude, or futures that exceed the temporal dimensions of Western thought" (Mitchell 2019), and ultimately, to craft a discussion between disparate knowledge traditions for "doing difference generatively" (Verran 2013: 141). In this way, by engaging with differing modes of 'futuring outer space' the chapter aims to bring attention to the need for critical scrutiny of hegemonic imaginaries grounded in linear neoliberal temporalities of capitalist expansion off-Earth.

Acknowledgements

This chapter developed from initial musings and conversations with colleagues to whom I am grateful and indebted: Matthew Kearnes, with whom we developed a paper for the 2022 Annual Meeting of the American Association of Geographers (AAG) in March 2022, and Tsvetelina Hristova, with whom we collaborated on an earlier paper presented at the *Methods for Researching Automated Futures* workshop convened by Sarah Pink at Monash University, Melbourne, in September 2021.

Funding

The author discloses receipt of financial support for the research, authorship, and/or publication of this chapter by the Australia Research Council Future Fellowship program, grant FT190100729.

Notes

1 The discussions offered in this chapter are intimately related to other chapters in this volume: those of Olson; Black Quantum Futurism; Triscott; Vermaylen; Gál and Armstrong; Noon et al.; Bawaka Country; and Smiles. Space feminisms is a generative figure coming out of contemporary art-science interventions and developed by Marie-Pier Boucher (2022) together with artist Nahum, curator Annick Bureaud and a number of other collaborators (Paré 2022; Boucher and Bureaud 2022). Audra Mitchell and Aadita Chaudhury use the term BIPOC futurisms where they acknowledge the term BIPOC (Black, Indigenous, People of Colour) refers "to people and communities who self-identify as such or are assigned this label within the racial taxonomies imposed by ongoing (settler) colonialism, capitalism, and other Euro-centric projects of domination" (2020: 309). Craig Henry Jones uses Ethnofuturism an umbrella term to refer to a "process by and through which histories that deviate from the hegemonic 'norm' are reinvigorated and mobilised to (re)produce alternative discourses of futurity". Examples of such futurisms for Jones, include among others Afrofuturism, Aotearoa futurism, Cambrofuturism, and Sinofuturism. Josh Rios uses the term Chicanafuturism to discuss technologies of resistance as a "possible future return to the past. (2017: 59). Blaire Topash-Caldwell, writes about Neshnabé futurisms which "guide Native American ecologists, theorists, and activists in the Great Lakes region in mitigating and surviving ecological destruction of their homelands" (2020:3). See also Deondre Smiles "Anishinaabe in Space", this volume.
2 Here I specifically use commoning to refer to outer space as a global commons, and to Blaser and de la Cadena's description of "the 'commons' as also those collective imaginaries sometimes called for by governments, industries, and social movements to frame extractivist and enclosing agendas and practices (Blaser and de la Cadena 2017). I wish to draw a distinction between this approach and the wealth of inspiring academic and activist work on processes and practices of commoning as transformative change,

as struggle against the enclosure of the commons, and as a postcapitalist politics (Gibson-Graham, Cameron, and Healy 2016). For Miller and Gibson-Graham (2019) commoning, or making-common, refers to the myriad ways in which complex relations of livelihood are rendered into explicit sites of ethical negotiation. For these authors these relations unfold as rupture and revolt against hierarchical relations and are enacted and renewed through institutional forms seeking to render livelihood relations into sites of democratic deliberation. As they put it: "Commoning, in all forms, is the ongoing production of a shared space of mutual exposure to the ethical demands of interdependence" (Miller and Gibson-Graham 2019: 15). The distinction I wish to make is this. In not all forms of commoning are the poetics of making-common rendered according to the same ethical frameworks. As Blaser and de la Cadena (2017) aptly ask in their invitation to consider the need to uncommon the commons that have been captured and co-opted: "How far does the shared domain that constitutes a community extend? What kinds of things does it include, and what kinds of responsibilities do these things demand?" (p. 186). If, as Miller and Gibson-Graham sustain, "particular ecosystems, diseases, experiences of shared oppression, cultural traditions, mutual relations with distant others, the planetary climate system—all may be commoned by their rendering as sites of connection and negotiation" (2019: 15), can outer space, the Moon, low Earth orbit, and asteroids also also be commoned? Yes. And no. NewSpace is a proposal for a common system for and vision of how "we all" should make use and make meaning of outer space, through the very narrow set of codified morals of technoutopianism in astrocapitalism.
3 Laura Bear uses the analytic of timescapes to trace "technologies of imagination" seeking to understand how time intersects with and affects social and nonhuman rhythms where "various kinds of action on and with time have the quality of poeisis or skillful making" (Bear 2016: 487).
4 As an established body of work on the geopolitics of outer space has shown, outer space has been subject to a futural mode of neoliberal and globalising capitalism (Ortner 2016). Dunnett et al. (2019) call it astrocapitalism. It is the dominant political and economic narrative—determined by forces of capital, extractivism, and profit and the enclosure of outer space (Jones 2021). In this context technoutopian visions of human expansion into space have been torqued toward explicitly privatised, capitalist, and extractivist narratives which are in varying degrees utopian and dystopian. The proposed extraction of minerals from near-Earth asteroids and the Moon (off-Earth mining), in anticipation of a future space economy and even settlements beyond the upper atmosphere, is widely being regarded as an emerging area of research investment, technological development, and capital speculation (Kearnes and van Dooren 2017).
5 In their introduction to a special issue on Trans Temporalities, Simon Elin Fisher, Rasheedah Phillips, and Ido Katri (2017) offer "original insight into the time(s) of trans life experience" (p. 2) and discuss original work on alternative and counter temporalities produced by a range of authors and activists including, among others, Jake Pyne, who argues that "Western queer and trans subjects were temporalized in ways that mimicked the temporalization of colonial subjects" (p. 3); or Josh Rios's work, which explores forms of Chicanx/feminism and "postcolonial speculative fiction as an experimental space for reshaping notions of technology and future and interrogating and reexamining historical hegemonic social structures (p. 10).
6 For a discussion of new-wave Indigenous-made media including short films, novels, comic books, artwork, video games, and podcasts, see Topash-Caldwell (2020).
7 For Scott, the distinction between Afrofuturism and Black Futurism "represents a theoretical rejection of the notion that the two concepts must be assumed to be functionally equivalent" (Scott 2021: 146).

References

Aït-Touati, Frédérique. 2019. "Récits de la Terre." *Critique, Vivre Dans un Monde Abîmé*, 1 (860–61): 5–16. https://hal.archives-ouvertes.fr/hal-02169959.

Amoureux, Jack, and Varun Reddy. 2021. "Multiple Anthropocenes: Pluralizing Space–Time as a Response to 'the Anthropocene.'" *Globalizations* 18 (6): 929–46. https://doi.org/10.1080/14747731.2020.1864178.

Bawaka Country including Audra Mitchell, Sarah Wright, Sandie Suchet-Pearson, Kate Lloyd, Laklak Burarrwanga, Ritjilili Ganambarr, Merrkiyawuy Ganambarr-Stubbs, Banbapuy Ganambarr, Djawundil Maymuru, and Rrawun Maymuru. 2020. "Dukarr Lakarama: Listening to Guwak, Talking Back to Space Colonization". *Political Geography* 81: 102218. https://doi.org/10.1016/j.polgeo.2020.102218.

Bear, Laura. 2016. "Time as Technique." *Annual Review of Anthropology* 45: 487–502. https://doi.org/10.1146/annurev-anthro-102313-030159.

Behrendt, Larissa. 2019. "Indigenous Storytelling: Decolonizing Institutions and Assertive Self-Determination: Implications for Legal Practice." In *Decolonizing Research: Indigenous Storywork as*

Methodology, edited by Jo-Ann Archibald, Q'um Q'um Xiiem Archibald, Jenny Bol Jun Lee-Morgan and Jason De Santolo, 175–86. London: ZED Books.

Berinstein, Paula. 2002. *Making Space Happen: Private Space Ventures and the Visionaries Behind Them*. Medford, NJ: Plexus Publishing.

Blaser, Mario, and Marisol de la Cadena. 2017. "The Uncommons: An Introduction." *Anthropologica* 59 (2): 185–93. https://doi.org/10.3138/anth.59.2.t01.

Blaser, Mario, and Marisol de la Cadena. 2018. "Pluriverse: Proposals for a World of Many Worlds." In *A World of Many Worlds*, edited by Marisol de la Cadena and Mario Blaser, 1–22. Durham and London: Duke University Press.

Bodkin-Andrews, Gawaian, Shannon Foster, Aunty Frances Bodkin, Uncle John Foster, Uncle Gavin Andrews, Aunty Karen Adams, Uncle Ross Evans, and Bronwynn Carlson. 2022. The colonial storytelling of good intent: Or the inspired erasure of our ancestors? *Griffith Review* 75: 110-122.

Boucher, Marie-Pier. 2022. "Indigenous Space Feminism: An Interview with Michelle A. McGeough." *Espace: Art Actuel* 130: 64–71.

Boucher, Marie-Pier, and Annick Bureaud. 2022. "Multispecies Space Witch: An Interview with Agnes Meyer-Brandis/Sorcière Spatiale Multi-espèces: Un Entretien Avec Agnes Meyer-Brandis." *Espace: Art Actuel* 130: 72–7.

Chua, Liana, Hannah Fair, Viola Schreer, Anna Stępień, and Paul Hasan Thung. 2021. "'Only the Orangutans Get a Life Jacket': Uncommoning Responsibility in a Global Conservation Nexus." *American Ethnologist* 48 (4): 370–85. https://doi.org/10.1111/amet.13045.

Collis, Christy. 2017. "Territories Beyond Possession? Antarctica and Outer Space." *The Polar Journal* 7 (2): 287–302. https://doi.org/10.1080/2154896X.2017.1373912.

Cornum, Lou. 2021. "Skin Worlds: Black and Indigenous Science Fiction Theorizing Since the 1970s." PhD Dissertation, City University of New York. https://academicworks.cuny.edu/gc_etds/4422.

Cornum, Lou, and Maureen Moynagh. 2020. "Introduction: Decolonial (Re) Visions of Science Fiction, Fantasy, and Horror." *Canadian Literature* 240: 8–18. https://doi.org/10.14288/cl.vi240.

Davis, Hodari B. 2022. "Black on Black Futures: A Call to Diversify the Discipline of Black Futuring." *Journal of Futures Studies* 26 (3): 89–96. https://doi.org/10.6531/JFS.202203_26(3).0008.

de la Cadena, Marisol. 2019. "Uncommoning Nature: Stories from the Anthropo-Not-Seen." In *Anthropos and the Material*, edited by Penny Harvey, Christian Krohn-Hansen and Knut G. Nustad, 35–58. Durham, NC: Duke University Press. https://doi.org/10.1215/9781478003311-003.

Demos, T. J. 2021. "Radical Futurisms: Documentary's Chronopolitics." *Trigger* 2: 58–64.

Dillon, Grace. 2012. *Walking the Clouds: An Anthology of Indigenous Science Fiction*. Phoenix, AZ: University of Arizona Press.

Doutreligne, Sophie. 2020. "From Critical Manifesto to Transformative Genderplay: Feminist Futurist and Dadaist Strategies Countering the Misogyny Within the Historical Avant-Gardes." *Documenta* 38 (2): 32–62. http://hdl.handle.net/1854/LU-8702762.

Dunnett, Oliver, Andrew S. Maclaren, Julie Klinger, K. Maria D. Lane, and Daniel Sage. 2019. "Geographies of Outer Space: Progress and New Opportunities." *Progress in Human Geography* 43 (2): 314–36. https://doi.org/10.1177/0309132517747727.

Eshun, Kodwo. 2003. "Further Considerations on Afrofuturism." *CR: The New Centennial Review* 3 (2): 287–302. https://doi.org/10.1353/ncr.2003.0021.

Fabian, Johannes. 1983. *Time and the Other: How Anthropology Makes Its Object*. New York: Columbia University Press.

Fisher, Simon D. Elin, Rasheedah Phillips, and Ido H. Katri. 2017. "Introduction: Trans Temporalities." *Somatechnics* 7 (1): 1–15. https://doi.org/10.3366/soma.2017.0202.

Freeman, Elizabeth. 2010. *Time Binds: Queer Temporalities, Queer Histories*. Durham, NC: Duke University Press.

Gibson-Graham, J. K., Jenny Cameron, and Stephen Healy. 2016. "Commoning as a Postcapitalist Politics." In *Releasing the Commons: Rethinking the Futures of the Commons*, edited by Ash Amin and Philip Howell, 192–212. London: Routledge.

Ginsburg, Faye. 2008. "Rethinking the Digital Age." In *Global Indigenous Media: Cultures, Poetics, and Politics*, edited by Pamela Wilson and Michelle Stewart, 287–305. Durham, NC: Duke University Press. https://doi.org/10.1215/9780822388692-020.

Grosz, Elizabeth. 1998. "Thinking the New: Of Futures Yet Unthought." *Symplokē* 6 (1/2): 38–55. https://doi.org/10.1353/sym.2005.0074.

Grove, Kevin, Lauren Rickards, Ben Anderson, and Matthew Kearnes. 2022. "The Uneven Distribution of Futurity: Slow Emergencies and the Event of COVID-19." *Geographical Research* 60 (1): 6–17. https://doi.org/10.1111/1745-5871.12501.

Gunkel, Henriette, and kara lynch. 2019. *We Travel the Space Ways: Black Imaginations, Fragments and Diffractions*. Bielefeld: transcript Verlag.
Harjo, Laura. 2019. *Spiral to the Stars: Mvskoke Tools of Futurity*. Tucson, AZ: University of Arizona Press.
International Astronautical Congress 2022. *Space for @ll: IAC Paris 2022 Sponsorship and Exhibitors Prospectus*. https://www.react-profile.org/upload/KIT/system/uploads/IAC_2022_sponsorguide_v10.pdf.
Jones, Craig Henry. 2021. "Enclosing the Cosmos: Privatising Outer Space and Voices of Resistance." *Society + Space Magazine*, 24 May 2021. https://www.societyandspace.org/articles/enclosing-the-cosmos-privatising-outer-space-and-voices-of-resistance.
Karuka, Manu. 2019. *Empire's Tracks: Indigenous Nations, Chinese Workers, and the Transcontinental Railroad*. Oakland, CA: University of California Press.
Kearnes, Matthew, and Thom van Dooren. 2017. "Rethinking the Final Frontier: Cosmo-Logics and an Ethic of Interstellar Flourishing." *GeoHumanities* 3 (1): 178–97. https://doi.org/10.1080/2373566X.2017.1300448.
Klein, Naomi. 2013. "Dancing the World into Being: A Conversation with Idle No More's Leanne Simpson." *Yes! Magazine*, 6 March. Accessed 25 April 2022 at http://www.yesmagazine.org/peace-justice/dancing-the-world-into-being-a-conversation-with-idle-no-more-leanne-simpson.
Latour, Bruno. 2004. "Whose Cosmos, Which Cosmopolitics? Comments on the Peace Terms of Ulrich Beck." *Common Knowledge* 10 (3): 450–62. https://doi.org/10.1215/0961754X-10-3-450.
Latour, Bruno. 2018. *Down to Earth: Politics in the New Climatic Regime*. Cambridge: Polity Press.
Law, John. 2015. "What's Wrong With a One-World World?" *Distinktion: Journal of Social Theory* 16 (1): 126–39. https://doi.org/10.1080/1600910X.2015.1020066.
Lempert, William. 2021. "From Interstellar Imperialism to Celestial Wayfinding: Prime Directives and Colonial Time-Knots in SETI." *American Indian Literature and Research Journal* 45 (1): 45–70. https://doi.org/10.17953/aicrj.45.1.lempert.
Loncon Antileo, Elisa. 2019. "Una Aproximación al Tiempo, el Pensamiento Filosófico y la Lengua Mapuche." *Árboles y Rizomas* 1 (2): 67–81. https://doi.org/10.35588/ayr.v1i2.4087.
lynch, kara, and Henriette Gunkel. 2019. "Lift Off… an Introduction." In *We Travel the Space Ways: Black Imagination, Fragments, and Diffractions*, edited by Henriette Gunkel and kara lynch, 21–44. Bielefeld: transcript Verlag. https://doi.org/10.1515/9783839446010-003.
Medak-Saltzman Danika. 2017. "Coming to you from the Indigenous future: Native women, speculative film shorts, and the art of the possible". *Studies in American Indian Literatures* 29(1): 139–171.
Miller, Ethan, and J. K. Gibson-Graham. 2019. "Thinking with Interdependence: From Economy/Environment to Ecological Livelihoods." *Draft Chapter for Thinking in the World: A Reader*, edited by Jill Bennett and Mary Zournazi. London: Bloomsbury. Accessed 13 November 2022 at http://www.communityeconomies.org/publications/chapters/thinking-interdependence-economyecology-ecological-livelihoods.
Mita, Merata. 2000. "Storytelling: A Process of Decolonisation." In *The Journal of Puawaitanga*, Special Issue: Indigenous Women and Representation, edited by Leonie Pihama, 7–9. Auckland: The University of Auckland.
Mitchell, Audra. 2018. "Outer Space." In *Security Studies: An Introduction*, 3rd edition, edited by Paul D. Williams and Matt McDonald, 569–82. London and New York: Routledge. https://doi.org/10.4324/9781315228358-39.
Mitchell, Audra. 2019. "Can International Relations Confront the Cosmos?" In *Routledge Handbook of Critical International Relations*, edited by Jenny Edkins, 51–64. London and New York: Routledge.
Mitchell, Audra, and Aadita Chaudhury. 2020. "Worlding Beyond 'the' 'End' of 'the World': White Apocalyptic Visions and BIPOC Futurisms". *International Relations* 34 (3): 309–32. https://doi.org/10.1177/00471178209489.
Nelson, Alondra. 2000. "Braving the New World—AfroFuturism: Beyond the Digital Divide." In *Race and Public Policy*, edited by Makani Themba, 37–40. Oakland, CA: Applied Research Center.
Nelson, Alondra. 2002. "Introduction: Future Texts." *Social Text* 20 (2 (71)): 1–15. https://doi.org/10.1215/01642472-20-2_71-1.
Nowotny, Helga. 1994. *Time: The Modern and Postmodern Experience*. Cambridge: Polity.
Olson, Valerie. 2018. *Into the Extreme: US Environmental Systems and Politics Beyond Earth*. Minneapolis: University of Minnesota Press.
Olufemi, Lola. 2021. *Experiments in Imagining Otherwise*. London: Hajar Press.
Oman-Reagan, Michael P. 2017. "Queering Outer Space." *SocArXiv*, Open Science Framework. Manuscript, submitted 22 January 2017. https://osf.io/preprints/socarxiv/mpyk6/.
Ortner, Sherry B. 2016. "Dark Anthropology and Its Others: Theory Since the Eighties." *HAU: Journal of Ethnographic Theory* 6 (1): 47–73. https://doi.org/10.14318/hau6.1.004.
Paré, André-Louis. 2022. "L'espace au Féminin/Space in the Feminine." *Espace: Art Actuel* 130: 2–11.

Phillips, Rasheedah. 2019. "The Nowness of Black Chronopolitical Imaginaries in the Afro/Retrofuture." *The Funambulist* (24), 19 June. https://thefunambulist.net/magazine/24-futurisms/nowness-black-chronopolitical-imaginaries-afro-retrofuture-rasheedah-phillips.

Phillips, Rasheedah. 2020. "Communal, Quantum & Afrofutures: Time & Memory in North Philly." In *Space-Time Collapse II: Community Futurisms*, edited by Black Quantum Futurism, 10–51. Philadelphia, PA: The Afrofuturist Affair/House of Future Sciences Books.

Phillips, Rasheedah. 2021. "Counter Clockwise: Unmapping Black Temporalities from Greenwich Mean Timelines." *The Funambulist* (36), 21 June. https://thefunambulist.net/magazine/they-have-clocks-we-have-time/counter-clockwise-unmapping-black-temporalities-from-greenwich-mean-timelines.

Raheja, Michelle H. 2011. *Reservation Reelism: Redfacing, Visual Sovereignty, and Representations of Native Americans in Film*. Lincoln, NE: University of Nebraska Press.

Redfield, Peter. 2002. "The Half-Life of Empire in Outer Space." *Social Studies of Science* 32 (5–6): 791–825. https://doi.org/10.1177/030631270203200508.

Rifkin, Mark. 2017. *Beyond Settler Time*. Durham, NC: Duke University Press.

Sage, Daniel. 2008. "Framing Space: A Popular Geopolitics of American Manifest Destiny in Outer Space." *Geopolitics* 13 (1): 27–53. https://doi.org/10.1080/14650040701783482.

Salazar, Juan Francisco (Producer and Director), 2015. *Nightfall on Gaia* [Motion Picture]. Australia/Chile: AQ Films and Western Sydney University.

Salazar, Juan Francisco. 2017a. "Speculative Fabulation: Researching Worlds to Come in Antarctica." In *Anthropologies and Futures*, edited by Juan Francisco Salazar, Sarah Pink, Andrew Irving and Johannes Sjöberg, 151–70. London and New York: Bloomsbury. https://doi.org/10.4324/9781003084570-10.

Salazar, Juan Francisco. 2017b. "Microbial Geographies at the Extremes of Life." *Environmental Humanities* 9 (2): 398–417. https://doi.org/10.1215/22011919-4215361

Salazar, Juan Francisco. 2017c. "Antarctica and Outer Space: Relational Trajectories." *The Polar Journal* 7 (2): 259–69. https://doi.org/10.1080/2154896X.2017.1398521.

Scott, Damion Kareem. 2021. "Afrofuturism and Black Futurism: Some Ontological and Semantic Considerations." In *Critical Black Futures: Speculative Theories and Explorations*, edited by Phillip Butler, 139–63. Singapore: Palgrave Macmillan.

Serres, Michel, and Bruno Latour. 1995. *Conversations on Science, Culture, and Time*. Ann Arbor, MI: University of Michigan Press.

Squire, Rachael, Oli Mould, and Peter Adey. 2021. "The Final Frontier? The Enclosure of a Commons of Outer Space." *Society and Space Magazine*. Accessed 31 May 2022 at https://www.societyandspace.org/forums/the-final-frontier-the-enclosure-of-a-commons-of-outer-space.

Stengers, Isabelle. 2005. "Introductory Notes on an Ecology of Practices." *Cultural Studies Review* 11 (1): 183–96. https://doi.org/10.5130/csr.v11i1.3459.

Time Zone Protocols n.d. *About*. Accessed 14 November 2022 at https://timezoneprotocols.space/about/.

Topash-Caldwell, Blaire K. 2020. *Neshnabé Futurisms: Indigenous Science and Eco-politics in the Great Lakes*. PhD Dissertation, University of New Mexico. https://digitalrepository.unm.edu/anth_etds/200.

Tutton, Richard. 2018. "Multiplanetary Imaginaries and Utopia: The Case of Mars One." *Science, Technology, & Human Values* 43 (3): 518–39. https://doi.org/10.1177/0162243917737366.

Tutton, Richard. 2021. "Sociotechnical Imaginaries and Techno-Optimism: Examining Outer Space Utopias of Silicon Valley." *Science as Culture* 30 (3): 416–39. https://doi.org/10.1080/09505431.2020.1841151.

Valentine, David. 2012. "Exit Strategy: Profit, Cosmology, and the Future of Humans in Space." *Anthropological Quarterly* 85 (4): 1045–67. http://doi.org/10.1353/anq.2012.0073.

Valentine, David. 2017. "Gravity Fixes: Habituating to the Human on Mars and Island Three." *HAU: Journal of Ethnographic Theory* 7 (3): 185–209. https://doi.org/10.14318/hau7.3.012.

Valentine, David, and Amelia Hassoun. 2019. "Uncommon Futures." *Annual Review of Anthropology* 48 (1): 243–60. https://doi.org/10.1146/annurev-anthro-102218-011435.

van Veen, Tobias C., and Reynaldo Anderson. 2018. "Future Movements: Black Lives, Black Politics, Black Futures—an Introduction." *TOPIA: Canadian Journal of Cultural Studies* 39: 5–21. https://doi.org/10.3138/topia.39.00.

Verran, Helen. 2013. "Engagements between Disparate Knowledge Traditions: Toward Doing Difference Generatively and in Good Faith." In *Contested Ecologies: Dialogues in the South on Nature and Knowledge*, edited by Lesley Green, 141–61. Cape Town: HSRC Press.

Vizenor, Gerald, ed. 2008. *Survivance: Narratives of Native Presence*. Lincoln: University of Nebraska Press.

Whyte, Kyle Powys. 2018. "Indigenous science (fiction) for the Anthropocene: Ancestral dystopias and fantasies of climate change crises". *Environment and Planning E: Nature and Space*, 1(1-2): 224-242.

Yusoff, Kathryn. 2019. "Geologic Realism: On the Beach of Geologic Time." *Social Text* 37 (1 (138)): 1–26. https://doi.org/10.1215/01642472-7286240.

13
FEMINIST APPROACHES TO OUTER SPACE

Engagements with Technology, Labour, and Environment[1]

Réka Patrícia Gál and Eleanor S. Armstrong

Introduction

Outer space exists both in the vast material reality of all of the cosmos beyond Earth and also as a social project. Engineering, scientific research, or the stories we tell ourselves about our future in the stars raise pressing questions pertaining to justice and power. Who has the right to outer space? Whose labour enables people to exercise this right? For whom is space technology tailored? How do these technologies affect our relationship with our terrestrial and extraterrestrial environments? Our aim in this chapter is to demonstrate how feminist approaches have been and continue to be valuable tools for research in the social studies of outer space. Such approaches critically unearth how social hierarchies have been both affected by and reinforced through engagement with outer space.

For this chapter, we selected three thematic areas in which work bedded in plural feminisms has developed salient interventions that make visible the power relations and ideologies that undergird the field: labour, technology, and the environment. Introducing feminist thought within science and technology studies, environmental studies, and media studies has proved a rich and fruitful avenue for novel areas and approaches to research. Such interventions have advanced critical understandings of how patriarchal power relations have underpinned epistemologies of science and technology (e.g., Cipolla et al. 2017). This includes understanding patriarchal relationships to so-called nature or the environment, as well as how these relations are connected to racial and class politics. For example, as Natalie Treviño (2020) shows, the US space programme has been embedded in a matrix of colonialism, capitalism,[2] and patriarchy that extends US exceptionalism and the notion of 'manifest destiny' beyond the terrestrial. This scholarly intervention highlights how elements of ongoing space colonisation reproduce binarised gender and heterosexuality in both fictionalised popular culture and imagined futures by aiming to populate interstellar space and other moons, stars, and planets with 'space cowboys' and reducing the function of women in space to reproduction (Deerfield 2019; Penley 1997; Rand 2014), and how these are part of a larger practice. Space colonisation is entangled with, as David Uahikeaikalei'ohu Maile (2019) argues, displacement of local Indigenous communities for the construction of launch sites and observatories, and, as Richard Tutton (2021) develops, the enlistment of exploitative environmental and labour practices as a means to its end.

The history of human engagement with outer space and the stars is vast and culturally varied. Yet "Western" (Hall 1992) astronomy's overreliance on ancient Greek and Roman genealogies of thought has served to bolster Euroamerican white supremacist ideologies underpinning engagement with outer space and simultaneously to underengage with and disregarded Indigenous (Simpson 2017), African (Holbrook, Medupe, and Urama 2008), Islamic, Chinese, and Indian, as well as other, astronomical knowledges (Selin and Xiaochun 2002). We continue to see this reflected in the contemporary discourse surrounding SpaceX's Starlink satellites' obstruction of the sky, which centres the constellations' detrimental impact on scientists' astronomical observations while glossing over how they also disrupt Indigenous wayfinding practices (Venkatesan et al. 2019). As feminist scholars have advanced, Western genealogies of thought, and specifically Western conceptions of *what* counts as science and *whose* knowledge gets to count as science, are bound up not only in whiteness but also in patriarchal and capitalist structures. These serve to reinforce the sorting of humans neatly into two opposing binarised genders in which "maleness" is tied to knowledge production, waged work, and technology and assigned an active role, while "femaleness" is tied to reproduction—and hence unwaged or lowly waged work—and to nature and assigned a passive, receiving role (Haraway 1991; Merchant 1989).

Reproductive justice and care work has been a central matter of feminist politics. bell hooks' (2001) work has illuminated how this history is further troubled by the convergence of misogyny and racism. Saidiya Hartman (2016) demonstrated how these can be seen intertwined through historical moments such as the enslaved Black women forced to be responsible both for the reproduction of white households (by serving as nannies, housekeepers, and wet-nurses) and for the reproduction of the enslaved Black people. Race and gender have a significant impact on the view of the individual, agential human—indeed, as Sylvia Wynter argues, dominant (scientific, fictional) narratives have been written through the perspective of the European white male (2003). As a result of these struggles both Indigenous and Black scholars have been reacting through desire-based (Gaudry 2015; Tuck 2009) and reparation-based frameworks (Patterson et al. 2016). We therefore recognise feminism here as plural and proliferating, encompassing queer, trans, transnational, Black, Indigenous, and de-, post-, and anti-colonial feminisms. Each of these provides a rich tradition of theory and unique vantage points for developing theoretical insights into the social studies of outer space. Through this chapter, we seek to engage with traditions of feminist research by thinking in community and writing and citing with care (Liboiron 2021; McKittrick 2021; Puig de la Bellacasa 2017) as we capture some of the multiplicity of work within the social studies of outer space. Throughout, we direct the attention of the reader to future directions in which feminist approaches can enrich the scholarship within the field.

Thinking with feminist scholarship on visibility politics and entrepreneurial labour (Banet-Weiser 2018; Hewa 2021; Singh 2020) and decolonial scholarship detailing and theorising Indigenous and Black resistance within settler states (Hartman 2020; Lorde 2003; Estes 2019; Maile 2019) can develop the field of outer space studies. Drawing on their theorising in other domains shows how a feminist approach to outer space does not end with demands for representation within the field or an encouragement to hire women into CEO positions at venture-capital-backed space corporations. Instead, we direct our readers towards a feminist tradition that attends to unpicking, untangling, and uncovering the structural and ideological systems that underpin *why* certain identities have been a subject of exclusion and oppression within the field. We think with *ESPACE art actuel*'s thematic issue *Space Feminism*, edited by Marie-Pier Boucher, which highlighted numerous artistic projects that reimagine the outer spatial futures through feminist perspectives (2022). Likewise, we engage with the research of Kat Deerfield (2019), who argues that social studies of outer space is pervaded by a presumption of heterosexuality, contributing to a culture of *heteronormativity* within the field that leads to marginalisations on the basis of both gender and sexuality, and Chanda Prescod-Weinstein (2021), who demonstrates the pervasive assumption of white empiricism that also underpins assumptions about knowledge and power within the field.

As two white and queer women from Europe, with one of us (Gál) living in Toronto on Turtle Island, on Dish With One Spoon treaty territory, and the other in Europe (Armstrong), our knowledge is limited by our geographical locations, our cultural and scholarly backgrounds, and notably also the languages we speak; this chapter is therefore not a collection of global engagements or an argument regarding universal human engagement with the cosmos. As engagements with outer space enter, arguably, a new space age through new space engagements in China, India, South America, and the African continent, we are limited by our use of anglophone scholarship at the expense of other languages. We look forward to thinking in community with feminist scholars from around the world and ultimately pluralising the anglophone discourse's dominance in the field in order to unsettle (feminist) outer space studies from its Euroamerican dominance. We turn now to what feminism has done, and can do, for the social studies of outer space, to both introduce some key works in the field and gesture to what future work in the field could achieve.

Labour

Space science research and practice is underpinned by many different types of labours. In this section, we draw attention to some types of labour documented in feminist research within and beyond the immediate purview of social science of outer space scholars and direct the reader to think further on this theme. Daniela K. Rosner (2018) demonstrates that feminist approaches to science studies can reject the focus on technoscience projects' "aggregation of individuals rather than ... a web of relationships ... that valorize the work of inventors and innovators" (12–13), instead focusing on collective and collaborative work, and for whom such technoscience projects are useful or beneficial. Picking up this thread in her research on Navajo women workers in technoscience, Lisa Nakamura demonstrates this as a case in the connection Haraway draws between the labour required to produce the technology and those the technoscience products empower:

> [T]echnoscience is, indeed, an integrated circuit, one that both separates and connects laborers and users, and while both genders benefit from cheap computers, it is the flexible labor of women of color, either outsourced or insourced, that made and continue to make this possible.
>
> *(Nakamura 2014: 919)*

Nakamura's work traces how this "flexible", "outsourced" labour is that of Navajo women at Fairchild Semiconductor, where the labour of racialised women, reduced to their temperament, their culture, and their gender, is essential to the construction of the semiconductor circuits. Elsewhere the labour beyond the bodies of cis white men that underpins the achievements we think of as 'space science' is made visible through a range of research projects. Work such as Margot Shetterly's *Hidden Figures* (2016) documenting of Black women (including Katherine Johnson, Dorothy Vaughan, and Mary Jackson) as the early computers of NASA's space programme at Langley is complemented in Charnell Chasten Long's (2019) work tracing, through the Black press of the USA, Black women working at Stouffer's Food Cooperation, including Julie Stewart and Sara Thompson, and in Osase Omoruyi's (2021) making visible the contributions of Black and brown labourers in images of the construction of Harvard's and Yale's observatories in South Africa. Such scholarship attends to what Chasten Long describes as the "periphery of the space race" (2019), using a feminist call to attention of who is *doing* the work to challenge narratives that only include the most privileged. Resurfacing work such as the analogue glass-observatory analysis at early observatories (Sobel 2016), developing computers (Light 1999), undertaking calculations (Holt 2016), or the "Little Old Ladies" stitching (Rosner 2018) for Apollo 8 provides an alternative trajectory of what labour has been required for space research. Such feminist labour histories provide a starkly contrasting narrative to hegemonic narratives of space science and open us to pluralising the folk who are valued within the field.

It's not only those who are hegemonically 'within' the field—particularly in the USA context—whose labours we should consider. At the base of Mauna Kea, a puʻuhonua (place of refuge) established in 2019 by Kanaka Maoli (Indigenous Hawaiians) works to care for the safety of kiaʻI (mountain protectors) against the building of the Thirty Meter Telescope (TMT). David Uahikeaikaleiʻohu Maile (2021) describes the actions of Lanakila Mangauil to frustrate the official groundbreaking; of Noelani Goodyear-Kaʻōpua, ʻImaikalani Winchester, and six others in binding themselves to the cattle grate; of ʻĀina traveling with Maile; of Maile's brother, Kapalikūokalani, creating a hoʻokupu of ʻohe wai (fresh water offering); of Jennifer Marley in her crafted baked-clay gift; of Pua Case and Kalani Flores to enduringly resist the TMT; of Paul Neves's litigation against the Hawaiian governor; of Kahoʻokahi Kanuha to orate ceremonies at the blockade; of Oli Kūkulu to pen a chant of resistance; and of Maile's own labour as Kanaka Maoli on the ground as well as his resistance through the scholarship method *"writing the land back"* (Maile 2021: 98, italics in the original). Maile makes it clear that labours of resistance require many actors, and all contributions are valuable to the effort. Resistance to space science activities takes place in many contexts. Terrence McCoy and Heloísa Traiano (2021), in their photographic and textual essay for the *Washington Post*, document the resistance of Maria José Lima Pinheiro and others in the quilombos (historically Black villages) against the expansion of the Brazilian Space Agency's site in Alcântara. May-Britt Öhman and Lilian Mikaelsson (2014) explore the use of Saami land in Sampi through the forced relocation of reindeer herders for the Swedish Defence Materiel Administration's Vidsel Test Range. NewSpace sites draw challenges too—both SpaceX's sites in Boca Chica, Texas, USA, and Rocket Lab's Aotearoa New Zealand Māhia Peninsula launch range have also drawn criticism from local communities where activist labour, described by Ollie Neas (2021), challenges the dual-use launches and environmental impacts of these space sites. These are but some of the globally distributed labours highlighting the tensions of communities with colonial-capitalist expansionist space science environments.

Throughout Maile's article is the tension of Indigenous temporality of action against the prescribed settler time of scientists and proponents of space science—the "alternative tempo" of kiaʻi (2021: 100), "waiting" (99), "lateness" or being "too late" to protest (102), being in "different times" (104), being "too slow" to explore or utilise the resource (108), preventing work happening in a *"timely manner"* (113, emphasis in original)—encouraging us to also ask *when* is resistance in social studies of outer space:

> In Hawaiʻi, the here and now of haole technoscientific conquest is a militarized prison house—it occupies and contains—and yet kiaʻi continue, despite claims it is not pragmatic and too utopian, to cruise for a decolonized then and deoccupied there.
>
> *(Maile 2021: 112)*

Consolidating Mark Rifkin's rejection of settler time as linear, straight, and heteronormative (2017) with José Esteban Muñoz's call for queer theory to think and feel a then and there (2009), Maile's employment of cruising as method challenges the heteronorms of settler colonial science in the research. This questioning of *when is space* (Deerfield 2013) can highlight the atemporality of both active and resistive labour, as well as bringing our attention to *when* different forms of labour are recaptured into scholarship and theory.

Early in the paper, Maile directs the reader's attention to the headquartering of the TMT in California, showing that "the astronomy industry benefits from militourism in Hawaiʻi, and vice versa" (Maile 2021: 96). This calls attention to the networks of economic capital that undergird all such labour practices, and the commensurate insistence of promissory economic capital expansion that facilitates the speculative development of NewSpace. Leveraging economic capital for labour is unequally distributed. Redfield describes the networks financing the transmutation of the "lead of empire into the gold of national entitlement" (2002: 800) by France in its overseas department currently known as Guyane through the input of labour of local Guianese workers and international scientists undertaken at the Guiana Space Centre.

Even a cursory focus on gender in the finance networks that underpin the commercial space age reveals Jeff Bezos, Richard Branson, and Elon Musk bankrolling this shift in our engagement with outer space. Further research could theorise commonalities that might characterise these 'astro-masculinities'—much as Cara Daggett describes locally specific petro-masculinities that in the USA are characterised by "rosy nostalgia" for the mid-twentieth century that sees a "convergence ... between climate change, a threatened fossil fuel system, and an increasingly fragile Western hypermasculinity" (2018: 29). Indeed, Daggett suggests that Elon Musk's public disposition may be characteristic of *ecomodernist* masculinities—where "technological solutions, often private and market-based, would solve any difficulties" (p. 33) of environmental issues here on Earth while ensuring that "[c]are and compassion remain subordinate to techno-rationality, toughness, and economic growth" (p. 34). Bronwyn Lovell (2021) documents that this manifests both as a significant underrepresentation of women in the workforce and a self-aggrandisement of men who do work in the field. Lovell observes that "being an astronaut is [perceived by them to be] perhaps an even more powerful sexual position for men [than being a celebrity], allowing both married and single astronauts alike to romp in a 'potpourri of pussy'" (p. 66, quoting Mullane 2007). Such expressions of power are borne out in the experiences of harassment and unwanted sexual attention that are rife within the space industry, in major companies (as documented by Abrams et al. 2021), by high-profile individuals (covered in Smith 2022), or in research expeditions (where Clancy et al. (2014) documented 70% of women and 40% of men experiencing sexual harassment in fieldwork). While "women's access to remote labour opportunities was bound up with broader processes of institutional change" (p. 331), Morgan Seag (2017) argues that both in Antarctica and Outer Space the stymying of women's participation in the workforce was primarily due to "ideological and strategic commitments to masculinity in remote spaces" (p. 332) which are upheld by institutions.

Thinking with Sara Ahmed's (2017) valuing of (feminist) care labour within the house and the home, Eleanor S. Armstrong (2022) demonstrates that both terrestrial field research today and speculative outer space futures need to more fully engage with the labours of care and pre-emptively prepare for the negative social dimensions within outer space communities. Elsewhere theorising of masculinities and femininities in space studies highlights pluralities. Daniel Sage argues that "NASA as an organization is complicit with the rehearsal of gendered identities through polarized binaries" (2009: 146). Casper and Moore (1995) have described the differential treatment of women, and they have similarly been singled out for traditionally feminised items for space flight such as makeup kits (Armstrong, 2023 Moving beyond this construction of people and their labours in research as being binarised (and centred on Euroamerican institutions) and seeing pluralities of gender explored would further improve our understanding of outer space in the social sciences.

Technology

Feminist, critical race, and crip approaches within media and science and technology studies offer particularly valuable insights for understanding the complex interplay between social difference, technology, and the space sciences. Critical perspectives on media and technology recognise that "the technological is a specific vector of power" (Sharma 2022: xi): far from being tools separate from politics, technologies introduce tangible changes to the relations between humans and other humans, and humans and their environment. Many such technologies have historically supported colonial-patriarchal dynamics (Atanasoski and Vora 2019; Benjamin 2019; Wajcman 1991). Incorporating these critical approaches into space studies scholarship unsettles dominant popular and scientific discourses surrounding engagements with space—which have tended to valorise technological development, innovation, and territorial conquest as a universal human good. Instead, these approaches allow us to unveil how the sociotechnical systems associated with space travel have shifted or reinforced an unequal distribution of power along various axes of identity.

As we have described in our previous section, discourses around space technologies have systematically sidelined the labour of people of colour and women and appropriated their knowledge, maintaining the perception that the field has been principally built by white men. In addition to how we discussed their labour, it is also important to value the technological, mathematical, and engineering knowledge Johnson, Vaughan, and Jackson brought to the Mercury and Apollo missions, making them possible (Shetterly 2016). Similarly, as ongoing research undertaken by Gál demonstrates, the construction of parasol that replaced Skylab's damaged thermal shield required the sewing knowledge of General Electric seamsteesses, and the design was likely influenced by the lead engineer's knowledge of his mother's sewing work. Yet in the end, only the male engineer received a NASA medal for his work and came to be remembered as "the man who saved Skylab" (Kinzler 1999: 14–45), ultimately reinforcing a narrative of technological solutions being borne out of the individual expertise of sole white male geniuses. As David Mindell's investigation of human–machine interaction during the Apollo programme (1961–1972) shows, the engineering choices for US spaceflight were themselves heavily influenced by masculinist worldviews—the designers had to make sure that the space shuttles were not too automated, because "frontiersmen could not be passengers" (2011: 12). While studies conducted on potential astronauts in the 1960s showed that women would be physiologically better suited for spaceflight than men, NASA's demand for astronauts to be qualified jet pilots automatically excluded them. Margaret Weitekamp argues that this was intentional, as "[t]he very qualifications required for NASA astronauts proved the complexity of US space achievements. Demonstrating that a woman could perform those tasks would diminish their prestige" (2004: 3). The cancellation of NASA's first all-female spacewalk in 2019 reveals that space technologies continue to reinforce gender hierarchies: the aerospace agency could not provide enough smaller suits on the ISS to fit the women going on space walks (Cantor 2019).

What Sarah Sharma calls "gender's tech problem" (2020: 172) is also reflected in the anthropomorphisation and gendering of specific space technologies. Tamara Szűcs (2015) describes how the scientific discourse created by the European Space Agency surrounding the Rosetta probe and Philae lander projected gendered roles onto the spacecraft. Rosetta was presented as a mothership, providing care and emotional support to its son, the Philae lander. Philae, gendered as a small boy, 'pioneered' into space on its mission to conquer the 67P/Churyumov–Gerasimenko comet. The comet was, in turn, assigned a passive and feminine role, and presented as awaiting the scientific probing by the male lander and scientists. Elsewhere, Janet Vertesi shows how the Mars rover teams reveal a regular referral to Opportunity and Spirit as a "she"—ostensibly due to nautical convention—but also because the rovers are seen as *cute* (2015: 187–88). Showing that gender is not a single dimension even in anthropomorphism, Vertesi describes how the two rovers are ascribed different class markers—one as a hard-working blue-collar labourer, the other a white-collar lucky labourer. Monica J. Casper and Lisa J. Moore (1995) demonstrate that the space sciences' construction of maleness as norm is tied to associating masculinity with stability, technology, and control, while seeing womanhood as inherently tied to nature, instability, and contamination. The construction of womanhood as a "problem" has to led some scientists wishing to shed their gender marking altogether:

> According to one scientist, they prefer to be identified as "just another piece of hardware" to avoid being gendered. Yet on the other hand, they are judged negatively by other NASA staff when they do not behave or act like women in essentialized ways.
>
> *(Casper and Moore 1995: 318)*

Being marked by gender differences was seen as less desirable than being seen as a technology, which further solidifies the historical construction of the field as being a domain of white men and their machines. A pluralised feminist lens encourages us to be critical about who is in the position of longing for a status that rejects not only gender but humanity as well: throughout history, racialised people have been repeatedly dehumanised into being technology. As Armond Towns shows, Black people have historically been seen as technologies (2020). Fred Scharmen demonstrates a similar tension in how Nazi aerospace engineer Wernher von Braun thought of technology as "the only means offered by God whereby we may strip off the curse of slavery", while his V2 rocket was built by the prisoners in the Dora-Mittelbau Nazi concentration camp (2021: 90).

Afrofuturist engagements, as Ytasha L. Womack (2013) describes, have used the themes of space and space technologies as avenues towards creative and material empowerment, liberation, counter-memory, and understanding. We see this reflected in, for example, the hip-hop group Public Enemy's tracks that use extraterrestriality and alien abductions to explore histories of forced dislocation (Eshun 2003), visual artist Yinka Shonibare's sculptures of the Refugee Astronaut—depicted in Salazar and Gorman's introduction to this volume introduction—that imagine technologies that could safely transport Black people through hostile environments (Hamilton 2017), Sun Ra's temporal and outer-spatial dislocation through sonic media and the abandonment of the confines of Earthly existence in favour of the "cosmic multi-self" (Brown 2021: 156), or Octavia Butler's use of an alien DNA manipulation to unsettle dominant understandings of a gender binary (Butler 1987).

Within crip scholarship, Ashley Shew has been working to unsettle what she calls "technoableism" (2017) in space exploration—a cultural glamorisation and framing of technologies as allowing humans to "overcome" bodily limitations. As crip scholars argue, living with technologies does not always mean an effortless integration between bodies and machines that inherently "fixes" bodies; rather, it is continuously labour-intensive and often a source of pain, requiring adaptation, negotiation, and technological maintenance (Kafer 2013; Shew 2018a). Shew contends that disabled people are particularly well suited for space travel, both because certain disabilities make people adept at navigating spaces and technologies in creative ways and also because some medical conditions can prove advantageous when adapting to space. For example, some types of deafness reduce motion sickness, while people with hearts closer to their brains can tolerate higher acceleration (Shew 2017, 2018b). The project AstroAccess (https://astroaccess.org/) is also making headway in promoting disability inclusion in spaceflight.

This interplay of technology and the human is a constant refrain in outer space studies. Interrogating the history of bioregenerative life-support systems designs in space cabins, Leah Aronowsky argues that while spaceflight has been discursively framed as an emblem of technoscientific—and by extension, masculine—supremacy, the reality is that human survival in space has always been "a thoroughly multispecies affair", one that highlights the interdependency between the human and their environment (2017: 361). David Valentine (2017) urges scholars to move away from settler colonial, patriarchal, control-seeking visions of space travel and consider instead the possibilities that open up when we grapple with the ethical obligations we have towards the machines that we are entangled within space. Thinking with these scholars, Réka Gál (2020) interrogates the politics of breakdown and repair in outer space and argues that rather than technological innovation alone, sustainable space travel is, and has always been, dependent on historically gendered and racialised maintenance, repair, and care labours. Such feminist approaches to critically understanding technology as a sociotechnical project that is always already part of the society from which it is created offer scholars fruitful avenues to thinking through the technoscientific project of outer space.

Environment

One of the key interventions of feminist technoscience has been demonstrating how distinctions between nature and technology (or culture) have fallen across gendered and racialised lines. By tracing the effects of these conceptions across the histories of science and technology—including the space sciences and engineering—such scholarship makes visible the implications of such actions. Lisa Messeri argues that exoplanet astronomy's search for habitable planets reflects nostalgic, colonial desires to recover an Edenic Earth elsewhere in the solar system—emerging especially strongly as increasingly "the prospect of repairing our own planet is daunting" (2017: 333). Pointing towards the figure of the mother astronomer as a recurring character in stories told at exoplanet astronomy conferences, in papers, and to the public, she contends that despite aiming to paint a progressive image of women in the sciences, it also reinforces conservative views of women as inherently tied to reproduction and to nature. Sarah T. Roberts and Mél Hogan also locate eschatological dimensions in contemporary space colonial desires, which they call "prepping for pleasure and for profit" (2019: 14). Ultimately, they contend, techno-utopian plans to colonise outer space are rooted in a desire to escape an Earth that is seen as no longer being able to assure a high quality of life for the élites and the vast majority of the population. Insofar as the search for an Edenic nature or a pristine "wilderness" (Cronon 1996) is the result of increasing industrialisation and capitalist extractivism, contemporary space colonisation is then framed as serving the complex dual purpose of extending capitalist markets, while simultaneously trying to escape what they have wrought. As Elizabeth Kessler (2012) shows, space science's relationship to the cosmic environment is informed by already existing aesthetic norms shaped by the representation of the US's 'American West' trope.

The colonial, and indeed explicitly Christian, worldviews reflected in space colonial and space exploration narratives are highlighted in their relationship to both gender and nature. Vanessa Watts (2013) argues that attending to the difference between Anishinaabe and Christian creation stories can help us understand the workings of sexism and environmental extractivism as co-constitutive. Where Christian creation myths see the 'fall' as being the fault of feminine Eve's interaction with the Tree of Knowledge and the Serpent, Anishinaabe creation myths see the feminine as the originator of Land and understand interspecies communication and mutually respectful engagement as an ethical obligation. Watts thus understands the workings of sexism and environmental extractivism as being co-constitutive, and writes: "[i]f you belong to a structure where land and the feminine are not only less-than, but knowingly irresponsible, violations against her would seem warranted" (2013: 26). These violations often manifest as desires for control over the environment, as a result of seeing only humans as possessing agency while seeing nonhumans and the environment as being merely passive recipients of human actions. This is clear even within the sciences that are aimed at understanding the systematic nature of environmental interactions. As Peder Anker (2005) has argued, even the influence of ecology on the scientific developments aimed to enable the colonisation of space reflects imperial traditions and is largely influenced by Cold War fears of nuclear disasters and militaristic hopes of creating wholly governable closed-world environments. Similarly, Valerie Olson's (2018) research highlights how the systems thinking of NASA engineers and scientists (articulated through various bodies such as the human as system, the environment as system, the solar system, etc.) ultimately serves to extend control and governance into a cosmic ecosystem.

The colonial undertones of space exploration discourses have been discussed by numerous scholars (Billings 2007; Treviño 2020; see also Treviño this volume), and recent discussions have turned towards investigating how the materiality of ground and off-ground infrastructure of space activities continues to serve colonial interests and engender environmental injustice across the world. In various places around the world, the sovereignty of Indigenous nations has been undermined, compromising their relationship to and stewardship of the Land in order to institute a capitalist, extractivist relation based on the promises of Enlightenment science and "development", which are positioned as inherently serving the good of a universal humanity. This is particularly visible in the framing of the Kānaka Maoli protests against the desecration and destruction brought by the TMT as futile, outdated, an obstruction of "the future". In contrast, Noelani Goodyear-Kaʻōpua argues that the "Protect Mauna a Wākea" movement is aimed at protecting the future, a project of "Indigenous resistance against industrial projects that destroy or pollute our territories [that] concerns the health of all people" (2017: 185). Asif Siddiqi (2021) demonstrates that the Indian government's forcible removal and resettlement of Yanadi people in Andhra Pradesh to make way for a new space centre in Sriharikota is marked by a similar colonial "logic of location". In this, we see how specific areas are operationalised as being most well suited to pursue science, such that *not* going forward with the project is framed as completely inhibiting the ability to pursue science, and hence, "progress".

Elsewhere, Megan Black (2018) argues that the pursuit of the "development" of the world's resources has been at the foundation of the US imperial project since the establishment of the US Department of Interior, namely the usage of the environment as the logic of US international intervention. Black shows how satellite technologies have played a central role in the mapping of Earth's resources and have been mobilised in the justification of US foreign intervention in attempts to "develop" areas of the world through extractive capitalism. This same thread is taken up in Julie Klinger's (2017) research, where this developmental agenda is explicitly exported into outer space in the international competition over the mining of the Moon's resources. Plural feminist orientation to the imaginaries of the material cosmos beyond Earth continues to help unpack and challenge the status quo of how contemporary power structures and ideologies are continued into outer space. The resources used in building rockets and telescopes have extractive origins (Riofrancos 2020). As Katheryn M. Detwiler shows, not only satellite but also radio telescope data continues to be instrumentalised for extractivist purposes: the data produced by the Atacama Large Millimeter Array (ALMA) in the Chilean Andes—built on the lands of the Lickan Antay Indigenous people (Lehuedé 2022)—is used to develop underground mining of the Atacama Desert (Detwiler 2021; see Detwiler this volume). At the other end of the use-chain, Valentina Marcheselli (2022) demonstrates how, after they are decommissioned, mines are reused by astrobiology as "Earthly analogues" for extraterrestrial locations, reconceptualising the mine—formerly the extractive site *par excellence*—as a literal rehearsal for the cosmic extractive frontier.

Feminist waste and discard studies can also help reshape the kinds of environmental engagements that take place in outer space by disrupting the ideas of infinities into which waste can be displaced. Lisa Ruth Rand's (2019) analysis of the 1978 nuclear reentry of the Soviet Kosmos 954 satellite into the territory of the Dene and Inuit communities in the Great Slave Lake area in the settler state of Canada demonstrates that space exploration, not only in moments of innovation but also in moments of its decay, has the potential to reinforce global geopolitical hierarchies and settler colonial ethics. The state's delay in and navigation of recovering the satellite clearly reflects Max Liboiron's definition of a type of pollution that is a function of colonialism, predicated on access to Indigenous Land, and based on viewing the land as "a sink, a place to store waste" (2021: 8). Tracing the history of containment protocols employed by the space sciences also shows that not only the Land but also oceans are implicated in these dynamics. For example, while the Apollo 11 astronauts were put in containment after their return from the Moon, their capsule itself landed in the Pacific Ocean, which Stefan Helmreich argues shows a view of the ocean as "outside of human geography", and hence, outside the need for containment (2009: 269). The ocean in its immensity and the island in its seeming fragility (but also its orientalist position of being exploitable—the duality of the island) frame the metaphors of outer space. Claire I. Webb (2021) shows that linking the "planet" with the "island" within exobiologists' imaginaries creates "cosmic archipelagos" that shape the narrativisation of contamination by biowaste, casting the (US) scientist as the paternalistic father figure who decides which extraterrestrial "sites [are] to be preserved, cared for, and protected" (p. 398), often in direct contrast to the treatment of sites designated for waste here on Earth. Elsewhere the waste and discard of the outer space project has been figured along archaeological lines, as Alice Gorman argues (this volume), where these items become a source of knowledge about the scientific past. Highlighting this increasing pollution of low Earth orbit and the collecting space debris at Point Nemo in the Pacific Ocean demonstrates how existing practices for theorising commodity chains from extraction to discard could equally trace the engagement of the environment in outer space and its enlistment in the colonial-capitalist ideology of space exploration in the twenty-first century.

A focus on the environment has highlighted how dominant epistemologies are reproduced *both* discursively and materially. By investigating the differential impacts of these reverberations on communities across the world, environmental scholarship, and indeed scholarship focusing on environmental justice, can as we have demonstrated here provide significant contributions to the social studies of outer space. With a move towards increased physical presence in outer space, rooted in increased extractivism and increased launch sites around the world, critically examining the impacts of these on both environmental and (neo)colonial dynamics is especially urgent.

What's Next?

In this chapter, we have demonstrated how key areas of feminist technoscience research interests—labour, technology, and environment—can be brought to bear on theorising about outer space. A recurring theme in these engagements is how the way we think about work, technology, and environments on Earth—whether in terms of producing them, using them, or repurposing them physically or metaphorically—shape the way we research the past, understand the present, or speculate about the future.

We contend that feminism is developing the field of outer space studies, and by continuing to engage with scholarship beyond our immediate subdiscipline the social studies of outer space will be all the better for it. While the work we have highlighted demonstrates a range of feminist methods, methodological commitments, and onto-epistemologies, we are cognisant that there are many and plural works that are bedded in other feminisms that we believe will enrich the field. Feminisms are not monolithic; nor should their entailed theorising be.

Acknowledgements

We thank the editors for asking us to contribute to this volume. We are also grateful for the support of our copyeditor in editing our piece. Any remaining errors are ours. All elements of this project (methodology, conceptualisation, original draft, review, and editing) have been equally shared between the authors.

Notes

1 Eleanor S. Armstrong and Réka Patrícia Gál have contributed equally to this piece and are joint first authors. Feminist thinkers have for long been discussing coauthorship and the issue of author order as part of feminist methodologies. For more on this see, for example, Liboiron et al. (2017).
2 For a longer discussion on the difference and interplay between (different types of) colonialism and capitalism, see Liboiron (2021), especially pp. 7–16.

References

Abrams, Alexandra, et al. 2021. "Bezos Wants to Create a Better Future in Space. His Company Blue Origin Is Stuck in a Toxic Past." *Lioness*, 30 September 2021. https://www.lioness.co/post/bezos-wants-to-create-a-better-future-in-space-his-company-blue-origin-is-stuck-in-a-toxic-past.

Ahmed, Sara. 2017. *Living a Feminist Life*. Durham, NC: Duke University Press.

Anker, Peder. 2005. "The Ecological Colonization of Space." *Environmental History* 10 (2): 239–68. https://doi.org/10.1093/envhis/10.2.239.

Armstrong, Eleanor S. 2022. "Cosmic Queeries: Queer Theory in Studies of Outer Space." *Online presentation given at Ethnographies of Outer Space: Methodological Opportunities and Experiments*, University of Trento, September 1–2, 2022. https://webmagazine.unitn.it/evento/sociologia/109969/ethnographies-of-outer-space.

Armstrong, Eleanor S. 2023. "Make-Up Kit." In *The Gender of Things: How Epistemic and Technological Objects Become Gendered*, edited by Maria Rentetzi. London: Routledge.

Aronowsky, Leah V. 2017. "Of Astronauts and Algae: NASA and the Dream of Multispecies Space Flight." *Environmental Humanities* 9 (2): 359–77. https://doi.org/10.1215/22011919-4215343.

Atanasoski, Neda, and Kalindi Vora. 2019. *Surrogate Humanity: Race, Robots, and the Politics of Technological Futures*. Durham, NC: Duke University Press.

Banet-Weiser, Sarah. 2018. *Empowered: Popular Feminism and Popular Misogyny*. Durham, NC: Duke University Press.

Benjamin, Ruha. 2019. *Race After Technology: Abolitionist Tools for the New Jim Code*. Cambridge: Polity.

Billings, Linda. 2007. "Overview: Ideology, Advocacy, and Spaceflight—Evolution of a Cultural Narrative." In *Societal Impact of Spaceflight*, edited by Steven J. Dick and Roger D. Launius, 483–99. NASA SP-2007-4801. Washington, DC: NASA.

Black, Megan. 2018. *The Global Interior: Mineral Frontiers and American Power*. Cambridge, MA: Harvard University Press.

Boucher, Marie-Pier. 2022. "Space Feminism." *ESPACE Art Actuel*, 130.

Brown, Jayna. 2021. *Black Utopias: Speculative Life and the Music of Other Worlds*. Durham. NC: Duke University Press.

Butler, Octavia E. 1987. *Dawn: Xenogenesis*. New York: Warner Books.

Cantor, Matthew. 2019. "Nasa Cancels All-Female Spacewalk, Citing Lack of Spacesuit in Right Size." *The Guardian*, 26 March 2019, sec. Science. https://www.theguardian.com/science/2019/mar/25/nasa-all-female-spacewalk-canceled-women-spacesuits.

Casper, Monica J., and Lisa Jean Moore. 1995. "Inscribing Bodies, Inscribing the Future: Gender, Sex, and Reproduction in Outer Space." *Sociological Perspectives* 38 (2): 311–33. https://doi.org/10.2307/1389295.

Chasten Long, Charnell. n.d. "The Black Women Food Scientists Who Created Meals For Astronauts." *Lady Science*. Accessed 27 August 2022. https://www.ladyscience.com/essays/black-women-food-scientists-who-created-meals-for-astronauts.

Cipolla, Cyd, Kristina Gupta, David A. Rubin, and Angela Willey. 2017. *Queer Feminist Science Studies: A Reader*. Seattle: University of Washington Press.

Clancy, Kathryn B. H., Robin G. Nelson, Julienne N. Rutherford, and Katie Hinde. 2014. "Survey of Academic Field Experiences (SAFE): Trainees Report Harassment and Assault." *PLoS One* 9 (7): e102172. https://doi.org/10.1371/journal.pone.0102172.

Cronon, William. 1996. "The Trouble with Wilderness: Or, Getting Back to the Wrong Nature." *Environmental History* 1 (1): 7–28. https://doi.org/10.2307/3985059.

Daggett, Cara. 2018. "Petro-Masculinity: Fossil Fuels and Authoritarian Desire." *Millenium: Journal of International Studies* 47 (1): 25–44. https://doi.org/0.1177/0305829818775817.

Deerfield, Kat. 2013. "Subversions of Time in (Outer) Space." Presented at Temporal Belongings, Cardiff, UK, 2 January. http://www.temporalbelongings.org/3/post/2013/01/kat-deerfield-cardiff-university.html.

Deerfield, Kat. 2019. *Gender, Sexuality, and Space Culture*. London; New York: Rowman & Littlefield.

Detwiler, Katheryn M. 2021. "Logistical Natures in Andean Worlds." In *Logistical Worlds: Infrastructure, Software, Labour; No. 3, Valparaíso*, edited by Brett Neilson and Ned Rossiter, 79–89. London: Low Latencies, an imprint of Fibreculture Books, Open Humanities Press.

Eshun, Kodwo. 2003. "Further Considerations of Afrofuturism." *CR: The New Centennial Review* 3 (2): 287–302. https://doi.org/10.1353/ncr.2003.0021.

Estes, Nick. 2019. *Our History Is the Future: Standing Rock Versus the Dakota Access Pipeline, and the Long Tradition of Indigenous Resistance*. London: Verso Books.

Gál, Réka Patrícia. 2020. "Climate Change, COVID-19, and the Space Cabin: A Politics of Care in the Shadow of Space Colonization." *Mezosfera*, October 2020. http://mezosfera.org/climate-change-covid-19-and-the-space-cabin-a-politics-of-care-in-the-shadow-of-space-colonization/.

Gaudry, Adam. 2015. "Researching the Resurgence: Insurgent Research and Community-Engaged Methodologies in 21st-Century Academic Inquiry." In *Research as Resistance: Revisiting Critical, Indigenous, and Anti-oppressive Approaches*, edited by Susan Strega and Leslie Allison Brown, 243–65. Toronto: Canadian Scholars' Press.

Goodyear-Kaʻōpua, Noelani. 2017. "Protectors of the Future, Not Protestors of the Past: Indigenous Pacific Activism and Mauna a Wākea." *South Atlantic Quarterly* 116 (1): 184–94. https://doi.org/10.1215/00382876-3749603.

Hall, Stuart. 1992. "The West and the Rest: Discourse and Power." In *Formations of Modernity*, edited by Stuart Hall and Bram Gieben, 275–32. Understanding Modern Societies 1. Cambridge, MA: Polity Press.

Hamilton, Elizabeth C. 2017. "Afrofuturism and the Technologies of Survival." *African Arts* 50 (4): 18–23. https://doi.org/10.1162/AFAR_a_00371.

Haraway, Donna. 1991. *Simians, Cyborgs, and Women: The Reinvention of Nature*. New York: Routledge.

Hartman, Saidiya. 2016. "The Belly of the World: A Note on Black Women's Labors." *Souls* 18 (1): 166–73. https://doi.org/10.1080/10999949.2016.1162596.

Hartman, Saidiya V. 2020. *Wayward Lives, Beautiful Experiments: Intimate Histories of Riotous Black Girls, Troublesome Women and Queer Radicals*. New York: W. W. Norton.

Helmreich, Stefan. 2009. *Alien Ocean: Anthropological Voyages in Microbial Seas*. Berkeley: University of California Press.

Hewa, Nelanthi. 2021. "The Mouth of the Internet, the Eyes of the Public: Sexual Violence Survivorship in an Economy of Visibility." Published online 5 May 2021. *Feminist Media Studies*, 1–12. https://doi.org/10.1080/14680777.2021.1922483.

Holbrook, Jarita C., Rodney Medupe, and Johnson O. Urama, eds. 2008. *African Cultural Astronomy: Current Archaeoastronomy and Ethnoastronomy Research in Africa*. Astrophysics and Space Science Proceedings. Berlin: Springer.

Holt, Nathalia. 2016. *Rise of the Rocket Girls: The Women Who Propelled Us, from Missiles to the Moon to Mars*. New York: Little, Brown.

hooks, bell. 2001. *Ain't I a Woman: Black Women and Feminism*. Reprint. Pluto Classics. London: Pluto Press.

Kafer, Alison. 2013. *Feminist, Queer, Crip*. Bloomington, IN: Indiana University Press.

Kessler, Elizabeth A. 2012. *Picturing the Cosmos: Hubble Space Telescope Images and the Astronomical Sublime*. Minneapolis, MN: University of Minnesota Press.

Kinzler, Jack. 1999. *Oral History 3 Transcript*. Interview by Roy Neal. Houston, TX: Johnson Space Center History Office. https://historycollection.jsc.nasa.gov/JSCHistoryPortal/history/oral_histories/KinzlerJA/JAK_4-27-99.pdf.

Klinger, Julie Michelle. 2017. *Rare Earth Frontiers: From Terrestrial Subsoils to Lunar Landscapes.*. Ithaca, NY: Cornell University Press..

Lehuedé, Sebastián. 2022. "Territories of Data: Ontological Divergences in the Growth of Data Infrastructure." *Tapuya: Latin American Science, Technology and Society*, published online 11 April 2022, article 2035936. https://doi.org/10.1080/25729861.2022.2035936.

Liboiron, Max. 2021. *Pollution Is Colonialism*. Durham, NC: Duke University Press.

Liboiron, Max, Justine Ammendolia, Katharine Winsor, Alex Zahara, Hillary Bradshaw, Jessica Melvin, Charles Mather, et al. 2017. "Equity in Author Order: A Feminist Laboratory's Approach." *Catalyst: Feminism, Theory, Technoscience* 3 (2): 1–17. https://doi.org/10.28968/cftt.v3i2.28850.

Light, Jennifer S. 1999. "When Computers Were Women." *Technology and Culture* 40 (3): 455–83.

Lorde, Audre. 2003. "The Master's Tools Will Never Dismantle the Master's House." In *Feminist Postcolonial Theory: A Reader*, edited by Reina Lewis and Sara Mills, 25–28. London: Routledge.

Lovell, Bronwyn. 2021. "Sex and the Stars: The Enduring Structure of Gender Discrimination in the Space Industry." *Journal of Feminist Scholarship* 18 (18): 61–77. https://doi.org/10.23860/jfs.2021.18.04.

Maile, David Uahikeaikaleiʻohu. 2019. "Resurgent Refusals: Protecting Mauna a Wākea and Kanaka Maoli Decolonization." *Hūlili: Multidisciplinary Research on Hawaiian Well-Being* 11 (1): 57–69.

Maile, David Uahikeaikaleiʻohu. 2021. "On Being Late: Cruising Mauna Kea and Unsettling Technoscientific Conquest in Hawaiʻi." *American Indian Culture and Research Journal* 45 (1): 95–122. https://doi.org/10.17953/aicrj.45.1.maile.

Marcheselli, Valentina. 2022. "The Exploration of the Earth Subsurface as a Martian Analogue." *Tecnoscienza: Italian Journal of Science & Technology Studies* 13 (1): 25–46.

McCoy, Terrence, and Heloísa Traiano. 2021. "A Story of Slavery—and Space." *Washington Post*, 26 March 2021. https://www.washingtonpost.com/world/interactive/2021/brazil-alcantara-launch-center-quilombo/.

McKittrick, Katherine. 2021. *Dear Science and Other Stories*. Durham, NC: Duke University Press.

Merchant, Carolyn. 1989. *The Death of Nature: Women, Ecology, and the Scientific Revolution*. New York: Harper & Row.
Messeri, Lisa. 2017. "Gestures of Cosmic Relation and the Search for Another Earth." *Environmental Humanities* 9 (2): 325–40. https://doi.org/10.1215/22011919-4215325.
Mindell, David A. 2011. *Digital Apollo: Human and Machine in Spaceflight*. Cambridge: MIT Press.
Mullane, Mike. 2007. *Riding Rockets: The Outrageous Tales of a Space Shuttle Astronaut*. New York: Simon and Schuster.
Muñoz, José Esteban. 2009. *Cruising Utopia: The Then and There of Queer Futurity*. New York: NYU Press.
Nakamura, Lisa. 2014. "Indigenous Circuits: Navajo Women and the Racialization of Early Electronic Manufacture." *American Quarterly* 66 (4): 919–41. https://doi.org/10.1353/aq.2014.0070.
Neas, Ollie. 2021. "Mahia, We Have A Problem." *North & South Magazine*, April 2021. https://northandsouth.co.nz/2021/03/14/rocket-lab-military/.
Öhman, May-Britt, and Lilian Mikaelsson. 2014. "When the Land Became a Testing Range: Nausta, Udtja and NEAT." In *Re: Mindings: Co-Constituting Indigenous/Academic/Artistic Knowledges*, edited by Johan Gärdebo, May-Britt Öhman and Hiroshi Maruyama, 245–54. Uppsala: The Hugo Valentin Centre. http://urn.kb.se/resolve?urn=urn:nbn:se:uu:diva-240362.
Olson, Valerie. 2018. *Into the Extreme: U.S. Environmental Systems and Politics Beyond Earth*. Minneapolis, MN: University of Minnesota Press.
Omoruyi, Osase. 2021. *The Extractive Gaze: Astronomical Southern Stations in South Africa*. Presented at the Annual Conference of the Society for Social Studies of Science, online, October 6.
Patterson, Ashley, Valerie Kinloch, Tanja Burkhard, Ryann Randall, and Arianna Howard. 2016. "Black Feminist Thought as Methodology: Examining Intergenerational Lived Experiences of Black Women." *Departures in Critical Qualitative Research* 5 (3): 55–76. https://doi.org/10.1525/dcqr.2016.5.3.55.
Penley, Constance. 1997. *NASA/TREK: Popular Science and Sex in America*. London: Verso.
Prescod-Weinstein, Chanda. 2021. *The Disordered Cosmos: A Journey into Dark Matter, Spacetime, and Dreams Deferred*. New York: Bold Type.
Puig de la Bellacasa, María. 2017. *Matters of Care: Speculative Ethics in More than Human Worlds*. Minneapolis, MN: University of Minnesota Press.
Rand, Lisa Ruth. 2014. "The Case for Female Astronauts: Reproducing Americans in the Final Frontier." *The Appendix*, 15 July 2014. http://theappendix.net/issues/2014/7/the-case-for-female-astronauts-reproducing-americans-in-the-final-frontier.
Rand, Lisa Ruth. 2019. "Falling Cosmos: Nuclear Reentry and the Environmental History of Earth Orbit." *Environmental History* 24 (1): 78–103. https://doi.org/10.1093/envhis/emy125.
Redfield, Peter. 2002. "The Half-Life of Empire in Outer Space." *Social Studies of Science* 32 (5–6): 791–825. https://doi.org/10.1177/030631270203200508.
Rifkin, Mark. 2017. *Beyond Settler Time: Temporal Sovereignty and Indigenous Self-Determination*. Durham, NC: Duke University Press.
Riofrancos, Thea N. 2020. *Resource Radicals: From Petro-Nationalism to Post-Extractivism in Ecuador*. Durham, NC: Duke University Press.
Roberts, Sarah T., and Mél Hogan. 2019. "Left Behind: Futurist Fetishists, Prepping and the Abandonment of Earth." *B2o: An Online Journal* 4(2). https://escholarship.org/uc/item/8sr8n99w.
Rosner, Daniela K. 2018. *Critical Fabulations: Reworking the Methods and Margins of Design*. Cambridge, MA: MIT Press.
Sage, Daniel. 2009. "Giant Leaps and Forgotten Steps: NASA and the Performance of Gender." *The Sociological Review* 57 (1): 146–63. https://doi.org/10.1111/j.1467-954X.2009.01822.x.
Scharmen, Fred. 2021. *Space Forces: A Critical History of Life in Outer Space*. Brooklyn, NY: Verso Books.
Seag, Morgan. 2017. "Women Need Not Apply: Gendered Institutional Change in Antarctica and Outer Space." *The Polar Journal* 7 (2): 319–35. https://doi.org/10.1080/2154896X.2017.1373915.
Selin, Helaine, and Sun Xiaochun. 2002. *Astronomy across Cultures: The History of Non-Western Astronomy*. Dordrecht: Springer. http://public.ebookcentral.proquest.com/choice/publicfullrecord.aspx?p=3566730.
Sharma, Sarah. 2020. "A Manifesto for the Broken Machine." *Camera Obscura: Feminism, Culture, and Media Studies* 35 (2 (104)): 171–79. https://doi.org/10.1215/02705346-8359652.
Sharma, Sarah. 2022. "Preface." In *Re-understanding Media: Feminist Extensions of Marshall McLuhan*, edited by Sarah Sharma and Rianka Singh, vii–xii. Durham, NC: Duke University Press.
Shetterly, Margot Lee. 2016. *Hidden Figures: The American Dream and the Untold Story of the Black Women Mathematicians Who Helped Win the Space Race*. New York: HarperCollins.
Shew, Ashley. 2017. "Technoableism, Cyborg Bodies, and Mars." *Technology and Disability* (blog), 11 November 2017. https://techanddisability.com/2017/11/11/technoableism-cyborg-bodies-and-mars/.

Shew, Ashley. 2018a. "Different Ways of Moving Through the World." *Logic Magazine* (5), 1 August 2018. https://logicmag.io/failure/different-ways-of-moving-through-the-world/.

Shew, Ashley. 2018b. "Disabled People in Space—Becoming Interplanetary." *Technology and Disability* (blog), 14 October 2018. https://techanddisability.com/category/technoableism/.

Siddiqi, Asif. 2021. *The Colonial Logic of Location: The Yanadi Community in India and the Violence of Spaceflight*. Paper presented at the Annual Conference of the Society for the History of Science, online, 19 November 2021.

Simpson, Leanne Betasamosake. 2017. *As We Have Always Done: Indigenous Freedom through Radical Resistance*. Indigenous Americas. Minneapolis, MN: University of Minnesota Press.

Singh, Rianka. 2020. "Resistance in a Minor Key: Care, Survival and Convening on the Margins." *First Monday* 25(5), 4 May 2020. https://doi.org/10.5210/fm.v25i5.10631.

Smith, Zachary Snowdon. 2022. "SpaceX Reportedly Paid $250,000 to Settle Sexual Harassment Accusation Against Elon Musk." *Forbes*, 19 May 2022. https://www.forbes.com/sites/zacharysmith/2022/05/19/spacex-reportedly-paid-250000-to-settle-sexual-harassment-accusation-against-elon-musk/.

Sobel, Dava. 2016. *The Glass Universe: How the Ladies of the Harvard Observatory Took the Measure of the Stars*. New York: Viking.

Szűcs, Tamara. 2015. "What Do Cyborgs Gossip About in (Cyber)Space? Tracing Posthuman Discourses in the Rosetta Space Mission." *Pulse: The Journal of Science and Culture* (Central European University) 3 (1): 161–75.

Towns, Armond R. 2020. "Toward a Black Media Philosophy." *Cultural Studies* 34 (6): 851–73. https://doi.org/10.1080/09502386.2020.1792524.

Treviño, Natalie. 2020. *The Cosmos Is Not Finished*. PhD Thesis, Western University, Canada. https://ir.lib.uwo.ca/etd/7567.

Tuck, Eve. 2009. "Suspending Damage: A Letter to Communities." *Harvard Educational Review* 79 (3): 409–27. https://doi.org/10.17763/haer.79.3.n0016675661t3n15

Tutton, Richard. 2021. "Sociotechnical Imaginaries and Techno-Optimism: Examining Outer Space Utopias of Silicon Valley." *Science as Culture* 30 (3): 416–39. https://doi.org/10.1080/09505431.2020.1841151.

Valentine, David. 2017. "For the Machine." *History and Anthropology* 28 (3): 302–7. https://doi.org/10.1080/02757206.2017.1291506.

Venkatesan, Aparna, David Begay, Adam J. Burgasser, Isabel Hawkins, Kaʻiu Kimura, Nancy Maryboy, and Laura Peticolas. 2019. "Towards Inclusive Practices with Indigenous Knowledge." *Nature Astronomy* 3 (12): 1035–37. https://doi.org/10.1038/s41550-019-0953-2.

Vertesi, Janet. 2015. *Seeing Like a Rover: How Robots, Teams, and Images Craft Knowledge of Mars*. Chicago: University of Chicago Press.

Wajcman, Judy. 1991. *Feminism Confronts Technology*. University Park: Penn State University Press.

Watts, Vanessa. 2013. "Indigenous Place-Thought and Agency Amongst Humans and Non Humans (First Woman and Sky Woman Go On a European World Tour!)." *Decolonization: Indigeneity, Education & Society* 2(1): 20–34 https://jps.library.utoronto.ca/index.php/des/article/view/19145.

Webb, Claire Isabel. 2021. "Gaze-Scaling: Planets as Islands in Exobiologists' Imaginaries." *Science as Culture* 30 (3): 391–415. https://doi.org/10.1080/09505431.2021.1895737.

Weitekamp, Margaret A. 2004. *Right Stuff, Wrong Sex: America's First Women in Space Program*. Baltimore, MD: Johns Hopkins University Press.

Womack, Ytasha L. 2013. *Afrofuturism: The World of Black Sci-Fi and Fantasy Culture*. Chicago, IL: Laurence Hill.

Wynter, Sylvia. 2003. "Unsettling the Coloniality of Being/Power/Truth/Freedom: Towards the Human, After Man, Its Overrepresentation—An Argument." *CR: The New Centennial Review* 3 (3): 257–337. https://doi.org/10.1353/ncr.2004.0015.

14
THE ICONOGRAPHY OF THE ASTRONAUT AS A CRITICAL ENQUIRY OF SPACE LAW

Saskia Vermeylen

Introduction

This chapter juxtaposes the iconography of the *astronaut* as the envoy of humankind with that of the *afronaut* as the harbinger of lost and regained utopias. The image of the astronaut as the white, male hero potentially sacrificing his life for the benefit of humanity is a trope that has informed space law. When appointing the first spacefarers, the National Aeronautics and Space Administration (NASA) selected military test pilots precisely for their daredevil qualities combined with that element of willingness to be in the service of the wider public and country (Hersch 2011: 74). The astronauts of the Apollo era shared the American values and ideologies that centred on "duty", "faith", and "country" (Launius 2008: 187). They represented the American "everyman". Understandably, the astronauts were celebrated by the public as "noble champions who would carry the nation's manifest destiny beyond its shores and into space" (p. 187). NASA, together with the media and political establishment, carefully crafted a portrait of the astronauts that, according to Launius, conveys the astronaut as (i) the ordinary American always willing to act as the good neighbour and perfect father and husband who worships God, (ii) a staunch defender of the nation protecting the American way of life against any foreign intrusion, and (iii) a fun-loving, virile, masculine representative of the American ideal (p. 194). In other words, the American astronaut is pictured as the all-American hero cultivating celebrity status in the media.

But the white, Protestant, and civic standards of the American space programme were questioned at the start of the second phase of America's spaceflight history (Spiller 2013: 66). African Americans and women united in the civil rights movement were seeking explicit recognition of the important role they played in the American space programme. Against the background of mounting racial and ethnic discontentment, the African American magazine *Ebony* featured reportages of African American women and men supporting the space programme as mathematicians and medical assistants. It opened a wider debate about the whiteness of NASA and the marginalisation of its nonwhite astronauts. Eventually, the first six women and three African Americans were recruited as astronauts in 1978.

The whiteness and masculinity of space travel's history in the 1960s stand in sharp contrast with the political and legal ideology that was and still is shaping international space law. The preamble of the Treaty on Principles Governing the Activities of States in the Exploration and Use of Outer Space, including the Moon and Other Celestial Bodies, or the Outer Space Treaty (1967), stipulates that "the exploration and use of outer space should be carried on for the benefit of all peoples irrespective of the degree of their economic or scientific development". This tension between the lofty ideals that space exploration should be for the benefit of all humanity and the simultaneous exclusion of women and people of colour from spaceflight programmes has provoked a cultural critique. Whereas cultural, political, and social studies of space have exposed how *race* matters in the space 'race', barely any attention has been given to the silencing of women and people of colour or minorities in space law.

In this chapter, I employ this cultural critique as a methodological tool to analyse the historical evolution of international space law and to propose future developments in international space law. While space law is regaining in popularity as a result of the expansion of the commercial space sector, most academic research has focused on analysing and exposing the shortcomings of international space law (for a recent publication see, e.g., Schrogl, Giannopapa, and Antoni 2021). While the Outer Space Treaty is the most important international legal instrument governing the exploration and use of outer space, it is clearly an instrument of the Cold War era. Therefore its effectiveness is rightly questioned in a vast range of academic papers across the social sciences and humanities. However, this story of an inadequate or outmoded international legal regime to govern the use of outer space has not yet been told through the lens of the astronaut. This chapter is one of the very few pieces that use the astronaut as an icon to reveal the ambiguity and contradictions in international space law when it comes to its ambition to protect outer space as a commons for the benefit of humankind. I propose that the iconography of the afronaut in Africanfuturist artworks can act as a moral compass to develop more effective and inclusive principles to govern the use of outer space in a more fair and equitable manner.

The astronaut's clothing was used to convey the image of the astronaut as simultaneously the everyman and heroic. As commented upon by Launius, the astronaut's immense and disproportional mythical power was symbolised through the spacesuit (2008: 202). For the astronauts, the spacesuit was like their protective armour allowing them to go into 'hostile' environments. For the wider public, the spacesuit became the symbol of the dreams and beliefs of humanity: who we are and what we can achieve. The spacesuit captured the imagination of the American dream. In the words of Launius, the spacesuit "symbolized and reified the utopian desire to colonize the Solar System and make a perfect society at a new and pristine place beyond the corrupt Earth" (p. 203).

But as I aim to expose the discriminatory and exclusive character of international space law, I am particularly interested in analysing the cultural counternarratives that expose the cultural and geopolitical history of colonialism, imperialism, and capitalism through the fabric of the spacesuit. While the spacesuit is meant to function as a protective layer against extreme temperatures, radiation, and dust (NASA 2018), African artists in the diaspora and on the continent have redeployed it as a site of contamination (most notably the work of Yinka Shonibare has contributed to this canon; for more on this see Vermeylen 2021a). Inspired by the methodological possibilities that Afrofuturism and Africanfuturism have to offer, the artworks that are analysed in this chapter become discursive sites showing the lacuna, prejudices, and weaknesses of our current space law as embodied in the spacesuit. But the artworks showing the astronaut as the afronaut also embody hope for a more inclusive, just, and progressive body of space law.

As Bourland (2020: 229) illustrates, the afronauts in their different guises have become a "powerful icon in Afrofuturistic narratives of what has been, what could have been, and what is yet to come". In a similar vein, I use the iconography of the afronaut as a critical trope to question what space law would look like if the first steps on the Moon were the imprints of, for example, the footsteps of an African female astronaut. As commented by Bould, the Afrofuturist archive has a triple methodological function: first, it remembers, "displays things that might have been lost of forgotten"; but second, while remembering it also "dislocates materials, wrenching them from contexts and fitting them into … other patterns"; and third, the past is erased and new futures can arise (Bould 2019: 178).

This chapter attempts to do something similar. It opens the Afrofuturist archive about space travel and law, first by turning the critical lens onto the iconic figure of the astronaut and how they are represented in space law, thereby erasing the voices and contributions of women and people of colour. Second, the figure of the afronaut is introduced to tell an alternative, progressive, and more inclusive history of space travel. The afronaut is deployed as a critical cultural envoy with a mission to decolonise, deracialise, and rehumanise space law.

The Astronaut in International Space Law

The status of the astronaut as a singular representative of humanity or a heroic explorer expanding American values in space was reflected in cultural symbols and popular nationalistic imaginaries (Sammler and Lynch 2021: 705). Good examples of this practice are the reportages in magazines such as *Life* and *Time*. *Life* in particular contributed to the production of the heroic status of the jet pilots selected to become the first astronauts on the Mercury Project (see, e.g., Hersch 2011; Launius 2008; Spiller 2013). But while grooming the heroic status, magazines and other popular cultural outlets were also used to perfect the image of the astronaut as the American everyman. NASA was keen to build this image of the astronaut as an everyman risking their life for the benefit of all in order to justify using taxpayers' money to support the spaceflight programme (Sammler and Lynch 2021: 710). Another tactic to glorify the heroic but simultaneously everyman status of the astronaut was to contrast this icon with the image of the scientists, engineers, and mathematicians as unreliable (p. 710).

Just like with any kind of propaganda, as Sammler and Lynch highlight, these popular images of the astronauts were also framing the development of space policy and law. According to Sreejith, it was the astronauts' heroic status that led to them being perceived as envoys of—in the language and prejudice of that time—mankind (2019: 133). But as Sreejith further explains, the prestigious role of being an envoy of mankind was not comparable to the formal position of diplomatic envoys that have clear duties and responsibilities towards the countries they represent in diplomatic missions (p. 133).

For example, the Declaration of Legal Principles Governing the Activities of States in the Exploration and Use of Outer Space (1963) promulgates that:

> States shall regard astronauts as envoys of mankind in outer space, and shall render to them all possible assistance in the event of accident, distress, or emergency landing on the territory of a foreign State or on the high seas. Astronauts who make such a landing shall be safely and promptly returned to the State of registry of their space vehicle.

Similar wording is also repeated in Article V of the Outer Space Treaty. According to Sreejith, the rather open-ended reference in the Declaration and the Outer Space Treaty that astronauts were envoys of mankind but with no specific legal function was intentional in order to protect "the transcendental purity of astronauts" (2019: 133). But the reluctance to attribute any legal duty to astronauts actually made them vulnerable subjects in the sense that they became more like cultural icons of the Cold War than ambassadors for humanity. According to Sreejith, by not specifying what kind of duties the astronaut had to fulfil in order to protect, in the wording of the Outer Space Treaty, "the common interest of all mankind in the progress of the exploration and use of outer space for peaceful purposes", astronauts became a hermeneutical propaganda tool for the two spacefaring superpowers (p. 133). Although presented as envoys of "mankind", astronauts, despite their travel to outer space, could not escape the "vernacular culture, [political] memory and ideology" of the Cold War (p. 130). The American astronaut represents the "star sailor in pursuit of playful adventure and inquisitiveness" (p. 130), while 'his' counterpart, the Soviet cosmonaut, is deeply entangled with the Leninist Soviet character of that era.

Interestingly, this tension between international law portraying astronauts as envoys for humanity and the reality that they were in fact the embodiment in space of opposing political ideologies on Earth can possibly explain the strong iconography of the white virgin spacesuit as the harbinger of neutrality and universality. The ideal of the astronaut as a faceless and nationless hero was perfected in the cultural image of the space traveller clad in a white spacesuit whose face was hidden behind the visors of the space helmet. It was an image that could accompany the promise in international space law that the astronaut was the envoy of humankind. But it also fulfilled other performative functions. The spacesuit also acted as a symbol of manhood, virility, and bravery. The spacesuit embodied the transformation from layperson to astronaut. According to Launius (2008: 203), the puffy spacesuit turned an average person into an individual that was portrayed as a hero, an individual larger than life, stronger and more virile than any other person on planet Earth.

The astronaut adorned in a white suit and space helmet with a darkened visor was also a useful symbol to hide or mask the military background of the first generation of astronauts. Rather ironically, the military force directed the selection of who should become the USA's first space explorers as envoys of humankind. This, seemingly, is a contradiction to one of the most important guiding principles that "States Parties to the Treaty shall carry on activities in the exploration and use of outer space, ... in accordance with international law, ... in the interest of maintaining international peace and security and promoting international co-operation and understanding" (Art. III, Outer Space Treaty 1967). The image of the astronaut as an 'everyman' is undeniably ambiguous (Sammler and Lynch 2021: 710), especially if we look further into the role of NASA and how they staged and layered the persona of the astronaut.

From the outside, it seemed that the first astronauts recruited for the Mercury programme by NASA were selected on the basis of their profile matching the ideal elements of the US space endeavour and the national character of the white, handsome, Protestant male. However, from the inside, this idea of the white American everyman was quickly busted as the Mercury Seven were in fact not civilian everymen but military test pilots selected for their reliability and discretion (Hersch 2013: 40). As a result, the military pilot culture became part of NASA's working environment. A rigid and hierarchical management programme was embedded in NASA's space programmes giving NASA the power to control the 'labour' of its astronauts. The military background of the astronauts diminished their status of being envoys of humankind to that of blue-collar workers controlled by a ruthless regime of rules and discipline (Sammler and Lynch 2021: 712). As I will show in the next section, a similar trend can also be traced in the evolution of international space law and the provisions that are being made towards the protection of astronauts.

As Sreejith explains, towards the end of the 1960s, space travel lost some of its mythical attraction and became more of a "mundane" activity. Once astronauts walked on the surface of the Moon, their position transitioned to one of being "participants in the burgeoning 'space work'" (2019: 134). This shift in their status was accompanied by a growing awareness that astronauts are exposed to a lot of danger, radiation being one of them, and that they required special protective measures. Concerns about the health and safety of astronauts prompted the UN's Committee on the Peaceful Uses of Outer Space (COPUOS) to adopt the 1968 Agreement on the Rescue of Astronauts, the Return of Astronauts and the Return of Objects Launched into Outer Space (hereafter the Rescue Agreement). It is in the Rescue Agreement that we see the shift from presenting astronauts as envoys of humankind in the Outer Space Treaty to focusing more on the humanitarian concern towards the safety of the astronauts who work in dangerous contexts.

While in the Outer Space Treaty astronauts were still described as envoys, in the preamble of the Rescue Agreement this status is reduced to *sentiments* of humanity. In full acknowledgement of the dangers that astronauts were exposed to, the Rescue Agreement calls in its preamble for the "rendering of all possible assistance to astronauts in the event of accident, distress or emergency landing, the prompt and safe return of astronauts, and the return of objects launched into outer space". But while in the preamble there is still mention of *astronauts*, in the remaining text of the Agreement, they are referred to as *personnel*. Article V of the Outer Space Treaty made State Parties duty-bound to rescue and return "astronauts as envoys of mankind in outer space", and the Rescue Agreement specifies throughout the legal text that States are duty-bound to rescue and return personnel on board a spacecraft. This raises the question: how significant is this change in wording from astronauts to personnel?

Addressing this question is somewhat speculative, but there are suggestions in the literature (see, e.g., Sreejith 2019) that the reference to personnel in the Rescue Agreement could have been part of a strategy to future-proof the Agreement and space law in general. The Agreement recognised that the semantic scope of an astronaut could prove to be problematic in the future when space travel becomes more common. Especially now with commercial space travel being a reality, astronauts seem like a very romanticised trope. Even personnel may prove challenging given that we are now in an era that embraces the idea of space tourism. As I will discuss later, extending the category of space traveller so it can also include the space tourist is somewhat anticipated in the Agreement Governing the Activities of States on the Moon and Other Celestial Bodies (1979, hereafter the Moon Agreement), which uses the very generic category of *persons*.

But putting that observation aside for a moment, the disappearance of astronauts and the downplaying of their status in the Rescue Agreement introduced already in the late 1960s a shift in our thinking about and perception of outer space. As Sreejith specifies, the introduction of personnel in space law created a new subject in international law. While the astronaut of the early 1960s was still perceived to be the hero and a political object of the Cold War era, within a decade that status had changed to personnel. This new subject represents, according to Sreejith, the "'person next door', [the] blue-collared proletarian" (2019: 135), and gone is the era of the astronaut as hero and envoy on behalf of humankind.

The moment when outer space, and especially the Moon, was perceived to be a conquered space, outer space lost its 'exotic' appeal. It was downgraded to a rather ordinary workplace where astronauts laboured (Sreejith 2019). Astronauts' status changed accordingly from envoy to employer. Their work environment also changed accordingly from ambassadorial to industrial. These changes were also sealed in international law. While the Outer Space Treaty was still concerned with protecting the status of the astronaut as envoy of humankind, the Rescue Agreement was focusing more on having procedures in place for their safe rescue and return, just like it also regulated the return of objects. As Sreejith observes, astronauts became 'thingified' in the Rescue Agreement precisely because its main function was to safeguard the return of astronauts *and* objects.

This downgrading to the status of blue-collar workers also affected the experience of the NASA astronauts on board the space stations. Despite the astronauts being used to a rigid working regime because of their military background, the disciplined labour regime and surveillance culture on board the spaceships led to discontented voices and labour disputes (Sammler and Lynch 2021). Illustrated by the account of Goemaere and colleagues (2019), astronauts' daily existence on board spaceships has always been dictated by what they refer to as schedule enslavement (p. 274). This made simple tasks very cumbersome and provoked occasional defiant behaviour on the part of the astronauts. These disputes highlight that astronauts' daily existence on board a spaceship was, despite NASA's attempt to glorify it, far from glamorous and heroic. The discontentment about labour further illustrates the point that over time the heroic position of the astronaut as representative of humankind is reduced to a more mundane position as labourer.

But the astronaut's loss of the heroic status has also a wider significance. Space was portrayed and protected in the Outer Space Treaty as the common interest of all humankind, and its use and exploration were limited to peaceful purposes. Astronauts were portrayed as the guardians of these ideals. But this was only half of the story. The fact that NASA, in reality, treated astronauts as an ordinary workforce is, I would argue, already a foreboding that space is not just there to be explored for scientific purposes but is also valued as a resource that can be exploited and used for commercial purposes. The changing profile of space travellers corroborates this preliminary observation.

As Hersch (2011) reports, the US scientific community was keen to put the spotlight on their own important contributions to the spaceflight endeavour. The recruitment of scientists as potential astronauts was quite challenging, and their profile as scientists with doctorates did not fit easily in NASA's culture that primed the ideal image of the astronaut as the American everyman. But eventually scientists' contribution was more explicitly recognised as important for the success of NASA's space endeavours. I argue that the inclusion of a wider workforce constituted another milestone for opening up and treating outer space not as a commons that should benefit humankind but rather as a space that can be explored and potentially exploited by a wider workforce. Although NASA was initially not keen to include scientists in the flight missions, more recently, NASA has further widened its access to space. It portrays space travel now as a public undertaking and seeks to recruit a wide group of people ranging from farmers, surveyors, and mechanics to teachers (Sammler and Lynch 2021: 711).

Opening up space to wider categories than the original military crew that was employed by NASA to lead spaceflights has taken a more dramatic turn now that we have entered the commercial space era. Although the Moon Agreement is not recognised as binding international law, it did foresee extending the categories of people who could travel to and stay on the Moon. This can be best illustrated by the wording in Article 10 that specifies that "States Parties shall adopt all practical measures to safeguard the life and health of persons on the moon". It then refers that any person shall be regarded as an astronaut within the meaning of Article V of the Outer Space Treaty and/or as personnel within the meaning of the Rescue Agreement. According to Sreejith (2019), the Moon Agreement amalgamated purposely the distinctive categories of astronauts and personnel under the rubric of *person*. It thereby killed off once and for all the prestigious and heroic status of the astronaut as the envoy of humankind. Furthermore, it also prepared the way for anybody to travel to the Moon and settle on it (p.136).

To conclude this section, the astronaut in international law has always been a flawed concept as it was crafted around the idea of the white masculine hero and everyman, which is a contradiction to the idea that space is for the benefit of humankind. The hollowing out of the role into personnel and then persons may actually further threaten the idea that space should be for the benefit of humankind as space is now accessible not just to the meritorious astronaut but to anyone who happens to be very rich. Therefore, I am suggesting that if we want to prevent space from becoming the next frontier whose commons become commodified, it is important to reinstate the importance of the astronaut. However, unlike the older model of the white universal astronaut clad in a white suit, I argue in the next section that it is crucial to imagine a more inclusive image of the astronaut.

Afrofuturism

I have outlined in the previous section that international law cannot be assumed to be universal and neutral. Therefore, I offer a more progressive and speculative reading of space law. As I have shown, in the Rescue Agreement, the role of the astronaut loses some of its earlier cachets as an envoy of humankind. I seek to reinstate the importance of the astronaut as the envoy of humankind. But unlike the Outer Space Treaty that envisions the astronaut in very gendered and racialist terms, I subvert this conservative worldview and replace the white male astronaut with the afronaut. The afronaut is modelled after and is conceived in response to a wider movement that is widely known as Afrofuturism.

Afrofuturism has been around for a few decades and is gaining in importance, and merits a more in-depth discussion within the context of space travel. I have already started this conversation elsewhere (Vermeylen 2021a, 2021b). But in order to keep this piece precise and to the point, I have to keep this introduction to Afrofuturism brief and refer interested readers to other excellent scholarship on this topic (e.g., Anderson and Fluker 2019; Anderson and Jones 2016; Womack 2013; Zamalin 2019). I find Bourland's introduction to the topic useful for this chapter as it is already applied to the issues of space travel. Bourland (2020: 212) defines Afrofuturism as a cross-media genre and an art form that challenges the future by questioning the past and exposing how modernity is steeped in colonial and neocolonial discourses that are represented in our cultural fabric. What Afrofuturism does is to critique these cultural symbols. The white male astronaut in *Life* magazine is a good example of this cultural hegemonic practice. Afrofuturism repurposes the figure of the white male astronaut and instead presents afronauts as "afronautical protagonists in the matrix of enslavement, segregation and postcolonial migration" (p. 212). In other words, what Afrofuturist artists are doing is to use an alternative imagining of the future to critique and rewrite the past in a more progressive and inclusive manner (Gaskins 2016: 30). Pioneers in the Afrofuturist movement, such as the artist Sun Ra, deploy science fiction as a trope to address the Atlantic slave trade. The trauma caused by the Middle Passage and the ongoing feeling of displacement and alienation is an important area of critique for African artists in the diaspora. For Afrofuturist artists and critics, the experience of the Middle Passage destabilises the Eurocentric ontological concept of the human. Humanism has lost its credibility as a result of the protracted dehumanisation that started with the trans-Atlantic slave trade but continues with the ongoing trauma that is still being suffered by those who lost their homeland, identity, and sense of humanness as a result of our capitalist system that still exploits a labour force in order to feed our hunger for continuous economic growth (Eshun 2003).

When deconstructing the idea of astronauts as envoys of humankind through the critical lens of Afrofuturism we unearth an entangled history of exploitation, enforced labour, displacement, and humiliation. Despite the history of enslavement, the Outer Space Treaty still believes in the universal good of humankind when it defines the status of astronauts as envoys of "mankind". But as Sinker (1992, quoted in van Veen 2016: 64) asks in the context of our planet's history of enslavement: "What does it mean to be human?" The answer cannot be found in the Outer Space Treaty because the astronaut is modelled after the image of the white, Christian man. From an Afrofuturist perspective, we know that our humanness has been tainted and corrupted by the slave trade, and our life on earth is already a version of, in Sinker's words, a post-apocalyptic dystopia (Sinker 1992, quoted in van Veen 2016: 64). Therefore, I analyse in this chapter the iconography of the afronaut to subvert the meaning of the astronaut in the Outer Space Treaty and to use the image of the afronaut as a source of inspiration for a new body of space law.

The Afronaut as the Harbinger of New Space Law

Unlike the white spacesuits and helmets with dark visors, the afronauts' spacesuits and helmets no longer represent (literally) a whitewashed history that negates the history and rich knowledge of the African continent. I have selected a combination of artworks from African artists from the continent because their works take us back to the roots of African epistemes and expose us to other ways of knowing and being in this world. These African worldviews and knowledges can reinstate humanity that, as the Afrofuturists argue, got lost in the trans-Atlantic slave trade. While Afrofuturists' artworks (see also Nicola Triscott's chapter in this volume) introduce an entangled view of the past and the future presented from the perspective of their experience of loss, mourning, and trauma, with the purpose to create "visionary end" (Bourland 2020: 212), Africanfuturists' (this is a term coined by the writer Nnedi Okorafor; see Okorafor 2019) artworks, I argue, also include these elements but simultaneously also remain closely embedded in, connected to, and celebratory of Africa's rich cultures and knowledge systems, which can still be witnessed and experienced on the African continent.

The first afronaut I present has walked the streets of Kinshasa clad in a silver suit made from recycled material with a silver-painted bucket as a space helmet. A member of the Kongo Astronauts collective, this afronaut[1] has also been featured on the cover of the debut album of Mbongwana Star, a Congolese band, whose first track is titled "From Kinshasa to the Moon". But this is just one 'entrance' of the afronaut amongst many others that have been made in different Kongo Astronauts performances across Kinshasa. Another example is the astronaut in a golden suit, plastered with digital debris made from minerals mined in the Congo, and standing in the vault of a cargo plane.[2]

Kongo Astronauts is a collective formed in 2013 in Kinshasa by multimedia artists Eléonore Hellio and Michel Ekeba. As an artist collective that is in constant flux, they reflect in their performances what it means to live in postcolonial Kinshasa and in the Democratic Republic of the Congo in general. They are part of the alternative cultural arts scene in Kinshasa, always critical of the forces that have created ghettos where people live in dire circumstances. But they also seize the opportunity that this environment offers to raise our awareness of our, in their words, "human fragility and … our own reflections as we struggle with the crisis of late capitalism and climate change" (Axis Gallery n.d.). Kongo Astronauts present their work in what they describe as a space station, and their "cosmic apparitions" and "polysemous fictions" in the city offer a critical look at "different forms of exile and survival tactics" (Axis Gallery n.d.). Travel is thus an important element in their arts practice, and their astronauts appear in different self-made spacesuits and helmets across different spaces that represent "interzones of digital globalization, wherein past, present and future collide, impacting politics of intimacy and identity in urban and rural settings alike" (Karachi Biennale 2017).

But looking into their performances in more depth, a clear message starts to emerge that is very relevant in the context of New Space or the exploration of outer space for commercial purposes. I will illustrate this with an example drawn from *Postcolonial Track #02*, which is a visual critique against extractivism. Against the background of screeching noises, the afronauts are showing the violence that is committed when mining resources such as coltan and precious and semi-precious gems. The injustice gets bigger when these resources are traded on a speculative market that leads to a radical instability between the wealth of some and the poverty of the majority. This instability is expressed in the film by mixing sounds, sights, and random cuts that make little sense, except that they capture in an eloquent manner the absurdity of extractivism. Through the radio waves and muffled satellite relays, a message is being transmitted that conveys, in Malaquais's words, that "technology is misappropriated and fails" (Malaquais 2013).

What the afronauts may be looking for becomes even more poignant in another series, *Predic(a) tion 2*. This series is based on a futurist-feminist perspective and is part of the exhibition *Kinshasa 2050: Les Femmes d'abord!*. The series follows a young singer, Céline Banza, who meets on her journey traditional healers, pastors, and mediums who tell her what Kinshasa will look like in 2050 and predict the role of women in it. The afronaut wears a red spacesuit and helmet, which in Congolese culture is the colour of the witch, a mystical figure capable of communicating with the cosmos (Grugier 2021). The red spacesuit that embodies traditional Congolese cultural practices, rituals, and belief systems particularly sparks my interest within the legal context of this chapter.

It is in contrast to the white and the red spacesuits that I relocate the astronaut as the envoy of humankind. While the white spacesuit stands for the Eurocentric technological and scientific advancements from which so many on this planet have been excluded from benefiting, the red spacesuit symbolises African knowledges and belief systems that are more relational. It is impossible to envision the astronaut of the Outer Space Treaty as the envoy of humankind because *he* only represents the white Eurocentric man. The afronaut in her red spacesuit, on the other hand, carries as her payload a strong critique and rejection of that white hegemonic worldview. But importantly, the red spacesuit also conveys a message that is linked to African rituals that existed before the rise of colonialism and capitalism. The spacesuit embodies, as Hellio reflects in an interview with Grugier, an alternative positioning of the future and symbolises "a positive wind of freedom" (Grugier 2021) that is connected to past rituals of *ngangas* (traditional healers). Hellio points out that the ritual masks of the past can no longer be donned: Congolese people no longer have access to them; they have been confiscated, pillaged, violently acquired, and hidden in the vaults of colonial museums. But maybe they can be replaced with the red space helmet, which epitomises a new future that is always intricately and intimately connected to a precolonial past.

I find this message of a future that is yet to come but simultaneously is intricately linked to history a productive proposition in thinking about the future of space governance. After all, as the Third World Approaches to International Law (TWAIL) movement argues, international law does not always deliver on its promises. On the contrary, it behaves more like a hegemonic power that seeks to protect the interests of the powerful (Gupta and Sanchez 2012). According to TWAIL scholars, international treaties are steeped in a legal tradition that is Euro-American-centric, which limits the options for genuine change. International law, for them, is a practice that universalises and institutionalises inequality and inequity on a global scale by prescribing standard economic solutions to fight against an unequal world (Gupta and Sanchez 2012; Rajagopal 2006). TWAIL scholars call for international lawyers to become more critical of the colonial discourses that are still embedded in and part of international law (Chimni 2006; Okafor 2005). Unfortunately, the same can be said for international space law. If we want to hold the Outer Space Treaty accountable to preserve and protect space for the benefit of *all* humankind, we also need to think about the role and the symbolism of the astronaut from a multicultural perspective. Therefore, I introduce in the next section another example of an afronaut in order to unpack further the proposition that is made by Africanfuturists that the future is connected to deeply rooted (in most cases precolonial pasts) historical African cultural traditions, religions, and spirituality.

Vodunaut is a series of artworks that merge the imagery of space exploration and science fiction with Yoruban cultural tradition (Buckley and Galbraith 2020). The *Vodunaut* series (2017) is, according to the Benin artist Emos de Medeiros, "born from a fascination for cowry shells, space navigation, the times to come, and this question: what if a future futurology was based on *Fa*?" (de Medeiros n.d.). As the artist explains further, Fa (or Ifa) is a West African philosophy and geomancy system using cowry shells as objects and symbols of wisdom in divination. Not only do the artworks describe future possibilities, but they also show how to achieve and navigate these futures through a spiritual pathway (de Medeiros n.d.). Unlike other forms of African divination, Ifa does not rely on a person to have oracular powers. Rather, the priest makes use of cowry shells, a corpus of texts, and mathematical formulas when advising on important matters that could range from politics and economics to personal health. The cowry shells provide, together with other objects and poetic verses, spiritual guidance in a variety of decision-making processes (for more details about the Ifa religion see, e.g., Bascom 1969).

The *Vodunaut* series presents space helmets that are an amalgamation of the traditional use of shells with the industrial design of a motorcycle helmet. The darkened visor of the NASA space helmet is replaced by smartphones showing material that is filmed on different continents and evokes premonitory dreams of electronic brains. For de Medeiros his art represents a link with spirituality and sacredness (Art Africa 2016). The space helmets symbolise an alternative future where Yoruba spirituality and cultural heritage are expanded into outer space (Now Look Here 2020).

The wider point that I am making is that the visual representation of afronauts offers moral and legal guidance on how to reclaim space for the benefit of humanity in an era of commercial space travel and exploitation. While non-Western cultural practices and religions are underexplored areas of research in outer space studies, within the context and the limited space in this chapter, I can only highlight a few relevant points when exploring the meaning of humanity from an African perspective.

Interesting links have been drawn between African belief systems and their relevance for sustainable development (see, e.g., Asuquo 2019). Although we must be careful not to romanticise or generalise, there are specific traits and moral values that regulate different aspects of African societies. In the discussion on sustainable development and African values, Awaonyi and others (see, e.g., the forthcoming edited collection by Chitando and Kamaara) make the point that values such as integrity, hard work, generosity, reciprocity, hospitality, truth, respect for others, tolerance, and solidarity guide not only the behaviour of individuals but also contribute to the social cohesion and smooth running of the community, including interpersonal relationships. As I will elaborate in the next section, being guided by these principles would bolster the core principle in the Outer Space Treaty that the exploration and exploitation of resources in outer space should be for the benefit of humankind.

Zooming into a more general meaning of African philosophy, the notion of communalism and how it has a bearing on what it means to be a person stands out. In broad lines, "the notion of 'personhood' or 'being a person' is understood in many African languages and societies as an acquired status that is dependent on people's relationship to their community" (Bell 2002: 61). Gaining this status of personhood is, according to the Nigerian philosopher Ifeanyi Menkiti, dependent on reaching an ethical maturity. But as the Ghanaian philosophers Kwasi Wiredu and Kwame Gyeke further explain, this ethical maturity must be understood as practising a moral life that is at the service of the community and must contribute to the well-being of the community (Bell 2002: 62). Without wanting to romanticise the difference between Western modernity with a focus on individual autonomy and traditional African communalism, the latter is still an important characteristic that defines the moral values in African societies and their institutions. This point is aptly made by Wiredu who argues that "[a] person is not just an individual of human parentage, but also one evincing in his or her projects and achievements an adequate sense of social responsibility" (Wiredu 1996 in Bell 2002: 63).

In its current form, the astronaut's position in the Outer Space Treaty is rather vague and undefined as the envoy of "mankind". If the astronaut is replaced by the afronaut, more diverse sets of moral values can be introduced when interpreting and applying the core principles of the Outer Space Treaty at the dawn of a new commercial space era. As a matter of fact, the most important idea in Article 1 of the Outer Space Treaty that "the exploration and use of outer space, including the moon and other celestial bodies, shall be ... the province of all mankind" carries more weight when interpreted from an African communal perspective rather than from a Euro-centric international law perspective. As I have argued elsewhere together with the Kenyan Africanfuturist artist Jacque Njere, Ubuntu, one of the most well-known and famously reinstated African principles that came embedded in South Africa's post-apartheid constitution, can offer, in contrast to international law, better guidance on what kind of rules could be used to protect space for the common interest of humankind (Vermeylen and Njere forthcoming).

In very generic terms, *ubuntu* is a Zulu-Xhosa word which can be roughly translated as humanness. Often its interpretation is reduced to the Nguni expression *umuntu ngumuntu ngabantu*, meaning a person is a person through other people. Ubuntu acknowledges otherness and restores the belief that it is possible for relational ethics to make their entry into the law. As the legal philosopher Cornell clarifies, Ubuntu "is not a contractual ethic. It is up to me. And, in a certain profound sense, humanity is at stake in my ethical action" (2014: 112). In other words, Ubuntu incorporates an ethics of duty, sharing, and generosity. Equitable principles are therefore at the heart of the African ethical principle of Ubuntu. This is in contrast to liberal individualism that usually defines justice in international law.

In their editorial piece for *New Space*, Cristian van Eijk and Timiebi Aganaba (2021) also make the point that it is timely that the meaning of space law is no longer interpreted through a Eurocentric canon such as the Kantian ideal of cosmopolitanism. Whereas Kantian cosmopolitanism seeks to protect the individual, Ubuntu focuses on the collective. As they rightly point out, in order for international space law to be effective in preserving and promoting space for the benefit of humankind, we must also address the issue of "who is able to participate in global governance" (p. 2). Just like the identity of the astronauts was historically one-sided, so are the values that underpin space law. What this chapter has demonstrated is that by replacing the astronauts with afronauts as envoys of humankind, we are able to inject other value systems into international law so that space law represents rather than restricts the diversity of governing rules. As we are entering into a new era of commercial space travel one of the most important tools that are inscribed into international law to protect the common heritage principle is the fair and equitable sharing of benefits. As I have argued within the context of biodiversity conservation, there is a desperate need for a more diverse understanding of what fair and equitable could mean (Vermeylen 2019).

So far, debates around what constitutes fair and equitable benefit sharing have been mostly influenced by a liberal agenda of distributive justice. As we are moving closer to the development of a commercial space industry that seeks to mine resources on celestial bodies and asteroids, it is very likely that the provisions in Article 11(5) in the Moon Agreement "to establish an international regime, including appropriate procedures, to govern the exploitation of the natural resources of the Moon" will be revisited. The failure to sign and ratify the Moon Agreement by most countries has been attributed to the stipulations in Article 11(7d) that the main purpose of the international regime to be established includes the regulation for "an equitable sharing by all States Parties in the benefits derived from those resources, whereby the interests and needs of the developing countries ... shall be given special consideration". Based on the analysis I made in this chapter, I would like to add a final point that the Moon Agreement, together with other international space law instruments, has perpetuated an epistemic violence by ignoring the history, experience, and cultural heritage of the afronaut. For space law to live up to its principle that the use of outer space should be for the benefit of humankind, it should first and foremost give space to the experiences and knowledge systems of *all* humankind.

Conclusion

As I have shown in this chapter, the role of the astronaut has become reduced, both in the wording in the Rescue Agreement and in the experience on board the space shuttles, to that of a blue-collar worker. As the 'frontier' of outer space has been unlocked for commercial space travel, I argue that to halt this vertical expansion of our capitalist labour exploitations, the international legal community (and others) should consider reinstating the prestige of astronauts as envoys of humankind. However, this time round, the iconography and the (popular) culture that should support this image of the astronaut as envoy of humankind must no longer be honed and crafted by NASA and its propaganda. Instead, as the artworks discussed in this chapter show, inspiration for the next image of the astronaut can be found in other places such as the neighbourhoods of Kinshasa. It is from the streets in Kinshasa that we can remake the past to create a better world on earth and preserve space as a cosmic and utopian space that lives in our imagination and inspires us to be better humans worthy of living relationally and connectedly with other humans, non-humans, and more-than-humans on this beautiful planet we call Earth.

Notes

1 Kongo Astronauts use the word cosmonaut, but in the context of this paper I refer to them as afronauts except when I quote directly from Kongo Astronauts.
2 Images of the afronauts can be found on https://www.makery.info/en/2021/10/12/kongo-astronauts-lastronaute-se-sent-etranger-sur-sa-propre-planete-un-homme-exile-par-la-force-des-choses/ or on the Kongo Astronauts' website, https://kongoastronauts.wordpress.com. Last viewed on 26 September 2022.

References

Anderson, Reynaldo, and Clinton Fluker. 2019. *The Black Speculative Movement: Black Futurity, Art+Design*. Lanham, MD: Lexington Books.

Anderson, Reynaldo, and Charles E. Jones. 2016. *Afrofuturism 2.0: The Rise of Astro-Blackness*. Lanham, MD: Lexington Books.

Art Africa 2016. *That Art Fair 2016: Participating Galleries & Artists Announced!*. Accessed 22 January 2022 at https://www.artafricamagazine.org/that-art-fair-2016-participating-galleries-artists-announced/.

Asuquo, Gabriel. 2019. "African Values and Institutional Reform for Sustainable Development in Africa." *International Journal of Humanities and Innovation* 2 (4): 136–42. https://doi.org/10.33750/ijhi.v2i4.56.

Axis Gallery. n.d. *Kongo Astronauts: Bio & CV*." Accessed 26 September 2022 at https://axis.gallery/kongo-astronauts-bio-cv/.

Bascom, William. 1969. *Ifa Divination: Communication between Gods and Men in West Africa*. Bloomington; Indianapolis: Indiana University Press.

Bell, Richard H. 2002. *Understanding African Philosophy: A Cross-Cultural Approach to Classical and Contemporary Issues*. New York: Routledge.

Bould, Mark. 2019. "Afrofuturism and the Archive: Robots of Brixton and Crumbs." *Science Fiction Film and Television* 12 (2): 171–93. https://doi.org/10.3828/sfftv.2019.11.

Bourland, W. Ian. 2020. "Afronauts: Race in Space." *Third Text* 34 (2): 209–29. https://doi.org/10.1080/09528822.2020.1733845.

Buckley, Alexander, and Hannah Galbraith. 2020. "African Contemporary Artists and SF." *Blog Post*, 24 November 2020. https://vector-bsfa.com/2020/11/24/african-contemporary-artists-and-sf/.

Chimni, Bhupinder S. 2006. "Third World Approaches to International Law: A Manifesto." *International Community Law Review* 8 (1): 3–27. https://doi.org/10.1163/187197306779173220.

Chitando, Ezra, and Eunice Kamaara. Forthcoming. *Values, Identities, and Sustainable Development in Africa*. Cham: Palgrave Macmillan.

Cornell, Drucilla. 2014. *Law and Revolution in South Africa: Ubuntu, Dignity, and the Struggle for Constitutional Transformation*. New York: Fordham University Press

De Medeiros, Emo. n.d. *Vodunaut 2017*." Accessed 26 September 2022 at https://www.emodemedeiros.com/vodunaut-1.

Eshun, Kodwo. 2003. "Further Considerations on Afrofuturism." *CR: The New Centennial Review* 3 (2): 287–302. https://doi.org/10.1353/ncr.2003.0021.

Gaskins, Nettrice. 2016. "Afrofuturism on Web 3.0: Vernacular Cartography and Augmented Space." In *Afrofuturism 2.0: The Rise of Astro-Blackness*, edited by Reynaldo Anderson and Charles E. Jones, 27–44. Lanham, MD: Lexington Books.

Goemaere, Sophie, Thomas Van Caelenberg, Wim Beyers, Kim Binsted, and Maarten Vansteenkiste. 2019. "Life on Mars from a Self-Determination Theory Perspective: How Astronauts' Need for Autonomy, Competence and Relatedness Go Hand in Hand with Crew Health and Mission Success—Results from HI-SEAS IV." *Acta Astronautica* 159: 273–85. https://doi.org/10.1016/j.actaastro.2019.03.059.

Grugier, Maxence. 2021. "Kongo Astronauts: 'The Astronaut Feels Like a Foreigner on His Own Planet, Exiled by Fate'." *Makery*, 12 October 2021. https://www.makery.info/en/2021/10/12/kongo-astronauts-lastronaute-se-sent-etranger-sur-sa-propre-planete-un-homme-exile-par-la-force-des-choses/.

Gupta, Joyeeta, and Nadia Sanchez. 2012. "Global and Green Governance: Embedding the Green Economy in a Global Green and Equitable Rule of Law Polity." *Review of European Community & International Environmental Law* 21 (1): 12–22. https://doi.org/10.1111/j.1467-9388.2012.00739.x.

Hersch, Matthew H. 2011. "Return of the Lost Spaceman: America's Astronauts in Popular Culture, 1959–2006." *Journal of Popular Culture* 44 (1) 73–92. https://doi.org/10.1111/j.1540-5931.2010.00820.x.

Hersch, Matthew H. 2013. "'Capsules Are Swallowed': The Mythology of the Pilot in American Spaceflight." In *Spacefarers: Images of Astronauts and Cosmonauts in the Heroic Age of Spaceflight*, edited by Michael J. Neufeld, 35–55. Washington, DC: Smithsonian Institution Scholarly Press.

Karachi Biennale. 2017. *Kongo Astronauts*." Accessed 26 September 2022 at https://kbcuratorial.com/artists/kongo-astronauts.

Launius, Roger D. 2008. "Heroes in a Vacuum: The Apollo Astronaut as Cultural Icon." *Florida Historical Quarterly* 87 (2): 174–209. https://doi.org/10.2514/6.2005-702.

Malaquais, Domunique. 2013. "Speculate This!" *Kongo Astronauts*. https://kongoastronauts.wordpress.com/2020/04/12/speculate-this-text-in-english/. Last viewed on 26 September 2022.

NASA 2018. "What Is a Spacesuit?" *NASA Knows!*, 2 August 2018. (Grades K-4) series. https://www.nasa.gov/audience/forstudents/k-4/stories/nasa-knows/what-is-a-spacesuit-k4.html.

Now Look Here: The African Art of Appearance 2020. "Emo de Medeiros." *Online Exhibition Programme.* Accessed 26 September 2022 at https://www.now-look-here.com/Participants/Emo-de-Medeiros.

Okafor, Obiora Chinedu. 2005. "Newness, Imperialism, and International Legal Reform in Our Time: A TWAIL Perspective". *Osgoode Hall Law Journal* 43 (1/2): 171–91. http://digitalcommons.osgoode.yorku.ca/ohlj/vol43/iss1/7.

Okorafor, Nnedi. 2019. "Afrofuturism Defined." *Blog post, Nnedi's Wahala Zone Blog,* 20 October 2019. Nnedi.blogspot.com/2019/10/africanfuturism-defined.html.

Rajagopal, Balakrishnan. 2006. "Counter-Hegemonic International Law: Rethinking Human Rights and Development as a Third World Strategy". *Third World Quarterly* 27 (5): 767–83. https://doi.org/10.1080/01436590600780078.

Sammler, Katherine G., and Casey R. Lynch. 2021. "Spaceport America: Contested Offworld Access and the Everyman Astronaut." *Geopolitics* 26 (3): 704–28. https://doi.org/10.1080/14650045.2019.1569631.

Schrogl, Kai-Uwe, Christina Giannopapa, and Ntorina Antoni. 2021. *A Research Agenda for Space Policy.* Elgar Research Agendas. Cheltenham: Edward Elgar Publishing.

Spiller, James. 2013. "Nostalgia for the Right Stuff: Astronauts and Public Anxiety about a Changing Nation." In *Spacefarers: Images of Astronauts and Cosmonauts in the Heroic Age of Spaceflight,* edited by Michael J. Neufeld, 57–80. Washington, DC: Smithsonian Institution Scholarly Press.

Sreejith, S. G. 2019. "The Fallen Envoy: The Rise and Fall of Astronaut in International Space Law." *Space Policy* 47: 130–9. https://doi.org/10.1016/j.spacepol.2018.10.004.

United Nations 1963. *Declaration of Legal Principles Governing the Activities of States in the Exploration and Use of Outer Space.* https://www.unoosa.org/pdf/gares/ARES_18_1962E.pdf.

United Nations 1967. *Treaty on Principles Governing the Activities of States in the Exploration and Use of Outer Space, Including the Moon and Other Celestial Bodies (Outer Space Treaty).* https://www.unoosa.org/pdf/gares/ARES_21_2222E.pdf.

United Nations 1968. *Agreement on the Rescue of Astronauts, the Return of Astronauts and the Return of Objects Launched into Outer Space (Rescue Agreement).* https://www.unoosa.org/pdf/gares/ARES_22_2345E.pdf.

United Nations 1979. *Agreement Governing the Activities of States on the Moon and Other Celestial Bodies (Moon Agreement).* https://www.unoosa.org/pdf/gares/ARES_34_68E.pdf.

van Eijk, Cristian, and Timiebi Aganaba. 2021. "Inspired by Africa: A New Approach to Global Space Governance." *New Space* 9 (1): 1–4. https://doi.org/10.1089/space.2021.0011.

van Veen, Tobias C. 2016. "The Armageddon Effect: Afrofuturism and the Chronopolitics of Alien Nation." In *Afrofuturism 2.0: The Rise of Astro-Blackness,* edited by Reynaldo Anderson and Charles E. Jones, 63–90. Lanham, MD: Lexington Books.

Vermeylen, Saskia. 2019. "Special Issue: Environmental Justice and Epistemic Violence." *Local Environment: The International Journal of Justice and Sustainability* 24 (2): 89–93. https://doi.org/10.1080/13549839.2018.1561658.

Vermeylen, Saskia. 2021a. "Space Art as a Critique of Space Law." *Leonardo* 54 (1): 115–24. https://doi.org/10.1162/leon_a_01990.

Vermeylen, Saskia. 2021b. "Space as a Source of Inspiration, Identity and the Arts." In *Research Agenda for Space Policy,* edited by Kai-Uwe Schrogl, Christina Giannopapa and Ntorina Antoni, 219–34. Cheltenham: Edward Elgar.

Vermeylen, Saskia, and Jacque Njere. Forthcoming. "African Space Art as a New Perspective on Space Law." In *Reclaiming Space,* edited by James Schwartz, Linda Billings and Erika Nesvold. Oxford: Oxford University Press. 113–125

Womack, Ytasha L. 2013. *Afrofuturism: The World of Black Sci-Fi and Fantasy Culture.* Chicago, IL: Lawrence Hill.

Zamalin, Alex. 2019. *Black Utopia: The History of an Idea from Black Nationalism to Afrofuturism.* New York: Columbia University Press.

15
DIVERSITY IN SPACE

Evie Kendal

Introduction

As billionaires in their giant, metal phalluses continue to drag race each other to the Kármán line, one thing has never been clearer: space has a diversity problem. Demographic studies of astronauts, cosmonauts, and taikonauts from 1961 to 2020 found only 11.4% of humans in space have been women, with people of colour also known to be severely underrepresented (Smith, Kelley, and Basner 2020: 292). The stringent selection criteria applied to astronaut candidates in terms of their mental and physical health has also been seen as a "gating process" intended to exclude neurodivergent and differently abled people from space exploration (Wells-Jensen, Miele, and Bohney 2019: 50). The combined result of these actions has led to what Wells-Jensen, Miele, and Bohney (2019) label a "cultural and physical homogeneity aboard space vessels which may, in certain contexts, decrease the survival chances of the overall mission", despite growing recognition in most other occupational environments that "diversity strengthens working groups" (p. 50). And it is not just those who get to travel in space that are affected by this homogeneity; the field of astronomy more broadly has been found to be particularly hostile to minorities, with widespread accusations of sexism, racism, and homophobia (Clancy et al. 2017).

The existence of this diversity problem in the space industry has not gone unnoticed by space agencies. NASA's five-year neurodiversity network programme, operating out of Sonoma State University, aims to "provide a pathway to NASA participation and STEM employment for neurodiverse learners, with a focus on those on the autism spectrum" (NASA Science 2022). NASA is also a regular partner organisation for Entry Point!'s STEM internship programme for students with disabilities (Ham 2021). Likewise, the European Astronomical Society's annual conference has continued to build its Equity and Diversity in Astronomy offering, while making other adjustments to support inclusivity, such as providing childcare subsidies and making disability accommodations for delegates (Jermak, Lucatello, and Woods 2018). Jermak, Lucatello, and Woods (2018) note that in their 2018 conference, the equity and diversity programme garnered the most registrations and included "discussions on equity, inclusivity, demographics, disability, sex, gender identity, mental health, neurodiversity, race, sexual orientation and unconscious bias in astronomy and in academia" (p. 523). While there are many contributing factors to the predominantly "pale, male, and stale" fields of astronomy and astrophysics, this chapter will focus on one of the identified solutions: increasing the number and visibility of minority role models in real and imagined space occupations.

DOI: 10.4324/9781003280507-17

The Role of Role Models in Choosing STEM Careers

In studies considering the underrepresentation of minority groups in science, technology, engineering, and mathematics (STEM) careers, the influence of key role models on educational and career choices is frequently noted (Cerinsek et al. 2013; Kricorian et al. 2020). Kricorian et al.'s (2020) survey of forty-eight adult learners in STEM fields, of which 71% were female and 96% identified as belonging to an ethnic minority, found 68% reported having a role model in a relevant STEM field of the same gender as them, and 66% of the same ethnicity. Fifty-four percent of respondents also reported that meeting a STEM professional of both the same gender and ethnicity would "be effective encouragement to pursue STEM", with 56% reporting they believed this role could also be filled by "media exposure to gender- and ethnicity-matched STEM professionals" (Kricorian et al. 2020). In their study of 1281 STEM undergraduates in Slovenia (861 male, 420 female), Cerinsek et al. (2013) found that the choice of a STEM degree after high school was influenced by many factors, including primary and high school education, family values, and out-of-school activities. Perhaps surprisingly, excursions and field work had minimal impact, while engaging with "popular science television channels and programmes" was listed as the most important influence of the nonschool activities, with engagement with "science fiction or fantasy books/films" also prominent, particularly among boys (pp. 3015–16). Despite significantly lower numbers of women pursuing STEM training in Slovenia, according to the 2018 Programme for International Student Assessment (PISA) student performance data for the country, girls in high school outperform boys in reading, mathematics, and science (OECD 2022). Cerinsek et al. (2013) conclude that it is not a lack of aptitude but the effect of socialisation and the presence of negative attitudes toward women in STEM that have led to the gender disparity seen in most STEM fields, noting similar patterns across Europe and the USA (p. 3000).

This disparity can also be seen in Ashar Johnson Khokhar's (2020) study of fifty-two female postgraduate students from Lahore, Karachi, and Rawalpindi in Pakistan. These women reported a lack of positive role models in school textbooks, agreeing that "if they had read stories of successful women in textbooks, working in different fields [including science] ... they would have thought about choosing it as their career" (p. 46). It was found depictions of women in these educational resources were typically restricted to those performing domestic duties, such as household chores and child-rearing. Khokhar (2020) concluded that "the lack of female role models working in different fields in textbooks, is affecting the career and academic choices" of women, by reinforcing traditional gender roles, including financial dependence on male partners (p. 47). This dependency is also seen when going beyond gender and ethnic minorities to consider educational and other media representations of people with disabilities. Studies have shown a prevalence of depictions of unemployed, socially and economically dependent individuals who rely on medical professionals for support, thereby erasing potential occupational role models from within disability communities (Zhang and Haller 2013).

Unfortunately, it is not just in primary and secondary school that such biases are seen in learning materials. Students from minority groups who do pursue higher education in STEM, including in space-related areas, are often faced with similar microaggressions. As Clancy et al. (2017) note:

> Gazing at the stars is an accessible introduction to science, one that gets many young children dreaming of being an astronaut, astronomer, or planetary scientist one day. ... At the same time, the accessibility and inclusive atmosphere within science, including astronomy and planetary science, has been called into question. Science syllabi use gendered language that not only can show women as incompetent but also normalizes masculine behaviors, belief systems, and priorities.
>
> (p. 1610)

For the space sector in particular, Amanda Keeler (2019) notes the "hegemonic imagery of space travel with its central image of the white male astronaut" perpetuates the idea that members of minority groups will only ever be on the periphery of the industry, quoting one article from a 1950s *Collier's* magazine that suggested women might participate "not as pilots ... but as radio and radar operators" due to their supposed ability to "perform monotonous and tedious tasks" for long periods of time (p. 127). She continues:

> While the hegemonic imagery of space travel remains unequal in its representation of gender, these images have begun to shift. The March 2018 issue of *National Geographic* magazine's cover story "Through an Astronaut's Eyes" features Peggy Whitson, who is credited with spending more days in space than any other American astronaut. Although Whitson and many other women have long participated in space flight programmes in countries around the globe, their visibility has not always been foregrounded in publicly disseminated images and narratives.
>
> *(pp. 127–28)*

Attempts to increase the visibility of women's contributions in the sector (such as Whitson's above) are not limited to real-world narratives either, with a concurrent increase in the representation of female astronauts in popular culture seen in recent times (Purse 2019: 54). The same can also be said for (incremental) increases in the racial diversity of casting choices for science fiction and fantasy cinema. However, this project has not been met with universal approbation, with many fan-based controversies arising regarding supposedly "woke" casting choices (Lawrence 2022). BBC's long-running science fiction series, *Doctor Who*, provides two recent examples: first, the #notmydoctor online campaign objecting to Jodie Whittaker's casting as the first female iteration of the spacefaring Doctor, a movement which media commentators Chelsea and Theresa Adams noted included such gems as "It's Time Lord not Time Lady", "Nobody wants a Tardis full of bras", and the doubly offensive "It's DOCTOR Who, not NURSE Who" (Adams and Adams 2017); and second, some online communities' racist responses to Ncuti Gatwa's casting as the fourteenth Doctor following Whittaker's departure (Lawrence 2022). The same level of opposition has not been seen when women and people of colour have been cast in the supporting role of the Doctor's companion. Thus, this chapter considers not only the number of diverse role models available but also their relative position in the real-world and fictional narratives where they are found. Seniority is one element that can continue to challenge outdated perceptions—like those seen in *Collier's* article—that assume minority groups will only ever perform junior or auxiliary functions in the space industry.

The Important Role of "Important" Role Models

There are two main reasons a lack of minority role models is important when attempting to promote diversity in STEM and the space sector in particular. Both are related to the unfortunate reality that underrepresentation begets underrepresentation. Both those self-selecting into STEM and space industry careers and the external committees selecting candidates for study and employment may be unduly biased by a lack of exposure to positive examples drawn from diverse groups. In other words, it may be harder to visualise a STEM career for those who have never seen someone like them succeed in such a field, and likewise for those selecting them. Relatedly, Kovacs and Shadden (2017) claim that the process of astronaut selection is "not transparent to the public nor easy to elucidate ... carried out predominantly by individuals selected through the same mechanisms" with "no known external oversight". Although there is minimal data available on the process, these authors note it is possible "inappropriate selection biases exist" (Kovacs and

Shadden 2017), which may include the exclusion of women, people of colour, older individuals, and people with disabilities.

There are numerous theories suggesting mechanisms by which role models affect attitudes, choices, and behaviour, including regarding study and career ambitions. One that appears frequently in the scholarly literature on the topic is Albert Bandura's social cognitive theory (SCT). SCT is primarily concerned with developmental learning through observation and imitation (Bandura 1986). Nancy Signorielli (2009) claims that according to this theory, media can provide "images and role models that viewers, particularly children, may use to develop scripts or schemas about different types of people" (p. 324). In her study of representations of racial minorities in prime-time television, she notes SCT suggests judgments about people of colour "rely on the images seen on television", and are particularly important when viewers do not typically interact with members of these communities in real life (p. 324). Regarding gender minorities, Steinke and Tavarez (2018) similarly note that SCT explains how stereotypes in fictional representations of STEM professionals may affect attitudes towards these careers; through "identificatory learning", if women and girls observe a pattern where they are absent or inferior in STEM professions, they may be encouraged to imitate alternative career aspirations portrayed as more feminine (p. 247). However, the corollary is that when these same viewers identify with female STEM characters—e.g., when they look or act similar to themselves—this may help them visualise themselves in similar occupations. The same applies to gender-diverse characters and those with disabilities. This directly connects to another theory from the same time period in developmental psychology, Markus and Nurius's (1986) possible selves theory (PST). According to these authors, "possible selves" represent an individual's "ideas of what they might become, what they would like to become, and what they are afraid of becoming" (p. 954). Thus, they are mental images furnished by personal experience and media exposure that influence personal motivation to pursue (or avoid) certain futures. In both SCT and PST, media representations provide a way for people from gender and racial minorities and differently-abled individuals to envisage a future in which people like them to fill roles within STEM in general, and the space industry specifically. Children often list films and television as a "primary source of information about what scientists are like", indicating they are susceptible to the influence of media bias when determining whether people like them belong in STEM careers (Cheryan et al. 2013). As such, Steinke and Tavarez (2018) suggest content creators should increase both the number and significance of diverse characters in popular media.

As will be demonstrated in the following sections, diverse role models are beneficial in their own right, but those fulfilling more senior, important roles are even more so. When it comes to fictional representations, while there is no scope here to attempt a comprehensive review of the many relevant examples available, those that are mentioned represent some of the most well-known and influential franchises.

Gender and Racial Diversity in Space

In her opening plenary for the 2018 European Astronomical Society's annual conference, British Labour Party MP Chi Onwurah provocatively asked: "Why is there a black hole where women should be?" (Jermak, Lucatello, and Woods 2018). With one study showing 91% of white women and 96% of women of colour in astronomy and planetary science employment reporting experiencing negative gendered comments, it is perhaps unsurprising that many do not stay in the profession (Clancy et al. 2017). As noted in the previous section, the problems reach back all the way to sexist science textbooks and a lack of female role models for young women in STEM (Cerinsek et al. 2013; Khokhar 2020). In the USA, for example, less than 25% of STEM roles are filled by women, and Hispanic, Asian, and African-American women each represent less than 5% of STEM undergraduate degrees conferred in the country (Kricorian et al. 2020). For members of the LGBTIAUQ+ community, the situation is even more dire, with the Out Astronaut Project reporting more than 40% of STEM professionals who identify as gay, bisexual, transgender, or queer are not publicly out, and none of the 560+ astronauts to date have openly identified as a member of this community (Out Astronaut 2021).

When comparing the demographics of male and female astronauts, Smith, Kelley, and Basner (2020) found that women were less likely to be military-trained or have any children (and when they did it was typically fewer than for their male counterparts), but more likely to be younger and possess a doctoral degree than the men (pp. 290–91). Overall, they report "astronauts were significantly less likely to be female with increasing age and with increasing numbers of children", concluding these women may have had to prioritise their careers over family plans in order to succeed (pp. 292, 297). They note only five astronauts lacked any college education and none of these were women (p. 292). While proportionately women's participation as astronauts has increased (2.1% in the 1960s to 20% in the 2010s), these authors note this increase is not statistically significant (p. 297). In his review of Karin Hilck's 2019 book *Lady Astronauts, Lady Engineers, and Naked Ladies*, former NASA chief historian Roger Launius claims:

> It should come as no surprise to anyone that NASA has a poor record of racial and gender equality. ... NASA trailed most of the nation as a heavily white male technical organization that reinforced stereotypical gender norms and resented pressure to adapt to changing mores.
> *(Launius 2019: 299)*

He further claims aerospace historians are "well aware" of the rampant discrimination, "public scandals" and "private indiscretions" that plagued the organisation, and how at the establishment of the Equal Employment Opportunity office at NASA Headquarters in 1971, the agency had the lowest level of workplace diversity of any federal agency (5%) (p. 300). This was despite the fact physiological testing of potential female astronauts since the 1960s—starting with the group of elite female pilots later named the Mercury 13—has demonstrated equal or superior performance to men (Hilck 2019). Differences in opinion regarding the precise definition of "astronaut" complicate things somewhat (Varga 2021), but by some accounts, one member of the Mercury 13, Wally Funk, did finally earn the title when at the age of eighty-two she was launched into space in Blue Origin's first crewed spaceflight in 2021 (Iati 2021).

In her article "Women Need Not Apply", Morgan Seag (2017) notes NASA's decision to recruit the first astronauts from within the cohort of military jet test pilots disqualified female candidates wholesale, as women were excluded at the time from all military test pilot schools. Despite claims of "unintentionality" in such discriminatory recruitment practices, Seag notes NASA's carefully curated public narrative of the astronaut as the idealised reflection of "white, masculinist middle-class values" served to construct an image of Outer Space as "a decidedly masculine arena" (p. 323). Over time the narrative intended to keep women out shifted from relying on (false) claims they were physically unfit for space travel to political and economic arguments that admitting women would "slow down" efforts to win the space race against the Soviet Union (Lathers 2009). As noted above, this degree of exclusion was not typical of many other industries at the time, leading some of the Mercury 13 to call out this "Outer Space exceptionalism" coming from an organisation far less socially than technologically progressive (Seag 2017).

Both gender and racial minorities face obstacles in pursuing space careers, and intersectional approaches identify that women of colour face a "double jeopardy"; the energy they could expend increasing their work output is instead redirected to navigating institutional sexism and racism, limiting their career advancement while also perpetuating stereotypes about their productivity in the field (Clancy et al. 2017). Clancy et al.'s (2017) study showed women of colour in astronomy and planetary science "are isolated and experience microaggressions—subtle, indirect, or unintentional acts of discrimination—in the workplace", including disparaging comments about their appearance, competence, and intelligence (p. 1611). Using the example of NASA again, the Equal Employment Opportunity Act of 1972 led to the admission of women and people of colour into the astronaut training programme in 1978, which Lisa Purse (2019) argues shifted "public perception of what an astronaut could be away from the longstanding figure of the white, cis-gendered military-trained male" (pp. 55–56). Nevertheless, she still notes very low total numbers of women in pilot and commander roles, and persistent media attention on gendered stereotypes of female astronauts, e.g., reporters asking Sally Ride if she would "cry during [her] flight" and concerns about women with children going into space (p. 56). It is also worth noting that the first woman and African-American hired to a senior manager role at NASA in 1971, Ruth Bates Harris, was unceremoniously fired two years later for highlighting the "near total failure" of the Equal Employment Program to actually increase employment of women and people of colour (Holden 1973; *New York Times* 1974). She later returned to NASA in 1974, following a Senate subcommittee hearing into her dismissal (*New York Times* 1974; Ruel, Mills, and Thomas 2018).

Importantly, concerns regarding the lack of diversity in space-related employment are not relegated to history, with a 2022 stakeholder report on Australia's space industry and recently established space agency exposing ongoing issues with inclusivity, particularly for women and Aboriginal and Torres Strait Islander peoples (Salazar and Castaño 2022). While there was a multiplicity of views and opinions on the topic of diversity, multiple interviewees in this study reported a dominance of white males in the sector at every level, from academic conference panels—the dreaded "manel"—to the Australian Space Awards, with one respondent also claiming a lack of support and recognition for Indigenous and "LGBTIQ people" (p. 120).

Gender and Racial Minority Role Models in Space-Related Fiction

While at present it looks like we will have to wait until the Artemis programme to place the first woman on the Moon in 2024, in the meantime there are many fictional representations of women and people of colour in space that warrant examination (Smith, Kelley, and Basner 2020). Things have come a long way since fictional NASA pilot Captain Buck Rogers had to rescue his miniskirted female companions seen gasping for air as (presumably) the only ones who needed oxygen in the *Buck Rogers* TV series' debut episode in 1950. Purse (2019) notes we now have a rich array of female astronauts fulfilling the "strong female protagonist" trope in science fiction, citing recent examples like those in *Sunshine* (2007), *Gravity* (2013), and *Interstellar* (2014), to name a few (p. 53). Keeler (2019) names Sonequa Martin-Green's character from *Star Trek: Discovery*, Michael Burnham, as a good example of a complex character that goes beyond just a "positive representation", to what Amanda Lotz might classify as one of a "multiplicity of images" of diverse populations that together serve to "dismantle" stereotypes, in this case of both women and people of colour (p. 136). Thus, it is not Burnham in isolation, but rather in concert with the other female, nonbinary, queer, and transgender characters that work to supplant the previously cisgender male-dominated vision of space in the genre.

Unlike in the real world, there are many female astronauts and commanders in science fiction films and television, dating back well before women were admitted into space programmes around the world. A classic example is the original *Star Trek* series (1966–1969), often lauded for including women, people of colour, and Asian-Americans at a time when these groups were mostly absent from both the space industry and popular television. Nevertheless, Keeler (2019) claims there is no doubt that the main characters are three white males: Captain James T. Kirk, Dr. Leonard "Bones" McCoy, and Lieutenant Commander (probably not S'Chn T'Gai, after all) Spock. In terms of providing positive role models, though, Keeler writes that Nichelle Nichols, who played Lieutenant Nyota Uhura, "has recounted a conversation with Dr Martin Luther King Jr, who convinced her to stay on *Star Trek* to serve as a role model for African-American girls and women" (p. 131). The actress also shared stories of meeting women at *Star Trek* conventions who attributed their pursuit of careers in physics or the military to Uhura's inspiration. As such, Keeler (2019) claims *Star Trek* "served as a blueprint for negotiating shifting norms in the 1960s and beyond ... predicting and possibly influencing the reality of increasing gender and race diversity in the real-world space programme" (p. 131). Later series in the franchise would continue this trend, increasing the prominence and rank of the female officers, notably including Captain Kathryn Janeway and Chief Engineer B'Elanna Torres (*Star Trek: Voyager*, 1995–2001), and Captains Philippa Georgiou and Michael Burnham (*Star Trek: Discovery*, 2017–). Purse (2019) claims that although there is an increase in representation, "these female screen astronauts look strikingly alike", with tightly bound or short-cropped hair and firm jawlines that she claims makes them look "consistently boyish" (p. 54). In seeming contradiction, she also notes that while the professional positions of these powerful women are not questioned, there is still the "tendency to manoeuvre female protagonists into a heterosexual romantic relation", reinforcing traditional gender expectations in their private lives (pp. 56–57).

In Kricorian et al.'s (2020) study, role models from the media were considered a viable substitute for real-life mentors when these were unavailable. While this study looked at real-world social media influencers, fictional role models might also serve this function, especially given the fact influencers are also only providing a fictionalised version of their real lives. Lindy Orthia's (2019) survey of 575 *Doctor Who* viewers found the show exerted some influence on educational choices among this population, most commonly the pursuit of scientific training, including in the fields of "physics, astronomy, mathematics, engineering", and various others. She concluded "engagement with a fictional television program can have a significant impact on some people's education and career choices" (Orthia 2019). Unfortunately, as seen in Bigler, Averhart, and Liben's (2003) study of ninety-two African-American children (forty-seven girls and forty-seven boys), this influence can also lead viewers to denigrate careers typically associated with disadvantaged groups, or influence children to pursue lower status occupations if these are the only ones they are familiar with from media representations of their own communities (p. 577). As such, it is important not just to have role models from minority backgrounds but for these to be afforded authority and respect in their roles. Whoopi Goldberg's famous quote after first seeing Uhura on *Star Trek* when she was nine demonstrates this well: "[T]here's a black lady on television and she ain't no maid! I knew right then and there I could be anything I wanted to be" (Mastro 2017: 415). That Goldberg followed Nichol's footsteps, not only as an actor but as a *Star Trek* actor, illustrates the interplay of SCT and PST when it comes to observing and emulating an identifiable role model.

Cheryan et al. (2013) and Steinke and Tavarez (2018) note that even though diverse representations of some STEM careers may have improved over the last few decades, including increasing numbers of female astronomers and astronauts, stereotypes still abound, particularly regarding fields like computing science and engineering, where women are the most underrepresented in the real world. Female characters are also more likely to be cast as romantic interests of, and research assistants to, leading male scientist characters (Steinke and Tavarez 2018: 245–56). Using Fujioka's (1999) concept of "vicarious contact", Steinke and Tavarez claim exposure to fictional STEM professionals may be particularly influential when "direct contact" opportunities are lacking, including for women in these most underrepresented STEM fields (Steinke and Tavarez 2018: 246). However, these authors relate a "symbolic annihilation" of women in STEM in popular film, noting that in a sample of 42 films released in the USA between 2002 and 2014 that were specifically chosen due to the presence of female STEM characters as "lead, co-lead or secondary characters", only 25% of the STEM characters with speaking roles were coded as "white/Caucasian" women and a mere 1% were "Black or African American" women (p. 251). This is compared to 55% white/Caucasian men, 5% Black or African American men, and vanishingly small or non-existent percentages of other racial groups, including the categories "Asian/Indian American", "Hispanic or Latino/a" and "Multiracial". Of the female STEM characters in the sample, 23% were working in astronomy, where they were typically seen in professional attire, such as a lab coat or spacesuit. However, the authors also relate:

> In some of the films, 31 per cent of female STEM characters were hypersexualized and shown as partially naked or with cleavage showing ... In one scene in the film *Star Trek: Into Darkness*, a female quantum physicist suddenly disrobes for no apparent reason, asking a male colleague to turn his back while she changes clothes.
>
> *(p. 256)*

They also note 95% of the female STEM professionals were "portrayed as attractive" with the remaining 5% typically appearing in comedies (p. 255). These results indicate there is still a long way to go before space-related fiction can reach its potential of improving gender and racial diversity in media representation.

Differently-Abled Bodies and Neurodivergent Minds in Space[1]

A lot of the concerns regarding homogeneity in the space workforce listed in the previous section also apply to the lack of disability representation. It is well-known that astronaut selection processes are often more demanding than those for elite athletes and military personnel. Even those who generally support inclusivity for different abilities tend to balk at the idea of an astronaut with a physical disability. According to Wells-Jensen, Miele, and Bohney (2019):

> Despite the increasing acceptance of diversity among spacefarers, the idea of astronauts with disabilities has yet to be taken seriously. While other minorities assume their place among elite crews and potential colonists, the presence of even the smallest physical disability still acts as an automatic barrier to space exploration.
>
> *(p. 51)*

However, these authors note that for any long-term space mission or human off-world settlement, disabling accidents will happen, necessitating that roles for differently abled people be established (p. 52). They claim adjusting to life with a disability would be challenging in such an environment and peer-mentoring from other crew members with disabilities would be a valuable therapeutic tool, best facilitated if the contributions of said members were already seen to be respected and valued by the rest of the mission (p. 52). They also note that there are situations where conditions typically considered disabling, like blindness, could be an asset on a space mission. For example, a blind person would be adept at navigating in darkness and would not need their eyes to adjust to a sudden loss of illumination if the lighting went offline, thereby potentially saving precious time during an emergency (p. 52). They note the same applies in terrestrial aircraft, where emergency exit rows are still reserved for able-bodied passengers, despite the fact a blind passenger would likely be more capable of finding a hatch in dark or smoky conditions (p. 52). Jermak, Lucatello, and Woods (2018) relate that in the final session of the European Astronomical Society's Equity and Diversity in Astronomy special session in 2018, Nicolas Bonne explained that "as all astronomers are visually impaired when looking at the Universe, more resources should be put in place to aid scientists with blindness and visual impairments to pursue a career in astronomy" (p. 523).

When it comes to mental health conditions, Smith et al. (2021) claim astronauts have been "reluctant to talk about psychological difficulties, partly because of the potential consequences for their future mission allocation" (p. 11). However, these authors also note a willingness to privately seek psychological services or engage in digital mental health services, indicating the stressors of working in space are adversely impacting wellbeing. Wells-Jensen, Miele, and Bohney (2019) note that when selecting the "best" candidates for space missions, "crew compatibility" and the ability of members to cooperate to achieve mission objectives is vital (p. 50). This suggests some psychological traits may be intrinsically relevant for selection; however, these authors note "insistence on physical uniformity ... artificially limits the pool of candidates", potentially threatening mission success (p. 53). Given that the stress of working off-world is likely to lead to some degree of psychological distress among astronauts and other spacefarers, disqualifying candidates with a history of mental health issues may not be a safe or appropriate solution. Smith et al. (2021) note that due to their "isolated and confined conditions" astronauts are "at risk of deteriorating behavioural and mental health" (p. 13). The rationale behind excluding those with previous mental health issues appears to be to ensure only the strongest are selected, in the hopes they will best be able to cope with stressful situations. However, when it comes to mental health, personal resilience and the psychological resources it bestows are rarely born from a lack of life challenges, and thus candidates who have previously managed mental health crises may be more capable of adapting to the unique stressors of working in the space environment. When it comes to the lack of diversity in the space sector, Aarnio et al. (n.d.) note, "microaggressions, aggression, overt racism, and disparagement of gender and sexual minority identities can negatively impact the mental health of astronomers of color and LGBTQIA+ members", highlighting that minority groups are often doubly excluded: first due to their identities, and then for any mental health issues arising from related discrimination and mistreatment.

The focus on selecting mission candidates "for their knowledge and ability to get along with one another" (Wells-Jensen, Miele, and Bohney 2019) also potentially neglects the contribution neurodivergent individuals can and do make to the space industry, often despite experiencing social issues. In 2015, then eighteen-year-old Homero Palaguachi announced to the world he wanted to be the first autistic astronaut (NASA 2015). While a diagnosis of autism spectrum disorder (ASD) might previously have disqualified his entry into the astronaut training programme, NASA's Neurodiversity Network is signalling a change in attitude with regard to neurodivergent individuals. Krzeminska and Hawse (2020) note that while autistic people have the "highest rates of unemployment among any group of people with or without 'disabilities'", the skills many autistic people possess are "essential to meeting current and future workforce needs, particularly in STEM areas" (p. 229). These authors include in this list a high capacity for focus, good attention to detail, enhanced memory, creativity, lateral thinking, and "affinity with technology", as well as heightened colour perception and auditory abilities (p. 235). All of these have immediate relevance to a space mission. Other forms of neurodivergence also correlate with valuable occupational skills, including attention deficit hyperactivity disorder (ADHD). Individuals with ADHD may or may not experience interpersonal or workplace organisational issues, and like people with ASD may or may not identify themselves as disabled. Studies show people with ADHD tend to perform well in high-stress environments and can be highly productive and creative when working in fields that support their mode of operation and thinking (Patton 2009). Again, the relevance to the space industry is clear.

Aarnio et al.'s (n.d.) white paper for the American Astronomical Society (AAS) on improving the accessibility of astronomy for people with disabilities found "physical, technological, and pedagogical barriers to access" and a lack of support for career progression and retention of astronomers with disabilities. Using labour statistics from the USA, these authors note people with disabilities are far less likely to be employed in STEM professions than their nondisabled peers (21% versus 70%), with this issue further compounded by the significant drop-offs seen in STEM higher education among disabled students: 9–10% at the undergraduate level reducing to 5% at the graduate level and a mere 1% at the doctoral level. They report the AAS membership demographic survey found only 3.2% of respondents reported deafness or significant hearing impairment, blindness or significant vision impairment, or mobility issues, with 94% of respondents selecting "none of the above" (Aarnio et al. n.d.). While limited in scope, these results indicate a lack of disability representation in the membership. This is perhaps unsurprising when considering these authors note less than 40% of people with disabilities in the USA attain a college degree and an "estimated 86% of students with psychiatric disabilities withdraw" from their studies before completion (Aarnio et al. n.d.). They note many neurodivergent students also get "forced out along the way", with those remaining often reporting feelings of isolation.

While not a disability, age discrimination is also a relevant consideration in the space industry. In their study of NASA astronaut selection processes, Kovacs and Shadden (2017) claim there is a lack of transparency regarding how long applicant lists are culled to produce first- and second-round interview candidate lists. They note that despite a diverse range of ages among potentials, those actually selected represent a very narrow age range, with many older people also just assuming they won't be considered so choosing not to apply in a form of "self-deselection". Overall, their analysis indicates significant age bias, with the authors recommending NASA conduct analyses of their selection process to ensure fairness.

Alongside the diversity projects already noted in various astronomy institutions and space agencies, the European Space Agency's (ESA) Parastronaut Feasibility Project is also worth mentioning here. This project recently recruited potential candidates for astronaut selection that would usually have been disqualified due to lower limb disabilities or short stature (ESA 2021). However, it is stated applicants must still be "psychologically, cognitively, technically and professionally qualified", presumably indicating those with intellectual disabilities or mental health issues would still be disqualified (ESA 2021). If this project demonstrates the feasibility, the recruited individuals will be the first astronauts not considered fully able-bodied at launch. As such, they will become the first role models for future candidates with physical disabilities, or as PST would have it, the embodiment of a possible "future self" imaginary for those who follow. Hopefully, with wider social acceptance, astronauts with invisible disabilities will also feel empowered to openly identify as disabled without fear of career disadvantage.

Disability Role Models in Space-Related Fiction

Again, aspiring astronauts and space scientists with disabilities may currently struggle to find real-world role models to inspire them in their chosen career path, but they will not lack options from popular culture. Keeping with the blindness example from the previous section, *Star Trek: The Next Generation*'s Lieutenant Commander Geordi La Forge, played by Levar Burton, is a talented engineer whose skills are enhanced by the ocular device he uses due to congenital blindness. It would not be a stretch to consider the socially inept Vulcan species an analogue for some forms of neurodivergence either, especially given the focus on these characters' skills in logical reasoning. When it comes to other physical disabilities, *Star Wars*'s Luke Skywalker is an amputee whose prosthetic limb allows him to continue his mission unchanged, while *Star Trek*'s lack of accessible starships leaves Admiral Christopher Pike unable to serve once he becomes a wheelchair user. In her article for the online news site *Gizmodo*, Marina Galperina (2018) reports the United Federation of Planets is not the only science-fictional employer failing to provide appropriate workplace accommodations, with Han Solo's *Millennium Falcon* from *Star Wars* (1977–), the Doctor's T.A.R.D.I.S. from *Doctor Who* (1963–), and Malcolm Reynolds's *Serenity* from the 2005 film of the same name and its preceding series, *Firefly* (2002–2003), all specifically mentioned as spacecraft with an inordinate number of staircases. It should be noted the latter series does contain a leading character with significant mental illness (River Tam), although this representation contains various stereotypes about such people posing a danger to the people around them.

Zhang and Haller's (2013) survey of 390 people with disabilities indicates media representations of disability are generally considered unrealistic by the disabled community, swinging between depictions of extreme underperformance and superhuman ability (p. 326). These authors recount that studies have demonstrated harmful representations in film media can "add to the oppression of people with disabilities" in the real world, while also risking disabled viewers themselves internalising these negative messages and thereby "preventing them from realizing their intellectual potential" (pp. 321–22). They claim this is because according to SCT, "people are not merely passive viewers of content but are cognizant consumers who reflect, regulate, and vicariously learn from materials projected on media" (p. 322). As such, the sometimes contradictory depictions of disabled characters in popular media mean they may not provide as many inspirational role models as the strong female astronaut characters mentioned in the previous section. Nevertheless, there are still many good examples, and greater visibility is an important step in promoting diversity of representation.

Allan and Cheyne (2020) relate that "[d]isability has been and still is absolutely central to the genre of science fiction" (p. 389). These authors list "fetishization of prosthesis and other adaptive technologies" as one of the many ways science fiction explores models of disability, noting Rosemarie Garland-Thomson's account that "we cannot make up positive disability identity out of nothing" highlights the way "stories can create or shut down the space necessary for disability identity" (p. 390). Katie Ellis (2016) argues some of this representation shows disability and disabled bodies as "monstrous" while also "adaptive and subversive" (p. 64). Thus, the representation of disability in science fiction and other popular culture provides an opportunity for meaning-making among disabled communities, even when the representations may sometimes be ambivalent. From the perspective of providing role models to enhance the participation of people with disabilities in the space industry, this is particularly valuable, as for many disabilities there may not be a single real-world example of a person with that disability working in the field. In other words, it might be some time before Geordi La Forge is supplanted by a real-world blind space engineer.

Conclusions

It is generally accepted that diversity increases innovation and creative problem-solving within groups, which is why the underrepresentation of minorities in the space sector, and STEM careers more broadly, needs to be urgently addressed. One identified barrier to pursuing study and employment in space sciences is the lack of role models available to inspire and mentor women, people of colour, and people with disabilities. Programmes currently aimed at enhancing training and employment opportunities for members of minority groups, such as NASA's Neurodiversity Network and Artemis Programme or ESA's Parastronaut Feasibility Project, will hopefully provide more real-world role models in the future. Fictional representations provide some alternative sources of inspiration when real-world role models might be lacking, demonstrating the importance of promoting diversity in popular media representations of astronauts and space scientists. Importantly, it is not just increasing the number of diverse role models available in fiction but also their significance that is expected to influence educational and career choices for members of minority groups. Social cognitive theory (SCT) and possible selves theory (PST) both support the idea that real and fictional role models can inspire individuals to pursue careers in STEM and the space sector, by helping them visualise themselves as people who belong in these industries. As such, consciously increasing diversity in representations of real and imagined space occupations is not "political correctness" or "wokeness", but rather an essential step toward the sector achieving its potential as an inclusive, collaborative, and therefore more productive, space.

Note

1 As a member of these communities the author is using their own preferred terms here but recognises these are not universally accepted.

References

Aarnio, Alicia, Nicholas Murphy, Karen Knierman, Wanda Diaz Merced, Alan Strauss, Sarah Tuttle, Jacqueline Monkiewicz, et al. n.d. "Accessible Astronomy: Policies, Practices, and Strategies to Increase Participation of Astronomers with Disabilities." *Bulletin of the American Astronomical Society* 51(7). Unpublished manuscript. Revision from 10 July 2019. https://doi.org/10.48550/arXiv.1907.04943.

Adams, Chelsea, and Adams, Theresa. 2017. "A Female Doctor Who: Nobody Wants a Tardis Full of Bras." *TheatreArtLife: The Global Media Site for Entertainment*, 1 August 2017. https://www.theatreartlife.com/lifestyle/nobody-wants-tardis-full-bras/.

Allan, Kathryn, and Ria Cheyne. 2020. "Science Fiction, Disability, Disability Studies: A Conversation." *Journal of Literary & Cultural Disability Studies* 14 (4): 387–401. https://doi.org/10.3828/jlcds.2020.26.

Bandura, Albert. 1986. *Social Foundations of Thought and Action: A Social Cognitive Theory*. Englewood Cliffs, NJ: Prentice-Hall.

Bigler, Rebecca S., Cara J. Averhart, and Lynn S. Liben. 2003. "Race and the Workforce: Occupational Status, Aspirations, and Stereotyping among African American Children." *Developmental Psychology* 39 (3): 572–80. https://doi.org/10.1037/0012-1649.39.3.572.

Cerinsek, Gregor, Tina Hribar, Natasa Glodez, and Slavko Dolinsek. 2013. "Which Are My Future Career Priorities and What Influenced My Choice of Studying Science, Technology, Engineering or Mathematics? Some Insights on Educational Choice—Case of Slovenia." *International Journal of Science Education* 35 (17): 2999–3025. http://doi.org/10.1080/09500693.2012.681813.

Cheryan, Sapna, Victoria C. Plaut, Caitlin Handron, and Lauren Hudson. 2013. "The Stereotypical Computer Scientist: Gendered Media Representations as a Barrier to Inclusion for Women." *Sex Roles* 69 (2013): 58–71. https://doi.org/10.1007/s11199-013-0296-x.

Clancy, Kathryn B. H., Katharine M. N. Lee, Erica M. Rodgers, and Christina Richey. 2017. "Double Jeopardy in Astronomy and Planetary Science: Women of Color Face Greater Risks of Gendered and Racial Harassment." *Journal of Geophysical Research: Planets* 122 (7): 1610–23. https://doi.org/10.1002/2017JE005256.

Ellis, Katie. 2016. *Disability and Popular Culture: Focusing Passion, Creating Community and Expressing Defiance*. New York: Routledge.

European Space Agency (ESA) 2021. *Parastronaut Feasibility Project*. https://www.esa.int/About_Us/Careers_at_ESA/ESA_Astronaut_Selection/Parastronaut_feasibility_project.

Galperina, Marina. 2018. "Staircases in Space: Why Are Places in Science Fiction Not Wheelchair-Accessible?" *Gizmodo*, 1 August 2018. https://www.gizmodo.com.au/2018/08/staircases-in-space-why-are-places-in-science-fiction-not-wheelchair-accessible/.

Ham, Becky. 2021. "Diversity in STEM Includes Scientists with Disabilities." *Science* 371 (6528, January 29): 475–76. https://doi.org/10.1126/science.371.6528.475.

Hilck, Karin. 2019. *Lady Astronauts, Lady Engineers, and Naked Ladies: Women and the American Space Community during the Cold War, 1960s–1980s*. Berlin: De Gruyter Oldenbourg.

Holden, Constance. 1973. "NASA: Sacking of Top Black Woman Stirs Concern for Equal Employment." *Science* 182 (4114): 804–07. https://doi.org/10.1126/science.182.4114.804.a.

Iati, Marisa. 2021. "In 1961, She Lost Her Chance to Go to Space. At 82, She Finally Got Her Shot." *The Washington Post*, 20 July 2021. https://www.washingtonpost.com/history/2021/07/20/wally-funk-astronaut-mercury-13/.

Jermak, Helen E., Sara Lucatello, and Paul Woods. 2018. "Equity and Diversity in Astronomy." *Nature Astronomy* 2 (7): 523–24. https://doi.org/10.1038/s41550-018-0514-0.

Keeler, Amanda. 2019. "Visible/Invisible: Female Astronauts and Technology in Star Trek: Discovery and National Geographic's Mars." *Science Fiction Film and Television* 12 (1): 127–50. https://doi.org/10.3828/sfftv.2019.07.

Khokhar, Ashar Johnson. 2020. "Women Representation in Textbooks in Pakistan: Impact on Career and Study Choices of Female Students Enrolled in the Postgraduate Programmes." *Pakistan Journal of Women's Studies: Alam-e-Niswan* 27 (2): 1024–256. https://doi.org/10.46521/pjws.027.02.0077.

Kovacs, Gregory T. A., and Mark Shadden. 2017. "Analysis of Age as a Factor in NASA Astronaut Selection and Career Landmarks." *PLoS One* 12(7): e0181381. https://doi.org/10.1371/journal.pone.0181381.

Kricorian, Katherine, Michelle Seu, Daniel Lopez, Elsie Ureta, and Ozlem Equils. 2020. "Factors Influencing Participation of Underrepresented Students in STEM Fields: Matched Mentors and Mindsets." *International Journal of STEM Education* 7(16): 1–9. https://doi.org/10.1186/s40594-020-00219-2.

Krzeminska, Anna, and Sally Hawse. 2020. "Mainstreaming Neurodiversity for an Inclusive and Sustainable Future Workforce: Autism-Spectrum Employees." In *Industry and Higher Education*, edited by Leigh Wood, Lay Peng Tan, Yvonne A. Breyer and Sally Hawse, 229–61. Singapore: Springer. https://doi.org/10.1007/978-981-15-0874-5_11.

Lathers, Marie. 2009. "'No Official Requirement': Women, History, Time, and the U.S. Space Program." *Feminist Studies* 35 (1): 14–40. https://www.jstor.org/stable/40607922.

Launius, Roger D. 2019. "Lady Astronauts, Lady Engineers, and Naked Ladies: Women and the American Space Community during the Cold War, 1960s–1980s by Karin Hilck (Review)." *Technology and Culture* 62 (11): 299–300. https://doi.org/10.1353/tech.2021.0036.

Lawrence, Briana. 2022. "Racism Is Always Right on Time with Black Casting Announcements and It's Exhausting." *The Mary Sue*, 10 May 2022. https://www.themarysue.com/the-predictable-backlash-for-black-castings/.

Markus, Hazel, and Paula Nurius. 1986. "Possible Selves." *American Psychologist* 41(9): 954–69. https://psycnet.apa.org/doi/10.1037/0003-066X.41.9.954.

Mastro, Dana. 2017. "The Role of Media in the Well-being of Racial and Ethnic Groups." In *The Routledge Handbook of Media Use and Well-being*, edited by Leonard Reinecke and Mary Beth Oliver, 409–21. New York: Routledge. https://doi.org/10.4324/9781315714752.

NASA 2015. *Teenager Strives to Become First Autistic Astronaut*, 31 July 2022. https://www.nasa.gov/langley/teenager-strives-to-become-first-autistic-astronaut.

NASA Science 2022. *NASA's Neurodiversity Network*, 6 January 2022. https://science.nasa.gov/science-activation-team/nasa-neurodiversity-network.

New York Times 1974. *NASA Defends Lag on Women's Jobs*, 12 January 1974. https://www.nytimes.com/1974/01/12/archives/nasa-defends-lag-on-womens-jobs-says-decline-in-work-force-is.html.

OECD 2022. *Education GPS*. http://gpseducation.oecd.org.

Orthia, Lindy A. 2019. "How Does Science Fiction Television Shape Fans' Relationships to Science? Results from a Survey of 575 Doctor Who viewers." *Journal of Science Communication* 18(4). https://doi.org/10.22323/2.18040208.

Out Astronaut 2021. *The Problem*. https://outastronaut.org/.

Patton, Eric. 2009. "When Diagnosis Does Not Always Mean Disability: The Challenge of Employees with Attention Deficit Hyperactivity Disorder (ADHD)." *Journal of Workplace Behavioral Health* 24 (3): 326–43. https://doi.org/10.1080/15555240903176161.

Purse, Lisa. 2019. "Square-Jawed Strength: Gender and Resilience in the Female Astronaut Film." *Science Fiction Film and Television* 12 (1): 53–72. https://doi.org/10.3828/sfftv.2019.04.

Ruel, Stefanie, Albert J. Mills, and Janice L. Thomas. 2018. "Intersectionality at Work: The Case of Ruth Bates Harris and NASA." *Ephemera: Theory & Politics in Organization* 18 (1): 17–49.

Salazar, Juan Francisco, and Paola Castaño. 2022. *Framing the Futures of Australia in Space: Insights from Key Stakeholders*. Paramatta, Sydney: Institute for Culture and Society, Western University of Sydney. https://doi.org/10.26183/ffm4-5k07.

Seag, Morgan. 2017. "Women Need Not Apply: Gendered Institutional Change in Antarctica and Outer Space." *The Polar Journal* 7 (2): 319–35. https://doi.org/10.1080/2154896X.2017.1373915.

Signorielli, Nancy. 2009. "Minorities Representation in Prime Time: 2000 to 2008." *Communication Research Reports* 26 (4): 323–36. https://doi.org/10.1080/08824090903293619.

Smith, Michael J., Michelle Kelley, and Mathias Basner. 2020. "A Brief History of Spaceflight from 1961 to 2020: An Analysis of Missions and Astronaut Demographics." *Acta Astronautica* 175: 290–99. https://doi.org/10.1016/j.actaastro.2020.06.004.

Smith, Nathan, Dorian Peters, Caroline Jay, Gro Mjeldheim Sandal, Emma Barrett, and Robert Wuebker. 2023. "Off-world Mental Health: Considerations for the Design of Wellbeing Supportive Technologies for Deep Space Exploration." *JMIR Formative Research* 7. https://formative.jmir.org/2023/1/e37784.

Steinke, Jocelyn, and Paola Maria Paniagua Tavarez. 2018. "Cultural Representations of Gender and STEM: Portrayals of Female STEM Characters in Popular Films 2002–2014." *International Journal of Gender,*

Science and Technology 9 (3): 245–76. https://genderandset.open.ac.uk/index.php/genderandset/article/view/514.

Varga, Ian. 2021. "What Is an Astronaut? The Untold Stories of Payload Specialists and Canceled Missions." *History: Review of New Books* 49 (6): 133–36. https://doi.org/10.1080/03612759.2021.1987106.

Wells-Jensen, Sherri, Joshua A. Miele, and Brandie Bohney. 2019. "An Alternate Vision for Colonization." *Futures* 110: 50–53. https://doi.org/10.1016/j.futures.2019.02.012.

Zhang, Lingling, and Beth Haller. 2013. "Consuming Image: How Mass Media Impact the Identity of People with Disabilities." *Communication Quarterly* 61 (3): 319–34. https://doi.org/10.1080/01463373.2013.776988.

16
MARE INCOGNITO
Live Performance Art Linking Sleep with the Cosmos through Radio Waves

Daniela de Paulis, Thomas Moynihan, Alejandro Ezquerro-Nassar, and Fabian Schmidt

Figure 16.1 Daniela de Paulis (Mare Incognito, 2022). Video still from Mare Incognito. Credits: Mirjam Somers, Bas Czerwinski.

Introduction

Mare Incognito is an interdisciplinary project, conceived and directed by media artist Daniela de Paulis, exploring the poetic and philosophical aspects of transitional states of consciousness during sleep. The project includes a series of live performances poetically highlighting the gradual dissolution of consciousness and of the thinking process while falling asleep, alternatively shifting from the subjective to the cosmic perspective. During each performance, the brain activity of sleep is transmitted into space, in real time, by a radio antenna of the Square Kilometre Array's prototype in Cambridge, United Kingdom. The project crosses various fields of research, including radio astronomy, neuroscience, performance art, cosmology, and intellectual history. *Mare Incognito* is a collaboration bringing together and stimulating intellectual exchange among researchers from renowned international institutions.

DOI: 10.4324/9781003280507-18

This chapter is a first-person account written by the artist in collaboration with some of the researchers who are working on the project. This chapter analyses the artistic and conceptual significance of the project and the cultural references that lead to its composition. It also describes the first performance hosted as part of the project and filmed at the Mullard Radio Astronomy Observatory in Cambridge in March 2022. The last section of this chapter traces the first stage of a global narrative on the philosophical and poetic connection between sleep, death, and the cosmos throughout human history.

Mare Incognito and Sleep in the Field of Performance Art

Mare Incognito broadens the ongoing exploration of brain-activity recording as an artistic medium within the field of live performance art. Specifically, the project links to some of the experimental practices employed by Alvin Lucier in his pioneering performance *Music for Solo Performer* (1965). As in Lucier's pivotal work, *Mare Incognito* highlights the moments of the preparation of the solo performer, with the fitting of the electrodes on the skull for the amplification of the brain waves. The preparation is a relevant part of the live performance, and by exhibiting the fitting of the electrodes on the skull, as well as the equipment and the methodology employed by scientists for revealing the brain activity through an electroencephalogram device, the scientific procedure acquires both materiality and artistic legitimacy within the piece. As in Lucier's performance, *Mare Incognito* employs scientific procedures and technological tools as accurately as in the laboratory setting, equalling the relevance of both scientific and artistic delivery within the narrative structure and presentation of the piece.

The rigorous use of scientific methodologies and technological devices within an artistic performance is also represented in *101 Nights—Dream Sessions* (2017–2018), a project by the Dream Sessions collective, composed of neuroscientists Guillaume Dumas and Roberto Toro, in collaboration with interdisciplinary artist Nathalie Regard. For the project, the neuroscientists recorded Regard's dreams, using a lab-grade electroencephalogram device, while stimulating her dreams with acoustic inputs. The auditory stimuli occasionally showed their influence on Regard's written account of the dreams that she experienced during these sessions. The comprehensive work by the Dream Sessions collective is one excellent example of an accurate scientific approach within performance art practices. As an artist, I acknowledge the importance of accuracy and integrity when using scientific methodologies and tools as part of my work. In my projects, science is a crucial component of the structure of the performance, and for me, it is important that the viewer or participant can trust the authenticity of their experience of the event.

Sleep, as an artistic practice, has been widely explored in other forms of contemporary performance works, not necessarily engaging with technology. One of the most poignant examples in the Western scenario is by Californian performance artist Chris Burden who presented *Bed Piece* in 1972, sleeping for twenty-two days in the Charles Eames Gallery in Venice Beach. The work proved to be confrontational for the audience as most people avoided getting close to the sleeper and seemed frightened, as reported by the artist in a 1974 film documenting the piece.[1] The minimalist and uncompromising set-up of the performance, consisting simply of a bed and the artist sleeping on it for twenty-two days without pause, allowed Burden to emphasise the subversive symbolism of sleeping in public, of exhibiting an action typically perceived as intimate and exposing the great vulnerability of the body during sleep.[2]

Within the broad diversity of artistic creations and practices that are informed and inspired by sleep, performance artworks that adopt the language and methodologies of science and technology are attentive to revealing the precise activity of the brain during sleep. During a performance, the electroencephalogram is able to reveal when sleep is an actual state of the brain as opposed to a simulated or staged event. Here technology can enhance the performative intensity of sleep by revealing its phenomenological presence as the true state of the mind of the performer during the artistic event.

Poetic and Scientific Views of the Project

Mare Incognito started conceptually in 2017, while I was completing my project *COGITO in Space* (De Paulis 2019) The first public presentation of the project was as part of a written conversation with Dutch gallery director Anke Bangma, for the programme TENT Online.[3] The first title of the project was *Dissolution in Sleep and Death*, an expression borrowed from one of the chapters in *Sleeping, Dreaming and Dying*, a collection of essays on sleep from both the Eastern and Western perspectives, compiled by biologist and neuroscientist Francisco Varela (1997).

COGITO in Space is an experiential performance during which the participant sends their brain activity into space as radio waves while watching a film in virtual reality showing experimental footage of the cosmos and Earth seen from space. *COGITO in Space* explores the possibility of physically extending the mind into the cosmos by using radio waves and thus creating a direct, albeit invisible, connection between the participant and the universe.

Mare Incognito started along this line of thought, continuing the same poetic exploration at the thresholds of consciousness and bodily presence, delving into fundamental questions regarding the human experience and its spatial and physical boundaries. *Mare Incognito* shifts the performative experience from waking life to the moment of falling asleep. The project explores the moment during the sleep cycle when awareness seems to dissolve and during which the self gradually minimises and detaches from the continuous life narrative. The perceived loss of consciousness during sleep is the only moment in daily life when the thinking process and self-awareness gradually shred into an unfathomable void: an experience plausibly similar to the moment of dying. *Mare Incognito* poetically explores and draws reflection upon the process of dying as a daily experience in human life. The performance conceptually links the dissolution and symbolic death of the self—as experienced during deep sleep—with the darkness, coldness, and vacuum of outer space, exploring how immeasurable expanses of space might poetically resonate with the emptiness of minimally conscious states. The title of the work hints at a journey into the obscure oceans of inner and outer space.

The experience of falling asleep engages the mind and the body in a form of dissolution that is both frightening and liberating. During these moments, thoughts disintegrate, overlap, and fade into memories and flickering associations in a non-sequential form, while the body dissolves the awareness of its spatial map and spatial boundaries, merging into an indefinite continuum of space. While falling asleep, the bodily limbs melt into darkness, as the lights of consciousness start fading. The mind and the body enter a timeless and boundless space in which the biographical self surrenders to the unfathomable. As a child, the moments of falling asleep were especially frightening. Talking with intellectual historian Thomas Moynihan, one of the collaborators in the project, I realised that my younger self used to experience something called 'hypnagogic micro- and macro-somatognosia', which is a form of hallucination for which the body is perceived as utterly out of scale, the size of a planet or the size of a pea: "Hypnagogic", he said, "refers to the transitional state between sleeping and wakefulness; 'macro' means large, 'micro' means small; 'soma' means body, and 'gnosia' means something like knowledge." We both were struck by how it seems that, as you approach the threshold of sleep, there appears to be a kind of sequential ablation of the different cognitive processes that, during waking life, provide a sense of a proportionate and coherent world.

In the liminal space between wakefulness and sleep, our experience of reality morphs into dreamlike visions. For a brief moment, our internal predictions of the world become unstable as our brain tries to make sense of external inputs, creating a collage of real and imagined objects. Perceptual time is distorted. A beeping sound from an alarm clock can smoothly blend into the story in our dream as if by magic, just at the right moment.

As awareness of our surroundings dissolves in dreamless sleep, so does our experience of a bodily self. Popular Western accounts of consciousness suggest that consciousness descends in levels, upon a kind of continuum: from being fully awake, to being asleep and dreaming, and then finally into dreamless sleep. In this linear view, consciousness is defined as that which disappears during dreamless sleep—a definition which has been adopted mostly by Western neuroscience. However, the Yoga and Advaita Vedānta schools of thought suggest that sleep is simply another mental state, and that through training, one can learn to witness sleep in the absence of dreaming. Such schools of thought propose that some form of experience can continue throughout sleep, even in the absence of perceptual objects and without the need for intentionality. In this state of being, the experienced self is unbound by bodily constraints and can exist purely as subjective time.

Mare Incognito seeks to explore the limitations of the human body as our primary interface with the external world, effectively asking whether removing the constraints of subjective bodily experience can liberate the self, uniting it with the cosmos as the fundamental continuity of matter. Does suspending bounded bodily awareness bring subjective perception closer to physical reality, where bodies exist in a boundless continuum?

The phenomenon of lucid dreamless sleep is debated among philosophers and consciousness scientists in the West. If we accept the Western definition of consciousness as that which is absent in dreamless sleep, the possibility of *lucid* dreamless sleep appears nonsensical. However, a multidimensional framework of consciousness would counter that conscious states are not linear, but rather can be better understood as a set of phenomenal properties that are partially dissociable from one another (Bayne, Hohwy, and Owen 2016). A nonlinear approach widens our taxonomy for describing conscious states and opens the door for different properties of consciousness outside of wakefulness and dreaming. When we transition from dreaming or wakefulness into dreamless sleep, we can think about the property "bodily self" diminishing, as phenomenal temporality takes precedence, manifesting as a state of lucid dreamless sleep.

In an attempt to provide an empirically grounded framework of the self, Blanke and Metzinger introduced the concept of *minimal phenomenal selfhood* (MPS), described as "the simplest form of self-consciousness" (Blanke and Metzinger 2009). *Mare Incognito* asks not what the simplest form is self-consciousness is, but rather, is MPS closer to harmony with the complexity of the cosmos? Could the MPS be more expansive than our full-waking-self model? In *Mare Incognito*, we record electroencephalographic (EEG) signals from electrodes positioned on the scalp and transmit them to space using a radio antenna. The EEG signal is the vehicle—the limb that extends towards outer space as we disintegrate into a minimal state of consciousness.

The scientific work for *Mare Incognito* is developed by Jarrod Gott, Çağatay Demirel, and Martin Dresler at the Donders Centre in the Netherlands, in collaboration with Alejandro Ezquerro-Nassar and Tristan Bekinschtein at the University of Cambridge. Cosmologist Fabian Schmidt at the Max Planck Institute in Germany is the scientific advisor for the astronomical references in the project. Eloy de Lera Acedo is the scientific advisor for the radio astronomical instruments at the Mullard Radio Astronomy Observatory.

Performance at the Mullard Radio Astronomy Observatory

Mare Incognito is a project divided in two stages and consisting of a site-specific performance and a live planetary, participatory performance. The first stage of the project began in September 2020, when the entire team started meeting online on a weekly basis. The research stage lasted for more than a year and allowed us to develop the scientific framework and identify the technical requirements for the EEG radio transmission into space as part of the live performance. The implementation of the research phase took place on 29 March 2022 with the film recording of the performance outdoors of the Mullard Radio Astronomy Observatory in Cambridge, a scientific site immersed in a vast forest surrounding, hosting a great diversity of plant and animal species. The main stage of the event was the Square Kilometre Array (SKA), a cluster of tree-shaped metallic antennas standing on a disc-shaped platform. Placed amongst the antennas were a reclining chair and a table with the equipment for monitoring the electroencephalogram device. A stage light brightened the circular area of the performance against the complete darkness of the soil, the surrounding forest, and the sky. Seen from some distance, the circular stage appeared like a faraway galaxy of events, emitting a dim light in the middle of a cosmic void. For the performance, I slept on the reclining chair for several hours during the cold night, wrapped in a sleeping bag (Figure 16.1). During sleep, my brain activity was recorded by a lab-grade electroencephalogram device, previously fitted on my skull by the neuroscientists, with conductive gel and wires cabled to a computer. While my brain activity was recorded, it was transmitted into space as radio waves in real time by one of the antennas forming the SKA cluster. During the entire transmission into space, the antenna remained in a fixed position, while the rotation of the Earth allowed the radio waves to spread across the sky. In my projects involving radio transmissions into space, I typically avoid tracking one specific celestial object in order to reduce the possible existential risks associated by the SETI (Search for Extraterrestrial Intelligence) scientific community with messaging a potential cosmic civilisation.

In *Mare Incognito*, the radio transmission into space is intended as a symbolic dissolution of the self into a greater unknown. In the project, radio waves provide a medium for transcending the physical identity, increasingly rarefying its matter and its boundaries while trailing onward into the cosmos.

My experience of the performance at the Mullard Observatory was a mystical one. With my eyes closed, gradually falling asleep, immersed in the surrounding wilderness, lying on the reclining chair and with my body projected towards the sky, I could abstract myself from the context of the performance and the filming, surrendering to the state of vulnerability in which I was gradually plunging whilst losing awareness. During these moments of a heightened sense of exposure to the unknown, while my brain activity was being recorded and transmitted into space, I could perceive my biographical self losing coherence in my mind and dissipating into the cosmos above, with the radio waves radiating my thoughts and merging with an immeasurable matter. Awakening from a deep sleep, I retained the experience of the performance, feeling profoundly transformed.

The performance was witnessed by the small project team, composed of neuroscientists Jarrod Gott, Tristan Bekinschtein, Alejandro Ezquerro-Nassar, cosmologist Fabian Schmidt, video artist Mirjam Somers, and photographer Bas Czerwinski, who filmed the event. The surrounding wilderness was felt as part of the observers, motionless in a surreal suspension during the cold night.

The site of the Mullard Observatory greatly affected the ambience of the performance and the photographic narrative of the film. Located next to a disused railway line that was partly embedded in the construction of some of the radio telescopes on site, the observatory is an open-air museum with obsolete radio telescopes and the ground for some of the most advanced antennas in the world, as well as the home for a rich wildlife, coexisting with human artefacts searching for cosmic phenomena.

The obsolete radio telescopes stand as imposing structures corroded by rust, and inside cabins once used to manoeuvre these colossal apparatuses, the air and time stand still, suspended in a mist of dust, as if all operators and scientists had suddenly evacuated the site, leaving their belongings behind and abruptly interrupting their experiments. Some of the results of the observations are still visible, printed in analogue form on long sheets of greyish, perforated paper, marked with the date of the last measurements, obtained sometime in the late 1980s when the radio telescopes were eventually retired. Next to the measurements are cigarette ends, metal scraps, paper notes, and various types of accidental objects. All over, the place feels like the vacated stage of a science fiction film, the set of a nuclear fallout, or a lucid dream, where the colours of reality become tinted with hallucinations, objects decay in the grip of helplessness, and time slips out of joint.

The *Mare Incognito* film combines the conceptual narrative of the sleep performance with the emblematic footage of the various scientific instruments inhabiting the observatory alongside the wildlife which makes its fleeting appearance during intervals of human activities. The film, completely shot at night and dusk, presents the various stages of the sleep cycle, including the moment of falling asleep, deep sleep, and the dream stage (REM sleep), ending with the moments that anticipate the awakening, when awareness is at the threshold of the self. This is perhaps the most evocative segment of the film as my intention was to highlight the crucial time when the biographical self is about to reemerge, after the complete numbness of deep sleep and the nonsensical wonderings of the dream stage. If deep sleep can be symbolically associated with death, the waking stage can be interpreted as a moment of suspension, during which the self hovers in a liminal space and finds itself at a gate, as if hesitating to reconnect with the biographical narrative of the previous day. This transitional stage of consciousness is vibrant with possibilities. What if one day I woke up as a different person? What if during these liminal moments, my biographical self was channelled into a different identity, or what if it simply disappeared altogether? These were some of the thoughts that led to the composition of the closing scenes of the film, influenced by *The Tibetan Book of the Dead* or *Bardo Thodol*. This ancient text is intended as a guide for the dying during the experience of leaving the physical world, whilst approaching the perilous moments after death, so as to advise the mind on how to navigate the interval (*bardo*) between death and possible rebirth. During the *bardo*, the dying person experiences the fear of departing from the physical world, and the guide brings support to negotiate these frightful moments and pursue the liberation and absolute light of the spirit. In the *Bardo Thodol*, however, death is intended as a physical as much as a symbolic occurrence: the *bardo* can be also interpreted as the intermission between two life events, during which some form of dissolution and despair is experienced.

According to the philosopher of mind Evan Thompson, one of the most compelling descriptions of the waking experience is by Marcel Proust at the beginning of his opus *In Search of Lost Time*:

> [M]y sleep was deep and allowed my mind to relax entirely; then it would let go of the map of the place where I had fallen asleep and, when I woke in the middle of the night, since I did not know where I was, I did not even understand in the first moment who I was; all I had, in its original simplicity, was the sense of existence.

Commenting on Proust's words, Thompson writes:

> What marks the first instant of awakening is not the self of memory but the feeling of being alive …. The moment of awakening thus reveals two kinds of self-experience. The first kind is the embodied self-experience of being alive in the present moment, or the experience of being sentient. The second kind of self-experience is the autobiographical experience of being a person with a storyline, a thinking being who mentally travels in time. The first kind of embodied sense of self we experience immediately upon awakening, but as we reach automatically for the second kind of autobiographical sense of self, it sometimes goes missing.
> *(Thompson 2015)*

Future Developments of the Project

The second part of the project consists of a live performance streamed on the web and involving participants from around the world who transmit their brain activity into space in real time while falling asleep and while the Earth rotates. Whereas the site-specific performance at the Mullard Observatory explores the intimate relationship of a single human with the unfathomable vastness of inner and outer space during the vulnerable state of sleep, the online performance amplifies this experience into a participatory happening shared at a planetary scale, highlighting the sleep cycle as a fundamental rhythm of all life, echoing the ancestral cycle of life and death, inextricably linked to our planetary and cosmic identity. The global performance allows participants to experience the intimate dialogue with the cosmos while falling asleep at their given location on Earth, while tangibly experiencing being part of a timeless planetary cycle of light and darkness, of dissolution and renewal. The terrestrial sleep performance allows people from around the world, equipped with an EEG device, to connect to an online platform purpose-built on the project's website, and to send their brain activity into space thanks to a remote connection with the Mullard Observatory. The performance takes place over a period of twenty-three hours and fifty-six minutes, the actual rotation period of the Earth relative to the fixed stars, highlighting the gradual darkening and brightening of the globe while sleep alternates with waking life and while different states of awareness fade into each other at a planetary scale. The online performance highlights the planetary cycle of sleep across cultures situated along the twenty-four terrestrial meridians.

In the *Mare Incognito* performances, the mind expands into the void of outer space during sleep, while cosmic phenomena observed in real time by the antennas at the Mullard Observatory are converted into sounds during the entire sleep cycle, producing a dialogue between the deep sleeper/dreamer and the universe, the inner and the outer worlds. The dialogue is made of electromagnetic signals produced both by the brain during sleep and by the cosmological phenomena observed at the Observatory in real time. The radio signals received by the SKA prototype antennas, including their cosmic component, are converted into an audible sound in real time throughout the entire sleep cycle.

The signal received in real time by the antennas is a radio noise that varies with a period of twenty-three hours and fifty-six minutes, indicating that the origin of this radio noise is outside our solar system. It is due in fact to an agglomeration of sources near the centre of our Milky Way galaxy in the constellation of Sagittarius. In addition, this small cosmic noise is emitted by energetic particles trapped by the Milky Way's magnetic field. These energetic particles in turn are remnants of dramatic cosmic events such as supernova explosions, which play an important role in the life cycle of stars and planets in our galaxy. Just like neurons firing generate new synaptic connections across the brain, supernova explosions eject and spread the components of fundamental matter across the universe, allowing for the formation of new celestial objects and, eventually, of life itself. "We are made of the same stuff as the stars" and are "part of a magnificent creation", as astronomer Harlow Shapley first articulated in the 1920s (Garbedian 1929). At higher radio frequencies, like in the case of the SKA antennas used for the project, a small contribution to the radio background also comes from the cosmic microwave background, the most ancient known signal of the cosmos, emitted a mere 380,000 years after the Big Bang.

Conceptual and Literary References

Mare Incognito is informed by a diversity of literary works and philosophical theories, exploring the poetics of sleep, dreams, death, and the desire of bridging a connection with the cosmos by allowing the mind to travel outside of the terrestrial boundaries.

The idea of travelling into space as a disembodied self has been addressed extensively in both Western and Eastern literature, perhaps the first example being Plato's *Myth of Er*, the earliest written account in human history of a possible journey of the soul into the cosmos after death. The novel *Solaris* (1961) by Stanisław Lem and the eponymous film (1972) by Andrei Tarkovsky have been very influential in my projects combining radio transmissions into space and neuroscience. In *Solaris*, a team of scientists studying a sentient planet composed of a global ocean, having failed all attempts to establish some form of communication with the liquid entity, resort to their last experiment: transmitting a stream of brain activity as an X-ray scan towards the surface of the emblematic world. The brain waves relayed towards the sentient ocean contain a stream of thoughts contaminated with memories and dreamlike visions, as in the process of falling asleep.

Philosopher Chelsea Haramia, also a collaborator in several of my projects, pointed me towards the extended mind thesis (EMT), in reference to my ongoing interest in transmitting brain waves into space. The EMT was conceptualised by Andy Clark and David Chalmers in 1998, proposing that the mind extends beyond its bodily limits into the physical surroundings that become part of an interchange with its cognitive development. In the EMT, the mind embodies space in a continuity of mutual interaction. In *Mare Incognito* the mind is converted into radio waves that move as its physical, yet invisible extension into outer space. Here the mind fuses with the cosmic distances, posing questions about the limits of human bodily presence. Travelling into space with the mind, etching the brain activity of sleep onto the infinite space medium for an immeasurable time, suggests the possibility of continuing one's life after death through a dream state.

In addition to the EMT, other perspectives in the philosophy of mind have been an important reference for my projects. *Mind and Cosmos* by Thomas Nagel (2012) has provided a valuable critical framework for my recent projects, in questioning the type of knowledge obtained by the scientific method through the materialistic approach. Nagel's argument on the limits of the scientific method in gaining a deep understanding of nature and the cosmos is especially relevant in reference to neuroscience and its objective to study and potentially explain a quality as imponderable as consciousness using mechanical procedures, such as electrical recordings of the brain. Nagel also points to the limits of the human mind in comprehending that which is much greater than itself. How can a mind that has evolved and adapted for survival on a limited planet with specific physical conditions truly understand the nature of the cosmos, which is beyond any possible experiential and spatial reference for such a mind? Thomas Nagel poignantly writes:

> Isn't it sufficient to try to understand ourselves from within—which is hard enough? Yet the ambition appears to be irresistible—as if we cannot legitimately proceed in life just from the point of view that we naturally occupy in the world, but must encompass ourselves in a larger world view. And to succeed, that larger world view must encompass itself.
>
> *(Nagel 2012: 23)*

In *Mare Incognito*, Nagel's perspective was instrumental in diverting the focus from the celebrated accomplishments and brilliance of science towards using scientific instruments and methodologies to highlight the precariousness of the human condition and human knowledge. In the project, the measurements obtained through sophisticated devices studying the brain and the cosmos become the emblematic language of the inner and outer worlds, creating a continuum of poetic resonance between these two forms of the unknown.

The cultural association of fundamental existential concepts such as sleep, death, and the cosmos is an ancient one, encompassing a diversity of civilisations across history. Eastern philosophy, for example, has been widely addressing the association of sleep, dream, and death in meditation, and the comparison between the Eastern and Western perspectives on this association has been an object of interdisciplinary studies. For example, in the aforementioned book *Sleeping, Dreaming and Dying*, biologist and neuroscientist Francisco J. Varela (1997) explores this association in both scientific Western and Tibetan traditions, addressing several aspects of sleep and death and approaching them from the fields of psychoanalysis, philosophy, and neuroscience.

For the project, I invited intellectual historian Thomas Moynihan to draw a chronology and a map of literary and philosophical works that have contributed to our symbolic collocation of sleep, minimal consciousness, death, and the cosmic depths of outer space. Moynihan's work attempts to map the changing ways in which people have thought about the position and placement of mind in the wider cosmos: how prior generations conceived of the relation of mind to the universe, in the broadest sense of each term, and how this conception has changed and mutated over time, in response to novel discoveries and building insights. Moynihan points out that one important way that the conceived relation of mind to cosmos has transformed was triggered by modern science's gradual discovery that the universe is far larger, emptier, and less hospitable than previously assumed. In our personal communication in 2021, he explains:

> Where once the Platonic tradition conscripted the image of an ascent toward the heavenly spheres as a metaphor for the culmination and apotheosis of lucid cogitation, because it assumed that the cosmos was itself constructed by mind and maximally suffused with spirits, modern cosmology has since revealed a cosmos much less obviously mindful or alive. In this way, it is less obvious that mind is 'at home' in the wider cosmos. But, despite this, many modern thinkers wanted to retain some sense of connection, filial or otherwise, between cosmos and mind. So, the imagined dilation of one's mind toward cosmic volumes still somehow represented a 'return home', but ground had to be ceded elsewhere: it could now no longer be so easily portrayed as an apotheosis of lucid wakefulness and conscious personhood; rather, it was now more comfortably thought of as a relapse towards more primordial and depersonalized modes of being.

Many were led to the idea that our eldest and most ancestral 'memories'—in the form of bodily instincts and reflexes—were thus a kind of internal isthmus to the ancient expanses of the cosmos. As a former contemporary dancer, I found these thoughts strangely fascinating and complementary to my line of thinking for *Mare Incognito*. In Moynihan's words:

> Many otherwise 'rational' and 'sober-minded' thinkers of scientific modernity, in their more romantic and poetical moments, remained too allured by the attractions and comforts of trying to find parallels between microcosm and macrocosm—as had been the habit of their pre-modern forebears—such that they stubbornly continued to seek out such parallels, *even after* modern science had heavily implied that consciousness is, in light of modern cosmology, not so easily represented as 'at home' within a universe that is vastly elder than all life, alongside being more inhospitable and empty than all prior generations could have assumed.

Moynihan continues:

> If you believe most of the cosmos is conscious and awake, as many prior generations did, then it is easy to imagine our consciousness 'at home', as a member of the wider cosmic family; but, after the discovery that the vast majority of the cosmos is unawake and inorganic, it becomes harder to so happily portray any filial relation between 'cosmos' and 'mind'; but due to the persistence of old habits of thought into new domains and contexts, as a kind of conceptual inertia, people didn't immediately give up on their desire to try to find such a relation. This led to a strangely persistent suggestion, among many philosophers and scientists in the nineteenth century, that this filial relation must be reconfigured along the lines of *forgetfulness* rather than *lucidity*. In other words, many believed that the entire history of the cosmos, in some sense, provides the unconscious prelude to consciousness and that we therefore are recapitulating, or returning to, these depths and 'prior states' in certain modes of altered consciousness: which provides a new sense of filial belonging, even if it has become obscured and related to the narcotic, intoxicated, and irrational.

In our exchanges, Moynihan pointed out that "the notion became very influential in psychoanalysis, which held that modes like sleep are temporary relapses toward elder evolutionary biology forms and, ultimately, even the dead expanses of the pre-organic cosmos".

Some Episodes Unveiling the Interconnection of Sleep, Death, and Cosmos throughout the Western Intellectual Tradition

Sleep has long been related to death. Heraclitus fused the two, Shakespeare further enshrined the conjunction—calling sleep the "ape of death"—and T.S. Eliot referred to "death's dream kingdom". Back in the 1600s, Thomas Browne put it bluntly:

> Sleepe is a death.

For obvious reasons, sleep has also long been collocated with night and the night sky. In Greek mythology, Hypnos, the embodiment of sleep, is sometimes thought to be sired by Nyx, goddess of night, and Erebus, god of darkness.

Thinking transitively, it is obvious to make the further connection: as sleep is related to death and the night sky to sleep, so it seems natural to relate death and the night sky. The intimacy between options of death and celestial domains becomes obvious: a link forged between the quietuses of space, of sleep, and of sentience itself. This intuitive connection has played out in the West since, at least, Plato's *Myth of Er*. Here, after death, the soul explores the celestial orbs. In Milton's *Paradise Lost* (1667: 3, 481–82), expired souls "pass the Planets seven,/ And that Crystalline Sphear". This was often seen, however, as the elevation—perhaps even apotheosis—of alertness and conscious presence, rather than its dissolution. This persists down into the eighteenth century, particularly in Platonic strains of poetry. Look to Edward Young's 1740s masterpiece, *Night Thoughts*, which narrates nocturnal visions of consciousness expanding to explore "Nature's universal orb". Young (1749: 163) claims the soul who "circles spacious earth" knows the planet is not the mind's true "home, but a "speck", and that the soul "feels herself at home among the stars". He imagines the soul-expanding, dilating beyond the Earth, until the narrator's sensorium comprehends and circumscribes cosmic volumes, where, finally, the soul is at home.

Similar strains are found, for another example, in Percy Shelley's staggering *Queen Mab* of 1813, which centres around another dream-enabled trip through outer space. Looking back on this pendant world from afar, Shelley (1813: 22) describes how "the Earth's distant orb appeared / The smallest light that twinkles in heaven". Here, again, Shelley—in Platonist mode—depicts the dreamtime dilation of mind, expansive enough to reach cosmic catchments, and he describes it as the apotheosis of alertness and awareness at the cost of the body. Because prior generations assumed that all other planets and suns are the seats of endless, interminable mind, it seemed natural to assume that cosmic volumes are the mind's true residence, our bodily existences but fleeting contractions of the spiritual whole.

Scientific discoveries in astronomy have played an important role in shaping the association of the human soul with the cosmos and consequently the correlation of sleep, the cosmos, and death. Where both Young and Shelley assumed this cosmos—of "countless and unending orbs" (Shelley 1813: 16)—was *full* of life and mind, such that it could comfortably beckon as the hearth of universal mind, the discoveries of science were set to slowly reveal a more alien, more inhospitable, more insensate cosmos. After this, the idea of the dreamtime dilation of the mind, to comprehend such cold spaces, slowly came to take on darker connotations: of the intoxicating lapse of awareness, of the drop into unconscious nadir and stillness.

If the universe in full is an extension of the mind, then it makes sense that cosmic dreams are a return home to the celestial whole; but if the universe is revealed to be seemingly largely devoid of intellectual activity, and largely empty, then one can continue to cling to the poetic metaphor of 'cosmic mind', but one must alter it to acknowledge that it must really be a *special type of unknowing*.

In the first half of the 1800s, large reflecting telescopes—such as the Leviathan of Parsontown—began revealing the lineaments of a far more alien galactic architecture. Where previously poets focused on the fullness of space, some now began highlighting its terrifying emptiness. Reacting to new images of distant nebulae, the writer Thomas De Quincey—in around 1845—spoke of the "dreadful magnitudes", and relayed the "silence", the "frost", and "eternities of death". Looking at images of spiral galaxies lately revealed, De Quincey (1846: 566–79) wrote of "the frightful magnitude [and] depth to which [they] are sunk in the abysses of the heavenly wilderness". Nothing on the human scale can compete with such scales, but what of the planetary scale? It fares little better, De Quincey mused: attempting to measure these "dreadful distances" in terms of "diameters of the Earth's orbit" would fail almost just as spectacularly, he concluded. Pondering the Orion Nebula he saw it as a parsec-wide "skull"—a giant avatar of "Death"—grimacing "in the very anguish of hatred", as "brutalities unspeakable sit upon the upper lip".

Things had begun to change: the deadliness of space, its sheer inimitability to life, was nascently beginning to be recognised. But what of sleep?

Elsewhere, in his *Suspiria de Profundis* (i.e., 'sighs of the deep'), De Quincey, famous for his addictions to opium, borrowed precisely this astronomical register—sublime yet deadly—to describe his experiences of intoxicated sleep. He wrote of how opium—inducing loss of consciousness, abrading selfhood strata by strata, and bottoming out into the profundity of sleep—seemed to dilate time such that the circadian melted into the cosmic. He wrote:

> Time becomes infinitely elastic, stretching out to such immeasurable and vanishing termini, that it seems ridiculous to compute the sense of it, on waking, by expressions commensurate to human life. As in starry fields one computes by diameters of the earth's orbit, or of Jupiter's, so, in valuing the virtual time lived during some dreams, the measurement by generations is ridiculous—by millennia is ridiculous; by aeons, I should say, if aeons were more determinate, would be also ridiculous.
>
> *(De Quincey 1874: 8)*

In sleep, he seems to say, we lapse into the cosmic, inasmuch as our consciousness—and its terrestrially structured proportions—lapses. It is telling that De Quincey saw it fit to relate cosmic dilations of mind not to high-minded cogitations but instead to his opium-induced stupors.

Other writers of the time, particularly in Germany, wrote of the "*Nachtseite der Naturwissenschaft*": the nightside of natural science, defined by somnolence and strangeness (von Schubert 1808). Given their protoevolutionary theories, imagining creation as a hierarchy of beings progressively arranged and developed over time, these writers immediately interpreted sleep as a relapse to evolutionarily 'earlier' stages of natural development, traced in a clean backwards arc from primate to protoplasm.

The physician Christoph Hufeland even spoke poetically of sleep as a return to "vegetative time". It had similarly been said by Georges Buffon (1774: 247), the French naturalist, that "un végétal n'est dans ce sens qu'un animal qui dort", or "a plant is in this sense but a sleeping animal". Classifying sessile animals like oysters as beings designed to "sleep always", Buffon said that as 'evolution' can be interpreted as an upward rise from sessile somnolence to cerebralised wakefulness, so too can we interpret our own ontogenetic maturation this way: "Our existence begins with sleep, the foetus sleeps almost continuously, and the child sleeps much more than he stays awake" (1774: 247). Sleep, then, could be interpreted as a return to oyster-like modes.

But why not relate the deepest slumber to even more primordial echelons or epochs than the vegetative? Some latter-day romantics and spiritualists suggested exactly this. The physician of nervous diseases Charles Bland Radcliffe, in 1875, put all the pieces together to rhapsodise that sleep, and dreaming, was the submersion of our fragile individuality within a "cosmical" ocean. He wrote:

> Dreaming? What is it? May it not ... show that man is *a part of* the universe in which he is placed, and not *apart from* it in the sense in which he appears to himself in the waking state, the revelation being not altogether unlike that by which the true relations of the earth to the universe are made evident at night, when 'the withdrawal of the veil of light' allows the stars to be seen? May it not be that in sleep, as in death, the portal of a fuller life is opened, and that Jacob's dream of a 'ladder reaching from earth to mysterious altitudes above the earth' is to show that the way to escape from the earth is in the dreaming rather than in the waking state? Life is renewed in sleep: the [individual body] is forgotten in sleep: and this forgetfulness, it may be, brings with it this renewal by letting the wearied sleeper—wearied because while waking he had only made use of a life which was self-contained, and, therefore, soon spent—fall into the ocean of cosmical life....
>
> *(Radcliffe 1875: 138, emphasis in original)*

Others, such as German spiritualist and parapsychologist Carl du Prel, suggested in the 1880s that our somnambulant and hypnagogic states, and even our "common dreams", may be signs of more advanced life forms, from other stellar systems, attempting to initiate communications with us, casting their experiences and memories to us via some sensory and perceptual modes that humans are only nascently evolving and mastering (du Prel 1889: 257–91).

During the 1910s and 1920s, a new generation of large-scale telescopes—such as the Hooker telescope at Mount Wilson—revealed an extragalactic universe yet larger and ever more empty. By this time, evolutionary modes of understanding had settled in, and Freudian psychoanalysis had become popular. It was only natural for adherents to relate these deepening spaces, then, to the depths of the somnolent unconscious that Freud had, supposedly, lately started sounding.

Following this thread, Ernst Trömner (1912: 1), a German psychoanalyst and neurologist, had written in 1911 that:

> Thus arise light and life out of the lap of night and nothingness. But the night does not dismiss its creatures for aye; it holds fast to them ... and ever again compels them back to its silencing bosom. ... Daily we must return again to the bosom of all-nourishing Night, in whose dark folds dwell the true nurturers of existence.

Responding to these words in 1924 (Ferenczi 1938), Freud's protégé, the Hungarian psychoanalyst Sándor Ferenczi, accordingly couldn't help but conclude that the "sleeping stage represents ... a repetition of long superseded modes of existence, nay, of an existence before life [itself] began. Sleep, so runs an old Latin proverb, is the brother of death" (p. 80). Ferenczi enthusiastically interpreted sleeping as our temporary "recapitulation" of the dead, inorganic "repose" of the cosmos prior to the abiogenetic awakening of life. For Ferenczi, the birth of life, as of the individual, is like a transient disturbance of the wider cosmic slumber: an emergence of self-consciousness within an otherwise enveloping ocean of unconsciousness and somnolence. With a characteristic flourish that collapsed the cosmic, evolutionary, and circadian rhythms, Ferenczi concluded, "embryogenesis too is like a sleep which is disturbed only by the palingenetic repetition of the history of the species, as by a biographical dream" (p. 80).

The relation between cosmic spaces and hypnagogic states had indeed changed since Young's time: this was an era wherein physicists had recognised, and had begun stressing, that outer space is an expanse filled with "torrential deluges of life-destroying radiation", where life is entirely "the accident" and titanic, abiotic death "the essential". It had only lately been realised, for example, that the Sun's ultraviolet rays would sterilise the Earth but for the thin, protective layer of ozone. In this setting, the symbolic linking of the inhospitable and inorganic expanses of space with the minimal selfhood of sleep, and with death's oblivion, could only grow yet stronger.

We can respond to a silent and unconscious cosmos by desiring to immerse ourselves in it, relapsing into primordial unconsciousness. But another response was brewing. Indeed, this was also the era when people—predominantly science fiction writers—started seriously imagining that 'mind' may somehow seep beyond Earth, on a rocket ship or otherwise. That is, these were the decades immediately before the Space Age, when speculators began prophesying that—through scientific ingenuity—people in the future may somehow be able to physically reach those abandoned spaces and "wake them up". Others have imagined that we might one day commune and converse with distant planets, through remote communication and messaging, thus connecting planets as distant "specks" of consciousness, to weave a wider "cosmical mind", just as countless neurons synthesise a consciousness. If the sky appears sterile and somnolent, why don't we instead imagine the possibility of one day "waking it up"?

In the late 1920s, the physicist James Jeans, in a contemplative mood, wrote the following:

[T]he universe which we study with such care may be a dream, and we brain-cells in the mind of the dreamer.

(Jeans 1928: 86)

We do not know what the true relation between mind and cosmos is, but we do know that it has changed mightily over time, and will probably change again. *Mare Incognito* focuses on the alluring collocation between sleep, death, and cosmos: responding to the ways in which, as our ideas about the universe have changed over time, people have been provoked to redefine the ways in which they assume that this interrelation plays out. As the universe has become emptier and more unconscious, some have responded by associating minimal states of consciousness with a lapse towards earlier and more primordial modes of being, seeking immersion and release in the "cosmical ocean". Others have responded, more proactively, by determining to find ways to bring consciousness to the somnolent firmament, and 'wake it up'. The latter response Lem (2013: 68–70) once described as the tendency to pursue a "heroic attack on the surrounding matter". We could say that the latter is proactive, the former passive. The beauty and profundity of *Mare Incognito*, perhaps, is that it holds together these contradicting and conflicting responses to a silent cosmos. It involves a passive lapse into unconsciousness, whilst at the same time actively broadcasting the mind into the depths. It involves a somnolent immersion into the still cosmos, whilst at the same time, at least symbolically, rippling the pulse of consciousness outwards into those unconscious depths.

Future Developments of Intellectual History in *Mare Incognito*

Moynihan's timeline and map of the connection between sleep, death, and the cosmos in the Western cultural tradition has delved so far into the human imaginary inspired and informed by scientific discoveries brought by large-scale telescopes in the field of optical astronomy, up to the early 1920s. Other pivotal scientific discoveries and new theories of nonvisible cosmic phenomena were discovered and proposed during the first decades of 1900. The dawn of quantum physics and the theory of relativity, for example, as well as the ongoing discovery of the electromagnetic spectrum and the development of astrobiology in more recent years, have possibly played an important role in how contemporary cultures around the world continued shaping the relation between sleep, death, and the universe. At the same time, the electroencephalogram was invented, advancing new methodologies for the understanding of brain functions. Has the poetic tradition linking sleep with death and the cosmos changed with the age of electrically lit cities, where waking life frenetically stretches throughout the night? The human relationship with the environment has dramatically changed over the past century, with increasingly fewer locations on Earth enjoying dark skies and the sounds of nature at night. Sleep is also becoming increasingly affected by the hectic urban environment. As humans, can we still experience sleep as a poetic dissolution into the cosmos at night, surrendering our biographical self into a much greater totality, embracing the vastness of the universe as our primary and ultimate cradle? Perhaps experiencing this form of dissolution and death through sleep on a daily basis would evoke once again in our species the sense of finitude and unfathomable vulnerability in relation to our planet and the cosmos, as for our visionary ancestors.

As *Mare Incognito* continues developing, the collaboration with Moynihan is ambitiously attempting to map a comprehensive intellectual history of the cultural association between sleep, death, and the cosmos across times and places around the globe. This map will progressively follow the terrestrial meridians, starting with the Greenwich prime meridian and chasing the gradual transition from daylight to darkness across the terrestrial sphere. The proposal would be to create a global map of the poetic association between sleep, death, and the cosmos for the live terrestrial performance, highlighting cultural differences and analogies across the globe while reinforcing the perception of humans being part of one single sky.

Conclusion

Mare Incognito is a very significant experience in my artistic journey for encompassing both a rigorous intellectual investigation and my personal, visceral fascination for the moment of falling asleep: as far as I remember, I have always regarded this seemingly mundane and brief time of daily life as mystical and inscrutable. As an artist with substantial experience creating and leading global-scale collaborative projects, I regard *Mare Incognito* as an effort in which the various collaborators truly engage and interact as *one mind* towards the accomplishment of the poetic objectives. It is remarkable to experience how researchers from the fields of neuroscience and cosmology expand ideas and theories from their specialist knowledge into much wider reasoning, having the opportunity to collaborate in a trans-disciplinary setting, such as the one for the project. *Mare Incognito* allows scientists to share their knowledge and methodology so that queries specific to one branch of knowledge can be reframed and expanded when confronted with fundamental debates from another area of research. In this context, principles from the field of neuroscience echo cosmological questions and vice versa, emphasising the unknown in both disciplines. This process feeds back into the artistic process as a catalyst for poetic ideas and layers of meaning.

The inclusion of an overview of intellectual history within the project has also been crucial in expanding the poetic links between sleep, death, and the cosmos from the subjective experience to that of numerous thinkers across cultures and centuries, suggesting this association deeply resonates with human nature.

Acknowledgements

Daniela de Paulis would like to acknowledge the intellectual contribution of all collaborators in the project, including Jarrod Gott, Martin Dresler, Tristan Bekinschtein, Çağatay Demirel, Eloy de Lera Acedo, Mirjam Somers, and Bas Czerwinski. We are grateful to each collaborator for bringing their unique perspectives and ideas as well as their specialist knowledge into the work.

Notes

1 "Chris Burden Documented Projects 71–74", posted to Vimeo by user "angelo", https://vimeo.com/29168858#t=552.
2 Jason Farago, "The Real Story behind Tilda Swinton's Performance at MoMA", *The New Republic* (28 March 2013), https://newrepublic.com/article/112782/real-story-behind-tilda-swintons-performance-moma.
3 "Dissolution in Sleep and Death", interview with Anke Bangma, *Tent Online*, https://www.tentrotterdam.nl/artikelen/dissolution-in-sleep-and-death/.

References

Bayne Tim, Jakob Hohwy, and Adrian M. Owen. 2016. "Are There Levels of Consciousness?" *Trends in Cognitive Sciences* 20 (6): 405–13. https://doi.org/10.1016/j.tics.2016.03.009
Blanke, Olaf, and Thomas Metzinger. 2009. "Full-Body Illusions and Minimal Phenomenal Selfhood." *Trends in Cognitive Sciences* 13 (1): 7–13. https://doi.org/10.1016/j.tics.2008.10.003.
Buffon, Georges-Louis Leclerc de. 1774. *Oeuvres Complètes de Buffon*, Vol. 5. Paris: Imprimerie royale.
Coleman, Graham and Thupten Jinpa, editors. 2007. *The Tibetan Book of the Dead*. New York: Penguin.
De Paulis, Daniela. 2019. "COGITO in Space." *Antennae: The Journal of Nature in Visual Culture* 47: 199–211.
De Quincey, Thomas. 1846. "System of the Heavens as Revealed by Lord Rosse's Telescopes." *Tait's Edinburgh Magazine* 13 (153): 566–79. ProQuest ID 4445840.
De Quincey, Thomas. 1874. *Suspiria de Profundis*. Edinburgh: Adam & Charles Black.
Du Prel, Carl. 1889. *The Philosophy of Mysticism*. Vol. 2. London: George Redway.
Ferenczi, Sándor. 1938. *Thalassa, a Theory of Genitality*. Translated by Henry Alden Bunker. New York: Psychoanalytic Quarterly.
Garbedian, H. Gordon. 1929. "The Star Stuff That Is Man." *New York Times*, August 11.
Jeans, James. 1928. *Eos: Or the Wider Aspects of Cosmogony*. London: Kegan Paul.
Lem, Stanisław. [1961] 1970. *Solaris*. London: Faber & Faber.
Lem, Stanisław. 2013. *Summa Technologiae*. Translated by Joanna Zylinska. Minneapolis, MN: University of Minnesota Press.
Milton, John. 1667. *Paradise Lost*. London: Samuel Simmons.
Nagel, Thomas. 2012. *Mind and Cosmos: Why the Materialist Neo-Darwinian Conception of Nature Is Almost Certainly False*. New York: Oxford University Press.
Radcliffe, Charles Bland. 1875. "Man Trans-Corporeal." *Contemporary Review* 25: 125–47. ProQuest ID 1294651455.
Shelley, Percy Bysshe. 1813. *Queen Mab: A Philosophical Poem*. London: R. Carlile. https://archive.org/details/queenmabphilosop02shel/.
Thompson, Evan. 2015. "Dreamless Sleep, the Embodied Mind, and Consciousness: The Relevance of a Classical Indian Debate to Cognitive Science." In *Open MIND*, edited by Thomas K. Metzinger and Jennifer M. Windt, Chapter 37. Frankfurt am Main: MIND Group. http://doi.org/10.15502/9783958570351.
Trömner, Ernst. 1912. *Das Problem des Schlafes: Biologisch und Psychophysiologisch Betrachtet*. Hamburg: Wiesbaden.
Varela, Francisco J., ed. 1997. *Sleeping, Dreaming, and Dying: An Exploration of Consciousness with the Dalai Lama*. Somerville, MA: Wisdom Publications.
von Schubert, Gotthilf Heinrich. 1808. *Ansichten von der Nachtseite der Naturwissenschaft*. Dresden: Arnoldsche Buchhandlung.
Young, Edward. 1749. *Night Thoughts on Life, Death, and Immortality*. London: R. Dodsley.

PART III

Colonial Histories and Decolonial Futures

17
CELESTIAL RELATIONS WITH AND AS MILŊIYAWUY, THE MILKY WAY, THE RIVER OF STARS

Bawaka Country, including Dr Laklak Burarrwanga, Ritjilili Ganambarr, Merrkiyawuy Ganambarr-Stubbs, Banbapuy Ganambarr, Djawundil Maymuru, Lara Daley, Sarah Wright, Sandie Suchet-Pearson, and Kate Lloyd with Naminapu Maymuru-White and Rrawun Maymuru

Sky Country

We write this together as the Bawaka Collective, an intercultural, Yolŋu and ŋäpaki (white/settler), human and more-than-human research collective led by Bawaka Country with Yolŋu artist Naminapu Maymuru-White and Yolŋu songman Rrawun Maymuru. We are a collective of four sisters, Dr. Laklak Burarrwanga, Ritjilili Ganambarr, Merrkiyawuy Ganambarr-Stubbs, and Banbapuy Ganambarr, their daughter Djawundil Maymuru, and four ŋäpaki human geographers—Lara Daley, Kate Lloyd, Sandie Suchet-Pearson, and Sarah Wright. In this essay, we write with Banbapuy, Dr. Laklak, Ritjilili, and Merrkiyawuy's son, songman Rrawun Maymuru. Rrawun is Wäŋa Wataŋu, custodian of the Guwak songspiral, which holds and frames this essay. We also write with the paintings of Naminapu Maymuru-White and the knowledges these share of Milŋiyawuy, the River of Stars. Naminapu is a contemporary artist of the Maŋgalili clan whose homeland is at Djarrakpi at the base of Cape Shield, the northern perimeter of Blue Mud Bay, Arnhem Land, in the Northern Territory. Her work references Maŋgalili country, particularly the 'outside story' or origin story of the Maŋgalili.

Bawaka Country is the lead author of this essay. Bawaka Country is a place in North East Arnhem Land, in the Northern Territory of Australia, and it is also Country. Country is an Aboriginal English word for the human and more-than-human beings and agencies that co-become as place/space (Bawaka Country 2016). Country includes rivers, rocks, people, animals, plants, sea, winds, and weather. Country also embraces atmospheres, the Moon, the Sun, stars, the Magellanic Clouds, and Milŋiyawuy, the Milky Way.

In this essay, we are sharing about Milŋiyawuy and some of its important connections with life on earth and life beyond, yet still connected to the earth. We travel with two men, Burrak and Yikawaŋawak, nurturing and demonstrating relations with the night sky through a series of four paintings by Naminapu Maymuru-White that tell their story. We also share about Guwak, a messenger bird, who travels the night sky. Guwak gave Maŋgalili people the way to the other world, the world of sky Country. Guwak's call, the resonating sound of *guuuuuu-wak*, affirms the link between sky and earth, between life and death, living and dead, leading spirits to the world beyond.

DOI: 10.4324/9781003280507-20

These stories and knowledges show ongoing Yolŋu connections with and as Milŋiyawuy and deeply challenge dominant imaginaries of 'outer' space and its exploration. However, we are only revealing some of the top layers of these knowledges. There are rules about who can know and talk about the deep layers of knowledge, even in the Yolŋu community. It is important that we, and you, be aware that there are limits to what we are sharing and acknowledge the many layers of Yolŋu knowledge, sovereignty and experience that underpin this telling.

In North East Arnhem Land there are many songspirals, also known as songlines. Songspirals are a sacred song, story, and ceremony. They are about knowing Country, singing the land, the sky, and the heavens. They are a deep mapping of the land and its many relations, above and below, around, in many layers and dimensions. The Guwak songspiral provides the map for spirits to travel safely through sky Country to their final destination among the stars (Bawaka Country 2020).

Guwak has many layers. Guwak is a songspiral, and a messenger bird, known as a koel in English. Guwak calls out in the night and travels across the land guiding spirits to the Milky Way. Guwak is the link between Yolŋu people and the River of Stars, sky Country. Each clan has its own place and songs, but some are shared, such as the Guwak songspiral. Guwak is shared by clans, but each has their own way of singing the song. The songspiral holds important relationships between people and sky Country, so they can continue across space and time, between the earth and sky, and through the generations. As we have previously shared:

> [Guwak] demonstrates that Sky Country is and always has been a richly known, mapped, governed and cared-for place. The Rom that governs it has always been there and never changes—regardless of developments in state or international law, or in the Western sciences.
> *(Bawaka Country 2020: 6)*

Beginning the Journey

Burrak and Yikawaŋawak announced to the Maŋgalili, that they would go hunting for turtle and would travel out to sea, to a place in the sky, where their spirits would remain with the stars which would shine out of the night sky. So, a canoe and paddles were made, and their journey began by paddling down the Milŋiya River which flows into Blue Mud Bay near Djarrakpi (Figure 17.1).

Sitting in their canoe, looking for turtles, making their journey to sky Country, the men are not alone; they are never alone. They are intimately connected to the worlds they are an integral part of. Through Rom—Yolŋu Law—they know how they are related to everything; they know their places and their obligations and responsibilities. Through gurruṯu, the Yolŋu kinship system, they know how they are related not only to other human beings but also to everything, to the currents and winds, to the seasons and cycles, to the land and sea and water, and to the stars and sky.

These connections, these intimate relationships guided by Rom, weave and bind together everything that is part of earth and ocean, and water. And they also weave earth and sky Country

Figure 17.1 Naminapu Maymuru-White, *Milŋiyawuy #1*. Reproduced with permission.

into a continuous whole. The men journey to sky Country through the ocean after padding down the Milŋiya River. What's done on earth is reflected in sky Country. What's done in sky Country is reflected in the oceans, in the seas, and on the land. Guwak, the messenger bird, guides all, reminding and invigorating this link. Rrawun tells us that the Milky Way is:

> in the sky, that everyone sees around the world, and [it is also] beneath the sea and it's called Muŋurru. The reason why Guwak was calling to the sea at Muŋurru is to let the spirits ... know that they are coming and that they are going to unite in one universe. Calling to the seas where the earth holds the sea and the echoes of Guwak will bring unity between those two spirits up to the universe and beyond. Because we've got two—our land here and then the other land, that is waiting, the spiritual land. Unseen, unheard, untouched, only the spirit will go there.

Rom has always been present. Legal fictions of Terra Nullius, caelum nullius, of the land, sky, and heavens belonging to no one, deny the presence of people–Country-Law. Guwak reminds us that there are always, already plural laws governing sky Country and that these laws have been here, and will always be here, in/through/as all time.

Water Rising, Darkness Falling

And somewhere in the middle of the ocean, there was water rising. In the bay at Yingalpiya, which is the nesting place of the freshwater crocodile, strong winds developed (Figure 17.2). The wind overturned the men's canoe. This same place is the spirit source for Maŋgalili people.

The two men kept going in the water until it got dark in the middle of the ocean. Still, they kept on. And then they were drowned.

There were many beings there under the sea during this journey. These beings can't be seen in the painting; they are there in the salt water. The men had many offers of help from these beings as they paddled in the darkness.

The special log called Bandumul that contains mangrove worms was passing by and said, "You two need help?" It offered itself as assistance, and the men said, "No".

And a sea monster, Dhäla, passed them and said, "Do you two need help?" And they said, "No".

And then the ancestral king fish Ŋoykal came to them and said, "Do you two need help?" And they said, "No". Even the rock cod they had caught offered assistance, but the two men refused help.

And so, all the beings left them and then they drowned in the water.

The story shares some of the ways that Country and its beings are agentic, powerful, and communicative. They are not imaginary. The beings of Country have knowledge and messages and Yolŋu Law. They act within their own communities, with each other, and they also act in ways that speak to human worlds.

Figure 17.2 Naminapu Maymuru-White, *Milŋiyawuy #2*. Reproduced with permission.

These beings of Country need to be taken seriously, especially as they send their warnings. The beings have the power to hurt, but in this case, they are offering warnings and help. As Dr. Laklak Burarrwanga et al. (2012: 24) explain:

> If you were hunting *maranydjalk*, stingray, for example, a Yolŋu hunter might rub the sweat from under his armpits all over your body and head. This is for your protection so that Country will recognise you, so that Country will acknowledge and know you. Country will protect you then. *Maranydjalk*, the stingray, will recognise the local scent and won't hurt you. You see, Country and animals have an active part to play in that relationship. You must ask permission from them, respect the relationships and behave correctly. They decide. The world looks different if you see it that way.

Behaving correctly, according to protocols and law, is something that has long been respected and understood in many diverse Indigenous cultures throughout the world (Kimmerer 2013; Poelina et al. 2020; RiverofLife et al. 2020; Tynan 2020). Instead of passive and in the background, all beings of Country, whether on the land, in the sky, under the sea, whether animal or plant or dream or weather or creation energy or more, have agency and law. As Anishinaabeg academic Vanessa Watts points out, "habitats and ecosystems are better understood as societies …; meaning that they have ethical structures, inter-species treaties and agreements" (Watts 2013). This includes sea Country and sky Country, inner and outer worlds.

And there are consequences if Country's warnings are ignored. Country can take dramatic action, floods, earthquakes, out-of-control fire, or Country may even withdraw from relationship if laws are broken (Smith et al. 2021; Watts 2013; Yandaarra 2022).

Yet, these big changes, the rise of the water and the weather, can bring new possibilities and new connections (Smith et al. 2021). Aunty Shaa Smith, storyholder for Gumbaynggirr Country, speaking as part of the Indigenous-led collective Yandaarra points out that, at times of big change, at times of destruction, there is also creation, the potential for new pathways and relationships. As she says:

> There is a crumbling of what was, but there is potential for creation to come through. Like the rainbow serpent, the serpent changes land as she moves across country, singing the clans and the languages into existence (Burarrwanga et al. 2019, 2013). In a sense, she is destroying what was as she creates the new. This transformation too happens within us, deep in ourselves, so we are not standing outside, observing what is happening; we are a part of it; it is transforming us.
>
> (Smith et al. 2021: 164)

In this case, the two men were undertaking a sacred journey nourishing relationships between themselves, their clan, their new homeland and sky Country. Following Guwak's call, binding sky and land—demonstrating the special link that others would follow, that continues to animate the world today.

They offered themselves to the night sky where their spirits will take their place in the River of Stars along with Maŋgalili spirits who will follow the connections.

Becoming Sky

The spirits of the men went up to the River of Stars to dwell there with other spirits of people who have died (Figure 17.3). These Maŋgalili spirits of the deceased attain their celestial position in the River of Stars by means of possum fur string Burrkun that connects Djarrakpi at the site of the Marawili tree to the night sky.

Milŋiyawuy, the River of Stars, is not caelum nullius: it is homeland for the spirits and souls of the Maŋgalili people and intimately connected to life here on earth. In sky Country, there are multiple connections. Sky Country is a river, not just a star or a planet with empty space/s between. The universe is full, full of connections and stories, and beings. Maŋgalili are related to the Milky Way, and they paint these relationships as part of their stories and part of their unknown heaven. From the land to the universe and beyond. Maŋgalili make the possum string on earth, and that is their passport through the River of Stars. We/They weave together connections between space, earth, and the journey of the spirit. As Rrawun says:

> The scared string that's my passport that will take me where I want to go. Also, my family, my daughters, sons, grandchildren, my sisters, and so on. It is not like building a spaceship, because when we are building a spaceship we are destroying things and then we are going to fly the spaceship and all the toxic waste is going to cover the land. That's why our ancestors knew that there is a way to explore the universe and beyond and they knew from the beginning. And that's why we have our own passport to explore the universe when we pass. And then we pass on that, and that's why we are passing on the knowledge to the younger generation—so they can go free to the other world.

For Yolŋu people, entering the heavens has strict protocols that must be followed and relationships that must be negotiated under Rom. Space is not for human beings that are alive. Space is for human beings that hold the right passport to go there. With that passport, it's like opening the gates to the heavens, to the universe, for the spirit who is carrying the string. Maŋgalili protocols are part of existing multiple and complex Indigenous governance systems and relations already governing the night sky.

Yolŋu relationships, and many other Indigenous relations, with and as Milŋiyawuy deeply challenge dominant imaginaries of 'outer space' and its exploration. Diverse Aboriginal and Indigenous nations globally have long-held relationships and systems of governance and law that have been in existence for millenia and include 'outer space' (Fuller, Norris, and Trudgett 2014; Hamacher 2022; Noon and De Napoli 2022; Watts 2013). The multiplicity and longevity of these relations, and their embeddedness in life on earth, means that discussions, plans, and protocols around entering 'outer space' must foreground Indigenous understandings and protocols of sky Country to respect and safeguard important prior and existing Indigenous relationships.

Indigenous knowledges of sky Country, of 'outer space', emphasise that space is already a known place, inhabited by animate spirits and beings, and is full of connections and law that play important roles in patterns of existence sustaining sky Country as well as life on earth. There

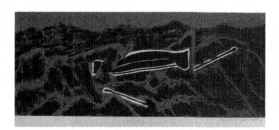

Figure 17.3 Naminapu Maymuru-White, *Milŋiyawuy #3*. Reproduced with permission.

is no boundary separating the River of Stars and the land. They are connected. When the stars are above, they shine on the rivers of the earth and the islands. As we have written elsewhere:

> There are so many stories and they are in relationship with each other. When we sing the stars, we sing about which direction the morning star comes from, which direction the moon comes from, from which place they come and where they go. There are so many layers.
> *(Burarrwanga et al. 2019: 131)*

Yet the current prevailing imaginaries, discussions, and ventures into space are underpinned by an extractive mindset, dominated by corporate and geopolitical interests. In Australia, the space industry is being positioned as an area of great opportunity and as playing an important enabler in Australia's post-covid economic recovery (Australian Government 2020). In 2021, the Australian Space Agency launched an AU$150 million Moon to Mars investment initiative to strengthen Australia's capability in the growing space economy, connecting with NASA's Artemis human exploration programme (Australian Government 2021). These programmes and initiatives set Australia on a path of participating in further human space exploration and potential resource extraction. Such activities have the potential to harm, disrupt, or destroy Yolŋu and other Aboriginal and Indigenous sky relations, connectivities, and lands. Celestial relations with and as Milŋiyawuy call for the respecting of existing laws, protocols, beings, and systems of relations which already inhabit the night sky. Heeding this call will be critical in preventing engagements in space from furthering processes and practices of ongoing colonisation.

Milŋiyawuy

Guwak, the two men, and the possum string are important celestial relations that speak back to colonising notions that space is distant, separate, lifeless, uninhabited, empty, or caelum nullius. Indigenous ways of knowing and being teach that there is nothing 'outer' about so-called 'outer space', that the Milky Way, constellations, and celestial bodies above are deeply connected to life on earth (Figure 17.4). These entities are an intimate part of daily existence through their connections with creation, story, navigation, time-telling, changing tides, and changing seasons, and as home to many spirits. Celestial entities and beings are intimate relations of Yolŋu people: they have agency, communicate, and are participants in complex systems of political and legal governance. They are part of Yolŋu sovereignties.

Disrespecting and disrupting these relations can cause great harm. The stakes are very real. Milŋiyawuy is the homeland of the Maŋgalili who have passed. At the same time, space exploration poses harm and further destruction of Indigenous lands on earth (e.g., Goodyear 2017; Gorman 2005; Peryer 2019). In North East Arnhem Land, a new space launch site in Gumatj clan lands is just near the second place Guwak went on her journey (Bawaka Country 2020). This is

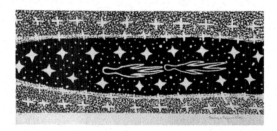

Figure 17.4 Naminapu Maymuru-White, *Milŋiyawuy #4*. Reproduced with permission.

a special area for the Guwak songspiral. Merrkiyawuy shares what can happen if the songspirals and Law are not respected:

> [T]he spiral can come tumbling down and burst. That's what we say, it will burst open and just float and you will be like a leaf floating in the air, nothing controlling you, that's what the old people say. So, the spiral is more than a thought, it's belief of a way of living, and understanding it and following it. And so, to have human beings have that belief of the spiral, it's the human beings who've got the voice of the songs of the land, so if that spiral is burst open, then the songs disappear.
>
> *(Bawaka Country 2022: 443)*

It is important to take seriously 'outer space' as already governed, connected to earth, and as a homeland peopled by spirits and celestial beings. This will require a big shift in perspective and an intercultural approach to understanding 'outer space', led by Indigenous knowledges, sovereignties, and Country itself. In sharing about Yolŋu celestial relations with and as Milŋiyawuy, we hope to open people's hearts, minds, and spirits to a more complex picture of what space is and how people might relate to it.

As we close the essay, you may like to listen to Guwak, as shared by Rrawun Maymuru. The Guwak songspiral talks about a person who has passed away. The spirit waits until Guwak calls out. Guwak and the person who has passed away will journey through the sky together. The story is connected to the stories of the paintings through Yolŋu relationships with and as Milŋiyawuy, the River of Stars, particularly through the relationships and sovereignties of the Maŋgalili clan (Figure 17.5).

Figure 17.5 QR Code to listen to Guwak.

Acknowledgements

The authors would like to acknowledge that this essay was written on the unceded lands and Country of Yolŋu, Gumbaynggirr, Awabakal, Worimi, and Dharug peoples, and pay our respects to their Elders past, present, and emerging. Thank you to Buku-Larrnggay Mulka Centre and the University Gallery (University of Newcastle) for their assistance with Milŋiyawuy artwork. Thanks to Juan Francisco Salazar for his support and efforts to include us in this volume. This research was partially supported by an Australian Research Council Discovery Project (DP190102202), the Social Sciences and Humanities Research Council (Canada) and Professor Sarah Wright and Professor Sandie Suchet-Pearson's of Australian Research Council Future Fellowships (FT160100353; FT210100320).

References

Australian Government, Department of Industry, Science and Resources 2020. "Australia Signs NASA's Artemis Accords." *Department of Industry* (website), 14 October. https://www.industry.gov.au/news/australia-signs-nasas-artemis-accords.

Australian Government, Department of Industry, Science and Resources 2021. "Moon to Mars Initiative: Launching Australian Industry to Space." *Department of Industry* (website), 16 February. https://www.industry.gov.au/news/moon-mars-initiative-launching-australian-industry-space.

Bawaka Country, including Laklak Burarrwanga, Ritjilili Ganambarr, Merrkiyawuy Ganambarr-Stubbs, Banbapuy Ganambarr, Djawundil Maymuru, Kate Lloyd, Sarah Wright, Sandie Suchet-Pearson, and Lara Daley. 2022. "Songspirals Bring Country Into Existence: Singing More-Than-Human and Relational Creativity." *Qualitative Inquiry* 28 (5): 435–47. https://doi.org/10.1177/107780042110681.

Bawaka Country including Audra Mitchell, Sarah Wright, Sandie Suchet-Pearson, Kate Lloyd, Laklak Burarrwanga, Ritjilili Ganambarr, Merrkiyawuy Ganambarr-Stubbs, Banbapuy Ganambarr, Djawundil Maymuru, and Rrawun Maymuru. 2020. "Dukarr Lakarama: Listening to Guwak, Talking Back to Space Colonization." *Political Geography* 81: 102218. https://doi.org/10.1016/j.polgeo.2020.102218.

Bawaka Country including Sarah Wright, Sandie Suchet-Pearson, Kate Lloyd, Laklak Burarrwanga, Ritjilili Ganambarr, Merrkiyawuy Ganambarr-Stubbs, Banbapuy Ganambarr, Djawundil Maymuru, and Jill Sweeney. 2016. "Co-becoming Bawaka: Towards a Relational Understanding of Place/Space." *Progress in Human Geography* 40 (4): 455–75. https://doi.org/10.1177/0309132515589437.

Burarrwanga, Laklak, Ritjilili Ganambarr, Merrkiyawuy Ganambarr-Stubbs, Banbapuy Ganambarr, Djawundil Maymuru, Sarah Wright, Sandie Suchet-Pearson, Kate Lloyd, and Bawaka Country. 2012. "They Are Not Voiceless." In *The 2013 Voiceless Anthology*, edited by J. M. Coetzee, Ondine Sherman, Wendy Were and Susan Wyndham, 22–39. Crows Nest: Allen & Unwin.

Burarrwanga, Laklak, Ritjilili Ganambarr, Merrikiyawuy Ganambarr-Stubbs, Banbapuy Ganambarr, Djawundil Maymuru, Sarah Wright, Sandie Suchet-Pearson, and Kate Lloyd. 2019. *Songspirals: Sharing Women's Wisdom of Country Through Songlines*. Crows Nest: Allen & Unwin.

Fuller, Robert S., Ray P. Norris, and Michelle Trudgett. 2014. "The Astronomy of the Kamilaroi and Euahlayi Peoples and Their Neighbours." *Australian Aboriginal Studies* 2: 3–27.

Goodyear-Kaʻōpua, Noelani. 2017. "Protectors of the Future, Not Protestors of the Past: Indigenous Pacific Activism and Mauna a Wākea." *South Atlantic Quarterly* 116 (1): 184–94. https://doi.org/10.1215/00382876-3749603.

Gorman, Alice. 2005. "The Cultural Landscape of Interplanetary Space." *Journal of Social Archaeology* 5 (1): 85–107. https://doi.org/10.1177/1469605305050148.

Hamacher, Duane. 2022. *The First Astronomers: How Indigenous Elders Read the Stars*. Crows Nest: Allen & Unwin.

Kimmerer, Robin. 2013. *Braiding Sweetgrass: Indigenous Wisdom, Scientific Knowledge and the Teachings of Plants*. Minneapolis, MN: Milkweed Editions.

Noon, Karlie, and Krystal De Napoli. 2022. *Astronomy: Sky Country*. Port Melbourne: Thames & Hudson.

Peryer, Marisa. 2019. "Native Hawaiians on Coverage of Mauna Kea Resistance." *Columbia Journalism Review*, 29 July. https://www.cjr.org/opinion/mauna-kea-telescope-protest-hawaii.php.

Poelina, Anne, Sandra Wooltorton, Sandra Harben, Len Collard, Pierre Horwitz, and David Palmer. 2020. "Feeling and Hearing Country." *PAN: Philosophy Activism Nature* (15): 6–15. Retrieved from http://panjournal.net/issues/15.

RiverOfLife, Martuwarra, Anne Poelina, Donna Bagnall, and Michelle Lim. 2020. "Recognizing the Martuwarra's First Law Right to Life as a Living Ancestral Being." *Transnational Environmental Law* 9 (3): 541–68. https://doi.org/10.1017/S2047102520000163.

Smith, Aunty Shaa, Neeyan Smith, Lara Daley, Sarah Wright, and Paul Hodge. 2021. "Creation, Destruction, and COVID: Heeding the Call of Country, Bringing Things into Balance." *Geographical Research* 59 (2): 160–68. https://doi.org/10.1111/1745-5871.12450.

Tynan, Lauren. 2020. "Thesis as Kin: Living Relationality with Research". *AlterNative: An International Journal of Indigenous Peoples* 16(3): 163–70. https://doi.org/10.1177/1177180120948270.

Watts, Vanessa. 2013. "Indigenous Place-Thought & Agency Amongst Humans and Non-Humans (First Woman and Sky Woman Go on a European World Tour!)." *Decolonization: Indigeneity, Education & Society* 2 (1): 20–34. https://jps.library.utoronto.ca/index.php/des/article/view/19145/16234.

Yandaarra with Gumbaynggirr Country including Aunty Shaa Smith, Uncle Bud Marshall, Neeyan Smith, Sarah Wright, Lara Daley, and Paul Hodge. 2022. "Ethics and Consent in More-than-Human Research: Some Considerations from/with/as Gumbaynggirr Country, Australia." *Transactions of the Institute of British Geographers* 47 (3): 709–24. https://doi.org/10.1111/tran.12520.

18
COLONIALITY AND THE COSMOS

Natalie B. Treviño

It is coloniality, rather than curiosity, that lies at the heart of westernised conceptions of space exploration. These conceptions were founded upon capitalist accumulation through colonial activity, language, and logic rather than human nature, exploration, and scientific endeavour. The future that mostly US-centric space advocates envision simply reproduces the norms, systems, and myths of oppression and violence of the European colonial order. This is what I call the cosmic order of coloniality, the final frontier. The cosmic order of modernity/coloniality separates nature from humanity, enforces a hierarchy of humans, and renders nature, and those denied personhood, as fully exploitable. Under this cosmic order, all relations and ways of being and knowing are reduced to relations of exploitation; the heavens are used to legitimise this. These norms and systems, such as the explorer gene, resource exploitation, or dehumanised labour, are not neutral as propagandised, nor is modernity an unending celebration of uplifting humanity. On the contrary, it is the uneven world order of exploitation. Traces of this exploitation are articulated—explicitly or indirectly—in the metaphors, logic, and ideas of space policy and advocacy, often through patriotic and celebratory scientific rhetoric. The very structure of the US cosmic order is bound to oppression and exploitation.

Coloniality is constitutive of the US cosmic order because the history and narrative of the United States are characterised by colonialism and capitalism. One of the deadliest aspects of modernity is the set of hegemonic assumptions that permeate all aspects of US space exploration, which limits the imagination of space exploration. The normative language of policy, both that of the US and of the international community, reaffirms assumptions that are rooted in coloniality, specifically the conceptions of "humankind, peace, nature", and economic relations. While seemingly standard in their use, this language carries colonial assumptions that produce coloniality within the realm of space exploration. As Silvia Rivera Cusicanqui writes, "Words have a peculiar function in colonialism: they conceal rather than designate" (2020: 12). Beyond language there are numerous examples of coloniality in space activities and rationales. These include the claimed "scientific necessity" of the location of the Thirty Meter Telescope on the island of Mauna Kea, Elon Musk praising an antidemocratic coup in Bolivia as it may lower lithium costs, and the very location of many space launch facilities being built and used on Indigenous land with little to no connection to the local community (Maile 2019; Prashad and Bejarano 2020; Redfield 2002). Even the futures that so-called space visionaries produce are locked into the logic of coloniality, repeated Eurocentric ideas rather than imagining something new—such as Gerrard O'Neill's L5 colonies that were reproductions of mid-century American suburbia featuring middle-class white families with manufacturing jobs and hobbies, or even Mars Society founder Robert Zubrin's insistence that space exploration will save western civilisation from disappearing. Whether they are intentional or not, these actions and ideas display values: what is important and what is not, who can be exploited and displaced, and who can exploit. These very actions are rooted in Eurocentric assumptions that western modernity is the "best" or only way forward, and yet it is this very paradigm that renders violence acceptable and the destruction of nature and life as necessary. This is based on five hundred years of colonial action and capitalist accumulation. The final frontier is Eurocentric in both ontological and epistemological ways and shackled to exploitation.

Coloniality is a fundamental part of western modernity, without the exploitation of peoples and the natural world, of the Americas, Africa, Oceania, and Asia, the modern world system would not exist. Yet, coloniality—as a logic—is a socioeconomic, political, and cultural structure that began with colonialism and continues to this day. This logic produces ways of being and thinking that are exclusive or exclusionary, rendering conceptions of humanity, gender, race, knowledge, authority, and nature that reinforce colonial norms and capitalist presents and futures. The philosophical values (including the scientific method), technological achievements, and secular governance are only one half of modernity; the other half, the dark side, is the genocide, the epistemicide, the expansion of European patriarchal norms to the rest of the world, the development of racism, and the capitalist system. Neither can exist—in their current forms—without the other. Modernity foregrounds European or North American sociocultural and economic norms as universal. It assumes that all humans use and (can) understand these norms, which display the myths of modernity, such as emancipation, rationality, and secularisation. Decolonial thinker Boaventura de Sousa Santos explains that modernity is based on social regulation and social emancipation, which, in turn, constitutes the nation-state, the (capitalist) market, and rationality, including instrumental rationality (science and technology) as well as ethical practices (Santos 2014). If this is modernity, then coloniality continues through practices of oppression in the Americas, Africa, Oceania, and Asia by destroying other sociocultural and economic forms and relations. These genocidal practices were essential for the emancipatory aspects of modernity that manifested in Europe and later North America (i.e., scientific and political revolutions).

This all can be seen as *colonial imagery* that masks the logic of coloniality in US space exploration. The concept of the Frontier and coded phrases like "peaceful purposes" and "benefit of all mankind" have no real meaning or power beyond their hegemonic use-value. The continuing modernity/coloniality world system abstracts humanity and subjectivity, then categorises humanness in Eurocentric terms. Although space policymakers and advocates alike proclaim that space exploration will be beneficial "for all mankind", those benefits are seldom distributed beyond the US settler nation-state or its European allies. The modernity/coloniality world system normalises dehumanisation and "war", as Maldonado-Torres (2020) explains, through the normalisation of exploitation and violence in becoming accepted and expected to be an aspect of governance and the economy. In this, the often-stated "peaceful purposes" of space exploration affirm capitalism and state violence as "peace" (Maldonado-Torres 2020).

According to the archaeoastronomer E. C. Krupp, ancient civilisations organised themselves in relation to the cosmos. This organisation reflected and historically justified governance and sociocultural norms. As Krupp (1983) states, "the way people look at the universe has a lot to do with how they behave" (p. 1). This dialectical pattern creates a unique, culturally specific cosmic order reflected in political organisation, religious structure, and ritual (Krupp 1997). A cosmic order, or cosmovision, is the worldview that frames cultural, social, and/or political relations within a given culture in terms of how that culture understands the cosmos. Cosmic orders not only reflect internal social and political structures but also govern how a culture relates to other cultures. Some cultures have conflicting theories of the cosmos or rival creation stories or visions of the universe (Blacker 1975). Although it may be tempting to believe that cosmic orders belong to the superstitious or unscientific social orders of the past, contemporary North American cultural hegemony also requires a cosmic order to understand its relation to the universe, which has evolved from the myth of Europe, Puritanism, and the material conditions of colonisation and capitalism in the Americas. Although administrative colonisation may have ended, the sociocultural and economic changes caused by it—by coloniality—shape political forces across a global context.

Cosmic orders reflect and reinforce the conditions of a culture (Dickens and Ormrod 2007). Consequently, cosmic orders regulate and ascribe meaning to relations through the power and status conveyed through symbolism, ritual, or astronomical predictions (Krupp 1983, 1997). Not only do they dictate societal structures, they also constitute the very essence of what it is to be human to that culture. Significantly, the arrangement of internally produced characteristics as "human" allows for a culturally specific set of characteristics to be deemed universal by way of colonisation (Wynter 2003).

Under the hegemony of western modernity, power is bound to colonial and capitalist structures. Cosmic power means that the sky has a place within this system. Yet, if cosmic power must be secular under the conditions of modernity, how does this power manifest? This cosmic power derives from the ability to understand the cycles and patterns of the sky (Krupp 1983, 1997). Cosmic orders are constantly reinforced through community identification and invested with authority through specialised knowledge of the sky. Cosmic meaning—written in the sky—is attributed to a community ideology that functions as a binding for internal relations and external boundaries. Although these ideologies are different for each culture throughout time, some common structural patterns are discernible. The cosmic order of ancient Egypt with *Maat* and the divine order of kings, a system overseen by the priesthood, may be vastly different from the European medieval Great Chain of Being, which ranked the hierarchy of creatures from God down to rocks (Dickens and Ormrod 2007), but both hierarchies were regulated by the religious order of their respective cultures.

Although these forms of cosmic power may seem distant from, and distinct to, "our" scientific, rational, objective understanding of the universe, our own cosmology is also linked to sociocultural and economic norms, which are conveyed to us by elites. Just as

> [K]nowledge and skills to discover the natural order, to structure and rate the world by measuring time, space and matter, and to associate with spiritual entities, gave rise to the expert power of the sage, magician, shaman, medicine man and later to the scientist.
>
> *(Rappenglück 2016: 1)*

the cosmic order of modernity/coloniality—a holistic understanding of the relationship between humans, their hierarchies and norms, and the environment—is presided over by a scientific and political cosmic elite and functions as a cohesive and commanding worldview. This highly scientific/objective view of the universe stems from the Enlightenment and its valuation of the scientific method. Yet, the lack of competing cosmic orders is not due to the pure "objectivity" of science. On the contrary, the diminishing number of other cosmic orders is linked to a broader reduction of ways of knowing that followed the historic epistemicides of the colonial project. Admittedly, there have been competing cosmic orders since the rise of technoscience. Indeed, the "Space Race" between the USSR and the United States was a competition to see which cosmic order—communism or capitalism—would rule supreme on Earth and in the heavens. The control of the cosmos was a continuation of political control through cosmic power. Yet, this conflict was not a matter of ritualistic or observational cosmic power, but, rather, emerged from a *contestation over access and use*, which was a new aspect of cosmic orders from the rise of technology under western modernity. In this sense, other cosmic orders—or forms of cosmic power—are only possible insofar as they conform to the hegemonic framework of modernity/coloniality.

The Colonial Matrix of Power

Coloniality, or the colonial matrix of power, is a framing theory in which changes to systems of authority, knowledge, and nature wrought by colonisation, and the accompanying violence, are understood as a continuing force of social, political, and cultural arrangements, even after the end of formal colonisation (Quijano 2000). Such changes to Indigenous societies were intended to enforce Eurocentric political and social structures. These changes—restructuring authority, for example—enabled the subjugation of peoples for the economic benefit of Europe. Such a violent transformation in relations, fostered on multiple levels and in multiple domains, caused European-ness to become the inspiration (Quijano 2007). What followed was the transformation of Indigenous cultures from their own ways of being and knowing in a variety of attempts at "developing" them towards the idea of Europe. Relations with the natural world were changed to match those of Europe. With Europe as the model, and with colonisation as the violence enforcing Eurocentric institutions and culture on Indigenous peoples, coloniality is the lasting effect on colonised people and their descendants. Yet, Europe's growth in political and social power was a consequence of siphoning off wealth from the indigenous population from around the world and of enslaved peoples. As the rich materials of colonial nations were exported from the "new world" to the European continent, vast wealth was accumulated from this exploitation of lands and peoples that allowed for the modernisation of Europe and later the United States. Coloniality is the basis of space exploration, not curiosity, or strategic political action without historical context. The relations produced through coloniality are still the functioning relation of the exploration of space as it is coloniality that determines how, why, and what we do and think about space.

What space is and what it is used for are not neutral, but rather colonial because of the foundational assumption produced under coloniality. I focus on the assumptions about the epistemology and ontological natures of nature and humanity under modernity because these constructions are both perceived as "givens". Consequently, the economy is one of the domains of the colonial matrix of power that intersects with both the conditions of "being" and of nature. In this way, "the complementary movement of land appropriation and labor exploitation meant, simultaneously, the dismantling and overruling of other existing relations between human beings, society, land, and labor" (Mignolo and Tlostanova 2008: 111). This overruling led to the supremacy of Eurocentric conceptions of these relations and reduced the ways in which peoples might relate land and labour to the capitalist relationship. As Macarena Gómez-Barris (2017) describes it, "before the colonial project could prosper, it had to render territories and people extractable" (p. 5). This "extractibility" occurred through the "catastrophic transformation of whatever we can consider as human space, time, structure, culture, subjectivity, objectivity, and methodology, into dehumanising coordinates or foundations that serve to perpetuate the inferiority of some and the superiority of others" (Maldonado-Torres 2016: 20). Beginning with colonisation and the co-development of capitalism as the world economic system, this transformation reduced or eradicated all other ways of being/seeing/doing. "Human and nonhuman multiplicity" was rendered mute (Gómez-Barris 2017). In short, it was more than just the colonisation of land; it was the "colonization of the imagination" (Quijano 2007). Not only does the colonisation of the imagination subdue beings in their own times and spaces, but it also eliminates the possibility of futurity (i.e., the future as *other* than the past or present).

The modernity/coloniality structure contains humans who are ranked as not-human, transforms nature into a stock of "natural resources", and regards western subjectivity as if it were universal objectivity. As Maldonado-Torres (2016) puts it, this "metaphysical catastrophe … turns a potential world of human relations into one of permanent forms of conquest, colonialism, and war" (p. 12). The normalisation of these forms through western hegemony for five hundred years means that this violence has become acceptable, and, in many cases, victims are considered at fault for their lack of "development" or for any number of racial, ethic, or religious associations. Due to this process, Europe created the myth of itself by way of the conditions of colonialism and modernity.

The modern/colonial being is a product of Cartesian "I think", which Dussel describes as a product of the previous 150 years of "I conquer, therefore, I am" (Dussel 2016; Grosfoguel 2013). Like Grosfoguel, Dussel (2000) argues that "the modern *ego cogito* was anticipated by more than a century by the practical, Spanish-Portuguese *ego conquiro* (I conquer) that imposed its will (the first modern 'will-to-power') on the indigenous populations of the Americas" (p. 471). To be a good human, then, was to be the "I think/I conquer". However, not all humans were able to claim this identity, as the violence of colonialism normalised systems of violence toward and stigmatisation of conquered people. As previously mentioned, the modernity/coloniality structure was enforced and reinforced through the four genocides/epistemicides that produced a cosmology of normalised violence against peoples who are closer to "nature" than to the imperial being, the human/man.

In addition to the overdeterminations of human/man as "I think/I conquer", the Cartesian "I think" replaces and secularises the Christian God's omnipotent position. As Grosfoguel (2013) explains:

> Although Descartes never defines who this "I" is, it is clear that in his philosophy this "I" replaces God as the new foundation of knowledge and its attributes constitute a secularization of the attributes of the Christian God. For Descartes, the "I" can produce a knowledge that is truth beyond time and space, universal in the sense that it is unconditioned by any particularity—"objective" being understood as equal to "neutrality" and equivalent to a God-Eye view.
>
> (p. 75)

This is how the European human/man can possess the only acceptable subject position and transform it into the only acceptable position of objectivity: such a God-like worldview seizes and produces the "right" to determine the inferiority or superiority of knowledges and ways of being and seeing and produces a cosmology that is determined to be Truth. The western acceptance of, and reliance on, dualism reinforces this, as does the accepted hierarchy of the cosmic order. If this is the construction of the human/man, then as Sylvia Wynter (2003) says, "it was to be the peoples of the militarily expropriated New World territories (i.e., Indians), as well as the enslaved peoples of Black Africa (i.e., Negroes), that were made to reoccupy the matrix slot of Otherness" (p. 266).

To be a "human", by Eurocentric standards, was impossible for the colonised, because they were neither "the rational" (in terms of "I think") nor Christian (later secularised and racialised). This exclusionary idea of human/man was transformed into the abstract "Man2", which rendered most of the world's population "exclusionable", extractable, and exploitable (Wynter 2003). This is the theoretical framework of the colonial matrix of power: the conquest of the Americas, Africa, and Asia by the European colonial powers transformed the world into a system of coloniser and colonised, reshaping the Indigenous relations of authority, gender/race/sex, economies (nature), and knowledge/subjectivity.

European and (later) US hegemony produced the structural influence necessary to normalise these hierarchies, through the world system of the nation-state as the sole political formation, and through the economy, which can only be based on capitalism or "war". This is still apparent today in contemporary forms of racism, sexism, transphobia, class oppression, and conceptions of disability and ability, as well as ethnic and religious identities. These forms of exclusion leave only the human/man as a direct descendent of the Cartesian "I think", and thus make the "conqueror" the only accepted "human" form under modernity/coloniality. This is the condition of "war" that Maldonado-Torres describes as normalised under the conditions of modernity/coloniality, wherein the mass genocide of living creatures and disregard for life are acceptable (Maldonado-Torres 2016). To be "human/man" is to be a death-oriented conqueror. This is the cosmology by which human/man thrives, while all others are subjected to the conditions of coloniality that regulate their lives: the normalised violence of the economy, the internal violence of the nation-state, and the acceptance of military violence on the part of the state. The structurally dualistic orientation of Eurocentrism means that all that is othered by the human/man becomes its opposite. Consequently, the human/man—the abstract universal human—is an imperial being, whose practices lead to the death of all others that can be exploited.

The logic of coloniality renders the natural world exploitable (Alimonda 2019; Dussel 2000; Dussel 1995; Gómez-Barris 2017; Grosfoguel 2013). The environment is the opposite of culture, which establishes human/man as superior to others. Through the access to materially rich lands, the mass enslavement of Africans by the Europeans, and the repressions of other epistemologies, the colonial matrix of power was constructed to benefit Europe through raw materials, epistemological dominance, and the normalisation of the conditions of war (Maldonado-Torres 2008). Subsequently, wealth, power, and access have become concentrated and centralised within the west. These are still the prevailing conditions, as modernity is built on the backs of those others. According to these conditions, the nation-state is the only legitimate political structure, and capitalism is the only legitimate economy for the west (Mignolo and Walsh 2018). What was once colonisation of lands through military force is now development, regulated by the market. The destruction of nature, including, but not limited to, the changes happening to the climate, threatens all living beings on Earth, yet this is not considered nearly as important by economic policies and systems, because most of those harmed by these systems are either not-human or not-human-enough (Gómez-Barris 2017; Grosfoguel 2013; Howell 2000). In this sense, I consider the human/man to be death orientated as he appropriates all things to an eventual point of destruction, even of the self.

This process of extractivism has always fuelled the oppression of Indigenous and African peoples, even after the so-called era of decolonisation after World War II. The reduction of nature to a source of human/man's riches produces a conception of nature that only exists for the use of and enslavement by human/man. Consequently, any other relationship between human/man and nature is suspect and holds no power, because the only legitimate relation is that of conqueror-or-to-conquered. While many other cultures have or have had intimate, dialectic, and integrative connections to nature, the west places culture outside of, and above, nature (Escobar 2008). These are the relations to nature that were exterminated or repressed through colonisation and after (Dussel 1995; Grosfoguel 2013; Howell 2000; Kheel 2008). It is through the coloniality of nature that human/man has cultivated his relationship with any form of space. This is a relationship and definition that limits the possibilities of humanity and how it encounters outer space. The Western conception of nature was outlined and influenced by Francis Bacon in his 1620 work *Novum Organum*. The ecofeminist Carolyn Merchant (1996) summarised Bacon's impact on the metaphors associated with man and nature: "Nature must be 'bound into service' and made a 'slave,' put 'in constraint' and 'molded' by the mechanical arts" (p. 81.) These exploitative metaphors express human/man's relation not only to the earth but also to racialised and gendered subjects—both colonised women and white women—and knowledge. As such, the condition of human/man as exploiter forces all things—living or dead—into the position of the exploited or exploitable. The idea that man and nature are opposed to each other, and that God placed man as the ruler of the natural world for his own needs, is a myth that cannot continue to be the foundation of the world.

> Since capitalist production can develop fully only with complete access to all territories and climes, it can no more confine itself to the natural resources and productive forces of the temperate zone than it can manage with white labour alone. Capital needs other races to exploit

territories where the white man cannot work. It must be able to mobilise world labour power without restriction in order to utilise all productive forces of the globe.

(Luxemburg 2003: 343)

In this quote, Luxemburg details the connection between the development of capitalism and the necessity of colonialism. Colonial administrations must destroy indigenous cultures and ways of knowing and implement forced labour to render colonised peoples "useful" to capitalism. This is how colonialism and capitalism produced modernity/coloniality. This reduction of ways of being can be seen in how space exploration is categorised: militaristic, exploitation of resources, the overemphasis on building a space economy rather than world building.

Cosmic Orders

Modernity/coloniality are not the only structures that affect epistemological and ontological forms: as discussed in the introduction, cosmic orders define how a culture or civilisation understands itself in relation to the cosmos. In the context of the United States, the conditions of modernity/coloniality produce a cosmic order that reinforces and reflects itself in a relationship to the cosmos reduced to a relation of exploitation. Unlike ancient and premodern medieval cosmic orders, the current hegemonic US cosmic order is not founded upon a cultural understanding of how the culture itself fits within the cosmic order as a natural component: rather, it conceives of itself—the United States—outside of it with the might and right to exploit nature. Before I explain how this occurred, it is important to detail cosmic orders and their forms. Cosmic orders do not only form the self-understanding of a society and the cosmos, but they also regulate other relations as well: what it means to be human, what sorts of authority are legitimate, ways of maintaining power, and religious significance. Unlike cosmology, the branch of astronomy that studies the origins and the evolution of the cosmos, cosmic orders or cosmologies denotes "the knowledge of a given society about the composition of the universe and the place of humankind within it" (Ossio 1997: 549). As such, a cosmic order is a composition not simply of the physical world but of the political, cultural, and social worlds as well.

As Krupp (1983) writes,

> People in organized societies trace the lineage of their institutions to sources with enough power to justify the way things are. We find it important to demonstrate that our ways of governing ourselves, of organizing ourselves, are part of the natural order.
>
> *(p. 90)*

This natural order is found in the heavens, in both astronomical phenomena and celestial signs regarding changes in seasons associated with agriculture. Living in accordance with the natural order is both practical and sacred: the wonder of the heavens, often associated with gods, and more agriculturally based observations coalesced into successful reassurance; following the astronomical signs, conveyed through the elite, brought bounty, thus reinforcing the need for the elites and sign reading (Krupp 1983).

According to Krupp (1997), the legitimacy of a cosmic order and the social and/or political order that it reflects was religious in nature. However, although the significant rationale of this ordering was religious, we can still find these structures in secular society. These culturally specific, yet structurally similar, aspects are "the Centre of the World", "Celestial Empires", "Mother Earth", and the most pervasive, "Cosmic Power" (Krupp 1997, 2015). They continue to function as the links between "the architecture of the universe, the pattern of nature, the fabric of society, and the personal environment" (Krupp 1997: 17)), even though the contemporary west is adamant that the knowledge of outer space is based solely on scientific and measurable observations (Beery 2016). Thus, our understanding of the universe orders and reorders the structure of our world. We understand our relation to the world around us by common consent regarding legitimate power. Although these hierarchies may seem disconnected from the cosmos, the cosmos continues to be a major source of legitimacy and power even today. To illuminate this point, Beery (2016) summarises the nature of cosmic orders in this way:

> Regardless of the socionatural practices of different communities, many societies affiliated cosmic (i.e., universal, "natural") power with the celestial realm. The celestial realm, as the site of power, informed and substantiated terrestrial power, but how the cosmos and the celestial realm were structured, as fixed, universal, and all-powerful as they were portrayed to be, were inescapably social constructions, productions of social organization, and corresponding institutions of power.
>
> *(p. 53)*

Krupp's anthropological work indicates that cosmic knowledge often legitimates state power. In ancient China, for example, the dynastic control of the calendar not only organised bureaucratic processes but also justified the power of the emperor (Krupp 1997). Power, empire, and sacred relationships with the gods derived from any given cosmic order. The legitimation of institutions, roles, norms, and relations through cosmic association exists across the globe in culturally specific forms with the sun, the moon, or constellations as the source.

Empires have legitimised themselves by mimicking the cosmic myth to establish and hold political power. There is also often a claim to sky divinity, as was seen in Imperial Japan's relation to the sun, and with the Mongols with their concept of Eternal Blue Heaven linked to their expression of power through territorial expansion (Krupp 1997). There were divine links between god(s) and the expansion of the empire, not unlike the Catholic Church's missionary work. Historical and cultural references to a celestial source of power that justifies the actions of a nation have been made throughout Asia, the Americas, the Pacific, Africa, and Europe (Krupp 1997). There could be a cosmic divine relation, an observational one, or both. The power of prediction can become a great advantage for a state, such as Imperial China (Sun 2015). In this context, celestial power derives from predictive knowledge, the establishment of timekeeping, or abilities to read cosmic omens (Krupp 1983, 1997, 2015). During the Space Age, power was still defined in relation to the cosmos as cosmic power became the ability to explore and exploit outer space (as the engineering prowess for sending rockets into space).

Philosopher Sylvia Wynter draws on Krupp to show how cosmological orders have influenced conceptions of the human and humanity (Wynter 2003: 273). According to Wynter:

> Archaeo-astronomy has shown that all human orders … have mapped their "descriptive statements" or governing master codes on the heavens, on their stable periodicities and regular recurring movements (Krupp, 1997). Because, in doing so, they had thereby mapped their specific criterion of being human, of what it was "to be a good man and woman of one's kind" (Davis, 1992), onto the physical cosmos, thereby absolutizing each such criterion; and with this enabling them to be experienced by each other's subjects as if they had been supernaturally (and, as such, extrahumanly) determined criteria, their respective truths had necessarily come to function as an "objective set of facts" for the people of that society—seeing that such truths were now the indispensable condition of their existence as such a society, as such people, as such a mode of being human.
>
> *(p. 270)*

In this rigorous interpretation of Krupp's cosmic order, Wynter interrogates the implications of the cosmic order. For Wynter, the relationship between society and the physical cosmos determines what it is to be human. The very idea of the human which is made material through the conditions of and connections to the cosmos is then reinforced through normative behaviours. In the case of coloniality, the conception of Human/man as exploiter is being mapped onto the cosmos in this same way. The cosmic condition is then only understood through the idea of the human that indicates the idea of the heavens. Human beings build their own worlds, then live in them as if they themselves did not construct them (Berger 1969). This displaces responsibility for oppression or hierarchy onto the cosmos, making it acceptable and mostly unchangeable.

Krupp's research on cosmovisions demonstrates an intimate relationship between culture and the cosmos. Whether the primary purpose was political or agricultural, there was always a relationship to the sky. These cosmic orders possessed some structural commonalities: the earth as life-giving, the sky as powerful, the mimicking of celestial patterns to foster success, and the use of the divinity of the sky for expansion. All these commonalities continue to animate the cosmic conceptions of modernity. And so, the overarching hegemonic forms of western modernity depend on a cosmic order generated by the patterns of colonialist and capitalist systems. These systems are then reflected in the sky. Yet, since the increase in astronomical and aerospace technologies, the relationships between society and sky are no longer just about power in understanding the cosmos but also about access, control, and exploitation. The colonial domination of the cosmos reflects the change toward secular power structures on earth and reconfigures those of the sky. Whereas celestial power was once reflected in the activities of a culture, the ruling forces on earth use the structures of cosmic power to justify their domination of sky. As such, colonial power structures have pivoted towards the sky to produce a different relationship. Under modernity, the dominant relationship between "Man2" and the cosmos is one of subjugation rather than reverence.

Cosmic orders are "humanity's imaginative relationship with the universe" (Dickens and Ormrod 2007: 13). The US cosmic order is a descendant of European Christendom and the Great Chain of Being. The Great Chain of Being was the cosmological order of the myth of Europe that ranked all material beings—living and lifeless—in a hierarchy from the most important and powerful to the least (Dickens and Ormrod 2007). This system of ranking included humans and transformed religious associations into racial divisions (Dickens and Ormrod 2007; Dussel 1995; Grosfoguel 2013; Nee 2005). This cosmology naturalised power relations, as it was "God-given". Throughout the conquest of the Americas, Africa, and Asia, and the development of capitalism through colonialism, mass genocide, and epistemicide, the Great Chain of Being was not only legitimised—as non-European people were uncivilised because they did not have faith in the Christian God, participate in Eurocentric forms of knowledge, or possess material goods—but also secularised through the Scientific Revolution (Dickens and Ormrod 2007; Grosfoguel 2013). The structure of this cosmological hierarchy continued despite the massive social, political, and cultural change.

Conclusion

Coloniality is the foundation of US (and, more broadly, Eurocentric) political, social, and cultural norms. Forms of oppression and privilege that emerge from colonialism and capital are transformed and perpetuated through coloniality, and the cosmic order of the final frontier is one way in which coloniality affects the present and the future. As both Wynter and Krupp have stated, cosmic orders produce the conception of the human/man. In the case of the final frontier, the imperial/patriarchal form of "human" is confused with a universal conception of humanity due to western hegemony (Dussel 2000). Human/man has the disposition of exploiter, and this is the only accepted relation between human/man and nature. Structurally, coloniality functions to reinforce colonial norms on a global level through the hegemony of the nation-state, the western control of knowledge, the economy, and norms of gender, race, and sexuality. Due to the history of genocides and epistemicides, the west has a monopoly on power, wealth, and knowledge, which, in turn, produces a cosmology that reproduces colonial norms. The exploitation of formerly colonised countries continues through economic practices that still ensure that vast wealth is funnelled to their former colonisers. Within this legacy, racialised peoples are not assigned the status of human/man, because historically in the United States, they were on the other side of the human/man and nature (for exploitation) relationship.

Historically, cosmic orders have enabled a culture to understand itself in relation to the universe. The various social and political formations of different cultures reveal how they understand the universe. In this sense, cosmic orders justify socioeconomic and political structures. Elements of cosmic orders include the conceptions of the earth as fertile, the power of the sky, the Centre of the World, and empire building through cosmic divinity. The European cosmic order was that of Christendom, which reflected a hierarchy from God down to rocks (Dickens and Ormrod 2007). Although this order was secularised through the emergence of modernity/coloniality, some formerly divine structures still echo within European hegemony. Cosmic orders are both epistemological—a way of knowing the world—and ontological—a way of being in the world. Cosmic orders construct what it means to be a "good human" within that order.

Coloniality, cosmology, and US exceptionalism merge to produce a uniquely US cosmic order, in which coloniality is bound to elements of previous Eurocentric cosmic orders, the hierarchy of humans, domination over nature, and the salvation narrative of the early Puritans. Extractivist practices normalise the exploitation of peoples and the expropriation of land; this extends into space through the capitalist motivation of mining celestial properties, defined as resources for profit rather than as possible relations, which is often justified by the expanse of the universe. Within this legacy, racialised peoples are not assigned the status of human/man, because historically in the United States, they were on the other side of the human/man and nature (for exploitation) relationship.

Coloniality within the Eurocentric cosmic order, the final frontier, cannot be overcome without full-scale systemic change. From its epistemological and ontological foundations, the final frontier is exploitative. Diversity and inclusion are about bringing in token individuals while not attempting to foster change within, or as Silvia Rivera Cusicanqui (2020) states, "change that changes nothing" (p. 57). This was easily seen when Jeff Bezos chose Wally Funk to accompany him into "space". A white woman who had hoped to be part of the Apollo programme during the 1960s finally realised her dream in the 2020s, but what is there to celebrate in women's liberation when at the same time as Wally went to space, a woman in one of Bezos's Amazon warehouses miscarried because of the rules regarding sitting down during shifts (Gurley 2021)? This is not feminism, while it may appear as such: this is the use of white women to legitimise a colonial-capitalist programme. How does space benefit the woman in the warehouse? Is she not human enough to benefit from space? Currently, the cosmic order of coloniality encompasses the vast majority of space activities, leaving little room for resistance. Forms of resistance that do emerge are often defanged by rendering them "ethical questions" rather that the social-political questions they are. Decoloniality is not a matter of ethics: rather, it is a practice of liberation; it is a matter of action. In the realm of space exploration, the cost of not pushing back is a future in which the oppressive assumptions about humans and the universe are always reproduced, often mutated. What I have presented in this chapter is a summary of the interconnected forms of oppression and violence that exist within the current sociocultural, economic, and political systems that produce the space activities of both the nation-state and of the private sector. Capitalism is colonial, the nation-state is colonial, the gender binary is colonial, and the westernised university system is colonial—while some aspects of these things can be decolonised, some cannot; there is no decolonising capitalism, there is only abolishment. In space, if the foundations of the sociopolitical are capitalist in nature, then they are colonial—producing and reproducing coloniality, as it adapts to the space environment. Treating extraterrestrial (and terrestrial) landscapes and worlds as nothing more than resources is a colonial view of the universe—the final frontier is founded on exploitation. The question we must ask ourselves is: "Are we imperial beings? Who is this 'we' and who is not? Or is being human so much more?"

References

Alimonda, Héctor. 2019. "The Coloniality of Nature: An Approach to Latin American Political Ecology." *Alternautas* 6 (1), (Re)Searching Development: The Abya Yala Chapter. https://doi.org/10.31273/alternautas.v6i1.1094.
Beery, Jason. 2016. "Terrestrial Geographies in and of Outer Space." In *The Palgrave Handbook of Society, Culture, and Outer Space*, edited by Peter Dickens and James S. Ormrod, 47–70. New York: Palgrave MacMillan. https://doi.org/10.5325/utopianstudies.28.2.0348.
Berger, Peter L. 1969. *The Sacred Canopy.* New York: Anchor Books.
Blacker, Carmen. 1975. "Introduction." In *Ancient Cosmologies*, edited by Carmen Blacker and Michael Loewe, 13–16. London: Allen and Unwin.
Dickens, Peter, and James S. Ormrod. 2007. *Cosmic Society: Towards a Sociology of the Universe.* London: Routledge.
Dussel, Enrique. 1995. *The Invention of the Americas: Eclipse of "the Other" and the Myth of Modernity.* Translated by Michael D. Barber. New York: Continuum.
Dussel, Enrique. 2000. "Europe, Modernity, and Eurocentrism." Translated by Javier Krauel and Virginia C. Tuma. *Nepantla: Views from South* 1 (3): 465–78.
Dussel, Enrique. 2016. "Transmodernidade e Interculturalidade: Interpretação a Partir da Filosofia da Libertação." *Sociedade e Estado* 31 (1): 51–73. https://doi.org/10.1590/S0102-69922016000100004.
Escobar, Arturo. 2008. *Territories of Difference: Place, Movements, Life, Redes.* Durham, NC: Duke University Press.
Gómez-Barris, Macarena. 2017. *The Extractive Zone: Social Ecologies and Decolonial Perspectives.* Durham, NC: Duke University Press.
Grosfoguel, Ramón. 2013. "The Structure of Knowledge in Westernized Universities: Epistemic Racism/Sexism and the Four Genocides/Epistemicides of the Long 16th Century." *Human Architecture: Journal of the Sociology of Self-Knowledge* 11 (1): 73–90.
Gurley, Lauren Kaori. 2021. "Amazon Denieda Worker Pregnancy Accommodations. Then She Miscarried." *Vice*, 21 July. https://www.vice.com/en/article/g5g8eq/amazon-denied-a-worker-pregnancy-accommodations-then-she-miscarried.
Howell, Nancy R. 2000. *A Feminist Cosmology: Ecology, Solidarity, and Metaphysics.* Amherst, NY: Humanity Books.
Kheel, Marti. 2008. *Nature Ethics: An Ecofeminist Perspective.* Lanham, MD: Rowman & Littlefield.
Krupp, Edwin C. 1983. *Echoes of the Ancient Skies: The Astronomy of Lost Civilizations.* New York: Harper & Row.
Krupp, Edwin C. 1997. *Skywatchers, Shamans & Kings: Astronomy and the Archaeology of Power.* New York: Wiley.
Luxemburg, Rosa. 2003. *The Accumulation of Capital.* London: Routledge.
Maile, David Uahikeaikalei'ohu. 2019. "Threats of Violence: Refusing the Thirty Meter Telescope and Dakota Access Pipeline." In *Standing With Standing Rock: Voices from the #NODAPL Movement*, edited by Nick Estes and Jaskiran Dhillon, 328–43. Minneapolis: University of Minnesota Press. https://doi.org/10.5749/j.ctvr695pq.30.
Maldonado-Torres, Nelson. 2008. *Against War: Views from the Underside of Modernity.* Durham, NC: Duke University Press.
Maldonado-Torres, Nelson. 2016. "Outline of Ten Theses on Coloniality and Decoloniality." *Frantz Fanon Foundation*, 23 October. http://fondation-frantzfanon.com/outline-of-ten-theses-on-coloniality-and-decoloniality/.
Maldonado-Torres, Nelson. 2020. "Notes on the Coloiniality of Peace." *Frantz Fanon Foundation*, 4 June. https://fondation-frantzfanon.com/notes-on-the-coloniality-of-peace/#_ftn1.
Merchant, Carolyn. 1996. *Earthcare: Women and the Environment.* New York: Routledge.
Mignolo, Walter, and Madina Tlostanova. 2008. "The Logic of Coloniality and the Limits of Postcoloniality." In *The Postcolonial and the Global*, edited by Revathi Krishnaswamy and John C. Hawley, 109–23. Minneapolis: University of Minnesota Press.

Mignolo, Walter., and Catherine E. Walsh. 2018. *On Decoloniality: Concepts, Analytics, Praxis*. Durham, NC: Duke University Press.

Nee, Sean. 2005. "The Great Chain of Being." *Nature* 435 (7041): 429. https://doi.org/10.1038/435429a.

Ossio, Juan M. 1997. "Cosmologies." *International Social Science Journal* 49 (154): 549–62. https://doi.org/10.1111/j.1468-2451.1997.tb00044.x.

Prashad, Vijay, and Alejandro Bejarano. 2020. "'We Will Coup Whoever We Want': Elon Musk and the Overthrow of Democracy in Bolivia." *MRonline*, 28 July. https://mronline.org/2020/07/28/we-will-coup-whoever-we-want-elon-musk-and-the-overthrow-of-democracy-in-bolivia/.

Quijano, Aníbal. 2000. "Coloniality of Power and Eurocentrism in Latin America." *International Sociology* 15(2): 215–32. https://doi.org/10.1177/0268580900015002005.

Quijano, Aníbal. 2007. "Coloniality and Modernity/Rationality." *Cultural Studies* 21 (2–3): 168–78. https://doi.org/10.1080/09502380601164353.

Rappenglück, Michael A. 2016. "Keepers of Time and Guardians of Space." In *Astronomy and Power: How Worlds Are Structured; Proceedings of the SEAC 2010 Conference, Oxford, United Kingdom*, edited by Michael A. Rappenglück, Barbara Rappenglück, Nicholas Campion and Fabio Silva, 1–10. Oxford, UK: British Archaeological Reports Publishing.

Redfield, Peter. 2002. "The Half-Life of Empire in Outer Space." *Social Studies of Science* 32(5–6): 791–825. https://doi.org/10.1177/030631270203200508.

Rivera Cusicanqui, Silvia. 2020. *Ch'ixinakax Utxiwa: On Practices and Discourses of Decolonization*. Translated by M. Geidel. Medford, MA: Polity Press.

Santos, Boaventura de Sousa. 2014. *Epistemologies of the South: Justice Against Epistemicide*. New York: Routledge.

Sun, Xiaochun. 2015. "Observation of Celestial Phenomena in Ancient China." In *Handbook of Archaeoastronomy and Ethnoastronomy*, edited by Clive L. N. Ruggles, 2043–49. New York: Springer. https://doi.org/10.1007/978-1-4614-6141-8_224.

Wynter, Sylvia. 2003. "Unsettling the Coloniality of Being/Power/Truth/Freedom: Towards the Human, After Man, Its Overrepresentation—An Argument." *CR: The New Centennial Review* 3 (3): 257–337. https://doi.org/10.1353/ncr.2004.0015.

19
SAFEGUARDING INDIGENOUS SKY RIGHTS FROM COLONIAL EXPLOITATION

Karlie Alinta Noon, Krystal De Napoli, Peter Swanton, Carla Guedes, and Duane Hamacher

Introduction

For the Indigenous peoples of the world, the stars are an integrated part of the world, inseparable from the land, water, animals, and people. The sky is described by Elders across the globe as a reflection of everything that occurs on the land. The stars serve as a map, a textbook, a law book, and a memory space. They are central to identity and spirituality and inform all aspects of culture, from ceremony and kinship systems to food economics, navigation, weather forecasting, and more. They are critically important and central to the lives of some 500 million people around the world who speak over four thousand languages (UNESCO 2021).

Despite this, Indigenous peoples' connections to the stars are being actively erased by colonial states pushing for the human colonisation and exploitation of natural resources in space with almost no consultation with First Nations peoples around the world, with thousands of satellites being launched into orbit and traditional lands and sacred sites being developed and destroyed for the construction of space facilities. All these matters increase light pollution that further impede the view of the sky. All of this is occurring as part of the ongoing process of extractive and destructive land use around the world that Indigenous peoples continue to pay for. As argued by Ojibwe geographer Deondre Smiles, a "scientific venture such as space exploration does not exist in a vacuum, but instead draws from settler colonialism and feeds back into it through the prioritization of 'science' over Indigenous epistemologies" (Smiles 2020). For many Indigenous peoples and communities, the colonisation of space is the continuation of the colonisation of their lands.

This article discusses each of these topics as a guide for understanding the issues and concerns and for proffering perspectives that can guide future practices in space while safeguarding Indigenous rights to the skies. At the core of this discussion is an acknowledgment of the United Nations Declaration of the Rights of Indigenous Peoples (UNDRIP) (United Nations 2007: Article 12):

> Indigenous peoples have the right to manifest, practise, develop and teach their spiritual and religious traditions, customs and ceremonies; the right to maintain, protect, and have access in privacy to their religious and cultural sites; the right to the use and control of their ceremonial objects; and the right to the repatriation of their human remains.

Each of the sections in this paper addresses this declaration with respect to pressing issues facing Indigenous communities around the world.

Space Colonisation: Challenging *Sphaera Nullius*

Whether it be motivated by a curiosity to see worlds beyond our own or by a sense of urgency to evade existential risk to humankind, space colonisation is becoming a frequently discussed topic. Space colonisation may refer both to the long-term settlement of our neighbouring planets and to space exploration and resource exploitation (Bawaka Country et al. 2020). Along with these discussions of space colonisation, there are a lot of questions centred around: *When will we do so? And, how?* It is also important to ask: *Why do we feel compelled to? What entitles us to colonise extraterrestrial bodies? Just because we can, does that mean that we should?*

Outer space is often regarded as lifeless and inanimate—a true wilderness of which the exploration does not risk the trampling of other life forms (Bawaka Country et al. 2020). It is sometimes regarded as not only an untapped resource that we are morally obligated to exploit to ensure humanity's survival (Munevar 2019) but also one that we should already be engaging in exploiting with the utmost urgency (Abney 2019; Green 2019). It could be regarded as *sphaera nullius* (the sphere of outer space belonging to no one) and therefore ripe for the taking. This contention that outer space is disjointed from Earth, and ours for exploiting, is not a unanimous point of view and is especially not representative of the ways of knowing the skies that belong to the many diverse cultures that inhabit our planet. To regard outer space as disconnected from the Earth is to disregard an Indigenous way of knowing the universe.

Sky Country is the fabric through which Indigenous Knowledge Systems are tightly woven. Celestial features, their variations, and their movements inform knowledge holders of processes on the ground that are vital for sustaining life and culture. Each and every bright star or patch of darkness in the Milky Way serves as a memory aid by which oral cultures encode and transmit science, Law, and history. Sky and land are one: they are dynamic, they are home to the ancestors, and they have life. In the words of the Bawaka Country group:

> Country includes lands, seas, waters, rocks, animals, winds and all the beings that exist in and make up a place, including people. It also embraces the stars, moon, Milky Way, solar winds and storms, and intergalactic plasma. Land, Sea and Sky Country are all connected, so there is no such thing as 'outer space' or 'outer Country'—no outside. What we do in one part of Country affects all others.
>
> (Bawaka Country et al. 2020: 2)

Current existential threats facing Earth and humanity are being used as justification for colonising upwards and outwards. Overpopulation and climate change are examples of unchecked exponential growth that put the certainty of humanity's long-term survival into question (Elvis and Milligan 2019). The misuse of nonrenewable energy resources to support our unsustainably increasing population is both directly and indirectly leading to increases in economic inequity and the inaccessibility of food and water sources. Humanity's consumption of ecological resources is currently exceeding Earth's biocapacity, using resources equivalent to approximately 1.75 Earths in order to meet population demands (Global Footprint Network 2022). What guarantee is there that our mismanagement of resources won't follow us into the cosmos? If the best predictor of future behaviour is past behaviour, what qualifies us as a species to colonise other celestial bodies?

There are only two international treaties that aim to guide the legality of space mining. The 1967 Outer Space Treaty (Treaty on Principles Governing the Activities of States in the Exploration and Use of Outer Space, including the Moon and Other Celestial Bodies), signed by 108 countries, states that the exploration of outer space shall be done to benefit all countries and that space shall be free for exploration and use by all the states (Ball 2007; "Sustainable Space Mining" 2019). However, this treaty is seen as outdated and vague, lacking the specificity that space colonisation and space mining would require in order to prevent exploitation and long-term resource depletion (Johnson-Freese 2017). The 1979 Moon Treaty (Agreement Governing the Activities of States on the Moon and Other Celestial Bodies) was created as a follow-up to the Outer Space Treaty in an effort to protect the solar system from this previous ambiguity, stating that the Moon and other bodies of the solar system should not have their environments disrupted ("Sustainable Space Mining" 2019). But these agreements have not been accepted unanimously by all states. In fact, none of the world's spacefaring nations have ratified the 1979 Moon Treaty agreement (United Nations Office for Disarmament Affairs 2022).

Without widespread adherence to these treaties, supporters of an eventual colonisation of other bodies in the solar system urge for a slow, thoughtful, and purposeful entry into space, motivated solely out of necessity (e.g., Delgado-López 2015; Schwartz 2019; Slobodian 2015; Torres 2018; Traphagan 2019), while others remain unconvinced that the nature of humanity could ever prevent the repeating of unsustainable practices on Earth from being perpetuated through resource extraction of other celestial bodies (Marino 2019). To continue proceeding with discussions as though space colonisation is an inevitability perpetuates an incorrect assumption that the interests of the intellectual and political elites supersede the majority of the Earth's population (Traphagan 2019).

The connection of Indigenous peoples to Sky Country and the Indigenous view that there is no conceptually separate 'outer Country' have been largely absent from conversations and decisions involving space activities in Australia and likely around the world. It is incorrect to think of Sky Country as lifeless, nor can it be regarded as *sphaera nullius* (adapted from the term *terra nullius*, which was used to justify claiming Australia for the British Crown). As expressed by Bawaka Country et al. (2020: 4):

> Terra nullius, a legal fiction which provided a foundation for the invasion and colonization of Australia and other First Nations territories globally, is not defined as a place with no people, rather it is a place that is deemed to have no Law/lore, no protocols and no constitutive relationships. To speak of Sky Country in this way, then, is an erasure of Indigenous Law, and of many, diverse legal orders, relationships and systems that extend to, and include, space.

Further colonisation of Sky Country should not happen without Indigenous voices central to the conversation. Attempting to declare outer space as *sphaera nullius* runs the risk of justifying the exploitation and polluting of space while disregarding the continuity of Country and Sky Country for Indigenous peoples.

Artificial Satellites: Impacts on Sky Sovereignty

Indigenous peoples all over the world have spent hundreds and thousands of generations observing, memorising, and tracking all the visible stars in the sky for the purposes of navigation, seasonal tracking, and cultural responsibility, to name a few. In very recent years, companies including SpaceX, Amazon, and OneWeb are competing in a modern-day telecommunications space race, with each striving to dominate Earth's outer orbits (Payne 2020), potentially permanently changing how the sky appears from Earth. Their goal is to launch thousands of small satellites into orbit to increase internet accessibility around the globe. However, despite claims of increased internet access, sky gazers, including Indigenous peoples are left asking, *at what cost?* And *to whose benefits?* As commented by author Ceridwen Dovey (2021) in her award-winning essay "Everlasting Free Fall", "What will it mean if all visible stars are speeding satellites?" Desecrating the skies has a direct impact on Indigenous sovereignty as it limits access to their knowledge systems, and in the same way desecrating the land has removed First Peoples from their countries, cultures, and ways of life.

The first Starlink satellites were launched in 2019, and as of the time of writing, the Starlink project run by US-based company SpaceX has launched approximately 1700 satellites into low Earth orbit, with plans to launch another 30,000 over the next decade (Sheetz 2021a). These "megaconstellations" are designed to range over nine different altitudes between 340 and 614 kilometres above the Earth's surface. The initial, operational satellites each measure approximately four metres in length and weigh 200–350 kilograms. Starlink has suggested that this size will likely increase in the future to allow for additional payloads. In a similar (albeit more conservative) effort, British company OneWeb has launched nearly 150 satellites with plans for another 6000 (Richards 2021). The American multinational conglomerate Amazon intends to launch an additional 3000 satellites into multiple orbits (Sheetz 2021b).

When news of Starlink's plans first became public, astronomers were immediately concerned about the impact the satellites would have on the skies due to the rapidly increasing number of human-made objects in orbit (Witze 2021). Few people, including experts or the public, had an opportunity to voice concerns before communication regulation bodies approved Starlink's plans. At first, humans around the globe began seeing highly reflective objects cross our skies. When these objects were photographed, they appeared as streaks (see Figure 19.1). These objects and streaks were unlike anything anyone had witnessed before, altering our collective view of the sky. The same skies that have been studied meticulously since time immemorial by Indigenous and non-Indigenous communities alike are at risk.

Two years after the initial Starlink launch in May of 2019, evidence started to emerge that validated concerns about the potential impacts of megaconstellations and how they are contributing to the destruction of dark skies. In March 2021, Kocifaj et al. (2021) published an article on how the proliferation of space objects is a rapidly increasing source of artificial night sky brightness. The paper considers the ways in which objects in orbit increase the overall brightness of the sky by considering data prior to Starlink's first megaconstellation launch. Artificial satellites' contribution to radio interference, loss of information in telescopic photographs (streaks), and increased skyglow were noted as major concerns for conducting ground-based astronomy (p. 1). Notably, they found that as the satellites orbit our planet, the sun's rays are being reflected and scattered into our atmosphere at a drastically increased rate (p. 4).

The study concluded that we are collectively experiencing a new type of skyglow due to the increase of artificial objects in our sky. Initial measurements indicate that this new source of light pollution is increasing the brightness of night skies by 10%. Currently, the upper limit of light pollution tolerable at observatories is 10% of the natural skyglow (Cayrel 1979: 215), meaning some scientific observations of the sky will be affected. Astronomical observatories, and dark skies in

Figure 19.1 Image of Venus and the Pleiades open star cluster featuring tracks of Starlink satellites. Credit Torsten Hansen/IAU OAE. Public domain.

general, were already threatened by numerous other sources contributing to light pollution before the emergence of megaconstellations.

The goal of megaconstellations is to provide high-speed, low-latency internet across the entire planet, leaving no place untouched. As stated by SpaceX's company president, Gwynne Shotwell:

> We hope after about 28 launches we'll have continuous coverage throughout the globe, and then the plan after that is to continue to add satellites to provide additional capacity. We will do some polar launches starting this summer to get connectivity over the poles as well.
>
> *(Shotwell 2021)*

If they are allowed to continue undirected, with little to no engagement with Indigenous or astronomical communities, these companies will likely radically brighten night skies worldwide. The potential use of these technologies is impressive and innovative, but is the potential for harm also being addressed?

Several companies have made attempts to reduce the impact of megaconstellations on professional astronomy. For example, OneWeb has opted for fewer satellites than what was initially proposed and designed them to be positioned at a higher altitude, meaning they can cover a larger area and are less visible to the naked eye (Mallama 2020: 4). However, the same satellites at a higher altitude would be visible to instruments for a longer duration, ultimately experiencing longer periods of illumination (Hainaut and Williams 2020: 4). With Starlink, SpaceX conversely intends to stay at the same altitude but has made attempts to reduce the satellites' luminosity by using a novel antireflective coating. While coating techniques demonstrated a reduction in reflected visible sunlight by up to 50%, unfortunately, not all wavelengths of light scatter were reduced (Horiuchi, Hanayama, and Ohishi 2020: 3), and the coating was found to cause other issues such as overheating. As such, no Starlink satellites currently in orbit (other than the initial test cases) employ coating techniques.

With the current trajectory of satellite approvals and injections, we are in the process of overpopulating an already contested space, and there are rising concerns for the consequences of orbital congestion. In the words of astronomer Aparna Venkatesan and colleagues, "the manner and pace of 'occupying' near-Earth space raises the risk of repeating the mistakes of colonization on a cosmic scale" (Venkatesan et al. 2020: 1043; see also Bawaka Country et al. 2020; Traphagan 2019; Williams 2010).

Indigenous histories teach us of the devastating consequences of the colonial agenda. For example, many Aboriginal and Torres Strait Islander cultures have no conception of 'outer space', only a continuous, connected reality where coexistence is paramount. As captured by the Bawaka Country group, "[t]o hurt Sky Country, to try and possess it, is an ongoing colonization of the plural lifeworlds of all those who have ongoing connections with and beyond the sky" (Bawaka Country et al. 2020: 1).

Indigenous cultures, traditions, and peoples show us that impacts of our actions can be minimised, and the health of Country and community can, and should, take first priority (AIATSIS 2011). 'Slowing down' is one of the great lessons modern technologists could take from Indigenous communities. A great example of this is *dadirri*, a Ngangikurungkurr term from Daly River in Northern Territory, describing a research technique employed by Aboriginal and Torres Strait Islander communities which prioritises deep listening to the internal and external environments (West et al. 2012: 1584). Indigenous astronomy is not just knowledge of the natural world. It also embodies the values, techniques, and histories of the communities from which it was born. Further, Indigenous sky sovereignty enables Indigenous peoples' voice and authority over matters that concern them, as opposed to assuming the interest of these corporations and colonial states are the same interests held by Indigenous peoples and communities (Traphagan 2019). Active Indigenous sky sovereignty acknowledges the interconnectivity between land and sky, and that caring for Country includes Sky Country, which disrupts the unimpeded sovereignty held by corporations (Maile 2019: 148). By understanding that the world (and indeed the universe) is interconnected and relational, we see that no living creatures—not even humans—are immune to the consequences of polluting the skies. By valuing the sustainability of our actions, we can create a reality where we are not a threat to our own survival.

Solutions are required to navigate our increasingly polluted atmosphere, particularly if the communication monopolies continue to have free rein over near-Earth space, resulting in the undervaluing of Earth's sensitive natural resources and Indigenous lives. Just as some companies have begun to consider mitigation tactics to avoid the increase in skyglow, all companies must be responsible for adding to an already polluted space. Guidelines such as those set out by the Inter-Agency Space Debris Coordination Committee offer solutions to this growing problem, such as lowering the height of a satellite's orbit at the end of its life to ensure it will disintegrate on its reentry to Earth (Witze 2018). However, as these are international guidelines, there is no legal framework to enforce such practices. Communication bodies can try and enforce such guidelines are adhered to; however, as commented by the senior space debris mitigation analyst at the European Space Agency, Stijn Lemmens, "it's only after launch that we know how responsible their behaviour was" with respect to Starlink's use of debris mitigation guidelines (Özden 2020). Given the near misses that have already taken place and the known tens of thousands—combined with the estimated millions—of pieces of space debris already floating above, orbital pollution reduction is required (Coldewey 2019; ESO 2022). Further, reducing air pollutants has been shown to drastically decrease natural sky brightness (Kocifaj and Barentine 2021: 2), offering potential solutions for both night sky visibility and cleaner-breathing air for all.

Land Rights: Space Facilities on Indigenous Lands

Indigenous sky rights are closely linked to Indigenous land rights. Historically, in Australia, land rights sit within the realm of the Native Title Act (1993) which, once granted, allows Traditional Owners access and use of their lands and waters in ways that are consistent with traditional laws and customs. However, one of the many issues related to land rights and native title is that traditional laws and customs postulate that Country includes everything: the lands, the waters, the animals, the rocks, the resources below the land, and of course the sky up above. With respect to the space sector, the major conflicts in this space have focused on the construction of astronomical and space facilities and launching sites on Indigenous lands. These lands, which are regarded as optimal and necessary by astronomers and space scientists, are also often sacred and culturally significant to Indigenous peoples. Since astronomical facilities can be used for space exploration, satellite tracking, and telecommunications, the field of astronomy also must consider its part in the development of the modern space race, space exploration, and space colonisation.

In Australia, the Commonwealth Scientific and Industrial Research Organisation's (CSIRO) Parkes Radio Telescope Observatory is used for astrophysics research and for tracking spacecraft for planetary missions. In Hawai'i, the Mauna Kea Observatories are focused on astrophysics research, space exploration missions, searching for near-Earth asteroids, and tracking space debris, and satellites with links to the military. Similarly, the Woomera Rocket Range, approximately 450 km north of Adelaide, South Australia, played a significant role in the development of the US, UK, and European space programmes (Morton 1989: 295), but resulted in many Aboriginal groups, including the Kokatha and Pitjantjatjara, being forcibly removed off their lands (Gorman 2005: 95). Both observatories exist on unceded Indigenous lands.

Over the last forty years, particularly in the Americas, conflict between Indigenous peoples wanting to control and protect their land and Western astronomers who wish to build research facilities on those lands has been a focal point of concern (see e.g., Swanner 2013). In 1980, astronomers planned the construction of three telescopes atop Dził Nchaa Sí'an (West Apache) or Mount Graham in Arizona, which is home to sacred sites of the Tsék'áádn (San Carlos Apache). This led to Indigenous and environmental activists banding together against the project (Hall 2015). The first two telescopes were constructed, but the third—designed to occupy much more land to the point that it would obscure the sacred peaks—faced forty lawsuits and eight federal appellate courts. After years of legal disputes, the astronomers won their case, and the telescope was allowed to be constructed.

Arizona's Kitt Peak National Observatory, built on Tohono O'odham lands, became the new site of controversy. In 2005, the Tohono O'odham fought against construction of the VERITAS (Very Energetic Radiation Imaging Telescope Array System) and won their case, stopping the development of VERITAS. In 2009, scientists selected Mauna Kea in Hawai'i as the future home of the Thirty Meter Telescope (TMT). Mauna Kea is protected by the National Historic Preservation Act, meaning that the mountain is a sacred site to kānaka 'ōiwi. Mauna Kea is a living temple, a site of numerous shrines and ceremonies, and an important burial ground. Hawaiian protectors of that land have been peacefully but assertively protesting the TMT for many years, delaying construction and forcing the astronomical community to consider the effects of its activities on Indigenous communities (Witze 2020).

Long-lasting and diplomatically exhausting conflicts between Indigenous peoples and Western astronomers tend to focus on two factors: (1) cultural incompatibilities around the use of the land and the meaning of 'sacred sites' for the Indigenous communities, and (2) the advancement of scientific and commercial progress for the benefit of Western astronomy and space exploration. Astronomers have been accused of being both insensitive and culturally incompetent, which leads to cultural destruction, traumatic experiences for both Indigenous peoples and Western astronomers, costly construction delays, and ruined financial partnerships with institutions (Guedes 2018).

The further development of the space industry must work for the mutual benefit of all stakeholders. This involves recognising sacred sites, which are areas of significance to Indigenous peoples that, as places of worship and remembrance, link to identity, knowledge, and spirituality (Oviedo, Jeanrenaud, and Otegui et al. 2005). They are often restricted by taboos to certain community members and follow unique protocols for activities. Some Indigenous sacred sites have a complex, troublesome, even traumatic history because of how they have been appropriated, destroyed, unacknowledged, or disrespected by Western society in general and the Western scientific community in particular, including astronomers (Heinämäki and Herrmann 2017).

Indigenous ontological concepts of 'building' are often inconsistent with concepts of that term in Western society (Ojanlatva and Neumann 2017). The variety and complexity of what is understood as 'sacred' and 'building' is diverse in Indigenous communities, of which there are thousands today. Indigenous sacred sites represent works of ancestral communities, such as ceremonial sites and sites of material culture. They can also be natural landscapes, including rivers, springs, deserts, forests, rocks, groves, coral reefs, coastal waters, mountains, and stars (Heinämäki and Herrmann 2017). Some sacred Indigenous deserts and mountains are the most desirable places to build astronomical and space facilities due to their clear, dry conditions and high elevation. It is crucial that an understanding of Indigenous land rights and culture be central to the development of space facilities at these locations. This requires cultural awareness/competency/responsiveness training and working closely with Indigenous communities to follow proper protocol to avoid perpetuating the colonial agenda.

It is essential to recognise that Indigenous leaders and community members have a wide range of views, and that proposed projects may be supported and opposed simultaneously by members of those communities, and obtaining unanimous community support is not always possible. The space sector must learn to acknowledge issues and accept a 'no', as it does not have an inherent right to develop Indigenous lands (Hamacher and Britton 2015) and risks seriously jeopardising or destroying future working relationships, support, and engagement with Indigenous communities.

Light Pollution: Impacts on Sky Country

Indigenous cultures across Australia, as well as around the world, have continually maintained a strong connection to the night sky, which is used to inform many aspects of culture and everyday life. This connection is represented through oral traditions which use objects in the night sky to encode important information of cultural significance, such as ceremony, customs, and social interactions, as well as scientific observations which inform navigation, weather forecasting, seasons, and animal behaviours (Nakata 2010; Norris 2016; Ruggles 2010).

Many celestial objects described in oral traditions are bright, easy-to-see natural light sources such as the Moon, the planets, conspicuous stars, and prominent constellations (like the Southern Cross, or Crux). However, some objects that feature in Indigenous astronomy are much fainter, such as the Small and Large Magellanic Clouds, star clusters, nebulae, and the dark constellations traced out by the dust lanes in the Milky Way. Light pollution, being human-made non-natural light, is reducing the visibility of these faint objects, particularly in and around areas of higher urbanisation, which in turn is disrupting Indigenous peoples' connections to the cosmos (Amir 2021). The ongoing erasure of the night sky by growing light pollution is a product of colonisation, an act of slow violence, and arguably an example of cultural genocide (Hamacher, De Napoli, and Mott 2020).

For the Gamilaraay and Yuwaalayaay people of northwest New South Wales, an example of both the cultural and scientific applications of Indigenous astronomy can be found in the dark regions of the Milky Way, a dark constellation representing the celestial emu, Gawarrgay. The celestial emu constellation comprises the dark dust lanes in the Milky Way from the Coalsack Nebula (located near the Southern Cross) along Centaurus through the Pointer stars (Alpha and Beta Centauri) and into the galactic bulge of the Milky Way in Scorpius and Sagittarius (Fuller et al. 2014). The depiction and position of Gawarrgay at various stages throughout the year inform the people about the behaviour of the land emu, dhinawan, on earth. From the celestial emu's first appearance around April, the people on the land know it is breeding season for the dhinawan, so they can go out and collect emu eggs as a source of food. Then the celestial emu changes position around June/July, where the legs of the celestial emu can no longer be seen, which means the eggs are beginning to hatch, so hunting them should stop. Later in the year, when you can no longer see the head of the emu, this means that the dry season has begun and the waterholes are no longer full, requiring protection from the thirsty dhinawans.

So how dark does the night sky need to be in order to see the Milky Way or the celestial emu? Because the Milky Way is not uniform and the ability to see such features varies based on individual people's vision, this can be hard to quantify. Crumey (2014) posited that a limiting magnitude for the visibility of the Milky Way could be found using empirical observations, where observers viewed the Milky Way through a series of variable filters until a select portion of the Milky Way remained just visible. Bigourdan (1917) reported that in the summer months at the Paris Observatory, the Milky Way was visible once the sun had reached thirteen degrees below the horizon, that *New General Catalogue of Nebulae and Clusters of Stars* objects became visible at fifteen degrees below the horizon, and the faintest objects in the night sky at sixteen degrees below the horizon (as cited in Crumey 2014: 2617). This criterion for the Milky Way then corresponds to a sky brightness of 20.2 to 20.3 mag arcsec^2 (Crumey 2014). Falchi et al. (2016) used their light pollution propagation software to create an atlas of sky brightness, which produced similar results, estimating that a sky brightness of 20.0 to 20.6 was the minimum range required in order to see the Milky Way. Falchi et al. also used population studies to estimate what percentage of a country's population lived under different levels of light pollution. Their results show that only 2–5% of Australia's population live in areas where there is low enough light pollution for the Milky Way to be clearly visible.

There are many different types of light pollution, but most of them can be attributed to various design choices in city planning. There are five main types of light pollution in urban areas: excessive illumination caused by the misuse of lighting; glare from light sources entering the eyes when it is not intended; light clutter from poor placement of lights, such as street lights or those from businesses; skyglow, which is the effective "light dome" that encompasses a city area; and light trespass, which refers to unwanted light entering the property of someone else (Conserve Energy Future 2021).

To combat light pollution, long-term plans and policies must be developed and implemented with the goal of preserving the dark night sky as a *limited natural resource*. Work in this area is ongoing around the world, with the International Dark-Sky Association (IDA) being the international authority. With the help of the IDA, communities can apply for areas to be designated a Dark Sky Place, with varying levels of requirements and significance depending on the type of designation. The base-level Dark Sky Place designation offered by the IDA—Dark Sky Park—requires the Milky Way to be readily visible to the naked eye as a minimum (International Dark-Sky Association 2018).

There is one such designation in Australia: Warrumbungle National Park in the state of New South Wales. Warrumbungle National Park has been designated as a Dark Sky Park due to its scientific importance based on the area remaining dark. It is home to Siding Spring Observatory, a world-class observatory hosting important research telescopes for optical and infrared astronomy. It is also a site of cultural and spiritual importance, with the park getting its name, Warrumbungle, from a Gamilaraay word meaning 'crooked mountain'. Local landscape features are described in local Aboriginal traditions linking it to the sky, such as 'the Breadknife' geological feature, which is related to a Seven Sisters (Pleiades) Songline (Fuller, Norris, and Trudgett 2014: 15).

It is also not only the planning of cities that contributes to light pollution. A rapidly growing threat comes in the form of mining and gas extraction. As an example, a report in 2014 showed that Siding Spring Observatory was in danger of being shut down due to light pollution as a result of coal seam gas developments around Boggabri, NSW, about 120 km away (Milman 2014). This was already affecting the observatory more than its larger neighbouring towns of Narrabri and Gunnedah. To get an idea of the sensitivity required for the telescopes, and to illustrate how pervasive light pollution is, Siding Spring Observatory is negatively affected by the lights of Sydney, over 400 km away (Milman 2014).

Light pollution has a detrimental impact on society as a whole, which Pothukuchi (2021: 165) states "is a threat to the health and well-being of humans and nonhuman species and the pristine night sky". It then requires that all aspects of society contribute to the effort of reducing and preventing light pollution. An awareness of the problem and its impacts is gaining momentum around the world and solutions are being developed (e.g., International Dark-Sky Association 2012). Including Indigenous peoples, knowledges, and perspectives in this process is integral in ensuring that our cultures maintain our continuing connection to the night sky.

Gunagala Galuma-Li (Care for Sky)

In light of the many struggles Indigenous peoples around the world face with respect to safeguarding their rights to land, water, and sky, there have been instances of successful and meaningful collaboration between Indigenous communities and the space sector. Here we briefly introduce two examples. One is the Square Kilometre Array and the other is an Aboriginal-owned satellite company.

The Square Kilometre Array (SKA), consisting of 3600 radio telescopes scattered across Western Australia and South Africa, is being constructed primarily on the lands of the Yamatji-Wajarri people of Western Australia. Astronomers have been consulting with those communities since day one to seek their permission and involvement as collaborators in developing an art project guided by respect and mutual benefits (Tingay 2018). One of the major outcomes of this collaboration was the *Ilgarijiri—Things Belonging to the Sky* exhibition, which brought together Aboriginal artists and radio astronomers to share knowledge and pave the way for a collaborative future. This resulted in a series of artworks as part of a travelling exhibition (Goldsmith 2014). This initial gesture of respect shown to the Yamatji-Wajarri people has benefited both parties in terms of generating a culturally inclusive collaboration between the local Indigenous peoples and the Square Kilometre Array project. During the process of building the observatory, sites of cultural significance and heritage to the Yamatju-Wajarri people were actively avoided thanks to rigorous consultation between the two parties (CSIRO 2021). Further, via a land use agreement, the SKA has vowed to offer enterprise agreements, training, and educational opportunities to the Yamatju-Wajarri people in exchange for using their land. The respectful collaboration between the Yamatju-Wajarri people and the SKA has ensured their cultural heritage sites remain intact and accessible, and also has the potential to provide mutual benefit to both parties. Further, this collaboration set a precedent for other observatories in Australia. The Parkes radio telescope was recently renamed Murriyang, a Wiradjuri word meaning 'skyworld', after consultation with local Wiradjuri knowledge holders. Similarly, the Australian Telescope Compact Array, which hosts six radio telescopes, is in discussions with local Aboriginal communities, including Gamilaraay Elders, to identify appropriate Aboriginal names for the six dishes.

In Alice Springs, Central Australia, the Centre for Appropriate Technology (CfAT), an Aboriginal-owned science and technology not-for-profit, became the first Indigenous-owned organisation to receive rights to manage a new ground-based telecommunications facility designed to track the influx of satellites in low Earth orbit, such as Starlink's megaconstellations. The data collected by this facility will contribute to scientific research, inform commercial projects, and monitor the environments of both the land and the sky. Notably, the station will provide high-resolution imagery in real time, offering significant improvements to disaster management such as bushfires or cyclones (Cross 2020). The Centre is providing Aboriginal Australians with first-hand experience and the opportunity to make contributions to the growing Australian space sector, whilst providing economic and skill-building opportunities for the local community ("Indigenous Australians to Lead Space Industry" 2019). Initiatives such as the Centre for Appropriate Technology assist Indigenous peoples around the world in becoming leaders in the satellite and space industry through ongoing investment into Indigenous communities, culture, and values.

These examples show how collaborations and proper engagement between the space industry and Indigenous peoples can provide a different approach, leading to positive outcomes for all. Whether it is through harm minimisation, as exemplified by the Yamatji-Wajarri and SKA collaboration, or through the localised, culturally relevant use of scientific instruments, as shown to us by the Centre for Appropriate Technology, Indigenous peoples and communities have solutions to the pressing issues affecting Indigenous sky rights and our collective view of the cosmos.

Acknowledgements

We recognise the Traditional Owners of the land on which we live and work and pay respect to their Elders, past and present: Ngunnawal and Ngambri (Karlie Noon and Pete Swanton), Boon Wurrung (Krystal De Napoli and Duane Hamacher), and Bedegal (Carla Guedes). Duane

Hamacher received funding from the Australian Research Council, Laby Foundation, Pierce Bequest, and Indigenous Knowledges Institute at the University of Melbourne. Duane Hamacher and Krystal De Napoli are Ambassadors of the Australasian Dark Sky Alliance.

References

Abney, Keith. 2019. "Ethics of Colonization: Arguments from Existential Risk." *Futures* 110: 60–63. https://doi.org/10.1016/j.futures.2019.02.014.

AIATSIS (Australian Institute of Aboriginal and Torres Strait Islander Studies) 2011. "The Benefits Associated with Caring for Country: Literature Review." *Report prepared for the Department of Sustainability, Environment, Water, Population and Communities*, edited by Jessica K. Weir, Claire Stacey and Kara Youngetob. Canberra: AIATSIS. https://aiatsis.gov.au/sites/default/files/research_pub/benefits-cfc_0_2.pdf.

Amir, Nikita. 2021. "Light Pollution Threatens Millennia-Old Indigenous Navigation Methods." *Discover Magazine* (online), 28 October. Accessed 3 November 2021: www.discovermagazine.com/environment/light-pollution-threatens-millennia-old-indigenous-navigation-methods.

Ball, Philip. 2007. "Time to Rethink the Outer Space Treaty." *Nature* (News), 4 October. Accessed 3 November 2021: https://doi.org/10.1038/news.2007.142.

Bawaka Country, including Audra Mitchell, Sarah Wright, Sandie Suchet-Pearson, Kate Lloyd, Laklak Burarrwanga, Ritjilili Ganambarr, Merrkiyawuy Ganambarr-Stubbs, Banbapuy Ganambarr, Djawundil Maymuru, and Rrawun Maymuru. 2020. "Dukarr Lakarama: Listening to Guwak, Talking Back to Space Colonization." *Political Geography* 81: 102218. https://doi.org/10.1016/j.polgeo.2020.102218.

Bigourdan, Guillaume. 1917. "Observations de 1907. Observations de Nébuleuses et D'amas Stellaires". Paris: Annales de l'Observatoire de Paris.

Cayrel, R. 1979. "50. Identification and Protection of Existing and Potential Observatory Sites." *Transactions of the International Astronomical Union, Series A* 17 (1): 215–23. https://doi.org/10.1017/S0251107X00010798.

Coldewey, Devin. 2019. "Near Miss between Science Craft and Starlink Satellite Shows Need to Improve Orbital Coordination." *TechCrunch*, 4 September. techcrunch.com/2019/09/03/near-miss-between-science-craft-and-starlink-satellite-shows-need-to-improve-orbital-coordination/.

Conserve Energy Future. 2021. *What Is Light Pollution?* www.conserve-energy-future.com/types-causes-and-effects-of-light-pollution.php.

Cross, Hannah. 2020. "New Satellite Facility Positions Indigenous Businesses to be Leaders in Satellite and Space Industry." *National Indigenous Times*, 10 July. Accessed 3 November 2021: nit.com.au/new-satellite-facility-positions-indigenous-businesses-to-be-leaders-in-satellite-and-space-industry/.

Crumey, Andrew. 2014. "Human Contrast Threshold and Astronomical Visibility." *Monthly Notices of the Royal Astronomical Society* 442 (3): 2600–19. https://doi.org/10.1093/mnras/stu992.

CSIRO 2021. *CSIRO and the Square Kilometre Array.* Updated 9 September 2021. Accessed 1 March 2022: https://www.csiro.au/en/about/facilities-collections/international-facilities/ska.

Delgado-López, Laura. 2015. "Beyond the Moon Agreement: Norms of Responsible Behavior for Private Sector Activities on the Moon and Celestial Bodies." *Space Policy* 33 (Part 1): 1–3. https://doi.org/10.1016/j.spacepol.2014.08.006.

Dovey, Ceridwen. 2021. "Everlasting Free Fall." *Alexander* (narrative storytelling app), 16 February.

Elvis, Martin, and Tony Milligan. 2019. "How Much of the Solar System Should We Leave as Wilderness?" *Acta Astronautica* 162: 574–80. https://doi.org/10.1016/j.actaastro.2019.03.014.

ESO (European Space Agency) 2022. *Space Debris by the Numbers.* Darmstadt, Germany: ESOC. https://www.esa.int/Safety_Security/Space_Debris/Space_debris_by_the_numbers.

Falchi, Fabio, Pierantonio Cinzano, Dan Duriscoe, Christopher Kyba, Christosphper Elvidge, Kimberly Baugh, Boris Portnov, Nataliya Rybnikova, and Richard Furgoni. 2016. "The New World Atlas of Artificial Night Sky Brightness." *Science Advances* 2 (6): 1–25. https://doi.org/10.1126/sciadv.1600377.

Fuller, Robert S., Michael G. Anderson, Ray P. Norris, and Michelle Trudgett. 2014. "The Emu Sky Knowledge of the Kamilaroi and Euahlayi Peoples." *Journal of Astronomical History and Heritage* 17 (2): 171–79. https://www.narit.or.th/files/JAHH/2014JAHHvol17/2014JAHH...17..171F.pdf.

Fuller, Robert, Ray Norris, and Michelle Trudgett. 2014. "The Astronomy of the Kamilaroi and Euahlayi Peoples and Their Neighbours." *Australian Aboriginal Studies* (2): 3–27.

Goldsmith, John. 2014. "The *Ilgarijiri* Project: A Collaboration between Aboriginal Communities and Radio Astronomers in the Murchison Region of Western Australia." *Journal of Astronomical History and Heritage* 17 (2): 205–15.

Gorman, Alice. 2005. "The Cultural Landscape of Interplanetary Space." *Journal of Social Archaeology* 5 (1): 85–107. https://doi.org/10.1177/1469605305050148.

Green, Brian Patrick. 2019. "Self-preservation Should Be Humankind's First Ethical Priority and Therefore Rapid Space Settlement Is Necessary." *Futures* 110: 35–37. https://doi.org/10.1016/j.futures.2019.02.006.

Guedes, Carla Bento. 2018. *Exploring Cultural Competence for Astronomers*. Master's Thesis. Faculty of Languages and Social Sciences, University of New South Wales, Australia.

Hainaut, Olivier, and Andrew Williams. 2020. "Impact of Satellite Constellations on Astronomical Observations with ESO Telescopes in the Visible and Infrared Domains." *Astronomy & Astrophysics* 636: A121. https://doi.org/10.1051/0004-6361/202037501.

Hall, Shannon. 2015. "Hawaii's Telescope Controversy Is the Latest in a Long History of Land-Ownership Battles." *Scientific American*, 11 December. https://www.scientificamerican.com/article/hawaii-s-telescope-controversy-is-the-latest-in-a-long-history-of-land-ownership-battles/.

Hamacher, Duane W., and Tui Britton. 2015. "Mauna a Wakea: Hawai'i's Sacred Mountain and the Contentious Thirty Meter Telescope." *The Conversation*, 21 September. https://theconversation.com/mauna-a-wakea-hawaiis-sacred-mountain-and-the-contentious-thirty-meter-telescope-46069.

Hamacher, Duane, Krystal De Napoli, and Bon Mott. 2020. "Whitening the Sky: Light Pollution as a Form of Cultural Genocide.". arxiv.org/ftp/arxiv/papers/2001/2001.11527.pdf.

Heinämäki, Leena, and Thora Martina Herrmann. 2017. *Experiencing and Protecting Sacred Natural Sites of Sámi and Other Indigenous Peoples*. Springer Polar Sciences. Finland: Springer International Publishing.

Horiuchi, Takashi, Hidekazu Hanayama, and Masatoshi Ohishi. 2020. "Simultaneous Multicolor Observations of Starlink's Darksat by the Murikabushi Telescope with MITSuME." *Astrophysical Journal* 905 (1): 1–13. https://doi.org/10.3847/1538-4357/abc695.

"Indigenous Australians to Lead Space Industry at New Alice Springs Earth Ground Station." 2019. *SBS News* (Australia), 11 June. Accessed 3 November 2021: www.sbs.com.au/news/indigenous-australians-to-lead-space-industry-at-new-alice-springs-earth-ground-station/b35811cc-1ecb-4a90-9be2-d6c1f4486e3b.

International Dark-Sky Association. 2018. *International Dark Sky Park Program Guidelines*. Tucson, AZ: International Dark Sky Association. https://www.darksky.org/wp-content/uploads/bsk-pdf-manager/2021/05/IDSP-Final-May-2021.pdf.

International Dark-Sky Association. 2012. *Fighting Light Pollution: Smart Lighting Solutions for Individuals and Communities*. Mechanicsburg, PA: Stackpole Books.

Johnson-Freese, Joan. 2017. "Build on the Outer Space Treaty." *Nature* 550: 182–84. https://doi.org/10.1038/550182a.

Kocifaj, Miroslav, and John C. Barentine. 2021. "Air Pollution Mitigation Can Reduce the Brightness of the Night Sky In and Near Cities." *Scientific Reports* 11: 14622. https://doi.org/10.1038/s41598-021-94241-1.

Kocifaj, M., F. Kundracik, J.C. Barentine, and S. Bará. 2021. "The Proliferation of Space Objects Is a Rapidly Increasing Source of Artificial Night Sky Brightness." *Monthly Notices of the Royal Astronomical Society: Letters* 504 (1): L40–L44. https://doi.org/10.1093/mnrasl/slab030.

Maile, David Uahikeaikalei'ohu. 2019. *Gifts of Sovereignty: Settler Colonial Capitalism and the Kanaka 'Ōiwi Politics of Ea*. PhD Dissertation, American Studies. The University of New Mexico.

Mallama, Anthony. 2020. *The Brightness of OneWeb Satellites*. Self-published. arxiv.org/ftp/arxiv/papers/2012/2012.05100.pdf.

Marino, Lori. 2019. "Humanity Is Not Prepared to Colonize Mars." *Futures* 110: 15–18. https://doi.org/10.1016/j.futures.2019.02.010.

Milman, Oliver. 2014. "Siding Spring Observatory Under Threat from Coal Seam Gas Light Pollution." *The Guardian*, October 21. www.theguardian.com/science/2014/oct/21/siding-spring-observatory-threat-coal-seam-gas-light-pollution.

Morton, P. 1989. *Fire Across the Desert: Woomera and the Anglo-Australian Joint Project, 1946–1980*. Canberra: Australian Government Publishing Service.

Munevar, Gonzalo. 2019. "An Obligation to Colonize Outer Space." *Futures* 110: 38–40. https://doi.org/10.1016/j.futures.2019.02.009.

Nakata, Martin. 2010. "The Cultural Interface of Islander and Scientific Knowledge." *The Australian Journal of Indigenous Education* 39: 53–57. https://doi.org/10.1375/S1326011100001137.

Norris, Ray P. 2016. "Dawes Review 5: Australian Aboriginal Astronomy and Navigation." *Publications of the Astronomical Society of Australia* 33: e039. https://doi.org/10.1017/pasa.2016.25.

Ojanlatva, Eija, and Antje Neumann. 2017. "Protecting the Sacred in the Finnish Sápmi: Settings and Challenges." In *Experiencing and Protecting Sacred Natural Sites of Sámi and Other Indigenous Peoples*, edited by Leena Heinämäki and Thora Martina Herrmann, 83–98. The Netherlands: University of Tilburg. https://doi.org/10.1007/978-3-319-48069-5_6.

Oviedo, Gonzalo, Sally Jeanrenaud, and Mercedes Otegui. 2005. *Protecting Sacred Natural Sites of Indigenous and Traditional Peoples: An IUCN Perspective*. Switzerland: Gland. https://www.iucn.org/sites/dev/files/import/downloads/sp_protecting_sacred_natural_sites_indigenous.pdf.

Özden, Nisanur. 2020. "A Space Law Matter: SpaceX Starlink and Minds-On Legal Concerns." *HERDEM Attorneys at Law*. Accessed 1 March 2022: https://www.lexology.com/library/detail.aspx?g=d2df66a7-1c9a-4308-8228-3afa0d75d602.

Payne, Miriam. 2020. "The Modern Space Race." *The Gist*, 19 June. https://the-gist.org/2020/06/the-modern-space-race/.

Pothukuchi, Kameshwari. 2021. "City Light or Star Bright: A Review of Urban Light Pollution, Impacts, and Planning Implications." *Journal of Planning Literature* 36 (2): 155–69. https://doi.org/10.1177/0885412220986421.

Richards, Isabella. 2021. "OneWeb to Reach Halfway Mark of Satellite Constellation Mission." *Space Connect*, 12 October. Accessed 3 November 2021: www.spaceconnectonline.com.au/launch/5111-oneweb-to-deploy-over-half-its-constellation-satellites-this-month.

Ruggles, Clive L. N. 2010. "Indigenous Astronomies and Progress in Modern Astronomy." *Proceedings of Science* 099: 1–8. https://doi.org/10.22323/1.099.0029.

Schwartz, James S. J. 2019. "Space Settlement: What's the Rush?" *Futures* 110: 56–59. https://doi.org/10.1016/j.futures.2019.02.013.

Sheetz, Michael. 2021a. "SpaceX Adding Capabilities to Starlink Internet Satellites, Plans to Launch Them with Starship." *CNBC*, 19 August. Accessed 3 November 2021: www.cnbc.com/2021/08/19/spacex-starlink-satellite-internet-new-capabilities-starship-launch.html.

Sheetz, Michael. 2021b. "Amazon Plans to Launch Its First Internet Satellites in Late 2022." *CNBC*, 1 November. Accessed 3 November 2021: www.cnbc.com/2021/11/01/amazons-project-kuiper-launching-first-internet-satellites-in-q4-2022.html.

Shotwell, G. 2021. "YouTube Livestream with Via Satellite magazine." 6 April 2021, since removed. Retrieved from Mike Brown, "When Will Starlink Be Available Globally? SpaceX Is About to Hit a Big Goal," *Inverse Inc*, 13 May 2021. www.inverse.com/innovation/spacex-starlink-global-coverage-when-available.

Slobodian, Rayna Elizabeth. 2015. "Selling Space Colonization and Immortality: A Psychosocial, Anthropological Critique of the Rush to Colonize Mars." *Acta Astronautica* 113: 89–104. https://doi.org/10.1016/j.actaastro.2015.03.027.

Smiles, Deondre. 2020. "The Settler Logics of (Outer) Space." *Society + Space*, 26 October. https://www.societyandspace.org/articles/the-settler-logics-of-outer-space.

"Sustainable Space Mining" 2019. "Editorial." *Nature Astronomy* 3: 465. https://doi.org/10.1038/s41550-019-0827-7.

Swanner, Leandra Altha. 2013. *Mountains of Controversy: Narrative and the Making of Contested Landscapes in Postwar American Astronomy*. PhD Dissertation, Harvard University.

Tingay, Steven. 2018. "Indigenous Australian Artists and Astrophysicists Come Together to Communicate Science and Culture Via Art." *Journal of Science Communication* 17 (4): CN02. https://doi.org/10.22323/2.17040302.

Torres, Phil. 2018. "Space Colonization and Suffering Risks: Reassessing the 'Maxipok Rule'." *Futures* 100: 74–85. https://doi.org/10.1016/j.futures.2018.04.008.

Traphagan, John W. 2019. "Which Humanity Would Space Colonization Save?" *Futures* 110: 47–49. https://doi.org/10.1016/j.futures.2019.02.016.

UNESCO. 2021. *Indigenous Peoples*. Accessed 3 November 2021: https://en.unesco.org/indigenous-peoples.

United Nations. 2007. *United Nations Declaration on the Rights of Indigenous Peoples*. A/RES/61/295. Accessed 1 November 2021: https://www.un.org/development/desa/indigenouspeoples/declaration-on-the-rights-of-indigenous-peoples.html.

United Nations Office for Disarmament Affairs. 2022. *Agreement Governing the Activities of States on the Moon and Other Celestial Bodies*. Accessed 23 August 2022: https://treaties.unoda.org/t/moon.

Venkatesan, Aparna, James Lowenthal, Parvathy Prem, and Monica Vidaurri. 2020. "The Impact of Satellite Constellations on Space as an Ancestral Global Commons." *Nature Astronomy* 4 (11):1043–48. https://doi.org/10.1038/s41550-020-01238-3.

West, Roianne, Lee Stewart, Kim Foster, and Kim Usher. 2012. "Through a Critical Lens: Indigenist Research and the Dadirri Method." *Qualitative Health Research* 22 (11): 1582–90. https://doi.org/10.1177/1049732312457596.

Williams, Lynda. 2010. "Irrational Dreams of Space Colonization." *Peace Review* 22 (1): 4–8. https://doi.org/10.1080/10402650903539828.

Witze, Alexandra. 2018. "The Quest to Conquer Earth's Space Junk Problem." *Nature* 561 (7721): 24–26. https://doi.org/10.1038/d41586-018-06170-1.

Witze, Alexandra. 2020. "How the Fight Over a Hawaii Mega-telescope Could Change Astronomy." *Nature* (News), 14 January. Accessed 3 November 2021: www.nature.com/articles/d41586-020-00076-7.

Witze, Alexandra. 2021. "Astronomers Push for Global Debate on Giant Satellite Swarms." *Nature* (News), 16 July; correction 19 July. Accessed 3 November 2021: www.nature.com/articles/d41586-021-01954-4.

20
ANISHINAABEG IN SPACE

Deondre Smiles

Introduction

Setting: A bright summer morning in northeastern Minnesota's Iron Range, some day in the not-too-distant future...

It is finally, at long last, launch day at the Anangoog Inaawanidiwaad spaceport in this remote part of northern Minnesota. The hard work, the dreams, the sacrifice of many Anishinaabeg scholars, scientists, astronomers, engineers, community members, elders, and even children are about to pay off, as after years of hard work and ingenuity, the Anishinaabe space programme is finally ready to launch with the first voyage of the Animiikii rocket, carrying the Bikwaakwad probe into space, to begin a voyage that will take it far beyond the limits of the solar system, much in the same vein as the Pioneer and Voyager satellites of historic lore. The goal of this first launch of what will become many as part of the broader Bikwaakwad programme is to investigate the limits of the solar system and the celestial bodies further afield, in what promises to provide great benefits for Anishinaabeg astronomical knowledge.

The platitudes are effusive and frequent. One elder speaks about the programme as providing a way to "engage with the stars in a good way, and to continue to provide our future generations with knowledge about the world beyond this Earth". An engineer on the programme speaks about this new Anishinaabeg engagement in space and NASA's eager collaboration with it as the realisation of the truth that Anishinaabeg scientific knowledge, especially about the stars, and the dominant "Western" form of astronomical knowledge are both valid, on their own merits. Other scientists comment on the fact that the data generated from this project will be collected through non-extractive means, and will be freely shared with communities and peoples across the globe— that the Anishinaabeg go to space not to conquer or to settle, but to better understand the spaces and places beyond Earth with which they must live in good relations. The various non-Indigenous dignitaries and scientists who have come are amazed at what they see. The more numerous representatives from other Indigenous nations are not only amazed but also filled with pride, because many non-Anishinaabe Indigenous peoples also helped with the development of this space programme, and their communities are hard at work developing their own engagements with space.

The launch site, constructed with sustainable materials, is placed within a reclaimed iron ore mine—the site chosen by Anishinaabe community elders as a reclaiming of stolen land that had been brutally exploited but would now serve as a site of Anishinaabeg resurgence. Construction on the site had not only provided jobs for many tribal members but also revitalised an area of Minnesota that had long struggled economically. The Animiikii rocket rises tall over the former mine site, its white body decorated with Anishinaabe floral beadwork patterns. The time has finally come for launch. The countdown begins. "*Midaaswi... zhaangaswi...*" the announcer begins counting down in Ojibwemowin. "*Niswi... niizh... bezhig...*" they finish, as the rocket takes off with a deafening roar amid the smoke and flame of liftoff. The rocket gains altitude quickly, moving through the atmosphere and its various stages, eventually crossing into outer space itself. The probe is launched from the rocket as the rocket begins to gracefully float back to Earth, and Bikwaakwad I begins its journey out into the stars...

The above narrative is a contrived piece of fiction, of course; a flight (no pun intended) of the author's (my) fancy. There is no Anishinaabeg space programme. While one could reasonably argue that there is never a *zero* chance, the actual chance of a spacecraft designed and built by Anishinaabeg being launched from the Iron Range—or, quite frankly, from anywhere—is probably very close to zero. But, that is not the point of the above story—it represents just one imagining of the potential futures for continued Indigenous engagement with the stars, couched within contexts that we understand very well in the so-called United States—the excitement surrounding space launches and the dreams and meanings that we attribute to space exploration, especially the desire to explore the unknown and make it knowable. It also represents a growing tradition of Indigenous engagement with futurisms and how these engagements apply to our broader environments, including by Anishinaabe writer Grace Dillon (Dillon and Marques 2021) and Kyle Powys Whyte (2017, 2018).

In an era of ever-increasing climate crisis, the stars are often presented as an avenue of potential for us to create a new beginning for humanity. However, in the context of the United States, there is also a darker legacy to engagement with space, one couched in questions of colonialism, exploitation, and hegemony (Werth 2004; Cornish 2019; Treviño 2020). Those legacies have also found their way into contemporaneous engagement with space in many ways, ranging from disregard and exploitation of Indigenous lands in the name of space exploration (Prescod-Weinstein et al. 2020; Smiles 2020) to questions about the exploitation of extraterrestrial spaces and places (Marshall 1995). These actions threaten to recreate the same logics of colonisation in space as has been done on Earth (Smiles 2020; Treviño 2020). So, what can be done about this?

In my previous foray into these topics, I positioned Indigenous conceptions of space as a potential counterweight to settler colonial logics of space, both terrestrially and extraterrestrially (Young 1987; Marshall 1995; Kahanamoku et al. 2020; Prescod-Weinstein et al. 2020; Smiles 2020). While that previous chapter focused on the United States' fraught history with these topics, in this chapter, I seek to bring my analysis both a bit deeper and a bit closer to home in exploring the ways that my own people, the Anishinaabe/Ojibwe nation, have engaged with the stars. I position my own people's astronomical knowledge and our systems of accountability and relation with the land and more-than-human kin here on Earth together to provide one potential way through which an ethical engagement with the cosmos might take place. Although we may never get our own space programme, our connections with the stars can still serve as a guide in how to conduct ourselves among them.

My narrative will proceed as follows. I begin by defining settler colonialism briefly and then return to existing threads on how settler colonialism functions in concert with imperialism and capitalism in certain aspects of contemporary space engagement, in particular questions of resource extraction and evading anthropogenic climate/environmental crisis. Next, I turn to Anishinaabe and other Indigenous ontologies of astronomy and space, defining the ways that these ontologies run counter to settler colonial logics of space exploration. Finally, I conclude by pointing out some ways that Anishinaabe people are engaging ethically with the stars in the present day, without having to leave Earth. In all of this, I seek to make the argument that we do not need to export ecological crisis to the stars to explore them or to expand humanity's reach beyond Earth.

Settler Colonialism in Space, Redux: Resource Extraction, Space Colonisation, and Climate/Environmental Crisis

To understand the ways in which logics of settler colonialism extend into space exploration and engagement, it is of course necessary to outline scholarship that has been written about it. While there is not one exact definition of settler colonialism, and it is experienced differently across geographies, there are some common traits of the phenomenon. I begin by turning to the noted settler colonial scholars such as the late Patrick Wolfe (2006), who defines settler colonialism as a unique form of colonialism which is built around the enduring occupation of land by a colonising power, at the expense of the displacement of any Indigenous peoples who may have been present on the land before. This form of colonialism is positioned as distinct from more extractive forms of colonialism as the land itself is central to the goals of colonialism in settler contexts, versus forms of colonialism where natural resources and other forms of material/economic gain were to be extracted and sent back to the colonial metropole (Wolfe 2006). To put it simply, as Wolfe does, "Land is life—or, at least, land is necessary for life" (2006: 387). However, recent scholarship within contexts of settler colonial studies begin to chip away at Wolfe's assertions about settler colonialism.

This critique is multifaceted. Scholars such as Tiffany Lethabo King (2019) have critiqued Wolfe and some of his white contemporaries, such as Lorenzo Veracini, as dominating discourse surrounding settler colonial studies at the expense of Black and Indigenous voices. King in particular describes the ways that settler colonial scholarship has historically centred the settler colonial relationship around an Indigenous–settler dyad, while ignoring the roles that other racialised peoples have played in broader settler colonial structures. Other scholars, such as Sai Englert (2020), have critiqued the ways in which settler colonialism engages with the question of exploitation in settler colonies, and this is the critique that is most important to our discussion. In particular, Englert asserts that by attempting to draw artificial boundaries between "settler" colonialism and "traditional" or "extractive" forms of colonialism, settler colonialism as a concept fails to engage with the ways that it functions through the dispossession of land from its inhabitants via the exploitation of Indigenous peoples (Englert 2020). In particular, Englert employs a Marxist analysis of how class in settler societies is defined chiefly through struggles over who exactly benefits from Indigenous dispossession and exploitation via primitive accumulation (Englert 2020).

This is important because it fundamentally shifts how we think about settler colonialism and its role in constructing and defining itself—if we follow Englert's model of how the settler state constructs and defines itself, it is not enough to violently dispossess Indigenous peoples of their land and engage in campaigns of cultural and physical genocide against them. Rather, the class structure of the settler state is predicated on who can exploit Indigenous lands and peoples the most.

This exploitation takes many different forms, in pursuit of a variety of different economic goals. For example, in North America, where I live, work, and research, there is scholarship that attends to the burgeoning petroleum industry and the way that it operates through the theft and pollution of Indigenous lands, as well as its accompanying effects on Indigenous bodies, alongside broader conversation about the ways that environmental injustice far too often breaks down along racialised lines, with the greatest effect on marginalised peoples (which includes Indigenous peoples and communities) (Preston 2013, 2017; Shadaan and Murphy 2020). Similar work focuses on contexts such as occupied Palestine (Jaber 2019). The implications from this scholarship are painfully clear—settler colonial development and articulation of settler colonial society are intrinsically tied with exploitation of Indigenous land and environment, a conclusion that grimly exists in lockstep with Englert's thoughts on the topic.

This must also be tied together with questions of resource extraction and resource contestation in broader global contexts. The work of Julie Klinger provides an important bridge by which we can turn these conversations toward exploitation in outer space. In particular, Klinger speaks on the ways in which the pursuit of rare-earth minerals, which has run rampant in a variety of terrestrial environments on Earth, now begins to look toward places beyond the Earth for new venues of exploitation, such as the Moon (Klinger 2015, 2017). In particular, Klinger invokes the concept of the frontier as being key to understanding why it is that we are eager to conduct mining on places like the Moon—the idea that rare-earth minerals are rare on Earth and therefore we must go to the Moon to mine them, while false, according to Klinger, can invoke strong emotions related to discovery and geopolitical rivalry, creating yet another "frontier" that must be discovered, conquered, and made use of by geopolitical competitions (Klinger 2017). Of course, the nature of space exploration as being intrinsically tied into questions of maintenance of empire/hegemony both on Earth and in extraterrestrial space makes sense, given the historical and contemporaneous role of this pursuit in the development of national pride and scientific superiority (Dunnett et al. 2019; Smiles 2020; Treviño 2020).

Conversations such as those had by scholars such as Klinger about the ethics of resource extraction in outer/uninhabited space are just one side of the coin, unfortunately. In recent decades (and even more frequently in recent years), there has been another scholarship that has presented resource extraction in outer space as something that not only is possible but can be presented ethically. Some works have approached this topic from legal frameworks, seeking to define what rights nations have in the exploitation of resources in "uninhabited" environments such as Antarctica, the ocean floor, and outer space, or whether wealthier, more powerful countries should share these resources with smaller, geopolitically "weaker" countries (Frakes 2003; Tennen 2010). Other articles muse on the ambiguity of law related to potential resource extraction in space, stating that clarity is needed, if only to ensure that humankind's engagement with the "frontier" of space can proceed unimpeded (Johnson 2011). These articles present the rapid scarcity of resources on Earth and the need to explore new spaces, such as extraterrestrial space, as a fait accompli (an argument that scholars such as Klinger poke holes in). Recent discoveries such as the existence of water on broader areas of the Moon than previously discovered (Wasser 2020) or of large quantities of gold inside a large asteroid, sixteen Psyche—large enough, says Smith (2019), for each person on Earth to get US$93 million from a hypothetical sale of all of it—show the growing public consciousness about resources in outer space, and the inevitability of the extraction and use of said resources. Smith (2019) writes not on the ethics of mining such an asteroid but rather on the economic impact of such a large quantity of gold hitting the market: the mining of asteroids like sixteen Psyche is seen as a done deal. Rather distressingly from an Earthbound perspective, Smith gives examples such as Spanish mining of gold in colonial Latin America or British/South African diamond mining, focusing on the economic impact of these activities versus the brutal human impact these activities brought about. But, this rationalisation isn't just couched in raw extractive logic. Questions about resource extraction centre around whether or not it can be done *ethically*, and the mechanisms through which that might be achieved (such as environmental impact assessments), not whether or not we should be doing it at all (Dallas et al. 2020; Dallas et al. 2021).

The marriage of economics and space exploration is coming together in other ways as well. Billionaires such as Jeff Bezos and Elon Musk have also turned their gaze towards the stars as a potential setting for humanity's future. Citing anthropogenic and socioeconomic factors, these tech moguls point towards a future in outer-space colonisation as a cure for these issues. "It's time to go back to the moon, this time to stay", said Bezos at the 2019 unveiling of a lunar lander that his company Blue Origin designed, going on to say that he believed heavy/extractive industries could be successfully carried out in extraterrestrial colonies, sparing the Earth from further anthropogenic change (Youn and Theodorou 2019). Bezos's trip to the edge of space in 2021 represents another step in his eventual goal of bringing humanity en masse into outer space to live and work (Bender 2021). While Bezos's vision focuses on the Moon and in potential self-contained colonies in space, dubbed O'Neill colonies, Musk has set his sights even further afield—Mars (Powell 2019; Hamilton 2021). Musk's company, SpaceX, minces no words when describing the potential for colonisation of Mars:

> At an average distance of 140 million miles, Mars is one of Earth's closest habitable neighbors. Mars is about half again as far from the Sun as Earth is, so it still has decent sunlight. It is a little cold, but we can warm it up. Its atmosphere is primarily CO2 [sic] with some nitrogen and argon and a few other trace elements, which means that we can grow plants on Mars just by compressing the atmosphere. Gravity on Mars is about 38% of that of Earth, so you would be able to lift heavy things and bound around. Furthermore, the day is remarkably close to that of Earth.
>
> *(SpaceX 2021)*

Of course, in the meantime, these men (alongside other tech moguls such as Richard Branson) are testing the technologies they believe will bring humanity beyond Earth via short-term flights/voyages (Ascott 2021; Bender 2021).

Compared to Earth, where questions of colonisation and exploration have become mired in ethical questions and conversations surrounding power and privilege, space presents an easy way to think about expansion and growth in a way that does not harm anyone. This thinking is not new, of course—the logical line of thought is that if there are no Indigenous peoples living in space to contend with, it makes outer-space exploration, from an ethical standpoint, not only possible but desirable. This logic underpinned the works of physicists such as Gerald K. O'Neill—a direct source of inspiration to Jeff Bezos in particular (Bender 2021)—who stated in 1974: "[W]e can colonize space and do so without robbing or harming anyone and without polluting anything" (O'Neill 1974: 32).

O'Neill continues:

> Space exploration so far, like Antarctic exploration before it, has consisted of short-term scientific expeditions, wholly dependent for survival on supplies brought from home. If, in contrast, we use the matter and energy available in space to colonize and build, we can achieve great productivity of food and material goods. Then, in a time short enough to be useful, the exponential growth of colonies can reach the point at which the colonies can be of great benefit to the entire human race.
>
> *(O'Neill 1974: 32)*

With reasoning such as this, colonisation of outer space takes on an altruistic tone. Men like Bezos and Musk appear at first glance to be motivated by a desire to ensure humanity has a future—Musk stated in 2020, "If there's something terrible that happens on Earth, either made by humans or natural, we want to have, like, life insurance for life as a whole" (Wattles 2020). The acceleration of anthropogenic climate and environmental change on Earth makes the situation more dire—according to Rebecca Lindsay and Luann Dahlman of NOAA (2021), our planet's temperature has risen by nearly 0.1°C since the late nineteenth century, and when viewed over the last forty years, that rise in temperature has more than doubled. But other individuals have pointed out that there is far more than meets the eye as far as these billionaires' desire to explore outer space. Some have pointed out the inherent danger in attempting to colonise places like Mars, given the environmental, logistical, and technological challenges that would be present, such as lack of atmosphere, exposure to space-bound radiation, and the outright lack of technology to even attempt to do things like terraform Mars (Hamilton 2021; Stirone 2021). Other critiques revolve around the lack of democracy that would exist in an extraterrestrial economy, or around the fact that even if there ended up being no resources to extract on a place like Mars, colonies would inherently become a money-making enterprise for men like Musk via tourism and other means (Stirone 2018; Wattles 2020).

These critiques, alongside the broader narratives and motivations that drive men like Bezos and Musk to push for colonisation in space, are in line with the thinking of Englert (2020)—it is spatial colonisation with land and resources in mind, and therefore, it is settler colonialism. Even if there are no Indigenous peoples to be found on planets such as Mars, it is already clear that settler colonial logics do not require the displacement of Indigenous peoples to function—in fact, it is desirable if they do not (Smiles 2020). The potential for prestige, both economically and socially, still exists in extraterrestrial space and allows its champions to ignore their own roles in anthropogenic change here on Earth (Abbruzzese 2019). But, in the face of apocalypse, is this form of engagement with space an inevitability?

Such a conclusion would suggest that the futures being presented by figures like Bezos and Musk are the only potential futures that are available to us. However, I argue that there exists a broader contestation over the potential futures of humanity in outer space, as well as different conceptions of what engagement might look like for humans and the environment alike. Returning to my opening vignette of what Anishinaabe engagements with outer space might look like, I now turn to the contemporary actions and viewpoints that Anishinaabe people express related to the stars.

Anishinaabe Ontologies of Environments and (Extraterrestrial) Space

Scholars such as Kyle Powys Whyte (2017, 2018) would respond to a presumed inevitability of colonial, extractive, and potentially apocalyptic futures for humanity with the answer that for Indigenous peoples, the apocalypse has already come and gone, and that Indigenous peoples are still here and are thriving in spite of the apocalypses that they have endured. While this chapter is not focused on how we can effectively combat climate crisis (an entire collection of books would be needed just to scratch the surface), I do want to use Whyte's work to make a key argument as to how we engage with outer space—that we do not need to replicate logics of capitalism and colonialism in outer space as we have created these logics here on Earth, and that systems of accountability and relation to land here on Earth can be applied to the stars.

Part of this comes from our own Anishinaabe creation story, which is something with which I begin every class or guest lecture that focuses on the environment. Our origin story, the creation of what we call Turtle Island, while too long to recount here, teaches the very important lesson that in our worldview, every part of the environment is interconnected. The animals who banded together to help create a new world out of the waters that inundated the old one were able to do so once they realised that they were stronger together than when they tried to do the work on their own. Of particular importance in the version of the story that I tell is that humans are not mentioned. To me, this is because as Anishinaabe, we are the least important part of the environment. This is not to say that we are not important as people but rather that because of the hard work of our more-than-human kin in creating the world we inhabit, we are bound by webs of relations to them and must do our best to protect them. These relations extend to the stars themselves and how we view them as Anishinaabe people. For example, many of the constellations in the night sky hold stories about our animal kin, as well as other culturally important stories and lessons for our people (Lee et al. 2014; Mitchell et al. 2020; Rajala 2020). The Anishinaabe concept of *mino-bimaadiziwin*, or living in a good way also applies to these relations—much as we try to live in a good, positive way with ourselves and one another as Anishinaabe, we also must live in a good way with our more-than-human kin, which includes the ways we engage—or do not engage—with them.

There are a growing number of Anishinaabe and Indigenous community members who are actively endeavouring to pass on this Anishinaabe knowledge of space and the stars to the younger generations. Individuals such as Annette Lee (Lakota), Carl Gawboy (Anishinaabe), Melanie Goodchild (Anishinaabe), and Michael Wassegijig Price (Anishinaabe) have made this knowledge available via a variety of means, such as star maps, publications, visual art, and even workshops and curricula designed for school-age children, hosted in particular by the Native Skywatchers project (Lee 2012, 2013; Lee, Rock, et al. 2013; Olson 2015; King 2014; "Our Manifest Galaxy" 2019; Gawboy et al. 2020; Lee, Maryboy, et al. 2020; Rajala 2020; Olson n.d.).

These scholars tie astronomical knowledge to the continued vitality of Anishinaabe/Indigenous culture. As Lee and others say: "As with many North American tribes much cultural knowledge, especially cultural astronomy, has been lost. The goal of the Native Skywatchers programming is to build community around the native star knowledge" (Lee, Rock et al. 2013: 153). Relationships between individuals and their environments, in this case, the stars, are central to Indigenous conceptions of space, they argue:

> Astronomy as presented in planetarium shows can be beautiful but ultimately distant with no way for audiences to link what they are viewing to their everyday lives. In contrast, Indigenous astronomy has people at its center. It is about people, relationships and the sky, not just about the sky.
>
> *(Lee, Maryboy et al. 2020: 76)*

This dissemination of Indigenous star knowledge is not limited to the classroom or the art exhibit, however. Indigenous nations have been collaborating with space agencies such as NASA for a long time (Bartels 2019; Bean 2018; Smiles 2020), and Anishinaabe astronomical knowledge has long featured in similar collaborations, in both terrestrial and extraterrestrial contexts. In 2011, Michael Wassegijig Price organised an internship with NASA at Minnesota's White Earth Tribal and Community College that focused on geospatial applications (Price 2011). Part of a broader collaboration between NASA and tribal colleges across the United States, the internship participants learned geospatial skills such as GIS and applied these towards research and work towards stewardship of vital community resources such as wild rice, or as we call it in Ojibwemowin, *manoomin* (Price 2011). Of course, Anishinaabe knowledge can be applied to NASA activities beyond the Earth. Native Skywatchers' pamphlet (Gawboy et al. 2020) entitled "Two-Eyed Seeing: Ojibwe Astronomy & NASA Moon to Mars" brings Anishinaabe terrestrial and extraterrestrial knowledge into conversation with NASA's efforts to return to the Moon as a pedagogical tool, using the concept of "Two-Eyed Seeing", or the bringing together of Indigenous and non-Indigenous perspectives, to provide students with a clearer picture of the ways that these two knowledge systems can collaborate in order to engage with the stars in a whole new way.

Conclusion

In my previous work, I presented Indigenous conceptions of space as a foil to colonial logics of space exploration—an engagement that I still feel can provide a way forward in how we engage with space. However, I want to challenge and expand my own previous thinking on this topic. Previously, I said that contending with Indigenous modes of astronomical knowledge could help the settler state and settler society practice self-reflexivity in the way that it conceptualises control and exploration of terrestrial and extraterrestrial space. It is worth asking why we go to space, not just whether or not it is possible, as well as who benefits from these actions and who is harmed. However, continuing events such as contestations over Earthbound spaces of space exploration such as Mauna Kea, as well as my own anxieties surrounding the role of Indigenous knowledge in the academy, lead me to think that it is not enough to simply acknowledge and pay heed to Indigenous astronomical knowledge when we talk about the future of humanity and our potential existence beyond Earth. Indigenous viewpoints and knowledges cannot be acknowledged simply for the sake of using them without allowing Indigenous peoples and communities active input and to have a stake in the work being done. This form of academic knowledge production trends close to what Indigenous scholars such as Glen Coulthard (2014) describe as politics of recognition, or the allowing of Indigenous sovereignty/power/perspectives/knowledge only as much prominence as is possible without threatening the structures of the settler colonial state/settler society. This represents a particularly extractive and damaging politics of recognition that acts against the words of other Indigenous scholars such as Devon Mihesuah and others (1998), who advocate that when our knowledges are being told, we must always try to make sure that we are the ones who are doing the telling.

What is clear about the work being done by Indigenous peoples such as Lee, Gawboy, Price, and others is that they are producing and promoting astronomical knowledge for Indigenous peoples, by Indigenous peoples. Instead of taking a supporting role or having to rely on Western academia and dominant science to tell these stories, they are doing so themselves, and the benefits flow directly to Indigenous peoples. And these benefits are not those of gaining yet another foothold onto space or beyond Earth, or making possible forms of environmental exploitation, or enriching entrepreneurs who use outer space as a pressure release valve for anthropogenic climate crisis on Earth. Instead, this engagement centres around the desire to preserve relationships between people and the environments around them. Rather than seeking to master extraterrestrial space or make it into something that materially benefits humanity, Anishinaabe astronomical knowledge seeks to educate and to remind us of the obligations that we've had since the creation of our world. Not only this, but it can represent a way to turn back inwards into how we engage with the Earth itself, and perhaps might represent another way forward out of climate crisis.

What might the end goal of all this look like? To return to the story at the beginning of this chapter, I still do not know if we will ever see an Anishinaabe space programme, as wonderful and exciting as it may be. But, if we do, the Anishinaabe thinkers and community members might very well point back to the work of folks such as Lee, Gawboy, and others as having made it possible to bring such a thing from dreams to reality. But, it is also clear that we do not need to replicate what settler society is doing in space exploration and exploitation in order to bring the stars closer to us—we are already doing so, and in fact, bringing the stars into conversation with our worldviews as Anishinaabe can also allow us to continue to make space for the other important participant in this conversation—the Earth itself.

References

Abbruzzese, Jason. 2019. "Amazon Employees Push for Company to 'Be a Climate Leader' to Combat Global Warming." *NBC News*, 11 April 2019. https://www.nbcnews.com/tech/tech-news/amazon-employees-push-company-be-climate-leader-combat-global-warming-n993076.

Ascott, Emma. 2021. "Destination Mars: Elon Musk's Plan to Colonize Space Starts with Test Flight This Month." *Signals*, 18 July 2021. https://www.signalsaz.com/articles/destination-mars-elon-musks-plan-to-colonize-space-starts-with-test-flight-this-month/.

Bartels, Meghan. 2019. "NASA and Navajo Nation Partner in Understanding the Universe." *Space.com*, 26 February 2019. https://www.space.com/nasa-partnership-with-navajo-nation.html.

Bean, Heather. 2018. "A Bridge between Indigenous Knowledge and NASA." *University of Waterloo*, 9 March 2018. https://uwaterloo.ca/stories/global-impact/bridge-between-indigenous-knowledge-nasa.

Bender, Bryan. 2021. "'A Much Grander Human Destiny': For Jeff Bezos, Space Travel Is about More Than Tourism." *Politico*, 20 July 2021. https://www.politico.com/news/2021/07/20/jeff-bezos-space-travel-philosophy-500300.

Cornish, Gabrielle. 2019. "How Imperialism Shaped the Race to the Moon." *Washington Post*, 22 July 2019. https://www.washingtonpost.com/outlook/2019/07/22/how-imperialism-shaped-race-moon/.

Coulthard, Glen Sean. 2014. *Red Skin White Masks: Rejecting the Colonial Politics of Recognition*. Minneapolis: University of Minnesota Press.

Dallas, J. A., S. Raval, J. P. Alvarez Gaitan, S. Saydam, and A. G. Dempster. 2020. "Mining Beyond Earth for Sustainable Development: Will Humanity Benefit from Resource Extraction in Outer Space?" *Acta Astronomica* 167: 181–88. https://doi.org/10.1016/j.actaastro.2019.11.006.

Dallas, J. A., S. Raval, S. Saydam, and A. G. Dempster. 2021. "An Environmental Impact Assessment Framework for Space Resource Extraction." *Space Policy* 57: 1–12. https://doi.org/10.1016/j.spacepol.2021.101441.

Dillon, Grace, and Pedro Neves Marques. 2021. "Taking the Fiction Out of Science Fiction: A Conversation about Indigenous Futurisms." *E-flux Journal* 120. https://www.e-flux.com/journal/120/417043/taking-the-fiction-out-of-science-fiction-a-conversation-about-indigenous-futurisms/.

Dunnett, Oliver, Andrew S. Maclaren, Julie Klinger, K. Maria D. Lane, and Daniel Sage. 2019. "Geographies of Outer Space: Progress and New Opportunities." *Progress in Human Geography* 43 (2): 314–36. https://doi.org/10.1177/0309132517747727.

Englert, Sai. 2020. "Settlers, Workers, and the Logic of Accumulation by Dispossession." *Antipode* 52 (6): 1647–66. https://doi.org/10.1111/anti.12659.

Frakes, Jennifer. 2003. "The Common Heritage of Mankind Principle and the Deep Seabed, Outer Space, and Antarctica: Will Developed and Developing Nations Reach a Compromise?" *Wisconsin International Law Journal* 21 (2): 409–34.

Gawboy, Carl, William Wilson, Jeffery Tibbetts, Jim Knutson-Kolodzne, Annette S. Lee, Lindsey Markwardt, Melissa Peterson, and Genie Turner. 2020. *Two-Eyed Seeing: Ojibwe Astronomy & NASA Moon to Mars*. Native Skywatchers. https://www.nativeskywatchers.com/articles/Booklet-Ojibwe-10-23-20-v9-screen-version.pdf.

Hamilton, Isabel Asher. 2021. "Jeff Bezos and Elon Musk Both Want to Colonize Space. Here Are the 6 Biggest Problems with Their Plans, from Thinning Bones to Toxic Plants on Mars." *Business Insider*, 22 July 2021. https://www.businessinsider.com/gaping-holes-elon-musk-and-jeff-bezos-space-plans-2019-7.

Jaber, D. A. 2019. "Settler Colonialism and Ecocide: Case Study of Al-Khader, Palestine." *Settler Colonial Studies* 9 (1): 135–54. https://doi.org/10.1080/2201473X.2018.1487127.

Johnson, David. 2011. "Limits on the Giant Leap for Mankind: Legal Ambiguities of Extraterrestrial Resource Extraction." *American University International Law Review* 26 (5): 1478–517.

Kahanamoku, Sara, Rosie ʻAnolani Alegado, Aurora Kagawa-Viviani, Katie Leimomi Kamelamela, Brittany Kamai, Lucianne M. Walkowicz, Chanda Prescod-Weinstein, Mithi Alexa de los Reyes, and Hilding Neilson. 2020. *A Native Hawaiian-Led Summary of the Current Impact of Constructing the Thirty Meter Telescope on Maunakea*. 3 January 2020 revision. https://doi.org/10.48550/arXiv.2001.00970.

King, Bob. 2014. "Make Way For The Wintermaker." *Sky & Telescope*, 12 November 2014. https://skyandtelescope.org/astronomy-blogs/make-way-wintermaker11122014bk/.

King, Tiffany Lethabo. 2019. *The Black Shoals: Offshore Formations of Black and Native Studies*. Durham, NC: Duke University Press.

Klinger, Julie. 2015. "A Historical Geography of Rare Earth Elements: From Discovery to the Atomic Age." *The Extractive Industries and Society* 2 (3): 572–80. https://doi.org/10.1016/j.exis.2015.05.006.

Klinger, Julie. 2017. *Rare Earth Frontiers: From Terrestrial Subsoils To Lunar Landscapes*. Ithaca, NY: Cornell University Press.

Lee, Annette S. 2012. "Building Community Around Native Knowledge." *Tribal College: Journal of American Indian Higher Education* 24 (2): 54–55.

Lee, Annette S. 2013. "Native Skywatchers and the Ojibwe Giizhig Anung Masinaaigan—Ojibwe Sky Star Map." *Communicating Science: A National Conference on Science Education and Public Outreach ASP Conference Series* 473.

Lee, Annette S., Nancy C. Maryboy, David Begay, Wilfred Buck, Yasmin Catricheo, Duane Hamacher, Jarita Holbrook, Kaʻiu Kimura, Carola Knockwood, Te Kahuratai Painting, and Milagros Varguez. 2020. "Indigenous Astronomy—Best Practices and Protocols for Including Indigenous Astronomy in the Planetarium Setting." In *Proceedings of the 25th International Planetarium Society Conference, Edmonton, 2020*, edited by Dale W. Smith, 75–83. https://cdn.ymaws.com/www.ips-planetarium.org/resource/resmgr/vcon2020/papers/IPS_2020rev1.pdf.

Lee, Annette S., Jim Rock, William Wilson, and Carl Gawboy. 2013. "The Red Day Star, the Women's Star and Venus: D(L/N)akota, Ojibwe and Other Indigenous Star Knowledge." *The International Journal of Science in Society* 4 (3): 153–66. https://doi.org/10.18848/1836-6236/CGP/v04i03/51398.

Lee, Annette S., William Wilson, Jeffrey Tibbetts, and Carl Gawboy. 2014. *Ojibwe Sky Star Map Constellation Guidebook: An Introduction to Ojibwe Star Knowledge*. Native Skywatchers.

Lindsey, Rebecca, and Luann Dahlmann. 2021. "Climate Change: Global Temperature." *NOAA*, 15 March 2021. Accessed 15 October 2021 at https://www.climate.gov/news-features/understanding-climate/climate-change-global-temperature.

Marshall, Alan. 1995. "Development and Imperialism in Space." *Space Policy* 11 (1): 41–52. https://doi.org/10.1016/0265-9646(95)93233-B.

Mihesuah, Devon, ed. 1998. *Natives and Academics Researching and Writing about American Indians*. Lincoln: University of Nebraska Press.

Mitchell, Audra., Sarah. Wright, Sandie. Suchet-Pearson, Kate. Lloyd, Laklak Burarrwanga, Ritjilili Ganambarr, Merrkiyawuy Ganambarr-Stubbs, Banbapuy Ganambarr, Djawundil. Maymuru. and R. Maymuru. 2020. Dukarr lakarama: Listening to Guwak, Talking Back to Space Colonization. *Political Geography* 81: 102218. https://doi.org/10.1016/j.polgeo.2020.102218.

Olson, Carolyn. *Ojibwe Seven Teachings Star Map and Stories*. University of Minnesota. Accessed 15 October 2021 at https://intersectingart.umn.edu/?lesson/64.

Olson, Dan. 2015. "Sacred Stories Burn Bright on Minnesotan's Ojibwe Star Map." *Minnesota Public Radio*, 18 September 2015. https://www.mprnews.org/story/2015/09/18/gawboy.

O'Neill, Gerald K. 1974. "The Colonization of Space." *Science Today* 27 (9): 32–40. https://doi.org/10.1063/1.3128863.

Powell, Corey S. 2019. "Jeff Bezos Foresees a Trillion People Living in Millions of Space Colonies. Here's What He's Doing to Get the Ball Rolling." *NBC News*, 16 May 2019. https://www.nbcnews.com/mach/science/jeff-bezos-foresees-trillion-people-living-millions-space-colonies-here-ncna1006036.

Prescod-Weinstein, Chanda, Lucianne M. Walkowicz, Sarah Tuttle, Brian Nord, and Hilding R. Neilson. 2020. "Reframing Astronomical Research Through an Anticolonial Lens—for TMT and Beyond." *White Paper*. https://arxiv.org/ftp/arxiv/papers/2001/2001.00674.pdf.

Preston, Jen. 2013. "Neoliberal Settler Colonialism, Canada and the Tar Sands." *Race & Class* 55 (2): 42–59. https://doi.org/10.1177/0306396813497877.

Preston, Jen. 2017. "Racial Extractivism and White Settler Colonialism: An Examination of the Canadian Tar Sands Megaprojects." *Cultural Studies* 31 (2–3): 353–75. https://doi.org/10.1080/09502386.2017.1303432.

Price, Michael Wassegijig. 2011. "White Earth Tribal and Community College Hosts NASA Geospatial Summer Internship." *Anishinaabeg Today* 16 (9): 13.

Rajala, Nikki. 2020. *The Night Sky from an Ojibwe Perspective*. 3 September 2020. Accessed 15 October 2021 at https://nikkirajala.com/2020/09/03/the-night-sky-from-an-ojibwe-perspective/.

Shadaan, Reena, and Michelle Murphy. 2020. "Endocrine-Disrupting Chemicals (EDCs) as Industrial and Settler Colonial Structures: Towards a Decolonial Feminist Approach." *Catalyst: Feminism, Theory, Technoscience* 6 (1): 1–36. https://doi.org/10.28968/cftt.v6i1.32089.

Smiles, Deondre. 2020. "The Settler Logics of (Outer) Space." *Society+Space* (blog), 26 October 2020. https://www.societyandspace.org/articles/the-settler-logics-of-outer-space.

Smith, Noah. 2019. "Giant Asteroid Has Gold Worth $700 Quintillion. But It Won't Make Us Richer." *The Print*, 9 July 2019. https://theprint.in/opinion/giant-asteroid-has-gold-worth-700-quintillion-but-it-wont-make-us-richer/260482/.

SpaceX. "Mars & Beyond." 2021. Accessed 15 October 2021 at https://www.spacex.com/human-spaceflight/mars/.

Stirone, Shannon. 2018. "The 'Escape to Mars' Plan Has a Fatal Flaw." *OneZero*, 14 November 2018. Accessed 15 October 2021 at https://onezero.medium.com/the-escape-to-mars-plan-has-a-fatal-flaw-a26e1b44282.

Stirone, Shannon. 2021. "Mars Is a Hellhole." *The Atlantic*, 27 February 2021. https://www.theatlantic.com/ideas/archive/2021/02/mars-is-no-earth/618133/.

Tennen, Leslie I. 2010. "Towards a New Regime for Exploitation of Outer Space Mineral Resources." *Nebraska Law Review* 88 (4): 794–830.

Treviño, Natalie B. 2020. *The Cosmos Is Not Finished*. PhD Thesis, Theory and Criticism, University of Western Ontario. https://ir.lib.uwo.ca/etd/7567.

Wasser, Molly. 2020. "There's Water on the Moon?" *NASA*, 5 November 2020. Accessed 15 October 2021 at https://moon.nasa.gov/news/155/theres-water-on-the-moon/.

Wattles, Jackie. 2020. "Colonizing Mars Could Be Dangerous and Ridiculously Expensive. Elon Musk Wants to Do It Anyway." *CNN*, 8 September 2020. https://www.cnn.com/2020/09/08/tech/spacex-mars-profit-scn/index.html.

Werth, Karsten. 2004. "A Surrogate for War—The U.S. Space Program in the 1960s." *Amerikastudien/American Studies* 49 (4): 563–87. http://www.jstor.com/stable/41158096.

Whyte, Kyle Powys. 2017. "Our Ancestors' Dystopia Now: Indigenous Conservation and the Anthropocene." In *The Routledge Companion to the Environmental Humanities*, edited by Ursula Heise, Jon Christensen and Michele Niemann, 206–18. London: Routledge.

Whyte, Kyle Powys. 2018. "Indigenous Science (Fiction) for the Anthropocene: Ancestral Dystopias and Fantasies of Climate Change Crises." *Environment and Planning E: Nature and Space* 1 (1–2): 224–42. https://doi.org/10.1177/2514848618777621.

Wolfe, Patrick. 2006. "Settler Colonialism and the Elimination of the Native." *Journal of Genocide Research* 8 (4): 387–409. https://doi.org/10.1080/14623520601056240.

Youn, Soo, and Christine Theodorou. 2019. "Blue Origin, Jeff Bezos Unveils Plans for Space Colonization." *ABC News*, 10 May 2019. https://abcnews.go.com/Business/blue-origin-jeff-bezos-unveils-lunar-lander-mission/story?id=62941981.

Young, M. Jane. 1987. "'Pity the Indians of Outer Space': Native American Views of the Space Program." *Western Folklore* 46 (4): 269–79. https://doi.org/10.2307/1499889.

21
EARTHLESS ASTRONOMY, LANDLESS DATASETS, AND THE MINING OF THE FUTURE

Katheryn M. Detwiler

In early July 2012, I attended a small conference, Research Networks and Cloud Computing for Astronomy and Mining, organised by the Universidad de Chile's Centre for Mathematical Modelling (CMM). The conference focused on two seemingly distinct industrial and scientific domains in northern Chile's Atacama Desert: megascale copper mining and radio astronomical observation. Visits to two sites bookended the conference, both located high in the western slopes of the south-central Andes, in El Loa province in Chile's second northernmost region of Antofagasta. The first site was Chuquicamata, one of the largest open-pit copper mines on the planet. The second, located about two hours east of the mine, on the Llano de Chajnantor (Chajnantor Plateau), near the international border of Chile and Bolivia, was the Atacama Large Millimeter Array (ALMA), one of the most ambitious ground-based astronomical projects in the world.

With a pre-Columbian history of copper mining at the hill of Chukutukut'a Mallku dating to at least AD 550,[1] the massive mine at Chuquicamata was, in 2012, nearly a century old in its industrial incarnation. It was a mine at the "end of its life", in the parlance of the industry. Ore grades were falling and production costs skyrocketing. In 2006, a partial collapse of the mine at Chuquicamata brought nearly 14 million tonnes of rock crashing down, temporarily freezing operations and costing Codelco (Corporación Nacional del Cobre), Chile's state-owned copper mining corporation, approximately US$100 million in production losses. The ALMA observatory, by contrast, was an observatory still in the making, in its final stages of construction nearly a decade after the observatory's "first stone" had been laid in 2003. When ALMA came into full operation in 2013, the US$1.4 billion project of the European Organisation for Astronomical Research in the Southern Hemisphere (ESO, formerly the European Southern Observatory), the US Association of Universities for Research in Astronomy (AURA), and the National Institutes of Natural Sciences (NINS) of Japan, operated in cooperation with Chile, became one of the world's four so-called "next generation" megatelescopes, three of which are located in Chile's Atacama Desert.

At over five thousand metres above sea level on Chajnantor, the ALMA radio telescope is an array of sixty-six one-hundred-tonne radio antennas, spread across some eighteen kilometres of the plateau. ALMA's distributed antennas collect light from the dry, thin atmosphere in wavelengths from the far infrared and radio portion of the electromagnetic spectrum. A supercomputer, also sited on Chajnantor, the ALMA Correlator, synchs the antennas to observe as one, yielding extremely high image-resolution capabilities. Performing up to 17 quadrillion operations per second to stitch the signals from the discrete antennas together, using one hundred 34 million processors, the ALMA Correlator can generate astronomical datasets corresponding to particular

DOI: 10.4324/9781003280507-24

observations at a rate of between one and five terabytes per day. The instrument is designed to be highly automated and "remotely" operated from the observatory's Operation Support Facility more than six thousand feet below. Together, the array and the supercomputer comprise the second-highest-altitude technical facility—and data centre—on the planet, second only to a Chinese cloud campus built in a high-tech area of Lhasa in the Autonomous Zone of Tibet.

"Mining and astronomy have a common cosmic origin as they look back into the history of the planet and the sky, respectively", remarked the then director of the CMM and the co-convener of the cloud computing conference I was attending. The conference brought together a group of experts in the computational aspects of both mining and astronomy, including the ALMA observatory's director of computation, theorists of the semantic web, graduate students in astroinformatics and computational modelling, machine learning experimentalists, and applied mathematics specialists. The conference co-convener was describing the premise of the conference to me as we travelled together from El Loa airport, on the outskirts of the city of Calama—the capital of El Loa province, a regional copper-mining hub, and a medium-sized city of just over one hundred fifty thousand people—to the city centre. The first several days of the conference were to be held at Codelco's northern headquarters.

Codelco is the largest copper-producing company in the world, holding around 11% of the world's copper assets, including the mine at Chuquicamata, located just outside of Calama. Codelco's sixth annual seminar on a "digital approach" to mining was then underway, a high-level international meeting gathering together hundreds of academics, policy experts, leaders of technology start-ups, mining executives, state officials from Chile, Peru, and Mexico, and representatives of international logistics firms like Cisco Systems under the theme of "Building the Mining of the Future".

"These disciplines show interesting overlaps", the CMM director said, continuing to discuss mining and astronomy as our taxi navigated Calama's narrow streets toward Codelco's headquarters, "as they both translate signals from the analogue to the digital world". The increasing accuracy and sophistication of physical measurements and the proliferation of sensor networks in both mines and observatories, he explained, was bringing forth a "data tsunami" in both domains. Both fields, in turn, were increasingly reliant on cutting-edge technologies of data storage, processing, and transmission with high processing power and high-density memory—up to petabyte-scale data storage and archiving capacities. It was these data storage, processing, and transmission technologies, gathered under the metaphor of "the cloud", that were creating new challenges and demands for expertise in astronomy and mining as well as the potential for new traffic between them.

The articulations then emerging between astronomy and mining in the Atacama Desert went beyond possibilities of mutual investment in network infrastructures that might serve both copper mines and astronomical observatories in northern Chile, which are often distant from the main transmission lines of public or private networks, and which require greater network capacities than existing networks tend to offer. Beyond such possible sites of technical interaction and exchange, these discussions also contained germinal, hypothetical, and even tacit connections between astronomy and mining in the Atacama Desert that, in the contemporary, would emerge and extend quite far beyond questions of shared network infrastructures. Large-scale astronomy and mining in the Atacama Desert were converging on a terrain configured by the practices, aspirations, expectations, and ideologies organised under the signs of optimisation and automation—of extraction, on the one hand, and observation, on the other.

This was not merely a symmetrical process of technological transformation unfolding in separate technoscientific domains. Rather, the conversations and connections fostered at the cloud computing conference were meant partly to identify and partly to propose a link between the ever more refined and computationally sophisticated extraction of the Atacama Desert's mineral underground and the precision observation of its sky. The proposition of the mathematicians, astroinformatics experts, modellers, and data scientists at the conference was that astronomy *is* the future, in some sense, of mining and of processes of datafication, automation, precision measurement, and advanced techniques for data storage, processing, and analysis more broadly, estimated to be between five and ten years ahead of the private technology sector (see Lehuedé 2021; also Data Observatory n.d.). Contemporary advances in astronomy are driving advances in cloud computing as much as being driven by them, just as, historically, astronomy was one of the first fields to experience the "avalanche of printed numbers" that gave rise to modern probabilistic and statistical tools and practices (Hacking 1982).

The question emerging was how "innovations" in mining might be enabled, in part, by the automated techniques for observation, planetary-scale computation, data processing, analysis, and management being developed in contemporary astronomy. At a then-formative register, the role of "next-generation" observatories like ALMA as drivers of advances in computational technologies was implied as a possible pathway to optimisation and automation elsewhere. Behind the formulations of "cloud computing for astronomy and mining" and "building the mining of the future" was, implicitly, the question of astronomy's role in building the mining of the future.

Building the Mining of the Future

Codelco's Building the Mining of the Future seminar showcased the use of distributed sensor technologies, machine learning, ubiquitous computing, Big Data, geological modelling facilitated by hypercomputation, and the integration of new, "smart" mining technologies at every level of the global mining industry, from extraction, to production, to the logistics of transport and circulation. From tiny biometric devices to be threaded into miners' work vests to systems that would speed up and routinise the delivery of extracted minerals to shipping ports, these were technologies designed not only to facilitate new mining projects, infrastructures, and processes but also to optimise and automate existing ones.

At the centre of Codelco's seminar was the company's strategy for converting the Chuquicamata copper mine from an open-pit mine to an expanded, underground mine. A costly measure to wring more from depleted earth, the US$5.6 billion Chuquicamata underground expansion unveiled at the Codelco seminar was to be a technical and logistical feat. It would require the construction of hundreds of kilometres of tunnels, ore passes, and ventilation shafts nearly a kilometre underground beneath the existing pit. The mine conversion would allow Codelco to reach what remained of the buried ore and facilitate the extraction of more than 60% of the amount of copper and molybdenum that has been exploited from the mine in the last century. The underground expansion would also be an opportunity to implement Codelco's "digital approach" to mining.

The new underground mine's tunnels would harbour automated conveyer belts to move ore. They would be traversed by autonomous trucks to haul ore. They would be studded with ubiquitous sensor networks to supply continuous streams of data that would inform the control of the mine. Representatives of Codelco and partnered technology firms and startups unveiled biometric devices that would continuously generate data about mine conditions and mine workers, theoretically improving safety and enabling automated decision-making while creating ever more tightly managed and precise movements of both ore and labour. It would make Chuquicamata "remotely" operated and one of the most sensor-laden and data-rich mines in the world. It would automate up to a third of Chuquicamata's workforce, increase productivity by 40%, and extend the life of the mine by thirty years.

Engineers and geologists presented different simulations of the Chuquicamata underground expansion to the conference attendees on a floor-to-ceiling hyperwall. These were supercomputed, crunched from huge amounts of data generated by remote sensing, geoimaging, and geological modelling to detect and visualise the location and density of ore blocks and the most efficient paths for extraction tunnels. On the screen of the hyperwall, the simulations rendered both a past and a future of the inner earth. Past geological processes by which magma flows were twisted into a deep vein of porphyry copper and traces of past industrial excavation were visualised alongside the infrastructures of the future mine, overlaid with modelled extractable units of remaining copper reserves. The cloud—itself a "resource-intensive, extractive technology that converts water and electricity into computational power", as Tung-Hui Hu (2015) has written—would be used not only to observe but also to more efficiently mine the earth.

In 2012, the Chuquicamata copper mine was both at the "end" of its industrial life and on the cusp of a geocomputational, data-rich, and optimised future, in which automation would be deployed to forestall decline, downsize labour, and reduce operating costs. The ALMA observatory, located several hours east of Chuquicamata on the Chajnantor plateau, was an observatory to be "born digital", designed to be one of the most sophisticated and highly automated observatories on the planet, a revolutionary leap in the automation of observation. Like the visual technologies and data practices that enable Codelco to visualise and optimise the subterranean for extraction, ALMA, too, is a powerful instrument for visualising the invisible. As anthropologists Rachel Douglas-Jones, Antonia Walford, and Nick Seaver point out, "new forms of visibility are also new arenas for calculation" (2021: 13).

ALMA's dishes collect light that ranges from 0.32 to 3.6 millimetres in wavelength, corresponding to frequencies between 31 and 1000 GHz. This low-frequency, long-wavelength cosmic radiation is a form of energy emitted by most objects in the universe. It is analogue data unavailable to either optical telescopes or human observers; the longest wavelengths are up to a thousand times longer than visible light. Through this window into the electromagnetic continuum, scientists observe cosmic processes and chemistries otherwise hidden, shrouded by clouds of interstellar dust and gas that block visible light, but through which radio light can pass. In the far infrared and radio portion of the electromagnetic spectrum, astronomers observe processes of planetary, stellar, and galactic formation and pursue studies of astrochemistry, including the formation and distribution of complex, even organic molecules in the universe.

In millimetre and submillimetre light, clouds of dust and gas can be seen to harbour stellar "nurseries" that incubate forming stars. ALMA has imaged "waterfalls" of gas flowing around a young star, indicating the presence of planets in formation, and has determined the orbital motion of a gas cloud circling a supermassive black hole in a galaxy 100 million light years away. Hidden behind clouds of cosmic dust, a team of astronomers identified in ALMA data two spiral galaxies that formed only 800 million years after the birth of the universe, two galaxies at the observable "edge of space and time".

ALMA has been used to detect ice in swirling disks of dust and gas from which planets, asteroids, and other rocky bodies form, and gas jets emanating from distant proto-stars. It has imaged storms on Jupiter and the cold, rocky rings surrounding Uranus. It has been used to detect clouds of vinyl cyanide swirling in the stratosphere of Neptune's moon, Titan, one hundred thirty miles above the methane rains of Titan's troposphere. In cocoons of interstellar dust, harbouring protostars, ALMA has detected abundant traces of methyl chloride, an organohalogen also known as Freon-40—a compound produced on Earth by common biological and industrial processes. It has located in the spectral signatures of light waves 1 quintillion tons of NaCl, ordinary table salt, in the disk surrounding a star fifteen hundred light years away. In its early science phase, spectral lines were detected in ALMA data corresponding to the frequency emitted by the simple sugar glycolaldehyde, a key ingredient in the formation of more complex molecules including RNA. These sugary traces were detected in the gas surrounding a young, sun-like binary star called IRAS 16293-2422, around four hundred light years from Earth.

Though capable of moving undistorted through interstellar dust clouds, the millimetre and submillimetre light waves that ALMA collects are easily absorbed by water in the atmosphere, which is one reason why ALMA was built in Chile's Atacama Desert, high up on the Chajnantor plateau in the Andean puna, the region of the highest altiplanic terraces, at five thousand metres above sea level, beyond nearly half of Earth's protective atmosphere, where the sky is highly transparent to cosmic radiation, and where there is almost zero atmospheric water vapour.

Through the ALMA instrument, radio light is funnelled by the antenna dishes into vacuum-sealed antenna interiors cooled to the cryogenic temperature of 4 kelvins, or −459°F, roughly the temperature of space. Antenna interiors are kept in this cryogenic state to minimise disturbances in the form of heat generated by their own electronic systems. This is close to true zero, where noise is suppressed, "the lowest possible temperature", as I would read in an ALMA educational pamphlet, "at which all molecular and atomic motion is at a minimum".

The telescope can resolve extremely fine measures and detect very weak, distant signals. It can detect the presence even of molecules forming in different regions of space, capable of signal-targeting across light years. Transforming the faint, fragile millimetre and submillimetre light waves through which ALMA observes into computational data requires that ALMA's sixty-six antennas, its electronics, and the ALMA Correlator function with a precision down to a millionth of a millionth of a second. When at full operation, the array observes for some four thousand hours annually, representing a little under half of what would constitute 24/7 operation. Even when not actively observing, ALMA's antennas and electronic systems can never be powered down. A permanent, uninterrupted supply of electricity flows from ALMA's three turbine generators, operated independently from the Chilean grid. ALMA consumes some twenty gigawatt hours of electricity annually and generates some fifty thousand tonnes of CO_2 each year, depending on the mix it employs of diesel fuel and natural gas, the latter provisioned by a pipeline from Chile's southern Bío Bío region.

Materialised as computational datasets, the fragile cosmic signals ALMA gathers from the atmosphere depart the high site of Chajnantor and eventually depart the Atacama, moving through a connectivity infrastructure installed in 2014 to handle high transmission capacities, ALMA's "digital highway". This public–private patchwork runs from an exclusive, high-speed fibre-optic link that travels from the supercomputer on Chajnantor one hundred fifty kilometres west to Calama. From there, the data travel an existing communication network that runs to the coastal port city of Antofagasta. They then enter a national university communications network, the Chilean fibre backbone called REUNA, and from there travel one thousand three hundred kilometres south to Santiago, arriving at ALMA headquarters within a few hours of collection as what are called "dirty maps".

In Santiago, ALMA's data are processed, reduced, or "cleaned" of any stray or distorting atmospheric effects, in an increasingly automated process of removal of traces of temperature flux and wind speed along with other variables or extraneous "noise" in an astronomical dataset. Data are clean when they become a science deliverable, with visualisable science products delivered to the PI of any given observation. The complete ALMA Science Archive (ASA) is stored in the data centre at ALMA's Santiago headquarters. From there, data are copied to ALMA Regional Centres, or ARCs, at ESO's headquarters in Garching bei München, Germany, in Charlottesville, Virginia, and in Mitaka, Japan. These data centres, in turn, are connected to a coordinated network of scientific support nodes equipped with computational facilities in Bologna, Bonn/Cologne, Grenoble, Leiden, Manchester, Ondřejov, Onsala, Lisbon, Taipei, and Daejeon. Data corresponding to any particular observation are, for one year, the intellectual property of the astronomers or research teams who proposed the observation. After that, these data go public, organised into vast databases that are increasingly searchable and available to be "scraped" for new investigations, queries, and data analytic experimentation.

Katheryn M. Detwiler

Figure 21.1 Event Horizon Telescope Collaboration: Supermassive black hole in M87 Galaxy, 2017.

Figure 21.2 Schematic of Chuquicamata block cave mine.
Source: *Mining Magazine,* May 21, 2020.

In 2017, ALMA's array of sixty-six radio antennas was linked with seven other arrays, spread across four continents, to create the Event Horizon Telescope, a synchronised global network of radio telescopes. This created a "virtual" telescope with a diameter the size of the planet and inaugurated the age of "multi-messenger astronomy", by which observations can be performed across multiple, distributed observing infrastructures operating together in real time. It captured the first-ever image of a supermassive black hole, located at the centre of the galaxy known as Messier 87, an elliptical galaxy in the Virgo constellation, 55 million light years from Earth, at the extreme limit of the computable and quantifiable (Figure 21.1).

Like the simulations of Chuquicamata's underground ore reserves, this image of an unimaginably distant supermassive black hole is also predicated on the extraction that sustains contemporary data practices and enables hypercomputation, linking astronomical observatories to extractive landscapes far beyond their specific sites of operation, including in the Atacama Desert (Figure 21.2). This feat of coordination and data collection captures the future-generating qualities of contemporary astronomy's computational technologies and techniques. It also registers its logistical capabilities, that is, the ability to enact planetary-scale infrastructure and coordinate far-flung sites and forms of work, ranging from manufacture to data analytics, to yield an effect of real-time, simultaneous observation. It renders observation as global infrastructural assembly, a logistical dream of interoperability and planetary coordination. It renders the earth itself, even if momentarily, a sensory apparatus (Halpern 2021).

On the Terrain of Contingency and Precision Measurement: "Free" Astronomical Big Data

The planetary-scale channels that coordinate earth-based observation, and which route centrally through Atacama-based observatories like ALMA, are not the only ways by which astronomical data increasingly circulate. They also circulate into sites of data science innovation and experimentation. They do so as a source of highly complex data, as astronomical Big Data, as nonmonetised, nonproprietary, nonsensitive, nonrivalrous datasets—supposedly free of both exploitable ends and ethical implication. Containing valuable traces of hypercontingency—like traces of sugar molecules in distant space—they circulate as "*free*" Big Data, not only highly complex but also politically "superclean", unconstrained by privacy considerations or proprietary claims, upon which, if marshalled, new capacities for data storage, processing, and analysis can be built and upon which new algorithms and data analytical techniques can be developed, tested, and refined.

It was in 2017 at the CMM—the sponsor of the cloud computing conference and a leading lab for applied mathematics for mining—that I glimpsed more concretely a formative conjuncture between the drive toward the optimisation of extraction and astronomy's technologies for automated observation, visualisation, and precision measurement. The CMM data centre, located in the chilled, climate-controlled basement of the Universidad de Chile in the centre of Santiago, was then hosting astronomical data from the Sloan Digital Sky Survey (SDSS) project. This was an astronomical megaproject to create three-dimensional, multicoloured maps of the universe from observatories all over the world. In its fourth phase, this included observations from the southern sky, using data from the Las Campanas observatory, operated by the Carnegie Mellon Institute for Science since 1969, located northeast of the coastal city of La Serena in Chile's Atacama region.

Through astronomical data generated at Atacama-based observatories and hosted on CMM servers, new data processing and storage capacities were being built and tested by CMM scientists and graduate students. New algorithms and analytical techniques were being invented and refined. CMM researchers had recently developed an algorithm that could analyse these Sky Survey data while they were en route from the Atacama to Santiago, travelling in a fibre-optic channel. The algorithm was designed to enable "real-time" astronomy, as they described, in which the algorithm could trigger an alert based on a particular identification in the SDSS data so that observatories around the world could respond, training their telescopes on the relevant region of the sky to follow up on the event or objects detected. Working upon the data almost instantaneously from their source, comparing sets of images to identify the presence of a change, it was an algorithm designed for the automated detection of supernova events.

To detect supernovae, images of a patch of sky are scrutinised for deviation, and the algorithm has a relatively simple problem to solve: does the sky look the same or different in the data over time; does a given star appear dimmer or brighter? This algorithm had also, in a trial phase, been set to work on another problem entirely. It was deployed in one of Codelco's century-old mines to analyse satellite imagery of the vast open pit and detect changes that might predict instability. There, the algorithm was used to detect signs not of an exploding star but of another kind of catastrophic event: slope collapse.

Just as the algorithm would register changes in the brightness emitted by a source in the sky over time, it could register subtle shifts in light and shadow in satellite images of the mine. These shifts would correspond to a changing angle of the ground, evidence of subsidence or instability that might be imperceptible to human observers but which the algorithm could register within degrees of probability and which could, at a certain threshold, trigger an alert to mine management—theoretically preempting disaster. Abstracted to be formally similar kinds of problems, some translatability is achieved between brightness that indicates stellar explosion and shifts in the shadow cast by the angle of a mine's slope that indicates collapsing earth.

Astronomical datasets are rich in both patterns and anomalies, containing, for example, arcs of orbital motion durable over unimaginably long periods and thus predictable over time, as well as signals from rare, contingent cosmic events like supernovae, asteroids, and comets. They can therefore serve as training environments for refining algorithmic techniques, particularly for identifying anomalous, contingent events in time-series data in increasingly automated ways. Hypothetically, the CMM researchers explained, the algorithm for the real-time detection of cosmic events could be applied in other domains as well, used to scan other sorts of visual data for signals predictive of trouble, breakdown, or failure. The algorithm, eventually named ALeRCE, an "early alert" algorithm now in wide usage in astronomy, processed 100 million real-time alerts in the two years after its adoption in the field, including the classification of 40 million images. It has reported more than six thousand supernovae, sixty thousand supermassive black holes, and eight hundred thousand variable stars.

The tools developed from Atacama-generated astronomical Big Data have potential applications not just for the identification of "anomalous" events but for the prediction and the preemption of them. This puts their value on the terrain of real-time detection and automated decision-making, serving aspirations for finer-resolution monitoring to trigger the near real-time management of disruption. This is in order to ensure the smooth functioning of systems and the continuous flow of work, production processes, and distribution circuits, secured through the preemption of accidents, infrastructural failure, work stoppages, and other such "logistical nightmares" (Rossiter 2016).

Monitoring for such contingencies and responding to them in near real-time requires knowledge practices of observation, data collection, measurement, signal-targeting, visualisation, and the detection of error, prospect, or anomaly. These are at the heart of the scientific, computational, epistemological, and political stakes of astronomical data as they move beyond astronomy itself as *astronomical Big Data* and as an experimental substrate for innovations that optimise and automate other processes and practices. Astronomical data are, among other things, materialised cosmic complexity, containing deep patterns and traces of rare, unpredictable events. The cosmic traces they contain are part of what makes them, as anthropologist Antonia Walford (2021) has written of data in a quite different context, a form of potential.

Data Observatory: Toward an Economy of Optimisation

The building of ALMA marked an expansion of an already dense amount of observing infrastructure in the Atacama Desert. The international science consortiums and ALMA project partners of ESO and AURA have predominated in developing and operating observatory installations in the Atacama since the early 1960s, an era in which European, Soviet, and US astronomers' southern hemispheric ambitions, postwar disciplinary currents, Cold War geopolitics, and deepening conflicts over the control of the Atacama's mineral resources, particularly of copper ore, collided in the arid mountains of northern Chile. When ALMA came into full operation in 2013, it joined—just on Chajnantor—Princeton's Atacama Cosmology Telescope, Berkeley's Huan Tran Telescope, and, at the summit, the one-metre mini University of Tokyo Atacama Observatory telescope. The twenty-five-metre Atacama Submillimetre Telescope, a project of Cornell and Caltech, was also then under construction on Chajnantor. At other mountaintop observatories in the Atacama, particularly in Chile's northern Antofagasta, Coquimbo, and Atacama regions, other astronomical infrastructures were also expanding.

At the Las Campanas Observatory in the Atacama region, which has been operated by the Carnegie Mellon Institute for Science since 1969, plans were underway in 2012 for the Giant Magellan Telescope, a US$1 billion dollar US-led project in partnership with Australia, Brazil, and South Korea that would build a telescope with a segmented mirror yielding a total optical surface of twenty-four metres. The construction of the summit facility for the telescope would begin in 2017. ESO's Paranal Observatory, established in 1999 and host to ESO's Very Large Telescope, was expanding to bring the nearby Cerro Armazones into the observatory complex, where in 2014 construction would begin of ESO's Extremely Large Telescope, to boast a primary mirror forty metres in diameter with a light-gathering area more than two hundred times greater than the Hubble Telescope.

In the early 2000s, AURA, which has operated the Cerro Tololo Inter-American Observatory since 1965, expanded its facilities to include the nearby Cerro Pachón, to be the site of the future Vera C. Rubin Observatory. A project of AURA, the US National Science Foundation, and the US Department of Energy, in collaboration with private funders, the Rubin Observatory's telescope will be equipped with a mirror 8.4 metres in diameter that will funnel light to a 3200-megapixel camera, the largest camera on earth. It will conduct a ten-year sky survey called the Legacy Survey of Space and Time (LSST), transforming optical light from some 37 billion cosmic objects into up to forty terabytes of data each night.

The completion of the Rubin Observatory in 2023 will bring to two-thirds the proportion of the world's infrastructure for astronomical data collection concentrated in the Atacama, that is, of the world's astronomical "seeing capacity", with more than US$6 billion invested. The quantity of astronomical data generated in the Atacama is to grow to an anticipated sixteen and a half petabytes of astronomical data per year by 2022, according to Chile's Ministry of the Economy, compared, for example, to fifteen petabytes of data per year by 2022 for the megaplatform YouTube (Data Observatory 2019; see Lehuedé 2021). The Rubin Observatory alone will deliver an estimated five-hundred-petabyte set of images and additional data products over a decade, generating the largest non-proprietary computational dataset in history.

In January 2020, a summit took place at the ALMA array. It brought together representatives from Chile's elite private business school, the Universidad Adolfo Ibáñez; the Chilean state Ministry of Science, Technology, Knowledge, and Innovation; the Ministry of Economy, Development, and Tourism; and representatives of Amazon Web Services. Amazon is the world's biggest provider of data storage and processing infrastructure, controlling 33% of the world's cloud industry. Standing for a photograph at the feet of ALMA's giant radio antennas, this group gathered to mark the one-year anniversary of the creation of a so-called Data Observatory.

The Data Observatory project is to build a vast "data lake", or repository of large-object, unstructured data, to be hosted by Amazon Web Services and stocked, initially, with Atacama-generated astronomical datasets, starting with data from the ALMA radio array. This "lake" of digitised desert light is designed to store data not only from the powerful ALMA observatory but hypothetically from *all* the telescopes in northern Chile. The Data Observatory, as Amazon's press release regarding the partnership stated when it was announced in early 2019, aims to "consolidate, analyze in real-time, and archive astronomy data streams from all wavelengths across all Chilean observatories in the Atacama Desert" (AWS Public Sector Blog Team 2019).

For Amazon Web Services, for whom the data will be encrypted, the Data Observatory gives the corporation further footing in the Latin American cloud services market; the project is part of Amazon's "long-term commitment" to promoting the "power of cloud computing services in order to foster IT modernisation, innovation, and workforce development" in Latin America (ibid.). For the Chilean state, the Data Observatory is part of a push to diversify the national economy away from its dependency on raw-resource extraction and to build a "knowledge and innovation" economy—and become Latin America's AI leader.

Just as ALMA data is only the initial source of "free" astronomical data for the Data Observatory, "free" astronomical data is only the initial substrate for building a massive repository eventually to include other sorts of "non-sensitive" data. Astronomy is a "capacity generator and market maker", a document summarising the aims of the Data Observatory states, and the Data Observatory is envisioned as a "neutral broker organization" that will enable transference between "data-centric fields (beginning with astronomy) and the IT industry, to foster the digital economy of the Latin American region". "As such", this document goes on, "the Data Observatory will not only provide and train the most capable human capital in data science, but it will also contribute to generating the markets of the future" (Data Observatory 2019).

At the confluence of prominent state and corporate discourses of data-driven economic development, data science, technology, artificial intelligence, machine learning, and global logistics, the data generated in Atacama-based observatories are potentialised as a source of nonmonetised, freely available Big Data through which to construct a new, data-driven vision of the Chilean economy. This positions astronomical Big Data as a driver *away* from an economy of industrial raw-resource extraction—based on mining as well as plantation forestry, industrial agriculture, and aquaculture—to a new mode of economy, one of optimisation, and toward what anthropologist Sebastián Lehuedé has described as an astronomical data-driven vision of Chile's "allegedly post-extractive future" (2021: 64).

At the ALMA summit, Carlos Jerez, acting CEO for the Data Observatory, described Chilean astronomical data as a form of "global value" that can and should be instrumentalised toward solutions in Chile's public and private sectors. "Astronomy is an ideal training field for Chile given the characteristics of the data generated by the observation of the skies", he said, "in terms of volume, quality, speed and diversity of this data. But we must focus these mechanisms on Earth to contribute to solutions that address problems such as global warming and water shortage" (ALMA Observatory 2020). It is not only that the scale and complexity of astronomical datasets render them valuable for "capacity building"—for constructing the infrastructures and technical expertise required for a national Big Data platform—but also the specific qualities of astronomical data that render them valuable training environments for algorithmic anomaly detection. As journalist Cassandra Garrison described for Reuters, "the particular tools developed for the astrodata project could be applicable for a wide variety of other uses, such as tracking potential shop-lifters, fare-evaders on public transport and endangered animals" (2018).

Echoing Codelco's vision of the "mining of the future", in which automation extends and intensifies extraction in part by refining existing methods for mitigating worker resistance and material recalcitrance, here astronomical datasets are envisioned as instrumentalisable for automating older logics of governance and techniques for surveilling "anomaly". In an optimisation economy, extractive modes, logics, and practices are *optimised*, not displaced.

Light Extraction: Automating Observation, Constructing Landless Datasets

As astronomical Big Data circulate as a "free" and politically "clean" resource for reimagining one particular future of the Chilean economy, they are explicitly placed within the Atacama Desert's history of mineral extraction (Lehuedé 2021: 124). They are positioned within a history of the exploitation of bird guano, nitrate fertiliser, copper ore, and lithium carbonate, as if atop an evolutionary sequence that moves from rudimentary, labour-intensive, dirty, and destructive modes of industrial extraction, with attendant forms of social, political, and environmental conflict, and toward more "advanced", light, less destructive, weightless, natural, and uncontested modes of extraction.

Astronomical data are positioned atop this progressive, evolutionary chain as light itself, while, as critical scholars from a wide range of disciplinary locations have extensively documented, computational media and cloud technologies are fundamentally "of the earth", made of "rocks and lithium brine and crude oil" (Crawford 2022: 31). Lithium carbonate, like astronomical Big Data, is entwined in this evolutionary sequence, currently bound up in this powerful, ideological story of "light" extraction. Lithium is the lightest metal and lightest solid element in the solar system. It formed, after helium and hydrogen, within an estimated three minutes of the Big Bang. The soft, highly reactive alkaline metal is valued for its very instability…" commodified as electromobility, and used to manufacture the ultralight metallic batteries that power electric cars, networked sensors, and electronic and computational devices—the future, supposedly, of data, optimisation, technology, and energy. Neither lithium nor astronomical data are, of course, weightless, nor their extraction uncontested or uncontestable.

The entrance gate to ALMA territory is sited at the edge of the 100-million-year-old basin of the Salar de Atacama, forming part of the ancestral territory of the Indigenous Likanantay people. The vast salt flat is hemmed in by the salt ridges, dunes, and geological formations of the

Cordillera de la Sal to the west, the Domeyko mountain range across the salt flat to the south, and the Andes to the north. Water draining from the western slopes of the Andes collects in the basin and percolates into underground aquifers of hypersaline brine, containing high saturations of sodium chloride, bromides, potassium, boron, magnesium, and some 27% of the planet's lithium reserves.

Deep in the Salar de Atacama are mines operated by the US Albemarle Corporation and Chile's Sociedad Química y Minera (SQM or Soquimich), two of the top lithium producers in the world. There, some of the largest lithium mines on the planet pump hypersaline brine from the salt flat's subsurface into enormous pools from which lithium is precipitated out and "harvested" for the global battery industry—a process that requires an estimated 2 million litres of water to yield one ton of lithium.

Hundreds of individual wells pump brine from the desert subsurface through thousands of kilometres of piping into purpose-built evaporation pools, covering thousands of acres of salar. The pools' walls are constructed from the salt surface—the desert recruited as infrastructure—while sunlight is used to precipitate substances out, the sky enrolled as a productive force and the means of extraction itself. Naturalising extraction as a capacity of the Earth itself, the salar and the sun form, as a manager at Soquimich put it to me, a "perfect reactor". Evaporation yields potassium chloride, potassium sulphate, boric acid, and magnesium chloride, salts used as fertiliser, for a variety of industrial processes, and as mediums of photovoltaic energy storage. Lithium is the final precipitate, harvested after fifteen months of evaporation.[2]

The mines are in constant motion. Rains and snowmelt from the high Andes leech salts into the salar; brines pool and percolate in subterranean channels; pumping creates depressions, new flows, and shifting concentrations of salts. A wide range of temporalities surface: the tectonic shifts of the Nazca and South American plates, which raised the Andes and initiated the compression of the salar 100 million years ago; the pace of evaporation; the pace of rapidly changing specs for custom blends in the battery and electronics industry; and the modelling of salar futures, which creates forms of speculation, prediction, and regulation that shape investments and production decisions in the present. Hyperdynamic, they are "living mines".

The sampling of wells and pools generates large amounts of data that feed both hydrogeological models and near- and long-term projections of brine compositions. Risk modelling anticipates hyperconcentrations of minerals that can slow down pumping, while weather monitoring seeks to anticipate and account for the contingent disruptions of brine-diluting rain or cloud cover that dims the sun, weakening its evaporative power. As flows of brine and flows of data become interactive at this living mine, it is managed as a "smart mine". The proprietary custom blends of different battery clients demand that the composition of each pool and each harvest of lithium is monitored and known to molecular, *ionic* specificity, a form of precision measurement and purification that rivals—and mirrors—that of the ALMA instrument overlooking the Salar de Atacama from thousands of metres above.

Chajnantor was designated as the site for the ALMA array in 2003, after nearly a decade of site testing across northern Chile by ALMA project partners. In 2004, land for the ALMA observatory was secured as a fifty-year cession from the Chilean state. Following a precedent established by a 1963 international treaty between Chile and ESO, this established Chajnantor and surrounding land as a scientific territory with many of the exemptions and immunities granted to a diplomatic embassy, free of legal process and execution and exempt from both import duties and direct taxation of income and property.

Shaped as non-Chilean, nonsovereign spaces of international science, these observatories function somewhat like what architectural critic Keller Easterling has called "spatial products", designed to propagate uninhibited flows and to be jurisdictionally ambiguous worlds unto themselves, "self-reflexive" and free from the "political inconveniences of location" (2005: 1).

Extending this territorial-juridical mechanism for controlling for worldly noise, ALMA secured a further cession from the Chilean Ministry for Radio and Telecommunications, which granted the observatory exclusive occupation of certain transmission bandwidths, limiting those that could be used in and around observatory territory. This created a protected zone of "radio quiet" extending over a 120-kilometre radius around Chajnantor.

Legally, territorially, and technically exceptionalised from both below and above, at the outset of the process through which Chajnantor was transformed into the operational world of the ALMA observatory, ALMA's project partners and those of ALMA's experimental forerunner, the Atacama Pathfinder Experiment (APEX), sought assurances from the Chilean military that ALMA territory was stabilised in an even more fundamental way: that it had been cleared of unexploded munitions left behind by Augusto Pinochet (Nyman 2019).

In 1979, Pinochet, who by then had ruled Chile as leader of a military junta for six years, laid landmines in quantities ranging in estimate from 200,000 to 500,000 to 1 million along Chile's northern border. Bolivia had severed diplomatic relations with Chile the year before and, additionally, had bitterly contested some of Chile's territorial claims since Chile's annexation of the Atacama and Tarapacá Deserts from Bolivia and Peru at the conclusion of the conflict known in Chile as the War of the Pacific, or the Saltpeter War (1879–1884). Pinochet sought to militarise the borders, believing that Bolivia would take the opportunity presented by a dispute between Chile and Argentina over a group of islands in the Beagle Channel to encroach upon Chile's territorial boundaries.

Many of these antipersonnel mines have been recovered and removed, while others loosed from the supposedly fixed time and space of the militarised border of the Pinochet dictatorship have shifted, travelled, and settled again. Occasional rainstorms and flash floods, along with regular mountain ice melt, can dislodge these mines, sending them sliding down the slopes of the Andes mountains to accumulate in dry riverbeds in the valleys below. With assurances that what would become ALMA observatory territory was clear of this most literal source of disruption and these most literal expressions of the state's territorial power, the construction of the ALMA observatory began.

The reorganisation of the Chajnantor plateau as the site of the revolutionary ALMA array required a decade of construction that involved spatial, territorial, juridical, material, categorical, infrastructural, and epistemological work. This was not only a process of massive-scale construction and political-territorial reconstitution but also one of material-semiotic transformation.

The access road to ALMA begins in the basin of the Salar de Atacama and then ascends through six distinct ecological zones to the Array Operation Site, located at 5400 metres in altitude on Chajnantor. With little vegetation besides lichens, the high puna zone, composed of the highest altiplano terraces of the Andean highlands, is marked by a few lakes and salars, surrounded by marshy grounds visited occasionally by vicuñas, rheas, foxes, pumas, flamingos, Andean geese, and crested ducks. Twenty-eight kilometres from the ALMA Operation Support Facility (OSF), the main hub of scientific activity from where the telescope above is "remotely" operated, Chajnantor affords vast views of the Salar de Atacama, the salt ridges, sand dunes, and geological formations of the Cordillera de la Sal, the Domeyko mountain range across the salt flat, and the Andean high peaks, the stratovolcanoes rising on either side of Chajnantor.

These are volcanoes, some conical and topped with crater lakes, some dormant, some active, but they are also *cabures* or *mallkus*, tutelary mountains or "earth beings" (de la Cadena 2015).[3]

In its construction and ongoing operation, ALMA negotiates Chajnantor as a place already enmeshed in an Andean "ecology of practices" (Stengers 2005; de la Cadena 2015). It articulates with a parallel and enmeshed world not organised by the extractive view's privileging of transparency, in which these mountains are not only mountains, are more than nature, and exceed the category of environment.

Likancabur rises to five thousand eight hundred metres, "the mountain of the people", central actor in regional Likantantay kinship networks, son of Laskar, brother of Jurikes, "the headless one", decapitated by a lightning bolt thrown by Likancabur's lover, Kimal, a water mountain exiled by Laskar to the Domeyko range across the salt flat, the lithium-rich salt itself a dried lake of the lovers' tears. They are among the broadly earthen and geological things in the Salar de Atacama, including hills and mountains (*cabures* or *mallkus*), stars, lightning, springs, the elements, and animals, that are "conveyed", as anthropologist Manuel Tironi (2020) puts it, as *"abuelos*, ancestors with spiritual and affective trajectories".

In this socioecological construction of Andean mountain cosmologies, Chajnantor is also Thaknatur. Translated from the traditional Kunza language of Likanantay collectives, Thaknatur is "the place of departure", "the place of flight", or "the place of reconciliation". It is a place already infrastructurally observational, already cosmological, and, critically, thoroughly cosmo-*geological* (Tironi 2020), where a "non-anthropocentric balance between the ground, the sky, and the human" makes both the geological and the cosmological partially available, not absent or withdrawn but "ethically present" (ibid.)

In 2002, just one year before ALMA selected Chajnantor/Thaknatur as the site of its revolutionary antenna array and just two years before it secured its territory as a concession from the Chilean state, controversy erupted over the installation of a radio antenna on the summit of Kimal, visible directly across from the plateau at the far side of the Salar de Atacama in the Domeyko range. The antenna was installed to facilitate communications at Codelco's Gaby mine. As anthropologist Anita Carrasco Moraga (2010) has detailed, Kimal and Likanantay representatives managed to assert political presence for the mountain *as* Kimal rather than in a subdued form of "nature" or "environment", successfully suing for the removal of the antenna on ontological grounds.

This regional precedent for the potential of parallel and enmeshed cosmogeologies to erupt on and against extractivist territory and to disturb the categorical assertions that sustain extraction—in which kinship claims are undercut such that "nature" is rendered passive, separate, and alienable—represents a potential disturbance to ALMA's operations and the operation of the array of radio antennas on Chajnantor. ALMA manages this disruptive potential, in part, through a parallel knowledge project and institutional investment in re-narrating its relationship to place.

A 2007 ALMA-sponsored regional "ethnoastronomy" project, led by Likanantay anthropologists, exemplifies how points of alignment are drawn between Andean cosmology and ALMA's radio astronomy with the effect of quieting political questions of ontology and territory. The text draws a connection between Thaknatur as "the place of departure" and the ALMA array as a revolutionary "departure" for radio astronomical observation. Working by analogy, "the place of departure" becomes a way in which ALMA asserts its continuity with place and rationalises its own emplacement on Chajnantor/Thaknatur. This commensurate framing becomes the ground for further cosmological translations:

> Unlike the Greek cosmovision and that of the western world, in which stars are grouped to form constellations, in the Andean cosmovision constellations are distinguished in the dark areas of the sky. These areas of the sky emit a light that is imperceptible to our eyes but becomes visible when we observe it with the ALMA antennas. Scrutinizing the secrets of that cold universe, where stars and planets are born, is the observatory's mission.
>
> *(ESO 2013)*

The constellations that are most prominent in the Andean world are the dark shapes that emerge in the bright band of the Milky Way, the hazy glow of light formed from a disk of billions of stars, all spiralling around the black hole at the centre of our galaxy, a luminous band given texture and dimensionality by massive interstellar formations of gas and dust. These dark constellations block starlight but allow radio and infrared light—that light which is observed by ALMA—to pass.

One of these fields of dust and gas that intercedes between the earth and the bright band of the Milky Way in the sky, as is detailed in the ethnoastronomy research, forms the llama constellation Yakana, which travels through a river of stars, the continuation of all rivers on Earth. Yakana grows darker and darker as it walks across the sky, eventually coming, every night, to the horizon, where it stops to drink all the water from the seas and streams of the Earth in order to prevent the world from drowning. It leaves behind wool that, if encountered by a person, transmits *kana* (soul) to them and, if they have llamas, ensures the proliferation of their herd (ESO 2013; see ALMA Kids n.d.).[4] The Magellanic Clouds—two dwarf galaxies visible in the southern night sky—form Yakana's wallowing grounds (ESO 2013).

The ethnoastronomy project was a gesture of recognition and inclusion, but such translations are also a way for ALMA to implicitly manage the territorial, political, ethical, and relational world of Thaknatur. ALMA's investment in the production of Likanantay "ethnoastronomy" as continuous with radio astronomy serves as a way to accrue legitimacy through multicultural respect while also leveraging that claim to garner consensus—if not innocence—to the complexity of its spectral and territorial occupation. It preempts other analogies that might be made drawn between ALMA and other regional extractive presences. Among the many political, technical, historical, territorial, and expert ways that ALMA's highly pure astronomical data are rendered "free" and "clean" are such unstable and partial acts of ontological reckoning and cosmological translation.

While Chajnantor and Thaknatur, radio astronomy and Andean cosmology, and interstellar dust clouds and constellations like Yakana may share, in Marilyn Strathern's terms, "partial connections" (2004), they do necessarily not refer to the same thing. Nor are they necessarily contradictory or mutually distinct, but they are, as Marisol de la Cadena (2015), following Isabelle Stengers (2005), might term them, divergent or "self-different".[5] The translation of Thaknatur as a site principally for the astronomical observation of the *sky* involves the partial un-earthing of Thaknatur. The effect of this commensuration is not one of Thaknatur's placelessness, erasure, or emptiness per se, but of a vision of cosmology as separate from cosmogeology. Moreover, *both* radio astronomy and Likanantay cosmology are abstracted to appear as something they are not: *Earthless*. It is an orientation that yields "seemingly landless datasets", as Indigenous science studies scholar Max Liboiron puts it in another context—datasets that circulate as if "free" and unmoored from social, political, ethical, and ecological life (2021:876)."

A year after ALMA's opening, its operations were brought to a halt by a labour strike and the occupation of the observatory by the union of ALMA workers against the Associated Universities, Inc. (AUI), the US nonprofit corporation in charge of operations at ALMA. In this strike, 195 striking workers occupied the observatory for seventeen days. They blocked the observatory entrance and demanded the right to unionise and to conduct contract negotiations with AUI.

The demands made by the union of ALMA workers included an across-the-board salary increase of 15%, a reduction in the work week from forty-five to forty hours, reflecting a reduction in shifts from twelve to eleven hours, and an hourly bonus for work conducted at the extremely high-altitude Array Operation Site—hazard pay. This emphasised the embodied nature of the work of running one of the world's most sophisticated and supposedly automated observatories. One communiqué from the union of ALMA workers insisted that the telescope not be understood as simply a machine, and that though it strives toward ever more highly automated observation processes, "human beings still work here". Three hundred kilometres to the southwest, workers at the Paranal Observatory (operated by ALMA partner ESO) demonstrated in support of the strike by putting down their radios for the night. They published a statement articulating the problems posed to workers by Atacama-based observatories' extraterritorial jurisdictions, the legal status granted to observatories since the mid-1960s that renders their workers unprotected by Chilean labour laws. During the strike and occupation of the ALMA observatory, the union of ALMA's Chilean workers removed the flags of ALMA's participating member states from the flagpoles that ring the observatory's basecamp control centre, overlooking the Salar de Atacama below. They replaced them with black flags that signal regional opposition to extractive industry and, in particular, to lithium mining.

The strike inverted the assumption of the observatory's "remote operation". It expressed a complex critique of how observatories occupy space in the Atacama Desert and the position of labour within this space of political exceptionality. The ALMA workers' strike not only theorised automation as both mythology and extraction but also conceptualised the observatory as extractive in multiple registers. Implicitly, the black flags raised on ALMA's flagpoles drew a parallel between the ALMA observatory's territoriality in the desert and its extractive relationship to observatory labour and other forms of mining and extraction, including from Indigenous territories and from the Earth.

In 2021, AUI leveraged its logistical and managerial expertise for running large-scale science infrastructures, both around the world and in the Atacama, in order to secure a contract from Chile's Production Development Corporation (Corporación de Fomento de la Producción de *Chile*), CORFO. This was to build and manage a new institute, the Chilean Institute for Clean Technologies, located, like the ALMA observatory, Codelco's Chuquicamata copper mine, and the US Albermarle and Soquimich lithium mines, in Chile's Antofagasta region.

This regional and national development initiative is focused on solar energy, "green" hydrogen, and the "sustainable" mining of copper, lithium, and other minerals, along with the optimisation of mining processes to enhance the value chains of these critical materials. It aims, by 2030, to be a world-class centre of technological expertise. Over the next ten years, it expects an investment of US$265 million, drawing 54% of these contributions from the Soquimich lithium mining corporation and 46% from ALMA's managing corporation, AUI (AUI 2021).

As astronomical Big Data are imagined as a driver toward a post-extractive Chilean economy, the *expansion* of mining—the mining of the future—comes to be routed through the scientific, infrastructural, and logistical expertise of large-scale astronomical observation. The de-sovereigned status and transformation of Chajnantor and the unstable translations of Thaknatur along with the embodied labour of operating one of the world's most "automated" observatories are background conditions of ALMA's functioning by which its astronomical data are produced and circulated as both "free" and "politically clean". They lie behind and anchor the subsequent labours and technical and political manoeuvres of producing clean astronomical data, while also shaping the implications of the subsequent uses of astronomical data as they move within and beyond networks of astronomical expertise. Echoing feminist science studies scholars Helen Pritchard, Jara Rocha, and Femke Snelting's (2020) critique of geological innocence in geocomputation: no astronomy contemplates that doesn't participate. No astronomy is Earthless.

For the ALMA observatory's official opening in 2013, the presence of Likanantay community leaders was requested so that they could conduct a *pago* (payment) ceremony on Chajnantor/Thaknatur (Figure 21.3). *Pago* is a Likanantay practice of reciprocity with the Earth that commonly accompanies ground-breaking and involves offerings of wine and coca leaves, which acknowledges and reproduces communal value and enacts the landscape and its elements as sacred. As distinct from elaborating "ethnoastronomy" as a separate sphere of difference to be made commensurate with radio astronomy's trajectories, categories, and desires, this episode points to a negotiated "cosmopolitics" or the presence of "uncommon nature", in which radio astronomy and Likanantay cosmogeologies could each be translated into some new articulation, each potentially transformed, and in which what *emerged* from ALMA, whether circulating as intellectual property, free Big Data, or cosmological images and models, would be acknowledged as partly constructed from Likanantay territory and knowledges, including of the land itself.[6]

The *pago* ceremony might indeed have referenced ALMA and its occupation of Chajnantor, but it also referenced Thaknatur, and might suggest other ways of thinking about the landedness of computational data—data as connected to land and social worlds—and the stakes of Big Data

Figure 21.3 *Pago* ceremony at the 2013 inauguration of the Atacama Large Millimeter/Submillimeter Array on Chajnantor/Thaknatur. Source: ESO.

vis-à-vis extraction in the Atacama Desert. The opening of ALMA was not the ground-breaking on Chajnantor, but all parties seem to have consented to this stretched equivalency between ground-breaking and opening. Or maybe not. *Pago* is reciprocal exchange with the Earth. It is not, then, necessarily a gift, or blessing, for ALMA. Or not, perhaps, for ALMA as such.

★ ★ ★

Though during the 2013 strike of ALMA workers AUI announced that it had "activated a contingency plan" to continue basic science operations, ensuring that the work of data collection and delivery would be uninterrupted, the ALMA workers won their demand for unionisation and sought and eventually received a contract renegotiation with AUI. The observatory returned to operation. The observatory's science operations were again halted by its workers in solidarity with the massive social protests that engulfed Chile in October 2019, when outrage about the ongoing authority of Pinochet's constitution bloomed at a scale not seen since the formal end of Chile's dictatorship. That year, the Soquimich lithium mine's plan to expand production on the salar was forestalled by a campaign of resistance mounted by Indigenous Likanantay collectives, their legal complaint upheld by a Chilean environmental court.

On 22 March 2020, the ALMA observatory was shuttered by the global COVID-19 pandemic. It would remain closed for more than a year. A team of thirty-five ALMA employees began working to restore ALMA's operations six months after the initial closure, in October 2020. As reported in *Science*, they confronted a wide range of logistical problems (Clery 2021). ALMA's water, power, and sewage systems had suffered minor damage from earthquakes in May and June 2020. Pipes had burst in the gas turbine generators that power the observatory, with its mix of diesel and natural gas, and which keep ALMA's antennas cooled to cryogenic temperatures, minimising noise from their own electronic systems. Each of ALMA's sixty-six antennas, which had been sitting idly, hunkered down in a position called "survivor stow", had to be cleared of layers of dust, which had clogged the bearings by which the dishes swivel into position. On 20 December 2020, the atomic clock that synchronises ALMA's antenna dishes and the ALMA correlator were powered up. By 1 January 2021, the first dish was able to be rotated again.

These quite disparate forms of disruption—worker resistance, mobilisations in solidarity and in defence of the salar, material recalcitrance, and crisis—exceed the automated preemption of disruption. They suggest that there are things that are bigger than planetary computation. There is dust in the engines of optimisation and automation that cannot easily or always be rendered anomalies to be reabsorbed as recursive learning. Logistical dreams are yet haunted by potential disruptions of the sort often consigned to a different mode of historical time—contingency.

Notes

1 In 1899, the mummified remains of a pre-Columbian miner were excavated from the pre-Columbian Chuquicamata copper mine nearly perfectly preserved in copper. The remains were purchased by John Morgan and installed in American Museum of Natural History in New York City. In 1978, radiocarbon dating placed his death at AD 550. For a discussion of Chukutukut'a Mallku as a female hill in a network of scared mountains, in which "the whole mountain chain 'is a provider for Chuquicamata,' in other words, it is the source of the wealth of this gigantic copper mine", see Castro and Aldunate (2003); see also Berenguer, Aldunate del Solar, and Castro (1982).
2 These salts percolate as agencies of renewal for an ailing Earth in what anthropologists Dominic Boyer and Cymene Howe (2020) call the "verdant optimism" that surrounds green capitalist aspirations, masking "hierarchies of access to renewable futures".
3 Elsewhere in the Andes described as *wak'as* (*guacas* or *huacas*), earth beings are entities that are integral to the constitution of the emplaced socionatural collectives of *ayllu* (kinship group). *Ayllus* are "socionatural collectives" at once singular and plural, and the entities that compose them "bring about the *ayllu* even when appearing individually" (de la Cadena 2019). "Nature and humans as such are not absent from *ayllu*", de la Cadena explains, "yet in corporate, extractivist territory, their imperative assertion makes impossible all that exceeds nature and humans and the relation that separates them" de la Cadena 2015: 281.
4 All translations are the author's own.
5 Thus conceptualised, the site where heterogeneous practices connect is also the site of their divergence, their becoming *with* what they are not without becoming what they are not (Stengers 2005, 2011; de la Cadena 2015: 280). The cosmopolitics these thinkers advocate is one that "recognizes and even fosters relations among divergent worlds as a decolonial practice of politics with no other guarantee than the absence of ontological sameness" (p. 281).
6 Chanda Prescod-Weinstein, writing of settler colonial resistance in Hawai'i, observes that a lot of what we know about cosmology and astronomy in general comes from the thirteen telescope facilities that have been built on Maunakea in the last seventy years as well as from facilities built elsewhere, for instance on Haleakalā on Maui. Thus our cosmology is already, in some sense, partly created from kanaka knowledge … One commonality in all of the stories of colonialism's relationship with indigeneity is the disconnection of Indigenous knowledge from its larger cosmology. For kānaka maoli, this includes the land itself, and not just the things in it (2021: 89). See also Casumbal-Salazar (2017).

References

ALMA Kids. n.d. "Atacameño Children Produce a Video on the Yakana Myth." Accessed 22 September 2022. https://kids.alma.cl/atacameno-children-produce-a-video-on-the-yakana-myth.
ALMA Observatory. 2020. "Data Observatory Members Celebrate First Year of Operations with Visit to ALMA." 10 January. https://www.almaobservatory.org/en/announcements/data-observatory-members-celebrate-first-year-of-operations-with-visit-to-alma.
AUI. 2021. "CORFO Selects AUI to Build and Manage the Chilean Institute for Clean Technologies." 5 January. https://aui.edu/corfo-selects-aui-to-build-and-manage-the-chilean-institute-for-clean-technologies/.
AWS Public Sector Blog Team. 2019. "AWS and Chile Launch the Data Observatory Project." AWS Public Sector Blog, 23 April. https://aws.amazon.com/blogs/publicsector/aws-and-chile-launch-the-data-observatory-project.
Berenguer, José, Carlos Aldunate del Solar, and Victoria Castro. 1982. "Orientación Orográfica de Las Chullpas en Likán: La Importancia de Los Cerros en la Fase Toconce." In *Simposio: Culturas Atacameñas, XLIV Congreso Internacional de Americanistas, Manchester, Inglaterra, 1982*, edited by Bente Bitteman von Holleufer, 175–220. Chile: Universidad del Norte.
Boyer, Dominic, and Cymene Howe. 2020. "Verdant Optimism." Dominic Boyer, 29 August. https://www.dominicboyer.org/post/verdant-optimism.
Castro, Victoria, and Carlos Aldunate. 2003. "Sacred Mountains in the Highlands of the South-Central Andes." *Mountain Research and Development* 23 (1): 73–79. https://doi.org/10.1659/0276-4741(2003)023[0073:SMITHO]2.0.CO;2.

Casumbal-Salazar, Iokepa. 2017. "A Fictive Kinship: Making 'Modernity', 'Ancient Hawaiians', and the Telescopes on Mauna Kea." *Native American and Indigenous Studies* 4 (2): 1–30. https://doi.org/10.5749/natiindistudj.4.2.0001.

Clery, Daniel. 2021. "After Long Shutdown, Giant Radio Telescope Array Set to Resume Observations." *Science*, 15 March. https://www.science.org/content/article/after-long-shutdown-giant-radio-telescope-array-set-resume-observations.

Crawford, Kate. 2022. *ATLAS OF AI: Power, Politics, and the Planetary Costs of Artificial Intelligence*. New Haven, CT: Yale University Press.

Data Observatory. n.d. "Historia Del DO." Accessed 10 August 2022. https://www.dataobservatory.net/sobre-do-nivel-superior/historia-del-do/.

Data Observatory. 2019. "Llamado a Propuestas de Valor." Ministerio de Economía, Fomento, y Turismo, Gobierno de Chile.

de la Cadena, Marisol. 2015. *Earth Beings: Ecologies of Practice Across Andean Worlds*. Durham, NC: Duke University Press.

de la Cadena, Marisol. 2019. "Extinction and Biocultural Conservation." Video posted to YouTube by Sydney Environment Institute. https://www.youtube.com/watch?v=ZiHLc_zEIWY.

Douglas-Jones, Rachel, Antonia Walford, and Nick Seaver. 2021. "Introduction: Towards an Anthropology of Data." *Journal of the Royal Anthropological Institute* 27 (S1): 9–25. https://doi.org/10.1111/1467-9655.13477.

Easterling, Keller. 2005. *Enduring Innocence: Global Architecture and Its Political Masquerades*. Cambridge, MA: The MIT Press.

ESO (European Organisation for Astronomical Research in the Southern Hemisphere). 2013. *El Universo de Nuestros Abuelos | The Universe of Our Elders*. Available online: https://www.eso.org/public/products/books/book_0029/.

Garrison, Cassandra. 2018. "Amazon Eyes Chilean Skies as It Seeks to Datamine the Stars." *Reuters*, 4 September. https://www.reuters.com/article/us-amazon-com-chile-telescopes-idUSKCN1LK0Y7.

Hacking, Ian. 1982. "Biopower and the Avalanche of Printed Numbers." *Humanities in Society* 5: 279–95.

Halpern, Orit. 2021. "Planetary Intelligence." In *The Cultural Life of Machine Learning: An Incursion into Critical AI Studies*, edited by Jonathan Roberge and Michael Castelle, 227–56. Cham: Springer International Publishing. https://doi.org/10.1007/978-3-030-56286-1_8.

Hu, Tung-Hui. 2015. *A Prehistory of the Cloud*. Cambridge: The MIT Press.

Lehuedé, Sebastián. 2021. "Governing Data in Modernity/Coloniality: Astronomy Data in the Atacama Desert and the Struggle for Collective Autonomy." PhD thesis, London School of Economics and Political Science (LSE). https://doi.org/10.21953/lse.00004321.

Liboiron, Max. 2021. "Decolonizing Geoscience Requires More than Equity and Inclusion." *Nature Geoscience* 14 (12): 876–77. https://doi.org/10.1038/s41561-021-00861-7.

Mining Magazine. 2020. "Chuquicamata Underground Hits 1Mt." 21 May 2020. https://www.miningmagazine.com/development/news/1387402/chuquicamata-underground-hits-1mt.

Moraga, Anita Carrasco. 2010. "A Sacred Mountain and the Art of 'Impression Management': Analyzing a Mining Company's Encounter with Indigenous Communities in Atacama, Chile." *Mountain Research and Development* 30 (4): 391–97. https://doi.org/10.1659/MRD-JOURNAL-D-09-00065.1.

Nyman, Lars-Åke. 2019. "APEX Safety Plan." Atacama Pathfinder Experiment, 1 June 2019, APEX-APX-PLA-0004. https://www.apex-telescope.org/safety/documents/docs/APEX%20Safety%20Plan%20signed.pdf.

Prescod-Weinstein, Chanda. 2021. *The Disordered Cosmos: A Journey into Dark Matter, Spacetime, and Dreams Deferred*. New York: Bold Type Books.

Pritchard, Helen, Jara Rocha, and Femke Snelting. 2020. "Figurations of Timely Extraction." *Media Theory* 4 (2): 159–88. https://hal.archives-ouvertes.fr/hal-03266402.

Rossiter, Ned. 2016. *Software, Infrastructure, Labor: A Media Theory of Logistical Nightmares*. New York: Routledge.

Stengers, Isabelle. 2005. "Introductory Notes on an Ecology of Practices." *Cultural Studies Review* 11 (1): 183–96. https://doi.org/10.5130/csr.v11i1.3459.

Stengers, Isabelle. 2011. *Cosmopolitics II*. Posthumanities 10. Minneapolis: University of Minnesota Press.

Strathern, Marilyn. 2004. *Partial Connections*. Updated edition. ASAO Special Publications 3. Lanham, MD: AltaMira Press.

Tironi, Manuel. 2020. "Rocks Have History." Theorizing the Contemporary, 22 September. *Journal of Cultural Anthropology*. https://culanth.org/fieldsights/rocks-have-history.

Walford, Antonia. 2021. "Data – Ova – Gene – Data." *Journal of the Royal Anthropological Institute* 27 (S1): 127–41. https://doi.org/10.1111/1467-9655.13484.

22
RECONSTELLATING ASTROENVIRONMENTALISM
Borders, Parks, and Other Cosmic Imaginaries

Alessandra Marino

> Just as none of us is outside or beyond geography, none of us is completely free from the struggle over geography. That struggle ... is not only about soldiers and cannons but also about ideas, about form, about images and imaginings.
>
> *Edward Said*

The New Space age is presenting us with what appears to be a dichotomy. On the one hand, fantasies of leaving our planet in ruins are igniting a 'space rush'. Space entrepreneurs promote space colonisation simultaneously as capitalism's ultimate "spatial fix" (Dickens and Ormrod 2007: 49) and as a response to the environmental catastrophe (Valentine 2012). Terraforming other planets and mining asteroids and other celestial bodies are promoted as ways of harnessing space benefits to secure a future for humanity (Abiodun 2013). On the other hand, and often as a response to the extractivist and colonising discourses of space capitalism, new calls for preserving pristine environments have been voiced by both activists and scholars. For example, organisations like For All Moonkind have vowed to protect human heritage in space, starting with safeguarding those landing sites on the Moon that have come to populate cultural imaginaries of what it looks like to step beyond Earth.

In line with this second trend, astrobiology—the interdisciplinary science that investigates the existence of life beyond Earth and is primarily concerned with planetary protection—has registered renewed interest. Recent articles have asked that the remit of astrobiology be widened beyond backward and forward contamination to engage with anti-imperialism and sustainability in space research and activities (Galli and Losch 2019; Vidaurri et al. 2020). In the context of the space debris crisis and other forms of 'pollution' beyond Earth's atmosphere, the discourse of astroenvironmentalism, with roots in astrobiology, has had a strategic role in directing public attention towards ethical and sustainable uses of outer space environments. Within this context, astroenvironmentalism is often posited as the positive answer to capitalist exploitation on a cosmic scale.

While astroenvironmentalism is often invoked to discuss a wide range of space-related issues, from deep space exploration to the cluttering of orbits (Morin and Richard 2021), it is seldom defined. Linda Billings, science communicator and consultant for NASA's Astrobiology Program, recently referred to it as "a call to preserve pristine extraterrestrial environments for their own sake" (Smith and Mariscal 2019: 246). Her description builds upon astrobiologist Charles Cockell's argument on the recognition of the intrinsic value of an undisturbed extraterrestrial body as an object of study and of microorganisms found on other planets (Cockell 2005). Like Cockell, astrobiologist Christopher McKay has long been interested in environmental ethics and has proposed that the existence of life and biological diversity enriches planetary bodies, making them more valuable than lifeless landscapes such as the Moon or the surface of current Mars (McKay and Marinova 2001). In envisaging governance mechanisms for environmental protection in space, astrobiologists have explicitly theorised the delineation of zones with specific designations for tourism, facilities, and special features (McKay 2021: 115), as well as planetary parks, which are protected areas on other celestial bodies modelled upon earthly heritage sites. But is this encircling of spaces a type of bordering practice that mirrors modes of territorial ordering of settler colonialism and the postcolonial nation-state?

In this chapter, I examine the ethics of thinking ecologically about outer space to probe the limits of astroenvironmentalism in its current scientific formulations. Instead of accepting or rejecting the two logics of appropriation and preservation of space environments as opposite choices, I look at the epistemologies that underpin both positions and reveal unexpected 'common ground'. I maintain that a dialogue between astrobiology and works of postcolonial, decolonial, and critical Indigenous studies urges us to rethink mainstream images and maps of outer space environments, as well as the relationships and practices that bring them into being. For this reason, I start with Edward Said's concept of "imaginative geographies" as a key to unveiling the performative power of scientific theories that construct space as an environment to be experienced, used, and even tamed.

By bringing anticolonial perspectives into dialogue with astrobiology, this chapter has a dual aim. First, it advances debates on the ethics of outer space exploration by presenting a critique that originates within postcolonial geographical and ecological thought. In other words, it contributes to the construction of an anticolonial genealogy for imaginative geographies of outer space. Second, it extends the reach of postcolonial thinking beyond the limits of colonial and postcolonial territorial configurations on our planet. It critiques the re-creation of a binary division between nature and culture through scientific knowledge and, at the same time, proposes an understanding of astrobiology as a speculative science. Speculative thought can transform the roots of environmentalism into new *routes*, or pathways, that challenge dominant scientific paradigms and may enable us to embrace the emergence of alien outer space imaginaries.[1]

Imaginative Outer Geographies

Edward Said's concept of "imaginative geographies", developed in his influential book *Orientalism* (1979), is a key tenet of contemporary geographical and geopolitical thought. In the book, building on philosopher Michel Foucault's investigation of the mutual creation of knowledge and power (1991), Said presented Orientalism as a western hegemonic discourse and a means of constructing images of the Orient to dominate and gain authority over it. The colonialist discourse that creates the Orient rests on three main elements: knowledge, power, and mapping. Maps create knowledge that is useful to assert, maintain, or justify power—a concept that is particularly clear in relation to the making of national borders. Arbitrary border lines drawn by colonial administrations in Africa, Asia, and the Middle East, largely based upon western presumptions about ethnic, religious, and cultural factors, have come to define modern nations and contemporary geopolitics. However, cultural representations, including art and literature, also had a creative or performative function: they produced images of the Orient that supported western governance over it.

Said's investigation of the intimate linkages between geography, geopolitics, and cultural representations is fundamental to discussions of how conceptions of space bear the mark of, and in turn influence, global power dynamics. Taking the concepts of imaginative geographies beyond our planet, one must ask: What words, representations, and mental maps are available to understand and represent outer space? What repertoires have come to constitute space 'common sense'? And what ideologies and modes of power operate through these representations?

Drawing upon Said, Derek Gregory suggested that space can be understood as a performance, as something people 'do' in the everyday (1998). Taking up Judith Butler's notion of performativity (2006), Gregory questions the existence of a material world as separate and unaffected by the viewing subject. When imagined, space is also produced through practices, relations, and creative works that engage with it. Crucially, in *The Colonial Present* (2004), Gregory demonstrates that in the context of the "war on terror" and politics after the 9/11 attacks in the United States, cultural constructions of difference have resorted to a renewed series of spatialisations that build upon colonial repertoires (p. 17): us/them, self/other, ours/theirs, Occident/Orient. Gregory discusses spatial representations as maps of belonging or contestation that get produced by cultural processes in a specific time, but whose heritage can be long-lasting. He states: "Culture involves the production, circulation, and legitimation of meanings through representations, practices, and performances that enter fully into the constitution of the world" (p. 8). In other words, when spatial representations that recall and rework colonial tropes and images become naturalised, "the performance of the colonial present" (p. 10) gets under our skin.

In the same vein, Simon Dalby and Gearóid Ó Tuathail, in "The Critical Geopolitics Constellation" (1996), maintain that "the ideological production and reproduction of societies can, in part, be understood as the mundane repetition of particular geopolitical tropes which constrain the political imaginary" (p. 452). Repetition enables the naturalisation of thoughts that constitute the building blocks of political constellations. Dalby and Ó Tuathail's invitation to be cautious about the mobilisation and repetition of tropes that can constrain our modes of relating with the world is particularly generative for thinking, or rethinking, outer space.

In the following sections, I discuss some of the geographical and cultural tropes that have come to constitute a constellation of images through which space environments are understood and acted upon in contemporary space culture. With Kat Deerfield, I understand space culture as the "culture found within space science and space industry settings and the broader culture that surrounds this" (Deerfield 2019: 4). More specifically, I primarily focus on the images that are invoked within astroenvironmentalist discourses, their underlying theories, and resulting governance mechanisms (proposed or existent) that attempt to support cosmic environmental protection. I do not take issue with or contest the objective of protecting outer space environments from the intensifying wave of activities taking place beyond the perceived border of our atmosphere. However, I do question the very possibility that cosmic environmental justice can be realised through mobilising images, tropes, and modes of thinking that are colonial in their histories and connotations.

For this reason, I suggest that astroenvironmentalism needs to be reconstellated. This means endorsing an approach that attends "to fissures, margins and breaks" (Karavanta and Morgan 2008: 2) within theories and texts, through which cultural criticism can enter a productive dialogue with science and science studies. By noticing critical affiliations and productive oppositions, I use a culturalist lens to weave a narrative between works of science, the social studies of outer space, and critical theory. In the following sections, first, I discuss how the astrobiological label of extreme environments can be extending forms of Orientalist imagination from Earth to space. Then, I point out that while wilderness is often seen as a benign alternative to the frontier metaphor, it is crucially intertwined with colonial misrepresentations of Indigenous territories. After looking at parks as proposed modes of bordering otherworldly environments, I suggest that an epistemological shift in understandings of astroenvironmentalism must start from unsettling border thinking when studying life and its place in the universe.

Space Orientalism

Anthropological discussions of astrobiology—also referred to as the study of the origins of life and life in extreme environments—have focused on the polysemy of 'extreme' and the ways in which this label has come to refer both to a limit that cannot be surpassed and to a horizon moving the line of what is possible a little further away. Extreme environments can provide a route to access alien biologies and grasp the unknowns that may make up *life as-we-don't-know-it* (Marcheselli 2019). For Valentine, Olson, and Battaglia (2012), extreme designates an analytic of limits and ever-opening horizons, which prompts radically new understandings of life on Earth.

While the science of extreme environments tries to objectify the meaning of 'extreme', by pointing to measurable characteristics such as temperature, pressure, pH, and others, it is important to note the dynamic character of this term. In a widely referenced scientific paper, Rothschild and Mancinelli note the anthropocentrism implicit in the use of this label, as some organisms thrive (and not merely survive) in conditions that are not favourable to humans. 'Extreme' would be better thought as a shifting signifier—one that gets reimagined every time we learn more about the possibilities of life in the deep oceans or in very arid or icy environments.

Valentine and colleagues refer to the trope of 'extreme-as-uttermost' to note the anthropological fascination with the "primitive, exotic, and extraordinary" (Valentine, Olson, and Battaglia 2012: 1013), which trickles into discussions of alien life. However, they do not dwell on how this image and the troubling language of primitivity surface in scientific discussions of extreme environments. The designation of extreme, in this sense, recalls the cultural constructions of lands unknown to European settlers during colonialism. Colonial discourses can be understood as giving rise to two positions towards environments: on the one hand, there is the branding of lands as wastelands, to be made productive or used as a dumping ground, and on the other, a form of extremophilic idealisation of some environments' biodiversity, which justifies enclosures and conservation, sometimes through dispossession of Indigenous lands. I posit these two trends as the result of 'space Orientalism' in which the commodification of extreme environments reasserts the western/European centre as the norm.[2] As Olson notes, extremes are "both dangerous and desirable" (Olson 2018: 69). In brief, rather than being antonyms, preservation, and extraction coexist in colonial discourses of land use. This inheritance is particularly visible in relation to extreme and marginal environments that come to occupy the scientific imagination of outer space.

Two examples from arid and icy environments can provide helpful illustrations. Firstly, in *The Arid Lands* (2016), geographer Diana K. Davis argues that colonially constructed ideas of deserts as extreme wastelands still affect environmental policy and practice today. For example, in Algeria the planting of trees at the edges of the Sahara to stop desertification was started in the nineteenth century by the French colonial administration and, even though this strategy failed to increase biodiversity, it gave rise to the idea of 'green dams' that remain popular in the region and beyond. The colonial dismissal of deserts as wasteland continues to echo today in the view of arid environments as deficient and in need of regeneration and reforestation. 'Extreme' is caught between the exoticism associated with the uniqueness of remote environments and their perceived inhabitability or uselessness, which recalls the infamous colonial trope of *terra nullius*.

Secondly, as anthropologist Juan Francisco Salazar outlines in relation to his fieldwork in Antarctica, the study and preservation of extreme environments are not incompatible with their use and extraction (2017). Referring to Helmreich's work on limit biologies (2011), Salazar notes that the exploration of microbial geographies at the extreme brings to the fore the question of the exploitability of knowledge about 'life' and its limits. Antarctica, like the Amazon in Veronica Davidov's anthropological work (2013), becomes a cornucopia of rich biological material. In this light, astrobiological knowledge is instrumental to bioprospecting and the extraction of value from extremophiles, living organisms that thrive under extreme conditions. Through astrobiology, analogue environments get mapped into a 'geography of life', existent or expected, that links Earth and outer space and subordinates both to special characteristics that can be observed and extracted. In scientific practices, this form of exceptionalism equates analogue environments to alien landscapes. When extreme environments become proxies for understanding life on other planets, the very conditions of their exploitability are favoured by the colonial echoes that fill the notion of extreme environments with the allure of promise and disdain for their diversity.

Extraction and exploitation are quite certainly not the aims of most astrobiologists and their research. However, the relation between the discipline and the rise of the biotechnology industry is well documented and matters when discussing environments and their 'value'. Melinda Cooper's *Life as Surplus* zooms in on the rise of astrobiology as a new discipline in which researching life (on Earth and beyond) is tied to the inherent promise of commercial exploitation of properties discovered in extremophiles. In her analysis of the scientific predicament towards "mobilizing life as a technological resource" (2008: 33), Cooper identifies the role of the NASA space biology programme as translational between speculative science and (post) industrial applications (p. 41). The science of life at the extremes is part of the wider rise of the 'bioeconomy'. Also, Rothschild and Mancinelli (2001) concede that "the discovery of extremophiles has also put vitality into the biotech industry and dreams of stock options in the minds of field biologists" (p. 1092).

In the topological connection that links extreme environments on Earth and space, the ways in which astrobiology, and science in general, treat analogue sites give us a glimpse of how our relationships with other planets are shaped. If the scientific production of analogue environments takes place in accordance with an anthropocentric, Eurocentric, and value-driven mindset, Orientalism is already folded within the ways in which we think of the cosmos. In this light, spatial Orientalism is a discursive tool that territorialises outer space: imagining extreme environments as wastelands or mines is a passport for overcoming the limits of what is known, not only for science but for the expansion of capitalism beyond planetary limits.

New Worlds' (B)orders

The trespassing of borders and frontiers, of knowledge, economy, and life, is a defining feature of space culture. For anthropologist Valerie Olson, extremes are frontiers built through innovative space activities, from scientific fieldwork in analogue sites to astronaut training camps. In Olson's ethnography of NASA, the colonial echo of the idea of progress inherent in the rhetoric of pioneers and frontiers does not go amiss:

> If frontier-making subjects such as pioneers embody settler colonial rhetorics of progress, beings associated with extreme environments—such as deep-sea microorganisms, astronauts, and aliens—have come to embody scientific and social fascinations with the biology of developmental capacity.
>
> *(Olson 2018: 27)*

A fascination with extremes sustains new pioneers' fantasies that create temporal (through the idea of progress) and spatial thresholds: frontiers constitute the spatial promise of new lands, territories, and resources—as well as more knowledge. The imperative to reach them is linked to the attainments of new stages of development and progress.

This image of the "final frontier", a phrase widely popularised by science fiction but still powerfully denoting the enticement of extremes, has not eluded criticism for implicitly invoking colonial and imperial histories and expansionist discourses (Billings 2006; MacDonald 2007; Smiles 2020; Treviño 2020). In *Dark Skies*, Daniel Deudney (2020) reflects on how space culture casts the frontier as both as an aspiration towards future achievements, often purporting a future of technological advancement, and a potential vacuum—a space of conflict:

> Frontier spaces are often described as 'power vacuums,' which core powers tend to seek to fill as best and as fast as they can. The absence of established territorial borders and property claims is also a potential source of conflict.
>
> *(pp. 281–82)*

While frontiers point toward continuous expansion, they are also marginal, even empty, spaces. Their role is to reassert the centrality of a core or a centre. In the case of space, Earth gets reaffirmed as the implicit centre of human activities; but the main centres of power coincide with older spacefaring nations, whose geographies stretch beyond territorial confines through satellites, missions, and commercial space activities.

Returning to Edward Said, his scholarship has demonstrated that modern geography is indissolubly tied up with "wider 'western' epistemology, deeply implicated in colonial-imperial power" (Sidaway 2000: 592). Understanding geography as a western-colonial science prompts a rethink of Euclidean categories that make up hegemonic spatial representations. Linda Tuhiwai Smith's *Decolonizing Methodologies* expands these considerations and powerfully outlines how the spatial vocabulary of colonialism has created a static understanding of space. Smith discusses three concepts: the line, the centre, and the outside, which are fundamental to the colonial marking and control of space (Smith 2012: 55). While the line is a tool of control that enables border creation, the centre determines an orientation for all that is deemed 'outside'. This same vocabulary is applied to outer space, well beyond the overused frontier metaphor.

I want to pay attention here to how these emerging geographical imaginaries, including centres and empty environments, reinforce anthropocentric and Eurocentric views of what constitutes extreme/normal (or in scientific texts mesophilic) conditions. But also, I want to dwell on how they repropose binary oppositions that are ingrained within a colonial cartographic mindset: here/there; core/frontiers; centre/peripheries. This language and imaginary are ubiquitous: they can be found in scientific literature on space and in commercial space settings, as well as in the law.

For example, much has been written about the spirit and the history of the Treaty on Principles Governing the Activities of States in the Exploration and Use of Outer Space, including the Moon and Other Celestial Bodies (also called Outer Space Treaty or OST) of 1969, which remains the main governance mechanism of space law. For my argument, it is relevant to note that its language may be analysed as part of this cultural repertoire that consolidates the imaginary of a spatial dimension based on a centre and its others. According to Article I, "the exploration and use of outer space shall be carried out for the benefit and in the interests of all countries ... and shall be the province of all mankind" (United Nations 2002). If activities in space are cast as "the province of mankind", space comes into being as a 'province'—or an expansion—when it is occupied and used.

In astroenvironmentalist texts, as I discuss in more detail in the next section, lines of control delimit the contours of what counts as the core and separate it from the rest—creating peripheries and wilderness. Parks or heritage sites get encircled and defined as areas of specific and scientific interest. The line that draws new borders becomes an epistemic ordering device that attempts to tame and classify the diversity of outer space environments. New borders create new orders. Legal scholar Nadine El-Enany joins these two terms in *(B)ordering Britain* (2020). Her book analyses the divisive imaginaries and practices of legal immigration law and demonstrates how British colonial categories, active through the law, continue to enable state violence. In this chapter, I borrow this idea of resistance against violent colonial imaginaries as tools of territorial control. However, I use (b)ordering to refer to how existing proposals for environmental governance in outer space can work as potentially harmful extensions of earthly politics. In taking to task colonial epistemologies and the creation of outer space geographies, I am supported by critiques of imperialism as an ecological enterprise (Crosby 2004) and by studies of the role of scientific knowledge in the creation of existing structures of power (Said 1994).

Wilderness and Parks

Borders aim to divide the core from the rest. If Spaceship Earth is the core and the atmosphere a border, all that lies beyond that limit is often cast as homogeneously untamed wilderness. The wilderness analogy has been endorsed and heavily used in space ethics since the 1980s when Eugene Hargrove published the collection of essays *Beyond Spaceship Earth* (1986). In the book, most papers in the section on environmental ethics refer to space as wilderness. More recently, this image has resurfaced as an alternative to the heavy reliance upon the frontier metaphor in the space sector. Linda Billings's long-standing concern with the frontier and its colonial connotations in the settler history of the United States led her to suggest swapping this image for that of wilderness:

> The wilderness metaphor has been suggested as an alternative to the idea of space as a frontier in the concept of astroenvironmentalism, the idea of applying the values of environmental protection and preservation to space exploration. Treating the solar system like a wilderness to protect rather than a frontier to exploit could keep nuclear weapons, nuclear power, humanmade debris, and environmental hazards out of space and prohibit private and sovereign property claims. The point … would be to avoid making the same mistakes in space as we have on earth.
>
> *(Billings 2006: 434)*

In this quote, Billings accepts that spatial thinking has a performative power. The promise implicit in the exchange of frontiers with wilderness is not repeating mistakes made on Earth. However, the environmental discourse of protecting wilderness has also historically been coterminous with colonial exploitation, expropriation of lands, and genocide.

In *Uncommon Ground*, environmental historian William Cronon highlighted that there is nothing inherently benign in the concept of wilderness (Cronon 1996: 79). Cronon pointed to the ways in which the creation of national parks as protected wilderness on Earth has been predicated on a model of territorial occupation that attempted to erase Indigenous people's ties to their lands. The very ideology of wilderness can be 'in contrast' with what it wants to protect. In this vein, and with reference to the settler logics of outer space use, Ojibwe scholar Deondre Smiles directly pointed to the fact that, for Indigenous people, frontier and wilderness are both signifiers of colonial viewpoints. He maintains that the "language surrounding 'frontier' is troubling because it perpetuates the rationale of why the American settler state even exists—it could make better use of the land than Native people would. After all, they lived in wilderness" (Smiles 2020).

There is a long tradition of critiques of wilderness from Indigenous, postcolonial, and Global South perspectives (see DeLoughrey and Handley 2011). Indigenous scholar Fabienne Bayet questioned wilderness as a western construct that posits humans and nature as fundamentally separate. It also fails to account for relational understandings of home, extended to the cosmos or not, in non-Euro-American knowledge systems. She states: "To Indigenous peoples the land is no abstract wilderness. The whole of Australia is an Aboriginal artefact" (Bayet 1994: 28). Malcom Ferdinand recently critiqued the blindness of ecological thought to colonial and imperial histories, summarising that wilderness "refers to an ideology, a dualist conception of nature, society, and history embedded in the settler-colonial and (post)slavery society of the United States" (Ferdinand 2022: 188).

In a nutshell, wilderness is a colonial and dehumanising construct: a tool of governance in support of western-oriented conservation thinking and approaches (Fletcher et al. 2021). As introduced in the previous section in relation to extreme environments, from deserts to Antarctica, wilderness reinforces the two attitudes towards environments: idealising areas for their high-value biodiversity and minimal human disturbances and dismissing this value to treat areas as wastelands. Discourses on environmentalism in outer space are endorsing these images of nature, possibly with little awareness of the long-standing and mounting critiques of environmentalist models that are steeped in narrowly western histories and understandings of nature.

When Indian historian Ramachandra Guha published "Radical American Environmentalism and Wilderness Preservation: A Third World Critique" in 1989, his aim was to question the spreading of deep ecology as a model for global environmentalism. He argued that national parks and wilderness preservation were specifically US preoccupations and ineffective or counterproductive as tools for dealing with environmental challenges in the Global South. Their establishment, and the exclusionary nature of drawing borders around protected areas, are infused with the legacies of colonialism and racism. Bordering practices marginalise not only people but also nonsettler or nonproprietary conceptions of relating with the land. For example, they are obstacles to the movement of pastoralist societies and disavow the existence of lands that are not privately owned but customarily used as a commons for grazing. Despite these critiques, the reach of these ideas became planetary: the "wilderness imaginary was vitally important to the American National Park concept and preservationist policies to follow in America and globally" (Ward 2019: 40–41). For parks, the export of the 'Yellowstone model' was characterised by Euro-American ideas on property rights, colonialism, and nature.

As anticipated, this same model is being proposed for space. Astrobiologist Charles Cockell refers to the US Wilderness Act of 1964 to situate the possible creation of "planetary parks". These are delimited areas on celestial bodies that get chosen because of their "scientific, historical and aesthetic importance" (Cockell and Horneck 2006: 256). Specific rules that apply to them would include: "no waste to be left in the park, no landing of robotic spacecraft, and movements of people or robotic vehicles only along specified routes" (p. 256). Cockell and Horneck pinpointed some suitable candidate areas to become Martian parks, such as Olympus Mons. Planetary parks preserve space wilderness in ways that are similar to national parks, that is, by exerting control over the types and frequency of activities that become permissible in tightly enclosed areas.

In this hypothesis, the perimeter of parks works as a border, out of which other practices become acceptable: in non-park areas "land can be transformed through labour into productive land by any individual or group of individuals that can find a use for it, and in so doing land becomes their property" (Cockell and Horneck 2006: 260). On Earth and in space, parks privilege a colonial-capitalist relationship with nature, functioning as mechanisms of colonial territorialisation and primitive accumulation (Coulthard 2014). Analysing the political economy of parks shows a clear similarity with space and a warning sign: "in East Africa, early wildlife preserves are understood to have been (and to an extent remain) 'rich men's playgrounds'" (Rashkow 2014: 819). With space being considered the new billionaire's playground, the establishment of parks raises questions about the production of wilderness within a worldview that "construct(s) certain humans and certain uses of nature as acceptable and conservation-friendly, and others not" (Youdelis et al. 2020: 235). Planetary parks may constitute an exception to the use and extraction of resources; however, that implicitly means condoning capitalist extraction on a cosmic scale.

Cockell and Horneck also admit that planetary parks are only a viable proposition if 'widely distributed' life is not found on a planet—in which case the whole planet *may* (my emphasis) become a park. However, the establishment of planetary parks may precede conclusive evidence of life, thus rendering their promise of protection ineffective. Cockell explicitly compares the eventuality of having to disregard the intrinsic value argument in regard to alien microbes to Attfield's

(1981) ethical view on felling trees: "we may be forced to disregard the interests of microbes in many situations (but not all), but this is not to make individual microbes of no ethical relevance in themselves" (Cockell 2016: 170–71). Resorting to this analogy, Cockell fails to account for the potentially devastating consequences of environmental changes that tree felling and permanent changes to planetary environments engender. National parks have not protected our planet from the consequences of anthropogenic activities, and planetary parks will not protect otherworldly environments from permanent changes derived from pollution and settlements.

In brief, planetary parks have not engendered a new imaginary for environmental protection. More specifically, they are emblematic of the ways in which astroenvironmentalism endorses western epistemologies that deny the complexity of environmental relationships and see planets as territories that can be parcelled and bounded. Smith's critique of the binding of Euclidean geography with colonising projects has been an important aid for thought. Planetary parks suggest that permanent changes can be made to parts of an ecosystem, but they can be controlled and delimited through acts of border creation. Under the guise of an environmentalist argument, this hypothesis entertains a settler future in outer space and legitimises colonial claims to property and extraction.

Cronon warned that "any way of looking at nature that encourages us to believe we are separate from nature—as wilderness tends to do so—is likely to reinforce environmentally irresponsible behavior" (Cronon 1996: 87). The fact that astroenvironmentalism bears residues of this western, Eurocentric, and Cartesian mode of thinking reveals that addressing the issue of colonialism in space is not an easy task. It requires a paradigm shift, a transformation that goes beyond simply expanding hegemonic environmentalist discourses beyond our planet. I call this shift "reconstellation".

Reconstellating Astroenvironmentalism: Planetary S/kin?

In *Negative Dialectics*, philosopher Theodor Adorno reads Walter Benjamin's *Origin of the German Tragic Drama* (2009) and dwells on the idea of constellations. These are clusters of thoughts that signify a concept:

> As a constellation, theoretical thought circles the concept it would like to unseal, hoping it may fly open like the lock of a well-guarded safe-deposit box: in response, not to a single key or to a single number, but to a combination of numbers.
>
> *(Adorno 1983: 163)*

Gaining awareness of a constellation is a bit like decoding a sequence that allows new light to be shed on a concept. If astroenvironmentalism is the concept in question, I have looked at the use of frontiers, borders, and wilderness as traces of the colonial roots of its epistemology. Planetary parks or the outlined preservation of extraterrestrial wilderness have two limits: first, they remain focused on views of planets as bounded Galilean objects, where the borders between inside and outside and borders drawn within their environments justify and support forms of capitalist governmentality. Second, they recentre Euro-American environmental knowledge and paradigms that have been ineffective in furthering environmental justice on Earth.

These two points are interconnected. Mainstream environmentalist discourses do not deconstruct the abstraction of planetary boundedness or displace 'the planet' enough to allow for the emergence of other imaginations of living with multiple ecologies on Earth, in lower Earth orbit, and beyond. On the contrary, they risk reproducing universalist narratives of what types of environments count as worthy of protection, and who are the subjects entrusted with protecting them. These views that separate humans and nature in turn affect and justify enclosures of outer space environments for capitalist extraction, their use as stations for more anthropogenic technologies, and dumping sites for waste. As exemplified by Earth's environmental crisis, this utilitarian ideology constitutes a significant barrier to a more just and future-oriented relationship with our place of dwelling.

However, I do not dismiss astroenvironmentalism as a rising movement or an aspiration towards more sustainable relationships with the cosmos. I welcome the growing interest and awareness in ecological approaches to outer space. For this reason, I call for astroenvironmentalism to be 'reconstellated' with other ideas, images, and analogies that bring about other nonextractive practices. Another astroenvironmentalism is possible if predicated upon resisting cartography based on bordering practices and the creation of new environmental others. A route for this enterprise is expanding astrobiological discussions on planetary protection beyond their current technoscientific remit. Embracing ethics in relation to planetary contamination and environmental justice involves listening to worldviews and voices that have historically been oppressed and marginalised in the production of scientific thought.

Writing about Aboriginal cosmological thought, Bawaka Country greatly contributes to this endeavour by revealing that the image of Spaceship Earth and its totalising narratives—one of which suggests that colonising space environments can be made to benefit humanity as a whole—conceal our planetary histories of injustice and racism. This erasure of earthly histories risks reproducing forms of environmental injustice:

> Treating space as a lifeless, uninhabited, un-governed wilderness and store of resources also allows proponents of space colonization to envision it as a dumping ground for pollution and ecologically-harmful activity, a move that echoes the racialized undertones of environmental injustices on earth.
>
> *(Bawaka Country 2020: 4)*

Against this image of Spaceship Earth, and its binary division between inside and outside taken to task by critiques of globalisation, the invitation to listen to Sky Country presents non-Indigenous audiences and advocates of colonisation with a view of environmental relations in which "Land, Sea and Sky Country are all connected, so there is no such thing as 'outer space' or 'outer Country'—no outside" (Bawaka Country 2020: 2). This intimate cosmic connection displaces the image of Earth as an enclosed globe, or a "sealed vessel" separated from space. It highlights the ways in which ecologies, on and off Earth, are entanglements of different lives as well as of life and nonlife. Such connections fundamentally resist space colonisation as an enterprise of occupation and primitive accumulation.

Working towards this shared anticolonial objective, thinkers, activists, and practitioners of speculative space science have different paths to follow. One of them involves unearthing and rerouting marginalised theories and images belonging to the wide repertoire of astrobiological thought. There are lineages of feminist science studies that can be traced and built upon. For example, philosopher of science Donna Haraway's rereading of the work of biologist Lynn Margulis and writer Dorion Sagan proposed a political commitment to multispecies cohabitation and justice.[3] Overthrowing the primacy of humans as cosmic subjects, this form of commitment requires getting attuned to the ways in which seemingly different entities "co-shape" (Haraway 2016) or "intra-act" (Barad 2007) with each other and the environments they are in. Situating my work in dialogue with this literature, I argue that concepts of biological interconnections can be read contrapuntally and as alternatives to the narratives about borders within and at the edges of planets and beyond.

In this sense, the title of a Cisco–NASA partnership to create one of the largest wireless networks of sensors, launched in 2009, provides a generative image: Planetary Skin. The 'skin' here refers to the encircling of the Earth by data transmitted from a myriad of datapoints and sensors, whose erratic trail—which leaves and comes back onto land—questions the existence of a self-evident outer layer of Earth coinciding with the atmosphere. In *Biospheres*, Sagan and Margulis suggest that the atmosphere is more like a giant circulatory system than a static border, as it supports the movement of a wide range of chemicals across the planet (Sagan and Margulis 1989: 13). We continually breathe out gases in the atmosphere, which actively contribute to the flow of chemicals and organic compounds that support Earth's dynamic harmony. In other words, the atmosphere is part of the same complex matter that makes up our planet:

> Many very unusual, highly unstable chemicals exist in Earth's air. These include all sorts of organic compounds from the scent of magnolia flowers to butyl mercaptan, the spray of skunks. Our complex atmosphere reflects the diversity of organisms living at the surface.
>
> *(p. 19)*

In this sense, the ecological feedback loops and complex interactions that materially constitute life urge us to question what borders can really obstruct, protect, or halt. Margulis's microbiology of relations informs philosopher Isabelle Stengers's idea of ecology as multiplicities and symbiotic tangles (Stengers 2010). Symbiosis is the phenomenon by which two organisms cooperate for their survival and evolution. In astrobiology, this is often referenced as a crucial mechanism to improve the chances of survivability in extreme environments. When rethinking ecological dependencies and kinship, however, symbiotic relations and practices of cooperation become central, and they are far from rare. Much like human and animal skin is teeming with the life of different microbial communities, making it a dynamic ecology, planetary skin could be understood as something other than a shield protecting the individuality of Earth. Rather, it could stand for the plurality and interrelatedness of life and be seen as active player in cosmic symbiosis (Margulis 1998). This refers to the dependency of life on Earth on several cosmic processes, including the tidal waves and solar energy which were crucial to the development of early living organisms (see also Klinger 2021).

Thinking of planetary s/kin has allowed me to enlist Margulis's, Haraway's, and Stengers's work on ecology as cohabitation with a difference in this cosmic reconstellation. Locating symbiosis on the planetary skin suggests focusing on the complex relations that make up life while recognising that the biocentricity of some scientific thought can itself be reproductive of an antiquated binary—life/nonlife—in which the latter gets read as less worthy. Instead, ecological thinking brings about the relationality intrinsic in what Gabrys calls "becoming planetary"—a way of living on the planet "otherwise" (Gabrys 2018). Making kin can be part of this reconstellation. In a recent article entitled "Making Kin with the Cosmos" writer Ceridwen Dovey wrote: "We must learn to [… see] space-nature not as a simple repository of raw materials or cosmically irradiated rocks with which we can do what we like, as possessions and property, but as our kin" (Dovey 2021). In this sense, s/kin provides more dynamic views of the possibilities of cosmic dwelling. The interactions between different organisms and the codependency of organic and inorganic substances prompt us to rethink ecologies as being, by definition, "intraplanetary".

Conclusion

This chapter looked at the interrelation between knowledge about extreme environments and outer space and suggested that forms of Orientalism are folded into cultural understandings of deserts and icy environments as either biologically deficient or a wilderness to protect. These environments are proxies for the ways in which scientific efforts conceptualise the possibilities of relating with the cosmos. In the context of environmental ethics, astrobiologists have advanced hypotheses for the protection of celestial bodies that are largely based on mirroring earthly governance tools, such as protected zones or parks. Through references to postcolonial and Indigenous critiques of western environmentalism and its epistemology, I have questioned the ways in which bordering processes, the encircling of parks, and the use of wilderness thinking can be tools for environmental justice in outer space. If astroenvironmentalism condones resource extraction, it becomes a form of ethics that serves the interest of capitalism and enables the continuation of a system of oppression that transforms labour and life into profit. Instead, I have suggested that new routes for astroenvironmentalism can be charted. Reconstellating astroenvironmentalism is an open project that can be premised upon anticolonialism, resistance to extraction, a relational ethos, and a wider ecology of knowledges. Fundamental starting points for these new routes are provided, among others, by Indigenous critiques of space colonisation and feminist science studies about ecological and material entanglements with the cosmos.

Notes

1 I borrow the roots/routes wordplay from Paul Gilroy's book *The Black Atlantic*, where it is used to refer to the ways in which Black culture and identity are intertwined with mobility and migration (1993: 19). I use the metaphor to highlight the ways in which scientific thought can be conceptualised as constantly in flux, thus charting new routes for investigation.
2 I am aided in this conceptualisation of space Orientalism referring both to environments and environmentalist claims to preservation by the work of Sawyer and Agrawal (2000). The authors point out that contemporary idioms of environmentalism that resonate with colonial attempts to sexualise, racialise, and control colonised geographies and bodies are instances of environmental Orientalisms.
3 For an exhaustive survey of the literature on multispecies justice and its promises and challenges, see Celermajer et al. (2021).

References

Abiodun, Adigun Ade. 2013. "We Must Harness Space for Sustainable Development." *Space Policy* 29 (1): 5–8. https://doi.org/10.1016/j.spacepol.2012.11.009.
Adorno, Theodor W. 1983. *Negative Dialectics*. New York: Continuum.
Attfield, Robin. 1981. "The Good of Trees." *Journal of Value Inquiry* 15 (1): 35–54. https://doi.org/10.1007/BF00136626.
Barad, Karen Michelle. 2007. *Meeting the Universe Halfway: Quantum Physics and the Entanglement of Matter and Meaning*. Durham, NC: Duke University Press.
Bawaka Country, including Audra Mitchell, Sarah Wright, Sandie Suchet-Pearson, Kate Lloyd, Laklak Burarrwanga, Ritjilili Ganambarr, Merrkiyawuy Ganambarr-Stubbs, Banbapuy Ganambarr, Djawundil Maymuru, and Rrawun Maymuru. 2020. "Dukarr Lakarama: Listening to Guwak, Talking Back to Space Colonization." *Political Geography* 81 (August): 102218. https://doi.org/10.1016/j.polgeo.2020.102218.
Bayet, Fabienne. 1994. "Overturning the Doctrine: Indigenous People and Wilderness—Being Aboriginal in the Environmental Movement." *Social Alternatives* 13 (2): 27–32.
Benjamin, Walter. 2009. *The Origin of German Tragic Drama*. Translated by John Osborne. London: Verso.
Billings, Linda. 2006. "To the Moon, Mars, and Beyond: Culture, Law, and Ethics in Space-Faring Societies." *Bulletin of Science, Technology & Society* 26 (5): 430–37. https://doi.org/10.1177/0270467606292504.
Butler, Judith. 2006. *Gender Trouble: Feminism and the Subversion of Identity*. Routledge Classics. New York: Routledge.
Celermajer, Danielle, David Schlosberg, Lauren Rickards, Makere Stewart-Harawira, Mathias Thaler, Petra Tschakert, Blanche Verlie, and Christine Winter. 2021. "Multispecies Justice: Theories, Challenges, and a Research Agenda for Environmental Politics." *Environmental Politics* 30 (1–2): 119–40. https://doi.org/10.1080/09644016.2020.1827608.
Cockell, Charles S. 2005. *Space on Earth: Saving Our World By Seeking Others*. London: Macmillan.
Cockell, Charles S. 2016. "The Ethical Status of Microbial Life on Earth and Elsewhere: In Defence of Intrinsic Value." In *The Ethics of Space Exploration*, edited by James S. J. Schwartz and Tony Milligan, 167–79. Cham: Springer. https://doi.org/10.1007/978-3-319-39827-3_12.

Cockell, Charles S., and Gerda Horneck. 2006. "Planetary Parks—Formulating a Wilderness Policy for Planetary Bodies." *Space Policy* 22 (4): 256–61. https://doi.org/10.1016/j.spacepol.2006.08.006.

Cooper, Melinda. 2008. *Life as Surplus: Biotechnology and Capitalism in the Neoliberal Era*. In Vivo. Seattle, WA: University of Washington Press.

Coulthard, Glen Sean. 2014. *Red Skin, White Masks: Rejecting the Colonial Politics of Recognition*. Indigenous Americas. Minneapolis, MN: University of Minnesota Press.

Cronon, William, ed. 1996. *Uncommon Ground: Rethinking the Human Place in Nature*. New York: Norton.

Crosby, Alfred W. 2004. *Ecological Imperialism: The Biological Expansion of Europe, 900–1900*. 2nd ed. Studies in Environment and History. Cambridge: Cambridge University Press.

Dalby, Simon, and Gearóid Ó Tuathail. 1996. "The Critical Geopolitics Constellation: Problematizing Fusions of Geographical Knowledge and Power." *Political Geography* 15 (6–7): 451–56. https://doi.org/10.1016/0962-6298(96)00026-1.

Davidov, Veronica. 2013. "Amazonia as Pharmacopia." *Critique of Anthropology* 33 (3): 243–62. https://doi.org/10.1177/0308275X13490309.

Davis, Diana K. 2016. *The Arid Lands: History, Power, Knowledge*. History for a Sustainable Future. Cambridge: The MIT Press.

Deerfield, Kat. 2019. *Gender, Sexuality, and Space Culture*. Radical Cultural Studies. London; New York: Rowman & Littlefield.

DeLoughrey, Elizabeth M., and George B. Handley, eds. 2011. *Postcolonial Ecologies: Literatures of the Environment*. New York: Oxford University Press.

Deudney, Daniel. 2020. *Dark Skies: Space Expansionism, Planetary Geopolitics, and the Ends of Humanity*. New York: Oxford University Press.

Dickens, Peter, and James S. Ormrod. 2007. *Cosmic Society: Towards a Sociology of the Universe*. London: Routledge.

Dovey, Ceridwen. 2021. "Making Kin with the Cosmos." Humans and Nature (online). https://humansandnature.org/making-kin-with-the-cosmos/

El-Enany, Nadine. 2020. *(B)ordering Britain: Law, Race and Empire*. Manchester: Manchester University Press.

Ferdinand, Malcom. 2022. "Behind the Colonial Silence of Wilderness: 'In Marronage Lies the Search of a World'." *Environmental Humanities* 14 (1): 182–201. https://doi.org/10.1215/22011919-9481506.

Fletcher, Michael-Shawn, Rebecca Hamilton, Wolfram Dressler, and Lisa Palmer. 2021. "Indigenous Knowledge and the Shackles of Wilderness." *Proceedings of the National Academy of Sciences* 118 (40): e2022218118. https://doi.org/10.1073/pnas.2022218118.

Foucault, Michel. 1991. *Discipline and Punish: The Birth of the Prison*. Penguin Social Sciences: Psychology. London: Penguin Books.

Gabrys, Jennifer. 2018. "Becoming Planetary." *E-Flux Architecture*. https://www.e-flux.com/architecture/accumulation/217051/becoming-planetary/.

Galli, André, and Andreas Losch. 2019. "Beyond Planetary Protection: What Is Planetary Sustainability and What Are Its Implications for Space Research?" *Life Sciences in Space Research* 23 (November): 3–9. https://doi.org/10.1016/j.lssr.2019.02.005.

Gilroy, Paul. 1993. *The Black Atlantic: Modernity and Double Consciousness*. New York Verso.

Gregory, Derek. 1998. *Geographical Imaginations*. Reprinted. Cambridge: Blackwell.

Gregory, Derek. 2004. *The Colonial Present: Afghanistan, Palestine, Iraq*. Malden, MA: Blackwell.

Guha, Ramachandra. 1989. "Radical American Environmentalism and Wilderness Preservation: A Third World Critique." *Environmental Ethics* 11 (1): 71–83. https://doi.org/10.5840/enviroethics198911123.

Haraway, Donna Jeanne. 2016. *Staying with the Trouble: Making Kin in the Chthulucene*. Experimental Futures: Technological Lives, Scientific Arts, Anthropological Voices. Durham, NC: Duke University Press.

Hargrove, Eugene C., ed. 1986. *Beyond Spaceship Earth: Environmental Ethics and the Solar System*. San Francisco, CA: Sierra Club Books.

Helmreich, Stefan. 2011. "What Was Life? Answers from Three Limit Biologies." *Critical Inquiry* 37 (4): 671–96. https://doi.org/10.1086/660987.

Karavanta, Mina, and Nina Morgan, eds. 2008. *Edward Said and Jacques Derrida: Reconstellating Humanism and the Global Hybrid*. Newcastle: Cambridge Scholars.

Klinger, Julie Michelle. 2021. "Environmental Geopolitics and Outer Space." *Geopolitics* 22 (3): 666–703. https://doi.org/10.1080/14650045.2019.1590340.

MacDonald, Fraser. 2007. "Anti-*Astropolitik*—Outer Space and the Orbit of Geography." *Progress in Human Geography* 31 (5): 592–615. https://doi.org/10.1177/0309132507081492.

Marcheselli, Valentina. 2019. "Life As-We-Don't-Know-It: Research Repertoires and the Emergence of Astrobiology." PhD thesis, University of Edinburgh. http://hdl.handle.net/1842/36070.

Margulis, Lynn. 1998. *Symbiotic Planet: A New Look at Evolution*. Science Masters. New York: Basic Books.

McKay, Christopher P. 2021. "Preservation of Static Lifeless Landscapes in the Antarctic Dry Valleys and the Atacama Desert and Applications to the Moon and Mars." *Ethics & the Environment* 26 (1): 105–20. https://doi.org/10.2979/ethicsenviro.26.1.05.

McKay, Christopher, and Margarita M. Marinova. 2001. "The Physics, Biology, and Environmental Ethics of Making Mars Habitable." *Astrobiology* 1 (1): 89–109. https://doi.org/10.1089/153110701750137477.

Morin, Jean-Frédéric, and Benjamin Richard. 2021. "Astro-Environmentalism: Towards a Polycentric Governance of Space Debris." *Global Policy* 12 (4): 568–73. https://doi.org/10.1111/1758-5899.12950.

Olson, Valerie. 2018. *Into the Extreme: U.S. Environmental Systems and Politics Beyond Earth*. Minneapolis: University of Minnesota Press.

Rashkow, Ezra D. 2014. "Idealizing Inhabited Wilderness: A Revision to the History of Indigenous Peoples and National Parks." *History Compass* 12 (10): 818–32. https://doi.org/10.1111/hic3.12190.

Rothschild, Lynn J., and Rocco Mancinelli. 2001. "Life in Extreme Environments." *Nature* 409 (6823): 1092–101. https://doi.org/10.1038/35059215.

Sagan, Dorion, and Lynn Margulis. 1989. *Biospheres from Earth to Space*. Hillside, NJ: Enslow.

Said, Edward W. 1979. *Orientalism*. New York: Vintage Books.

Said, Edward W. 1994. *Culture and Imperialism*. London: Vintage.

Salazar, Juan Francisco. 2017. "Microbial Geographies at the Extremes of Life." *Environmental Humanities* 9 (2): 398–417. https://doi.org/10.1215/22011919-4215361.

Sawyer, Suzana, and Arun Agrawal. 2000. "Environmental Orientalisms." *Cultural Critique* 45: 71–108. https://doi.org/10.2307/1354368.

Sidaway, James D. 2000. "Postcolonial Geographies: An Exploratory Essay." *Progress in Human Geography* 24 (4): 591–612. https://doi.org/10.1191/030913200100189120.

Smiles, Deondre. 2020. "The Settler Logics of (Outer) Space." *Society and Space*, 26 October 2020. https://www.societyandspace.org/articles/the-settler-logics-of-outer-space.

Smith, Kelly C., and Carlos Mariscal, eds. 2019. *Social and Conceptual Issues in Astrobiology*. New York: Oxford University Press.

Smith, Linda Tuhiwai. 2012. *Decolonizing Methodologies: Research and Indigenous Peoples*. 2nd ed. London: Zed Books.

Stengers, Isabelle. 2010. *Cosmopolitics*. Posthumanities 9–10. Minneapolis: University of Minnesota Press.

Treviño, Natalie B. 2020. "The Cosmos Is Not Finished." PhD thesis, Western University, London, Ontario, Canada.

United Nations Treaties and Principles on Outer Space. 2002. New York: United Nations.

Valentine, David. 2012. "Exit Strategy: Profit, Cosmology, and the Future of Humans in Space." *Anthropological Quarterly* 85 (4): 1045–67. https://doi.org/10.1353/anq.2012.0073.

Valentine, David, Valerie A. Olson, and Debbora Battaglia. 2012. "Extreme: Limits and Horizons in the Once and Future Cosmos." *Anthropological Quarterly* 85 (4): 1007–26. https://doi.org/10.1353/anq.2012.0066.

Vidaurri, Monica, Alia Wofford, Jonathan Brande, Gabriel Black-Planas, Shawn Domagal-Goldman, and Jacob Haqq-Misra. 2020. "Absolute Prioritization of Planetary Protection, Safety, and Avoiding Imperialism in All Future Science Missions: A Policy Perspective." *Space Policy* 51 (February): 101345. https://doi.org/10.1016/j.spacepol.2019.101345.

Ward, Kim. 2019. "For Wilderness or Wildness? Decolonising Rewilding." In *Rewilding*, edited by Nathalie Pettorelli, Sarah M. Durant, and Johan T. du Toit, 34–54. Cambridge University Press. https://doi.org/10.1017/9781108560962.003.

Youdelis, Megan, Roberta Nakoochee, Colin O'Neil, Elizabeth Lunstrum, and Robin Roth. 2020. "'Wilderness' Revisited: Is Canadian Park Management Moving Beyond the 'Wilderness' Ethic?" *The Canadian Geographer/Le Géographe Canadien* 64 (2): 232–49. https://doi.org/10.1111/cag.12600.

23
DIVERGENT EXTRATERRESTRIAL WORLDS
Navigating Cosmo-Practices on Two Mountaintops in Thailand

Lauren Reid

On two separate occasions during my year-long field research in Thailand, I climbed into a minivan to go on excursions to sites of extraterrestrial discovery. The first excursion was with an exoplanet astronomer to an observatory on Thailand's tallest mountain. The second was with the Buddhist group UFO Kaokala to a 'stargate' on a not-quite-so-high mountain. Atop these two mountains, I learned about two different technologies: one is a spectrograph used by space scientists at the National Astronomical Research Institute of Thailand (NARIT) to find exoplanets (planets that orbit a sun-like star outside Earth's solar system), and the other is an invisible technology implanted into the mind via Buddhist practices to establish a line of communication with extraterrestrial beings. In this chapter, I juxtapose these two searches for life and life-supporting worlds off-Earth that are rooted in two different ontologies—exoplanet astronomy and ufological Buddhism.

The astronomical observatory for exoplanet research and the Buddhist 'stargate' for extraterrestrial communication exemplify that—depending on one's cosmological order—there are numerous techniques and technologies to discover and reach extraterrestrial worlds. There are also numerous ways of conceptualising extraterrestrial worlds and potential life forms that may inhabit them. Such divergent cosmic engagements take shape through a multitude of actors, matter, phenomena, interactions, and imaginaries that compose dramatically different realities. Given the plurality of cosmological compositions in motion at any given moment, it can be difficult to make sense of coexisting yet completely disparate ways of imagining, relating to, and searching for extraterrestrial worlds. Moreover, why might we even want to?

First, renewed promises of human expansion beyond Earth in the form of tourist trips to the Kármán line, robot explorations of Mars, and proposals to mine asteroids contribute to a persuasive contemporary imaginary that it is human 'destiny' to inhabit, excavate, and profit from extraterrestrial terrains. This dominant discourse obscures the myriad outer spatial practices happening on and off Earth every day. Attending to diverse ways of knowing and being can complexify, add more nuance to, and challenge hegemonic space exploration narratives and practices (see also Gorman 2005; Johnson 2020; Traphagan and Traphagan 2015).

Second, divergent ways of knowing and engaging with the cosmos can be frictious (Tsing 2005). A modern Western ontology tends to separate and revere the technoscientific over religious and speculative, as well as Indigenous knowledges and fringe worldings related to, for

DOI: 10.4324/9781003280507-26

example, extraterrestrial intelligence. This hierarchical separation is connected to the general understanding that space exploration is a scientific and technological problem (Traphagan 2020), the modernist philosophical assumption that technoscientific progress moves in step with the diminishment of religious and so-called magical interpretations of the world, and the tendency for fringe worldings to not be taken seriously (Pasulka 2019). Even within scientific fields, practices associated with questions of extraterrestrial intelligence like SETI (search for extraterrestrial intelligence) and METI (messaging extraterrestrial intelligence) struggle to be taken seriously due to their long-term connection with campy, pop cultural science fictions (Wright and Oman-Reagan 2018).

Yet Western doctrines of progress have been widely challenged by theorists who demonstrate that modernisation is not linear; nor are science and religion inevitably dichotomous and incompatible realms (e.g., Latour 1993; Harding 2008; Stengers 2010; Szerszynski 2005). Additionally, practices like 'astronomy', 'ufology', or 'Buddhism' are neither static, discrete entities nor beholden to uniform categories: they are instead fluid and intertwined and mutually inform each other (see also Behrend and Zillinger 2015; Jasanoff 2004; Wright and Oman-Reagan 2018). Many space scientists, for example, frame and structure their work, projects, or institutions around science fiction books, films, and music—*Star Trek* (series since 1966), *2001: A Space Odyssey* (1968), and *Dr. Strangelove* (1964) are perennial favourites (Messeri 2017; Vertesi 2019). More subtly, US American Christian salvific narratives are inextricably tied to outer space through imaginaries of the 'final frontier' and rhetoric that it is our 'manifest destiny' to expand beyond Earth to ensure the survival of the human species (Kearnes and Van Dooren 2017; Newell 2014; Sage 2008; Smiles 2020).

How then to avoid reinscribing limiting categories like 'science' and 'religion' in the study of human engagements with outer space? And how to take different cosmo-practices seriously, especially those that are marginalised or fall outside the frame of 'big science'? Recent scholarship related to Indigenous cosmopolitics has offered productive frameworks and concepts to actively work with a wide variety of actors (e.g., Blaser 2016; de la Cadena 2010, 2015; Escobar 2020; Tsing 2000; Verran 2001, 2002; Viveiros de Castro 2004). Such theorists identify that the modern West assumes there is a singular reality onto which multiple perspectives are projected (Latour 2005; Stengers 2010). Since one 'perspective' or 'world view' is presumably more accurate than another, certain forms of knowledge like science are privileged over others, as I have roughly sketched above. To counter this representational paradigm, scholars argue that encounters between multiple ways of knowing and being "must be understood as a meeting of divergent realities rather than in terms of an opposition between cultural world views and an objective reality" (Morita 2017: 228). Furthermore, instead of working with Western-rooted concepts like 'science', 'religion', 'nature', and 'culture', attending to everyday relations, particularly performance, agency, and process, offers an analytic lens that does not presuppose how different worlds work or reduce difference(s) within and between them (Omura et al. 2019; Pickering 2017).

In what follows, I work with such conceptual tools offered by theorists who think through difference to approach the two separate yet cosmically connected mountaintops as active sites of ongoing, intricate relations between entities—human, nonhuman, technological, environmental. I will first narrate the excursions to the observatory at Doi Inthanon and the stargate at Kaokala as disjointed fragments to attune to their idiosyncrasies. Following a reflection on the relationships between the technologies, the practitioners, and their methods at each site, I then locate some partial overlaps between them. The purpose of symmetrically analysing these disparate realities is twofold: to advance an understanding of the plurality of outer spatial practices, while also reorienting away from modernist presuppositions and dualistic categories to cultivate a generative space that takes seriously alternative modes of engaging with outer space such as ufological Buddhism.

Emergence and Hybridity in Thailand

Before I begin, a few words about what led me to go on these two mountaintop excursions in the first place. For twelve months over 2018–2019, I researched how futures beyond Earth are envisioned and planned for in Thailand from the perspectives of space scientists, artists, and religious groups—including the subjects of this chapter, NARIT, and UFO Kaokala. Given that Thailand is not currently a leader in the field of space exploration, it may seem like a rather peripheral location from which to investigate extraterrestrial worldings and space technologies. Thailand's space science sector only seriously took off in the early 2000s when NARIT, Thailand's first astronomical research institute, officially opened in 2009. The field has since been in the process of rapidly developing and establishing itself, providing an opportunity to study how international outer spatial practices travel and transform on Thai soil.

My motivation to research in Thailand, however, is not primarily because its space science sector is relatively peripheral and emergent. This project is driven by a broader aim to think outside colonialist, extractivist, and capitalist space exploration imaginaries and practices that are embedded in Western-rooted ontologies. A short walk down the street in Bangkok invites encounters with high-rise skyscrapers towering above vacant lots that burst with overgrown tropical plants; spirit-shrine altars built in the form of miniature houses dot the streets to honour and host the local spirits; Buddhist monks roam the tech aisles of a mall, shopping for high-speed 5G-network-connected mobile phones. These are just a few kaleidoscopic sights among many in which persistent nature, high technology, religiosity, and capitalism seem to break down nature/culture, religion/science, tradition/modernity, and the other modernist dualisms that domino onward (Chua 2021; Morris 2000), at least to my Euro-Australian senses.

Flowing through this terrain are diverse religious milieus, the majority of which centre around Thailand's official religion, Theravāda Buddhism. Theravāda Buddhism originally came to Thailand from Sri Lanka around the third century BC and today incorporates elements from Hinduism, Brahmanism, Chinese religious traditions, and Tai folk animist traditions. At the same time, Thailand's religious landscape proliferates with hybridised forms of this already-hybrid religion, including spirit cults, amulet cults, and a "parade of supernaturals" (Tambiah 1970; see also Kitiarsa 2005). UFO Kaokala's form of extraterrestrial-infused Buddhism (or what I call ufological Buddhism, for lack of an official name) is one form of contemporary hybridisation that I will explain in more detail in this chapter. Such pluriversal cosmic relations provide rich terrain for generatively thinking through an array of alternative outer spatial imaginaries, practices, and instruments. But before I tread too far, let me first tell the story of the excursions to Doi Inthanon and Kaokala.

Mountaintop 1: Doi Inthanon, Chiang Mai, Thailand, 15 March 2018

On a characteristically bright and sweltering day in Chiang Mai, Thailand's second most populous city, I meet up with two exoplanet researchers, David and Alec. Alec is an amateur exoplanet astronomer visiting Chiang Mai from Canada, where he is usually based. David is a senior researcher at NARIT specialising in both astroseismology and exoplanets. Astroseismology involves the study of stars' internal structures, which are measured by how they change shape or pulsate. Exoplanet astronomy involves the search for planets beyond our solar system. David's warm and welcoming yet decisive manner, in combination with cropped hair and slim *Matrix*-esque sunglasses, lends him an air of the military. Indeed, David previously worked on ballistic missiles in his home country of Ukraine during military service before entering astronomy. Alec meanwhile is wearing typical 'tourist-in-the-tropics' garb with a muted khaki Hawaiian shirt and cargo shorts. Both he and I are somewhat wilted, pink, and puffy, so far unaccustomed to Chiang Mai's humid heat.

As I climb into the back of a new leather-lined van, David matter-of-factly tells me, "We will sit in the front because we will talk about science." Both researchers are originally from Odesa, so they have much to share. They begin speaking in Ukrainian, and I do not know if they speak about science, but the occasional "NARIT" and "teleskop" seem to indicate that they do. That's fine by me as I feel lucky to come along for the ride. Today we are going on an excursion to Doi Inthanon, the highest mountain in Thailand and the site of the Thai National Observatory (TNO).

———

At some two hours' drive, Doi Inthanon National Park, with its abundant forests, waterfalls, and wildlife, is a lush oasis compared to Chiang Mai, which has been engulfed in thick smog. This yearly phenomenon usually runs from January until April. The source of air pollution is not entirely understood since the region is made up of 70% forest with a relatively small city centre. Some speculate that dust whipped up from the preceding dry season is the pollution culprit, or worse, farming chemicals and pesticides. Others blame the noxious smoke on nearby slash-and-burn farming practices in northern Thailand and neighbouring Laos and Myanmar. It is likely a combination of all of the above (Pardthaisong et al. 2018).

Doi Inthanon's 2,565-metre elevation above sea level makes it the ideal location for the TNO and its optical reflecting telescope. At the time of writing, the TNO is one among sixteen observatories with telescopes in Southeast Asia, and it has been the most advanced facility for optical astronomy in the region since it opened in 2013. On a global scale, the telescope's location near the equator puts it in a prime position for observing both the northern and southern hemispheres. Yet its 2.4-metre aperture size—while impressive—falls short of at least fifty-five other operational optical reflecting telescopes around the world, the largest of which is the Gran Telescopio Canarias (GTC) at 10.4 metres. The TNO is also home to a robotic telescope and a small exhibition area for the public to learn about NARIT's development and work.

What I do not initially see, but what David must instead explain to me, is that Thailand's monsoon season, extreme storms, and dust problems render the clear sky unviewable for some months of the year, despite Doi Inthanon's ideal location. The TNO is, therefore, connected to an international network of observatories in Australia, Chile, China, and the USA to enable astronomers from each location to overcome their local terrestrial conditions and study the night sky twenty-four hours a day, three hundred and sixty-five days a year (if they wish to!). Zooming in, the TNO is also part of a national network of six observatories built by NARIT in provinces throughout Thailand to educate and give access to astronomers where there were none before. Increasingly interconnected relations are formed between earthly infrastructures near and far, as well as the celestial bodies and phenomena that they observe and sense.

Mountaintop 2: Kaokala, Nakhon Sawan, Thailand, 31 March 2018

On a characteristically smoggy and sweltering day in the province of Nakhon Sawan, central Thailand, I wait on the curbside. A white minivan pulls up. As the door slides open, I am greeted by five smiling faces—Noiy, Ukrin, Jaejoob, Aume, and Ann, all core members of the group UFO Kaokala. Everyone is wearing matching black nylon T-shirts with a neon green outline of an alien's face at its centre or a variation of it. Today we are in Nakhon Sawan, on our way to camp overnight on a nearby mountain, Kaokala. Its name translates to 'heavenly city'; however, it is neither angels nor gods that we are here to encounter—it is extraterrestrials.

Each member in the van has a unique role to play. Noiy is a healer who can channel extraterrestrial technology to cure illnesses. Ukrin has multiple phones and cameras to capture supernatural phenomena. Aume is newer to the group; for this trip, he is providing his van. His friend Jaejoob is also a new member and seems yet to carve out a defined role for herself. Finally, Ann has been part of the group since 2010. As a stylish twenty-something-year-old who is fluent in English, she is the main point of contact for curious foreigners like me and often finds herself as UFO Kaokala's public face for the local and international media that occasionally come to document the seemingly strange group of extraterrestrial communers on the mountain.

As I climb into the back of the van, I take the last seat next to Ann among the piled-high luggage. She immediately starts quizzing me: "Everyone here wants to know your story. What are your beliefs? Why are you interested in UFO Kaokala?" I tell Ann that I have never had an extraterrestrial encounter, but I am interested in learning about different ways of thinking about humankind's potential futures both on and off Earth. Ann eventually seems satisfied by my response and for the rest of the drive, she unfolds UFO Kaokala's history for me.

UFO Kaokala was initially founded on 17 December 1997, after then-retired Sergeant Major Cherd Chuensamnaun unexpectedly received telepathic communication from extraterrestrials (a.k.a. ETs). Not believing in his own experience, the ETs told him to check the skies outside his home for the following seven nights. If he saw UFOs, he would know that the extraterrestrial communication was real. On the following nights, his inner experience was confirmed when he saw bright lights over his home, situated on the concrete outskirts of Nakhon Sawan's centre. Following his ET experience, the Sergeant Major formed and grew UFO Kaokala until his death, when he passed on the leadership to three of his adult daughters—Somjit, Wassana, and Sonjai.

After about one hour's drive from the city centre of Nakhon Sawan, our minivan makes its way along a gravel road up the mountain, soon arriving at the campsite. Here, some group members are cooking dinner for us under a covered pavilion. A few wooden benches are placed on the edge of the steep slope to admire the farmland below. Some further steps lead up to the official peak of the mountain, which is a flattened concrete square with an altar that rises to form a sharp peak of its own. Here, a golden Buddha sits on top of a coiled *nāga*, a semi-divine serpent found in Hindu, Buddhist, and Jain traditions. The nāga's seven heads fan out and around the Buddha, framing and protecting him.

It is under the watchful gaze of the nāga at 2:17 a.m. that I and other first-time visitors to Kaokala will scrape together chairs, hold hands, and meditate to receive extraterrestrial technology into our minds. I am not told why 2:17 a.m. is significant nor exactly what the ET technology will be or do. Based on what Ann told me earlier, it is an invisible, internal device, possessed by ancient civilisations of extraterrestrials who either come from Pluto or live below the crusted surface of Lokukataapakadikong, a planet that is yet to be discovered by 'capital S' Science. For some group members, the mind device enables communication and potentially beyond-human abilities like X-ray vision, healing powers, or telepathy.

What I do not initially see, but what Ann must instead explain to me, is that the mountain is alive with invisible forces and supernatural phenomena. Two large indents in a rock have been painted gold to honour the giant who left them as footprints. Two sleepy flea-ridden dogs who were formerly humans have been condemned to staggering around the parking lot for their immoral behaviour in their previous life. A year or so earlier, a 'transformer' (a tall robotic figure in white) had walked through the rice fields at Kaokala's base. Noiy, the healer from the van, saw a nāga standing bolt upright in the centre of a nearby lake. Apparently, there is a cave underneath the mountain inside which Sergeant Major Cherd Chuensamnaun built an altar. No one dares search for it for fear of snakes.

Familiar Fragments and Unusual Patterns

In the narration of these two mountain excursions, I have taken some poetic licence by laying out each site's key players, infrastructures and various at-times-invisible phenomena in a somewhat symmetrical manner. The intention behind pairing up these disparate extraterrestrial relations is akin to anthropologist Peter Redfield's method of bringing "familiar fragments into an unusual pattern as a strategy" to tease out what is "otherwise too often lost between the fault lines of knowledge" (Redfield 2000: xv). Redfield did this by juxtaposing French Guiana's penal colony with the Ariane rocket launchpad to tell the colonial stories of global technologies. In a similar spirit, philosopher and sociocultural theorist Martin Savransky proposes that "by attending to stories where other worlds remain ongoing and unfinished, by experimenting with the possible beginnings such worlds might open up, the impossible itself can crack open" (2021: 2). But what is the impossible here? For Redfield, it is to destabilise generalised understandings of modern development and "the certainty of the present" (2000: 17). For Savransky, it is to foster alternative modes of thought and life amid "catastrophes of capitalism, colonialism, and extractivism" (2021: 4). For me, it is a combination of the two.

As emphasised by Redfield and Savransky, encounters between different ways of knowing and being are often deeply intertwined with neocolonial practices, marginalisation processes, and global power asymmetries. This is explicit in the recent work of three scholars who have similarly documented divergent worldings on mountains: geographer Adam Bobbette figured the active volcano Mt. Merapi in Java, Indonesia, as a "battleground of ideas" between scientists and shamans "about what geology is" (2018: 169); anthropologist Marisol de la Cadena has explored the entanglements of Indigenous and non-Indigenous activist worlds connected to Ausangate—the Earth Being that is also a mountain—in Cusco, Peru (2015); most relevantly for the social studies of outer space, Iokepa Casumbal-Salazar has interrogated the struggle between Kanaka ʻŌiwi (Indigenous Hawaiians) activists and "big science" advocates over the contested Thirty Meter Telescope on the sacred site of Mauna a Wākea in Hawaiʻi (2017). Although their locations and agents vary, Bobbette, de la Cadena, and Casumbal-Salazar demonstrate that infrastructures like geological research stations, mines, and telescopes have significant consequences for underprioritised forms of knowledge. Although the exoplanet astronomical and ufological Buddhist worlds atop Doi Inthanon and Kaokala can unfold comparatively unhindered (there is no direct conflict between the two), I aim here to resist the marginalisation processes at stake when incongruous cosmologies coexist, by actively giving value to their multiple realities and emphasising a kind of democracy of objects—humans, weather phenomena, technologies, animals, distant locales.

Technologies: A Spectrograph and a Receiving Device

Back at the Thai National Observatory, David, Alec, and I find ourselves standing in front of a narrow reflective glass door near the Control Room. David dramatically declares: "This is where the magic happens!" The door is labelled SPECTROGRAPH. We squeeze into a cupboard-sized room that is roughly painted black with two large air conditioners mounted on the wall to keep it cool. On top of a table sits a large stainless steel box with wires passing into it from a rough hole in the roof. David explains that the wires are connected to the telescope outside.

This spectrograph allows David to find and study exoplanets via the Doppler method, which relies on observing stars for potential planets that may be rotating around them. The idea is that as a planet orbits a star, its gravitational pull creates small variations in the star's movement. Therefore, a star with the right movement can indicate the presence of a planet. Exoplanets are currently almost impossible to 'see' directly with technology, let alone the naked eye. They emit little light and orbit around a brighter star like our Sun that obscures any direct view, and therefore, the majority of exoplanets are found via their star rather than a view of the planet itself.

While it is not possible for me to see exoplanets directly, I can see the spectrograph that David uses to find them, unlike UFO Kaokala's internal technology, implanted inside the mind. The group's methods to see UFOs and commune with extraterrestrials depend on Theravāda Buddhist concepts and practices. According to the UFO Kaokala group, the extraterrestrials that they communicate with consider Kaokala the spiritual centre of Earth, since Theravāda Buddhism is the closest earthly religion to their cosmic one. Like UFO Kaokala group members, the extraterrestrials are embedded in cycles of rebirth and share the fundamental Buddhist understanding that everything is interconnected in an "unending cycle of growth and decay, integration and disintegration" (Ratanakul 2007: 234). Accordingly, the ETs follow Buddhist precepts that include abstaining from killing living beings, stealing, sexual misconduct, lying, and intoxication. Group members, in turn, strive to improve their Buddhist practice to better connect with the extraterrestrials.

Stemming from Buddhist practice, the central mechanism to operate group members' mind-implanted ET technology is meditation. As Somjit, one of UFO Kaokala's leaders, explained to me, "meditation and mind-focus practices are basic to the understanding of how to receive extraterrestrial knowledge, including telepathy". In a YouTube video, Somjit instructs beginners to imagine their mind as a film screen and 'reality' as just pictures and sounds projected onto that screen. Through the mind-as-film-screen image, one is more easily able to detach oneself from the stresses, distractions, and seductions of 'reality'. More technically, UFO Kaokala works with a 'five-aggregate' model of the mind in which "all our experience involves material form, feelings, perception, volition, and sensory consciousness" (Karunamuni 2015). Practitioners work to dismantle these conditions and reach an existential understanding that the self is not stable or a bounded entity (Cassaniti 2015). In doing so, UFO Kaokala members seek to release their affective attachments, dissolve their ego, break the cycle of rebirth, and transcend the planetary constraints of Earth.

Multiple Worlds and Partial Connections

Given that NARIT's exoplanet astronomy and UFO Kaokala's extraterrestrial-infused Buddhism both employ technologies to engage with extraterrestrial realms, it can be tempting to fall into a modernist representational understanding that these disparate cosmo-practices are the outcome of two different views on a singular reality—what John Law describes as a "one-world world" (2015). If operating under the assumption that there is a 'real' world out there with numerous perspectives projected onto it, then presumably one perspective is more accurate than another. As seen in the mountaintop conflicts on Mt. Merapi in Indonesia, Ausangate in Peru, and Mauna a Wākea in Hawai'i, this is dangerous because you can rank these perspectives according to some supposedly factual world, marginalising or destroying some (Blaser 2016). How then to attend to the two mountaintop practices without reproducing one-world-world presuppositions? A first step can be to break the two cosmo-practical sites into rough components:

At Kaokala, a ufological Buddhist world takes shape through UFO Kaokala members with unique roles to play, an altar for offerings, a campsite to connect with ETs, internal technologies that expand the practitioner's biosensory capacities, and an array of entities that are visible only to some. This world is ordered according to cycles of rebirth and operates across interconnected external and internal planes of the cosmos and consciousness.

At Doi Inthanon, an exoplanet astronomical world takes shape through the working scientists, a mountaintop that depends on the right weather, a network of international telescopes, and the movements of distant celestial bodies that are translated by the observatory's technologies. This world is ordered along a linear trajectory of scientific progress that spans out from Earth and towards potentially Earth-like planets.

As technologies transform, research practices shift, or different components come and go, each mountaintop reality emerges indefinitely through the ongoing "collective action" of intricately interdependent agents and forces (Verran 2014: 528). Understanding that the exoplanet astronomical and ufological Buddhist compositions generate themselves through a complex array of interrelated and always-changing entities offers a first opening out of the representational one-world world. Unlike representations, relations need not be true or false. In turn, Western-rooted distinctions between religion or science, nature or culture, knowledge or belief can melt away. There are always multitudes of ways to perform, interact, and engage with the many entangled and active elements, agents, and forces inside various realities (Pickering 2017).

With that in mind, I can follow a second analytic move and focus on "multiplicities of relation" (Jackson 2018: 14; see also Bauman 2015). I already began attending to relations between technology and practitioner at each site in the previous section. Going further into relations—or specifically "gestural relations" (Messeri 2017)—David's spectrograph 'gestures outwards' to yet-to-be-discovered exoplanets. At first glance, Ann's alien technology similarly seems to gesture outwards towards extraterrestrials on the yet-to-be-discovered planet of Lokukataapakadikong. However, as Ann conspiratorially whispered to me late into the evening on Kaokala, the group's goal is not really to find aliens but to expand consciousness. UFO Kaokala's orientation, therefore, conversely gestures inward to the practitioner's mind via Buddhist practice. Rather than building a material, representational world in the way that the TNO's ever-emerging exoplanet astronomy does, UFO Kaokala's extraterrestrial-infused Buddhism transforms the individual to build an inner neuro-practical world.

When broken down into rough components (which are by no means exhaustive) and thinking through relations or practices, David and Ann can be understood as active agents within different realities. That is, they inhabit entirely different worlds (plural), rather than having entirely different interpretations of a world (singular). It does not make sense to compare or translate across these entirely different yet coexisting cosmic compositions because there is no common referent. Attempting to equivocate between the two worlds would reduce their differences (de la Cadena 2015; Stengers 2011; Viveiros de Castro 2004) and misappropriate or minimise the "entities, agencies, situations, substances, relations, experiences" from which they emerge (Latour 2005: 29).

At the same time, the worlds generated through the TNO and UFO Kaokala are ever-emerging, unbounded, and entangled with other worlds of various scales. Thus, one world can be "constituted by more worlds inside, and may be itself part of another world" (Omura et al. 2019: 2). Even the so-called Western scientific community is far from unified when it comes to imaginaries and cosmological presuppositions. So while David and Ann's cosmo-practices gesture towards completely different things, some partial connections can inevitably be found between their disparate realities (Haraway 1991; Strathern 2004). These connections are only partial because the components and relations of each world are incommensurable (de la Cadena 2015). For this chapter's final two sections, therefore, I focus on some partially connected or overlapping points in the worlds atop Doi Inthanon and Kaokala in the relationships between their cosmo-technologies, -imaginaries, and -practices.

Connection 1: Instruments for Sensing the Invisible

The first partial overlap emerges from active engagements with technologies. The complex cosmo-practices at Doi Inthanon and Kaokala involve vast sensing infrastructures to reach and study entities that are neither directly experienceable nor sensible. As specialised experts, David and Ann decode, translate, interpret, and transform the information that they receive from their technologies that interface with an array of complex matter and phenomena beyond the scope of current human sensory capacities (exoplanets, star movements, extraterrestrial communications, thought waves). For Ann at Kaokala, the technology resides in the body, and thus sensory experiences are directed inward and only made palpable to the cosmo-practitioner. For David at Doi Inthanon, entire planets cannot be viewed directly. Instead, the seismic measurements of stars are translated into data sets like radial velocity curves. As Bruno Latour writes, science

> builds extraordinarily long, complicated, mediated, indirect, sophisticated paths so as to reach the worlds—like William James I insist on the plural—that are invisible because they are too small, too far, too powerful, too big, too odd, too surprising, too counterintuitive, through concatenations of layered instruments, calculations, models
>
> *(2005: 36)*

Such translation and transformation of distant, invisible worlds into scientific 'fact' is not a neutral endeavour but involves artistry and active world-building. Astronomers rely on a "cosmic imagination" and aesthetic style to depict and describe the cosmos (Praet and Salazar 2017). For example, images taken by the Hubble Space Telescope, when digitally processed, tend to be rendered in an aesthetic style reminiscent of nineteenth-century paintings and photographs of the American West. This in turn reinforces notions of an "astronomical sublime" and space as a frontier (Kessler 2012).

> Co-productive dynamics like these emphasise how scientific knowledge is not just an objective representation of reality. It is produced by and produces a wide variety of ways of seeing, doing and seeing, as well as infrastructures and environments.
>
> *(Jasanoff 2004)*

In turn, the mediated paths to other worlds can only be interpreted by experts trained in exoplanets and astroseismology like David. The gap in expertise was made obvious to me when David signalled that I would not be able to follow his and Alec's conversation "about science" at the start of our excursion. Similarly at Kaokala, extraterrestrials and access to ET-powered abilities can only be interpreted, verified, and harnessed via an internal technology used by those who have practised and honed their Buddhist craft. Although I passed a seemingly invisible test of trust in the van, as a nonexpert, I cannot access their technologies and methods unless I learn, test, and experiment for myself—as Ann frequently encouraged.

Connection 2: Apocalyptic Imaginaries and Planetary Futures

The second partial overlap can be found within imaginaries and "projectories" about worlds ending and emergent worlds in the making (Messeri and Vertesi 2015; see also Jasanoff and Kim 2009).

Both Ann and David's searches for either habitable planets or extraterrestrial life unfold within a conceptual framework of Earth's finitude. NARIT's research and technical coordinator, Suparerk, explained the astronomical institute's underlying motivations for exoplanet research to me in an interview:

> [Firstly], is there really life on another planet or another solar system? Secondly, is it possible for us to have another colony? What happens if Earth is full of garbage, with not enough energy, no more food? We would need to relocate, right? To somewhere else. You cannot stay on a ship—you need to settle down on a new planet, right? I think they're the two things that astronomers are thinking: either survival or to find other intelligent life.

In tandem, UFO Kaokala group members envision an apocalyptic future of natural disasters and nuclear catastrophe that will culminate in extraterrestrial lifeforms coming to save at least some of the human population. Unlike the exoplanet astronomy community's desire to secure human futures, UFO Kaokala group members are ambivalent about the continuation of human life since their world is based on transience, impermanence, and karmic cycles of rebirth.

Due to their future-oriented engagement with potential extraterrestrial life, David and Ann also hold precarious positions in the larger realities in which they operate. A semi-famous actor shared with me that he feared losing work due to his connection to UFO Kaokala since in Thailand, the concept of extraterrestrials tends to be relegated to US American pop culture fantasies and alt-right conspiracy theorists. At the same time, the group sometimes leans into ET culture's "giggle factor" (Wright and Oman-Reagan 2018). Driving in a van on the way to Kaokala, prominent UFO Kaokala member Ukrin pointed and shouted, "UFO!" "UFO!" before bursting into high-pitched laughter. It turned out he was pointing at a concrete water tower that did indeed resemble an archetypal disc or saucer-like UFO.

As an astronomer operating within the broader realm of Science, it might seem that David would have no such problems with being taken seriously. Yet scientists who engage with potential extraterrestrial life or life-supporting planets in fields like astrobiology, SETI, METI, and exoplanet research are often derided by not only broader publics but also fellow scientists, partly because of the same kind of 'giggle factor' faced by UFO Kaokala's actor (Wright and Oman-Reagan 2018). To avoid too closely associating with the question of extraterrestrial life and its connection to imaginaries of 'little green men', space anthropologist Lisa Messeri identifies that exoplanet astronomers tend to carefully frame their work as searching "for the conditions of life, rather than life itself" (2017: 330; see also Losch 2016). Messeri's observation is echoed in David's explanation of the potential steps in his field:

> The first step is to detect [an exoplanet], and the second step is to detect the atmosphere, to study, to find the chemical components … if it is a gas planet. So at this moment, we are searching for evidence of atmospheres on the planets. And I think the next step will be to find the indicators of life. So step by step you have to move.

When I asked David what the next step after that would be, he ponders, "Maybe I think about this but not seriously", ultimately dismissing the prospect as "ufology". Here, exoplanet astronomy works along a distinct trajectory from Earth toward the pursuit of not just any yet-to-be-discovered planet but a planet that contains indicators of life. However, an invisible threshold from 'serious' to 'unserious' thought is crossed when there is a question of engagement with extraterrestrial life.

Looking towards the future, if David's step three is reached and another life-supporting planet is discovered, any ideas about Earth being a unique exception in the cosmos would be destroyed. Just as Copernicus radically decentred Earth by showing that the sun—not the Earth—is the solar system's stable centre, the discovery of habitable planets would knock Earth from its central position as a supporter of life and reposition it into new relations with other potential living entities and worlds (Messeri 2017). Meanwhile, Somjit's mind-as-film-screen image is a first step in teaching ufological Buddhist practitioners that their thoughts are simply enduring, ever-changing projections onto a blank screen. From here, one aims to understand that both the self and all of existence are transient and impermanent. The ongoing Buddhist project, therefore, hinges on overcoming attachments to various conditions, including the idea of a stable and bounded self (McMahan and Braun 2017; Stonington 2020). In this sense, radically decentering and destabilising the human self are potential key outcomes of both UFO Kaokala and NARIT's work. However, I want to be careful about treading too far into this partial connection since the composition of Ann's world is fundamentally different to David's world. In contrast to Buddhism's constantly changing and precarious reality (Aulino 2019), exoplanet astronomy and the broader modernist doctrine in which it is embedded continues to stabilise itself with each new discovery.

Inventing Anew and Spatialising Differently

This chapter began with the question of how to take different cosmo-practices seriously. If written in a modernist philosophical framework, this chapter would likely have played out as a classical battle between science and religion, reason and belief, global and local forms of knowledge, and so on. Yet I have sought to offer an antidote to the marginalising impulse embedded within dualistic thought by breaking exoplanet astronomical and ufological Buddhist cosmo-practices into components and attending to a multiplicity of relations within them. In doing so, it becomes clear that the practices at the TNO are external and their technologies are directed outward towards material celestial bodies. Conversely, UFO Kaokala's practices are internal and their technologies are directed inward to transform the practitioner. Through this recomposition, exoplanet astronomy and ufological Buddhism emerge as incommensurably different worlds rather than different perspectives projected onto a singular world. Each world is only partial, unfinished, and always in transformation. One is no more 'right' than the other. One is no more stable than the other.

Thinking within the social studies of outer space, this generative approach of juxtaposing an array of outer spatial practices can be experimented with further by taking into account a multiplicity of extraterrestrial engagements. This would, in turn, contribute towards a robust social scientific practice that incorporates wider information, complexity, and nuance. Furthermore, a focus on emergent, interdependent, and dynamic relations helps to estrange and render certain aspects of divergent worlds more clearly. In this chapter, the different motivations and methods that underpin David and Ann's worlds invite speculative questions such as, how might meditation and other mind practices be used as methods for space exploration? What if decentring the self, and by extension, the human, was an explicit motivation in future-oriented astronomical cosmo-practices the way that it is in Buddhist ones?

The point in working to take disparate worlds seriously and refracting them through an array of emergent relations, then, is not just to affirm a plurality of cosmo-practices but to open up a generative space that enables us to "invent anew and spatialise differently" (Jackson 2018: 14). Like both David's and Ann's cosmo-practices, this chapter unfolds against a backdrop of potential worlds ending, and potential new worlds beginning. Released from the confines of a modernist one-world world, we can know and imagine other worlds are possible, and in turn, other modes of human space endeavours.

Acknowledgements

I would like to thank the Emslie Horniman Anthropological Scholarship fund for support in my fieldwork. I also thank Milan Kroulík, Andrea Coyotzi Borja, and the editors for reviewing and commenting on this chapter, as well as my supervisors Thomas Stodulka and Bronislaw Szerszynski for their guidance and professional support.

References

Aulino, Felicity. 2019. "Everyday Care and Precarity: Buddhaghosa and Thai Social Story-Making." *Medical Anthropology* 39 (4): 305–18. https://doi.org/10.1080/01459740.2019.1589465.
Bauman, Whitney. 2015. "Religion, Science, and Globalization: Beyond Comparative Approaches." *Zygon* 50 (2): 389–402. https://doi.org/10.1111/zygo.12170.
Behrend, Heike, and Martin Zillinger. 2015. "Introduction: Trance Mediums and New Media." In *Trance Mediums and New Media: Spirit Possession in the Age of Technical Reproduction*, edited by Heike Behrend, Anja Dreschke, and Martin Zillinger, 1–24. New York: Fordham University Press. https://doi.org/10.2307/j.ctt1287g07.5.
Blaser, Mario. 2016. "Is Another Cosmopolitics Possible?" *Cultural Anthropology* 31 (4): 545–70. https://doi.org/10.14506/ca31.4.05.

Bobbette, Adam. 2018. "Cosmological Reason on a Volcano." In *Political Geology: Active Stratigraphies and the Making of Life*, edited by Adam Bobbette and Amy Donovan, 169–99. Cambridge: Springer International. https://doi.org/10.1007/978-3-319-98189-5_6.

Cassaniti, Julia. 2015. *Living Buddhism: Mind, Self, and Emotion in a Thai Community*. Ithaca, NY: Cornell University Press.

Casumbal-Salazar, Iokepa. 2017. "A Fictive Kinship: Making 'Modernity', 'Ancient Hawaiians', and the Telescopes on Mauna Kea." *Native American and Indigenous Studies* 4 (2): 1–30. https://doi.org/10.5749/natiindistudj.4.2.0001.

Chua, Lawrence. 2021. *Bangkok Utopia: Modern Architecture and Buddhist Felicities, 1910–1973*. Honolulu: University of Hawai'i Press.

de la Cadena, Marisol. 2010. "Indigenous Cosmopolitics in the Andes: Conceptual Reflections beyond 'Politics'." *Cultural Anthropology* 25 (2): 334–70. https://doi.org/10.1111/j.1548-1360.2010.01061.x.

de la Cadena, Marisol. 2015. *Earth Beings: Ecologies of Practice across Andean Worlds*. Durham, NC: Duke University Press.

Escobar, Arturo. 2020. *Pluriversal Politics: The Real and the Possible*. Translated by David Frye. Durham, NC: Duke University Press.

Gorman, Alice. 2005. "The Cultural Landscape of Interplanetary Space." *Journal of Social Archaeology* 5 (1): 85–107. https://doi.org/10.1177/1469605305050148.

Haraway, Donna. 1991. *Simians, Cyborgs, and Women: The Reinvention of Nature*. New York: Routledge.

Harding, Sandra. 2008. *Sciences from Below: Feminisms, Postcolonialities, and Modernities*. Durham, NC: Duke University Press.

Jackson, Mark, ed. 2018. "Introduction: A Critical Bridging Exercise." In *Coloniality, Ontology, and the Question of the Posthuman*, edited by Mark Jackson, 1–17. London: Routledge.

Jasanoff, Sheila. 2004. *States of Knowledge: The Co-production of Science and Social Order*. London: Routledge.

Jasanoff, Sheila and Sang-Hyun Kim. 2009. "Containing the Atoms: Sociotechnical Imaginaries and Nuclear Power in the United States and South Korea." *Minerva* 47 (2): 119–46. https://doi.org/10.1007/s11024-009-9124-4.

Johnson, Anne W. 2020. "Space Cultures and Space Imaginaries in Mexico: Anthropological Dialogues with the Mexican Space Agency." *Acta Astronautica* 177: 398–404. https://doi.org/10.1016/J.ACTAASTRO.2020.08.002.

Karunamuni, Nandini D. 2015. "The Five-Aggregate Model of the Mind." *Sage Open* 5 (2): 1–7. https://doi.org/10.1177/2158244015583860.

Kearnes, Matthew, and Thom van Dooren. 2017. "Rethinking the Final Frontier: Cosmo-Logics and an Ethic of Interstellar Flourishing." *GeoHumanities* 3 (1): 178–97. https://doi.org/10.1080/2373566X.2017.1300448.

Kessler, Elizabeth. 2012. *Picturing the Cosmos: Hubble Space Telescope Images and the Astronomical Sublime*. Minneapolis: University of Minnesota Press.

Kitiarsa, Pattana. 2005. "Beyond Syncretism: Hybridization of Popular Religion in Contemporary Thailand." *Journal of Southeast Asian Studies* 36 (3): 461–87. https://doi.org/10.1017/S0022463405000251.

Latour, Bruno. 1993. *We Have Never Been Modern*. Translated by Catherine Porter. Cambridge, MA: Harvard University Press. First published 1991.

Latour, Bruno. 2005. "'Thou Shall Not Freeze-Frame', or, How Not to Misunderstand the Science and Religion Debate." In *Science, Religion, and the Human Experience*, edited by James D. Proctor, 27–48. Oxford Scholarship Online. https://doi.org/10.1093/0195175328.003.0003.

Law, John. 2015. "What's Wrong with a One-World World?" *Distinktion: Journal of Social Theory* 16 (1): 126–39. https://doi.org/10.1080/1600910X.2015.1020066.

Losch, Andreas. 2016. "Astrotheology: On Exoplanets, Christian Concerns, and Human Hopes." *Zygon: Journal of Religion and Science* 51 (2): 405–13. https://doi.org/10.1111/zygo.12252.

McMahan, David, and Erik Braun, eds. 2017. *Meditation, Buddhism, and Science*. New York: Oxford University Press.

Messeri, Lisa. 2017. "Gestures of Cosmic Relation and the Search for Another Earth." *Environmental Humanities* 9 (2): 325–40. https://doi.org/10.1215/22011919-4215325.

Messeri, Lisa, and Janet Vertesi. 2015. "The Greatest Missions Never Flown: Anticipatory Discourse and the 'Projectory' in Technological Communities." *Technology and Culture* 56 (1): 54–85. https://doi.org/10.1353/tech.2015.0023.

Morita, Atsuro. 2017. "In Between the Cosmos and 'Thousand-Cubed Great Thousands Worlds': Composition of Uncommon Worlds by Alexander von Humboldt and King Mongkut." *Anthropologica* 59 (2): 228–38. http://dx.doi.org/10.3138/anth.59.2.t05.

Morris, Rosalind C. 2000. "Modernity's Media and the End of Mediumship? On the Aesthetic Economy of Transparency in Thailand." *Public Culture* 12 (2): 457–75. https://doi.org/10.1215/08992363-12-2-457.

Newell, Catherine L. 2014. "Without Having Seen: Faith, the Future, and the Final American Frontier." *Astropolitics* 12 (2–3): 148–66. https://doi.org/10.1080/14777622.2014.964126.

Omura, Keiichi, Grant Jun Otsuki, Shiho Satsuka, and Atsuro Morita. 2019. *The World Multiple: The Quotidian Politics of Knowing and Generating Entangled Worlds*. London; New York: Routledge.

Pardthaisong, Liwa, Phaothai Sin-ampol, Chanida Suwanprasit, and Arisara Charoenpanyanet. 2018. "Haze Pollution in Chiang Mai, Thailand: A Road to Resilience." *Procedia Engineering* 212: 85–92. https://doi.org/10.1016/j.proeng.2018.01.012.

Pasulka, D.W. 2019. *American Cosmic: UFOs, Religion, Technology*. New York: Oxford University Press.

Pickering, Andrew. 2017. "The Ontological Turn: Taking Different Worlds Seriously." *Social Analysis* 61 (2): 134–50. https://doi.org/10.3167/sa.2017.610209.

Praet, Istvan, and Juan Francisco Salazar. 2017. "Introduction: Familiarizing the Extraterrestrial/Making Our Planet Alien." *Environmental Humanities* 9 (2): 309–24. https://doi.org/10.1215/22011919-4215315.

Ratanakul, Pinit. 2007. "The Dynamics of Tradition and Change in Theravada Buddhism." *Journal of Religion and Culture* 1 (1): 233–57.

Redfield, Peter. 2000. *Space in the Tropics: From Convicts to Rockets in French Guiana*. Berkeley: University of California Press.

Sage, Daniel. 2008. "Framing Space: A Popular Geopolitics of American Manifest Destiny in Outer Space." *Geopolitics* 13 (1): 27–53. https://doi.org/10.1080/14650040701783482.

Savransky, Martin. 2021. *Around the Day in Eighty Worlds: Politics of the Pluriverse*. Durham, NC; London: Duke University Press.

Smiles, Deondre. 2020. "The Settler Logics of (Outer) Space." *Space and Society* [online], 26 October. Accessed 17 Jan. 2022 at https://www.societyandspace.org/articles/the-settler-logics-of-outer-space.

Stengers, Isabelle. 2010. *Cosmopolitics I*. Translated by Robert Bononno. Minneapolis: University of Minnesota Press.

Stengers, Isabelle. 2011. "Comparison as a Matter of Concern." *Common Knowledge* 17 (1): 48–63. https://doi.org/10.1215/0961754X-2010-035.

Stonington, Scott D. 2020. "Karma Masters: The Ethical Wound, Hauntological Choreography, and Complex Personhood in Thailand." *American Anthropologist* 122 (4): 759–70. https://doi.org/10.1111/aman.13464.

Strathern, Marilyn. 2004. *Partial Connections*. New York: Altamira.

Szerszynski, Bronislaw. 2005. *Nature, Technology and the Sacred*. Malden: Blackwell.

Tambiah, Stanley J. 1970. *Buddhism and the Spirit Cults in North-East Thailand*. Cambridge: Cambridge University Press.

Traphagan, John. 2020. "Religion, Science, and Space Exploration from a Non-Western Perspective." *Religions* 11 (8): 397. https://doi.org/10.3390/rel11080397.

Traphagan, John, and Julian Traphagan. 2015. "SETI in Non-Western Perspective." In *The Impact of Discovering Life beyond Earth*, edited by Steven J. Dick, 299–307. Cambridge: Cambridge University Press. https://doi.org/10.1017/CBO9781316272480.024.

Tsing, Anna Lowenhaupt. 2000. "The Global Situation." *Cultural Anthropology* 15 (3): 327–60. https://doi.org/10.1525/can.2000.15.3.327.

Tsing, Anna Lowenhaupt. 2005. *Friction: An Ethnography of Global Connection*. Princeton: Princeton University Press. https://doi.org/10.1515/9781400830596.

Verran, Helen. 2001. *Science and an African Logic*. Chicago; London: University of Chicago Press.

Verran, Helen. 2002. "A Postcolonial Moment in Science Studies: Alternative Firing Regimes of Environmental Scientists and Aboriginal Landowners." *Social Studies of Science* 32 (5/6): 729–62. https://doi.org/10.1177/030631270203200506.

Verran, Helen. 2014. "Working with Those Who Think Otherwise." *Common Knowledge* 20 (3): 527–39. https://doi.org/10.1215/0961754X-2733075.

Vertesi, Janet. 2019. "'All These Worlds Are Yours Except …': Science Fiction and Folk Fictions at NASA." *Engaging Science, Technology, and Society* 5: 135–59. https://doi.org/10.17351/ests2019.315.

Viveiros de Castro, Eduardo. 2004. "Perspectival Anthropology and the Method of Controlled Equivocation." *Tipití* 2 (1): 3–22.

Wright, Jason T., and Michael P. Oman-Reagan. 2018. "Visions of Human Futures in Space and SETI." *International Journal of Astrobiology* 17 (2): 177–88. https://doi.org/10.1017/S1473550417000222.

PART IV

Objects, Infrastructures, Networks, and Systems

24
A GLITCH IN SPACE

Juan Francisco Salazar

A glitch is usually a malfunction caused by a spike or change in voltage which takes place when the circuit suddenly has a new load put on it and which can cause a temporary setback. An early use of the term comes from US astronaut John Glenn, who in his 1962 book *In Orbit* explains a brief unexpected surge of electrical current. *In Orbit* was Glenn's reflections as the first person from the United States to orbit Earth as part of NASA's three-orbit Mercury-Atlas 6 mission, aboard a spacecraft named *Friendship 7*.

But the term also has a parallel history. It can be found in glitch art, the practice of using digital or analogue errors for aesthetic purposes by either corrupting digital data or physically manipulating electronic devices. Len Lye was experimenting with these visual art techniques as early as 1935 in the film *A Colour Box* (1935). This continued decades later during the 1960s, when the Fluxus art movement played an important role, in the origins of noise music, and during a time when Nam June Paik was crafting his video sculpture *TV Magnet* (1965), corrupting electronic images. In the 1990s the term *glitch* also became associated with genres of contemporary experimental electronic music.

In "Glitch Studies Manifesto", Rosa Menkman (2011) makes the following provocation: "The dominant, continuing search for a noiseless channel has been—and will always be—no more than a regrettable, ill-fated dogma" (p. 346). The seed of this *Handbook* draws on this provocation and attempts to bring together a diversity of perspectives which in one way or another challenge dominant, noiseless narratives, and imaginaries of outer space, shaped by ill-fated dogmas of colonisation that could turn out to be no more than regrettable. Menkman puts it this way:

> the glitch is a wonderful experience of an interruption that shifts an object away s its ordinary form and discourse. For a moment I am shocked, lost and in awe, asking myself what this other utterance is, how was it created. Is it perhaps…a glitch?
>
> *(pp. 340–41)*

The images were produced using an AI "text to image" image generator and editor (Figures 24.1 and 24.2). The glitching not only speaks to a mere technical error or a malfunction within every space infrastructure, network, and system. The glitch works as a device to speak metaphorically of a malfunction in contemporary hegemonic imaginaries of human bodies in outer space. A humble provocation to call for a glitching of space futures, against dominant and normative narratives of humanity in space.

Figure 24.1 Space Glitch Astronaut #3. Image by Juan Francisco Salazar, 2022.

Figure 24.2 Space Glitch Afronaut #5. Image by Juan Francisco Salazar, 2022.

Reference

Menkman, Rosa. 2011. "Glitch Studies Manifesto." In *Video Vortex Reader II: Moving Images beyond YouTube*, edited by Geert Lovink and Rachel Somers Miles, 336–47. Amsterdam: Institute of Network Cultures.

25
PREPARING FOR THE "INTERNET APOCALYPSE"

Data Centres and the Space Weather Threat

A. R. E. Taylor

Introduction

It is October 2018. I'm sitting in the audience for a talk on data centre security at a cloud computing expo in London. This is one of the biggest information technology trade shows in the world, attracting international technology vendors specialising in cloud infrastructure, cybersecurity, and data centre development. Over the course of the two-day event, a number of talks are organised by different IT specialists. The speaker for the talk I am attending is a data centre professional in his early fifties named Mark Cooper. His presentation begins with a close-up image of the Sun published by NASA. The image depicts a violent-looking loop of plasma spurting outwards from the Sun's outer atmosphere (the solar corona) and seemingly reaching—in what appears to be a whipping motion—towards a tiny Earth that NASA has superimposed in the lower left-hand corner of the image to provide a sense of scale. Standing in front of this dramatic image, Cooper begins his talk by calling for the audience to "forget cyberterrorists—it's space weather that's going to bring the digital world crashing to its knees".

Cooper's talk, it turned out, was not about the security issues that are often associated with the internet—cyberattacks, viruses, phishing scams, etc. Rather, he discussed the need to protect the data centres that underpin the internet from the disruptive and destructive effects of "space weather". Space weather refers to disturbances of Earth's upper atmosphere and near-space environment that can disrupt technology. The Sun regularly experiences periods of intense magnetic activity (often referred to as "solar storms") during which highly charged particles and magnetised plasma are ejected from the solar corona. These solar events are known as coronal mass ejections (CMEs) and are often accompanied by explosive solar flares that emit large amounts of radiation across the electromagnetic spectrum. According to one popular science website, a single solar flare can "release the equivalent energy of millions of hydrogen bombs" (Gaughan 2017). The electromagnetic radiation emitted by solar flares is capable of causing dayside radio blackouts, while the energetic particles released during a CME can ionise the fragile microelectronics and memory circuits found in space-based and airborne infrastructure like satellites and aircraft, potentially causing component failure and leading to loss of service. If a CME is ejected in an Earth-facing direction, the solar material released can also disturb and weaken our planet's magnetic field, producing geomagnetic storms, which are often indexed by auroral displays. Space weather poses a risk not only to infrastructure situated in outer space but also to terrestrial infrastructure (Taylor 2020). As Cooper explained during his talk, the geomagnetically induced currents (GICs) produced by space weather can damage or even destroy the components of grounded systems, such as railway track circuits, oil and gas pipelines, and the electricity transmission networks that data centres rely on.

In his fifteen-minute presentation, Cooper outlined the threat posed by space weather to critical infrastructure. He highlighted that the internet services that data centres enable are now essential to the functioning of industrialised societies and, as such, data centre operators must take measures to ensure that their mission-critical services can withstand a space weather event. He described various measures that data centres can adopt to better protect themselves from space weather, from fitting surge protectors to investing in power supply equipment that can operate off-grid. Explaining to the audience why it is important that data centres begin to address space weather, Cooper said: "With people becoming more dependent on data centres every day, it is vital [that] we begin to better protect these buildings. ... without them, the digital world will simply switch off". Cooper's talk was seasoned with the rhetoric of preparedness that has become commonplace in discourse on the space weather threat, particularly within the popular press, where phrases like "it's only a matter of time", "it's not a question of *if* but *when*", and "before it's too late" frequently abound. He cited an article that concluded Earth has a one-in-eight chance of being hit by a "catastrophic solar megastorm" before 2020 (fortunately, this scenario never materialised).[1] To conclude his presentation, he clicked the wireless remote and text flew in from the side of the PowerPoint slide saying: "Don't get scared, get prepared!"

In this chapter, I trace the emergence and construction of space weather as a threat to internet infrastructure through a focus on the data centre industry. I draw from news articles in the data centre press and fieldwork and interviews conducted with staff at VMCloud, a cloud computing provider that operates a "space weather-proof" data centre based in London. In doing so I explore how the data centre community considers the issue of the space weather risk, what measures they are taking to address this, and what role this plays in their marketing. I argue that, in the ethnographic context of the data centre industry, space weather arises as both a threat and a marketing opportunity, generating preparedness measures but also providing data centres with a means to showcase and promote their security.

The discussion in this chapter contributes to a growing body of interdisciplinary scholarship exploring linkages between terrestrial geographies and outer space. Amidst a wider "turn to space" (Dunnett et al. 2017: 2; Olson and Messeri 2015) that has taken place across the arts, social sciences, and humanities, there has been growing interest in terrestrial sites through which outer space and earth are brought into relation (Battaglia, Valentine, and Olson 2015; Klinger 2017; MacDonald 2007: 593; Valentine 2016). A range of ground-surface sites dedicated to space activity have been explored, including spaceports (Redfield 2000; Siddiqi 2015), radar dish arrays that are used for space science (Taylor 2022), observatories (Hoeppe 2020; Merron 2020), and the spaces and places of scientific institutions such as NASA (Messeri 2016; Olson 2018). A significant body of scholarship has also examined the ways in which extreme terrestrial landscapes, such as deserts, oceans, and mountains, have been mobilised as "analogue" sites for conducting space research or simulating alien worlds (Helmreich 2006; Collis 2016; Messeri 2016; Praet and Salazar 2017). To date, this literature has predominantly focused on sites that are directly related to space activity and are often associated with space organisations. In this chapter, I expand this focus by exploring how the space weather threat is enfolding the operators of infrastructures that have no immediate association with outer space into relation with the solar system.[2] Through this analysis, I trace an expanding cosmology of critical infrastructure protection, whereby the material and energetic environment of near-Earth space plays a growing role in how internet infrastructure providers think about, imagine, and enact security. I predominantly concentrate on the UK, where the majority of my fieldwork in the data centre industry has taken place and where space weather has become a growing target of infrastructure security and policymaking.

Space Weather Becomes a Policy Object

Space weather moved onto the UK national security agenda in 2010, after the government conducted a review of emergency scenarios that might have been overlooked by previous risk assessments. The review recognised space weather as a threat to space-based and ground-based critical infrastructure in need of urgent attention (House of Commons 2011). Space weather was added to the UK's National Risk Assessment in 2011 and was included in subsequent National Risk Registers. In July 2014 the UK government published its Space Weather Preparedness Strategy. Later that year, in October 2014, as part of a £4.6 million investment programme, the Met Office Space Weather Operations Centre (MOSWOC) was launched in Exeter, southwest England. More recently, in September 2021 the UK government published the UK Severe Space Weather Preparedness Strategy. Beyond the UK, space weather has also become a key target of preparedness for China, Japan, India, the United States, and a number of European countries, many of whom have now invested in infrastructure and research programmes in efforts to build national and international preparedness for space weather events. In 2010 the Asia-Oceania Space Weather Alliance (AOSWA) was formed, consisting of organisations from thirteen countries across Asia and Oceania. The following year, the World Meteorological Organization (WMO) released its Statement on Global Preparedness for Space Weather Hazards, calling for the coordination and implementation of near-term and long-term plans among all WMO members for addressing the space weather risk. In 2015 the White House released its National Space Weather Action Plan and National Space Weather Strategy, while in 2016 the European Commission published its policy paper on Space Weather and Critical Infrastructures. In November 2019, the United Nations launched a 24/7 space weather network to provide real-time updates for global aviation.

As space weather becomes a global security project, it is also attracting media attention, spawning dystopian visions of social and economic collapse. TV shows like Sky's *Cobra* (2020) provide viewers with a post-apocalyptic vision of the UK descending into anarchy after a severe space weather event shuts down power grids across Europe. News articles about the threat that solar storms pose to social life on Earth have become a regular occurrence in the British tabloid press. These usually take the form of dramatic warnings about the societal disruption that could be caused if a predicted solar storm causes power grid failures or satellite outages. The imagined technological and societal disruption is typically configured temporally as a violent "return" to an earlier stage of pre-industrial being, with news headlines frequently proclaiming that a severe space weather event would send humanity back to the "Dark Age" (Waghorn 2021).

The basis for these apocalyptic imaginaries is a space weather event that occurred in the late summer of 1859, when a series of CMEs erupted from the Sun, producing dramatic auroral displays that were reported across Europe and North America. Strong geomagnetic currents were also generated, which greatly affected telegraph systems. The currents disrupted the sending of messages and in some cases produced power surges that gave operators electric shocks and caused fires in telegraph stations (Clauer and Siscoe 2006). Today, this event is known as the Carrington Event. It was named after the nineteenth-century English astronomer Richard Carrington (1826–1825), who happened to witness a series of solar flares erupting on the Sun during this period and suggested that a connection might exist between the solar eruptions and the ensuing terrestrial magnetic disturbances. The Carrington Event occurred when electrical infrastructure was in its infancy and recurrently arises in discourse on the space weather threat today as a "reasonable worst case scenario" (RWCS), which policymakers, infrastructure operators, and insurance providers use as a benchmark to imagine and assess the potential impact of a severe solar storm occurring today. An article written by space weather historians Sten Odenwald and James L. Green (2008: 80) warns us that "[a] recurrence of the 1859 solar superstorm would be a cosmic Katrina, causing billions of dollars of damage to satellites, power grids and radio communications". A 2013 study released by the insurance company Lloyd's (2013: 4) estimated that if a Carrington-scale event affected the US power grid today it could leave 20–40 million people without power over a timescale that could stretch from sixteen days up to two years (Lloyd's note that the outage duration will depend largely on the availability of replacement transformers). The report calculated the total economic cost for such a scenario at US$0.6–$2.6 trillion.

The Carrington Event is not the only large-scale space weather event that has affected Earth. The largest geomagnetic storm in the last century took place in May 1921. This storm generated "violent levels of geomagnetic disturbance" (Love, Hayakawa, and Cliver 2019: 1281) that caused widespread interference to the telephone and telegraph systems in New York. Like the Carrington Event, this solar storm took place before widespread electrification. More recent space weather events that occurred in the second half of the twentieth century have been less magnetically powerful, but their economic consequences have exceeded the 1859 and 1921 events due to increased societal reliance on electrical infrastructure. For example, in March 1989, a geomagnetic storm tripped circuit breakers on Hydro-Québec's power grid, causing a nine-hour outage of the electricity transmission system, "which affected three million people and cost an estimated $2 billion in gross domestic product" (Odenwald 2007: 1). Between mid-October and early November 2003, a series of solar flares and coronal mass ejections damaged—and in some cases permanently disabled—spacecraft and satellites, affecting terrestrial GPS and communications systems. Aeroplanes had to be diverted to avoid high altitudes, while interference with over-the-horizon radio communications forced cancellations of airline polar routes. These space weather events also affected terrestrial power grids. In Malmö, Sweden, a power outage was triggered and transformers at a nuclear power plant overheated, while in South Africa it was also reported that "storm-induced surges fried transformers" (Witze 2016: 458; NASA 2008).

While the natural phenomena underlying space weather (e.g., the solar wind, geomagnetic activity, and solar energetic particle events) have thus existed since the Earth and the Sun formed, it was only in the nineteenth and twentieth centuries, amidst increasing societal reliance on electrical technology systems, that this naturally occurring electromagnetic activity was constructed as a risk. In this sense, space weather might be described as a 'technonatural' or 'envirotechnical' risk. Environmental historian Sara B. Pritchard (2012) uses the term 'envirotechnical disaster' to describe threats that arise from the conjunction of ecological and technological systems. The space weather risk arises from a tangled web of natural, technical, and social relationships, whereby the energetic conditions of the near-Earth space environment exacerbate vulnerabilities arising from societal dependencies on electro-digital technologies. A growing number of studies have now explored the large economic impacts arising from the adverse effects of space weather on electricity transmission networks (Forbes and St. Cyr 2008; Oughton et al. 2017). In addition to electricity supplies, efforts to model, assess, and quantify the impact of space weather have also focused on railway circuits (Krausmann et al. 2015), pipelines (Viljanen et al. 2006), aircraft (Jones et al. 2005), and satellites (Hapgood 2017). All of these critical sectors are, in turn, increasingly reliant upon and mediated by internet infrastructure. However, only recently has attention begun to turn towards the internet (Jyothi 2021).

The Internet Apocalypse

Data centres form the operational backbone of the "cloud" internet, interconnecting and enabling an ever-increasing range of infrastructures and services across business, government, and society. These buildings store and process the data that is now central to the everyday operation of online systems. Financial services (banking and insurance), transportation systems (air traffic controls, road and rail signals, driverless cars), global logistics, communications (telephone networks, satellites, messaging apps, videoconferencing platforms), government and emergency services, and utility providers (gas, water, electricity) are just some of the key sectors that rely on data centres. These buildings are now perceived to connect such an incredible range of services and utilities that, we are told, "It's the data centre that makes our modern world possible" (Coors 2016). As one data centre professional states in an industry magazine: "Without data centers, our world would pretty much grind to a halt in a very short time. ... No banks, no traffic lights, no shipping, no petrol stations, no food in a very short while" (Rayner 2016). For this reason, the UK's Centre for the Protection of National Infrastructure (CPNI 2010) has recognised data centres as "essential to the overall running of the country".

Unplanned data centre downtime can cause significant societal disruption. In 2017, the failure of two data centres in London led to the cancellation of 672 British Airways flights at an estimated cost of £58 million (Judge 2018). Data centre failure events like this have provided a window onto the chaos that can ensue when these buildings are momentarily unable to deliver their services. With the internet services provided by data centres increasingly understood as essential to everyday life, imaginaries of the catastrophic potential of internet outages are gaining traction. Novels like Tim Maughan's *Infinite Detail* (2019) provide a glimpse of what life may look like after the collapse of the internet. An increasingly complex network of providers and interdependencies now underpins internet infrastructure, which has led to a number of significant downtime events in recent years. In October 2021, Facebook and its subsidiary services became globally unavailable for a period of six to seven hours (Morris 2021a). In June 2021, some of the world's most visited websites, including Amazon, PayPal, and Reddit, were left inaccessible after Fastly, a global content delivery network (CDN) that provides cloud computing services, suffered a major outage. For technology correspondents and cybersecurity analysts, the blackout highlighted the "fragility of the internet's current architecture" (Associated Press 2021) and served as "a stark reminder that the Internet can fail" (Miller 2021). Not long after this event, in July 2021, another internet outage occurred, disabling banking, retail, and online videogame services (Morris 2021b).

In addition to causing societal disruption, if a data centre should go offline, even for a few seconds, it can have major financial and reputational implications for the provider. Considerable effort is thus invested in the security of these buildings, with data centres promising to protect their clients' data from an ever-multiplying range of threats, including cyberattacks, hurricane-level winds, brute force breaches, car bombs, and, in some cases, space weather (Taylor 2021, 2023).

Joining cyberattacks and software bugs, space weather has surfaced as a growing threat to the continuity of the internet. In August 2021, Sangeetha Abdu Jyothi, a computer scientist based at the University of California, Irvine, presented a paper at the annual Special Interest Group on Data Communication (SIGCOMM) conference on the risk that a severe space weather event potentially poses to internet infrastructure. The paper, dramatically titled "Solar Superstorms: Planning for an Internet Apocalypse", generated considerable attention in the popular press (Figure 25.1). Reporting on Jyothi's paper, *Wired* magazine proclaimed that "A Bad Solar Storm Could Cause an 'Internet Apocalypse'", noting that "[e]ven if the power comes back after the next big solar storm, the internet may not" (Newman 2021). Jyothi's paper was published in the proceedings of the conference and continued to be picked up by the news media, generating alarming headlines. The UK newspaper *The Independent* published an article titled "Once-in-a-Century Solar Superstorm Could Plunge the World into 'Internet Apocalypse', Study Says" (Sankaran 2021). The popular science news website LiveScience posted an article titled, "An 'Internet Apocalypse' Could Ride to Earth with the Next Solar Storm, New Research Warns" (Specktor 2021). Forbes published an article headlined "Why America Should Suddenly Prepare for a Billion-Dollar 'Internet Apocalypse' Caused by the Sun" (Carter 2021).

Jyothi's study examined the potential impact of space weather effects on land and submarine cable networks, internet exchange points (IXPs), data centres, and DNS root servers. In particular,

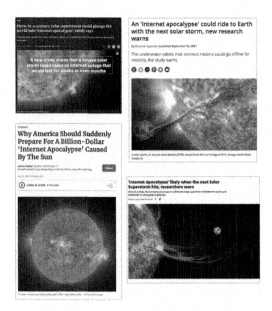

Figure 25.1 News coverage of the threat that space weather poses to the internet. Screenshots by author.

it highlighted that long-distance submarine fibre-optic cables are potentially vulnerable to damage from the geomagnetically induced currents produced by coronal mass ejections and geomagnetically induced currents: "Based on the strength of the CME, in extreme cases, GIC has the potential to enter and damage long-distance cables that constitute the backbone of the Internet" (Jyothi 2021: 692). Others have also voiced concerns about the impact of space weather on the internet. In an article on solar storms published in *The Conversation*, David Wallace (2022), a professor of electrical engineering at Mississippi State University, highlights that, in addition to power grid failures, "communications would be disrupted on a worldwide scale", adding that "Internet service providers could go down". Wallace goes on to highlight that a large-scale geomagnetic storm

> could produce geomagnetically induced currents in the submarine and terrestrial cables that form the backbone of the internet as well as the data centers that store and process everything from email and text messages to scientific data sets and artificial intelligence tools. This would potentially disrupt the entire network and prevent the servers from connecting to each other.[3]

The impact of space weather on internet infrastructure has been a matter of discussion and debate within the data centre community long before the publication of Jyothi's study. Indeed, data centre industry news articles were discussing the space weather risk even before it moved on to the UK government's security agenda (Miller 2009). A 2009 article by IT journalist Rich Miller warned industry professionals about the risk to data centres posed by solar storms. Miller observed that "data center operators are being encouraged to educate themselves about the issue [of space weather]" and discussed a range of "common-sense preparations" that data centre operators can take to protect their facilities from space weather, asking readers, "Is your data center ready?" In the article, Miller invoked the eschatological visions that were being prompted by the end of the Mayan calendar in December 2012. He noted that 2012 was not only when the Mayan calendar was ending but also when the next peak in the eleven-year cycle of solar activity was predicted to take place. In solar physics, magnetic activity on the solar surface (indicated by sunspots) is understood to wax and wane in cycles, with a period length of approximately eleven years. The mid-point of a solar cycle, when the Sun is at its most active, is known as the "solar maximum". The year 2012 was the mid-point of Solar Cycle 24, which began in 2008 and ended in 2019. Space weather garnered attention in the data centre press around this time (Clark 2013; Verge 2013). Data centre journalist Jason Verge (2013) highlighted that solar storms "can wreak havoc on infrastructure" and noted, "While the chances of a direct hit from a solar flare are small, it's something data center managers should be preparing for." In the next section I draw from a field visit to a data centre to explore space weather preparedness in practice.

Space Weather Preparedness

During a visit to a data centre in London, the various measures that can be taken take to "solar-proof" (Brown 2015) a facility were explained to me. The data centre is operated by the cloud computing provider VMCloud, which predominantly provides cloud resources and data storage services for businesses and corporate clients. As part of their security marketing, they promise to protect the data and equipment their facilities house from a range of disaster scenarios, including cyberattacks, hurricane-level winds, and the effects of space weather. Gary Kellner, the director of business continuity, showed me around the site and talked me through the structural features that make the data centre space weather-proof.

"Contingencies for space weather are similar to the standard measures that most data centres will have in place to ensure they can maintain uptime in the event of a lightning storm or power grid disturbance", Kellner told me.[4] This includes fitting and regularly testing circuit breakers, trip switches, and fuses, as well as investing in emergency generators, developing a surge suppression strategy and robust disaster recovery plans, and regularly testing blackstart procedures (a blackstart is when power is restored without relying on an external electricity transmission provider). Kellner informed me that one of the biggest challenges space weather poses to a data centre is "voltage transients"—short-duration power surges of electrical energy that can be generated by geomagnetically induced currents. He explained that mission-critical equipment in data centres, such as control electronics, power generation and distribution equipment, switchgear, flywheels, and heating, ventilation, and air conditioning (HVAC) systems must be safeguarded from these "overvoltage events". The simplest way to do this, Kellner told me, was by fitting specialist surge protectors known as transient voltage surge suppressors (TVSS) at multiple strategic points throughout the data centre. He showed me a TVSS in one of the power rooms. The room contained some of the data centre's switchgear (the electrical disconnect switches, fuses, and circuit breakers that are used to protect and isolate the facility's electrical equipment). He opened up wall-mounted steel cabinet in which a surge protector was installed and explained that these devices are fitted to all of VMCloud's service entrance switchgear and distribution switchgear, and that they are relatively inexpensive (usually costing around £1000). These surge suppressors monitor the voltage of the incoming electricity feed from the National Grid (the UK's electricity transmission network operator) and divert any surges they detect on the incoming voltage line. He told me that VMCloud goes beyond these standard security measures by also incorporating "blocking capacitors" into their electrical circuity, which help to block the flow of geomagnetically induced currents. A single blocking capacitor can cost £100,000 alone, he highlighted. "It's expensive", said Kellner, "but nowhere near as expensive as downtime".

Space weather invites data centre providers to confront their relationship to the power grid. There is a tight interdependence between power grids and the internet. "It's not so much space weather that's that threat", Kellner explained, "but the industry's dependence on the electrical grid, which could easily go down during a severe space weather event, taking data centres with it". As data centre industry journalist Jeff Clark (2013) surmised in a news article on the space weather threat: "Any event that harms part of the power grid is a potential threat to data centers". The most important thing, Kellner highlighted, is ensuring that back-up generators are connected to mission-critical equipment and that there is plenty of stored fuel so the facility can survive in the event of a power collapse. "This includes ensuring that the back-up generators are well maintained, have an adequate supply of diesel fuel, and that fuel supply agreements are in place to cover an extended outage", he informed me. He explained that electrical outages caused by a major solar storm could be long term and that even these measures might be insufficient in the event of outages that extend to weeks or even months. Space weather thus throws into relief the relations of dependency that characterise the data centre industry's connectivity to the power grid.

In addition, Kellner explained that "data centres should have uninterruptible power supply (UPS) systems installed—not just backup generators—as part of their preparedness strategy". UPS systems are battery-powered devices that provide an immediate power source while generators warm up, ensuring there is no break in the power supply to critical equipment. Kellner highlighted that preparedness measures like this are standard practice, especially for data centres located in regions where earthquakes or hurricanes are relatively commonplace.

Figure 25.2 VMCloud's "space weather-proof" server room. Photo by author.

The big problem for data centres in places like the UK and Europe is that they can fall short of providing these basic disaster preparedness measures, simply because they don't really have to deal with natural disasters on a regular basis.

He explained that "with space weather we are all in the risk zone so we should all be adopting these preparedness practices, and solar storms should really be factored into every data centre's risk assessment". Through these practices, data centres become "space weather-proof" (Figure 25.2).

Anticipating the Inevitable

A characteristic feature of preparedness is its anticipatory orientation (Anderson 2010; Keck 2016; Lakoff 2017). Based on a distinctly modern vision of the future as a time-space filled with threat (Horn 2018), preparedness structures the space and time of the present in relation to an unexpected future event, cultivating a sense of unease and anxiety in order to mobilise action and produce a state of readiness. These threatening future events are understood to be largely inevitable and unpreventable, but potentially manageable if the right measures are taken to anticipate them. If action is not taken, "a threshold will be crossed and a disastrous future will come about" (Anderson 2010: 780).

One of the key difficulties that space weather poses for infrastructure operators and preparedness practitioners is the uncertainty surrounding when an event will occur. While small-scale space weather events take place on a regular basis, it is estimated that Carrington-level events occur once every one hundred to two hundred years. The 2013 Lloyd's risk assessment highlights that

> [a] Carrington-level, extreme geomagnetic storm is almost inevitable in the future. While the probability of an extreme storm occurring is relatively low at any given time, it is almost inevitable that one will occur eventually. Historical auroral records suggest a return period of 50 years for Québec-level storms and 150 years for very extreme storms, such as the Carrington Event that occurred 154 years ago
>
> *(Lloyd's 2013: 4)*

The Lloyd's assessment has become a key document that is regularly cited in the domain of space weather preparedness. Here the assessment works to generate an affective state of readiness by presenting a severe space weather event as already four years overdue at the time the article was published (writing today in 2023 this anticipated event is now twelve years overdue), configuring the present as a form of borrowed time. More recent publications have similarly reproduced the affective register of emergency that is characteristic of preparedness discourse, with Jyothi observing that "a Carrington-scale event can occur in the next couple of decades, we need to prepare our infrastructure now for a potential catastrophic event" (Jyothi 2021: 694).

Analyses of archival records have shown that these events do not only occur during the maximum of a solar cycle when the Sun's magnetic activity is at its peak. The Carrington event is a case in point. A 2012 report published by the UK government's Defence Committee (House of Commons 2012: 10) foregrounds that "space weather events do not necessarily obey this cycle; the Carrington event of 1859 occurred in the middle of a cycle". This irregularity makes space weather a threat "that can happen at any time" (House of Commons 2011: ev110). Space weather events are thus seen to occur relatively regularly but also randomly, producing an ever-present threat riddled with anywhere-anytime potential. Jyothi's (2021: 694) article on the space weather threat to internet infrastructure mobilises the language of preparedness, reproducing a sense of impending doom and calamity if action is not taken to prepare. Citing a November 2020 report that suggested the current solar cycle twenty-five "has the potential to be one of the strongest on record", Jyothi reminds readers that "[t]he past 2–3 solar cycles, which coincided with the birth and growth of the Internet were very weak" and that "current Internet infrastructure has not been stress-tested by strong solar events" (p. 694).

During my visit to VMCloud, Kellner talked me through some strategies in place for managing the uncertain timescape of space weather. "The first thing our security team do with each shift rotation is check out the latest space weather forecast", he told me. He explained that data centre providers should subscribe to a space weather forecasting service if they want to improve their preparedness. Space weather forecast services are now offered by a range of organisations, including the Met Office Space Weather Operations Centre (MOSWOC) and the National Oceanic and Atmospheric Administration's (NOAA) Space Weather Prediction Center (SWPC). These forecast services compile space weather reports from data collected by spacecraft stationed between the Sun and Earth to monitor solar activity, such as NASA's Solar and Heliospheric Observatory (SOHO) and Solar Dynamics Observatory (SDO), the Indian Space Research Organisation's Aditya-L1 satellite, and NOAA's soon-to-be-launched Space Weather Follow On-Lagrange 1 (SWFO-L1), with the aim of providing forecasts and early warnings of incoming space weather (Poppe and Jorden 2006). While the radiation from solar flares travels at the speed of light (reaching Earth in eight minutes), the charged and magnetised material from CMEs can take between thirteen hours to three days to travel to Earth (Jyothi 2021: 701). This provides infrastructure operators with a window of time in which they can make decisions about whether to shut down their systems in order to minimise connectivity loss during and after impact. Kellner explained to me that "data centre personnel should monitor these services so they are aware of any incoming solar activity". He showed me a number of space weather alert apps on his mobile phone that automatically send him notifications if a solar storm is going to take place. He also explained that he receives geomagnetic disturbance alerts from the British Geological Survey. "You need to keep track of space weather just as you keep track of the regular weather", he said.

As well as these temporal considerations, the space weather threat also has spatial implications that preparedness practitioners must take into account in their planning. As a UK government policy document states:

> Space weather is a global threat and may affect many regions and countries simultaneously. This means that there is scope for mutual assistance, but also that there is no safe place from which it can be assumed that help will come.
>
> *(House of Commons 2012: 35)*

For Kellner, the potentially extensive spatial impact of a space weather event reinforced his conviction that data centres must be self-reliant and have robust plans in place to survive off-grid for an extended period of time. As he showed me VMCloud's redundant generators he further highlighted the importance of infrastructure independence and warned me about the industry's overreliance on back-up data centres. "Most data centres heavily rely on their secondary sites" he told me, "but if a severe space weather event occurred you can't guarantee these will be unaffected. … Recovery sites should never come at the expense of investments in the physical security of primary sites."

Conclusion

VMCloud has taken a range of measures to increase the likelihood of ensuring that its data centre remains operational during a severe space weather event. While Kellner noted that the precautions most data centres will have in place to withstand power grid disturbances should enable them to survive the effects of a small-scale solar storm, he was sceptical that many would be able to withstand a Carrington-level event. For Kellner, the space weather protection measures in place at the data centre demonstrated VMCloud's "next-level security offering ... that goes beyond the standard threats to data centres" and "shows that we take security seriously". By promoting these measures as forms of 'space weather-proofing', Kellner sought to highlight VMCloud's expansive security thinking.

Discourses and practices of space weather preparedness in the data centre industry must be seen within the political-economic context that Naomi Klein (2007) has termed "disaster capitalism". Klein uses this phrase to describe the economic-industrial complex that converts disasters into profitable opportunities. Elsewhere I have highlighted how data centre providers conjure threats in their marketing and tours in order to promote the security affordances of their sites to prospective clients (Taylor 2021). While waiting for the anticipated space weather event to occur, the marketing teams of space weather-proof data centres expend considerable effort on raising awareness of the solar storm threat in order to promote themselves as offering a level of security that their competitors do not possess. Kellner does not just inhabit a cosmos of threatening electromagnetism but was actively engaged in bringing this cosmology into being for prospective clients and other industry professionals. Like Mark Cooper, who we met at the beginning of this chapter, Kellner is a regular speaker at the expos, trade fairs, and other events that make up the data centre professional's calendar. These events provide an opportunity to increase awareness of the space weather issue and to promote the security affordances of VMCloud's data centre. Kellner voiced concern about the lack of public and industry awareness of the urgency of space weather threats. He talked me through a "near miss" CME that took place in 2012. "If the eruption had occurred just a few days earlier it would have hit Earth", he explained, "NASA said it would have been the worst solar storm in two hundred years, maybe bigger than the Carrington event: we'd still be picking up the pieces". NASA reported on this event—and the lack of attention it garnered in the press—by comparing it to another planetary end-times scenario in the form of the asteroid:

> If an asteroid big enough to knock modern civilization back to the 18th century appeared out of deep space and buzzed the Earth-Moon system, the near-miss would be instant worldwide headline news. Two years ago, Earth experienced a close shave just as perilous, but most newspapers didn't mention it. The 'impactor' was an extreme solar storm, the most powerful in as much as 150+ years
>
> *(NASA 2014)*

Echoing the predications in scientific and policy literature, Kellner informed me that a large-scale space weather event is certain to occur in the not-too-distant future: "it's only a matter of time", he told me, "and we all need to be prepared". Discourse on space weather in the data centre industry merges the "prophetic with the profitable" (Comaroff and Comaroff 1999: 281). Space weather-proof data centres don't just provide potential clients with a solution to a security problem, but actively perform considerable work in persuading people that there is a problem and that this problem can be mitigated by storing data in their facilities. While awareness of the space weather threat is growing among clients, Kellner informed me, many people remain unaware of this obscure electromagnetic threat. With solar cycle twenty-five expected to reach its maximum around 2025, we will no doubt see increasing media coverage of the space weather threat and more data centres taking measures to protect themselves and promote their security.

Beyond the profit motives of disaster capitalism, by tracing discourses and practices of space weather preparedness in the data centre industry, we can also see that perceptions of Earth's location within a dynamic (and threatening) solar system are increasingly crucial for how critical infrastructure protection and internet security is imagined and enacted. Technological systems are always embedded within material environments, and data centre providers increasingly recognise these environments as stretching beyond the boundary of Earth's atmosphere. Here, the internet is perceived as a complex, interdependent, and porous technological configuration that is situated within (and subject to) the energetic conditions of near-Earth space. At the same time, while Earth's surrounding electromagnetic topography is being factored into the security thinking of data centre professionals, efforts to "space weather-proof" a data centre nevertheless assume that a boundary can be established between technology and the space environment. Space weather-proof data centres, as self-reliant and shielded systems, strive to operate as material barricades against envirotechnical risk. Space weather preparedness in the data centre industry is just one way that outer space and the internet are now being brought together materially, imaginatively, and discursively. With satellite systems increasingly delivering internet connectivity, with Wi-Fi now installed on the International Space Station (ISS), and with tech start-ups currently competing to build an internet for the Moon, outer space and the internet are becoming ever more overtly entangled.

Notes

1 Cooper was citing an article published in *Wired* magazine in 2012, he told me when I spoke with him afterwards (see Mann 2012).
2 There are, of course, data centres with direct links to outer space. Observatories and Earth stations, as well as space science organisations like NASA and ESA, construct their own dedicated data centres (or rely on external colocation data centres) in which they house servers that contain the data related to research projects or that is downlinked from satellites or other space-based equipment.
3 It should be noted that there is debate in the space weather community about the findings of Jyothi's 2021 paper. Space weather scientist and risk advisor to the UK Government Mike Hapgood questioned some of the paper's conclusions on Twitter (Hapgood 2021).
4 After a lightning storm in Belgium in August 2015, Google lost some of the data in its Belgium facilities (Greenberg 2015). A major cloud outage also occurred in early September 2018, when a lightning strike affected Microsoft's data centres (Moss 2018).

References

Anderson, Ben. 2010. "Preemption, Precaution, Preparedness: Anticipatory Action and Future Geographies." *Progress in Human Geography* 34 (6): 777–98. https://doi.org/10.1177/0309132510362600.
Associated Press. 2021. "Government, News and Commercial Websites Affected as Fastly Outage Causes Large-Scale Global Internet Disruption." *Market Watch*, June 8. Accessed 30 Mar. 2022 at https://www.marketwatch.com/story/government-news-and-commercial-websites-affected-as-fastly-outage-causes-large-scale-global-internet-disruption-01623158092.
Battaglia, Debbora, David Valentine, and Valerie Olson. 2015. "Relational Space: An Earthly Installation." *Cultural Anthropology* 30 (2): 245–25. https://doi.org/10.14506/ca30.2.07.
Brown, Michael. 2015. "Are Your Cloud Data Centers Solar Proof?" *Channel Futures*, September 29. Accessed 15 Mar. 2022 at https://www.channelfutures.com/uncategorized/are-your-cloud-data-centers-solar-proof.
Carter, Jamie. 2021. "Why America Should Suddenly Prepare for a Billion-Dollar 'Internet Apocalypse' Caused by the Sun." *Forbes*, August 31. https://www.forbes.com/sites/jamiecartereurope/2021/08/31/why-america-should-suddenly-prepare-for-a-billion-dollar-internet-apocalypse-caused-by-the-sun/?sh=4ee2f9bc52f9.
Clark, Jeff. 2013. "Solar Flares: Risk to the Data Centre." *Data Centre Journal*, July 25. Accessed 16 Nov. 2021 at http://www.datacenterjournal.com/solar-flares-risk-data-center/.
Clauer, C. Robert, and George Siscoe, eds. 2006. "The Great Historical Geomagnetic Storm of 1859: A Modern Look." *Advances in Space Research* 38 (2): 117–18. https://doi.org/10.1016/j.asr.2006.09.001.
Collis, Christy. 2016. "Res Communis? A Critical Legal Geography of Outer Space, Antarctica, and the Deep Seabed." In *Palgrave Handbook of Society, Culture and Outer Space*, edited by Peter Dickens and James S. Ormrod, 270–91. Basingstoke: Palgrave Macmillan.
Comaroff, Jean, and John L. Comaroff. 1999. "Occult Economies and the Violence of Abstraction: Notes from the South African Postcolony." *American Ethnologist* 26: 279–303. https://doi.org/10.1525/ae.1999.26.2.279.

Coors, Lex. 2016. "A Brief History of Data Centres." *Interxion*, September 7. Accessed 12 Apr. 2022 at https://www.interxion.com/blogs/2016/09/a-brief-history-of-data-centres.

CPNI. 2010. "CPNI Viewpoint: Protection of Data Centres.", *CPNI*, April 2010. Accessed 9 Apr. 2022 at https://www.frontierpitts.com/wp-content/uploads/Documents/2010006-vp_data_centre.pdf.

Dunnett, Oliver, Andrew S. Maclaren, Julie Klinger, K. Maria D. Lane, and Daniel Sage. 2017. "Geographies of Outer Space: Progress and New Opportunities." *Progress in Human Geography* 43 (2): 314–36. https://doi.org/10.1177/0309132517747727.

Forbes, Kevin F., and O. C. St. Cyr. 2008. "Solar Activity and Economic Fundamentals: Evidence from 12 Geographically Disparate Power Grids." *Space Weather* 6 (S10003): 1–20. https://doi.org/10.1029/2007SW000350.

Gaughan, Richard. 2017. "How Long for a Solar Flare to Reach Earth?" *Sciencing*, April 25. Accessed 12 Apr. 2022 at https://sciencing.com/long-solar-flare-reach-earth-3732.html.

Greenberg, Alissa. 2015. "Google Lost Data After Lightning Hit Its Data Centre in Belgium." *Time.com*, August 20. http://time.com/4004192/google-data-lightning-belgium/.

Hapgood, Mike. 2017. "Satellite Navigation—Amazing Technology but Insidious Risk: Why Everyone Needs to Understand Space Weather." *Space Weather* 15 (4): 545–48. https://doi.org/10.1002/2017SW001638.

Hapgood, Mike. 2021. @space_weather, 8 September 2021. Sorry @independent. This report is nonsense. The authors of the underlying scientific study do not understand how solarstorms create voltages on undersea cables, or using basic physics (Ohm's Law) to calculate currents in those cables. If you do that, the threat goes away. Twitter. Accessed 8 Mar. 2022 at https://twitter.com/space_weather/status/1435581927638061057.

Helmreich, Stefan. 2006. "The Signature of Life: Designing the Astrobiological Imagination." *Grey Room* 23 (4): 66–95. https://doi.org/10.1162/grey.2006.1.23.66.

Hoeppe, Götz. 2020. "A Sky to Work With: Astronomers, Media, Infrastructures." *Roadsides* 3: 15–22. https://doi.org/10.26034/roadsides-202000303.

Horn, Eva. 2018. *The Future as Catastrophe: Imagining Disaster in the Modern Age*. New York: Columbia University Press.

House of Commons. 2011. *Scientific Advice and Evidence in Emergencies: Third Report of Session 2010–11*. Volume I: *Report, Together with Formal Minutes, Oral and Written Evidence*. Science and Technology Committee, March 2. HC 498. London: Stationery Office. https://publications.parliament.uk/pa/cm201011/cmselect/cmsctech/498/498.pdf.

House of Commons. 2012. *Developing Threats: Electro-Magnetic Pulses (EMP); Tenth Report of Session 2010–12. Report, Together with Formal Minutes, Oral and Written Evidence*. Defence Committee, 8 February. HC 1552. London: Stationery Office. https://publications.parliament.uk/pa/cm201012/cmselect/cmdfence/1552/1552.pdf.

Jones, John Bryn Lloyd, R. D. Bentley, R. Hunter, D. J. Thomas, Roger Iles, and Graeme Charles Taylor. 2005. "Space Weather and Commercial Airlines." *Advances in Space Research* 36 (12): 2258–67. https://doi.org/10.1016/j.asr.2004.04.017.

Judge, Peter. 2018. "BA to Sue CBRE over £58m Data Center Outage." *Data Center Dynamics*, November 20. Accessed 10 Apr. 2022 at https://www.datacenterdynamics.com/en/news/ba-to-sue-cbre-over-58m-outage/.

Jyothi, Sangeetha Abdu. 2021. "Solar Superstorms: Planning for an Internet Apocalypse." In *SIGCOMM '21: Proceedings of the 2021 ACM SIGCOMM 2021 Conference*, August 23–27, 2001 (Virtual), 692–704. New York: Association for Computing Machinery. https://doi.org/10.1145/3452296.3472916.

Keck, Frédéric. 2016. "Preparedness." Fieldsights, *Cultural Anthropology*, September 30. Society for Cultural Anthropology. Accessed 12 Mar. 2022 at https://culanth.org/fieldsights/preparedness.

Klein, Naomi. 2007. *The Shock Doctrine: The Rise of Disaster Capitalism*. London: Allen Lane.

Klinger, Julie Michelle. 2017. *Rare Earth Frontiers: From Terrestrial Subsoils to Lunar Landscapes*. Ithaca, NY: Cornell University Press.

Krausmann, Elisabeth, Emmelie Andersson, Terry Russell, and William Murtagh. 2015. "Space Weather and Rail: Findings and Outlook." JRC Science and Policy Reports. Luxembourg: European Union.

Lakoff, Andrew. 2017. *Unprepared: Global Health in a Time of Emergency*. Oakland, CA: University of California Press.

Lloyd's. 2013. "Solar Storm Risk to the North American Electric Grid." Report. https://www.lloyds.com/news-and-risk-insight/risk-reports/library/natural-environment/solar-storm.

Love, Jeffrey J., Hisashi Hayakawa, and Edward W. Cliver. 2019. "Intensity and Impact of the New York Railroad Superstorm of May 1921." *Space Weather* 17 (8): 1281–92. https://doi.org/10.1029/2019SW002250.

MacDonald, Fraser. 2007. "Anti-*Astropolitik*—Outer Space and the Orbit of Geography." *Progress in Human Geography* 31 (5): 592–615. https://doi.org/10.1177/0309132507081.

Mann, Adam. 2012. "1 in 8 Chance of Catastrophic Solar Megastorm by 2020." *Wired*, February 29. https://www.wired.com/2012/02/massive-solar-flare/.

Messeri, Lisa. 2016. *Placing Outer Space: An Earthly Ethnography of Other Worlds*. Durham, NC: Duke University Press.

Merron, James. 2020. "Placing the Cosmic Background: The Ghana Radio Astronomy Observatory as an Ambient Infrastructure." *Roadsides* 3: 73–81. https://doi.org/10.26034/roadsides-202000310.

Miller, Neil. 2021. "Inside the Fastly Outage: A Firm Reminder on Internet Redundancy." *Data Center Dynamics*, June 22. Accessed 20 Nov. 2021 at https://www.datacenterdynamics.com/en/opinions/inside-the-fastly-outage-a-firm-reminder-on-internet-redundancy/.

Miller, Rich. 2009. "2012: No Apocalypse, but Space Weather Threat?" *Data Centre Knowledge*, November 10. Accessed 15 Mar. 2022 at https://www.datacenterknowledge.com/archives/2009/11/10/2012-no-apocalypse-but-space-weather-threat.

Morris, Chris. 2021a. "Facebook's Outage Cost the Company Nearly $100 Million in Revenue." *Fortune*, October 4. https://fortune.com/2021/10/04/facebook-outage-cost-revenue-instagram-whatsapp-not-working-stock/.

Morris, Chris. 2021b. "Massive Outage Hits Major Sites Across the Internet." *Fortune*, July 22. https://fortune.com/2021/07/22/internet-outage-psn-website-playstation/.

Moss, Sebastian. 2018. "Microsoft Publishes Preliminary Analysis of Major Cloud Outage." *Data Center Dynamics*, September 18. Accessed 19 Mar. 2022 at https://www.datacenterdynamics.com/en/news/microsoft-publishes-preliminary-analysis-major-cloud-outage/.

NASA. 2008. "Halloween Storms of 2003 Still the Scariest." October 28. Accessed 14 Apr. 2022 at https://www.nasa.gov/topics/solarsystem/features/halloween_storms.html.

NASA. 2014. "Near Miss: The Solar Superstorm of July 2012." *NASA Science*, July 23. Accessed 18 Mar. 2022 at https://science.nasa.gov/science-news/science-at-nasa/2014/23jul_superstorm.

Newman, Lily Hay. 2021. "A Bad Solar Storm Could Cause an 'Internet Apocalypse'." *Wired*, August 26. https://www.wired.com/story/solar-storm-internet-apocalypse-undersea-cables/.

Odenwald, Sten. 2007. "Newspaper Reporting of Space Weather: End of a Golden Age." *Space Weather* 5 (S11005): 1–17. https://doi.org/10.1029/2007SW000344.

Odenwald, Sten F., and James L. Green. 2008. "Bracing for a Solar Superstorm." *Scientific American* 299 (2): 80–87. https://doi.org/10.1038/scientificamerican0808-80.

Olson, Valerie. 2018. *Into the Extreme: U.S. Environmental Systems and Politics Beyond Earth*. Minneapolis, MN and London: University of Minnesota Press.

Olson, Valerie, and Lisa Messeri. 2015. "Beyond the Anthropocene: Un-Earthing an Epoch." *Environment and Society: Advances in Research* 6: 28–47. https://doi.org/10.3167/ares.2015.060103.

Oughton, Edward J., Andrew Skelton, Richard B. Horne, Alan W. P. Thomson, and Charles T. Gaunt. 2017. "Quantifying the Daily Economic Impact of Extreme Space Weather due to Failure in Electricity Transmission Infrastructure." *Space Weather* 15 (1): 65–83. https://doi.org/10.1002/2016SW001491.

Poppe, Barbara B., and Kristen P. Jorden. 2006. *Sentinels of the Sun: Forecasting Space Weather*. Boulder, CO: Johnson Books.

Praet, Istvan, and Juan Francisco Salazar. 2017. "Introduction: Familiarizing the Extraterrestrial/Making Our Planet Alien." *Environmental Humanities* 9 (2): 309–34. https://doi.org/10.1215/22011919-4215315.

Pritchard, Sara B. 2012. "An Envirotechnical Disaster: Nature, Technology, and Politics at Fukushima." *Environmental History* 17 (2): 219–243.

Rayner, Christine. 2016. "Data Protection." *South East Business*, June 18, 2016. https://www.southeastbusiness.com/section/features/data-protection.

Redfield, Peter. 2000. *Space in the Tropics: From Convicts to Rockets in French Guiana*. Berkeley, CA: University of California Press.

Sankaran, Vishwam. 2021. "Once-in-a-Century Solar Superstorm Could Plunge the World into 'Internet Apocalypse', Study Says." *The Independent*, September 13. https://www.independent.co.uk/space/solar-storm-cme-internet-apocalypse-b1915462.html.

Siddiqi, Asif A. 2015. "Science, Geography, and Nation: The Global Creation of Thumba." *History and Technology* 31 (4): 420–51. https://doi.org/10.1080/07341512.2015.1134886.

Specktor, Brandon. 2021. "An 'Internet Apocalypse' Could Ride to Earth with the Next Solar Storm, New Research Warns." *Live Science*, September 6. Accessed 3 Mar. 2022 at https://www.livescience.com/solar-storm-internet-apocalypse.

Taylor, A. R. E. 2020. "Space Weather as Threat to Critical Infrastructure." *Roadsides* 3: 63–72. https://doi.org/10.26034/roadsides-202000309.

Taylor, A. R. E. 2021. "Future-Proof: Bunkered Data Centres and the Selling of Ultra-secure Cloud Storage." *Journal of the Royal Anthropological Institute* 27 (S1): 76–94. https://doi.org/10.1111/1467-9655.13481.

Taylor, A. R. E. 2022. "Building Planetary Preparedness: The Arctic Circle as Space Weather Sentinel Territory." In *More than "Nature": Research on Infrastructure and Settlements in the North*, edited by Doris Friedrich, Markus Hirnsperger, Stefan Bauer, 209–37. Munich: LIT.

Taylor, A.R.E. 2023. Concrete Clouds: Bunkers, Data, Preparedness. *New Media & Society*, 25(2): 405–430.

Valentine, David. 2016. "Atmosphere: Context, Detachment, and the View from Above Earth." *American Ethnologist* 43 (3): 511–24. https://doi.org/10.1111/amet.12343.

Verge, Jason. 2013. "Space Weather and the Data Centre: The Risk from Solar Storms." *Data Centre Knowledge*, August 9. Accessed 21 Sep. 2022 at https://www.datacenterknowledge.com/archives/2013/08/09/space-weather-and-the-data-center.

Viljanen, A., A. Pulkkinen, R. Pirjola, K. Pajunpää, P. Posio, and A. Koistinen. 2006. "Recordings of Geomagnetically Induced Currents and a Nowcasting Service of the Finnish Natural Gas Pipeline System." *Space Weather* 4 (S10004): 1–9. https://doi.org/10.1029/2006SW000234.

Waghorn, Mark. 2021. "Devastating Solar storm 'Could Send Mankind Back to Dark Age' in Doomsday Forecast." *The Mirror*, December 9. https://www.mirror.co.uk/news/uk-news/solar-storm-dark-age-nasa-25656345.

Wallace, David. 2022. "A Large Solar Storm Could Knock out the Power Grid and the Internet—An Electrical Engineer Explains How." *The Conversation*, March 18. https://theconversation.com/a-large-solar-storm-could-knock-out-the-power-grid-and-the-internet-an-electrical-engineer-explains-how-177982.

Witze, Alexandra. 2016. "US Sharpens Surveillance of Crippling Solar Storms." *Nature* 537 (7621): 458–59. https://doi.org/10.1038/537458a.

26
SPACE INFRASTRUCTURES AND NETWORKS OF CONTROL AND CARE

Katarina Damjanov

Introduction

For over sixty years, many beings and things have left the comforts of the terrestrial environment to facilitate a range of scientific, commercial, and military activities across the solar system and beyond. Hundreds of astronauts, several space tourists, thousands of technologies, and countless specimens of plants and animals have been sent forth to partake in space flight, orbit celestial bodies, reside within space stations, and observe and traverse planets and their moons, often never to return. Great efforts are taken to keep them safe and sound amidst the perils of space. From their departure to the end of their missions, they are encased within extensive infrastructures of ground and in-situ support, relying upon intricate arrangements of sophisticated technical apparatus, precise logistic protocols, and pools of expert labour. Their precarious circumstances situate these space envoys within the ambits of a vigilant attention that extends from their command-and-control centres to the watchful scrutiny of competitors, regulators, and partners across national and international space sectors and further out into the attentive realms of global media and public cultures. The endeavour to facilitate their extraterrestrial presence is necessarily grounded in elaborate technical and organisational forms of control, involving comprehensive surveillance grids and meticulous regimes of upkeep and maintenance. At the same time, the attempts to secure their activities and wellbeing in space envelop these humans and nonhumans within a host of relational and affective practices of taking and extending care. These concurrent investments of control and care condition the manners by which terrestrial societies 'pay attention' to their pursuits of life in space.

Attending to the increasing proliferation of Earth-born bodies and objects outside the planet, this chapter addresses the infrastructures of control and care that undergird and sustain their exploits out there. In doing so, I highlight the centrality of infrastructures to the ongoing human endeavour to propel its enterprise outside the terrestrial confines, approaching them as vital to attempts to assert its productive, reproductive, and destructive courses into the fundamentally inhuman environment that is outer space. As military-industrial complexes continue to invest in various off-Earth ventures, the development of space infrastructures steadily extends the reach of the technological structures of power that seek to harness the circumstances of human life while refining the tactics deployed to direct its sociotechnical processes across inhospitable space environments. These extraterrestrial configurations of the earthly regimes of life-governance lie at the crux of my interests in outer space. My work has engaged with the more-than-planetary evolution of biopolitical approaches to governance, exploring how the species' technologic involvements with space inflects their rationalities, practices, and effects (Damjanov 2015, 2017; Damjanov and Crouch 2019, 2020). In this chapter, I extend this line of inquiry to account for the ways in which the infrastructural envelopment of humans, nonhumans, and space environments gives rise to formations of more-than-planetary networks of control and care. In the following sections, I situate the extraterrestrial unfolding of infrastructures within the evolving arena of human life and explore how the expansions of its precincts into space conditions approaches to life-management, conflating the governmental apparatus of security and strategies of risk management with the affective netting of concern and care. I suggest that this ongoing merging is not only a result of the evolving methods and means by which human societies attempt to grasp space, but itself inflects the processes of the species' making and remaking of its living domain.

Attending to Infrastructures of the Space Age

Infrastructures occupy a special place within human aspirations to progress their pursuits of power, knowledge, and wealth beyond their home planet. They are what makes the species' space endeavours possible. Down here on Earth, infrastructures have for long sustained attempts to consolidate and extend human activities within the natural world. Configured, as Brian Larkin puts it, into "built networks that facilitate the flow of goods, people, or ideas and allow for their exchange" (Larkin 2013: 328), they have themselves become a distinct component of the human environment, taking on the role of intermediaries that enable the species to align with, and overcome, the givens of space and time. Gradually, infrastructures have come to undergird a host of global politico-economic and socio-environmental processes, facilitating the routes of movement, contact, and exchange at a planetary scale (Hannam, Sheller, and Urry 2006; Larkin 2008; Easterling 2015; Parks and Starosielski 2015). From the undersea cables laid deep down on the ocean floor to the constellation of satellites in Earth's orbital space (Parks and Starosielski 2015), infrastructures have become a constitutive feature of the human terrestrial domain. However, their physical distribution is not only limited to Earth's environs. Their support networks progressively spread out onto other celestial bodies and regions across the solar system and beyond—all the way to the Voyager missions currently traversing interstellar space. Engaging with this extraterrestrial protraction of infrastructures, my work examines their role in configuring human material and social relations at more-than-planetary scales. Outside the Earth, where any and all activity must be technologically mediated, infrastructures do not merely expedite the encounters of earthlings with space. Rather, they are pivotal for making their space exploits possible.

Space endeavour accentuates the strategic role of infrastructures in the ongoing technological conditioning of the human domain. The design, operations, and maintenance of space infrastructures mobilise substantial creative and financial investments of governmental and private sectors, entwining scientific expertise within technical and political forms of power and control (Olson 2018), changing the rationalities and tenets of governance (Damjanov 2015) and fuelling economic and cultural imaginations (Tutton 2018; Dunnett 2019). From Sputnik onward, their extraterrestrial forms and operations have progressively become a part and parcel of human enterprise. Alongside the historical development of space infrastructures, various legal, technical, political, economic, social, and environmental issues surrounding their creation, operations, and destruction have also gained attention (Bichsel 2019), in particular those matters relating to the prominent and provocative accretion of satellites and their debris in Earth's orbit (Gorman 2005; Damjanov 2017; Clormann and Klimburg-Witjes 2022). Arising from various scientific, commercial, military, and cultural practices, the unfolding of space infrastructures is simultaneously the outcome of attempts to advance the strategic management of human life and a resource for its further development. As such, their formation underscores what Ash Amin describes as the inherent "liveliness" of infrastructures, highlighting them as at once a "gathering force and political intermediary" (Amin 2014: 137). Opening up novel directions of technological progress, space infrastructures enliven the human drive to advance its grasp upon the world, while themselves gradually maturing as a lively matter of species' concern.

My research into space infrastructures concerns their impact upon the evolution of governmental regimes obsessed with seizing power over the arena of human life. Technological innovations have progressively enhanced the extent and effectiveness of the infrastructure that supports the biopolitical operations of contemporary "societies of control" (Deleuze 1992), enabling them to assert their preoccupations with the systematic management of life processes across a multitude of scales, agendas, and techniques (Galloway 2004; Chun 2006; Thacker 2009). Grounded within precise technological engineering, calculative procedures of informatics, and pervasive networks of surveillance, communication, and exchange, the high-tech infrastructures of the terrestrial societies of control steadily advance in space. Yet, the endeavour to assemble earthly ways of life in some order outside the planet not only extends the rationalities and practices of their control but also tests them under new environmental settings, resituating them within exceedingly more "extreme" conditions (Olson 2018). The extraterrestrial situation of infrastructures offers a challenge to high-tech modes of governance, as each claim to control is tenuous and difficult to uphold. Set in a risk-abundant situation in which any venture is exposed to potential disturbance and disorder, space investitures require constant attention, unceasing monitoring, guidance and maintenance, and adjustments and adaptation to all sorts of interferences. Such interruptions are integral to the 'lives' of infrastructures. Their physical set-up and capacity to assemble secure networks of circulation and exchange are, as Brian Larkin notes, fundamentally shaped by their "vulnerability to breakdown" (Larkin 2013: 328). Given over to unforgiving space, infrastructures radically extend the reach of terrestrial networks of connection and control but also expose their fractures and limitations. Out there, communication links regularly fail, rockets explode, spacecrafts disappear from sight, and the intricate systems of life-support are perennially under threat of collapse. The endeavour to propel the species' prospects outside the terrestrial zones of security is entirely determined by its infrastructural dependencies and vulnerabilities.

The susceptibility of space infrastructure to breakdowns and disturbances brings their inherent liveliness and impact upon the modes of exercising power over life into sharp relief. At the core of governmental concerns with the effective control of life lies the problematics of the careful steering of its multiple courses towards their projected political and economic ends. Fuelled by the imperatives to ensure the orderly conduct of human bodies and populations, the regimes of public and self-care (Foucault 1988, 1990, 2007, 2008) have evolved to encompass the entirety of the species' relationship with the world, gradually expanding their focus from the regulation and management of the activities and behaviours of human individuals and groups onto the multitude of animate and inanimate nonhumans and all manner of cohabitations of a shared planet (Haraway 1991, 2008; Latour 1999, 2005; Tsing 2015; Puig de la Bellacasa 2017). As technological progress refines the techniques of life-governance, its momentum deepens the blurring between the operations of control and care (Bauman and Lyon 2012), enabling the logic and apparatus of the former to work in tandem with the cooperative and affective forces of the latter (Richardson et al. 2017; Andrejevic et al. 2021; Hjorth and Lupton 2021). The extraterrestrial placements of infrastructures further resituate the ongoing merging of the realms of control and care. Positioned in inhospitable space, infrastructures not only are the instruments with which to envelop earthly forms of life under the auspices of controlling and caring but also become the central object around which to design their strategic implementation. The necessity of establishing comprehensive protocols of control and care alongside the development of space infrastructures emphasises their tendency to act as a 'gathering force', as an 'intermediary' that fuels the historical evolution of biopolitical regimes.

The extraterrestrial integration of the governmental diagrams of control and care reassembles their terrestrial features into novel sociotechnical configurations. Their entwining off Earth emerges alongside the creation and establishment of space infrastructure and within the objectives of upholding its integrity through efficient construction, use, and repair. The rationalities behind this merging are distilled in the imperatives of securing the activities and wellbeing of those humans and nonhumans in space, who are themselves the integral system component of space infrastructures, entirely embedded in their designs and operations. These mutually constitutive encounters between control and care are replicated across different extraterrestrial environments and specific agendas and approaches to their exploration and exploitation. The endeavour to govern the extraterrestrial courses of life actualises the multifaceted disposition and meanings of care as "a concrete work of maintenance, with ethical and affective implications, and as a vital politics in interdependent worlds" (Puig de la Bellacasa 2017: 5). In this sense, the infrastructural groundings and organisational operations of care places are at the root of questions concerning the politico-ethical and socio-affective dimensions of the human drive to extend the species' exercise of power and control over the more-than-human worlds.

The human conquest of space has progressed alongside continually shifting modes of attention, and is inseparable from the political, economic, ethical, and affective conducts that shape the technologically driven processes of taking care and securing control. As Bernard Stiegler reminds us, all societies

> are characterised by types of attention: types of attentional forms and knowledges that are also types of concern, systems of care, of techniques for care of the self and of others, together constituting ways of life that characterise cultures and civilisations.
>
> *(2012: 3)*

The Space Age calibrates very particular forms of attention through which human societies take care of themselves. As the technological incorporation of affective gestures and practices into the calculative economies of attention acquires its cosmic disposition, it opens up a range of questions about the place (and ultimate range) of care as a "species activity that includes everything that we do to maintain, continue, and repair our 'world' so that we can live in it as well as possible" (Fisher and Tronto 1990: 40). Directed by explorative and exploitative agendas of military-industrial complexes, space endeavour brings to the fore the human determination to upend the boundaries of its living domain, posing and re-posing concerns about the possibilities and limitations of assembling and nurturing inclusive forms of care amidst rigid and exclusive systems of control. The politico-ethical and socio-environmental issues surrounding the species' investments of control and care increasingly demand our attention. After all, attending to the world is just as much a matter of controlling it as it is about caring for it—or not caring at all.

Upholding Life in Space

Terrestrial forms and ways of life are apparently destined to tread carefully outside the planet. Tentative and circumspect, space forays are wary of small failures that could swiftly become spectacular disasters. With no recourse to rescue services, backup generators, or emergency response units, they demand extreme precaution and exhaustive control over all minute aspects. Missions are planned years and decades in advance, every vital detail is tested and trialled and each likely scenario considered and weighed up. Human crews are recruited for their prowess and expertise, usually from military and science backgrounds, and must pass rigorous physical and mental health requirements and undergo exhaustive preparations. The approved specimens of the particular animals, plants, fungi, and bacteria required for space-based experiments are carefully chosen and prepared. Technologies such as spaceships, space stations, orbiters, landers, and rovers are likewise thoughtfully designed, constructed from choicest materials, and engineered to perform precise functions. Space exploits are highly considered and exact but also highly exclusive enterprises, thus far involving only a handful of states and private companies and providing only a limited pool of participants with the opportunity to depart to a specific destination. Only select images and information about their proceedings are available to the terrestrial public. The restrictive access to space environments and regimented procedures associated with all in-situ activities lay bare the elaborate control diagrams through which technological structures of power set out to forge the species' prospects in space. The products of particular political, economic, scientific, and cultural contexts, the itineraries of space enterprises reinforce particular outlooks, ideas, and imaginaries about the direction and manners in which life as we know it will proceed off its home planet, privileging specific biological, technological, organisational, and affective forms and traits.

Myriad space ventures disperse in many directions from Earth, each requiring a different set of infrastructures and strategies for its adaptation to a particular setting. Each crewed or uncrewed mission has its own distinct technological and logistic choreography to accommodate its presence in an alien surrounding, demanding precise calculation of all its technological elements and environmental variables, acute awareness of its proceedings, and even accurate estimates of its future conditions. At the same time, each must also conform to the broader administrative and logistic context in which it transpires—including various national and international funding and regulative frameworks, industry standards and procedures, and shared facilities such as launching sites or deep-space communication networks—and carefully align in regard to all external actors, events, and variables. Space exploits at once are minutely defined but also must remain flexible. Such a twofold disposition informs the strategic designs of their support infrastructures. Various interwoven overlapping and conflicting governmental agendas, political and economic interests, technical and scientific procedures, legal and engineering principles, and community values and aspirations inflect their formations, requiring them to remain at once complete and malleable, firmly enclosed within their prescribed protocols, and open to absorbing any external influences.

The delicate balances and disruptive imbalances surrounding space infrastructure come to the fore aboard one of its true masterpieces, the International Space Station (ISS) (NASA 2015). A habitable laboratory designed to host a range of technoscientific, biological, and social experiments, the station is a space infrastructure *par excellence*. Tonnes of hardware and software have been deployed and intricately arranged to provide living and working conditions, from systems that regulate levels of oxygen, gravity, and temperature to those that facilitate all contact and communication inside and outside the station (NASA 2014). The station, including all human and nonhuman activities on board, is continuously overseen by internal and external cameras, sensors, and monitoring devices. This elaborate system of surveillance captures a vast amount of diverse information, from data on the wellbeing of astronauts and the progress of plant experiments to responses of chemicals and the health of collision detection systems. The complexities of tending and attending to life on the ISS heighten what is involved in ongoing impositions of "surveillance as care" (Bauman and Lyon 2012). Continuous scrutiny of all elements and variables inside and around the ISS envelops its human and nonhuman residents and further refines the practices of "careful surveillance" (Richardson et al. 2017), entangling acts of watching, caring, and controlling within affective and calculative techniques of life management. The comprehensive surveillance systems of the ISS make acute a situation in which relentless control blurs into and then appropriates the connectivity of attentive care.

The complex life-support infrastructures of the ISS are also extended to various uncrewed spacecrafts and missions. With human agency removed from the site, both the imperatives of control and the rationalities of care become more delicate. A remotely located spacecraft is given a high degree of autonomy to traverse its designated environment and execute prearranged and impromptu tasks, but it needs to remain continually supervised and in connection with Earth. Yet, its movements and activities are ultimately hard to keep under control as all the components and instruments are attenuated by harsh environmental conditions, while the communication signals that connect it to its ground control have to travel vast distances and are distorted by environmental disturbances along the way. A complex purview of careful surveillance develops around distant spacecraft such as those to be found on Mars, where for example, the Curiosity rover sends reports about its activities and wellbeing to the Mars Reconnaissance Orbiter that oversees it from above, which then passes the information through the Deep Space Network to a rover control centre at NASA's Jet Propulsion Laboratory (JLP) in Pasadena (NASA n.d.). In response, Curiosity's operators at JLP process and closely analyse reports, check the rover's vital functions and workflow, issue commands, and adjust instructions (Wall 2012). These remote exchanges between the rover and its Earth-based 'drivers' distil the envelopment of humans and technologies within the governmental diagrams of the society of control. Attempts to achieve 'controlled' autonomy of uncrewed missions amidst high-latency environments rely upon the human ability to incorporate all the noise that emerges within the communicative networks between Earth and space. These new technical arrangements and logistic configurations condition the liveliness of space infrastructures and refine their ability to manage unforeseen circumstances, while also widening their potential for sustaining and extending networks and dispositions of care and concern.

The work of caring for and controlling space activities is distributed across individual missions, but also encompasses an array of political and economic actors and benefactors, professional partners and competitors, and broader social and public forms of attention. The world keeps a watchful eye upon the goings-on in space. Extensive monitoring systems deployed to control the satellites in Earth's orbit, for example, keep their operators and owners immediately aware of their health and occupations but also supply wider surveillance networks that seek to oversee all orbital traffic and inform the systems of national and global security. The public too is kept aware of orbital events through services such as those like Satellite Tracker (Vito Technology 2022) which feature satellites' positions and movements. The real-time streaming of the activities on the ISS are also available to the terrestrial audiences (NASA TV n.d.). The live broadcasts of space launches and landings such as the Apollo 11 arrival on the Moon or descents of Mars rovers on the red planet likewise attract breathless TV and internet audiences. Various forms of public and private attention gather around the ongoing conquest of space, sculpting its symbolic, affective, and sociocultural registers. Images of distant planets and their moons, comets, stars, and galaxies shape the vision of space as the species' frontier (Kessler 2012). The graphic representations of orbital debris prompt an awareness of its environmental imprints (Damjanov 2015; Tutton 2021). Tragedies such as Laika and *Challenger* spotlight the fragility and the tentativeness of earthlings' presence in space. Already a domain of human concerns, the conquest of space increasingly becomes a testing ground for reframing control of sociotechnical assemblages as "matters of care" (Puig de la Bellacasa 2011).

As space activities grow in range and complexity, more lively infrastructures are recruited to sustain them and enable more stable connections with Earth. For example, the implementation of state-of-the-art optical communications on the ISS is destined to substantially increase the traffic of data and information between the station and its ground control. Such improved communication exchanges would also enhance internet connections with the Earth-bound public, encouraging even further and more intimate interactions with the crew through social media. Amidst continuous and ongoing developments of technical components, guidance systems, regulations, and logistic coordinations, space infrastructures increasingly pose and re-pose questions of care amidst the systems of control. They involve the ever more careful management of humans, nonhumans, and technologies, but also reveal and put forward care as a "'species activity' with ethical, social, political, and cultural implications" (Puig de la Bellacasa 2017: 3). Such infrastructural animations of care bring it into focus as an underlying material and relational agency in the ongoing processes of making 'our world' on and off the globe.

Concerns of Risk and Security

The species' exploits off Earth are destined to contend with numerous inhospitable environments and cope with local weather extremes, alien gravities, and atmospheres. Adaptation to extraterrestrial conditions is technically challenging, organisationally demanding, extremely expensive, and requires extensive resources. A space venture depends upon a range of available assets for establishing its comprehensive systems of control, all capable of continuous adjustments in order to better absorb the internal and external risks. Yet, choreographing all its components, actors, and actions into a flawlessly functioning whole is not always possible, as unforeseen problems often arise, whether due to human errors, technical glitches, or sudden environmental disturbances. Amidst all manner of jeopardy, prone to breakages, corrupted and interrupted relays, and losses of external supervision, a satellite falls from its orbit, the carefully plotted route of a rover can be mistimed, and uninvited microbes can stow away on spacecrafts and escape the Earth. Space endeavour puts the strategies through which we maintain, support, control, and care for life to the test, refining their adaptive responses through a programme of intensive exercises in resolving a host of "logistical nightmares" (Rossiter 2016). Reinforcing alertness to risks, these 'logistic nightmares' hone the species' approaches to the strategic management of its living domain, aligning its infrastructural dependencies and interdependencies around the imperatives of security and progress.

At the centre of human cosmic aspirations is the species itself and the problematics of making it at home in inhuman space. The efforts to enable human bodies to safely reside in any extraterrestrial environment, for a while at least, have required substantial financial and logistic investments, and thus far, only a small number of people have had an opportunity to leave the Earth, including several hundred astronauts and members of support crews and a handful of space tourists. To smooth out the way and mitigate risks, extensive safety practices and procedures are drawn up to secure human enclosures within carefully controlled settings. Astronauts are swathed in ergonomic spacesuits and fail-safe spacecraft designs. They use special tools and instruments created to function in space through human hands, and they take advantage of innovations that enable continuous and stable connections with the control centres, colleagues, friends, and families they leave on Earth. And even when they return, they receive regular monitoring and check-ups of physical and mental wellbeing. Research into the health impact of space travel identifies its various side effects including muscle atrophy, anaemia, immune system changes, and flatulence (Akiyama 1993; Kanas and Manzey 2008). Yet the dangers of space travel are far more concerning than a few farts. Humans in space fall under constant and immediate threat of obliteration. For example, the ISS must continually navigate amidst the risk of orbital debris, and at times there is an urgent manoeuvring of the station employed to avoid destructive impact (Reuters 2021). But not all such strategies are successful. While fatal space disasters are still relatively rare, they occasionally do happen, sometimes in full view of captivated terrestrial audiences, such as was the fate of the *Challenger* mission carrying a crew of seven that exploded during the live TV broadcast of its launch in 1986, swiftly becoming the main topic of global media coverage and gaining general recognition as a shared tragedy of the species.

Other living beings accompany the species outside the planet. Laika and several other dogs were sent to pioneer spaceflight before humans. A range of biosatellites launched within NASA's Bion programmes have carried various specimens, including primates. Seeds have been flown to the Moon and back. A whole menagerie of nonhuman earthlings has come to reside on the ISS: various insects, amphibians, rodents, fish, and vegetables have all been drafted to participate in the activities on board. While nonhuman space explorers have been recruited to trailblaze endeavours in space from their very beginnings, it took decades to bring their plights to public and institutional attention and acknowledge the importance of exercising care; it was not until 1996 that the NASA Principles for the Ethical Care and Use of Animals addressed concerns regarding the treatment and conditions of their extraterrestrial presence (Damjanov 2018). Although the launches of nonhumans continue, the safety infrastructures sustaining them have improved alongside those that support humans. From Laika's one-way journey in a small capsule which enabled her to survive for a few days, nonhumans have been gradually encapsulated into elaborate life-support systems, such as those at work on the ISS. The various living plants and animals brought to the ISS to participate in scientific experiments are placed under highly controlled laboratory conditions, residing in specialised environments such as rodent and insect habitats, aquariums, and terrariums. Like their human cohabitants on board the station, their health and activities are continually under scrutiny, closely observed, analysed, tended to, and regularly reported to ground control. Immured in laboratory conditions intricately arranged through the multilayered logic of control, their ongoing presence in space continues to shape the sociotechnical networks of careful attention that the species extends to those with which it cohabits the world.

The uncrewed spacecraft are also subject to inordinately sophisticated controls, and they too are burdened with the baggage of the species' self-expectations. They are sent far further than the living bodies of human or nonhuman earthlings, commissioned to stay longer in even trickier environmental situations. Once dispatched, a spacecraft rarely returns. Aside from those tasked with transporting astronauts and retrieving samples, they usually leave for good. If they are not well-provisioned and cared for, problems arise in remarkable fashion—such as with the prominent 'trouble' with the Hubble space telescope, which was spectacularly launched to deploy is probing gaze into distant cosmic events, but its vision apparatus contained a faulty mirror and the repair efforts took years until it was finally fixed and started to fully operate (Cubitt 1998). Like humans and other living beings in space, a craft is also continually exposed to threats posed by various command errors, technical failures, and environmental conditions. Over the course of their probes on Mars, rovers such as Spirit, Curiosity, and Opportunity have each encountered various unforeseen situations that endangered their operational status and exploratory activities, from an occasional failure of power supply systems to getting stuck in the soft soil after a tempestuous Martian storm. When a rover experiences such a 'life-threatening' event, its ground control mobilises resources to remotely resolve the problem, trying to remove the obstacle, repair the rover and postpone the loss of its important functions, or even delay the end of the whole mission. But ultimately each mission reaches its end. For its ground control, this is a poignant moment: people who have been working alongside a rover for years are emotionally caught up in its demise. The ends of spacecraft also become national and even global tragedies, and the information about their activities and achievements are featured in the mainstream news and shared and discussed on social media. While the complex choreography of humans and technologies that makes it possible to retain control over distant spacecraft is perhaps most central, the sociocultural and affective economies invested in and emerging from these exploits are also crucial for determining the species' collective cosmic disposition.

Calculating possibilities, estimating risks, weighing costs, making vital and strategic decisions—the conquest of space involves a precarious balancing of control and care. Sometimes missions take an unplanned turn or intentions can radically change. Such was the fate of the Cassini spacecraft mission to Saturn. The spacecraft was sent on a long journey to probe into the Saturn system, and during its exploratory wandering it had made many scientific discoveries, amongst them collecting data indicating that Enceladus, one of Saturn's moons, could harbour the conditions to sustain organic forms of life. However, from being one of greatest space explorers of all time, Cassini quickly became a liability. It was suspected that the spacecraft may have picked up microorganisms from Earth and carried them on its way, and so it was deliberately crashed into Saturn to avoid the possibility of Enceladus's biological contamination. The assessment and management of the risks involved in the exploration of outer space require calculative interference with the courses and continuations of life—attentive negotiations and arbitration of its desired and undesirable directions, promising and harmful destinations, and decisions to let one of its threads safely prosper over another. These intercessions are not only limited to a single activity but are also expressed in their relation to a broader context of other space programmes and their overlapping and competing agendas and itineraries, modulating both immediate proceedings of a separate mission and the long-term visions of the species' conquest of space. If risk management is an "(institutionalized) attempt" to "colonize the future", plans and procedures designed to "foresee and control" (Beck 1999: 3) certain risks in outer space indicate both the imperial and institutional shape of the infrastructures by which the species paves a way to its cosmic futures.

The future conquest of space will also have to contend with—remedy or absorb—the risks associated with the technological and infrastructural impacts invariably left upon environments. Not only is space infrastructure already scattered across the solar system, the Moon, Mars, and beyond, but also its remnants; various pieces of human-made space debris mar a range of off-Earth locations. This by-product of the species' extraterrestrial advances is most notable in Earth's orbit, where every outward journey must first pass through a swirling swathe of waste, rockets, parts of spacecrafts, defunct satellites, and miscellaneous particles of abandoned and obliterated technologies. Orbital debris disturbs the circulation to and from space, as all launches, crewed and uncrewed missions, and their operations and support, are influenced by it in one way or another. It has direct and immediate effects on the satellite infrastructures that are crucial for planetary security systems such as Earth monitoring, communications, and surveillance, those which sustain the political, economic, and sociocultural processes of terrestrial societies and their governmental logics of control. As it accrues exponentially, it has the increasing potential to prevent any future venture in orbit or beyond. The question of mitigating, or coexisting with, orbital debris has received growing and more urgent attention, expressions of concern, and subsequent provisions and organisations of care, from strategies to avoid its unruly pieces and policies to prevent its accumulation to plans for reducing the consequences of its effects (Damjanov 2017). The tenuous controls, shared concerns, precise coordination, and complex cooperation demanded by space activities take the trajectories of security and risk management to new heights. Conflating the grids of surveillance, safety, and support, technological advances in space herald the evolution of governmental regimes that structure the species' politico-ethical and socio-environmental orientation.

Conclusion

The Earth's exterior is certainly not a place 'to be'. Despite the broadening and accelerating interest of terrestrial societies in outer space, its vast expanses remain remote and inhospitable. Various enterprises nevertheless continue to venture out into space, seeking to domesticate its expanses as a promising site in which the biological, technological, and social threads of human life would advance and prosper. Vital for enlivening the horizon of such expectations are the infrastructures deployed to cultivate these prospects amongst the unwelcoming space environments. Space infrastructures spur the species' ambitions to progress its grasp over the world, un-earthing their familiar rationalities and techniques, and resituating them into new configurations. Their progression marks a radical change in the human biopolitical condition, inflecting the designs of its security apparatus, calculations of risk management, and approaches to the logistics and strategies of life maintenance. This chapter has engaged with some of the key features of the more-than-planetary evolution of the governmental regimes that assemble around the species' manoeuvres to take hold of space. Highlighting the crucial role of infrastructure in heralding the extraterrestrial courses of life, I have sought to capture the circumstances in which the widening and hardening of its support networks give birth to novel interplays between calculative regimes of power and control and the affective expressions of care. The extraterrestrial entwining of the purviews and practices of control and care distils the manners by which the species attends to its living domain, tempering the futures of the human infrastructural occupation of their environments, both on Earth and in outer space.

References

Akiyama, Toyohiro. 1993. "The Pleasure of Spaceflight." *Journal of Space Technology and Science* 9 (1): 21–23. https://doi.org/10.11230/jsts.9.1_21.

Amin, Ash. 2014. "Lively Infrastructure." *Theory, Culture & Society* 31 (7/8): 137–61. https://doi.org/10.1177/0263276414548490.

Andrejevic, Mark, Hugh Davies, Ruth DeSouza, Larissa Hjorth, and Ingrid Richardson. 2021. "Situating 'Careful Surveillance'." *International Journal of Cultural Studies* 24 (4): 567–83. https://doi.org/10.1177/1367877921997450.

Bauman, Zygmunt, and David Lyon. 2012. *Liquid Surveillance: A Conversation*. Cambridge: Polity.

Beck, Ulrich. 1999. *World Risk Society*. Cambridge: Blackwell.

Bichsel, Christine. 2019. "Introduction: Infrastructure On/Off Earth." *Roadsides* 3: 1–7. https://doi.org/10.26034/roadsides-202000301.

Chun, Wendy. 2006. *Control and Freedom: Power and Paranoia in the Age of Fiber Optics*. Cambridge, MA: MIT Press.

Clormann, Michael, and Nina Klimburg-Witjes. 2022. "Troubled Orbits and Earthly Concerns: Space Debris as a Boundary Infrastructure." *Science, Technology, and Human Values* 47 (5): 960–85. https://doi.org/10.1177/01622439211023554.

Cubitt, Sean. 1998. *Digital Aesthetics*. London: Sage.

Damjanov, Katarina. 2015. "The Matter of Media in Outer Space: Technologies of Cosmobiopolitics." *Environment and Planning D: Society and Space* 33 (5): 889–906. https://doi.org/10.1177/0263775815604920.

Damjanov, Katarina. 2017. "Of Defunct Satellites and Other Space Debris: Media Waste in the Orbital Commons." *Science, Technology, & Human Values* 42 (1): 166–85. https://doi.org/10.1177/0162243916671005.

Damjanov, Katarina. 2018. "Accounting for Non-Humans in Space Exploration." *Space Policy* 43: 18–23. https://doi.org/10.1016/j.spacepol.2018.01.001.

Damjanov, Katarina, and David Crouch. 2019. "Orbital Life on the International Space Station." *Space and Culture: The Journal* 22 (1): 77–89. https://doi.org/10.1177/1206331217752621.

Damjanov, Katarina, and David Crouch. 2020. "Mooring a Space Station: Media Infrastructure and the Inhuman Environment." *Roadsides* 3: 7–14. https://doi.org/10.26034/roadsides-202000302.

Deleuze, Gilles. 1992. "Postscript on the Societies of Control." *October* 59: 3–7. https://www.jstor.org/stable/778828.

Dunnett, Oliver. 2019. "Stairway to Heaven? Geographies of the Space Elevator in Science Fiction." *Roadsides* 3: 42–7. https://doi.org/10.26034/roadsides-202000306.

Easterling, Keller. 2015. *Extrastatecraft: The Power of Infrastructure Space*. New York: Verso.

Fisher, Berenice, and Joan C. Tronto. 1990. "Toward a Feminist Theory of Caring." In *Circles of Care: Work and Identity in Women's Lives*, edited by Emily K. Abel and Margaret K. Nelson, 35–62. Albany, NY: State University of New York Press.

Foucault, Michel. 1988. "Technologies of the Self." In *Technologies of the Self: A Seminar with Michel Foucault*, edited by P. H. Hutton, H. Gutman, and L. H. Martin, 16–49. Amherst: University of Massachusetts Press.

Foucault, Michel. 1990. *History of Sexuality*. Vol. 1. New York: Vintage Books.

Foucault, Michel. 2007. *Security, Territory, Population*. New York: Palgrave Macmillan.

Foucault, Michel. 2008. *The Birth of Biopolitics*. New York: Palgrave Macmillan.

Galloway, Alexander. 2004. *Protocol: How Control Exists after Decentralization*. Cambridge: MIT Press.

Gorman, Alice C. 2005. "The Archaeology of Orbital Space." In *The Fifth NSSA Australian Space Science Conference*, 338–57. Melbourne: RMIT.

Hannam, Kevin, Mimi Sheller, and John Urry. 2006. "Mobilities, Immobilities, and Moorings." *Mobilities* 1 (1): 1–22. https://doi.org/10.1080/17450100500489189.

Haraway, Donna. 1991. "A Cyborg Manifesto: Science, Technology, and Socialist-Feminism in the Late Twentieth Century." In *Simians, Cyborgs, and Women: The Reinvention of Nature*, edited by Donna Haraway, 149–81. New York: Routledge.

Haraway, Donna. 2008. *When Species Meet*. Minneapolis: University of Minnesota Press.
Hjorth, Larissa, and Deborah Lupton. 2021. "Digitised Caring Intimacies: More-Than-Human Intergenerational Care in Japan." *International Journal of Cultural Studies* 24 (4): 584–602. https://doi.org/10.1177/1367877920927427.
Kanas, Nick, and Dietrich Manzey. 2008. *Space Psychology and Psychiatry*. El Segundo, CA; Dordrecht, Netherlands: Microcosm Press and Springer.
Kessler, Elizabeth. 2012. *Picturing the Cosmos: Hubble Space Telescope Images and the Astronomical Sublime*. Minneapolis: University of Minnesota Press.
Larkin, Brian. 2008. *Signal and Noise: Media, Infrastructure, and Urban Culture in Nigeria*. Durham, NC: Duke University Press.
Larkin, Brian. 2013. "The Politics and Poetics of Infrastructure." *Annual Review of Anthropology* 42: 327–43. https://doi.org/10.1146/annurev-anthro-092412-155522.
Latour, Bruno. 1999. *Pandora's Hope: Essays on the Reality of Science Studies*. Cambridge, MA: Harvard University Press.
Latour, Bruno. 2005. *Reassembling the Social: An Introduction to Actor-Network Theory*. Oxford: Oxford University Press.
NASA. 2014. "International Space Station: Environmental Control and Life Support System." FS-2004-12-175-MSFC. http://www.nasa.gov/centers/marshall/pdf/174687main_eclss_facts.pdf.
NASA. 2015. "About the Space Station: Facts and Figures." http://www.nasa.gov/mission_pages/station/main/onthestation/facts_and_figures.html;
NASA. n.d. "Mars Curiosity Rover: Communications with Earth." https://mars.nasa.gov/msl/mission/communications/.
NASA TV. n.d. "Live ISS Stream." http://www.ustream.tv/channel/live-iss-stream.
Olson, Valerie. 2018. *Into the Extreme: U.S. Environmental Systems and Politics Beyond Earth*. Minneapolis: University of Minnesota Press.
Parks, Lisa, and Nicole Starosielski, eds. 2015. *Signal Traffic: Critical Studies of Media Infrastructures*. Chicago: University of Illinois Press.
Puig de la Bellacasa, María. 2011. "Matters of Care in Technoscience: Assembling Neglected Things'." *Social Studies of Science* 41 (1): 85–106. https://doi.org/10.1177/0306312710380301.
Puig de la Bellacasa, María. 2017. *Matters of Care: Speculative Ethics in More Than Human Worlds*. Minneapolis: Minnesota University Press.
Reuters. 2021. "International Space Station Swerves to Dodge Space Junk." 3 December. https://www.reuters.com/lifestyle/science/international-space-station-swerves-dodge-space-junk-2021-12-03/.
Richardson, Ingrid, Larissa Hjorth, Yolande Strengers, and William Balmford. 2017. "Careful Surveillance at Play: Human–Animal Relations and Mobile Media in the Home." In *Refiguring Techniques in Digital Visual Research*, edited by Edgar Gómez Cruz, Shanti Sumartojo, and Sarah Pink, 105–16. London: Palgrave Macmillan. https://doi.org/10.1007/978-3-319-61222-5_9.
Rossiter, Ned. 2016. *Software, Infrastructure, Labor: A Media Theory of Logistical Nightmares*. New York: Routledge.
Stiegler, Bernard. 2012. "Relational Ecology and the Digital *Pharmakon*." *Culture Machine* 13: 1–19.
Thacker, Eugene. 2009. "The Shadows of Atheology: Epidemics, Power and Life After Foucault." *Theory, Culture & Society* 26 (6): 134–52. https://doi.org/10.1177/0263276409347698.
Tsing, Anna. 2015. *The Mushroom at the End of the World: On the Possibility of Life in Capitalist Ruins*. Princeton, NJ and Oxford: Princeton University Press.
Tutton, Richard. 2018. "Multiplanetary Imaginaries and Utopia: The Case of Mars One." *Science, Technology, and Human Values* 43 (3): 518–39. https://doi.org/10.1177/0162243917737366.
Tutton, Richard. 2021. "Sociotechnical Imaginaries as Techno-Optimism: Examining Outer Space Utopias of Silicon Valley." *Science as Culture* 30 (3): 416–39. https://doi.org/10.1080/09505431.2020.1841151.
Vito Technology. 2022. "Satellite Tracker." https://vitotechnology.com/apps/satellite-tracker.
Wall, Mike. 2012. "Martian Curiosity: How Do You Drive a $2.5 Billion Mars Rover?" *Space.com*, August 22. https://www.space.com/17220-mars-rover-curiosity-martian-driving.html.

27
MEXICO DREAMS OF SATELLITES

Anne W. Johnson

Mexico, I Will Come On Board Your Ship!

The canvas is painted black and covered in white dots: a starry night in outer space (Figure 27.1). The artist has placed the Moon in the upper left-hand corner: a greyish-white sphere with washes of pale colours. The larger Earth, with pastel blue oceans that surround the American continent, painted with warmer greens, oranges, and yellows, occupies the lower half of the canvas. But this is all background; the protagonists of this space scene are the girl, the ship, and the satellites.

Figure 27.1 "México... ¡Me subo a tu nave!" by Federica Sánchez y Carrillo Bernal. 1er. Concurso de Arte Espacial "México Hacia la Luna", Agencia Espacial Mexicana. Used with permission.

DOI: 10.4324/9781003280507-31

The girl wears a grey-and-pink space suit with a shoulder patch—a small Mexican flag—and she clings with one hand to a ladder that undulates from its base on the Earth up to the ship: a futuristic caravel like the ones Christopher Columbus's crew used on their transatlantic journey. Its sails, marked with another Mexican flag and the initials of the Mexican Space Agency (AEM), billow, but it seems to be propelled by rockets with jets that shoot bright flames. The scene is inhabited, as well, by three objects that orbit the Earth: a representation of the defunct space station Skylab, a resupply ship for the International Space Station (ISS), and a satellite that seems to be an image of Solidarity, the second satellite system launched by Mexico in the 1990s. The eleven-year-old artist has titled the work "Mexico, I will come on board your ship!"

I first encountered this image, the winning submission in the juvenile category of the first Space Art Contest sponsored by the Mexican Space Agency, when I arrived at the office of the agency's Science and Technology Outreach department, in October of 2018. When I told the department head of my desire to develop a research project about Mexican imaginaries of outer space, he exclaimed, "I have the perfect image for the cover of your book!" And certainly, the image eloquently evokes the imaginary of the Mexican space industry characterised by, among other things, the belief that space technoscience has the potential to drive the country's progress and social development. The space sector deposits its faith in the satellites that expand national frontiers outward and upward into Earth orbit, at the same time as they allow for the visualisation of Earth itself as part of processes of communication and observation.

It All Started with Sputnik

The "Fellow Traveller" looks like an odd, large bug. One of them hangs from the museum's ceiling, unmistakable: a round metallic ball with four spidery appendages. The National Polytechnic Institute in the north of Mexico City houses this Sputnik within the planetarium named after Mexican astronomer Luis Enrique Erro. According to one of the museum guides, it was donated to Mexico by the Soviet Union at the end of the 1980s, and it's "one of the satellite's three original prototypes". It didn't make to space, obviously, "but it came close". The original antennas were lost at some point, so the extensions on display are replacements.

"Sputnik is essential", artist Juan José Díaz Infante tells me, "in order to change our imaginary" (interview, January 2022). And Annick Bureaud characterises this first artificial satellite as "an all-round object (political, ideological, demiurgic, technical, performative, utopian, and aesthetic)" (2021: 79). Its 1957 launch marked the first time that humanity (or a part of humanity) would escape Earth's gravity through the use of technology, and it stunned the world. As an object, continues Díaz Infante, Sputnik was relatively simple: "Really, Sputnik is a battery, a radio, and an antenna. You could have a Sputnik in your house. Sputnik's mission lasted twenty-eight days. It just beeped. And three hundred kilometres. Acapulco is closer." What was really important, he concluded, was Sputnik's symbolic power, because the "space bug" didn't just change how humans imagined outer space, but how they imagined the Earth itself.

In Mexico, Sputnik's launch was reported on the same day of the event, at the beginning of the General Motors news programme, and for most Mexican viewers, this was the beginning of the space race. Mexican journalists began to speculate about the possible military uses of satellite technology in the context of the Cold War, which they described as "a balance of terror" (González de Bustamante 2012: 121). Viewed from Mexico, human activities in space provoke profound ambivalence. On the one hand, Sputnik, the effervescence sparked by the flight of Yuri Gagarin, and the Apollo moon landings inspired a flurry of space-related activities, including the construction of ground tracking stations, suborbital rocket launches, the consolidation of university science programmes, and participation in the debates around international space-use treaties (Johnson 2020). During the 1950s and 1960s, Mexican architects designed sleek skyscrapers and imaged modernist "satellite" cities, expanding urban life outward and upward.[1] And Mexican artists depicted space exploration in hopeful terms, as the logical outcome of social development tied to technological processes.[2] But on the other hand, Mexico's complicated relationship with both the United States and the Soviet Union, as well as its precarious position with regard to "modernity", created a context in which the discourse of "for all mankind" was viewed with suspicion and, in some cases, hostility. The tracking station built in Guaymas, Sonora, in support of NASA's Mercury human spaceflight programme, for example, was hailed by some as an example of a Mexican "modernising project", but others feared that the collaboration with the United States went against Mexico's "pledge to remain neutral in the face of international conflict" and that the station could fulfil military, and not just scientific, purposes (González de Bustamante 2012: 25).

Mexico in Orbit

It seems obvious now, but one of the statements that most struck me when I went to the Mexican Space Agency in search of outer space imaginaries was: "People here don't understand the importance of space in their daily lives. After all, Uber is a space tech company!" My interlocutor was right, of course. Transport, communication, entertainment, mapping, planning, finance, and many other services, as well as more sinister surveillance applications, today depend on the orbitalisation of infrastructure. The region around the Earth, by January 2021 occupied by 6542 active and inactive satellites (Mohanta 2021), has become, as Gärdebo, Marzecova, and Knowles argue, a kind of second atmosphere, a mesh that these authors have termed the "orbital technosphere" (2017). Satellites produce new perspectives, new relations, and new scales, connecting the surface of Earth with outer space as they pass through the "imperceptible and multiple 'spheres' (atmosphere, stratosphere, ionosphere) through which satellite-to-Earth transactions move and world histories unfold" (Parks and Schwoch 2012: 2).

Various writers have detailed the ways in which the view of Earth from above, represented by photographs such as *Earthrise* (1968) and *Pale Blue Dot* (1990), radically transformed how humans view our planet (Lazier 2011; DeLoughrey 2014). Other authors have written of the global debates over space, national sovereignty, and access to satellite technology that have arisen as a result of the human occupation of low Earth orbit (Collis 2012; Barker 2005). In what follows, I will concentrate on the particularities of Mexican space access to and occupation of low Earth orbit, as I argue that the use, development, and launch of satellites are central to the Mexican space sector's sociotechnical imaginaries (Jasanoff 2015) and dreams for the future.[3]

In 1968, Mexico hosted the Olympic Games, an event that motivated the Mexican government to affiliate itself with the global satellite network INTELSAT in order to transmit the games to the public. But renting communication satellites and buying Landsat images from NASA for the purposes of Earth observation proved to be a short-term solution, given the increasing importance of satellite data from the latter half of the twentieth century. International collaboration and sharing of images had served its objectives, like the successful eradication, thanks to remote satellite observation, of a screwworm plague that had attacked Mexican livestock, but there were concerns over the consequences of allowing foreign countries access to Mexican data. In September 1971, the Mexican government demanded that the United Nations agree that "no data would be collected over Mexican territory from the air or space without prior permission" (Mack 1990: 187).

Worried about this lack of control over national data, as well as the telecommunications gap between urban and rural populations, the Mexican government negotiated the obtention of two geostationary satellite positions in 1979. The national satellite project was also supported by the communications company Televisa, as the colocation of satellites in the newly acquired positions would allow for the transmission of its television programmes throughout its principal markets: Central America, the Caribbean, and part of South America. Although their concerns were mainly economic, both Televisa and the government publicised their efforts as part of an attempt to resist the "Americanization" of Mexican values by means of the production of regional and national television content (Borrego and Mody 1989: 271). The project was also publicly justified by appealing to the possible social uses of the new satellites, although no major social agency participated in the decision-making process (ibid.).

Three years later, at a cost of US$92 million, Mexico's secretary of communication and transportation hired Hughes Space and Communications (later Boeing) to construct Mexico's first satellite system, consisting of two satellites, Morelos 1 and 2, and a ground control centre in the Iztapalapa area of Mexico City. The state-run company TELECOMM would take charge of the satellites' operation, but the design and delivery of the new technology, as well as training and maintenance, would be undertaken by international experts. This strategy was the object of critique by some, as it meant that Mexico would continue to be technologically dependent on the United States instead of moving toward national sovereignty and autonomy, unlike countries such as Brazil and India, which invested in the longer-term strategy of consolidating national human and technological resources (Borrego and Mody 1989). In 1985, through an agreement with NASA, the Mexican government put its two satellites in orbit and sent Mexican citizen Rodolfo Neri Vela into space on board the space shuttle *Atlantis*. Morelos I was disorbited in 1994, while Morelos II lasted for another decade. Both are now considered unlocatable and inoperable space junk.

The Morelos satellite system was replaced by the Solidarity system, also constructed by Hughes, at a cost of US$300 million. After the privatisation of the telecommunications industry in 1997, a series of satellites financed by transnational companies were put into orbit (SATMEX), as well as another government-controlled satellite system (MEXSAT). The academic sector has also participated in satellite development; notably, scientists at the National Autonomous University (UNAM) launched the first satellites developed in Mexico, UNAMSAT-1, and UNAMSAT-B, from Russia in the 1990s. UNAMSAT-1 was destroyed in a launchpad explosion, while UNAMSAT-B was successfully placed in orbit, although it failed after one year due to a problem with its batteries. Several decades would pass until the next successful Mexican satellite launch.

Satellite Dreams in Miniature

The amount of economic and technological resources needed for the operation of national space programmes has been a major impediment to the incorporation of countries from the Global South in space exploration and commercialisation projects. The combined budget of all Latin American space agencies represents about 2% of NASA's budget, or 6% of the European Space Agency's budget.[4] Therefore, none of these countries is able to invest in expensive technological projects. But the transformation of the space industry projected for "emerging countries" will depend on three factors: the "democratisation of space", the reduction of the costs of space technology that is resulting from processes of miniaturisation, and the private sector's increasing presence in the space industry.[5]

Despite the "democratisation of space", Latin American countries continue to have little impact on or participation in the megaprojects planned for the exploration of the solar system. As several of my interlocutors have stated, "the floor is uneven": that said, low Earth orbit has become an important possibility for expansion, especially given the development of microsatellite technology, with much more minimal requirements than the massive satellite infrastructures that underlay systems such as Morelos and Solidarity. The Mexican Space Agency, therefore, has set its sights on the construction of CubeSats, which are literal "black boxes": small, standardised satellites that weigh one kilogram, take up one litre of volume, and measure ten cubic centimetres per unit. The development, launch, and operation of a CubeSat tends to cost less than ten thousand dollars, a fraction of the cost of a large satellite, and the price goes down when various satellites share a rocket's payload space. The standardisation of the design also allows a developer to buy many of the satellite's components off the shelf and later adapt them to the project's requirements. For this reason, aside from their scientific value, CubeSats are also considered to be valuable teaching tools for students and citizens (Pang and Twiggs 2011: 50).

The most basic CubeSats don't do much more than Sputnik did six decades ago: they emit a "beep" which is transmitted by radio to confirm that they continue to function in orbital conditions. But missions may also be more complex, complying with objectives that can include detecting changes in Earth's magnetic field, testing advanced technology, measuring climate change, observing atmospheric layers, and imaging the Earth's surface, among other things (ibid.). And although the quality of CubeSat communication systems cannot compare with those of larger satellites, their potential does increase when they are designed as part of a satellite constellation. Because of their size, they can be designed to automatically deorbit when their functions cease and burn up in the Earth's atmosphere, instead of becoming more pieces of space junk. Advocates of CubeSats have emphasised their utility in the new space economy, given that both risk and investment are relatively low (ibid.).

But for my interlocutors in Mexico, the importance of CubeSats goes beyond their pedagogic, scientific, economic, or ecological benefits: they seem to promise a future of independence from the hegemonic centres of power, a kind of epistemic sovereignty (Litfin 1999) that may assure national control not just over territorial borders and natural resources but also over knowledge and information produced in and about the nation, a latent worry since the days of Landsat. It is argued that the "formation of talents"—a phrase I heard many times—that is understood as another consequence of the development of CubeSats is another factor that, in the long term, will help to achieve this autonomy.

"Satellites are noble", Genaro, a young engineer, told me in 2018; "they are agnostic" (Genaro Grajeda, pers. comm., Dec. 2018).[6] These "invisible friends high up above us" provide a wealth of benefits, he and other participants in the Mexican space sector argue, including connecting people, rendering visible a variety of processes that occur on the Earth's surface, and contributing to the dream of seeing a greater Mexican presence in outer space. Three recent CubeSat projects have competed for the title of "first Mexican satellite" (after UNAMSAT). The first to be launched was Painani-1, developed at the Ensenada Centre for Scientific Research and Higher Education in Baja California (CICESE), at the request of the University of the Mexican Army and Airforce.

Painani-1 was launched from New Zealand by the private company Rocket Lab in June 2019. According to the Mexican secretary of national defence Painani-1 was merely meant to be an educational project for CICESE students, as well as a rehearsal for the development of Earth observation technology; however, given military involvement, the government asked Rocket Lab not to publicise the mission.[7] Although the military has not been seen as the primary user of satellite technology in Mexico, it seems that the armed forces may seek a stronger space presence in the future. In an article for the journal of the Mexican navy, for example, Rivera Parga argues for the military importance of satellites to "increase the national power of the Mexican state" (2017: 33). After enumerating the social, economic, and political benefits of satellites, the author appeals to the rights of each state to "defend its sovereignty, not just within the terrestrial atmosphere, but outside it", given that "if we as a sovereign State do not exercise sovereignty in our own air space and outer space, who will?" (2017: 57). In the last decade, the Mexican government has turned to satellites for at least some of its surveillance activities, tracking, for example, the movement of undocumented immigrants and the activities of delinquent groups.[8]

The second Mexican satellite to be launched in the twenty-first century was accompanied by much greater national press coverage. AzTechSat-1 was undertaken at the Popular Autonomous University of the State of Puebla (UPAEP) and relied on technical advice by experts from NASA. The satellite, whose name combines a recognition of the pre-Hispanic past with the appropriation of modern technology, was a one-unit CubeSat designed to test communications between small satellites and commercial satellite constellations belonging to the company Globalstar. AzTechSat-1 was launched to the ISS from Cape Canaveral on a SpaceX Dragon capsule in

December 2021, contributing one kilogram to a payload of 2585 kilograms that included genetic experiments from NASA, Anheuser-Busch experiments on the germination of seeds in space, and an ISS experiment on the use of spectrometers to detect gas leaks in space. AzTechSat-1's short life ended when it unexpectedly deorbited, disintegrating upon contact with the Earth's atmosphere.

The launch was broadcast on the Mexican Space Agency's YouTube channel, which retransmitted NASA's live feed. One public official who spoke at the event characterised AzTechSat-1 as "the first nanosatellite made in Mexico and probably, depending on how it is defined, also the first satellite made in Mexico".[9] However, the satellite's "true nationality" continues to be debated; several of my interlocutors mentioned that AzTechSat-1 was bought as a "kit" from the United States, although its payload design and assembly took place in Mexico. But quibbling aside, the coordinator of the Space Studies Programme at the UNAM told me that at least the experience "served as training" and was an important step for the "development of talents" and the achievement of "technological independence" that would eventually "let us see what we want". He went on to state the importance of being able to observe "our own territory, our forests, our urban growth", track earthquakes, diseases, and volcanic eruptions, and improve communication. In the future, he concluded, these "transformative technologies" and the information they provide will generate wellbeing and development (José Francisco Valdés, pers. comm., February 2020; ass also *El Financiero* 2021): the government, the academy, and the private sector.

However, promotors of the space industry may be overly optimistic about satellite technology. As Australian archaeologist Alice Gorman argues, countries with low GDP "are in this position because of systemic and historic inequities relating to colonialism and capitalism …. Additional Earth observation data isn't going to fix global inequalities, without radical political change, too" (Gorman in Howell, 2020).

Satellite Entanglements

The third satellite project I will mention here is the one I know best. NanoConnect-2 (NanoConnect-1 was only launched suborbitally) was developed in the UNAM's Space Instrumentation Laboratory (LINX) with a payload designed to test technology in low Earth orbit and connectivity with Earth monitoring stations. In February 2021, NanoConnect-2 was placed in orbit at a height of 504 kilometres by the Indian Space Research Agency (ISRO). As was the case for AzTechSat-1, this satellite shared its flight on the Polar Satellite Launch Vehicle with international projects, on this occasion as part of a package whose main payload was the Brazilian satellite Amazonia-1. According to Gustavo Medina Tanco, the head of LINX, NanoConnect-2 (unlike AzTechSat-1) is "one hundred percent Mexican in its technology, design and conception; it was made on our own initiative, with our students"[10]: of course "100 percent Mexican" is something of a misnomer, given the number of intricate international agreements required to launch a satellite.

I visited the laboratory in August 2019, as various members of the NanoConnect-2 team were checking the satellite so that it could undergo the battery of tests needed for launch. In my notes, I wrote "objects, objects everywhere, a bit of chaos": the lab was filled with containers, computers, printers, boxes, cables, and a large quantity of equipment I couldn't identify. Students in white lab coats worked in front of screens. Some were doing calculations, others used specialised software to analyse information, and still others put together or adjusted instruments. Near the entrance was a small darkroom, with a device that had something to do with photons, and a series of 3-D printers. At the front of the lab, Medina Tanco explained with pride, was a piece of equipment that cost several million dollars, used to test instruments in extreme conditions.

During the time I observed the lab's activity, the satellite had some problems: first, it wouldn't turn on, so it was connected directly to a power source. Then NanoConnect-2 had to show it could transmit and receive information. After various tries and the use of several different computers, communication was established. The next step would be acquiring liquid nitrogen for the cooling tests. I felt the intense pressure on everyone's time: "This has to happen today." Conversations focused on the resolution of concrete problems; no one was debating the philosophy or the ethics of space exploration, or the social uses of technology (at least while I was there). But there was no lack of emotion. A few days after this visit, I received a short video through WhatsApp, in which various lab-coated students surrounded NanoConnect-2, seen without its shell, its innards exposed. A green light blinked. I heard "5-4-3-2-1…" and jubilant shouts when the satellite's antennas deployed with a whip-like movement.

After its successful launch, NanoConnect-2 communicated successfully with the ground station located in the laboratory. At the time of this writing months later, the satellite lives on, as Eduardo, one of the students at the LINX, showed me. He has been a satellite fanatic for a long time; he has mounted do-it-yourself antennas on the house where he lives with his parents so that he can "hunt" satellites. In this way, he says, "you can be in space, even if it's just through satellites" (interview, Eduardo Salazar, June 2022). Eduardo built his antennas with "things you can buy in your neighbourhood hardware store", and, following YouTube tutorials, he attached them to his house and combined them with a radio and a cheap computer to create his own ground monitoring station, a necessary part of a satellite's infrastructural assemblage. One afternoon, chatting in an outside courtyard at the UNAM, he showed me how to follow a satellite by means of an online platform that allows anyone to access the observations undertaken by members of the network of ground stations that belong to the SatNOGS project, [11] which include Eduardo and the official LINX monitoring station.

NanoConnect-2 appears on the platform as an image that visually represents the transmission of its signal, a long rectangle in tones of blue and green: "the cascade" (Figure 27.2). If I understood correctly, the wavy neon green line represents the tracking of the satellite during the period of observation. Other, more tenuous lines cut through the image from top to bottom: "noise" in the transmission. Data can also be seen as numbers or heard as audio: a high-pitched squeal with slight changes in intensity that make me think of bats and echolocation. Sounds appear onscreen in purple waves as if they were tracing the satellite's frenetic heartbeat, proof that "it's still alive".

The Satellite Sublime

> I saw two shooting stars last night
> I wished on them, but they were only satellites
>
> *Billy Bragg, "A New England"*

However practical a satellite might be, however much it promises to fulfil dreams of progress and technological inclusion on diverse scales, its potential is not limited to its instrumentality. The poetic potential of satellites started to come into focus when, in 2019, Medina Tanco sent me the image of a multicoloured parabola that I couldn't at first identify: the representation of NanoConnect-2's potential orbit.

> I see my satellite revolving in space—I'm calculating orbits to see the level of insolation the solar panels will receive in relation to time—and I imagine it up there, where I always longed to go … turning in the darkness of space, looking at the stars, and the continents, in an endless dance, immersed in the most absolute silence … tiny in the immensity of the universe.
> *(Gustavo Medina Tanco, pers. comm., Sept. 2019)*

As I have stated, those involved in the Mexican space industry repeat over and over what they consider to be the benefits of satellites: fomenting talents, testing space technology, driving economic and social development, connecting people, and observing Earth processes. But at least for those

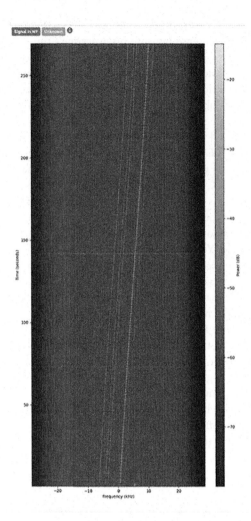

Figure 27.2 NanoConnect-2 appears on the platform as an image that visually represents the transmission of its signal, a long rectangle in tones of blue and green: "the cascade".

intimately involved in their creation, satellites exceed their practical functions, becoming human prostheses in space. They cannot merely be reduced to technophilic fetishes (although they are also that); for some, satellites are a means of achieving cosmic dreams. Medina Tanco's satellite is the consequence of "my desire to navigate infinity … to fuse myself with the darkness of the cosmos … of my crazy mix of angst and fascination when faced with the emptiness that defines our ephemeral and absurd existence" (pers. comm., June 2022).

"Space is a blank canvas", one young engineer told me in 2018, enthusiastic about what he considered the infinite possibilities of space exploration. But for artists that have worked with satellites, "space is a *black* canvas" (interview, Nahum Romero, Jan. 2019), data production or communication, but rather reflects the desire "to create something on the scale of the cosmos by placing a new celestial body within it" (Bureaud 2021: 80). On the other hand, as the produce of citizen science, artistic satellites highlight the process of their own creation outside institutional channels. They defy the notion that access to space should be restricted to commercial or governmental actors; as such, the construction of an artistic satellite is both a political and a poetic act.

According to Mexican artist Juan José Díaz Infante (interview, Jan. 2022), it is all about "changing the conversation": "What I do is generate frames of thought around space and how to see the world from above". The satellite Ulises I began its life in Díaz Infante's imagination in 2010, partly in the context of the bicentenary of Mexico's independence from Spain, partly because the artist was turning 50 and, in his own words, "needed a reengineering". Not long after, he found an article in *Scientific American* about citizen satellites (Pang and Twiggs 2011), and so he decided to create a citizen space agency called the Mexican Space Collective (CEM) in order to challenge governmental and industrial hegemony and include other visions and voices in space, an action that he felt was particularly important to undertake as a Mexican citizen. The collective built Ulises I with the intention of appropriating "the poetic energy of Sputnik. The beep as a poem, a pixel as a masterpiece. This small object the size of a basketball, this little sound, became a trigger of the imagination" (Garciandia 2017: 31).

At first, the artists who collaborated on the project thought of it as an homage to soccer (a universal language), meant to evoke teamwork and a triumphal spirit, but the sport was gradually pushed aside. The group of works of art that were eventually included ranged from visual art to poems to musical compositions, and the transmission of the satellite's signal would translate to "I love the road" in Morse code. The project was exhibited in artistic festivals around the world, but the practical engineering, as well as the process of financing the satellite's launch, were more complicated. After a series of intricate negotiations with Mexican and international institutions (and the complexities were felt on both sides, according to those involved), Ulises I was launched into the stratosphere during the Guadalajara Book Fair in 2015, although the signal was quickly lost. Other Ulises are being developed.

According to Díaz Infante (2017), poetic satellites are transcendent because of their capacity to achieve the sublime "overview effect", a term created by Frank White in 1987 to describe the radical transformation of perspective reported by some astronauts after seeing Earth from space. White claims, based on a series of interviews with US astronauts who participated in diverse missions, that the overview effect offers a correction to egocentric and anthropocentric points of view by offering the possibility of a planetary perspective. Those of us who have not had the opportunity to experience the overview effect for ourselves, argues White, may be able to have a similar experience by communicating with astronauts who describe their transformations, or, alternatively, by simulating that experience by means of technology. White writes that

> Earth-orbiting satellites provide a technological parallel to the Overview Effect experienced by astronauts in orbit, building the Overview Effect as part of our collective reality on a continuing basis. …When astronauts see the Earth from space, they comprehend that it has a natural unity. Satellites embody the message that the planet is also becoming a social unity.
> *(2014: 58)*

For White, the goal is the creation of a species of "terranauts", humans who have "achieved astronaut awareness without going into orbit or to the Moon. They realize that the Earth is a natural spaceship … and all of us are, in a very real sense, astronauts who make up its crew" (2014: 70.).

White's mission is certainly seductive, and Díaz Infante and many other space artists articulate some version of it, often mentioning what they perceive as the apocalyptic ecological, social, political, and economic scenarios that characterise the contemporary age. For these artists, the potential for "seeing like a satellite" (Rothe 2017) is a call to connection, communication, and an ethics of care for the Earth and its creatures. The satellite sublime is a call to reenchant technology and, in doing so, reenchant outer space and Earth's place in it. But as Jordan Bimm reminds us, the overview effect that astronauts (and terranauts, one assumes) are said to experience is a product of a cybernetic vision of Earth as a closed system that emerged after the Cold War and was linked to notions such as James Lovelock's Gaia and Buckminster Fuller's Spaceship Earth (2014: 42).[12] Also worrisome in White's conceptualisation is the idea that the overview effect is seen as a kind of sign from the universe that justifies the belief in an evolutionary human need to leave Earth and colonise the universe, echoing the US doctrine of manifest destiny (Bimm 2014: 40). The overview effect, while it questions the artificial nature of national frontiers and evokes the possibility of a world without wars and inequalities (invisible from space, but not nonexistent), has the effect of rendering invisible cultural textures and differences (Bimm 2014: 43). And as Dovey argues, the overview effect, "while a nice idea", has "a rather dystopian underbelly", as it often serves to romanticise the human presence in outer space and justify the privatisation of space activities (2020).

On the other hand, an older cosmic perspective still makes itself known in Mexico and other territories with a precolonial history of stargazing. In fact, satellites (sublime or mundane) may be a threat to the cosmic sublime that results from finding oneself enveloped in the night sky, a blanket of black peppered with bright points of light. The "right to dark skies" proposed by UNESCO is being taken up in many countries, including Mexico, and specifically names satellites and satellite constellations as threats to this experience of the universe, not necessarily mediated by technology (UNESCO 2016; see Noon et al. this volume for their discussion on dark skies and Aboriginal and Torres Strait Peoples in Australia). Space artists, too, begin to question the need to launch more stuff into space, even in the name of poetry. "Do we have the right to put objects in other people's skies, even for pacific and cultural purposes, without asking them first? To whom does the sky belong?" (Bureaud 2021: 80; see also Triscott in this volume and her critical overview of perspectives on space in contemporary arts).[13]

Conclusions: How to Do Things with Satellites

Satellites challenge categorisation. They are located outside the lower levels of Earth's atmosphere, but they remain trapped in terrestrial orbits by the force of gravity. They are entangled in the planetary, even as they signal the possibility of thinking outside the planet's limits. They are part of the orbital technosphere that confuses the categories of the celestial and the terrestrial. They also represent ontological challenges. They are assemblages of objects that depend on a complex interdependence between earthly technology and satellite components in orbit; but in each phase of their design, construction, launch, operation, and disposal, they also depend on abilities and knowledge, economic investment, and political agreements. They become ocular or imaginative prosthetics. They are invisible to most of us, unless they fall out of the sky, although we can also feel the repercussions of their failure when "the system goes down". For many, satellites and their discourses perform a future marked by progress and wellbeing.

Looking at satellites as sociotechnological assemblages, and not just looking through them, is a way of bringing into focus historical processes, political and economic forces, and temporal and geographic imaginaries. This implies taking astrogeopolitics as a starting point (Graham 2019: 219) and taking seriously the global inequities that are brushed aside when representatives of the international space sector claim that "space is for everyone". But it also implies imagining alternative uses for satellite technology by diverse social actors, as in the cases of anticapitalist and anticolonialist cartographic practices that are beyond the scope of this article, and may be called community mapping, ethnocartography, Indigenous cartography, or participatory cartography. In these cases, satellite images may be reinscribed with graphic traces that emerge from the lived experience of inhabiting a particular territory: narratives, the location of natural resources to be protected, the tracing of extractivist megaprojects and their effects, militarised zones, or instances of different kinds of violence.

As opposed to "the satellite gaze" that pretends to present an objective perspective, unconnected to territorial processes, community mapping and its related practices explicitly incorporate subjectivity and political situatedness in the production of territorial representations. Like artistic satellites and other forms of space art, they also represent a call to think about the potential of satellites to perform diverse futures.

Finally, each satellite gaze is a gaze from somewhere in particular. Thinking about satellites from Mexico, like thinking about Mexico through satellites, offers an essential corrective to the study of technology, infrastructure, and modernity from *los lugares de siempre*.

Notes

1 In fact, ads attempting to entice homebuyers to invest in apartments in Ciudad Satélite, or Satellite City, featured cartoon space aliens to illustrate the futurist aspirations of these projects (for an example see "Anuncio ciudad Satélite", posted on YouTube by fomentoculturalsatel, https://www.youtube.com/watch?v=BsF9n48eIw8&t=3s). The "city outside the city" was soon swallowed up in Mexico City's urban sprawl.
2 Muralist David A. Siqueiros's monumental *The March of Humanity on Earth and Toward the Cosmos* is one example of mid-century modernist techno-optimism.
3 Of course, not everyone is fascinated with satellites. While many Mexicans have feelings of awe, nostalgia, or curiosity about outer space or the cosmos, they may also have serious reservations about space technology, and about technology in general. I would characterise Mexican astroculture, outside the microculture of the space sector, as being marked by (1) an interest in pre-Hispanic astronomical knowledge; (2) ambivalence toward technology and distrust in government institutions; (3) belief in alien intelligence; and (4) the idea that a future in space is only for rich individuals or nations.
4 Global Conference on Space for Emerging Countries (GLEC), Quito, Ecuador, 2022. According to representatives of NASA present at the conference, the US space administration had a budget of US$21.5 million in 2019.
5 For more on "merging space countries", see the studies on Indonesia's satellite program (Barker 2005) and Australia's space agency (Salazar and Castaño 2022).
6 Genaro, like many other STEM students of his generation, was inspired by the International Astronautical Congress that had been held in Guadalajara, Mexico, in 2016. It was here that Elon Musk publicly laid out his plans for the human occupation of Mars.
7 Tom Pullar-Strecker, "Rocket Lab's Secret Payload Owned by Mexican Defence Agency", *Stuff*, 22 July 2019, https://www.stuff.co.nz/business/114387492/rocket-labs-secret-payload-owned-by-mexican-defence-agency.
8 See, for example, "Mexico to Use Satellites to Track Migrants' 'La Bestia' Trains", 26 Aug. 2014, https://www.nbcnews.com/storyline/immigration-border-crisis/mexico-use-satellites-track-migrants-la-bestia-trains-n188861. On the other hand, some middle- and upper-class Mexicans have turned to satellite technology as a way of protecting themselves against kidnapping (Mica Rosenberg, "Satélites rastrean con chips a víctimas de secuestro en México", *Reuters*, 24 Aug. 2008, https://www.reuters.com/article/internet-delito-mexico-chips-sol-idLTAN2342313920080823). Citizens' fears of tracking technology are common; during the COVID-19 pandemic, conspiracy theories regarding the perceived use of vaccines to inject tracking chips were widespread in Mexico.
9 "Lanzamiento del Aztechsat-1 (transmisión en vivo)", streamed live on YouTube by Hacia el Espacio, 6 Dec. 2019, accessed 19 June 2022 at https://www.youtube.com/watch?v=YbMcHO_xuoQ&t=1271s.
10 "Refrenda la UNAM su potencial científico con lanzamiento de nanosatélite al espacio", DCGS–UNAM, 26 Feb. 2021, https://www.dgcs.unam.mx/boletin/bdboletin/2021_176.html.
11 https://network.satnogs.org.
12 Notably, Díaz Infante's father was well-known architect Juan José Díaz Infante Núñez, the designer of the building that now houses the AEM, a NASA consultant, and a student of Buckminster Fuller's.
13 Another Mexican contribution to space art is being proposed by Emilié Estrada, cofounder of the Interplanetary Creative Society. Instead of launching objects into space, Estrada proposes a "museum of space junk", including the remains of defunct satellites. See www.interplanetarycs.org.

References

Barker, Joshua. 2005. "Engineers and Political Dreams: Indonesia in the Satellite Age." *Current Anthropology* 46 (5): 703–27. https://doi.org/10.1086/432652.
Bimm, Jordan. 2014. "Rethinking the Overview Effect." *Quest: The History of Spaceflight Quarterly* 21 (1): 39–47. https://www.spacehistory101.com.

Borrego, Jorge, and Bella Mody. 1989. "The Morelos Satellite System in Mexico: A Contextual Analysis." *Telecommunications Policy* 13 (3): 265–76. https://doi.org/10.1016/0308-5961(89)90009-8.

Bureaud, Annick. 2021. "It's a Beautiful Name for a Satellite: Paradoxical Art Objects Somewhere between Politics and Poetics." *Leonardo* 54 (1): 79–91. https://doi.org/10.1162/leon_a_01987.

Collis, Christy. 2012. "The Geostationary Orbit: A Critical Legal Geography of Space's Most Valuable Real Estate." In *Down to Earth: Satellite Technologies, Industries, and Cultures*, edited by Lisa Parks and James Schwoch, 61–81. New Brunswick, NJ: Rutgers University Press.

DeLoughrey, Elizabeth. 2014. "Satellite Planetarity and the Ends of the Earth." *Public Culture* 26 (2): 257–80. https://doi.org/10.1215/08992363-2392057.

Díaz Infante, Juan José. 2017. *Ulises I: An Art Mission to Space by the Colectivo Espacial Mexicano*. Mexico: Concitep/Arizona State University.

Dovey, Ceridwen. 2020. "Pale Blue Dot." *The Monthly*. Accessed 24 Aug. 2020 at https://www.themonthly.com.au/issue/2020/december/1606741200/ceridwen-dovey/pale-blue-dot#mtr.

El Financiero. 2021. "México quiere llegar sí o sí al espacio y lo hará con ¿Rusia?" 28 Sep. 2021, accessed 24 Aug. 2022, https://www.elfinanciero.com.mx/nacional/2021/09/28/mexico-quiere-llegar-si-o-si-al-espacio-y-lo-hara-con-rusia/?fbclid=IwAR0-wIcDpmuF64mSqCteq09iLCtNS3JmYpDprLsjzdC9PZRAy7pEIxZ3rhU.

Gärdebo, Johan, Agata Marzecova and Scott Gabriel Knowles. 2017. "The Orbital Technosphere: The Provision of Meaning and Matter by Satellites." *The Anthropocene Review* 4 (1): 44–52. https://doi.org/10.1177/2053019617696106.

Garciandia, Laura. 2017. "The Interplanetary Human: The Sputnik Mission." In *Ulises I: An Art Mission to Space by the Colectivo Espacial Mexicano*, by Juan José Díaz Infante, 31. Mexico: Concitep/Arizona State University. Downloaded from https://www.ulises1.org/.

González de Bustamante, Celeste. 2012. *"Muy Buenas Noches": Mexico, Television, and the Cold War*. Lincoln: University of Nebraska Press.

Graham, Stephen. 2019. "Enigmatic Presence: Satellites and the Vertical Spatialities of Security." In *Spaces of Security: Ethnographies of Securityscapes, Surveillance, and Control*, edited by Setha Low and Mark Maguire, 206–30. New York: New York University Press.

Howell, Elizabeth. 2020. "63 Years after Sputnik, Satellites Are Now Woven into the Fabric of Daily Life." *Space.com*, 29 Sep. 2020. https://www.space.com/satellite-technology-daily-life-world-space-week-2020.

Jasanoff, Sheila. 2015. "Future Imperfect: Science, Technology, and the Imaginations of Modernity." In *Dreamscapes of Modernity: Sociotechnical Imaginaries and the Fabrication of Power*, edited by Sheila Jasanoff and Sang-Hyun Kim, 1–33. Chicago and London: University of Chicago Press. https://doi.org/10.7208/chicago/9780226276663.003.0001.

Johnson, Anne W. 2020. "A Mexican Conquest of Space: Cosmopolitanism, Cosmopolitics, and Cosmopoetics in the Mexican Space Industry." *Review of International Studies* 13 (2): 123–44. https://doi.org/10.31261/rias.9808.

Lazier, Benjamin. 2011. "Earthrise; or, The Globalization of the World Picture." *American Historical Review* 116 (3): 602–30. https://doi.org/10.1086/ahr.116.3.602.

Litfin, Karen T. 1999. "The Status of the Statistical State: Satellites and the Diffusion of Epistemic Sovereignty." *Global Society* 13 (1): 95–116. https://doi.org/10.1080/13600829908443180.

Mack, Pamela Etter. 1990. *Viewing the Earth: The Social Construction of the Landsat Satellite System*. Boston: MIT Press.

Mohanta, Nibedita. 2021. "How Many Satellites Are Orbiting the Earth in 2021?" *Geospatial World*. https://www.geospatialworld.net/blogs/how-many-satellites-are-orbiting-the-earth-in-2021/.

Pang, Alex Soojung-Kim, and Bob Twiggs. 2011. "Citizen Satellites: Sending Experiments into Orbit Affordably." *Scientific American* 304 (2): 48–53. https://doi.org/10.1038/scientificamerican0211-48.

Parks, Lisa and James Schwoch. 2012. "Introduction." In *Down to Earth: Satellite Technologies, Industries, and Cultures*, edited by Lisa Parks y James Schwoch, 1–18. New Brunswick, NJ: Rutgers University Press.

Rivera Parga, José Ramón. 2017. "La exploración espacial: una oportunidad para incrementar el poder nacional del estado mexicano." *Revista del Centro de Estudios Superiores Navales* 38 (4): 33–62.

Rothe, Delf. 2017. "Seeing Like a Satellite: Remote Sensing and the Ontological Politics of Environmental Security." *Security Dialogue* 48 (4): 334–53. https://doi.org/10.1177/0967010617709399.

Salazar, Juan Francisco, and Paola Castaño. 2022. *Framing the Futures of Australia in Space: Insights from Key Stakeholders*. Sydney: Western Sydney University.

UNESCO. 2016. *The Right to Dark Skies/El derecho a los cielos oscuros*. Mexico and Paris: UNESCO.

White, Frank. 2014. *The Overview Effect: Space Exploration and Human Evolution*. 3rd edition. Reston, VA: American Institute of Aeronautics and Astronautics.

28
SPACE CODES
The Astronaut and the Architect

Fred Scharmen

Introduction

This chapter is about the hidden rules that make visible space. I will survey existing recommendations, regulations, codes, and standards that apply to the design and construction of human habitable spaces in outer space. I will connect these spatial codes to precedents and principles that obtain within the history of spatial practice on Earth and speculate about how they might evolve forward in time as standards and practices develop and change, on our planet and off of it. I will address these spatial codes as they interact with the work of designers at four scales. First, *codes of conduct* regulate the professional roles that designers play. As practitioners, they have certain legally mandated responsibilities to the public that go along with their title. Second, *building codes* dictate the specifics about how the designer's responsibilities are translated into built form, with special attention to the way that structures and spaces present affordances to the human bodies that use them. Third, *zoning codes* prescribe the limits and manner of the interactions and obligations between private and public spaces. Fourth and finally, *codes of law* organise situations and spaces at the highest scale, dictating the status of public commons, and the nature of the human worlds that depend on them. In the last portion of this chapter, I bring the largest and smallest scales together, collapsing personal responsibility to worlds and publics back into a cosmopolitan composite of two figures with distinct but overlapping legal definitions and obligations, the astronaut and the architect.

Understanding Spatial Practice

The forms and spaces of built environments on Earth look and act the way they do because they are the result of complicated negotiations between many heterogeneous types of things. The myth of the singular heroic architect was always just that: a myth (Miller 1988). In what I'll call broadly the "spatial practice disciplines"—especially architecture, landscape architecture, and city and regional planning—the intentions of individual designers matter less than the interconnections of constraints through which those intentions are filtered. Successful designers are skilled at synthesising the needs of collaborators, clients, constituencies, users, and public audiences, but they must also interface with other actors. Laws and treaties, regulations and boundaries, zoning and safety, rights and responsibilities, means and methods ... all of these also determine the shape and functions of the constructed worlds that humans occupy. All of these are solidified into what I'll label here "spatial codes".

These codes are a kind of record of past failures, and a set of anticipations about future hopes. Structures collapse, disasters occur, and practitioners learn from those mistakes and seek to codify practices that will prevent or mitigate these breakdowns, whether they are due to accident or negligence. Codes exist to safeguard the long-term public good and public safety against private interests focused on profit and short-term gain. In outer space—in territories and worlds away from Earth—safety in the short and long term becomes an even more pressing concern than on our home planet. Spatial practice in space is, in these places, one of the sole means of protection for the humans there. Artificial designed and built environments are the only thing standing between the fragile biological creatures that we are and the harsh conditions outside. Disasters lurk in the present, past, and futures of these spaces. The existing environment offers constraints, and so do the realities of biology and behaviour. How are spatial codes in outer space constructed to mitigate the dangers associated with these constraints? What kind of relationships do they have to the codes that regulate spatial practice on Earth? And how might these constructions and relationships change as human presence in outer space expands, along with our knowledge base about the hazards and opportunities?

Codes of Conduct: Who the Architect Is

In the United States and several other nations, the term "architect" is a protected professional title. Like lawyers and medical doctors, no one working in the built environment industries may call themselves an "architect" in a professional capacity unless they have met certain criteria, as certified by a central authority. In the US, the National Council of Architectural Registration Boards (NCARB) coordinates requirements for architectural licensure among the states and territories. These include standards for schooling, professional experience, and a series of exams. But other touchstones apply as well. Since 1977, NCARB has compiled and updated a set of *Model Rules of Conduct* for architects. In states that adopt these rules, the penalty for violating them could be as severe as the revocation of the architect's licence, and the loss of their valuable ability to practise the profession under that legal title.

NCARB's *Model Rules of Conduct* specify that architects should act with competence, avoid conflict of interest, and practise truth telling and full disclosure when it comes to violations and conflicts. They should comply with laws, and they should carefully exercise their professional role as the signatory for construction documents. The *Model Rules* recognise that the architect has a responsibility to their client, but also that they have obligations to the people who use the projects they work on, and to the world at large. The first guiding principle in the document states that these rules are not aspirational, but rather mandatory, for the profession. The second guiding principle in the *Model Rules* sets the architect's primary duty out clearly: "The objective of these *Model Rules of Conduct* is the protection of the public health, safety, and welfare". Further, the fifth principle specifies that sometimes, in order to protect that public interest, architects might have to "insist on positions that are not in their clients' interest". And even further still, the sixth guiding principle stipulates that an architect observing unsafe conditions or practices at any time must report them to their state board, even if those conditions are the result of another architect's work (NCARB 2018: 5, 7).

Similar standards are obtained within other related spatial practice disciplines in North America. In landscape architecture, they are codified by the field's professional organisation, the American Society of Landscape Architects (ASLA). The *ASLA Code of Professional Ethics* calls out the importance of "public health, safety, and welfare", and beyond that, "protection of the land and its resources". The *Code of Professional Ethics* breaks down its standards into some that are *aspirational* and some that are *required* (ASLA 2017). The American Institute of Certified Planners (AICP) also upholds an *aspirational* obligation to "serve the public interest", and it has the authority to strip violators of their professional certification (AICP 2016: 2). Only NCARB, in its ability to centrally regulate the profession of architecture, links a direct requirement *for* (not just an aspiration *towards*) responsibility to a broadly defined public good with the power to expel violators from legally recognised participation in a spatial practice discipline.

In the nascent field of space architecture, the obligations and responsibilities of the architect are no less fraught. In architectural education in the US, the National Architectural Accrediting Board (NAAB) ensures that schools of architecture offering professional degrees are delivering the kind of education necessary for eventual practice in the field. At the time of this writing, one institution, the Sasakawa International Center for Space Architecture (SICSA) at the University of Houston, offers the only master's degree in space architecture in the US, or indeed the world. Their programme was accredited in 2002 by the Texas Higher Education Coordinating Board (THECB). No design-specific organisation like NAAB accredits schools offering degrees in space architecture, and SICSA relocated in 2015 away from the University of Houston's College of Architecture and was integrated instead into the university's College of Engineering. In North America at least, this creates a gap in the way that space architects are professionally accredited for practice in the field.

No doubt there are issues pertaining to architecture in space that are specific to that domain, but a commitment to public health, safety, and welfare should be universal, as aspirational ideals and, for certain figures, as professional obligations. In the construction of spaces on Earth, even the engineers are usually—within the organisational structures laid out in the model contracts of the American Institute of Architecture (AIA)—subcontractors of the architects, with whom the primary responsibility for the work lies. As these roles are constructed today, the engineers simply don't have the level of overarching responsibility that is necessary.

NCARB's *Model Rules of Conduct* are codes that construct the architect as a particular kind of figure, whose advocacy on behalf of the public users of the built environment even extends, in theory, to the architect's daily life and the conditions they observe while going about it. The explicit prioritisation of that responsibility before the demands of the architect's client, and beyond the scope of work that the architect directly contributes to, is particularly important. However, the system is also open to corruption: studies have suggested that self-regulating professions such as architecture tend to favour their own interests over public interests, despite the existence of codes of ethics or conduct (e.g., Adams 2017). The sanctions allowed for in the codes are applied unevenly and may not be effective in eliminating poor practice (Perlis and Shannon 2012).

In space, the reduction of health, safety, and welfare to "human factors" is all too common; this approach is outlined in more detail in the following section. The clients who commission living space for humans in space may, given the high levels of capital investment involved, be incentivised to minimise these factors and the standards for living, comfort, and habitability in the environments they ask architects to design, especially if those clients are private actors. The space environment presents many new hazards, but many more are all too familiar to architects working on Earth. The protections offered by these codes of conduct and their construction of the architect as public advocate are all the more important here. The figure of the architect, in NCARB's *Model Rules*, is expected to act not only with competence but with "care" (NCARB 2018: 6). Space architecture is Earth architecture with the volume turned up. What's necessary here is more than the minimum. Spatial practice in outer space is the mitigator of extreme threats to the welfare of the spacefaring and Earthbound public, and it needs a corresponding set of empowered and caring individuals who are charged with upholding and defending that welfare.

Building Codes: Who the User Is

The history of contemporary building codes goes back at least as far as Hammurabi. In that Babylonian ruler's legal text, composed in the 1750s BCE, the importance of the builder's responsibility to health, safety, and welfare is made clear (Hammurabi [c. 1772 BCE] 1910). The designer of a house that collapses is liable for damages, and the most severe penalty is death. In the Christian Bible, the book of Deuteronomy, written between the seventh and fifth centuries BCE, also has instructions for building safe structures.

The stipulations in contemporary building code break down broadly into two types: those that guide the behaviour of the designers, requiring them to ensure that the building is constructed in a way that is stable, sturdy, and reasonably protected from dangers like fires or earthquakes, and secondarily those that guide—and to no small extent, condition—the behaviour of the users, anticipating and influencing the way that they might act in the event of an emergency and in ordinary daily life.

The International Building Code (IBC), for example, sets key dimensions for elements of the built environment: door opening widths, railing heights, stair rise and run, handrail and handle locations, ramp slopes, and clearances for head heights (ICC 2021). These are standards for the interaction between architecture and the human body. They are based on assumptions about the aspects and abilities of imagined bodies, including maximum reach, eye height, centre of gravity, mobility, energy, and strength levels. If professional codes of conduct construct the subjectivity and personhood of the designer, then building codes construct the embodiment of the user. And they literally concretise the specifics of that assumed embodiment into the built environment. If those assumptions are wrong, or if they fail to address the needs and abilities of some portion of potential users, then the space will exclude them from access (Taylor 2008).

Perceptual psychologist James J. Gibson names these aspects of the built environment *affordances*.

> The *affordances* of an environment are what it *offers* the animal, what it *provides* or *furnishes*, either for good or ill ... I mean by it something that refers to both the environment and the animal in a way that no existing term does. It implies the complementarity of the animal and environment.
>
> *(Gibson 1979: 127; italics in original)*

This complementarity is taken for granted in building code, especially when it comes to any possibility of a difference between perception and action. The spirit of these codes dictates that nothing should look like a stair unless it also functions as one, that is, that it should present vertical and horizontal surfaces to the user that are uniform and at a proportional relationship to each other that affords safe and comfortable ascent and descent, lest someone stumble in haste or fear.

During the design process, designers following building codes move through their hypothetical projects with the kind of attention that new parents bring to baby-proofing a home with a toddler in it. Anything that could be a hazard, through accident, misuse, or malice, is removed or mitigated. Slopes and steps get handrails, anticipating a stumble and grasp. Deep drops get guardrails, against the possibility of a wander off the edge, and these guardrails themselves must in turn be made safe. Building code warns against the potential "ladder effect" of railings that are easily climbable and proscribes against any openings large enough to pass "a soft four-inch sphere" (as architects colloquially summarise it) through them that might then get stuck. Even though the public who use the space, and the developers that pay for it, often resent these impositions, they are necessary. Each safety feature is a monument to a past tragedy and the code that prescribes it is a message to a hopeful future. Every successful design is littered with hypothetical ghosts. The human user constructed here is one that is sometimes unable or unwilling to perceive danger in front of them or one that is destructive enough to invite it. And after the efforts of the designer implementing building code are done, the structure itself seems to exhibit a certain kind of *care* towards the vulnerable, fallible—and sometimes even malignant—humans inside it.

Building Codes and the Body

Recognition of the principle of complementarity between organism and environment, the way each creates and interacts with the other, is also present in the very titles of NASA's own key specification documents for affordances in space, the *Space Flight Human-System Standard* (SFHSS) and the *Human Integration Design Handbook* (HIDH). These documents use terms like "human-system integration" and "human-centered design" to refer to the "procedure for including the human in the design process" (NASA 2014: 20). The process begins with specifications about the human population intended to occupy the spaces. The baseline information for human size and abilities used for NASA's Orion spacecraft (designed to take humans to the Moon and beyond), for example, was collected from US military databases, "because the obesity rate of civilian databases outpaces the foreseen obesity rate of an astronaut population" (NASA 2014: 40). The *Handbook* specifies that system designers should derive linear regression equations from the database for key body metrics. Rather than base dimensions of the built environment on static minimums and maximums, like building code does on Earth, each system or structure is designed dynamically around these statistical analyses of likely population characteristics, once the engineering capabilities of the vehicle are established. There is flexibility here, but only within predetermined bounds. If codes on Earth go from the structure inwards, conditioning and limiting the behaviour of the user and their body, codes in space go from the statistically constructed body of the user at the centre, outwards to the physical affordances of the structure.

Writing in the 1950s about his universal "Modulor" system for translating human dimensions into space and structure at all scales, the influential modernist architect Le Corbusier explained that he had started with a six-foot-tall male figure because that was the height of English policemen in detective novels (Le Corbusier 1954: 56). Similarly, the notional astronaut is first conceived as a statistically variable authority figure in this "human-centred" schema. Fraught analyses of the average or ideal human abound.

Today, in the 2020s, the US-led Artemis programme, the system that will return humans to the Moon, with the Orion module as a centrepiece, will also be built around the statistically filtered dimensions of militarised authority figures. These imagined bodies will literally condition the nature of the space around them. Orion's design specifications are based on population databases that exclude people with obesity and people with disabilities, who would be denied military training and thus be omitted from the databases. Linguist and disability studies scholar Sheri Wells-Jensen makes the case that leaving behind people with disabilities in space exploration would be a mistake (Wells-Jensen 2018; Eveleth 2019). Besides basic ethics and equity concerns, people with mobility issues would not necessarily be any more encumbered in space than able-bodied people. And, in situations where hearing or sight is restricted, people with sensory and other disabilities might find themselves at an unexpected advantage. In 2021 the European Space Agency (ESA) launched its parastronaut feasibility project, actively seeking astronaut candidates with certain disabilities (ESA 2021). After all, says ESA astronaut Samantha Cristoforetti, "We did not evolve to go to space. So, when it comes to space travel, we are all disabled" (Baker 2021).

Space is not just one place—it contains multitudes. And these different places have different characteristics, especially when it comes to gravity. The International Space Station (ISS) is in low Earth orbit, only on average about 400 kilometres up. The station is in free-fall, that is, it is falling in a roughly circular orbit around Earth. Although there is a gravity field here in space, the people and objects inside it don't feel the influence of its force due to this trajectory. During launch and reentry, those who are on the way to, or returning from, the ISS will experience forces that are several times stronger than Earth's gravity. On the Moon, they would be under the influence of weaker gravity, about one-sixth as strong as Earth's, and on Mars, a little more than a third of Earth's gravity. Design in space will encompass environments that help humans deal with radically different forces than the ones they are used to experiencing, sometimes more, sometimes less. The effect on the design of handrails for gripping with hands and feet and the material surfaces of bulkheads, walls, and ceilings that people might bump into will be different for different locations and times, depending on the gravity. The same push that might not have any effect at all in one place might send a person flying across the room in another. Human-proofing for variable gravity will remain a large part of the designer's job. Space is an arena in which predicting human behaviour and capabilities based on the statistical modelling of idealised human bodies could go drastically wrong in several ways.

Escape Routes

An important aspect of building code is emergency egress. In a worst-case scenario, when the basic integrity of the structure is existentially threatened by fire, earthquake, or other disaster, building codes ensure that there are safe travel paths to exits. The codes that describe how these exit paths should be designed take into account the potentially erratic and confused behaviour of humans when presented with chaotic and dangerous fast-moving situations. Visibility might be low and people who don't have experience with impaired eyesight need clear visual signals, so exit signs light up, but other cues are spatial and material in nature. Individual rooms lead to corridors that lead to stairs that then let out of the building entirely. The general principle is that each space you enter, as you move along an exit path, should be a little safer than the space you just left. So corridors are rated to withstand fire outside of them for longer than most rooms, and stair towers are even more protected than that. Most scenarios require that two potential exit paths should be available to people when they enter a corridor, both to mitigate confusion and to provide a backup in case one is blocked (Barber 2019).

The culmination of an exit path on Earth should be outside the building or structure, theoretically safer than anywhere within. In outer space, this is obviously not possible, given the harsh and deadly character that the external environment presents. There is no safety outside. Rather than using an emergency exit paradigm borrowed from building egress principles, contemporary structures in space use a lifeboat model adapted from ships at sea. Most large oceangoing cargo ships today are required to carry at least enough lifeboat capacity to evacuate all crew and passengers. In case the emergency has caused the ship to roll or capsize, this 100-% capacity is duplicated on both the port and starboard sides of the vessel. On the ISS enough spacecraft are docked at all times to evacuate all persons on board the station in the event of an emergency. This craft would find ultimate safety by going not out but down, reentering Earth's atmosphere. In the event that crew had to perform an emergency landing in a place outside their country of origin, the 1967 Outer Space Treaty (more on that below), also building on principles from maritime law, stipulates that they must be rescued and returned home.

The concept of hallways is no less a technological invention than the concept of the life raft. Hallways are relatively uncommon in western architecture before the eighteenth century (Jarzombek 2010). Structures would either be too humble and small or too large and luxurious to set aside space that existed only for people to move through and circulate, with no other practical purpose. Hallways and corridors are part of "gross" calculations of interior square footage. Gross area includes all of the floor plate that is unleasable, along with the "net" square footage that realises a direct financial return on investment. Making space like this is counterintuitive, and it tended to be limited to the servant spaces of large structures so that the more formal spaces could be served as unobtrusively as possible. A different class of people was, in a sense, living behind the walls. These spaces were liberated and somewhat democratised when new technologies, like electric lights and steel frames, allowed buildings to grow taller and wider.

After, again, a series of tragedies in tenements and factories like the Triangle Shirtwaist fire in New York City in 1911, in which 146 mostly female garment workers died (to this day one of the deadliest industrial disasters in the US), the need to create new spaces and new protocols for emergency egress became clear. These protections for the health, safety, and welfare of the public were written into building code, sometimes against the protests of private interests that saw their leasable floor plate get eaten up by safe paths to exit. Now that new dangers were present in these larger crowded structures, the hallway was pressed into a new service, contributing to access both in daily life and in emergencies.

Similarly, the lifeboat, a boat for a boat, is not at first an obvious solution to an obvious problem. Sometimes it's necessary, in a dangerous situation, to escape into the outside world in a small craft that's even more vulnerable than the larger one you are leaving. Exit corridors and lifeboats are both a kind of technology, spatial inventions that solve problems and make places safer. In space, there will almost certainly be the necessity for habitable structures to have "storm shelters", special areas like panic rooms deep inside them that are well shielded from radiation by extra mass, where the inhabitants can hide from outbursts of solar radiation. The appropriate response to danger is not always an egress to an outside but sometimes a retreat to the centre. What other spatial technologies will be necessary for life in these newly dangerous places? What new dangers will humans bring, accidentally or on purpose, to these places?

Zoning Codes: Where the Space Is

The proliferation of hallways within the enlarged structures newly enabled by electric lighting and steel structure, especially in North America and Europe at the turn of the twentieth century, gave rise to a new kind of interior life within architecture. Where formerly spaces had often been arranged "enfilade", with private life and public life intermingling as people went from room to room directly through connecting doors, the technology of the hallway allowed for private activity to remain tucked away. Hallways also created the opportunity for a more explicit public life and public space within the building, as corridors became something like internal streets, facilitating encounters and gatherings that had not arisen before (Gieryn 2002). Meanwhile, as contemporary egress and fire protection protocols were written into the building code that dictated the design of the building's interior, these newly possible tall, deep buildings were also threatening the actual streets outside them. A different kind of code for urban design, zoning code, had to be constructed in order to protect this exterior public realm from private development that verged on overwhelming it.

Zoning codes find their roots in customs that restricted what kinds of activities, and therefore what kinds of building types, could exist in different areas of cities. These laws separated out work that was noisy, dirty, or noxious, like tanning, agricultural slaughtering, or milling, from the centres of cities where people lived, worked, and gathered. Zoning by use type is the contemporary descendant of this mode. But another kind of zoning created and protected the street. Streets, too, are a kind of technology. Some of the oldest cities recognised as such by archaeologists, like Çatalhöyük in modern-day Turkey, from around 7500 BCE, had no streets in their earliest phases (Düring 2001). Buildings were built right next to one another, with shared, closed walls. To go from space to space, inhabitants would climb a ladder through a hole in the ceiling, and move around on a shared roof level. Streets, like hallways, are counterintuitive. They create and enable economic activity through secondary, nonobvious, effects. They have both no function and every function. And if they were to continue to exist on the ground plane of a growing, changing city, they had to be recognised as part of a public commons whose borders and characteristics were written into code.

In the early twentieth century, skyscrapers, a new building type, began to undermine the quality of life in the public realm of the street below and between them. To maximise their return on investment in valuable urban land in Manhattan, developers would again seek to maximise their leasable floor plate. In many sites, like the triangular plot that New York's Flatiron Building is on, this logic led to a simple extrusion of the lot line into the sky, building upwards as tall as the elevators and steel of the day would allow, in order get the most rent money from the resulting habitable space (Koolhaas 1978: 88). Planners in New York eventually realised that if every property owner followed this logic, the streets, and plazas left on the ground would eventually become dark and dank, dreary places unfit for the exterior public life, transportation, and commerce that the city depended on. In 1916 New York implemented a new zoning code that ensured the ground plane's access to light and air. Tall buildings, under this code, would have to step back from their lot lines if they exceeded certain heights. Unchecked vertical expansion, limited only by technological feasibility, was restricted to the centres of large blocks. This code curtailed the high-flying potential profits of private real-estate developers while protecting the health, safety, and welfare of the public realm below.

Outer space, with the possibility for easy access to large supplies of energy and material and seemingly limitless volume to dispose of waste, might be an ideal place for industrial zoning. Proposals for settling and living in space, even from the early twentieth century, included the possibility that heavy industry from Earth could and should be relocated there along with a large human population (Tsiolkovsky [1920] 1960). In the 1970s, Princeton physicist Gerard O'Neill made the case for space industry and space living in a NASA workshop, in testimony before a US congressional committee, and in a popular book, *The High Frontier* (O'Neill 1977) (Scharmen 2019). A lifelong follower of Gerard O'Neill's ideas about space "colonisation", Amazon and Blue Origin founder Jeff Bezos is also a proponent for specific zoning use types for space and Earth. As high school valedictorian in 1982, Bezos gave a speech advocating for moving first millions, then eventually most humans, off Earth, to "see it turned into a huge national park" (Huddleston 2018). In 2016, Bezos told a conference interviewer that "[i]n at least a few hundred years ... all of our heavy industry will be moved off-planet" and that "Earth will be zoned residential and light industrial" (Kulwin 2016).

In 1933 the International Congresses of Modern Architecture (Congrès Internationaux d'Architecture Moderne, or CIAM) published the influential *Athens Charter*. This document outlined a zoning programme for cities that would dominate urban planning around the world for the next fifty years. The *Charter* reduces cities to "The Four Functions": dwelling, recreation, work, and transportation. These functions and their subcategories, the *Charter* recommends, should be clarified, organised, and, when desirable, separated from one another. Recreational space should be connected to residential space, and it should be used to keep industrial space away from housing. Commercial and office space should be adjacent to, but not necessarily mixed with, residential districts. Transportation, especially via private automobile, should be prioritised, and it should be made as efficient as possible, in order to link all of this separated fabric back together (CIAM [1933] 1973).

Meant to be egalitarian in theory, in practice, this mode of single-use or "Euclidean Zoning", as it came to be known, was often used to separate and even segregate people of different races, classes, and genders. Using zoning as a tool, planners and municipalities could artificially maintain a neighbourhood at a lower than optimal density, keeping out multifamily buildings that would bring more racial and economic diversity. They could place poorer residential neighbourhoods in areas that were nearer to industrial zones than wealthier housing districts. They could restrict access between neighbourhoods, limiting mobility for those, like many of the women of the day, who might not be able to drive or have access to a car. They could also wield power, in conjunction with the strategic deployment of building code, that would allow them to condemn poorer or Blacker neighbourhoods when they were useful for other purposes, displacing legacy residents who would then be forced to move to even more undesirable areas (Pietila 2010).

In outer space, all space is expensive. The economic incentive to realise a direct return on investment into the production of space often becomes overriding once more, and spaces within habitats that can't justify their own existence in those terms get cut from planning sessions. There are no hallways in the ISS; the capsules and modules are arranged enfilade again, returning to the earlier mode of house design. With the exception of the private crew quarters, each smaller than a phone booth, all living and working takes place within the same spaces that people use to circulate and travel around the station. And when the Habitation Module—that would have separated out living, sleeping, eating, and toilet space away from work areas—was cancelled in 2006, zoning on the ISS effectively moved from single-use to mixed use.

If the public space of corridors and atriums is priced out in outer space already, the future is murky with regard to the viability of larger-scale places like streets and public plazas in space. Zoning codes in outer space should enable and protect these public spaces that give rise to culture and secondary economic activity that will be a necessary part of life here. But zoning in space should not be used, as it has on Earth, as a tool to segregate and alienate space-based populations of people from one another. In these harsh environments, the participation and cooperation of everyone with a stake in health, safety, and welfare is crucial, and space zoning should support that solidarity.

Codes of Law: What a World Is For

In 1967, the United Nations put a new document up for the international community to consider and possibly ratify. Most of the world's nations are now parties to the Treaty on Principles Governing the Activities of States in the Exploration and Use of Outer Space, including the Moon and Other Celestial Bodies. A product of the unique period during the Cold War and the Space Race between the United States and the Soviet Union, when it wasn't clear which country would make it to the Moon first, the Outer Space Treaty, as it is more popularly known, is surprisingly optimistic and even utopian in the way it frames a human future in space. The Outer Space Treaty is a document that is a first of its kind. Here, the representatives of the governments of one world are creating a model in international law for the production of other worlds outside of it. These codes operate at the largest scale of all, as they define the basic parameters that humans from Earth should follow when making new worlds in space.

The foundational principles of the Treaty are rooted in the recognition of common inspiration, common interest, and common benefit, and in the necessity of cooperation and friendly relations between nations and people. The Treaty describes the nature and qualities that these new worlds in space should have. In this way, the Treaty takes its place among other codes above that prescribe methodologies for spatial practice in general. Exploration of these worlds "shall be the province of all mankind [*sic*]", and these worlds are "not subject to national appropriation by claim of sovereignty ... or by any other means". Flag or not, the Americans did not and could not claim the Moon as their territory during the Apollo missions. There can be no military installations or manoeuvres, and no weapons of mass destruction are permitted. Astronauts, in particular, as people who are "carrying on activities" in these new worlds, have certain special rights and responsibilities. They must warn one another of danger and render any necessary mutual aid to each other if they are able to. They also have the right to be returned to their home base or home country if they go astray or get lost (UNOOSA 1967).

The Outer Space Treaty further stipulates that nations are responsible for the actions of their nonstate actors in space, like private spaceflight companies. And even though no nation can claim sovereignty over territory in outer space, the Treaty implies that the use of resources in space is allowed, and that individual countries retain jurisdiction over their hardware and installations in space. In order to further the cause of cooperation, states should inform the international community of their activities in space and open one another's installations in space to mutual inspection. If activities carried out by one nation result in damage to objects or activities from another nation, then the parties are liable for that harm.

Some of the ambiguities in the Treaty, such as the right to claim the material results of activities like mining as private property, have later been clarified (or perhaps exploited) in national law. In the US, at least since the SPACE Act of 2015, mining in space, and the exploitation of space resources, is considered legal under that law's interpretation of the Outer Space Treaty. Other terms, like the point above Earth where outer space officially begins or the legal definition of the word "astronaut", are yet to be defined in US law. But however untested in practice, some legal scholars assert that at least some portions of the Outer Space Treaty have by now transitioned into the status of *customary law*. Under these conditions, the Treaty would bind the actions of any state or nonstate actor in space, even if they weren't signatories. And if states who have signed later decide to withdraw, then (under this theory) the Treaty's terms would still obtain (Lyall and Larsen 2020: 63–73).

The environment of outer space presents many unknown hazards and opportunities, and the potential consequences of these cannot be totally anticipated or captured in advance by international codes of law. Two interrelated discoveries about the Moon illustrate the nature of some of these unknowns and how international law and custom might deal with them. In a place with low gravity and no atmosphere or erosion from wind and water, the material that makes up the ground surface of the Moon—known broadly as regolith—can easily get disturbed and fly around at dangerous velocities. Many common activities that might eventually take place on the Moon, like mining and rocket ship take-offs and landings, can send regolith long distances, and its particles have such sharp jagged edges that they can effectively sandblast and destroy anything they hit, like equipment or people, even possibly going into lunar orbit (Metzger 2020). Meanwhile, it has recently been confirmed that craters at the lunar poles in perpetual darkness contain reserves of water ice that are billions of years old, useful for making rocket fuel, among other things. This confirmation has sparked new and urgent interest in the kind of landing and mining activities that could create exactly this kind of dangerous abrasion from flying regolith, a threat from private activity that could effectively damage the public realms of the Moon.

To mitigate this danger and others, the creators of the international Artemis programme to return humans to the Moon, led by the United States and European Union, have drafted a set of accords that could become a framework for safe cooperation in this other world. Like the planners of the twentieth century, they will use zoning. Language in Section 11 of the Artemis Accords creates provisions for the mutual establishment of "safety zones" on the Moon and elsewhere, in order to avoid conflict between activities like science, transportation, and resource extraction. This is a direct response to discovery of new dangers as mining potentially interacts with aspects of the lunar environment (Artemis Accords 2020). The further possible conflict, the effective difference between a nation's establishment of a "safety zone" (encouraged by the Artemis Accords) and a claim of "sovereignty" (forbidden by the Outer Space Treaty), remains relatively unexamined.

Codes of international (and interplanetary) law in space are part of an ongoing project still in progress. But documents like the Outer Space Treaty provide a foundational basis for further elaboration, and the general principles and practices enshrined in the Outer Space Treaty, especially mutual aid and peaceful cooperation, should not be abandoned lightly as new technical realities or material opportunities become apparent. The public on the Moon and in space must be protected by new codes of law. These are the protocols for shared space in new worlds, and they represent, like all of these other codes, a template for spatial practice in general that many disciplines could learn from, in space and on Earth.

Conclusion: The Architect and the Astronaut

The four types of codes outlined here act at a range of scales, from the individual person in a professional capacity to a possible new world or worlds shared by uncountable types of future people. The presentation of the figure of the astronaut in the Outer Space Treaty points towards a possible role model for anyone navigating these scales. In an age of growing private spaceflight opportunities, new questions about who has the right to claim the title of "astronaut" have arisen (Lyall and Larsen 2020: 117). According to some interpretations of the Outer Space Treaty, the closest that document offers to a definition of the term "astronaut" is any person who is "carrying on activities in outer space and on celestial bodies" (UNOOSA 1967) (Scharmen 2021). The American Federal Aviation Administration uses a default term, "spaceflight participant", to describe most people engaging in privately organised trips to space. At the time of this writing, they reserve the term "commercial astronaut" for only those who are conducting work in space that benefits the public broadly or contributes to astronaut safety specifically (FAA 2021). This is a possible recognition of the Outer Space Treaty's requirement that space activities should benefit humankind generally, that astronaut safety is paramount, and that astronauts are also "envoys" of humanity (UNOOSA 1967).

This is also cognate with the role of the architect in the built world. In NCARB's *Model Rules of Conduct,* the architect's obligation to the health, safety, and welfare of the public extends even into their daily life. Following these rules strictly would mean reporting any unsafe condition—anything designed or built that does not meet the spirit or the letter of building code—at any time, even if the condition is the work of someone else, and even if they are acting outside of their professional role on the clock and just going about their ordinary activities (NCARB 2018: 5, 7). The penalty for failing to observe this obligation could be the loss of their professional title and role.

Architects and astronauts both are defined by their responsibilities and by their actions. They are the embodiments of past tragedies and future hopes captured by spatial codes. The subject of those responsibilities, choices, and actions is the welfare of the public at large, in both cases. Activities that astronauts undertake in space should, as the Outer Space Treaty stipulates, "be carried out for the benefit and in the interests of all countries" (UNOOSA 1967). This is maybe the broadest possible definition of the "public" that architects are obligated to care for. Both architects and astronauts are spatial practitioners that protect the public from dangers outside, they protect the public from harm they might do themselves, and they protect the public from private interests that might seek to undermine the principles of mutual aid, cooperation, and commons that worlds and people depend on generally. At the scale of a building, and at the scale of a world, these same obligations obtain. Spatial practice is ultimately something that even the public itself, the nominal subject of these codes, is no stranger to. The public is conditioned, and, as we've seen, even produced by these space codes, on or around any body, celestial or otherwise, and in documents like the Outer Space Treaty, the blurred line between spatial occupant, spatial user, and spatial producer is explicitly acknowledged. The public makes space too. Whether personal, structural, territorial, or universal, these spatial codes regulate our responsibilities to one another whenever space is made or shared.

References

Adams, Tracey L. 2017. "Self-Regulating Professions: Past, Present, Future." *Journal of Professions and Organization* 4 (1): 70–87. https://doi.org/10.1093/jpo/jow004.

AICP (American Institute of Certified Planners). 2016. *AICP Code of Ethics and Professional Conduct.* Chicago, IL: AICP.

ASLA (American Society of Landscape Architects). 2017. *ASLA Code of Professional Ethics.* Washington, DC: ASLA.

Artemis Accords. 2020. *The Artemis Accords: Principles for Cooperation in the Civil Exploration and Use of the Moon, Mars, Comets and Asteroids for Peaceful Purposes.* Washington, DC: NASA.

Baker, Sam. 2021. "ESA Welcomes Parastronauts: In Space We're All Disabled." *DW*, 18 February 2021. https://www.dw.com/en/esa-welcomes-parastronauts-in-space-were-all-disabled/a-56617337.

Barber, Daniel A. 2019. "Emergency Exit." *e-flux Architecture*, September 2019. https://www.e-flux.com/architecture/overgrowth/284030/emergency-exit/.

Congrès Internationaux d'Architecture Moderne (CIAM). [1933] 1973. *The Athens Charter.* Translated by A. Eardsley. New York: Grossman Publishers.

Düring, Bleda S. 2001. "Social Dimensions in the Architecture of Neolithic Çatalhöyük." *Anatolian Studies* 51: 1–18.

ESA (European Space Agency). 2021. *Parastronaut Feasibility Project.* Paris: ESA. https://www.esa.int/About_Us/Careers_at_ESA/ESA_Astronaut_Selection/Parastronaut_feasibility_project.

Eveleth, Rose. 2019. "It's Time Rethink Who's Best Suited for Space Travel." *WIRED*, January 27, 2019. https://www.wired.com/story/its-time-to-rethink-whos-best-suited-for-space-travel/.

FAA (Federal Aviation Administration). 2021. *FAA Commercial Human Spaceflight Recognition.* Washington, DC: FAA. https://www.faa.gov/space/human_spaceflight/recognition.

Gibson, James J. 1979. *The Ecological Approach to Visual Perception.* Boston, MA: Houghton Mifflin.

Gieryn, Thomas F. 2002. "What Buildings Do." *Theory and Society* 31 (1): 35–74. https://doi.org/10.1023/A:1014404201290.

Hammurabi. [1772 BCE] 1910. *The Code of Hammurabi.* Translated by L. W. King. https://avalon.law.yale.edu/ancient/hamframe.asp.

Huddleston, Tom, Jr. 2018. "Valedictorian Jeff Bezos Said He Wanted to Build 'Space Hotels and Colonies' in His 1982 High School Graduation Speech." *CNBC Make It*, 3 September 2018. https://www.cnbc.com/2018/08/31/amazon-jeff-bezos-proposed-colonizing-space-high-school-graduation-speech.html.

ICC (International Code Council). 2021. *The International Building Code.* Washington, DC: ICC.

Jarzombek, Mark. 2010. "Corridor Spaces." *Critical Inquiry* 36 (4): 728–70. https://doi.org/10.1086/655210.

Koolhaas, Rem. 1978. *Delirious New York: A Retroactive Manifesto for Manhattan.* New York: Monacelli Press.

Kulwin, Noah. 2016. "Jeff Bezos Thinks We Need to Build Industrial Zones in Space in Order to Save Earth." *Vox*, 1 June 2016. https://www.vox.com/2016/6/1/11826514/jeff-bezos-space-save-earth.

Le Corbusier. 1954. *The Modulor.* Translated by Peter de Francia and Anna Bostock. London: Faber & Faber.

Lyall, Francis, and Paul B. Larsen. 2020. *Space Law: A Treatise.* 2nd edition. Abingdon-on-Thames: Routledge.

Metzger, Philip T. 2020. "Dust Transport and Its Effects Due to Landing Spacecraft." Presented at the second NASA Engineering and Safety Center's Lunar Dust workshop, 11–13 February 2020, Houston, TX.

Miller, Ross. 1988. "Burnham, Sullivan, Roark, and the Myth of the Heroic Architect." *Art Institute of Chicago Museum Studies* 13 (2): 87–95. https://doi.org/10.2307/4115893.

NASA (National Aeronautics and Space Administration). 2014. *Human Integration Design Handbook.* Washington, DC: NASA.

NCARB (National Council of Architectural Registration Boards). 2018. *Model Rules of Conduct.* Washington, DC: NCARB.

O'Neill, Gerard K. 1977. *The High Frontier: Human Colonies in Space.* New York: Morrow.

Perlis, Clifford, and Noah Shannon. 2012. "Role of Professional Organizations in Setting and Enforcing Ethical Norms." *Clinics in Dermatology* 30 (2): 156–59. https://doi.org/10.1016/j.clindermatol.2011.06.002.

Pietila, Antero. 2010. *Not in My Neighborhood: How Bigotry Shaped a Great American City.* Lanham, MD: Rowman & Littlefield.

Scharmen, Fred. 2019. *Space Settlements.* New York: Columbia University Press.

Scharmen, Fred. 2021. "A Billionaire Space Tourist by Any Other Name." *Slate*, 16 November 2021. https://slate.com/technology/2021/11/space-billionaires-tourist-astronaut-bezos-branson-shatner.html.

Taylor, Astra, dir. 2008. *Examined Life.* Film. 1 h 25 min. https://www.youtube.com/watch?v=8rEgcLMamZE.

Tsiolkovsky, Konstantin. [1920] 1960. *Beyond the Planet Earth.* Translated by Kenneth Syers. New York: Pergamon Press.

UNOOSA (United Nations Office for Outer Space Affairs). 1967. *Resolution 2222 (XXI). Treaty on Principles Governing the Activities of States in the Exploration and Use of Outer Space, including the Moon and Other Celestial Bodies.* New York: United Nations.

Wells-Jensen, Sheri. 2018. "The Case for Disabled Astronauts." Blog post. *Scientific American*, 30 May 2018. https://blogs.scientificamerican.com/observations/the-case-for-disabled-astronauts/.

PART V

Cultures in Orbit/Life in Space

29
COSMIC WATERS

Julie Patarin-Jossec

Cosmic waters. The underwater and outer space worlds have commonalities. Access to both is dependent on technology, techniques, and *savoir-faire*. They extricate bodies from their otherwise gravitic docility. They are dangerous for these bodies. They are fantasised and exploited for greed and control. They are an Otherness of which eerie aesthetics initiate phantasmatic meditations (*Figure 29.1*).

Spatial knowledge. The oddness, yet somehow familiarity, of some obscurities is a way to deploy new senses and comprehension about how bodies interact with what surrounds them and the signals they send. A pain in the inner ear signals descending or ascending, and the need for the body to equalise eardrums. Darkness prevents relying on vision, while stability in weightness is not only the result of successful transmission from the inner ear to the brain, like in earthly circumstances, but of successful osmosis with fluids. What the body exhales paves the way towards the surface—the ground where bodies lie and survive without artefacts. When this happens, water and the cosmos strangely become a new, odd world where human anatomy transcends its condition through plasmatic liquidity (*Figure 29.2*).

Weighted floatation. The first feeling space and underwater travellers experience coming back to earthly ground is weight. Bodies and artefacts no longer float, as they had learned to do for a while, but are, once again, disciplined by the force of gravity. Only through artifice can conditions not ruled by weightiness be somewhat reproduced. And yet, the feeling is not there. It disappears as soon as the feet can walk again (*Figure 29.3*).

Soaring corporeality. Cardinal orientation is a framework—among others. When weightness doesn't force verticality according to mathematical axes, positions follow the flow. Bodies adjust—even if they have to unlearn to do so. Minds might never adapt—habits are comforting. Accessing new worlds strangely relies on excessive rise or fall from the surface, and then by the liminality of buoyancy—where experimenting and empowering are governing movements (*Figure 29.4*).

Recording the invisible. Out-of-this-world bodies are closely monitored by life support system sensors. How bodies react, where they are located, and everything happening to them along the way are expressed, materialised, and visualisable through biometrics. Descending or rising from the surface is visible, and controllable, through screened data. These technological artefacts oversee the exploration—both its characteristics (depth or altitude, distance, surrounding temperature, and pressure) and how bodies react to these features (bpm, nitrogen saturation in body tissues, or pulmonary oxygen rate). Biometrics unveil an otherwise invisible world, materialised by bizarre lines, colloquial numbers, and algorithmically generated notices. Cosmic physicalness is a matter of narrative (*Figure 29.5*).

Julie Patarin-Jossec

Figure 29.1 Cosmic Waters #1. Image by Julie Patarin-Jossec, 2022.

Cosmic Waters

Figure 29.2 Cosmic Waters #2. Image by Julie Patarin-Jossec, 2022.

Julie Patarin-Jossec

Figure 29.3 Cosmic Waters #3. Image by Julie Patarin-Jossec, 2022.

Cosmic Waters

Figure 29.4 *Cosmic Waters #4.* Image by Julie Patarin-Jossec, 2022.

Figure 29.5 Cosmic Waters #5. Image by Julie Patarin-Jossec, 2022.

30
UNEARTHING BIOSPHERE 2, BIOSPHERE 2 AS UN·EARTHING

Ralo Mayer

In summer 1991, a curious theatrical performance took place a few miles southwest of Oracle, Arizona. Recorded on Hi8 video tape, we see a stage and a hand-painted backdrop suggesting a geodesic structure. In front of a small audience, eight people in outlandish costumes and colourful makeup frenetically dance and sing. Their slapstick routines follow the misfortunes of a crew of peculiar astronauts inside a closed self-sustaining ecosystem. The troupe runs out of oxygen and food, people start to quarrel, and they begin a rebellion against mission control. Everything that can go wrong goes wrong. The skit, called *The Wrong Stuff*—taking a shot at Tom Wolfe's book about the first US astronauts—received standing ovations.[1]

A few weeks later, on 16 September 1991, a crew of eight left Earth's atmosphere for real. Under the blazing sun of the Sonoran Desert, dozens of professional camera teams and thousands of visitors witnessed the spectacle, which for some time had spurred considerable attention in the US as well as international media. When their mission launched, the crew did not ride on top of a fiery pillar of burning fuel, their bodies would not be accelerated to escape velocity and no rocket science was involved. Some even argued no science was involved at all, and that this was rather a theatrical stunt (Maugh 1991). The eight so-called *Biospherians*, who had now swapped their carnivalesque costumes for smart, dark blue jumpsuits, waved towards the audience and stepped through an airlock. They entered another biosphere, a small, self-containing world that they and their group, countless workers, and scientists had built since 1987.

The experiment of Biosphere 2 was set in a futurist greenhouse, designed and constructed to be materially closed and energetically open. For two years, the crew would live and work inside a 1.3 ha miniature world, the closed system providing recycled air, water, and food. Biosphere 2 housed eight of our planet's major biomes, including its own rainforest, marsh, coral reef, and small agricultural farm. The eight humans were one among 3,800 species of plants and animals. They interpreted their human roles as stewards, trying to foster the ecological equilibrium the new artificial ecosystem would hopefully establish (Alling, Nelson, and Silverstone 2020; Reider 2009). Designed to be inhabited by changing crews over a period of one hundred years (Allen 1990), Biosphere 2 had two main research goals: to test the feasibility of humans living in self-sustaining settlements in outer space and on other celestial bodies, and to learn more about the Earth's own complex ecological cycles via a miniaturised model of its major interconnected biomes (Allen and Nelson 1999).

In my artistic research and resulting works of the past fifteen years, I have explored Biosphere 2 primarily through its performative and cultural aspects. These lesser-known aspects situate the project as much within the Earth–Space complex as do its experimental setups of biophysics, ecological engineering, or psychology of small isolated groups. The Biosphere 2's founders' background in 1960s counterculture and avant-garde theatre (Reider 2009; Poynter 2006; Mayer 2016) catalysed an entanglement of the experiment within wider sociopolitical, ecological, and cultural transformations of the past decades (Mayer 2016). While the space race made the Moon an arena of the Cold War, Biosphere 2 is situated within a variety of changes of the 1990s often broadly generalised as "globalisation".

As the beginning of this text hopefully helps to establish, my methods of artistic research are informed by forms of storytelling between fact and fiction, and an exploration of multiperspective and fragmentary narratives crossing disciplinary fields as well as artistic and popular media. This practice includes the use of essayistic approaches as hybrid forms interlinking fragments of science, subjective experience, ephemeral observations, and transient textures (Adorno 1991) and its critical reflection within contemporary art and artistic research (Steyerl 2017). My work is also based within theories of ecology and nature-cultures as proposed for instance by Bruno Latour, Isabelle Stengers, Timothy Morton, or Donna Haraway; these theories integrate and encourage modes of speculation and fabulation, and at the same time correspond to the very setup of Biosphere 2's artificial ecological system.

Since 2007 I have researched Biosphere 2 through several visits of the site as well as through interviews and exchange with key people of its founding and construction group. I've approached the experiment primarily via an anecdote related to the weight loss of the Biospherian crew during the first mission. Due to difficulties in farming and food production, the eight crew members would lose up to 20% of their individual body mass. As this lost weight remained inside the closed system, they joked about a potential ninth Biospherian that might have formed from their individual losses (Mayer 2018). This imaginary ninth crew member and their whereabouts after the experiment are the subject of the fictitious novel *The Ninth Biospherian*. Through a series of works I have "translated" this fabulated work of literature into installations, films, and texts, the eponymous phantom and nonhuman ecological entity becoming a narrative device of my performative research and its dissemination.

As I will outline in the following, Biosphere 2 and its multilayered stories feature key characteristics of what I call un·Earthing, a multiplicity of transformations that humans undergo when leaving Earth and the change of human cultures by and in outer space. While developed in the context of artistic research, I would like to propose un·Earthing as a sketch for a conceptual framework to investigate, speculate, and fabulate about these transformations across disciplines, fields, and in exchange with various audiences. This delineated framework is inherently ambivalent, displays contradictory traits and points towards conflicting futures and struggles on and off Earth, and is also relevant for current discussions and contested narratives of the Anthropocene.

Unearthing an Experiment

Built between 1987 and 1991, Biosphere 2 was financed and run by Space Biosphere Ventures, a private joint enterprise of the founding group and Texan oil dynasty heir Ed Bass. The experiment was set in a futurist greenhouse, designed and built to be airtight and based on geodesic structures that had been popularised by R. Buckminster Fuller, science fiction films, and vernacular architecture of 1960s counterculture.[2] The experiment's scientific background was based on the new discipline of systems ecology and on Soviet research, specifically geochemist Vladimir Vernadsky's concept of *biospherics* and related closed-system experiments undertaken by the Institute of Biophysics in Krasnoyarsk in the 1970s and 1980s (Marino and Odum 1999; Gitelson and Lisovsky 2008; Allen 1990).

Despite collaborations with major institutions and established scientists, the project's scientific credibility was being questioned already before its first mission began in September 1991.

Journalists researching the background of Biosphere 2 criticised a lack of academic credentials—none of its founders had a PhD at the time of the experiment. Articles also sensationalised the founders' theatre background as well as their communal lifestyle at the Synergia Ranch in Santa Fe and Biosphere 2s site in Oracle.[3] Public and academic criticism, compounded by a lack of forecast economic profits, led to a change of ownership amidst the second mission in 1994. The facilities were taken over by Columbia University, which stopped human involvement in the ecosystem. After Columbia withdrew in 2003, all closed-system experiments stopped and the site was briefly up for sale on the real estate market. Since 2007, the University of Arizona has undertaken various ecological research in the now materially open greenhouse.

Largely forgotten by the broader public after the first mission, the experiment has been examined since the 2000s by historians of science and environmental sciences in relation to ecology, environmental thinking, space exploration, and cybernetics (Anker 2010; Höhler 2010; Reider 2009). More recently, its controversial and changing image in the media has been the subject of media analysis (Brooks, Juanals, and Minel 2022), and Biosphere 2's theatre and performance background has become of increasing interest for researchers at the intersection of art, science, and technology (Ivison, Tcharfas, and Sadler 2018). Artists and filmmakers have likewise begun to unearth Biosphere 2, reflecting on its now retro-futurist architecture and its relation to global warming and other contemporary ecological discourses (Rivers 2016; Wolf 2020), and it has become a source of inspiration and reference for novels (Boyle 2016; Lillemose 2021). In my own work in film, installation, and performances, I have traced its parallels to ecological narratives and motives on and off Earth in fiction, the arts, and the public imagination (Mayer et al. 2008; Mayer 2018).

Not unusual for research-based artistic practices, my investigation of Biosphere 2 parallels established methods from academic and scientific disciplines, like archival research, interviews, or on-site surveys. Time and again, I felt like I was digging up futures from the past, imaginary

Figure 30.1 Collapsed model of Biosphere 2 at the abandoned visitor centre. Photo: Ralo Mayer/Bildrecht, 2009.

futures in outer space that had been lost (or unrecognisably repurposed in the digital realm), like so many other departures and utopias of the 1960s and 1970s. This pseudo-archaeological romantic sentiment became most apparent during early visits at the site of Biosphere 2 in 2007 and 2009 when I encountered Biosphere 2 and its surrounding infrastructure in varying degrees of neglect, decay, and redefinition. The Ninth Biospherian, as an ephemeral figure of collective loss, was indeed haunting the physical site of Biosphere 2.

The entire area was an epitome of Ballardian landscapes. My exploration of it felt like exploring ruins—not ruins of the space age, but leftovers from a later era, an era that had already historicised the fading memories and imaginations of the 1960s and 1970s. I stumbled across several artefacts telling the ambivalent story of the site's recent past between science, tourism, and institutional struggles. Inside the abandoned former visitor centre, I found a detailed miniature of Biosphere 2 that had cost around US$100,000 in the 1990s. Once slowly revolving to impress arriving tourists, it had partly collapsed and was covered in faeces of local wildlife that now inhabited the ruins (Figure 30.1). Boxes of 35mm slides, once part of a sophisticated 1990s-state-of-the-art multimedia show, lay strewn around an empty auditorium. In an unconscious, Schliemann-esque reflection of my romanticising performance as archaeologist, I took some of these boxes with me and later integrated them into an installation work.

From Unearthing to Un·Earthing

While I had been unearthing the history of Biosphere 2 for years, it was not until 2018, during an art residency in Japan, that I realised a potentially different interpretation of this term in a serendipitous moment during an otherwise inconclusive artistic investigation. I had been trying to visit a futurist tower, built by Metabolist architect Kiyonori Kikutake for Expo '70 in Osaka (Koolhaas et al. 2011; Shikata 2019), which had inspired the eco-spaceship Valley Forge in the movie *Silent Running* (Trumbull 1972), a fictional precursor to Biosphere 2. As I found out all too late, the tower had been demolished more than ten years earlier, and the only traces I could find were some dark outlines of its foundation on an abandoned plot next to Expo Memorial Park. My aerial drone images of this fading shadow reflected my frequent work about lost futures; the photos looked like an archaeological survey. Once again, I thought, I am unearthing past futures. *But what about un-earthing?*

"To unearth" is often used as a metonym for a quasi-archaeological activity. It is a transitive verb, referring to acts of digging something up, revealing objects from the past covered by layers and sediments of time and space. Unearthing means to bring things to light, to uncover and rediscover hidden objects and their stories and histories, which could very well describe the basic approach of many contemporary artistic projects, including my own. "Un-Earthing", or as I prefer to write, *un·Earthing*,[4] could be used as an intransitive verb. Un·Earthing offers a multidisciplinary perspective towards a range of processes and transformations that humans and human cultures (and quite likely other species) undergo when they leave Earth as their planetary home (Mayer 2021). These processes are shaped by both real-life events and fictional accounts concerning life in space as much as on Earth. I argue that un·Earthing is not limited to astronauts or dependent on space travelling, and has been a broader phenomenon—by way of mediated and collectivised experiences and imagery like the photos of Earth from space—at least since the late 1950s.[5] Instances of un·Earthing are driven by a multitude of narratives which engage a multidimensional situatedness of transformed temporal and spatial relations, imply concepts of ecology beyond nature as a paradigm of multispecies performance, and feature uncanny hauntings of what appears to be all too familiar on Earth.

Some aspects of un·Earthing could be understood as closely related to notions of unlearning and decolonising (Danius, Jonsson, and Spivak 1993; Tlostanova and Mignolo 2012), but while humans might unlearn earthly habits and structures of oppression, un·Earthing might as well (and most probably will) include yet inconceivable new forms of colonialism and violence. Un·Earthing is an area of ambivalence and ambiguities; it refuses to be pinned down in unambiguous classifications. Like the notion of the pharmakon and its meanings of remedy, poison, and scapegoat, un·Earthing is a process of destabilisation, questioning foundations and fixed points, features of the pharmakon that Isabelle Stengers has described in reference to ecology, in that ecology "refers to questions of process, namely, those likely to include disparate terms" and is "the science of multiplicities, disparate causalities, and unintentional creations of meaning" (Stengers 2010: 33, 34).

Un·Earthing favours an entanglement of facts and fictions oscillating between Earth and space. Consider, for instance, the first Apollo missions of the late 1960s, the astronauts being military test pilots that became the first humans to travel to another celestial body. Nobody had previously come closer to the barren landscape of lunar craters. And despite all the excitement of this pioneering trip what actually blew their minds was the view looking homeward, the blue disc in the distance, of which they took a photo, which some countercultural protagonists then turned into an ecological icon (Poole 2008; Mayer 2012; Turner 2006). The story and impact of the photos of the whole Earth from space are a superb example of un·Earthing and its unintentional and ambivalent implications. Un·Earthing is full of serendipity. As Robert Merton and Elinor Barber delineate in their history of the term's invention and circulation, the "accidental sagacity" of serendipity is rarely an individual phenomenon but mostly involves multiperspective storytelling driven by narrative transfers and accidents of translation (Merton and Barber 2006). This can found be found in most research approaches, including artistic research, or space exploration. While startup culture and its mantra of innovation and creativity have brought about a tiring ubiquity of the term (Olma 2016), the concept was also invoked by participants of Biosphere 2 in the early 1990s to explain and defend the experiment's processual and unorthodox approaches. The experiment was not designed as a hypothesis-driven experiment and its crew regularly referred to the importance of serendipity in their research, comparing it for instance to Charles Darwin's voyage of the Beagle (Walford 2002).

Following Hans-Jörg Rheinberger's discussion of experimental setups and the relation of technical and epistemic things (1997, 2008), Biosphere 2 was built as a technical object, an experimental apparatus, with which to investigate Earth's ecology and test the feasibility of self-sustaining future settlements in space. While the validity of this experimental apparatus has been subject to controversy, often due to its foundations in theatre, counterculture, and new ecological disciplines, it is mostly this multifaceted background which has turned the experiment itself into an epistemic object beyond the natural sciences. Biosphere 2 not only was an unprecedented technical apparatus for experiments in biospherics and closed ecological life support systems but also constituted a miniature model of a unique mélange of intertwined sociocultural, ecological, and economic developments situated right at the beginning of a period in the early 1990s that was globally transformational (Mayer 2018).

Serendipity redraws, if not erases, the lines between technical and epistemic objects, its accidental and unplannable nature catalyses their proliferating dialectic. After the original experiment had ended, Biosphere 2 became an epistemic object itself, an object of academic, artistic, and documentary investigations. It is a storied place and narrative machine that continues to connect itself to contemporary issues, from global warming and the new space race by private companies to the US presidency of Donald Trump and the COVID-19 pandemic.[6] Although the original experimental setup was shut down after 1994, its founders have since stated that their experiment is, in many ways, ongoing (pers. comm. Kathelin Gray; Mark Nelson). Their "greatest performance", as several protagonists called the experiment in our talks, continues in the public imagination, as well as through various transformations on-site. In 2007, when I told John Allen, regarded as

Biosphere 2s inventor, about the decaying state of the site that he had not been able to visit since 1994, he said they had anticipated the experiment's uncertain future and possible demise. With a laugh, he explained that they had deliberately employed styles reminiscent of famous archaeological sites and poured a foundation of several meters of concrete that should be hard to remove for centuries to come.

Mining Plots

In their research about the European Space Agency's artificial life-support system MELiSSA, Céline Granjou, and Jeremy Walker delineate a genealogy of artificial systems as characterised by "life's dislocation from its prior rootedness in ground, soil and earth: an increasing 'de-grounding' and de-territorialisation of select multi-species communities" (Walker and Granjou 2017: 66). As closed-system life-support systems are a central element enabling human life in space, this "de-grounding" of various species reveals un·Earthing as a process that is not limited to humans but is an inherently interspecies phenomenon. Just like the "colonial and imperial roots & routes" of science fiction (Haraway 2013), artificial biospheres evoke colonial Wardian cases used to transport plants to plantations as well as research greenhouses (Keogh 2022), and they contain speculations and fabulations about futures in outer space.

The biomes of Biosphere 2 housed animals and plants collected all over the globe, organisms that had never encountered one other within an ecosystem before. As would seem natural for such an artificial world, a frequently invoked narrative concerning this human-curated system was one of modernity's original myths—Mary Shelley's *Frankenstein* (1818) and its derivations in various media.[7] Like the story's creature, Biosphere 2 was patched together from unearthed elements, explored artificial nature and the role of humans in it, and was met with controversial reactions. Related to yet differing from this narrative of Frankenstein, the figure of the Ninth Biospherian also tells a story of a bricolage of fragments, of loss and decay assembling surprising new formations. The Ninth Biospherian is a myth of transformation and a blurring of human and nonhuman. The experiment is no longer a mining operation but the afterlife of leftovers of planetary mining. The Ninth Biospherian is a figuration of un·Earthing in that it tells the story of collective loss that constitutes something new and unforeseen.

Travelling the US Southwest is a Grand Tour of what in German is called *Western von Gestern* (yesterday's western), and mining plots are abundant everywhere. Oracle, the site of Biosphere 2, was named after a mine that had attracted the first European settlers to the area. The first and ongoing ecological project of Biosphere 2s founders was the revitalisation and reforestation of a ranch outside of Santa Fe, New Mexico. This, too, was a place that miners had ecologically devastated by cutting down vegetation in the late nineteenth century. During my first visit, John Allen, who had studied metallurgy and worked for a mining company prior to founding the group that would later build Biosphere 2, took me on a walk through the eroded landscape and gave me a hands-on introduction to the ecological approach.[8] When the Synergia group moved to the ranch in 1972, rather than clearing out the miners' trash they made regular use of it to fill in eroded trenches. Slowly, through the decades, this little routine would stop further erosion and reenable diverse plant growth.

The notion of unearthing is not limited to a romanticising metonym of archaeology; it could also be considered in relation to the extraction of natural resources in a global industrial capitalist context. The past which is unearthed in this sense ranges from carbohydrates of long-gone biospheres to metals and rare earths whose formation long precedes the emergence of Earth's biosphere, if not Earth itself. Mining rare earths provides raw material for electronics used in space, and histories of extractivism and colonialism are often ground for and complicit with space-related research on Earth, like in the Atacama Desert in Chile (Detwiler 2021; see also

Detwiler this volume). Contemporary imaginaries of mid- and long-term exploration of the solar system, mostly but not exclusively propagated by private entrepreneurs, point to the potential exploitation of extraterrestrial resources. While such ideas have long been a background to science fiction stories, from pulp stories to movies spanning Fritz Lang's *Frau im Mond* (1929) to Ridley Scott's *Alien* (1979), the economic rationale behind commercial exploitation of space resources has already transformed fabulation into legislative text in many countries. Asteroid mining, or "mining the sky" (Lewis 1997), is a curious and paradoxical twist on un·Earthing: it is an unearthing of material that has never been earthly in the first place. Today, it is a narrative used to mobilise for colonisation once more. As Ursula K. Le Guin so aptly states as critique of the origins of male techno-heroic narratives: "It wasn't the meat that made the difference. It was the story" (Le Guin 1996).

Unearthing Biosphere 2 both at and from a site of science implies digging into layers of cultural plots and economic plotting: is this a theatre piece about ecology or an asset's unfriendly takeover orchestrated by an investment banker named Steve Bannon? In this detective work the uneasy interferences between ecology and conspiracy theories become obvious once again. Everything seems to be connected; there is "a latent criminality" to this theatre/archaeology (Pearson and Shanks 2001: 62). Experimental systems are related to traps, and Biosphere 2 was a trap, too—only in this case its setup became blurry: who or what was to be trapped? A trap is "the simplest form of the plot", in that it builds upon and against other plans and creates a not-quite-deliberate or -conscious collaboration of narratives (Singleton 2015). As Hans-Jörg Rheinberger observes, models, as epistemic things, "participate in the game of switching media" and "thrive from the tension created by the fact that they always leave something to be asked" (Rheinberger 2008: 26).

If the research question is about un·Earthing, an unearthed Biosphere 2 can once more be employed as a technical object. The apparatus of Biosphere 2 is no longer a 250-million-dollar, airtight greenhouse housing 3,800 species and countless machines, computers, and sensors; Biosphere 2's technical apparatus is now a setting for performative experiences, imaginaries, and narratives of un·Earthing. The experiment is a laboratory for storytelling. Such a story apparatus could take the form of an imaginary novel revolving around the figure of the Ninth Biospherian. There would be no need for a hero in this novel. It would rather be a bag of things,

> full of beginnings without ends, of initiations, of losses, of transformations and translations, and far more tricks than conflicts, far fewer triumphs than snares and delusions; full of space ships that get stuck, missions that fail, and people who don't understand.
>
> *(Le Guin 1996: 153)*

Such rethinking of Biosphere 2 as an ecosystem of narratives of un·Earthing is, of course, closely related to Donna Haraway's concept of science fiction as multispecies worlding practice. SF can be "science fiction, speculative feminism, science fantasy, speculative fabulation, science fact" (Haraway 2016: 10). If we take up Haraway's proposal of SF's meanings and engage in its string-figure patterning, Biosphere 2 as un·Earthing could be space fabulation and space fact. The conceptual framework of un·Earthing itself might be a string figure for "giving and receiving patterns, dropping threads and failing but sometimes finding something that works, something consequential and maybe even beautiful, that wasn't there before, of relaying connections that matter, of telling stories in hand upon hand" (Haraway 2016: 10). As Juan Francisco Salazar remarks concerning his approach for researching the extreme environment of Antarctica, an entanglement of fact, fiction, and fabulation "enables research to follow forked directions, to both respond and anticipate phenomena that may not simply be held, observed and acted upon" (Salazar 2020: 154) (Figure 30.2).

Figure 30.2 Crew of Biosphere 2 and Biospherian trainer Kathelin Gray after a performance of *The Wrong Stuff*, 1991. Photo courtesy of the Institute of Ecotechnics.

Biosphere 2 as Plot and Performance of Un·Earthing

Outer space, like Biosphere 2, is not a mere site. Formations of un·Earthing are characterised by fundamental shifts in human perception of time and space, and these shifts could perhaps best be approached through the multivalent notion of plot—a term that bears various and conflicting meanings between fictional narratives, mathematical graphs, organisational intention, and economic exploitation (Singleton 2015). While site-specific practices have been crucial for critical art since the 1960s and can be seen as fundamental for discursive and institutional critique and for conceptual and research-based art (Kwon 1997), the notion of plot favours narrative approaches towards and multidimensional storytelling about places against the more territorial idea of "site". Rather than being limited to physically delineated places, un·Earthing takes shape as multiple exposures and perspectives of locations, indicating multispecies storied places (Van Dooren and Rose 2012) and interplanetary storytelling between physical reality, fiction, and fabulation.

It is a well-known anecdote of the relationship between science fiction and space exploration that the countdown was invented by Fritz Lang as a dramaturgical device to spice up the rocket launch scene for *Frau im Mond*. While the Biospherians publicly acknowledged systems ecology and Soviet biospherics as their references, they also followed the advice of their close friend, avant-garde writer William S. Burroughs, and included Galago primates in Biosphere 2. Inside their crew quarters, they watched Freeman Lowell in *Silent Running* (Trumbull 1972) killing his crewmates and teaching ecology to robots. Biospherian Linda Leigh told me she thought *Bio-Dome*, the notoriously bad 1996 stoner comedy set in a closed ecosystem, was actually quite an accurate depiction of certain aspects of their life inside. Un·Earthing is the performative realisation and reinterpretation of plots, plots of reenactments, and preenactments. Un·Earthing is both fact and fiction; it is a multitude of trajectories, or as the artist and activist group AAA described their alternative space programme in the late 1990s, "moving in several directions at once" (Inner City AAA 1997).

For performance theorist Jon McKenzie, in the twentieth century, the paradigm of performance has permeated into diverse areas beyond the theatre stage, such as technology, organisational and economic structures, and broader cultural contexts. In *Perform or Else* (2001) McKenzie explores this growing significance through notions of effectiveness (technology), efficiency (organisations and economy), and efficacy (culture). McKenzie conceives a common ground of "performance" through a case study of the explosion of Space Shuttle *Challenger* in 1986, which "brought together cultural, organisational, and technological performances" (McKenzie 2001: 140). McKenzie tracks the shuttle's iconic mission and the disaster through a failure of performances and their political, public, and cultural aftermath. Such a deep entanglement of performances, and their failures, in technology and science and in organisational structure, as well as in the cultural and public imaginary, can likewise be found in Biosphere 2. The effectiveness of its technological and scientific performance has been discussed in scientific publications (Marino and Odum 1999), its efficiency and efficacy for ecological thinking have been contextualised in science and technology studies (Höhler 2010; Anker 2010), and its background in theatre and counterculture has been described in memoirs, personal accounts (Alling, Nelson, and Silverstone 2020; Poynter 2006), and academic and artistic research (Reider 2009; Mayer 2016; Ivison, Tcharfas, and Sadler 2018).

While the effectiveness of its scientific and technological performance was initially the main focus of discussion around the experiment, and its organisational efficiency was subject to internal as well as external conflicts and evaluations, I would argue that Biosphere 2's most influential performance was linked to its enormous cultural efficacy as a narrative machine. From early on, and unanticipated by its founders,[9] the media and public were enthralled by the small world under glass and its human crew, drawing comparisons to religious myths, science fiction, and space age promises. The "Frankensystem", as it was called by its own crew (Alling, Nelson, and Silverstone 2020), had not only come to life but had also begun to spawn its own stories. Biosphere 2 has been and still is a hothouse of narratives; it is an ecosystem of storytelling about nature-cultures on Earth and possible futures in space. Biosphere 2 is a performative plot of un·Earthing, a "multi-form worlding practice" (Haraway 2013) within a "laboratory of ideas for thinking life in extra-terrestrial Earths, but at the same time an extra-terrestrial mode of thinking Earth", as Juan Francisco Salazar writes about research stations in Antarctica (2020).

Tales of futures are recycling plots of hauntings from the past. While staying at the site, I became strongly aware of the ongoing repercussions of several changes in ownership, of scientific goals and methodologies, and of economic and organisational transformations inside as well as outside the project. In my interviews, as well as personal talks, I almost always felt some sort of ghosts lurking around, in between carefully chosen words and phrasing in conversations, between the plants and steel struts, and within the cracks in the concrete. The Ninth Biospherian is that which comes from in between; it is an entity of ecology. This phantom is neither sinister nor benevolent. It is at the same time familiar and alien, all around us and yet intangible. Following Mark Fisher's concept of hauntology, this is the "agency of the virtual, with the spectre understood not as anything supernatural, but as that which acts without (physically) existing" (Fisher 2013: 26).

Already during the first test mission in the smaller prototype system, John Allen, or "Vertebrate X"—the first human subject—wrote in his journal about a "strange partnership building between my body and the plants" (Allen and Blake 1991, 29). Similar feelings and perceptions of physiological changes were observed by further test subjects and the Biospherian crew. The closed system transforms human understanding of ecology as an environment surrounding us (the *Um-welt*) into a system blurring boundaries between humans and nonhumans, culture, and nature. The familiar becomes the *un-heimlich*, the uncanny. If Earth is our home, then space is that which is not home.[10] Biosphere 2s biosphere is familiar, yet different. A Martian landscape looks alien, but familiar too, like a rocky desert on Earth. During a video call from the test module in the Arizona desert,[11] "Vertebrate Y", Linda Leigh, told astronaut Buzz Aldrin, "I could visualise a different terrain on the outside and I was pretending that maybe it was a Martian or lunar terrain" (Allen and Blake 1991: 31). Unfortunately, the term "uncanny", as the common English translation of Sigmund Freud's concept of the unheimlich, drops the original relation to the home. In my essay film *Extra-Terrestrial Ecologies* (Mayer 2018) I suggest the use of unsettling instead in order to maintain this connotation. Biosphere 2 was a prototype for a space settlement, and as a space un·settlement, it triggers narratives and performances of un·Earthing.

Ecologies without Earth

Biosphere 2s intricate meshwork of species, machines, computers, and sensors is an evident demonstration of an "ecological cyborg", a concept that has originated in plotting space exploration since the 1960s (Clynes and Kline 1960; Anker 2010). Such a setup goes beyond a back-to-nature conservationist naturalism and includes technological and informational cycles. In a filmic paraphrasing of Richard Brautigan's 1967 poem "All Watched Over by Machines of Loving Grace" (Brautigan 1989), the plot of *Silent Running* runs through this development: the robot takes over the stewardship of Earth's remaining trees in the spaceship's biosphere. Biosphere 2's imagery of idyllic waterfalls, sensors, electronics, and computer monitors at first goes along Brautigan's poem: "a cybernetic meadow/where mammals and computers/live together in mutually/programming harmony/… a cybernetic forest/filled with pines and electronics". The Biospherian self-representation (and daily experience) as farmhands contrasted with its last part: "a cybernetic ecology/where we are free of our labors/and joined back to nature,/returned to our mammal/brothers and sisters,/and all watched over/by machines of loving grace."

Space, widely regarded as rather dead and empty, has been quite full of ecological plots for over a century, including, for instance, Konstantin Tsiolkovsky's sketches for greenhouses, cosmonauts growing wheat on the space station Mir, or the resourceful botanists of *E.T. The Extra-Terrestrial* (1982) and *The Martian* (2015) (Mayer 2016). Plants and gardening have been proposed as crucial elements not only for long-term life support systems but also as a psychological element in the architecture of space stations and long-term missions (Häuplik-Meusburger, Peldszus, and Holzgethan 2011), an approach that was also actively argued for by the Biosphere 2 group as an alternative to NASA's "reductionist" approach in closed ecological life-support systems.[12] The history of the whole-Earth image represents an entire complex of transforming environmental consciousness and cybernetic ideas (Turner 2006), what Peder Anker has called the "ecological colonization of space" (Anker 2010).

The contemporary ecological issues of our own planet are still often negotiated separately to the environment beyond Earth's atmosphere. In regard to the current geological epoch of the Anthropocene, Lisa Messeri and Valerie Olsen have examined this separation of inner and outer environment (Olson and Messeri 2015). They point to the role of satellite sensing in environmental sciences as well as to exoplanetary sciences as the origin of ecological concepts such as the Gaia hypothesis. Consequently, they propose to "un-Earth the Anthropocene ... to question terracentric boundaries presently attached to the concept, to perceive the environment as polymorphous, and to bring together productive examinations of human relations with both inner *and* outer environments" (Olson and Messeri 2015: 42, emphasis in original).

If we consider ecological meshworks to include the outer environment of space, their distribution across vast ranges of time and space in a way becomes more obvious than on Earth. Timothy Morton's notion of a "hyperobject" becomes more tangible when it is presented as a distant black hole than through the description of the future of a nuclear waste repository under a German village (Morton 2013; Gorman 2019; Oman-Reagan 2016). This is not a question of distance in space or time but one of narratives and popular imaginaries. Biosphere 2 was explicitly built as a research *and* educational facility, to study and communicate the hyperobject of Earth's biosphere. The experiment itself is not a hyperobject, but it proliferates storytelling which potentially offers an understanding of what is outside the limits of human perception. Its ecological cycles followed an accelerated rhythm, akin to the filmic apparatus of the time-lapse, as an extension of human perception in order to see environmental processes such as plant growth. Biosphere 2 was designed as a "time microscope" (Alling et al. 2005: 251; Alling, Nelson, and Silverstone 2020: 79). Within the setup, accelerated ecological and biophysical cycles of the atmosphere, water, and inhabitants could be followed in temporal close-up. This extension of perception also included the very personal and emotional involvement of the crew, which was confronted with the impact of their own actions and behaviour on a daily basis through water recycling, air quality, and food production.

I would argue Biosphere's design as time microscope or "cyclotron for ecology" (Alling, Nelson, and Silverstone 2020: 22, 178–79) was not limited to accelerated biophysical cycles. Its situatedness in the early 1990s and its public and media reception are a unique crystallisation of crucial transformations of that time—from a growing awareness of planetary environmental problems and the global political changes after the disintegration of the Soviet Union to the rising role of real-time telecommunication and the World Wide Web. The reference to and exchange with Soviet scientists was only possible within the larger geopolitical changes during the end of the Cold War. The performance of Biosphere 2 was a reenactment of space-age promises and countercultural upheaval, and a preenactment of planetary and global issues that have only become palpable more recently, from ecological issues to private spaceflight. Its performance was that of a temporal joint between past and future.

Un·Earthing involves a fundamental change in the perception of spatial surroundings as well as of time. Astronauts on board the International Space Station experience sunrise every ninety minutes; the lunar surface offers 13.5 days of daytime. In *Red Mars*, Kim Stanley Robinson contrives the "Martian Time Slip", a daily quasi-heterotopian timeslot that the settlers come up with as an answer to the extra thirty-nine minutes and forty seconds of the Martian day (Robinson 1993). Obviously, Biosphere 2 was subject to the same solar cycle and circadian rhythms as Earth, yet to deal with immense workloads, food scarcity, decreasing oxygen levels, and group dynamics, the Biospherians staged regular festivities of feasting, theatrical performances, and partying. These were heterotopian time-outs within tight schedules of scientific, technical, and organisational

Figure 30.3 Biosphere 2 at night. Still from *Extra-Terrestrial Ecologies*. Photo: Ralo Mayer/Bildrecht, 2018.

procedures in the experiment.[13] The plots of un·Earthing are fragmentary manifestations of hyper-objects that emerge through the changes and challenges that come along with everyday human life beyond the Earth (Figure 30.3).

A Scent of the Future

The experiment of Biosphere 2 presents a wide range of features and stories that run parallel to processes of un·Earthing. These include an entangled relationship between Earth and space and the distinct roles of ecology and performance of humans in exchange with nonhuman species and inanimate actors. Un·Earthing can also be understood through its frequent contiguity of forms of extractivism, deterritorialisation, and mining. Biosphere 2 not only featured temporal shifts within its miniature closed ecological cycles that had a direct physical and psychological impact on the human crew but also oscillated between narratives of the past and tracing stories of future developments that had not yet become fully apparent. The performance of Biosphere 2 is what Jon McKenzie calls *perfumance*, a scent of the future.[14] Biosphere 2s situatedness can best be approached through the multivalent notion of plot, a term whose various meanings between fictional narratives, mathematical graphs, organisational intention, and economic application could also be employed in transdisciplinary discussions of human futures in outer space. Like Biosphere 2, the space of un·Earthing is not a specific site, but rather a set of plots.

While all of these traits of un·Earthing can be found in Biosphere 2, two major elements were necessarily missing, elements that have likewise been all too often ignored in science fiction. The first, gravity, is perhaps the most influential background for humans and any other life on Earth, and even slight variations in its force will most possibly yield yet unforeseeable implications in the human condition off-Earth. In the late 1920s, an engineer in Vienna changed his name from

Herman Potočnik to Hermann Noordung and designed a revolving space station. Although the meaning of Potočnik's pen name is unknown, I would argue the German-sounding name reflects his thoughts about the significance of changed gravity scenarios. He describes microgravity as a lack of *Ordnung* (order):

> The force of the Earth's gravity pulling all masses down to the ground and thus ordering them according to a certain regularity is no longer active. ... These unusual conditions must ... lead to the result that all bodies show a completely altered behavior and that, in accordance with this behavior, our unique actions and inactions will develop in a manner entirely different from previous ones.
>
> *(Potočnik et al. 1995: 80–81)*

The second missing element are babies and children. While more or less disguised questions about sex were asked almost every time a crew member was being interviewed about life in an artificial Garden of Eden, one of the more outlandish and ephemeral stories was about actual human reproduction, as several project participants told me. The rumour was that a crew member had become pregnant and given birth inside, which mission control kept secret in order to continue the experiment (Nelson 2018; Alling, Nelson, and Silverstone 2020). Once more, the figure of the Ninth Biospherian is a paraphrase of such a creation, as much as Mary Shelley reflected on reproduction and childbirth in Frankenstein. Yet, the fabricated baby story points to a step which I would argue to be perhaps the most radical transformation of un·Earthing. The first child born and raised in space would change unfathomable layers of the human condition, altering foundations of physiological, psychological, and cultural aspects of childhood.[15]

Serendipity often springs from the entanglement of personal and social circumstances; it thrives in situatedness; and I consider it a wonderful potentiality and privilege of artistic research to openly embrace the role of (inter)subjectivity. Countless times over—for what has now been, at the time of writing, two years of the COVID-19 pandemic—I've spent time at home in lockdowns or quarantines with our now two-year-old toddler. While thinking about un·Earthing the baby question accompanied me all the time. I heard a babbling infant over the baby monitor and imagined listening to an accidental transmission from a baby on a space station. I tried to imagine dressing a toddler for a walk in the Martian hills, which can only be all the more difficult than getting them ready for a winter stroll through the Viennese Prater Park. The big leap in un·Earthing won't be a SpaceX suburb on Mars, nor a Weyland-Yutani asteroid-mining prison facility.[16] The small step that changes everything will be changing diapers in microgravity.[17] This is the perfumance of un·Earthing.

Notes

1. Author's archival view of the video recording and interview with Biospherian trainer and advisor Kathelin Gray, 2009.
2. The "dome-like" appearance also reflected the founding group's 1960s/1970s background, resonating with other vernacular architecture of the counterculture and self-building's links to self-education (Linortner 2021).
3. The most infamous and influential media bashing was probably the *Village Voice*'s "Take This Terrarium and Shove It" in April 1991(Cooper 1991). For an overview of media reports of the time, see also Ivison, Tcharfas, and Sadler (2018) and Brooks, Juanals, and Minel (2022).
4. In typography, the interpunct · is also called the space dot.
5. Hannah Arendt made an at once compelling and impartial argument that a *Conquest of Space* would only be possible by humans leaving the planet themselves, not through instruments on robotic missions. At the same time, this becoming "an observer poised in free space" would destroy the stature of humans (Arendt 2006).

6. In 2017, Biosphere 2 was popping up in the context of Donald Trump's presidential campaign, when his advisor Steve Bannon was discovered to have been in charge of Biosphere 2 after 1994 (Mayer 2017). The global COVID-19 pandemic in March 2020 prohibited a wide cinematic release of the documentary *Spaceship Earth*, whose streamed premiere was consequently marketed relating to notions of quarantine, lockdowns, and isolation.
7. Tellingly, the common blurring of creator and monster can also be found in Biosphere 2.
8. A similar tour of the Synergia Ranch is described in Reider (2009: 13).
9. "We expected Biosphere 2 to be a quiet research facility. Southern Arizona can top 100 degrees Fahrenheit for months on end in summer, so the choice of Oracle, Arizona, for the site was a poor one if the aim was to attract visitors" (Nelson 2018).
10. See also Alice Gorman's discussion of the uncanny on the International Space Station (Gorman 2020).
11. The video call, as a frequent setting and trope in space movies, tells a story of distance and isolation, narratives of un·Earthing that suddenly became commonplace during the COVID-19 pandemic (Mayer 2021).
12. With some amusement one day, several of us [Biospherians] watched a TV news story about some NASA-sponsored research …. They were attempting to engineer three species of plants … in order to supply astronauts with a minimum, nutritionally complete, diet. This may look good in theory, if you ignore trace elements and some enzymes, but some basic points seem to have been missed. One is that with only three crops, a failure of any one of them means disaster. Another provides more important lessons we can offer to those involved with space exploration, though we are perhaps not the first to learn it: variety and diversity in cuisine is essential to human well-being. If you consider living off the planet for a long time—not just a few days or weeks in a space capsule where the effort is focused simply on achieving a short-term goal—then you must design a life style that can support you not just physiologically but psychologically as well

    (Alling, Nelson, and Silverstone 2020: 83)

13. See also Sabine Höhler's description of closed spaces as heterotopias (Höhler 2010: 44).
14. A perfumance is a displaced, disjointed performance, a minor performance that breaks with the sociotechnical system producing it and enters into recursive communication from other systems, thereby displacing their discourses and practices as well as their systemic limits. …Not only are its forces and intensities too diverse, too dispersed, too disseminated, but perfumance is anachronistic, untimely; if anything, *it belongs to the future*. More accurately: perfumance emits emissions of the future

    (McKenzie 2001: 228, 232, emphasis in original)

15. In relation to an approach of "*queer* modalities of reproduction and living *with* other worlds" (p. 22), Michael Oman-Reagan discusses the case of David Phillip Vetter, who was born with severe combined immunodeficiency and needed to be isolated in an isolation chamber provided by NASA (Oman-Reagan 2019).
16. Weyland-Yutani is an interplanetary megacorporation in Ridley Scott's fictional *Alien* universe (Scott 1979).
17. See also Walker and Granjou's discussion of human waste in closed systems in space: "Governing the messy complexity and discomfort of proximity to 'shit' (which connects waste-making indelibly to consumption and self-care) is critical for colonisation to continue into the vastness of deep space" (Walker and Granjou 2017: 63).

References

Adorno, Theodor W. 1991. "The Essay as Form." In *Notes to Literature*, Vol. 1, 3–23. New York: Columbia University Press.

Allen, John P. 1990. "Historical Overview of the Biosphere 2 Project." In *Biological Life Support Technologies: Commercial Opportunities*, edited by Mark Nelson and Gerard Soffen, 12–22. Washington, DC: NASA.

Allen, John P., and Anthony G. E. Blake. 1991. *Biosphere 2: The Human Experiment*. New York: Viking.

Allen, John P., and Mark Nelson. 1999. "Overview and Design Biospherics and Biosphere 2, Mission One (1991–1993)." *Ecological Engineering* 13 (1–4): 15–29. https://doi.org/10.1016/S0925-8574(98)00089-5.

Alling, Abigail, Mark Nelson, and Sally Silverstone. 2020. *Life under Glass: Crucial Lessons in Planetary Stewardship from Two Years in Biosphere 2*. 2nd edition. Santa Fe, NM: Synergetic Press.

Alling, Abigail, Mark Van Thillo, William Dempster, Mark Nelson, Sally Silverstone, and John Allen. 2005. "Lessons Learned from Biosphere 2 and Laboratory Biosphere Closed Systems Experiments for the Mars On Earth Project." *Biological Sciences in Space* 19 (4): 250–60. https://doi.org/10.2187/bss.19.250.

Anker, Peder. 2010. *From Bauhaus to Ecohouse: A History of Ecological Design*. Baton Rouge: Louisiana State University Press.
Arendt, Hannah. 2006. "The Conquest of Space and the Stature of Man." In *Between Past and Future: Eight Exercises in Political Thought*, 260–74. Penguin Classics. New York: Penguin Books.
Boyle, T. Coraghessan. 2016. *The Terranauts*. London: Bloomsbury.
Brautigan, Richard. 1989. "All Watched Over by Machines of Loving Grace." In *Trout Fishing in America; The Pill Versus the Springhill Mine Disaster; and, in Watermelon Sugar*. Boston, MA: Houghton Mifflin/Seymour Lawrence. http://www.brautigan.net/machines.html#28.
Brooks, Catherine Francis, Brigitte Juanals, and Jean-Luc Minel. 2022. "Trends in Media Coverage and Information Diffusion Over Time: The Case of the American Earth Systems Research Centre Biosphere 2." *Journal of Creative Communications* 17 (1): 88–107. https://doi.org/10.1177/09732586211056109.
Clynes, Manfred E., and Nathan S. Kline. 1960. "Cyborgs and Space." *Astronautics*, September 1960: 26–27 and 74–76.
Cooper, Marc. 1991. "Take This Terrarium and Shove It." *Village Voice*, April 2, 1991.
Danius, Sara, Stefan Jonsson, and Gayatri Chakravorty Spivak. 1993. "An Interview with Gayatri Chakravorty Spivak." *Boundary 2* 20 (2): 24–50. https://doi.org/10.2307/303357.
Detwiler, Katheryn M. 2021. "Logistical Natures in Andean Worlds." In *Logistical Worlds: Infrastructure, Software, Labour: No. 3, Valparaíso*, edited by Brett Neilson and Ned Rossiter, 79–90. London: Low Latencies, an imprint of Fibreculture Books, Open Humanities Press.
Fisher, Mark. 2013. *Ghosts of My Life: Writings on Depression, Hauntology and Lost Futures*. Winchester: Zero Books.
Gitelson, I. I., and G. M. Lisovsky. 2008. "Creation of Closed Ecological Life Support Systems: Results, Critical Problems and Potentials." *Journal of Siberian Federal University (Biology)* 1 (1): 19–39. https://elib.sfu-kras.ru/handle/2311/630.
Gorman, Alice. 2019. *Dr. Space Junk vs. the Universe: Archaeology and the Future*. Cambridge: The MIT Press.
Gorman, Alice. 2020. "The Geometry and the Uncanny in the Interior of the International Space Station." In *Interior Space: A Visual Exploration of the International Space Station*, edited by Roland Miller and Paolo Nespoli, 53–57. Italy: Damiani Editore.
Gray, Kathelin, dir. 1991. *The Wrong Stuff (Archival Recording of Theatrical Performance)*. Arizona: Oracle.
Haraway, Donna. 2013. "SF: Science Fiction, Speculative Fabulation, String Figures, So Far." *Ada: A Journal of Gender, New Media and Technology* 3. https://doi.org/10.7264/N3KH0K81.
Haraway, Donna. 2016. *Staying with the Trouble: Making Kin in the Chthulucene*. Experimental Futures: Technological Lives, Scientific Arts, Anthropological Voices. Durham, NC: Duke University Press.
Häuplik-Meusburger, Sandra, Regina Peldszus, and Verena Holzgethan. 2011. "Greenhouse Design Integration Benefits for Extended Spaceflight." *Acta Astronautica* 68 (1–2): 85–90. https://doi.org/10.1016/j.actaastro.2010.07.008.
Höhler, Sabine. 2010. "The Environment as a Life Support System: The Case of Biosphere 2." *History and Technology* 26 (1): 39–58. https://doi.org/10.1080/07341510903313048.
Inner City AAA. 1997. "We Have a World to Leave Behind!" Association of Autonomous Astronauts. http://aaa.t0.or.at/documents/3aaa04.htm.
Ivison, Tim, Julia Tcharfas, and Simon Sadler. 2018. "Biosphere 2s Experimental Life." In *Laboratory Lifestyles: The Construction of Scientific Fictions*, edited by Sandra Kaji-O'Grady, 169–94. Leonardo. Cambridge: The MIT Press.
Keogh, Luke. 2022. *The Wardian Case: How a Simple Box Moved Plants and Changed the World*. Chicago: University of Chicago Press.
Koolhaas, Rem, Hans Ulrich Obrist, Kayoko Ota, and James Westcott. 2011. *Project Japan: Metabolism Talks…*. Köln; London: TASCHEN GmbH.
Kwon, Miwon. 1997. "One Place after Another: Notes on Site Specificity." *October* 80: 85–110. https://doi.org/10.2307/778809.
Le Guin, Ursula K. 1996. "The Carrier Bag Theory of Fiction." In *The Ecocriticism Reader: Landmarks in Literary Ecology*, edited by Cheryll Glotfelty and Harold Fromm, 149–54. Athens: University of Georgia Press.
Lewis, John Simpson. 1997. *Mining the Sky: Untold Riches from the Asteroids, Comets, and Planets*. Reading, MA: Helix Books.
Lillemose, Jacob. 2021. *Architecture Zero*. København: A Mock Book.
Linortner, Christina. 2021. "Learning to Live Against the Norm: Strategies of Self-Building in US Back-to-the-Land Communes|Lernen, Gegen Die Norm Zu Leben. Strategien Des Selbstbaus in U.S.-Landkommunen." In *GAM 16: Gewohnt: Un/Common*, edited by Daniel Gethmann, Petra Eckhard, Urs Hirschberg, Andreas Lechner, and Petra Petersson, 152–73. Vienna: De Gruyter. https://doi.org/10.1515/9783868599480-010.

Marino, Bruno D. V., and Howard T. Odum, eds. 1999. *Biosphere 2: Research Past and Present*. Amsterdam: Elsevier Science.

Maugh, Thomas H., II. 1991. "2 Years Inside a Living Lab—Is It Science or a Stunt?" *Los Angeles Times*, 23 September 1991. https://www.latimes.com/archives/la-xpm-1991-09-23-mn-2048-story.html.

Mayer, Ralo, dir. 2012. *Warum sehen wir das Bild der Erde so oft (dass wir es gar nicht mehr sehen)?* Austria: Digital video 1080p.

Mayer, Ralo. 2016. "Beyond the Blue Marble: Artistic Research on Space and Ecology." *Acta Astronautica* 128: 573–79. https://doi.org/10.1016/j.actaastro.2016.08.015.

Mayer, Ralo. 2017. "How Steve Bannon Wrecked a World Well Before He Went for This One." *Multiplex Fiction* (blog). 4 March 2017. http://was-ist-multiplex.info/2017/03/how-steve-bannon-wrecked-a-world-well-before-he-went-for-this-one/.

Mayer, Ralo, dir. 2018. *Extra-Terrestrial Ecologies (Retroflectors: The Astronaut, the Robot, the Alien)*. Austria: Sixpackfilm.

Mayer, Ralo. 2021. "An Index of Un·Earthing: Log Entries towards the Decolonization of Outer Space." Online presentation given at the 12th SAR Conference on Artistic Research. https://www.researchcatalogue.net/view/1564288/1564271.

Mayer, Ralo, András Pálffy, Annette Südbeck, Eva M. Stadler, and Vereinigung Bildender KünstlerInnen Wiener Secession, eds. 2008. *Multiplex Fiction/Ralo Mayer: Das Muster der Schatten des Spaceframe der Biosphere 2, ...; September 19 to November 9, 2008*. Secession. Exhibition catalogue. First edition. Vienna: Wiener Secession.

McKenzie, Jon. 2001. *Perform or Else: From Discipline to Performance*. London; New York: Routledge.

Merton, Robert King, and Elinor Barber. 2006. *The Travels and Adventures of Serendipity: A Study in Sociological Semantics and the Sociology of Science*. Princeton, NJ: Princeton University Press.

Morton, Timothy. 2013. *Hyperobjects: Philosophy and Ecology after the End of the World*. Posthumanities 27. Minneapolis: University of Minnesota Press.

Nelson, Mark. 2018. *Pushing Our Limits: Insights from Biosphere 2*. Tucson: The University of Arizona Press.

Olma, Seb. 2016. *In Defence of Serendipity*. London: Repeater Books.

Olson, Valerie, and Lisa Messeri. 2015. "Beyond the Anthropocene: Un-Earthing an Epoch." *Environment and Society* 6 (1). https://doi.org/10.3167/ares.2015.060103.

Oman-Reagan, Michael P. 2016. "Unfolding the Space Between Stars: Anthropology of the Interstellar." Preprint, last edit 2 July 2018. SocArXiv. https://doi.org/10.31235/osf.io/r4ghb.

Oman-Reagan, Michael P. 2019. "Politics of Planetary Reproduction and the Children of Other Worlds." *Futures* 110 (June): 19–23. https://doi.org/10.1016/j.futures.2019.02.015.

Pearson, Mike, and Michael Shanks. 2001. *Theatre/Archaeology*. London; New York: Routledge.

Poole, Robert. 2008. *Earthrise: How Man First Saw the Earth*. New Haven, CT: Yale University Press.

Potočnik, Herman, Ernst Stuhlinger, John D. Hunley, Jennifer Garland, and Frederick Ira Ordway. 1995. *The Problem of Space Travel: The Rocket Motor*. Washington, DC: National Aeronautics and Space Administration, NASA History Office.

Poynter, Jane. 2006. *The Human Experiment: Two Years and Twenty Minutes inside Biosphere 2*. New York: Thunder's Mouth Press.

Reider, Rebecca. 2009. *Dreaming the Biosphere: The Theater of All Possibilities*. Albuquerque: University of New Mexico Press.

Rheinberger, Hans-Jörg. 1997. *Toward a History of Epistemic Things: Synthesizing Proteins in the Test Tube*. Writing Science. Stanford, CA: Stanford University Press.

Rheinberger, Hans-Jörg. 2008. "Epistemic Objects/Technical Objects." In Research Colloquium "Epistemic Objects." Technical University Berlin: Max Planck Institute for the History of Science, Berlin.

Rivers, Ben, dir. 2016. *URTH*. USA. Super 16mm film.

Robinson, Kim Stanley. 1993. *Red Mars*. New York: Bantam Books.

Salazar, Juan Francisco. 2020. "Speculative Fabulation: Researching Worlds to Come in Antarctica." In *Anthropologies and Futures*, edited by Juan Francisco Salazar, Sarah Pink, Andrew Irving, and Johannes Sjöberg, 151–70. London; New York: Bloomsbury Academic. https://doi.org/10.4324/9781003084570-10.

Scott, Ridley, dir. 1979. *Alien*. Los Angeles: 20th Century Fox.

Shikata, Yutaka, ed. 2019. *Reprint Edition: Expo '70 = Sairoku EXPO '70*. The Japan Architect, 113 (Spring 2019). Tokyo: Shinkenchiku-Sha.

Singleton, Benedict. 2015. "The Long Con." In *When Site Lost the Plot*, edited by Robin Mackay, 105–20. Redactions 005. Falmouth: Urbanomic Media Ltd.

Stengers, Isabelle. 2010. *Cosmopolitics*. Posthumanities 9–10. Minneapolis: University of Minnesota Press.

Steyerl, Hito. 2017. "The Essay as Conformism? Some Notes on Global Image Economies." In *Essays on the Essay Film*, edited by Nora M. Alter and Timothy Corrigan, 276–85. Film and Culture. New York: Columbia University Press. https://doi.org/10.7312/alte17266-020.

Tlostanova, Madina V., and Walter D. Mignolo. 2012. *Learning to Unlearn: Decolonial Reflections from Eurasia and the Americas*. Transoceanic Studies. Columbus, OH: Ohio State University Press.

Trumbull, Douglas, dir. 1972. *Silent Running*. Universal City, California: Universal Pictures.

Turner, Fred. 2006. *From Counterculture to Cyberculture: Stewart Brand, the Whole Earth Network, and the Rise of Digital Utopianism*. Chicago, IL: University of Chicago Press.

Van Dooren, Thom, and Deborah Bird Rose. 2012. "Storied-Places in a Multispecies City." *Humanimalia* 3 (2): 1–27. https://doi.org/10.52537/humanimalia.10046.

Walford, Roy L. 2002. "Biosphere 2 as Voyage of Discovery: The Serendipity from Inside." *BioScience* 52 (3): 259–63. https://doi.org/10.1641/0006-3568(2002)052[0259:BAVODT]2.0.CO;2.

Walker, Jeremy, and Céline Granjou. 2017. "MELiSSA the Minimal Biosphere: Human Life, Waste and Refuge in Deep Space." *Futures* 92 (September): 59–69. https://doi.org/10.1016/j.futures.2016.12.001.

Wolf, Matt, dir. 2020. *Spaceship Earth*. New York City: Neon.

31
LIVING AND WORKING IN "THE GREAT OUTDOORS"

Astronautics as Everyday Work in NASA's Skylab Programme

Phillip Brooker and Wes Sharrock

Introduction

Often overlooked in spaceflight history, Skylab was the USA's first space station, launching in May 1973 and occupied by three three -person crews until February 1974. Skylab was a product of the Apollo Applications Program (AAP), a NASA initiative for repurposing existing hardware into innovative but cost-effective new vehicles and systems in a context of shrinking government funding (Hitt, Garriott, and Kerwin 2008). Thus, Skylab's design incorporated machinery from earlier programmes into a space station, within which the possibilities of long-duration spaceflight and the human potential for living and working in space could be explored (Brooker forthcoming). This included a vehicle system for return travel to low Earth orbit and an orbital workshop—an emptied third-stage Saturn IV rocket booster compartment approximately the volume of a three-bedroom house, furnished with scientific laboratory equipment and living amenities for missions that would ultimately stretch up to eighty-four days.

During missions, Skylab crews would undertake application-oriented science that could not be achieved on Earth, with a research programme comprising over three hundred experiments across four themes: astronomy, Earth observations, zero-gravity technology, and "the reaction of man[1] to space" (Belew and Stuhlinger 1973: 114). The latter refers specifically to biomedical research incorporating monitoring and supporting astronaut health and wellbeing aloft, but also investigating the habitability of the station itself in terms of the fit between the station, its human occupants, and the strange environment of low Earth orbit (i.e., zero gravity). It is within this research strand that NASA hoped to learn about the social life of a space station, via scientific studies such as their M151 time and motion study (Kubis and McLaughlin 1975; Kubis et al. 1977). M151 used crew-captured video data to measure and compare task performance on Earth (the "control" setting) and in orbit, applying Taylorist methods of 'scientific management' to empiricise the work of doing astronautics (Brooker, Castaño, and Le Moignan 2021; Brooker forthcoming).

This belies NASA's overarching aim of exploring, understanding, and providing strong—empirically rigorous and scientifically replicable (Newell 1980)—arguments for opening up space as a social environment in which greater numbers of humans might ultimately live and work long term. Skylab's role in pioneering living and working in space was to form the basis for an emerging space infrastructure that would develop orbital shuttle systems during the 1980s and the construction and occupation of permanent and much larger factories and bases in space and on the Moon and/or Mars from there (Froehlich 1971; see Heppenheimer 1977; O'Neill 1976, 1981).[2] Arguments as to whether such ambitions should be pursued at all notwithstanding (Deudney 2020; Scharmen 2021), that these grand visions have not materialised is perhaps in part due to how NASA and Skylab designated human life and work in rigidly scientific and empiricist ways. This chapter follows Brooker, Castaño, and Le Moignan's (2021) recommendation of repurposing the data produced by Skylab to explore what we might learn about the practical work of doing astronautics if we begin with a different focus and use different tools and methods to explore it.

This chapter, then, demonstrates the use of ethnomethodology as an approach to studying data of audio recordings of a spacewalk undertaken by the Skylab 4 crew on 29 December 1973. The description of these data points primarily to how the interactional, physical, and technological features of the setting combine in 'getting the work done'. The overarching argument speaks to the role that qualitative research might play in describing and understanding how life and work is possible in space; while qualitative approaches are typically overlooked in spaceflight research as 'non-scientific', they can nonetheless provide a parallel mode of enquiry that engages with and reflects the lived work of doing astronautics in different but useful ways. Ethnomethodology, with its track record in detailed descriptions of technical practice, is ideally placed to provide this, and the aim of this chapter is to demonstrate as much through presenting an ethnomethodological study of astronautics activities and discussing the affordances the approach offers.

Applying Ethnomethodology to NASA Audio and Conversation Transcripts

This research is informed by ethnomethodological studies of work (Garfinkel 1986). Ethnomethodology concerns itself with the local everyday methods by which members—those involved in any given setting—order and organise their work in accountable ways (i.e., in ways which both 'do' and 'display the doing of' the production of social order) (Garfinkel 1984). As Button (2012) stresses, ethnomethodological studies of work is more than the application of ethnographic methods to workplace settings; rather, the term 'work' more broadly refers to all forms of 'doing' and practical activity. This is especially apposite for Skylab's joint research focus on living *and* working, providing a tonic to NASA's own research in the area which characteristically (and continuously since Skylab) construes life and work in purely quantifiable metrics amenable to the scientific method (see DeChurch et al. 2019; Kubis and McLaughlin 1975; Kubis et al. 1977; Mesmer-Magnus et al. 2021). Hence, a major question to be addressed through the ensuing demonstration and discussion will be: just what activities comprise 'living and working in space'? It is increasingly commonplace that qualitative (ethnographic and sometimes also ethnomethodologically influenced) approaches are applied to the social study of spaceflight and space science missions (see Messeri 2016; Mirmalek 2020; Vertesi 2015, 2020). Whilst situating the present study amongst these may seem natural at this point, it is in keeping with the spirit of Garfinkel's (1984) insistence that ethnomethodology must be demonstrated and practised rather than elaborated in abstract that we refrain from saying more here. Instead, the chapter will *begin* with a descriptive demonstration, to be analysed-along-with by readers working with this text as well as the original audio and transcriptions that produce the analysis here, only later returning to discuss features relevant to applying these tools elsewhere. This ethnomethodological strategy of *showing* rather than *telling* is designed to foreground an understanding of just what ethnomethodology might bring to the study of spaceflight and astronautics, as an intended *outcome* of the research rather than a matter to be established *a priori* of it.

The context of an event (wrongly) alleged to have taken place during the Skylab 4 mission also proves ethnomethodological inquiry of this kind apposite—the astronaut crew were said, by sensationalising journalists and others (e.g., Balbaky and McCaskey 1981; Cooper 1976), to have engaged in a 'strike in space', whereby they downed tools and forced a day-long radio silence with their ground support team in response to their unrealistic workload demands. That this was a 'strike' is disputed by various NASA personnel and space historians (see Burns and Gibson 2021; Hitt, Garriott, and Kerwin 2008). It is, however, acknowledged in mission conversation transcripts (Brooker forthcoming) and post hoc accounts of relevant NASA personnel (Carr 2000; Gibson 2000; Pogue 2000) that the ground teams scheduling the astronauts' scientific labours were doing so on the basis of metrics that proved unreasonable for a crew learning to adapt to their peculiar environment on what was at the time the longest-duration mission ever (eighty four days). This issue came to a head on 28 December 1973 when Commander Gerald Carr recorded and sent a tape to the ground team voicing the crew's concerns regarding their unsustainable workload. The ground team resolved these concerns in a mutually agreeable way by paying greater care to how various tasks were scheduled and giving the astronauts (slightly) more autonomy over the scheduling of their scientific experimentation work alongside the regular 'housework' of the station (repairing and maintaining equipment, unstowing and stowing equipment, etc.).

Given this dispute and the availability of documents capturing insights on the everyday work of astronautics as the Skylab 4 crew undertook it, questions arise as to just what work these astronauts were tasked with, and how did they make it happen? The events of 28 December 1973 cast the issues in sharp relief, demonstrating that NASA's typical scientific/scientist insistence on quantifications of human behaviour is sometimes counterproductive (here, it created and exacerbated Skylab 4's scheduling problems), in ways which encourage a different engagement with these and other mission 'data'. In other words, this 'breach' (Garfinkel 1984) in the order and organisation of the setting provides a moment of analytic interest, motivating a focal shift from a demonstrable failure in NASA's metric-oriented accounting of astronautics to something more attentive to the lived work involved therein.

The 'data' in question pertains to an EVA (extra-vehicular activity; a 'spacewalk' outside of Skylab) undertaken by Commander Gerald Carr and Science Pilot Ed Gibson on 29 December 1973, with Pilot William Pogue remaining inside Skylab to support the EVA team. EVAs are amongst the most physically demanding, complex, and hazardous tasks an astronaut carries out, requiring constant intense attention for long periods of time (the EVA described below lasted three hours twenty-nine minutes). Yet, for Skylab astronauts, EVAs were also a routine and highly prescribed (i.e., planned/trained-for/knowable-in-advance) aspect of their scientific work. Hence, describing EVA work provides much insight into how 'normal' routine operations are carried out in this extraordinary context.

The materials covered here are audio recordings and written conversation transcripts produced and made available by NASA as part of their science research and public relations (Holder et al. 2022). The radio-only communications setup between the astronaut crew and ground support teams is useful, since the work the astronauts do in collaboration with their colleagues (the ground team, their pilot) *must be made accountable verbally*. It is these aspects on which the ensuing analysis centres, since this brings the relevant features of the work being done to the fore of the audio and transcripts, for the astronauts and mission control but also for those analysing the audio and transcripts post hoc (i.e., us, and you).

The description elaborates one sixteen-minute excerpt of the audio recording of the full EVA operation, beginning approximately one hour into the EVA and chosen on the basis of its exemplification of recurring themes found throughout the entire recording. The audio reflects communications delivered, via the air-to-ground channel (Channel A), between two EVA astronauts (Commander Jerry Carr and Science Pilot Ed Gibson, designated CDR-EVA and SPT-EVA), Pilot William Pogue (PLT) aboard the ship, and Story Musgrave as Capsule Communicator (CapCom, or CC)—the astronauts' point of contact in the ground team. The excerpt reflects one 'communications pass'—a period where Skylab was in radio contact with the ground team, beginning with the ground's acquisition of Skylab's signal and ending as the signal is lost. There are four relevant conversation transcripts, two for each of Skylab's two communications channels—the Channel A air-to-ground channel, and Channel B as an internal communications loop and tape-recording facility for the astronauts to use. Whilst Channel B was, at least in principle, accessible by the astronaut crew at all times, a communicable signal on Channel A was dependent on the ship being in the aerial vicinity of one of thirteen communications relays located across Earth; a working signal could be attained for approximately twenty minutes out of every hour. Hence, the use of four transcripts is required, since the two channels (A and B) are used in different ways. This analysis uses the transcripts as supplementary to the audio recording, producing a description of the work that speaks to four themes: who can hear who (and why), the astronauts' bodily expositioning, the sequencing and pacing of tasks, and the notions of 'good enough' and 'normal troubles'. All relevant data is available at the following link, and readers should engage with the below description alongside the audio and transcripts themselves: https://github.com/phillipbrooker/TheGreatOutdoors. The timestamps given below are drawn from the air-to-ground transcript unless otherwise stated, and are in the following format: day of year; hour; minute; second (e.g., the opening timestamp of the excerpt is 363 18 03 03: a little after 6 pm on the 363rd day of the year).

Living and Working in "The Great Outdoors"[3]

The excerpt begins as the astronauts are already working on an EVA task—setting up a camera for photography-based experiments—and come into radio contact with the ground via the Honeysuckle and Carnarvon communications relay stations. Here, the astronauts are already talking with one another prior to the connection being announced by CC (SPT-EVA: "They got some beautiful thunderstorms down there. Okay." (363 18 03 03)). CC introduces its presence by stating the locations of its communications relays and noting the time remaining before the signal will be lost again ("14 minutes"). SPT acknowledges and affirms the communications connection with the ground by stating "Roger, Story".

Introductions complete, SPT-EVA turns back to the task at hand, requesting that Bill (PLT, inside Skylab) continue reading from the instructions that guide the camera setup task ("Okay, that's locked. Go ahead, Bill. Read on"). Neither the Channel A transcript nor audio features PLT's reply—both of these refer only to the air-to-ground channel, whereas PLT is talking via Channel B (the internal communications loop). In the Channel B transcripts, PLT provides the next instruction from his checklist: "EV-2, unstow T025 filter case and pass to EV-1"—this nominates CDR-EVA (taking the role of EV-2) to give SPT-EVA (EV-1) a piece of equipment relevant to the present task. The non-availability of PLT's talk to the audio and Channel A transcripts is significant for reasons to be elaborated throughout the analysis, but importantly here, the "silence" in the audio, and SPT-EVA's seemingly disconnected "That's affirmative", is not indicative of a 'missing instruction'/'unanswered question', but rather a feature of how the astronauts and ground teams manage their communications across the two Channels, A and B, at their disposal.

At 363 18 04 07, SPT-EVA blocks out time to undertake the next instruction by talking expositionally about his bodily orientation ("Okay, just stand by. Let me get back in my foot restraint here"). Throughout, the astronauts provide regular constant commentary on where they are, where they want to be, where they are going, what they can and can't see, etc. One feature of SPT-EVA's comment, therefore, is that it reflects the operational requirements of an EVA for participants to narrate what they are doing in terms unambiguous to non-EVA colleagues with only audio reportage to rely on, or EVA colleagues whose vision and mobility are hampered by their pressure suit equipment. A second feature of SPT-EVA's comment is that it paces the task at hand by indicating SPT-EVA's position in the sequence of instructions, effectively telling PLT to pause reading the instructions until the previous one is complete.

CDR-EVA's simultaneous commentary on *his* particular task ("Okay, there it is and safety tethered") is also significant, demonstrating that PLT carries a set of interlocking though discrete instructions, and that EVA work comprises tasks that SPT-EVA must do independently of but collaboratively with CDR-EVA, and vice versa. Hence, monitoring the pace of instructions is important to an EVA—PLT's role is not just transmitting instructions over radio, but cohering the activities of his two EVA crewmembers and helping make their position in the task and schedule accountable. In this sense, it is not only bodily expositioning that is crucial to the astronauts' work but also sequential expositioning—elaborating *what* has just been done and *when*.

At 363 18 05 07, SPT-EVA details his travails in tethering the T025 camera filter to the ship to prevent it from floating away as he frees his hands to do other work. CDR-EVA watches and suggests ways he can support this (e.g., by offering a second tether). SPT-EVA elaborates, noting the difficulties are in part due to the design of the one-point tethering system—without a second tethering point, there is an unavoidable risk of dropping the item as there will always be a period between the item being tethered to the pressure suit or to the ship. CDR-EVA suggests putting the item or the tether attachment point (this is ambiguous) in the other way, and SPT-EVA notes that he has never tried this before—despite the stringency of their on-the-ground training in completing instruction sets such as these, the practicalities of delivering those instructions in the lived context of a spacewalk make the proposal uncertain. This points to the notion of the 'normal troubles' of the EVA, with the astronauts commenting on the obstacles to following their instructions straightforwardly, and the workarounds they develop in situ to complete their tasks. This also demonstrates that rather than merely following instructions capably, doing astronautics requires expertise, skill, and knowledge in the objectives that the instructions are designed to achieve, to see how they might be met with some flexibility. The astronauts do not get stuck, but rather find ways to bend the instructions to meet the requirements of the task at hand. This reinforces (see Garfinkel 1984) that the instructions guiding the Skylab astronauts do not comprehensively detail the work that must be done to enact those instructions. Rather, they give precise specifications on what the intended outcome should be and idealised steps to get there, but do not preclude the exertion of autonomy and expertise—an important point especially for the Skylab 4 crew in light of the workload issues flagged the previous night.

From here (approx. 363 18 06 03), PLT summarises the task that SPT-EVA and CDR-EVA are about to undertake: installing the T025 camera filter, adjusting the camera to point in the right direction, then taking pictures with it. After this, they will undertake a similar task with the nearby S020 camera. As astronomy-oriented equipment, PLT suggests SPT-EVA (a scientist with expertise in astronomy) decide which camera to attend to first. SPT-EVA selects the S020 as it requires a longer exposure period, making it more time-efficient to set the S020 off first.

Following the decision to begin with the S020 task, at 363 18 07 39 CDR-EVA offers to support SPT-EVA by securing himself in the available restraints and holding SPT-EVA as he carries out the camera work. Restraints are important when working in zero gravity, as without being fixed to some other object (the spacecraft) any movements the astronauts make—pushing, pulling, twisting—would move the astronauts themselves with an equal and opposite reaction to their efforts. The request is accepted by SPT-EVA "because it looks as though I'm—even though I've grown a little, I'm still about a foot too short to make my head over there". This constitutes further bodily expositioning and task sequencing—SPT describes a bodily property (height) in terms of its situational relevance to the task at hand, whilst also announcing (to PLT, to CC and the ground team, and to CDR-EVA) that he is not yet in a position to begin the camera work. Of course, changeability of height is typically not a relevant feature for colleagues on Earth to discuss. In space, however, an astronaut's spine will decompress in the absence of a constant downward gravitational pull, and while this adds a few inches to their height, SPT-EVA comments he is still not tall enough to do the job without support. This has parallels with an episode reported in Garfinkel (1964) of two parents discussing how their child has become able to put a coin in a parking meter. The point here is that these matters are invariably indexical (i.e., referential points are contingent on the context in which these statements are situated); hence, you cannot understand the parents' story unless you know that their child has been trying to reach the parking meter for a while but has only just grown tall enough to do so, and you cannot understand SPT-EVA's statement unless you know that changeable height is a situationally relevant thing for an astronaut to report as they are manoeuvring to better handle awkwardly placed equipment.

The camera remaining out of SPT-EVA's reach presents a practical obstacle to task completion, and CDR-EVA adds to his earlier proposal: "Well, I could hold you like a sausage, a loaf of bread under my arm, you know, and you could just kind of go where you wanted" (363 18 07 39), which the two put to practice. As above, the capacity for one colleague to pick another up and hold them under their arm is not normally feasible on Earth, but in this context, it is possible and helpful. Again, there is a juxtaposition between what the astronauts are doing as a mundane collaborative task of finding ways to enact a set of instructions that don't completely specify how to respond to the situational context they encounter, and the peculiar set of environmental resources (e.g., weightlessness) in which their collaboration is embedded and which they can draw on.

As SPT-EVA approaches a workable bodily position, the team must wait for the instruction to be completed before moving on, providing an opportunity to discuss ancillary/non-operational matters; namely, the weather as can be seen on Earth below, the astronauts' pressure suit telemetry, and the potential visibility of Mercury as it appears to rise above Earth's horizon (363 18 08 31 to 363 18 10 16). Meanwhile, SPT-EVA is attempting to point the S020 camera in the correct direction as specified by the instructions, a task which causes him some trouble. SPT-EVA and CDR-EVA subsequently discuss SPT-EVA's troubles and strategies for working around them.

As elaborated at 363 18 11 25, the attendant problems for SPT-EVA are that the space within which he needs to place his head to adjust the S020[4] camera through its sighting device is tight; another camera (the T025) is also in that space and SPT-EVA risks disturbing it; and that it is difficult to practically deliver the required adjustments at the fine granularity required. SPT-EVA's reporting on these normal troubles does double duty—first, keeping CDR-EVA and PLT informed on his progress to pace further instructions, and second, flagging the troubles to the ground team as a 'human factors' matter. On this latter point, the Skylab astronauts were *expected* as a matter of scientific enquiry to produce data on the difficulties experienced with their equipment, such that ground teams could feed these insights into the design and development of future spacecraft (Hitt, Garriott, and Kerwin 2008). Also noteworthy is that SPT-EVA's efforts are less about precisely delivering the instructions given (which stipulate the use of the camera's sighting tool; SPT-EVA has already instead proposed to "sight it in coarsely" (363 18 10 16)) than they are about making sure the job is done 'good enough'. SPT-EVA settles for pointing the cameras *accurately enough* given the time available and the awkward spatial organisation of the environment in which to do it—in SPT-EVA's professional judgement this provides a workable solution that will not hamper the capacity of the S020 camera to capture its scientific data despite the process having diverged from the instruction checklist.

The next section of the audio and transcripts (approx. 363 18 12 42 to 363 18 13 59) capture an increasingly complex use of Channel A, where PLT raises an issue about the orientation of the ship with CC, whilst CDR-EVA and SPT-EVA continue their own collaborative efforts (which, as above, involves talking *about* those efforts) simultaneously. Throughout this period, SPT-EVA and CDR-EVA continue their bodily expositioning in regard to the task of adjusting the S020 camera, whilst PLT checks with CC as to whether mission control has noticed odd telemetry on the ship's orientation systems and whether a correctional process (an "H-cage") is required. This is relevant to both the maintenance of the ship generally (whose orbit must be monitored continually) and the undertaking of the scientific photography forming a focus of the EVA (inasmuch as the ship's orientation must be kept stable for the cameras to stay pointed at the right objects). While the overlapping audio results in a complex period of interaction for the listener/analyst, there is a civil inattention exerted by the two pairs of speakers—PLT/CC and CDR-EVA/SPT-EVA—enabled by the nominating of addressees that help them disentangle which utterances are salient to them specifically. For instance, PLT nominates CC as the listener for his query ("Story, are you looking at the outer gimbal angle on gimbal 3?" (approx. 363 18 12 42)), giving effective grounds for SPT-EVA and CDR-EVA to ignore that conversational thread and continue with their own.

A point to raise here is while this period (and its accompanying audio and transcription) reflects a complex use of an already complex multi-channel communications setup, there are commonplace interactional means of mitigating confusions and conflicts. Again, whilst the work the astronauts do is in some ways thoroughly extraordinary, the interactional tools at their disposal are recognisably ordinary—nominating conversational partners is not just something that people do in space or over radio (Sacks 1992). Another ancillary point pertains to the communications setup of Skylab more broadly—PLT's featuring in the audio recording and on the Channel A transcripts (whereas PLT's talk had previously been visible only in the Channel B internal loop transcripts) shows he has actively switched from Channel B to A. It is, then, PLT's judgement to exert as to which channel his communications are best delivered through. Here, the operational need to speak to the ground team provides a reason for PLT to switch channels, despite the conversational complexity this might entail (indeed, PLT's default position on Channel B feasibly constitutes a strategy for keeping Channel A clear).

Upon resolving his issue with CC, PLT switches back to Channel B as the EVA crew begins to take pictures with their newly calibrated cameras (approx. 363 18 15 38). At this point, PLT's talk is once more *visibly and audibly absent* from Channel A, in SPT-EVA's request and acknowledgment of a "mark" (an instruction to begin the exposure on the S020 photography task) that the transcript does not show is ever given, and in CDR-EVA's apparent conversation with no conversant ("Go ahead", "Yes", "Yes, on the next night pass right after sunset", etc.). Hence, not only is the communications setup complex, it is also *dynamic*—it can be used in different ways to achieve different objectives and meet different requirements. As such, the doing of astronautics requires some mastery of the various interactional media through which that work is to be achieved.

The final events of the communications pass are for CC to sign off on behalf of the ground team as Skylab travels out of radio contact and the astronaut crew continues their EVA work (approx. 363 18 17 23 to 363 18 18 44). This sign-off period encapsulates the different features of the interaction thus far, beginning with CC helping pace the astronauts' work by noting the imminent thirty-eight-minute loss of radio signal. PLT switches back to Channel A to respond to CC's update on the ship's orientation systems, whilst SPT-EVA and CDR-EVA continue expositioning of their bodily movements as part of the collaborative sequential organisation of their EVA tasks. The signal distorts and fades.

Discussion

There have been four major (interrelated) themes to the description/demonstration: the dynamic nature of the communications system and the work required to navigate it; the operational need for bodily expositioning by the EVA crew; how talk sequences and paces tasks; and reporting 'normal troubles' as scientific labour where 'good enough' is a working standard. These themes have been unpacked as they were encountered. Here, however, an opportunity is provided to look closely at the overarching notion of a spacewalk as being routine work in an extraordinary setting. In doing this, we also aim to discuss the potential (and requirements) for ethnomethodological study, in line with its self-characterisation as a parallel mode of enquiry to the 'formal analysis' of sociology and the social sciences (Garfinkel 2002), to contribute to furnishing social science's repertoire with additional tools for accounting for astronautics and human spaceflight.

As noted, Skylab's intentions to study 'living and working in space' were hampered at the outset owing to the rigidly scientistic way in which life and work were construed. Taking the M151 experiment ("Time and Motion Study") (Kubis and McLaughlin 1975; Kubis et al. 1977) as exemplary of NASA's habitability research, M151 tasked Skylab astronauts with various activities reflecting everyday living and working in orbit—donning and doffing spacesuits, handling large volumes of equipment, preparing food—and instructed them to time their efforts comparative to measurements made previously on Earth (the 'control' setting). The goal was to observe, systematically and scientifically, the difference in seconds, using time taken as a proxy for 'efficiency'. This rigidly quantitative approach, it is worth noting, persists even in latter-day research. It is found in DeChurch et al.'s (2019) and Mesmer-Magnus et al.'s (2021) work on scheduling and sequencing astronautics tasks—Skylab 4's bugbear issue as well as the object of the M151 experiment—which seek to quantify, mathematically formalise, and computationally model astronautics activities to identify optimal forms of organisation for future human spaceflight missions. This draws a direct and unbroken line between the scientistic (Taylorist) approaches of NASA's early astronautics research and the methods deployed today.

What we have seen above, however, indicates that there is far more to the lived work of doing astronautics that is unaccounted for, and unaccountable at all, in the scientific schema of M151 and Skylab's other habitability studies, and their scientific methods as latterly pursued by DeChurch et al. (2019) and Mesmer-Magnus et al. (2021). Furthermore, there is more than a Taylorist notion of 'efficiency' serving to organise the astronauts' efforts. The activities elaborated above are precisely what these scientistic approaches obscure or ignore altogether. Hence, repurposing existing 'data' produced by human spaceflight missions—conversation transcripts, audio, video, scientific/technical reports, astronaut diaries (Castaño n.d.), post-mission debriefs and interviews, etc.—and exploring them from different perspectives stands to yield much new insight on what the work of doing astronautics comprises (Brooker, Castaño, and Le Moignan 2021).

It is, of course, not an inevitability that humans will or should have a permanent presence outside of Earth—there are convincing arguments to the contrary (Deudney 2020; Scharmen 2021). However, rather than focus on the big, broad conceptualisations of what is at stake, important though that is, this chapter has aimed to advocate and begin a different navigation of the issues— one which zones in on the lived work of doing astronautics. This provides a sense of the interactional work required to make doing astronautics happen, something which is typically assumed a priori (both by space agencies including NASA and by social scientists) rather than investigated directly. Others working along these lines include Messeri (2016), Mirmalek (2020), and Vertesi (2015, 2020), who conduct ethnographic (and ethnomethodologically inflected) work in NASA's planetary science research activity and their Mars Exploration Rover missions (in regard to both the technical design and delivery of those missions, and the temporal synchronising of operations on Mars with Earth). Whilst these studies do not deal with astronautics specifically, they are relevant here in that what the astronauts above are engaged in is organised collaborative scientific work—each of our studies reflects the exigencies of this as the activities play out in their situational context.[5] While there are key differences between our research and that of Messeri (2016), Mirmalek (2020), and Vertesi (2015, 2020)—chiefly the possibilities of our undertaking participant observation in our setting are limited by chronology (Skylab 4 launching twelve years to the day before the birth of the principal author) and expertise (neither author being a trained astronaut)—we hope to have demonstrated value in bringing an ethnomethodological/ethnographic practice-oriented approach to the texts and data that *are* available. Furthermore, the demonstration of this value might, we hope, close the feedback loop on the qualitative research that NASA endorses and find ways to more programmatically build it into the planning and conduct of future spaceflight missions (where typically, this has been reserved for quantitative studies premised on the application of a scientific method (Brooker, Castaño, and Le Moignan 2021)). The intention here, then, is to help furnish social studies of space with close and detailed understandings of the practical lived work involved. Ethnomethodology, with its long history of studies of work in high-tech settings (see Garfinkel 1986), is ideally placed to do this.

To help demonstrate (such that we can now evaluate/situate) the contribution an ethnomethodological approach could make, the account above provides descriptions local to and locatable in astronautics practices as recorded in transcript and audio. Whilst characteristic of ethnomethodology, this tendency to resist theorising and generalisation (as a typical objective of explanatory sociology) is sometimes cast as reductionist and neglectful of broader social structures (e.g., Gordon 1976). As it is not within the scope of this chapter to fully explicate these long-standing debates, we defer to Hutchinson, Read, and Sharrock (2008), Winch (1990), and Woolgar (1981) as proxies for our position on this—sociology's status as an empirical discipline notwithstanding, the explanations it produces must necessarily rely on the production of stable descriptions to form the basis of a generalisable and theoretical analysis. The key move for ethnomethodology, which we apply above, is instead to treat the production of descriptions—accounts of the work of astronautics as given by astronauts *as an integral part of that work*—as a topic rather than a resource of investigation. In this sense, keeping the focus on the local rather than the general becomes a virtue that keeps our understandings of social life grounded *in* social life. This is something, we contend, that is glossed over too readily in social studies of space that seek to rigidly formalise human life and work by leveraging the scientific method to produce a 'God's eye view', and where a description of constituent practices is assumed rather than investigated/demonstrated (e.g., DeChurch et al. 2019; Kubis and McLaughlin 1975; Kubis et al. 1977; Mesmer-Magnus et al. 2021).[6]

What makes the ethnomethodological approach apt is, in some respects, ethnomethodology's indifference to the work under investigation. This is not to say that it doesn't matter that these activities take place on a space station orbiting the Earth every ninety-three minutes. Indeed, the description/demonstration above points directly at how the space environment inflects and intersects with the astronauts' work as its fundamental relevant context. Ethnomethodology acknowledges this fantastical context whilst simultaneously attuning to the ordinary ways in which these activities are *recognisable as* collaborative work. These two things (the extraordinary and the ordinary) are not exclusive of one another; as Elliot notes: "Science inevitably starts from the experiences of everyday life as the phenomena to be investigated. Where else could it start?" (1974: 23). Elaborating on this, one of the difficulties in understanding the activities of the Skylab 4 astronauts is that we may not recognise the esoteric terms they use—S020s, T025s, gimbal outer angles, nominal H-cages, etc. However, as Caton notes, "technical language is always an *adjunct* of ordinary language" (1963: viii, emphasis in original), and referential descriptions of technical work (as we have provided above) are often all that is required for us to see the sense in technical talk since the *form* of that talk is already legible to us as ordinary conversation:

> [P]hysicists and mathematicians, for example—people who necessarily employ large amounts of very technical language—do not find it necessary to devise new kinds of questions in order to cause their colleagues to explain what they are saying: new questions, to be sure, but not new *kinds* of questions... "Do you mean *rings* or *commutative* rings?" differs from "Do you mean *rings* or *engagement* rings?" only in that the things the person may have meant are different. The "Do you mean... or...?" is not different.
>
> *(Caton 1963: ix, emphasis in original)*

This, then, opens up the possibility for ethnomethodology to engage closely with all manner of technical activity, since there is lots we can already get our teeth into (e.g., that much of what astronauts and ground teams do is talk with one another and make their work accountable through that talk) and 'known unknowns' we can address to fill in the gaps (e.g., What is the S020 experiment? How does a gimbal work? Why is working in a pressurised suit difficult? etc.). Rather than portraying astronautics as 'only' ordinary work with technical attachments, the intention here is simply to note that the "the 'technical' cannot be divorced from the 'ordinary', and... their relationship invites not criticism, from either side, but... investigation" (Turner 1974: 9). Hence, rather than critiquing the Skylab 4 EVA team above for their 'failure' to precisely enact instructions pertaining to sighting a camera using the correct device and procedure, we point at how it is possible to complete this work successfully and effectively *even when* the completion of those instructions is prohibited by their assumption of a context different than that encountered. This, then, is an attempt at clarifying how the work of doing astronautics is possible, without relying (as much popular culture does) on the assumption that the work is only achievable by superhumans with the rarefied and fabled qualities of the "right stuff".

If we are to bring ethnomethodology to this domain, however, we acknowledge that a claim to explore the lived work of doing astronautics relies on the acquisition of requisite knowledge to identify and understand the technical language and work alluded to in relevant data. This is no insignificant matter. While these are knowledges that trained astronauts have as a matter of course, they are (and have to be) approached differently by ethnomethodologists sitting at their desks with only documentation to draw from. We do not claim that somehow by engaging with documents such as audio and transcripts we are de facto capable astronauts—there is a world of difference between reading and praxis. But as we have shown above, these documents can be used to satisfy a weak use of the "unique adequacy requirement of methods" (Garfinkel and Wieder 1992: 182), where the analyst is capable of identifying/recognising and describing the order and organisation of a setting in terms that are coherent with members' own accounts of the same. The adoption of members' methods of knowing the scene is vital:

> "[O]bserving" computer programmers designing software, or "recognizing" that a question delivers an insult to its interlocutor requires the investigator to be privy to the competent performances being "observed". Practices of "observation" (seeing, recognizing, making intelligible, reacting appropriately) already are on the scene. There is no avoiding them if one aims to render an account of the actions "observed".
>
> *(Lynch 2006: 511)*

As we have shown, this can be achieved through close attention to relevant documents as NASA (and other space agencies) are so completist in their approach to record-keeping (Holder et al. 2022). Interestingly, even in the highly specialised realm of space science, it is not impossible to fulfil the unique adequacy requirement strongly, as the work of Messeri (2016), Mirmalek (2020), and Vertesi (2015, 2020) exemplifies; each of these did not merely observe, but were competent practitioners actively participating in the scientific teamwork their studies investigate. Though we suggest that there would be interesting work resulting from the placement of a (strongly uniquely adequate) ethnomethodologist aboard a space station, in line with the spirit of the astronautics described above *this* chapter presents its weak fulfilment of the requirement proudly, as a 'good enough' tool for getting some useful work done despite the limitations. And, broadly, our hope is that this work suggests to those interested in the study of social life in space—space agencies and social scientists alike—that ethnomethodological analysis provides a useful and interesting supplementary alternative inroad.

Notes

1 A fuller treatment of the problematic gendering characteristic of NASA in their historical documentation is given in Brooker (forthcoming), paying particular regard to NASA's "standardisation" of the human for the purposes of scientific enquiry.

2 Emblematic of this was the creation of a new "science pilot" role in NASA's astronaut corps, enabling applications from civilians (rather than only military personnel) with no requirement for previous flight experience but with qualifications in science and engineering—ideal occupants of the space factories and bases of the future.
3 The phrase "The Great Outdoors", as used here, comes from Science Pilot Ed Gibson's first utterance upon exiting the airlock for this EVA: "There it is. The great outdoors again." This is an apt summary of the simultaneously extraordinary and mundane/routine nature of astronautics—profoundly impressive, but seen before.
4 The transcription in the air-to-ground transcript, which gives S022 as the camera in question, is erroneous—SPT-EVA is referring to the S020 camera, as corroborated by other transcripts and the original audio.
5 It is worth mentioning that Messeri (2016), Mirmalek (2020), and Vertesi (2015, 2020) conduct their ethnographic research as *participants* under NASA's employ. Hence, there is evidently some appetite on NASA's part for qualitative study elaborating just how scientific research happens, though our contention here and elsewhere (Brooker, Castaño, and Le Moignan 2021; Brooker, forthcoming) is that for astronautics and human spaceflight operations specifically, these more practice-oriented qualitative approaches have been overlooked in favour of exclusively quantitative formalisations of life and work in space.
6 As Woolgar (1981) details, ethnomethodological descriptions of practice could indeed be delivered in support of sociological explanations that seek to generalise and add theoretical focus, for instance on the political–military context of the post-Apollo period and/or the construction and flow of scientific knowledge in a quasi-governmental organisation, in which these astronautics activities are embedded. However, Woolgar's (1981) position (shared by Hutchinson, Read, and Sharrock (2008), Winch (1990), and ourselves) is that grounded descriptions can also stand alone as illuminating accounts that are useful for other purposes too; for instance, in the planning and conduct of spaceflight missions where a purely quantitative approach to task-scheduling has had demonstrable failings.

References

Balbaky, E. Mary Lou, and Michael B. McCaskey. 1981. "Strike in Space." Case Study. *Harvard Business Review*, 1 November 1981. 16 pp.
Belew, Leland F., and Ernst Stuhlinger. 1973. *Skylab: A Guidebook*. Huntsville, AL: George C. Marshall Space Flight Center, National Aeronautics and Space Administration.
Brooker, Phillip. Forthcoming. *Living and Working in Space: An Ethnomethodological Study of Skylab*. Manchester: Manchester University Press.
Brooker, Phillip, Paola Castaño, and Effie Le Moignan. 2021. "Living and Working in Space: Expanding the Human Factors Framework." *The Sociological Review Blog*, Accessed 18 May 2021 at https://www.thesociologicalreview.com/living-and-working-in-space-expanding-the-human-factors-framework/.
Burns, Lucy, and Edward G. Gibson. 2021. "The 'Strike' in Space" (podcast episode). *Witness History* (podcast), 6 January 2021. Accessed 17 February 2021 at www.bbc.co.uk/sounds/play/w3cszmsv.
Button, Graham. 2012. "What Does 'Work' Mean in 'Ethnomethodological Studies of Work?': Its Ubiquitous Relevance for Systems Design to Support Action and Interaction." *Design Studies* 33 (6): 673–84. https://doi.org/10.1016/j.destud.2012.06.003.
Carr, Gerald Paul. 2000. *NASA Johnson Space Center Oral History Project: Oral History Transcript*. Interviewed by Kevin M. Rusnak, 25 October 2000. 64 pp.
Castaño, Paola. n.d. "Beyond the Lab: The Social Life of Experiments on the International Space Station." Unpublished manuscript.
Caton, Charles Edwin. 1963. "Introduction." In *Philosophy and Ordinary Language*, edited by Charles Edwin Caton, v–xii. Urbana, IL: University of Illinois Press.
Cooper, Henry S. F., Jr. 1976. *A House in Space*. New York: Holt, Reinhart and Winston.
DeChurch, Leslie A., Ashley A. Niler, Jessica R. Mesmer-Magnus, and Noshir S. Contractor. 2019. "Task Management in Space Multiteam Systems." *Presented at the 2019 NASA Human Research Program Investigators' Workshop Annual Conference*, 22–25 January 2019. Galveston, TX.
Deudney, Daniel. 2020. *Dark Skies: Space Expansionism, Planetary Geopolitics, and the Ends of Humanity*. New York: Oxford University Press.
Elliot, Henry C. 1974. "Similarities and Differences Between Science and Common Sense." In *Ethnomethodology: Selected Readings*, edited by Roy Turner, 21–26. Middlesex: Penguin Education.
Froehlich, Walter. 1971. *Man in Space: Space in the Seventies*. Washington, DC: National Aeronautics and Space Administration.

Garfinkel, Harold. 1964. "Studies of the Routine Grounds of Everyday Activities." *Social Problems* 11 (3): 225–50. https://doi.org/10.2307/798722.

Garfinkel, Harold. 1984. *Studies in Ethnomethodology*. London: Polity.

Garfinkel, Harold, ed. 1986. *Ethnomethodological Studies of Work*. London: Routledge.

Garfinkel, Harold. 2002. *Ethnomethodology's Program: Working Out Durkheim's Aphorism*. Oxford: Rowman & Littlefield.

Garfinkel, Harold, and D. Lawrence Wieder. 1992. "Two Incommensurable, Asymmetrically Alternate Technologies of Social Analysis." In *Text in Context: Contributions to Ethnomethodology*, edited by Graham Watson and Robert M. Seiler, 175–206. London: SAGE.

Gibson, Edward George. 2000. *NASA Johnson Space Center Oral History Project: Oral History Transcript*. Interviewed by Carol Butler, 1 December 2000. 91 pp.

Gordon, Raymond. 1976. "Ethnomethodology: A Radical Critique." *Human Relations* 29 (2): 193–202. https://doi.org/10.1177/001872677602900208.

Heppenheimer, Thomas A. 1977. *Colonies in Space*. New York: Warner Books.

Hitt, David, Owen Garriott, and Joseph Kerwin. 2008. *Homesteading Space: The Skylab Story*. London: University of Nebraska Press.

Holder, Alexander, Christopher Elsey, Martina Kolanoski, Phillip Brooker, and Michael Mair. 2022. "Doing the Organisation's Work—Transcription for All Practical Governmental Purposes." *Frontiers in Communication* 6 (797485): 1–20. https://doi.org/10.3389/fcomm.2021.797485.

Hutchinson, Phil, Rupert Read, and Wes Sharrock. 2008. *There Is No Such Thing as Social Science: In Defence of Peter Winch*. Hampshire: Ashgate Publishing Limited.

Kubis, Joseph F., and Edward J. McLaughlin. 1975. "Skylab Task and Work Performance (Experiment M151—Time and Motion Study)." *Acta Astronautica* 2 (3–4): 337–49. https://doi.org/10.1016/0094-5765(75)90100-9.

Kubis, Joseph F., Edward J. McLaughlin, Janice M. Jackson, Rudolph Rusnak, Gary H. McBride, and Susan V. Saxon. 1977. "Task and Work Performance on Skylab Missions 2, 3 and 4: Time and Motion Study—Experiment M151." In *Biomedical Results from Skylab*, edited by Richard S. Johnston and Lawrence F. Dietlein, 136–54. Washington, DC: National Aeronautics and Space Administration, Science and Technical Information Office.

Lynch, Michael. 2006. "The Origins of Ethnomethodology." In *Philosophy of Anthropology and Sociology*, edited by M.W. Risjord and S. P. Turner, 485–515. London: North Holland. https://doi.org/10.1016/B978-044451542-1/50015-5.

Mesmer-Magnus, Jessica, Alina Lungeanu, Alexa Harris, Ashley Niler, Leslie A. DeChurch, and Noshir Contractor. 2021. "Working in Space: Managing Transitions Between Tasks." In *Psychology and Human Performance in Space Programs: Extreme Application*, edited by Lauren Blackwell Landon, Kelly J. Slack and Eduardo Salas, 179–203. London: CRC Press.

Messeri, Lisa. 2016. *Placing Outer Space: An Earthly Ethnography of Other Worlds*. Durham, NC: Duke University Press.

Mirmalek, Zara. 2020. *Making Time on Mars*. London: The MIT Press.

Newell, Homer E. 1980. *Beyond the Atmosphere: Early Years of Space Science*. Washington, DC: National Aeronautics and Space Administration, Scientific and Technical Branch.

O'Neill, Gerard K. 1976. *The High Frontier: Human Colonies in Space*. New York: Bantam Books.

O'Neill, Gerard K. 1981. *2081: A Hopeful View of the Human Future*. New York: Simon and Schuster.

Pogue, William Reid. 2000. *NASA Johnson Space Center Oral History Project: Oral History Transcript*. Interviewed by Kevin M. Rusnak, 17 July 2000. 58 pp.

Sacks, Harvey. 1992. *Lectures on Conversation: Volumes I and II*. Malden, MA: Blackwell.

Scharmen, Fred. 2021. *Space Forces: A Critical History of Life in Outer Space*. London: Verso.

Turner, Roy. 1974. "Introduction." In *Ethnomethodology: Selected Readings*, edited by Roy Turner, 7–12. Middlesex: Penguin Education.

Vertesi, Janet. 2015. *Seeing Like a Rover: How Robots, Teams, and Images Craft Knowledge of Mars*. London: University of Chicago Press.

Vertesi, Janet. 2020. *Shaping Science: Organizations, Decisions, and Culture on NASA's Teams*. London: University of Chicago Press.

Winch, Peter. 1990. *The Idea of a Social Science, and its Relation to Philosophy*. 2nd ed. London: Routledge & Kegan Paul.

Woolgar, Steve. 1981. "Critique and Criticism: Two Readings of Ethnomethodology." *Social Studies of Science* 11 (4): 504–14. https://doi.org/10.1177/030631278101100406.

32
ADAPTING TO SPACE
The International Space Station Archaeological Project

Justin St. P. Walsh

Introduction

The International Space Station Archaeological Project (ISSAP), co-directed by Alice Gorman and me, is the first full-scale, systematic archaeological investigation of the material culture from a site of human activity in space. We started in late 2015, in response to a number of phenomena, including a growing desire to move the focus of space archaeology away from heritage studies and purely theoretical discussions and towards deep interpretation of material culture and more practical applications of archaeological effort. The obstacles to carrying out archaeological research in space have been discussed Alice Gorman elsewhere in this volume. This chapter tells the story of ISSAP from concept to execution, providing a view into space archaeology as a social science in the early twenty-first century.

ISSAP was inspired by the National Aeronautics and Space Administration's (NASA's) announcement of a new recruitment of astronaut candidates on 4 November 2015 (NASA Johnson Space Center 2015). Michael Oman-Reagan, in a since-deleted post on Twitter, drew attention to the list of qualifications, which included at least a bachelor's degree in science, engineering, or mathematics fields. He noted that the document explicitly excluded candidates with "degree fields [which], while related to engineering and the sciences, are not considered qualifying: [such as] …degrees in social sciences (geography, anthropology, archaeology, etc.)" (NASA 2015). On the one hand, it was surprising that NASA was thinking enough about subjects like archaeology to prohibit them; on the other hand, it was deeply frustrating to see that the agency was apparently sure that archaeological training, experience, and perspectives would be useless as part of their space missions.[1] After all, archaeologists are surely among the scientific groups most used to living and working in small, isolated, often confined groups far from home, and having to respond to trying circumstances using only the resources immediately at hand. It seemed particularly strange to exclude social scientists given that NASA's plans included a three-year-long round-trip journey to Mars—how could they expect to have a successful mission of such duration without understanding how space crews relate to each other socially and culturally, or how they interact with the material culture surrounding them, adapting it to their needs or adapting themselves to it?

The recruitment announcement led me to think about what kind of project could possibly convince space agencies and the space industry of the value of archaeology. What site could be studied, and how? My first idea was the International Space Station since it's the most intensively inhabited site so far—more than 250 people have visited it, with at least two people on board continuously since 2 November 2000. But the problem of how to study a site that I couldn't visit seemed difficult to overcome. An answer came in the form of a book that had been published only the previous month, Jason De León's *The Land of Open Graves: Living and Dying on the Migrant Trail* (2015). In this remarkable work, De León adapted existing anthropological and archaeological methods, and developed new ones, to allow him to study the phenomenon of migration across the Sonoran Desert between Mexico and the United States. One of his methods was to give disposable film cameras to migrants on the Mexican side of the border, which they would use to document their journeys before he retrieved the cameras on the US side. This allowed De León to observe events that were otherwise hidden from him. It occurred to me that astronauts and cosmonauts on ISS had been taking photos constantly since occupation of the station began. The coincidence of the beginning of habitation of ISS with the rise of digital photography meant that far more photographs had been taken there than on any previous space station—and that the images' metadata would allow them to be put in chronological order. If I could extract key archaeological data from the images, most notably where in ISS the images were taken, what crew members were present, and what items were also visible, it would then be possible to trace out the patterns of activity, use of spaces and items, and relationships between people, places, and things over the entire history of the station's occupation. This was the start of ISSAP (Walsh and Gorman 2021).

I invited my colleague Alice Gorman to join me in this work because I knew it was too much to take on alone. We have co-directed ISSAP and developed our approach for the last seven years. Our first move was to strategise how to get access to the photographic data—and what we would do with it when we received it. Given NASA's evident bias against archaeology, a cautious approach seemed advisable. We first reached out to the NASA History Office at headquarters in Washington, since it seemed likely that staff there would be more sympathetic to our plans. After meetings in person in November 2016, they directed us to the NASA ISS Outreach Office, especially Gary Kitmacher, who had previously helped to design major ISS components such as the US Laboratory module and the Habitation module. Mr. Kitmacher facilitated an introduction to the ISS Research Integration Office (RIO), which manages all research activities on the station. It was clear that the staff in RIO didn't know what to make of us and our plans, but they allowed us to submit an unsolicited proposal requesting access to the historic images and other relevant data sets. By March 2017, we received a positive response from RIO stating that they would be able to provide access—once we had obtained external research funding. We were ineligible for applying to NASA itself for grant support because, although its Human Research Program (HRP) states that its focus is "human health and performance countermeasures, knowledge, technologies, and tools to enable safe, reliable, and productive human space exploration", in reality, it funds only biomedical and psychological studies (another indication of disciplinary bias on the part of the agency) (NASA n.d.a). We would have to focus on other sources.

Developing a Methodology for Space Archaeology

The disposition of artefacts and structures provides the entrée into understanding the human behaviours and post-depositional factors which shaped the site. The ISS photographs provided a great advantage in that they showed the crew in the process of using the site. This, however, necessitated developing methods for recording the crew in relation to objects and interior spaces.

At this point, our idea was to take the historic photos and place them within a three-dimensional model of ISS. We wanted to put the photos virtually in/over the locations which they depicted, as "layers" (in both the stratigraphic sense and the sense of layers within image-editing software such as Adobe Photoshop or Illustrator). A timeline bar would allow a moment in the space station's history to be chosen, with all relevant images becoming visible. In this way, individual moments in the station's life could be examined. As we honed this idea, however, it became clear that it was a dead end: a potentially wonderful didactic tool for showing a public audience change on ISS over time, but not very useful for capturing data and making it analysable. We needed another way to analyse the photos.

We began to practise with publicly available images from ISS, posted by NASA Public Affairs on its Flickr page (NASA n.d.b). The first iteration was a Microsoft SharePoint database with tables for information about each photograph (date, time, expedition number, module) and about the people and things in it. The challenge was how to extract archaeological data from photographs and in the microgravity environment. Following standard archaeological methods, the location of each item and person should be recorded within a grid superimposed on the photograph as well as in the physical space of ISS. For the latter, we couldn't adopt a standard coordinate system such as latitude-longitude or the Universal Transverse Mercator system, since the ISS is not only off-Earth but also in constant motion. So we developed a relative system for each module, dividing them into 27 three-dimensional volumes derived from positions on the three-dimensional axes: forward-centre-aft, starboard-centre-port, and zenith-centre-nadir (we adopted nautical terminology, following the system crew use to navigate around the station). For example, an item could be located in the upper left quadrant of a photograph, as well as in the forward-centre-nadir volume of a module, as shown in the photograph.

We recorded the general activity depicted in the photograph (arrival, departure, experiment, maintenance, exercise, communication, eating/drinking, leisure, other). People were assigned random numerical identifiers to provide the necessary privacy. Items were assigned categories (media, personal item, storage, equipment, electronics, toy, religious item), types (container, photography, pen, icon), and then descriptions (toiletry bag, black pen, checklist, Mother of God of Kazan icon). Then we needed to represent a status for the item or person—attached/holding on to a wall or floating. If the items were associated with a person, the relationship was described by a verb (holding, using, eating, drinking, observing, giving, taking, throwing, etc.). If objects were simply present in the image but not associated with a person, they were recorded in a separate table together with their location. Experimenting with several images indicated that it could take two or three hours to record all relevant information in a single photo. Since there were 8,000 photos of the ISS interior on Flickr alone, with an unknown but presumably much larger number still unpublished, it was clear that manual entry alone would present logistical problems relating to the time required for data collection.[2]

Pilot Study—Visual Displays in Space Habitats

While examining the photos from Flickr, I noticed an intriguing phenomenon in one of the Russian modules. On the aft wall of the service module Zvezda, I saw a wide variety of things on display, everything from standard mission patches and flags to paintings and photographic portraits of Soviet-Russian space heroes, to religious items like Orthodox crosses, sacred texts, and icons. There were even several toys. I wondered whether these items were always on the wall—if they changed, moved around, or were static. Looking at earlier photos, I could see clearly that there were numerous changes. To track the changes, I created a simple database in Microsoft Access, again with a table for metadata about the photographs and another with information about the items. I identified forty-eight photographs in the Flickr set, dating from 2000 to 2014, that showed a different arrangement or a change in the group of items displayed from previous images. For this work, I ignored the presence of people in the photos. I divided the wall into different zones, especially noting the difference between the top of the wall, around the air vents, and what I labelled the "niche"—a small space below and slightly recessed from the top area.

In all, I captured identifying and locational information for seventy-eight unique items that appeared 441 times across the forty-eight photographs (Walsh, Gorman, and Salmond 2021). A simple statistical analysis showed the pattern of display for all items, and for religious items compared to secular ones. It became clear that the wall display underwent significant changes, both as Russian crews changed and as important events happened on Earth. Only one item could truly be said to be static: a famous 1961 portrait of Yuri Gagarin holding a dove, which first appeared in 2002 and has been in every photograph of the wall since that date (all but once in the niche, which is the preferred location for all of the portraits of space heroes). Its continuing presence underlines the supreme symbolic importance of Gagarin for cosmonauts; he has become a kind of secular saint watching over the crew. Icons, on the other hand, tended to appear in the top area, as did flags and mission patches. Religious items appeared most frequently in 2005, 2008, and 2013–2014, possibly associated with celebrations of the sixtieth anniversary of the end of the Second World War, the Russian invasion of Georgia, and the lead-up to the Russian invasion of Ukraine. Growing connections between the Russian Orthodox Church and the Russian state, military, and cosmonaut corps have been documented since the fall of the Soviet Union, and especially the rise to power of Vladimir Putin (Adamsky 2019). News reports have described how some icons have been official visitors to ISS, managed by the Russian space agency Roscosmos, while others have been brought to space due to personal relationships between devout cosmonauts and the clergy.

These results represented the first archaeological interpretation of human culture in space. In order to take the analysis further, we collaborated with art historian Wendy Salmond, a specialist in Russian icon studies. We first examined the patterns of display within the cultural geography of ISS as a space station with crew and modules from many nations (Walsh, Gorman, and Salmond 2021). When compared to American and European displays on ISS, the Zvezda one stands out for its complexity, duration, and public visibility. We also established that the phenomenon of using the aft wall of the service module for this purpose had a longer history than ISS itself. Cosmonaut crews used an identical space on Mir for the same purpose (including the display of Soviet space heroes and, after 1991, religious icons), and there are numerous examples of displays in other locations of the previous series of seven Salyut stations going back to at least 1976. In other words, visual displays are a cosmonautic tradition, passed down from generation to generation—probably through the mixing of individual cosmonauts on a variety of missions to multiple space stations.

We next interpreted the presence of icons on ISS through the lens of *hierotopy*, or the bringing into being of a special religious space (Lidov 2006; Salmond, Walsh, and Gorman 2020). The cosmonauts imbued the aft end of Zvezda with sacred qualities, delimiting it by confining the presence of religious objects (especially icons) to this area and not others. They did this in a space that was not designed for the purpose, adapting it to their needs. The display of religious items happened within the specific historic context of the reestablishment of the Orthodox Church as a major force in Russian life and the integration of its beliefs with Konstantin Tsiolkovsky's early-Soviet-era concept of cosmism to redefine the purpose of Russian expansion into space—spreading Orthodoxy and Russian nationalism into low Earth orbit.

Machine Learning and Space Archaeology

As exciting as it was to develop new and unexpected results from observation of the historic photographs, the problem remained of tagging each image with information about the people, places, and objects depicted in them. We could not afford the time in hours per image to do this work manually for the roughly 8,000 images that the space agencies had made publicly available, never mind for the thousands or even millions more unpublished ones to which we hoped to gain access. We turned to a colleague in computer science, Erik Linstead, who specialises in artificial intelligence, specifically machine learning (ML) algorithms that are focused on problems in computer vision; he is the principal investigator of Chapman University's Machine Learning and Affiliated Technology laboratory. The best-known examples of such algorithms are probably the facial recognition and object recognition tools used by social media platforms such as Facebook to automatically recognise users, their friends, and the brands with which those people associate (holding a can of Coca-Cola, for example) in photos posted to the network. The promise of ML is that a trained algorithm can perform high-quality identifications in the thousands per second, vastly diminishing the amount of time needed for large photo sets. We began to seek grant funding to develop a tool for this work, applying to the National Endowment for the Humanities and the National Science Foundation. We argued that a generic tool that could work with historic sets of photos to identify similar locations, people, and objects would open up exciting new possibilities for researchers across the humanities and social sciences. Unfortunately, these proposals were not accepted—perhaps not the worst outcome for us, because they would have diverted our time and attention to making a tool that worked for others, not ourselves. But a generic tool like the one described above could add fascinating new data for humanists and social scientists to study.

Erik's doctoral student Rao Hamza Ali joined the team in 2020 and started working on the particular problems of the image data set. He developed solutions using the Flickr photos' captions, written by NASA Public Affairs, to train a neural network to recognise specific modules and individual ISS crew members in the photographs with high accuracy. We used these identifications to map relationships between crew members who appeared together (Ali et al. 2022).

Unpublished Images and the Inventory Management System

As mentioned earlier, NASA had committed to providing unpublished photos and other data once the project was funded. We applied for a Discovery Program research grant from the Australian Research Council in 2018, and were successful, with funding from 2019 to 2021. This allowed us to hire a database engineer, Amir Kanan Kashefi, to design and build a database to hold the unusual kinds of data and relationships identified in our pilot studies. It also began the process of gaining access to unpublished data from ISS. The first step was a review by NASA's HRP Institutional Review Board to assess the risks posed by our research to the crew, and proposed methods of mitigating those risks (we simultaneously underwent a review by Chapman's IRB). The limitations of the HRP system quickly became evident, since they had never seen a study using photographs before, or assessed a project outside biomedical or psychological research. We were initially told the review process would last about six weeks. After ten months of submitting forms, responding to questions, and resubmitting forms, we were (to our equal surprise and chagrin) finally and officially determined to be "not human research"—that is, that our work simply did not fall under their scrutiny. We were still required to adhere to NASA requirements regarding crew privacy, including anonymisation and aggregation of data, and had to agree not to publish any previously unpublished material without permission. But NASA could give us imagery, and we could study it. We also were exempted from gaining consent from crew members to use photos of them—a development of major importance, since we would have had to ask for permission for each photo individually, and, in the case of retired crew, NASA regulations permit only three total consent requests for research participation once the crew member has left employment (more than this would be considered an unethical imposition). Finally, we had to send emails to relevant contacts at ESA, JAXA, and CSA to gain their approval for the use of images of their crews (none of these messages were answered).

In October 2019, we started receiving images in chronological order by expedition. We were now officially an ISS research "payload", as any project associated with the space station is known. It is important to be clear that we did not receive every image of the ISS interior that exists in NASA's archives. We only received unpublished images that were not considered "sensitive" according to several criteria:

- The image did not show a crew member in a state of undress or some other "embarrassing" situation, as judged by NASA.

- The image did not show a research activity whose investigators had not approved release of the image.
- The image did not show proprietary technology on ISS which NASA had agreed to protect from release.

The consequence of implementing the criteria was that every single image we received had to be individually selected by our payload manager. This created an enormous amount of work for her and also meant that the tranches of photos appeared slowly. By late 2021, we had only received the approved images for the first seventeen expeditions and part of the eighteenth. Even so, we worked to define how we could work with these photographs.

Another data source which we were able to access was the ISS Inventory Management System (IMS), the database built and used by the five international partner agencies to keep track of precisely which items were on board. By the middle of 2020, over 332,000 items that had been sent to the space station were recorded in the IMS. The records for some 77,292 of these were considered "active" on station, according to the database managers (personal communication). Of the remainder, 247,766 items had either been returned to Earth or were destroyed in a deorbiting cargo craft. An additional 7,000 items, or more than 2%, were simply considered "lost". The IMS exists in multiple installed instances, including on the station and at each of the terrestrial mission control centres, that update daily. From the perspective of an archaeologist, the prospect of receiving a list of all the artefacts present at a site prior to excavating was obviously enticing. We were given copies of the archived IMS versions from the first ten years of the station's habitation. We quickly learned, however, that as a document of ISS material culture, IMS was deeply flawed. It was never intended to be used in a forensic analysis, so it was initially impossible to search for changes over time. It also had no clear data validation, meaning that the same kind of item, such as a certain size of resealable plastic bag, or a urine collection device, might be written with varying numbers of capital letters, different spellings, typographic errors, or in different languages (both English and Russian are used; sometimes both are given for the same item, other times just one language is used, depending on which agency the item belongs to). This means that queries must try to account for all possible variations to generate complete results.

From this experience, we learned that the space agencies' attitude towards their activities is focused almost exclusively on the present and the future, with hardly any attention given to what might be learned from the past. This was another way in which our research might have a positive impact—directing attention towards lessons to be learned from the past. Amir set to work on making the IMS searchable and quantifiable, with a user interface that integrates Google Translate for Russian language queries and results. We plan to integrate our transformed version of IMS with the ML algorithm training for the next step in our image tagging: object recognition. IMS data allows the algorithm to constrain its attempt to identify items only to the kinds of things known to be on board, making it faster, less expensive, and more accurate. We also now have the possibility of identifying patterns of supply that can be associated with specific missions (and their crew) or with specific cargo spacecraft, using a graph-database version of the IMS built by Amir that displays relationships as edges that connect nodes.

Cargo Processes

We reported the results of the Zvezda pilot study to ISS RIO in 2017. Our contact was surprised, remarking that he had looked at the display wall for fifteen years, and knew that there were items there—but not what they were or that they changed. These revelations seemed to change his attitude about the potential of archaeological methods, making him more supportive of the project. As a result, when we had a new idea, he responded positively. Even though we could not go to ISS, some material culture from ISS did return to Earth, almost exclusively (since the end of the Space Shuttle programme in 2011) on the SpaceX Cargo Dragon supply vehicle. A variety of archaeological questions came to mind. What were these items? How were they selected for return? What happened to them? What did they mean, in the context of ISS culture? We reached out to our RIO contact in August 2017 to see whether it might be possible to observe the return of items on a future flight. He wrote to the Cargo Mission Contract officer and the management of the two contractors who handled the cargo return (what NASA refers to as "deintegration"), Leidos and Jacobs Engineering Group. Everyone involved was supportive, so in January and May 2018, I was able to watch the return process for two cargo resupply missions, CRS-13 and CRS-14, in Houston and Long Beach, California, respectively.

I shadowed the contractors, documented their actions with photography and video, and interviewed two dozen of them about their work and their understandings of what the things associated with ISS meant to them and about life in space (Walsh, Gorman, and Castaño 2022). Methodologically, of course, this work shares more with anthropological ethnography than archaeology. We were not able to work directly with the items from ISS—not even, for the most part, able to touch them. However, we learned that the items which come back from space are primarily scientific samples and research equipment, other kinds of equipment which are broken and need to be repaired or examined on Earth, and crew personal items and other memorabilia. These items together are taken to justify the creation and enactment of elaborate processes, the formation of various teams of workers, and the use of hugely expensive and specialised equipment. It therefore seems clear that these items have extraordinary symbolic value in the eyes of the space agencies and their owners.

This value is especially clear relative to other items sent to ISS and used there, which are either stowed in bags wedged into corners, sometimes to be forgotten there, or packed into other cargo supply craft which do not survive atmospheric reentry, incinerating their contents; anything which might survive falls into the ocean. We interpreted this difference in attribution of value through the metaphor of discard, that is, the removal of the items from their systemic context, as described by Michael Schiffer fifty years ago (Schiffer 1972). Archaeologists are highly experienced in the interpretation of discard practices, given that trash forms one of the most common kinds of evidence found through excavation and survey. The "royal treatment" given to the ISS items that return can be compared to the rich arrays of burial goods often interred with high-status individuals in ancient societies (Walsh, Gorman, and Castaño 2022). The abandonment or destruction of the other items which do not return would, in this interpretation, be similar to the practices associated with the discard of quotidian or cheap, replaceable things like broken pottery. Combining this concept with the *chaîne opératoire* of André Leroi-Gourhan (Sellet 2016), we focused on the steps in the return process as creating meaning. The cargo analysis provided significant insights into the regulated, documented, and scheduled nature of life on the station, and the small degree of autonomy that ISS crew members have in relation to most objects and spaces in their lives. In a context where every action seems to entail a procedure and every object is part of an inventory, the astronauts' selection of the personal items they want to bring and return is the only activity that remains discretionary and confidential. In space, their own few belongings are the only direct reminders of home; following a return to Earth, the same items become the only tangible connection to their experience of space.

For the analysis we collaborated with sociologist Paola Castaño, whose research focuses on scientific practices on ISS, such as an experiment to grow plants in space (see Castaño this volume). She introduced an additional interpretative lens from forensic science, the "chain of custody", as a way to understand the meanings attributed to the returned items. The chain of custody is particularly important for scientific samples, as it ensures the integrity of the scientific results from such costly experiments. However, a similar level of care is devoted to ensuring that the return of personal crew items is done in such a way to preserve their privacy and dignity. Interviews with the cargo staff revealed a sense of pride in upholding the chain of custody, both for the experiments and crew.

Population Distributions

These initial efforts tried to grapple with how we could undertake archaeological research on a remote, unvisitable site. They also started to ask the kinds of questions archaeologists are often interested in answering—what items are present at a site, and how were they arranged or used; or, what are the meanings behind the discard of certain items? Another basic question arose from examining the photographs published on Flickr: who was using which parts of the site? In other words, how were different subgroups within the overall population distributed around ISS? Could we identify patterns for women and men, or people of different nationalities, or members of different space agencies—what Erik called "the low-hanging fruit"? We decided to use the captions supplied by NASA for each photo, which typically identified the location where the image was taken and the identities of the people in it. We automated the extraction of relevant content, using the Flickr API and web scraping software developed by Amir and Rao, allowing us to collect the metadata for the 8,219 photos published from the first sixty-three expeditions (2000–2020). Of these, 6,262 photos included information in their caption for both a location and an individual, yielding 10,346 identifications of 217 individuals (89% of the total who had visited ISS by that time) in twelve modules. For example, a caption might read, "Drew Morgan and Jessica Meir work on the Waste and Hygiene Compartment in Tranquility." The scraper accessed the Flickr site, parsed the content of each page, found the data of interest (in the example above, "Drew Morgan", "Jessica Meir", and "Tranquility"), and finally structured the data as needed. Because the gender, nationality, and agency affiliation of every ISS visitor is readily available, it was easy to attribute those variables to each identification: Drew Morgan is a male, American, NASA astronaut; Jessica Meir is a female, American, NASA astronaut; Tranquility is Node 3 in the US Orbital Segment of ISS. Therefore, one man and one woman, two Americans, and two NASA crew occupied this module. This process was repeated for all of the identifications.

We plotted charts for each of the three categories of population—gender, nationality, and space agency affiliation—comparing them to the overall population for the space station (Walsh et al. 2021). The charts revealed extremely interesting, and in some cases, quite surprising results. For gender, women were hardly represented in the Russian Orbital Segment—perhaps unsurprising, since Russia has only sent one female cosmonaut to ISS in the station's first twenty years—but they were also somewhat underrepresented in parts of the US Segment associated with eating and hygiene. Women were vastly overrepresented in one location: the US observation module known as the Cupola. In this space, they represented 24% of all identified people, a proportion 50% higher than in the overall population. We suggest that this phenomenon may be evidence of a bias in the NASA Public Affairs Office in choosing to publish images of women in an aesthetically pleasing location, looking out the window at Earth, rather than others associated with less pleasant (or less stereotypically "feminine") activities. This result indicates how important access to the unpublished photos of life on ISS, presumably free of this bias, will be to our future studies.

The result of the analysis of gender distribution does not necessarily mean that nothing can be learned from this first approximation. The distributions for nationality and agency affiliation (which tend to mirror each other, apart from the combination of European nationalities under the ESA rubric for agencies) do reveal some important phenomena. In broad strokes, the Russians dominate in their four modules and Americans in the eight modules which comprise the US Segment (although there is greater mixture in this zone). Notably, Japanese crew are the second-largest contingent in their module, Kibo, and Italians make up the second-largest contingent in the European module (reinforced by other ESA citizens). In other words, ISS may not be as international as it seems from its name and from public relations pronouncements. Instead, the usage of different spaces seems directly related to their ownership and management at the level of space agencies. For what is likely to be the most expensive building project in the history of humanity, it seems surprising that there is not a more even—and efficient—distribution of crew. We might imagine that all crew are used to performing every necessary task, but this is not the case. Future space stations might want to consider how they can more equitably distribute work and other activities.

Square

From the beginning of the project in 2015, we wanted to develop experimental work that the crew of ISS could perform on our behalf. This kind of activity, we learned, required sponsorship—by a space agency, for example, or by some other group with access to ISS resources. One such group is the Center for the Advancement of Science in Space (CASIS), a nonprofit organisation chartered by the US Congress to facilitate research in what is referred to as the ISS National Laboratory. CASIS provides funds to selected research groups, as well as crew time and the capability to launch equipment to the station and return samples. Once again, the inherent bias of existing structures towards physical and biological sciences, medicine, technology, and engineering worked against us. We first met with CASIS staff in late 2018, and while they were excited and wanted to see our research happen, we did not fit into the mission statement and goals of the organisation as they were formulated, so they could not provide funding. We continued to engage with them, sharing details of various ideas we had for experiments. Some, we were told, were not feasible, such as removing selected experimental racks to see what items may have become stuck or lost behind them, analogous to removing a soil matrix to reveal artifacts. Since this action would require turning off power to the racks, they would jeopardise other researchers' work, so the idea was rejected. We ultimately settled on a suite of seven experiments that we were told could actually be performed if funding were found to support them:

1 Systematic archaeological recording of objects in sample locations around the station to record the dynamic nature of spaces.
2 Video recordings to examine astronauts' accounts of their spaces.
3 Directed photography to document various spaces, including storage areas and, if feasible and according to informed consent, private crew berths.
4 Sampling of surfaces in various modules with cotton swabs for the accretion of "soil" (dirt, skin cells, hair, body oils, food, and other materials).
5 Sampling of the air in various modules to identify the cultural origins of airborne particles in a microgravity environment.
6 Audio recording, sound metering, and photography to investigate distinctions between public and private spaces.
7 Placement of radio-frequency identification (RFID) tag readers at module thresholds, with the crew wearing tags, to identify how different spaces are occupied and used.

We also recruited a multidisciplinary team of experts to help us design, implement, and analyse results from these tasks. The team includes Paola Castaño, Wendy Dunn (a design anthropologist), Erick Jones (an industrial engineer), Marit Meyer (an aerosol scientist), Daniel Richter (a soil scientist), and Frederick Scharmen (an architectural designer). With CASIS's preliminary approval of the proposed experiments, we submitted a grant proposal to the National Science Foundation. As we were waiting to hear a response, in February 2021, our liaison at CASIS reached out to say that some other experiments planned for the end of the year had dropped out, and there was now an excess of crew time. He asked if we had an experiment which could be performed without sending anything to the ISS. We responded by proposing the first of our experiments, which involved designating sample locations with adhesive tape and photographing them every day for a sixty-day period. The core concept, which Alice Gorman developed, was derived from the standard archaeological technique for systematically sampling a site through excavation of one-metre-squared test pits. Each photo of a sample location would be equivalent to a stratigraphic layer, representing a moment of time and a specific activity. Within a week, CASIS had approved the proposal and began to help us find an implementation partner—a required role to be filled by a commercial entity that would manage the technical and logistical aspects of the work in collaboration with NASA. Axiom Space, a company that plans to build a private space station by attaching modules to ISS, agreed to take on this role.

By September, our experiment was formally designated a payload by CASIS. Meetings began immediately to plan its integration into the station timeline, led by NASA staff and contractors at Johnson Space Center and Marshall Spaceflight Center. We needed an official name, preferably one that could be condensed to a snappy acronym (since it has become cultural tradition to abbreviate everything associated with space). We settled on the name Sampling Quadrangle Assemblages Research Experiment or SQuARE. Over the next four months, we determined our sample locations, met with NASA's Astronaut Office to gain their approval and acknowledgment of potential privacy issues and collaborated with NASA to write the specific procedures that would be used. This process proved to be almost as important for us in understanding how ISS functions as the experiment itself, revealing as it did the culture on the ground, complete with its own language, processes, relationships, roles, and more (Figure 32.1).[3]

Figure 32.1 NASA astronaut Kayla Barron takes a photograph of one of the sample areas for the SQuARE experiment in the US Node 1 galley area (dotted lines indicate the sample area boundaries). Credit NASA.

SQuARE began formally on 14 January 2022, when NASA mission specialist Kayla Barron placed the first pieces of tape to designate the corner of a sample location in the Japanese module Kibo. It was one of the fastest experiments from proposal to execution (eleven months) in the history of the space station programme, and probably the cheapest. It demonstrated the importance of being nimble and prepared, and of laying the foundations for a working relationship with NASA and CASIS far in advance. Over the following two months, we received 358 images of the six locations, which we are now processing by identifying every item and its location in a database. The tool we used for the database was the product of another collaboration, this time with digital archaeologist Shawn Graham and his graduate student Chantal Brousseau. Chantal identified an open-source image-tagging tool that she could modify for our needs (Dutta, Zisserman, and Gupta n.d.), which included extracting the recorded data from the database in a format that can be used for training Erik Linstead and Rao Hamza Ali's machine-learning algorithm for ISS objects in the historic photos.

Future Directions—Restraints, Stowage

We have begun to identify new areas of research using archaeological methods to illuminate life in space. One is how the crew of ISS attempts to mitigate the lack of gravity (and the effects of gravity which humans adapted for and are habituated to) through use of various means of attachment. The technical term for these attachments is "restraints"; they include handrails, elastic "bungee" cords, Velcro, cable ties, resealable plastic bags, plastic or metal clips, and articulable "Bogen" arms. Alice Gorman has coined the term "gravity surrogates" for these items since they serve to keep items in a specific place, just as we expect them to stay in place when we put them down on a table in a terrestrial, one-g context. The accumulation of restraints such as many Velcro patches in a given location over time can be interpreted as meaning that this location is one which requires a lot of "gravity" (but the need for this gravity was not originally foreseen by ISS's designers). We have started to catalogue the various restraints and their changes in drawings of different ISS modules. We are also comparing different solutions originating in the disparate engineering cultures of ISS, especially Russian and American approaches.

Another critical issue is stowage, a problem that has plagued ISS from the beginning. Items that are kept on board are stored in generic white fabric bags that are crammed or wedged into every available corner. Two entire modules (Leonardo and BEAM) are filled with these bags, as is the so-called "attic" of the Kibo module. The bags are cumbersome to manipulate and hard to distinguish from one another, and it is difficult to find the correct item inside them if it has been a long time since they were last opened. Finding the correct bag often means moving dozens of others first. Space agencies have tried for decades to impose technological solutions, such as using machine-readable barcodes or inserting RFID tags that correspond to items in the bags. We are interested in whether low-tech cultural design changes might produce positive effects as well.

Conclusion

After almost seven years of work on this project, we feel we have demonstrated the utility of an archaeological approach to studying a space habitat. Major challenges remain in the form of identifying adequate funding sources that are open to a project like this and breaking down disciplinary boundaries that exist in space bureaucracies. There have been other obstacles, too—for example, in May 2022, the ISS Research Integration Office withdrew its support of the historic photo archive delivery, stating that it did not have the resources to continue devoting our payload manager's time to selecting appropriate imagery for us to use. Intensified security measures recently taken by the Russian government deny us access to that country's historic photo archive of life on ISS, too. Yet the highly positive responses of individual people in space agencies and in the space industry when they learn about our work have been gratifying and allow us to maintain hope that we can achieve our goals.

To close this narrative, in addition to revealing important and novel insights into long-duration life in space through individual tasks, our project as a whole is something like a grand experiment that identifies key aspects of doing social sciences in the space world. The complex, time-consuming, and often-frustrating processes of getting the archaeology done—all the small details of our story, from developing a general concept to identifying specific tasks to relationship-building, proposal, execution, and dissemination of results—indicate the hard disciplinary boundaries that exist in human space activity and the blind spots created by those boundaries. The ultimate effects of that grand experiment remain to be seen, but we think that its performance is already showing results.

Notes

1. It is worth noting that until the Japanese Aerospace Exploration Agency (JAXA) announced an astronaut recruitment in November 2021 (JAXA 2021) that was open to people of all educational backgrounds, no space agency accepted applications from outside science or engineering. There has, accordingly, never been an astronaut with a social science specialisation. On February 28, 2023, the two new JAXA astronaut candidates were announced: a physician, and a disaster risk specialist with a background in geosciences. There has, accordingly, never been an astronaut with a social science specialisation.
2. In a presentation in 2022, one of the NASA staff who works with ISS photography revealed that the current total of photographs made by crew is over 4 million (pers. comm.).
3. In an email to our Payload Manager two weeks before SQuARE began, I wrote,

> I am completely amazed and fascinated by this process—I am learning so much from being a part of it. I don't have any concerns, but I would say that being new in the payload integration process is like visiting a foreign country for the first time. Even knowing what I already did about ISS, there is so much I don't fully understand and therefore have difficulty responding to. I don't know what any of the acronyms refer to (and don't want to take up people's valuable time by asking), I'm not sure what most people's precise roles are, and I didn't have a clear sense of the roadmap as the process has developed. I also don't know whether I'm performing my role as PI correctly—am I interfering too much? Am I not providing enough feedback or background info? Am I asking for too much, or stepping on people's toes? I honestly have no idea, and I don't know how the experience of this payload compares to all the other ones everyone else has worked on before.
>
> (author pers. comm., 28 Dec. 2021)

References

Adamsky, Dima. 2019. *Russian Nuclear Orthodoxy: Religion, Politics, and Strategy*. Palo Alto, CA: Stanford University Press.

Ali, Rao Hamza, Amir Kanan Kashefi, Erik Linstead, Justin Walsh, and Alice Gorman. 2022. "Automated Identification of Astronauts onboard the International Space Station: A Case Study in Space Archaeology." *Acta Astronautica* 200: 262–69. https://doi.org/10.1016/j.actaastro.2022.08.017.

De León, Jason. 2015. *The Land of Open Graves: Living and Dying on the Migrant Trail*. Los Angeles: University of California Press.

Dutta, Abhishek, Andrew Zisserman, and Ankush Gupta. n.d. "VGG Image Annotator (VIA)." *Visual Geometry Group*, University of Oxford. Accessed 13 July 2022 at https://www.robots.ox.ac.uk/~vgg/software/via/.

JAXA 2021. "年度 宇宙飛行士候補者 募集要項 2021" *Recruitment Guidelines for Astronaut Candidates for the Year 2021*. Accessed https://astro-mission.jaxa.jp/astro_selection/item/Application.pdf.

Lidov, Alexei. 2006. "Creating the Sacred Space: Hierotopy as a New Field of Cultural History." In *Spazi e Percorsi Sacri: I Santuari, le Vie, I Corpi*, edited by Laura Carnevale and Chiara Cremonesi, 61–89. Padua: Libreriauniversitaria.it Edizioni.

NASA n.d.a. "HRP Research Announcements." *NASA*. Accessed 13 July 2022 at https://www.nasa.gov/hrp/research/announcements.

NASA n.d.b. "NASA Johnson." *Flickr*. Accessed 13 July 2022 at https://www.flickr.com/photos/nasa2explore/.

NASA Johnson Space Center 2015. "NASA Facts: Astronaut Selection and Training." *NASA*. Accessed 18 November 2022. https://www.nasa.gov/centers/johnson/pdf/606877main_FS-2011-11-057-JSC-astro_trng.pdf.

Salmond, Wendy, Justin Walsh, and Alice Gorman. 2020. "Eternity in Low Earth Orbit: Icons on the International Space Station." *Religions* 11: 611. https://doi.org/10.3390/rel11110611.

Schiffer, Michael B. 1972. "Archaeological Context and Systemic Context." *American Antiquity* 37 (2): 156–65. https://doi.org/10.2307/278203.

Sellet, Frédéric. 2016. "Chaine Opératoire; The Concept and Its Applications." *Lithic Technology* 18 (1–2): 106–12. https://doi.org/10.1080/01977261.1993.11720900.

Walsh, Justin, and Alice Gorman. 2021. "A Methodology for Space Archaeology Research: The International Space Station Archaeological Project." *Antiquity* 95 (383): 1331–43. https://doi.org/10.15184/aqy.2021.114.

Walsh, Justin, Alice Gorman, and Paola Castaño. 2022. "Postorbital Discard and Chain of Custody: The Processing of Artifacts Returning to Earth from the International Space Station." *Acta Astronautica* 195: 513–31. https://doi.org/10.1016/j.actaastro.2022.03.035.

Walsh, Justin, Alice Gorman, and Wendy Salmond. 2021. "Visual Displays in Space Station Culture: An Archaeological Analysis." *Current Anthropology* 62 (6): 804–18. https://doi.org/10.1086/717778.

Walsh, Justin, Rao Hamza Ali, Alice Gorman, and Amir Kanan Kashefi. 2021. "A First Approximation of Population Distributions on the International Space Station." SocArXiv. Accessed 18 November 2022https://doi.org/10.31235/osf.io/ra4c3.

33
AN ETHNOGRAPHY OF AN EXTRATERRESTRIAL SOCIETY
The International Space Station

David Jeevendrampillai, Victor Buchli, Aaron Parkhurst, Adryon Kozel, Giles Bunch, Jenia Gorbanenko and Makar Tereshin

Introduction

The International Space Station (ISS) is a modular habitat that orbits the Earth at a speed of 7.66 kilometres per second relative to the Earth's surface at an altitude of around 400 kilometres. This means it orbits the Earth roughly every ninety-three minutes, around 15.5 times a day. It comprises modules that interconnect, reflecting international cooperation between five space agencies: NASA (United States), Roscosmos (Russia), JAXA (Japan), ESA (Europe), and CSA (Canada). The space station was initially launched in 1998 and has seen a series of developments and additions. It reached its fully operational size supporting six crew members in 2009. More than two hundred astronauts, cosmonauts, and civil participants from nineteen different countries have visited the ISS, which has allowed a range of activities from scientific research to media engagements, teaching exercises, and even the shooting of a feature film. The station cost an estimated $150 billion to develop and build with operations expected to run until around 2030 (Sheetz 2021). NASA has described the station as "one of the greatest technological, geopolitical and engineering achievements to benefit humanity" (Nixon 2016: 29). The NASA 2019 *International Space Station Benefits for Humanity* book states that the ISS has seen over 2135 scientific works published from the research carried out on board, representing the work of over five thousand scientists. It notes that the impacts of this research are predominantly in the fields of chemical, mechanical, and civil engineering, health and disease, electrical engineering, computer science, and medical research.

This unique extraterrestrial environment has received little attention from mainstream anthropology. Whilst, as this volume attests, there is a significant and growing interest in the social and anthropological study of outer space (see Dickens and Ormrod 2016; Messeri 2016; Olson 2018; Valentine, Olson, and Battaglia 2009; Battaglia, Valentine, and Olson 2015), there has been little direct attention on the ISS as a sociocultural object of ethnographic inquiry. Gorman and Walsh's (Gorman and Walsh Forthcoming; Gorman 2009) work on the archaeology of gravity and the material culture of the ISS is a notable exception to this, but their disciplinary approach differs from the ethnographic. This chapter outlines the approaches of the ETHNO-ISS team, who are conducting a multisituated, large-scale anthropological study of the ISS. The five-year project, running from 2019 to 2024, is funded by the European Research Council, and it partners with a number of associated academics with funding from other sources (see Acknowledgements). This chapter outlines the approaches taken by each of these contributing academics. In doing so, we present the ways in which such a study can be approached methodologically, and how an ethnography of the ISS talks back to core theoretical concepts and ideas in anthropology.

Each ethnographic contribution to the ETHNO-ISS project explores distinct and individual anthropologies that stand alone as contributions that both build upon and further the discipline through a focus on the ISS. However, the ethnographies compose a purposeful partnership, unified through the shared practice of 'worlding'. It is this concept of worlding, taken from Martin Heidegger, that positions the ETHNO-ISS research agendas as able to highlight the ways in which people attune to the fabrics of society in constant dialogue with the social and material worlds around them. The ISS presents a milieu in which the standard terms of engagement between the bodily and the material, the intimate and far-reaching, are reconvened. One's relationship with one's body, and with one's cosmology, are recalibrated to make new affective natures, in what Kathleen Stewart (2014) refers to as senses of "legibility" (p. 119), particularly as they relate to the widely diverse scales of habitation and gravity that are at play between the Earth and low Earth orbit. As she writes, "Some assemblage of affects, effects, conditions, sensibilities, and practices throws itself together into something recognisable as a thing. Disparate and incommensurate elements ... cohere and take on force as some kind of real, a world" (p. 119). Martin Heidegger himself refers to such worlding processes as nothing short of the "uprooting of man" (cited in Oliver 2015: 152), implying that Earth has both a physical and social soil from which the human figure drinks nutrients and knowledge. Cultural practices, knowledges, and movements, and the theories and analytics the anthropological discipline has developed to understand them, can then be understood as also deeply earthbound and terrestrial.

The ISS as a 'nexus' enables this form of metaphorical anthropic gardening, challenging us to think through the ways in which the ISS and human activity in outer space may provide disruptions that either pull up established roots of our being or make new fertile ground from which humans can construct their worlds. The ETHNO-ISS project shows how such disruptions and newness that outer space provides seep into all the colourful foundations of being human that have so long fascinated anthropology: cosmology and religion; biology and well-being; a sense of home and a sense of belonging; what it means to be local and what it means to be global; freedom, individualism, collective behaviour, and the nature of control. These human conditions and frameworks of knowing are made anew in lower Earth orbit—sometimes powerfully, and sometimes subtly, and often in ways unanticipated and unexpected, what Debbora Battaglia has partly referred to as "exo-surprise" (2012). The ETHNO-ISS mission is to systematically trace this worlding.

Lastly, in presenting these ethnographic explorations, ETHNO-ISS asks its readers to return this 'sense of legibility' to their earthbound worlds. It furthers the Anthropocenic call to challenge the notion of the Earth as a concrete and stable stage upon which actors carry out life and enact their social milieu, what Stefan Helmreich has described as a form of qualitative weight (2011: 1236). Ethnographies of the ISS illustrate and evidence, perhaps ironically, the principles of what Buckminster Fuller (1963) famously referred to as "Spaceship Earth", our terrestrial world itself as actor and agent providing nurture, movement, and a sense of home more fragile than it is often given credit. In doing so, the ethnographies ultimately highlight these processes of attunement that are central to living on and constructing any world, and which are always in the making.

When telling people that we are undertaking an ethnography of the ISS we often meet with some version of a now-familiar joke: "How big is your travel budget?!"[1] or "So you are going to space then!?" The jokes highlight two things. First, space is an incredibly difficult and expensive place to which to travel. Second, as a disciplinary practice, social anthropological fieldwork is traditionally considered as an exploration of the 'other', conducted in places peripheral to the anthropologist. The anthropologist must travel, dwell amongst the ethnographic 'other', and return to their home. Many anthropologists are able to state that they do fieldwork in *a* place with *a* people, that is, they study a particular cultural group that is located in a specific place. Many methodological trends in ethnography in the last decades have challenged this anthropological orthodoxy, including principles of multisited ethnography (Marcus 1995), in which the researcher's field site is defined by mobility, fluidity, and lines of flight which the ethnographer must 'follow'. This methodology creates new freedoms for its practitioners, and freedoms as well for the people and places of its study, though these methods are not without its analytical dangers and limitations (see Van Duijn 2020). Because of a biographical emphasis on objects, material culture studies anticipated these trends in its emphasis on 'following the object', and that subdiscipline continues to push the boundaries of ethnographic method (Carroll, Walford, and Walton 2021). As our project is situated in both cutting-edge material culture studies and social anthropology, we employ both traditional and recent methods to engage with the cultures of lower Earth orbit. Our study starts with an eponymous object and is attentive to the multiple communities that have significant relations with the ISS as an object. As such, the groups of people with whom we engage and the social relations we study are wide and varied, incorporating, among a great many things, notions of religion and transcendence in Russia, materiality and utopia in the United States, or enthusiasm and energy in online communities. The commonality here is the ISS itself and its novel position as an extraterrestrial habitat that facilitates particular modes of social relations.

As Buchli (2020) states, the ISS presents new methodological challenges for fieldwork. Taking a lead from anthropological studies of social media and digital cultures, Buchli argues that communities such as mission controls in Moscow, Houston, and Tsukuba, or Orthodox Christians tracking relics on the ISS, or enthusiasts monitoring rocket launches are all coterminous with the ISS site, "simultaneously constituting and occupying the same 'field' of co-presence" (2020: 18). As Anne Beaulieu (2010) argues, an emphasis on co-presence produces different formulations of the anthropologist to the field site more than a focus on co-location does. Beaulieu asserts that the "field is constituted in the interaction" (p. 463). So, whilst we may not be spending all (and then some) of our grant on a ticket to the ISS, we are able to feel its effect, and be attentive to the ways in which it produces social relations through the practices of the communities that relate to the ISS. As this chapter will demonstrate, such attentiveness relies on traditional ethnographic participant observation as well as innovative methodologies involving online or dispersed communities. The chapter considers each researcher's work in turn, leading us through anthropological issues of the body in space, rapid manufacturing technologies and novel materialities, notions of universal humanity, utopia, the apocalypse, God, transcendence, and more.

We start with the work of the principal investigator, **Victor Buchli**, whose work examines the new manufacturing economy and material culture of low Earth orbit (LEO) aboard the ISS. The terrestrial locus of this research is Silicon Valley and its wider communities. Buchli, through his participant observation with a number of companies and communities of makers involved in the development of 3D printing and other forms of manufacturing aboard the ISS, examines the ways in which microgravity is exploited as a resource in the creation of a new and distinctive extraterrestrial material culture and its novel scales. The methodology involves following an artefact as it is designed, rendered, coded, provisioned, and printed and further how it is used, talked about, and employed in not only a utilitarian way but as an object that elicits narratives of exciting and expansive futures and the creation of new terrestrial communities and the materialisation of novel moral orders. The 3D-printed objects are used in education and public outreach as they are perceived to symbolise a potential for a future where the conditions of manufacturing and making are radically different as well as creating the basis for new desired forms of democratisation. But alongside, the research also examines how new forms of exclusion are suggested both terrestrially and extraterrestrially as they emerge within this new manufacturing economy in microgravity.

In particular, Buchli's research examines the relationship between this new manufacturing economy with its terrestrial and extraterrestrial uses and the new communities and diverse emergent oecumenes it strives to engender. It examines how the extraterrestrial manufactured object is to be integrated into terrestrial daily life and how this suggests challenges to our understanding of the terrestrial body and the very conditions of terrestrial daily life itself.

One of the emerging issues of this research is the role of the 'extreme' that characterises the extreme environment of LEO and how this notion of the 'extreme' is instrumental in producing a distinctive manufacturing economy in LEO and in particular new understandings of extraterrestrial craftsmanship and their geographies and attendant moral orders as they emerge in LEO. Alongside the manufacturing case studies examined, the research is positioned to understand ethnographically and historically the transition from centralised state-sponsored and developed space technologies and their communities to decentralised commercial technologies that characterise the historical shift taking place at present in the transition from nation-state–sponsored space sectors to commercial ones. This current moment, seen as a 'tipping point' within manufacturing communities, is examined historically against the backdrop of Alexander MacDonald's (2017) proposal of a "long space age". Tensions between state and private interests going back to the nineteenth century and earlier and in particular in relation to the invocations of settler narratives of expansion and infrastructural development are echoed in current narratives of commercial space communities as they emerge in Silicon Valley and its wider penumbra.

Aaron Parkhurst approaches the ISS as a medical anthropologist and a scholar of the anthropology of the human body. The human body, with its biological limitations and needs, its sociality and materiality, and its politics, serves as a profound ethnographic nexus that brings together and entangles cultures of medicine, ecology, technology, and well-being. The human body in space is no different from the body on Earth in this regard. Yet, low Earth orbit, and the vast potentials and challenges of other worlds, provide novel conditions and contexts within which one can test, witness, and challenge the parameters of the body and the ways in which it moves through complex systems of social relations.

Parkhurst's research broadly explores the social anatomy of the human body as it is constructed and envisioned by extraterrestrial living and space futurism. It is, at first, anatomical—in as much as its starting points are the biological structures and material of the human body and form, and the challenges that the complex material ecology of outer space creates for human biology. However, the anthropological purpose of charting this anatomy is threefold. Such an ethnographic project affords the opportunity to chart new trajectories for biosocial thinking, and to continue to develop work in "medical materialities" (Parkhurst and Carroll 2019) and material culture studies. In addition, however, the body in space, and life-science research conducted on the ISS, positions the study of human anatomy and biological processes as analogues for the future of human exploration of the cosmos. Embedded in such science and research are, ultimately, the complex systems of social, medical, political, and economic relations on Earth which flow through and emanate from the human body. Parkhurst's research demonstrates how the body, medicine, and life-science research on the ISS is as much an analogue of Earth itself as it is for off-world living on the Moon, Mars, and beyond.

Parkhurst is conducting ethnographic fieldwork on bodily practice and research on the ISS, with grounded partner institutions and laboratories that run experiments and collect data on medical and life-science projects on board the station, and with industry and culture that finds itself intersecting with the human body in space in complex and often unpredictable ways. These laboratories focus on cognition, nutrition, adaptation to gravity, smell and taste, cell biology, arthritis, lung function, and other bodily functions and activity in space. Parkhurst's research takes particular purchase in Scheper-Hughes and Lock's (1987) important prolegomenon on the mindful body. A study of the human body in space offers new directions and challenges for this call. The effects of space exploration on the human body are profound. There is an extensive field of aerospace medicine that focuses on the extensive physiological and neurological effects of long-term space travel. Similarly, life-science research on the ISS offers a future for medicine on Earth and interventions on the human body. An anthropology of the body places the human figure in space as central to the cultivation of systems of social relations. However, the relationship between these systems and the body is reciprocal. That is to say, a study of the parameters of the human body, indeed even its anatomy and medical needs, informs the environment of the ISS, just as the ISS itself cultivates and makes the human body. The prolegomenon, and its attention to "the body politic", reminds its readers of this partnership. The affective turn within anthropology and geography of the last few decades is also challenged and furthered by the context of outer space living. Parkhurst and Jeevendrampillai (2020) have begun to answer this challenge in what they frame as an *"anthropology of gravity"*, showing how the ISS offers "a unique vantage point through which to consider the human relationship to emotion, cognition, and the curation of social relations via experiences of the body in different gravitational environments". In this way, Parkhurst's research borrows and extends Valerie Olson's framework of *ecobiopolitics* (2010), testing these ideas further through a study of space medicine, space psychology, and analogue curation.

Finally, Parkhurst's research aims to further the interdisciplinary dialogue between medical anthropology and material culture studies. There are many potential aspects of this dialogue to explore, not least because of the hybrid forms of living that arise between the human body and the built environment in space, but also because of the way the human body on the ISS is captured in data and countless research projects within life sciences and then transformed into applications, politics, and economic activity back on Earth. In this regard, the body aboard the ISS undergoes complex transformations, movements, and disjunctures as it weaves through systems of social relations on Earth. Through methodologically 'following the object', Parkhurst's ethnography charts and follows these movements to uncover the gambit of social interactions and productivities that might arise. Parkhurst's ethnography is, then, at its core, a social life of the spacefarer's body.

Giles Bunch's work considers the labour undertaken by ground teams supporting operations on the ISS. Bunch's ethnography follows the training programme for ground support personnel (GSP) and analyses the organisational cultures at two key European human spaceflight centres: the European Astronaut Centre in Cologne and the Columbus Control Centre in Oberpfaffenhofen, Germany. Bunch's ethnography is analytically focused on two core processes. The first seeks an understanding of how GSP working on the Columbus project (Europe's main contribution to the ISS) are trained to support the operations and science conducted within this module of the ISS. The second seeks to develop an organisational ethnography of the culture of European human spaceflight projects.

Bunch is currently conducting ethnography within ESA training centres and control rooms operated by DLR (Deutsches Zentrum für Luft- und Raumfahrt, the German Aerospace Centre), participating in training events, observing simulations, and learning about the lives of the trainees and instructors. Employing participant-observation methods, Bunch is following the journey taken by GSP trainees from their recruitment to learning about spaceflight systems and operating procedures, participating in simulations and role-plays, and finally their certification, from a trainee's perspective. This data, taken alongside surveys and interviews with trainees and experienced GSP, will illuminate the training processes within the elite world of human spaceflight and consider them through anthropological lenses of learning and practice and themes of games and play, role-play, and care.

For example, Bunch participated in classes that gamified the training process. These events relate to sociological arguments on the nature of games and play such as those found in Caillois (2001), which have also been developed by Woodcock (2019). Aligning with Caillois's description of play as consisting of elements of choice, uncertainty, rules, and separation from other forms of work, these gamified simulations complexify such elements when 'play' becomes a means for delineating and reinforcing desired behaviours in training events. The study speaks to recent scholarship on practice and material culture (Mohan and Douny 2020), in its examination of the ways that GSP's engagement with control-room equipment, understanding of 'procedures', communication 'over the loops' (a term applying to the method of voice communication between console positions, operations centres, and the ISS), and understanding of each system changes over the course of a training cycle. Further, Bunch's fieldwork is conducted in the second year of the Coronavirus pandemic and provides details of how national, organisational, and personal protective measures altered GSP training into what his informants call an "off-nominal" state. His informants describe the diminishing of what Hutchins and Klausen name as "distributed cognition", where "intersubjective understanding" (1996: 23) would otherwise be fostered through gesture and nonverbal cues both in training settings and in control rooms.

The second key theme in Bunch's study takes his experiences of GSP training at the European Astronaut Centre and Columbus Control Centre as a point of entry for developing an organisational ethnography of human spaceflight in the European context. This aspect of the study adapts methods of the workers' inquiry (Marx 1880; Woodcock 2014) to analyse the social composition and labour relations within and across the different centres. Recent debates in organisational anthropology (Caulkins and Jordan 2013) and recent sociological accounts of spaceflight projects in the United States (Vertesi 2020) are developed in the European context to better understand how organisational cultures shape the material and political qualities of mature and future human spaceflight projects.

This two-fold ethnography examining the GSP training processes for ESA's human spaceflight project and the organisational culture of the centres in which this takes place addresses a gap in the literature. Recent scholarship looking at the European spaceflight project has focused on the Moon as a target for future exploration (Alvarez 2020) or on the astronaut and the work of control rooms (Patarin-Jossec 2021). Bunch's ethnography contributes to this work through its close examination of a training cycle for teams working on a mature project, as well as attending to the organisational cultures of the centres in which this activity takes place.

Adryon Kozel's work considers how the ISS is constituted through its wider publics, particularly through social media channels and enthusiast groups. While the ISS is inhabited by a small group of astronauts and cosmonauts in constant contact with the respective mission controls of the ISS, the station is also experienced vicariously through social media platforms by a large and diverse online public. Many millions of individuals follow the combined social media feeds of astronauts, cosmonauts, and agencies on Instagram, Twitter, YouTube, and other platforms on a daily basis. Participatory social media events, such as livestreams, 'watch parties', amateur radio contacts, and astronaut Q&As occur around such things as launches, spacewalks, and dockings. In these events, large terrestrial populations of space enthusiasts are co-present and co-temporal with the inhabitants of the ISS even if they are not co-local.

Through such events, the ISS is felt through social energy, shared enthusiasm, and emotional experiences. Kozel's work is attentive to how enthusiasm is generated, sustained, and experienced in these more attenuated forms of inhabitation of the ISS. Considering how the ISS may be conceptualised through such experiences, which are deeply emotional, corporeal, and social, expands our conception of inhabitation of the ISS in ways that consider wider publics and social imaginaries. This develops existing work in the social sciences, particularly the research of geographer Hilary Geoghegan (2008, 2013) on technology enthusiast groups and emotional geographies, demonstrating how enthusiasm moves beyond a biological 'feeling' for something and becomes intentional and measurable through such practices as collecting, curating, communicating, and performing enthusiasm in social settings. This harnessing of enthusiasm through social and cultural practice has also been explored in studies of fandom communities (Jindra 1994;

Shefrin 2004) and of national space programmes, including the Mexican Space Agency (Johnson 2020, this volume), NASA (Launius 2017), the European Space Agency (Detsis and Detsis 2013), Roscosmos (Siddiqi 2011), and the Indian and Chinese space programmes (Abraham 2020).

Kozel has embedded herself in space-enthusiast organisations and communities of media producers both online and offline. Her fieldwork involves extended field visits to sites of rocket launches such as Cape Canaveral in Florida and the SpaceX launch facility in Boca Chica, Texas. From here Kozel works with key influencers to trace how the experience of witnessing rocket launches is captured, curated, and circulated through social media to wider public. Inspired by Durkheim's writings on the forms of social energy, or "collective effervescence", generated around particular events and gatherings of people (2008 [1912]), this methodology traces forms of social energy from the event of the launch through various media to wider publics. These publics, who are predominantly but not exclusively North American, are able to form common bonds and affiliations through shared experiences and excitement about common space futures.

Further to social media influencers and launch events, Kozel will also consider the social media of astronauts and space agencies in terms of how such outputs are received, engaged with, and generative of enthusiasm, or not, amongst a wider public and space communities. Enthusiasm for ISS-related events is contextualised within a wider lineage of enthusiasm about space inhabitation that looks forward to habitats on the Moon or Mars, for which the ISS is often seen as a stepping stone.

In its engagement with dispersed communities that rely predominantly on polymedia outputs, the work builds upon an existing body of work in digital anthropology and participatory digital methods (Madianou and Miller 2012; Gubrium and Harper 2016). This research investigates how online communities of enthusiasts develop around scientific events and projects such as rocket launches and analogue missions, and intersects with wider discussions in the social sciences about how space science generates and engages with particular demographics and publics, and in doing so, advances narratives of inclusion, participation, and democratic accountability (cf. Messeri 2017).

In his consideration of the implications of the ISS for notions of territory, belonging, and humanity, **David Jeevendrampillai** engages with another group of space enthusiasts who call themselves the 'Overviewers'—people who advocate for the widespread public engagement and shared experience of the 'overview effect'. Frank White, the journalist who coined the term, defines the overview effect as the theory that an astronaut's experience of spaceflight fundamentally changes their worldview (1998). The overview effect is premised on an embodied response to seeing Earth from space. It is understood as consisting of a psychological shift in thinking via a realisation and recalibration of relations to the planet, to other humans, and to existence brought about through seeing from a particular perspective—outer space.

A lineage in this form of perspectivism can be drawn back to the early images of Earth from space, namely from the Apollo mission. On 24 December 1968, NASA astronaut Bill Anders, aboard Apollo 8, captured NASA image AS08-14-2383, a photograph popularly known as *Earthrise*. The image shows the three-quarters-illuminated Earth rising over the Moon's surface. It was described by nature photographer Galen Rowell (1999) as "the most influential environmental photograph ever taken". The image is perhaps only matched by NASA image AS17-148-22727, or *The Blue Marble*, an image of the whole Earth from eighteen thousand miles away, captured by the crew of Apollo 17 on 7 December 1972. These images of Earth are purportedly the most widely circulated and viewed photographic images in history (Poole 2008). Bill Anders (2018) himself has stated that "we set out to explore the Moon and instead discovered the Earth". Today, imagery of the Earth from space is everywhere—as desktop backgrounds, in advertising, featured in movies. Seeing the Earth from space has gone from being a novel experience to an ingrained part of the popular imagination. Staring at the Earth from the ISS cupola window is reportedly the favourite pastime of the crew aboard the ISS. A recent study of crew photography of Earth showed that around 84.5% of the almost two hundred thousand photos taken over eight expeditions on the ISS were taken by the crew in their free time (Robinson et al. 2011).

Historian Benjamin Lazier (2011) argues that imagery of the Earth from space has filtered into the popular imagination and given rise to new scales of social relations. This can be seen in what he calls 'globe talk'. Here, a global sense of relation to other humans is carried by concepts and conversations around such things as globalisation, global climate change, global citizenship, cosmopolitanism, and the Anthropocene. The planetary scale of social relations that perspectives of Earth from space enable are central to the concerns of the Overviewers. The group's members have various projects such as working with schools, releasing public media such as podcasts, books, blogs, VR experiences, and art projects that foreground the overview effect in order to bring about a particular relationship to the planet and humanity. The influence of such imagery on planetary imagination has been written about by geographers (Cosgrove 1994; Jazeel 2011), philosophers (Chakrabarty 2021; Oliver 2015; Sloterdijk 2014), and many others. However, Jeevendrampillai's work offers an ethnographic tracing of how concepts such as global cosmopolitanism, utopian space futures, and ecological planetary thinking inform a sense of planetary subjectivity within the Overviewers, brought about through a direct engagement with the visual cultures of spaceflight.

Whereas Jeevendrampillai examines a secular ideology of spaceflight, **Jenia Gorbanenko** is interrogating a religious perspective on the ISS and space exploration. Of the religious traditions in space, those of the Russian Orthodox Christians are particularly prominent, and they are the focus of her work. Cosmonauts travel on rockets that are blessed by Russian Orthodox priests from the temples near cosmodromes. Icons and saints' relics are regularly sent up to the ISS together with cosmonauts or cargo. Frequently appearing in photographs of the ISS, the space icons have been examined systematically by the International Space Station Archaeological Project (ISSAP) (Salmond, Walsh, and Gorman 2020). In LEO, these icons and relics orbit the Earth in what some consider a religious procession called a *krestnyy khod* (Rus., lit. cross procession). Historically, these processions have taken place on foot to mark significant celebrations or to pray in times of hardship. More recently, with the development of new technologies of mobility, the processions have also been taken on cars, motorbikes, and planes. Now the ISS allows for a procession around the entirety of the globe. Most icons and relics are eventually brought back down to Earth after a few months of a continuous *krestnyy khod*. Consequently, they are either returned or gifted to terrestrial Russian Orthodox communities or individuals. For instance, the newly built temple in Star City, where cosmonauts train and the Russian ground control centre is located, hosts many of these religious objects returned from space. Cosmonauts attend services there, and some of them even assist in the altar.

In the social sciences, the question of the relationship between space exploration and religion is most frequently discussed from the standpoint that treats and critiques space exploration as akin to religion (Bjørnvig 2018; Geppert 2018; Harrison 2013; Siddiqi 2008, 2010; Traphagan 2014, 2016). Gorbanenko, in contrast, follows in the steps of a growing group of anthropologists of religion in space looking at the dialogue between space exploration and religion (Bialecki 2020; Bielo 2020; Weibel 2019) and new space religious practices (Weibel 2015, 2016, 2017).

Gorbanenko's ethnographic research traces the objects, people, and sites that tie the ISS to the Russian Orthodox terrestrial communities. She considers how through religious practices, religious material culture in space, and new religious sites the Church initiates a dialogue between the scientific and the religious cosmology. She explores how they function as interfaces that invite the cosmonauts, space scientists, engineers, and other members of the space community to contemplate their space and scientific pursuits from within the perspectives of religious cosmology.

As part of this project, Gorbanenko seeks to unpack how the Church foregrounds the primacy of religious cosmology over the scientific. In his autobiography, Yuri Gagarin—a Soviet cosmonaut and the first human in space—described how upon his return home he was asked by the villagers if he had seen God in the skies and how he had to disappoint them (Gagarin 1961). Over the years, many variations of the phrase "Gagarin flew to space and didn't see God there" have been used for Soviet scientific atheism propaganda. Today, rather than disputing the claim that Gagarin did not see God in space, Russian Orthodox voices often quote Gagarin's contemporary, Iosif Chernyy, a metropolitan of Alma-Aty and Kazakhstan, for saying that Gagarin could not have seen God there, but "God saw him. And blessed him" (Koroleva 2012). With this simple perspectival shift—and other religious practices that Gorbanenko observes in the field—the Russian Orthodox Church underlines the constraints of the human condition and the unknowability of God, thus emphasising the limits of the scientific way of knowing.

The scientific and technological discoveries of the space age prompt the Church to respond to the changing times, in some cases incorporating them into religious practices, such as *krestnyy khod*. Russian Orthodoxy is neither a static nor a homogeneous religious tradition, and there have not been any top-down directives on the Church's position with regard to space exploration yet, so this incongruous, slowly creeping process of adjustment is uncentralised. It is mostly the clergy and laypeople, at the interfaces between religion and the space community, who interrogate the space age on religious terms. In her work, Gorbanenko is focusing on these discursive practices through which the Russian Orthodox dispel with beliefs deemed outdated and incorporate modern inventions.

Space debris has been a much-discussed topic and problem in LEO (Damjanov 2017; Gorman 2019; Rand 2019; Reno 2020). **Makar Tereshin**'s work examines a little-known aspect of the space economy revolving around terrestrial communities in Kazakhstan who make their living by salvaging space rocket boosters discarded after the launches from Baikonur Cosmodrome. In particular, Tereshin examines the communities and economies that form around the space debris and the manner in which salvaging links scavengers within the wider nexus of space societies. At the heart of this project is the relationship of modernising national space narratives, both Russian and Kazakh, that literally 'touch down' in these marginal communities and the way in which space debris and hazardous waste shape these terrestrial communities between Earth and LEO. Here utopian ideals of spaceflight come into stark contrast with these emergent practices.

For those who live in the vicinity, the rocket debris fallout zones present a profoundly ambiguous landscape, which simultaneously threatens their health and well-being through invisible pollution and offers the means to sustain one's household by salvaging rocket boosters or making health claims on the state. After the dissolution of the Soviet Union and the abrupt state restructuring that followed, local communities have had to rely on precarious formal employment and state subsidies, coupled with seasonal work and other informal economic activities. In this context, the space debris complements the villagers' attempts to navigate their lives amidst social and political uncertainty. At the same time, as they encounter the debris, scavengers have to negotiate their exposure to the toxic fuel residuals. Although it is certain that some boosters were fuelled with highly toxic heptyl, it remains unclear whether propellant residuals in the salvaged wreckage are heptyl or kerosene. These toxic exposures often transform communities' subjectivities and engage them in ongoing political and ecological debates between Kazakhstan and Russia.

Tereshin's research explores how local communities inhabit and negotiate such indeterminate borders, spaces, and materials, and what such edgework can tell us about the larger polities to which they belong. Post-Soviet crisis and uncertainty are intensified in the fallout zones where the edges of imperial histories, nation-states, outer space, and pollution coalesce (cf. Stoler 2008). Space debris points to the material, ecological, and technological processes that support the work of the ISS and creates the possibility for critiquing the reliance of space exploration on waste and sacrifice of lands. Bringing the focus of space exploration back down to Earth demonstrates that outer space's frontiers are also firmly grounded in geopolitical borders. Space infrastructure is typically built in lands that are geographically and politically marginal—or made so through processes of evacuation and ruination (cf. Lerner 2010; Redfield 2000; Mitchell 2017). This provides us with a chance to investigate if and how such space materials and technologies mediate different moral-political projects at different scales: advancing space exploration, subjecting remote communities to systematic inequality and environmental injustice, and providing a livelihood. Through a focus on scavengers' encounters with the space debris within fallout zones one can consider space exploration through the analytical lenses of modernity, mobility, ecology, and pollution, as well as forms of spatial, political, and ecological alienation.

Conclusions

The work presented here outlines the ongoing research conducted by the core ETHNO-ISS group and its associates. Dr. Jo Aiken, an earlier member of the core team, examined the organisational culture of NASA at the Johnson Space Center and how the ISS in LEO is integrated within the terrestrial infrastructure at Johnson. She continues with the project now as an Honorary Research Fellow while working as a Senior Researcher for Google. Paddy Edgley has also contributed to the project's research community through his work on his LAHP[2]-funded PhD project, which considers the ways in which amateur astronomers in London engage with the cosmos, the ISS, the city, and the Earth through stargazing. Soon, Aliça Okumura-Zimmerlin, building on her current doctoral research as embedded anthropologist on JAXA's Hayabusa 2 mission, will join the team as a postdoctoral researcher based in Tsukuba examining JAXA's Kibo module and the way in which JAXA and its affiliates shape the future beyond LEO at the ISS.

Whilst no researcher is aboard the ISS in person, many are co-present with it through studies of its emergent material economies, whether through manufacturers with their independent 'mission controls'; the ways in which the ISS challenges conceptions of the body; how it is understood and engaged with by its staff and controllers; its publics and social media image; the communities that engage with its contributions to the visual cultures of Earth; the way it intersects and affects religious practices and the economies of debris; and related positions of state and subject formation. Overall this is a study of the ways in which the ISS has exerted, and continues to exert, influence over terrestrial social life and expands it. The ETHNO-ISS project does not claim to be an exhaustive study of the ISS; rather we aim to refract the phenomenon of the ISS to show the multitude of ways in which the ISS can orientate rich ethnographic engagements with the forms of social relations that emerge from outer space activity. In this regard, the project works within an exciting lineage and burgeoning field of space anthropology which has seen rapid growth over recent years, in particular, due to influential works from authors such as Lisa Messeri (2016), Valerie Olson (2018), Deborah Battaglia (with Valentine and Olson 2015), Janet Vertesi (2015, 2020), David Valentine (with Olson and Battaglia 2009), and many more (see references). However, our perspectives are heavily influenced by our location and training at UCL anthropology. In particular, we have a strong analytical focus on material culture, the digital, the body, and infrastructure. Through teaching, we have spawned a range of master's dissertations and projects that go to demonstrate the breadth of opportunity that thinking about the anthropology of space, as an understudied anthropological region, can provide.

Acknowledgements

The work of the authors is funded by the European Research Council Advanced Grant "ETHNO-ISS: An Ethnography of an Extra-terrestrial Society: The International Space" Station (grant agreement number 833135), with the exception of Makar Tereshin's work, which is supported by the UK Arts and Humanities Research Council (grant number AH/R012679/1) and is affiliated with ETHNO-ISS.

Notes

1 Our travel budget falls rather short. At the time of writing, one 'night' in the ISS costs a tourist 35,000 USD. The bulk of the cost is the taxi ride: travelling with SpaceX costs US$55 million.
2 London Arts and Humanities Partnership: https://www.lahp.ac.uk/student/patrick-edgley/.

References

Abraham, Itty. 2020. "The Future of a Promise and the Promise of a Future: China and India." *Inter-Asia Cultural Studies* 21 (1): 93–98. https://doi.org/10.1080/14649373.2020.1720390.

Alvarez, Tamara. 2020. *The Eighth Continent: An Ethnography of Twentieth-First Century Euro-American Plans to Settle the Moon*. PhD Dissertation, The New School for Social Research.

Anders, William. 2018. *50 Years After 'Earthrise,' A Christmas Eve Message from its Photographer*. Accessed 18 November 2021. https://www.space.com/42848-earthrise-photo-apollo-8-legacy-bill-anders.html.

Battaglia, Debbora, 2012. "Coming In at an Unusual Angle: Exo-Surprise and the Fieldworking Cosmonaut." *Anthropological Quarterly* 85 (4): 1089–106. https://doi.org/10.1353/anq.2012.0058.

Battaglia, Debbora, David Valentine, and Valerie Olson. 2015. "Relational Space: An Earthly Installation." *Cultural Anthropology* 30 (2): 245–56. https://doi.org/10.14506/ca30.2.07.

Beaulieu, Anne. 2010. "Research Note: From Co-location to Co-presence: Shifts in the Use of Ethnography for the Study of Knowledge." *Social Studies of Science* 40 (3): 453–70. https://doi.org/10.1177/0306312709359219.

Bialecki, Jon. 2020. "Future-Day Saints: Abrahamic Astronomy, Anthropological Futures, and Speculative Religion." *Religions* 11 (11): 612. https://doi.org/10.3390/rel11110612.

Bielo, James S. 2020. "Incorporating Space: Protestant Fundamentalism and Astronomical Authorization." *Religions* 11 (11): 594. https://doi.org/10.3390/rel11110594.

Bjørnvig, Thore. 2018. "Transcendence of Gravity: Arthur C. Clarke and the Apocalypse of Weightlessness." In *Imagining Outer Space: European Astroculture in the Twentieth Century*, edited by Alexander C. T. Geppert, 141–62. London: Palgrave Macmillan.

Buchli, Victor. 2020. "Extraterrestrial Methods: Towards an Ethnography of the ISS." In *Lineages and Advancements in Material Culture Studies*, edited by Timothy Carroll, Antonia Walford and Shireen Walton, 17–32. London: Routledge.

Caillois, Roger. 2001. *Man, Play and Games*. Translated by Meyer Barash. Urbana; Wantage: University of Illinois Press.

Carroll, Timothy, Antonia Walford, and Shireen Walton, eds. 2021. *Lineages and Advancements in Material Culture Studies: Perspectives from UCL Anthropology*. New York: Routledge. https://doi.org/10.4324/9781003085867.

Caulkins, Douglas, and Ann Jordan, eds. 2013. *A Companion to Organizational Anthropology*. Hoboken, NJ: Wiley.

Chakrabarty, Dipesh. 2021. *The Climate of History in a Planetary Age*. Chicago, IL: University of Chicago Press.

Cosgrove, Denis. 1994. "Contested Global Visions: One-World, Whole-Earth, and the Apollo Space Photographs." *Annals of the Association of American Geographers* 84 (2): 270–94. https://doi.org/10.1111/j.1467-8306.1994.tb01738.x.

Damjanov, Katarina. 2017. "Of Defunct Satellites and Other Space Debris: Media Waste in the Orbital Commons." *Science, Technology, & Human Values* 42 (1): 166–85. https://doi.org/10.1177/0162243916671005.

Detsis, Bianca and Emmanouil Detsis. 2013. "The Benefits Brought by Space—General Public versus Space Agencies Perspectives." *Acta Astronautica* 88: 129–37. https://doi.org/10.1016/j.actaastro.2013.03.021.

Dickens, Peter, and James S. Ormrod, eds. 2016. *The Palgrave Handbook of Society, Culture and Outer Space*. Basingstoke: Palgrave Macmillan.

Durkheim, Émile. 2008 [1912]. *The Elementary Forms of Religious Life*. Oxford: Oxford University Press.

Gagarin, Yuri. 1961. *Doroga v Kosmos: Rasskaz Letchika-Kosmonavta SSSR*. Moscow: Pravda.

Geoghegan, Hilary. 2008. *The Culture of Enthusiasm: Technology, Collecting and Museums*. PhD Dissertation, Royal Holloway, University of London.

Geoghegan, Hilary. 2013. "Emotional Geographies of Enthusiasm: Belonging to the Telecommunications Heritage Group." *Area* 45 (1): 40–46. https://doi.org/10.1111/j.1475-4762.2012.01128.x.

Geppert, Alexander C. T. 2018. "European Astrofuturism, Cosmic Provincialism: Historicizing the Space Age." In *Imagining Outer Space: European Astroculture in the Twentieth Century*, edited by Alexander C. T. Geppert, 3–28. London: Palgrave Macmillan.

Gorman, Alice. 2009. "The Gravity of Archaeology." *Archaeologies* 5 (2): 344–59. https://doi.org/10.1007/s11759-009-9104-1.

Gorman, Alice. 2019. *Dr Space Junk Vs the Universe: Archaeology and the Future*. Cambridge: MIT Press.
Gorman, Alice, and Justin Walsh. Forthcoming. "Archaeology in a Vacuum: Obstacles to and Solutions for Developing a Real Space Archaeology." In *Archaeology Out-of-the-Box*, edited by Hans Barnard and Ran Boytner. Los Angeles, CA: Cotsen Institute of Archaeology Press. https://doi.org/10.48550/arXiv.2009.02471.
Gubrium, Aline, and Krista Harper. 2016. *Participatory Visual and Digital Methods*. London: Routledge.
Harrison, Albert A. 2013. "Russian and American Cosmism: Religion, National Psyche, and Spaceflight." *Astropolitics* 11 (1–2): 25–44. https://doi.org/10.1080/14777622.2013.801719.
Helmreich, Stefan. 2011. "From Spaceship Earth to Google Ocean: Planetary Icons, Indexes, and Infrastructures." *Social Research* 78 (4): 1211–42. https://doi.org/10.1353/sor.2011.0042.
Hutchins, Edwin, and Tove Klausen. 1996. "Distributed Cognition in an Airline Cockpit." In *Cognition and Communication at Work*, edited by Yrjö Engeström and David Middleton, 15–34. Cambridge: Cambridge University Press.
International Space Station Program Science Forum. 2019. *International Space Station Benefits for Humanity*. Edited by Julie Robinson and Kirt Costello. Houston, TX: NASA. 3rd edition. https://www.nasa.gov/sites/default/files/atoms/files/benefits-for-humanity_third.pdf
https://www.nasa.gov/sites/default/files/atoms/files/benefits-for-humanity_third.pdf.
Jazeel, Tariq. 2011. "Spatializing Difference beyond Cosmopolitanism: Rethinking Planetary Futures." *Theory, Culture & Society* 28 (5): 75–97. https://doi.org/10.1177/0263276411410447.
Jindra, Michael. 1994. "Star Trek Fandom as a Religious Phenomenon." *Sociology of Religion* 55(1): 27–51. https://doi.org/10.2307/3712174.
Johnson, Anne. 2020. "Space Cultures and Space Imaginaries in Mexico: Anthropological Dialogues with the Mexican Space Agency." *Acta Astronautica* 177: 398–404. https://doi.org/10.1016/j.actaastro.2020.08.002.
Koroleva, Vera. 2012. *Svet Radosti v Mire Pechali: Mitropolit Alma-Atinskij i Kazakhstanskij Iosif*. Moscow: Palomnik.
Launius, Roger. 2017. "NASA's Quest for Human Spaceflight Popular Appeal." *Social Science Quarterly* 98(4): 1216–32. https://doi.org/10.1111/ssqu.12473.
Lazier, Benjamin. 2011. "Earthrise; or, The Globalization of the World Picture." *American Historical Review* 116 (3): 602–30. https://doi.org/10.1086/ahr.116.3.602.
Lerner, Steve. 2010. *Sacrifice Zones: The Front Lines of Toxic Chemical Exposure in the United States*. Cambridge: MIT Press.
MacDonald, Alexander. 2017. *The Long Space Age*. New Haven, CT: Yale University Press.
Madianou, Mirca, and Daniel Miller. 2012. "Polymedia: Towards a New Theory of Digital Media in Interpersonal Communication." *International Journal of Cultural Studies* 16 (2): 169–87. https://doi.org/10.1177/1367877912452486.
Marcus, George E. 1995. "Ethnography in/of the World System: The Emergence of Multi-sited Ethnography." *Annual Review of Anthropology* 24 (1): 95–117. https://doi.org/10.1146/annurev.an.24.100195.000523.
Marx, Karl. 1880. "A Workers' Inquiry." *La Revue Socialiste*, 20 April 1880. https://www.marxists.org/archive/marx/works/1880/04/20.htm.
Messeri, Lisa. 2016. *Placing Outer Space: An Earthly Ethnography of Other Worlds*. Durham, NC: Duke University Press.
Messeri, Lisa. 2017. "Extra-terra Incognita: Martian Maps in the Digital Age." *Social Studies of Science* 47 (1): 75–94. https://doi.org/10.1177/0306312716656820.
Mitchell, Sean T. 2017. *Constellations of Inequality: Space, Race and Utopia in Brazil*. Chicago, IL: The University of Chicago Press.
Mohan, Urmila, and Laurence Douny, eds. 2020. *The Material Subject: Rethinking Bodies and Objects in Motion*. London: Routledge.
Nixon, David. 2016. *International Space Station: Architecture beyond Earth*. London: Circa Press.
Oliver, Kelly. 2015. *Earth & World: Philosophy After the Apollo Missions*. New York: Columbia University Press.
Olson, Valerie. 2010. "The Ecobiopolitics of Space Biomedicine." *Medical Anthropology* 29(2): 170–93. https://doi.org/10.1080/01459741003715409.
Olson, Valerie. 2018. *Into the Extreme: U.S. Environmental Systems and Politics Beyond Earth*. Minneapolis: University of Minnesota Press.
Parkhurst, Aaron, and Timothy Carroll, eds. 2019. *Medical Materialities: Toward a Material Culture of Medical Anthropology*. London: Routledge.
Parkhurst, Aaron, and David Jeevendrampillai. 2020. "Towards an Anthropology of Gravity: Emotion and Embodiment in Microgravity Environments." *Emotion, Space and Society* 35: 1–7. https://doi.org/10.1016/j.emospa.2020.100680.

Patarin-Jossec, Julie. 2021. *La Fabrique de L'astronaute: Ethnographie Terrestre de la Station Spatiale Internationale.* Europes, terrains et sociétés. Paris: Editions PETRA.
Poole, Robert. 2008. *Earthrise: How Man First Saw the Earth.* New Haven, CT: Yale University Press.
Rand, Lisa Ruth. 2019. "Falling Cosmos: Nuclear Reentry and the Environmental History of Earth Orbit." *Environmental History* 24 (1): 78–103. https://doi.org/10.1093/envhis/emy125.
Redfield, Peter. 2000. *Space in the Tropics: From Convicts to Rockets in French Guiana.* Berkeley, CA: University of California Press.
Reno, Joshua O. 2020. *Military Waste: The Unexpected Consequences of Permanent War Readiness.* Oakland, CA: University of California Press.
Robinson, Julie A., Kelly J. Slack, Valerie A. Olson, Mike H. Trenchard, Kim J. Willis, Pam J. Baskin, and Jennifer E. Boyd. 2011. "Patterns in Crew-Initiated Photography of Earth from the ISS—Is Earth Observation a Salutogenic Experience?" In *Psychology of Space Exploration: Contemporary Research in Historical Perspective,* edited by Douglas A. Vakoch, 79–101. Washington, DC: NASA History Program Office. https://history.nasa.gov/SP-4411.pdf.
Rowell, Galen. 1999. "The Earthrise Photograph." *Australian Broadcasting Corporation.* Accessed 1 November 2021. https://www.abc.net.au/science/moon/earthrise.htm.
Salmond, Wendy, Justin Walsh, and Alice Gorman. 2020. "Eternity in Low Earth Orbit: Icons on the International Space Station." *Religions* 11 (11): 611. https://doi.org/10.3390/rel11110611.
Scheper-Hughes, Nancy, and Margaret M. Lock. 1987. "The Mindful Body: A Prolegomenon to Future Work in Medical Anthropology." *Medical Anthropology Quarterly* 1 (1): 6–41. https://doi.org/10.1525/maq.1987.1.1.02a00020.
Sheetz, Michel. 2021. "NASA Wants Companies to Develop and Build New Space Stations, With Up to $400 Million Up for Grabs." *CNBC,* 27 March. Accessed 20 November 2021. https://www.cnbc.com/2021/03/27/nasa-commercial-leo-destinations-project-for-private-space-stations.html.
Shefrin, Elana. 2004. "Lord of the Rings, Star Wars, and Participatory Fandom: Mapping New Congruencies Between the Internet and Media Entertainment Culture." *Critical Studies in Media Communication* 21 (3): 261–81. https://doi.org/10.1080/0739318042000212729.
Siddiqi, Asif. 2008. "Imagining the Cosmos: Utopians, Mystics, and the Popular Culture of Spaceflight in Revolutionary Russia." *Osiris* 23 (1): 260–88. https://doi.org/10.1086/591877.
Siddiqi, Asif. 2010. *The Red Rockets' Glare: Spaceflight and the Soviet Imagination, 1857–1957.* Cambridge: Cambridge University Press.
Siddiqi, Asif. 2011. "Cosmic Contradictions: Popular Enthusiasm and Secrecy in the Soviet Space Program." In *Into the Cosmos: Space Exploration and Soviet Culture,* edited by James T. Andrews and Asif A. Siddiqi, 47–76. Pittsburgh: University of Pittsburgh Press.
Sloterdijk, Peter. 2014. *Globes: Macrospherology.* Translated by Wieland Hoban. South Pasadena, CA: Semiotext(e).
Stewart, Kathleen. 2014. "Tactile Compositions." In *Objects and Materials: A Routledge Companion,* edited by Penny Harvey, Eleanor Casella, Gillian Evans, Hannah Knox, Christine McLean, Elizabeth B. Silva, Nicholas Thoburn and Kath Woodward, 119–27. London: Routledge. https://doi.org/10.4324/9780203093610.
Stoler, Ann Laura. 2008. "Imperial Debris: Reflections on Ruins and Ruination." *Cultural Anthropology* 23 (2): 191–219. https://doi.org/10.1111/j.1548-1360.2008.00007.x.
Traphagan, John W. 2014. *Extraterrestrial Intelligence and Human Imagination.* New York: Springer.
Traphagan, John W. 2016. *Science, Culture and the Search for Life on Other Worlds.* New York: Springer.
Valentine, David, Valerie A. Olson, and Debbora Battaglia. 2009. "Encountering the Future: Anthropology and Outer Space." *Anthropology News* 50 (9): 11–15. https://doi.org/10.1111/j.1556-3502.2009.50911.x.
Van Duijn, Sarah. 2020. "Everywhere and Nowhere at Once: The Challenges of Following in Multi-sited Ethnography." *Journal of Organizational Ethnography* 9 (3): 281–94. https://doi.org/10.1108/JOE-12-2019-0045.
Vertesi, Janet. 2015. *Seeing Like a Rover: How Robots, Teams, and Images Craft Knowledge of Mars.* Chicago, IL: University of Chicago Press.
Vertesi, Janet. 2020. *Shaping Science: Organizations, Decisions, and Culture on NASA's Teams.* Chicago, IL: University of Chicago Press.
Weibel, Deana L. 2015. "'Up in God's Great Cathedral': Evangelism, Astronauts, and the Seductiveness of Outer Space." In *The Seductions of Pilgrimage: Sacred Journeys Afar and Astray in the Western Religious Tradition,* edited by Michael A. Di Giovine and David Picard, 233–56. Farnham: Ashgate Publishing.
Weibel, Deana L. 2016. "Pennies from Heaven: Objects in the Use of Outer Space as Sacred Space." In *Touching the Face of Cosmos: On the Intersection of Space Travel and Religion,* edited by Paul Levinson and Michael Waltemathe, 33–44. New York: Fordham University Press.

Weibel, Deana L. 2017. "Space Exploration as Religious Experience: Evangelical Astronauts and the Perception of God's Worldview." *The Space Review*, 21 August. Accessed 15 July 2021. http://www.thespacereview.com/article/3310/1#idc-cover.

Weibel, Deana L. 2019. "Astronauts vs. Mortals: Space Workers, Jain Ascetics, and NASA's Transcendent Few." *The Space Review*, 8 April. Accessed 15 July 2021. https://www.thespacereview.com/article/3690/1.

White, Frank. 1998. *The Overview Effect: Space Exploration and Human Evolution*. Reston, VA: AIAA.

Woodcock, Jamie. 2014. "The Workers' Inquiry from Trotskyism to Operaismo: A Political Methodology for Investigating the Workplace." *Ephemera* 14 (3): 493–513.

Woodcock, Jamie. 2019. *Marx at the Arcade: Consoles, Controllers, and Class Struggle*. Chicago, IL: Haymarket Books.

34
PLANT BIOLOGISTS AND THE INTERNATIONAL SPACE STATION
Institutionalising a Scientific Community

Paola Castaño

Introduction

The International Space Station (ISS) is commonly defined as a laboratory in low Earth orbit for hundreds of experiments, and scientific research is one of the main justifications for its existence. According to NASA's official numbers and categorisations, 2354 experiments have been conducted to date on the ISS across biology and biotechnology, technology development and demonstration, educational activities and outreach, human research, physical sciences, and Earth and space sciences. For biology, there is a dual purpose in the study of microbes, plants, and animals on the ISS: to understand how they respond to the space environment, and to enable "significant scientific and technological advances that enable exploration and benefit life on Earth" (NASA 2022b).

Faced with the diversity of fields and the breadth of the objectives, this chapter focuses on one group of scientists that conducts experiments funded by NASA on the ISS: plant biologists. The chapter shows how their work is embedded in the multifaceted processes of justification, experimental activities, and valuation of the station as a setting for their research, and follows one key process that institutionalises their role: the Decadal Survey on Biological and Physical Sciences Research in Space 2023–2032. The chapter provides a sociological characterisation of these scientists' work in relation to the ISS and the Decadal process. From there, it addresses the broader issue of how to conceptualise communities of scientists, a long-standing object of interest in social studies of science.

The Decadal is a report commissioned by NASA to the National Academies of Sciences, Engineering, and Medicine (NASEM) where "the community"[1] in a scientific field funded by the agency comes together in a two-year process to define and recommend "a compelling research portfolio for the coming decade that represents prioritised activities" (presentation by committee chair, NASEM 2020a). The Decadal presupposes the existence of scientists actively invested in conducting research on the ISS (and beyond) and prescribes a particular type of cohesiveness in their research programme amenable to considerations of relevance and priority. The process also presupposes and prescribes a commitment amongst them to get involved in writing white papers, attending forums and workshops, listening to briefings from NASA about capabilities and restrictions, and participating in committees and panels to craft and review the report.

The concept of institutionalisation points to stabilisation, and even formalisation, of roles, practices, and understandings in particular organisational forms (Johnson 2007; Stinchcombe 1965), and the Decadal certainly serves those purposes, as I illustrate. However, these processes are not "once-and-for-all events", entail "diverse degrees of openness or closure" (Benzecry 2014:

DOI: 10.4324/9781003280507-39

170), and require ongoing validations (Glaeser 2014). Along these lines, the examination of plant space biologists and of the Decadal that I propose here invites a more processual and open-ended understanding of scientific communities, seeing them in motion through their multiple interdependencies and as simultaneously embedded in various social worlds.

There is a recent and lively social-scientific interest in the ISS that, with diverse methods and emphases exemplified in this volume, converges in studying the station as a habitat with a subsequent focus on crew members and ground operations teams and an interest in the use of the ISS for scientific research (Buchli 2020; Damjanov and Crouch 2019; Jeevendrampillai et al. this volume; Patarin-Jossec 2018, 2021; Walsh and Gorman 2021; Gorman this volume). The use of the ISS for scientific research is certainly mentioned in these studies, but there are currently no social scientific studies dedicated to the ISS as a platform for science, the actual process of conducting those experiments, or the scientists who engage in this peculiar line of research. My work (Castaño 2021, in preparation) has centered on NASA experiments on the ISS expanding the notion of the laboratory to grasp the social life of experiments, which includes processes of justification, design, execution, and value assessment. From this background, in this chapter, I shift attention to research communities as another point of entry into the sociological study of science on the ISS.

Regarding space scientists, the spotlight has been on the work of astronomers, planetary scientists, and astrobiologists (Burton this volume; Messeri 2016; Thomson this volume; Vertesi 2015, 2020). In the few exceptions that have looked at the life sciences in space (Mackowski 2022; Olson 2018), plant biologists do not play a prominent role. Their work, however, presents a very illuminating case because it exemplifies some enduring tensions—in human spaceflight and in scientific research more broadly—between big promises, heterogeneous activities, and operational constraints.

The chapter is based on NASA's and the Decadal's official documents and white papers, and observations during public online events held in 2020 and 2021. In what follows, first, I provide an overall characterisation of plant biology on the ISS in terms of its promises, the challenges in the execution of experiments, various framings of assessment, and timeframes. Second, I examine the 2023 Decadal process in terms of how it summons and formalises "the community" as a collective with a research programme that can be projected into the future (at least the next decade), and as part of a much larger set of interconnected institutional strains. Third, drawing on processual and formal sociology, I outline a framework for the characterisation of scientific communities and consider its pertinence for the study of this and other research communities. Finally, I propose some potential directions for the continuation of research about scientific communities in space science.

Plant Biology on the ISS

Many of the ambitious aspirations of human spaceflight converge in the study of plants on the ISS. Research in this field is multipurpose and aims to cover the spectrum from fundamental to applied science, with applications both for space exploration and for life on Earth. Regarding fundamental science, the key questions are about the effects of the multiple stressors of spaceflight on living organisms. One of those stressors, gravity, has been at the centre of the research agenda in studies of model organisms, particularly *Arabidopsis thaliana* (Wyatt and Kiss 2013; Cannon et al. 2015). Regarding applications for space exploration, promises around plants are far-reaching. As stated by a prominent researcher in the field, "plants allow us to be explorers" (Paul 2020), a phrase that conveys the projected role of plants in habitation of low Earth orbit (LEO), the Moon, and Mars in various fronts: the provision of fresh food and pharmaceuticals, bioregenerative life-support systems, and psychological well-being (Johnson et al. 2021; Kordyum and Hasenstein 2021). And regarding Earth, space plant science promises applications in controlled-environment agriculture

(Wheeler 2012), plant resilience amid climate change (Philips 2013; Chandler et al. 2020[2]), and public engagement with science through educational and citizen-science activities (Raymond and Rubinson 2020).

While the predominant imagery is overconfident regarding the various and significant roles of plants, the realities of experimentation on the ISS are more modest. The station is not just the extraterrestrial extension of laboratory practices "as we know them" but a qualitatively different endeavour that requires multiple compromises from all sides. From the researchers' standpoint, sending plant experiments to the space station is, as described during an interview, "an endurance sport". More specifically, in the words of an experienced researcher in the field: "Compared to typical laboratory research, spaceflight research is difficult and typically requires a significant effort of time on the part of investigators. PIs [principal investigators] can wait many years before their experiment flies in space" (Kiss 2015: 274). Additionally, growing plants in a multi-stressor environment require laborious experimental designs to disentangle the biological effects of the concomitant and atypical conditions of airflow, irrigation, gravity, and radiation on the plants.

Alongside their data-collection activities for hundreds of experiments in diverse fields, crew members on the ISS must perform tasks of physical preservation with exercise routines, cleaning, maintenance of hardware and facilities inside and outside the station, cargo management, and public engagement. In consequence, the execution of experiments takes place in a context of significant limitations in which researchers also have to minimise their requirements in terms of crew time and skill, hardware size, and sample return.

Next to these operational complexities, the diversity of its aims and activities situates the ISS at the intersection of various stakeholders and audiences with their diverse criteria of assessment. The scientific element of the ISS brings together fields that diverge in terms of logistical requirements, but also of meanings of scientific achievement and recognition. Even though "firsts" make it to the news (Yuhas 2015), most of the key elements of work in this field have been part of incremental—and often heterogeneous—processes of elucidation of systems and processes.

As horticulturists, botanists, plant physiologists, plant pathologists, molecular biologists, and microbiologists, researchers sending plants to the ISS belong to their laboratories at various universities and research centres, and to their field and subfield communities. And, in consistency with the Earth-bound goals, some of them also have intersections with the fields of controlled-environment agriculture, climate-change agriculture, and education. They are also part of larger constituencies of space science, mainly the American Society for Gravitational and Space Research (ASGSR), the Committee on Space Research (COSPAR), and the NASEM committees and panels where they advocate for their research in the larger policy world of human spaceflight.

And to add one last element to this landscape, there is a pressing fact for these scientists: the ISS has a finite lifespan determined by the endurance of its physical structure and the political agreements that sustain the programme. As the estimated end of the ISS in 2030 draws nearer, and with the uncertain move to "commercial destinations" in LEO (NASA 2021), plant scientists confront the need to complete as many investigations as possible on the station, while working already on what will come next, and contributing to archiving and curating the resulting data for experimental design and future reutilisation. The asynchronous ticking clocks marked by these horizons imbue the ISS scientific programme with a sense of urgency to "deliver" in its many fronts.

From the ISS side, accommodating the operational demands of everyday life on the station with research across multiple fields is an intricate process. This endeavour involves actors at all levels of the programme issuing calls for proposals, assembling review panels, assessing operational feasibility and safety aspects of selected experiments, developing hardware and instructions for the execution of data-collection tasks on board, scheduling those tasks, and arranging the preservation and return samples. And before all those tasks, there is the fundamental question about the science worth doing out there in the first place given the scarce opportunities and high costs. In this last regard, the Decadal offers the due process to answer that question through a "community-driven" process that aims to formulate "a consensus on the most compelling science questions for the decade ahead in each of the disciplines" (NASEM 2020a). The Decadal is a momentous instance where the expectations of the scientists and the possibilities of NASA and the ISS meet and engage in a mutually shaping negotiation.

Decadal Survey on Biological and Physical Sciences Research in Space 2023–2032

In the words of the head of the Committee on Biological and Physical Sciences in Space (CBPS) at NASEM, the Decadal represents "an important moment in our community's business, in our science, and the way we conduct our science" and a rare instance "when we do have control over our future" (NASEM 2020a). The Decadal is a textbook case of what some scholars call "instruments to govern science" (Gläser and Laudel 2016: 155): it provides a formally structured procedure with rules for participation, it stabilises some key definitions, and its outcome is treated by all parties involved as a guide for action. The key question is, of course, how the governing process takes place considering the particularities of plant science and the scope of the Decadal.

The Decadal's statement of task sets a high bar:

> The study will generate consensus recommendations to implement a comprehensive strategy and vision for a decade of transformative science at the frontiers of biological and physical sciences research in space. The results of the study will assist NASA in defining and aligning biological and physical sciences research to uniquely advance scientific knowledge, meet the needs of human and robotic exploration missions, and provide terrestrial benefits.
>
> *(NASEM 2020b)*

NASA's reliance on "the community" to identify and prioritise "leading-edge scientific questions" (NASA SMD 2022) is an elaborate process in all fields, but alignment in this context is even more demanding because of the disciplinary breadth: microbiology, animals, plants, materials, biophysics, combustion, complex fluids, fluid physics, and education, diversity, equity, and inclusion. The report is written by a committee supported by input from panels on biology; physics; engineering and science interface; and technical, risk, and cost evaluation. In other words, "the science case" cannot exist in isolation from exploration goals, costs, risk, technological readiness, and the balance between the numerous elements of the portfolio.

Decadal surveys in scientific fields supported by NASA[3]—the first of which started in 1964—are firmly established in astronomy and astrophysics, with seven to date, resulting in the recommendation of programmes like the Hubble and James Webb space telescopes. Planetary science and heliophysics have three Decadals, the first starting in 2003, and Earth Science and Applications from Space has three starting in 2007. In this context, the one for biology and physics in space is a newcomer, with only one report in 2011 as the antecedent for the 2023–2032 one.

The 2011 Decadal represented NASA's effort to bring back researchers to the agency after a series of major budget cuts that almost eradicated entire research portfolios (Mackowski 2022: 260–9). That report was framed along the lines of research that enables space exploration—i.e., "that is needed to develop advanced exploration technologies and processes, particularly those that are profoundly affected by operation in a space environment"—and research enabled by access to space—i.e., "that takes advantage of unique aspects of the space environment to significantly advance fundamental scientific understanding" (Committee for the Decadal Survey 2011: 2). The recommendations for plant science were mostly outlined in relation to microbiology and included the use of the ISS as a "Microbial Observatory"; the implementation of cell and molecular biology studies "to monitor evolution of genomic changes … in spaceflight"; "a systematic suite of plant biology experiments to elucidate mechanisms by which plants respond and adapt to spaceflight, and to facilitate their eventual use in Bioregenerative Life Support Systems"; and a major move towards open science "facilitating open public and scientist access ... to data and results by building data archives and data management tools, especially in the area of [omics]" (Sato, Malarik, and Kundrot 2020: 6).

Six years after this publication, NASA requested a midterm assessment of the Decadal's implementation. This report, published in 2018, stated some actions taken by the agency: a "modest" budget increase for life and physical sciences, a broader engagement with "the U.S. science community outside NASA to join in this research" (Committee on a Midterm Assessment 2018: 2), and the start of a new division. The Space Life and Physical Sciences Research and Applications Division (SLPSRA) was created within the Human Exploration and Operations (HEO) Mission Directorate to organise and centralise research opportunities, and began the implementation of GeneLab, viewed by the report as an "extremely positive outcome in support of open science within NASA" (ibid.: 35). Amongst the setbacks identified, NASA continued to have "dissimilar and often confusing" approaches to fund investigations given the little coordination between the directorates managing them, and that "frequent exploration strategy changes result in unclear traceability between research investigations and exploration needs" (ibid.: 3).

And then it was time for another Decadal with more changes. In 2020 the biology and physics portfolio moved from HEO to the Science Mission Directorate (SMD). This change also entailed the dissolution of SLPSRA and the creation of the new Division of Biological and Physical Sciences (BPS) while the Human Research Program (HRP) remained under HEO. The display of acronyms here explains the absence of "life sciences" from the title of the Decadal and the fact that it does not cover human research. BPS now sits next to astrophysics, planetary science, heliophysics, and Earth science at SMD, divisions that have not only a long tradition when it comes to this process but much more focused research portfolios and far more resources.[4] In one of his early addresses to the BPS community, the associate administrator at SMD, an astrophysicist, exemplified "transformative science" and missions that "move to the unknown" with the Parker Solar Probe mission that, at the time, was on its way to meet the Sun. Beyond this not-reading-the-room moment, the effort to align the BPS Decadal with the rest of SMD was clear throughout the Decadal process with astronomers and planetary scientists providing advice and lessons learned to the biologists and physicists (NASEM 2021a).

Communications about the 2023 Decadal began during the ASGSR's annual meeting in November 2019 where representatives of the CBPS and NASEM's Space Studies Board encouraged "community participation". Soon after, this participation faced the challenge of the first two years of the COVID-19 pandemic and the move to online interactions. This fact allowed for a larger number of participants than in the previous Decadal, with up to 450 attendees in some of the public webinars and workshops.

But of course, the number of online attendees is not—per se—an indicator of participation, and the process required some "community-gathering" resourcefulness. ASGSR, assisted by the consultant firm Knowinnovation, took on this task creating a series of online materials and organising town halls and interactive writing workshops for the ten fields pertinent to the Decadal. The format for the town halls involved a series of short "Plus 10" talks where researchers were asked to predict their work in the next ten years as a basis for generating discussions about the most important ideas or future directions and to bring people together to develop white papers (ASGSR 2020).

But white papers also came with some changes in this Decadal. The major novelty was the concept of "research campaigns" (RC) which involve the "integration of multiple missions, disciplines, and platforms to tackle an overarching scientific or exploration goal" pointing to "transformative science" (NASEM 2020a). While the process also called for the traditional format for topical single-project white papers, researchers were encouraged to team up and make proposals for these RCs with projected costs of up to US$100 million. This language—and these budgets, while still very small compared with other SMD divisions—are certainly new for these fields alongside the Directorate's push to "invest more and more directly toward breakthroughs", even leading, in the words of its director, to Nobel-prize science (ibid.).

Substantive agreement on what "pioneering scientific discovery" and "transformative science" mean across all the BPS disciplines is almost impossible, as the director of the division acknowledged when introducing the concept: "Are things driving to a goal? Should there even be a goal in one area? Some areas are quite mature, others are nascent, and for others, the goal-driven aspect might not be in play" (ibid.). Rolling up his epistemological sleeves, he described three ways of conceiving "transformative science". First is "when you change a paradigm and things begin to operate in a different manner than was conceived before one launched the line of research". Second is when "you are making a substantial update to an understanding that opens up a whole line of research". Third, for exploration "this could mean the difference between something you couldn't do yesterday but you can do tomorrow". In sum, the goal of RCs is "not incremental progress" but "moving the boundaries forward. It's more disruptive" (ibid.).

By the December 2021 deadline, seventy[5] RC papers were submitted and nine of them were about plants. Two stood out because of the groups that came together to write them and the way in which they provided diagnoses of the current state of their field and projections about what is required for "transformative science".

The first addressed plant diseases in space with a focus on crop production (Schuerger et al. 2021). The fifteen authors included the two PIs with more research experience in crops and model organism research respectively on the ISS alongside experts in omics, flight operations, plant pathology, and virology, and two astrobiologists. After identifying seventeen knowledge gaps (KGs) about the increasing virulence of pathogens in space and the decreasing mechanism of resistance in plants, the authors called for an acceleration of this research: "There are too many KGs related to disease development in space to continue at the pace that is currently funded" (ibid.: 5). The paper proposes that plant biology and pathology become a coordinated effort between ground and flight research and across flight investigations. And, certainly thinking big beyond current ISS operations, it proposed a dedicated flight RC with astronauts "trained in the operation of all plant biology hardware during one, 6-month mission … [2028–2032; US$30 million for a dedicated RC mission]" (ibid.: 6).

The second paper was authored by twenty-two members of the GeneLab Plants Analysis Working Group (AWG). They included a former SLPSRA director, two of the most awarded PIs in model organism experiments, and the core group of participants in this group. In their view:

> Our current knowledge of plant spaceflight responses is drawn from a disparate series of experiments performed by a wide range of experimenters, each pursuing a particular hypothesis or goal. This kind of analysis remains important, but a complementary systematic research approach is needed to make even more rapid progress in our understanding of plant spaceflight responses in order to deliver the critical science required to engineer for the coming near-term exploration opportunities.
>
> *(Porterfield et al.: 2)*

Their RC proposal centred on reference experiments for multi-omics studies covering model organisms, through leafy greens and tuber crops to cereals, aiming for "a series of well-replicated studies of some carefully chosen model plants and crops where the latest analytical approaches, including omics-level analyses, could be employed to provide a comprehensive view of how these plants respond to growing in space" (ibid.: 2). This proposal also stressed the need for ground-based research and the rapid release of data "for community-wide analyses" following the principles of open science.

From these two examples, "frontiers", "disruption", and "transformation" mean something different from SMD standards for other space sciences and even from what the director of BPS was outlining as he introduced the RC concept. For the most part, the goal in these papers is integration across the disparate elements of the research portfolio and a more systematic research programme with reproducible activities, systematic ground studies, sustained funding, and implementation of open science data management.

By early 2022, with panels formed and papers submitted, the public part of the Decadal ended as "deliberations are held in closed sessions to ensure independence from external influence" (NASEM 2020a). As I write, it is unclear if or how any of the white papers' ideas will make it to the final document. Like all agreements involving people with different aims and finite resources, the one that will materialise in the report will likely be imperfect, yet much better than a unilateral imposition. Thus, the institutionalising work achieved by the Decadal is threefold: it provides a formally structured procedure with rules for participation, it stabilises some key definitions, and its outcome is treated by all parties involved, particularly by NASA, as a guide for action.

Alongside these elements of stabilisation, the Decadal also has different moments of uncertainty and openness. While there are formal procedures, they also incorporate ways to update the process itself and expand the actors involved. While aiming to stabilise definitions, RCs, for instance, were interpreted differently by the various actors. And, while the Decadal is a guiding instrument, it is not a fully binding one since NASA, in response to governmental directions, can change goals and along with them the terms of pertinence for the science it funds. In consequence, the multifaceted aspects of plant science, the Decadal, and the scientists participating in these processes provide a good standpoint to reexamine the conceptualisation of scientific communities.

The Key Word Is "Community"

The expression "scientific community" is used loosely throughout the Decadal process on different scales: it is used to treat those who study quantum entanglement and the determination of the virulence of bacteria as part of a collective, and—in the case of plant science—to group those who study crops and model organisms. Then, of course, when we turn to sociology things do not get much clearer given that "definitions of community are almost as varied as the number of sociologists attempting to deal with the concept" (Bates and Bacon 1972: 371).

To restate that scientific knowledge is the product of people working together in a volume about social research is like making a statement about the existence of water amongst marine biologists. But that apparently obvious fact about the social nature of scientific knowledge carries enormous complexity and has involved social scientists in vastly different interpretive and explanatory tasks.[6] There are two common threads in the scholarship about scientific communities: first, the preoccupation with boundaries, demarcations, and identities; and, second, the appearance that some modes of practice operate to the exclusion of others (norms/counter-norms, collaboration/competition), disregarding the fact that "researchers can and do move between different approaches and models of work, depending on circumstances, including making smaller-scale changes and using more than one approach simultaneously" (Ankeny and Leonelli 2016: 20).

The case of space plant scientists is sensitising to the fact that scientific communities are not bounded units with features, and that a shift of focus in our conceptualisations can be fruitful. I find my grounds for that shift of focus in two central ideas in processual and formal sociology: Norbert Elias's concept of figurations and Georg Simmel's intersection of social circles. For Elias, figurations are dynamic "webs of interdependencies formed among human beings" that connect them. By interdependencies, he meant structures of mutually oriented and dependent roles that emerge from plans and intentions but not directly from any single one of them (Elias 2000 [1939]: 312). The concept represents a way out of the static category of society and incorporates the fact that the nature and intensity of these interdependencies change with context and time, and that these webs are also made up of power imbalances. And here some of Simmel's views come in handy as a way to represent those figurations. Conceived to conceptualise individuality, his image of the multiplicity of human associations represented by social circles is useful to think about the specificities of groups at the intersections of those circles. The more circles there are, the more unlikely that a group or an individual will "manifest the same combination of groups, that this many circles would ... intersect at one point" (Simmel 2009 [1890]: 372).

Along these lines, my schematic understanding of plant biologists as a research community around the ISS places them at the intersection of, at least, eight circles that are, broadly conceived, social worlds. In alignment with the characterisation I provided about plant biology on the ISS, each circle[7] can be described in terms of its promises and expectations, practices, criteria of valuation, and timeframes. What is specific about space plant scientists is the unique and irreplicable overlap of circles in their work, and what is common—and typical—with respect to other scientists is that there are those circles (Figure 34.1).

To put some of these pieces in motion, for instance, there are different forms of interaction amongst plant scientists. Researchers growing crops on the station can rely more on collaborative work with microbiologists, behavioural researchers, and fluid physicists for issues of food safety, psychological benefit, and irrigation (Massa 2021a, 2021b) than with researchers exploring the molecular biology guiding the altered growth of plants in microgravity (Gilroy 2021). Whereas for the first, achievement is an *Escherichia coli*–free lettuce leaf (Dixit et al. 2021) eaten by a smiling astronaut accustomed to packaged foods, for the others it is gaining some clarity about the role

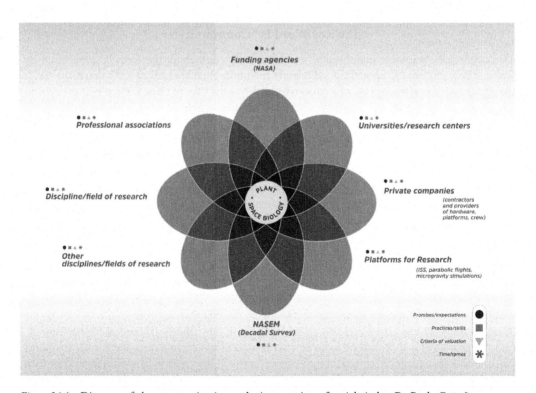

Figure 34.1 Diagram of plant space scientists at the intersection of social circles. By Paola Castaño.

of epigenetic DNA methylation in guiding the adaptive responses of *Arabidopsis* seedlings in the ISS (He et al. 2022). When summoned at another institutional level, for example joining forces for an RC in the new Decadal, plant scientists (like many other scientists and scholars) efficiently become compatriots of a cause. A prominent scientist in this field can testify before Congress to support the extension of the space station representing the entire ISS research community sitting next to representatives of the programme (Castaño 2021: 687–8), and in another instance, like the Decadal he can sit across them discussing opportunities given many restrictions for their experiments.

Whereas the ISS as a platform for experiments comes with an expiration date and criteria for allocating resources at NASA can shift in relatively short timescales, a university is a more constant infrastructure for research, and there are traceable genealogies of mentorship in this field. And the temporalities of these processes coexist in the careers of these scientists with their own ticking clocks regarding processes like completion of doctorates, career stability, and tenure. In fact, there is a running comment amongst plant biologists who have worked on the ISS about the fact that it is hard to get tenure only based on experiments in space.

In terms of criteria of valuation, whereas assessments of accuracy and originality can only be made by a small subset of colleagues, there are other modes of recognition. Alongside their academic awards, prominent members of this community have received NASA Exceptional Public Service medals (Murray 2022) and awards at the ISS R&D conference for significant scientific results (Huot 2015). However, in the shifting balances between these worlds, some of these scientists have moved out of academia to work for commercial providers, private companies, or NASA itself as staff scientists. Finally, some researchers in this field have given their TED talk about growing plants in space. In that context, the audience is likely to be more impressed by an asteroid named after the speaker (COSPAR 2021) than by their "Spaceflight Studies Identify a Gene Encoding an Intermediate Filament Involved in Tropism Pathways" article finally being published after two rounds of review in *Plant Physiology and Biochemistry* (Shymanovich et al. 2022).

The sociological implications of these observations seem obvious but are not without consequence. First, they require moving away from the notion of scientific communities sharing "a culture" because, next to the substantive expertise in their specialties, in each one of the worlds in which they participate, diverse norms, theories, trust, skill, collaboration, and competition matter differently. Second, the more productive focus is thus not on boundaries and demarcations but in the shifting interdependencies of scientists with heterogeneous social worlds. And, third, grasping these shifting interdependencies requires an intersituational approach (Tavory 2016: 95) observing concrete settings to grasp the changing equilibria amongst their interdependencies. In sum, thinking intersituationally entails following the many moving pieces of these worlds in the work of scientists, and doing so without dwelling in the complexities, but with some tools and principles of navigation at hand.

Final Considerations

The world of spaceflight is full of undaunted uses of the word "we" to universalise particular standpoints. The most prevalent one is the invocation of "humanity" in depictions of futures in space as presumably desired by all members of our species. But pretty much any other form of existing or invoked human grouping is susceptible to the "we" move. This plasticity of uses is a matter of serious consequence and significant interest for many social scientists. In the case of plant biologists, the goal of this chapter has been to see their "we" in motion considering their work in terms of its far-reaching promises, opportunities and constraints, diverse criteria of assessment, and timeframes.

The study of scientific communities, with all our conceptual disagreements about them in the social sciences, will remain central to understanding the social nature of knowledge production. The approach proposed here identified some principles and levels of analysis, which I expect to use and refine in my ongoing work with plant space biologists. One component of this study entails detailed attention to what these scientists, in their various realms of belonging, accept or question morally and politically about the nature of their work and its societal impact. This is the realm of ideas about what is inevitable, what is desirable and possible, and what is not even worth arguing about across their various social worlds. Scientists sending plants to space can seem too niche for big questions about values in science, but this is a field where "colonisation", "multiplanetary species", "climate change", "food security", "planet B", and "dinosaurs became extinct because they didn't have a space programme" are part of the available vocabularies of pertinence.

The approach suggested here can provide a way to examine some of the key puzzles of two processes that are shaping space science: commercialisation and open science. The first is a hazy term that covers the spectrum from space agencies contracting companies that build and sell hardware to the expansion of the aerospace industry towards ownership of infrastructures and a single billionaire enforcing his vision of life on another planet just because he can afford the rockets to get there. What this uncertain and seemingly inexorable scenario means for scientific research opens key questions that require attentiveness to the who, where, and how: In what specific arrangements do commercial platforms in space increase opportunities and expedience for the execution of experiments? Is this a path towards even more heterogeneity, with researchers becoming paying customers of private companies without many of the review procedures that currently characterise the process of sending an experiment to space? Will consensus-building instruments like the Decadal become obsolete in these scenarios? Does the increasing number of academic researchers in biology that become biotech entrepreneurs—some of them panel members in the Decadal (NASEM 2021b)—imply the transition of this field towards "industrial science" or "post-academic science"?

Open science is another polysemic concept that intersects with crucial issues for scientific practice (Levin et al. 2016) and is increasingly an institutional mandate to guarantee public access to data and publications from federally funded research (Holdren 2013; Nelson 2022). Alongside existing programs like GeneLab for space biology, in 2022 NASA started a multiyear effort to "Transform to Open Science" across all the disciplines it supports. Under which forms of governance can science be "open" across the agency and particularly in plant space biology? What are the implications of "opening science" for research on plants in terms of standardisation across experiments and more collaborative work amongst scientists? How would these processes reshape "the community" and expand the social worlds that constitute it?

Just like the organisms they study, plant biologists' survival in space depends on adaptations to many changing conditions of their environment. This survival is fundamentally tied to their actions, visions about the future, and concomitant value commitments. Thus, a research agenda in the social sciences about them needs less attributions of coherence and more traceable paths through the shifting interdependencies that make up their work.

Acknowledgements

This work was supported by the Newton International Fellowship from the British Academy (grant no. NF171553, 2018–2021) and by the Philosophy of Open Science for Diverse Research Environments project funded by the European Research Council under the European Union's Horizon 2020 research and innovation programme (grant no. 101001145, 2022–2025).

Notes

1 "Community" ranks high on the list of the malleable vocabularies of the social sciences. At the core of this malleability is both the fact that the term is used by the actors in the fields of practice under study and that we sociologists cannot give it up as an analytical category. This chapter lives with that fact trying to distinguish the "emic" and "etic" (Mostowlansky and Rota 2020) uses of the term.
2 "Rocket Science: The Effect of Spaceflight on Germination Physiology, Ageing, and Transcriptome of *Eruca sativa* Seeds" is surely the best paper title in the history of plant space biology.
3 For a description of the structure of the process and the configuration of committees in Astronomy, which also applies to the Biology and Physics Decadal, see Groswald and Smith (2013).
4 For Fiscal Year 2022, the NASA Science Mission Directorate budget is US$7,614 million, out of which $3,120 is for Planetary Science, $2,061 for Earth Science, $1,393 for Astrophysics, $778 for Heliophysics, $175 for the James Webb Space Telescope, and $82.5 for Biological and Physical Sciences (NASA 2022a).
5 All papers are public, and the complete database has been published by NASA and NASEM. While the database lists 89 RC papers, seven of them are repeated and twelve, most from the same author, fall remarkably outside the boundaries of the Decadal, addressing issues like God, the nature of men and women, and shoe design for Space Shuttle astronauts (the Shuttle was retired from operations in 2011).
6 There is significant diversity of approaches in the study of scientific communities ranging from the foundational and influential concern with the institutional norms shared by scientists (Merton 1942; Polanyi 1962) and contestations of that framework in terms of counter-norms (Mitroff 1974) to dismissals altogether that normative commitments are the right level of analysis to engage with the communitarian nature of scientific research and that norms are no more than "vocabularies of justification" (Mulkay 1976). There are also theory-based understandings of scientific communities in terms of thought collectives (Fleck 2008 [1935]) and paradigms (Kuhn 2012 [1962]). Other social scientists have focused their inquiries on communities around the issue of social ties expressed in publications (Crane 1972), networks (Mulkay, Gilbert, and Woolgar 1975), trust (Shapin 1994; Collins et al. 2022), competition for prestige and control over their fields (Bourdieu 1975), and gift-based exchanges (Hagstrom 1975).
7 For purposes of the illustration, the circles have the same size and can appear as coherent wholes, but they differ and each one is also the product of its own unique intersections. Acknowledgment to Andrés Barriga who turned my rudimentary hand drawing into that graph.

References

Ankeny, Rachel A., and Sabina Leonelli. 2016. "Repertoires: A Post-Kuhnian Perspective on Scientific Change and Collaborative Research." *Studies in History and Philosophy of Science Part A* 60 (December): 18–28. https://doi.org/10.1016/j.shpsa.2016.08.003.
ASGSR, American Society for Gravitational and Space Research 2020. *ASGSR Decadal Survey Workshop Series*. https://asgsr.org/decadal-talks/.
Bates, Frederick L., and Lloyd Bacon. 1972. "The Community as a Social System." *Social Forces* 50 (3): 371–79. https://doi.org/10.2307/2577041.
Benzecry, Claudio E. 2014. "An Opera House for the 'Paris of South America': Pathways to the Institutionalization of High Culture." *Theory and Society* 43 (2): 169–96. https://doi.org/10.1007/s11186-014-9214-7.
Bourdieu, Pierre. 1975. "The Specificity of the Scientific Field and the Social Conditions of the Progress of Reason." *Social Science Information* 14 (6): 19–47. https://doi.org/10.1177/053901847501400602.
Buchli, Victor. 2020. "Extraterrestrial Methods: Towards an Ethnography of the ISS." In *Lineages and Advancements in Material Culture Studies*, edited by Timothy Carroll, Antonia Walford, and Shireen Walton, 17–32. London: Routledge. https://doi.org/10.4324/9781003085867.
Cannon, Ashley E., Mari L. Salmi, Gregory Clark, and Stanley Roux. 2015. "New Insights in Plant Biology Gained from Research in Space." *Gravitational and Space Research* 3 (2): 3–19. https://doi.org/10.2478/gsr-2015-0007.
Castaño, Paola. 2021. "From Value to Valuation: Pragmatist and Hermeneutic Orientations for Assessing Science on the International Space Station." *The American Sociologist* 52 (4): 671–701. https://doi.org/10.1007/s12108-021-09515-y.
Castaño, Paola. "Beyond the Lab: The Social Life of Experiments on the International Space Station." In preparation.

Chandler, Jake O., Fabian B. Haas, Safina Khan, Laura Bowden, Michael Ignatz, Eugenia M. A. Enfissi, and Frances Gawthrop, et al. 2020. "Rocket Science: The Effect of Spaceflight on Germination Physiology, Ageing, and Transcriptome of *Eruca sativa* Seeds." *Life* 10 (4): 49. https://doi.org/10.3390/life10040049.

Collins, Harry, Robert Evans, Martin Innes, Eric B. Kennedy, Will Mason-Wilkes, and John McLevey. 2022. *The Face-to-Face Principle: Science, Trust, Democracy and the Internet*. Cardiff: Cardiff University Press. https://doi.org/10.18573/book7.

Committee for the Decadal Survey on Biological and Physical Sciences in Space, National Research Council 2011. *Recapturing a Future for Space Exploration: Life and Physical Sciences Research for a New Era*. Washington, DC: National Academies Press. https://doi.org/10.17226/13048.

Committee on a Midterm Assessment of Implementation of the Decadal Survey on Life and Physical Sciences Research at NASA, Aeronautics and Space Engineering Board, Space Studies Board, Division on Engineering and Physical Sciences, and National Academies of Sciences, Engineering, and Medicine 2018. *A Midterm Assessment of Implementation of the Decadal Survey on Life and Physical Sciences Research at NASA*. Washington, DC: National Academies Press. https://doi.org/10.17226/24966.

COSPAR, Committee on Space Research 2021. *International Cooperation Medal*. Last modified 2 June 2021. https://cosparhq.cnes.fr/awards/international-cooperation-medal/.

Crane, Diana. 1972. *Invisible Colleges: Diffusion of Knowledge in Scientific Communities*. Chicago, IL: University of Chicago Press.

Damjanov, Katarina, and David Crouch. 2019. "Orbital Life on the International Space Station." *Space and Culture* 22 (1): 77–89. https://doi.org/10.1177/1206331217752621.

Dixit, Anirudha R., Christina L. M. Khodadad, Mary E. Hummerick, Cory J. Spern, LaShelle E. Spencer, Jason A. Fischer, and Aaron B. Curry, et al. 2021. "Persistence of *Escherichia coli* in the Microbiomes of Red Romaine Lettuce (*Lactuca sativa* Cv. 'Outredgeous') and Mizuna Mustard (*Brassica rapa* Var. Japonica)—Does Seed Sanitization Matter?" *BMC Microbiology* 21 (1): 289. https://doi.org/10.1186/s12866-021-02345-5.

Elias, Norbert. 2000 [1939]. *The Civilizing Process: Sociogenetic and Psychogenetic Investigations*. Malden, MA: Blackwell Publishers.

Fleck, Ludwik. 2008 [1935]. *Genesis and Development of a Scientific Fact*. Chicago: University of Chicago Press.

Gilroy, Simon. 2021. "Spaceflight-Induced Hypoxic-ROS Signaling (APEX-05), 2017–2019." *NASA Space Station Research Explorer*. Last modified 14 May 2021. https://www.nasa.gov/mission_pages/station/research/experiments/explorer/Investigation.html?#id=1775.

Glaeser, Andreas. 2014. "Hermeneutic Institutionalism: Towards a New Synthesis." *Qualitative Sociology* 37 (2): 207–41. https://doi.org/10.1007/s11133-014-9272-1.

Gläser, Jochen, and Grit Laudel. 2016. "Governing Science: How Science Policy Shapes Research Content." *European Journal of Sociology* 57 (1): 117–68. https://doi.org/10.1017/S0003975616000047.

Groswald, Lewis, and David H. Smith. 2013. *Lessons Learned in Decadal Planning in Space Science: Summary of a Workshop*. Washington, DC: National Academies Press. https://doi.org/10.17226/18434.

Hagstrom, Warren O. 1975. *The Scientific Community*. Carbondale: Southern Illinois University Press.

He, Li, Huan Huang, Mariem Bradai, Cheng Zhao, Yin You, Jun Ma, Lun Zhao, Rosa Lozano-Durán, and Jian-Kang Zhu. 2022. "DNA Methylation-Free *Arabidopsis* Reveals Crucial Roles of DNA Methylation in Regulating Gene Expression and Development." *Nature Communications* 13 (1): 1335. https://doi.org/10.1038/s41467-022-28940-2.

Holdren, John. 2013. *Memorandum for the Heads of Executive Departments and Agencies: Increasing Access to the Results of Federally Funded Scientific Research*. Washington, DC: Executive Office of the President, Office of Science and Technology Policy. https://rosap.ntl.bts.gov/view/dot/34953.

Huot, Daniel. 2015. "ISS R&D Conference." *NASA Blogs*, 7 July 2015. https://blogs.nasa.gov/spacestation/tag/results/.

Johnson, Victoria. 2007. "What is Organizational Imprinting? Cultural Entrepreneurship in the Founding of the Paris Opera." *American Journal of Sociology* 113 (1): 97–127. https://doi.org/10.1086/517899.

Johnson, Christina M., Haley O. Boles, LaShelle E. Spencer, Lucie Poulet, Matthew Romeyn, Jess M. Bunchek, Ralph Fritsche, Gioia D. Massa, Aubrie O'Rourke, and Raymond M. Wheeler. 2021. "Supplemental Food Production With Plants: A Review of NASA Research." *Frontiers in Astronomy and Space Sciences* 8 (November): 734343. https://doi.org/10.3389/fspas.2021.734343.

Kiss, John. 2015. "Conducting Plant Experiments in Space." In *Plant Gravitropism: Methods and Protocols*, edited by Elison Blancaflor, 255–83. New York: Springer. https://doi.org/10.1007/978-1-4939-2697-8_19.

Kordyum, Elizabeth, and Karl H. Hasenstein. 2021. "Plant Biology for Space Exploration—Building on the Past, Preparing for the Future." *Life Sciences in Space Research* 29 (May): 1–7. https://doi.org/10.1016/j.lssr.2021.01.003.

Kuhn, Thomas S. 2012 [1962]. *The Structure of Scientific Revolutions*. Chicago: University of Chicago Press.
Levin, Nadine, Sabina Leonelli, Dagmara Weckowska, David Castle, and John Dupré. 2016. "How Do Scientists Define Openness? Exploring the Relationship Between Open Science Policies and Research Practice." *Bulletin of Science, Technology & Society* 36 (2): 128–41. https://doi.org/10.1177/0270467616668760.
Mackowski, Maura Phillips. 2022. *Life in Space: NASA Life Sciences Research During the Late Twentieth Century*. Gainesville: University of Florida Press.
Massa, Gioia. 2021a. "Veggie Hardware Validation Test (VEG-01), 2014–2016." *NASA: Space Station Research Explorer*. Last modified 14 May 2021. https://www.nasa.gov/mission_pages/station/research/experiments/explorer/Investigation.html?#id=842.
Massa, Gioia. 2021b. "Pick-and-Eat Salad-Crop Productivity, Nutritional Value, and Acceptability to Supplement the ISS Food System (VEG-04B), 2019–2020." *NASA: Space Station Research Explorer*. Last modified 14 May 2021. https://www.nasa.gov/mission_pages/station/research/experiments/explorer/Investigation.html?#id=7895.
Merton, Robert. 1942. "The Normative Structure of Science." In *The Sociology of Science: Theoretical and Empirical Investigations*, edited by Norman W. Storer. 267–78. Chicago, IL: University of Chicago Press.
Messeri, Lisa. 2016. *Placing Outer Space: An Earthly Ethnography of Other Worlds*. Durham, NC: Duke University Press. https://doi.org/10.1515/9780822373919.
Mitroff, Ian I. 1974. "Norms and Counter-norms in a Select Group of the Apollo Moon Scientists: A Case Study of the Ambivalence of Scientists." *American Sociological Review* 39 (4): 579–95. https://doi.org/10.2307/2094423.
Mostowlansky, Till, and Andrea Rota. 2020. "Emic and Etic." In *Cambridge Encyclopedia of Anthropology*, edited by Joel Robbins, Rupert Stasch, Matei Candea, Andrew Sanchez, Sian Lazar, Hildegard Diemberger, and Felix Stein. December. https://doi.org/10.29164/20emicetic.
Mulkay, Michael J. 1976. "Norms and Ideology in Science." *Social Science Information* 15 (4–5): 637–56. https://doi.org/10.1177/053901847601500406.
Mulkay, Michael J., Nigel Gilbert, and Steve Woolgar. 1975. "Problem Areas and Research Networks in Science." *Sociology* 9 (2): 187–203. https://doi.org/10.1177/003803857500900201.
Murray, Samantha. 2022. "Rob Ferl Receives NASA Exceptional Public Service Medal." *University of Florida News*, 27 April 2022. https://news.ufl.edu/2022/04/rob-ferl-receives-nasa-medal/.
NASA 2021. "Commercial LEO Destinations." Announcement 80JSC021CLD. Final. Amendment 3. 5 August 2021. https://www.nasa.gov/jsc/procurement/cld.
NASA 2022a. *FY 2022: Spending Plan for Appropriations Provided by P.L. 117-103, July 2022*. https://www.nasa.gov/sites/default/files/atoms/files/fy_2022_spend_plan_july_2022.pdf.
NASA 2022b. *International Space Station Research*. https://www.nasa.gov/mission_pages/station/research/nlab/index.html.
NASA SMD, Science Mission Directorate 2022. *Decadal Survey: Decadal Snapshot*. https://science.nasa.gov/earth-science/decadal-surveys.
NASEM, National Academies of Science, Engineering, and Medicine 2020a. *Decadal Survey on Biological and Physical Sciences Research in Space 2023–2032*. Webinar. https://www.nationalacademies.org/event/09-29-2020/designing-research-campaigns-for-the-next-decade-of-biological-and-physical-sciences-in-space.
NASEM, National Academies of Science, Engineering, and Medicine 2020b. *Statement of Task*. https://www.nationalacademies.org/our-work/decadal-survey-on-life-and-physical-sciences-research-in-space-2023-2032#sectionProjectScope.
NASEM, National Academies of Science, Engineering, and Medicine 2021a. *Biological and Physical Sciences in Space Decadal: Early-Career Webinars*. https://vimeo.com/showcase/8836575.
NASEM, National Academies of Science, Engineering, and Medicine 2021b. *Decadal Survey on Biological and Physical Sciences Research in Space 2023–2032. Committee and Panels Bios*. www.nationalacademies.org/our-work/decadal-survey-on-biological-and-physical-sciences-research-in-space-2023-2032-physical-sciences-panel#sectionWebFriendly.
Nelson, Alondra. 2022. *Memorandum for the Heads of Executive Departments and Agencies: Ensuring Free, Immediate, and Equitable Access to Federally Funded Scientific Research*. Washington, DC: Executive Office of the President, Office of Science and Technology Policy.
Olson, Valerie. 2018. *Into the Extreme: U.S. Environmental Systems and Politics Beyond Earth*. Minneapolis: University of Minnesota Press.
Patarin-Jossec, Julie. 2018. Le vol habité dans l'économie symbolique de la construction européenne. Doctoral Dissertation, Université de Bordeaux.
Patarin-Jossec, Julie. 2021. *La Fabrique de L'astronaute: Ethnographie Terrestre de la Station Spatiale Internationale*. Europes, Terrains et Sociétés. Paris: Éditions PETRA.

Paul, Anna-Lisa. 2020. "Plant Molecular Genetics in Space Exploration." *ASGSR Decadal Survey Town Hall Talks,* 14 November 2020. YouTube video, 8:51. https://www.youtube.com/watch?v=TCxO2CUp55I.

Philips, Tony. 2013. "Glow-in-the-Dark Plants on the ISS." *NASA Share the Science.* https://science.nasa.gov/science-news/science-at-nasa/2013/06may_arabidopsis/.

Polanyi, Michael. 1962. "The Republic of Science: Its Political and Economic Theory." *Minerva* 1: 54–73. https://doi.org/10.1007/BF01101453.

Raymond, Catherine, and Amy Rubinson. 2020. *Growing Beyond Earth STEM Education Program Evaluation Results Summary 2016–2020.* Fairchild Botanical Garden and Raymond Consulting. https://resources.informalscience.org//growing-beyond-earth-evaluation-results-summary-2016-2020.

Sato, Kevin, Diane Malarik, and Craig Kundrot. 2020. *NASA Space Biology Science Plan 2016–2025.* Last modified 21 December 2021. https://science.nasa.gov/science-pink/s3fs-public/atoms/files/NASA_Space_Biology_Science_Plan_2016_2025_TAGGED.pdf.

Schuerger, Andrew, et al. 2021. *Plant and Phytopathogen Interactions in Altered Gravities: Integrated Research into the Stability of Plant-Based Crop Production Systems in Space.* Research Campaign White Paper, Decadal Survey on Biological and Physical Sciences Research in Space 2023–2032. https://science.nasa.gov/biological-physical/whitepapers.

Shapin, Steven. 1994. *A Social History of Truth: Civility and Science in Seventeenth-Century England.* Chicago: University of Chicago Press.

Shymanovich, Tatsiana, Joshua P. Vandenbrink, Raúl Herranz, F. Javier Medina, and John Z. Kiss. 2022. "Spaceflight Studies Identify a Gene Encoding an Intermediate Filament Involved in Tropism Pathways." *Plant Physiology and Biochemistry* 171 (January): 191–200. https://doi.org/10.1016/j.plaphy.2021.12.039.

Simmel, Georg. 2009 [1890]. "The Intersection of Social Circles." In *Sociology: Inquiries into the Construction of Social Forms,* edited by Anthony J. Blasi, Anton K. Jacobs, Mathew Kanjirathinkal, and Horst Jürgen Helle, 363–408. Boston, MA: Brill.

Stinchcombe, Arthur. 1965. "Social Structure and Organizations." In *Handbook of Organizations,* edited by James March, 142–93. Chicago, IL: Rand McNally.

Tavory, Iddo. 2016. "Interactionism: Meaning and Self as Process." In *Handbook of Contemporary Sociological Theory,* edited by Seth Abrutyn, 85–98. Springer International Publishing. https://doi.org/10.1007/978-3-319-32250-6_5.

Vertesi, Janet. 2015. *Seeing like a Rover: How Robots, Teams, and Images Craft Knowledge of Mars.* Chicago: University of Chicago Press.

Vertesi, Janet. 2020. *Shaping Science Organizations, Decisions, and Culture on NASA's Teams.* Chicago, IL: University of Chicago Press.

Walsh, Justin St P., and Alice C. Gorman. 2021. "A Method for Space Archaeology Research: The International Space Station Archaeological Project." *Antiquity* 95 (383): 1331–43. https://doi.org/10.15184/aqy.2021.114.

Wheeler, Raymond. 2012. "Controlled Environment Agriculture (CEA) for Space: Some Observations from NASA Studies." *NASA Technical Reports Server,* 26 September 2012. https://ntrs.nasa.gov/citations/20120016670.

Wyatt, Sarah E., and John Z. Kiss. 2013. "Plant Tropisms: From Darwin to the International Space Station." *American Journal of Botany* 100 (1): 1–3. https://doi.org/10.3732/ajb.1200591.

Yuhas, Alan. 2015. "NASA Astronauts Take First Bites of Lettuce Grown in Space: 'Tastes Like Arugula'." *The Guardian,* 10 August 2015. https://www.theguardian.com/science/2015/aug/10/nasa-astronauts-lettuce-vegetables-grown-space.

35
WHITEBOARDS, DANCING, ORIGAMI, DEBATE

The Importance of Practical Wisdom for Astrophysicists and Instrument Scientists

Fionagh Thomson

Introduction

The reliability (and nature) of human senses in rigorous scientific observations has been questioned since the ancient Greeks (Figure 35.1). Contemporary philosophy of science and the wider education system continue to portray the work of astrophysicists in terms of "objectivity" and a removal of the personal equation. Drawing on ethnographic fieldwork with astrophysicists (from instrument scientists to observers and cosmologists in the UK), I offer a different view of how

Figure 35.1 Above the clouds: Cumbrecita Ridge (2,426 m), Parque Nacional de la Caldera de Taburiente, La Palma, location of sixteen observatories. Photo by author.

DOI: 10.4324/9781003280507-40

the astrophysics communities make sense of the world "up and out there", where variables cannot be altered, and uncertainty abounds. I explore the everyday scientific (and creative) practice of deciding "what is real". I focus on the temporary, fluid, and dynamic interactions, through and with technologies, and the importance of being human and getting it wrong. I draw on Aristotle's practical wisdom, reimagined through Hans-Georg Gadamer's dialogue-as-play that moves beyond individual bodies and embraces thinking through doing.

Setting the Scene 1: A Cosmologist, an Astrophysicist, and an Ethnographer Walk into a Room...

"Do they not care ... that I care ... what they think?" asked a cosmology colleague after a Philosophy of Dark Matter e-conference. After a long pause Sam quietly said, "Well, I didn't say who I was ... maybe I should have". I was also revisiting what had happened, through my ethnographic fieldnotes, and pondering why I had felt surprised and perplexed at what had unfolded. Sam and Helen, both astrophysicists, had attended the e-conference, after I'd emailed, "Come along ... It'll be fun". Sam agreed once he'd noted an "interesting" presentation in the agenda, that transpired to be a critique of a particular method(ology) (and a topic in which Sam is a world-leading specialist). The presenter, a philosophy PhD student with a degree in (astro) physics, gave a succinct confident analysis of the method's failings. As soon as the screen-sharing stopped and the Q&A started, I noticed Sam's virtual raised hand and thought, "Great, he's engaging".

SAM: "Can you go to slide 3 ... plot 4, can you tell me more ... why did you do it this way?"
PRESENTER: "... That's how they do it."
SAM: "But why ... up to that point on the vertical axis?"
PRESENTER: "That's ... how they ... do it?"
SAM (QUIETLY): "But what made you decide to ...?"
PRESENTER (LOWERED VOICE): "Uhm, well ... I think that ..."
SAM: "It's okay, oh I probably ... haven't asked the question correctly."

The presenter, looking unnerved, was immediately surrounded by a chorus of reassuring voices (from philosophy colleagues): "It's a good paper ...", "Yes, it's really interesting ...". Sam seemed equally unnerved by the interaction. Over four years, I had never seen Sam falter, pause, or hesitate when asking questions. I knew they suspected something was wrong with the method, not because I can read the formulas but because I know their particular questioning style and I have learnt the (informal) unspoken conventions of question-asking in the community. In this instance, Sam was inviting the presenter to "work backwards", while looking for a common point of understanding to start a dialogue. I understood Sam was interested in the methodology (i.e., what were the assumptions that guided them to do it that way) through asking about the method (the mechanics of developing the plot). I also knew there was no trickery afoot. During the Q&A, a message popped up on my computer screen from Helen: "Aren't you going to say anything?" I replied, "No, this is your gig." Helen knew I thought that there was a disconnect between contemporary philosophy of astrophysics and contemporary astrophysics as practised. Two years earlier, I was muttering to myself while reading at my desk, head in hands, when Helen stopped for a chat. Instead of engaging in polite chit-chat, I turned the open book towards her and said, "Read this. Do you recognise what they are saying?" The book was open at a chapter from a philosophy of science book by a group of eminent scholars on the aesthetics of knowledge that critiqued and dismissed the field of dark matter (DM), through analysing a 3-D map of DM that turned out to be Helen's work. Later that day, Helen returned a photocopy of the chapter, with scribbled green annotations in the margins, in the style of a written dialogue with the author (that included a few "WTFs"). One example:

AUTHOR: "But in some strange way, mapping dark matter acts as proof that dark matter exists and even brings it into existence."
HELEN: "NO! We are very conscious of the (external) evidence for and against DM. This is a map constructed under the working hypothesis that it exists."
A.: "Where previously mapping was two-dimensional, the dark matter map has a temporal dimension a well as three spatial dimensions."
H.: "No, it is only 3 dimensions. The link between distance and time is a limitation we have to work within, even if we/I sometimes spin it as a glass half full."

During this conference presentation, I had listened intrigued by what had unfolded and suddenly realised why I was perplexed. The world I worked in and the world that they were critiquing were poles apart. I had initially thought it was a misunderstanding of the methods, and definitely the methodology (the historian's analysis that embedded frozen, unyielding meaning within the 3-D DM map). But this was more: this was a cosmology that had been invented, created, and critiqued, from significant hard work and experience, where the philosophers' and historians' criticisms held sway. But this was not the world I had inhabited for the past four years. This was a whole other (epistemological) world.

In this chapter, I invite the reader to glimpse an alternative world, where scientific knowledge is never absolute and is always contingent, in particular in a discipline that foregrounds, acknowledges, and manages (embraces) near-unimaginable levels of uncertainty and known unknowns.[1] This contingency plays out through dialogues that occur in the moment, across time and space in corridors, in Google chats, over coffee, in the pub. These dialogues are not linear or confined to one person but transcend physical bodies and go beyond the spoken or written word, and static, unyielding meaning is not embedded within visual images (plots, graphs, diagrams). I encountered these dialogues through extensive immersive time in the field with the community, where physically being in the field does not equate to accessing the field. In contrast to other fieldwork (in fast-paced A&E departments, quiet consultation spaces, or remote humid rainforests), I had to learn not to be a silent observer, as the way in is to engage, not to stand back (though I still had to move at high speed with working instrument scientists on mountaintop observatories, running up and down stairs and jumping into cars).

I approach this topic as an ethnographer and human geographer working within the everyday world, which I understand to be complex, unfolding, and entangled (more than the sum of its parts). My interest is in what people do rather than what they think they do as they move through the everyday world. I focus on the minutiae, the detail, the seemingly mundane, and view the field of study to be historically and materially situated—that is, not confined by the four walls of the immediate environment. As my work is immersive, I rarely engage in formal prearranged interviews or preempt what I will encounter in the field.

Building Spaces for Dialogue

For five years, I have been based in a three-storey building, designed by an award-winning international architect, and housing close-knit international communities of instrument scientists and astrophysicists. The building was designed for the residents around principles of light and movement and has, in theory, created spaces for dialogue both informally (corridors, sofas, kitchens) and formally (small glass-fronted meeting rooms and break-out corners).[2] On every floor, in every office, and in key public spaces, whiteboards are carefully positioned and are usually covered in drawings, sketches, and formulas.

On the first floor are observers (experimental astrophysicists) who work mainly in extragalactic astronomy, studying the universe far beyond our own Milky Way galaxy and stellar mass billions of light years away, including black holes, dark matter, white dwarfs, and light from the first stars. Working on desktop computers, the observers analyse and interpret data taken from astronomical instruments hosted at mountaintop observatories (e.g., the Spanish Canary Islands, Chile, and Hawai'i) and on space-based telescopes (e.g., Hubble, Spitzer, James Webb). On the top floor are cosmologists and theoretical astrophysicists, who develop computer simulations of different astronomical phenomena. On the ground floor are instrument scientists, who are all trained astrophysicists, and a few space science engineers. Core time is spent walking between offices (where they create computer simulations) and windowless laboratories in the adjacent building (to test their simulation results with on-bench models), before shipping instruments overseas to test on sky (in astronomical observatories).

A key part of everyday life in the building are daily talks, journal clubs, informal discussions, and meetings, and I attend as many as I can. Discussions are highly technical and, unlike other sciences I've worked in, few images/plots are in a standard format; many are colourful creations, a phenomenon I return to later in the chapter, and almost none have detailed standardised labelling. A question-and-answer session usually ensues to clarify the details. But these objects are rarely held up as self-contained sources of knowledge, and seeing does not equate to knowing or understanding.

Seeing Is Not Knowing: Rejecting Authenticity and Crafting Networks of Dialogue

Until the twentieth century, astronomers/"natural philosophers" could only make their observations within the visible (optical) part of the electromagnetic (EM) spectrum, which forms only a tenth of the spectrum as known today.[3] Contemporary images gathered from all telescopes (ground- or space-based) are constructed, created, and often enhanced through colour, and, unlike previous generations of astronomers (such as Galileo, Copernicus, or Hypatia), today few professional observers personally look through telescopes and see objects in the night sky.[4] Even in the optical, to human eyes, the raw data is a blur of white light and grainy images (background noise). Raw data from all telescopes require extensive post-processing in order to extract the signal from this background noise before any scientific interpretations can begin and meanings be inferred.[5] Recently, in an attempt to create richer data sources, images from different telescopes have been superimposed on each other (multi-message observations). The colour palette is bright, human-made, and intended to create contrast between the different structures in the astronomical objects observed. The colouring of telescope images is not new, nor is debate about the appropriateness of altering these images (Hannam 2009). The nineteenth-century astronomer T. H. Webb stated that his eighteenth-century predecessor William Herschel was "rather too 'partial to red tints'" (Webb quoted in Holmes 2008: 87).

Consequently, to identify, differentiate, and infer meanings from processed telescope images is a skill in astronomical qualitative data (image) analysis, learned on the job and inaccessible to the uninitiated. Professional astronomers and instrument scientists, guided by modern physics, also view unmediated human vision as unreliable, unreplicable, and untestable. Hence, the image (qualitative data) is further transformed, often creatively, into various graphs, plots, and diagrams (quantitative data) that are considered to be more transparent and reliable. Example: it is 3:20 a.m. during an on-sky all-night session, early in a two-week slot at a Spanish mountaintop observatory; Abe, a seasoned instrument scientist, is reviewing raw data from their guest instrument on the telescope. He hears me close the door from the outside platform.

ABE (EYES FIXED ON SCREEN): "Fionagh, any photos from a couple of hours ago?"
FT (WALKING QUICKLY OVER): "Yep ... have a look."

ABE (SCROLLING THROUGH PHOTOS): "Where's the plot?"
FT (TAKING OFF JACKET): "What plot?"

To his bemusement, I had taken a photo of the telescope image and ignored the adjacent power spectrum plot. He explained (as we munched popcorn to keep awake):

> When you first looked at [my computer screen in the observatory control room] you saw an image and assumed that was the most important part. But that's the *least* important part of the data. We have to try and process this data in order to decide if something is real or not or ... if it's an artefact or which component fits into which, and then compare it to theory. If it doesn't fit with theory ... then ... something is wrong.

Constructing Reality/Trustworthiness through Conventions of Dialogue

Experienced astrophysicists/instrument scientists rarely accept the reliability (accuracy or precision) of an image/plot/simulation based on (blind) trust. Any object under analysis must prove worthy of trust (be trustworthy). This trustworthiness may be built through a close collaborator's written analysis or through calculated opinion during a work meeting. But more often, informal conventions of rigorous questioning are set in motion and a complex, multilayered dialogue begins. Silently, often tacitly, the question asked is: does this seem plausible (based on our current understanding of what we believe to be true)? Here, the concept of what is true or "the truth" corresponds to current accepted theories in the field (of which there can be many). But while these theories offer guidance during the analytical dialogue, when Abe says "if it doesn't fit with theory then something is wrong", he is not implying that the theory is inherently correct and the image is incorrect. The community is continually on high alert for different types of known errors, known unknowns or unknown unknowns. Potential sites of systematic and systemic errors are visited and revisited through dialogues, alone and with their past selves through work diaries or in groups, in person, or virtually, sharing written text, spoken prose, or embodied dialogue, in locations from formal to informal.

What triggers this process is noticing that something is not quite right, and the immediate reaction is often visceral: a sudden straightening of the back, drawing back of shoulders, peering into a computer screen, and/or a long deep sigh, placing head in hands. But before they can conclude whether or not the image/graph is "real", a foundational question must be answered: why should we trust the data (raw or analysed)? Working backwards, everything is put under the spotlight and no stone is left unturned.

Once the reliability of the information source is established, then the overriding analytical concern (between observers and cosmologists) is: does the theoretical model fit the empirical observations? Identifying and foregrounding known and potential errors is also key to building trust in a group's work. During presentations on new ways of modelling the universe, if a presenter fails to highlight any errors or unknowns, it is common for seasoned cosmologists to ask, rhetorically: "Well, your model is elegant, but can it cope with the messiness and chaos of the real universe?" Similar analytical discussions occur between cosmologists, who debate the reality of theoretical simulations, some aspects of which cannot be ratified by observational data, as the instrumentation has not yet been developed to collect the faint light that has travelled from distant astronomical structures. Intense debates can break out over whether the error is systematic or systemic—a necessary distinction to effectively mitigate these errors in the final analysis.

For instrument scientists, the questioning arises in their labs, at their office desks, or in a mountaintop observatory at night. Through testing every working part, from simulations to on bench and finally on sky, data collected at every step must be precise, although not necessarily accurate. It can even be wrong (inaccurate). The term accuracy becomes important at levels of high technology readiness, when instruments are considered ready for observers to begin using on sky, which can take decades. Knowing the precision, accuracy, and sensitivity of the instrumentation is paramount (and calibration is everything). In contrast to other experimental sciences (e.g., microscopy), observers/instrument scientists cannot carry out traditional lab experiments. The astronomical observatories atop mountains or in space are, in effect, their labs, and variables cannot be perturbed or controlled within the vastness of the night sky (or the day sky, for solar telescopes). But even this knowledge remains contingent as bespoke highly sensitive ground-based instruments, built and tested in environmentally controlled labs, have to survive high-altitude mountaintops and endless sources of vibration from wind, rain, and the nightly rotation of the telescope platform as it tracks objects across the night sky, while space-based instruments need to survive the high temperatures and (be cushioned from) violent vibrations of launch and then the extreme cold and high radiation levels of space.

And so endless analytical dialogues continue at every stage of the communities' work, in every moment, checking and double-checking, questioning, with the guiding questions of "What I am observing? And is this plausible?" These analyses are inherently human-centred endeavours (albeit supported by multiple sources of information curated by different groups across time and space). Transparency of method(s) and methodology is also key to building trust from the community, which is one reason Sam was questioning the philosophy student's understanding of the methodology (not just the method). The recent introduction of AI (artificial intelligence) analysis tools into astrophysics to analyse the tsunami of raw data (petabytes) from large sky surveys has sparked many a discussion around the potential lack of transparency in locating systematic errors.

Computational simulations and models are also rarely perceived to be pure, authentic representations of the world "up there"; trade-offs always exist between simplicity and usefulness, complexity and time-efficiency. As one mathematician told me after a talk on the role of the human in Bayesian statistics in astronomy, "using sophisticated AI tools or Bayesian maths does not mean we put aside our analytical faculties—in fact we need them more". Many cosmology colleagues spend hours of devotion and pour love into these mathematical (and philosophical) creations. As one cosmologist told me, with each model crafted, "it's like losing a little of your soul".[6]

Thinking through Doing: Whiteboards, Dancing, Origami, Debate

Dialogues in the sciences have always been studied and researched by historians, in detail, and with great skill, since antiquity. A recent example includes the Bohr–Einstein debates: a series of public discussions lasting over forty years on the nature of quantum mechanics between the elder Albert Einstein and the younger Niels Bohr, who throughout remained firm friends. In contrast, the types of dialogues that I encounter during fieldwork evolve within the informal and ephemeral spaces of the everyday world (lifts, pubs, corridors). The great philosopher of science Ian Hacking views extragalactic astronomy's methods to be observations and models (Hacking 1989). For me, observations and models—or any visual, auditory, or tactile representation of their research findings—are not their methods but are instead carefully crafted tools for analytical discussions. Their methods are complex, intuitive, iterative, dialogic, and often temporary, with no written record left behind. These types of dialogue are also often embodied and can remain unspoken, as rather than *thinking then doing*, the instrument scientists and astrophysicists are frequently *thinking through doing*, through rituals embedded into everyday practices.

Throughout my time in the field, the physicists that I spent time with would often begin explaining an idea to me, then pause, pick up a whiteboard marker, and ask, "May I?" I would nod, and they would start to draw, sketching out ideas considered too difficult to describe verbally. Or, as I observed, they were often thinking through their ideas as they drew/sketched. At times,

I found myself completely outside a whiteboard conversation (or a whiteboard party, as my colleague Cillian calls them), not because I lacked knowledge of a specific concept or couldn't read the mathematical formulas (which I can't) but because the astrophysicists (cosmologists, observers, and instrument scientists) would communicate in half-sentences. One speaker would begin a sentence and after a few words, the listener would say "oh yes" or "you mean, like this" and draw a sketch. One memorable moment occurred when an observer and a cosmologist, who work closely together, solved a thorny problem through a high-speed dialogue composed of words, hand and body movements, and silent mutual staring at the board, interspersed with sketches and formulas that covered a wall-sized whiteboard in a matter of minutes. In remembering this episode, I am reminded of watching a video of the abstract artist Jackson Pollock at work. Pollock covered expansive canvases in streaks of seemingly random brushstrokes and splashes of paint, in no particular linear order, working close to the canvas, but not stopping in one position for long. When he finished and the camera zoomed back, the work, to me, formed a harmonious whole. At the time, while watching the observer and cosmologist, I was fixed to the spot, mesmerised, in particular, as their individual bodies, speech, and hands appeared to merge into one being.

I have encountered similar experiences of being with instrument scientists in the mountaintop observatories when they were commissioning (testing out) new instruments. They work between two observatories, located 426 metres apart, jumping in a car to make the five-minute journey. Once at the observatory, they run up and down stairs and through a maze of rooms performing tasks (for example, searching for or testing, tracing, or installing cables) that require a keen understanding of the instrument, the observatories, and the research project. If additional knowledge/experience is needed to solve a problem, no matter how small, they call a friend in the community. Moving at high speed, they communicate almost telepathically. At times they left me scrabbling to gather my things (camera, bag, coat) as, after pondering a problem together, they suddenly got up and sprinted out the door. I have numerous photos of them working together. At times, it is difficult to tell which hands or arms belong to which body; the biological and the technological merge as they work out the problem. Afterwards, when we review fieldwork photos, they have limited memory of what has happened.

One theoretical astrophysicist in the building uses origami, the Japanese art of paper folding, to explain the nature of the cosmic web. Commentators compare his use of origami to an analogy, a scientific show and tell, to explain to others the interconnected foldings in different galaxies. But when we spoke together about how he developed this concept, it emerged that endless hours of paper-folding (he taught himself from online videos) and experimenting/playing with different patterns of folding had enabled him to think through the layered nature of the cosmic web. This embodied way of being/thinking mirrors the work of the foundational astronomer William Herschel, who was also a professional musician, composer, and teacher. It is thought that Herschel composed symphonies as a way of exploring his thinking on the complex and unknown nature of the universe. Herschel's younger sister Caroline, who won the Royal Astronomical Society's Gold Medal for her astronomical work and who remains woefully underrecognised, was an accomplished astronomer and singer. The twentieth-century physicists Max Planck and Albert Einstein were outstanding musicians who extolled the virtues of music in their working lives. Perhaps unsurprisingly, many of the physicists in the building are also highly accomplished musicians, singers, photographers, or dancers, some to professional standards. When explaining concepts in talks or over coffee, they frequently use their hands, arms, or upper or whole body to imitate the dynamic nature of different astronomical structures and processes. Many engage in a form of interpretive dance.

To (try to) understand the specialised nature of an astrophysicist's/instrument scientist's work, I rarely ask, "What do you do?" Instead, I ask, "Where do you find beauty?" With hardly a pause, everyone I have met in this field gives answers (in great variety) that often link together their specialist work and choice of art form. For example, an instrument scientist and theorist who works on the largest optical telescope in the world finds beauty in playing around with fine optical measurements that, I then discovered, can morph into improvised jazz piano pieces. One professor of radio astronomy has an exquisitely embroidered dress that she designed, crafted, and wore at her PhD viva. The dress is black silk with minimalist patterns in white thread to represent different aspects of her research. For me, the understated black-and-white elegance of the design also represents the visual representations created by the radio astronomy community to communicate their work. In contrast, recently at the end of an e-meeting with an optical astrophysicist, as we shifted to informal chit-chat, I asked: "Do you have an art, a craft?" Without pausing, she smiled and held up a slim A4 paper folder. On the front was a perfectly drawn circle, filling the page, within which were two concentric circles of geometric symbols, a coloured spectrum from violet, orange, and green to red and blue, that reminded me of water lilies. Susan explained that crafting mandalas helps her think through ideas, and each project folder was adorned with different coloured geometric patterns.[7]

This concept of thinking through doing[8] with and through the material world has been well documented, in particular in the arts. The anthropologist Tim Ingold (2013) has written about thinking through making, although he extends this concept only to his definition of "makers" (artists, architects, and craftspeople) and excludes all scientists (see Ingold 2016). Ingold's unyielding viewpoint has, I would argue, evolved from a lack of immersion within, and of direct experience of, contemporary sciences, a topic I return to at the close of this chapter. Numerous commentators have also developed various concepts of inter- and intra-materiality. See, for example, Bruno Latour's Actor-Network Theory (2007) and Annemarie Mol's (2002) seminal work on multiple bodies in medicine. Many commentators who wrote during the cultural turn, the performative turn, the material turn, and now, the post-humanist turn aimed (and aim) to redress the logocentric view of western knowledge and dominance of the word (spoken or written). Consequently, in their work, with the exception of Mol, spoken language is often pushed to the background in order to highlight the material and the embodied.

Latour, for example, views the creation of knowledge (observational data) as the "inscription" of ideas into writing, in forms such as diagrams, lab notes, proposals, etc., that are tools in negotiating emerging knowledge within the relevant community of scientists, while the historian David Turnbull (2017) frames scientific images, including the 3-D DM map mentioned at the start of this chapter, as objects in motion, similar to the concept of the boundary object (Leigh Star 2010), where meaning shifts and changes depending on the interlocutors. But in each instance, the role of dialogue is subsidiary and instrumental in nature (or absent).

In extragalactic astronomy, however, dialogue is not instrumental but rather transformational in nature, and thinking through doing includes the spoken word. Precision in choice of words is also a prized skill. Words matter, and playing with words (often turning static nouns into dynamic adverbs) is part of these astrophysicists' and instrument scientists' everyday practice. For me, the concept of thinking through doing is widened (and better explicated) through the work of the German philosopher Hans-Georg Gadamer, and his lesser-known concept of dialogue-as-play (see Thomas 2018). This dynamic concept and form of practical wisdom illuminate the nature of many rigorous analytical dialogues in deciding which information is real/trustworthy—as I encountered in the everyday practices of extragalactic astronomy.

Dialogue-as-Play as Spinning Plates: Everyday Practical Wisdom Beyond Spoken Words

Hans-Georg Gadamer (1900–2002) was a leading continental philosopher and the founder of philosophical hermeneutics, which refers to the detailed examination of human understanding. In his 1960 book *Truth and Method* (Gadamer 1975 [1960]), Gadamer drew together many of the previously discussed insights from Schleiermacher, Dilthey, Husserl, and Heidegger to provide an extensive and innovative description of understanding how we make sense of the world around us. Key to his work is a belief that our perception of the world is not primarily theoretical but practical and performed through everyday activities. Unlike Heidegger, who viewed the hermeneutic process as cycles of self-reference that situate our understanding in a priori prejudices (Heidegger 1962 [1927]), Gadamer transformed the enclosed and private hermeneutic circle into an open iterative process (Lammi 1991) exploring the detail of everyday existence through shared dialogue.

Gadamer employed the analogy of play, in which the players are caught up with, and lose themselves in, their experiences—a dynamic that holds the potential to transform all players by radically changing our understanding of the world around us.[9] This form of dialogue moves beyond words as instrumental and engages all our human senses (Jütte 2005), beyond the contemporary five. These dialogues are not between human beings alone and engage with the material world (including the somatic body and everyday tools/technologies) (Thomson 2018). Dialogue-as-play is dynamic, never-ending, and often based on tacit knowledge, and therefore remains partially or wholly unspoken. Importantly, it is through the playing of the game that meaning is co-created (Dallmayr 2000) and, following Aristotle, privileges listening above seeing/speaking that continues to dominate western philosophy (Di Cesare 2013; Vilhauer 2010). Underpinning dialogue-as-play is the practice of approaching dialogue knowing that one does not and indeed cannot know everything (Barthold 2010).

Gadamer offers us an open-ended methodology, rather than a method, for how to create a successfully shared dialogue, the exact details of which we need to work out ourselves through ongoing experience and practical wisdom. No amount of persuading or eliciting can create an open dialogue; as many of us have experienced in our own lives, successful dialogue as play requires the active participation of all players (Malpas et al. 2002). For Gadamer, to engage in iterative experiences can widen our horizons, but only by first overturning an existing perspective that we can accept is erroneous or at least narrow. Its effect is not simply to add to our "stock of information" but to broaden our perspectives and to come to understand our own limits that constitute non-dogmatic wisdom. At the heart of these experiences is our ability (and willingness) to engage in open dialogue in which we actively listen to (and hear) the everyday world (across time and space). According to Gadamer's biographer, Jean Grondin (2003), this concept underpins Gadamer's choice of a poem by Rainer Maria Rilke for the introductory epigraph in *Truth and Method*:

> Catch only what you've thrown yourself,
> all is mere skill and little gain;
> but when you're suddenly the catcher of a ball
> thrown by an eternal partner
> with accurate and measured swing
> towards you, to your centre, in an arch
> from the great bridgebuilding of God:
> why catching then becomes a power—
> not yours, a world's.

The above poem beautifully encapsulates the role of dialogue-as-play as a shared human endeavour, which, if successful, leads to transformative understanding and practical wisdom.[10] For Gadamer, human beings must *continually* interpret their everyday world, as we are neither neutral, independent, nor objective observers, and so we are existential finite interpreters—in dialogue within the hermeneutic world we inhabit, and always within the unending flow of dialogue that has no clear beginning or end (Zabala 2009). For me, extragalactic astronomy embodies this description, which I consider ubiquitous in academia. Multiple and simultaneous dialogues are set up like spinning plates and continually spin. If nobody is discussing the topic, then the plate slows down, loses momentum, and eventually falls away from view. In other fields that I've worked in, when ideas/

concepts/objects cease to be critically discussed, they often become naturalised and embedded in policies, laws, regulations, rituals, or instrument design, often framed as common sense, with no one asking "but why?" In contrast, extragalactic astronomy creates no policies, nor do its practitioners build prototypes, as instrument scientists are the haute couturists of the instrumentation world. Nothing is replicated, all is bespoke and designed for a specific purpose—and critical and creative dialogue is everywhere. But this world remains hidden to many researchers (outside the field looking in), for a number of reasons that are beyond the scope of this chapter, although I invite the reader to revisit the scenario at the start of the chapter and consider my closing thoughts.

Closing Thoughts: Islands of Specialist Knowledge: Spinning Plates Together in a World of Deep Uncertainty

To (begin to) understand the foundational (and hidden) role of analytical dialogue-as-play in extragalactic astronomy, it is useful to acknowledge its similarities and differences with the worlds of pre-industrial revolution astronomers (those of Hypatia, Galileo, Copernicus, and Isaac Newton). They lived before the carving up of world knowledge into silos through academic disciplines (Harvey 2000) and hence were also instrument scientists, observers, cosmologists, and natural philosophers. Contemporary astronomy continues to use the language of geometry and trigonometry, but many modern-day astronomers are trained in one highly specialised field of astrophysics and study a specific astronomical structure or phenomenon (using data from a bespoke instrument that has been designed to *capture* targeted wavelengths at a specific point along the EM spectrum). Contemporary astrophysics is notably different from the isolated world of astronomers such as Galileo and instead has morphed into numerous islands of specialist knowledge with "coastlines" that increase yearly. As one observer asked (as we chatted over coffee about this book chapter): "Do you think it's *because* we're so specialised that we *have to talk* with each other?" I think so, but also working within unfathomable uncertainty (expanding islands of knowledge, increased specialisms, with new instrumentation to observe further back in time), astrophysics is a complex field of study that holds more unknowns than knowns. In this field, knowledge is inherently contingent and slippery, so continually seeking errors and being vigilant against *fallacies of misplaced concreteness* is a way of being not a pleasantry, created by necessity rather than choice.

But the miscommunications in the scenario that starts this chapter (the student unaware of and untrained in the community's conventions of question-asking; the historian's interpretation of the 3-D dark matter map, from their own isolated standpoint) also stem from the way in which extragalactic astronomy presents itself to outsiders. For example, the 3-D dark matter map is not one of the trusted information sources used by observers and cosmologists for rigorous analyses. It is an outreach image chosen for being engaging and attractive that was sent out into the public domain, like many other extragalactic astronomy images. And therein lies the sting in the tail. The very activity that the community excels at—critical and creative dialogue-as-play—is hidden away from sight. In place, the historians' and philosophers' unspoken assumption—that the community assigns (blind) faith to the meaning of an image/plot/graph—appears to hold true. However, as outlined throughout this chapter, this is not the case.

This practice of hiding the important role of humanness in rigorous research is an omnipotent oxymoron across the sciences (Thomson 2019). Scientific practices are framed as a human endeavour, but one that views human senses and sensibilities as inherent weaknesses, even vices, in rigorous scientific practice. These weaknesses and vices must be overcome or mediated through various practices, including machine learning and automated systems. Moreover, while the scientific argument is lauded as the epitome of good scientific practice, the humanness of dialogue and interpretation is deemed inappropriate and is often removed from formal discussions, educational curricula (Thomson and McGhee 2015), and academic publications in the sciences.

This oxymoron can be traced back to different key events over centuries, one being the removal of "rhetorick" from science by a Royal Society Charter in the eighteenth century, that called for members to

> separate the Knowledge of *Nature* from the Colours of *Rhetorick*, the Devices of *Fancy*, or the delightful Deceit of *Fables*, [and] the only Remedy for this *Extravagance* ... (is) to reject all the Amplifications, Digressions, and Swellings of Style: to return to the primitive Purity, and Shortness, when Men deliver'd so many *Things*, almost in an equal number of words ... bringing all things as near the Mathematical plainness as they can.
>
> *(Sprat 1722: 62, 113)*

Another key event in the history of astronomy is the removal of the personal equation from analyses of astronomical calculations,[11] which began in 1796, when Neville Maskelyne, the Astronomer Royal, sacked his assistant of over thirty years after discovering that the assistant had recorded notably different transit times of stars from his own timings. In place of his assistant, Maskelyne employed untrained/uneducated young boys to take measurements following a strict protocol, and so began the implementation of vigilant surveillance of subordinated astronomers across all the large observatories. John Pond, Maskelyne's successor as Astronomer Royal, continued the tradition, stating:

> I want indefatigable hard working & above all obedient drudges ... men who will be content to pass their day using their hands & eye in the mechanical act of observing & the remainder of it in the dull process of calculation.
>
> *(Pond cited in Croarken 2003: 286)*

With the removal of trained and experienced astronomy assistants, the "problem" of the personal equation in astronomical analyses was considered solved. But Maskelyne was unaware that the astronomy assistants, who he had replaced with what he thought were unthinking human automatons, often discussed their measurements in detail and altered their findings accordingly (Schaffer 1988). My fieldwork findings indicate that the personal equation and the key role of dialogue-as-play in rigorous analysis did not disappear but instead became hidden—and arguably remains alive and kicking after two hundred years.

Acknowledgements

The chapter was written through intense discussions with co-participants in the field; these, for me, reflect the ethnographic process of engaging in dialogue-as-play, with all its glorious thorny challenges. A heartfelt thank you to all the philosopher-physicists for sharing their thoughts, stories, and time with me—and for questioning me critically, continually, relentlessly, mercilessly—and for making me laugh (a lot). Thanks to Ariadna Calcines Rosario, Paula Chadwick, James Osborn, Richard Massey, James Nightingale, Andrew Robertson, and Matt Townson. A special thank you to Rayna Rapp (New York University) for unflinching encouragement, and wisdom during the early years of this fieldwork. And finally, thank you Polly Poet-Palmer.

Notes

1 Dark matter makes up about 27% of our universe and 67.8% is dark energy. The rest, everything on Earth and ever observed, is 5.2% of the universe (Giagu 2019).
2 When the building opened there was a cacophony of complaints about the noise and acoustic panels were installed throughout.

3 Almost all contemporary astronomical images are crafted from information (light/photons) captured from targeted frequencies along the breadth of the EM spectrum. Each wavelength of photons offers different information and also (re)acts differently. For example, capturing fast-moving gamma rays is akin to chasing a rare species of tiger that runs like lightning and moves around, over, and through every trap set in its path. It is difficult. If you don't know where to observe, using a carefully crafted instrument, and you blink—it's gone. In contrast, radio waves are more abundant. But while these wavelengths are easier to capture, they are also wider, and can only be collected by telescopes with large apertures the size of football fields.

4 Contemporary astronomers, or more accurately astrophysicists, observe through computer screens, either in the observatory through the hands-on skill and knowledge of a resident telescope operator and a resident night-time astronomer or, increasingly, in their offices hundreds or thousands of kilometres away.

5 All ground-based telescopes have an added complication of atmospheric seeing. Looking up through the atmosphere, the images are distorted. To human eyes, the stars appear to move back and forth (known to astronomers as "wobble") and the light intensity alters ("twinkles"). Adaptive optics corrects the former by reconstructing the image in the telescope, but currently there is no solution to stopping the stars from twinkling.

6 I often meet PhD students exhausted after a night's work of searching for a particularly slippery error. The difference in attitude between new and experienced astronomers is how they respond to errors, which shifts from "oh no, what have I done!" to "now that's interesting".

7 Buddhist monks use mandalas to focus the attention, establish a sacred space, and guide meditation. Mandalas are found in art around the world (e.g., in Celtic crosses) and are echoed in nature in flowers, snowflakes, and seashells.

8 I have observed this embodied way of working in every fieldwork setting, from forests to hospitals.

9 This is different from the concept of flow, where the meaning-maker is not transformed. See Csíkszentmihályi (2003).

10 There is one potential point of discord between Gadamer's work and my fieldwork. Gadamer viewed dialogue-as-play as a form of solidarity and partisan ways of being, while intense debate and disagreement is (not un)common during high-energy discussions in astrophysics. However, dialogue-as-play is not about achieving consensus. It is about coming together to agree on the matter under discussion, which requires listening. Through his questions, Sam was trying to create a fusion of horizons with the philosophy student.

11 A person's characteristic reaction time, or a correction for it, was first investigated after an incident in which Neville Maskelyne (1732–1811), the eighth Astronomer Royal at Greenwich, reported in 1799 that he had found discrepancies averaging 0.8 seconds between his own observations of the transit times of stars across a hair line, measured by counting the ticks of a pendulum clock, and those of his assistant, whom he had therefore fired. But in 1820 the German astronomer and mathematician Friedrich Wilhelm Bessel (1784–1846) followed up this report and discovered that even skilled astronomers vary consistently in the transit times that they report. On the basis of this finding he introduced the personal equation for calibrating individuals to reflect these differences, in what later came to be called reaction time (Hoffman 2007).

References

Barthold, Lauren Swayne. 2010. *Gadamer's Dialectical Hermeneutics*. Plymouth: Lexington.

Croarken, Mary. 2003. "Astronomical Labourers: Maskelyne's Assistants at the Royal Observatory, Greenwich, 1765–1811." *Notes and Records of the Royal Society of London* 57 (3): 285–98. https://doi.org/10.1098/rsnr.2003.0215.

Csíkszentmihályi, Mihaly. 2003. *Good Business: Leadership, Flow, and the Making of Meaning*. New York: Penguin.

Dallmayr, Fred. 2000. "*The Enigma of Health*: Hans-Georg Gadamer at 100." *Review of Politics* 62 (2): 327–50. https://doi.org/10.1017/S003467050002948X.

Di Cesare, Donatella. 2013. *Gadamer: A Philosophical Portrait*. Translated from Italian by Niall Keane. Bloomington: Indiana University Press.

Gadamer, Hans-Georg. 1975 [1960]. *Truth and Method*. Translated from German by Garrett Barden and John Cumming. New York: Seabury Press.

Giagu, Stefano. 2019. "WIMP Dark Matter Searches with the ATLAS Detector at the LHC." *Frontiers in Physics* 7: 75. https://doi.org/10.3389/fphy.2019.00075.

Grondin, Jean. 2003. *Hans-Georg Gadamer: A Biography*. New Haven, CT: Yale University Press.
Hacking, Ian. 1989. "Extragalactic Reality: The Case of Gravitational Lensing." *Philosophy of Science* 56 (4): 555–81. https://doi.org/10.1086/289514.
Hannam, James. 2009. *God's Philosophers: How the Medieval World Laid the Foundations of Modern Science*. London: Icon.
Harvey, David. 2000. "Cosmopolitanism and the Banality of Geographical Evils." *Public Culture* 12 (1): 529–64. https://doi.org/10.1215/08992363-12-2-529.
Heidegger, Martin. 1962 [1927]. *Being and Time*. Translated from German by John Macquarrie and Edward Robinson. Malden, MA: Blackwell.
Hoffmann, Christoph. 2007. "Constant Differences: Friedrich Wilhelm Bessel, the Concept of the Observer in Early Nineteenth-Century Practical Astronomy and the History of the Personal Equation." *British Journal for the History of Science* 40 (3): 333–65. https://doi.org/10.1017/S0007087407009478.
Holmes, Richard. 2008. *The Age of Wonder: How the Romantic Generation Discovered the Beauty and Terror of Science*. New York: Pantheon.
Ingold, Tim. 2013. *Making: Anthropology, Archaeology, Art and Architecture*. Milton Park: Routledge.
Ingold, Tim. 2016. "From Science to Art and Back Again: The Pendulum of an Anthropologist." *Anuac* 5 (1): 5–23. https://doi.org/10.7340/anuac2239-625X-2237.
Jütte, Robert. 2005. *A History of the Senses: From Antiquity to Cyberspace*. Translated from German by James Lynn. Malden, MA: Polity Press.
Lammi, Walter. 1991. "Hans-Georg Gadamer's 'Correction' of Heidegger." *Journal of the History of Ideas* 52 (3): 487–507. https://doi.org/10.2307/2710048.
Latour, Bruno. 2007. *Reassembling the Social: An Introduction to Actor-Network-Theory*. Oxford: Oxford University Press.
Leigh Star, Susan. 2010. "This is Not a Boundary Object: Reflections on the Origin of a Concept." *Science, Technology, & Human Values* 35 (5): 601–17. https://doi.org/10.1177/0162243910377624.
Malpas, Jeff, Ulrich Arnswald, and Jens Kertscher, eds. 2002. *Gadamer's Century: Essays in Honor of Hans-Georg Gadamer*. Cambridge: MIT Press.
Mol, Annemarie. 2002. *The Body Multiple: Ontology in Medical Practice*. Durham, NC: Duke University Press.
Sprat, Thomas. 1722. *The History of the Royal Society of London: For the Improving of Natural Knowledge*. London: Samuel Chapman.
Schaffer, Simon. 1988. "Astronomers Mark Time: Discipline and the Personal Equation." *Science in Context* 2 (1): 115–45. https://doi.org/10.1017/S026988970000051X.
Thomson, Fionagh. 2018. "The Mirror and the Lake: (Creating a Space to Speak for) Gadamer's Philosophical Hermeneutics to Explore the Role of Dialogue as Practical Wisdom—During the 'Good' Medical Consultation." *Philosophy, Theology and the Sciences* 5 (2): 239–64. https://doi.org/10.1628/ptsc-2018-0018.
Thomson, Fionagh. 2019. "Telescopes, Microscopes, and Simulations: The Everyday Scientific Practice Of Deciding 'What Is Real?'." In *Virtue and the Practice of Science: Multidisciplinary Perspectives*, edited by Celia Deane-Drummond, Thomas A. Stapleford and Darcia Narvaez, 56–76. Notre Dame: University of Notre Dame, Center for Theology, Science, and Human Flourishing. https://curate.nd.edu/show/5712m616f9d.
Thomson, Fionagh, and John McGhee. 2015. "Seeing Me: The Role of Transparent Bodies in the Medical Consultation." *Studies in Material Thinking* 13 (6): 3–14.
Turnbull, David. 2017. "Mapping Dark Matter and the Venice Paradox." In *Aesthetics of Universal Knowledge*, edited by Simon Schaffer, John Tresch and Pasquale Gagliardi, 203–31. Cham: Palgrave Macmillan. https://doi.org/10.1007/978-3-319-42595-5_9.
Vilhauer, Monica. 2010. *Gadamer's Ethics of Play: Hermeneutics and the Other*. Lexington, KY: Lexington.
Zabala, Santiago. 2009. *The Remains of Being: Hermeneutic Ontology after Metaphysics*. New York: Columbia University Press.

36
UNDERSTANDING THE QUESTION OF WHETHER TO MESSAGE EXTRATERRESTRIAL INTELLIGENCE

Chelsea Haramia

Introduction

Either aliens exist or they don't. If they do exist, we do not know where they are, and they do not seem to know we are here. To date, we have no confirmed evidence that aliens are trying to communicate with us. In fact, we have no confirmed evidence that any intelligent life exists elsewhere in our solar system, galaxy, or universe. And yet, the following question has been the subject of legitimate debate in the astrobiological community and beyond: Should we be trying to communicate with aliens? This question is worth addressing despite the dearth of evidence. If humans ever find and communicate with extraterrestrial intelligence (ETI), the effects will almost certainly be radical, global, intergenerational, and deeply profound. In this chapter, I will situate this central question within the history of and the search for ETI and explore it through a critical philosophical analysis of the assumptions, implications, social dynamics, and mysteries that structure the communication debate.

Absence

The term 'SETI' stands for 'search for extraterrestrial intelligence'. SETI scientists devote their research to the project of exploring the cosmos for signs of intelligent life. Notably, they appeal to a quite circumscribed sense of 'intelligence' and acknowledge that it is a purely functional definition used for scientific purposes (Wright and Oman-Reagan 2017). For these practitioners, 'intelligence' simply refers to having technological capabilities that we humans would be able to detect.[1]

Contemporary SETI searches began in 1960 with Project Ozma when Frank Drake pointed a radio telescope at two nearby, sun-like stars, Tau Ceti and Epsilon Eridani. Giuseppe Cocconi and Philip Morrison (1959) had just shown that humans' radio-receiving technology would soon be capable of detecting humans' radio broadcasts at interstellar distances, which uncovered the potential for scientists to use radio technology to search for extraterrestrial broadcasts. Soon after Project Ozma, Frank Drake, and Carl Sagan organised the first-ever SETI conference at which the famous Drake equation materialised (Drake 1965).[2] This equation offers a means of computing the number of alien societies that theoretically are both capable of transmitting electromagnetic signals and are also transmitting their signals to Earth (Shostak 2021). The Drake equation establishes a number of parameters on which to focus our speculation, but the actual parameters cannot be fixed without further analysis of the variables or actual observation of ETI. The equation was presented as a tool rather than an answer, and the scientific terrain is far more complicated than the equation allows. Our current lack of knowledge prevents us from making any determinations based solely on the Drake equation, but it has nonetheless proved an invaluable heuristic and a useful indication of where to direct scientific inquiry and exploration.

The equation allows for the possibility that alien intelligence is quite common. Given empirical facts like the number of sun-like stars and potentially habitable planets in our galaxy alone, the following question arises: Where is everybody? This is the basis of the famous Fermi paradox (Hart 1975).[3] While the Fermi Paradox leaves open what conclusions we should draw about the existence of extraterrestrial intelligence, the facts remain that extraterrestrial intelligence is possible and potentially highly probable, and humans have observed no concrete evidence of the existence of any particular ETI.

Reference

Referring to Aliens

Let's begin by thinking about the referential assumptions within the question 'Where is everybody?' 'Everybody' here refers to other, alien societies, and, while the colloquial connotation of 'everybody' is surely meant to be quite open-ended, the term 'body' narrowly denotes the discrete, morphological form of an individual organism. This comports nicely with how we typically understand the individuals that comprise human societies and many nonhuman animal social groupings. But it is very easy for us to fall back on common anthropocentric, terrestrial, and cultural concepts of what comprises a society when we are looking for unknown, extraterrestrial others.

Humans have already created and encountered a number of fictional aliens—famous Western examples include the various Martian aliens imagined by authors such as Orson Welles and Ray Bradbury, the endearing alien visitor in the movie *E.T.* (1982), and the hostile aliens of cinema blockbusters such as *Alien* (1979) and *Independence Day* (1996). There are also relatively famous works that depict fictional instances of messaging and communication per se, such as Cixin Liu's award-winning novel *The Three Body Problem* (2008), the film *Arrival* (2016), and Carl Sagan's own SETI-inspired novel *Contact* (1985) and its film adaptation (1997). In turn, such fictional speculations can end up informing real-world scientific explorations. Jason T. Wright and Michael P. Oman-Reagan (2017) point out that cultural and anthropocentric biases are built into our concept of 'alien', and that this leads to a myriad of presumed risks and hopes that extend beyond the fictional and into actual social and scientific analyses. However, every one of our presumptions about potential alien attributes is derived directly from humans and human understandings. And many think there is good reason to resist importing our biased assumptions into nonfictional science.

The idea of aliens with individual bodies and autonomous minds that comprise societies is just one possibility among others. As Carlos Santana (2021) notes, perhaps an extraterrestrial society will not resemble a typical human society composed of discrete, physical individuals at all and will instead be some kind of evolving superindividual, or a eusocial hive whose individual members lack autonomy. Or, perhaps ETI have reached the kind of post-body or post-biological stage, as posited by philosopher Nick Bostrom (2003), where their consciousness has been uploaded to an artificial substrate.

Perhaps we should even question whether humans themselves can justifiably be described as discrete, autonomous individuals. Melford E. Spiro (1993) explores the Western concept of the individual self and challenges its presumed applicability beyond Western culture. Jonathan Beever and Nicolae Morar (2016) argue that human beings are best described as nonautonomous ecological communities, given the extent to which our constitution and behaviours are shaped by the microbiomes and microscopic organisms on which our existence relies. Their work was preceded and shaped by Lorraine Code's (2006) deconstruction of the concept of the autonomous individual that highlights humans' necessary interdependence on ecological surroundings. Furthermore, there are philosophical theories of extended minds, starting with the work of Andy Clark and David Chalmers (1998). And there are anthropological theories of distributed consciousness, such as Alfred Gell's (1998) work on the complex intentionalities in art objects that mediate social agency. With these critiques in mind, we may include in our analyses the possibility that aliens are like us, but we should also recognise that the quality of being-like-us might provide reason to search for ETI who lack discrete physical, mental, and social boundaries.

There may, of course, be many other assumptions and biases to uncover and many other alternatives to the potential forms that ETI may take, and our critical and creative faculties are probably not capable of imagining all of the possibilities. Evidently, even our own understanding of the nature of humans may not be accurate or complete.[4]

Uncritically importing our biases into scientific investigations may hinder good science, but open exploration of biased assumptions can be useful. That a belief arose from bias does not entail that it must be false. Similarly, it may be true that at least some ETI have attributes to which we can relate, even if we are not justified in concluding this with certainty from our current knowledge. Objective facts about ETI do not depend on our biases, and we can acknowledge the possibility that our biases may happen to align with the truth.

Another reason to allow these biases into our speculations is that we do in fact have at least some evidence of how intelligent life can evolve in the cosmos. We are that evidence.[5] Our existence, along with our knowledge of evolutionary processes on Earth, lends credence to the claim that ETI *could* be like us in relevantly important ways, even if this evidence falls far short of determining any particular attributes of ETI. When we are unsure what is true, as we are in the search for extraterrestrial intelligence, we should consider the evidence available.

A third reason to allow these biases into our speculations is that this is a way of acknowledging our ignorance and limitations while also providing a scientific path forward. Starting with what we know is justified under these circumstances, especially accompanied by the recognition of all that we don't know. Undetectable life and intelligence may exist, and SETI scientists are quite aware that we cannot search for such life. At the same time, we can acknowledge that human capabilities typically grow and expand. The natural and technological evolution of humans shows that our capabilities are not static, so what qualifies as detectable by humans is likewise not static. Human ingenuity and potential coupled with careful reflection and epistemic humility are, therefore, the ingredients of an appropriately biased search.

And at the end of the day, when we refer to 'ETI', some features of this referent are fixed simply by our referring to it. The ETI must be life that did not originate on Earth and that is capable of producing detectable technology. These are very general, qualifying features. All ostensible, particular features, however, are open. Only confirmed evidence of ETI's existence will allow us to determine that our referent exists and to begin the project of discovering particular attributes; hence the value of the search itself.

The Drake equation focuses on the probability of the existence of ETI that are *transmitting signals to Earth*. However, it's possible that ETI are both detectable and *not* transmitting their signals to us. Why might an ETI fail to send signals to Earth? One answer is that they don't know we're here, and that they themselves are merely searching, not signalling. Another is that they know we're here, but they are waiting for some sign from us before attempting to signal us. Possibilities like these have motivated a specific kind of search known as 'messaging extraterrestrial intelligence' (METI).

METI (also known as 'active SETI') is the project of sending intentional, directed messages into space in an explicit attempt to communicate with anyone who detects the signal. Proponents of METI maintain that passive detection measures are likely to be insufficient. Notable figures in this arena include Douglas Vakoch of METI International and Alexander Zeitsev of the Russian Academy of Science's Institute of Radio Engineering and Technology. Sending out signals could jump-start communication with extraterrestrial others, by getting ETI either to notice us or to realise that we're ready to communicate. METI proponents often point to the potential benefits of communication with ETI as justification for their messaging attempts. I will explore those potential benefits and competing considerations in the next section, but first, let's briefly turn to the other referents involved in our original question: humans.

Referring to Humans

METI proponents want ETI to realise that we are ready to communicate. But whom are they referring to with the pronoun 'we'? The potential for equivocation here is strong. Certainly, *they* are ready to communicate. 'They' here refers to the relatively small subset of radio operators who engage in METI projects. But those practitioners have presented their particular interest in messaging as a human interest. And as Kathryn Denning notes, scientists "tend to develop syntheses that pull all human experience together into a single narrative" (2009: 66–67). However, not only does 'they' fail to accurately represent all humans, it does not even refer to the narrower astrobiological community, as there is significant disagreement and debate within that community regarding this matter (Denning 2010). Some are amenable to the arguments of the current METI proponents (e.g., Korbitz 2014; Shostak 2015). Others criticise current METI practices while remaining open to the possibility that messaging could be acceptable under different circumstances (e.g., Billingham and Benford 2011; Haramia and DeMarines 2019; Traphagan 2021). Still others argue that METI itself is ethically inadvisable (e.g., Gertz 2016). There is no uniform agreement on messaging even among those researching and studying extraterrestrial data.

Furthermore, there is no uniform agreement among humans on the topic of METI, making it difficult to maintain that the 'we' above successfully refers to humans in general. Of course, many people are simply unaware that messaging has been taken up, but some who are aware have expressed ethical concerns on behalf of humanity in general (Smith 2020). And in a very important sense, these messages speak for all of humanity. Since we don't know what even the majority of humans think about messaging, it's difficult to maintain that *we* are ready to communicate if 'we' refers to humans.

The temporal issues inherent to searches and messaging also affect these referential concerns. Given the presumably vast distances involved, no one who currently exists will be directly affected by any messaging successes. Instead, these effects would be felt by future generations, and it's safe to say that people who do not yet exist have not agreed to any specific activities such as messaging extraterrestrial intelligence. This confounds the question of the referent of 'we' even further.

The original question asks: Should we be trying to communicate with aliens? As we've seen, both 'we' and 'aliens' here are thoroughly ambiguous terms. The merit of a given answer depends in part on the particular attributes of whoever legitimately fills in for 'we' and for 'aliens'. It also depends heavily on what the effects of messaging might be. So, let's turn now to an exploration of the merits of answering the question by appealing to the *outcomes* of communication.

Risk

Despite our wholesale ignorance of the actual details of extraterrestrial intelligent life, we seem to successfully refer to 'aliens', 'extraterrestrial life', and 'ETI'. In a very general sense, these prospective entities are the legitimate subjects of both philosophical deliberation and scientific inquiry. As I indicated above, the ETI referred to must be extraterrestrial life that is capable of producing detectable technology. Furthermore, ignorance and uncertainty are not uncommon in referential discourse. Biologists may refer to and speculate about undiscovered species before discovering them in nature. Environmentalists and others may refer to and speculate about future generations when none of the people they reference exists yet.

However, there is a notable difference between partial ignorance and wholesale ignorance of a particular referent. Biologists can safely assume that undiscovered species will have arisen via Earth's natural evolutionary processes. These evolutionary processes entail that at least some actual details are set (e.g., any species found will be carbon-based). Environmentalists can safely assume that future humans will have human DNA and organs, and this means that they will typically possess various physical and mental capabilities such as fine and gross motor skills, consciousness, interests, and critical thinking skills. But there is little that we may safely assume about the likely or actual details of ETI. How should this lack of knowledge affect our philosophical and scientific deliberations?

Outcomes

To answer the preceding question, this ignorance significantly undercuts our ability to perform a risk analysis. Many are concerned about the existential risk to humanity and our planet of contacting or messaging ETI. No doubt inspired at least in part by popular science fiction imaginings of hostile extraterrestrial encounters, this risk of global catastrophe cannot be ignored. There is a non-zero chance that intentionally messaging ETI will end our existence in one way or another. Hostility from ETI is not even required for this outcome. An otherwise benign or altruistic attempt by ETI to communicate with humans could unintentionally harm us if, for example, their means of communication were somehow deadly to humans. It is reasonable to think that a non-zero risk of global catastrophe or of the end of humanity is enough to justify a prohibition on the activity that creates that risk. Therefore, since contacting extraterrestrial intelligence creates a catastrophic risk, it seems reasonable to conclude that we should not attempt to contact ETI.

But the issue is not so simple. To attempt a comprehensive risk analysis, we must also consider the risks involved in not contacting ETI. Some METI proponents have argued that we are unduly affected by fears of alien invasion brought on by popular fictional imaginings (Vakoch 2016). Cold War-era anxiety and its effects have fuelled such fears, and SETI as a scientific practice was born in and heavily influenced by Cold War-era politics and international relations (Charbonneau 2022). And for an ETI to invade Earth, they would have to overcome serious challenges posed by the presumed distances involved, along with the laws of physics as we know them. METI proponents aren't as interested in invasion risks as they are in the risks involved in *not* communicating with ETI.

It is true that failing to communicate with ETI *also* entails a non-zero risk of global catastrophe (Korbitz 2014). Consider the catastrophic risks we already face. Some are anthropogenic, such as climate change or nuclear disaster. Some are part of nature, such as a supervolcano explosion or an asteroid impact. Other unknown risks may arise in the future. For all of these possible catastrophes, ETI might have the knowledge, tools, or capabilities to help us forestall such existential harm. Contacting ETI might be the very thing that saves us from these other kinds of catastrophe. Aliens might know how to reverse climate change, or they might have instruments that can redirect asteroids on a collision course. They might be able to share their scientific and technical knowledge, tools, and capabilities with humans. If this kind of outcome occurs and prevents some existential catastrophe, then it's at least possible that we would not have been able to prevent that catastrophe had we not tried to contact ETI. Therefore, not contacting ETI also presents a non-zero risk of global catastrophe or the end of humanity.

Missed opportunities for benefits to both ourselves and ETI is another worry that follows from the decision not to message. The 'SETI paradox' is a version of this worry, and it has been presented as justification for immediate messaging (Zaitsev 2006.).[6] If messaging is risky, then ETI are in a position to recognise this risk as well. If they recognise this risk, then they will merely listen and not attempt communication. If everyone merely listens and no one sends messages, then everyone is left wondering if they are alone in the universe. While this is one potential explanation for the apparent silence we are encountering as we explore the cosmos, it is not immune to criticism. There are various critiques to consider, but one of the most serious is that the SETI paradox is self-defeating.[7] It relies on the assumption that ETI reason like we do. But if we assume that ETI reason like we do, and if recognising the reasoning in the SETI paradox is enough to justify active communication, then we may assume ETI recognise that as well and find messaging to be justified. That is, if the assumptions in the SETI paradox are true, the problem it outlines does not arise. Nonetheless, discovery of extraterrestrial others could be enormously beneficial—for us and for aliens—and someone's decision to message could be the act that precipitates those benefits.

Ultimately, both attempting to contact and not attempting to contact ETI present serious existential and global risks along with potential missed opportunities for benefits. But that exhausts the available options; we cannot avoid either attempting or not attempting contact with ETI. However, not all risks of harm are equally risky. One potential way to adjudicate between the available options would be to assess which option carried *greater* risks. Then, the less risky option would become the advisable route. However, this is where the unique nature of the search for extraterrestrial intelligence sets it apart from other more common risk-based analyses. We simply know nothing about these extraterrestrial others. We don't know how they evolved or where; their capabilities; what form they might take; even whether 'they' is an accurate or appropriate way to refer to any actual ETI.

This is not your typical uncertainty. Currently, we have no concrete, extraterrestrial evidence around which to structure our speculations. And these details are precisely what is needed to even begin to assign higher or lower probabilities to the potential outcomes of our available options. So, we are prevented from legitimately designating any one option as more or less risky than the others. Each of our available options carries a non-zero risk of catastrophe; that is true. But that is all we may legitimately conclude, and so our available options appear to be on equal footing, risk-wise.

But there are two other important considerations. The first involves the assessment of risks *inherent* to the activities in question. This can be contrasted with the above assessment of the risky *outcomes* of those activities. The second involves questions of our own *detectability* and whether messaging affects how noticeable we are.

Inherent Risk and Detectability

Let us begin with questions of inherent risk. SETI searches have been commonly focused on the passive approach of detecting a signal of extraterrestrial intelligence. Only recently have METI practitioners begun active messaging attempts. Successful active messaging guarantees contact, whereas successful detection does not require contact. Moreover, successful messaging entails that we notify ETI of our presence before we can confirm any concrete details about that ETI. Mere detection, on the other hand, allows for the opportunity to gather as many concrete data as we can and to then decide whether to communicate with others.[8] These competing features of SETI searches versus METI searches indicate that METI searches are inherently riskier.

When a risk is inherent to an activity, it is a fundamental part of the activity itself. Built into all current messaging projects is the attempt to intentionally signal our presence to a completely undetermined referent. This is not a fundamental feature of passive SETI projects aimed at mere detection. Intentional communication with a completely undetermined referent is in and of itself risky because it entails that harmful outcomes cannot be ruled out or minimised through discretion. While not completely risk-free, passive SETI searches do not carry this inherent risk, given that passive searches are equipped to allow us to exercise discretion regarding communication. Because of this, typical SETI searches are likewise equipped to provide us with a crucial opportunity to evaluate the evidence of ETI that we find and to use that concrete information to better inform the question of how probable a given outcome of contact might be. Successful METI attempts automatically prevent us from making more informed choices regarding communication (Haramia and DeMarines 2021).

To be clear, passive SETI searches do not *guarantee* that we may evaluate concrete data on ETI before contact. These searches simply provide that opportunity, and they lack the inherent risk involved in intentionally signalling an undefined referent. At the same time, this risk inherent to METI searches does not guarantee that the outcomes of messaging will be automatically worse than not messaging. Depending on future details that are completely opaque to us now, it is possible that messaging could bring rewards that mere detection would not. But until we uncover some concrete details of ETI, we simply cannot assign higher or lower probabilities of risk or reward to any of our available options. The opacity of the future effects of contact means that we cannot appeal to concerns about risky outcomes to adjudicate the question of whether to message ETI. All of our available options are equally concerning in that respect.

Messaging is an irreversible action. Signals sent out into space cannot be taken back or deleted, even if we later discover good reasons not to announce ourselves. All else equal, then, it is better to maintain flexibility in our options. Passive SETI searches allow such flexibility without removing the possibility of contacting ETI and potentially benefiting from communication. These searches simply better equip us to make more informed decisions about whether and when to send irreversible signals and attempt intentional contact.

But I have not yet addressed the question of our current detectability and how that might affect the riskiness of different searches. One thing that human astrobiologists look for when searching for life in the universe is life-supporting conditions. Detecting evidence of water or an atmosphere on another planet would provide some reason to think that the planet could house life (Jones and Lineweaver 2010; McKay 2014). If extraterrestrial others are searching, they may be searching for such conditions as well. Earth has displayed these biosignatures for billions of years. And more recently, human-technological advancements have arguably added to our detectability (Haqq-Misra et al. 2013). Some claim that intentional messaging creates no new risks because unintentional signals—such as radio and television broadcasts and satellite communication—have been travelling into space for generations (Shostak 2013). If these unintentional signals are as noticeable as the intentional beacons sent out by METI researchers, then this fact contributes directly to SETI debates about detectability. Unfortunately, this matter is empirically unsettled at this time, and more research is needed regarding the strength, decay, and detectability of our unintentional signals (Brin 2019; Haqq-Misra et al. 2013; Haramia and DeMarines 2019).

METI messages are nonetheless distinct from unintentional signals. They are typically targeted and intentional, and they aim to be highly noticeable. But what if METI messages were intentional but no more targeted or noticeable than the unintentional leakage of our television and radio broadcasts? João Pedro de Magalhães (2016) has suggested a creative approach to messaging that fits these criteria. Instead of sending out high-powered cosmic beacons, we could embed messages to ETI in our radio and television signals that are already being emitted for other purposes. So, a radio or television broadcast could broadcast a show to its audience and at the same time include a message to anyone of extraterrestrial origin who happens upon that broadcast. One virtue of this approach is that it creates no new risks in terms of detectability. Another virtue is that it might jump-start the benefits of communication—assuming that ETI can somehow successfully parse and interpret our broadcasts—by signalling that we are ready to communicate.

Of course, whether such communication would actually be beneficial instead of mixed, harmful, catastrophic, or simply missed or misinterpreted by ETI depends on concrete details of which we are unaware. An important difference between METI signals and background radio leakage is *intentionality*. METI messages are intended to communicate with ETI. Current commonplace broadcasting activities are not intended to become messages to ETI.[9] If a project involves intentionally speaking for others, distinct considerations apply. Let us look finally at some details surrounding the messages themselves and at our history of knowingly attempting communication with ETI.

Messages

A variety of messages have been sent into space to date. I have focused primarily on the targeted, high-powered radio signals of current METI projects. These are explicitly intended to "elicit a reply" (Vakoch 2011a), but others have not been so narrowly focused. Some of the very first messages were more about communication or capabilities among humans than they were about communication with ETI. The Morse message sent by the Soviet Union to the planet Venus in 1962 was primarily a Cold War demonstration of Soviet capabilities, though it was at the same time humans' first attempt at extraterrestrial messaging. The Arecibo message, sent to globular star cluster M13 in 1974, was more a demonstration of astronomers' newly achieved scientific capabilities than a genuine attempt to get the attention of an extraterrestrial intelligence. And neither the Pioneer plaques (1972) nor the Voyager Golden Records (1977) were standalone messaging attempts. These messages were extensions of other space exploration projects. The Pioneer and Voyager spacecraft were designed to gather information about our solar system and send it back to Earth. The knowledge that these spacecraft would eventually leave our solar system and travel indefinitely far into interstellar space made the prospect of messaging a foreseen side effect, but the goal of including the plaques and records was certainly not to maximise efficacy in alerting ETI to our presence.

While the Pioneer plaques and Golden Records amounted to dropping a metaphorical message in a bottle into the cosmic ocean, current METI projects may be better compared to spotting a plane and firing a flare gun in its direction. For example, in 2017, METI practitioners beamed a message to GJ273, Luyten's Star, precisely because one of the planets orbiting this star may be capable of supporting life (Wall 2017). By targeting areas of our galaxy with potentially habitable exoplanets and sending signals that should be noticeable with the right kind of technology, METI practitioners are doing what they can to increase the possibility that their messages reach extraterrestrial others. Again, their goal is to elicit a response. In reaction to such activities, many members of the SETI community signed on to a statement responding to METI/active SETI which included the following claim:

> Intentionally signaling other civilizations in the Milky Way Galaxy raises concerns from all the people of Earth, about both the message and the consequences of contact. A worldwide scientific, political and humanitarian discussion must occur before any message is sent.[10]

The concerns target the consequences of successful messaging as well as the message itself. Since we have already examined salient concerns regarding the consequences of messaging, let us turn to some detailed concerns regarding the content of the messages.

One obvious concern is intelligibility. There is little ground for assuming that an extraterrestrial species will be able to understand any messages that we construct. Consider the dearth of interspecies communication here on Earth. Some terrestrial nonhuman species are arguably intelligent or social, yet there is no evidence that humans have managed more than very rudimentary communication with any of these other species. And of course, humans often find it difficult or impossible to understand one another. An apt example of this is the Arecibo message. This message, sent from the now-defunct Arecibo Radio Telescope in Puerto Rico, relayed, among other things, our solar system, human DNA, a stick figure of a human, some of the biochemicals of Earthy life, and the Arecibo telescope itself (Figure 36.1). Again, this low-resolution image was intended to signify human technological advancement far more that it was intended to actually and effectively signal ETI, but it is notable that the content of the message is not immediately evident to all humans. The problem remains that even communication as basic as the Arecibo message can be confusing or undecipherable among members of humanity themselves, which does not bode well for the prospect of sending messages that are comprehensible to alien others.

Proper representation is another messaging concern. We can think about proper representation in terms of both accuracy and justice. With respect to accuracy, proper representation would require true representation of humans. METI messages imply to the cosmos that humans consent to messaging, but no one who is messaging has sought global consent, and there are potentially insurmountable practical hurdles to securing consent or human-wide consensus on messaging. Without consent or consensus, messaging could inaccurately present humanity as ready to communicate when that is not the case. In response to this, Vakoch claims that we are unlikely to reach consensus on the matter, given that cross-cultural and interpersonal disagreement among humans seems to be rampant, including, but not limited to, disagreement regarding cosmic projects (Vakoch 2011b). As an example, when the Pioneer plaques were launched, they contained images of a nude woman and man. Not only was there disagreement about whether this nudity was appropriate, there was disagreement among those who thought it was inappropriate about

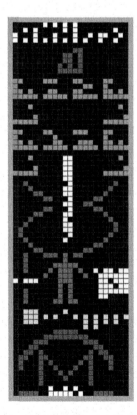

Figure 36.1 The Arecibo message sent in 1974 from the Arecibo Observatory. Author Arne Nordmann. Public Domain. Wikimedia Commons.

what exactly was inappropriate about it (Capova 2021). Vakoch argues that accuracy requires us to represent ourselves as a species whose members disagree, with a diversity of attitudes and aspirations. Properly representative messaging, then, would represent this discord, and, according to his argument, consensus is not needed, given that accuracy demands that we portray ourselves to ETI as diverse. Notably, this begs the question against those who call for a halt to messaging on grounds of inaccurate representation. Answering the question of whether to present ourselves as cohesive versus diverse presumes that presenting humanity to ETI is acceptable to humans. Even the representation that Vakoch calls for is still potentially inaccurate insofar as humans do not consent to be represented to ETI.

With respect to justice, proper representation would involve representing humanity without producing or reinforcing oppressive conditions. Messaging necessarily involves speaking for others—METI practitioners are speaking on behalf of humans and for our entire planet. It is remarkably easy to introduce or reinforce injustice—even and especially unintentionally—whenever an activity involves speaking for others in an attempt to benefit them. For example, various attempts by Western feminists to represent women in the Global South facing oppression have led these theorists to perpetuate the misapprehension of what Uma Narayan (1997) calls "death by culture". This happens when those who speak out decontextualise actual circumstances and then incorrectly recontextualise them according to detached assumptions and stereotypes, effectively reinforcing the oppression those stereotypes engender while misrepresenting those they are attempting to benefit. This happens in part because the social location of those who speak for others always bears on the impact and meaning of their words, and the METI practitioners who speak for humanity are socially located in historically privileged domains. They occupy roles in the relatively prestigious areas of academia and Western science, performing work primarily in the Global North, and exercising an enormous amount of power and autonomy when deciding for all of humanity that we will unequivocally engage in intentional, representational communication with potential ETI. These concerns indicate the potential for oppressive colonialist and paternalist attitudes to be reinforced within messaging practices.[11] Thus, we may worry that the foundations of current METI activities reinforce hierarchical and unjust assumptions, such as assumptions about whose interests take priority.

Linda Alcoff (1991) acknowledges how often the motivations of privileged members of humanity to speak for others stem from an interest in mastery and domination of the discourse. METI practitioners have control over everything that their messaging attempts convey on behalf of humanity, and they do not always share the details of these messages with SETI scientists or the general public.[12] Gayatri Spivak (1988) treats this kind of discussion as inherently misrepresentative insofar as privileged speakers maintain a closed discussion with themselves and fail to subvert presumed hierarchies of Western superiority. Alcoff prescribes that the impetus to speak for others be carefully analysed, as a desire for control of the narrative is often a reason to reject one's desire to speak. This does not mean that speaking for others is always inadvisable or oppressive. As Alcoff (1991) notes, there may be conditions under which there is a strong responsibility to speak for others, and such conditions could arise with the project of messaging. And as Alison Jaggar (2005) notes, Western-led representations of others can aim to be immersed rather than detached in order to undermine the potential for cultural imperialism. Similarly, Rebecca Charbonneau writes, "with a critical eye, analysis of SETI concepts and messages can help reveal truths about power and culture" (2021: 88). This means that, with sufficient critical and immersive achievements, properly representative messaging may be possible, but current messaging conditions raise specific concerns regarding unacknowledged oppression and unjust representation.

One important concern arises from the fact that the context surrounding communication acts is never static, and the potential for contextual shifts to follow messaging is immense. There are great distances involved in messaging, and both success and our knowledge of that success would presumably not occur until a significant amount of time had passed. Luyten's Star, for example, is twelve light years away, and decades will pass before it is reasonable to hope for a response. Much has already changed for humanity since METI practitioners beamed their signal toward this star in 2017, and much more will change in the decades to come. Radical change is a common phenomenon. For example, since the early messaging of the 1970s, human technology underwent a large-scale and radical shift from analogue to digital. In all likelihood, current messaging attempts, if successful, will affect future generations of humans who do not yet exist and who may exist under much different circumstances. The context under which current messages are sent undoubtedly plays a role in the content of the messages and the intentions behind them, and these details could significantly affect other features of the messages, such as intelligibility, accuracy, and how they are interpreted. As Stuart Hall's reception theory indicates, a speaker can easily lose control of a message and how it is interpreted once it is conveyed (Hall 1980). And, as Hall, Alcoff, and others have outlined, the audience itself plays a role in the meaning of messages and is part of the dynamic context of the project of speaking for others.

ETI are not the messengers' only relevant audience. Current (and future) humans are also part of the audience of present-day messaging attempts. Speech acts themselves can change the context into which they are delivered. By speaking for humanity, METI practitioners are changing the context surrounding messaging and constructing a particular deliberative dynamic. As we saw, SETI members called for a "worldwide scientific, political and humanitarian discussion" to take place *before* messages are sent.[13] This call encourages listening, and it allows for careful deliberations to inform the intentions behind, and content of, any messages sent.

But that discussion has not happened. Because METI practitioners have bypassed this process and have begun engaging in intentional, high-powered messaging attempts, they have shifted the power dynamics. METI proponents are messaging at a time when the answer to the question of whether we should message is crucially unsettled. Now, messaging is part of the status quo, and the burden of proof is on METI detractors to convince METI proponents and others to take their concerns seriously. METI proponents' messages control humanity's intentional extraterrestrial speech acts at the same time that the act of messaging itself establishes a status quo and exercises power and control over the METI discussions here on Earth. Because there is currently no authority on Earth to regulate messaging, METI practitioners have gained de facto authority on the matter simply by messaging. With authority comes accountability and responsibility. METI practitioners have a responsibility not to create or reinforce injustice, and there is good ethical reason for them to take this responsibility seriously, even when there is no one to hold them accountable for their actions.[14]

Conclusion

The answer to the question of whether we should be trying to communicate with aliens must start with a careful analysis of the question itself. This analysis requires that we consider not only facts about extraterrestrial others but also the absence of facts regarding these targets of our searches. We must also consider what constitutes proper representation of humanity to these mysterious, alien others. We are in a unique position as we consider communication with a referent whose actual features are entirely unknown to us. But we are also treading on familiar analytical terrain as we question our assumptions and biases, assess the implications of our ignorance, and challenge decisions that stand to create or reinforce unjust power dynamics among humans. The search for extraterrestrial intelligence continues, and those who conduct this search by sending messages to ETI face important hurdles and challenges, both empirical and philosophical. While this chapter falls short of exhaustively presenting all of the relevant considerations, our exploration here demonstrates that the question of whether we should be trying to communicate with ETI is thoroughly unsettled at this time.

Notes

1. For SETI practitioners, the ability to produce detectable technology is typically considered a sufficient but not necessary condition for possessing intelligence. That is, it's enough to qualify as intelligent, but it's not presumed to be a requirement for intelligence.
2. For a quick reproduction of the Drake equation, see https://www.seti.org/drake-equation-index.
3. Technically speaking, the Fermi paradox is a puzzle, not a paradox. It does not contain a logical contradiction, which is what a true paradox comprises.
4. For evidence of this, see debates about 'behavioural modernity' in archaeology by, for example, Garofoli (2016).
5. This is reminiscent of the anthropic principle insofar as Earth's evolution and our resulting existence is proof that the universe is at least capable of producing organisms like us, though this does not necessarily mean that the universe was created *for* us.
6. This, too, is not a true logical paradox but rather a point that the goals of mere listening may not be universalisable.
7. Self-defeating arguments possess a fatal logical flaw and must be revised or abandoned.
8. Notably, these benefits of mere detection do not address other relevant concerns. See, for example, Shorter (2021), who raises questions about the ethical concerns surrounding the act of listening to or observing others.
9. This of course doesn't mean that such broadcasting activities could never unintentionally message others, and the 1999 sci-fi comedy film *Galaxy Quest* is a vivid fictional example of this possibility.
10. https://setiathome.berkeley.edu/meti_statement_0.html.
11. See Shorter (2021) for more specific concerns within Indigenous scholarship of the "settler science" that forms the basis of both SETI and METI projects.
12. And in truth, anyone with access to strong enough radio equipment can send messages and may currently do so without providing the public with any information regarding those messages.
13. https://setiathome.berkeley.edu/meti_statement_0.html.
14. The majority of philosophers are moral realists (see https://philpapers.org/surveys/results.pl), and virtually all moral realists will agree that the truth of a moral requirement does not rely on whether you will be held accountable for meeting that requirement nor on whether you want to follow that requirement.

References

Alcoff, Linda. 1991. "The Problem of Speaking for Others." *Cultural Critique* 20: 5–32. https://doi.org/10.2307/1354221.

Beever, Jonathan, and Nicolae Morar. 2016. "The Porosity of Autonomy: Social and Biological Constitution of the Patient in Biomedicine." *American Journal of Bioethics* 16 (2): 34–45. https://doi.org/10.1080/15265161.2015.1120793.

Billingham, John, and James Benford. 2011. *Costs and Difficulties of Large-Scale 'Messaging', and the Need for International Debate on Potential Risks*. Unpublished manuscript, last revision 23 April 2011. https://arxiv.org/abs/1102.1938.

Bostrom, Nick. 2003. "Are We Living in a Computer Simulation?" *Philosophical Quarterly* 53 (211): 243–55. https://doi.org/10.1111/1467-9213.00309.

Brin, David. 2019. "The 'Barn Door' Argument, the Precautionary Principle, and METI as 'Prayer'—an Appraisal of the Top Three Rationalizations for 'Active SETI'." *Theology and Science* 17 (1): 16–28. https://doi.org/10.1080/14746700.2018.1557391.

Capova, Klara Anna. 2021. "Introducing Humans to the Extraterrestrials: The Pioneering Missions of the Pioneer and Voyager Probes." *Frontiers in Human Dynamics* 3: 714616. https://doi.org/10.3389/fhumd.2021.714616.

Charbonneau, Rebecca. 2021. "Imaginative Cosmos: The Impact of Colonial Heritage in Radio Astronomy and the Search for Extraterrestrial Intelligence." *American Indian Culture and Research Journal* 45 (1): 71–93. https://doi.org/10.17953/aicrj.45.1.charbonneau.

Charbonneau, Rebecca. 2022. "Historical Perspectives: How the Search for Technosignatures Grew out of the Cold War." In *Technosignatures for Detecting Intelligent Life in Our Universe: A Research Companion*, edited by Anamaria Berea, 1–32. Beverly, MA: Wiley-Scrivener. https://doi.org/10.1002/9781119640738.ch1.

Clark, Andy, and David J. Chalmers. 1998. "The Extended Mind." *Analysis* 58 (1): 7–19. https://doi.org/10.1093/analys/58.1.7.

Cocconi, Giuseppe, and Philip Morrison. 1959. "Searching for Interstellar Communications." *Nature* 184: 844–46. https://doi.org/10.1038/184844a0.

Code, Lorraine. 2006. *Ecological Thinking: The Politics of Epistemic Location*. New York: Oxford University Press. https://doi.org/10.1093/0195159438.001.0001.

de Magalhães, João Pedro. 2016. "A Direct Communication Hypothesis to Test the Zoo Hypothesis." *Space Policy* 38: 22–26. https://doi.org/10.1016/j.spacepol.2016.06.001.

Denning, Kathryn. 2009. "Social Evolution: State of the Field." In *Cosmos and Culture: Cultural Evolution in a Cosmic Context*, edited by Steven J. Dick and Mark L. Lupisella, 63–124. Washington, DC: NASA History Office.

Denning, Kathryn. 2010. "Unpacking the Great Transmission Debate." *Acta Astronautica* 67 (11–12): 1399–405. https://doi.org/10.1016/j.actaastro.2010.02.024.

Drake, F. D. 1965. "The Radio Search for Extraterrestrial Intelligent Life." In *Current Aspects of Exobiology*, edited by G. Mamikunian and M. H. Briggs, 323–45. London: Pergamon.

Garofoli, Duilio. 2016. "Cognitive Archaeology without Behavioral Modernity: An Eliminativist Attempt." *Quaternary International* 405, Part A: 125–35. https://doi.org/10.1016/j.quaint.2015.06.061.

Gell, Alfred. 1998. *Art and Agency: An Anthropological Theory*. Oxford: Clarendon Press.

Gertz, John. 2016. "Reviewing METI: A Critical Analysis of the Arguments." *Journal of the British Interplanetary Society* 69: 31–36. Unpublished manuscript, last revision 8 June 2021. https://arxiv.org/abs/1605.05663v3.

Hall, Stuart. 1980. "Encoding/Decoding." In *Culture, Media, Language*, edited by Stuart Hall, Dorothy Hobson, Andrew Lowe and Paul Willis, 117–27. London: Routledge.

Hart, Michael. 1975. "Explanation for the Absence of Extraterrestrials on Earth." *Quarterly Journal of the Royal Astronomical Society* 16: 128–35.

Haqq-Misra, Jacob, Michael W. Busch, Sanjoy M. Som, and Seth D. Baum. 2013. "The Benefits and Harm of Transmitting into Space." *Space Policy* 29 (1): 40–48. https://doi.org/10.1016/j.spacepol.2012.11.006.

Haramia, Chelsea, and Julia DeMarines. 2019. "The Imperative to Develop an Ethically-Informed METI Analysis." *Theology & Science* 17 (1): 38–48. https://doi.org/10.1080/14746700.2019.1557800.

Haramia, Chelsea, and Julia DeMarines. 2021. "An Ethical Assessment of SETI, METI, and the Value of Our Planetary Home." In *Astrobiology: Science, Ethics, and Public Policy*, edited by Octavio A. Chon Torres, Ted Peters, Joseph Seckbach and Richard Gordon, 271–91. New York: Wiley-Scrivener. https://doi.org/10.1002/9781119711186.ch13.

Jaggar, Alison. 2005. "Global Responsibility and Western Feminism." In *Feminist Interventions in Ethics and Politics: Feminist Ethics and Social Theory*, edited by Barbara S. Andrew, Jean Clare Keller and Lisa H. Schwartzman, 185–200. Lanham, MD: Rowman & Littlefield.

Jones, Eriita G., and Charles H. Lineweaver. 2010. "To What Extent Does Terrestrial Life 'Follow the Water'?" *Astrobiology* 10 (3): 349–61. https://doi.org/10.1089/ast.2009.0428.

Korbitz, Adam. 2014. "The Precautionary Principle: Egoism, Altruism, and the Active SETI Debate." In *Extraterrestrial Altruism: Evolution and Ethics in the Cosmos*, edited by Douglas Vakoch, 111–27. Berlin: Springer-Verlag. https://doi.org/10.1007/978-3-642-37750-1_8.

McKay, Christopher P. 2014. "Requirements and Limits for Life in the Context of Exoplanets." *Proceedings of the National Academy of Sciences of the USA* 111 (35): 12628–33. https://doi.org/10.1073/pnas.1304212111.

Narayan, Uma. 1997. *Dislocating Cultures: Identities, Traditions, and Third World Feminism*. New York: Routledge.

Santana, Carlos. 2021. "We Come in Peace? A Rational Approach to METI." *Space Policy* 57: 101430 (1–9). https://doi.org/10.1016/j.spacepol.2021.101430.

Shorter, David Delgado. 2021. "On the Frontier of Redefining 'Intelligent Life' in Settler Science." *American Indian Culture and Research Journal* 45 (1): 19–44. https://doi.org/10.17953/aicrj.45.1.shorter.

Shostak, Seth. 2013. "Are Transmissions to Space Dangerous?" *International Journal of Astrobiology* 12 (1): 17–20. https://doi.org/10.1017/S1473550412000274.

Shostak, Seth. 2015. "Should We Keep a Low Profile in Space?" *New York Times*, 27 March 2015. https://www.nytimes.com/2015/03/28/opinion/sunday/messaging-the-stars.html.

Shostak, Seth. 2021. "Drake Equation." *The SETI Institute*. Last updated July 2021. https://www.seti.org/drake-equation-index.

Smith, Kelly. 2020. "METI or REGRETTI: Ethics, Risk, and Alien Contact." In *Social and Conceptual Issues in Astrobiology*, edited by Kelly Smith and Carlos Mariscal, 209–36. New York: Oxford University Press. https://doi.org/10.1093/oso/9780190915650.003.0013.

Spiro, Melford E. 1993. "Is the Western Conception of the Self 'Peculiar' within the Context of the World's Cultures?" *Ethos* 21 (2): 107–53. https://doi.org/10.1525/eth.1993.21.2.02a00010.

Spivak, Gayatri Chakravorty. 1988. "Can the Subaltern Speak?" In *Marxism and the Interpretation of Culture*, edited by Cary Nelson and Lawrence Grossberg, 271–313. Urbana and Chicago: University of Illinois Press.

Traphagan, John W. 2021. "Should We Lie to Extraterrestrials? A Critique of the Voyager Golden Records." *Space Policy* 57: 101440. https://doi.org/10.1016/j.spacepol.2021.101440.

Vakoch, Douglas. 2011a. "Asymmetry in Active SETI: A Case for Transmissions from Earth." *Acta Astronautica* 68 (3–4): 476–88. https://doi.org/10.1016/j.actaastro.2010.03.008.

Vakoch, Douglas. 2011b. "Responsibility, Capability, and Active SETI: Policy, Law, Ethics, and Communication with Extraterrestrial Intelligence." *Acta Astronautica* 68 (3–4): 512–19. https://doi.org/10.1016/j.actaastro.2010.01.008.

Vakoch, Douglas. 2016. "In Defence of METI." *Nature Physics* 12: 890. https://doi.org/10.1038/nphys3897.

Wall, Mike. 2017. "Interstellar Message Beamed to Nearby Exoplanet." *Scientific American*, 16 November 2017. https://www.scientificamerican.com/article/interstellar-message-beamed-to-nearby-exoplanet.

Wright, Jason T., and Michael P. Oman-Reagan. 2017. "Visions of Human Futures in Space and SETI." *International Journal of Astrobiology* 17 (2): 177–88. https://doi.org/10.1017/S1473550417000222.

Zaitsev, Alexander. 2006. "Messaging to Extra-Terrestrial Intelligence." Unpublished Manuscript, last revision 5 October 2006. arXiv:physics/0610031.

37
ASTROBIOLOGY AND THE IMMANENCE OF LIFE AMIDST UNCERTAINTY

Dana Burton

When Viking touched down on the surface, weather reports started streaming their way to Earth. Martian weather was clear, cold, uniform, repetitious. Seymour L. Hess, meteorology team leader, reported on conditions at Chryse Planitia on sols 2 and 3:

> Winds in the late afternoon were again out of a generally easterly direction but southerly components appeared that had not been seen before. Once again the winds went to the southwesterly after midnight and oscillated about that direction through what appears to be two cycles. The data ended at 2:17 PM (local Martian time) with the wind from the ESE, instead of from the W as had been seen before. The maximum mean wind speed was 7.9 meters per second (18 mph) but gusts were detected reaching 14.5 meters per second (32 mph).
>
> The minimum temperature attained just after dawn was almost the same as on the previous Sol, namely −86°C... The maximum measured temperature at 2:16 PM was −33°C... This [was] 2° cooler than measured at the same time on the previous Sol.
>
> The mean pressure was 7.83 mb, which is slightly lower than previously. It appears that pressure varies during a Sol, being about 0.1 mb higher around 2:00 AM and 0.1 mb lower around 4:00 PM.
>
> Edward Ezell and Linda Ezell, *On Mars: Exploration of the Red Planet, 1958–1978*

Dwelling on Ambiguity

At 4:53 a.m. PDT on 20 July 1976, the first spacecraft to land successfully on another planet paused (Ezell and Ezell 1984). Dust motes caught the western light, upswept when an unfamiliar entity arrived among them. Following a choreographic cue drilled into it several months before, at twenty-five seconds after touchdown Viking 1 snapped two pictures.[1] The first was of its foot—footpad 3 to be exact—to visually confirm its position. The second was of the landscape it was now a part of. The sun cast the shadow of the lander upon the ground. Low dunes stretched far into the distance, undulating with small dips and hollows. Modest-sized rocks were strewn across the sand, most no larger than the size of a fist, all the same, bright rusty red. It made the terrain look motley and jagged. The horizon was obscured by haze, a combination of particles suspended in the atmosphere struck by rays of light. A bit of the lander itself—the camera colour calibration charts, an antenna, and the sampling arm—were captured in the picture frame.[2] Viking promptly sent the images back to Earth. And this is when it paused. Before the dust had completely settled from the spacecraft's soft alighting via parachute upon the surface. Before the scientists at Mission Control in Pasadena, California, could acknowledge the sent data file because of the approximately twenty-minute transmission delay between Earth and Mars. And certainly before the initiation of the diagnostic testing of the instruments. Prior to any of those moments of direct linkage with home, Earth, it was just Viking and Mars, and all the possibilities immanent in their encounter (Deleuze and Guattari 1983).

This chapter is an invitation to imagine the encounter of Viking and Mars beyond the technical reports and media impressions. In these accounts, the fact that Viking's biological experiments did not definitively ascertain the existence of life on Mars divided the scientific community. As a result, the Viking biological mission as a whole was seen as inconclusive, leading to ambiguity as to which scientific perspective was "right".[3] To address the inconclusive results on an operational level, NASA, in the 1980s, moved away from astrobiological missions, instead focusing on accruing information about planetary bodies' potential habitability and other environmental data (NRC 2007). To delve into this ambiguity that has continued to linger into the present, I analysed the archival records at NASA Headquarters as well as conducted two years of ethnographic research with NASA scientists. Importantly, I dwell on the details of Viking's technical designs and the processed results of the mission for determining the existence of life on Mars.

Taking a critical description approach (Tsing 2013), I ask, what other forms of knowledge were generated through Viking's encounter with Mars? In particular, I focus on the sensory—the touch, textures, and sensations—in the moments of interaction between Viking's biological instruments and the Martian environment as a method of tuning into and attuning to what emerged from that interaction (Stewart 2011). Attending to the emergent or immanent is an opportunity to reassess the narratives around Viking's results—the ambiguity that became a decades-long source of uncertainty. Although the results of the experimentation may be up for debate, their inconclusiveness revealed underlying assumptions scientists made about the construction of Viking itself. This piece takes ambiguity as the starting point for unravelling the scientific conceptualisations of biology and its relation to the environment that gave rise to Viking. Additionally, it provides a retrospective look at the future that unfolded after Viking, the legacy of planetary science missions that have dominated NASA—until now. In a time when NASA is again prioritising astrobiology in its missions for the 2020s–2030s, what possibilities are immanent in moments when science cannot claim a result with certainty? How does critically engaging with the Viking spacecraft as the first representative of Earth, rather than a technical measuring machine, allow us to imagine interplanetary exploration otherwise going forward?

A Matter of Design

Feet shaped like "an inverted sailor's hat" (Tillman and LeCompte 1991) sank slightly into the loose powdered red soil. There were three legs; one had penetrated the surface farther than the other two. Scientists pondered over this when they received images of each footpad later in the sol, or Martian day. The first sol began at the time of Viking's landing; even measuring time emerged as a result of the Viking–Mars interaction. As the diagnostic tests began to get a sense of the spacecraft's health, there was a realisation that the sampling arm was stuck in an undeployed position. Engineering efforts were immediately activated to address this. Viking's tripod legs stretched widely along the ground, their near-horizontal angle designed to keep the spacecraft upright when sandstorms swept the surface. Unlike future rovers, Viking couldn't walk to another location. Rather, this spacecraft architecture was supposed to settle and also to settle in.

This act of settling recalls histories of discovery ventures that for their faceted reasons of profit, power, and prestige justified the extension of certain people, countries, and rationalities through territorial acquisition, technoscientific infrastructure development, and population control, often through explicit and systematic violence (Lowe 2015; Povinelli 2016; Redfield 2000; Sharpe 2016; Simpson 2014; Smiles 2020). NASA, newly founded as an offshoot of the Air Force in the late 1950s, was no stranger to aeronautics and atmospheric science for the purpose of military dominance and authority (Kaplan 2015; Leslie 1993; Neufeld 1995; Turchetti and Roberts 2014). However, the scientific and philosophical pursuit of biology in space, which seemingly prioritised nonhuman species as the core subject of its research, began to shift the construction of missions away from military (and astronaut-centric) interests towards conducting science for science's sake (see Wolfe 2002 for complications to this story). In the 1960s and 1970s, activities orchestrated by NASA's growing expertise in managing operations in outer space and the United States' anxiety to "beat" other countries (especially the Soviet Union, see Siddiqi 2000) in an international space race had the effect of transforming outer space into an environment that humans could access and govern. Through processes of ecobiopolitics (Olson 2018), the extraterritorialisation of governance was coordinated under the guises of maintaining national technoscientific expertise, manufacturing resources, and developing biomedical products and techniques for humans in extreme environments (McKinson 2020; Olson 2018; Rand 2016; Valentine 2017).

There is no doubt that Viking was a part of this legacy of exploration. Originally called Voyager, the mission to land on Mars came from an initiative led by the Jet Propulsion Laboratory (JPL) to devise a new class of spacecraft. As the primary engineering hub of NASA activities, particularly spacecraft design, and assembly, JPL created Voyager to advance missions to Mars and Venus, the two closest planets to Earth. Unlike the Ranger (1961–1965) and Surveyor (1966–1968) missions that constructed and tested spacecraft architectures for landing, and the Saturn architectures that were the basis of the astronaut programme on the Moon (1968–1972), Voyager was intended to be a more streamlined spacecraft that incorporated manufacturing innovations to allow it to carry a heavier payload[4] (Siddiqi 2018; for concurrent developments in launch vehicles see Launius and Jenkins 2002). The advantage of this was that more instruments could be flown, thus increasing the amount of science that could be conducted. Voyager was specifically being pitched as a biological mission, to definitively answer the question of whether Earth was the only planet with life in the inner solar system. The design of Voyager was left to contractors in commercial and private industries—such as Martin Marietta (later to merge with another company and become Lockheed Martin) and Celesco Industries—who wrote bid proposals for the position in 1963. While looking through the archives, I was taken aback that the spacecraft design was being created before the mission design. This was somewhat of an opposite approach to how missions are typically designed now, where the science steers the spacecraft construction (cf. the role of planetary protection in constraining spacecraft design, discussed in depth in Meltzer 2011; also DeVincenzi, Race, and Klein 1998). Skimming the pages of a folder filled with memos of technical propositions, I found a letter from the Biosciences division that, in 1964, asked to be a part of the design endeavour. They argued that it would be beneficial to include their expertise earlier in the manufacturing, as the systems for biological testing would be expensive to add after major architecture decisions were made. In 1975, two orbiters with accompanying landers were launched to Mars. With such technically motivated beginnings to this mission, it seems like an addendum that Voyager-made-Viking's purpose was life detection.

As such, Viking was a kind of double experiment. On the one hand, Viking itself was designed as a trial in interplanetary operations; the mission would demonstrate the capacities of NASA to conduct landed scientific investigations. On the other hand, Viking's innovative configuration allowed for the experiments it carried to analyse a particular environment and potential biological inhabitants through an assortment of sample manipulations. Life detection, the methodological term for what some astrobiologists do, supports the study of the origin, evolution, distribution, and future of life in the universe. At astrobiology's core are three fundamental directives: (1) to determine the origin of life—specifically when complex prebiological chemistry becomes biology, (2) to find a second genesis of life, unrelated to biology on Earth, and (3) to determine the future of life in the universe. One of the persistent challenges of astrobiology is that it only has one biological subject, Earth life. Thus, in order to conduct their work, astrobiologists must acknowledge that life beyond Earth may have formed or developed functions that are radically different from what is known here. Experiments at analogue sites on Earth—such as the Atacama Desert in Chile or under the ocean near hydrothermal vents—are efforts to fix some of the limits of life's ability to survive in extreme environments (A. Davila, pers. comm. 2020; Hoehler, Bains et al. 2020; Hoehler, Brinckerhoff et al. 2021). Originally called exobiology, astrobiology emerged entangled with the national Cold War politics surrounding the launch of Sputnik and concerns about regulating cosmic exploration in the 1950s[5] (Bertka 2009; Dick and Strick 2004; Meltzer 2011). It is a deeply interdisciplinary field despite its emphasis on biology, attracting chemists, geologists, and bioinformatists as well as oceanographers and instrument scientists. The search for evidence of life draws on multiple kinds of scientific expertise because the form extraterrestrial biology may take is unknown, nor is it currently very well constrained by knowledge of planetary environments. Calculating the limits of life (Helmreich 2009, 2011; Hoehler, Bains et al. 2020), that mutable threshold between complex chemistry (or nonliving processes) and biology (or living systems), became a crucial factor in determining where to look for life and the kinds of measurements that would be most conducive to that environment.

After years of atmospheric evaluations of Mars, which provided images as well as meteorological and geological data about the Martian geography, the NASA of the late 1960s felt it was ready to embark on a mission that included biological investigations. At the time, the accepted strategy of conducting such research on Earth was through in-person fieldwork that allowed for the physical manipulation and preparation of samples as a method for generating data to be articulated into scientific knowledge. In outer space, this translated into a landed mission with a spacecraft that hosted a suite of instruments that stood in for the scientist. Effort to code the scientist's intuition and creativity in the field or lab into instrument technologies was an imperfect procedure. It sought to amalgamate data gathered remotely from previous flyby and satellite missions at Mars, cross-disciplinary scientific hypotheses that predicted the composition of the Martian environment, and scientists' own experiences of extreme environments on Earth (Davila et al. 2020; Ezell and Ezell 1984). However, despite all this preparation, astrobiologists could only speculate about how a biological mission should unfold and to what degree it could succeed at its goal to find life (see also abductive reasoning, as per Helmreich 2009). Thus, scientists had to design experiments that balanced the instruments' ability to be sensitive to difference while also communicating information intelligible to an Earth-informed conceptualisation and experience of biology.

Working Out Those Space-Legs

In the moment Viking landed on Mars, the spacecraft and the planet were, quite literally, connected. Taking this interaction seriously is an exercise of attention or attunement (Stewart 2011). Tuning into the Viking–Mars encounter invites curiosity about what may come into being in excess of mission plans and instrument results, especially, I argue, in this more-than-human relation (Tsing 2013; also see complementary approaches from multispecies anthropology, non-representational theory, and object-oriented ontology). Therefore, what happened beyond the conceptual and programmatic imaginaries of what Viking was supposed to deliver? Well, before the biological experiments could be initiated, Viking ran diagnostic tests of the various instruments and systems to ensure that they had not been damaged in the cruise and landing[6] (Ezell and Ezell 1984; Tillman and LeCompte 1991). Immediately, it was realised that the soft, fine-grained landscape had compromised the sampling arm, and it took three days to diagnose and regain the capacity to use it. Additionally, the seismometers had not been deployed, and these were a significant part of the environmental context science that would provide information about the planet's core and whether it had tectonic plates like Earth.[7] Remember the footpads, particularly the one that sank deeper than the other two? Mounted on footpad 2 was a temperature sensor. As Viking was passing through the atmosphere in its descent to Mars, the sensors, although designed to do entry science, were also used to get a basic measurement of surface and near-surface temperatures (Huber 2021). The report that summarised the instrument additionally described the challenges of this alternate application. Data gathered had to be recalibrated to account for elevated levels of conductivity from the ground, inconsistent radiation exposure due to seasonal changes, and the shadow of the lander itself artificially decreasing the temperature. As the legs upon which the lander stood settled into place, its difficulty getting a read on Mars thwarted the apparatus's core purpose: to take accurate measurements of the environment. Simultaneously, the inopportune occurrences allowed for the creative implementation of the footpad sensor. The seismometer, as it turns out, also ended up being used unconventionally to measure wind speed and dynamics (Ezell and Ezell 1984). Despite the instruments' inability to record detections within the scope of their design, through experimentation, these instruments did sense the environment. Particularly, in outer space, generating knowledge about the environment is something that is necessarily open-ended, prompting scientists towards alternative, resourceful operations spurred by wondering: "What else can be done? Will this work?"

Next, preprogrammed instruments were deployed, such as the meteorological suite, to begin gathering data about the environment. Two 360-degree cameras mounted on the spacecraft transmitted via antenna allowed scientists on Earth to experience the Martian terrestrial surface for the first time, up close. Almost immediately, the Martian landscape troubled what scientists had believed the surface of Mars would be like. While much had been learned from the Viking orbiters about the appearance of the surface, the resolution of the pictures made these aerial representations indistinct, and unplaceable (Messeri 2016). As an example, the significance of ground-level images is best captured by a report which described how the first colour picture was released to the public within eight hours of having been received by NASA. In the rush to release it to the public, the sky was incorrectly filtered, making it appear blue, like Earth's. When the scientists in charge of the camera instruments spoke up to correct the colour of the sky in the media, saying it was not blue but a light pink, the crowd supposedly hissed. The images simultaneously shattered what Mars was imagined to be, as it had been described in past astronomical observations as well as in fantasies witnessed in the dark of movie theatres. Carl Sagan is reported as saying in response, "The sort of boos given to Jerry Pollack's pronouncement about a pink sky reflects our wish for Mars to be just like the Earth" (Ezell and Ezell 1984). In what other ways would our Earth-centric perceptions of interpreting Mars be shaken?

Once the sampling arm was functioning, scientists performed a series of digging and piling exercises to understand the weight, density, and various other properties of the soil. They also used the arm's digging capacity to get below the top layer of surface material, which was heavily irradiated by UV rays from the sun. The decision of where to land on Mars had not been an easy one. Scientists' eventual agreement on Chryse Planitia in the northern equatorial region was after years of debates about the advantages of choosing the polar regions or the equatorial region, a decision centred around scientists' desire to access water (either present or past)[8] (Ezell and Ezell 1984). Water is one of three requirements for life. Or rather, it is equivalent to the more general life requirement: a liquid solvent to facilitate chemical reactions in, across, and with it as a medium. The other two are an energy source and nutrients. Thus, another part to deciding a landing spot was calculating the chemical elemental composition of the landscape. Biology on Earth is made up of organic compounds, primarily composed of the elements carbon, hydrogen, nitrogen, oxygen, phosphorus, and sulphur, or CHNOPS for short. The most prevalent is carbon, which is a crucial building element and source of energy utilised across living entities (Hoehler,

Bains et al. 2020). However, it's not enough for carbon to be present in an environment. Carbon is also used in abiotic, or nonbiological, processes. For carbon to be an indicator of life, it must be used in certain functions—such as metabolism or respiration—that are themselves evidence of living organisms. One point of concern was that scientists were not sure they could differentiate between biological, nonbiological, and prebiological (or complex chemistry that was on the threshold of becoming biology) processes with enough confidence. This effort is made more difficult when time is factored in, and scientists had to contend with degradation or destructive forces (such as solar radiation or cosmic rays) that could further obscure observations (Davila et al. 2020; Hoehler, Bains et al. 2020).

In those first few sols, Viking's settling into the routine of data gathering was also an opportunity to appraise itself in its new space. As a technoscientific extension of human scientists on Earth, on Mars, its significance was predicated on its ability to sift, sort, and scoop. To move. Playing in the dirt, tumbling pebbles that may have been sitting on the Martian surface undisturbed for years, invites us to recognise the excitement and thrill of being present in a place that is unknown. As an experiment in interplanetary encounters, Viking proved not only that such an interaction was possible, but that it was generative on multiple levels. Additionally, as a designed experiment for specific scientific objectives, regardless of the results, its operation on the Martian surface opened up space for the troubling of prior conceptions about Mars. Viking, as a double experiment, became a node around which the possibility of finding life—and knowing the secret of its origin—became immanent to every interactive act between Mars and Viking.

(Dis)entangling the Environment?

The biological instrument payload or package included three components[9] (Geosciences Node 2001). These were a pyrolytic experiment, a gas exchange experiment, and a labelled release experiment. On a basic level, all three required a soil sample to be introduced into a chamber and an agent (liquid or gas) to be added, with the expectation that any organisms present in the soil would react. Attuning to the sample intake of each experiment is a method for parsing the relation between the potential biological organisms in the soil and the soil as an environment. As the detectors sought to make sense of the soil, they were also part of a process that highlighted a central tension of astrobiology. The work of doing astrobiology necessitated scientists to attempt to constrain the unknowns of outer-space exploration by learning from and simultaneously suspending their knowledge about Earthly biology. At the Woods Hole meeting in 1970 to discuss the current state of Viking's construction, a lead scientist of the project, Joshua Lederberg, commented that the biological experiments were Earth-biased in their approach to identifying the limits of life. He said that there had not been sufficient time and resources to be more agnostic or attuned to the different ways life could have formed in a divergent Martian environment. In fact, beyond testing the instruments during their manufacture, the completely constructed instrument package arrived too late to be tested for full functioning end to end once it was installed on the spacecraft. Moreover, engineers admitted that testing should be discouraged because cleaning the experiments would require disassembly, incurring an expense way beyond the budget margin.[10] What did that mean for how Viking was trained to sense? One way to look at this is as an operational failure on the part of Viking scientists. But that doesn't explain why scientists even now talk about Viking with a mixture of reverence, warning, longing, anxiety.

In the moment of encounter, between the Martian sample and the nutrient or radioactive agent, before any data had been gathered or interpreted, was the possibility that life could exist on Mars. In action: the sampling arm would scoop soil from the surface and deposit it in a funnel that was connected to a piping mechanism leading to each experiment. One can imagine that the sample flowed smoothly through the apparatus, like sand in a timekeeper. A sieve filtered out pebbles to ensure that nothing got clogged and that each cycle of experimentation had exactly the same sample size. The instruments themselves were housed in an environmentally controlled chamber to keep the sample at a consistent temperature throughout the mission. The chamber could be heated up to 160°C to sterilise the unit after each sample was run. Part one of the experiment consisted of mixing soil with the nutrient agent. Then, after a certain time period, a detector was activated, to measure the rate of reaction. Based on the parameters set to give meaning to the information gathered, scientists could use the data to interpret whether or not evidence of life existed in the sample.

The experiment that was the most controversial (and still is) is the labelled release (LR) experiment (Levin and Straat 1976, 2016). Primarily, the difficulty in evaluating the LR results was that the experiment involves elements about the environment that scientists could not explain. The experiment was performed by introducing a liquid nutrient containing organic molecules like glycine (an amino acid common in living organisms) to a soil sample taken from the sandy dunes beside the lander. When the nutrient was introduced to the soil sample, a detector measured the gas that was produced when the two substances interacted. A positive result for the experiment would be that any organisms in the soil would ingest or otherwise metabolise the nutrients and create a by-product made of certain carbon compounds that scientists recognised. After two cycles of the experiment, scientists noticed a pattern, a very sharp spike of reactivity, followed by a plateau of flat activity. The manipulation of temperature across a range of 50°C–160°C also had an effect on the sample that scientists could not explain because the temperature-induced reactions were inconsistent across instruments. In an effort to contextualise what they were seeing on Mars, scientists compared the reactions to the same trials conducted on Earth soils, including a sample of sterilised Antarctic material. None quite fit. Unable to determine the source of the inconsistency and incomparability, scientists began to wonder: did these unusual results come about because of biological processing or nonbiological chemical reactions, or was it an unknown function of the environment?

Reflecting on these grapplings with trying to translate or categorise Mars, I became curious. Is the environment distinguishable from biology? Where does one end and the other begin? Don't they form a close-knit system, in which they exchange parts of themselves as they constitute the other? Scientists would agree: the line between the biological and ecological is very thin if it exists at all. Viking experiments brought home the reality of Earth's deep ecological entanglement. Biology doesn't happen in a vacuum—it interacts. Evidence of biology is present on a geological level. Think about coal and limestone: both are the result of the decomposition of organic matter—dead plant matter and fossilised shells, respectively—that become "rock" over hundreds of thousands of years. In fact, scientists are hard pressed to find any surface on Earth that hasn't been affected by biology. On Mars, however, that was not the case (at least not anymore, if there was life in the ancient past). The biological instruments in question did what they were supposed to do—look for life within a spectrum that would capture biological diversity on Earth. Yet, they were frustrated by a Mars that refused to be read as similar. It was already divergent; the effects of time, a gravity one-third of that on Earth, and relentless exposure to radiation had taken care of that—how could it be otherwise? Could the instruments be other than themselves, Earth-centred and geobiologically biased? The inability to distinguish the environment on Mars became a problem to address in the lab. The logic was that if they could mimic what the data was telling them was present, they could parse out the processes that produced the results they were seeing on Mars.

While some solutions were found to explain the reaction results, none were satisfactory, though that didn't stop scientists from trying to figure it out. What scientists could recognise was that the untranslatability of the Martian environment through an Earth instrument filter was always going to lead to ambiguity. Or put another way, the Earthly perspective was unable by itself to make sense of the Martian milieu. As Viking sat there sensing, taking measurements, and running experiments, it attended to the environment in a way that elicited from Mars a resonance or at least a "recognition" that Viking was there (recall: the shadow cast by the lander shifted the temperature just slightly; the soil there must have reacted ever so slightly, perhaps due to this shift in exposure to solar radiation). There was no immediate translation or perfect exchange that allowed Earth to "know" Mars fully and vice versa. Think back to how Viking is a double experiment, first, in its purpose as a life detection mission and second, through the operation of its biological instrument suite. Viking is shown to be generative beyond its ability to produce results towards determining whether life existed on Mars. The doing of experimentations—and the happenstances which occurred in excess of mission plans—revealed that other knowledges about Earth could be immanent in the interactions between Mars and Viking. Thus in more ways than one, the significance of the biological results' inconclusiveness, for the scientific community and for the conceptualisation of biology itself, reverberated well after the mission ended.

A Persistent Legacy

Across my fieldwork at NASA centres from 2018 through 2021, scientists in the present muttered about, exclaimed, ruminated, or sought to surmount this unsettling Viking legacy. When I first began asking about the details of this first astrobiological mission, I was surprised that it was the only such mission. The follow-up Viking-style lander missions to Mars, set to launch in 1984, were cancelled. Astrobiology became a secondary goal in the 1980s and onwards, with the rationale that habitability was a more reasonable goal. Habitability is the ability of an environment to host life. The planetary science community's decision to prioritise science that would survey, contextualise, and characterise the solar system's environmental system was in part in reaction to Viking's ambiguous results (Young 1978). Planetary science would fill the dearth of information about the solar system until astrobiological programmes were "ready", both fiscally and scientifically, to embark on another mission. This space science trajectory became manifested in public reports such as the Astrobiology Roadmap and NASA's Follow the Water strategy, documents with residual power today (Des Marais et al. 2008; Hoehler, Brinckerhoff et al. 2021; NRC 2007).

Pivotal in the way of a rock shifting the course of a river, Viking's effect was most significantly felt in mission selection and funding. Reviewing the list of missions since Viking, the trend from biology to geology couldn't be more stark. Among the popular or most recognised missions are Voyager 1 and 2 (1977) to interstellar space beyond the solar system, Magellan (1990) to map Venus's clouds, Galileo (1990) to do orbital science around Jupiter and its moons, Mars Pathfinder/Sojourner (1996) to land on Mars and test rover technology, Cassini-Huygens (1997) to do orbital and flyby science in the Saturnian system, Spirit and Opportunity rovers (2003) to conduct geological investigations and find evidence of ancient water on Mars, Phoenix (2007) to "follow the water" in the polar region of Mars, and the most more recent cadre of Mars missions: Curiosity (2011), InSight (2018), and Perseverance (2021) (Siddiqi 2018). All these missions and so many more that were launched across the world, by Russia, Japan, India, Europe, and now commercial enterprises, have been geared towards gathering data about the environment and habitability as their primary mission objectives. It is only now in the current Decadal Survey for 2023–2032, organised by the Space Studies Board of the National Academies of Sciences to get community input on the next ten years of mission priorities, that astrobiology is positioned as a central mission objective along with the planetary sciences.

As I followed the Decadal proceedings in the last year, Viking continued to be brought up, haunting mission proposal meetings and flitting across measurement selection debates. Uncertainty, unbound, abounded. In Viking's "present", scientists wondered whether refining variables that may affect the soil—how long the nutrient sat with the soil before it was tested by the detector, or whether soil collected from a deeper subsurface level was less damaged by sunlight exposure—may explain why the results after two of three cycles were perplexing (these inquiries continue, i.e., Quinn et al. 2013). In Viking's "future", scientists from the 1980s onward took to heart the inability of astrobiology to account for the data conclusively and restructured the trajectory of NASA missions accordingly. If the Viking mission is only evaluated for its end—for its results—its inability to disentangle the environment from what it hosts, whether biological or abiotic, only becomes significant because it throws doubt on processes of scientific certainty and knowledge production. Yet, returning to the Viking–Mars encounter, Viking's physical presence, experimental resourcefulness, excessive creativity, and persistence across time has shown to offer a different resolution beyond the inconclusive—not one of doubt or anxiety but rather of possibility.

Immanence and Interplanetary Attunement

Can we ever know what is immanent at the moment of encounter? Or are we only able to perceive partialities that give us the possibility to imagine multiple futures otherwise? In my time in the archives, the moments I remember the most were when I would suddenly get swept away by a provocative line in a memo, or the urgency of a voice in a correspondence. Amidst the grey cardboard boxes that housed hundreds of thousands of pages of material, I would attempt to trace the circumstances around the report or memo. But oftentimes, I would be left sifting through folders, thread lost, because that story was continued off the page, perhaps in a phone call or an unofficial meeting. But the feelings evoked by those lines of text moved me, and as I walked home, I'd often imagine what the rest of that story could have been. Curiosity kept me coming back to the archives, in wonder of what other partial lives I could encounter and carry with me.

What if Mars and Viking when they touched created an opportunity for interplanetary attunement? Delving into the fact that Earth and Mars have been exchanging geological material in the form of meteorites for eons, it's evocative to think about what those interactions have generated. Starting during the formation of the planetary bodies, the transference of materials hints at the sharing not only of minerals and metals but possibly the seeds of life—organic molecules. In discussions held by the Prebiotic Chemistry and Early Earth Environments research unit of NASA, it is generally accepted that the direction of impacts was from Mars to Earth. Embodied, emboldened, bouldered—these impacts between Earth and Mars shatter the illusion that there had ever been separation. Perhaps we are Mars's kin. In the genealogical sense, our Earthly present may be the result of Martian biology that travelled via meteorites to Earth. Even if that is not the case, the Viking mission to Mars is another kind of kinship (Haraway 2016), one based on circumstances that have brought Earth via Viking into relation with Mars. In the catch-up session of a long tease, in which Earth sent orbiters to fly by and become familiar with Mars, what a different kind of impression Viking must have made, when it actually landed and survived (USSR Mars 2 spacecraft probes had been sent earlier in the decade and crashed; Siddiqi 2018). Did the metallic presence remind Mars of its past, of a potential life form in ancient times moving across its surface? We will probably never know. What we do know is that when the dust settled after Viking landed, two once separate (or should I say separated) entities came into ecological relation (Salazar 2017; Tsing 2017).

Dwelling on the interaction of Viking on Mars through a method of attunement invites us to ponder what futures are immanent when two entities meet on an interplanetary scale. What I propose is not that we "attain" a Martian perspective, mastered through setting detection limits and measurement standards. Rather, I hope that the efforts to understand Mars on its own terms, as astrobiologists do when they suspend their Earth bias and simultaneously embrace the richness of it as they dream up missions, acknowledge the importance of relating, and our capacity to relate despite differences. Whether there is a Martian way of being that may be beyond Earth-based ones, striving towards understanding is important in and of itself. Grappling with this messy, uncertain process is a way to slow the fast flows and frictions of colonial and capitalist settling, and attune ourselves to an interplanetary way of living.

Notes

1. NASA. 2021a. "Viking Lander 1." NSSDCA/COSPAR ID: 1975-075C. NASA Space Science Data Coordinated Archive, v. 5.1. https://nssdc.gsfc.nasa.gov/nmc/spacecraft/display.action?id=1975-075C.
2. NASA. 1976a. "First Panorama Picture of Mars." https://nssdc.gsfc.nasa.gov/imgcat/hires/vl1_p17045.jpg.
3. Alfonso Davila, pers. comm., 2022. Dr. Davila contributed greatly to my knowledge of astrobiology and the Viking mission through regular meetings during the course of my fieldwork.
4. NASA History Division. Historical Reference Collection. Box 64, Space Probes Subject Files. "Mars Voyager (Viking)." #5549.
    NASA History Division. Historical Reference Collection. Box 97. "Viking Organization—Science." Space Probes Subject Files. #5490–92.
5. NASA History Division. Historical Reference Collection. Box 6. "Satellite Systems, Sterilization." #6696–97.
6. NASA History Division, box 97.
    NASA History Division. Historical Reference Collection. Box (unknown). "Folder 1–2: Voyager, Sterilization." #16603.
7. NASA. 2021a. "Viking Lander 1." NSSDCA/COSPAR ID: 1975-075C. NASA Space Science Data Coordinated Archive, v. 5.1. https://nssdc.gsfc.nasa.gov/nmc/spacecraft/display.action?id=1975-075C.
    NASA. 2021b. "Viking Lander Labeled Release Experiment Archive (PDS)." NSSDCA ID: PSBI-00001. NASA Space Science Data Coordinated Archive, v. 5.1. https://nssdc.gsfc.nasa.gov/nmc/dataset/display.action?id=PSBI-00001.
8. NASA. 1976b. "Viking Press Handbook." Document ID: 19760019036. NASA Technical Reports Server. https://ntrs.nasa.gov/archive/nasa/casi.ntrs.nasa.gov/19760019036.pdf.
9. NASA Historical Division, box 97.
10. NASA History Division. Historical Reference Collection. Box 95. "Viking General—Costs: Folder 2–5, Miscellaneous Viking Materials." Space Probes Subject Files. #5481–83.
    NASA History Division. Historical Reference Collection. Box 96. "Viking General—Costs: Folder 2–5, Miscellaneous Viking Materials." Space Probes Subject Files. #5485–89.
    NASA History Division, box 97.

References

Bertka, Constance M., ed. 2009. *Exploring the Origin, Extent, and Future of Life: Philosophical, Ethical and Theological Perspectives*. Cambridge: Cambridge University Press.
Davila, A., M. A. Kahre, R. Quinn, and D. J. Des Marais. 2020. "The Biological Potential of Present-Day Mars." In *Planetary Astrobiology*, edited by Victoria S. Meadows, Giada N. Arney, Britney E. Schmidt and David J. Des Marais, 169–84. Space Science Series. Tucson, AZ: University of Arizona Press. http://www.jstor.org/stable/j.ctv105bb62.13
Deleuze, Gilles, and Félix Guattari. 1983. *Anti-Oedipus: Capitalism and Schizophrenia*. Minneapolis: University of Minnesota Press.
Des Marais, David J., Joseph A. Nuth III, Louis J. Allamandola, Alan P. Boss, Jack D. Farmer, Tori M. Hoehler, and Bruce M. Jakosky, et al. 2008. "The NASA Astrobiology Roadmap." *Astrobiology* 8 (4): 715–30. https://doi.org/10.1089/ast.2008.0819.
DeVincenzi, Donald L., Margaret S. Race, and Harold P. Klein. 1998. "Planetary Protection, Sample Return Missions and Mars Exploration: History, Status, and Future Needs." *Journal of Geophysical Research* 103 (E12): 28577–85. https://doi.org/10.1029/98JE01600.
Dick, Steven J., and James E. Strick. 2004. *The Living Universe: NASA and the Development of Astrobiology*. New Brunswick, NJ: Rutgers University Press.
Ezell, Edward Clinton, and Linda Neuman Ezell. 1984. *On Mars: Exploration of the Red Planet, 1958–1978*. NASA SP-4212, NASA History Series. Washington, DC: Scientific and Technical Information Branch, NASA.
Geosciences Node 2001 (updated). "Viking Biology Instrument." NASA *Planetary Data System*. https://pds-geosciences.wustl.edu/viking/vl1_vl2-m-lr-2-edr-v1/vl_9010/extras/vbioinst.htm.

Haraway, Donna. 2016. *Staying With the Trouble: Making Kin in the Chthulucene.* Durham, NC: Duke University Press.
Helmreich, Stefan. 2009. *Alien Ocean: Anthropological Voyages in Microbial Seas.* Berkeley: University of California Press.
Helmreich, Stefan. 2011. "What Was Life? Answers from Three Limit Biologies." *Critical Inquiry* 37 (4): 671–96. https://doi.org/10.1086/660987.
Hoehler, Tori, William Bains, Alfonso Davila, Mary Parenteau, and Andrew Pohorille. 2020. "Life's Requirements, Habitability, and Biological Potential." In *Planetary Astrobiology*, edited by Victoria S. Meadows, Giada N. Arney, Britney E. Schmidt and David J. Des Marais, 37–69. Tucson, AZ: University of Arizona Press. http://www.jstor.org/stable/j.ctv105bb62.8.
Hoehler, Tori, William Brinckerhoff, Alfonso Davila, David Des Marais, Stephanie Getty, Danny Glavin, Andrew Pohorille, and Richard Quinn, et al. 2021. "Groundwork for Life Detection." *Bulletin of the American Astronomical Society* 53 (4): 1–8 https://doi.org/10.3847/25c2cfeb.bd9172f9.
Huber, Lyle (curator). 2021 (updated). "Welcome to the Viking Lander Archive." *NASA Planetary Data System.* https://atmos.nmsu.edu/data_and_services/atmospheres_data/MARS/viking/viking_lander.html.
Kaplan, Edward. 2015. *To Kill Nations: American Strategy in the Air-Atomic Age and the Rise of Mutually Assured Destruction.* New York: Cornell University Press.
Launius, Roger D., and Dennis R. Jenkins. 2002. *To Reach the High Frontier: A History of U.S. Launch Vehicles.* Lexington: University Press of Kentucky.
Leslie, Stuart W. 1993. *The Cold War and American Science: The Military-Industrial Academic Complex at MIT and Stanford.* New York: Columbia University Press.
Levin, Gilbert V., and Patricia Ann Straat. 1976. "Viking Labeled Release Biology Experiment: Interim Results." *Science* 194 (4271): 1322–29. http://www.jstor.org/stable/1743818.
Levin, Gilbert V., and Patricia Ann Straat. 2016. "The Case for Extant Life on Mars and Its Possible Detection by the Viking Labeled Release Experiment." *Astrobiology* 16 (10): 798–810. https://doi.org/10.1089/ast.2015.1464.
Lowe, Lisa. 2015. *The Intimacies of Four Continents.* Durham, NC: Duke University Press.
McKinson, Kimberley D. 2020. "Do Black Lives Matter in Outer Space?" *Sapiens*, 30 September 2020. https://www.sapiens.org/culture/space-colonization-racism/.
Meltzer, Michael. 2011. *When Biospheres Collide: A History of NASA's Planetary Protection Programs.* NASA SP-2011-4234. Washington DC: National Aeronautics and Space Administration. https://www.nasa.gov/connect/ebooks/when_biospheres_collide_detail.html.
Messeri, Lisa. 2016. *Placing Outer Space: An Earthly Ethnography of Other Worlds.* Durham, NC: Duke University Press.
NASA 1976a. *First Panorama Picture of Mars.* https://nssdc.gsfc.nasa.gov/imgcat/hires/vl1_p17045.jpg.
NASA 1976b. "Viking Press Handbook." Document ID: 19760019036. *NASA Technical Reports Server.* https://ntrs.nasa.gov/archive/nasa/casi.ntrs.nasa.gov/19760019036.pdf.
NASA 2021a. "Viking Lander 1." NSSDCA/COSPAR ID: 1975-075C. *NASA Space Science Data Coordinated Archive*, v. 5.1. https://nssdc.gsfc.nasa.gov/nmc/spacecraft/display.action?id=1975-075C.
NASA 2021b. "Viking Lander Labeled Release Experiment Archive (PDS)." NSSDCA ID: PSBI-00001. *NASA Space Science Data Coordinated Archive*, v. 5.1. https://nssdc.gsfc.nasa.gov/nmc/dataset/display.action?id=PSBI-00001.
NASA History Division. Historical Reference Collection. Box 6. *Satellite Systems, Sterilization.* #6696–97.
NASA History Division. Historical Reference Collection. Box 64, *Space Probes Subject Files.* "Mars Voyager (Viking)." #5549.
NASA History Division. Historical Reference Collection. Box 95. "Viking General—Costs: Folder 2–5, Miscellaneous Viking Materials." *Space Probes Subject Files.* #5481–83.
NASA History Division. Historical Reference Collection. Box 96. "Viking General—Costs: Folder 2–5, Miscellaneous Viking Materials." *Space Probes Subject Files.* #5485–89.
NASA History Division. Historical Reference Collection. Box 97. "Viking Organization—Science." *Space Probes Subject Files.* #5490–92.
NASA History Division. Historical Reference Collection. Box (unknown). "Folder 1–2: Voyager, Sterilization." #16603.
Neufeld, Michael J. 1995. *The Rocket and the Reich: Peenemünde and the Coming of the Ballistic Missile Era.* New York: Free Press.
NRC (National Research Council) 2007. *An Astrobiology Strategy for the Exploration of Mars.* Washington, DC: The National Academies Press. https://doi.org/10.17226/11937.

Olson, Valerie. 2018. *Into the Extreme: U.S. Environmental Systems and Politics Beyond Earth*. Minneapolis: University of Minnesota Press.

Povinelli, Elizabeth. 2016. *Geontologies: A Requiem to Late Capitalism*. Durham, NC: Duke University Press.

Quinn, Richard C., Hana F. H. Martucci, Stephanie R. Miller, Charles E. Bryson, Frank J. Grunthaner, and Paula J. Grunthaner. 2013. "Perchlorate Radiolysis on Mars and the Origin of Martian Soil Reactivity." *Astrobiology* 13 (6): 515–20. https://doi.org/10.1089/ast.2013.0999.

Rand, Lisa Ruth. 2016. *Orbital Decay: Space Junk and the Environmental History of Earth's Planetary Borderlands*. PhD Dissertation, University of Pennsylvania. Publicly Accessible Penn Dissertations. 1963. https://repository.upenn.edu/edissertations/1963.

Redfield, Peter. 2000. *Space in the Tropics: From Convicts to Rockets in French Guiana*. Berkeley: University of California Press.

Salazar, Juan Francisco. 2017. "Antarctica and Outer Space: Relational Trajectories." *The Polar Journal* 7 (2): 259–69. https://doi.org/10.1080/2154896X.2017.1398521.

Sharpe, Christina. 2016. *In the Wake: On Blackness and Being*. Durham, NC: Duke University Press.

Siddiqi, Asif A. 2000. *Challenge to Apollo: The Soviet Union and the Space Race, 1945–1974*. NASA History Series 2000-4408. Washington, DC: National Aeronautics and Space Administration, NASA History Division, Office of Policy and Plans.

Siddiqi, Asif A. 2018. *Beyond Earth: A Chronicle of Deep Space Exploration, 1958–2016*. NASA SP-2018-4041. Washington, DC: NASA History Division.

Simpson, Audra. 2014. *Mohawk Interruptus: Political Life Across the Borders of Settler States*. Durham, NC: Duke University Press.

Smiles, Deondre. 2020. "The Settler Logics of (Outer) Space." *Society+Space*, 26 October 2020. https://www.societyandspace.org/articles/the-settler-logics-of-outer-space.

Stewart, Kathleen. 2011. "Atmospheric Attunements." *Environment and Planning D: Society and Space* 29 (3): 445–53. https://doi.org/10.1068/d9109.

Tillman, James E., and George F. LeCompte. 1991. "Exercise 2: Feeling Dirt or Soil at the Lander 1 Site." *Live from Earth & Mars*. www-k12.atmos.washington.edu/k12/resources/mars_data-information/EX2.html#footpad%202.

Tsing, Anna Lowenhaupt. 2013. "More-than-Human Sociality: A Call for Critical Description." In *Anthropology and Nature*, edited by Kirsten Hastrup, 27–42. London: Routledge. https://doi.org/10.4324/9780203795361.

Tsing, Anna Lowenhaupt. 2017. *The Mushroom at the End of the World: On the Possibility of Life in Capitalist Ruins*. Princeton: Princeton University Press.

Turchetti, Simone, and Peder Roberts. 2014. *The Surveillance Imperative: Geosciences During the Cold War and Beyond*. New York Palgrave Macmillan

Valentine, David. 2017. "Gravity Fixes: Habituating to the Human on Mars and Island Three." *HAU: Journal of Ethnographic Theory* 7 (3): 185–209. http://doi.org/10.14318/hau7.3.012.

Wolfe, Audra J. 2002. "Germs in Space: Joshua Lederberg, Exobiology, and the Public Imagination, 1958–1964." *Isis* 93 (2): 183–205. https://doi.org/10.1086/344962.

Young, Richard S. 1978. "Post-Viking Exobiology." *BioScience* 28 (8): 502–05. https://doi.org/10.2307/1307296.

38
A POST-GEOCENTRIC GRAVITOGRAPHY OF HUMAN CULTURE

Alice Gorman

Introduction

With the exception of a small group of people currently orbiting Earth in space stations, all human activities take place against the backdrop of one unit of Earth's gravity. This is such a ubiquitous feature in terrestrial life that its effects on human culture are barely remarked upon (Gorman 2009). And yet Earth's gravitational disposition has not been constant throughout the evolution of the planet; human understandings of gravity have undergone many iterations; and even within the narrow band of atmosphere and pressure occupied by life on Earth, there are many situations where humans experience variable or inconstant gravities. Add to this social and cultural responses to gravity, and it is easy to make the case that gravity is far more complex than Isaac Newton's universal force (1846) or Einstein's deformable spacetime (1905, 1916). Forces, particles, waves, and quantum uncertainty are insufficient to capture how creatures with memories, emotions, and bodies experience gravity.

Soon, however, more humans are likely to engage with variable gravity environments outside Earth. The predicted growth in the space tourist market for suborbital flights will increase the number of people who have experienced higher gravity to free-fall, in a flight of approximately fifteen minutes. "Spacefaring" nations such as the US, Russia, and China are planning crewed missions to lunar orbit and eventually the lunar surface. Perhaps, someday, people will live on Mars. So understanding human engagements with gravity has direct applications to the future of space endeavours.

These different gravity environments create challenges for the health and growth of human bodies, and for the design of the habitats and infrastructure that allow humans to survive off-Earth. However, this is only half the story. Gravity also plays a role in structuring social relations, the emotions, and the embodied experience of an environment. This includes aspects of class, gender, and post-humanity. Taking the high-gravity worlds of science fiction writer Stephen Goldin as a starting point, this chapter is an exploration of the different ways we can understand the influence of gravity on human cultures both on and beyond Earth.

Falling, and Falling in Love

The ten Family d'Alembert science fiction novels were written by Stephen Goldin between 1976 and 1985, based on a 1964 novella by E. E. "Doc" Smith. The novels are set four hundred years in the future and feature a family of circus performers from the planet DesPlaines, which has three times Earth's gravity. As falling could be fatal in this much gravity, DesPlainians have evolved bodies with lightning reflexes and exceptional strength. Their bones are denser and their physiques shorter and stockier than is typical for humans from Earth. These qualities make them excellent bodyguards, labourers, and circus performers. The hereditary rulers of DesPlaines, the d'Alembert[1] family, operate and perform in the Circus of the Galaxy as a cover for their deep involvement in the secret Service of the Empire (SOTE).

In the galactic empire, only a few high-gravity planets have been colonised by humans. They include DesPlaines, Newforest, and Purity. The original settlers of these planets, in the carving up of the galaxy, were marginalised groups in terrestrial society: carnies, "gypsies", and, in the case of the planet Purity, religious fanatics. They've drawn the short straw in the lottery of habitable worlds. The problems of adaption to "high-grav" means that Earth-normal humans rarely visit these planets, although their inhabitants roam the galaxy freely. They are instantly recognisable as high-grav bodies unless they take pains to disguise their robust musculature.

The societies of the high-grav worlds tend to be endogamous. When galactic secret agent Yvette d'Alembert falls in love with an Earth-normal man, he is duly killed off, and she can pair herself more suitably with a native of Newforest, which was colonised by Roma people. Her brother Jules has sensibly fallen in love with one of his d'Alembert cousins, a former circus performer, as he and his sister also were. Cross-gravity love is seen as problematic because bodies have different capabilities, and one member of the couple must necessarily make a sacrifice to live in the gravity regime of the other.

While the Family d'Alembert series is a vastly entertaining read with an appealing gender-equal universe, Stephen Goldin's galaxy shows some of the ways in which gravity is not socially neutral. The gravitational landscape of the Galactic Empire shapes social norms which determine allowable marriages, suitable professions, and the routes of interplanetary travel. When there is more than one type of gravity, cultural variation should be expected. This, of course, is the future, whereas human experience in the present day is with only one type of gravity. Or is it?

"Gravity: It's Not Just a Good Idea, It's the Law"[2]

At this point, we should consider what this force that we all experience, and that we distil into equations and teach children about at school, actually is. Gravity is invisible: we know it only by its effects. It is universal: there is no existence without some relationship to it. And it is understood according to which theory is applied in a given circumstance.

Isaac Newton's law of universal gravitation unified a set of disparate phenomena. Before him, it wasn't obvious that gravity was equally the cause of, for example, planetary motion and fruit falling from trees. The concept of universal gravitation states that every object in the universe exerts a gravitational force on every other object, expressed in the equation $F = G\dfrac{M_1 M_2}{R_2}$, where F is the gravitational force acting between two objects, G is the gravitational constant, m_1 and m_2 are the masses of the two objects, and r is the distance between their centres of mass. First published in the *Principia* in 1687, the theory wasn't proved until over one hundred years later.

Einstein reformulated gravity in the theory of general relativity. Gravity was not a force, but a geometry in spacetime. As theoretical physicist John Wheeler famously said, "Space-time tells matter how to move; matter tells space-time how to curve" (2010: 235). The effect of gravity, i.e., the attraction between objects, was a consequence of bodies moving along invisible geodesic lines in a curved spacetime caused by the uneven distribution of mass. Instead of Einsteinian gravity replacing Newtonian gravity, Bohr's correspondence principle is applied: at a large enough scale, the two models produce the same outcome. However, at the quantum scale, the theoretical and practical effects of quantised gravity, such as the graviton particle, are still elusive.

In general, daily life on planet Earth is described well enough by Newton's classical mechanics. There is not always such agreed accommodation between different paradigms, however. The mathematical and experiential are often considered to be opposed or mutually exclusive. This is exemplified in a famous rivalry between the colour theories of Goethe and Newton (Ribe 1985). Mathematically, Newton's model of colour as different wavelengths of light is objectively true. Goethe, however, explored the role of light and shade in human colour perception (Goethe 1840). While Newton has traditionally been considered "right" and Goethe "wrong", in fact, they are describing different facets of the same phenomenon. In this chapter I want to take Goethe's position in relation to gravity, moving beyond the equations and into the realm of human experience.

Beyond the Equation

Newton made gravitation a universal that we are used to thinking of as a fixed quantity; but just a brief inquiry demonstrates that gravity is not invariant in space or time. First, western science has characterised gravity as something that can exist as multiples of a base unit. In what I might call Late Geocentrism, the standard unit of measurement of gravity is 1*g*, the average gravity of Earth. In other places, gravity can be more or less: the Moon has one-sixth the "quantity" of Earth's gravity, and Mars one-third. Larger planets, like Jupiter, are over 2.5 times greater (Table 38.1). We tend to interpret these numbers in human bodily terms: whether we will be lighter or heavier. The Apollo Moon landings in the 1960s were a powerful visual demonstration of what it meant to be lighter, as the television camera enabled millions of the Earthbound to watch the astronauts gambolling about the lunar terrain like lambs.

There are also terms for what is experienced as the absence of gravity, although universal gravitation tells us that it is not at all absent: freefall, zero gravity, microgravity, and even antigravity. There are countless science fiction accounts of antigravity mechanisms which remove the force of gravity from a limited environment by mysterious technology, while regular gravity holds sway everywhere else. The earliest known version of this is the gravity-lowering Ebelus stone[3] in Francis Godwin's 1638 tale of Domingo Gonsales's trip to the Moon.

While each celestial body has its own gravitational field, these bodies are not perfect isotropic spheres. Many have an uneven distribution of mass within them, creating variation in the strength of gravity. The orbit of the Vanguard 1 satellite around Earth in 1958 was affected by this unequal distribution, which perturbed the spacecraft from its predicted path and revealed a planet as lumpy as a rotting plum. There are also mascons, areas of higher mass concentration or density, which exert a greater gravitational attraction than the surrounding areas. Mascons render the Moon gravitationally lopsided in a way that makes it hard for satellites to achieve a stable orbit (e.g., Murphy and Siry 1970).

Gravity has also changed over the history of the planet itself, as it underwent various transformations. The protoplanetary mass initially grew by accumulation of orbital materials, coalescing into a planet around 4.6 billion years ago. From 4.5 to 3.9 billion years ago its mass increased through bombardment by asteroids and planetoids, culminating in the Late Heavy Bombardment (during this time icy bodies likely delivered the oceans to Earth). Since stabilisation, it has accumulated approximately 40,000 tons of extraterrestrial material per year (Peucker-Ehrenbrink and Schmitz 2001)—this is 120,000 million tons since human ancestors evolved approximately 3 million years ago—but also is losing 50,000 tons per year as elements leach out into space. So the Earth is getting smaller at a barely perceptible rate all the time; and its gravitational attraction, or the way it bends spacetime, is decreasing as well.

Human activities have played their own small part in this exodus, as spacecraft made of Earth materials remove them from the planet and deposit them elsewhere in the solar system. The Moon (formed 4.51 billion years ago) may soon be part of this redistribution if plans to mine water ice to use as fuel to travel to Mars eventuate. People often express the fear that lunar mining will reduce the Moon's mass to the point that its gravitational effect on Earth, principally the tides, will be negatively affected. This is a very far-future scenario indeed, and even then, extremely unlikely. In the shorter term, however, both Earth and the Moon are slowly eroding into space by natural and human agencies. Their level of gravity is not a stable characteristic even though it appears so to us.

Changes in planetary gravity may take place at a time scale beyond human perception; but gravity can also be a temporary state of affairs fluctuating over minutes or months, like in a fairground roller coaster ride, a zero-g flight, or suborbital spacecraft which moves between 1g and freefall, or a spacecraft which journeys to the surface of the Moon and back. Some gravities, like the higher gs resulting from acceleration and deceleration, are created in the process of making the journey; they are epiphenomena of leaving the planet. This gives us a distinction between "natural" or ambient gravity—what we find in the environment—and "artificial" gravity created by technology. Antigravity technology nullifies gravitational attraction, but there is also a need to replicate 1g gravity in orbit so that biological and chemical functions evolved on Earth can continue. This is achieved by spinning. The as-yet-unrealised rotating space station, first described from an engineering perspective by Hermann Potočnik Noordung in 1929, creates an island of 1g gravity in the freefall of orbit (Noordung [1929] 1995).

In all of this, 1g is taken as the standard by which we describe the gravity of celestial bodies and even assess their "habitability" when they occur in other solar systems (Rodríguez-Mozos and Moya 2017). Table 38.1 shows gravity according to a planet's distance from the Sun and multiples of 1g. It tells us something about how the planets are conceptualised, but perhaps not as much about gravity itself. Are there other ways of expressing this gravitography? Perhaps it makes more sense to take zero g as the standard and work outwards from there, or express the gravity as a multiple of the Sun's instead of Earth's. We could take some hypothetical equilibrium point as zero on our scale. Or we could make gravity a continuous curve threading the solar system and assign values according to location. No doubt there are reasons why such scales are mathematically unworkable. Nonetheless, it remains interesting that the Copernican revolution has barely touched Late Geocentric attitudes to gravity.

In inhabiting this and other solar systems, we seek planets close to 1g that enable the human body to translate itself easily to the new environment. As the artist Ralo Mayer has said, "the human body is a habit of gravity" (2022a). This alone says something about how the future is imagined. If the Late Geocentric commitment to 1g is eroded, then we must also abandon the idea of the human body in its current form.

Table 38.1 Comparative gravity of solar system bodies. Source: edited from Wikipedia

Body	Multiple of Earth gravity (g)	m/s^2	Time to fall 100 m and maximum speed reached	
Sun	27.90	274.1	0.85 s	843 km/h
Mercury	0.3770	3.703	7.4 s	98 km/h
Venus	0.9032	8.872	4.8 s	152 km/h
Earth	**1**	**9.8067**	**4.5 s**	**159 km/h**
Moon	0.1655	1.625	11.1 s	65 km/h
Mars	0.3895	3.728	7.3 s	98 km/h
Jupiter	2.640	25.93	2.8 s	259 km/h
Saturn	1.139	11.19	4.2 s	170 km/h
Uranus	0.917	9.01	4.7 s	153 km/h
Neptune	1.148	11.28	4.2 s	171 km/h
Pluto[4]	0.0621	0.610	18.1 s	40 km/h

The Evolutionary Relationship to Gravity

Just as taking a deeper perspective on Earth's history demonstrates how its intrinsic gravity has varied over time, so too we can look at the evolution of the human body and how its relationship to gravity has changed.

Humans and their ancestors have occupied different gravitational niches, starting with an arboreal or aerial phase, followed by "coming down from the trees" around 4 million years ago (a big mistake according to some in Douglas Adams's 1980 *The Hitchhiker's Guide to the Galaxy*). A few million years of terrestrial bipedality ensued. But perhaps it was more complicated than that. In the "Aquatic Ape" theory, humans took to the water at some point in this period (Morgan 1982). Once widely decried, a new scholarship is emerging around the aquatic ape (e.g., Vaneechoutte, Kuliukas, and Verhaegen 2011), which interrogates the human relationship to water. There is a nice symmetry in this, as water is often used as a simulated microgravity environment to train astronauts (Figure 38.1).

Archaeological evidence does not reveal much about human engagement with gravity during most of the terrestrial bipedal phase, until perhaps the first non-perishable antigravity technologies in the form of staircases, scaffolds, ladders, and towers, probably around six thousand years ago. The eighteenth century of the Common Era (CE) saw the emergence of mobile technologies for attaining the "footless halls of air" (Magee 1941), such as balloons in China and Europe. In the twentieth century, the invention of aeroplanes made the atmosphere a domain of war; then rockets pierced the clouds, and the upward movement continued with satellites in microgravity and spacecraft using moons and planets as mere devices for the "gravity assist", to fling them into interplanetary trajectories. Now we were really playing with gravity, using robots as human avatars.

The changing evolutionary relationship to gravity could be summarised as having three aspects:

1. The disposition of limbs, e.g., losing a tail, becoming bipedal;
2. The change in the centre of gravity entailed;
3. The use of gravitational prostheses in architecture and locomotion to enlarge the range of gravities accessible, and nullify the effects of the "work" created by gravity.

In the Newtonian gravity-worlds, everything has a centre of mass, and human bodies are no exception. Bipedality has meant that human bodies have a comparatively high centre of mass (COM) compared to other animals. Two-thirds of the body mass is located two-thirds of the height from the ground (Winter 1995). The risk of falling is far greater than for quadrupeds, which have a much lower COM. The entire apparatus of musculature is mobilised into counteracting the effects of gravity and maintaining balance in order to remain upright (Boughen, Nitz, and Johnston 2017). This feature was used by the US choreographer Stephen Paxton to create the "small dance", utilising the resting upright position or "quiet stance" to feel the minute movements of the body to maintain stability (Gorman 2019: 274; Paxton 1975). For Paxton, gravity was a partner in the dance.

Standing up in $1g$ gravity requires constant work. And, as Boughen, Nitz, and Johnston (2017) point out, the relationship to gravity changes with the passage of time from birth to old age, as the child develops from quadrupedal to bipedal locomotion, perhaps eventually relying on a prosthetic as the bones and muscles lose their strength: the riddle of the Sphinx reinterpreted through a gravitational lens.

Noordung hinted at a future stage of microgravity evolution where $1g$ habits would necessarily be discarded:

A Post-Geocentric Gravitography of Human Culture

Figure 38.1 Crew training in the Marshall space flight center neutral buoyancy simulator, 1967. Image courtesy of NASA.

> These unusual conditions [of zero gravity] must ... lead to the result that all bodies show a completely altered behavior and that, in accordance with this behavior, our unique actions and inactions will develop in a manner entirely different from previous ones.
>
> *([1929] 1995: 80–81)*

Without the pull of 1*g*, the body assumes the "neutral posture" (Mount, Whitmore, and Stealey 2003), curling up like a spider on its back or a floating foetus. Different gravities are a challenge to bipedality, the much-vaunted achievement of human evolution. In microgravity, legs and feet are superfluous. The soles of the feet return to the state of the newborn who has not yet set foot on terra firma (Pomeroy 2017) and the shoe becomes a cultural affectation rather than an essential. The astronaut swims through the cylinders of the space station like a mermaid, using feet and hands to attach themselves to the walls where an anchorhold presents itself. Perhaps we can read Hans Christian Andersen's tale of the little mermaid as a gravitational metaphor as she mutilates her body to adapt to bipedality in 1*g*—another example of the perils of cross-gravity love.

In the one-sixth gravity of the Moon, the 1*g* stride is abandoned for the much more effective skipping (Ackermann and van den Bogert 2012). This hypogravity gait mimics quadrupedal motion (Pavei, Biancardi, and Minetti 2015). Pavei, Biancardi, and Minetti's measurements "show that unilateral skipping, an expensive gallop-derived bipedal gait on Earth used by lemurs and (perhaps vestigially) by humans, has a central role in low-gravity locomotion" (2015: 99). Earlier evolutionary modalities of locomotion thus resurface in a case of ontogeny recapitulating phylogeny.

Fear of Falling, Fear of Flying

The only environments where falling is impossible are one- or two-dimensional, where there is no up or down. In Edwin Abbott's 1884 fable of the two-dimensional Flatland, the three-dimensional Sphere has a terrible business trying to explain verticality to the Flatlanders, and the one-dimensional denizens of Lineland are equally flummoxed by the concept of the plane in which you can travel in four directions. In three-or-higher-dimensional worlds, falling is always a possibility. We're afraid of falling and injuring ourselves, breaking bones, and tearing muscles, although we'd probably never say it was gravity itself that we feared.

Flying, on the other hand, is associated with excitement and joy. The spectacle of watching circus aerialists captures the exhilaration and the fear simultaneously. Their gravity-defying feats have been a human fascination since the origins of the art form in the 1700s. The courage and skill needed to nullify the risks of falling experienced by ordinary humans demonstrate both the adaptability of the human body and a desire to be free of gravity. Fox (2016) calls it "a disconcerting pact with gravity".

In his 1929 exploration of space travel, Noordung noted that falling causes anxiety on Earth, and in microgravity or free-fall, the sensation of constant falling would likely have psychological effects ([1929] 1995: 79). However, he also reasoned that pilots and ski jumpers adapt to falling, so one can be trained out of the negative emotions. He turned out to be wrong: astronauts have not reported feeling as if free fall was actually falling. By contrast, the early twentieth-century Russian pioneer of spaceflight Konstantin Tsiolkovsky associated free fall with a feeling of happiness. Gravity's absence produced high spirits: the ability to fly was the source of joy and mirth ([1920] 1960: 220).

Another experience which melds these emotions is known as the High Place Phenomenon, or the *call of the void*: the urge to jump off a high place. Research has shown that it is not strongly correlated with suicide ideation (Hames et al. 2012; Teismann et al. 2020); but its relationship to gravity has not been examined. The few studies of this phenomenon start with the assumption that no one in their right senses would want to jump off a cliff; but what if we interpret it as a perfectly natural desire to act as if gravity didn't exist?

Even when asleep, this desire is present. Flying and falling dreams are categorised as typical dreams, which are consistent across time, region, and gender (Maggiolini, Persico, and Crippa 2007; Schredl et al. 2004). A survey by Nielsen et al. (2003) of typical dreams among Canadian students showed that the most common were falling (73%), flying or soaring (48%), and swimming (34%). In Schredl et al.'s study of German participants, about 60% had flying dreams. Falling dreams, however, are not necessarily the reverse of flying dreams. They seem to be associated with activities in the vestibular system during sleep (Maggiolini, Persico, and Crippa 2007).

In Freud's interpretation of dreams ([1899] 1913), the appearance in dreams of the aerial machines of the early twentieth century, such as balloons, zeppelins, and aeroplanes, were symbols of erection. No doubt he would have included rockets in this, had he lived to see their advent. Inconveniently for this theory, women also had flying dreams. Freud's explanation was penis envy, evidence of a pathology rather than a symbolic desire to be free of the domestic constraints which weighed them down. Many women would perhaps take issue with Freud's assertion that an erection "cannot fail to be impressive, involving as it does an apparent suspension of the laws of gravity" (Freud 1913: 394). In the Freudian tradition, the emotional correlates of defying gravity were pride (for men) and envy (for women).

Freud's interpretation raises the gendered nature of experiences of gravity. He notes:

> Dreams of falling are most frequently characterised by fear. Their interpretation, when they occur in women, is subject to no difficulty because women always accept the symbolic sense of falling, which is a circumlocution for the indulgence of an erotic temptation.
>
> *(1913: 239)*

The fear of falling is the opprobrium and social exclusion that accompanies the sexually active woman—the "fallen woman"—in a moral system which strongly circumscribes her freedom. The US novelist Erica Jong played with this metaphor in her 1973 novel *Fear of Flying*, which opens with the protagonist, Isadora Wing, on a flight to Vienna filled with psychoanalysts. The fear of flying represents the dangers associated with being a woman outside the confines of patriarchal relationships. Flying represents the soaring of the creative self, which Jong likens to a spaceship journeying within, and sexual liberation, which she compares to a journey to the Moon "where you would live totally satisfied forever" (Nitzsche 1978). Even if sexual liberation is not all it's cracked up to be by the end of the novel, the power of the metaphor remains.

Gravity can inspire a moral fear as well as a physical one, it seems. This can also be provoked by the chaos of free-fall floating objects out of their proper order. Anderwald and Grond, in their exploration of dizziness, speak of how the resulting "space-time of ambiguity includes elements of order and elements of disorder" (2019: 46). Mayer (2022b: 62) points out that Noordung interpreted microgravity as a lack of order, perhaps even deriving his pseudonym from this: no order (German *ordnung*).

Technology, Masculinity, and Femininity

As the preceding section demonstrates, social responses to gravity are highly gendered. In the nineteenth and twentieth centuries, men reserved for themselves the gravity-defying technologies of the air and space. Speed, and hence high gs, were inimical to the female body. Hence we find the strongly masculine associations of sports cars (an overdetermined symbol in space, as in Elon Musk's red Tesla launched in 2018), civil and military aeroplanes (especially high altitude), rockets, zero-g flights, and space habitats are all domains into which women have had to fight to gain access. One of the reasons women were prevented from being pilots or astronauts was because it was thought weak female bodies couldn't withstand higher gs from acceleration. Women were the monogravity gender while men could roam freely across gravitational realms.

Gravity is the literal enemy of women because it causes their [our] bodies to "sag", an English word with a particular pejorative meaning when applied to women. "Perky" breasts, defying gravity in their own way, start to point towards the centre of Earth with age and the rigours of breastfeeding. The signs of youth by which women are valued are eroded as if Newton himself, the notorious misogynist, were determined to keep women in their place. We're meant to resent gravity: another emotional response.

There's a passage in Arthur C. Clarke's 1973 novel *Rendezvous with Rama*, which shows how women can't win with gravity:

> Some women, Commander Norton had decided long ago, should not be allowed aboard ship; weightlessness did things to their breasts that were too damn distracting. It was bad enough when they were motionless; but when they started to move, and sympathetic vibrations set in, it was more than any warm-blooded male should be asked to take. He was quite sure that at least one serious space accident had been caused by acute crew distraction, after the transit of a well-upholstered lady officer through the control cabin.

Even in an academic publication, I am sure I will not be condemned for expressing an "euuw".

Sports bras were not invented until the 1980s; but bras have long been advertised as anti-gravity devices. A 1947 advertisement in the *Perth Daily News* sings the virtues of a new American bra which "defies the force of gravity". The "secret of this engineering marvel", the ad declares, is "wire, firmly anchored at both sides like an arch-span bridge". The bra is a clothing item which is multifunctional across different gravities and recalls the fact that the Apollo spacesuits were initially designed and sewn by Playtex (Monchaux 2011). As an antigravity technology, its function is to control and regulate the female body as a spectacle for the male gaze in which the relationship between gravity and time is negated.

Bras are not the only traditional female clothing item which has to be reassessed in different gravity. Microgravity causes skirts to rise, revealing what is supposed to remain hidden. It is only in this context that we see how the skirt relies on gravity for its functionality. Tsiolkovsky considered the material culture responses to this problem. On his orbiting habitats,

> The ladies have tied tape round the lower part of their skirts, because they had little use for their legs, and also because the situation was embarrassing. Some were wearing male clothing—emancipation of a kind!
>
> *([1920] 1960: 76)*

Without gravity, these clothes become immodest and women have to adopt men's dress or become microgravity mermaids, with one lower limb. A different degree of gravity bends gender, making one of its primary social signifiers impractical. Thus Tsiolkovsky prefigures the unisex jumpsuits of the 1960s and 1970s that are favoured for space uniforms. Trousers, it turns out, are gravity-invariant because the legs prevent the rise of the fabric.

Traditionally, gravity is good for men—they can have gravitas, which gives them authority and seriousness. Women are left to be gravid, weighed down by pregnancy, and unable to leave Earth. The effects of microgravity on fertility and gestation are barely understood. However, some research suggests that late pregnancy could be made easier by living in microgravity (Merati et al. 2006). In another objectionable science fiction space opera, Robert A. Heinlein's *Time Enough for Love* (1973), higher gravity is generated by a machine to aid the process of birth on board a spaceship, allowing the baby to slip through its mother's body with ease. In space, gravity thus remedies the curse of Eve.

Gravity and Social Class

Love it or hate it, gravity must be reckoned with. Tsiolkovsky left us in no doubt: he hated it. Chapter 4 of his 1920 classic *Outside the Earth* was called "The Gravity Hater". Speaking as the gravity hater, Tsiolkovsky pointed out the work or labour that gravity created. He accused gravity of being the cause of death and broken bones. Gravity is a malevolent character in his universe.

As well as playing the role of the Grim Reaper, Tsiolkovsky argued that gravity held back social progress. As he expressed it, lack of gravity

> Makes the poor equal to the rich, for it gives both a comfortable carriage with wonderful horses which need no fodder and are tireless. Everyone sits, sleeps and works where he chooses, needing no ground and using fine furniture of comfort quite beyond compare. Houses of any size can be built everywhere, on a hill or mountain, where there is a tremendous advantage in many respects; they don't have to be strong and, at the same time, they can serve as airships carrying, inside or outside, as many passengers and as much cargo as space will permit.
>
> *([1920] 1960: 81)*

In his orbiting habitats, the temperature would be regulated at an even thirty to thirty-five degrees Celsius. The class distinctions brought about by clothing would be erased as everyone could go about naked. With no seasons, abundant food would be produced in the pest-free greenhouses all year round. No one would starve in this vegetarian hippie paradise. The weak, sick, and elderly would no longer be bed-bound, too weak to fight against gravity. Tsiolkovsky hated gravity, whether "natural" or "artificial" produced by rotation—what was the point of recreating this force which only held people back?

If gravity weighed people down and oppressed the proletariat, the only point on which Tsiolkovsky conceded that gravity might confer some advantage was the process of washing and using the toilet, another remarkably prescient view ([1920] 1960: 235). Noordung, in his rotating space station, was also sensible of the opportunity artificial gravity offered to have regular baths, although he noted that the surface of the bathwater would be curved ([1929] 1995).

By the year 2017, Tsiolkovsky imagined thousands of people living their best lives in space habitats in geosynchronous orbit. But the Space Race was won by the capitalists, not the cosmists or communists. His egalitarian vision has been eclipsed by a future where access to other gravities is brokered by billionaires. It takes money to get out of the gravity well, and poverty keeps most of the world at the bottom.

Intergravities: Love Between Worlds

It is clear from this unstructured excursion through the worlds of fiction and reality that gravity has profound effects on bodies, societies, and cultures. Beyond the equation, gravity has history. At the planetary scale it mostly, but not always, changes at a rate outside the range of human memory and perception. But every physical adaptation in the evolution of the current human body has had the effect of altering our relationship to gravity. This does not entail a sort of gravitational determinism. Far from passively reacting, gravity has been actively incorporated into material responses and belief systems. At the daily and personal scale, gravity has as many gradations and nuances as Goethe's coloured shadows. Gravity haunts our dreams and elicits emotional reactions; but although a universal presence, it is not experienced in the same way across the "species". It has been used to symbolise the moral and psychological characteristics of genders in contemporary western patriarchal society. Gravitational mobility, for example between $1g$ and zero g, is made possible by access to wealth, thus exposing fractures in the concept of humanity as a homogeneous entity, as it is presented in the UN space treaty system.

An important part of adapting to space is learning what aspects of human material and social culture are gravity-invariant. Shoes, as we have seen, are not, although the toothbrush is

Table 38.2 Post-geocentric gravitography

No. of Earth gs	Location	No. of humans	No. of robots	Nonhuman life	Dimensions	Date CE
0	Lineland	0	0	Unknown	One	1884
0	Flatland	0	0	Unknown	Two	1884
0	Planetary orbits	7	7500	Microbial	Three	2022
1/6	Moon	0	Four	Tardigrades	Three	2022
1/3	Mars	0	Seven	Unknown	Three	2022
1	Earth	8 billion	Indeterminate	Indeterminate	Three	2022
2.6	Jupiter	0	0	Unknown	Three	2022
3	DesPlaines	7,500,000	Indeterminate	Indeterminate	Three	2440
3.5	Unknown	0	0	Unknown	Three	TBD
Unknown	Unknown	0	Unknown	Unknown	Four	TBD

(Gorman 2021). Is the core of what it means to be human what survives when transplanted into the gravity environments of other worlds? To investigate this further, I make an attempt to move away from the Late Geocentric gravitography.

Table 38.1 ordered gravity in multiples of 1*g* and according to distance from the Sun, as is commonly done. In Table 38.2, I have attempted, somewhat imperfectly, to re-map gravity to take account of different bodies and modes of being. The level of gravity starts at zero and the number of dimensions at 1. Planetary orbit includes all planets in the solar system, with by far the majority of robots resident in Earth orbit. The robots on the Moon and Mars are rovers capable of locomotion (although only a few are still working). Of necessity, many of the cells are populated by "unknown", data we don't have or can't get, and "indeterminate", data it would be impossible to ascertain. The last row of the table takes the post-Geocentric gravitography into higher dimensions, about which most of our knowledge is purely theoretical (e.g., Lü and Pope 2011; Zumino 1986).

The limits of the average human body in its current form are about 3.5 × 1*g* (Poljak, Klindzic, and Kruljac 2019). The highest gravity found among the five thousand or so known exoplanets is 200*g*, with 125 exoplanets at over 50*g*, so at the galactic scale, humans can be classified as a low-grav organism (Poljak, Klindzic, and Kruljac 2019). At 3*g*, the home planet of the Family d'Alembert is nudging the upper limit of human habitability.

In the 2014 film *Interstellar*, the character Dr Amelia Brand makes a statement that has always resonated with me: "Love is the one thing we're capable of perceiving that transcends dimensions of time and space". But can we perceive it? In the microgravity of Earth-orbiting space stations, blood pools in the upper body and faces become congested and puffy. As Parkhurst and Jeevendrampillai (2020: 6) observe,

> Gravity, or the lack of it, radically changes all of the subtle movements and queues [*sic*] by which people have come to "know how to feel"; to recognise instinctively when another is frustrated, happy, impatient, cynical, or … enamoured.

In the Galactic Empire of the Family d'Alembert novels, the gulf between the 1*g* of Earth and the 3*g* of DesPlaines is an obstacle to love, but not because they can't recognise love when they see it. In some ways, gravity in the year 2440 maps onto race and gender in nineteenth-to-twenty-first-century Earth: it becomes a visual marker of socially sanctioned relationships. It is hard to know how far love can remain invariant between the gravities and dimensions of Table 38.2. Perhaps those at zero *g* will be eternally sundered from those who, instead of falling forever, only fall.

Notes

1 D'Alembert is not a random name. Jean d'Alembert (1717–1783) was a famous French *philosophe* and *Encyclopédiste* who created what is known as d'Alembert's principle, which applies to falling masses in Newtonian gravity.
2 Taken from a well-known meme by Gerry Mooney: http://www.mooneyart.com/gravity/historyof_01.html.
3 The *Lunar* Colour is so exceeding beautiful, that a Man would travel a thousand Leagues to behold it, the Shape is somewhat flat, of the Breadth of a Piece of Eight, and twice the Thickness, one Side is of a more orient Colour than the other, which being clapt to a Man's bare Skin, takes away all the Weight and Ponderousness of his Body, but turning the other Side, it adds force to the attractive Beams of the Earth either in this World or that, and makes the Body half as heavy again: Do you wonder now, why I should so overprize this Stone?

(from the Project Gutenberg edition)

4 I make no apologies.

References

Abbott, Edwin. 1884. *Flatland: A Romance of Many Dimensions*. London: Seeley and Co.
Ackermann, Marko, and Antonie J. van den Bogert. 2012. "Predictive Simulation of Gait at Low Gravity Reveals Skipping as the Preferred Locomotion Strategy." *Journal of Biomechanics* 45 (7):1293–98. https://doi.org/10.1016/j.jbiomech.2012.01.029.
Adams, Douglas. 1980. *The Hitchhiker's Guide to the Galaxy*. New York: Harmony Books
Anderwald, Ruth, and Leonhard Grond. 2019. "Dizziness—a Resource?" In *Dizziness—a Resource*, edited by Ruth Anderwald, Karoline Feyertag and Leonhard Grond, 22–53. Berlin: Sternberg Press.
Boughen, Jill, Jennifer Nitz, and Venerina Johnston. 2017. "Centre of Gravity: Relevance of Behaviour and Location in Bipedal Stance in Older Adults." *Physical Therapy Reviews* 22 (3–4): 186–96. https://doi.org/10.1080/10833196.2017.1283831.
Clarke, Arthur C. 1973. *Rendezvous with Rama*. New York: Harcourt Brace Jovanovich.
Einstein, Albert. 1905. "Zur Elektrodynamik Bewegter Körper" [On the Electrodynamics of Moving Bodies]. *Annalen der Physik* 322 (10): 891–921. https://doi.org/10.1002/andp.19053221004.
Einstein, Albert. 1916. "Die Grundlage der Allgemeinen Relativitätstheorie" [The Foundation of the General Theory of Relativity]. *Annalen der Physik* 354 (7): 769–822. https://doi.org/10.1002/andp.19163540702.
Fox, Renée. 2016. "A Disconcerting Pact with Gravity: Nineteenth-Century Acrobats and the Failure of Transcendence." *Nineteenth-Century Contexts* 38 (2): 79–92. https://doi.org/10.1080/08905495.2016.1135291.
Freud, Sigmund. [1899] 1913. *The Interpretation of Dreams*. Translated by A. A. Brill. New York: Macmillan and Co.
Godwin, Francis. 1638. *The Man in the Moone: Or a Discourse of a Voyage Thither by Domingo Gonsales*. London: John Norton.
Goethe, Johann Wolfgang von. [1810] 1840. *Goethe's Theory of Colours*. Translated by C. L. Eastlake. London: John Murray
Gorman, Alice C. 2009. "The Gravity of Archaeology." *Archaeologies* 5 (2): 344–59. https://doi.org/10.1007/s11759-009-9104-1.
Gorman, Alice C. 2019. *Dr Space Junk vs the Universe: Archaeology and the Future*. Cambridge, MA: MIT Press.
Gorman, Alice C. 2021. "Don't Leave Earth Without It!" *BRAVE Lecture*, Flinders University, 13 April. https://www.youtube.com/watch?v=Gv61pvER8m4.
Hames, Jennifer L., Jessica D. Ribeiro, April R. Smith, and Thomas E. Joiner Jr. 2012. "An Urge to Jump Affirms the Urge to Live: An Empirical Examination of the High Place Phenomenon." *Journal of Affective Disorders* 136 (3): 1114–20. https://doi.org/10.1016/j.jad.2011.10.035.
Heinlein, Robert A. 1973. *Time Enough for Love*. New York: G. P. Putnam's Sons.
Jong, Erica. 1973. *Fear of Flying*. New York: Holt, Rinehart and Winston.
Lü, H., and C. N. Pope. 2011. "Critical Gravity in Four Dimensions." *Physical Review Letters* 106 (18): 181302. https://doi.org/10.1103/PhysRevLett.106.181302.
Magee, John. 1941. "High Flight." *Pittsburgh Post-Gazette,* November 12.
Maggiolini, Alfio, Anna Persico, and Franca Crippa. 2007. "Gravity Content in Dreams." *Dreaming* 17 (2): 87–97. https://doi.org/10.1037/1053-0797.17.2.87.

Mayer, Ralo. 2022a. *Un-Earthing*. Video presented in partial completion of PhD, University of Applied Arts, Vienna.

Mayer, Ralo. 2022b. *Space Un-Settlements*. Unpublished PhD Thesis, University of Applied Arts, Vienna.

Merati, G., S. Rampichini, M. Roselli, E. Roveda, and G. Pizzini. 2006. "Gravity and Gravidity: Will Microgravity Assist Pregnancy?" *Sports Sciences for Health* 1 (3):129–36. https://doi.org/10.1007/s11332-006-0023-x.

Monchaux, Nicholas de. 2011. *Spacesuit: Fashioning Apollo*. Cambridge, MA: MIT Press.

Morgan, Elaine. 1982. *The Aquatic Ape: A Theory of Human Evolution*. New York: Stein and Day.

Mount, Frances E., Mihriban Whitmore, and Sheryl L. Stealey. 2003. "Evaluation of Neutral Body Posture on Shuttle Mission STS-57 (SPACEHAB-1)." *NASA* No. S-793 (TM-2003-104805).

Murphy, James P., and Joseph W. Siry. 1970. "Lunar Mascon Evidence from Apollo Orbits." *Planetary and Space Science* 18 (8):1137–41. https://doi.org/10.1016/0032-0633(70)90207-2.

Newton, Isaac. [1642–1727] 1846. *Newton's Principia: The Mathematical Principles of Natural Philosophy*. New York: Daniel Adee.

Nielsen, Tore A., Antonio L. Zadra, Valérie Simard, Sébastien Saucier, Philippe Stenstrom, Carlyle Smith, and Don Kuiken. 2003. "The Typical Dreams of Canadian University Students." *Dreaming* 13 (4): 211–35. https://doi.org/10.1023/B:DREM.0000003144.40929.0b.

Nitzsche, Jane Chance. 1978. "'Isadora Icarus': The Mythic Unity of Erica Jong's *Fear of Flying*." *Rice University Studies* 64 (1): 89–100. https://hdl.handle.net/1911/63311.

Noordung, Hermann. [1929] 1995. *The Problem of Space Travel: The Rocket Motor*. Edited by Ernst Stuhlinger and J. D. Hunley with Jennifer Garland. NASA SP-4206. Washington, DC: NASA History Office.

Parkhurst, Aaron, and David Jeevendrampillai. 2020. "Towards an Anthropology of Gravity: Emotion and Embodiment in Microgravity Environments." *Emotion, Space and Society* 35: 100680. https://doi.org/10.1016/j.emospa.2020.100680.

Pavei, Gaspare, Carlo M. Biancardi, and Alberto E. Minetti. 2015. "Skipping vs. Running as the Bipedal Gait of Choice in Hypogravity." *Journal of Applied Physiology* 119 (1): 93–100. https://doi.org/10.1152/japplphysiol.01021.2014.

Paxton, Steve. 1975. "Contact Improvisation." *The Drama Review* 19 (1): 40–42. https://doi.org/10.2307/1144967.

Peucker-Ehrenbrink, Bernhard, and Birger Schmitz. 2001. *Accretion of Extraterrestrial Matter Throughout Earth's History*. New York: Springer Science+Business Media.

Poljak, Nicola, Dora Klindzic, and Mateo Kruljac. 2019. "Effects of Exoplanetary Gravity on Human Locomotion Ability." *The Physics Teacher* 57: 378–406. https://doi.org/10.1119/1.5124276.

Pomeroy, Ross. 2017. *Why Space Travel Can Be Absolutely Disgusting*. https://www.space.com/36056-why-space-travel-can-be-absolutely-disgusting.html.

Ribe, Neil M. 1985. "Goethe's Critique of Newton: A Reconsideration." *Studies in History and Philosophy of Science Part A* 16 (4): 315–35. https://doi.org/10.1016/0039-3681(85)90015-9.

Rodríguez-Mozos, J. M., and A. Moya. 2107. "Statistical-likelihood Exo-Planetary Habitability Index (SEPHI)." *Monthly Notices of the Royal Astronomical Society* 471 (4): 4628–36. https://doi.org/10.1093/mnras/stx1910.

Schredl, Michael, Petra Ciric, Simon Götz, and Lutz Wittmann. 2004. "Typical Dreams: Stability and Gender Differences." *The Journal of Psychology* 138 (6): 485–94. https://doi.org/10.3200/JRLP.138.6.485-494.

Teismann, Tobias, Julia Brailovskaia, Svenja Schaumburg, and André Wannemüller. 2020. "High Place Phenomenon: Prevalence and Clinical Correlates in Two German Samples." *BMC Psychiatry* 20 (1): 478. https://doi.org/10.1186/s12888-020-02875-8.

Tsiolkovsky, Konstanin. [1920] 1960. "Outside the Earth." In *The Call of the Cosmos*, edited by V. Dutt, 161–332. Moscow: Foreign Languages Publishing House.

Vaneechoutte, Mario, Algis Kuliukas, and Marc Verhaegen, eds. 2011. *Was Man More Aquatic in the Past? Fifty Years after Alister Hardy-Waterside Hypotheses of Human Evolution*. Sharjah: Bentham Science Publishers. https://doi.org/10.2174/97816080524481110101.

Wheeler, John Archibald. 2010. *Geons, Black Holes, and Quantum Foam: A Life in Physics*. New York: W. W. Norton & Company.

Winter D. A. 1995. "Human Balance and Posture Control during Standing and Walking." *Gait Posture* 3: 193–214. https://doi.org/10.1016/0966-6362(96)82849-9.

Zumino, Bruno. 1986. "Gravity Theories in More than Four Dimensions." *Physics Reports* 137 (1): 109–14. https://doi.org/10.1016/0370-1573(86)90076-1.

INDEX

Note: **Bold** page numbers refer to tables; *italic* page numbers refer to figures and page numbers followed by "n" denote endnotes.

Aarnio, A. 193
Abbott, A. 96
Abbott, E. 486
Aboriginal-owned science 247
academic knowledge production 259
acceleration 1, 99, 164, 256, 432, 483, 487
accidental sagacity 375
actor-network theory 448
Adams, C. 187
Adams, D. 484
Adams, T. 187
adapting to space: anthropological and archaeological methods 401; biomedical and psychological studies 401; cargo processes 405–7; degree fields 400; digital photography 401; individual tasks 411; machine learning and space archaeology 403–4; material culture 400; population distributions 407–8; restraints, stowage 410; space archaeology 401–2; space bureaucracies 410; square 408–10; unpublished images and inventory management system 404–5; visual displays, space habitats 402–3
adaptive optics 452n5
Aditya-L1 satellite 322
aerospace technologies 234
affordances 323, 351, 354, 355
Africanfuturism 173
Africanfuturist artworks 173
Afrofuturism 8, 38, 122, 126–27, 143, 150, 153n1, 173, 177–78
Afrofuturist engagements 164
Afrogalactica 126
afronauts' spacesuits 9, 178
Aganaba, T. 181
age discrimination 194
Agrawal, A. 292n2
Ahmed, S. 162

Aït-Touati, F. 146, 147
Alcoff, L. 463, 464
Aldunate, C. 279n1
Aldunate del Solar, C. 279n1
ALeRCE algorithm 270
Ali, R.H. 404, 410
Allan, K. 195
allochronic distancing effect 146
All Time is Local 139
ALMA Regional Centres (ARCs) 267
ALMA Science Archive (ASA) 267
Álvarez, T. 15n5, 62
Amazon Web Services 271
American Astronomical Society (AAS) 193
American Federal Aviation Administration 361
American Institute of Architecture (AIA) 353
American Institute of Certified Planners (AICP) 352
American National Park 288
American Society for Gravitational and Space Research (ASGSR) 429
American Society of Landscape Architects (ASLA) 352
American space programme 172
Analysis Working Group (AWG) 432
Anders, W. 419
Animiikii rocket 252, 253
Anishinaabeg space programme: astronomical knowledge 252, 258; colonialism 253; environmental exploitation 259; environments and extraterrestrial space 257–58; extraterrestrial spaces and places 253; Iron Range 253; non-Indigenous dignitaries and scientists 252; resource extraction, space colonisation and climate/environmental crisis 254–57; space exploration 258, 259; sustainable materials 252
Anker, P. 15n5, 36, 165

493

Index

anthropic principle 465n5
Anthropocene 12, 28, 37, 49, 372, 381, 420
Anthropological Research into the Imaginaries and Exploration of Space (ARIES) project 81n2
anthropology 7, 33, 51, 57, 60–62, 72, 73, 80, 104, 105, 110, 117, 413, 414, 416–19, 422, 471
anthropology of gravity 417
anthropology of nature 66
anthropomorphism 163
anti-Blackness 152
anti-capitalists 140
anticolonial 88, 142, 152, 282, 290
anticipating space futures 9
anti-imperialism 281
Aotearoa futurism 153n1
Apollo Applications Program (AAP) 388
Apollo missions 47, 163, 359, 375, 419
Apollonian gaze 90
Apollonian vision of globe 130
Apollo programme 89, 121, 163, 235
aquatic ape theory 484
Arab futurism 127
Arabidopsis thaliana 428
Arboleda, M. 14
archaeo-astronomy 233
archaeological enquiry 48
archaeological record of space technology 46–47
archaeology: anthropological ethnography 406; behavioural 50; decolonise space 50; field-based discipline 7; fieldworkers 34; gravity 413; latent criminality 377; materials 44; NASA's evident bias 401; social spaces 33; unearthing 376; value 400
Arecibo Observatory *462*
Arecibo Radio Telescope 462
Ariane rocket system 88
The Arid Lands 284
Armstrong, E.S. 9, 162, 167n1
Arnould, J. 16n13, 110, 111, 112
Artemis human exploration programme 222
Artemis missions 15n3
artificial ecological system 36, 372
artificial intelligence (AI) 12, 47, 271, 403, 446
artificial satellites 240–43
art-making process 132
Asia-Oceania Space Weather Alliance (AOSWA) 315
Associated Universities, Inc. (AUI) 276
asteroid-impact mitigation projects 37
asteroid mining 377
AstroAccess project 164
astrobiological programmes 475
astrobiology 13, 118, 212, 281, 282, 284, 285, 291, 471
astrocapitalism 154n2, 154n4
astro-colonialism 10
astroenvironmentalism 11; anticolonial perspectives 282; cosmic scale 281; imaginative outer geographies 282–83; new worlds' (b)orders 285–87; planetary protection 281; reconstellation, planetary skin 289–91; resource extraction 292; scientific formulations 282; space Orientalism 284–85; space-related issues 281; space rush 281; speculative thought 282; wilderness and parks 287–89
astrofuturism 17n16
astro-masculinities 162
astronomical areology 35
astronomical datasets 269
astronomical revolution 30
astronomical sublime 303
astronomical technologies 234
astrophysics 442
astrosociological imagination 97
astrosociology 15n5, 96–99
Astrosociology Research Institute (ARI) 97
Atacama Desert 264, 268, 270
Atacama Large Millimeter Array (ALMA) 166, 263, 265–67, 276
Atacama Pathfinder Experiment (APEX) 274
Atacama Submillimetre Telescope 270
athwart theory 16n11
attention deficit hyperactivity disorder (ADHD) 193
Attfield, R. 288
Augé, M. 44
Australian Space Agency 222
Australian Telescope Compact Array 247
authenticity 200, 444–45
autism spectrum disorder (ASD) 193
automation 11, 117, 264–66; automated systems 450
Autonomous Zone of Tibet 264
Averhart, C.J. 191
Axiom Space 13
ayllus 279n2
AzTechSat-1 343–44

Bahamas Aerospace and Sea Exploration Center (BASEC) 125
Baikonur Cosmodrome 421
Baird Callicott, J. 16n13
Bardo Thodol 204
Basner, M. 189, 193
Battaglia, D. 15n5, 35, 284, 422
Bawaka Country 217, 239, 240
Bear, L. 146, 147, 154n3
Beaulieu, A. 415
Becker, J. 62, 67
Beever, J. 455
behavioural archaeology 50
behavioural modernity 53, 465n4
Benjamin, W. 289
Berenguer, J. 279n1
Berkeley's Huan Tran Telescope 270
Bertoni, F. 62
Beyond Spaceship Earth 287

Index

Big Data 265, 268–70, 277
Bigler, R.S. 191
Bigourdan, G. 245
big science 300
Billings, L. 110
biodiversity conservation 182
bioeconomy 285
Biological and Physical Sciences (BPS) 431
biological interconnections 290
biometric devices 265
biomimetic lamp model 62
biopolitical regimes 330
bioregenerative life-support systems 164, 431
biosociality 60
Biosphere 2 86; artificial ecosystem 371; artistic research 372; collapsed model *373*; ecologies without earth 380–82; elements 382; farming and food production 372; globalisation 372; human cultures 372; microgravity 383; mining plots 376–77; performative and cultural aspects 371; physical and psychological impact 382; plot and performance 378–80; self-sustaining ecosystem 371; time microscope 381; unearthing an experiment 372–74; unearthing to un-Earthing 374–76
Biospherians 371
biospherics 372, 375, 379
Black futurist liberation 139
Black, Indigenous, People of Colour (BIPOC) 153n1
Black liberation movements 140
Black, M. 166
Black Quantum Futurism (BQF) 8, 139, 141n1, 147, 152, 153n1
Black queer feminist physics 38
Black Space Agency 8, 141n1
Blaser, M. 146, 152, 153n2
Blue Marble 26, 130
Bohney, B. 185, 192, 193
The Bombing of Rafah 130
(B)ordering Britain 286
Bostrom, N. 455
Boucher, M.-P. 153n1
Bourland, W.I. 173, 178
Boyer, D. 279n2
brain-activity recording 200
brine compositions 273
British Interplanetary Society 92
Brooker, P. 104, 389
Buchli, V. 13, 415, 416
building codes 351, 353–54
Bunch, G. 13, 417, 418
Burarrwanga, L. 220
Burawoy, M. 101, 103
Bureaud, A. 16n14, 153n1
Burton, D. 13
business-school styles 104
Butler, J. 283

Button, G. 389
Byzantine complexity 48

Cambrofuturism 153n1
capacity building 272
Capelotti, P.J. 47, 48, 49
capital accumulation 100
capital expansion 143, 161
capital speculation 154
capitalism 4, 6, 11, 35, 36, 100, 142, 148, 158, 173, 180, 226, 228, 229, 235, 257
capitalist labour exploitations 182
capitalist system 227
Capsule Communicator (CC) 390, 391
Caputa, J. 76
cardinal orientation 365
career aspirations 188
Cargo Mission Contract 406
cargo processes 405–7
cargo resupply missions 406
Carrington Event 315, 316
Carrington, R. 315
Carrizo/Comecrudo Tribe of Texas 77
Casper, M.J. 162, 163
Castaño, P. 8, 13, 39, 104, 389
Castro, V. 279n1
Casumbal-Salazar, I. 61, 279n5
CDR-EVA 391–93
Celermajer, D. 292n3
celestial relations: becoming sky 220–22; journey 218–19; Milŋiyawuy 222–23; sky Country 217–18; skyworld 247; water rising, darkness falling 219–20
Center for the Advancement of Science in Space (CASIS) 408
Centre for Appropriate Technology 247
Centre for Mathematical Modelling (CMM) 263, 264, 269
Centre for the Protection of National Infrastructure (CPNI) 317
Centre national d'etudes spatiales (CNES) 145
centre of mass (COM) 484
cephalopods 66
Cerinsek, G. 186
Chajnantor plateau 274
Challenger disaster 112
Chalmers, D.J. 456
Cheryan, S. 191
Cheyne, R. 195
Chicanafuturism 153n1
Chile: Atacama Desert **144,** 264, 376, 471; Chajnantor Plateau 270; Chile's Production Development Corporation (CORFO) 277; Chuqicamata 265; Codelco 264; Salar de Atacama 274; Sloan Digital Sky Survey (SDSS) project 269; War of the Pacific 274
China National Space Administration (CNSA) 145
chronology 395

chrononormativity 148
chronopolitics: capitalist value 142; colonial linear temporalities 143; divergent futurisms 147–52; dualism 142; emancipatory qualities 152–53; futurity as method 143–44; NewSpace 145–47; politics of time 142; radical futurisms 143; technoutopian social imaginaries 142
chronotope 142
chrono-topos 142
Ćirković, E.E. 128, 129
Cisco–NASA partnership 290
civil rights 8, 139, 140, 172
Clancy, K.B.H. 186, 189
Clark, J. 319
Clark, N. 5
class markers 163
climate change 162, 179, 239, 343, 429, 436, 458
climate coloniality 16n10
climate/environmental crisis 254–57
closed system 36, 347, 371, 372, 373, 380
close-knit system 474
cloud computing 264
cluster concepts 148
Cockell, C. 110, 111, 281, 288
Code, L. 456
codes of conduct 351, 352–53
codes of law 351, 359–60
COGITO in Space 201
cognitive development 206
collision detection systems 332
colonial cartographic mindset 286
colonial discourses 284
colonial histories/decolonial futures 10–11
colonial imagery 227
colonialism 6, 9, 49, 85, 86, 92, 122, 123, 126, 142, 158, 166, 173, 180, 226, 230, 253, 257, 286, 288
coloniality: capitalist accumulation 226; colonial matrix of power 229–32; conceptions 226; cosmic order of modernity 226; cosmic orders 227–28, 232–34; display values 227; diversity and inclusion 235; elements 235; ethical questions 235; extractivist practices 235; extraterrestrial and terrestrial landscapes 236; genocides and epistemicides 235; hegemonic use-value 227; instrumental rationality and ethical practices 227; scientific necessity 226; socioeconomic and political structures 235; space exploration 226; western modernity 227, 228
colonial matrix of power: death-oriented conqueror 231; economy 229; epistemological dominance 231; extractability 229; extractivism 231; human and nonhuman multiplicity 229; Indigenous peoples 229; metaphysical catastrophe 229; modernity/coloniality structure 230; normalisation 231; objectivity 230; restructuring authority 229; theoretical framework 230
colonial-patriarchal dynamics 162
colonisation 7, 11, 30, 32, 34, 39, 78, 98, 99, 149, 358

colonizing impulse 15n5
colonizing space 126
commercial astronaut 361
Committee on Biological and Physical Sciences in Space (CBPS) 430
Committee on Space Research (COSPAR) 429
Commonwealth Scientific and Industrial Research Organisation's (CSIRO) 243
communalism 181
communication bodies 243
communications pass 390
communications satellites 90
communism 228
community mapping 348
community participation 431
computer vision 403
Conflict Minerals 131, 134n11
congenital blindness 194
Congolese culture 179
conjuncture 2; *see also* space conjuncture
consciousness 10, 99, 130, 199, 201, 202, 204, 208, 209
consequentialist approach 109
contact zone 6
contemporary scientific placemaking 35
content delivery network (CDN) 317
conversion concept 131
Cooper, M. 285
copper mining 263–66
co-productive dynamics 303
Cornum, L. 63, 150
coronal mass ejections (CMEs) 313
corporate transnationalism 5
Cosgrove, D. 89
cosmic apparitions 179
cosmic capitalism 100
cosmic mind 209
cosmic multi-self 164
cosmic narcissism 123
cosmic orders 232–34
cosmic societies 15n5, 99
cosmic waters: invisible recording 365; phantasmatic meditations 365; plasmatic liquidity 365; soaring corporeality 365; spatial knowledge 365; weighted floatation 365
Cosmic Waters 12
cosmic web 447
Cosmographies 144
cosmopoetics 39
cosmopolitanism 181, 420
cosmopolitics 39, 144, 277, 279n4, 296
Cosmos Connections 60
cosmos nullius 33
counter-futuring 9
crafting networks 444–45
The Crisis 5
critical Indigenous studies 6
critical zone 26–28, 30
Cronon, W. 287, 289

crop production 432
Crumey, A. 245
cryogenic temperature 267
Csíkszentmihályi, M. 452n9
CubeSats 342–43
cultural astronomy 57
cultural imperialism 463
cultural landscape approach 50
cultural meteorites 47
cultures in orbit/life in space 12–14
Cumbrecita Ridge *441*
Cusicanqui, S.R. 235
cyberattacks 317
cyclotron for ecology 381

Dalby, S. 283
d'Alembert's principle 491n1
Damjanov, K. 12, 17n20
Daniel, S. 145
Dark Age 315
dark matter (DM) 442, 451n1
darkness 38
darkness falling 219–20
data-centric fields 271
Data Observatory 270–72
Davidov, V. 284
Davis, H. 152
death's dream kingdom 208
debates 446
Decadal process 427, 428
Decadal survey 430–33
DeChurch, L.A. 395
decoloniality 235
decolonial speculation 150
decolonisation 8, 36, 39, 122–26, 149; decolonising space 122
deep uncertainty 450–51
Deerfield, K. 159
deintegration 406
De la Cadena, M. 6, 16n8, 146, 152, 153n2, 276, 279n2
DeLoughrey, E. 130
De Magalhaes, J.P. 460
DeMarines, J. 17n18
democratisation 145
democratisation of space 342
Demos, T.J. 148, 150–52
De Napoli, K. 10
Denning, K. 17n18
De Paulis, D. 199
Despret, V. 66
detectable technology 465n1
Detwiler, K.M. 11, 166
Deudney, D. 285
dialogue: authenticity and crafting networks 444–45; building spaces 443–45; constructing reality/trustworthiness 445–46
dialogue-as-play 448–51, 452n10
Díaz Infante, J.J. 347

Dickens, P. 99, 100, 104, 123, 133n1
Dick, S.J. 111
digital cultures 415
digital globalization 179
digital highway 267
Dillon, G. 253
Dillon, G.L. 128
dirty maps 267
disability role models 194–95
disaster capitalism 323
disaster management 247
discrimination 190
The Disordered Cosmos 9
disruptive imbalances 332
distributed sensor technologies 265
distributive justice 182
The Dithering 5
diversity in space: demographic studies 185; differently-abled bodies and neurodivergent minds 192–94; disability role models 194–95; equity 185; gating process 185; gender and racial 188–90; gender and racial minority role models 190–92; identified solutions 185; important role models 187–88; occupational environments 185; STEM careers 186–87
Doi Inthanon National Park 298
Donaldson, M.W. 49
Doppler method 300
Douglas-Jones, R. 266
Dovey, C. 240, 291, 348
Drake equation 455, 456, 465n2
dreamless sleep 201
Duemler, D. 108, 111
Duner, D. 111
Dunnett, O. 8, 154n4
Du Prel, C. 210
Dussel, E.D. 230

earthly analogues 85, 166
earthly politics 14, 34, 287
Earthrise 89, 130
Earth's biocapacity 239
earth-writing 84
ecobiopolitics 417, 470
ecological colonization of space 381
ecological cyborg concept 381
ecological resources 239
ecomodernist masculinities 162
Economic Geography 75
economic liberalism 1
economic resources 99
economy optimisation 270–72
Edge, D.O. 15n5
Edgeworth, M. 46
Einsteinian gravity 481
electricity transmission networks 316
electricity transmission system 316
electro-digital technologies 316
electroencephalogram device 200, 203

electroencephalographic (EEG) signals 202
electromagnetic signals 205, 454
electromagnetic spectrum 211, 263, 266, 313, 444
electromagnetic threads 46
El-Enany, N. 286
Ellis, K. 195
ELSI community 110
Englert, S. 254, 257
environmental degradation 11
environmental determinism 52
Environmental Ethics 108
environmental extractivism 165
environmental injustice 254, 290
environmentalism 11, 288
environmental justice 11, 131, 167
environmental management 5, 11
environmental sociology 100
environmental studies 158
envirotechnical disaster 316
epistemic disconcertment 81
epistemic sovereignty 343
epistemic violence 182
Equal Employment Opportunity Act 189, 190
equatorial geostationary orbits 90
ESA's Parastronaut Feasibility Project 195
Escherichia coli 434
Eshun, E. 126
Eshun, K. 142–44, 147, 150, 151
esotericism 85
Eternal Blue Heaven 233
ethical disposition 81
ethical theory 113
ethnoastronomy project 275–77
ethnocartography 348
Ethnofuturism 153n1
Ethnography 7, 34–37, 61–62, 71–72, 102–3, 132, 406, 413–15, 442; ethnographic concept 16n8; ethnographic studies of NASA 102, 285, 469; of the ISS 104, 414; thick description 103
ETHNO-ISS project 413–14, 422
ethnomethodological approach 104
ethnomethodology 396, 397; NASA audio and conversation transcripts 389–91; spacewalk 389; technical practice 389
Euclidean zoning 358
Euroamerican dominance 160
Eurocentrism 147
Eurochronology 150
European Christendom 234
European Organisation for Astronomical Research in the Southern Hemisphere 263
European Research Council 413
European Southern Observatory (ESO) 263; EParanal Observatory 270
European Space Agency (ESA) 47, 88, 110, 163, 194, 243, 355, 419
Event Horizon Telescope 268, *268*
Evocations of a Forgotten Voyage 124, 125

exobiology 471
exoplanet astronomy 295
exoplanets 92, 295, 297, 300–2, 461, 490
exo-surprise 414
extended mind thesis (EMT) 206
extraction-assimilation system 146
extractive gaze 11
extractivism 78, 165, 179, 231, 376; mineral extraction 272
extraplanetary imaginaries 11
Extra-Terrestrial Ecologies 380, *382*
extraterrestrial environments 281
extraterrestrial intelligence (ETI): absence 454–55; critical philosophical analysis 454; inherent risk and detectability 459–61; messages 461–64; outcomes 458–59; power dynamics 464; referring to aliens 455–57; referring to humans 457; risk 457–58
extraterrestrial life 457
extraterrestrial society: anthropology 413, 414; Apollo mission 419; craftsmanship and geographies 416; distributed cognition 418; enthusiasm 418; ethnographic inquiry 413; European human spaceflight centres 417; fieldwork 415; GSP training 418; legibility 414; life-science research 417; lower Earth orbit 415; manufacturing communities 416; material economies 422; medical and life-science projects 416; medical materialities 416; microgravity 415; multisited ethnography 415; national space programmes 419; nexus 414; online and offline media producers 419; overviewers 419, 420; physiological and neurological effects 417; rocket debris fallout zones 421; scales 422; social media channels and enthusiast groups 418; social media influencers and launch events 419; social relations 420; space agencies 413; space age prompt 421; spaceflight 420; space futurism 416; training process 417
extraterrestrial spaces 34
extraterrestrial worlds: apocalyptic imaginaries and planetary futures 303–4; cosmological compositions 295; disparate realities 296; emergence and hybridity, Thailand 297; excursions 295; familiar fragments and unusual patterns 300; human expansion 295; intelligence 296; inventing anew and spatialising differently 305; invisible sensing instruments 302–3; mountaintop 297–99; multiple worlds and partial connections 301–2; ontologies 295; scientific and technological problem 296; spectrograph and a receiving device technologies 300–1; uniform categories 296
extra-vehicular activity (EVA) 390
extreme environments 284, 288
extremophiles 61, 284
Ezquerro-Nassar, A. 10

Index

facial recognition 403
Falchi, F. 245
Farago, J. 213n1
Fear of Flying 487
feminist approaches: anglophone scholarship 160; astronomical knowledges 159; binarised gender and heterosexuality 158; desire-based and reparation-based frameworks 159; environment 165–67; futurist-feminist 148, 179; heteronormativity 159; human engagement 158; Indigenous wayfinding practices 159; labour 160–62; manifest destiny 158; patriarchal and capitalist structures 159; reproductive justice and care work 159; salient interventions 158; space cowboys 158; technology 162–64; technoscience research interests 167
feminist science studies 277, 290, 292
feminist theory 6, 7
Fermi paradox 455, 465n3
fibre-optic channel 269
fields 7–8, 31–33
fieldwork 12, 31, 33, 51, 72, 81, 144, 284, 314, 415, 418, 443, 446, 451, 475
Finney, B.R. 48
Firefly series 195
footpad sensor 472
For All Moonkind 281
forensic architecture 130–32
Fox, R. 486
Freeman, E. 148
Freon-40 266
Friendship 7 spacecraft 311

Gadamer, H.-G. 448, 449, 452n10
Gaia 16n12, 27, 348; hypothesis 381
Gaia-graphy 27
Galperina, M. 194
Gál, R.P. 12, 17n20, 164, 167n1
Garofoli, D. 465n4
Geertz, A.W. 65
Gell, A. 456
gender distribution 407
gender diversity 188–90
gender's tech problem 163
general relativity theory 481
gentrification 141
Geoghegan, H. 418
geographic fieldwork centre 33
geography 35, 84–85, 471
geography of life 285
geomagnetically induced currents (GICs) 313
geomagnetic disturbance 316
geosociality 60
geostationary orbit 45
Geppert, A.C.T. 15n5
gestural relations 302
gestures outwards 302
Gibson-Graham, J.K. 152, 154n2

Gibson, J.J. 354
giggle factor 304
Gilroy, P. 292n1
glitch 2, 311–12; digital/analogue errors 311
global citizenship 420
global climate 37
global climate change 420
Global Conference on Space for Emerging Countries (GLEC) 349n4
globalisation 1, 44, 130, 372, 420
global south space programmes 39
global worming 62
Goemaere, S. 176
Gómez-Barris, M. 229
González-Ruibal, A. 44
Gorbanenko, J. 13, 420, 421
Gorman, A.C. 5, 7, 12, 14, 15n1, 16n7, 17n20, 34, 49–51, 129, 400, 409
Granjou, C. 384n17
Gran Telescopio Canarias (GTC) 298
gravitational mobility 489
The Gravity Hater 488
gravity-lowering Ebelus stone 482
gravity surrogates 410
Great Chain of Being 234
Great Divide 97
The Great Outdoors 391–94, 398n3
Green, B. 111
green dams 284
Green, J.L. 315
Gregory, D. 283
Grondin, J. 449
Grosfoguel, R. 230
Grosz, E. 143
ground support personnel (GSP) 417
Guedes, C. 10
Guiana Space Centre 162
Gunagala Galuma-Li 246–47
Gunkel, H. 148
Guyane 162

habitability 62, 284, 353, 388, 395, 469, 475, 483
habitable-zone planets 92
Habitation Module 359
hair-washing 65
Haller, B. 195
Hamacher, D. 10
Haramia, C. 14, 17n18
Haraway, D. 377
Harding, S. 15n5
Harjo, L. 39
Harkins, A.M. 15n5
Hartmann, W. 118n1
Hartman, S. 159
Hassoun, A. 146
hauntology 380
Hawse, S. 193
Haynes, R. 110, 118n2

Index

H-cage process 393
heating, ventilation, and air conditioning (HVAC) systems 319
hegemonic commoning agents 152
Heidegger, M. 414, 449
Helmreich, S. 15n5, 16n11, 35, 60
Hersch, M. 177
Hersch, M.H. 37
heterogeneous assemblages of life 152
heteronormativity 159
High Place Phenomenon 486
Hilck, K. 189
historical materialism 99–100
Hobart, H.J. 35, 36
Hokowhitu, B. 127
Homo sapiens 64
hooks, b. 159
Hopi cosmology 57, 59, 65
Hopi Indians 58
Hopi ladders: amateur cosmonautics 63; ceremonialism 57; clusters 62; colonial imaginaries 63; conviction 64; cosmic loneliness 64, 65; cosmological science 60; cultural astronomy 61; cultural astronomy approach 59; epistemic virtue 60; extreme environments 63; facial expressions 67; heliosphere 61; heroic masculinity 63; human exceptionalism 57, 64–67; humanoid abundance principle 66; Indigenous peoples 63; macrocosm and microcosm 60; mapping and visualising 61; mesocosm 62; metaphysical cathedral 64; metaphysical troublemakers 59; off-Earth anthropology 59; plumbing system 60; rockets/high-tech spacecraft 59; self-evident 66; sense of urgency 67; space exploration 61; technological device 64
Horneck, G. 288
Houdart, S. 60
Howe, C. 279n2
Hubble Space Telescope 303, 335
human-centered design 355
human culture: deformable spacetime 480; dreams 486; Earth's gravity 480; equation 482–83; evolutionary relationship to gravity 484–86; gender-equal universe 481; gravity 481–82, 487, 488–89; intergravities 489–90; opprobrium and social exclusion 487; social class 488–89; spacefaring 480; space travel 486; technology, masculinity and femininity 487–88; terrestrial society 481; universal force 480; variable gravity environments 480
Human Exploration and Operations (HEO) 431
Human Integration Design Handbook (HIDH) 355
humanism 178
human–machine interfaces 52
human material culture 46, 47
humanness 450
Human Research Program (HRP) 401, 431
human spaceflight 62, 395

human-system integration 355
Hutchinson, P. 396, 398n6
Hu, T-H. 266
Hydro-Quebec's power grid 316
hypercomputation 265
hypersonic weapons 131
hypnagogic micro- and macro-somatognosia 201

iconography of astronaut: African Americans 172; Africanfuturist artworks 173; Afrofuturism 177–78; American values and ideologies 172; civil rights movement 172; cultural critique 173; disproportional mythical power 173; economic/scientific development 172; harbinger of new space law 178–82; international legal instrument 173; international space law 173–77; media and political establishment 172; methodological function 173; whiteness and masculinity 172
identificatory learning 188
imaginative geographies 282–83
Imperial China 233
imperialism 34, 36, 100, 173
Indian Space Research Agency (ISRO) 344
indigeneity 7, 32
Indigenous cartography 348
Indigenous communities 86, 88, 158
Indigenous intersections 16n5
Indigenous knowledges 221
Indigenous land rights 243–45
Indigenous perspectives 8, 122, 127–29
Indigenous science fiction 63, 149
individualism 100, 122, 414
Ingold, T. 448
INSIDE 25–28, *25–27*, 147
intentional communication 459
Inter-Agency Space Debris Coordination Committee 243
inter- and intra-materiality 448
intergenerational poverty 141
International Astronautical Congress (IAC) 145
International Astronautical Federation (IAF) 9, 145
International Astronautical Federation's Technical Activities Committee for the Cultural Utilisation of Space (ITACCUS) 124
International Building Code (IBC) 354
International Congresses of Modern Architecture (CIAM) 358
International Dark-Sky Association (IDA) 246
international space law 173–77
International Space Station (ISS) 4, 13, 39, 51, 57, 62, 91, 104, 324, 332, 340, 355, 381, 384n10, 413, 427–30
International Space Station Archaeological Project (ISSAP) 13, 49, 51, 400, 420
internet apocalypse: anticipatory orientation 321–22; asteroid 323; catastrophic solar megastorm 314; common-sense preparations 318; coronal mass ejections 318; cyberattacks

Index

and software bugs 317; cyberterrorists 313; data centre industry 318; data centre security 313; electromagnetic radiation 313; industry magazine 317; large-scale geomagnetic storm 318; material environments 323; online systems 316; policy object 315–16; political-economic context 323; self-reliant and shielded systems 324; societal disruption 317; space weather 313–14; space weather effects 317, *318*; space weather preparedness 319–21; space weather-proof data 323; terrestrial infrastructure 313; unplanned data centre downtime 317; whipping motion 313
internet security 314
Inter-Pacific Ring Tribunal (INTERPRT) 130
interpersonal/workplace organisational issues 193
interplanetary space 16n7
intersectional interventions 8–10
inventory management system (IMS) 404–5
invisible recording 365
IRAS 16293-2422 266
ISS Inventory Management System 49
ISS National Laboratory 408
Ivison, T. 383n3

Jaggar, A. 463
Jamestown 149
Japanese Aerospace Exploration Agency (JAXA) 411n1
Jason-3 satellite 90
Jeevendrampillai, D. 13, 62, 417, 419, 420, 490
Jermak, H.E. 185, 192
Jet Propulsion Laboratory (JPL) 333, 470
Johnson, A.W. 12, 39
Johnson-Schwartz, J. S. 8, 111
Jones, C.H. 143, 153n1
Jungen, C. 60

Kamili, L. 62
Kant, I. 114
Kármán line 4
Katri, I.H. 154n5
Kavka, G. 118n1
Kearnes, M. 63
Keeler, A. 187, 190, 191
Kelley, M. 189, 193
Kendal, E. 9, 10
Kessler, E. 165
Khokhar, A.J. 186
Kibo module 410
Kilgore, D.W.D. 17n16
King, T.L. 254
Kite, S. 36
Klein, N. 323
Klinger, J.M. 11, 16n6, 166
knowledge gaps (KGs) 432
Kocifaj, M. 241
koel in English 218
Kosmica 123, 126

Kovacs, G.T.A. 187, 194
Kozel, A. 13, 419
krestnyy khod 420, 421
Kricorian, K. 186, 191
Krupp, E.C. 227, 232–34
Krzeminska, A. 193
Kwast, S. 116
Kyba, C.M. 39

labelled release (LR) 474
labour 160–62
labour-intensive products 102
ladder effect 354
Lane, K. 35
Latour, B. 5–7, 16n12, 25, 26–28, 147, 303, 372, 448
launching sites/deep-space communication networks 332
launch sites 34
Launius, R.D. 175, 189
Lazier, B. 420
Legacy Survey of Space and Time (LSST) 271
Le Moignan, E. 389
Lempert, W. 17n18
Lem, S. 205, 211
Leviathan of Parsontown 209
Liben, L.S. 191
Liboiron, M. 167n1, 167n2
lifeboat model 356, 357
life-governance techniques 330
life-support systems 332, 335, 376
life-threatening event 325
light extraction: Andean mountain cosmologies 252; antipersonnel mines 274; astronomical data 272; cosmological translations 275; disruption 278; ecology of practices 274; ethnoastronomy 275, 276; geocomputation 277; global battery industry 273; high-altitude Array Operation Site 276; hydrogeological models 273; Indigenous Likanantay people 272; lithium carbonate 272; logistical and managerial expertise 277; material-semiotic transformation 274; occasional rainstorms and flash floods 274; *pago* ceremony 277–78, *278*; political exceptionality 277; political inconveniences of location 273; radio antenna 275; radio quiet 274; regional and national development 277; remote operation 277; smart mine 273; spatial products 273; spectral and territorial occupation 276; temporalities surface 273; territorial-juridical mechanism 274; verdant optimism 279n2; volcanoes 274; water draining 273
light pollution 245–46
limit biologies 284
linear regression 355
Little Old Ladies 160
Livingston, D. 16n13
living the cosmos *124*
Lock, M.M. 416

Index

logical reasoning 194
logistical nightmares 270, 334
Lovell, B. 162
Lovelock, J. 28, 348
low Earth orbit (LEO) 415, 428
Lower Rio Grande Valley 72, 78
low-hanging fruit 407
Lucatello, S. 185, 192
Lunar Embassy 126
Lunar Gateway 1
lunar landing sites 16n5
Lunar Legacy Project 51
Lunar Reconnaissance Orbiter (LRO) 51
lunar surface, Surveyor 3 47, *48*
Lupisella, M. 110
Lynch, C.R. 35
lynch, k. 148

MacDonald, A. 416
Macdonald, F. 52
machine learning (ML) 47, 51, 265, 403–4
macrocosm 207
macro-kivas 66
Magellanic Clouds 276
magic of irrigation 75
Magic Valley: Boca Chica beach 74; broken dreams 77; development-led growth 74, 77; downtown revitalisation 73; economic incentives 73; fracked-gas export terminal 77; images 75; local economic development 73; local residents 73; natural factors 76; poor people's beach 74; public utilities 75; qualities 75; segregated Hispanic workers 75; self-employment/contract 78; transportation facilities 75; utility system 76
Maile, D.U. 36, 158, 161
mainstream environmentalist discourses 289
Maldonado-Torres, N. 227, 229
Malina, F. 16n14
Malina, R. 124
Mancinelli, R. 285
Mandel, S. 15n5
Marcheselli, V. 62, 166
Mare Incognito: brain activity of sleep 199; conceptual and literary references 205–8; consciousness and thinking process 199; falling asleep 212; intellectual history 211–12; Mullard Radio Astronomy Observatory 202–4; poetic and scientific views 201–2; project developments 204–5; sleep 200; sleep, death and cosmos 208–11; trans-disciplinary setting 212
Margulis, L. 7, 28, 290, 291
Maria, D. 35
Marino, A. 11
Mariscal, C. 111
market values 1
Mars Reconnaissance Orbiter 333
Mars sample-return (MSR) mission 1
Martian society 98

Martian Time Slip 381
Martin, E.C. 9
Maruyama, M. 15n5
Marxism 104
masculinist worldviews 163
material culture 244, 400, 405, 415, 417, 418; agriculture/iron-working 44; archaeological record in space 46–47; creative re-imaginings 50–51; definition 44; development of space archaeology 47–49; human behaviour 44; interpretations, potentials and theoretical approaches 49–50; investigative disintegration 53; mobility 53; orbital industries 44; post-Medieval growth 45; research directions 51–53; spacecraft 45–46; spacefaring and non-spacefaring 50; supermodernity 44; time and identity 44
materialistic approach 206
materiality 6, 50
Mayer, R. 12, 13, 487
Maymuru, R. 223
McCoy, T. 161
McCray, W.P. 36
McKay, C.P. 110, 118n2, 282
measurements of absence 35
media studies 158
megaconstellations 241, 242
Menkman, R. 311
mental health 193
Merchant, C. 231
Mercury 13 189
Mercury Project 174
Mesmer-Magnus, J. 395
messaging extraterrestrial intelligence (METI) 17n18, 296, 456–57, 460, 464
Messeri, L. 35, 37, 61, 165, 395, 397, 398n5, 422
Messier 87 galaxy 268, *268*
metaphysical troublemakers 7
Met Office Space Weather Operations Centre (MOSWOC) 315, 322
Mexican Space Agency (AEM) 340, 342
Mexican Space Collective (CEM) 347
Mexico: anticapitalist and anticolonialist cartographic practices 348; ontological challenges 348; orbit 340, 341–42; satellite dreams in miniature 342–44; satellite entanglements 344–45; satellite sublime 345–48; sociotechnological assemblages 348; Sputnik 340; technoscience 340; territorial representations 348
Mezzadra, S. 6
microaggressions 186, 190
microbes 35, 98, 288, 290, 334, 427
Microbial Observatory 430
microbiomes 456
microcosm 207
microgravity 17n21, 50, 383, 415, 434, 484
microsatellite technology 342

Index

microscopic organisms 456
Miele, J.A. 185, 192, 193
Mihesuah, D. 259
Mikaelsson, L. 161
militarisation 78
militarism 34
Milky Way 10, 205, 217–19, 221, 239, 245
Miller, E. 154n2
Milligan, T. 8, 16n13, 111
Mill, J.S. 114
Milŋiya River 218–19
Milŋiyawuy 221, 222–23
Mind and Cosmos 206
Mindell, D.A. 52
minimal phenomenal selfhood (MPS) 202
mining rare earths 376
mining the sky 377
mino-bimaadiziwin 257
Mirmalek, Z. 61, 395, 397, 398n5
miscommunications 450
mission candidates selection 193
mission-control conversations 34
Mitchell, A. 127
Mitchell, S.T. 17n19
mobilising futurity 144
Model Rules of Conduct 352, 353
modern geography 35
modernity 39, 226, 227, 230, 341
modulor system 355
Mol, A. 448
Moon Agreement 177, 182
Moonscape 126
Moore, L.J. 162, 163
Moraga, A.C. 275
Morar, N. 455
Morelos satellite system 342
more-than-terran spaces: conceptual 31; earthliness and terrestriality 32; field and fieldwork 31–33; material-semiotic power 32; outer space studies 31; refielding 31, 33; relationalities 36–37; social experience 40; social groups 32; social science concepts 32; space-times 38–39; structures 33–36; subjectivities 37–38; surface geographies 32; temporal existence 32; theoretical and political tasks 32
Morrison, P. 454
Morton, A. 111
moving Earths *28,* 28
Moynihan, T. 10
Mulkay, M.J. 15n5
Mullard Radio Astronomy Observatory 200, 202–4
multi-instrumental collectivism 102
multi-messenger astronomy 268
multi-omics studies 432
multiplicities of relation 302
multispecies anthropology 471
Munevar, G. 118n1

Murphy, M. 254
music 27, 73, 122, 124, 139, 447; from Earth xiv; noise and electronic music 311; Southern music from the US 98
Music for Solo Performer 200
Musk Foundation 73

Nagel, T. 206
Nahum 123–25, 132, 153n1
Naminapu Maymuru-White *218, 219, 221, 222*
NanoConnect-2 344–45, *346*
Narayan, U. 463
NASA astronaut selection process 187, 194
NASA's Astrobiology Program 281
NASA's Neurodiversity Network 193
NASA's Neurodiversity Network and Artemis Programme 195
NASA's organisational system 101
NASA Space Science Data Coordinated Archive (NSSDCA) 49
National Academies of Sciences, Engineering and Medicine (NASEM) 427
National Aeronautics and Space Administration (NASA) 172
National Architectural Accrediting Board (NAAB) 353
National Astronomical Research Institute of Thailand (NARIT) 295
National Autonomous University (UNAM) 342
National Council of Architectural Registration Boards (NCARB) 352
National Institutes of Natural Sciences (NINS) 263
National Oceanic and Atmospheric Administration's (NOAA) 322
national parks 287–89
National Risk Registers 315
National Science Foundation 408
National Space Weather Action Plan 315
National Space Weather Strategy 315
Nation's food problem 75
Native Skywatchers programming 258
Native slipstream 149
natural resources 229
Neas, O. 161
Neilson, B. 6
Neilson, H. 128, 129
Nelson, A. 143, 146, 151
neocolonialism 140
neoliberal imaginaries 9
neoliberal subjectivities 14
neurodiversity network programme 185
neutral broker organization 271
neutral buoyancy simulator *485*
NewSpace 14, 142–46, 152, 153, 161
New Space Economy 143
Newtonian gravity 481, 484
next generation megatelescopes 263
Nielsen, T.A. 486

503

Nigerian cultural heritage 2
Nightfall on Gaia 144, *144,* 150, *151*
Ninth Biospherian 372, 374, 376, 380, 383
nonautonomous ecological communities 455
non-Euro-American knowledge systems 287
non-Indigenous communities 88
nonrenewable energy resources 239
non-representational theory 471
Noon, K. 10
normalization of deviance 101
normative ethical theory 109
Nowotny, H. 140, 143

objectivity 60, 228, 230, 441
object-oriented ontology 471
object recognition 403, 405
occupational environments 185
octopuses 66
Odenwald, S.F. 315
off-Earth architecture 62
off-Earth spaces 2, 4, 5, 46
Ohman, M.-B. 161
O'Leary, B.L. 49, 50
Olson, V. 5, 7, 15n5, 61, 146, 165, 422
Olson, V.A. 284
Olympus Mons 288
Oman-Reagan, M.P. 4, 16, 148, 455
Omoruyi, O. 160
on Earth spaces 2
O'Neill, G.K. 256, 358
OneWeb 242
one-world world (OWW) 2, 153
ontogenetic maturation 209
Operation Support Facility (OSF) 274
Operation Wetback 76
optical telescope 448
orbital circulation 89
orbital debris 5, 16n5, 336
orbital panopticon 100
Orbital Reflector 132
orbital shuttle systems 388
orbital space 34
orbital technosphere 341
organisational cultures 417, 418
organisational sociology 101–3
organism 65
orientalism 11, 282, 291
orion module 355
Ormrod, J. 99, 100, 104
Ormrod, J.S. 123
Orthia, L.A. 191
orthodox historical materialist perspectives 104
orthostatic tolerance 125
Ó Tuathail, G. 283
outer space as environment 5
outer space exceptionalism 189
outer-space knowledges 85
outer-space mobilities 89

Outer Space Treaty (OST) 286
overpopulation 239
overview effect 347, 419, 420

PACT systems 131
pago ceremony 277–78, *278*
Painani-1 343
Pálsson, G. 60
Paranal Observatory 276
Parkhurst, A. 13, 62, 417, 420, 490
participatory cartography 348
participatory social media events 418
Pass, J. 97, 98
Patarin-Jossec, J. 12, 63, 104
payload 404–5
Penley, C. 35
Pérez, P. 64
performativity 283
periphery of space race 160
personal communication 207
personnel astronauts 176
Persson, E. 111
petro-masculinities 162
Phillips, R. 142, 143, 151, 154n5
Pilot William Pogue (PLT) 390
Pinkus, R. 112, 113
Pioneer plaques 461, 462
planetarity 8, 34, 122, 129–32
planetary climate system 154n2
planetary ethnography 72, 80–81, 81n2
Planetary Mine 14
planetary parks 288–89
planetary science 2, 6, 9, 37, 66, 102, 103, 108, 188, 190, 395, 430, 469, 475
Planetary Science and Astrobiology Decadal Survey 103
planetary skin 289–91
planet-scale power 34
plant biologists: community 433–35; considerations 435–36; Decadal survey 430–33; institutionalisation 427; ISS 428–30; planetary scientists and astrobiologists 428; social circles *434*; social-scientific interest 428; sociological characterisation 427
poetics of tomorrowing 144
policy science 102
policy sociology 103
Polish-language radio programmes 76
Polish newspapers 76
political art techniques 2
political correctness/wokeness 196
political ecology 2, 5, 16n5, 61
political economic theory 39
political economy 61
political geography 16n5, 61
politico-ethical issues 331
politics of recognition 259
polysemous fictions 179

poor people's beach 74
population distributions 407–8
positivist ideology 33
possible selves theory (PST) 188, 195
post-geocentric gravitography 490, **490**; of human culture (*see* human culture)
Pothukuchi, K. 246
power 232, 256, 259, 274, 282, 286–87, 300, 329–31, 340, 343, 434; colonial matrix of power 228–32; cosmic power 228
power grid disturbance 319
power vacuums 286
practices of spacemaking 4–5
Praet, I. 16n9
Prescod-Weinstein, C. 6, 9, 17n17, 38, 159, 279n5
Princeton's Atacama Cosmology Telescope 270
principle of charity 115
Pritchard, S.B. 316
production of space 100
Programme for International Student Assessment (PISA) 186
Progress Aerospace Enterprises (PAE) 8, 139, 140
psychological distress 193
public perception 190
public–private patchwork 267
Purse, L. 190, 191

quantum physics 139, 211
queer futurisms 9, 148
queering 16n15
queer theory 161

raceless future paradigm 146
Race, M. 17n18, 110
racial diversity 188–90
racial inequities 38
racialised segregation 141
racial justice 140
racism xiv, 1, 6, 159, 185, 193, 227, 288
Radcliffe, C.B. 210
radio astronomical observation 263
radio astronomy 15n5, 448
radio-frequency identification (RFID) 408
radio telescopes 203, 268
radio transmission 202
Rahder, M. 11, 61
Rand, L.S. 166
Rappaport, M.B. 111
rare-earth minerals 255
Rathje, W. 48
Read, R. 396, 398n6
reasonable worst case scenario (RWCS) 315
reception theory 464
record-keeping approach 397
Redfield, P. 15n5, 49
reductionist approach 381
re-earthing 6
refining algorithmic techniques 269

refugee Astronaut II *3*
Regis, E. 118n1
remote sensing 45, 51, 61, 90
Republic of the Moon 128, 133n8
Rescue Agreement 176, 177, 182
research campaigns (RC) 431
Research Integration Office (RIO) 401
reservation realisms 149
resource community 110
resource extraction 254–57
resource frontiers 5
REUNA 267
Rheinberger, H.-J. 375, 377
Robinson Crusoe on Mars 86
Robinson, K.S. 5
robotic space missions 38
robust reevaluation 9
rocketry's accelerating sublime 86
Rocket science 97
Rocketship X-M 86
Rolston, H. 16n13
Rose, D.B. 4
Rosner, D.K. 160
Rothschild, L.J. 284
Rowell, G. 419
Rubin Observatory 271
Rummel, J. 110
Russian Orbital Segment 407
Russian Orthodox terrestrial communities 420
Russian Space Agency (Roscosmos) xiv, 88, 124, 145, 403, 413, 419

Sadler, S. 383n3
safeguarding Indigenous sky rights: artificial satellites 240–43; Gunagala Galuma-Li (care for sky) 246–47; land rights 243–45; light pollution 238, 245–46; natural resources 238; space colonisation 239–40
Said, E.W. 282, 283, 286
Salazar, J.F. 12, 15n4, 16n9, 36, 62, *151*, 284, 312
Salmond, W. 12
Samatar, S. 38
Sammler, K.G. 35
Sampling Quadrangle Assemblages Research Experiment (SQuARE) 409, *409*, 411n3
Santana-Acuña, A. 8
Santana, C. 455
Sasakawa International Center for Space Architecture (SICSA) 353
satellite-based activism 131
Satellite Devotion 128, *129*
satellite gaze 12, 348
Satellite Tracker 333
SatNOGS project 345
Saturnian system 475
Savransky, M. 300
Sawyer, S. 292n2
scenic essays 7, 25

Scharmen, F. 12, 164
Scheper-Hughes, N. 416
Scherer, D. 118n1
Schmidt, F. 10
Schwartz, J. 118n2
science and technology studies (STS) 6, 15n5, 32, 33, 50, 102, 158, 162, 379
science fiction 5, 30, 35, 47, 86, 100, 121–22, 149–50, 152, 178, 180, 186–87, 190, 195, 376, 377, 379, 480, 488
Science Mission Directorate (SMD) 431
science of Society 97
science, technology, engineering and mathematics (STEM) 186–87
scientific community 177, 433, 436
scientific knowledge 10, 61, 91, 127, 252, 282, 303, 433, 471
scientific management 388
scientific occupation 33
scientific organisations 102
Scientific Revolution 234
scientific visualisation 102
Scott, D.K. 150, 154n7
Scott, R. 377
Seag, M. 162
search for extraterrestrial intelligence (SETI) 17n18, 203, 296, 454, 458–59, 463
Seaver, N. 266
seismometers 471
self-aware robots 47
self-consciousness 202, 210
self-deselection 194
self-experience 204
self-reflexivity 258, 273
sensor networks 264
Sercel, J. 115, 116
Serres, M. 147
Service of the Empire (SOTE) 481
SETI paradox 458
SETI-style interstellar communication 66
settler colonialism 254–57
sexism 165, 189
Shadaan, R. 254
Shadden, M. 187, 194
shadow humanities 67
Shaping Science 102
Sharrock, W. 396, 398n6
Shelley, P.B. 208
ship's orientation systems 394
Shonibare, Y. 2–3, 164, 173
Shorter, D.D. 465n11
Siddiqi, A. 166
Siding Spring Observatory 246
Signorielli, N. 188
Silent Running 379
Silicon Valley 104
Simberg, R. 112

Sinofuturism 153n1
sipaapu 64
67P/Churyumov–Gerasimenko comet 163
sky Country 88–89, 150, 217–19, 221, 239, 245–46, 290
Skylab 104, 388–89, 390, 395
Skylab 4 mission 389, 390
skyrocketing 263
sky sovereignty 240–43
Sloan Digital Sky Survey (SDSS) 269
Sloterdijk, P. 130
smart mining technologies 265
Smiles, D. 10, 38, 63
Smith, K. 111
Smith, M.J. 189, 193
Smith, N. 255
Snelting, F. 277
soaring corporeality 365
social class 488–89
social cognitive theory (SCT) 188, 195
social equity 140
social hierarchies 9
social inequality 49
social injustices 77
social justice 6
social media 98, 415
societies of control 330
sociocultural research 14
socio-environmental issues 331
sociological approaches: astrosociology 96–99; causal analysis 96; commercialization 104; cross-domain intelligibility 105; disciplinary research problems 105; geographical domain 105; goal 96; historical materialism and cosmos 99–100; lines of inquiry 96; multiparadigmatic discipline 96; NASA organisations and science 100–3; research 104; space stations 104; unfolding of history 104
sociotechnical assemblages 333
sociotechnical configurations 331
sociotechnical imaginaries 4, 142, 341
sociotechnical systems 163
software bugs 317
Solar and Heliospheric Observatory (SOHO) 322
Solar Dynamics Observatory (SDO) 322
Solaris 205
solar maximum 319
solar-proof 319
solar storms 313
solar systems 46, 89, 91, 92, 165, 240, 328, 482, *483*
songlines *see* songspirals
songspirals 218, 223
Space Age 329–31
space analogues 34
space archaeology 401–2, 401–2; development 47–49; methods 50–51

space art xxviii, 4, 7–8, 16n14, 121, 340, 349, 349n13
space as method 6–7
Space Biosphere Ventures 372
space codes: architect and astronaut 361; body, building codes 355–56; building codes 351, 353–54; codes of conduct 351, 352–53; codes of law 351, 359–60; escape routes 356–57; spatial practice 351–52; zoning codes 351, 357–59
space colonisation 239–40, 254–57
space community 12, 47, 145
space conjuncture: critical thinking and making 2; lunar orbiting space station 1; pluriversal articulations 2; political-ecological 2; practices of spacemaking 4–5; predicaments 2; refugee astronaut 2; resource frontier 1; Zapatista communities 2
space ethics: balancing value considerations 114; classroom discussions 111; community 117; disclosure and consent 113; enhancing decision-making 114–16; ethical assessment 113; exploration 117–18; history 108–11; human activity 112; influence 112; informed consent 113; justice and injustice 113; liberal individualist assumptions 111; ongoing ethical engagement 116–17; philosophical/ethical theory 111; productive disagreements 114; progressive space activism 112; risk aversion/hostility 113; scientific disciplines 118; stress-testing concepts and frameworks 116; transformative process 118
Space Feminism 159
Space Flight Human-System Standard (SFHSS) 355
spaceflight participant 361
Space for @ll 145, 146, 152
space habitats 402–3
space heroes 49
space humanities 2
space industry development 244
space infrastructures/networks: command-and-control centres 328; envelopment 329; human biopolitical condition 336; life-management 329; military-industrial complexes 328; pay attention 328; risk and security 334–36; sociotechnical processes 328; Space Age 329–31; upholding life 331–34
Space Life and Physical Sciences Research and Applications Division (SLPSRA) 431
space media 12
space Orientalism 284–85, 292n2
Spaceport America 87
Spaceport America tourism 35
space ports 34
space race model 1, 15n1, 50
Space Refugee 125, 133n4
space refugee II 2
spacescape 34
space scepticism 112

space sciences 15n5
Spaceship Earth 290, 414
Spaceship Earth 384n6
space society 98
spaces of outer space: dead satellite with nuclear reactor 87; earth and cosmos writings 92–93; geography and language 84–85; mobility and circulation 89–92; place and landscape 85–89
spacesuit fabrication techniques 37
spacetime 38, 481; Indigenous spacetime 149; space-time mapping 143
space weather 313, 314, 315–16, 317, *318*
Space Weather Follow On-Lagrange 1 (SWFO-L1) 322
Space Weather Hazards 315
Space Weather Prediction Center (SWPC) 322
space weather preparedness 315, 319–21
space weather-proof *320*, 321, 323
SpaceX: aerospace industry 71; beyond concept 72; border wall in Brownsville *79*; fieldwork 72; Magic Valley 73–78; multivocality 72; planetary ethnography 72, 80; porous borders and beyond 78–80; socioeconomic issues 71; Starlink 128
Spanish mountaintop observatory 444
spatial inequality 141
spatial knowledge 365
spatial products 273
Special Interest Group on Data Communication (SIGCOMM) 317
speculative fiction 144, 148, 150
Spennemann, D.H.R. 47
sphaera nullius 239–40
Spiro, M.E. 455
Spivak, G.C. 129, 463
SPT-EVA 391–94
Sputnik 89, 340
Square Kilometre Array (SKA) 62, 203, 246–47
Sreejith, S.G. 176, 177
Starbase 78
Starlink satellites *241*, 241–42
Starship system 71
Star Trek 35, 190, 191
Steinke, J. 188, 191
Stengers, I. 152, 375
Stewart, K. 414
Strachan, T. 125, 132
stress-testing 116
strike in space 390
Suleiman, L. 127
Sultana, F. 6, 16n10
surface bias 5
survivor stow 278
sustainability 281
sustainable development 181
Swanson, G.E. 35
Swanson, H.A. 60
Swanton, P. 10

symbiosis 291
Szűcs, T. 163
Szocik, K. 111

Taiwo, O.O. 7
targeted disinvestment 141
Tavarez, P.M.P. 188, 191
Taylorist management techniques 104
Tcharfas, J. 383n3
technoableism 164
technology not-for-profit 247
technonatural/envirotechnical risk 316
technoscience 228
technoscientific domains 264
technoscientific outer spaces 34
technoutopianism 154n2
telecommunications 49
telecommunications gap 341
telepathy 301
telescopes 244, 269
temporal disjunction 147
Tereshin, M. 13, 421
terra nullius 36, 127, 240, 284
Terrestrial Trilogy 25
Texas Higher Education Coordinating Board (THECB) 353
Texas Open Beaches Act 73
Thailand: Doi Inthanon, Chiang Mai 297–98; emergence and hybridity 297; Kaokala, Nakhon Sawan 298–99
Thai National Observatory (TNO) 298, 300
theory of relativity 211
thinking-with space 6, 14
Third World Approaches to International Law (TWAIL) 180
Thirty Meter Telescope (TMT) 161, 244
time-space 38–39
Tironi, M. 275
Titan's troposphere 266
Topash-Caldwell, B.K. 154n6
Traiano, H. 161
Tranquility Base 49
transcendental purity of astronauts 174
transformative science 431, 432
transformative technologies 344
transient voltage surge suppressors (TVSS) 319
trans-temporality 148, 154n5
Trevino, N. 158
Trilogie Terrestre 7, 25–30
Triscott, N. 8
trustworthiness 445–46
Tsing, A.L. 5, 15n2
Tsiolkovsky, K. 489
Tucson garbage project 48
Turnbull, D. 448
Tutton, R. 11, 158

TV Magnet 311
Two-Eyed Seeing 258

ubiquitous computing 265
Ubuntu 181–82
UFO culture 85
ufological Buddhism 295, 296
UK government's Defence Committee 321
UNAMSAT-1 342
UNAMSAT-B 342
uncertainty: ambiguity 468–69; design 469–71; environment 473–75; immanence and interplanetary attunement 476–77; persistent legacy 475–76; space-legs 471–73
unconsciousness 211
un Earthing 12
unemployment 193
unheimlich concept 380
uninterruptible power supply (UPS) 320
United Nations Declaration of the Rights of Indigenous Peoples (UNDRIP) 238
universal gravitation 481
universalising impetus of Anthropocene 5
universalism 2
Universal Transverse Mercator system 402
universe within 60
University of Tokyo Atacama Observatory telescope 270
Un Mundo Donde Quepan Muchos Mundos 2
unpublished images 404–5
UN's Committee on the Peaceful Uses of Outer Space (COPUOS) 175
urban renewal 140
US Army's rocket development team 121
US Association of Universities for Research in Astronomy (AURA) 263
US Department of Interior 166
US-led Artemis programme 355
US Wilderness Act 288

Valentine, D. 15n5, 35, 61, 145–48, 164, 284
Van Dooren, T. 63
Van Eijk, C. 181
Varela, F.J. 201, 206
Vaughan, D. 101–4, 112
vegetative time 209
Venkatesan, A. 131
Verge, J. 319
Vermeylen, S. 9
Vertesi, J. 15n5, 38, 395, 397, 398n5, 422
Very Energetic Radiation Imaging Telescope Array System (VERITAS) 244
vicarious contact 191
VIRAL 25, *29*, 30
virtual reality 201
visual art techniques 311

Index

VMCloud 314, 319, *320*, 322, 323
Vodunaut series 180
voice communication method 418
voltage transients 319
Voyager Golden Records 461
Voyager mission 470

Walford, A. 266, 270
Walker, J. 384n17
Walkowicz, L. 6
Walking the Clouds 149
Wallace, D. 318
Walsh, J.P. 12
war on terror 283
water rising 219–20
Watts, V. 165
weather 91
Weibel, D.L. 35
weighted floatation 365
Wells-Jensen, S. 185, 192, 193
Western intellectual tradition 208–11
Western scientific community 302
Western scientific culture 85
Western von Gestern 376
Westwood, L. 49
whiteboard conversation 447
Whitey on the Moon 121
Whyte, K.P. 253, 257

wilderness 165, 287–89
Williamson, M. 16n13
Winch, P. 396, 398n6
Wired magazine 317, 324n1
Wolfe, P. 254
Womack, Y.L. 164
Woodcock, J. 417
Woods, P. 185, 192
Woolgar, S. 396, 398n6
Woomera 50, 88, 243
World Meteorological Organization (WMO) 315
writing the land back method 161
The Wrong Stuff 371, *378*
Wynter, S. 230, 233, 234

Yamatju-Wajarri people 247
Yellowstone model 288
Yolŋu kinship system 218
Young, E. 208, 211
Young, M.J. 38
Yusoff, K. 5, 147

Zabusky, S.E. 15n5
Zhang, L. 195
Zion Gardens Apartments 140
zoning codes 351, 357–59
Zubrin, R. 112

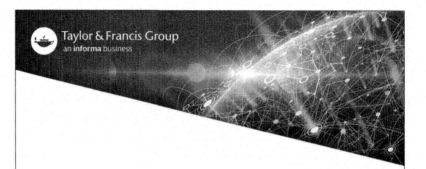